THE BLUE GUIDES

Austria
Belgium and Luxembourg
California*
Channel Islands
China*
Corsica
Crete
Cyprus
Egypt
England
France
Germany
Greece
Holland

Hungary*
Ireland
Mexico*
Morocco
Northern Italy
Portugal
Scotland
Sicily
Southern Italy
Spain
Switzerland
Turkey: Bursa to Antakya
Wales
Yugoslavia

Boston and Cambridge
Florence
Istanbul
Jerusalem
London
Moscow and Leningrad
New York
Oxford and Cambridge
Paris and Versailles
Rome and Environs
Venice

Cathedrals and Abbeys of England and Wales
Churches and Chapels of England*
Literary Britain and Ireland
Museums and Galleries of London
Victorian Architecture in Britain

*in preparation

The Torre Nueva, Zaragoza, demolished in 1894, drawn by Richard Ford on 19 October 1831

BLUE GUIDE

SPAIN

Ian Robertson

Atlas, maps and plans by John Flower

A & C Black
London

W W Norton
New York

Fifth edition 1989

Published by A & C Black (Publishers) Limited
35 Bedford Row, London WC1R 4JH

© A & C Black (Publishers) Limited 1989

Published in the United States of America by
W W Norton & Company, Inc.
500 Fifth Avenue, New York, NY 10110

Published simultaneously in Canada by
Penguin Books Canada Limited
2801 John Street, Markham, Ontario, LR3 1B4

British Library Cataloguing in Publication Data
Robertson, Ian, 1928-
    Spain.—5th ed.—(Blue guide).
    1. Spain—Visitors' guides
    I. Title II. Series
    914.6'0483
    ISBN 0–7136–2967–3

ISBN 0-393-30476-0   USA

Ian Robertson was born in Tokyo in 1928 and educated in England at
Stowe. After spending several years in publishing and bookselling in
London, he began working on *Blue Guides* when he was commissioned
to rewrite *Blue Guide Spain* in 1970. He has since revised the Blue
Guides to *Ireland, France, Paris, Portugal,* and *Switzerland,* as well as
writing *Blue Guide Austria* and *Blue Guide Cyprus.* He has also written
introductions to reprints of Richard Ford's *Hand-Book for Travellers in
Spain,* Joseph Baretti's *Journey from London to Genoa* and Gleig's *The
Subaltern.* He now lives in Spain.

Printed and bound in Great Britain by
Anchor Press Ltd, Tiptree, Essex

PREFACE

This fifth edition of *Blue Guide Spain* follows the successful pattern set by the last two editions, likewise concentrating on the mainland. It is the first time to be published since the country entered the European Economic Community. It is intended for the traveller wanting to take a close look at the country as a whole, for as Joseph Baretti observed over 200 years ago: 'Innumerable are the objects of curiosity up and down this large kingdom that deserve to be seen, examined and described'. This edition has been radically revised in several respects, and many of its routes—104 compared to 70 in the last edition—have been entirely re-written. *Gibraltar* is included for the first time since the edition of 1964. The Balearics and Canaries are *not* included, as most travellers visit the islands separately.

The introduction of autonomies, entailing the partial self-government of historical regions or groups of provinces—indeed in some cases of individual provinces—has posed several problems, not all of them satisfactorily resolved, particularly in the field of culture, for each autonomy goes its own way, and many have yet to find their feet. Although endeavouring to keep abreast of all the most recent changes and re-arrangements of museums, inevitably the latest facts are not forthcoming, and getting advance information accurate enough to print is virtually impossible. Times of admission to monuments and museums, other than in Barcelona and Madrid, are not included: to do so would inevitably misinform the traveller in a high proportion of cases. To avoid disappointment make advance enquiry at any Tourist Information Office.

In several ways this disintegration or decentralisation has been fruitful in that many disparate areas now have the opportunity to indulge their provincial pride in the publication of books on local topics, and in restoring or improving regional monuments and museums. Some have considered that any reversion to parochialism is a retrograde step and merely a temporary reaction to the former stranglehold of Castile and the cultural inertia of the Franco regime. Regrettably, the administration of cultural programmes has in some cases fallen into the hands of functionaries who have a very slight notion of what constitutes culture; but future developments are awaited with interest. Some autonomies have raced ahead, notably in Catalunya, which of course has its separate historical background; but even there over-reaction has taken place.

The routes in this volume have been arranged in seven sections, with occasional overlappings. It need hardly be emphasised—especially in the case of the longer routes—that it is virtually impossible to visit all the monuments described and hope to cover the route (or the particular town) in the same day. While the Editor has travelled very extensively throughout Spain on numerous occasions over the years, and again recently for this edition, not every location in so large a country can be visited for every edition; but a substantial proportion of the descriptions have been revised in the light of personal observation on the spot and familiarity with actual conditions. However, he knows from experience that sudden and unexpected changes can occur immediately he has turned his back. Not infrequently, in spite of illusion-dispelling experience, he has been disappointed by expecting too much of some 'local lion', and would rather save others the wasted journey by assuring them that it is not worth the time or trouble. Indeed, he would as much welcome a recommendation from a reader to delete a church—for example—which in his view did not merit inclusion, as having an omission pointed out to him.

One specific problem encountered during the last few years is that of gaining entry to churches, both in towns and villages. The excuse is that too many have been vandalised or robbed of their treasures. While several such instances have occurred, with certain exceptions those responsible for such losses might be sought nearer home (see p 91). With fewer priests around, even more time than formerly may be lost locating someone with the key; and in many cases it has been impossible to verify whether or not the objects previously listed as notable in their interiors are still to be found. However, unless the contents of a church—architecturally or artistically—are remarkable (such as the paintings at Arcenillas, near Zamora) they will not be described in detail. Nevertheless, the Editor would welcome information from readers who have gained admittance to any church whose contents have not been included, if in their opinion they deserve notice, together with any reliable information on the whereabouts of the key.

Any such constructive suggestions for the correction or improvement of future editions will be gratefully received and acknowledged by the Editor, who alone is responsible, as he has been held, for all inexactitudes, shortcomings, inconsistencies, and solecisms. No one is better aware of the difficulty of avoiding errors of omission and commission; in extenuation, he can quote Henry Swinburne, writing in the 1770s after his tour of Spain, for one may be 'detected in many mistakes, because a foreigner must often be exposed to receive partial accounts of things from the natives, who have an interest in hiding the nakedness of their country, and exaggerating its advantages'.

Like others in the Blue Guide series, this edition sets out to provide the traveller with a balanced account of certain characteristics of a country which will make a visit to it that much more rewarding. It does not omit (except perhaps deliberately) anything that will be conspicuous by its absence which might appeal to the intelligent visitor, but it is not so exhaustive as to leave no opportunity of discovering many additional pleasures.

At the same time the Editor feels obliged to warn the traveller that although there is now much more widely spread material prosperity, the cost of living has also risen dramatically, and what was once the comparatively low cost of a holiday in Spain is no longer a consideration. And the romantic concept of building castles in Spain has also taken on a new and unequivocal meaning, for in the last three decades the Spanish obsession with 'urbanización' has altered out of all recognition a large number of once attractive townscapes, entirely destroying the equilibrium of a place. This has likewise disfigured extensive stretches of the already over-exploited coast. Too many fine and characteristic vistas have been irremediably blighted by unsightly and perfunctorily controlled speculative development; and too often the Philistine erection of a brash new block of a bank, offices, or apartments has been left stranded for an interminable time in a sea of plastic, rubble, and refuse. This lack of civic pride is also noticeable in the non-disposal of garbage in many places, often obvious at the entry and exits of towns and villages, apart from car cemeteries; but this trait, together with the pollution of the sea in the vicinity of many resorts, is just one of several problems of civilisation to be solved as Spain becomes more integrated into Europe.

Hotels and restaurants are to be found throughout most of Spain, although in some areas they are thinner on the ground. Tourist Offices in Spain and abroad can provide up-to-date lists of various types of accommodation available, and individual hotels are therefore not indicated in this edition, with the exception of the State-run *Paradores*. Among several annual publications listing a selection of hotels and restaurants is the *red* Michelin Guide to Spain and Portugal—a useful companion to the present volume—which also contains numerous town plans giving detailed indications of the points of entry or exit, oneway streets, carparks, garages, etc. It is essential that the traveller has a good general map of Spain, and more detailed motoring maps of the areas through which he intends to tour or explore. Advice on these is given on p 69.

In addition to those who have assisted with previous editions of this Guide the Editor must express his gratitude to *Amado Jímenez Preciosa, Juan Sanchez Lorenzo,* and *María Luisa Fernández Lázaro* at the Secretaria General de Turismo for easing his path; this organisation has also kindly provided the majority of the illustrations. He must also thank *Horace Zammitt* and *Joseph Viale* and their staff at Gibraltar; and while it may be invidious to list individuals among the many who have gone out of their way to offer assistance or advice, special thanks are due to *P.J. Rhodes; Maria Carme Farré i Sanpera* in Barcelona; *Ana Barceló Calatayud* in Cádiz; *Bernard Bevan;* and *Heather Waddell,* while **John Flower** has again undertaken most of the cartography.

Arthur and Marion Boyars have again generously provided the Editor with a second home while on his travels, and whose unstinting hospitality can never be sufficiently acknowledged.

David M. Jones and Gemma Davies have shown their customary patience during the preparation of this edition for the press, which could not have been completed without the help of my wife, who has again driven many thousands of kilometres throughout Spain, and has shared the vexations and pleasures of intensive travel and the many secluded months of the Guide's gestation.

A NOTE ON BLUE GUIDES

The *Blue Guide* series began in 1918 when Muirhead Guide-Books Limited published 'Blue Guide London and its Environs'. Finlay and James Muirhead already had extensive experience of guide-book publishing: before the First World War they had been the editors of the English editions of the German Baedeckers, and by 1915 they had acquired the copyright of most of the famous 'Red' Handbooks from John Murray.

An agreement made with the French publishing house Hachette et Cie in 1917 led to the translation of Muirhead's London Guide, which became the first 'Guide Bleu'—Hachette had previously published the blue-covered 'Guides Joanne'. Subsequently, Hachette's 'Guide Bleu Paris et ses Environs' was adapted and published in London by Muirhead. The collaboration between the two publishing houses continued until 1933.

In 1931 Ernest Benn Limited took over the Blue Guides, appointing Russell Muirhead, Finlay Muirhead's son, editor in 1934. The Muirheads' connection with the Blue Guides ended in 1963, when Stuart Rossiter, who had been working on the Guides since 1954, became house editor, revising and compiling several of the books himself.

The Blue Guides are now published by A & C Black, who acquired Ernest Benn in 1984, so continuing the tradition of guide-book publishing which began in 1826 with 'Black's Economical Tourist of Scotland'. The Blue Guide series continues to grow: there are now more than 35 titles in print with revised editions appearing regularly and many new Blue Guides in preparation.

'Blue Guides' is a registered trade mark.

CONTENTS

EXPLANATIONS

Type. The main routes are described in large type, as are some sub-routes. Smaller type is used for most sub-routes, detours, excursions, etc.; for historical and preliminary paragraphs and (generally speaking) for descriptions of greater detail or minor importance.

Asterisks indicate points of special interest or excellence.

Distances are measured in kilometres; total route distances are also given in miles. Road distances along the routes themselves record the approximate distance between the towns or villages, etc. described, but it should be emphasised that with the re-alignment of many roads it is almost certain that these distances will vary slightly from those measured on milometers.

Population figures are given in round numbers, based on those of the census of March 1981, but they are now likely to be higher for the large towns. These include those normally resident; tourists can swell the numbers very considerably in the season. Figures are not given for places with fewer than 5000 inhabitants. It should be noted that these figures are for municipalities and often include a number of nearby villages, while in highly populated conurbations they will *not* take into account adjacent municipalities. See also p 65 .

Anglicisation. Most place-names retain their usual Spanish form (but see below), except in a few cases where the English equivalent is much more familiar.

Place-names. With autonomy, very many more place-names, particularly in Catalunya, and to a lesser extent in Valencia, in the Basque provinces, and in Galicia, have reverted to former spellings (some contrived), and these are incorporated in the text of this edition. In certain cases the Castilian form is also given (and indexed), although certain discrepancies may remain. Travellers should have little difficulty in recognising the names of others on the new signposts. Except in a few outposts of reaction or inertia, street names commemorating martyrs of the Franco regime, including the late *generalissimo* himself, have long been changed, and an attempt has been made to include all such changes.

Abbreviations. In addition to the generally accepted and self-explanatory abbreviations, the following occur in the guide.
Av.   *Avenida*, avenue (*Avinguda* in Catalan)
C   century
C.   *Calle*, street or road (*Carrer* in Catalan)
Cap.   *Capilla*, chapel
Conv. Convent
M   Michelin map number
N.S.   *Nuestra Señora*, Our Lady
Pal.   *Palacio*, palace (*Palau* in Catalan)
Pl.   *Plaza*, square or place, *or* Plan. The *Pl. Mayor* is always the main square of a town or village
R   Room
Rte   Route
S. or *Sta., San., Santa*   Saint (*Sant* in Catalan); SS.   Saints

See p 67 for Glossary of architectural and allied terms.

INTRODUCTION TO SPANISH HISTORY

Traces of prehistoric man in the Iberian Peninsula are many and varied, and the caves in which they have left their mark are widely distributed. Important Neolithic sites exist in the province of Almería, specifically at *Los Millares* (dated by radio-carbon tests to 2340–85 BC) and at *El Algar*. In the neighbourhood of Antequera are several Megalithic monuments, such as the *Cueva de Menga*, while of the Magdalenian period the murals at *Altamira* (near Santander) are outstanding.

Among the emerging culture groups were the LIGURIANS, related to those of Northern Italy, who are thought to have settled in the centre; the IBERIANS, who may have come from North Africa, and settled in the southern half of the country before spreading to the centre, and the CELTS, who penetrated Spain via France in the 6C BC, and settled in the North and West. The term Celtiberian, which was given to the inhabitants of the centre, does not indicate any fusion of the races. From the earliest times these peoples lived in tribes and did not unite to form a nation, a lack of union that was to be a marked characteristic throughout their history. Some tribes left their trace in the names of districts, such as the ASTURES in the Asturias. Of the BASQUES, who have to a large extent preserved their language, it is not possible to state their origin, although some have been tempted to connect them with the Iberians on account of certain affinities between the Basque language and that of the native tribes in North Africa, and the similarity between the unusual blood groups of the Berbers and Basques.

The first people known to have had commercial relations with Spain were the PHOENICIANS, who founded the port of *Cádiz* c 1100 BC, establishing further settlements at *Abdera* (Adra), *Malaca* (Málaga), *Onuba* (Huelva), and *Tarsis* (Tharsis), etc. Others attracted by the mineral wealth of the country were the CARTHAGINIANS, who also settled in the Guadalquivir valley at *Corduba* (Córdoba) and *Hispalis* (Sevilla), and at *Carteia* (near Algeciras). Meanwhile, from 630–570 BC the GREEKS had settled along the E coast, specifically at *Emporion* (Empúries) and *Dianium* (Denia).

Expelled from Sicily by the Romans, the Carthaginians adapted Spain as a base of action against their rivals, *Hamilcar Barca* eventually subjugating much of the country S of the Ebro, while *Hasdrubal* founded *Nova Carthago* (Cartagena). In 221 BC Hasdrubal was succeeded by *Hannibal*, who precipitated the Second Punic War by attacking Rome through its ally *Saguntum*, an action which was to bring about the ruin of the Carthaginian Empire. Rome, now the predominant power, endeavoured to colonise the peninsula, but it took almost 200 years to pacify the intractable tribes of the centre and North, who continued to resist imperialist expansion and exploitation with inflexible stubbornness. *Viriathus* defied Rome for six years until assassinated c 140 BC, while the defence of *Numancia* (near Soria), eventually reduced by *Scipio Æmilianus* in 133 BC, became legendary.

Nevertheless, Roman Spain prospered both commercially and politically. Under Augustus, the two earlier provinces of HISPANIA CITERIOR and HISPANIA ULTERIOR were rearranged to form *Tarraconensis* (the N, NW, and central area), *Lusitania* (roughly modern Portugal), and *Baetica* (S Spain). Spain produced four emperors (*Trajan, Hadrian, Theodosius I*, and *Honorius*, and *Marcus Aurelius* was of Spanish parentage); the two *Senecas, Lucan*, and *Columella* were also born in Spain of Roman parents, and both *Martial* and *Quintilian* were probably of Hispanic stock.

Between AD 264 and 276 the Hispanic provinces were devastated by the FRANKS and the SUEVI, and in 409 these raids were followed by significant invasions by the Suevi, ALANS, and VANDALS, who after pillaging the country, turned to fighting among themselves. The VISIGOTHS, operating from Toulouse, undertook to restore order on behalf of Rome, but when they were themselves defeated by the Franks in Gaul they sought refuge S of the Pyrenees, and eventually set up their capital at *Toledo*. There were at this time between 80,000 and 100,000 Visigoths occupying the N part of the central plateau. Under *Leovigild* (568–86) they unsuccessfully attempted to assimilate the 3 or 4 million Hispani who lived along the Mediterranean coast and in Baetica, for basically they remained an exclusive military aristocracy and would not mix with the natives. Their own tenuous unity was destroyed by civil war between religious factions, which continued in a desultory manner until 585 when Leovigild's son *Hermenigild*, the leader of the Catholic Party, was executed. Leovigild's successor *Recared* renounced Arianism, and at the Third Council of Toledo in 589, Catholicism became the officially enforced religion of the Visigothic kingdom. Nevertheless, in spite of apparent religious unity, the country was still prey to political disturbances for which the elective system of the monarchy was partially responsible.

The Caliphate and Moorish Rule. In 711, at the invitation either of the political opponents of *Roderic* (who had been elected king the previous year), or of *Count Julian* (whose daughter had been seduced by Roderic), an expeditionary force of some 7000 Berbers under *Tariq*, a lieutenant of *Musa*, governor of Mauretania, landed near Gibraltar, and was soon reinforced. The Visigothic army was defeated at the battle of the *Guadalete*, and the 'Moors', reinforced by Arabs of two rival tribes, rapidly extended their conquest over almost the entire country, leaving only scattered remnants of the Christian army in the inaccessible mountains of the Asturias. They subsequently invaded Gaul, but in 732 were decisively repulsed at *Poitiers* by *Charles Martel*. The Moors were generally welcomed, and the majority of the Christian inhabitants submitted to their tolerant masters. Those choosing to retain their faith were known as *Mozárabes*, but were subjected to a capitation tax. To avoid this many become Moslems, forming a class known as *Muladies*.

In 756 *Abderrahman*, sole survivor of the OMAYYAD dynasty at Damascus, took possession of Córdoba and obtained recognition of his independent emirate from the Caliph of Baghdad. His reign (until 788) was filled with a succession of wars with rebellious Berber states and minor chiefs, and it was not until the caliphate of *Abderrahman II* (912–61), a man of great political and military energy, that some semblance of unity was established in Moslem Spain. During this reign and that of *Hakam II* (961–76) Córdoba became perhaps the most civilised city in Europe: encouragement was given to literature and science; schools of philosophy and medicine were founded, and libraries formed. Military glory was gained by *Almanzor*, the prime minister of *Hisham II* (976–1013). He arrogated to himself all the power, and conducted numerous summer campaigns (*aceifas*) in which he ravaged Barcelona, León and Santiago de Compostela, and again forced back the Christians to the Pyrenees and into the mountain ranges of the NW. It is supposed that Almanzor was eventually defeated at *Calatañazor* (near Soria), but there is little evidence that such a battle ever took place. He died in 1002, to the relief of the northern kingdoms, but the militarism fostered by him was continued by his successors. Anarchy, however, soon set in. Provinces declared themselves independent and split up into petty *taifas*, but these, themselves distracted by perpetual civil wars, never consolidated their power, and were often obliged to pay tribute to Castile and León. Eventually the Moors turned to N Africa for aid, and towards the end of the 11C a contingent of ALMORÁVIDES, Berber tribes united by religious fanaticism, entered Spain, to be followed in 1147 by another dynasty, the ALMOHADES, even more fanatic, but hardly less so than the religious leaders of Christendom.

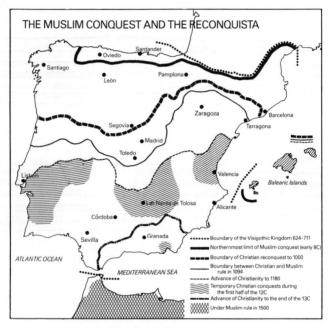

THE MUSLIM CONQUEST AND THE RECONQUISTA

······· Boundary of the Visigothic Kingdom 624–711

▬▬▬ Northernmost limit of Muslim conquest (early 8C)

▬ ▬ ▬ Boundary of Christian reconquest to 1000

▭▭▭ Boundary between Christian and Muslim rule in 1094

------- Advance of Christianity to 1180

Temporary Christian conquests during the first half of the 12C

━━━ Advance of Christianity to the end of the 13C

▨▨▨ Under Muslim rule in 1500

The Reconquest. Following the symbolic victory of *Covadonga* in 718 (in which a small probing force of Moors was repulsed), the Christians, led by *Pelayo*, rallied, and set up the kingdom of the Asturias with their capital first at Cangas de Onís, and later at Oviedo. *Alfonso I, the Catholic* (739–57), crossed the Cantabrian mountains and descended on León, but the Christian capital was not established there until 914. *Alfonso II, the Chaste* (791–842), continued with the slow acquisition of territory, and at his death the kingdom of León consisted of the Asturias, Cantabria, Galicia, N Portugal, and part of the province of Burgos. The reputed discovery of the body of Santiago in Galicia started a great cult which later grew to be an important contributory factor in the reconquest, Santiago 'Matamoros' (the Moorslayer) becoming a redoubtable Christian champion. Meanwhile *Ramiro I* (842–50) beat back attacks made on the Spanish coast by the Normans, and castles (which later gave the name to Castile) were constructed as bastions against fresh Moorish incursions. Counts were appointed by León to govern this new territory, and by the middle of the 10C *Count Fernán González*, one of many who had gradually tended to assert their independence, obtained a measure of autonomy for Castile. His son married *Sancha*, sister of *Bermudo III* of León, and received the title of King as dowry. Sancha, soon widowed, then married a son of Sancho the Great of Navarre, who as *Fernando I* reigned as king of Castile from 1037 to 1065. He also seized his father-in-law's kingdom of León, and extended his own to the S, making the Moorish kings of Toledo and Zaragoza his vassals.

Another focus of resistance against the Moors was in the Pyrenees. The Basques, beating off both Moors and Franks, had set up the kingdom of Navarre in the 9C. Under *Sancho the Great* (1000–35), whose territories stretched as far as Catalunya, this was for a time the most powerful of the northern kingdoms. The boundaries of Catalunya itself, set up as a march or border county by Charlemagne, were extended by *Ramón Berenguer I* (1035–76), while *Ramón Berenguer III* (1096–1131), opening relations with Italy, laid the foundations of Catalan naval power in the Mediterranean. *Ramón Berenguer IV* (1131–62) married *Petronila*, heiress of Aragón, and their son, who took the name of *Alfonso II* (1162–96), united Aragón with Catalunya.

Meanwhile Fernando I of **Castile** who, like his father, had divided his territory among his children, had died, precipitating a fratricidal war finally won by *Alfonso VI* (1072–1109), during whose reign Toledo fell to the Christians (1085). Nine years later Valencia was captured, temporarily, by the followers of the *Cid Campeador (Rodrigo Díaz de Vivar*, c 1043–99). Shortly afterwards the dependency of Portugal, given by Alfonso to his daughter *Teresa* on her marriage to *Count Henry of Burgundy*, became a separate kingdom. Castile continued to be ravaged by civil war, both during the reigns of queen *Urraca* (1109–26) and of her son *Alfonso VII* (1126–57), order being eventually restored by *Alfonso VIII* (1158–1214). Alfonso, united with the kings of León, Aragón, and Navarra in a general crusade, was able at the battle of *Las Navas de Tolosa* (between the pass of Despeñaperros and Bailén) to cripple Moorish power in the peninsula for good. Castile was finally united with León in the person of *Fernando III* (1217–52), son of Alfonso IX of León and Berenguela, daughter of Alfonso VIII of Castile. The reign of Fernando III, who was later canonised, was decisive in the long-drawn-out reconquest. In 1236 Córdoba fell; in 1241 Murcia; and in 1248 Sevilla. Universities were founded, and the building of the cathedrals of Burgos and Toledo started.

Concurrently, the kings of **Aragón** had been active. In 1118 *Alfonso I, el Batallador* (1104–34) entered Zaragoza, and later captured Tarazona, Calatayud, and Daroca, while Tortosa and Lleida, among other towns, fell to *Ramón Berenguer IV. Alfonso II* gained possession of Albarracín and founded Teruel. He was succeeded by *Pedro II* (1196–1213), who, involved in the Albigensian Wars, was killed at the battle of Muret. The long reign of *Jaime I, el Conquistador* (1213–76), was one of the most brilliant in the history of Aragón. The Balearics fell to him in 1229; he regained control of Valencia in 1238, and by 1266 Alicante was in his hands. His son *Pedro* or *Pere III* (1276–85) inherited Aragón, Catalunya, and Valencia; another son, *Jaime*, was left the Balearics, Roussillon, and the Cerdagne. In 1282, after the massacre of the French known as the 'Sicilian Vespers', Pedro became king of Sicily at the Sicilians' invitation, a consequence of which was a French invasion of Aragón. This was unsuccessful, and the French fleet was defeated by the Aragonese at Las Hormigas. On the death of his brother, Jaime inherited Sicily, while Pedro's son *Alfonso III* (1285–91) inherited his Spanish possessions. During the following reign, of *Jaime II* (1291–1327), a Catalan expedition to Constantinople and Asia Minor was undertaken. Although successful against the Turks, this aroused the jealousy of the Greeks, and Paleologos had its leaders assassinated. Later, however, the Catalans gained control of Athens, and formed a Grand Duchy of Athens which was to survive until the end of the 14C. *Pedro* or *Pere IV, the Ceremonious* (1336–87), was able, after the battle of Épila, to discipline the recalcitrant Aragonese nobles who had forced concessions from Alfonso III, and did much to strengthen royal authority. Majorca and Roussillon were united with Aragón. *Juan I* (1387–95) was succeeded by *Martín* (1395–1410), who left no male heirs, and the Infant of Castile known as *Fernando de Antequera* was elected king (1410–16). His son *Alfonso V, the Magnanimous* (1416–58), invited by Joanna II of Naples to help her to defend her kingdom against Louis of Anjou, was adopted by her as heir to Naples. Although defeated by the French at the naval battle of Ponza, Alfonso was able to regain Naples, and his illegitimate son Fernando was recognised as king. On the death of Alfonso V, the crown of Aragón passed to his brother *Juan II* (1458–79), who was involved in a quarrel with his own son, the *Príncipe de Viana*. The latter died in mysterious circumstances, at which the Catalans rose up in revolt, while Louis XI of France took possession of Roussillon. Juan died in 1479, leaving as his heir *Fernando V*, who had already, in 1469, married Isabel of Castile.

The history of **Castile** from the death of Fernando III to the accession of the Catholic Kings is one long record of civil war. The reign of Fernando's son, *Alfonso X, el Sabio* ('the Learned, but *not* Wise'; 1252–84), was more memorable for the lustre of his literary court than for political success, although he captured Cartagena, Cádiz, and Sanlúcar. *Sancho IV, el Valiente* (1284–95) was followed by *Fernando IV* (1295–1312) and *Alfonso XI* (1313–50), but the minorities of the last two were again periods of political turmoil. In 1350 *Pedro I, the Cruel*, succeeded to the throne. After quelling an insurrection stirred up in Castile by his bastard brother *Enrique de Trastámara*, he declared war on Pedro IV of Aragón. The latter, in conjunction with Enrique, called in the White Companies from France led by *Du Guesclin*, while Pedro the Cruel obtained assistance from the English under the *Black Prince*. Pedro defeated Enrique at *Nájera* (or *Navarrete*) in 1367, but lost the battle of *Montiel* (1369), and was murdered in De Guesclin's tent.

Enrique de Trastámara, as *Enrique II* (1369–79), was forced to grant concessions to the nobles in order to maintain his position, but was strong enough to refuse the demands of *John of Gaunt*, who claimed the throne through his wife, a daughter of Pedro the Cruel. *Juan I* (1379–90) legitimised his line by marrying his son (*Enrique III*, 1390–1406) to John of Gaunt's daughter. He also attempted to unite Portugal with Castile, but was beaten by the Portuguese at *Aljubarrota* in 1385. In 1391 there was a pogrom of Jews in Spain. *Juan II* (1406–54) preferred to leave the government of Castile in the hands of *Alvaro de Luna*, Grand Master of the Order of Santiago, who aimed at making the monarchy supreme. The refractory nobles were defeated at *Olmedo* (1445), but a later intrigue, supported by the queen, was successful, and the favourite was seized and executed (1453). *Enrique IV* (1454–74) was likewise faced with rebellion by the nobles, who proclaimed his brother Alfonso king, but a compromise was reached on Alfonso's death, when Enrique— ignoring his daughter *Juana ('La Beltraneja')*, whose legitimacy was disputed—named his sister *Isabel* heir to the throne. She refused to accept the crown during the lifetime of her brother, who, offended by her marriage with her cousin Fernando, heir of Aragón, annulled the pact and left the succession uncertain.

THE IBERIAN PENINSULA IN 1460

The Catholic Kings. The joint rule of *Isabel I of Castile* (died 1504), 'la Católica', and *Fernando V of Aragón* (died 1516), 'el Católico, partially unified the country: both kingdoms were considered of equal importance although their populations were very different. It has been estimated that in 1530 the population of Castile was 4,485,000; Aragón had 290,000 inhabitants, and Catalunya 312,000. By 1591 these had risen to 6,617,000, 348,000, and 373,000 respectively.

Civil war broke out between the partisans of 'La Beltraneja', whose claim was supported by the king of Portugal, but after the indecisive battle of *Toro* (1476) the Portuguese withdrew, leaving Fernando and Isabel firmly established. Numerous reforms were introduced, especially with regard to justice and legislation, and the revival of the *Santa Hermandad* constituted an effective police force which also formed the nucleus of a standing army. Although Councils were formed for the government of the kingdom, which met for consultation, the final decision rested with the sovereigns, and in accordance with the same centralising policy the grand-mastership of the military orders was vested in the crown. Royal revenues were reorganised, and encouragement was given to the *Mesta*, a powerful

guild of sheep owners. (The sheep had been crossbred with Moroccan sheep of the Banū Marīn, and were known for their 'merino' wool
as early as 1307.) A political and commercial treaty with England was
signed at Medina del Campo in 1489. The extreme bigotry of the
rulers and their ardour for the purity of the Catholic faith was attested
by the establishment of the Inquisition (in Castile in 1480; in Aragón
in 1487), which was to become another powerful and predatory arm
of the crown.

Once order had been established, the Catholic Kings turned their
attention to the conquest of the Nasrid kingdom of Granada, the only
surviving possession of the Moors in Spain. The subsequent war of
attrition lasted ten years, until, finally isolated, *Boabdil* capitulated,
and on 2 January 1492, the Catholic Kings entered Granada in
triumph. At first religious toleration was shown to the Moors, but
sterner measures were later advocated. In Castile, the MUDÉJARES
(Moors under Christian rule) were in 1502 confronted with the
alternative of accepting Christian baptism or expulsion. A similar
edict had been issued against the Jews in 1492, when between
150,000 and 400,000 were forced to abandon their country or suffered
persecution. The Moors who conformed were known as MORISCOS:
converted Jews were known as CONVERSOS, or New Christians;
those expelled from Spain (and from Portugal in 1497) were known
as SEFARDIES. An ostensibly Christianised Jew, but who was a
practising Jew in private or reverted to Judaism, was known as a
MARRANO.

In the same year as the conquest of Granada, the Genoese
navigator *Columbus* discovered America, thus opening a vast new
field for Spanish enterprise. In Europe, the foreign policy of the
Catholic Kings was to form strong alliances by skilfully arranged
marriages. *Isabel*, their eldest daughter, became queen of Portugal;
Juana, the second, married Felipe of Burgundy, son of the Habsburg
emperor Maximilian; *Catherine of Aragón*, the youngest, was the
first wife of Henry VIII of England. In 1494 Charles VIII of France
invaded Italy and took Naples. Later, the Spanish agreed to join the
French in dismembering the country, but quarrelled with them over
the division of territory.

The Spaniards, under the leadership of *Gonzalo de Córdoba (el
Gran Capitán)* were everywhere victorious, and Naples remained
under Spanish control. At the death of Isabel in 1504, her daughter
Juana (known as *la Loca*, 'the Mad'; 1479–1555) being considered
mentally unfit to rule and her son, *Carlos*, being only four years old,
Fernando of Aragón became regent. In 1512 Fernando took possession of southern Navarra, the territory to the N of the Pyrenees
passing to the House of Albret. As Carlos was not 20 years old, and in
Flanders, when his grandfather died, *Cardinal Cisneros* was
appointed regent of Spain, while *Adrian of Utrecht* (later Pope
Adrian VI) represented the young prince, who had shrewdly insisted
on being proclaimed king during the lifetime of his mother.

The House of Habsburg. On his accession, *Carlos I* (1516–56)—
perhaps better known as *Charles V*, and referred to as such in this
guide—inherited Flanders, the Low Countries, Artois, the Franche-
Comté, all the possessions of the crown of Aragón, and Castile,
together with the empire in America. Once comparatively isolated
from the rest of Europe, and almost exclusively occupied with its own
territorial problems, Spain now became the centre of European
politics, and after the election of Charles as Emperor in 1520 she was

linked for 36 years with the interests of the German Empire. Charles, born at Ghent, was a complete stranger to his Spanish subjects, and when he arrived in Spain in 1517 with a train of Flemish favourites, trouble soon ensued. The reign was disturbed first by the revolt of the COMUNEROS (1519–20), in which the 'cities' were supported by disaffected nobles. The insurgents under *Acuna, Bishop of Zamora*, and *Juan de Padilla* (1484–1521) came near to success against Adrian of Utrecht, but were subsequently defeated at *Villalar* (1521). Charles was then able to turn his attention against his rival, François I of France. Hostilities between them opened in Italy, where the campaign ended to the advantage of Charles, François being taken prisoner at *Pavia* (1525), but war with France continued intermittently until 1547. Meanwhile, perturbed by the growing influence of the Ottoman Turks, and by the activity of the Barbary pirates in the Mediterranean, Charles endeavoured to sever all contact between the Moors of N Africa with those still in the Peninsula, and in 1535 led a successful expedition to Tunis against Barbarossa; but an attempt to reduce Algiers six years later ended in disaster. Charles abdicated at Brussels in 1556, and passed the last two years of his life in the monastery of Yuste, near Plasencia, where he died.

Concurrently, the opening up of the New World progressed with astonishing rapidity. The bloody exploits of *Hernán Cortés* (1485–1547) in Mexico, and of *Francisco Pizarro* (1476–1541) in Peru in 1531–32, added extraordinary lustre to the reign. Chile was conquered by *Pedro de Valdivia* and *García de Mendoza*; Buenos Aires was founded in 1534. In 1519 the Portuguese navigator *Magellan* had set sail from S. Lucar with a fleet of five ships, and after doubling Cape Horn, reached the Philippines, where he was murdered by the natives; but one ship returned, commanded by *Sebastián Elcano*, the first to circumnavigate the world. This was also the age of *Sta. Teresa of Avila* (1515–82) and *S. Juan de la Cruz* (1542–91), both of *converso* descent.

Felipe II (1556–98), although free from the burdens of the German Empire, inherited many political problems including continued rivalry with France, and growing discontent in the Low Countries. Born at Valladolid, he was essentially a Spaniard. At first allied with England through his marriage with Mary Tudor (died 1558), possessing Milan and Naples, and with all the wealth of the Indies, he was in a most advantageous position when hostilities broke out in Italy. The seat of war was later transferred to the frontier of Flanders, where the Spaniards won notable victories at *St. Quentin* (1557) and at *Gravelines*. Peace was signed at *Cateau-Cambrésis* (1559), and Felipe married Elizabeth of Valois. The two main objects of his policy were to maintain his inheritance intact and to stamp out heresy. In 1559, leaving Flanders under the regency of Margaret of Parma, Felipe returned to Spain, which he never left again. In 1571 the Spaniards under *Don Juan of Austria*, Felipe's illegitimate half-brother, and the Genoese *Admiral Doria*, won a decisive victory over the Turkish fleet at *Lepanto*. In 1580, on the death of the aged Cardinal Henrique, king of Portugal, Felipe claimed the Portuguese crown through his mother, the eldest daughter of Manuel I. Meanwhile, the situation in the Low Countries grew more serious. At first the king paid little attention to the demands of his Flemish subjects, but when they reacted to his indifference by desecrating churches, the *3rd Duke of Alba* was sent to crush the rebellion. The introduction of a special tax caused members of both religions to unite to resist, supported by the Protestants of England, France, and Germany. The Northern

Provinces declared themselves an independent republic at The Hague in 1581, even if only recognised as such in 1609. The religious question, the assistance given to the insurgents, the unchecked piracy of English sea captains, together with Spanish plots in favour of Mary, Queen of Scots, led inevitably to war. Felipe decided to invade England. At great expense, an *Armada* was fitted out and was ready to sail in 1588, but incompetently led by *Medina Sidonia*, and encountering adverse weather, it fell an easy prey to the superior seamanship of the English, and the expedition ended in disaster.

During Felipe's reign the Moriscos also revolted. In spite of the milder measures proposed by *Mondéjar*, the king persisted in his intransigence, and in 1568 the Moriscos, after seeking the support of the king of Fez, prepared to resist in the Alpujarras and the mountains of Granada. Don *Juan of Austria*, after a difficult campaign, was able to suppress the rising in 1570 and the survivors were dispersed.

Felipe III succeeded his father in 1598, but preferred to leave the management of the State entirely in the hands of the *Duke of Lerma* (1553–1625), the first of a succession of unscrupulous royal favourites who were to exercise their baneful influence on Spain. In 1609 Philip decreed the expulsion of some 296,000 Moriscos (who comprised some 500,000 of the estimated total population of c 9,000,000), while the Thirty Years War in Germany, during which Spain supported the house of Austria, was an additional drain on its diminishing resources with no compensating benefits.

In 1596–1602 and in 1647–52 large parts of the country were decimated by plagues.

Felipe IV (1621–65) handed over the direction of affairs to the ambitious *Conde-Duque de Olivares* (1587–1645), who struggled to maintain the authority of the dynasty, but in spite of the victories of *Spinola* in the Low Countries, Spain was rapidly losing ground. In 1630 its hold over Italy was seriously undermined, and the victory of the French at *Rocroi* in 1643 destroyed the prestige of the Spanish infantry or *tercios*. In 1640 Olivares was faced with a serious rebellion in Catalunya, while in the same year Portugal, after 60 years of forced union, also revolted, and its subsequent separation from Spain hastened his downfall. The Catalans ostensibly capitulated in 1643, but it was not until 1659 that the province was completely pacified. By the *Treaty of the Pyrenees*, signed in that year on the marriage of the Infanta María Teresa with Louis XIV, the French king renounced all claims to the Spanish throne for his descendants, but the obligations undertaken by Spain were never completely carried out, and the treaty became a dead letter.

Felipe left one legitimate son, the sickly *Carlos II* (1665–1700), who succeeded at the age of four. The eleven years of his minority were disturbed by feuding between the regent Mariana of Austria and the king's half-brother Don Juan, while Carlos's marriage to Marie-Louise of Orléans caused equally bitter rivalry between the French and Austrian factions at court. On her death (1689), he married Maria of Neuburg. It seemed likely that the Austrian cause would triumph, but through the ability of d'Harcourt, the French Ambassador, Carlos, who was childless, was persuaded to bequeath his throne to Philippe, Duc d'Anjou, grandson of Louis XIV and María Teresa.

The House of Bourbon. With the accession of the Bourbons (or Borbones, as they are called in Spain) in 1700 there began a century during which Spain was to be dragged into nearly all the political conflicts of Europe. *Felipe V* (1700–46) entered Madrid in February 1701 without opposition, but the **War of the Spanish Succession** broke out in May 1702. The *Archduke Charles of Austria* invaded Spain, assisted by British troops commanded by *Peterborough, Galway*, and *Stanhope*, and naval forces commanded by *Rooke, Byng, Leake*, and *Shovel*. Gibraltar fell into British hands in 1704. The war was carried on with varying fortunes until the death of the emperor in 1711. At the *Peace of Utrecht* (1713) Felipe was recognised by the Powers as King of Spain. French methods and institutions were introduced, and a number of reforms were carried out. The *Duc de Saint-Simon* visited the court at Madrid in 1721–22, of which he left an amusing account.

But Spain was at a low ebb. The Church was still powerful, and in 1748 *Macanaz* was imprisoned for trying to curb its secular activities; even as late as 1778 *Olavide* was tried by the Inquisition. In an unenlightened age *Benito Feijóo* attacked the superstitious ignorance into which the Spanish people and clergy had fallen—for by then culture and Judaism had become synonymous terms—while any interest in scientific research was viewed with suspicion.

Fernando VI (1746–59) was succeeded by *Carlos III* (1759–88), who had been reigning in Naples, and the country enjoyed a period of comparative prosperity. Considerable improvements in the administration were made by a succession of able ministers, including *Aranda, Campomanes*, and later, *Floridablanca* and *Jovellanos*. In April 1767 the Jesuits, after decades of attempting to stifle any intellectual curiosity, were expelled from Spain, their schools abolished, and their revenues seized.

Between 1764 and 1821 some 70 Economic Societies (*Sociedades Económicas de Amigos de Amigos del País*) were established throughout the country. In the census of 1797, the population of Spain is given as 10,541,120, living in 21,120 *pueblos*; among them 168,248 secular and regular clergy; 181,321 employees in civil and military departments; 1,677,172 peasant farmers; 533,769 artisans; 25,685 merchants; 174,095 servants; 13,507 sick in public hospitals; 11,902 poor in hospices; and there were also c 400,000 who described themselves as 'nobles'; and anything from 100,000 to 140,000 vagrants.

Spain entered into a closer alliance with the Bourbons by a Family Compact in 1762, but was drawn again into intermittent war with England. However, it recovered Minorca and Florida at the *Peace of Versailles* (1783).

Among travellers from England during the latter half of the 18C, who wrote descriptions of the country were *Edward Clarke* (1760–61); *Joseph Baretti* (1760, and again in 1768–69); *Richard Twiss* (1773); *Henry Swinburne* (1775–76); and *Joseph Townsend* (1786–87).

Soon after *Carlos IV* (1788–1808) succeeded to the throne, Spain came into conflict with revolutionary France. Carlos and his minister Godoy—the favourite of *María Luisa*, his lascivious queen—were unable to save Louis XVI from the scaffold. Godoy, entitled 'Prince of the Peace' after his negotiations at the Peace of Basle (1795), was no match for Napoleon, and by degrees Spain was involved in Napoleonic schemes to the extent of active co-operation, which led, in 1805, to her fleet being shattered by *Nelson* at *Trafalgar*. Popular indignation led eventually to the overthrow of Godoy at Aranjuez (1808), which was followed by the abdication of Carlos IV. The royal family was decoyed to France. Meanwhile Murat was sent to Madrid, where, on 2 May 1808 ('el Dos de Mayo') he suppressed a popular rising with the utmost brutality. Napoleon's next step was to place his brother Joseph on the Spanish throne.

Meanwhile revolutionary *juntas* had been set up in the provinces, numerous pockets of resistance defied the French, and so commenced the sanguinary **Peninsular War**, known in Spain as the *War of Independence*. After their initial success at *Bailén*, the Spaniards carried on the war largely by guerrilla methods. At their invitation, a small British army under *Sir John Moore* entered Spain, but was forced back to *La Coruña* by *Soult* (1809). It was replaced by another expeditionary force commanded by *Wellesley*, known after the battle of *Talavera* (1809) as *Wellington*. In Spain, other famous battles of the war were those of *Fuentes de Oñoro* and *Albuera* (1811), *Salamanca* (1812), *Vitoria* and *Sorauren* (1813). The sieges of *Zaragoza* (1808 and 1809) and *Girona* (1809) are memorable for the extraordinary tenacity of the Spanish defenders. Later sieges of significance were those of *Badajoz* and *Ciudad Rodrigo* (both 1812) and *San Sebastián* (1813).

Meanwhile, the Spanish American colonies began to assert their independence, and one by one detached themselves from Spain. In 1812 the Cortes at Cádiz had enacted a constitution for a limited monarchial government, but on his restoration in 1814, this was repudiated by *Fernando VII*. He was more preoccupied in stifling all Liberal aspirations, and to this end his obnoxious administration enforced a rigid censorship, re-established the effete Inquisition, and readmitted the Jesuits. A revolt broke out in 1820 under *Gen. Riego*, and there followed a Liberal government until 1823, when Fernando was restored to power by the armed intervention of the French led by the *Duc d'Angoulême*. Fernando continued to persecute the Liberals and the country continued to suffer under his repressive absolutism until 1833. On Fernando's death, his brother *Don Carlos*, basing his claim to the throne on the Salic Law, contested the rights of his niece *Isabel II* (1833–68), then a child under the regency of her mother Cristina.

In the **First Carlist War**, the civil war which followed, Don Carlos was supported by the Church party, the reactionaries, and the Basques, whereas Cristina could rely on the Liberals and the army, but for some time the issue seemed doubtful. A British Auxiliary Legion, commanded by *de Lacy Evans*, also fought for Cristina in the Basque Provinces. The Carlists possessed some good guerrilla leaders, among whom were the ferocious *Cabrera* and *Zumalacárregui*, but eventually the Cristino generals *Espartero* and *Narváez* were able to bring the war to a successful conclusion after the *Treaty of Vergara* (1839). Cristina resigned the regency in 1840, and for three years the country was under the dictatorship of Espartero.

Literacy, merely 10 per cent in 1841, rose to 25 per cent in 1860, and progressively to 47 per cent by 1901. The population of Spain in 1857, according to the first official census, was 15,500,000.

Among English visitors to Spain during the post Peninsular War period were *Samuel Cook*, later *Widdrington* (1829–32, and again in 1843), *Richard Ford* (1830–33; author of the famous 'Hand-Book for Travellers in Spain', first edition published in 1845), and *George Borrow* (1836–40; author of 'The Bible in Spain').

In 1843 *Isabel II* was declared of age, but the remainder of her reign was a period of political confusion and constitutional crises. The conservative policy of Narváez was followed by the liberal régime of *O'Donnell*. The government, being at the mercy of any *pronunciamiento*, was unstable, and popular dissatisfaction increased. In 1868, when *Prim* and other liberal generals raised a rebellion in the South, the queen was forced to abdicate. After a brief interregnum, *Amadeus of Savoy* was invited to the throne, but abdicated three years later, in 1878. For a short period Spain tried the experiment of a Republic (1874–75), but anarchy in the South made it impossible for the successive presidents, *Pi y Margall*, *Salmerón*, and *Castelar*, to carry their progressive theories into practice.

Meanwhile the **Second Carlist War** had broken out in the North, but by a *pronunciamiento* at Sagunto, *Martínez Campos* restored the Bourbon dynasty in the person of *Alfonso XII* (1874–85), the eldest son of Isabel. In 1876 a new constitution was formed, establishing a limited monarchy with power vested in two chambers. Alfonso died in 1885, leaving the country under the regency of *María Cristina*. During this period of comparative calm Spain was ruled by the alternating governments of the conservatives under *Cánovas del Castillo* and the radicals under *Sagasta*. In 1898, as a result of the war with the United States of America, Cuba, the Philippines, and Porto Rico were lost to Spain. At this time the Spanish army had one general for every 100 men. *Alfonso XIII* was declared of age in 1902, and the alternating party system continued, with the conservative ministries of *Silvela*, *Maura*, and *Dato*, and the radical ministries of *Canalejas* and *Romanones*.

During the Great War of 1914–18 Spain remained neutral. In 1921 an insurrection broke out under *Abd-el-Krim* in the Riff, a Spanish protectorate, which was not brought under control until 1926. Meanwhile, in 1923, *Gen. Primo de Rivera* had established a military dictatorship, abolished the Cortes, and governed with a council of ministers. Although there was an increase in material prosperity, the imposition of a strict censorship of the press caused deep dissatisfacton, especially among the intellectuals, and opposition to the regime increased.

Although various attempts to supplant the dictators failed, the devious and hostile attitude of the king made his fall inevitable, and he was compelled to resign in 1930, and died soon after. But support for the crown also disintegrated rapidly, and new political factions began to take shape: the Liberal Republican Right was founded by *Alcalá Zamora*, while the Socialists were grouped under *Largo Caballero*. The result of the municipal elections of April 1931 were indeed largely anti-monarchist, and upon the proclamation of a republican régime in Barcelona, Sevilla, and other centres, Alfonso acceded to Alcalá Zamora's demand that he should abdicate.

The **Civil War**. A *Constituent Assembly* was elected and empowered with the function of drawing up a new constitution, which was completed and ratified in December 1931, when Alcalá Zamora was duly elected president of the Republic. Meanwhile, Catalunya had declared itself independent of the Madrid government and proclaimed itself a republic, while strong movements in favour of home rule sprang up in the Basque Provinces and in Galicia. The rigorous reforms introduced by the Constituent Assembly provoked discontent, and resulted in the formation of various conflicting parties, notably Acción Popular and Acción Católica, which greatly contributed to the undermining of the strength of the regime. Recent research has also confirmed that political activists of the Spanish Church were also very largely responsible for fomenting the later rebellion against the government. Long-overdue reforms affecting the structure of the army, introduced by the Minister for War *Manuel Azaña*, aroused resentment among the officers. In spite of sweeping agrarian reforms, and a new Law of Labour Contracts brought in by Largo Caballero, such measures did little to appease the various factions.

A general state of unrest accompanied by widespread strikes set in throughout the country. An insurrection in Sevilla sponsored by *Gen. Sanjurjo* was quickly suppressed. A far more serious rebellion of miners and workers flared up in the Asturias in October 1934 and, after much loss of life and damage, the movement was brutally stamped out by *Gen. López Ochoa* and *Col. Yagüe*, directed from Madrid by *Gen. Francisco Franco* (1892–1975). After the elections of February 1936 Azaña again became Prime Minister: Alcalá Zamora was compelled to resign and was succeeded as president by Azaña with *Casares Quiroga* as Prime Minister. But disorders became increasingly frequent, and numerous strikes virtually paralysed normal activity. The imprisonment of *José Antonio Primo de Rivera*, son of the late dictator and leader of a militant right-wing organisation, the *Falange*, and the assassination of the monarchist leader *Calvo Sotelo*, increased the tension between the rival parties.

On 17 July 1936 the garrison in Morocco rebelled under the leadership of *Gen. Franco*, and this was followed by military risings against the government throughout the country—notably under *Gen. Queipo de Llano* in Sevilla and by *Gen. Mola* in Pamplona. Franco captured Algeciras with airborne troops, and within a short time, after subjugating Badajoz and Mérida with his legionaries and 'moros' he was able to join forces with Mola, but the intended attack on Madrid was delayed in order to relieve the beleaguered *alcázar* at Toledo.

Although at first the European powers had agreed to adopt an attitude of non-intervention, arms and equipment poured into Spain from all sides, and soon the Civil War ceased to be a strictly national affair. The right-wing Nationalists received considerable military aid from Nazi Germany and Fascist Italy, both in men (c 17,000 and 75,000 respectively) and material, while the Republican government obtained equipment from Communist Russia and manpower in the form of 'International Brigades' (some 35,000, including c 2000–3000 Russians). After the initial successes of the Nationalists, the territories held by the two sides were roughly equal in extent.

Gen. Franco installed himself by a 'coup d'état' as Head of State, confirmed 'by decree' at Burgos on 1 October, while on 20 November José Antonio was shot at Alicante. Although it retained Madrid (which was to be defended to the last), Valencia, Barcelona, Murcia, Almería, Alicante, Santander, and Bilbao, the government withdrew to Valencia. Largo Caballero was ousted to make way for *Negrín*, while by now Azaña was virtually a prisoner in the hands of Communist extremists. Vigorous attempts made by Franco to storm the capital and cut the Madrid–Valencia road failed. After the capture of Málaga in February 1937 the Italian brigades launched a lightning attack on Guadalajara, only to be routed, but in the North, shortly after the bombing of Guernica by the German Condor Legion on 26 April, Bilbao and Santander fell. At the end of the year Republican government troops entered Teruel, which was recaptured by Franco in February 1938. In the July of that year Republican forces attacked with success along the Ebro and were able to maintain important strategic positions until November, but fell back before Franco's counter-thrust into Catalunya, Barcelona capitulating the following January. Shortly after these events the situation in Madrid became desperate. *Col. Casado*, commander of the central forces, was in favour of opening negotiations with Franco, but *Gen. Miaja*, insisted that opposition should continue, although by the end of March 1939 organised armed resistance had ceased. Pope Pius XII sent the dictator a telegram in which he 'thanked God' for 'Spain's Catholic victory'.

Although some 50,000 civilians had been killed by the Nationalists during the first six months of the war alone, once the conflict was over vindictive reprisals followed under a series of bloodthirsty police chiefs and military governors. Franco showed as heinous a lack of magnaminity as had his revengeful Nationalists at the fall of any town or village, when barbaric proscriptions were the order of the day; but—to quote the late Gerald Brenan—'in class wars it is the side that wins, that kills most'. In addition, some two million Republicans were to pass through concentration camps or prisons during the next three years alone, in the process of '*limpieza*' (cleaning up) or extirpating the 'unclean heresies of liberalism, socialism, communism, anarchism, and freemasonry' (Hugh Thomas, whose 'The Spanish Civil War' is essential reading).

During the war the Republicans had for their part executed c 55,000 'fascists' in an attempt to stem the tide of totalitarianism. Among them, such was the anticlericalism which had been engendered, were some 6832 religious, including 12 bishops, 4184 priests, 2365 monks, and 283 nuns (of the 60,000 nuns then in Spain).

Not directly involved in the Second World War, Spain was able to attend to its disrupted internal affairs undisturbed. Corruption was rife, the *estraperlo* (black market) flourished, and there was much suffering. However, Franco was able to withstand German pressure (interview with Hitler at Hendaye, 23 October 1941), and apart from the anti-Communist gesture of sending the 'Blue Division' to fight against Russia, Spain was able to remain in a state of non-belligerency; indeed it was too weak to do otherwise.

The new regime maintained order by authoritarian methods, which in the course of decades were progressively relaxed, although there was little political freedom as understood by Western democracies. Only one party, known as the '*Movimiento*', was permitted, and various forms of censorship were rigidly enforced. By a Law of Succession, Franco continued as head of state (*caudillo*), governing with a Council of the Realm. The *Cortes*, consisting of a single chamber composed ostensibly of representatives of the main national institutions, including the Catholic Church, the universities, professional syndicates, labour unions, etc., was reintroduced in 1942. In 1956, independence was granted to Spanish Morocco, which in 1957 itself appropriated Spanish Sahara.

In 1969 *Juan Carlos*, grandson of Alfonso XIII (who had died in Rome in 1941), was nominated heir to the vacant throne, an expedient considered anachronistic by some, but which met with the approbation of others as being preferable to the alternatives. In December 1973 *Adm. Carrero Blanco*, the reactionary President of the Government, was assassinated by ETA. After a valedictory exhibition of inflexibility in convicting impatient 'extremists' without any proper trial (at Burgos; 1970), and again in August 1975, which exposed him to the execration of the world, Gen. Franco died in November 1975.

Juan Carlos was invested with the trappings of sovereignty after an interregnum of almost 45 years. He was accepted by the populace in general, knowing the monarchy to be limited. The myth of the senile dictator being the saviour of his country very rapidly evaporated, his fly-blown portraits being replaced overnight by the new Head of State. Juan Carlos has maintained his popularity (particularly after 23 February 1981).

Fraga Iribarne, the heavy-handed minister of the interior in Arias Navarro's government, fulminated against all forms of opposition, but in December 1976 a referendum overwhelmingly confirmed the wish of the much-abused Spanish people for political reform. Press censorship was lifted in April 1977, and in June of that year the first general election for over 40 years returned a government professing to be 'of the Centre'. Nevertheless, demands for political amnesty were only partly granted. Eventually a measure of autonomy was conceded to Catalunya, and—to a more limited extent—to the Basque Provinces. The latter had long been humiliated by repressive measures too rigorously enforced by the military and police. Few tears were shed when the more aggressive members of these forces were assassinated by the militant group known as ETA (*Euzkadi Ta Azkatasuna*, or Freedom for the Basques), which surfaced as early as 1967, and with whom a high proportion of Basques were in sympathy, although perhaps less so when they started demanding funds to further their activities.

Meanwhile such fanatic organisations as the ultra-Right *Fuerza Nueva* and GRAPO, suspected of being infiltrated by *agents provocateurs*, endeavoured to destabilise the country by behaving in an obnoxious and irresponsible fashion rather than coming to terms with reality.

The government of *Adolfo Suarez* was returned to power (but with less enthusiasm) in March 1979 under the new 'Democratic' Constitution, with a strong Socialist opposition. It still governed 'by decree'. The voting age had meanwhile been lowered to 18. The general election of October 1982 proved a landslide victory of the Socialist party (PSOE), under the leadership of *Felipe Gonzalez* aided by Alfonso Guerra, his mordant deputy, with *Manuel Fraga Iribarne* in opposition as leader of Alianza Popular. Meanwhile the country had been rocked by the abortive coup of 23 February 1981, engineered by *Col Antonio Tejero* of the Guardia Civil and *Gen. Milans del Bosch*, among other military conspirators who had attempted to implicate the king in their insensate plot. Any tarnished prestige the Armed Forces may have enjoyed under the dictatorship rapidly plummeted, and demands were made to reduce their numbers: in 1980 there had been over 400 generals in active service. The influence of the para-ecclesiastical 'Opus Dei', which had too long followed its devious course, and of the Church itself, is progressively weakening. Progressive forces are slowly attempting to drag the country out of the intellectual, economic and political desert left behind by Franco, and in January 1986 Spain, which in so many fields had for so long lagged behind the rest of Europe, joined the European Economic Community. Much lost time has to be made up before full integration is achieved and one may say with more reason: 'Il n'y a plus des Pyrénées'.

Whether the present and future governments will be able to harness the not inconsiderable powers of the Spains—now again fragmented by the establishment of numerous autonomies, not all of which may prove viable—remains to be seen: it has never been an easy task. As Edward Clarke astutely observed in 1763: in Spain they travelled in a 'clumsy coach, drawn by six mules, with *ropes* instead of traces', and 'as the last two only are reined, or rather roped, they run on with the coach with their heads pointing four or five different ways. This is but a trifling circumstance, yet even the merest trifles may sometimes serve to shew the turn and genius of a people'.

The first official visit to Spain of a reigning British monarch was made by Elizabeth II in October 1988. (Charles I, when Prince of Wales, made an unofficial—and what was at first an incognito—visit to Madrid from March to October 1623, in an abortive attempt to conclude negociations to marry the infanta María. He was indulged in cripplingly expensive festivities, but the difficulties encountered in ironing out the religious differences proved insurmountable.)

INTRODUCTION TO SPANISH ARCHITECTURE

Compared with Spain, few countries have preserved so much evidence of their medieval greatness. Its artistic patrimony has survived comparatively unscathed, and an immense number of fine churches, castles, and palaces remain, although many buildings have suffered from neglect, which has probably caused more loss than the ravages of war. For although Spain's history has been stormy, and the Napoleonic invasion robbed it of many more portable treasures, it has been spared upheavals comparable to the Protestant Reformation or the French Revolution, as well as both World Wars. Even the Civil War did surprisingly little damage to ancient buildings, although there were some serious losses, such as at Sigena, and at Alcalá de Henares. It has been estimated that only 150 churches were entirely destroyed and about 1850 others seriously damaged. Whether many of these had sufficient architectural merit for their destruction to be considered a cultural loss rather than a loss to the cult is a matter of speculation.

Spain, partly for climatic reasons, is almost a continent in itself. While the storks of the chilly north cling obstinately to the chimneys of the Escorial, and an icy wind beats against the soaring pinnacles of the cathedral at León, the narrow winding streets of Toledo, the troglodyte villages near Guadix, and the sun-scorched, flat-roofed, mud-built houses of the south are purely African. In Spain, the meeting point of Christian and Moslem civilisations, one will find, built at the same time, such masterpieces as the Pórtico de la Gloria at Santiago de Compostela, a superb example of late Romanesque, and the Giralda at Sevilla, one of the finest minarets in existence; while among the many other Moorish relics the Mezquita at Córdoba and the Alhambra at Granada are world famous.

Moorish Spain possessed a higher civilisation than Christian Spain: Córdoba, the capital, was one of the largest cities in the world, and the centre of a tradition, both cultural and material, compared with which the level of the Christians in the north was almost barbarous. Nevertheless, the story of Christian architecture in Spain is equally fascinating. In the first place, in the 9–10C, in almost the only corner left to them in the Peninsula, the rulers of the kingdom of the Asturias produced in and around Oviedo a number of remarkable little churches and other buildings the like of which is to be found in no other country. They are far superior to contemporary Saxon work in Britain or to anything of that date in France. In the period immediately following, Spain should no longer be thought of as merely two countries divided by race and religion, for Christian Spain was subdivided into several states with constantly changing frontiers open to various influences from abroad. Thus, while a slowly decreasing portion of southern Spain remained Moslem for over 700 years, and open only to African or Near Eastern influences, for some four centuries Castile and the north in general became architecturally a French province, while Catalunya looked to Italy for inspiration and itself became a centre of a traditional style spreading into Languedoc.

The position has been well summed up in the phrase: 'The art of Spain is alluvial'—implying not only that waves of foreign influence broke upon her shore, left their impress and receded, but also that the Spaniards failed to take advantage of the new learning. It is certainly true that French monasteries dictated the usual sequence of Romanesque and Gothic, while later, Renaissance, Mannerist, and Baroque, were imported from Italy, largely through the influence of architectural treatises. It is also true that in no other Western country were so many foreign artists employed. In the 12th and 13Cs their names usually proclaim them as French. By the 14C, Frenchmen, Burgundians, Flemings, Germans, Italians, and even a few Englishmen—skilled architects, sculptors, ironworkers, glass-workers, or silversmiths—jostled one another in the race to supply this 'new' country with expert techniques. In the Renaissance and later ages, first Italians and then Frenchmen formed the bulk of these foreign technicians, while many Spaniards went to Italy for instruction.

The Spaniards, with a peculiar and immensely vital creative spirit of their own, inevitably found a way to adapt and modify the various styles imported, which soon became characteristically Spanish. No one, standing in the cathedrals of Burgos or Toledo, whose interiors are predominantly French, could suppose he was anywhere but in Spain. Spanish Renaissance and Baroque also have a flavour very different from the Renaissance and Baroque of Italy.

The Spanish were intensely conservative in architecture. This is due, perhaps, not so much to a question of temperament as to the subdivision of the Peninsula into disunited provinces, separated from each other by arid wildernesses and mountain ranges, both thinly populated, and to the subsequent extreme difficulties of contact and transport in so vast a country. Whatever the precise explanation, fashion in architecture changed very slowly and, once implanted, underwent little spontaneous or conscious development. This is most noticeable with Romanesque, which survived for more than three centuries, and long after the introduction of Gothic. Here one cannot resist the conclusion that most Spaniards, not without reason, felt that Gothic, developing towards walls of glass, was wholly unsuited to a country of blinding sunlight. But when Gothic was supplanted by Renaissance, they were equally loath to change—for example, the Gothic cathedrals at Salamanca and Segovia were not begun until well into the 16C, the latter only being finished in 1592, seven years after the completion of the Escorial, a monument of the High Renaissance.

This was further complicated by the existence of two hybrid styles peculiar to Spain: firstly, the *Mozarabic*, brought by Christian refugees fleeing from persecution in Cordoba, whose beautiful mosque-like churches, founded on the great *mezquita* in their former home, comprise one of the most curious chapters in Western art. Their horseshoe and lobed arches were even reproduced in France before the style was cut off in its prime by Cluniac Romanesque. The second hybrid, *Mudéjar*, is a whole family of styles, regional and chronological, brought to Christian Spain as the reconquest developed by captured Moslems and their descendants who stayed on in their native towns after surrendering, or who, as artisans and workmen particularly skilled as bricklayers, plasterers, and carpenters, migrated, in some cases, to the north. Their style of work, although originating mainly in pure Moorish building, is usually blended, according to period and region, with Romanesque, Gothic, or Renaissance. The precise degree of blend differs in almost every building and has a charm entirely its own. It appealed so much to the Christians that several of even the greatest 15th and 16C architects and decorators—foreigners as well as Spaniards—succumbed to its spell and included typically Moorish elements in their designs. It is thus because of Mudéjar that one finds obvious Moorish workmanship and taste in northern Spain, e.g. in the vaulting, plasterwork, and ceilings at Las Huelgas at Burgos. Mudéjar likewise explains the curiously Arabic appearance of Toledo, although in Christian hands since 1085. And to this day, in almost the whole of Aragón, Moorish taste, as translated for us by the Mudéjars, is still the dominant feature of the landscape; indeed the national taste is perhaps more deeply permeated with this tradition than is often willingly admitted.

Spanish buildings undoubtedly possess a unique 'atmosphere'. The essential characteristics can be summarised as follows: first, a predilection for solidity of construction: hence, the heaviness and austerity of Spanish Romanesque together with its long duration; hence, too, the massiveness of the Herreran, much of the Baroque, the Neo-Classic, and domestic architecture throughout.

Secondly, a curious partiality for square blocks: buildings as lofty and wide only as they are long, or precisely twice the length of their height and width. Or again, a preference for squareness in decoration; for instance, rectangular frames for anything, such as octagons, equilateral triangles, stars, and round-headed arches, that can be fitted into a square. Such proportions lead to a sense of calm and repose, an absence of fussiness in even the most ornate and ostentatious interiors. This squareness, noticeable in the Alhambra, in many Renaissance works, and in all forms of decoration, is the very antithesis of French Gothic with its emphasis on the vertical. It accounts for what might be called Horizontal Spanish Gothic, for the solid squareness of Spanish towers, for twin windows arranged in pairs (*ajimez*) and for the characteristic square dripstone (*alfiz*) over doorways.

Thirdly, an inclination to divide a space into compartments. Long, uninterrupted vistas do not appeal to Spaniards. Whether in the Alhambra, in churches, or in lengthy rooms, such vistas are broken up by series of columns, by screens or curtains, and alcoves become a predilection. Hence too, perhaps, the custom of alternating the barest plain surfaces with squares or bands of rich surface decoration, as in Moslem work, and in low relief, as in Isabelline and Plateresque.

Finally, a curious tendency towards hanging decoration. It originates, possibly, from Moslem stalactite ceilings and fringed arches; it appears in veritable tapestries of stone, stucco, or marble hanging from ceilings, vaults, and domes. Again, ornament seems to hang with no visible support from carved altarpieces, from façades and portals. Examples include the 16C façades of *S. Gregorio*, Valladolid, the *University* at Salamanca, and the Baroque *Hospicio de S. Fernando*, Madrid.

To generalise, perhaps the most striking feature is contrast: austerity with exuberance; massive stone buildings decorated with lacelike plasterwork; the simple grandeur of plain surfaces contrasted with sumptuous and extravagant decoration. It is true also that one finds a certain theatrical exaggeration and ostentation: exaggerated formality in the Herreran and Neo-Classic; exaggerated ornament in Late Gothic and Plateresque; and pure sensationalism in the Churrigueresque. There is no denying that for rich, and even sumptuous effects Spanish architecture has no parallel, and it also has unrivalled dignity.

Roman and pre-Romanesque. The history of architecture in Spain begins in Roman days, although the Cossetani, an Iberian tribe, are remembered for their cyclopean walls of unhewn stone at *Tarragona*, and the Greeks have left vestiges of colonies of the 6C BC at *Empúries* and elsewhere on the Levant coast. In comparison with earlier civilisations the Romans are well represented, although remains are scarce considering the importance and duration of their dominion. The best preserved are those for which succeeding ages found a use. Temples and theatres fell into ruin, but engineering works were constantly repaired and long served their original purpose. The aqueduct at *Segovia* is, with the possible exception of the Pont du Gard, the finest Roman aqueduct surviving. Others are seen at *Tarragona* and at *Mérida*, and smaller ones at *Almuñécar*, and between Sevilla and Alcalá de Guadira. *Mérida* is a complete Roman city, with a theatre (its proscenium now completely rebuilt), and amphitheatre, a trimphal arch, the longest bridge in the Roman Empire, a circus, a stadium, an artifical reservoir, and temples dedicated to Diana and Mars. Amphitheatres or theatres are also to be seen at *Itálica*, *Tarragona*, *Clunia* (Coruña del Conde), and *Ronda*. That at Itálica was, after the Colosseum, the largest in the Empire, but the best preserved is at *Sagunto*. City walls remain at *Tarragona*, *Astorga*, and *Lugo*; there are remains of a bridge at *Martorell*, and other works at *Barcelona*, *Valencia*, and *Vic*. The bridge spanning the Tagus at *Alcántara* is one of the most remarkable examples of civil engineering and the loftiest Roman bridge in existence. There remain also a few triumphal arches such as that at *Medinaceli*, and the *Arco de Bará* near Tarragona. Mausoleums exist at *Tarragona*, *Fabara* (near Caspe), and *Sádaba*. Inevitably these buildings were pillaged by later builders, and Roman columns and capitals became normal features in almost all pre-Romanesque churches.

The **Visigoths**, with their close relations with the Near East, brought to Spain a medley of influences. Traffic in small objects, particularly consular ivories, had some effect upon Visigothic decoration, but local constructional ideas were in part based upon monuments in Persia, Syria, and the N coast of Africa, at this time Christian (Arian), and in part upon Roman works they found in Spain. They were also conversant with contemporary works in Italy. There are remains of 5C baptisteries at *Gabia la Grande* (Granada) and at *Centelles* (Tarragona), but the best example is that now called *S. Miquel* at *Terrassa*, which recalls both Roman work and early Christian buildings at Ravenna.

Examples of Visigothic sculpture may be found at the old museum at *Mérida*, housing lintels, pilasters, and bands of ornament of typical decadent Roman type, some of them markedly Eastern Roman rather than Western. Here one finds the earliest *ajimez* or twin horseshoe window in Spain, with the lights divided by a colonnette, as well as the 'Maltese' cross, helices, stars, and the 'cable border', all of which are regarded as the most characteristic features of Visigothic ornamentation. It was not the Moslems who introduced the horseshoe arch into Spain, although they adopted it, modified it, eventually giving it a point, and used it almost to the exclusion of all other forms. It is to be found (always round-headed) as a decoration on nearly 60 Spanish Roman stelae of the 2nd to 5Cs, and the Visigoths, owing to their contact with the Near East, where it was known as early as 300 BC, used it constructionally and also in plan. But there is a subtle difference between the Visigothic and Moorish horseshoe, which is highly technical and has been explained in several conflicting ways, but is fairly obvious to the eye, for the Moorish horseshoe appears to be carried down further, and therefore to be more 'pinched' at the base than the Visigothic. One of the finest Visigothic churches is that of *S. Juan* at *Baños de Cerrato* (Palencia), although it contains little in decoration that foreshadows Moslem taste beyond tiny horseshoe windows and a nave arcade of slightly horseshoe arches. They spring from bastard Corinthian capitals and Roman columns taken from the neighbouring baths, and it appears that the whole interior of the church was originally veneered with marble. Of other Visigothic churches one need only mention four: the crypt of *Palencia Cathedral*, possibly built in 673; *Sta. Comba de Bande*, remotely situated in the province of Ourense; *S. Pedro de la Nave*, near Zamora; and *N.S. de las Viñas* at Quintanilla de Lara, near Salas de los Infantes.

Asturian. In the 8C nearly all Spain was in Moslem hands, but in Galicia and in the Asturias, shielded from the invaders by the Cantabrian mountains, the Christians reorganised their forces and set up a kingdom with Oviedo as their capital. Here, in a concentrated area, they erected a group of pre-Romanesque buildings of the highest interest. In style, they continue the Visigothic tradition, with debased classical ornament, but carved in a a manner perhaps even more rustic than that used by the Visigoths themselves. The earliest of these are the Cámera Santa, now incorporated into the *Cathedral* at *Oviedo*, and *S. Julián de los Prados*, or *Santullano*, both built by an architect named Tioda for Alfonso the Chaste (791–842), while from the reign of Ramiro I (842–50) there remain *S. Miguel de Lillo*, and *Sta. María de Naranco*, originally perhaps a royal hunting lodge, just outside Oviedo. Among later Asturian buildings should be mentioned *Sta. Cristina de Lena* (912), *S. Salvador de Valdedios* and *S. Salvador de Priesca*. One may well inquire how so vital and robust a style should have come to an untimely and sudden end. The answer is that with the moving of the capital from Oviedo to León, and the increasing importance of regions easily accessible from France, the importation of French Romanesque soon stifled it. But first there came an artistic invasion from the south.

Mozarabic. For over a hundred years after the Moorish invasion, the Christians of S Spain were permitted to keep their religion, to elect bishops, and to build churches. They spoke Arabic, dressed as Moors, and they assimilated Moorish culture. Unfortunately, there now survives, it seems, only two churches thus built under Moslem domination: *Sta. María de Melque*, near S. Martín de Montalbán (SW of Toledo), and *Bobastro*, N of *Alora* (Málaga). All other examples of Mozarabic architecture are the work of refugees who fled from Córdoba in the 9–10C to Aragón, Galicia, the Asturias, and León, and they naturally brought with them the style of architecture of their former home. This exodus of 'arabised' Christians had the effect of enriching the N of Spain, where the finest examples of their art are to be found, and not, as one would expect, in the S. They vary greatly in type, but nearly all include features borrowed direct from the Mezquita at Córdoba, and the typically Moorish horseshoe arch is almost universal both in construction and decoration. It is used in the nave arcades, which are often supported on monolithic columns with 'broken palm-leaf' capitals, and the chancel arches (also horseshoe) are usually copies from *mihrab* fronts; while the sanctuaries, horseshoe in plan and roofed with 'melon' domes, are copies from the mihrab itself. Other domes have parallel ribs as in the *maqsurah* at Córdoba, and windows and doorways are framed with the typical Moorish rectangular label known as an *alfiz*. Wooden roofs are often supported on curious corbels or eaves brackets decorated with stars and helices. One of the most accessible of these churches is *S. Miguel de Escalada*, SE of León, consecrated in 913. Other striking examples are *S. Cebrián de Mazote* (Valladolid), and *Sta. María de Bamba*; *Santiago de Peñalba*, and *Sto. Tomás de las Ollas*, near Ponferrada; *S. Miguel de Celanova*, S of Ourense, and *Sta. María de Lebeña*, near Potes. In Catalunya, there remain the less striking examples of *S. Quirze de Pedret*, *Sta. María de Marquet*, and *S. Miquel de Olérdola*, all of them 10C. More interesting are those in Castile, namely *S. Millán de la Cogolla*, and *S. Baudel*, near Berlanga del Duero. Small decorative features of Mozarabic art, such as lobed arches and miniature horseshoe arches, occasionally persisted in Spanish Romanesque, and are found in Southern France in buildings, for instance at Le Puy, and in Limoges enamels, while Mozarabic manuscripts were to influence French manuscript painting almost until the Gothic period. It is noticeable how many modern Spanish words concerning buildings are of Arab derivation, apart from the builder (*albañil*), and architect (*alarife*) themselves. Houses were often made of sun-dried bricks (*adobe*), adorned with blue tiles (*azulejos*), with terraces (*azoteas*), alcoves (*alcobas*), portico (*zaguán*), and provided with culverts (*alcantarillas*) and water conduits (*algibes*), etc.

Moorish Architecture Islamic or Moslem art covered a larger area of the world than medieval Christianity, and had as many subdivisions, including such well-defined regional variations as the Syrian, the Egyptian, the Persian, the Ottoman, the Indian, and the Moroccan. But to only two of these belong the so-called Moorish buildings in Spain. The first style, as shown at Córdoba, originates primarily from buildings in Syria, Egypt, and on the N coast of Africa. The second style, as shown in the Alhambra, is that of the Maghreb, which included Tunisia and Algeria as well as Morocco and Southern Spain. The Alhambra is in fact the principal monument of the Maghreb.

Art of the Caliphate. Once the invaders of the early 8C, Berbers and Arabs, settled down in the land of their adoption, Córdoba became the capital of the Western Moslem world. It soon rivalled Baghdad and Constantinople in the splendour of its monuments, and was in fact, after the latter, the largest town in Europe, with a population estimated at between 500,000 and a million. Its bronze founders, gold- and silversmiths, and ivory carvers produced some exquisite work which is still preserved in the treasuries of Spanish cathedrals and the principal museums of Europe and America. There was a direct trade in textiles and pottery with Baghdad (such textiles being also imported from Andalucía by the Christian monarchs of the north), while Near Eastern pottery exercises an influence upon Spanish peasant pottery to this day.

The importance of Córdoba stems from the fact that in 756 Abderrahman made a deliberate attempt to fix the religious centre of Islam in the West, after breaking away from the Baghdad Caliphate. Architecturally, the *Mezquita* or Mosque of Córdoba incorporated a number of audacious constructional features, based chiefly on Damascus and Kairawan (in Tunisia), among which may be mentioned first the double rows of arches supporting the wooden roof; all of them of ultra-semicircular horseshoe form, and of white stone alternating with red brick. Secondly should be noted the 10C innovations in the *maqsurah* or vestibule of three bays in front of the *mihrab*; these include intersecting arches, lobed and multifoil arches, true composite piers and lofty domical vaults with massive coupled ribs intersecting to form star patterns in the centre. All these features eventually found their way into Christian Spain, where in both Romanesque and Gothic one can continue to trace their descendants for centuries. Similar vaulting, but on a diminutive scale, can be seen in the miniature mosque in Toledo which was converted on the recapture of the city into *Sto. Cristo de la Luz*.

The only great civil monument of this period, the summer palace of the Caliphs at *Medina Azahara*, just W of Córdoba, was destroyed in the 11C, but recent discoveries and reconstructions show that its decoration was quite as rich as anything in the mosque. Among other surviving monuments may be mentioned the sovereign's private mosque in the *Aljafería* at *Zaragoza*, with various richly decorated halls (under restoration). On the decline of the Caliphate and the rise of the warring *taifa* kingdoms, much rebuilding of city walls took place. These usually consisted of a double enceinte, and the towers, square or polygonal, were built either of stone, brick, or cement encrusted with pebbles, and the crenellations are of a distinctive Moorish type. To this epoch we owe much of the surviving fortifications of Córdoba, Sevilla, Almería, Jaén, Ronda, Málaga, and the castle of Alcalá de Guadiara.

Art of the Maghreb. With the coming of the Almohades (1147–1235), the capital was transferred temporarily to Sevilla, and we fortunately retain from this period the *Giralda*. With its trellis-like diaper of pink brickwork (reminiscent of Marrakesh and Rabat in Morocco), this is by far the finest minaret not only in Spain, but in the whole Maghreb. According to tradition, Fernando III, during the siege of Sevilla of 1248, threatened the Moorish population with annihilation if one brick of the Giralda was loosened. On the fall of Sevilla, Moslem Spain became concentrated in the kingdom of Granada. Pleasure and repose rather than vitality became the keynote of their style, and their monuments show them to have been ornamentalists rather than architects. Even the late 12C *Patio del Yeso* surviving from the original Sevilla *Alcázar* already exhibits the arabesque and stucco decoration typical of the Alhambra. Henceforward the Andalusian interiors are as sumptuous as their exteriors, for fear of the Evil Eye, are bare. The walls of the *Alhambra* (1232–1408), embroidered in plaster, hung with gesso tapestries below delicate stalactical pendendives and surrounded by dados of richly coloured *azulejos*, produce an insinuating sensation of splendour and voluptuousness rarely experienced in occidental buildings.

Romanesque Architecture By the end of the 9C **Catalunya** had developed close contact with Languedoc, Provence, and N Italy, and it is here that the earliest Romanesque churches in the Peninsula are to be found. There remain at least 75, but most are small, aisleless, built of undressed masonry and roofed with timber, and they have little sculpture. Where aisles occur, single columns or plain rectangular piers support equally plain round-headed arches. Their exteriors are distinguished by Lombard blind arcading and pilasters, and by tall square belfries, also typically Italian. Fine examples survive at *S. Miquel de Cuxá* (1040), *Breda*, and *S. Miquel de Fluvià*. There are also examples of unorthodox planning, such as trefoil-shaped apses, while stone barrel vaults were already known before 950 and certain vaulting improvements seem to have been made before their adoption in either France or Italy. The five-aisled basilica of *Ripoll*, with its worn but richly sculptured W doorway, is the largest example of the style. Others are *S. Vicente de Cardona* and *S. Llorenc del Munt*, with their typically Lombard polygonal cupolas. In neighbouring Aragón, the castle and chapel of *Loarre*, and the monastic church of *Leyre*, are also important. Indeed sculpture plays an integral part in later Catalan Romanesque. There are many fine 12C cloisters, for example at the *Cathedral* and *S. Pere de Galligants* at *Girona*, *S. Cugat del Vallès*, *Estany*, *Ripoll*, and *S. Benito de Bages*, in which one finds capitals splendidly carved with interlacing floral ornament or with figures and scenes, the workmanship very like that at Arles.

Castile. In contrast to Catalunya, Romanesque influence in Castile was a comparatively sudden penetration. During the reign of Sancho the Great of Navarre (1000–35), the Benedictine monks of Cluny entered the country, immediately set about the reorganisation of the Spanish Church, and fostered a series of crusades. Before 1100 some 14 such expeditions set out from France, and another 15 before 1150. They also established on an international scale the pilgrimage to Santiago de Compostela, which before had only been a local concern. With royal support, the Benedictines constructed roads from Bordeaux and Toulouse, via Roncesvalles and the Somport respectively, to Nájera, Sto. Domingo de la Calzada, Burgos, and León. They dotted this road with monasteries, churches and hospices, so that pilgrims could make the 800km journey along the *Camino Francés*, as it was known, significantly—in Spanish the *Camino de Santiago*, or the 'Milky Way'—in 13 full-day stages from the frontier. At the beginning and at the end of the road they built at precisely the same time two great churches almost identical in their chevets and general proportions, St. Sernin of Toulouse and *Santiago de Compostela*. The latter, although masked outside with Baroque trappings, remains comparatively unaltered inside and is the earliest and most uniform Cluniac work in Spain, begun in 1075 and materially completed in 1128. Other early churches on the Pilgrimage Road are the *Cathedral* at *Jaca*, *S. Martín* at *Frómista*, and *S. Isidoro* at *León*. By the beginning of the 12C N Spain had become the most flourishing province of the Cluniac Order outside France. Fernando I himself became a lay brother, and gave to the Order three important monasteries, *Carrión de los Condes*, *Sahagún*, and *Frómista*. His son, Alfonso VI, self-styled 'Sovereign of the Three Religions' and father-in-law of Raymond of Burgundy, appointed his confessor, a Frenchman named Bernard de Sédirac, first abbot of Sahagún (to which eventually 130 Spanish monasteries became subject) and later as first archbishop of Toledo and Primate of Spain. In his turn Sédirac appointed 13 French bishops in the country.

One would expect the Cluniac monks to have planted innumerable derivatives of their mother church at Cluny, or at least to have introduced Burgundian Romanesque; and it is true that they have left a few examples in Spain such as *S. Vicente* at *Ávila*. But curiously enough they introduced much more often the variants of Romanesque found in W and SW France. For instance, at *Sto. Domingo* at *Soria* and at *Sangüesa* one finds the arcaded W fronts of Poitou, at *Salamanca* the stone shingled spire from Poitiers itself, and at *Silos*, at *León*, and on the Puerta de las Platerías at *Compostela* a type of sculpture typically Toulousain. But there are also a great number of churches in which the origins are inextricably confused and difficult to identify.

At a somewhat later stage one finds local Spanish schools of

Romanesque, eclectic in origin but sufficiently individual to be classed as new variants, which is not surprising considering that over 700 Romanesque churches are said to survive in Spain. Outstanding among these variants are the Galician, often with remarkable rose windows not unlike the Sicilian; the Segovian, with large W and lateral porches; the Zamoran, with curiously massive sculpture; and finally the several regions where brick was the only building material—Sahagún, Arévalo, Cuéllar, etc.—in which Mudéjar features make their first appearance. Here, too, one should note the 12C cloister at *Silos*, in which, although the bas-reliefs are Toulousain, the capitals, unsurpassed for their wealth of invention and their perfect execution, are so finely chiselled that they are attributed often to Moorish slaves.

In due course each important cathedral set a local fashion and had its derivatives. For instance, in Galicia, the model of Compostela served for those of *Lugo*, *Ourense*, and *Tui*, the last partly fortified as was Compostela at one time. The only essential difference was the introduction of pointed instead of round barrel-vaulting, but the transverse ribs remained as massive as before. As remarked earlier, the Spaniards were strangely conservative. Although the pointed arch was occasionally introduced in connection with vaulting almost as early as in France—at *La Oliva*, begun in 1164, and *Veruela*—its constructional advantages do not seem to have been appreciated. There was no obvious evolution from Romanesque to Gothic. While it is understandable that the Spaniards did not want to build churches of glass as in France, it would seem that they preferred a ponderous solidity of construction to forms that 'fly'. The result is that Spain has a number of magnificent but massive churches which, although Transitional and employing the pointed arch, are still Romanesque in spirit, among them the *Old* Cathedral at *Salamanca*, and those at *Zamora*, *Toro*, and *Ciudad Rodrigo*. The first three also have remarkable central lantern towers, derivatives of which are also found in the chapter house at *Plasencia* and in the Cathedral at *Évora* in Portugal. In the late 12th and early 13C there rose in NE Spain another series of massive Transitional cathedrals: *Tarragona*, *Lleida*, *Sigüenza*, *Sto. Domingo de la Calzada*, and *Tudela*. All have Gothic vaulting and pointed arches, but are still Romanesque in their solidity, their small windows, and their fortress-like aspect. There is no doubt that in these the influence of the Cistercians was of great importance. Just as former sovereigns had summoned the Cluniac Benedictines to Spain, so Alfonso VII imported the Cistercians. The first monks from Clairvaux arrived in 1131 at *Moreruela*, and there began a Cistercian 'invasion' almost as thorough as that of the Cluniacs. Few countries can claim so fine a collection of Cistercian abbeys. Altogether, more than 60 were founded, and more than half are still standing in whole or in part, among them *Fitero*, *La Oliva*, *Veruela*, *Piedra*, *Rueda*, *Gradéfes*, and *Las Huelgas*; *Osera*, *Melón*, *Meira*, and *Oya* in Galicia; and in Catalunya the two great monasteries at *Poblet* and *Santes Creus*, which have preserved their conventual dependencies almost complete. Most of the simplicity, sobriety, and vigour of later Spanish Romanesque is due to the Cistercians, who also introduced quadripartite, sexpartite, and octopartite vaulting. But the Spaniards made no attempt to act on the new building principles involved. Walls remained massive and windows small, and flying buttresses were not constructed.

Early Gothic Architecture. French Gothic in Castile. By the 13C the influence of the Benedictine and Cistercian monks had waned, although there are a few minor masterpieces of early Gothic for which the Cistercians were directly responsible, such as the refectory at *Sta. María de la Huerta*. The secular bishops, many of whom travelled abroad, now took the place of the monastic orders as patrons of art. Another generation of French architects entered the country, and the foundations were laid of three immense cathedrals: *Burgos*, *Toledo*, and *León*. They belong to the great cosmopolitan Gothic style which had been founded in the Domaine Royale of France and which spread throughout Western Europe. The Spanish examples may not be as lofty as those of France, nor as long as those of England, but they are magnificent expressions of French Gothic and none the less inspiring for being set as exotic flowers on the barren plains of Castile. Apart from *Cuenca* cathedral, which has many northern features, the first Gothic cathedral in Spain was *Burgos* (1221). Six years later *Toledo* cathedral, the metropolitan church, was begun. The cathedral at *León*, completed c 1303, was the first in Spain to have a glazed triforium throughout, in which the clerestory windows fill the whole space between the vaulting shafts, fulfilling the French ambition to construct a church with walls entirely of glass. Curiously enough the beauties of León created no architectural tradition in Castile and there are no important derivatives. Burgos, on the other hand, had many—such churches as *Támara*, *Aguilar de Campóo*, *Sta. María del Campo*, *Sasamón*, and the cathedral of *El Burgo de Osma*, and *Palencia* cathedral, another fine example of later French Gothic, completed, however, in Flamboyant. Finally *Sta. María* at *Castro-Urdiales* and *Pamplona* cathedral are both rich in fine French sculpture of a type repeated at *Vitoria*.

Catalan Gothic. In the late 13C Barcelona was the capital of a great Mediterranean Empire. An expansion in trade and population led to an increase in building activity and to the patronage of art on a generous scale. Here there was no direct importation of northern French architects as in Castile. Catalan architects, rational and sophisticated, soon evolved a purely regional, scientifically-planned variation of Gothic.

Neither in Catalunya nor in Castile did they cover their cathedrals with the high-peaked roofs which add so much to the grandeur of those in N Europe. The vaulting is usually covered with almost flat overlapping slabs of stone invisible from ground level, the rain pouring down runnels in the flying buttresses. *Lleida*, *Ávila*, and *León* are typical examples, while the later cathedral of *Sevilla* has no roof at all, and the vaulting is open to the sky.

As in many other parts of Europe where the 'hall church' was beginning to appear, the great Catalan churches were built for public, not monastic worship, and the prime objective in construction was to make the high altar visible to the entire congregation. The Catalans found two ways of doing this; first to build very wide aisleless churches with no columns to block the view, and secondly, churches with immensely wide central naves divided by tall slender columns from very narrow collaterals. For both types a wide vault was necessary and to support this massive oblong buttresses were provided, between which were placed side chapels, their outside walls flush with the ends of the buttresses. These buttresses do not show from the outside except above the aisle roof and hence become 'internal'. Artistically it was not a happy solution and the long unbroken wall surfaces of Catalan churches cannot vie with the picturesquely broken outline of northern churches, but they are remarkably capable works of engineering. The earliest example of the aisleless type, Sta. Catalina in Barcelona, begun in 1223, no longer exists, but there remain many others, including *Sta. María del Pi*, and *SS. Justo y Pastor* in *Barcelona* itself, and the plan was copied throughout southern France, where the outstanding example is at Albi.

The foremost Catalan architect was **Jaime Fabre**, a Mallorquin, who seems to have been the genius responsible for the *Cathedral* at *Barcelona*, and *Sta. María del Mar*, in turn used as models for other churches such as *La Seo* at *Manresa*, and *Tortosa* cathedral. In every one the triforia and clerestories are sacrificed in order to give added height to the main arcade, and the columns, often octagonal, rise unbroken to nearly twice the height of those in any northern church of this period. The supreme example of Catalan constructional engineering is *Girona* cathedral. Here, to a three-aisled chevet with a corona of radiating chapels, **Guillem Bofill** or *Boffy* added a gigantic single nave with a clear span of 22m, the widest vault of any Gothic church.

Catalan civil architecture was also noteworthy, beginning with the *Tinell Hall* of the Royal Palace in *Barcelona* and the *Hall of the Hundred*, which have wooden roofs supported on wide semicircular arches. Then comes a series of *Lonjas* or Exchanges, such as those at *Barcelona*, the earliest, at *Valencia*, *Palma*, and, later, at *Zaragoza*.

Mudéjar Architecture. We must retrace our steps to deal with the *Mudéjar* style. Although between the 12th and 14C the Christians had recovered almost the whole country, Moors and Jews continued to live on their native soil. More than a hundred towns possessed ghettos or *aljamas* in which these subject Mudéjars (and Jews) were segregated, and although not allowed to build or possess mosques, many clung to their religion and were not converted until the 16C. Yet the Christians showed toleration towards Moorish art, using it even for their tombs. The lace-like canopies of that at *Cuéllar*, and the chapel of the Annunciation in *Sigüenza* cathedral are outstanding examples of Mudéjar blended with Florentine Renaissance, and proof of the sentiment 'they lack our faith but we their works', expressed by Card. Cisneros (remember also Charles V's rebuke on seeing the new cathedral erecting in the Mezquita at Córdoba). While the great cathedrals and abbeys were built largely in the French styles, the Mudéjars were employed mainly on the smaller churches, to which their art was more suited. Of this class are the *Casa de Mesa*, the *Taller del Moro*, and the two *synagogues* at *Toledo*. The earlier of these, *Sta. María la Blanca*, with its octagonal pillars and round-headed horseshoe arches, is derived from the Caliphate style, but the rich plasterwork of the second, *El Tránsito*, recalls later Andalusian buildings. Toledo alone preserves no less than nine Mudéjar churches, their apses and towers with trefoil, horseshoe, and intersecting arches, as well as the *Puerta del Sol*.

A second medium of influence was the court. Christian kings had seized Moslem palaces at Toledo, Huesca, Zaragoza, Lleida, and Valencia, and found them more comfortable than Romanesque or Gothic dwellings, and Pedro the Cruel actually rebuilt and restored an earlier palace at Sevilla in imitation of the Alhambra. This predilection for Moorish art is also seen in the north, in the convent-palaces of *Astudillo*, and *Tordesillas*; and all through the 14C it was the custom for nobles, even in the far north, to decorate the interiors of their castles with Mudéjar brick and plasterwork. In the south, Mudéjar decoration in stucco persisted until it gradually merged with that of the Renaissance as in the so-called *House of Pilate* (Sevilla), built in the reign of Charles V. The garden pavilion, also of this date, at the Alcázar, still preserves perfectly the proportions of a Moorish building, and throughout southern Spain Mudéjar work remained remarkably pure in style. At *Sahagún*, one of the first northern towns to employ Mudéjars, two Romanesque churches, *S. Tirso* and *S. Lorenzo*, are decorated with simple recessed panels of bricks. Almost contemporary are *S. Lorenzo* at *Toro*, *La Lugareja* at *Arévalo*, and *S. Salvador* at *Cuéllar*, all with towers that slope slightly inwards like many minarets. Other strange examples are the 13C cloisters of *S. Juan de Duero* at *Soria*, with their interlacing and horseshoe arches, and the cupola of *S. Miguel* at *Almazán*, with coupled ribs derived from the *maqsurah* at Córdoba.

Of Mudéjar mingled with Gothic there are numerous examples in Castile; one of the most interesting is the brick cloister at *Guadalupe*. Even more curious than Castilian Mudéjar is that of Aragón. Here the belfries, often detached, like minarets, from the buildings they serve, form a striking feature of the landscape. The earliest (13C) are square, and at *Teruel* some of their wall surfaces patterned in brick and decorated with coloured tiles stand astride the streets, forming town gates as well as belfries. The 14th and 15C towers are usually octagonal, and survive at *Tarazona*, *Daroca*, *Alarcón*, *Ateca*, *Utebo*, *Tardienta*, and *Calatayúd*. At *Tobed*, *Torralba de Ribota*, and *Morata de Jiloca* there are windows of two or three lights with flamboyant tracery in the heads but stone jalousies below, and the walls are lined with patterned gesso.

Of the Spanish minor arts due to the Mudejáres none was so important as ceiling construction. Although of many varied types— flat, peaked, polygonal, deeply coffered and in the form of domes, usually called '*media naranja*'—the designs upon them are made from tiny pieces of wood to form interlacing geometrical patterns. Extremely rich in effect, for they are also painted and gilded and sometimes rise from stalactite cornices, they are found all over Spain.

Military and Later Gothic Architecture. Castles. That 'châteaux en Espagne' should be synonymous with chimeras appears to be due to the unfulfilled expectations of foreign knights whom the Spaniards urged to help them in local crusades against the Moors. The phrase is found in French literature as early as the 13C and in English in the 14C. Spain is particularly rich in castles, often crowning rugged peaks. Some 2000 of them have their principal walls in fair preservation. However, comparatively few of those still standing were built by the Christians to prevent the return of the Moors, and of purely Moorish citadels not many survive. First and foremost should be mentioned the *Alhambra*, then *Alcalá de Guadaira*, *Málaga* with its castle of *Gibralfaro*, *Carmona* with its horseshoe gateway, *Tarifa*, *Almería*, and *Almodóvar del Río*. All these are in the south, while in the north *Gormaz* (SW of Soria) is outstanding. It is believed that there were some 400 Moorish castles in Spain, and what little remains is sufficient to suggest that in the art of fortification the Moors were more advanced than the Christians, and that certain features first adopted in Palestine by the Crusaders (e.g. pentagonal towers) were repeated in Spanish castles earlier than elsewhere in Western Europe. Particularly striking is the Moorish appearance of many Christian castles near Toledo, for instance *Almonacid*, and the use made, as at *Escalona* and *Montalbán* in the same region, of colossal wedge-shaped towers projecting from the inner walls right over the outer walls, lofty pointed arches allowing communication through the 'lices'.

Romanesque military architecture is represented by the unrivalled monument of *Ávila*, which still looks like the city of an illuminated manuscript, girt with battlemented walls in perfect preservation, dating from the last decade of the 11C. At *Astorga*, *León*, and *Lugo* are other Romanesque city walls, in part on Roman foundations. The fortified monastery of *Loarre* is also of the 11th and 12C, while the fine stretch of curtain wall at *Berlanga de Duero* appears to date from the 13C. At *Madrigal de las Altas Torres* the walls formed a perfect circle c 700m in diameter. *Sevilla* and *Niebla* have also preserved stretches of wall and several gateways. Later walled towns include *Albarracin*, and *Morella*, and *Daroca*, where the gates are Mudéjar. *Toledo* retains gateways and two fortified bridges over the Tagus; other examples are those of *Valencia*, *Burgos* and *Vivero*.

Most of the great castles now to be seen in Spain—and they form a very impressive array—date from the 15C and even the 16C, and were erected either by kings or by powerful nobles jealous of royal and other interference. Of the royal castles the most imposing is the vast castle-palace, somewhat of the type of the Papal Palace at Avignon, erected by Carlos el Noble of Navarra at *Olite* (now a Parador). Of the many castles erected later in the 15C, two of the most famous are the Fonseca strongholds of *La Mota* at *Medina del Campo*, and *Coca*, both of brick. Nearly all the internal decoration of these castles is Mudéjar, with patterns in stucco, also repeated in the neighbouring castle of *Segovia*. Near by at *Turegano*, built by the Knights Templar, is another exceptional castle enclosing a three-aisled church. Two other outstanding castles are those of *Manzanares el Real* and *Belmonte*, but many lesser-known fortresses were equally formidable: *Valencia de Don Juan*, *Ampudia*, *Montealegre*, *Barco de Ávila*, *Davalillo*, *Fuensaldaña*, *Torrelobatón*, *Villafuerte*, *Peñafiel*, *Barciense*, *Illescas*, and *Grajal de Campos*. Most of these have imposing square or oblong keeps known as *Torres de Homenaje*, with bartizan turrets and heavy machicolations.

National Gothic and Isabelline. One final and magnificent burst of Gothic, this time of Flemish-Burgundian origin, was reserved for the 15–16C. Contemporary with Flamboyant in France and with Perpendicular in England, it became a National Gothic despite its northern sources, and the difference, characteristically Spanish, is immediately evident in the stress given to horizontal rather than vertical lines. The cathedral at *Sevilla*, begun in 1402, was the first to show Flemish influences. By the middle of the century, Flemish, Dutch, and German architects flocked to Spain as Frenchmen had done before them. Outstanding among them were Jan van der Eycken of Brussels, whose name became hispanicised as *Anequín de Egas*, and Hans of Cologne, who became known as **Juan de Colonia**. Anequín had worked on the town hall of Louvain and is chiefly remembered for the lofty spire that he added to *Toledo* cathedral, assisted by Juan Güas (or Wass; see below) who became one of the most original Isabelline architects. Anequín was also the father of a still greater architect, *Enrique de Egas*. Hans of Cologne was brought to *Burgos* by the converso bishop, Alonso de Cartagena, on his return from the Council at Basle. He is chiefly known for the spires of Burgos cathedral (which recall those of Freiburg in Germany); he was also the founder of a dynasty of architects, and with the help of his son, *Simón*, and another foreigner named *Gil de Siloé* (of *converso* origin—Siloé = English Siloam), introduced the star-patterned vaults for which Burgos is famous. Their successor here was a Burgundian from Langres named *Felipe Biguerny* or *Vigarni*.

With the marriage in 1468 of Fernando and Isabel, the final conquest of the Moors at Granada in 1492, and the discovery of America, there followed an era of intense building activity. The hall-church cathedrals of *Astorga* and *Plasencia* date from this period, and work on the new cathedrals of *Salamanca* and *Segovia* commenced, the chief architects for both being **Juan Gil de Hontañón** and his son *Rodrigo*. Displaying full stellar vaulting derived from Germany, they were the final expression of Gothic in Spain, unless we include the cathedral planted in the Mezquita at *Córdoba*, and the imposing 16C hall-churches of S. *Millán de la Cogolla, Berlanga de Duero*, and *Barbastro* cathedral, in which the details are frankly Renaissance. Isabelline ornament, as derived from Flanders and Burgundy, consists of highly naturalistic sculpture in rather low relief, accompanied by lace-like ornament, often beneath ogee or other curiously shaped arches and elaborately fringed canopies. Perhaps the best example in Spain is the portal (attributed to *Enrique de Egas*) of the *Capilla Real, Granada*. Another, attributed to *Simón de Colonia*, is the façade of *Sta. María* at *Aranda de Duero*, not Siloé, who is chiefly remembered for his superb tomb of Isabel's parents at *Miraflores*.

Before the recapture of Granada, the Catholic Kings had intended Toledo to be their burial place, and **Juan Güas**, pupil of Anequin, had already begun the Chapel Royal there, known as S. *Juan de los Reyes*. The work of Güas provides the most fantastic and Spanish variation of this over-rich Isabelline ornament. His real name was *Wass*, and he—or his parents—came from St. Pol-de-Léon in Brittany. As an architect he added to the typically Flemish-Burgundian repertory of florid Gothic an extreme emphasis on heraldry and at the same time a strange medley of Mudéjar designs. Thus in S. Juan de los Reyes there are not only vast heraldic achievements but also stalactite cornices, and his Gothic tracery has a distinctly Moorish look. Moreover, his work shows so great an antipathy to plain surfaces that walls are covered with a sort of tapestry in plaster or stone. He is known to have designed also the castle of *Manzanares el Real* and the *Infantado Palace* at *Guadalajara*. In much the same style are the retablo-like façades of S. *Gregorio* and S. *Pablo* at *Valladolid* (both of these built for the Dominican *converso*, Fray Alonso de Burgos, also Bp of Palencia), and a palace at *Úbeda*. The *Medinaceli palace* at *Cogolludo* is now given to *Lorenzo Vázquez*, architect of the central portion of the façade of the College of *Sta. Cruz* at *Valladolid*, and the mighty castle of *La Calahorra*. The *Casa de las Conchas* at *Salamanca* is now also attributed to Vázquez.

The Isabelline style, which recalls the Manueline of Portugal, is bizarre and opulent rather than beautiful. Perhaps all that can be said for it is that it set the stage for the next development, the introduction of Renaissance ornament in rather the same manner; the style known as 'Plateresque'.

Renaissance Architecture. Plateresque. Early in the 16C it became fashionable for Spanish nobles and ecclesiastics to commission their tombs in Italy, particularly at Genoa. Both tombs and sculptors were imported, and soon the delicately sculptured *amorini*, garlands, fruit, flowers, medallions, grotesques, and candelabra with which the effigies were surrounded were copied by Spanish silversmiths and architects.

With silver and gold pouring in from the New World, silverwork or *platería* for shrines, *custodias*, and church ornaments in general became exceedingly important, but it is untrue to say that early Renaissance architectural ornament was derived from silverwork. Both came from the same source, Lombard sculpture; the architects called their work '*obra del Romano*' and the term Plateresque, not applied to architecture until later, was perhaps derisive. The important point is that both silversmiths and architects used the new carefully chiselled ornament in much the same way: as an appliqué decoration. The structure of neither silver tabernacles nor of stone buildings was affected. The sole difference was that the new Lombard repertoire took the place of the florid Gothic crockets and finials beloved by Isabelline architects, and was indiscriminately applied, but often with immense charm.

Although several 'schools' were formed, the principal architects of the period travelled all over the country, and were at work on several buildings at the same time. The two greatest Plateresque architects from Toledo were **Enrique de Egas**, son of Anequín, and **Alonso de Covarrubias**, who married Enrique's niece and succeeded him as master of the works at Toledo cathedral. Both Egas and Covarrubias were members of an architectural commission for Salamanca cathedral, and Egas was probably responsible for the plan (in Gothic) of *Granada* cathedral, where he was succeeded by *Diego de Siloé*.

The first patrons of Plateresque were the Catholic Kings and the prelates Mendoza, Cisneros, and Fonseca. For the former Enrique erected the royal hospitals of *Santiago de Compostela* and *Granada*, where he was also in charge of the *Capilla Real*. He began the *Hospital de Sta. Cruz* at *Toledo*, completed by *Covarrubias*, who made an almost identical but finer replica of its monumental stairway at *Alcalá de Henares*, destroyed in the Civil War.

Most of the work of Egas is a subtle blend of Gothic construction with Italian ornament. *Alonso de Covarrubias*, on the other hand, was an architect in whom the evolution of style can be easily traced. Among his Plateresque works are the *Cap. de los Reyes Nuevos* in *Toledo* cathedral, and the *Sacristy* in *Sigüenza* cathedral.

Salamanca is a museum of 16C architecture, and the superb façade of the *University* is a masterpiece of Plateresque. No architect has yet been credited with the design, nor with that of other outstanding Plateresque works in this town: the *Escuelas Menores*, the two *Fonseca palaces*, and the *Monterrey palace*. Other fine Plateresque works are the façade of the *University* at *Alcalá de Henares*, by *Rodrigo Gil de Hontañón*, and the façade of *S. Marcos* at *León*. In Andalucía, we should note particularly the *Ayuntamiento* at *Sevilla*, begun by *Diego de Riaño*, the '*House of Pilate*', and the collegiate church at *Osuna*.

At *Burgos* the chief architect of the period was **Francisco de Colonia** (son of Simón and grandson of Hans of Cologne) to whom are due the sacristy doorway of the *Constable's Chapel* and the *Puerta de la Pellejería*, in Pseudo-Florentine style but with ungainly bell-shaped capitals and arches decorated with acanthus— peculiarities found also at the above-mentioned palaces at Cogolludo and Peñaranda de Duero. The *Hospital del Rey* at Burgos, the belfy at *Sta. María del Campo* (an early work by *Diego de Siloé*), and the palace at *Saldañuelo* also come within this group. Burgos is important also as the birthplace of **Diego de Siloé** (c 1495–1563), son of the sculptor and perhaps a pupil of Simón de Colonia. His first known work is the Plateresque '*Golden Staircase*' in the Cathedral. In 1524 he accompanied Bartolomé Ordóñez, the sculptor, to Florence and Naples, and his work thereafter is very different. First he was occupied with *S. Jerónimo* at *Granada*, which he took over from a certain *Jacobo Florentino L'Indaco*, who is said to have been a pupil of Michelangelo. Siloé also succeeded Enrique de Egas as master of the works at *Granada* cathedral, and he designed a number of important works, including the *Great Sacristy* at *Sevilla* cathedral, *El Salvador* at *Úbeda* (which was actually built by **Andrés de Vandaelvira**, chief architect of *Jaén* cathedral), and the courtyard of the *Irish College* at *Salamanca* (executed by *Pedro de Ibarra*). He also had a hand in the design of the cathedrals at *Málaga* and *Guadix*. None of these later works can be classed as Plateresque and, in fact, in Granada cathedral, the Classical repertoire is used constructionally. While the ground plan with nave, double aisles, and ambulatory is still Gothic, despite a central dome, the details are all Classical. The cathedrals of Málaga, Guadix, Jaén, and Cádiz all show the influence of this renaissance in the architecture of Granada, the half-way step to full comprehension of the Italian principles.

The High Renaissance. The first building in Spain of true Classical inspiration is the huge square palace which Charles V erected in the Alhambra. The architect chosen was **Pedro Machuca**, a Spaniard who, trained in Rome, had absorbed many of the best principles of the Italian Cinquecento. The next work is the *Tavera Hospital* at *Toledo* (1541–99) by *Covarrubias*. The same architect designed the courtyard of the *Alcázar* at *Toledo*. There are, of course, many lesser examples of Classical inspiration by the middle of the century such as the Palladian windows· of the *Ayuntamiento* at *Baeza* and the Corinthian *Ayuntamiento* of *Jerez de la Frontera*, but all these are of little account compared with the *Escorial*. Its first architect was *Juan Bautista de Toledo*, who had worked with Michelangelo on St. Peter's in Rome, and was summoned from Naples in 1559 to make the plans. In 1563 the corner stone was laid, but he died four years later and was succeeded by his assistant **Juan de Herrera** (1530–97), not a trained architect but a member of the royal bodyguard, eminent mathematician, inventor of clever mechanical devices, and superb draughtsman.

Although the Escorial was his life work, Herrera also designed the courtyard of the *Lonja* at *Sevilla* (executed by *Juan Mijares*), the *Puente de Segovia* at *Madrid*, and he may have had a hand in the design for the unfinished cathedral at *Valladolid*. For a long time Herrera, who enjoyed an awesome reputation for his energy in carrying out Juan Bautista's plan for the Escorial, was royal inspector of monuments, and everywhere there appeared churches, palaces, and public buildings in the dominating '*estilo desornamentado*', often reproducing the Escorial's corner towers capped with sharply-pointed, slate-roofed spires. Examples on the grand scale are the *Ducal Palace* at *Lerma*, built by *Francisco de Mora*, the façade of the ruined palace formerly at *Renedo de Valdeteja*, and now re-erected near the cathedral at León, and the *Ayuntamiento* at *Toledo*, by *Jorge Theotocopulos*. But in general it was the frigidity of the style that was reproduced, and not its grandeur.

Mannerism and Baroque. A reaction to the austerity of this style came spontaneously, and found its expression in Mannerism and

Baroque. The Baroque of Spain was perhaps the most sensational and most imaginative of all European variations and was surpassed in these respects only by that of its own colonies, in particular Mexico.

In many places it was Italian Mannerism that first held sway, for instance in the pantheon of the Escorial, entrusted by Felipe III to *Giovanni Battista Crescenzi*, and his style was followed in the church planned for the Jesuits at *Loyola*, their founder's birthplace. In *Madrid*, the plan of the Gesù at Rome was copied for *S. Isidro el Real.* In eastern Spain, again under Jesuit influence, the Neapolitan style is often recognisable, for instance in nearly all the churches of Valencia, but these influences are very mixed. The lavish stucco decoration in *Los SS. Juanes* at *Valencia* was due to a Milanese, *Jacopo Barthesi*, the W Front of the *Cathedral* to *Conrad Rudolf*, a German pupil of Bernini, the tower of *La Seo* at *Zaragoza* to another Italian, *Contini*, and the Borrominesque façade of *Murcia* cathedral to *Jaime Bort*, perhaps also a foreigner.

But these Italianate works are outside the main stream of Spanish tradition. During most of the 17C comparative simplicity reigned (from lack of money due to inflation); for instance in several Madrid churches of this epoch, and in the work of *Juan Gómez de Mora*, who designed the *Pl. Mayor* at *Madrid* and the *Jesuit College* at *Salamanca*. The same simplicity, indeed heaviness, is found in *Alonso Cano's* work, above all in the W Front of *Granada* cathedral. A minor masterpiece of interior decoration is the sacristy of *Guadalupe*, with its perfect co-ordination of ornament.

Far more interesting is the Baroque of the 18C, especially the variations of what is loosely termed *Churrigueresque*. Its originality is unquestionable; it is emotional, an architecture of fantasy, sometimes inspired, sometimes merely intoxicated. But it was a most successful protest against the rules of Vitruvius and the ascetic Herreran, and in its use of striking ornament in bold relief, often crowded on to one small portion of a building—usually the portal—it showed true appreciation of light and shade.

José Churriguera (1665–1723) after whom the style is named, and who was later said to have defiled stone with his pernicious and ill-directed genius, was a comparatively mild innovator, and his own work, for instance the planned village of *Nuevo Baztán*, was restrained. However, himself the son of a sculptor of retablos, he had four brothers, all of them architects or sculptors, and at least three of his sons followed the same profession. Their works have not yet been disentangled and moreover they often collaborated with another dynasty of architects, the **Quiñones**, and it is to this group as a whole that we owe the style, Churrigueresque. They specialised in huge gilt polychromed retablos peopled with ecstatic saints, but also produced a number of other dramatic and distinguished works, particularly at *Salamanca*, where *Joaquín Churriguera* and *Andrés Garcia Quiñones* completed the cathedral dome, while *Alberto Churriguera* carved the choir stalls. To Quiñones and the younger Churrigueras we owe the *Pl. Mayor* at *Salamanca*, one of the finest squares in Europe, and to Alberto Churriguera the partial completion of *Valladolid* cathedral.

In *Madrid* an architect perhaps equally original, **Pedro Ribera** (1683–1742) constructed the *Puente de Toledo* and the portal of the *Hospicio Provinciál*, while at Valencia a painter named *Hipólito Rovira* erected for the Marqués de Dos Aguas a palace with a remarkable portal carved by *Ignacio Vergara*. At *Santiago*, **Fernando**

Casas y Nóvoa dressed the W Front of the cathedral in Baroque trappings, and here too was evolved a sort of 'Plattenstil' with abstract ornament—the *Conv. de Sta. Clara* by *Simón Rodriguez* is the best example—a kind of protocubist fantasy. One of the most extraordinary compositions of the age is the *Transparente* by *Narciso Tomé* in *Toledo* cathedral.

Meanwhile, in *Sevilla* another dynasty, the *Figueroas*, was responsible for many attractive but unorthodox buildings, including *S. Luis Rey*, the *Archbishop's Palace*, and the *Pal. de S. Telmo* with its imposing portal. But the most revolutionary Andalusian was **Francisco Hurtado Izquierdo** (1669–1728), who died at *Priego*, where numerous Baroque works by his pupils survive. Among his rich interiors is the Sancta Sanctorum at *El Paular*, where he introduced a motive inspired by the interlacing arches of the Mezquita at Córdoba, and the Sacristy of the *Cartuja* at *Granada*, a fantastic domed hall surrounded by fretted pilasters surging with delirious ornament—this last executed by pupils after his death.

The styles at court in this period were very different. To the Bourbon Felipe V (grandson of Louis XIV) and his Italian queen Isabella of Parma, Spanish fashions in dress and architecture must have seemed outmoded, and in their new palaces they immediately attempted to rival the splendours of Versailles, and called in foreigners to do the work. The old Habsburg palace of *Aranjuez* was taken in hand in 1715, and later Carlos III added further wings, and a porcelain cabinet designed and executed by Neapolitans, the most remarkable example of Chinoiserie decoration in Spain. Next came the mountain palace of *La Granja*, begun in 1721 by a German, *Theodor Ardemans*, where the garden front was rebuilt in 1735 by the Italians *Juvara* (a pupil of Bernini) and *Giovanni Battista Sacchetti*. The gardens in the style of Le Nôtre were planned by *Etienne Boutelou*, with ornamental statuary by several other Frenchmen. Juvara and Sacchetti were responsible also for the *Royal Palace* at *Madrid*, rebuilt between 1738 and 1764, while its interior was decorated by other foreigners, mainly Italians, the greatest of whom was *Giambattista Tiepolo* (1696–1770)—fresh from Würzburg. But the style remained a fashion of the Court only, and in architecture Spain never appreciated the taste of the Bourbons.

The Neo-Classic. Despite the fact that Spain remained curiously aloof from the French styles in architecture and interior decoration that swept over most of Western and Central Europe, the Bourbons were in a sense responsible for the Classic Revival in Spain. By founding academies of art modelled on the Academy in Paris—a national school for architects (1744) and the Royal Academy of San Fernando (1752)—they set new standards in art and exercised virtual control. A royal decree prohibited the erection of any public building for which the plans had not been approved by the Royal Academy, where the professors of architecture were *José Hermosilla*, the translator of Vitruvius, and *Ventura Rodríguez*, an architect steeped in Classicism. As a result, buildings as severe and massive as those by Herrera rose on every side. By *Rodríguez* himself may be mentioned the church of the *Augustinian Convent* at *Valladolid*, the façades of *Lugo* and *Pamplona* cathedrals and significant alterations to the basilica of *El Pilar* at *Zaragoza*. In *Madrid* some of the best work of the period was by *Francesco Sabatini*, who built the *Ministerio de Hacienda*, and by *Juan de Villanueva*, who built the *Prado Museum* and the *Observatory*. The *Casita del Principe* at the

Escorial, another at the *Pardo*, and the *Casa del Labrador* at *Aranjuez* were decorated in the Pompeian style for Carlos IV.

The Peninsular War saw the destruction or dilapidation of a number of ancient buildings, while in the mid 1830s when church property was expropriated, many monasteries—including Santes Creus and Poblet—fell into ruin, but to balance this there was little loss by excessive and unscholarly restoration. The late 19C and early 20C saw tremendous building activity and a revival of many styles—including for instance Moorish and Mudéjar for bullrings and railway stations—but few individual buildings display any great originality, except for certain works by *Antonio Gaudí* (1852–1926).

Both before and after the Civil War a grandiose neo-Herreran style was imposed on many of the newly erected ministerial and university buildings, while conventional modern blocks of flats, banks, offices, barracks, and hotels continue to proliferate unchecked.

Strenuous efforts are being made to preserve Spain's architectural heritage, and legislation has gone some way in an attempt to protect individual buildings—often tastefully converted into museums, or State-owned Paradores—apart from 'monumental districts' of towns, picturesque villages, archaeological sites, and panoramic views. Much remarkable work of restoration of damaged or derelict buildings of historic or architectural interest has been carried out in recent years. Also, one should add, some churches have also been virtually rebuilt, which hardly deserved such attention.

Advertisement hoardings, TV aerials, a profusion of cables and wires, and an extraordinary number of road signs, etc. still scar most townscapes. Too many 'monumental districts' and villages of character are still crammed with cars. A special note of admiration should be recorded for the important work of preservation being done (for instance the transformation of the Infantado palace façade at Guadalajara, and the rebuilding of the city walls and castle at Almería) and every encouragement should be given to those entrusted with the task, even if, in their enthusiasm they may, in over restoring, destroy the patina of ages.

A revised and extended edition of Bernard Bevan's 'History of Spanish Architecture' (first published in 1938) is in preparation. The Editor must here acknowledge the considerable help and advice he has received from the author when revising this article, adapted from his own contribution to the first edition of this Guide.

INTRODUCTION TO SPANISH ART

'Spain, if visited by some of our artists, would, I am persuaded, open new, astonishing, and unexamined treasures to their view . . . '. Such was the reaction of Edward Clarke, who entered the country in 1760; an impression confirmed by the small but growing number of English travellers, collectors, and amateurs who traversed Spain in succeeding decades. But the depredations of the French during the Peninsular War—both in actual destruction and blatant appropriation—the sequestration of ecclesiastical property in the mid 1830s when some, but by no means all, works of art found their way into museums, the blight of unskilled restoration, the iconoclastic proclivities of extremists and the church-burnings of the early 1930s, the Civil War, sheer neglect and decay over the decades; all have taken their toll.

Certainly the Spain depicted in the lithographs of John Frederick Lewis, David Roberts, and George Vivian—to name but three English artists of the Romantic period—and in the topographical drawings of Richard Ford himself, is no longer. Ford described its unplundered treasures to English readers in his great *Hand-Book for Travellers in Spain* of 1845. He was following in the footsteps of J.A. Ceán Bermúdez (whose *Diccionario histórico de los más ilustres profesores de las bellas artes en España*, published in 1800, was a godsend to the French in search of canvases). Three years later Sir Edmund Head's *Hand-Book of the History of the Spanish and French Schools of Painting* appeared, as did William Stirling's *Annals of the Artists of Spain*. Spanish painting was no longer the great unknown. In spite of the gradual dissipation of its works of art, a very high proportion remained in Spain, and did not cease to astonish by its splendour and variety.

Now a new spirit of conservation has set in. Old collections are being reformed and new museums opened; and there is today a more general appreciation in Spain itself of the quality of its artistic heritage, which, due to the strenuous efforts of scholars, is being properly described and catalogued, and questionable attributions corrected.

Many pages could be devoted to the arts of Spain—to sculpture; to leatherwork, textiles, and tapestries; furniture, both ecclesiastical and domestic; glass and ceramics; jewellery, ivories, and jet; the art of the metalworker, armourer, and silversmith; miniatures and illuminated manuscripts—but to describe each facet would make this introductory study unwieldy; and many are the subject of specialised monographs.

Apart from such cave paintings as those at *Altamira*, perhaps the earliest known surviving examples of mural decoration that the traveller will come across, from the pre-Romanesque period, is that in *S. Julián de los Prados* or *Santullano* (Oviedo) of c 830, in which the traditional Byzantine splendour of effect secured by the use of mosaic was reproduced by elaborate fresco decoration, unfortunately much decayed. Northern Spain was indeed in the vanguard of European Romanesque painting, and a relatively high percentage of this 12C painting to survive is unrivalled outside Spain. One masterpiece is the apse of *S. Climent, Taüll* (now in the *Museu d'Art de Catalunya*, Barcelona), dated by an inscription 1123, where the basic colours of the Mozarabic art of illumination, red and yellow, are emphasised by strong black outlines. But the largest and most important example is the decoration of the *Panteón de los Reyes* in *S. Isidoro* (León), probably executed in the reign of Fernando II, who is portrayed in the painting.

Altar frontals conformed to international standards. They were often built of wooden panels on which were moulded stucco or gesso in low relief. The intention was to imitate as closely as possible with paint and gold and silver leaf certain frontals executed for the few wealthy sees by Limoges enamellers in solid gold, enamel, and precious stones. These painted substitutes, which almost alone survive, are usually designed to show Christ in Majesty or the Virgin Enthroned, within a mandorla, occupying the centre, while rows of saints or apostles, or scenes from religious legends are arranged in static groups on either side. These frontals gradually gave way to *retablos*, which grew in size as the crucifix was placed higher above the altar upon a painted panel. The panel became a diptych, then a triptych, and by the end of the 14C the Spanish retablo proper had evolved, rambling and asymmetrical, to occupy the entire eastern end of the church.

Spanish medieval art has only recently become the subject of serious study. We know little about the early artists, and half the extant works from before the mid 15C remain anonymous despite the labours of scholars, who have rescued scores of paintings and painters from oblivion. In signing his wall paintings in the Old Cathedral in Salamanca in 1262, *Antón Sánchez* of Segovia was one of the first to prove the existence of an individual artist proud of his personal achievement. These Castilian murals are in a marked Franco-Gothic style, found also in the majority of paintings executed about 1300 both in Aragón and Catalunya.

The artistic impulse of Catholic Spain moved slowly south in the wake of the intermittent reconquest of Moorish Spain, and schools of painting developed from the Catalan in Valencia, and later in Sevilla, with the shifting of commercial activity. Eventually they waned, for when the court was centred on Madrid, the capital became the focus of interest and seat of patronage. If Salamanca, Ávila, Toledo, and Granada are omitted from such a brief summary, it is because the relative importance of the various centres can be judged only by the works that have survived.

CATALAN SCHOOLS. By the 14C Barcelona had developed a rich, independent merchant class which vied with the king and Church in fostering local talent, with the result that Catalan artists enjoyed almost a monopoly of work in the realm of greater Aragón until the 15C. The recognised head of the Catalan school was **Ferrer Bassa** (active 1324–48), whose frescoes have survived in the *Convent of Pedralbes* in Barcelona. He was a versatile artist, having ten years earlier been engaged by Alfonso IV as a miniaturist. His manner and style are a blend of the art of Giotto, Simone Martini and Lorenzetti, and it is presumed that he was trained at Florence and Siena. But the Giottesque element was not handed on to his successors, *Arnau de la Penna* (1355–85), *Jaume* and *Pere Serra* (active 1363–99), and their pupil *Lluís Borrassà* (active 1388–1424), who may all be studied in Barcelona and Vic. Their works show more the influence of the French, Avignon, and Sienese Schools. They retain a somewhat naïve provincial character, but are marked by a rich display of contemporary costume and a taste for genre. It was in this century that towering retablos, with their gilded pilasters and pinnacles encasing innumerable panels of bright tempera and gold, came into their own. The artist who transformed the international Gothic style practised by Borrassà and his successor *Ramon de Mur* into a genuine Catalan Gothic, which was to survive until the end of the 15C, was *Bernat Martorell* (active 1427–52). He combined the naturalistic elements of Gentile da Fabriano in Italy with those of the Franco–Flemish movement centred in the Limburg brothers at the court of Jean, Duc de Berri.

Three years after Jan van Eyck's visit to Spain in 1428, Alfonso V sent **Lluís Dalmau** (active 1428–60), one of his court painters, to Flanders, where in Ghent he probably saw Van Eyck's great 'Adoration of the Lamb', then newly unveiled. Years after his return, Dalmau, in his one certain work executed for the city councillors of Barcelona in 1443–45, defied tradition by substituting a typically Flemish landscape for the customary gold background. It is largely through Dalmau that the realism of the Flemish School was introduced to **Jaume Huguet** (c 1414–92), who dominated the Catalan School from the 1460s. The workshop of *Rafael Vergós* and his brother *Pau*, artist of the 'Retablo of Granollers' (of 1495), merely reflected the models of Huguet, their master. Even contemporary painting in ARAGÓN was merely a provincial ramification of his style, which, inherited from Martorell, also incorporated many Flemish elements. But Huguet was unable to rid himself of the Catalan predilection for covering backgrounds with gilded motifs in stucco relief, and his work incorporates and summarises most of the qualities, styles, defects, and idiosyncrasies of the mature Catalan School, colourful, realistic, and robust.

Meanwhile, in adjacent VALENCIA, where Alfonso V had established his court, there developed a flourishing school of painting, more Italianate, in the persons of *Lorenzo Zaragoza* (1365–1402) and *Pere Nicolau* (fl. 1390–1410). Perhaps inspired by the Florentine *Gherardo Starnina*, whose frescoes once decorated the walls of Valencia cathedral, their brilliantly coloured altar pieces introduced the international Gothic style into the region. *Andrés Marçal de Sax* (active 1394–1410), who probably came from Germany and who collaborated with Nicolau, brought with him a tendency towards exaggerated realism, which corresponded to an inherent trait in the Spanish character, and was soon assimilated by their artists. Recent research has clarified the main lines of development of the Valencian School, although exact identification of painters is not always possible, the difficulty being to connect the commissioning contracts which have been unearthed with the altar pieces they prescribe, now so often dismembered. One of the principal figures was *Jacomart* (*Jaime Baço*; active 1409/17–61), who was court painter to Alfonso V for ten years in Naples, where he introduced the Hispano–Flemish style. One of his surviving works is in the Diocesan Museum at Segorbe, but the 'Cati Altarpiece' has now been proved to be by *Joan Reixac* (1431–84/92). In these we find superficial Italian Renaissance borrowings as in the architectural niches, and the Flemish love of counterfeiting jewellery and textiles, together with the Northern landscape backgrounds.

Bartolomé Bermejo (active 1474–95), a Cordoban painter who lived successively in Daroca, Zaragoza, and Valencia before settling in Barcelona in 1486, greatly encouraged the transformation of the Gothic to the Renaissance style in Aragón and Valencia. It was once customary to link his name with another Cordoban, *Master Alfonso*, whose fame rested on the 'Martyrdom of S. Cucufat' (in the Museu d'Art de Catalunya), which has now been proved to be the work of a German painter, *Ayne Bru*. Bermejo was one of the first exponents of oil-painting in Catalunya, although he exploited this strange medium more as an adjunct to than instead of tempera, which he controlled with such finesse that it is sometimes difficult to decide which medium he has used, or, when both are present, where tempera ends and oil begins.

With the partial unification of Spain under the Catholic Kings, a programme of public building was initiated together with attendant commissions to artists both foreign and indigenous. In CASTILE, the two foreign influences—Flemish and Florentine—were also at work. *Starnina*, already referred to in Valencia, was painting for Juan I at Salamanca in 1380, and was followed there by his compatriot *Nicolás Florentino* (active in Spain 1433–70), whose altar piece of 1455 in the *Old* Cathedral, is outstanding. In León, the partially reassembled retablo mayor of 1434, clearly inspired by Italian trecento models, was painted by a French artist, *Nicolás Francés* (1425–68). One of the first works of definitely Flemish character to be produced in Castile was executed in 1455 by *Jorge Inglés*, an artist of uncertain nationality, despite his name; while in Zamora and elsewhere **Fernando Gallego** (active 1466–1507) was imitating the technical skills of Roger van de Weyden, Campin, and Dirk Bouts. His altar pieces are Flemish in character, with the addition of a certain angularity of form and heightened sense of drama. Throughout the century there was a steady importation of devotional paintings of these masters, of Gerard David, and Isenbrandt, and their influence was dominating, except perhaps in Valencia, geographically nearer to Italy and Naples. In 1472 the cathedral chapter invited two Umbrian artists to settle in Valencia, where the influences of the Renaissance affected the styles of local painters, among them *Rodrigo de Osona* (father and son; active 1464–1513).

The Castilian **Pedro Berruguete** (active 1477–1504) set the fashion for Spanish artists to visit Italy, not always with happy results. In 1477 Berruguete was working in Urbino under Justus of Ghent and Melozzo da Forli, and influenced by Signorelli. He later became court painter to Fernando and Isabel, settling at Toledo (1483–95) before moving to Ávila, where he worked on the high altar in the cathedral. His son *Alonso Berruguete* (1486–1561), who had also trained in Italy under Michelangelo, became court painter to Charles V.

The altar piece of Valencia cathedral (1507), by *Fernando de los Llanos* and *Fernando Yáñez*, is another example of the influence of a great tradition—in this instance that of Leonardo da Vinci and the Florentines who they studied in Italy—which lacks any indigenous Spanish character. They were succeeded by another hybrid, *Juan Vicente Macip* (c 1475–1550) and his son **Juan de Joanes** (1523–79), whose altar pieces abound in Valencia.

SEVILLA. A great number of Sevillian paintings still hang in the city's churches, convents, hospitals and in the Cathedral, and a representative collection can be seen in the *Museo de Bellas Artes*. Among the first artists to achieve popular success was *Alejo Fernández* (active 1498–1543), who introduced the Renaissance style into his own serene and balanced compositions with their elegant idealised types. Apart from being a miniaturist, he also superintended the decoration of Sevilla for the entry of Charles V in 1526. His contemporaries *Pedro de Capana* (*Kempeneer* of Brussels, 1503–80), *Fernando Sturm* (active 1537–57), and *Frans Frutet*, also trained in Italy, were for a few years at work in Sevilla. There, after 28 years' travel in Italy, they were joined by *Luis de Vargas* (c 1502–68), a native of Sevilla, who had also absorbed the art of the Roman Mannerists. *Luis de Morales* ('el Divino', active 1546–86) from Badajoz, similarly subjugated his own natural capacity for religious expression to the fashionable mannerisms of the moment.

Another artist whose style sprang from Italian Mannerism was **El Greco** (*Domenico Theotocopoulos*, 1540–1614), a Greek from Candia (Crete). He received his 'Western' training directly from Titian in Venice. He later travelled to Spain, possibly in the hope of securing lucrative employment at the Escorial, and in 1575 settled for life in Toledo. Towards 1580 he entered into competition with some of the established favourites—*Carvajal, Sánchez Coello, et al.*—but his unorthodox drawing and design, and vivid, indeed too frequently livid colouring, was more than Felipe II could bear. His only other commission for the Escorial, the 'Gloria de Felipe II', with its ochrous reds and greys, is low in tone by comparison. Every eccentricity of his style is foreshadowed in another of his early masterpieces, 'The Burial of the Count of Orgaz', painted for Sto. Tomé at Toledo in 1586/8, where it still hangs. It is remarkable for the row of *hidalgos* across the lower half of the composition, which reveals El Greco as a portrait painter of rare mastery and insight. It was one of the few paintings which impressed George Borrow— admittedly no connoisseur—who considered it a work by a 'most extraordinary genius'. The Prado contains another series of individual portraits in which El Greco has depicted the pride and aloof temper of these Castilian gentlemen. His repetition of favourite designs at different periods, and consequent reversion to earlier types and elongated proportions make his work difficult to arrange chronologically. It was not until comparatively recently that there has been any general appreciation of his qualities. El Greco handed on little to his pupil *Luis Tristán* (c 1585–1624) or to his son *Jorge Manuel*, who was mainly an architect and sculptor.

One of the most powerful factors in the evolution of the Spanish school of the so-called 'Golden Age' of painting (lasting roughly from 1550 to 1650) was the formation of the Royal Collections under Charles V, Felipe II, and Felipe IV—the last acquiring a number of masterpieces sold from the collection of Charles I of England. The cosmopolitan emperor patronised Titian to the exclusion of all other 'face-painters', and began that magnificent collection of the Venetian's portraits and scriptural and mythological works which Felipe II continued in the Titian nudes. Felipe, having failed to entice Veronese from Venice to decorate the Escorial, and not appreciating El Greco, still would not trust to native talent. This neglect may have retarded progress in Castile but, much as his unpatriotic and expensive importations of such representatives of Italian Mannerism as Zuccaro, Cambiaso, and Tibaldi has been deplored, it seems true that this importation was only of slight significance. Even the failure of *Juan Fernández Navarrete*, 'el Mudo' (1526–79) to justify to the king his title of the 'Spanish Titian' cannot be wholly attributed to the noxious influence of these Italians among whom he worked. Nevertheless, he did help to translate Italian Mannerism into the Spanish idiom, and he and his ESCORIAL SCHOOL were the first of the '*tenebrist*' painters, so famous in the 17C, especially in Sevilla.

But the true founder of the SEVILLIAN SCHOOL was *Francisco Pacheco* (1564–1654), an Andalusian who in 1611 met El Greco in Madrid, and in the following year returned to Sevilla. There until 1617 he was the master of young Velázquez, to whom the shrewd Pacheco married his daughter, as he relates with engaging complacency in his *Arte de la Pintura*, a curious blend of useful biography and rules for religious painters. In 1623–25 Pacheco was in Madrid, accompanying Velázquez, and his house became an informal meeting place for writers and painters, who there copied engravings, studied the painting of still life, and painted directly from nature, a reaction against Mannerism. Even *Herrera the Elder* (c 1576–1656) was basically under this influence, which can also be observed in his contemporary *Juan de las Roelas* (1558/60–1625), who, from being an apostle of the Venetian, Bolognese and Roman Mannerists, became the exponent of a broader technique and a Baroque style. His insistence on naturalistic details in his subsidiary figures led to the genre pictures of the 17C Sevillian School.

It is convenient to consider here the impact on this school of the Catalan *Francisco Ribalta* (1551–1628), and the Valencian, *Ribera*. Ribalta spent his youth in Barcelona, and later, from 1582, painted in Madrid, until he settled in Valencia in 1599. His use of chiaroscuro, realistic details, and 'tenebrism' is a development of the Escorial School of Navarrete and the Italian Mannerists. Only after 1615 do his works in Valencia show the true impact of the Caravaggesque style, by which time the works of the Caravaggesque School were in Spain. His latest works show the influence of Ribera, who cannot ever have been his pupil.

José Ribera, *'el Españoleto'* (1591–1652), who was born at Xàtiva, went to Italy at an early age, and after a prolonged study of Titian, Correggio in Parma, and the Carracci in Rome, settled for life in Naples in 1616. He arrived at exactly the right moment to cull from Caravaggio those qualities of sensational lighting and unshrinking realism which were best calculated to display his dramatic gifts and to gratify the taste of the Neapolitans (and Spanish residents) for savage and sinister martyrdoms. His influence and great fame reached Spain with his works sent over by Spanish viceroys, and had a share in the formation of Murillo and his fellow painters in Sevilla. Unlike most Spaniards, Ribera was a daring and able designer and an accomplished figure draughtsman, and his method of placing the great bodies of his saints and their tormentors right across the foreground gives great force and verisimilitude to his grim representations. His 'Martyrdom of St. Bartholomew' (1630; the year he was visited by Velázquez), which is in the Prado, admirably illustrates this; while at Salamanca, in the *Augustinas*, one can see Ribera's celebrated 'Conception' of 1635, whose tall Virgin and golden glow appear later in the works of Alonso Cano and Murillo respectively.

In Sevilla itself—and excepting *Velázquez* (see below), whose work done in his native city has long since gone elsewhere—the most important figure, and perhaps the finest representative of Spanish religious painters, was **Francisco Zurbarán** (1598–1664). He travelled extensively in Spain, moving from cloister to cloister, illustrating saintly legends for the monks whose aspirations he shared. The dissolution of the monasteries scattered most of these works, but at least three series are still fairly complete and accessible: one devoted mainly to the Life of St. Jerome, which has remained at Guadalupe since 1639; another depicting Carthusian legends, now removed from the Cartuja at Jérez to the Cádiz Museum, and (attributed to his school) a number of female saints to be seen at the Museo de Bellas Artes at Sevilla. His early acquaintance with polychrome sculpture in the studio of *Pedro Diaz de Villanueva* in Sevilla, where he was apprenticed in 1614–16, strongly affected his practice, as may be seen in the Crucifixions in the Museum and in the S. Pedro

Nolasco series divided between Sevilla Cathedral and the Prado, in which figures and draperies resemble painted wood sculpture rather than human beings and woven stuffs. Later he was a pupil of Juan de las Roelas, but he was also greatly influenced by the 'tenebrists', by Ribera, and even by the young Velázquez. The application of Ribalta's chiaroscuro to his early training in naturalism produced Zurbarán's characteristic style of composition and side lighting. He borrowed, more than any other Spanish painter, new ideas from early 17C Antwerp engravings by Theodor Galle, Schelte, and Bolswert, a pupil of Rubens. Many of his compositions derive from 16C German prints by Dürer, Beham, and Salomon, as in the series of 'The Labours of Hercules' (in the Prado), painted in Madrid in 1634. Among his more attractive and original creations are the two large canvases in the Sevilla Museum depicting Carthusian brothers respectively kneeling beneath the wings of the Virgin's cloak and visited in their refectory by St. Hugo; in particular the Refectory with its cool fresh colours, still life paintings of loaves and blue and white pottery. Many of his single figures, ostensibly of saints in meditation, are portraits of his monkish friends: his solitary monks at prayer are more obviously creatures of his imagination.

A striving after realism had been a particular characteristic of the Sevilla School and the secret of it independent existence. **Bartolomé Esteban Murillo** (1617–82) arrived as an anticlimax, and just when the possibilities seemed greatest, reinstated academic standards and, indirectly, Italian idealism. He introduced the mawkish and 'picturesque' note which, in contrast to the force of Zurbarán, contributed so much and for so long to his popularity—the urchins, beggars, and flower girls of both his genre and religious compositions—and gave him an unrivalled place in public affections. He was long held in great esteem, and was highly regarded by Reynolds. He was also perhaps the first of the Spanish Baroque painters to achieve a convincing effect of figures floating up to heaven. A bitter theological controversy having provoked demonstrations in favour of the doctrine of the Immaculate Conception, Murillo, with easy conviction, took up the profitable role of 'Pintor de Concepciónes' to 'La Tierra de María Santísima', as the Sevillians called their province. But his success was his undoing. Possessing little imaginative power or creative invention, his run of commissions involved him in endless repetition of well-worn themes. In his later years his compositions are blurred by his 'estilo vaporoso', in which an enveloping yellow haze seems to suffuse every part. Perhaps the most impressive late examples are the paintings executed for the church of the *Caridad* at Sevilla in 1670–74.

Murillo's contemporary, *Juan de Valdés Leal* (1622–90), copiously represented in Sevilla, used the 'estilo vaporoso' a technical method derived from the Venetians. The most prominent and unpleasant feature is the tricky use of a hot red ground, which has since forced its way to the surface. But inequalities of handling and design, and a love of violent movement mar his works, and the Sevillian School virtually ended with *Esteban Márquez*, a heavy-handed academic imitator of Murillo's late work, and *Clemente Torres*, who reverted to the standards and tastes of the 16C.

Alonso Cano (1601–67), who was also an architect, studied sculpture with *Montañes* and painting under Pacheco, and, with his assistants, composed the short-lived SCHOOL OF GRANADA. His first signed known work in Sevilla is dated 1624, but in 1638 he was summoned to Madrid by the Conde-Duque de Olivares, and here he continued to train himself on the Titians, Rubenses, Van Dycks, and Riberas in the royal collections and churches. He later moved to Granada, his birthplace, where his canvases illustrating the Life of the Virgin (in the Cathedral) are among his most important paintings.

Many huge dull votive paintings in Sevilla are enlivened by portraits of their donors, but portraiture as a distinct branch did not exist in the early 16C outside the capital, where it was introduced on the accession of Felipe II, who brought *Antonio Moro (Anton van Dashort Mor*; active 1544–76), a Dutchman from Utrecht and a pupil of Scorel, to be his court painter. Mor is hard to find in England, despite the fact that he painted Mary Tudor in 1554, but he is superbly represented in the Prado, where he deserves careful study both for his own sake and because he established a tradition lasting until Velázquez, and even affecting the latter's youthful works. Mor's pupil *Sánchez Coello* of Valencia (c 1531–88), of Portuguese descent, who had been with him in Flanders, succeeded him as painter-in-ordinary to Felipe. The division between Mor and Sánchez Coello is sometimes difficult to mark, so deeply imbued with his master's spirit was Coello and so well trained in the transparent Flemish technique and the Flemish tradition of drawing. After Mor's departure, however, and under the influence of the king's Venetian portraits, Coello considerably broadened his handling and strengthened his colour; moreover, in his authentic works he has a very individual and engaging sense of aristocratic disdain and insolent humour which is quite different from Mor's burgher gravity. *Juan Pantoja de la Cruz* (1553–1608) studied under Coello, and stepped into his shoes during the next reign; Pantoja's successor was his imitator *Bartolomé González* (1564–1627).

The first visit to the Velázquez rooms at the Prado is an exciting experience, for nowhere else is there such an array of his masterpieces, from the naturalism and sombre tones of 'The Adoration', of 1619, painted in Sevilla, to his 'Las Hilanderas', painted nearly 40 years later. In his early years **Diego Velázquez de Silva** (1599–1660), also of Portuguese descent, was much influenced by Caravaggio and Rubens, whom he met in Madrid the year before he set out for Venice.

During his first visit to Italy (August 1629 to early 1631) Velázquez found much that was inspiring in Titian, Tintoretto, Guido Reni, and Massimo Stanzioni. In Italy he painted 'The Forge of Vulcan' and 'Joseph's Coat', and later, on returning to Madrid, he started work on 'Las Lanzas' (or 'The Surrender of Breda'), completed in 1640 (the composition of the two last derive from two woodcuts by Bernard Salomon in a book printed in Lyons in 1553). From 1649–51 Velázquez was in Rome, and on his return his work shows a steadily growing emphasis on colour, and, as exemplified in 'Las Meninas', his range and power, his subtlety and resource in his last phase can hardly be overestimated. And last of all, about 1660, is the enchanting unfinished portrait of the little Infanta, in her coral pink and flashing silver gown. Almost all his full-dress portraits of the royal family were copied, sometimes more than once, for presentation to foreign courts. These replicas, which are not always easily distinguished from the originals, were chiefly the work of his studio assistant and son-in-law *J.B. del Mazo* (?1612–67), and *Juan Carreño* (1614–85). For a painter trained under the eye of Velázquez, del Mazo in his original work is strangely uncertain in draughtsmanship, dull in colour, and weak in design, but his most serious defect is the faulty proportions of his figures, which are quite inadequately supported by their tapering legs and absurdly small feet. Carreño shows much more enjoyment of people, and more understanding of Velázquez, whom he took as his model when he turned to professional portraiture after long practice of religious painting in the manner of Van Dyck.

Strictly speaking, Velázquez did not belong to the SCHOOL OF MADRID, which had an independent origin and existence and pursued different ends. It was a numerous and prolific school, devoted mainly to historical, allegorical, and religious painting, and was grounded upon the Prado Titians, Rubenses, and Van Dycks which were then in various royal palaces—hence its conflicting aims and lack of local character. But one of the painters most affected by Velázquez was *Juan Bautista Maino* (1578–1649), who became a member of the Dominican monastery in Toledo in 1612. Other individual members of the school were *Antonio de Pereda* (1608–78) and *Jusepe Leonardo* (?1605–56) and, primarily religious painters, *José Antolínez* (1635–75) and *Mateo Cerezo* (1626–66), who were able draughtsmen and admirable colourists in the tradition of Van Dyck. Last in the line is *Claudio Coello* (1642–93), who is reputed to have spent seven years on his elaborate masterpiece, 'Carlos II worshipping the *Sagrada Forma'*, now in the Sacristy of the Escorial.

Felipe V, a Bourbon, who built the 'Spanish Versailles' at La Granja, brought *Michel-Ange Houasse* from Paris, and later came *Jean Ranc* and *Michel Van Loo*; from Italy *Luca Giordano* (1632–1705) had already reached Madrid by 1692. These artists and their fellows were so pampered, and their performances so exalted, that the listless native craftsmen simply aped them as paragons. In 1761 the Bohemian **Antón Rafael Mengs** (1728–79) settled in Madrid, and for the next two decades was the arbiter of taste. His portraits, which have perhaps been underestimated, were to influence Goya. Among the more important Spanish painters of the epoch may be mentioned the Catalan *Antoni Viladomat* (1678–1755), *Luis Meléndez* (1716–80), whose still lifes or *bodegones* are remarkable, *Luis Paret y Alcázar* (1746–99), an elegant painter of landscapes and court subjects, *José del Castillo* (1737–93), *Mariano Maella* (1739–1819), *Antonio Carnicero* (1748–1814), and *Agustin Esteve* (1753–1820?). Meanwhile, in the 1740s, a Royal Academy of Arts had been established in the capital, and later others were set up in some of the main cities of Spain, which did much to improve the general standard of work in the arts and crafts. The growing merchant class began to commission and collect paintings, and artists were no longer so dependent on royal patronage and the dictates of the Church.

Between 1776 and 1790 **Francisco de Goya** (1746–1828), encouraged by Mengs, was designing cartoons for the royal tapestry factory, illustrating popular outdoor scenes, which were remarkable for their variety, originality, and colour. Some were influenced by the French School of the period, and perhaps by prints of Hogarth's works; others by *G.B. Tiepolo* (1696–1770), who had come to Madrid in 1762 to decorate the new royal palace. Goya had also, in collaboration with his brother-in-law *Francisco Bayeu* (1734–95), worked on ceiling frescoes in Zaragoza between 1772 and 1783. He then started painting portraits, of which one of the earliest, and characteristic of his personal 'grey' style, is that of the Osuna family of 1787, to be followed by one of Bayeu (in the year of his death), and of the actress 'La Tirana' (1799). In 1799 Goya was made first painter to Carlos IV, but the devastating veracity of his portraits of the king, María Luisa, and the court, were very far from flattering. They are, however, suffused by a new richness of colour, while the composition and pose of some other examples, such as of Gen. Urrutia (1798) and Doña Tomasa Palafox (1804), recall Reynolds and Gainsborough. His later portraits are more sombre in style, but are no less impressive.

The entry of the French into Madrid, and the atrocities Goya witnessed at first hand in May 1808 and later, were to be the basis of some of his most dramatic paintings, and also inspired a grim series of etchings, 'The Disasters of War'. An earlier series—satires on the licentious nobility and the ignorant and unprincipled priesthood—known as 'The Caprichos', were followed by a bullfighting series, 'The Tauromachia', and by the so-called 'Proverbs'. Goya also decorated his house, the *'Quinta del Sordo'* (he had been almost stone deaf since the age of 47) with a remarkable series of saturnine murals, known as the 'Black Paintings', which have been transferred to the Prado. Whether they were the fruit of his own despair and isolation is hypothetical. In 1824 Goya retired to Bordeaux where he died. His remains were brought back to Madrid in 1919, where they rest in *S. Antonio de la Florida*, frescoed by himself in 1798, and which is now his mausoleum. The range, vitality, and impact of his work is indeed immense. Gautier remarked that in Goya's tomb was buried ancient Spanish art: 'all the world, which has now for ever disappeared, of torreros, majos, manolas, monks, smugglers, robbers, alguazils, and sorceresses; in a word, all the colour of the Peninsula. He came just in time to collect and perpetuate these various classes. He thought that he was merely producing so many capricious sketches, when he was in truth drawing the portrait and writing the history of the Spain of former days. . .'.

Among 19C painters, many of them portrait or genre painters (*Costumbristas*), were *Vicente López* (1772–1850), *José* and *Federico de Madrazo* (1781–1859 and 1815–94 respectively: from 1838–57 the former was a director of the Prado Museum, which had opened in 1819); *Antonio Esquivel* (1806–57); *José Elbo* (1804–44); *Leonardo Alenza* (1807–45); *Genaro Pérez Villaamil* (1807–54), and *Francisco Parcerisa* (1803–75), both best known for their topographical works; *Joaquin Espalter* (1809–80); *Eugenio Lucas* (1817–70); *José Casado del Alisel* (1832–86); *Eduardo Rosales* (1836–74); *Mariano Fortuny* (1838–74) and *José, Joaquin*, and *Valeriano Domínguez Becquer* (1809–41, 1817–79, and 1834–70 respectively). A later generation included the impressionists *Aureliano de Beruete* (1845–1912), and *Dario de Regoyos* (1857–1916); the Valencian *Joaquín Sorolla* (1862–1923), who achieved popularity with his sunny beach scenes; and a Catalan contingent, including *Santiago Rusiñol* (1861–1931), *Ramón Casas* (1866–1932), *Isidro Nonell* (1873–1911), *Joaquin Mir* (1873–1940), *Francesc Xavier Nogués* (1873–1941), and *Joaquim Sunyer* (1874–1956). *Ignacio Zuloaga* (1870–1945) exploited two distinct branches, fashionable portraiture and peasant genre scenes in combination with turbid landscapes. Also notable were the mural painter *José María Sert* (1874–1945); *Daniel Vázquez Díaz* (1882–1969); **José Gutiérrez Solana** (1886–1945), and the Cubist *Juan Gris* (1887–1927).

20C SPANISH ART. The most internationally famous, prolific and versatile (and some would say overrated) 20C Spanish artist was undoubtedly **Pablo Ruíz Picasso** (1881–1973), long exiled from his native country. He lived mostly in France from 1904, where numerous museums contain examples of his works, among them that in Antibes and the Musée Picasso in the Hôtel Salé in Paris, although the quality of the latter collection is uneven. Much of his earlier work may be seen in the Museu Picasso in Barcelona, which includes paintings of his 'Blue' and 'Pink' periods. This was followed from 1909 to 1917 by his involvement in the Cubist movement, and in 1924–29 with Surrealism. His huge painting of 1937 based on the bombing of Guernica during the Civil War (now displayed in Madrid) brought him further fame, while he also produced a quantity of prints during later decades, as well as sculptures and ceramics, and he continued to paint until well into his 80s.

The colourful art of **Joan Miró** (1893–1983), who also settled in Paris, in 1920, was at first much influenced by the folklore of his native Catalunya. Like Picasso, he was also a print maker, ceramicist and sculptor, and a selection of his output may be seen at the Miró Foundation in Barcelona.

Another Catalan was **Salvador Dalí** (1904–), with an international reputation as a Cubist, and later as a Surrealist, a movement with which he became disillusioned. (Gala, his wife, had been married previously to Paul Eluard, the Surrealist poet.) In 1928, together with Lluis Montanyà and the art critic Sebastià Gasch, Dalí signed the 'Manifest Groc' (or 'Yellow Manifesto'), attacking the Catalan culture of the time in Surrealist terms. In 1929 he collaborated with Luis Buñuel in making the Surrealist film 'Un Chien Andalou', which had a considerable impact. Dalí's art later descended into exhibitionism, but he remained an influential and provocative figure. A Dalí museum may be visited at Figueres.

In the 1950s the Catalan groups known as the 'Dau Al Set' came to the fore, with *Antonio Tapiès*, known for his textural paintings, its leading member. In Madrid the 'El Paso' group included the formalist and abstract artists *Manuel Millares, Antonio Saura, Rafael Canogar, Luís Feito*, and *José Guerro*. In the 1960s 'Pop Art' was fashionable, with the 'Equipo Cronico' contributing to the scene. Other important artists of the post Civil War period were *Fernando Zóbel* and *Eusebio Sempere*, who died in 1984 and 1985 respectively.

While it may be invidious to name contemporaries, among the more accomplished are the following; how many will survive the fluctuations of fashion remains to be seen: *Juan Genovés, José Guinovart, Ginés Liebana, Antonio López García, César Manrique, Lucio Muñoz, Pablo Palazuelo, Benjamin Palencia, Manuel Rivera, Ramiro Tapia* and *Gustavo Torner*.

In the 1980s *Zush, Féderico Amet, Miguel Barcelo* and *José-Maria Sicilia* have continued the Post-Modern tradition, showing their works both in Spain and abroad, and continued to develop the Spanish use of colour, form and image.

Notable among sculptors are *Miguel Ortiz Berrocal, Eduardo Chillida, Julio López Hernández, Jorge de Oteiza*, and *Pablo Serrano*.

Key to Basque Provinces
1 Vizcaya
2 Guipúzcoa
3 Aláva

SCONGADAS
(BA)SQUE PROVINCES

FRANCE

NAVARRA

ANDORRA

RIOJA

Huesca

Lleida

Girona

CATALUNYA

ria

Zaragoza

Barcelona

ARAGÓN

adalajara

Teruel

Tarragona

Castellón

Cuenca

-MANCHA

VALENCIA

Valencia

Albacete

Alicante

MURCIA

Almería

The Autonomias and Provinces

GEOGRAPHICAL INTRODUCTION;
THE AUTONOMIES; DEMOGRAPHY

Spain is the second most elevated and *mountainous* country in Europe (after Switzerland), with an average height of c 600m above sea-level, a point to be taken into consideration when planning a tour; see p 76–78.

Its main physical feature is a vast elevated plateau or *meseta*—two-fifths of the country—divided by a central chain of mountains (the sierras of Guadarrama, Gredos, and Gata) running W from the Iberian mountains. It has been estimated (in the 1960s) that 33.7 per cent of the soil produced virtually nothing. The northern section comprises a large area of Castilla y León; the southern part includes most of Castilla-La Mancha and Extremadura. The northern meseta, also known as the Duero basin, is cut off from the Atlantic coast to the N by the Picos de Europa and the Cantabrian mountains, a westward extension of the main Pyrenean chain, while to the NW the Montes de León combine to make remote Galicia difficult of access.

Between France and Spain is the formidable barrier of the Pyrenees, c 400km long and well over 1500m high for most of its length, and with a maximum height of 3404m (*Pic d'Aneto*). On the Spanish side, foothills of the range extend some distance into Aragón and Catalunya before reaching the wide depression of the Ebro valley. To the W and S of the Ebro a further range, the Iberian mountains, runs SE from Burgos to the coast near Valencia, providing a watershed between the Duero and Ebro, and including in its complex the Sierra de Demanda, Sierra de Moncayo, the Montes Universales, and the Sierra de Gúdar.

S of Madrid, the rivers Tagus and Guadiana run W through the southern meseta, separated by the lower Montes de Toledo and Sierra de Guadalupe. To the S, beyond the broad and broken Sierra Morena, extends the wide low-lying valley of the Guadalquivir. Still further S, rising abruptly from the Mediterranean coast and running roughly parallel to it for over 550km, are the complex ranges composing the Betic Cordillera, the main chain of which, the Sierra Nevada, rises SE of Granada to 3482m (*Mulhacén*), the highest summit in Spain. All these mountain ranges provide a variety of scenery amply compensating for the occasional monotony of the undulating plateaux.

The Pyrenees may be crossed at a number of points, and are passed with ease at either end. From its western extremity, travellers must climb through the broken and mountainous Basque provinces before reaching the Castilian plateau NE of Burgos, while from Barcelona the Ebro valley is ascended as far as Zaragoza before the road climbs through the Iberian mountains to approach Madrid. Almost all these ranges are traversed by reasonably surfaced and improved roads, and although during winter months some passes or *puertos* are intermittently blocked by falls of snow, there is now little difficulty in getting about the country.

In the past the problems of communication contributed to the localism of towns and separation of provinces. Climatic conditions further emphasise the physical divisions. The Basque Provinces, the Asturias, and Galicia—humid, green and often thickly wooded—are in striking contrast to the calcined plains and keen air of adjacent

Castilla y León. Modern methods of irrigation, reafforestation, etc. have combined to obscure these differences, but they still remain.

After a difficult period of *'pre-autonomia'*, the country has for administrative purposes been split into 15 mainland **Autonomies**, partly for historical reasons (particularly in the cases of the Basque provinces and Catalunya), and partly because of these physical barriers. In many cases their borders conform to the frontiers of former kingdoms, although the provinces of Logroño and Santander were previously part of what was Old Castile, which has now merged with León. The province of Albacete, formerly part of Murcia, has been annexed to New Castile to form Castilla-La Mancha, but that of Madrid has separated from it.

The autonomies are:

Autonomy	*including the provinces of*	*Administrative capital*
Andalucía	Almería, Cádiz, Córdoba, Granada, Huelva, Jaén, Málaga, Sevilla	Sevilla
Aragón	Huesca, Teruel, Zaragoza	Zaragoza
Asturias		Oviedo
Cantabria		Santander
Castilla y León	Ávila, Burgos, León, Palencia, Salamanca, Valladolid, Segovia, Soria, Zamora	Valladolid
Castilla-La Mancha	Albacete, Ciudad Real, Cuenca, Guadalajara, Toledo	Toledo
Catalunya	Barcelona, Girona, Lleida, Tarragona	Barcelona
Extremadura	Badajoz, Cáceres	Mérida
Galicia	A Coruña, Lugo, Ourense, Pontevedra	Santiago
Madrid		Madrid
Murcia		Murcia
Navarra		Pamplona
País Vasco/ Euskadi	Alava, Guipúzcoa, Vizcaya (Araba, Gipuzkoa, Bizkaia, in Basque)	Vitoria/Gasteiz
La Rioja		Logroño
Valencia	Castellón, Alicante, Valencia	Valencia

The correct titles of certain autonomies are: the *Principado de Asturias*; the *Comunidad Valenciana*; the *Comunidad Foral de Navarra*; the *Comunidad de Madrid*, and the *Región de Murcia*.

The movement of population from the smaller towns and villages of Spain to the larger urban areas and provincial capitals continues. Of the total population of *mainland* Spain, 35,540,000, some 39 per cent live in the capitals of provinces or autonomies. A continuous decline in population has taken place in the provinces of Ávila, Badajoz, Ciudad Real, Cuenca, Jaén, León, Lugo, Ourense, Segovia, Soria, Teruel, and Zamora. With the exception of Ciudad Real, Jaén, and León, they all have less population than in 1920, when the total population of mainland Spain was only 22,008,000. The provinces of Guadalajara, Huesca and Palencia also have a lower population than they did in 1920, but without showing a recent decline. The total population of Spain (in 1981) was 37,682,000. The provincial capitals (which do not include several other large towns) account for a total of

13,692,000 inhabitants. The figure in 1920 was a mere 4,055,000 and in 1950 only 7,457,000.

Those interested in past statistics may note that the population of Spain in 1715 was approx. 6,000,000, which by 1768 had risen to 9,307,000 (of which 176,000 were monks, nuns, friars, and secular clergy) and by 1791 had reached the figure of 10,143,000. Among these were 27,500 foreign *heads of families*, including 13,332 French, 1577 Germans, and 140 English. By 1800 the total population was estimated at 12,000,000.

Glossary

Acotado, preserve (shooting or fishing)

Adarve, wall walk

Ajaracas, brickwork in trellis pattern

Ajimez, two-light Moorish window divided by slender column

Alameda, promenade, usually tree-lined

Alcázaba, Moorish citadel

Alcázar, Moorish fortified place

Alfiz, rectangular moulding, often above a horseshoe arch

Alhóndiga, corn exchange or public granary; also *Almudin*

Alicatado, mosaic of glazed tiles

Alto, a height

Arroyo, a spring

Artesonado, wooden coffered ceiling

Atalaya, watch-tower, often coastal

Atarazanas, ship yards; *Drassens* in Catalan

Audiencia, law courts

Avenida, avenue; *Avinguda* in Catalan

Avitolado, imitation of brick courses, noticeable in Sevilla

Ayuntamiento, town hall; also *Casa consistorial*; *Ajuntament* in Catalan

Azulejo, glazed tile

Balneario, spa

Barranco, ravine

Barrio, district or suburb; an *ensanche* is usually a newly built extension to a town; *Barri* in Catalan

Bocacalle, side street

Bodega, cellar or warehouse, often also a wine bar

Bodegón, a still life

Boveda, vault

Calle, street; *calleja* or *callejón*, alley, often blind; *Carrer* in Catalan

Camarín, shrine of an image

Camino, road

Campo, countryside, field, or plain

Capilla, chapel; *capilla major*, chancel containing the high altar

Carretera, route, highway

Cartuja, Carthusian monastery

Castillo, castle; *Castell* in Catalan

Cerrado, shut

Chorro, waterfall

Churrigueresque, name given to an extreme form of Baroque architecture (after *José Churriguera*, 1650–1723, and members of his family)

Cimborio, cupola, lantern

Circunvalación, bypass

Ciudad, town, *Ciutat* in Catalan

Claustro, cloister

Colegiata, collegiate church

Comedor, dining room

Converso, a Jew converted to Catholicism

Coro, choir, usually in the centre of the nave, but sometimes over the W entrance (*coro alto*); *Cor* in Catalan

Cortes, Parliament

Cortijo, farm or estate

Coto de Caza, shooting preserve

Crucero, crossing of a church, transept

Cuartel, barracks, military or police

Cubo, semicircular tower in town walls

Cuesta, a slope

Cueva, cave

Custodia, monstrance

Dehesa, pasture land

Desfiladero, pass or defile

Despoblado, uninhabited place

Embalse, reservoir

Ermita, hermitage or chapel

Esmalte, enamel

Fachada, façade

Facistol, lectern

Ferrocarril, railway

Finca, farm

Feria, annual fair

Frontón, court with one high wall, in which the Basque ball game of *pelota* is played

Fuente, fountain, or spring

Fuero, charter of civic privileges

Garganta, gorge

Glorieta, roundabout

Herreran, a post-Plateresque and pre-Baroque style of architecture, named after *Juan de Herrera* (1530–97)

Hórreos, farm storehouse ubiquitous in Galicia and (less so) in the Asturias; see p 222

Huerta, highly cultivated land

Iglesia, church; *Església* in Catalan

Infante, a prince; *Infanta*, a princess

Isabelline, a style of architecture in fashion during the reign of the Catholic Kings

Judería, ghetto; *Call* in Catalan; also *Aljama*

Lago, lake

Lonja, exchange building; *Llotja* in Catalan

Mampostería, rubble masonry

Marfil, ivory

Marisma, marsh

Marmol, marble

Media naranja, half-orange (of cupola)

Ménsula, corbel or console

Mercado, market; *Mercat* in Catalan

Meseta, plateau

Mesón, inn; also *fonda* or *venta*

Mirador, balcony, belvedere or viewpoint

Molino, mill

Monte, mountain

Morería, Moorish quarter of a town after the Christian reconquest

Morisco, Moor nominally baptised as a Christian

Mozárabe, Christian subject to the Moors; the term *Mozarabic* extended to their architecture

Mudéjar, Moslem subject to the Christians; a term extended to their architecture

Muelle, quay

Muwallad or *Muladi*, a Christian converted to Islam

Obispo, bishop; *Bisbe* in Catalan

Palacio, royal mansion or palace; in the Asturias, any mansion; *Palau* in Catalan

Pantano, reservoir

Páramo, moor or heath

Paseo, promenade; also a stroll or walk; *Passeig* in Catalan

Pasos, religious sculptures taken in procession at Easter

Patio, courtyard; *Pati* in Catalan

Paço or *Pazo*, country manor, in Galicia

Peaje, toll

Peña, rock, or summit

Pico, a peak

Plateresque, an exuberant and ornate form of Renaissance architecture in Spain influenced by that of Lombardy

Playa, beach; *Platja* in Catalan

Plaza, town square or place; *Plaza mayor*, the main square; *Plaça* in Catalan

Población, town, populated place

Posada, inn

Presa, dam

Pueblo, village; *Poble* in Catalan

Puente, bridge; *Pont* in Catalan

Puerta, gate or doorway; *Portal* in Catalan

Puerto, mountain pass, or harbour

Rambla, boulevard, or dry riverbed

Reja, iron grille, guarding window, or a chapel

Respaldos, exterior side wall of the choir

Retablo, large altar piece, sculptured, carved, or painted (or all three); *Retaule* in Catalan

Ría, estuary, in Galicia

Río, river

Rollo, a pillory

Ronda, circular boulevard

Rúa, street, in Galicia

Sagrario, sacristy; also sanctuary, or monstrance

Salida, exit

Seo, cathedral, in Aragón and Catalunya

Sierra, range of hills or mountains

Sillería, choir stalls; also ashlar masonry

Solar or *casa solariaga*, old town mansion

Tajo, gorge

Tancada, shut (in Catalan)

Tapia, a sunbaked brick wall

Torre, tower

Trasaltar, wall behind altar, facing the ambulatory

Trassagrario, back of the high altar; ambulatory behind the *Capilla mayor*

Travesía, lane

Vega, alluvial plain

Verja, railing round a tomb

Villa, small town

Yacente, recumbent effigy

Zócalo, base, plinth, or dado

Maps

The latest edition of the *Michelin Map* of *France* (No. 989) or the
Carte Routière of France published by the *Institut Géographique
National*—both at 1:1,000,000—are recommended for motorists dis-
embarking at the Channel ports. Travellers entering from Portugal
should obtain *Michelin* No. 437 at 1:400,000. *Blue Guides* for France
and Portugal will not come amiss.

The Spanish *Instituto Geográfia Nacional* (IGN; C. Gen. Ibañez de
Ibero 3, 28003 Madrid) publishes numerous maps of varying quality
and scale, but they are not easy to find at short notice. There is now
less excuse for the traveller to find 'by chance' (as did Widdrington in
1843) a good plan of Granada in Málaga, although no bookshop in
Granada had heard of it. A *Centro de Información y Documentación*
is adjacent to the IGN offices. A general map published by IGN
entitled *Peninsula Ibérica* at 1:1,000,000, can be useful, and gives a
good idea of physical features (but not road distances).

The *Mapa Oficial de Carreteras* (in atlas form), published by the
Min. de Obras Publicas y Urbanismo (MOPU) at the same scale, with
an index and additional information, indicates many minor roads and
hamlets, but it is by no means as reliable as it should be, and no
contour is indicated.

Spanish military maps of varying quality are available from the
Servicio Geográfia del Ejército, and details may be obtained from the
Spanish IGN.

For general purposes the *Michelin* No. 990 at 1:1,000,000, covering
the whole of the Peninsula, is recommended as giving an overall
view for planning a tour. The new *Michelin* series of seven maps
(Nos 441–447; at 1:400,000), each of which include an index with
map co-ordinates, are essential supplements for anyone travelling off
the main roads. Although they are superior in many ways to most
maps at similar scales, they can be misleading occasionally, particularly in mountainous districts, when a road shown to have a few
small bends and a zigzag, in the event climbs up and down, twisting
and turning almost continually.

These, and other maps of a more specialised nature, should be
available from, or may be ordered through *Stanfords*, 12–14 Long
Acre, London WC2, or *McCarta*, 122 Kings Cross Road, London WC1,
or any good bookshop.

A variety of maps may be brought in Spain at *Phoebe, S.A.*, C.
Fernández de los Ríos 95, 28015 Madrid (metro Moncloa); and C.
Balmes 6, Barcelona.

Bibliography

Grouped below are a number of books in English about Spain; many
contain bibliographies for further reading. The *Spanish Institute
Library*, 102 Eaton Square, the *Hispanic Council Library*, 2 Belgrave
Square, London SW1, and the *Library of the Hispanic Society of
America*, 613 West 155th St, New York, should not be overlooked.

TOPOGRAPHICAL AND GENERAL. Among older works of particular value are: *Joseph Baretti*, A Journey from London to Genoa (1770, reprinted 1970); *Richard Ford*, Gatherings from Spain (1846, reprinted 1970), Hand-Book for Travellers in Spain (1845); the latter, of outstanding importance, was reprinted in its entirety in 1966; *George Borrow*, The Bible in Spain (1843), and The Zincali, or Gypsies of Spain (1841), are frequently reprinted.

Among later works of some interest are *Havelock Ellis*, The Soul of Spain (1908); *Hilaire Belloc*, The Pyrenees (1909); and *Rafael Shaw*, Spain from Within (1910). The once-restricted British Naval Intelligence Geographical Handbooks (1941; 1944) contain much curious information.
  Among the earlier descriptions of Spain, the following are the most notable: Private Correspondence of *Sir Benjamin Keene* (1933); *Henry Swinburne*, Travels through Spain (1779); *Joseph Townsend*, A Journey through Spain (1792); *Alexander Jardine*, Letters from Barbary (1788); *F.A. Fischer*, Travels in Spain (1802); *J. Bourgoing*, The Modern State of Spain (1808); *Lady E. Holland*, The Spanish Journal of (1910); *J. Blanco White*, Letters from Spain (1822); *A. Sliddell-Mackenzie* (the 'Young American'), A Year in Spain (1831), and Spain Revisited (1836); [?*Henry Southern*] Madrid in 1835 (1836); *S.E. Cook*, later *Widdrington*, Sketches in Spain (1834), and Spain and the Spaniards (1844); *C. Rochfort Scott*, Excursions in the Mountains of Ronda and Granada (1838); *G. Dennis*, A Summer in Andalucia (1839); and *T.M. Hughes*, Revelations of Spain (1845).
  A revised edition of *Ian Robertson*, Los Curiosos Impertinentes, a study of English travellers in Spain between 1760 and 1855 was published, in Spanish only, in 1988.

More recent works include: *Gerald Brenan*, The Face of Spain, and South from Granada; *V.S. Pritchett*, the Spanish Temper; *Sacheverell Sitwell*, Spain; *H.V. Morton*, A Stranger in Spain; *Robin Fedden*, The Enchanted Mountains (Pyrenees); *H. Myhill*, the Spanish Pyrenees; *Walter Starkie*, Spanish Raggle Taggle, The Road to Santiago, and Don Gypsy; *Rose Macaulay*, Fabled Shore; *J. Langdon-Davies*, Gatherings from Catalonia; *Fernand Braudel*, the Mediterranean; *P.E. Russell* (Ed.), Spain, a Companion to Spanish Studies (6th revised edition); *A. Boyd*, Madrid and Central Spain, and Essence of Catalonia.

GENERAL HISTORY. *H.N. Savory*, Spain and Portugal, the Prehistory of the Iberian Peninsula; *Simon J. Keay*, Roman Spain; *C.H.V. Sutherland*, The Romans in Spain, 217 BC–AD 117; *H.V. Livermore*, The Origins of Spain and Portugal; *E.A. Thompson*, The Goths in Spain; *R. Menéndez Pidal*, The Cid and his Spain; *Roger Collins*, The Basques (Peoples of Europe Series), Early Medieval Spain, 400–1000; *Américo Castro*, The Structure of Spanish History (revised edition entitled The Spaniards); *G. Jackson*, The Making of Medieval Spain; *W. Montgomery Watt*, History of Islamic Spain; *D.W. Lomax*, The Reconquest of Spain; *Peter Linehan*, The Spanish Church and the Papacy in the Thirteenth Century; *Sir Thomas Kendrick*, St. James in Spain; *J.F. O'Callaghan*, History of Medieval Spain; *J.N. Hillgarth*, The Spanish Kingdoms 1250–1516; *Angus Mackay*, Spain in the Middle Ages; *P.E. Russell*, The English Intervention in Spain and Portugal in the time of Edward III and Richard II; *J. Vicens Vives*, Economic History of Spain, and Approaches to the History of Spain; *W.R. Childs*, Anglo-Castilian Trade in the later Middle Ages; *J.H. Elliott*, Imperial Spain, 1469–1716, The Revolt of the Catalans, 1598–1640, and The Count-Duke of Olivares; *T.N. Bisson*, The Medieval Crown of Aragon; *H. Kamen*, The Spanish Inquisition, Inquisition and Society in Spain, The War of the Succession in Spain (1700–15), the political and economic background, Spain 1469–1714, a Society in Conflict, and Spain in the later seventeenth century 1665–1700; *G. Mattingly*, The Defeat of the Spanish Armada; *J.H. Parry*, The Spanish Seaborne Empire; *J. Lynch*, Spain under the Habsburgs, 1516–1700; *A.W. Lovett*, Early Habsburg Spain, 1517–1598; *A. Domínguez Ortiz*, The Golden Age of Spain, 1516–1659; *R. Herr*, The 18th Century Revolution in Spain; *G. Marañon*, Antonio Perez; *A.A. Neuman*, The Jews in Spain; *Y. Baer*, History of the Jews in Christian Spain; *T.F. Glick*, Islamic and Christian Spain in the Early Middle Ages; *E. Ashtor*, The Jews of Moslem Spain; *Salvador de Madariaga*, Christopher Columbus; *G.W.C. Oman*, History of the Peninsular War (7 vols), and Wellington's Army; *J. Weller*, Wellington in the Peninsula; *David Gates*, The Spanish Ulcer; *E. Longford*, Wellington, the Years of the Sword; *A. Bryant*, The Great Duke; *Julia V. Page* (ed.) Intelligence Officer in the Peninsula (Edward Charles Cocks); *E. Holt*, The Carlist Wars in Spain; *R. Carr*, Spain, 1808–1975; *H.J. Chaytor*, History of Aragon and Catalonia; *A.D. Francis*, the First Peninsular War, 1702–1713; *J. Read*, the Moors in Spain and Portugal; *W.N. Hargreaves-Mawdsley*, Eighteenth Century Spain; *C.E. Kany*, Life and Manners in Madrid, 1750–1800; *S. Harcourt-Smith*, Alberoni, or the Spanish Conspiracy; *Michael Glover*, The Peninsular War, 1807–14; *George Hills*, Rock of Contention (Gibraltar); *J.F. Coverdale*, The Basque Phase of Spain's First Carlist War; *R.A. Stradling*, Philip IV and the Government of Spain 1621–1665; *Julian Rathbone*, Wellington's War.

Among earlier works of interest are: *W.H. Prescott*, History of Ferdinand and Isabella (1842), and History of Philip II (1878); *Butler Clarke*, Modern Spain (1906); *A. Parnell*, The Wars of the Succession in Spain (1888), and *R. Dozy*, Spanish Islam, trans. by F. G. Stokes (1913).

MODERN HISTORY. *B. Bolloten*, The Grand Camouflage; *F. Borkenau*, The Spanish Cockpit; *Gerald Brenan*, The Spanish Labyrinth; *Gamel Woolsey*, Death's Other Kingdom; *G. Hills*, Spain; *G. Jackson*, The Spanish Republic and the Civil War; *Salvador de Madariaga*, Spain; *George Orwell*, Homage to Catalonia; *S.G. Payne*, The Falange, The Spanish Revolution, Politics and the Military in Modern Spain; *Hugh Thomas*, The Spanish Civil War (1977 edition); *R.A.H. Robinson*, The Origins of Franco's Spain; *D.T. Cattell*, Communism and the Spanish Civil War; *P. Broué* and *E. Témime*, The Revolution and the Civil War in Spain; *Arturo Barea*, The Forging of a Rebel (autobiography); *Paul Preston*, Spain in Crisis, The Coming of the Spanish Civil War, and The Triumph of Democracy in Spain; *David Gilmour*, The Transformation of Spain; *Robert P. Clark*, The Basque Insurgents, ETA 1952–80; *Ronald Fraser*, Blood of Spain; *Raymond Carr* and *J.P. Fusi*, Spain: Dictatorship to Democracy.

ART AND ARCHITECTURE, ETC., but not including works on specific artists or picture books. *Bernard Bevan*, History of Spanish Architecture, the standard work in English, an extended edition of which is in prepartion; *W.M. Whitehill*, Spanish Romanesque Architecture of the 11th Century; *J.H. Harvey*, The Cathedrals of Spain; *A.N. Prentice*, Spanish Renaissance Architecture and Ornament, 1500–1560 (rev'd edition, 1970); *Pedro de Palol* and *M. Hirmer*, Early Medieval Art in Spain; *C. Oman*, The Golden Age of Spanish Silver, 1400–1665; *A.W. Frothingham*, Spanish Glass; *J. Lees Milne*, Baroque in Spain and Portugal; *G. Kubler* and *M. Soria*, Art and Architecture in Spain and Portugal and their Spanish Dominions, 1500–1800; *Sacheverell Sitwell*, Southern Baroque Art, and Spanish Baroque Art; *Royall*

Tyler, Spain, a Study of her Life and Arts (1909); *C.R. Post*, A History of Spanish Painting (14 vols); *J.W. Waterer*, Spanish Leather; *D. and H. Kraus*, The Gothic Choirstalls of Spain; *Oleg Grabar*, The Alhambra; *Jonathan Brown* and *J.H. Elliott*, A Palace for a King; *Arts Council of Great Britain*, Homage to Barcelona, the city and its art (1888–1936).

Among earlier works is *G.E. Street*, Some Account of Gothic Architecture in Spain (1855; rev'd edition 1914, since reprinted); also of interest for the large number of plates they contain is *Muirhead Bone*, Old Spain (folio ed.; 1936).

LITERATURE. *W.J. Entwistle*, The Spanish Language; *Gerald Brenan*, The Literature of the Spanish People; *E. Allison Peers*, The Romantic Movement in Spain; *N. D. Shergold*, History of the Spanish stage (to 1700); *R.O. Jones* (Ed.), A Literary History of Spain (in 8 vols); *George Ticknor*, History of Spanish Literature (1849; reprinted 1965); *D.L. Shaw*, The Generation of 1898 in Spain; *José Alberich*, Bibliografía Anglo-Hispánica, 1801–50; *Philip Ward* (Ed.), The Oxford Companion to Spanish Literature.

MISCELLANEOUS. *M. Defourneaux*, Daily Life in Spain in the Golden Age; *J. Pitt-Rivers*, The People of the Sierra; *Rodney Gallop*, Book of the Basques; *A. Livermore*, Short History of Spanish Music; *J. Read*, The Wines of Spain; *Abel Chapman* and *W.J. Buck*, Unexplored Spain (1910), and Wild Spain (1893), both reprinted in Spain.

PRACTICAL INFORMATION

Formalities and Currency

Passports are necessary for all British and American travellers entering Spain. *British Visitors' Passports* (valid one year), available from Post Offices in the UK, are also accepted. No visa is required for British or American visitors.

Custom House. Except for travellers by air, who have to pass Customs at the airport of arrival, or those travelling on international expresses, where their luggage is examined in the train, luggage (*equipaje*) is scrutinised at the frontier or port of disembarkation. Provided that dutiable articles are declared, bona fide travellers will usually find the Spanish customs authorities (*aduaneros*) reasonable. It is as well to check in advance with Spanish Consulates or Tourist Offices for the latest regulations on the importation of firearms.

Embassies and Consulates in Spain. *British*, C. Fernando el Santo 16, 28010 Madrid (the Embassy); Av. de la Fuerzas Armadas 11, 11202 Algeciras; C. Duquesa de Parcent 4, 29001 Málaga; Pl. Nueva 8, 41001 Sevilla; Pl. de Compostela 23–6°, 36201 Vigo; Pl. Calvo Sotelo 1/2–1°, 03001 Alicante; Diagonal 477–13°, 08006 Barcelona; C. Real 33, 43004 Tarragona; Alameda de Urquijo 2–8, 48008 Bilbao; and Paseo de Pereda 27, 39004 Santander.
  USA Consulates will be found at C. Serrano 75, Madrid (the Embassy), with consulates at Via Laietana 33, Barcelona; Paseo de las Delicias 7, Sevilla; and Av. del Ejército 11, Deusto-Bilbao 12. The *Canadian* Embassy is at C. Nuñez de Balboa 35, Madrid, with consulates at Via Augusta 125, Barcelona; Plaza de la Malagueta 3, Málaga; Av. de la Constitución 24, Sevilla.

The addresses of the **Spanish Embassy** in London is 24 Belgrave Square, SW1 (Consulate at 20 Draycott Place, SW3).

Medical Advice. British travellers in Spain, covered by the British National Insurance Scheme, may obtain free medical assistance under the Spanish Health Service during their stay; but for further information apply to your local Health Authority Office.

Security and Hazards. Travellers should take care: robbery, sometimes with violence, is on the increase in several major cities and *costas* of Spain. Luggage, at airports, stations, and on ferries, should not be left unattended. Cars, even if parked for a moment, should *always* be locked, and preferably parked in a well-lit position at night, if not in hotel garages. It is tempting providence to leave *any* valuables, packets, suitcases, coats, etc. visible in cars, whether by day or night. Foreign number plates are very obvious. Be very cautious when collecting cash from autobanks. Do not flourish bundles of notes. Jewellery should not be displayed. Beware of bag snatchers (*tiron*), some on motorbikes. Straps of bags should be worn *across* the body, not just over one shoulder, but a belt is preferable. Particular care should be taken of credit cards, driving licences and passports. A note of their numbers, and of emergency telephone numbers for the cancellation of cards, should be kept in a safe place. Valuables sould be deposited with the manager of one's hotel against receipt, although a personal safe may be hired in some hotels.

Apart from the common pickpocket and sneakthief (*ratero*), there are organised gangs preying on tourists in several of the larger cities—Barcelona, and Sevilla are notorious, but likewise Granada, Málaga, Córdoba, Valencia, and Madrid, among others. Should one suffer any loss, or be attacked, apply to the *Comisaría de policía* immediately, and ask for a copy of your statement, as this may be required by your insurance company. There are usually overworked translators at the main police stations of the main towns. The police themselves are often unsympathetic and unhelpful, and may not even have the address to hand of local consulates. Their usual excuse is that such robberies take place because of the *paro* (unemployment), or that the *ladron* needs money to buy drugs, and that there is nothing they can do about it. It is unwise to travel without having taken out suitable insurance before leaving home.

Women are warned to expect some form of sexual harassment—often merely some impudent personal comment—from *macho* Spaniards, who will assume that they are irresistible, and that any foreign female is fair game. The best way to counter such approaches, notably in Andalucía, is to ignore them entirely—however persistent.

Currency Regulations. There is no restriction on the amount of sterling the traveller may take *out* of Great Britain, nor any limit to the amount of foreign currency which may be brought into and taken out of Spain (provided proof is shown that the visitor entered with such an amount), but such regulations are in the process of radical revision.

Money. The monetary unit is the *peseta*, divided into 100 *céntimos* (now rarely seen). Bank notes for 100, 200, 500, 1000, 2000, and 5000 pesetas are issued by the Banco de Espáñna, together with coins of 1, 5 (still referred to as a '*duro*'), 10, 25, 50, 100, 200 and 500 pesetas.

Exchange. Branches of Spanish banks and foreign banks in Spain are to be found near the centres of most towns, and are open from 9.00 to 14.00 only from Monday to Friday, and 9.00–13.00 on Saturday. A sign is usually displayed outside that change (*cambio*) is given, and there is now less difficulty than there was in changing travellers cheques etc., although there is an unconscionable delay in some banks. Exchange Bureaux are also to be found at airports and points of entry into Spain, often providing a 24-hour service. It is advisable to obtain a supply of Spanish change for incidental expenses before leaving home, particularly if travelling at weekends. Motorists are advised to carry sufficient money to cover minor expenses on the road, apart from petrol, as most garages only accept cash.

Major *credit cards* are now usually accepted, but it is as well to check in advance, when booking into hotels.

The Banco Popular and Banco Atlantico are primarily interested in speculating to the profit of the 'Opus Dei'.

Approaches to Spain; Transport and Motoring in Spain

There are several rapid rail and ferry services from London to the Channel ports, and beyond (see below), while the quickest means of transit is by air. Car hire facilities are available at airports, main railway stations, and elsewhere in Spain, but it is preferable to book in advance from the UK.

Travel Information. General information may be obtained gratis from the *Spanish National Tourist Office* at 57–58 St. James's Street, London SW1, while in most of the larger towns of Spain there are National, Regional, or Municipal Tourist Offices. They can provide information on accommodation, admission to museums, entertainment, festivals, etc.

The Spanish National Tourist Offices in *New York* is at 665 Fifth Av., N.Y. 1022, with branches at Water Tower Place, Suite 915 East, 845 N Michigan Av., *Chicago*; 5085 Westheimer, 4800 The Galería, *Houston*; 8383 Wilshire Blvd, Suite 960, *Beverly Hills*; and Casa del Hildalgo, Hipolita & St. George Streets, *St. Augustine*, Florida. In *Toronto*, it is 60 Bloor Street West, Suite 201.

There are numerous and frequent **Passenger** and **Car Ferry Services** between England and the Continent. Enquiries should be made to the **Car Ferry Centre**, 53 Grosvenor Gardens, London SW1. Hovercraft services may be erratic in adverse weather conditions.

The only direct ferry between England and Spain at present (1988) in operation is that between *Plymouth* and *Santander* (Brittany Ferries; Millbay Dock, Plymouth).

British Rail can provide full details of the variety of rail services available, together with their cost, and information with regard to Motorail (car carrier) expresses (*auto-expreso* in Spain), any special reductions, etc. on British, French, and Spanish Railways (RENFE—*Red Nacional de Ferrocarriles Españoles*).

Regular **Air Services** between Britain and Spain are maintained by *Iberia*, working in conjunction with *British Airways*. Full information regarding flights from London and elsewhere in the UK, and of internal services, may be obtained from Iberia, 169 Regent Street, London W1 or from British Airways, 75 Regent Street. A variety of services are also available from charter companies.

There are regular direct services from the USA, Canada, from most European capitals and larger cities to a number of destinations in Spain, and also from many other non-European countries.

From airports there are bus services to the town termini, and in many cases coach connections with other towns or resorts in the area. Taxis meet planes, and many car-hire firms have offices at airports. Services available at some Spanish airports have considerable room for improvement before they approach the standard set by many others of similar international importance. Few have any left luggage office (*consigna*) at the time of writing, with the excuse of 'terrorism', and will not accept luggage until the normal booking-in time.

In addition to a number of international through coach services from London to several destinations in Spain, there are numerous regular **Bus Services** (*Coches de Linea; autobuses*) between the main towns in Spain, apart from additional tourist services during the season. Fares are comparatively moderate.

Inquiry should be made in advance from local tourist offices as to the times and place of departure, but is always as well to have this confirmed and booked in advance at the bus station (*Estación de autobuses*), as seating is limited. Tickets are usually for a numbered seat, and can sometimes be booked for the return journey (*ida y vuelta*—there and back).

Taxis, pronounced *Tassi*, no longer inexpensive, display the sign 'LIBRE' ('LLIURE' in Catalunya) when free. Surcharges apply for drives outside town, to stations, airports, luggage placed in the boot, on Sundays, and late at night, etc. A tip of 10 per cent of the fare is more than enough.

Horse cabs can still be found in some Andalucian cities, but a very definite bargain should be made beforehand as to the duration of the drive and the total cost.

Local tourist offices in the main cities can advise on what tickets are available, and where, for municipal bus services, and also for the underground or *Metropolitano*, when applicable.

Motorists driving to Spain will save much trouble by joining the *Automobile Association* (Fanum House, Basingstoke, Hants RG21 2EA), the *Royal Automobile Club* (83 Pall Mall, London SW1), or the *Royal Scottish Automobile Club* (17 Rutland Square, Edinburgh); or the *American Automobile Association* (8111 Gatehouse Road, Falls Church, Virginia 22042), etc. These organisations can provide any necessary documents, as well as information about rules of the road abroad, restrictions regarding caravans and trailers, and arrangements for delivery of spare parts, bail bonds, insurance, etc. Motorists who are not the owners of their vehicle should possess the owner's permit for its use abroad. The insurance facilities provided by *Europ Assistance* should be considered.

Travellers should equip themselves in advance with good maps; see p 69. There are tolls to pay on motorways in France and Spain. Motorways (*autoroutes* in France) can become expensive. The latest edition of the *Michelin Map of France* (No. 989) should be studied before deciding on a convenient route to the Spanish frontier.

According to the published project (Plan General de Carreteras 1984–91) the main stretches of moterway or dual carriageway to be constructed, extending the present system, are: Bilbao to Santander and Torrelavega; Burgos to Valladolid and Tordesillas; Burgos to Madrid; the extension of the NVI from Madrid to Tordesillas and Benavente; Zaragoza to Madrid (long overdue); Madrid to Trujillo, Mérida and Badajoz; Madrid to Bailén, Córdoba and Sevilla; Madrid to Almansa, for Valencia or Alicante; Alicante to Murcia and Baza, and via Granada and Antequera, to Sevilla; Antequera to Málaga, and along the coast to Algeciras. Other shorter stretches are planned from Madrid to Toledo; Murcia to Cartegena; Utiel to Valencia, and the Valencia bypass; Lleida to Martorell, and the completion of the motorway from Santiago to Tui; and S from Oviedo: that from Sevilla to Huelva is virtually completed.

The main **frontier posts** (at Irún, on the A1 motorway, and at La Jonquera) are permanently open; most of the other important crossing points are open from 7.00–24.00, but may open later and close earlier in winter. If one is intending to cross elsewhere, it is as well to check beforehand when the border is open. Cars are likely to be stopped at police checkpoints inside the Basque country.

It is often a problem to plan an itinerary which will take in a representative selection of historic towns and monuments, at the same time passing through regions of scenic beauty or grandeur; this is partly because of the sheer size of the country, which is only very slightly smaller than France. But it should be reiterated that Spain is also very mountainous, a point not usually appreciated, and the time required to cover a particular route can easily be underestimated.

The quality of roads has improved considerably in recent years, although in some areas there is still much work to be done. Too often an important road has been allowed to deteriorate, while a rarely used mountain road has been entirely resurfaced. Long overdue has been the doubling of the N1 between Burgos and Madrid, still under way; while the improvement of the road between Zaragoza and Madrid—also one of the main routes to the capital—is still a project. The network of motorways (*autopistas*) is being slowly extended as part of the general European system, which has done a great deal already to facilitate communications. They are prefixed with an A (eg. A2), and their position is best seen on the latest *Michelin map of Spain* (No. 990).

Although there are usually sufficient exits and entrances, obviously the motorways will not be used by travellers wishing to explore sites and monuments in towns and villages which they deliberately bypass. Of course, motorways can often be combined with the older main roads, and in certain areas they are recommended, in spite of the cost of the toll (*peaje*). They can provide an interesting, attractive, and less tiring journey, for instance between San Sebastián and Bilbao, or they may avoid a comparatively dull coast and bypass several ugly towns (as between Tarragona and Sagunto), and in the latter case both Tortosa and Peñiscola can be approached with ease. A stretch which may be followed by travellers wishing to avoid some of the worst excesses of coastal development is that from S of Valencia to Alicante. Others recommended are between Sevilla and Jérez; La Jonquera (from Perpignan) to Girona; and from Girona to Barcelona; the stretch between Barcelona and Lleida (from which Santes Creus and Poblet may be visited); and from Lleida to Zaragoza; likewise from Bilbao to Burgos; from S of Oviedo to León; and from A Coruña to Santiago; and in particular during the season when crossing the frontier to approach San Sebastián from N of Bayonne.

The main highways radiating from Madrid forming part of the national network are prefixed with an N (*carratera Nacional*), and are given Roman numerals (eg. NIV), some of which are in part dual carriageways (*autovias*). Other main roads have the prefix N and are given Arabic numerals (eg. N234), while the more important local roads are classed C (*Comarcales* eg. C456). The general condition of by-roads, often marked *Camino Rural* or *Camino Forestal*, can usually be relied on, but the surface of some minor crosscountry roads still leaves much to be desired. Many are in a perfectly satisfactory state, even if narrow and winding, but occasionally they deteriorate unaccountably into rough stony tracks. Some roads are prefixed by the local provincial initials.

The apparently direct road between two points is by no means always the easiest or fastest, particularly off the beaten track. Some roads (indicated as reasonably good on maps) wind and climb through hilly country for hours, while others will lead for considerable distances across the level *meseta* in half the time.

As few maps indicate the contour of the area to be traversed, or how mountainous and broken up it may be, ascertain if possible the quality of the road to be followed from someone likely to have travelled on it in the recent past: the police or a garage are the most reliable judges, but few will admit that they don't know when asked such a question or even when asked directions. Some maps (such as those published by the Min. de Obras Públicas y Urbanismo) are inexcusably misleading, indicating a winding road as being straight, and a steep and tortuous mountain road as having merely a few wriggles.

In some villages the surface is non-existent, a situation aggravated by rain washing away the dust and rubble that has accumulated in its potholes. Many roads are hilly and even mountainous, and brakes (*frenos*) should be checked. Although there are many new garages and petrol stations on the main roads, elsewhere they are still few and far between, and it is advisable to top up where one can. It is often convenient to ask for so many pesetas-worth of petrol (*gasolina*) rather than by the litre. The 96-octane 'Super' is always preferable. A request to fill up the tank is 'Rellenar (pron. rel-yen-ar) por favor'.

When traversing mountainous districts in winter, and even as late as May, ensure in advance that the passes are open. Signs are displayed at the beginning of the ascent of many indicating whether they are closed (*cerrado*) or open (*abierto*). Chains (*cadenas*), which are *obligatory*, may be required. The weather on any high mountain road can suddenly deteriorate, and the driver may find himself in a blizzard within minutes. The police can often advise the motorist of road or snow conditions, while a telephone advisory service is also available.

When travelling in summer avoid if possible driving due W during the late afternoon. Towards evening the glare of the setting sun can be most unpleasant and even dangerous. And while most tourists will plan to reach their destination in daylight, particularly if travelling off main roads, when driving at dusk or after dark a sharp look-out should be kept for unlit carts, bicycles, and donkeys, etc. Lorry drivers are usually co-operative in allowing overtaking. Passing motorists invariably stop to assist a car in trouble, but should the breakdown (*averia*) be serious, it is advisable to contact the nearest *Auxilio en Carretera*, or garage.

The Highway Code conforms to the general Continental system. The use of seat belts is compulsory outside towns. A high proportion of the drivers of private cars in Spain will not have had their cars for long; many have comparatively little experience, and they are not always as considerate on the road as they might be.

On entering towns, and parking. Most large towns and many of the smaller ones are unpleasantly congested, particularly in the centre, where most of the monuments of interest to the traveller, and hotels, are likely to be. This area will be marked 'Centro Ciudad' at the approach to the town, but such directional signs may well peter out later. Having once found a vacant site for parking, it is as well to remain there, as long as it is conveniently near where one wishes to make one's base, for with the proliferation of one-way streets, an excess of traffic lights, and cars, it is no longer a pleasure to drive in towns.

Some car parks are attended (*vigilado*), at least during the day. Underground parking (*subterráneo*) is available in some of the larger cities. Do not leave visible any articles of value in a parked car; see Security, p 73. In Blue Zones (*zona azul*) a parking disk, obtainable at some garages, should be set at the hour one parked or a parking ticket (available at tobacconists) suitably marked. Wardens are usually more lenient with tourists. *Ill-parked* foreign cars are towed away by the *Grua* as ruthlessly as native ones and may take hours to recover. In addition, there will be a fine to pay.

When planning a tour, do not assume that many provincial capitals, even if written large on maps—especally Spanish maps—are necessarily of any great interest or importance if one is seeking a city replete with old-world charm. Many, whatever their past history, are now little more than administrative centres of regions, and as such are very likely to have been marked by recent development. Although it may be invidious to particularise, the following—described briefly in the text, which should be scanned first for what *may* be seen—can be bypassed without missing very much: *Albacete, Badajoz, Castelló, Ciudad Real, Guadalajara, Huelva,* and *Teruel* (in spite of some Mudéjar churches). *Santander,* were it not for its position, and *Lleida,* were it not for its restored cathedral, would be included in this list.

Postal and other Services

Postal Information. The main Post Office (*Correos*) in Madrid operates a limited 24-hour service; others are usually open from 8.00 to 12.00 and from 17.00 to 19.30. Correspondence marked '*lista de correos*' or '*poste restante*' (to be called for) may be addressed to any post office and is handed to the addressee on proof of identity (passport preferable). The surname of the addressee, especially the capital letter, should be clearly written, and no 'Esq.' added. Letters (*cartas*) of importance should be registered (*certificado*). A postcard is a *tarjeta postal*. Postage stamps (*sellos*) may also be obtained from tobacconists (*estancos*). Pillar or post boxes are painted bright yellow.

Telephones. The Spanish telephone service is maintained by the *Compañia Telefónica Nacional,* or *Telefónica,* which is a private monopoly. It is distinct from the postal services, although they will accept telegrams dictated over the telephone for dispatch. All towns have an office from which local, trunk, and international calls (*conferencias*) may be made. Many of these offices have recently been moved from a convenient central site to an obscure suburb, and their whereabouts are unknown by most citizens, and much time can be wasted trying to locate them. There are, however, more telephone cabins to be seen in the streets from which calls can be made, apart from call box instruments in bars and restaurants, etc. Spain is now, except in some rural areas, in automatic or STD communicaton with the rest of Europe, etc.

In telephone directories and other alphabetical lists names beginning with Ch are printed in a separate section after the Cs. It is also advisable to make sure you know the full name of the person required; e.g. Federico *Garcia* Lorca, as this will be indexed under the second name, which is the first part of the surname.

 When answering the telephone the expression *Diga* or *Digame,* literally 'Speak to me', should be used, while *Oiga* (listen) meaning 'hallo!' or 'are you there?' is the usual interrogation.

Hotels and Restaurants

Hotels. The standard of comfort, efficiency, and cleanliness of Spanish hotels is now comparatively high. All are officially graded and listed in an annual *Guía de Hoteles*, which is available at Tourist Offices. Tourist Offices can also advise on suitable accommodation and provide information about *Campsites* and *Youth Hostels*). The availability of accommodation is not indicated in this Guide, except in the case of the national network of *Paradores*; see below.

It is advisable to book in advance if visiting a town during a *fiesta* or *feria*, and it is sensible to check on the exact whereabouts of the hotel, as it may be further from the centre than expected. The usual European star system of categorisation is followed, charges varying according to the season.

The **Paradores Nacionales**, which have a central booking service in Madrid (tel. 435/9700, 9744, 9768, or 9814), often occupy historic buildings, or premises specially adapted or constructed in positions of outstanding scenic beauty or cultural interest. Some are strategically placed on main roads. (*Hosterías* are restaurants only, with no sleeping accommodation.) Bedrooms (with private bathrooms) and public rooms are comfortable and usually tastefully furnished. Their safe 'international' menu usually introduces several regional dishes to the cautious traveller, for not all are like Joseph Baretti, who remarked: 'Let it be dinner time, and I care not a fig for the difference between macaroni and roast beef, herring and frogs, the olla and the sourcrout; a very cosmopolite in the article of filling one's belly'. Nevertheless, the menu can pall if Paradores are resorted to habitually, and the quality of food rarely merits the prices now charged.

Unfortunately some of the more recent Paradores (among them Segovia and Salamanca) are large modern buildings some distance from town centres, of very little intrinsic interest, and in striking contrast to the discreet and intimate character of some earlier establishments. Also similar in style to the paradores are the luxury hotels of 'Los Reyes Católicos' at *Santiago*; 'San Marcos' at *León*, and 'De Reconquista' at *Oviedo*, among others.

The recession of the tourist boom has had the effect of improving the quality of many hotels—the fittest have usually survived, although regrettably a number of shoddy establishments remain. Some have turned their restaurants into bingo halls, and will only provide breakfast. And some of the internal walls of many of the newer buildings are embarrassingly thin, lacking any sound insulation.

In the main cities and coastal resorts there are large luxury hotels providing cosmopolitan comfort at corresponding charges, while the ordinary first class hotels in the medium-sized towns are usually excellent. Hotels are still few and far between in many inland areas, but satisfactory accommodation can almost always be found. In areas frequented by tourists—particularly package tourists—hotels are likely to be crowded during the season.

An increasing number of comparatively modest hotels have bathrooms (*cuarto de baño*), and running water in the bedrooms, and the lower category establishments with one or two stars only (which were in certain cases known previously as *Fondas*, *Posadas*, or *Ventas*) should not be scorned. Although simple, they are usually clean, however inelegant the décor and uninviting their exterior appearance, and they often serve food in the traditional local style. There may be a lack of comfort in the public rooms (where the ubiquitous television is often the centre of attraction), a disadvantage against which may be placed the opportunity of seeing a characteristic side of Spanish life.

Should no accommodation be found in the only local hotel or boarding house (*Casa de Huéspedes*—C.H.), a bed in a nearby

The Castillo de Sta. Catalina, Jaén, now a Parador

private house may be found. If food is required, an omelette (*tortilla*) or eggs and bacon (*huevos con jamón*) can almost always be produced at short notice.

Every bedroom (*habitación*) must display a notice giving details of the maximum price applicable to the room, and this is *inclusive* of all service charges and taxes. Rarely are the prices lower than the maximum, although in theory this is allowed. Extra gratuities are *not* normally expected, although porters, etc. in some of the larger hotels, may hang about hopefully, but (to quote Baretti again) 'where every trifle may be turned into money, money will be expected for every trifle'. A notice of prices must also be displayed at the reception desk. No charges higher than the maximum may be made for reasons such as festivals, special local events, etc., except in certain very specific cases (such as at Sevilla during Semana Santa and the Feria).

Any customer staying more than 48 hours in a hotel has the right to receive the full-board rates from the time of arrival. All hotels are allowed to charge the minimum price for a continental breakfast, whether or not the guest has it. More substantial breakfasts can be provided if requested.

Hotels *still* demand the traveller's passport on arrival, when it might be convenient to request garage space, at least when staying in towns, as parking facilities near hotels are rarely adequate. Request the return of passports soon after arrival.

Guests are not obliged to accept full board except in the case of Pensions. 1-star hotels and 1- or 2-star Hostels or Pensions are entitled to charge an additional 20 per cent over the maximum price for the room if the customer fails to have at least one of the two main meals on the premises. A demi-pension system sometimes operates, details of which may be discussed with the management.

If no single room (*sencilla*) is available, a double room may be offered, for which the price is less 20 per cent of the maximum. Some (even well-known) hotels dishonestly choose to assume that single tourists prefer the latter, and this point should be checked. Comparatively few Spanish hotels have actual double beds (*camas matrimoniales*). When accommodation is limited, it may be convenient to ask for an extra bed to be moved into a room; the additional charge for this may not be higher than 35 per cent of the price of the double room. The management must inform guests as to any reduced prices available in the case of children, servants, etc.

Despite the official categorisation, the quality of hotels can still vary widely. At the more popular resorts and tourist-conscious towns it will often be found that a hotel of lower category is superior in comfort and service than one flaunting four or five stars. The independent traveller will realise that here, as elsewhere, many hotels are geared to package tours and coach groups, the result being a standard stabilised at a mediocre or take-it-or-leave-it level.

An **official complaints book** (*Libro de Reclamaciones*) is a requirement of every establishment offering accommodation, and in the case of serious irregularity or indifferent service should be requested without compunction.

Restaurants. Spaniards have always eaten to live rather than lived to eat, and the general standard of Spanish cooking will not please the gourmet. Nevertheless there are many good restaurants, often providing palatable regional dishes, and there is often better value for money in the less pretentious establishments. Unfortunately there is a tendency for restaurants of all categories, particularly in areas frequented by tourists, to serve stereotyped meals of a mediocre quality for the price charged. As in hotels, an official complaints book (see above) is at the disposal of dissatisfied customers. Likewise, all restaurants in Spain have been officially graded into four classes plus De Luxe establishments, but often the categorisation refers to the number and variety of dishes available and the maximum price to be charged for the Touristic Menu, rather than to the *quality* of food and service provided. It should be noted that the bill (*la cuenta*) includes service, but it is still customary to leave a small gratuity to the *Camarero* or *Camerera* for good service.

The restaurants of all Paradores and many hotels are open to non-residents. Breakfast (*desayuno*), from 7.00 to 11.00, may be served—usually with a supplementary charge—in one's room if requested. Lunch is usually served between 13.00 and 16.00, and dinner between 20.30 and 23.00, both à la carte and at a fixed price, or on a 'Menu Turistico', and the bill of fare is displayed at the entrance. This may or may not not include tax or IVA (VAT).

Portions are often generous, particularly with the hors d'ouevre (*entremeses*), and one *ración* is often enough for two. Spanish cookery is apt to contain rather more olive oil (*aceite de oliva*) than the visitor is used to, and should be treated with respect; however the

From the Ceramic Museum, Valencia

local wine is often a good counter–agent. Although tap water (occasionally over-chlorinated) is usually safe, some tourists are induced to drink mineral water, which may be ordered '*con gas*' or '*sin*' (without) gas. Light Spanish beer (*cerveza*) may be ordered by the small bottle (*botellin*), large size (*doble*), or draft (*caña*). Cider (*sidra*) should be sampled along the N coast of Spain, regarded as the original home of cider making, whence the process was derived by the Normans, who brought it to England.

There is no lack of smaller and more convivial establishments—*bars, tascas, tabernas, cervecerias*, etc.—open throughout the day, many of which display a selection of dishes from which one may choose *tapas*, eating them at the bar or adjacent table. The charge for food and drink at a table, or out in the open, is often more expensive. The word *aperitivos* or *tapas* always applies to appetisers, not just drinks, and covers an occasionally bewildering range of hot or cold dishes, from smoked ham, cheese, salted almonds, olives (*aceitunas*), sardines, *chorizo*—a dried spiced pork sausage—mushrooms, tunny, peppers, etc., to more exotic prepared dishes such as *salpicón de mariscoes*, with eggs, onion, peppers, olive oil, and shellfish, etc. *Marisquerias*, restaurants serving only seafood, are likely to be expensive.

Refreshments are also available at most cafés. All are popular points of rest, particularly during the heat of the midday sun and the evening *paseo*, and remain open late. They are usually found in or near the main square, and many entertaining hours may be spent sitting in the open, but in the shade, observing the passing throng. It is also likely to be less noisy, and the TV and inevitable background music may be avoided. (Do not hesitate to ask for the music to be turned down.) Here one may have a snack (*merienda*) or sandwich (*bocadillo*), meet friends, and rest one's weary feet. Coffee may be ordered black (*solo*), with a dash of milk (*cortado*), or white (*con leche*); a large cup is a *doble*.

Food and Wine. While the *Paella Valenciana* is not always found at its best in Valencia, the traveller should have no hesitation in savouring most regional dishes, preferably in establishments used by local people. When touring, much time and money may be saved by having picnics en route, sampling the local bread, cheese, sausage, and wine, etc. It is as well, however, to wash first all fruit and vegetables. 'Spanish Tummy' is usually caused by over eating and a higher consumption of wine than normal, and the heat, or an over indulgence in cold drinks during excessive heat. Alka-Seltzer will usually clear it up, while the advice of a chemist (*farmacéutico*) is generally reliable. The increasing pollution of some shellfish nurseries has had unpleasant results.

Wine (*vino*) is the national drink, and wines of quality may be found in almost every bar, *tasca, taberna*, and restaurant in the country. Almost every region produces wine, much of it now controlled by a 'Consejo Regulador de la Denominación de Origen', similar to the French 'Appellation Controlée'.

The majority of the wines (white, *blanco*; red, *tinto*; and rosé, *clarete* or *rosado*) are regional, and will be found only in the area of their production. Probably the only wine which is sold throughout Spain (with the exception of *Sherry*; cf. Jerez de la Frontera), is the *Rioja*, more expensive than the regional wines. It is normally only available in bottles or half-bottles, not usually sold by the glass as are the local *vinos 'del pais'* or *'de la casa'*.

In the Rioja, now an autonomous province situated in the Ebro valley between Pancorbo (to the NW) and Alfaro (to the SE), with Logroño as its centre, wines of great quality are produced. They are similar to a Bordeaux or Burgundy, but with a higher alcoholic content, one of the characteristics of most Spanish wines compared with those of most other European countries. There are some dozens of companies producing Riojas (mostly red) at various prices. In the Rioja itself one may drink the young wines *'de cosechero'*, good and inexpensive. A local connoisseur can advise, but in general quality and price are reasonably balanced.

Among the better-known wines of Spain are the following: in Galicia and León, the dry white *Albariño*, the white *Condado*, and also the *Ribeiros* (a heavy red, and white), *Cacabelos* (red and rosé), and the red *Bierzo* or *Valdeorras*. The Asturias produce only cider (*sidra*).

Further S, in the Duero valley, are the red wines of *Toro*, the white *Rueda*, and those of *Cigales* (rosé) and *Las Navas* (white). Further up the Duero, E of Valladolid, is the famous (and dear) *Vega Sicilia* (red). The rosés of *Ribera de Duero*, which are less expensive, are found between Peñfiel and Aranda.

Returning to the N, in the Basque Provinces is *Chacolí* (both red and white), somewhat acid and an acquired flavour. Adjacent Navarra and Aragón, abutting the Rioja, are both important wine growing areas, producing strong red and rosé wines such as *Campanas*, *Murchante*, *Cariñena*, *Jalón*, and *Barbastro*.

Continuing E, we reach Catalunya, and the Mediterranean coast, where a great variety of wines is available. The best known are those of *Ampordá* (red and rosé), *Alella* (dry or sweet whites), the white *Penedés*, and the wines of *Tarragona*, such as the *Priorat* (with a high alcoholic content). Among the specialities of Catalunya are the champagne-like sparkling wines, produced *brut*, *sec*, and *demi-sec*, and some of them are quite good. Once again, the choice should be based on price if there is no other source of information.

Further along the coast, the old provinces of Valencia and Murcia produce a variety of wines such as *Manchuela* (red and white); those of *Utiel* and *Requena* (reds), *Monóvar* (red), and *Jumilla* (strong reds).

Towards *Málaga* are the famous sweet dessert wines; while inland Andalucía, near Córdoba, the white *Moriles* and *Montilla* are similar to those less known white wines of *Condado*, near Huelva.

Lastly there is the extensive central region, dominated by the wines of La Mancha, especially the cheap *Valdepeñas* (reds and whites), the largest producers of wine in Spain. Also in this area are interesting wines for their price such as *Mentrida* (reds) in Toledo, and the red and rosé *Cebreros*; and nearer Madrid, those of *Navalcarnero* (red). In Extremadura to the W are the light red *Aloque* and *Montánchez*, *Almendralejo* and *Salvatierra* (reds).

In general, it is suggested that the traveller drinks the wines *'de la casa'* or *'del pais'*, and on occasions in restaurants a good bottle of Rioja or other *'reserva'* of any of these regions.

A wide range of good Spanish brandies, and other spirits (*aguardientes*) are available. They vary from province to province, from the *Orujos* of Galicia and Santander to the *Anis de Chinchón*, *Cazalla*, or *Ojén*, *dulce* (sweet) or *séco* (dry).

Spanish-produced 'whisky' is best avoided.

Sangria is a summer cup composed basically of red wine, lemon juice, sugar, brandy, soda water, cinnamon, and ice (*hielo*)—a cool, refreshing, but somewhat heady drink.

Bota and **Porrón**. The *bota* is a large pear-shaped leather pouch for wine. At the neck is a turned wooden cup in which a small hole is stopped by a spigot. By raising the neck of the *bota* to the level of the mouth—without touching the lips—and then gradually raising the bag, a thin stream of wine flows out. Similarly with the *porrón*, found mainly in Catalunya, which is a cone-shaped glass bottle with a long narrow spout. Both require a little practice, otherwise wine will flow down one's neck rather than into one's mouth.

The following list includes a selection of the more common dishes, with their English equivalents.

Mesa, table; *Cuchillo*, knife; *Cuchara*, spoon; *Tenedor*, fork; and *Vaso*, a glass.

Entremeses, Hors d'œuvre

Spaniards often sustain themselves with *tapas* (see above) at a bar before returning home or going on to a restaurant, where they may continue to pick at similar dishes, or sliced sausages (*embutidos*). These include:

Chorizo, a hard dry spiced pork sausage
Longaniza, a longer and darker variety
Salchicha, fresh pork sausage
Salchichón, large hard dry sausage with paprika
Jamón (pronounced Hamón) *Serrano*, lean ham, which with *lomo*, sirloin of pork, are both cured in salt
Butifarra, Catalan pork sausage
Morcilla, fresh black pudding
Sobresada, soft lard and pimento
Fiambres, cold meats

Sopas, Soups

Gazpacho, a refreshing cold soup, originally from Andalucía, made from tomato, cucumber, olive oil, vinegar, garlic, pimento, bread, water, and ice.
Ajo blanco is a white gazpacho from Córdoba, with a base of ground almonds
Caldos, broths or consommés
Sopa de ajo, a substantial soup of garlic, bread and paprika (*pimentón*)
Caldo gallego, containing white beans, potatoes, cabbage, dried bacon fat, and pig's trotters
Sopa de fideos, noodle soup

Huevos, Eggs

These may be ordered *pasado por agua*, lightly boiled, *cocido* or *duro*, hard-boiled
frito, fried
escalfado, poached
revuelto, scrambled
à la Flamenca, fried with peas and *chorizo*, etc.
Tortilla, potato omelette; a plain omelette is a *Tortilla francesa*

Pescados y Mariscos, Fish and Shellfish

Anquila, eel; *Angulas*, elvers
Boquerónes, fresh anchovies, often provided as a *tapa*

Sardinas, sardines, delicious grilled
Pulpos, octopus
Sepia, cuttlefish
Calamares (called *Chipirones* in the Basque Provinces) *en su tinta*, squid in its own ink, or *à la Romana*, fried in egg and flour.

A wide variety of fresh fish, both on the coast, and brought inland by overnight lorries, is to be seen, including:
Besugo, sea bream
Chanquetes, whitebait
Lenguado, sole
Lubina, bass
Merluza, hake
Mero, brill
Rodaballo, turbot
Salmonetes, red mullet
Pez espada, swordfish
Bonito, tunny; also *atún*, see below
Trucha, trout
Arenque, herring
Rape, monkfish
Rayo, skate
Atún à la plancha, grilled tunny fish, or *Marmitako* (a Basque dish), stewed with tomatoes, potatoes, green peppers, and bread
Bacalao, dried—or occasionally fresh—cod, *al pil-pil*, slowly simmered, or *à la Vizcaina*, with garlic and red peppers

Of shellfish, also known as **moluscos** or **crustáceos**, there is a great variety, often known by other names in different regions. These include:
Quisquillas, shrimps
Gambas or *Camerones*, prawns
Cigalas, Dublin Bay prawns
Langostinos, larger prawns; a variety is *Carabineros*
Langosta or *Bogavante*, lobster
Cangrejos del rio, crayfish
Cangrejo or *Nécora*, sea crab
Centolla or *Changurro*, spider crab
Almejas, clams
Mejillones, mussels
Ostras, oysters
Percebes, goose barnacles
Vieiras, scallops
En escabeche means pickled, soused, or marinaded.

Carne, Meat

In Castile, particularly, you will find *Cordero*, lamb; *chuletas* are chops
Ternera, veal
Cerdo, pork, and *Cochinillo*, suckling pig, usually served *asado*, roasted
Choto, young beef (which is rarely hung in Spain)
Meats are also prepared *à la chilindrón*, stewed with tomatoes and paprika; *al horno*, baked or roasted; *à la parrilla* or *à la plancha*, grilled, etc.

There is a variety of stews, *cazuelas*, *calderetas*, *cocidos*, *guisadas*, *pucheros*, etc., and also the *olla podrida*, hotpot, while the *Fabada*

Asturiana, butter beans stewed with *chorizo*, *morcillas* and *lacón* (partially salt-cured pig's trotters) should not be overlooked
Callos, tripe, *à la Madrileña*, is always very appetising
Riñones, kidneys
Higado, liver
Vaca, beef
Solomillo, sirloin

Aves y Caza, Poultry and Game

Pollo, chicken, also *gallina*
Pavo, turkey
Pato, duck
Faisán, pheasant
Perdiz, partridge
Cordoniz, quail
Conejo, rabbit
Liebre, hare
Jabali, wild boar

Verduras, vegetables

Ensaladas, salads: *lechuga*, lettuce
Pisto, fresh vegetables slightly and slowly fried in oil
Menestra, similarly stewed, but with the addition of ham
Pulses are basic ingredients of a number of *potajes*, stews, and include *Judias blancas*, haricot beans; *judias verdes* are French beans
Grelos, turnip tops (in Galicia)
Ajo, garlic
Col, cabbage
Rábano, radish
Acelgas, Swiss beet, chard
Remolacha, beetroot
Cebolla, onion
Puerros, leeks
Setas, mushrooms
Habas, broad beans, often served with chopped ham
Alubias, dried beans; *alubias blancas*, butter beans
Garbanzos, chickpeas
Lentejas, lentils
Alcachofas, artichokes
Espinacas, spinach
Berejenas, aubergines
Pepino, cucumber
Zanahorias, carrots
Aguacate, avocado
Aceitunas, olives
Guisantes, peas

Quesos, Cheeses

While they cannot compare in quality or variety with those of France, Spain's cheeses are full-flavoured and worth investigating. They range from the soft white *queso de Burgos*, and *Villalón*, and the breast-shaped Galician *Tetilla*, to the smoked *Idiazabal*, hard *Roncal*, and ubiquitous *Manchego*, which is found *fresco*, fresh, *curado*, smoked, and *en aceite*, somewhat oily. *Cabrales* is a strong Asturian cheese.

Postres, Sweets, etc.

When asked what *postres* are available, a brief litany is usually repeated by waiters. Perhaps surprisingly in a country in which the Arab influence is so strong, most restaurants show an astonishing lack of imagination in providing puddings.

Flan, cream caramel
Arroz con leche, rice pudding
Nata, whipped cream
Natillas, custard
Carne de membrillo, a rich sweet quince cheese
Yemas, a rich sweet candied yoke of egg
Churros, a confection, usually eaten in the morning, of dough mixture piped into boiling olive oil, and often served with hot chocolate together with a glass of cold water
Turrón de Jijona, a nougat-like confection of ground almonds and honey; *Turrón de Alicante* is much harder, containing whole almonds
   There is also any number of sweet confections, such as *polverónes*, *mantecadas*, etc., which may be bought at *Pastelerias* and *Confiterías*.
Mermelada is merely jam. Those preferring marmalade for breakfast should ask for *Mermelada de naranja*; even 'Old English' marmalade *mermelada de naranja amarga* (bitter) is now being manufactured in Spain
Miel, honey
Mantequilla, butter

Frutas, Fruit

Fresas, strawberries; also *Fresón*
Frambuesas, raspberries
Higos, figs
Peras, pears
Uvas, grapes
Manzanas, apples
Cerezas, cherries
Ciruelas, plums or prunes; *Claudias*, greengages
Melocotón, peach; *en almibar*, in syrup
Sandia, water melon
Albaricoques, apricots
Pomelo (or *Toronja*), grapefruit
Piña, pineapple
Plátanos, bananas
Nueces, nuts
Naranjas, oranges; *jugo de naranja*, fresh orange juice.
Chirimoya, custard apple
Nispero, medlar

Visiting Monuments and Museums

Guides. Henry Swinburne in the 1770s complained that 'one of the greatest vexations a curious person experiences in travelling in Spain, is the scarcity of tolerable *ciceroni*; those you meet are generally cobblers, who throw a brown cloak over their ragged apparel, and conduct you to a church or two, where they cannot give you the least satisfactory information concerning its antiquities or curiosities'. Baedeker, equally cynical, remarked, when describing the Alcázar at Sevilla some 75 years ago: 'The traveller should reject the services of the official guides, who are always in too much of a hurry'—indeed, only too often one would do better being escorted by the famous Cornelio (the well-informed but blind guide of the Escorial in the second quarter of the last century) who would describe one picture and point to the next! With few exceptions, little has changed.

Travellers requiring the presence of an English-speaking official guide (who will have passed some form of examination) should apply to the local Tourist Offices. Be warned that all articles bought at 'recommended' shops are likely to have their prices inflated to cover the guide's commission. Do not be taken in by unofficial guides— plausible and insinuating individuals—who may attempt to guide one around the sites or museums, and then charge exorbitantly. Ask to see their credentials first.

Churches. Those of importance, including the larger cathedrals, are generally open all day except for c 2–3 hours in the early afternoon, although some may remain shut in the afternoon in winter. The less-visited churches are now usually kept locked. Although the priest or sacristan may be found by the persistent, the time incurred in locating him is a serious factor to be taken into account. Not infrequently all attempts to gain entry will be disappointed.

It will be noticed that the altars of many churches have been moved from their traditional place to a more central position nearer the crossing, in accordance with recent liturgical reform.

Twiss, visiting Sevilla in 1773, complained that the friars, who he had hoped might direct him to some paintings in the churches, 'were either asleep, or so lazy that they would not give themselves the trouble of shewing them . . . '. On visiting the museum at Segorbe, the present editor, having had to listen to the sacristan's patter, was informed that he might take photographs, *but not notes.*

But do not be too easily dissuaded, for difficulties have always risen up before the traveller in Spain. Richard Ford, in one of many brilliant passages, reiterated that whatever apparently impregnable barriers, unexpected obstacles, and impediments official keepers might make, the search should not be given up. 'No', may be assumed to be their natural answer; not even if you have a special order or permission, is admission by any means certain. The keeper, who here as elsewhere, considers the objects committed to his care as his own private property and source of perquisite, must be conciliated: often when you have toiled through the heat and dust to some distant church, museum or library, after much ringing and waiting, you will be drily informed that it is shut, can't be seen, that it is the wrong day, that you must call again tomorrow; and if it is the right day, then you will be told that the hour is wrong, that you are come too early, too late; very likely the keeper's wife will inform you that he is out, gone to mass, or market, or at his dinner, or at his *siesta*, or if he is at home and awake, he will swear that his wife has mislaid the key, "which she is always doing". If all these and other excuses won't do, and you persevere, you will be assured that there is nothing worth seeing, or you will be asked why you want to see it? As a general rule, no one should be deterred from visiting anything, because a Spaniard of the upper classes gives his opinion that the object is beneath notice . . . '. Elsewhere he attests to the absence of any *disinterested* appreciation of the beautiful by the incurious pococurante Sapniards, who lacked the organs of veneration and admiration 'for anything beyond matters connected with the first person and the present tense'.

The ecclesiastical authorities follow the practice of collecting together paintings and any other moveable objects in their cathedrals and churches and placing them in a so-called museum, for which admission charge is made. This system, which is particularly noticeable on routes frequented by tourists, may apply to locked chapels, choirs, cloisters, towers, and treasuries, etc., indeed to *anything* that can be used to extract money. The quality of the 'treasures' displayed rarely merits even the moderate charge imposed. In some churches and convents a charge is made at the end of an accompanied visit.

The most blatant examples of such rapacity are the sealing off of such outstanding buildings as the Capilla Real at Granada, and the *old* Cathedral at Salamanca. There seems to be considerable doubt as to whether these are now places of worship or museums: if the latter, they should, with their contents, pass into the more secure and competent hands of the secular authorities: indeed, there is a strong move to place the conservation of the fabric also of all cathedrals, convents, and churches in more qualified hands than those of the clergy. The quantity of religious art carefully stored up, but of no aesthetic quality whatsoever, has to be seen to be believed. And even when the items are of some interest and value, little has been done in the past to protect them, with the inevitable consequence that they have become a tempting prize (as at Murcia, and Burgos) or objects of vandalism (as at Oviedo). At Zamora the beautiful tapestries are hung in conditions which should embarass a bishop. There are of course exceptions, such as the cathedral museum at León.
  In extenuation, there are now perhaps fewer canvases rotting on damp walls than there were. In waves of anticlericalism—in Barcelona in 1909 and in many areas just prior to the Civil War—certain 'works of art', much of it of a very meretricious nature, were destroyed. Before that the cupidity of their custodians was such that even Baedeker complained that 'Every year art treasures find their way out of the country without the fact being generally known. Thus objects mentioned in our Handbook may sometimes have disappeared'. Indeed, the acquisitive tendencies of delinquent *dilettanti* would not demur at gutting buildings, Romanesque churches of their murals and absconding with paintings by the score.
  Few visitors would baulk at contributing to the upkeep of the fabric of such monuments as the Mezquita at Córdoba, among many others. But only too often one has the impression that as little as possible is spent on the ecclesiastical buildings concerned, which are invariably unkempt and often—as at Toledo—the retablo mayor is hidden under a shroud of dust, while grass-grown precincts—as at Segovia—are as unsightly as the display of political symbols and *Vitores* (panegyrical epitaphs) to be seen on many façades.

Museums. Much has been done in recent years to improve the quality of museums in Spain, to modernise and reform the older establishments, and work is still in progress. In these, exhibits are well displayed and labelled, and the entry charge (for foreign visitors) is correspondingly increased. In smaller towns, particularly those off the beaten track, the official opening hours are not always adhered to, and when the custodian lives on the premises, visitors may be admitted outside the prescribed hours, if any.

There are a small number of buildings which were once royal property, such as the Pal. Real and the Conv. de las Descalzas Reales (Madrid), and parts of the Escorial, which have been expropriated by and are now conserved and patrolled by a doctrinaire organisation known as the *Patrimonio Nacional*. These buildings may only be visited in dragooned 'groups', taken on a conducted tour by a guide (often English-speaking) with a basic knowledge of the exhibits, who expects, but should not receive, a gratuity. Time must be allowed for such a group to accumulate, after which, invariably, it is herded round the building at a breakneck speed. While it it appreciated that the supervision of crowds presents a problem of organisation, this stultifying expedient is quite deplorable, and all attempts by a guide to hurry one past the exhibits should be strongly resisted. Regrettably, this organisation (which has recently been criticised for its policies) seems to assume that all visitors are perfectly satisfied by a cursory glance at the objects displayed, and the uniformed functionaries concerned are not authorised to grant any facilities to those wishing to study undisturbed.
  Until there is a radical change in policy, one may apply in person, or write

well in advance, to the *Inspección General de Museos*, Palacio Real, Madrid, specifically requesting permission to visit the museums, etc. of the Patrimonio Nacional *'con detenimiento'*—without restraint and at leisure—at the same time giving a valid reason for wishing to do so. Sadly the reply is usually negative.

Although visitors are allowed to use their own guide books, cameras must be handed in at the entrance, or an additional fee charged.

Some of these properties have—not before time—been handed over to municipalities or autonomies.

General Information

Season. Climatically the best seasons for visiting Spain in general are the spring and autumn, although the Atlantic coast enjoys a comparatively temperate summer, and the Mediterranean coast a mild winter. The elevated central *meseta* has a continental climate, parched and dusty in summer, and mainly dry but often bitterly cold in winter, although fine crisp days are frequent. Then, even when the sun is shining, visitors to Madrid, for example, should be on their guard against the biting wind descending from the nearby snow-clad sierras. For winter travelling, an overcoat is essential, while even in summer some warm clothing should always be carried as a precaution against sudden drops in temperature.

Between June and September, when light clothes are equally essential, many towns of obvious historic or artistic interest are crowded, and the heat can be stifling. It is often better to avoid staying in the larger centres, which may be visited from smaller towns, where it is still possible to observe a more characteristic and provincial way of life. Almost all forms of dress or undress are now seen in all but the remotest regions. There is no longer officious supervision on the beaches, where the briefest costumes are common, but sun lovers are *warned* against over exposure, which can be both unpleasant and dangerous, but perhaps less so than bathing in the cloacal Mediterranean, which can result in some nasty skin complaints, etc.

Manners and Customs. It is customary to open conversations in shops, etc., with the courtesy of *buenos días* (good day), *buenas tardes* (good afternoon), and the phrases *digame usted* (please tell me), and *deme usted* (please give me), *tiene usted* (have you got), and *muchas gracias* (many thanks) should be used. The greeting *adiós*, literally 'goodbye', is used on occasions when we would say 'hallo'. In shops and offices a certain amount of self-assertion is taken for granted, since queues are not the general rule, and it is incumbent on the inquirer or customer to get himself a hearing. The handshake at meeting and parting is less usual than in France, and such ceremony is becoming progressively relaxed in many circles.

Sightseeing. Whether visiting monuments or museums, or when driving from one town to another, an early start is strongly advised. Not only will the traveller be able to see far more during the morning before such buildings close for their midday *siesta*, and before the heat of the sun becomes overpowering, but accommodation for the night may be found in good time.

Many tourists may be at a loss in some towns during the early afternoon. But by this time, particularly in the South in summer, the heat may force one to remain indoors. Even in the 18C, according to

Thomas James, the Spanish had a saying 'that none but a dog and an Englishman will be seen out in those four hours: which is literally true, for I have been barked at, from one end of the village . . . to the other'!

Also very time-wasting is the present anarchy in opening times of museums, cathedrals, and other monuments. An attempt to list such times of admission as far as they apply to Madrid and Barcelona has been made. In both almost all museums are closed on Mondays. One will find doors closed when one would expect them to be open, and vice versa, and while the local tourist offices should be applied to, they also may be shut. It is hoped that some simple rule will be laid down before long, which may also be applied to municipal and ecclesiastical museums, and those in private hands.

A pocket compass may be found helpful at times, also a pocket torch when exploring the darker recesses of some churches and cathedrals, which are rarely lit by more than weak light bulbs or guttering candles. A small pair of field glasses will also be of value.

Begging, which is still occasionally met with, and the importunate demands of gypsies, who can be a nuisance, and touts, together with uninvited offers of guidance, should be refused with firmness but without rudeness.

Language. While a knowledge of Spanish is not essential in the main tourist resorts, the attempt to speak it is always appreciated.

Castilian (*Castellano*) is spoken and understood throughout the country, although less so now in Catalunya, but visitors will often hear accents or dialects which can be confusing. 'Colloquial Spanish' by A. Bryston Gerrard, is a useful guide to general usage.

Vowels in Castilian are pronounced (a=ah, i=ee, etc.); in the syllables *gue, gui, que, qui,* the *u* is silent, unless marked by a diaeresis. *Consonants* are pronounced more or less as in English, with the following exceptions: *c* before e or i like th in think; *ch* as in chapter; *d final* is scarcely sounded; *g* before e or i as a guttural h (e.g. Gijón=Hijón); *h* is mute; *j* is roughly aspirated (Jaén=high-en); *ll* like the French l-mouillé (as in cotillon); *ñ* like the French gn (señora=senyora); *r* is trilled; *s* is sharp, *z* like th in think.

It has been estimated that over 4000 words in Castilian derive from the Arabic, including most commencing with al-, including *alcohol* (for make-up), *alcalde* (mayor), etc.; see also p 36.

Accents. Words of more than one syllable ending in a vowel, in ia or io, regarded as diphthongs, or in n or s are accented on the penultimate syllable; those ending in other consonants, on the last syllable. Exceptions to these rules are indicated by an acute accent.

The complex *Basque* language, known as *Vascuence* to the Spaniards, but as *Euskera* to the Basques, and still frequently spoken in the northern Basque provinces, is an idiom of no known derivation, but it is believed to be a relic of the Iberian tongue spoken throughout the Peninsula before the Roman conquest.

The *Catalan* language, a form of Provençal, spoken with some variations along the Mediterranean seaboard from Perpignan to beyond Valencia, is subject to rules of pronunciation different from the Castilian: *c, g,* and *j* are pronounced as in French; *ch*=k; *ny,* even at the end of a word, is pronounced as the Spanish ñ; *x*=sh; in *ll* the l-sound almost disappears, leaving a strong consonantal y-sound; *ig* at the end of a syllable=tch. E.g.: *xampany*=champagne; *puig*=putch; *Ripoll*=ripó-ye; *Bell-lloch*=bey-yók; *Vich*=Vick, now written Vic.

The signs *Dones* and *Homes,* in Catalan, indicate 'Women', and 'Men' respectively and *Tancada* means 'shut'.

Although a pocket dictionary and/or phrase book is recommended, listed below are the Castilian and Catalan for the days of the week, and numerals, and one or two other useful expressions. See also p 67 for a general glossary, mostly of topographical and simple architectural terms, etc., and under Food and Wine, p 86.

Monday	*Lunes*	Dilluns
Tuesday	*Martes*	Dimarts
Wednesday	*Miércoles*	Dimecres
Thursday	*Jueves*	Dijous
Friday	*Viernes*	Divendres
Saturday	*Sábado*	Dissabte
Sunday	*Domingo*	Diumenge
1	*un, uno, una*	un, uno, una
2	*dos*	dos, dues
3	*tres*	tres
4	*cuatro*	quatre
5	*cinco*	cinc
6	*seis*	sis
7	*siete*	set
8	*ocho*	vuit
9	*nueve*	nou
10	*diez*	deu
Do you speak English?	*Habla Inglés?*	Parleu anglès
Speak a little more slowly, please	*Hable más lento, por favour*	Parleu una mica més a poc a poc, si us plau
Where is . . .?	*Dónde está . . .?*	On és . . .?
I am looking for . . .	*Busco . . .*	Cerco . . .
I should like . . .	*Quisiera . . .*	Voldria . . .
How do I get to . . .?	*Par ir a . . .?*	Per anar a . . .?
Is it far/close?	*Está lejos/cerca?*	És lluny/a prop?
How much?	*Cuánta cuesta?*	Quant val?
What is your name?	*Cómo se llama usted?*	Com us dieu?
My name is . . .	*Me llamo . . .*	Em dic . . .

THE LANGUAGES OF SPAIN

With the lifting of censorship and granting of autonomy there has been a marked increase in the number of titles published in Catalan and Basque, as well as those in the Galician dialect, or *Gallego*.

Public Holidays. Official holidays are now 1 January; 6 January (*Día de los Reyes*; Twelfth Night or Epiphany); 19 March; Good Friday (*Viernes Santo*); Easter Sunday (*Día de Pascua*); 1 May; Corpus Christi; 25 July (Santiago); 15 August; 12 October; 1 November; 8 December; 25 December (*Navidad*/Christmas Day). Whenever these fall near a weekend a *puente* (a bridge or long weekend) is taken. These holidays vary in certain parts of the country, Catalunya, for instance, celebrating 11 September.

Working Hours. Offices and shops are normally open on weekdays from 9.00 to 13.00, and from 16.00 to 19.30, but from May to October from 16.30 to 20.00. In summer many offices work a *jornada intensiva*, i.e. they open earlier and close at 15.00. Some of the larger shops are now open during the lunch hour. There is a tendency towards following the European pattern (except perhaps in the summer), but habits in this respect are hard to change.

Newspapers. Foreign newspapers and magazines are only found, at an inflated price, at kiosks in the main tourist areas of the larger towns, but stocks are usually small.

Hikers and Mountaineers in the Pyrenees should carry their passports. Although there is no specific regulation prohibiting the crossing of the range in remote zones, the authorities do not recommend it.

Tobacco. The manufacture and sale of tobacco is a state monopoly. Many brands of cigarettes (*cigarrillos* or *pitillos*) and cigars (*puros*) are available in the *tabacaleras* or *estancos*, which display the Spanish colours—red, yellow, red—above their entrances. Foreign tobaccos, cigarettes, etc., are also available at these *estancos*, and from most hotels, restaurants, bars, etc. Matches are *cerillas*.

Tobacconists also sell postage stamps (*sellos*). Some have a post box (*buzón*) inside the shop, although they are now usually in the street, and are painted yellow.

Entertainment. *Theatre* performances, details of which may be found in the daily papers, often begin at a late hour and last until after midnight. *Tablao Flamenco*, exhibitions of authentic gypsy dancing, start even later, and end in the early hours. *Cinemas* are found in most towns, and a few specialise in showing foreign films (*salas especiales*), which are usually dubbed.

Police. Although Spain no longer admits to being a police state, the Guardia Civil being under civilian control, the police are still much in evidence. In most towns traffic is controlled by *Municipal police*, who may be mounted on motorcycles, as are the *Cuerpo de Vigilantes de Carreteras*, patrolling the main highways.

In the contryside their place is taken by the ubiquitous olive-green-uniformed *Guardia Civil*, always patrolling in pairs and known familiarly as '*La Pareja*', the couple. Their distinctive and incongruous patent leather tricorn hats are not now so frequently seen.

Formed in 1844, members of this strong but singularly ineffective arm of the law, raised originally to combat rural banditry, and who have since regularly intimidated the peasantry, are seldom officious, but are not invariably civil. Within their limited capacity they try to be helpful when their advice or assistance is required. As *Auxilio en Carretera*, they also patrol roads in Landrovers.

Normally only seen in urban areas, particularly when students, crowds, demonstrations, or 'manifestations' may in their opinion require supervision, are the autocratic police *armada*, now known as the *Policía nacional*. They also guard embassies, nervous capitalists, stations, banks, and post offices, etc. Some have been known to fire on the municipal police, thinking that they might be emissaries of ETA in disguise. All Spanish police are obtrusively armed. Some have met with a violent death in recent anti-authoritarian disturbances, notably in the Basque provinces, where their duties are being taken over by a specially formed Basque police force.

Passports and proofs of identity are occasionally demanded by the police, but this has been a feature of Spanish life under most political regimes and, however intolerable, is best accepted while it lasts as a mere formality.

Briefly seen in Madrid were several green-helmeted police, on the lookout for vehicles further polluting the already contaminated streets, but they did not survive long.

Serenos, a dying race of night watchmen, were first established in Valencia in 1777, and in Madrid 20 years later. Together with *porteros* (doormen), they also acted as police informers during the Franco regime.

Sports. Tourist Offices should be able to provide information on different sports, hunting and shooting (*caza*) and fishing (*pesca*); mountaineering; and also on National Parks, and the regulations of the *Instituto Nacional para la Conservación de la Naturaleza* (ICONA), etc.

Bullfights (*Corridas de toros*) are part of the sub-culture of Spain, and should be condemned just as fox hunting may be condemned, with the difference that while the odds are heavily against the bull, which is invariably killed, the danger to human life is considerable. It is still a favourite sport of the populace—apart from football—and all attempts in the past to abolish it have failed. Lady Holland wrote that such was the rage for the sport that women sold 'their shifts, and finally *persons*, to procure a seat'. Jardine stigmatised those who took part in the unedifying spectacle as 'hired gladiators, who are generally butchers by profession'. Most civilised people consider it a brutal and depraving activity. Nevertheless, as many travellers feel that it is incumbent on them to attend at least one before deciding for themselves, the bullfight—otherwise as incomprehensible to the British as cricket is to a Spaniard—is explained below.

Every town of any consequence—and many of no consequence—has its bull ring (*Plaza de Toros*), in which *corridas* take place from Easter until mid October. *Novilladas*—fights between young bulls and less experienced *toreros*—should not be confused with the *corrida* proper. An *encierro*, in which bulls are driven through the streets from an enclosure in the suburbs to the *corral* of the *plaza de toros*, is again different, the most vaunted occuring at Pamplona during the fiesta of S. Fermín (5–16 July). The side streets are barricaded off, and those that take part run before the bulls. Serious accidents are not infrequent, and only the most foolhardy tourist will participate.

The bull ring is an open amphitheatre with the arena separated from the rising tiers of seats by a stout stockade with narrow openings through which the *toreros* may escape when hard pressed.

(Occasionally a bull will leap over this barrier into the passage behind.) In hot weather it is preferable to get seats in the *sombra* or shady side of the ring.

The leading *torero* (*not* 'toreador'), the *matador* or *espada* (who eventually kills the beast), often an extravagantly paid idol, is assisted by his *cuadrilla*, consisting of *banderilleros*, who attempt to plant darts into the bull's shoulders, and *picadors*, or mounted lancers. Other *toreros*, occupied in wearying the bull with their *capas* or cloaks, or distracting his attention at critical moments, are known as *chulos* or *monos*.

The *corrida* opens with the processional entry of the group to the strains of a *paso-doble*, led by mounted *alguazils* (in late 16C costume), followed by the mule team whose later function it is to drag out the dead bull. The president, who occupies a central box facing the *toril* or enclosure, tosses its key to the *alguazil*; the *toril* is opened, and the bull, decorated by the *devisa* or colours of the *ganadería* or ranch on which it was bred, charges in. Fighting bulls are now usually between three and five years old, younger and lighter than the huge beasts used previously (as illustrated in Ernest Hemingway's 'Death in the Afternoon', first published in 1932, and now a dated curiosity). Usually six bulls are slaughtered at each *corrida*, the fate of each being settled in c 20 minutes; the evening's entertainment lasting 2½–3 hours.

The bull is first tired by playing him with magenta, yellow-backed, *capas*; the bull (which is colour blind) invariably attacking the moving cloak and not the man. *Picadores*, their legs protected by greaves, and mounted on blindfolded hacks, now enter the ring armed with short steel-pointed lances (*puyas* or *varas*). The bull is incited to charge the horse's protected right side, and irritated by the stab of the lance, lunges furiously, occasionally lifting both mount and rider and sending them sprawling in the sand. In such cases his attention is immediately distracted by the *chulos*, while a second *picador* enters. The intention is to damage and weaken the bull's neck muscles, while the loss of blood will further exhaust him.

(The great blot is the treatment of the horses, usually worn-out crocks, formerly exposed unprotected to be gored by the infuriated bull. They are now provided with padded plastrons or *petos*, but harrowing scenes still occur, and one must be prepared for the nauseating sight of trailing entrails. It is difficult to judge to what extent Gautier was exaggerating when he wrote that he saw 24 bulls and 96 horses killed in three days.)

The beast is next manoeuvred into the centre of the arena to encounter the *banderilleros*, which he charges while they skip aside after plunging two barbed darts, ornamented with streamers, into its shoulders. Three pairs should be thus planted.

Then the *matador*, after playing the bull with his cape, exchanges this for a scarlet cloth or *muleta*, attached to a short rod, and prepares to dispatch the bull with his *estoque* or short sword. Inviting but evading attack, his aim is to kill at a blow by thrusting his sword between the shoulders or withers to the heart, but this is only possible when the bull's feet are close together and its head held low. Several bloody thrusts are often necessary before the bull succumbs; or it may have to be killed by plunging a special sword, the *verdugillo*, into the nape of the neck, an action known as the *descabello*. Usually the coup de grâce is given to the prostrate beast with a dagger by the attendant *puntillero*. The carcase is dragged out; the sand is raked smooth; and the next victim enters.

Not the least curious features of the *corrida* are the reactions of the *aficionados*, swift to greet a sluggish bull or clumsy *torero* with whistles, catcalls, and ironical clapping in a slow triple time (*palmas de tango*); while a display of dexterity will receive an hysterical ovation, shouts of '*olé*', waving of handkerchiefs, etc. A good kill is rewarded by the president with one or two ears and the tail of the bull, which are cut off and presented to the *torero* as trophies, like a bush to a foxhunter, but often the reward is hardly deserved.

In recent years interest in an older form of *corrida* has gained ground, the main difference being that it is a mounted combat calling for dextrous horsemanship on the part of the *rejoneador*. The quality of the mount in no way compares with the poor hacks of the *picadores*.

There is an extensive vocabulary of the bull ring, naming with precision all the *pases*, as well as the age, colour, horns, and temper, etc. of the bull. And every season there is much argument among the fraternity and in the press regarding abuses, such as shaving the bull's horns, causing it to aim short, etc., but like boxing or wrestling, it attracts corrupt practices.

I PAIS VASCO/EUSKADI (IN BASQUE); NAVARRA; LA RIOJA

The Spanish **Basque Provinces** (*Las Provincias Vascongadas* or **Pais Vasco**) of *Guipúzcoa*, *Álava*, and *Vizcaya* (in Basque, *Gipuzkoa*, *Araba*, and *Bizkaia*), together with northern **Navarra** (anglicised as *Narvarre*), provide an unexpected view of Spain to most travellers entering the country at the western extremity of the Pyrenees. The countryside is exceedingly hilly and thickly wooded when not mountainous, and communications are not easy, although the main roads are good, and the state of repair of minor roads is improving continually. Solid wide-gabled farms or *caseríos*, their doors and shutters often painted dark green or maroon, are seen dotted over the steep green slopes of the broken ranges that form here a natural barrier between France and the Castilian plateau, and overlook the highly-populated industrial valleys to which they offer a strong contrast.

Many of the older stone-built houses still display carved escutcheons, a proud reminder of the Basques assumption of nobility, which was secured for them by the mere fact of being born in these provinces. Even in the smallest villages, and often abutting the churchyard—some of which preserve their characteristic discoidal tombstones—one will see an open court with one high wall, the ubiquitous *frontón*. Here is played their national ball game of *pelota*, resembling fives, utilising in one of its forms, a large basket-work glove or *chistera*. The Basque national costume is now represented only by their beret or *boina*, and rope-soled shoes or *alpargatas*. Their language (*Euskera*; see p 93) is still frequently heard in Guipúzcoa, eastern Vizcaya, and northern Navarra, but less so in Álava. Guipúzcoa, with its capital at San Sebastián, is perhaps the most completely Basque area, although the northern half of Navarra, with Pamplona as its capital, also remains Basque in customs. Álava, with Vitoria-Gasteiz, the administrative capital of the provinces, is relatively poor in natural resources, and with a less abundant rainfall, produces excellent wine along the N bank of the Ebro, the Rioja Alavesa; while Vizcaya possesses rich mineral deposits. The Basque provinces are also rich in agricultural produce, in fruit, and timber, while from time immemorial Basque fishermen have sailed from her ports into the Bay of Biscay and far beyond to the Cod fisheries of Newfoundland, and their whaling industry was famous.

The industrious, enterprising, materialistic, and intensely individualistic and hard-headed Basques, the autochthonous inhabitants of this rugged corner of Spain, a race of unknown origin, have always been energetic in preserving their independence, enjoying certain privileges of self-government, safeguarded by ancient *fueros*, or code of law, which they jealously maintained over the centuries against the centralising policy of their autocratic Castilian overlords.

The Basques, or *Vascones*, who long resisted Roman incursions, later gained themselves notoriety for plundering travellers in the western Pyrenees, and it was they who brought about the disaster at Roncesvalles. The influx of pilgrims to the shrine of Santiago de Compostela also brought them much booty. From the 11C onward the three northern provinces were restless vassals of Castile, but it was not until the 19C that they played a prominent part in Spanish history. In the Carlist Wars of 1833–39 and 1872–76 the Basques

ROUTE
MAPS

Key

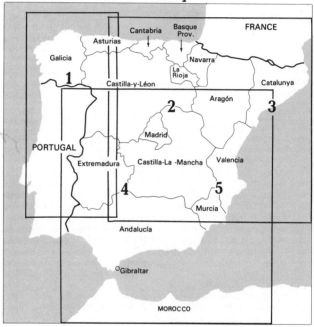

supported the rebels and showed some of their skill in guerrilla warfare in defence of a hopeless cause; as a punishment many of their *fueros*, including the cherished right of exemption from military service, were revoked. Until then, in Jardine's words (1777), these provinces were 'the only remaining asylums in the peninsula for liberty'.

During the last Civil War the majority of the autonomous Basques were cut off from the rest of the Republican zone, as reactionary Navarra adhered to the Nationalists, and suffered severely in the campaign mounted by Gen. Mola. The destruction of Guernica by German bombers was an atrocity which excited the sympathy of the non-fascist world. Basque nationalists claim that over 21,000 Basques died in the post-war repression. A small militant extremist group known as ETA (*Euzkadi Ta Azkatasuna*, or Freedom for the Basques) agitated too violently for home rule, which invited repressive counter measures instituted by Franco, causing world-wide recrimination. Although some regional autonomy was granted in 1980, this was not considered sufficient by the militant *Herri Batasuna* party, which formed ETA's political front. More recent measures against ETA, which still has considerable local support from Basques on both sides of the frontier, have spectacularly failed, underlining the incapacity of the Madrid government, who still think that a show of force can cow rather than exacerbate nationalist feelings.

Members of the Guardia Civil, who—apart from the military—have been the main target for assassination by ETA, not only acted with extreme brutality during the Franco regime, but have continued to do so since, and there is repeated evidence that they have tortured their suspects, and therefore have been picked out for retribution, whether justified or not. Although most Basques condemn the more violent forms of terrorism carried out by ETA, particularly when affecting innocent civilians, or when extorting a 'revolutionary tax', there is little sign of this dying down, and many suspect that it will *not* until the national police are entirely replaced by Basque police (a measure now being instituted), and the military presence is withdrawn.

Herri Batasuna have also endeavoured to incorporate the northern half of adjacent **Navarra** (*Nafarroa* in Basque) into the Basque provinces, with which it is very similar physically, although the former kingdom, established there in the 9C, has had a somewhat different history. Despite Frankish and Moorish attacks, it reached its zenith under Sancho the Great (el Mayor; 1000–35), after which its political importance declined. (Berengaria, daughter of Sancho VI, in 1191 married Richard I 'cœur de Lion' at Limassol in Cyprus).

For a time a dependency of Aragón, it eventually separated and was ruled by its own kings until Sancho VII died in 1234 without heirs. The Navarrese elected Thibaut V, Count of Champagne, and this dynasty ruled until 1285, when it became a dependency of the French crown. In 1328 it passed to the House of Évreux. In 1434 Leonor of Navarra married Gaston de Foix, and later the throne passed to the house of Albret. In 1512 Fernando the Catholic annexed the whole of Navarra south of the Pyrenees. It was anciently divided into six '*merindades*', with capitals at Pamplona, Sangüesa, Tudela, Estella, Olite, and St.-Jean-Pied-de-Port, the last representing French Navarra, which was eventually united to France at the accession of Henri IV.

Navarra remained a stronghold of Carlism, and the reactionary Navarrese militia or *requetés* earned themselves an unenviable reputation for ferocity during the Civil War, while in 1952 an 'Opus Dei' University was founded in Pamplona. The S half of the province (or *Comunidad Foral*) is indeed much more like Aragón as the Ebro valley is entered, while to the SW of Pamplona is broken country which as imperceptibly merges with **La Rioja**, famous for its wines, and which, W of Logroño, its flourishing capital, abuts Alava. Until recently the province formed part of Old Castile.

Without taking into account the many who have emigrated or who have sought asylum elsewhere, the Basques number approximately 2,000,000, including those in the French Basque provinces. The total population of the Spanish Basque provinces is 2,141,800 (782,000 in 1920), of which 189,500 of Alava's 257,850 are concentrated in Vitoria alone; while almost a million of Vizcaya's 1,189,300 live in the conurbation of Bilbao, but a high proportion of this increase is due to the organised influx of Spaniards from poorer provinces, an expedient considered by some Basques as a deliberate attempt to dilute their blood.

The population of Navarra is now 509,000 (339,000 in 1920); and of La Rioja, 258,350 (199,000 in 1920), 109,500 of which are in Logroño itself.

1 (Bayonne) Behobia and Irún to Burgos

A. Via San Sebastián, Tolosa and Vitoria

252km (156 miles). N1. 22km **San Sebastián**—27km *Tolosa*—44km *Alsasua*—46km **Vitoria**—49km *Pancorbo*—64km **Burgos**.

Maps: M 442.

Motorway. The French A63 autoroute, which bypasses *Bayonne*, *Biarritz*, and *St. Jean-de-Luz*, crosses the Bidasoa a short distance E of the *Behobia* border crossing (Customs), and is recommended, particularly during the summer when the two coastal roads are congested. The N1 (described below) may also be avoided by continuing on the motorway (*autopista*), from which *San Sebastián* may easily be approached.

Travellers wishing to remain on the motorway to *Burgos* will find the road as far as Pancorbo described in Rte 1C. This is recommended in winter as preferable to the main road climbing the Puertos de Echegarate and de la Brújula.

From **Bayonne** (see *Blue Guide France* for the Pays Basque, the French Basque region) the N10 drives SW to **St. Jean-de-Luz** before climbing a spur of the PYRENEES, with a good view to the left of *La Rhune* (900m), before descending to *Behobia* and crossing the Bidasoa, which forms the frontier.

An ALTERNATIVE road skirts the rocky coast from St. Jean through *Ciboure* to *Hendaye*, there crossing the *International Bridge* (Customs) immediately N of Irún, with a view (left) of the triple peak of the *Peñas de Haya* (806m), and (right) *Monte Jaizkibel* (448m). Below the latter is *Fuenterrabia*, at the mouth of the Bidasoa; see below.

Between the two frontier bridges lies the unprepossessing *Ile des Faisans* or *Île de la Conférence*, on neutral ground in the riverbed. Here negotiations between Louis XIV and Felipe IV put an end to hostilities between France and Spain in the Thirty Years' War (1659). When fitting up the conference saloon Velázquez contracted a fever from which he later died. Earlier international meetings had taken place between Louis XI and Enrique IV of Castile in 1468; and in 1615 between Isabelle, daughter of Henri IV, destined to marry Felipe IV, and Felipe's sister Ana (of Austria), who was on her way to Paris to marry Louis XIII.

For the road from Spanish *Behobia* to *Pamplona* see Rte 2. **Irún** (53,350 inhab.), damaged in 1936 and since much rebuilt, retains a 16C *Ayuntamiento* in the Pl. de S. Juan, the centre of the old town. Beyond it stands *N.S. de Juncal* (1508), typical of the Renaissance architecture of Guipúzcoa.

FROM IRÚN TO PASAJES VIA FUENTERRABÍA AND MONTE JAIZKIBEL (c 20km). **Fuenterrabía** (*Hondarribia*; 11,400 inhab.), some 3km N of Irún, is a characteristic old fortified town, somewhat spoilt by a series of tower blocks buttressing the sea flank of Jaizkibel. It was strong enough to withstand a siege by the French under the Prince of Condé in 1638, but was taken by François I in 1521, and in 1719 by the Duke of Berwick. Crossing the Bidasoa from near here by an unsuspected ford, Wellington was able to surprise and turn the strongly defended French right flank on 7 October 1813, when invading France 3½ months after the Battle of Vitoria. Whistler got this far only on his projected journey to Madrid in 1861. From the *Puerta de Sta. María* in the 15C walls the picturesque C. Mayor climbs past the *Ayuntamiento* and several ancient mansions to *N.S. de la Asunción*, 11C but altered during the Renaissance. At the upper end of the street is the *Palacio de Carlos V*, mainly 14–16C on 10C foundations, restored to house a Parador. From the lower town a road goes on to a lighthouse on *Cabo Higuer*, passing the remains of the *Castillo de S. Telmo*.

The main road climbs past *N.S. de Guadalupe* to run along the spine of *Monte Jaizkibel* (448m), providing a panoramic view over the valley of the Bidasoa towards the W foothills of the Pyrenees, before descending steeply to **Pasajes** (*Pasaia*) **de S. Juan**. The village is threaded by a single narrow street, and a visit on foot is preferable. From the 10th to the 16C it was a centre of the Biscay whaling industry, together with St. Jean-de-Luz and San Sebastián. Lafayette embarked for America in 1776 from here, while during the closing stages of the Peninsular War it was Wellington's main port of supply. Victor Hugo lived at No. 59 in the main street in 1843. This street continues past the 16C church to a ruined fort of 1621 and the narrow mouth of the land-locked bay, the safest harbour between Bordeaux and Bilbao. On the opposite bank lies *Pasajes de S. Pedro*.—The N1 may be regained by bearing left through adjacent *Lezo*, with old houses and the *Basilica de Santo Cristo*, rebuilt in the 17C.

Leaving Irún, the N1 leads SW below *Monte Jaizkibel*, and after crossing a ridge descends towards Renteria, first passing a turning (left) to **Oyarzun** (7750 inhab.), the ancient *Oeasso*, a Basque capital during the Roman occupation. It stands on the former post road to Madrid, and has a 17C church.

A road climbs SE from Oyarzun to a tunnel below the ridge dividing Guipúzcoa from Navarra, near the summit of the *Peñas de Haya* or *Las Tres Coronas* (806m), and winds through the mountains before descending to (27km) *Lesaca*; see Rte 2.—The old post road may be followed to the W via (9km) *Astigarraga* and, 3km beyond, **Hernani** (30,450 inhab.), its C. Mayor retaining several old mansions with striking balconies and escutcheons. The church contains the tomb of Juan de Urbieta (died 1553), who captured François I at Pavia (1525). The British Auxiliary Legion was defeated here by the Carlists in 1837 and the town suffered severely during the Carlist War of 1874. *San Sebastián* is 9.5km N.

Industrial **Renteria** (46,500 inhab.), with a 16C fortified church containing a jasper retablo designed by *Ventura Rodríguez* (1784), merges with the land-locked port of *Pasajes de S. Pedro* (20,750 inhab.; see above). After a short climb, the road descends below *Monte Ulia* (right; 234m) to approach the E suburbs of San Sebastián.

SAN SEBASTIÁN (**Donostia** in Basque; 172,300 inhab.; 63,000 in 1920; 111,000 in 1950), capital of Guipúzcoa, was from 1886 the most fashionable summer resort in Spain, with the Spanish royal family spending their holidays here. It has not lost its cachet, but in recent years it has been somewhat slighted and over policed. The *Parte Vieja* or old town, commanded by *Monte Urgull* with its castle, stands on a rocky peninsula. It was formerly a strong fortress, but its landward defences on the isthmus were demolished by 1866. To the W is the sandy semicircular bay of *La Concha*, protected from the open sea by the *Isla de Sta. Clara*; to the E flows the Urumea. It enjoys a mild climate, but sudden showers, or a '*siri-miri*' (Scotch mist), are not infrequent, and in winter it is depressingly damp.

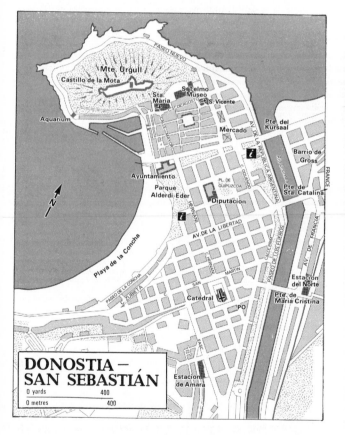

DONOSTIA – SAN SEBASTIÁN

0 yards 400
0 metres 400

Its early history is obscure. It received its *fuero* in 1180; and its former Basque name would seem to have been *Izurum*. With the union of Guipúzcoa with Spain it became a bulwark against French incursions. Among its many sieges the most disastrous was that of 1813, when Gen. Rey with 3000 veterans held out for six weeks against Gen. Graham with an Anglo-Portuguese force of 10,000. After several fruitless assaults involving great loss, they succeeded in fording the Urumea under cover of a heavy bombardment and entered the breaches. Rey withdrew to the castle, surrendering some days later, having set fire to the town to keep the besiegers at bay, and the English were later reproached for doing so out of commercial jealousy. Between 1835 and 1837 it was successfully defended against the Carlists, the garrison aided by the British Auxiliary Legion under the command of de Lacy Evans.

Among natives of San Sebastián were Adm. Antonio de Oquendo (1577–1640); Catalina de Erauso (1585–c 1650), known as 'La Monja Alférez' (the nun-ensign), who, after escaping from a convent, had a military career in Spanish America without her sex being discovered; and Pío Baroja (1872–1956), the novelist.

W of the *Puente del Kursaal*, spanning the Urumea, extends the ALAMEDA, laid out on the site of former fortifications. At its far end is the *Ayuntamiento* (previously the Casino), beyond which is the fishing port, with a terrace of fishermen's cottages sheltering under the bulk of Monte Urgull. Pass through an archway by the port to enter the **Parte Vieja**. Many of the more characteristic bars and restaurants are in this area of thronged narrow streets, preferably explored on foot. On reaching the C. Mayor, to the left is the elaborate sculptured façade of *Sta. María*, a hall-church recon-structed in 1743–64; it contains sculptures by Diego Villanueva and Juan de Mena.

Monte Urgull is best climbed by a path immediately W of the church, which later passes the *English Cemetery*, with tombs of officers of the British Auxiliary Legion. Above rises a monument to British troops who fell in the Peninsular War. The *Castillo de la Mota* on the summit, containing a disappointing military museum, is a good example of the 16C transition from the castle to the bastioned fortifications of the Renaissance. The views are extensive, although less attractive than they once were; the hill itself is disfigured by a monumental statue.

From Sta. María the C. 31 de Agosto leads E to Gothic *S. Vicente* (1507), N of which stands the former convent of *S. Telmo* (1551), housing the **Municipal Museum** (under reformation). The Renais-sance cloister contains early discoidal tombstones characteristic of the Basque provinces.

Among the paintings on the First Floor are *El Greco*, St. Domingo; *Vicente López*, Fernando VII; *Goya*, Portrait of Gen. Alexander O'Reilly (see Cádiz); and several works by *Zuloaga*. Upper galleries display archaeological and historical collections, with rooms devoted to the Carlist Wars. Another section contains Basque Ethnography. The former church, with recumbent effigies of the founder (Alonso de Idiáquez, secretary of state to Charles V) and his wife, has been decorated by *Josep María Sert* with paintings depicting the life of the Basque people.

Walking S from S. Vicente along the C. Narrica, one may turn right to enter the PL. DE LA CONSTITUCÍON with the old *Ayuntamiento* (1832).

S of the Alameda are the wider streets of the newer town, lined with shops and cafés, particularly in the Av. de la Libertad, reached by any street running S. To the W is the PARQUE ALDERDI EDER, and two streets to the E is the arcaded PL. DE GUIPÚZCOA, flanked by the *Diputación*.

From the W end of the Av. de la Libertad we approach the PASEO DE LA CONCHA, an esplanade overlooking the beach, in summer resplendent with *toldos* (sun shades); while the C. Hernani leads S from the avenue to the *Cathedral* (El Buen Pastor; begun 1888). To the E is the *Puente de Sta. Catalina*, and upstream the *Puente de María Cristina* crossing to the Railway station.

The C. Zurbieta, leading W, later skirts the beach and tunnels below the garden of the *Pal. de Miramar* (1893; designed by the English architect Selden Wornum), the former royal residence, standing on a cliff separating La Concha from the *Playa de Ondar-reta*. The main road bears SW, resuming its course as the Av. de Tolosa and N1.

The Av. de Satrústegui forks right just beyond the tunnel to approach the foot of *Monte Igueldo*, and climbs steeply to its summit, now surmounted by a hotel (also reached by funicular). Some distance beyond is the village of *Igueldo*, with a 12C church. After 7km the road peters out at the foot of *Mendizorrotz* (407m), with extensive views from its summit.

The N1 shortly reaches the interchange for the motorway to *Bilbao* (see Rte 1C), and later the N634; see Rte 1B. We bear S, following the wooded valley of the Oria, unfortunately polluted by paper mills, to bypass (left) **Andoain** (16,350 inhab.) with a Renaissance church, and the birthplace of Manuel de Larramendi (1690–1766), the Basque grammarian.

The valley becomes more industrial as the road skirts *Villabona* to approach (27km) **Tolosa** (18,900 inhab.), in which *Sta. María*, *S. Francisco*, and the 12C *Armería*, are notable. For the road to *Pamplona* see Rte 3.

The C6324 diverges right on leaving the town, crossing the mountains via *Régil* (views from the *Balcón de Guipúzcoa*) to 25km) *Azpeitia*; see p 116.

Legorreta, *Ordizia* and, beyond a short tunnel, industrial *Beasain*, are bypassed.

BEASAIN TO ESTELLA (69km). The C130 turns left beyond this tunnel to ascend the Argaunza valley through *Ataun* to the *Alto de Lizarrusti* (620m), before descending to meet the N240 at (29km) *Echarri Aranaz*. The N111 then climbs S to the *Puerto de Lizarraga* (1090m), commanding splendid views, and crosses the SIERRA DE ANDIA (rising to 1493m at the *Beriain*, to the E), and at 31km reaches *Abárzuza*. Some 3km NW is the Cistercian abbey of *Iranzu*, mainly 12–13C. Parts of the ruined dependencies (over restored) have been re-occupied.—9km *Estella*; see Rte 4.

BEASAIN TO VITORIA VIA BERGARA (c 70km). This sub-route follows the old coach road (C6322), turning right for *Ormaiztegi*, birthplace of the Carlist guerrilla leader Tomaso Zumalacárregui (1788–1835).—**Zumarraga** (11,800 inhab.), bypassed (right), on the left bank of the Urola, and the birthplace of Adm. López de Legazpi (c 1510–72), retains an attractive PL. MAYOR and 16C church. On the opposite bank lies *Urretxu*, with a late 16C hall-church, overlooked by *Monte Irimo*, and the castle of *Ipenarrieta* (1605).—The C6317 descends the wooded gorge of the Urola to (12km) *Azkoitia* (see p 117), while the main road climbs W to the *Puerto de Descarga* (585m) for *Bergara*, passing near *Antzuola*, in the hamlet of *Uzárraga*, an ancient Templar church.—A left turn SW of Zumarraga leads through *Legazpia* (10,650 inhab.) for (19.5km) *Oñati*; see below. *La Asunción* at Legazpia has a notable porch. The road then crosses the *Alto de Udana* (521m), with *Aloña* or *Gorgomendi* (1321m) rising to the SW.

Bergara (formerly *Vergara*; 16,050 inhab.) is famous as the scene of the Convention which brought an end to the first Carlist War in 1839. Here in 1756, under the auspices of Francisco Munibe e Idiáquez, Conde de Peñaflorida (1729–85), was founded the Real Sociedad Bascongada de los Amigos del País. This was the first of a number of Economic Societies which flourished throughout Spain in the late 18C, and did much to foster interest in education, agriculture, commerce and industry. Bergara preserves several old houses, including the *Casa de Jáuregui*, and a 17C *Ayuntamiento*. Among other buildings of some interest are *S. Pedro*, Gothic *Sta. Marina*, beyond the lower bridge across the Deva, the *Seminario* (1776), and outside the town, the mid 16C *Pal. de Olazaeta*.

The C6213 bears SW. At 5km a road turns SE up the Arantzazu valley to (7km) **Oñati** (10,900 inhab.), with the imposing buildings of its former *University*, founded by Bp Zuázola of Ávila in 1539. His Renaissance tomb of Parian marble is in 15C *S. Miguel*, which also contains those of the Counts of Oñati, and a Plateresque cloister; its tower of 1783 is by *Manuel de Carrera*. The Franciscan *Conv. de Bidaurreta* (1509), and the convents of the *Sacro Corazón* and *Sta. Ana*, and the *Ayuntamiento*, facing the *Pl. Mayor*, are of interest. The town, birthplace of Lope de Aguirre (c 1511–61), the *conquistador*, retains several old mansions and tower-houses, notably along the Arantzazu road, to the S.—This leads 9km up the valley to the modern convent of *Arantzazu*, from which *Aitzgorri* (1540m) may be ascended.

Not far beyond the turning for Oñati we enter (bypass projected) *Arrasate* or **Mondragón** (26,300 inhab.), noted for an iron mine that has been worked from remote antiquity. It was the birthplace of the Basque historian Esteban de Garibay (1439–99). Its *Ayuntamiento* dates from 1746.—We pass the spas of *Aretxabaleta* and *Eskoriatza*, and climb through woods to the *Puerto de Arlaban* (617m), 7km beyond which the N240 is reached 11.5km N of *Vitoria* at a point not far S of *Villareal*; see p 136.—A left-hand fork beyond the *puerto* skirts the *Ullivarri reservoir* and enters Vitoria via *Durana*, with an early Gothic church, the scene of a defeat of the Comuneros in 1521. For **Vitoria**; see below.

Beyond Beasain the N1 starts to climb. (Off it the old road across the *Alto de Sta. Bárbara* diverges right via *Zegama*, in the church of which is the tomb of Zumalacárregui; cf. Ormaiztegi.) Later it ascends in sweeping curves to reach the *Puerto de Echegarate* (658m), before descending gently to 28km) *Alsasua* (7300 inhab.) recently provided with a bypass, and overlooked from the SE by the barren SIERRA DE URBASA. The chapel of *S. Pedro* to the NE is the legendary place of election in 717 of Navarra's first king, García Jiménez.

ALSASUA TO PAMPLONA (49km). The N240 drives due E along the Araquil valley, now bypassing almost all villages en route, including (8km) *Echarri-Aranaz*, *Arbizu*, with a good church and large tower-house, and *Huarte-Araquil*, between the SIERRAS DE ARALAR (N; 1343m) and DE ANDIA (1493m), with Romanesque *S. Marcial*.—A path climbs N, passing the Romanesque church of *Zamarce* and, further on, a dolmen (one of numerous prehistoric remains in the district), to Romanesque *S. Miguel* (cons. 1098; containing a retablo in Limoges enamel of c 1200): also approached by road from *Lecumberri*; see Rte 3.—*Echarren*, with old houses, is traversed (near by is the Romanesque church of *Chisperri*), before meeting the A15 motorway and the N240 at (21km) *Irurzun*, for which and for *Pamplona*, 20km SE, see Rte 3.

At Alsasua the N1 bears almost due W, with the *Peña Araz* rising to the N (1445m), later passing a turning (right) to *Zalduendo*, where a mansion with a classical frontal and carved arms is notable. The dolmen of *Eguilaz* is passed to the right on approaching the formerly walled village of **Salvatierra** (bypassed). Arcaded streets lead to the *Pl. Mayor*, the *Pal. Municipal* of 1606, and the *Casa de los Eulates*. *Sta. María* is late 15C; *S. Juan* has a Renaissance porch and tower.

Gaceo, 3km W, has a Transitional church. 2km beyond, at *Ezquerecocha*, the early Gothic church has exuberant carvings and a stone reredos.—*Contrasta*, c 12km SE of Salvatierra beyond the

Puerto de Opacua (1020m), once a frontier town, has a fortified church and Romanesque *N.S. de Elizmendi.*

The N1 approaches the *Ulivarri reservoir*, passing near (right) the ruined castle of *Guevara*, modelled in the 15C on that of Sant'Angelo at Rome, but burnt out in 1889.

To the left at *Argómaniz* is the Parador, beyond which a left turn leads to *Alegria*, Roman *Tullonius*. *S. Blas* has an 18C tower by *Olaguibel*; *N.S. de Ayala*, an unspoilt Transitional 13C chapel, has a pointed barrel vault and arcaded S portico.—At *Gauna*, S of Alegria, with an ancient church, the *Ayuntamiento* is the former palace of the Counts of Salvatierra.

VITORIA (**-Gasteiz**; 189,550 inhab.; 36,000 in 1920; 69,000 in 1960), capital of Álava, and now the administrative capital of the Spanish Basque Provinces, is divided into an upper quarter of narrow lanes and old mansions, with a rapidly growing industrial and residential town surrounding it. The old nucleus, 'El Campo Suso', stands on a height (524m; Basque, *beturia*) which gives the town its name.

The settlement of *Gasteiz*, perhaps of Visigothic origin, lay on the hill. After the victory of Las Navas (1212) it was enlarged and surrounded by a new wall, and remained independent until the union of Álava with Castile in 1332. From 1366 to 1413 it passed to Navarra. Near Vitoria a battle was fought in 1367 between Pedro the Cruel, supported by English troops, and Enrique de Trastámara. For the more famous battle of Vitoria of 1813 see below. Sherer, in his 'Recollections of the Peninsula' (1823), records that a bookseller here assured him that in the fortnight after the battle he sold more books to the British than he disposed of in two years to the French who were constantly passing through the place. During the First Carlist War many men of the British Auxiliary Legion perished here of cold and fever.

Pero López de Ayala (1332–1407), the chronicler, and chancellor of Castile; Fray Francisco de Vitoria (c 1483–1546), defender of the Indians of America; Gen. Álava (1771–1843), aide-de-camp to Wellington; and Ramiro de Maeztu Whitney (1874–1936), the militant Catholic philosopher and essayist, were born here.

Several roads converge on the gardens of La Florida (with a Tourist Office) not far SW of the centre, from which the Prado approaches the PL. DE LA VIRGEN BLANCA. The partially pedestrian C. Dato leads N from the railway station to the arcaded PL. DE ESPAÑA (1791). Steps ascend from the adjoining PL. VIEJA to 14C *S. Miguel*, with a Baroque retablo by Gregorio Fernández. To the E in the PL. DE MACHETE is the *Pal. de Villasuso*, with a Renaissance doorway, and adjacent is 15C *S. Vicente*, with a tower of 1865.

Following the ancient *Cuchillería*, we pass (right) the *Casa del Cordón* (No. 24, restored) and the *Pal. De Bedaña* (Nos 58–60), both of c 1500, before reaching the 14C Gothic **Sta. María**, its vaulted W portico sheltering a *Doorway of c 1400 in the Franco-Navarrese style.

The church contains several works of art of doubtful attribution, and a retablo mayor by Olaguíbel with an Assumption in high relief by Valdivielso. The sacristy preserves a Descent from the Cross probably by Gaspar de Crayer, and a Conception by Juan de Carreño.

To the NW is the *Casa del Portalón* (Correría 151), an old timbered house with overhanging storeys, containing a small museum devoted to the Battle of Vitoria. At No. 116, opposite, are collections of armour and archaeology.

The concentric streets of the old town, on the E side of which stood the *Judería*, are flanked by ancient houses and mansions, notably in the *Correría* and the *Herrería*, in the *Cuchillería* and the *Zapatería*. Notable are the Plateresque *Pal. de Escoriaza-Esquivel* and the

Episcopal Palace, with Renaissance windows, in the C. del Fray Zacarías Martínez, while near the N end of the *Pintorería* is the façade of the *Conv. de la Santa Cruz*. The *Hospicio* has a Renaissance door.

Returning from Sta. María along the W side of the old town, to regain the Pl. de la Virgen Blanca, we pass 14C *S. Pedro*, with a fine portal, a Plateresque retablo, and two 16C bronze effigies (cast in Milan) of members of the Álava family.

From the *Canciller Ayala hotel*, on the S side of the *La Florida gardens*, a path leads shortly to the Paseo de Fray Francisco, in which the *Casa de Álava* (N side) houses the **Provincial Museum**.

It contains representative paintings by Alonso Cano and by Ribera, and others attrib. to Murillo and to Morales; a collection of polychrome statues (14–15C); a marble Goddess (2C) from Iruña, and other Roman carvings, altars, and mosaics; Romanesque sculpture, including a Column from *Zurbano* (c 5km NE) bearing grotesque figures (?c 1200).—A collection of *Arms* may be seen in a mansion almost opposite.

There are several churches and chapels of specialist interest in the vicinity of Vitoria. They may be difficult to find in the still-growing conurbation, and the Tourist Office may be able to advise on the easiest approaches. Among them are those at *Landa, Nanclares de Gamboa, Mendizábal, Arbubiaga*, and *Ullivarri-Arrazua* (all to the NE); *Betoño, Gamarra Mayor*, and *Menor* (to the N); *Lopidiana* (W); *Lasarte* (SW on the Trevino road); *Otazu* (SE); and *Monasterioguren* (SW of Otazu); see also p 136.

3km SW, to the left of the N1 in the hamlet of **Armentia**, *S. Andrés* (c 1181), unfortunately rebuilt in 1776, retains remarkable reliefs in its porch, carved capitals in the choir, and statues of the Evangelists at the crossing.—4km SW, to the right of the N1, lies *Zuazo de Álava*, with a pure Romanesque church, while another turning (right, 4km beyond) leads past *Iruña*, ancient *Suisacio*, with Roman remains.—Further W lies *Badaya*, with ruins of a 15C Hieronymite monastery. There are dolmens in the neighbourhood.—After 4km, at *Mendoza* rise the tower-houses of the Duke of Infantado (restored) and of the Count of Orgaz. Other churches may be seen to the NW at *Urrialdo, Hueto de Arriba*, and *de Abajo*.

For roads from Vitoria to **Estella** and **Logroño** see Rte 6.

Driving W and then SW from Vitoria the N1 passes (right) the battlefields of 1367 (*Inglesmendi*, where English troops, commanded by Sir William Felton, fought for Pedro the Cruel) and of 1813. On the right are the ancient bridges over the Zadorra of *Trespuentes* and *Villodas*.

The **Battle of Vitoria** (21 June 1813), in which Wellington defeated Jourdan and secured the mastery of the Basque Provinces, took place W of the town on either side of the road to Nanclares. After a day's heavy fighting, during which the French lost over 8000 compared to the Allies' 5000, the French army, with Joseph Bonaparte and his court, retreated E, leaving behind 143 guns and a prodigious amount of plunder which delayed the pursuit. The pictures from the royal Spanish collection found in King Joseph's carriages are now in Apsley House, London.

At 10km *Nanclares de Oca*, with a Romanesque church, lies 2km right.—We descend the Zadorra valley, with the castle of *Arganzón* to the right, to bypass *La Puebla de Arganzón* and, later, *Armiñon*, with a picturesque bridge, to enter the upper valley of the Ebro.

The entrances to the A1 motorway (for Burgos; see Rte 1C), off which the A68 for Zaragoza turns SE and the N232 for **Logroño** diverges left, are soon reached; see Rte 6.

The N1 bears SW, shortly entering *Castile y León* and traversing **Miranda de Ebro** (37,050 inhab.), an important railway junction, commanded by a ruined castle, but of slight interest. It was the site of a transit and concentration camp set up by the Nationalists towards the end of the Civil War for political prisoners, later used for refugees, and for Allied servicemen escaping from France.—We cross the Ebro, and after 8km leave the Cistercian convent of *Bugedo*, with a Romanesque apse (1172) and 17C dependencies, to the left. Soon after crossing the motorway the N625 from Bilbao via Orduña enters from the N, and the N1, the A1, and the Madrid railway line converge to traverse the narrowest part of the impressive **°Pass** (or *Desfiladero*) **of Pancorbo**, cutting through the MONTES OBARENES and tunnelling through an immense splintered cliff before skirting the village of *Pancorbo* (635m). Above the pass are a ruined Moorish castle and remains of a fort of 1794.—The N232 bears left for *Logroño*; see p 137.

THE EXCURSION TO OÑA AND FRÍAS may be made from Pancorbo by forking right off the N1 after *Sta. Maria Ribarredonda* (6km W), with a hall-church of 1583, and (left) *Cubo de Bureba*, with a star-vaulted hall-church rebuilt in 1734, to skirt the S flank of the sierra. At (22km) *Cornudilla*—5.5km W of which are the castle ruins of *Poza de la Sal*—turn right for (8.5km) **Oña**. There the former Benedictine abbey of *S. Salvador*, founded in 1011, has a remarkable church with Romanesque remains, a 13C nave containing restored 13–14C murals, Gothic choir stalls, royal tombs, and an Isabelline cloister.—One may either follow the N232 to the NW for c 32km, there turning right for (4.5km) *Villarcayo*, 8km W of *Medina de Pomar*; or, by crossing the Ebro by a single-arched bridge, bear NE to (11.5km) *Trespaderne*, 17.5km SE of Medina. At **Medina de Pomar** (5450 inhab.) the 15C *Castle*, with its two towers, contains ruins of a palace with Mudéjar stuccowork, and in the *Conv. de Sta. Clara* the Renaissance tombs of the Dukes of Frías.—19km NE of Trespaderne is late Romanesque *S. Pantaleón de Losa*, with carvings dated 1207.—By turning right 10.5km E of Trespaderne the Ebro is shortly re-crossed to approach **Frías**, picturesquely situated with its rock-set castle and a rare °*Bridge* retaining its central gate tower. Passing through a defile and crossing a ridge (views) we regain the N1 to the SE.

The landscape changes character as the N1 crosses the monotonous plain of LA BUREBA, part of the Castilian plateau. Many will agree with William George Clark, who (traversing the gorge in 1849) remarked that 'it is only on emerging from the Defile of Pancorbo that the traveller feels himself to be indeed in Spain'.

Berzosa (right), with a Romanesque church, is bypassed, before approaching (right at 25km) **Briviesca** (5100 inhab.). Here in 1388 Juan I established the title of Prince of the Asturias for the king's eldest son, first held by Enrique (later Enrique III), who was married to Catherine of Lancaster the same year. Several old mansions flank its streets, and a picturesque *Ayuntamiento* stands in the arcaded PL. MAYOR, on the N side of which is *S. Martín*, with star-vaulting. To the E is the *Hospital de Sta. Clara*, its *Church* (1525–65; begun by Juan Gil de Hontañón and completed by Pedro de Rasines), with a single nave and polygonal sanctuary covered by a wide stellar vault. *Sta. María la Mayor*, further S, has a Neo-Classical W front.

The motorway twice crosses the N1, which shortly starts the long climb up to (c 22km) the *Puerto de la Brújula* (981m) before making the gentler descent towards the sprawling E suburbs of (21km) Burgos, passing (left), at *Gamonal*, *N.S. de la Antigua*, begun c 1296 in a markedly English style, with a square buttressed tower and ridge-ribbed vaults. The towerless *Cartuja de Miraflores* may be seen on a ridge to the left, and the twin spires of the *Cathedral* ahead. For **Burgos** see Rte 8.

Those wishing to bypass Burgos are advised to enter the motorway 9km beforehand. This regains the N1 3km S of the city. The N620 for *Valladolid* may be reached by continuing due W from that junction.

B.   Via Bilbao and Pancorbo

298km (185 miles). N1. 22km **San Sebastián**—7km. N634. 44km *Deba*—68km **Bilbao**—N625. 93km *Pancorbo*—N1. 64km **Burgos**.

Maps: M 442.

For the motorway, which is recommended if speed is essential, see Rte 1C. This provides several exits at convenient points, and may be used in conjunction with the old main road, described below.

For the road from the frontier to the turning onto the N634 7km S of **San Sebastián**, see Rte 1A. We follow the wooded valley of the Oria, bypassing (right) *Usurbil*, with the *Casa de Soroa* and *Pal. de Samaniego*.—The fishing village of *Orio* on its estuary is skirted before crossing the ALTOS DE ORIO and descending to **Zarautz**, a fashionable resort (15,350 inhab.) at the foot of *Monte Sta. Bárbara*, with old houses in the C. Mayor, notably the early 15C *Torre Luzea*, with a half-ruined tower. *Sta. María la Real* is 18C. Overlooking the W end of the beach is the 15C *Pal. del Marqués de Narros*, where Isabel II in 1868 received the news of her deposition.—Hence a road climbs SW across the *Alto de Meagas* to (17km) *Zestoa*; see below.

The road clings to the rocky coast and at 5km enters **Getaria**, another fishing village, connected by a breakwater to the *Isla S. Antón*, known as the *Ratón* (mouse). It was the birthplace of Juan Sebastián de Elcano (died 1526), whose ship, the first to circumnavigate the globe (1519–22), was the sole survivor of Magellan's fleet of five. *S. Salvador* was largely rebuilt c 1429; the inner porch is of 1605; the tower, begun in 1526, was still unfinished in 1673.

At 5km the Urola is crossed. At its mouth is the resort of **Zumaia** (7850 inhab.), of Roman foundation. Gothic *S. Pedro*, *S. Telmo*, and *N.S. de Arritokieta* are notable, while among several mansions are those of *Ubillos*, *Olozábal*, and *Uriarte*.

Zumaia was the home of Ignacio Zuloaga (1870–1945). The *Villa Zuloaga*, E of the river, contains the 12C chapel of *Santiago Echea*, with a small cloister. The museum displays several of Zuloaga's own paintings; five by El Greco; portraits by Goya of the Marquesa de Baena, of Gen. Palafox, and of the artist's brother; and two santas attributed to Zurbarán.

ZUMAIA TO ELGOIBAR VIA AZPEITIA AND AZKOITIA (34km). The C6317 bears left not far S of the town, to skirt *Zestoa (Cestona)*, with the imposing Gothic *Pal. de Alércia* or *Lili*, to (16km) **Azpeitia** (13,200 inhab.). In its 16C hall-church of *S. Sebastián* is the font at which S. Ignacio de Loyola was baptised (the silver cover was carried off by the French in 1794). Opposite is the 15C *Casa de Anchieta* with brick façades in the Moorish style. The *Casas de Emparán* and *de Bazozábal*, beside the Urola, are notable, as are 16C *N.S. de la Soledad* and the *Conv. de la Concepción*. The composer Juan Anchieta (died 1523) was born here.—Bearing W, the **Sanctuario de Loyola** is shortly reached, the birthplace of Iñigo López Recalde (1491–1556), canonised as S. Ignacio in 1622, and the founder of the Jesuit Order, a society (in the words of Baretti) whose members were 'indefatigable accumulators of riches they do not want'. The so-called *Santa Casa*, a fragment of the tower-house (1387–1405) of the Loyola family, is entirely enclosed in the huge convent. Over its entrance is an effigy of a bear. A room containing reliefs illustrating Loyola's life is shown. In it he recovered from the wounds received at Pamplona, and began those studies which led to his missionary projects. The overdecorated *Church* which impressed Saint-Simon, who made a detour to see it in 1721, was designed by *Carlo Fontana* for Mariana of Austria, wife of Felipe IV, and built in 1686–1738.

6km **Azkoitia** (11,050 inhab.), in which there are several fine old mansions of its *caballeros* or gentlemen. The *Pal. de Balda* includes an ancient tower-house. *Sta. María la Real* contains a retablo incorporating eight Sevillian paintings of 1568. The *Ayuntamiento* is notable.

Manuel Ignacio de Altuna (1722–62), an enlightened mayor, had met and corresponded with Rousseau, while an academy founded here in 1748 was the precursor of the first of the Basque Sociedades Económicas de Amigos del País, established at *Bergara* (cf.).—The Bilbao road may be regained 12km NW by following the C6324 across the *Puerto de Azcárate* (396m).

On leaving Zumaia the main road crosses the motorway, climbing to *Iciar*, with a 14C church, before descending towards the coast again at (15km) **Deba** (5000 inhab.), attractively situated and built on a regular plan. *Sta. María* has a fine 13C portal and graceful 15C cloister, but most of the church dates from the rebuilding completed in 1629.

DEBA TO BILBAO BY THE COAST ROAD TO BERMEO (90km). Although offering numerous impressive land and seascapes, it should be emphasised that the winding road is narrow and hilly, and the going will be slow. The C6212 bears NW through **Mutriku** (*Motrico*; 5250 inhab.), named after the rocky spur (Basque *tricu*, hedgehog) that commands it, surrounded by wooded hills. It was the birthplace of Adm. Churruca (1761–1805), who fell at Trafalgar.—8km **Ondarroa** (12,400 inhab.), a fishing port, preserves several picturesque houses and a 14C church raised on arcades.

The BI140 leads across country to the SW via *Berriatúa*, with a tower-house, and close to the curious polygonal sanctuary of *S. Miguel de Arrichinaga*, before reaching (9.5km) *Markina-Xemein*, with a 16C hall-church containing a retablo that belonged to Charles V.—At *Aulesti* (8km NW) is a crenellated tower-house.—Continuing SW from Markina, at *Iruzubi* turn right onto the BI130, passing near *Cenarruza*, with a collegiate church of c 1380 and mid 16C cloister.—At *Arbacegui* turn left to approach the view point known as the *Balcón de Vizcaya, beyond which, at *Urruchua*, one may turn NW to *Gernika* (see below) or SW towards the N634.

Continuing to hug the coast road, at 12km the fishing village of **Lekeitio** (7200 inhab.) is entered, with several old houses, among them the picturesque *Casa de Adán*. *Sta. María* was rebuilt in 1488–1508. A fine single-arched bridge spans the river.—A DETOUR (12.5km longer than the direct C6212) follows the coast through *Ea*, and *Elanchove* with its old church of *S. Nicolás*, and then skirts the E bank of the *Ría de Gernika*, to *Gauteguiz de Arteaga* (with a 15C castle partly restored by the Empress Eugénie), 17km W of Lekeitio.—The main road there turns S through *Cortézubi*, near which the *Cueva de Basondo* contains rock paintings.—6km **Gernika** (*Guernica*; 18,150 inhab.), standing in the valley of the Mundaka, was the seat of the Basque Parliament until the repudiation of the *fueros* in 1876. Their meeting place had been beneath a venerable oak (the 'Guernikako Arbola', which gave its name to the Basque national anthem, by José María de Iparraguirre); a fragment of this tree has been preserved beside a younger one. The town has been rebuilt since its devastation by German bombs on 26 April 1937 and is now of little interest. The hall-church of *Sta. María* dates from c 1470–1518.—The N634 may be regained at *Amorebieta*, 14km S.

The C6315 now descends the left bank of the ría to (14km) **Bermeo** (18,300 inhab.), in which the *Torre de Ercilla* survives. The kings of Castile used to swear to uphold the Basque *fueros* in *Sta. Eufemia*.—The coast road continues past *Cabo Machichaco* to (12km) *Bakio*, with a castellated mansion, and (22km) *Plentzia* (see p 140), but the C6313 climbs inland to the ALTO DEL SOLLUBE (340m; the peak of Sollube rising to the S to 707m), descending to (17km) **Mungia** (11,350 inhab.), with the tower of the *Pal. de Abajo* (1360) and Gothic *S. Pedro*. 16km **Bilbao**; see Rte 7.

From Deba the N634 turns inland along the valley to (14km) **Elgoibar** (13,850 inhab.), beyond which the C6213 forks left to (15km) *Bergara* via *Placencia*, a village long famous for its damascened iron and manufacture of firearms.—7km **Eibar**, an industrial town of 36,900 inhab., hemmed in the valley, and largely rebuilt since 1937, was likewise long reputed for its arms. It was the birthplace of Ignacio Zuloaga (1870–1945), the artist.—The road soon enters the province of Vizcaya and, crossing a ridge, is several times spanned by the motorway.

A left turn leads to *Elorrio* (8000 inhab.), preserving several Renaissance mansions and a 16C hall-church containing the early tombs of the Arguineta family (6–11C).—To the W is *Apatamonasterio*, with an old church. From here the main route may be reached at Durango, first traversing *Abadiño* (6600 inhab.), with a tower-house, the abbey of *S. Torcas*, and the *Pal. de Trana-Jaúregui*.

18km **Durango** (26,500 inhab.), birthplace of Fray Juan de Zumárraga (c 1475–1548), the first bishop of Mexico. *S. Pedro de Tavira* is among the oldest churches in the Basque Provinces, containing two curious tombs and a Plateresque retablo. Adjacent is an arcaded *Market Hall*. The high altar in *Sta. Ana* is by Ventura Rodríguez (1774). Baroque *Sta. María de Ulibarri* contains a richly ornamented late 16C coro. A remarkable stone Cross of c 1442 stands in the suburb of *Crutziaga*.

DURANGO TO VITORIA (41km). A picturesque road (C6211) leads S through *Izurza* with its tower-house, later climbing steeply through the mountains separating Vizcaya from Álava to the *Puerto de Urquiola* (700m; views). Beyond *Ochandiano*, with the old church of *Sta. Marina*, we meet the N240 c 15km N of Vitoria.

10km **Amorebieta** (15,650 inhab.), the Baroque steeple of its church rising picturesquely above the river Ibaizábal, is traversed, and later, **Galdakao** (*Galdacano*; 26,800 inhab.), where 13C *Sta. María* has a notable doorway and additions of c 1500.—We enter the industrial SE suburbs of **Bilbao**. Central Bilbao is perhaps best approached by forking uphill—bypassing the old town—later descending steeply and crossing the Nervión. The town centre is entered at the N end of the Alameda de Recalde; see Rte 7.

Travellers wishing to continue W towards *Santander* (see Rte 7) are advised to join the motorway at Galdakao. On meeting the A68 motorway, those driving to *Burgos* will swing S; see Rte 1C.

A sharp look-out should be kept for the N625, turning left along the right bank of the Nervión, passing *Arrigorriaga*, with an 11C church erected in memory of a battle between the Basques and Ordoño, Infante of Castile (848). The road continues to ascend the narrowing valley through industrial **Llodio** (20,900 inhab.). It bypasses (right) *Amurrio* (9050 inhab.), retaining a Romanesque church and ancient houses, including the *Pal. de Guinea*, with a Gothic front. At *Murga*, on the NW outskirts, are the restored remains of a palace of 1270.

At *Lezama*, 5km SE, is a Romanesque church and Renaissance mansion; while W of *Respaldiza* (NW of Amurrio) is *Quejana*, where the 14C fortified church contains tombs of the Ayalas, including that of the Chancellor Pero López de Ayala (died 1407) and his wife.—Further NW (15km from Amurrio) is *Arceniaga*, with a Plateresque palace, and the castle keep of *Sojoguti*, to the S.

Beyond Amurrio we enter the fertile CONCHA DE ORDUÑA, a broad basin dotted with prosperous farms, to approach (7km) **Orduña** (283m), an ancient town with a picturesque *Plaza* from which ten streets diverge. Buildings of interest include the old *Aduana*, *Sta. María la Antigua*, *S. Juan Bautista*, and the Jesuit *Colegiata*, with a 16C front.

The C6210, climbing E, provides an approach to *Unzá* (right), *Oyardo*, and

Gujuli (left), and *Belunza*, all with Romanesque churches, the last with richly carved windows and an early Gothic doorway of five orders.

Not far S is the *Tertrago gorge* and the cascade of the Nervión, and the S extremity of the Orduña gradient, where at one point the railway track, making a sweeping curve round the valley, can be seen high up on the left only 550m from its starting point.

The N625 climbs steeply S in a series of zigzags to the *Puerto de Orduña* (900m), with fine retrospective views.—14.5km *Berberana*.— 10km *Villanañe* (right) has a fortified palace and the chapel of *N.S. de Angosto*, while further NE is the 14C *Colegiata of Valdepuesta*.— After 4.5km the Romanesque chapel of *Tuesta* lies to the left. Further E are the curious salt pans of *Salinas de Añana*, its church with a remarkable early triptych.

Just before reaching the Ebro (with the *Sobrón reservoir* to the W), the C122 turns left through *Fontecha*, with the *Orgaz palace*, and to the prehistoric site of *Molinilla*, and *Cambriana*, with Roman ruins, to approach (12km) *Miranda de Ebro*; see Rte 1A.

The main road soon skirts *Santa Gadea del Cid*, with a restored plaza, dominated by the ruins of a castle and preserving a Romanesque church and part of its town walls.—The N1 is reached just N of the defile of *Pancorbo*; see p 115, and for the road on to **Burgos**.

PANCORBO TO HARO (26km). The N232 turns left just beyond the defile, bearing SE to (17km) *Cuzcurrita del Río Tirón*—to the right of the main road—with a castle, the Gothic chapel of *La Sorejana*, and Baroque *S. Miguel* (1753–1800).— 4km N is *Sajazarra*, its picturesque castle with a turreted curtain wall and keep.—A Gothic tower-house may be seen at *Anguciana*, to the E of this road.— 4km *Casalarreina*, where there is the Plateresque *Conv. de Dominicanas* (1508), with a remarkable portico, and the Renaissance *Pal. of the Constables of Castile*, among other mansions.—*Sto. Domingo de la Calzada* is 13.5km S; see Rte 4. At *Zarratón*, 4km SE, is the monastery of *Herrera*, retaining a Romanesque cloister, and a parish church with a notable coro. For **Haro**, 6.5km NE, beyond the motorway, see Rte 6.

C. Via the Motorway

270km (168 miles). A1/8. 25km **San Sebastián** exit—91km **Bilbao** exit—A68. 38km exit for **Vitoria** (23km SE)—33km *Miranda de Ebro* exit—A1. 22km *Pancorbo* exit—51km exit for (10km) **Burgos**.

Maps: M 442.

From the frontier to Bilbao the motorway follows more or less the same line as the main road (see Rte 1B), and there are sufficient exits to get to most of the main points of interest en route. It certainly provides a much smoother and more rapid drive. Bilbao may now be reached from San Sebastián in approx. one hour. The motorway drives W through some magnificent scenery, and a number of tunnels, crossing the deep wooded gorges of the region in a series of remarkable viaducts, with several plunging views, and—in the first section—occasional views of the sea. The stretch of the A1 projected between Eibar and Vitoria appears to have been shelved, Vitoria now having an approach off the A68, although with the improved N1 it will be as easily reached (except when the Puerto de Echegarate is blocked by snow) by that highway.

The motorway is recommended between *Behobia* and *San Sebastián*, but—unless in a hurry—travellers may take the old road, later skirting the coast, to an entrance beyond *Zumaia*. The motorway may be followed through the industrial valley past *Eibar* and *Durango*, to meet the A68 just S of *Bilbao*.

Its continuation W towards *Santander* is still partly under construction; see Rte 7.

Turning S from **Bilbao**, the A68 soon bears away from the valley of the Nervión to commence the long but gradual ascent up the green valley of the Altube to the *Puerto de Altube* (638m), following roughly the old C6210, with several views ahead of the SIERRAS DE GORBEA, and (SW) DE ORDUÑA. For the approach road to *Vitoria*, turning off 38km from the Bilbao junction, see Rte 6.

The motorway later follows the valley of the Bayas, passing (right) *Andagoya*, with a Romanesque church, and (left) *Zuazo de Cuartango*, with an early Gothic church. We pass through the *defile of the Techas*, through which Wellington manoeuvred a body of his forces at a critical moment before the battle of Vitoria (cf.).—There is an exit at *Subijana*, linked by an ancient bridge with *Morillas*, the former with the *Pal. de Anda*.—Continuing S, we meet the junction with the A1 not far NE of *Miranda de Ebro* and bear SW.—For the road on to *Haro* and *Logroño* see Rte 6.

The motorway again runs approximately parallel to the N1 (see Rte 1A), and is recommended if there is a lot of traffic on the old road, and particularly on the stretch between *Briviesca* and *Burgos*, as it provides an easier crossing of the *Puerto de la Brújula* in winter.

Travellers bypassing **Burgos** will remain on the motorway, which veers S of the city (see Rte 8), with an exit onto the N1 driving S to *Madrid*; see Rte 12.—Continue W to gain the N620 for *Valladolid*; see Rte 10.

2   Behobia to Pamplona

87km (54 miles). C133. 12km *Vera de Bidasoa*—26km *Oronoz-Mugaire*—N121. 16km *Puerto de Velate*—33km **Pamplona**.

Maps: M 442.

We drive SE from the motorway exit on the border just S of *Behobia*, following the narrow left bank of the Bidasoa, which here forms the frontier, passing below the heights of *S. Marcial*. This was the site of a battle during the latter stages of the Peninsular War, in which a Spanish force led by Gen. Freire, not supported by British troops, repulsed Soult's attempted relief of San Sebastián (31 August 1813). Perched high on the French bank is the village of *Biriatou*, long the haunt of smugglers. When the road crosses the river at *Enderlaza* we enter Navarra, where both precipitous banks are in Spanish territory.

12km **Vera de Bidasoa**, an attractive village, lies in a green valley below the S flank of *La Rhune* (900m). It was defended by French troops and taken by Wellington's forces ascending the Bayonet ridge in October 1813. The church, old bridge, the *Ayuntamiento* (1776), and ruined castle of *Alzate* are of interest, while 'Itzea', the home of Pío Baroja (1872–1956) and Julio Caro Baroja, is one of the many attractive houses to be seen.

A road climbs E to (6km) the *Puerto de Lizuniaga* (Customs) for *Sare*, 6km beyond, see *Blue Guide France*.

At 4km *Lesaca* is 3km to the right. It was Wellington's headquarters during the crossing of the Pyrenees, and contains several tower-houses. In the church are medieval carvings covered with gold plating in the 16C.—The next left turn leads through the village of *Echalar*, before climbing to the *Puerto de Lizarrieta* (441m; Customs) for *Sare*.

We shortly pass (right) *Ventas de Yanci*, scene of fierce skirmishing during Soult's retreat from Sorauren (see below), and follow the windings of the river to picturesque *Sumbilla*, with an ancient *Bridge*, before skirting (right) *Santesteban*.—The villages of *Donamaría* (3km S), with a fine tower-house and round-towered church, and *Zubieta* (7km W) remain almost entirely Basque in this wild and mountainous corner of Navarra.

Both road and river turn abruptly E. We soon bypass (left) *Oyeregui*, with old houses and bridge, to enter *Oronoz-Mugaire*, meeting the N121 from *Dancharinea* (see below), and turn S again.

ORONOZ-MUGAIRE TO DANCHARINEA (33km): the **Val de Baztán**. This road can provide—in the reverse direction—an alternative approach to Pamplona from *St. Jean-de-Luz* or *Cambo*; and from here a pleasant circuit may be made from the frontier through *Sare* to regain the road at *Vera*.—6.5km *Irurita*, with señorial mansions, is passed to reach **Elizondo**, the main village of the valley, once an independent republic, with the 16C *Pal. de los Gobernadores*.—Skirting adjacent *Elvetea*, with a curious church and solidly-built houses, we shortly reach a turning (right) for *Ariscun*.
From this picturesque village, the NA260 climbs E through *Errazu* (Customs) to (12km) the *Puerto de Izpegui* (672m), marking the frontier. 8km below, in the *Vallée des Aldudes*, lies *St. Étienne-de-Baïgorry*, and 11km further E, *St. Jean-Pied-de-Port*; see *Blue Guide France*. Near Ariscun lived an ostracised community in previous centuries, known as Cagots. It is believed to have descended either from an isolated settlement of Visigoths or, more probably, from ancient leper colonies.
The main road climbs N past (right) *Maya del Baztán*, with a ruined castle, to reach the *Puerto de Otxondo* or *Col de Maya* (570m), fiercely but unsuccessfully defended by part of Wellington's forces at the start of Soult's advance to the relief of besieged Pamplona. Good views over France, and of *Urdax* in the valley below, with a 15C church, are obtained as the road descends steeply to the frontier at *Dancharinea* (*Dancharia*; Customs).—A road leads SW just short of the border to picturesque *Zugarramurdi*, once renowned for its witches.—*Ainhoa* lies on the D20 leading NE to (14km) *Cambo*; *St. Pée-sur-Nivelle* is 11km NW, 13km from *St. Jean-de-Luz*; *Sare* is approached by turning left off the St. Pée road: see *Blue Guide France*.

Beyond Oronoz the main road starts to climb steeply through the mountains to (16km) the *Puerto de Velate* (847m), with castle ruins, before descending to (12km) *Olagüe* (*Anué*).—A mountain road climbs E from here across a pass (894m) to *Zubiri*, on the Roncesvalles–Pamplona road; see Rte 4.—The N121 continues S down the valley, at c 12km passing the site of the sanguinary **Battles of Sorauren** (28–30 July 1813), fought on the ridges to the E, when Soult's thrust across the Pyrenees in an attempt to break the Allied blockade of Pamplona was successfully repulsed by Wellington. (The Allies lost 2652 men; French losses have been estimated at 4000. In the 'Battles of the Pyrenees', in which Soult's nine-day offensive failed to relieve either San Sebastián or Pamplona, his total losses were at least 13,500 of his original 60,000 men; the Allies lost 7100 of about 40,000 actually in action.)

PAMPLONA (415m; 177,900 inhab.; 33,000 in 1920; 93,000 in 1960), capital of the ancient kingdom of Navarra and of the present autonomy, stands on rising ground above the Arga in the midst of the CONCHA DE PAMPLONA, a broad valley among the Pyrenean foothills. Part of its fortifications have been levelled to make room for the extension of the fast-growing city.

A settlement of the Vascones, Pamplona was re-founded c 77 BC by Pompey and renamed *Pompelo* or *Pompeiopolis*. It was taken by Euric the Goth in 466, and by the Frankish king Childebert in 542. It was held by the Moors (who corrupted its name to *Bambilonah*) from c 738 to 748, when it was captured by Count García Iñiguez. Charlemagne, who had been called into Spain apparently to settle a dispute between two Moorish factions, sacked the city in 778 by way of payment for his services, in revenge for which the Navarrese Basques massacred his rearguard at Roncesvalles (cf.). In the mid 9C Pamplona became the capital of the county of Navarra, which was raised to the dignity of a kingdom by Sancho I in 905.

The city prospered during succeeding centuries, notably under Sancho III (1004–35) and Carlos III (1387–1425), although the cathedral was sacked by French troops in 1276. In 1512, during the reign of Catalina, wife of Juan de Labrit (Jean d'Albret), Spanish Navarra was overrun by Castile, and Pamplona became the seat of a viceroy. In 1521 Jean d'Albret, aided by the French, attempted to regain his former capital, and at this siege the young captain Iñigo López de Recalde, received the wound which had so momentous an effect upon the history of the church (cf. Loyola).

Felipe II, by erecting the citadel in 1571, made Pamplona the strongest fortress in N Spain and relieved the town from further assaults, until in 1808 Gen. d'Armagnac's division treacherously seized the place. In 1813 it fell to Wellington after a four-month blockade, in spite of Soult's attempt to relieve it (cf. Sorauren, above). It was never captured by the Carlists, and in the fortress ditch Santos Ladrón de Guevara was shot in 1839 for proclaiming Don Carlos king at Estella. Yet it remained a centre of Carlism, and in 1936 6000 Carlist *requetés* in red *boinas* (or berets) rose to support Gen. Mola. Another aspect of its reactionary proclivities was the foundation there in 1952 of a university by the devious para-ecclesiastical cult known as 'Opus Dei'.

Among natives of Pamplona are St. Firminius (S. Fermin; martyred at Amiens c 300); Pablo de Sarasate (1844–1908), the violinist; and Gen. Sanjurjo (1872–1936).

The boisterous fiesta of S. Fermin (5–16 July) is the most exploited; but see p 96.

The N121 enters the modern town from the E by the Av. de la Baja Navarra, from a central point in which the Av. de Carlos III bears right to approach the arcaded *Pl. del Castillo*, the main square of the older centre. This is flanked to the S by the *Diputación* (1847).

A later wing houses the *Archivo de Navarra*, containing the ancient book of *fueros*, and other objects relating to the history of Navarra, including an illuminated MS of the English Coronation Ritual sent to Carlos III by Richard II, whose portrait appears as an initial.

The short Chapitela leads N from the square, at the end of which the Curia turns right to approach the Gothic *•Cathedral*, with an unprepossessing W front, but with several details strongly reminiscent of the French 14C style.

The first cathedral on this site (1023–1102) fell into decay c 1390, and the present edifice was begun in 1397 and completed c 1525. The Classical façade, by *Ventura Rodriguez*, was completed in 1783 and replaced the only remaining part of the original Romanesque church. Baretti, who passed this way in 1768, remarked that the arches over the later gates of the cathedral exhibited 'many small naked figures of men and women placed in such postures, as it is not fit to tell'.

The coro has been removed from the nave and the Stalls (1597; by *Miguel de Ancheta*) have been placed in the Cap. Mayor, enclosed by a grille of 1517. The nave contains the *•Tomb of Carlos III* and his queen, Leonor (of Castile; died 1416), by *Jean de Lomme* of Tournai, a fine example of the Burgundian type. Several painted and sculptured retablos are in the side chapels, notably those in the ambulatory. The apse has a curious plan, with one advancing and two re-entrant angles.

The *Cloisters* date from the early 14C. On the N side is the tomb of Don

Leonel (died 1443), son of Carlos II (*el Malo*; the bad), and his wife Epifania de Luna. On the S side is the *Sala de la Preciosa*, once the meeting place of the Cortes de Navarra. On the W side of the cloister is the tomb of the guerrilla general Espoz y Mina (1781–1836). The Refectory of the Canons is now the *Diocesan Museum*; the adjacent *Kitchen* has a central chimney.

Leaving the cathedral by the N door, we soon reach the *Ramparts* (views over the Arga valley), which may be followed to the left to the *Puerta de Francia* (or *Zumalacárregui*) of 1553, the only survivor of the 16C town gates.

By turning half-right at the N end of the Chapitela, we reach the Baroque *Ayuntamiento* of 1741, behind which is 16C *Sto. Domingo*, with a brick cloister. Adjacent is the *Col. de S. Juan* (1734) housing the *Museo Histórico*, with mementoes of the Carlist Wars.

A short distance NW of the Ayuntamiento is the **Museo de Navarra**, being reformed, with archaeological and ethnographical collections, carved capitals from the Romanesque cathedral, armour, and 14–18C paintings, including Goya's Portrait of the Marqués de San Adrián.

From the Ayuntamiento the C. Mayor leads W past *S. Saturnino* (13–14C), built on the spot where St. Saturninus is said to have baptised 40,000 pagan citizens. The N door, with a Last Judgement in relief, is its most remarkable feature. Beyond the W end of the street extend the *Taconera gardens*. Turning S here, one may follow the C. de Eslava E towards the Pl. S. Francisco, in which is the *Cámara de Comptos* (c 1364), the former royal treasury. Two streets further S is *S. Nicolás*, with 12–13C details, flanking the Paseo de Sarasate.

A few steps SE of the Pl. del Castillo is the *Plaza de los Toros*. The Av. de S. Ignacio leads SW from the square to the Pl. del Príncipe de Viana, one of the main hubs of the town.

A short distance to its W rises the **Ciudadela** or citadel, a pentagonal fortress built for Felipe II by *Jorge Palearzo* in imitation of that at Antwerp, and now largely surrounded by gardens.

For roads from Pamplona to **Zaragoza**; **Burgos** via **Logroño**; and to **Soria**, see Rtes 3, 4, and 5 respectively; and to **Huesca**, Rte 67E.

3 San Sebastián to Zaragoza via Pamplona and Tudela

272km (169 miles). N1. 27km **Tolosa**—N240. 44km *Irurzun*—21km **Pamplona**—N121. 34km *Tafalla*—51km to the junction with the N232.—14km **Tudela**—81km **Zaragoza**.

Maps: M 442.

Motorway. This may be entered at *Irurzun*. It runs roughly parallel to the route described, with exits for *Pamplona*, *Tafalla* and *Olite*, *Tudela*, etc., and *Zaragoza* has a bypass. A bypass is planned for *Pamplona*, while it is expected that the motorway will be extended NW from *Irurzun*, and will eventually join the dual carriageway N1 at *Tolosa*.

An ALTERNATIVE ROUTE as far as Lecumberri, but a slow mountain road, is that following the valley of the Urumea SE from *Hernani*, climbing into Navarra. At 14km, perched on a height to the right is *Arano*, commanding extensive views, with *Monte Urdaburu* (588m) to the N. We shortly turn S up the valley through (8km) *Goizueta*, with ancient timbered houses, and meet the NA403

at the *Puerto de Usateguieta* (695m), with *Ezcurra* in the wild valley of the
Basaburúa Menor to the E. Turning right, we traverse (17km) *Leiza*. Crossing
the ALTO HUICI (802km), the N240 is reached just E of the *Puerto de Azpiroz* and
enters (13km) *Lecumberri*; see below.

Follow the N1 as far as Tolosa; see Rte 1A. Here turn SE up the
Araxes valley to (20km) *Betelu*, with ancient houses and a 15C
church. After crossing the *Puerto de Azpiroz* (617m) **Lecumberri** is
entered, with a Gothic church and picturesque streets. Descending
the valley of the Larráun, we pass between the craggy peaks of the
Dos Hermanas to approach (24km) *Irurzun*, with an old church.
  The N240 is now followed to the SE. It bypasses (left) *Larumbe*,
with an important 13C church, and skirts *Erice*, with an old church
and palace, and *Sarasa*, with a notable Cross, and later *Berrioplano*,
with Romanesque and Gothic churches.
  20km **Pamplona**; see Rte 2. For an alternative route from here to
Zaragoza via *Sangüesa*, *Sos*, *Sádaba*, and *Tauste*, see Rte 67E.
  The N121 drives S, off which the N240 shortly turns SE for *Huesca*
(off which the C134 turns to *Jaca*, see Rtes 67E and 67F). Beyond
Noáin we pass an 18C *Aqueduct* by Ventura Rodríguez, which
crosses the Río Elorz on the site of a Roman bridge. *Tiebas* (left), with
a Transitional church and ruins of a 13C castle, is later bypassed.
  32km **Tafalla** (9950 inhab.), an ancient capital, known as 'La Flor
de Navarra', is dominated by the *Fortress of Sta. Lucía*. Little remains
of the 15C palace of the kings of Navarra, although several old
mansions survive. *Sta. María* contains a Renaissance retablo by
Miguel de Ancheta, and the *Conv. de la Concepción* a retablo from
La Oliva (see below) by Rolam de Moys.

The NA603 leads 11km NW to *Artajona*, an impressive medieval town with a
remarkable circuit of *Walls* and tall square towers known as *El Cerco*; mid 13C
fortified *S. Saturnino*, with a sculptured front; *S. Pedro*, with a Transitional
porch; and 17C *N.S. de Jerusalén*.

The C132 leads E from Tafalla to (10km) *S. Martín de Unx*, with old walls, in
whose Gothic church there survives an earlier crypt.—9km beyond is the hilltop
village of *Ujué*, where late 14C *Sta. María* preserves earlier apses (c 1089 and
1150), and contains the heart of Carlos II of Navarra (died 1387), responsible for
the nave of a single wide span. The tower commands extensive views.

7km **Olite**, a large village, was the Roman *Ologicus* and preserves
remains of Roman walls. Here is the principal *Castle* (c 1400–19) of
the kings of Navarra, an imposing (much restored) rambling ruin,
with numerous square towers, and now housing a Parador. In
addition to huge vaulted halls, it once possessed a roof garden, a
lions' den, and an aviary. 12C *S. Pedro* has a Romanesque portal and
cloister, and Gothic spire; *Sta. María* preserves a richly sculptured
portal and remains of a 14C cloister, and an organ of c 1780, its case
conforming to the shape of the vault.

At 14km the C124 leads E along the bank of the Aragón to (9km) *Santacara*,
commanded by a Roman tower, and SE of *Carcastillo*, 9km beyond, the
Cistercian abbey of *La Oliva*. Founded in 1134, and completed in 1198, the
Church with its pointed arches is regarded as the earliest example of Gothic in
Spain. Note the sculpted band above the main door, and the capitals in the
austere interior. The *Chapterhouse* is 13C; the *Cloister* 15C. The abbey's
dependencies have been restored and re-occupied by Cistercians.—*Sádaba* lies
19km SE of Carcastillo; see p 421.

The main road shortly crosses the Aragón some 7km E of *Marcilla*,
with a fine but over-restored castle, and remains of a monastery. It
bypasses (right) *Caparroso*, with an 11C castle, while the hilltop

church of *Sta. Fe* has a ruined Gothic nave and 16C Mudéjar tower. The road now traverses the deserted region of the BÁRDENAS REALES, and at 20km reaches a road junction.

The N121, turning left here, provides a fractionally shorter approach to (19km) *Tudela*, passing through *Valtierra*, with castle ruins, and *Arguedas*, where *S. Miguel* is a converted mosque. The district is rich in prehistoric sites, while a track leads N past hilltop *N.S. del Yugo* to the ruined *Castle of Doña Blanca de Navarra*, some distance to the NE. To the E just beyond Arguedas are the remains of a Roman town.—At *Murillo de las Limas* is Romanesque *N.S. de la Huerta*.

The main road (briefly the C101) shortly crosses the Ebro to meet the N232, where we turn left. For the road on to **Soria** via *Agreda* see Rte 5.

14km **TUDELA** (24,950 inhab.), lying between the N232 and the Ebro, here crossed by a curious 13C *Bridge* of 17 irregular arches, and formerly fortified, is the second city of Navarra.

Its origins go back to a remote past. Taken by the Moors in 716, it was recovered by Alfonso I of Aragón in 1114 and passed to Navarra in the reign of his successor. It was the last place in Spanish Navarra to yield to Fernando the Catholic in 1512. After those of the Basque Provinces, the first Economic Society in the rest of Spain was established here in 1770 (cf. Bergara).
Among its natives were the poet Judah Ha-Levi (c 1075–after 1140); Abraham ben Meir ben Ezra (1092–1167), the poet, astronomer, and biblical scholar; Benjamin of Tudela (1127–73), the traveller; Sancho VII of Navarra ('*el Fuerte*', the Strong; 1194–1234); and Miguel Servet (Michael Servetus; 1511–53), forerunner of Harvey in the discovery of the circulation of the blood.

The ***Colegiata** (1194–1234) is an attractive early Gothic church, with a *W Door* of 1260 whose 116 sculptured groups depict the Last Judgement.

Internally well proportioned, it has important contents, notably a retablo mayor painted by Pedro Díaz of Oviedo (1494); 16C stalls by Étienne d'Orbray; and in the S chapel of the transept, closed by a 15C reja, the *Tomb* of the Chancellor Francisco de Villaespesa (died 1422) and his wife, by Jean de Lomme of Tournai, and two 15C painted retablos of 21 and 28 panels. The Romanesque *Cloister*, with admirably carved capitals, contains the tomb of Don Fernando, son of Sancho 'el Fuerte', and remains of a 9C mosque.

Near by is the *Ayuntamiento*, with notable archives and the 18C travelling coach of the Marqués de S. Adrián. Close to the Colegiata, at No. 13 C. de Sáinz, is the Renaissance *Casa del Almirante*; among other notable mansions are Nos 3, 9, and 29. At the N end of the street is *S. Nicolás*, where Sancho 'el Fuerte' lay from 1234 until his reburial at Roncesvalles. Largely rebuilt c 1733, it retains a 12C carved tympanum and retablos of some interest. At the head of the bridge is *La Magdalena* (13–16C), with a sculptured door of c 1200 and Romanesque tower.

To the SE of the Colegiata are the picturesque C. del Portal and, at No. 10 in the C. de Magallón, the *Pal. of the Marqués de S. Adrián*, with a Renaissance patio and superb staircase. Other buildings of note are the Plateresque *Bishop's Palace* adjacent to the Colegiata, the *Hospital* (1549), and *S. Jorge* with Baroque retablos, and among several mansions, now shops or tenements, No. 14 C. Villanueva.

For the DETOUR to Tarazona, 21km SW, and to the monastery of *Veruela*, see Rte 5.

Beyond Tudela the MONCAYO massif (2313m) rises to the SW, as we turn SE, bypassing (left) *Fontellas*, with the 16C church of *S. Carlos*

Borromeo, and at *El Bocal del Rey* the intake of the *Imperial Canal* from the Ebro, begun in 1528, with a palace.—At *Cortes* (left) is a castle-palace of the Dukes of Granada. At 30km from the Tudela junction we meet the N122 from *Tarazona* and *Borja*; see p 131; 132; *Gallur*, 5km E, has a conspicuous church tower. *Tauste* is 9km beyond; see p 421.

At 18km we bypass (left) *Pedrola*, where Don Quixote and Sancho Panza were entertained in the palace of the Duke of Villahermosa; at nearby *Alcalá de Ebro* occurred the adventure of the Enchanted Barque.—The road shortly crosses the motorway, passing (left) *Alagón*, with an octagonal brick church tower, and *Utebo*, where Mudéjar *Sta. María* (1514–44) has a brick tower and glazed tiles, to approach **Zaragoza**; see Rte 71.

4 (St. Jean-Pied-de-Port) Roncesvalles to Burgos via Pamplona and Logroño

281km (174 miles) from St. Jean. D933. 8km *Arnéguy*—C135. 22km *Roncesvalles*—46km **Pamplona**—N111. 43km **Estella**—49km **Logroño**—N232. 8km.—N120. 19km *Nájera*—20km **Sto. Domingo de la Calzada**—66km **Burgos**.

Maps: M 442.

This route follows part of one of the main medieval pilgrimage routes from SW France to *Santiago de Compostela*, and is continued by Rtes 9A and 35. It is a slow road as far as Logroño.

For *St. Jean-Pied-de-Port* see *Blue Guide France*. Bearing SW, Customs are passed at *Arnéguy*, and the road starts the long winding ascent from the *Defile of Valcarlos* to the *Puerto Ibañeta* or *Pass of Roncesvalles* (1057m), with the remains of the early chapel of *S. Salvador*.

It was in the pass of Roncesvalles in 778 that the rearguard of Charlemagne's army, retreating from Pamplona and led by Roland, was cut off and overwhelmed with rocks hurled by the Basques from the crags above. Louis le Debonnaire preserved his army from a like fate in 810 by forcing the wives and children of the peasantry to accompany him through the gorge. The Black Prince led his troops this way in February 1367 before the battle of Nájera; and in July 1813 Soult's army attempted to relieve Pamplona after forcing its way over the pass.

The hamlet of **Roncesvalles** (French, *Roncevaux*) lies just beyond the summit, with the restored *Augustinian Abbey* founded by Sancho 'el Fuerte' of Navarra in c 1230. The zinc-roofed church contains his tomb and that of his wife, Clemencia.

The treasury preserves a gold-embroidered cope given by Elizabeth of Portugal, a Holy Family by Morales, a Flemish triptych, and several reliquaries. The cloisters were rebuilt after a fire in 1400. The 12C chapel opposite was altered in the 15C.

Here also is the parish church of *Santiago* and an ancient church known as *Itzandegula*, now a barn.

Beyond *Burguete*, with old houses, the NA202 leads E through the mountains to (9km) *Arive*, in the Irati valley, and, 25km beyond, to *Ochagavía* in the Valle de Salazar; see Rte 67E.

Shortly after, the C127 turns S down the valley of the Urrobi past *Arce*, with a

Romanesque church, to (24km) *Aóiz* in the Irati valley, and on towards *Lumbier;* see Rte 67E.

The main road bears W to *Erro*. Crossing a ridge, it reaches *Zubiri*, with a Roman bridge, and continues down the Arga valley, passing *Urdániz*, with a 13C church, and *Huarte*, to approach **Pamplona** from the E; see Rte 2.

The N111 leads SW past (left) *Cizur Mayor*, with ruins of a 12C castle, 4km W of which, at *Gazolaz*, is a curious Romanesque church of c 1100. (Further NW, at *Ororbia*, the Gothic church contains good retablos; and Roman mosaics have been found at *Ibero*, near the confluence of the Araquil and Arga.)

We skirt *Astráin*, with the sanctuary of *N.S. del Perdón*, before crossing the *Puerto del Perdón* (679m) and descending into the Arga valley. On approaching (23km) *Puente la Reina*, it is worth making the brief DETOUR by turning left past *Obanos*, with old mansions, and (left) *Muruzábal*, with a Renaissance palace, to (right) the remarkable 12C Templar church of *Sta. María, Eunate*, octagonal in plan and surrounded by a cloister arcade.

Puente la Reina itself, with an old main street and relics of 13C walls, preserves a fine medieval *Bridge* over the Arga, well seen from the modern bridge. *Santiago* (12th, 15th, and 18Cs) has a good porch; *S. Pedro* is Romanesque; *Del Crucifijo* (c 1150, rebuilt 15C) is a Templar church; *La Trinidad* is ruined.

The NA603 runs S to (13km) *Artajona* (see p 124) via *Mendigorria*, with an old bridge and imposing church with a good tower.

The main road now runs due W through *Mañeru*, with ancient señorial houses and Neo-Classic *S. Pedro*, with a fine tower. There are several Romanesque chapels in the area.—*Cirauqui* is shortly passed (left), with *Sta. Catalina* and *S. Román*, the latter with a richly carved doorway. Here also are remains of a Roman road and bridge. On approaching Estella we skirt *Villatuerta*, with Romanesque *S. Miguel*.

ESTELLA (12,250 inhab.), the ancient *Gabala*, and a residence of the kings of Navarra throughout the Middle Ages, was a Carlist headquarters during the civil wars of 1833–39 and 1872–76. It contains several notable churches, particularly *S. Pedro de la Rua*, SW beyond the bridge over the Ega, with a 12C Poitevin front and a restored Romanesque cloister; and Romanesque *S. Miguel*, its doorway with a carved tympanum and original doors with 12C wrought-ironwork. *S. Juan Bautista*, in the Pl. de los Fueros, has a Romanesque N porch and Baroque and other retablos. *Sta. María Jus del Castillo* retains its Romanesque apse. The Gothic doorway (1328) of derelict *Sto. Sepulcro* survives below the ruined *Conv. de Sto. Domingo* (13C) on the right bank of the Ega. Also worth visiting are the *Capuchin Convent*; 12C *N.S. de Rocamadour*; and, on a height above the town, *N.S. del Puy*. Later religious houses include 17C *S. Benito* and *Sta. Clara*, and the 18C *Monjas Recoletas*. The *Audiencia*, formerly the palace of the Dukes of Granda de Ega, is one of the more remarkable 12C secular buildings to survive in Europe. The *Ayuntamiento* (1571) and the Renaissance *Pal. of the Counts of S. Cristóbal* are noteworthy among the mansions which range from the 14th to the 18C. The old *Judería* retains some picturesque alleys.

We pass, 3km W, the monastery of **N.S. de Irache**, a foundation of c 1200, which sheltered a university until 1833. The church is Transitional Gothic with Romanesque apses, and has a remarkable *media-naranja* Cupola (like that at Zamora) over the crossing, a Plateresque cloister, and tombs of interest.—*Igúzquiza*, with the *Pal. of the Marqués de Vessolla*, is passed to the right, and later, *Villamayor*, with the ruins of the castle of *Monjardín* on an eminence.

17km **Los Arcos**, with a picturesque *Plaza* surrounded by brick houses, entered through a 17C gateway. *La Asunción*, with a 15C cloister, contains a Baroque retablo and very beautiful organ, possibly by Juan Otorel, and paintings and woodwork of interest.

At *Sorlada*, some 9km NW, is the 17C basilica of *S. Gregorio Ostiense*, with a Baroque portal.

The main road now traverses a group of towns known as *Las Cinco Villas de Sansol*, among which (left) is *Torres del Río*, where the octagonal Templar church of *El Sepulcro* has a late 12C Mudéjar dome.—The church at *Azuelo*, 10km NW, dates from the first half of the 12C.

We cross a series of ridges before skirting **Viana**, formerly of some importance as the capital of the principality formed in 1423 by Carlos III of Navarra as the apanage of heirs to the throne. The town gave its title to the Prince of Viana (1421–61), son of Juan II of Aragón (Juan I of Navarra). It retains several old mansions, ruined walls, and the *Torre de S. Pedro*. Caesar Borja, killed in a skirmish in 1507, is buried in *Sta. María*, restored in the 16C, but his tomb has been violated. The imposing Renaissance portal dates from 1549–67.

Oyón, 3km to the right on approaching Logroño, has an Isabelline church with a good portal and 18C tower.

LOGROÑO (109,550 inhab.; 28,000 in 1920), the Roman *Julia Briga*, and now the capital of the autonomous region of **La Rioja**, has grown rapidly in recent decades, and its industrial suburbs have not improved its appearance. The rich wine-growing district takes its name from the Río Oja, which flows into the Tirón just above Haro; it also produces cereals and olive oil.

Logroño was the birthplace of the artist Juan Fernández Navarrete (1526–79; nicknamed 'El Mudo', the Dumb), and Martín Zurbano (1788–1845), the guerrilla leader. Gen. Espartero (1792–1879) resided here after his marriage to a local heiress and is buried in the cathedral.

Logroño has a bypass to the S, but its old centre, retaining several old mansions, is entered by crossing the Ebro by the *Puente de Piedra* of 1770, parallel to the iron bridge of 1884. On the S bank, between the two, is an arch of a bridge of 1138. To the right beyond the far end of the stone bridge stands *Sta. María del Palacio*, founded in the 11C, rebuilt at the end of the 12th, and enlarged in the 16C. Its 13C spired tower is known as *la Aguja* (the Needle). It contains a Renaissance retablo by Arnao de Bruselas, and its restored Gothic cloister has 17C frescoes.—Further S is *S. Bartolomé* (early 13C) with a 14C W Doorway in the Franco-Navarrese style, a 17C brick tower, and noteworthy tombs.

Adjacent to the SW is the cathedral, **Sta. María la Redonda**, a 15–16C hall-church with star vaults springing from tall shafts without capitals, and side chapels between the buttresses in the Catalan style. Later additions have been made at both ends: the W end has a Churrigueresque portal between twin towers (1769). In the *Cap. de la Cruz*, by the S door, is the Renaissance monument of Diego Ponce de León. In the *Chapterhouse* is a retablo by Pantoja de la Cruz.

To the NW, near the *Puente de Hierro*, is *Santiago*, with a wide and lofty single nave (early 16C).

LOGROÑO TO SORIA (106km). This road via the Puerto de Piqueras is often snowbound for some months in winter; check before setting out. The N111 ascends the valley of the Iregua, after crossing the motorway passing (left) a road leading to (12km) *Clavijo*, with castle ruins, and the site of a battle said—on no historical foundation—to have taken place in 844 between Ramiro I and the Moors, and famous for the legendary apparition of St. James, 'Santiago Matamoros'.—Bearing SW, we pass (left) at *Viguera* an ancient bridge, and later bypass (right) *Torrecilla en Cameros*, birthplace of Práxedes Sagasta (1872–1903), founder of the Spanish Liberal party.—At *Villanueva de Cameros* a road leads 4.5km W to picturesque *Ortigosa de Cameros*, below the *Puerto Hiricado* (1412m).

After 5.5km a mountain road leads 33km W through the Cameros nature reserve to meet the C113 from Nájera to *Salas de los Infantes* (see below), at 10km reaching *Montenegro de Cameros*, the starting point for climbs to the *Pico de Urbión* (SW; 2229m) and its lagoons. A mountain road leads S from Montenegro across the *Puerto de Sta. Inés* (1753m) and Urbión reserve to meet the N234 at 46km, 18km W of *Soria*.

The N111 now climbs SE in zigzags to the *Puerto de Piqueras* (1710m) in the austere SIERRA CEBOLLERA, rising to the SW to 2164m at *La Mesa*. We cross a high-lying, wind-swept district, slowly descending the valley of the Tera to *Garray*, with a Romanesque chapel of 1231.—A track here climbs to the hilltop site of **Numancia**, the Iberian city which resisted Scipio Æmilianus and his Roman legions for almost a year in 134–135 BC. Excavations have laid bare its regular plan, but most of the antiquities discovered date from the Roman town which rose on the ruins of the Iberian one, beneath which are traces of a prehistoric settlement.—7km **Soria**; see Rte 5.

Driving SW, we shortly bear off the N232 onto the N120, crossing the motorway (A68) to bypass (left) *Navarrete*, a village of ancient houses with a 16C church containing a Churrigueresque retablo.—At 12km **Nájera** (6150 inhab.), with a ruined castle, is bypassed. *Sta. María la Real* was formerly a burial place of the royal house of Navarra, and here Fernando III, 'el Santo', was crowned in 1217. The Church, consecrated in 1056, was rebuilt in 1453; its cloisters date from 1528. Its most important tomb is that of Blanca (queen of Sancho III), who died in 1155 giving birth to the future Alfonso VIII.

To the NE of Nájera took place the battle of early April 1367 in which the Black Prince helped Pedro the Cruel to regain his throne by defeating Enrique de Trastámara and his ally Du Guesclin. The van of the English contingent was led by Lancaster and Chandos.

NÁJERA TO SALAS DE LOS INFANTES (92km). The C113, a slow, winding, and partially mountainous road, climbs S before circling SW between the SIERRA DE LA DEMANDA (right; rising to 2262m) and the SIERRA DE URBIÓN (2228m), following for the main part the valley of the Najerilla.—At 5km a minor road forks right to (12km) **S. Millán de la Cogolla**, with a Benedictine abbey founded in 537, rebuilt on its present site in 1554, and known as the 'Escorial de la Rioja'. The retablo of the hall-church (1504–40), by Juan Rizi, depicts the life and miracles of S. Millán (died c 564).—Near by at a higher level the more interesting Mozarabic church of *S. Millán de Suso* (923–29), partly dug out of the mountainside, contains the tombs of the Infantes de Lara. Gonzalo de Berceo (c 1190–c 1264), the earliest known Castilian poet, was a native of Nájera and a priest at S. Millán.—Hence a road leads 18.5km NW to *Sto. Domingo de la Calzada* (see below), passing at 5km near the Cistercian nunnery of *Sta. María de Cañas*, founded in 1171 and begun in 1236. Only a presbytery and transepts were built, with a vaulted chapterhouse containing the tomb of the abbess Urraca López de Haro (c 1260). The C113 may be regained 12km E (7.5km S of the deviation).—At 16.5km a by-road diverges right 5km to the Benedictine monastery of *Valvanera*, rebuilt in 1883.—11km. The L0802 climbs left through the villages of *Viniegra de Abajo* and *de Arriba* to (23km) *Montenegro de Cameros*; see above.—We skirt the N bank of the *Mansilla reservoir* to (18km) *Canales*, with a Romanesque church, climb to the *Puerto el Collado* (1240m), and descend the valley of the Pedroso to approach (36km) *Salas de los Infantes*; see Rte 13.—For *Sto. Domingo de Silos*, 18km SW, see p 168.

The N120 leads due W from Nájera to (19km) **Sto. Domingo de la Calzada** (5700 inhab.; Parador), dominated by its *****Cathedral**, begun in 1168 and completed in 1235, with a detached Baroque *Belfry* (1767) by *Martín Beratúa* beside the ancient chapel of *N.S. de la Plaza*. The W Doorway has seven orders of mouldings carried round the arch without capitals.

Entering by the S door, we approach the shrine (1517) of the saint, a local hermit, beneath the huge vault of the transept, enlarged when the presbytery was reconstructed in 1529 by *Juan Rasines* to the designs of *Felipe Vigarni*. The 13C vaults of the nave have ridge-ribs, suggesting English influences. The retablo mayor of carved walnut (1541) was the last work of Damián Forment, while the stallwork of the coro was made by Andrés de Nájera (in 1531–36) after patterns by Guillén de Holanda. There is a Plateresque screen to the chapel of *La Magdalena*, and several other chapels contain retablos of interest. Other chapels surround the *Cloister* (c 1380), and by the door of the *Chapterhouse* is a monument recording the heart burial of Enrique de Trastámara, who died here in 1379. Within are two triptychs of the late 15C, one Flemish, the other German.

The great curiosity of the cathedral is the chamber opening from the W wall of the S transept and closed by a grille, in which are kept a live cock and hen (killed and replaced each 12 May), perpetuating a miracle in which a youth's innocence was proved by a roasted cock crowing on the table (as did another at Barcelos in Portugal).

Beside the cathedral is the *Hospital del Santo*, a hostelry built for the reception of pilgrims to Compostela.—At the W end of the town is the 16C *Conv. de S. Francisco*, by Juan de Herrera; the church contains a stone retablo and the alabaster tomb (1587) of the founder, Bernardo de Fresneda, confessor of Felipe II. In the *Conv. de Bernardas* is a tomb of the Manso de Zúñiga family. Remains of town walls and towers built in 1367 by Pedro the Cruel can be seen here, and also ancient houses.

14km S is *Ezcaray*, a summer resort with a 15C Gothic church. From Ezcaray a road climbs SE to *Valdezcaray* (1550m) on the flank of the peak of *S. Lorenzo* (2271m).—*Bañares* (5km NE of Sto. Domingo) contains Romanesque *Sta. Cruz* and *Sta. María*, with a Gothic nave.

Continuing W, at 6km *Grañón* is passed to the left, with remains of walls and the castle of *Mira-Villa*.—15km *Belorado*, with an arcaded plaza and remains of walls and gates.—11.5km *Villafranca-Montes de Oca*, with a good parish church and two chapels, beyond which we climb to the *Puerto de la Pedraja* (1130m).—15.5km *S. Juan de Ortega*, 6km right, whose church (c 1138; restored in the 15C) contains the saint's Flamboyant shrine. The marble of the district was once reputed.—The main road shortly passes (left) *Zalduendo*, 5km N of which, at *Atapuerca*, took place the battle of 1057 in which García de Navarra was killed by his brother, Fernando I of Castile. It is also the site of recent paleontological excavations which have brought to light human remains dating back to c 250,000 BC.

14.5km **Burgos**; see Rte 8. For the continuation of the pilgrimage road to Compostela see Rte 9.

5   Pamplona to Soria via Ágreda

178km (110 miles). N121. 34km **Tafalla**—51km to the junction with the N232.—C101. 42km **Ágreda**—N122. 51km **Soria**.

Maps: M 442.

For the road from Pamplona to the junction with the N232 see Rte 3; also for the first part of the recommended detour via Tudela, some 8km longer. For the road on via *Tarazona* see below.

TUDELA TO ÁGREDA VIA TARAZONA (40km). Driving SW and crossing the N232 and A68 motorway, at 9km *Cascante*, ancient *Cascantum*, is passed to the right. At Cascante a curious covered way leads to 17C *N.S. del Romero*, while Plateresque *La Asunción* contains a retablo of the school of Miguel Ancheta. We continue through *Tulebras*, with the oldest convent of Cistercian nuns in Spain, founded in 1215, and *Monteagudo*, with a brick church tower, a centre of Roman ruins and prehistoric sites.

12km **TARAZONA** (11,000 inhab.), an ancient episcopal city, famous as *Turiaso*, where a handful of Romans defeated a Celtiberian army. Reconquered from the Moors in 1118 by Alfonso I of Aragón, it remained a frontier town of importance and a royal residence until the 15C. Alfonso VIII of Castile married Eleanor of England (daughter of Henry II) here in September 1170.

The *Cathedral (1152–1235; enlarged and reconstructed between 1361 and 1500) is surmounted by a curious lantern of 1545 made of patterned brick by Juan Botero. The *Cloisters* (1504–29) are likewise a remarkable example of brickwork, as is the Mudéjar *SW Tower*, begun c 1500 by *Ali el Darocano*, and finished in 1588.

Internally, the brick nave with its star-vaulting is a fine example of the Aragonese style. The *Cap. Mayor* of 1560 contains a retablo of 1603. The chapels preserve several objects of interest including 16C tombs, among them two Gothic alabaster examples, and painted retablos. The Library is rich in illuminated MSS.

On the hill to the S is the *Conv. de Sta. Ana*, with a Renaissance N door. To the NW is the *Pal. of the Counts of Algira* and, further on, the old *Plaza de Toros*, converted into dwellings but retaining its three arcaded and balconied stages above the arena. Adjacent is brick *N.S. del Río* (16C), with curious cupolas. 13C *S. Francisco* has a single nave and brick steeple, late Gothic stellar vaulting, Renaissance side chapels, and a good retablo mayor.

Most of the old city is on the opposite bank of the Queiles, dominated by the Mudéjar tower of *La Magdalena*, which has a Romanesque E end. The adjoining *Bishop's Palace* (14–15C) was formerly an *alcázar* of the Kings of Aragón. Not far off is late Gothic *La Concepción*, and on the hill top, early 16C *S. Miguel*, with another brick belfry and Plateresque retablos. *La Merced*, near by, is 17C. Halfway up the hill is the 16C *Ayuntamiento, with decoration in high relief, and a frieze of figures running the whole length of the building, representing the taking of Granada.

TARAZONA TO BORJA AND THE N232 (39km), described for those making

the detour en route to Zaragoza. The N122 leads SE, the landscape dominated
by the MONCAYO massif (2313m), off which at 13.5km a right-hand turning
approaches (4km) the fortified abbey of *Veruela, one of the oldest Cistercian
houses in Spain (1171–1224), with an early Gothic church and chapterhouse,
and 14C cloisters. The Baroque sacristy door is notable. Many of the capitals are
notable, and a number of early tiles are preserved. Parts of the dependencies
now incongruously house a collection of modern art.

The road goes on to *Añón*, with its castle; another ruined castle (15C) is at
Trasmoz, NW of Veruela.—The N122 continues E through (12km) **Borja**, with
the ruined castle of the Borja family, which after migrating to Xàtiva (cf.) in the
14C, acclimatised itself in Italy as the Borgias. An old palace has been restored
here.—5km beyond is *Magallón*, with two Mudéjar churches, and the A63 and
N232 are reached not far beyond, 50km NW of Zaragoza.

The N122 climbs W from Tarazona to meet the C101 at 15km, 4km
before reaching *Ágreda*; see below.

The improved (and improving) main road from Pamplona, on crossing the N232 and A68, shortly bypasses (right) **Corella** (6300 inhab.),
containing several old mansions, notably the *Casa de las Cadenas*. S.
Miguel is 13C; *N.S. del Rosario* dates from 1579. The Carmelite
church contains several patrician tombs; that of the Benedictine
Nuns (1671); an Assumption by J.A. de Escalante.—*Cintruénigo*
(5250 inhab.), with the 16C church of *S. Juan Bautista*, is crossed.

After 5km a DETOUR may be made up the Alhama valley to **Fitero**,
5km W. Its church was formerly the Cistercian abbey of *Sta. María la
Real* (1152–1287), and contains notable tombs, a square Chapterhouse of nine bays, and an early 16C cloister; its treasury preserves a
10C ivory coffer.—The hot springs of *Los Baños de Fitero* and the
cold springs of *Grávalos* are further W.

The C101 climbs S to join the N122 4km before reaching **Ágreda**,
Iberian *Ilurci* and Roman *Graecubis*, an old frontier town dominated
by the *Castillo de la Muela*. It was burnt by Sir Thomas Trivet in the
winter of 1378–79 after his unsuccessful attack on Soria. The artist
Joaquín Inza (c 1736–after 1808) was born here.

It retains fragments of Moorish walls, with a horseshoe-arched
gateway (mid 10C), a single-arched bridge, picturesque remains of
its *Judería*, and the Barrio de los Castejones, with a medieval watch-
tower and ruined mansions. The 12C *Pal. de los Castejones* in the C.
Tudor is crowned with brick towers. Near the *Puerta de Añaviejo* is
another fortified tower.

Most of the churches contain retablos of some interest. *N.S. de la
Peña* (1193) has twin naves; 15C *S. Miguel* retains its Romanesque
tower; 15C *S. Juan* has a Baroque high altar; *N.S. de Magaña* has
three naves with Gothic ribbed vaults; *N.S. de los Milagros* is 16C.

In the *Conv. de la Concepción*, S of the town, is the tomb of Sor María (1602–65),
a mystic, and the valued adviser of Felipe IV. He visited her in 1643 and
corresponded with her on state affairs for 22 years, although it is now assumed
that she was merely acting as the mouthpiece of her Franciscan confessor.

Ágreda is a base for the ascent of the **Sierra del Moncayo** (2313m), providing
a distant view of the Pyrenees. Cars can ascend to the sanctuary on the E flank
of the massif, c 1½ hours' climb from the summit.

The N122, continuing W, shortly passes (left) *Muro de Ágreda*, with
Roman walls and a Romanesque church.

An ALTERNATIVE minor road to Soria (c 50km) turns right 10km from Ágreda to
Trévago, 7km NW of which is the 13C castle of *Magaña*, providing panoramic
views.—Driving W from Trévago, we approach *Suellacabras*, with an Iron Age

site, and the Visigothic cemetery of *Los Castillares*, and later the picturesque village of *Narros*. At *Almajano* turn SW for Soria.

The main road climbs to the bleak *Puerto del Madero* (1160m) before entering the basin of the Duero and commencing the gradual descent to Soria.

SORIA (30,350 inhab.; 19,000 in 1960; Parador), standing at 1050m, is the capital of a province noted for the coldest climate in Spain. It contains a number of medieval buildings, but modern development has impaired its once considerable charm, as celebrated in the poems of Antonio Machado (who lived here in 1907–13) and Gerardo Diego.

Of ancient foundation, Soria was restored after the Moorish invasions by Alfonso 'el Batallador' of Aragón, but later, ceded to Alfonso VII, it became a capital of the march, ruled by 12 noble families. It was largely untouched by the troubles of later centuries, although Du Guesclin captured the place and resided here in 1369–70, and it beat off an attack by Sir Thomas Trivet during the winter of 1378–79. It was part of the dowry of Catherine of Lancaster. In 1808 it was sacked by Ney. Soria long retained a strong provincial atmosphere; in 1920 its population was a mere 8000. It was the home of the brothers Gustavo Adolfo and Valeriano Becquer, the 19C poet and painter respectively.

On the N side of the Alameda de Cervantes (just W of the central Pl. Mariano Granados) is the **Museo Numantino**, with important material (badly displayed) from the excavations at *Numancia*, 8km NE; see p 129.—Opposite stands the 16C *Ermita de la Soledad*.

The C. Collado, the main street of the old town, leads E, passing (left) the C. de la Aduana Vieja (where Romanesque S. Clemente has been torn down and replaced by the Telefónica). Among remaining mansions are the Renaissance *Casa de los Ríos* (now a bottle warehouse) and the 16C *Pal. del Visconde de Eza. Sto. Domingo* (see below) is at the upper end of the street.

To the S is a small plaza and the 16C *Pal. de Alcántara*, beyond which is the *Diputación*. Adjacent is *S. Juan de Rabanera* (c 1200), with a good S front, apse, and internal cupola of Byzantine type, and containing a Plateresque retablo.—Following the C. de Caballeros SE through the former Judería, we pass what was the *Conv. de Sta. Clara* (16C) and, beyond, *El Espino* (in which Leonor, Machado's wife, is buried), with 16C vaults and a Churrigueresque retablo of 1686.—Hence a road climbs steeply to the ruined castle and the Parador (views).

From El Espino turn right to reach the *Pl. Mayor*, with a 19C *Ayuntamiento*, and the former *Audiencia* (1796) bearing an inscription dated 1621 recording the privileges of the city. *N.S. de Mayor*, mainly 16C Gothic, retains fragments of Romanesque *S. Gil*.—From the Pl. de S. Blas, to the W, the C. de Aguirre leads NE to the huge *Pal. de los Condes de Gómara* (1577–92), with a balustraded front, restored to house the new Audiencia.

Below, in the Pl. de Ayllón, is the *Conv. del Carmen* (in the *Pal. de Beaumonte*) where Sta. Teresa lived in 1580; the 17C church has Churrigueresque retablos. The C. Obispo Agustín leads downhill past the *Colegiata de S. Pedro*, a well-vaulted Gothic hall-church of 1520–73, with three remaining walks of a Cloister of 1150–1205.

Crossing the Duero by a stone bridge, turn left to ***S. Juan de Duero**, a ruined house of the Knights Hospitallers. The nave altars of the 12C church are flanked by singular canopies (one domed, the other conical) of c 1200, while the nave is occupied by a collection of relics from the province including 13C Jewish tombstones; note the well-preserved capitals. The curious *Cloister*, of which only one interlaced arcade remains, is one of the latest Romanesque buildings in Spain (13C). The columns change their character not at each corner but in the middle of each walk, with intersecting and horse-shoe arches in which Mudéjar and Romanesque features are combined.

A short distance along the river in the other direction, beyond the 13C Templar chapel of *S. Polo*, is the picturesque *Ermita de S. Saturio*, with restored 18C frescoes and a rock-cut crypt and staircase.

Regaining S. Pedro, one may climb the C. Tirso de Molina, named

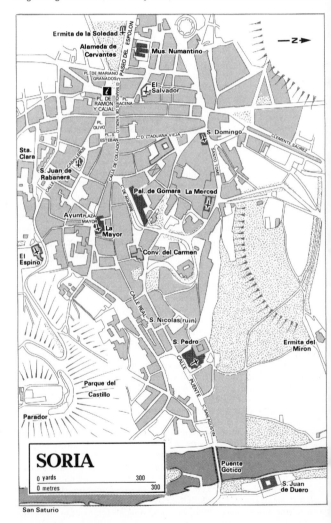

San Saturio

after the dramatist (1571–1648) who, as Fray Gabriel Téllez, was at one time at the late Gothic convent of *La Merced*. The *Hospicio* retains a 16C front. The C. Sto. Tomé leads W, with (left) *Sto. Domingo (late 12C), with one of the finest Romanesque façades in Spain, including a deeply recessed wheel window; note the musicians, the Massacre of the Innocents, etc. The interior, partly rebuilt in the 16C, has Gothic vaults and Baroque retablos.—The centre is regained by descending the C. de la Aduana Vieja, passing the *Instituto* in the 18C *Casa de los Castejones*, with a Baroque doorway.

Detail of the West Front of Sto. Domingo, Soria

For roads from Soria to **Calatayud**, or *Almazan*, see Rte 14; for **Atienza**, **Segovia**, and **Aranda**, Rtes 15, 16, and 17 respectively; and for **Burgos**, Rte 13 in reverse.

6   Bilbao to Zaragoza via Vitoria, Haro and Logroño

323km (201 miles). N240. 66km **Vitoria**—N1. 25km—N232. 19km *Haro*—41km **Logroño—48km** Calahorra—42km **Tudela**—81km **Zaragoza**.

Maps: M 442

The A68 **Motorway** provides the more rapid and shorter road, the first section of which is described on p 120. At 38km the new approach road to (22km) **Vitoria**

(C6210) turns SE, bypassing (left) *Olano*, with a Romanesque church, and *Manurga*, with the *Berástegui palace*. The *Sierra de Gorbea* rises to 1481m to the N. We pass (right) the airport before reaching the peripheral bypass of Vitoria; see Rte 1A. Travellers avoiding Vitoria will continue S on the A68, crossing the junction with the A1 near *Miranda de Duero* (for Burgos; see Rte 1A), and can exit 19km beyond for *Haro* (4km NE); *Sto. Domingo de la Calzada* (see Rte 4) lies 16km SW. The motorway bears SE roughly parallel to the N232, with exits for *Logroño*, *Calahorra*, and *Tudela*, among others, to approach *Zaragoza*, which may also be bypassed by those continuing E towards *Lleida* on the A2.

The improved main road (N240) bears away from the N634 some 11km SE of Bilbao, and ascends the wooded valley of the Arratia, bypassing (right) *Elebeitia*, with a curious church, and *Villaro*, where *La Piedad* and the *Pal. of the Marqués del Riscal* are of interest; and (left) *Ceanuri*, with an old church.—We climb steeply to the *Alto de Barazar* (604m), with views of the *Peña Gorbea* (1481m; right) and *Amboto* (1327m) to the E, and traverse *Legutiano/Villareal*, on the *Urrunaga reservoir*.

We pass *Urbina* 3km S, close to *Gojain*, with a simple church of great age. At *Urrúnaga*, to the W, is a Transitional church with a richly carved doorway. Adjacent *Nafarrate* also has an early church, while at *Miñano Mayor*, S of Urbina, is the notable Romanesque and early Gothic church of *S. Vicente*. For **Vitoria** see Rte 1A. A bypass is under construction to meet the N1 some 10km to the W.

VITORIA TO LOGROÑO VIA LAGUARDIA (61km). Following the L122 S, at 3km we pass *Gardélegui*, with a church of great antiquity. A track leads to the *Campo de los Palacios*, with remains of a Romanesque chapel, and to the prehistoric site of *Olárizu* or *Crucimendi*. The road crosses the *Puerto de Vitoria* in the MONTES DE VITORIA to (17.5km) the *Ventas de Armentia* and a crossroad leading SE to *Bernedo*; see below. The valley of the Ayuda is crossed and we again climb through picturesque country to (10km) walled *Peñacerrada*, with notable tombs in its church, to approach the **Puerto de Herrera** (1100m) in the SIERRA DE CANTABRIA, providing a magnificent *View over the Ebro valley and the Rioja Alavesa. The road descends steeply to meet the N232 just N of *Leza*, with a 15C gateway and late Gothic *S. Martin*, and after passing *Páganos*, with a curious church, at 6km reaches the hilltop village of *Laguardia*, surrounded by walls and towers, surmounted by castle ruins and containing numerous ancient houses. Gothic *Sta. María de los Reyes* has a fine 15C *Porch* with polychrome sculpture, and a Retablo of 1632 by Juan de Arismendi, Juan de Iralzu, and Juan Vascardo. *S. Juan* or *El Pilar* has vestiges of Romanesque work, but was transformed in the Churrigueresque style in the 1730s.—At *Elvillar* (6km NE) is the largest dolmen of the Pyrenean region, while at nearby *Berrena* are Roman remains.—We descend the Ebro valley and, after passing the Roman site of *Assa* and the ruins of the Roman bridge of *Mantible*, approach (17km) **Logroño**; see Rte 4.

VITORIA TO LOGROÑO VIA BERNEDO (63km). From (17.5km) *Ventas de Armentia* (see above) we follow the valley of the Ayuda SE through the enclave of the Condado de Treviño past *Albaina*, NE of which, at *Marquinez*, *S. Juan* of 1226 is a dated example of the transition from Romanesque to Gothic. Beyond Albaina the road crosses the MONTES DE IZQUIZ, a region of caves and ancient chapels to (21.5km) *Bernedo*, with castle ruins and a parish church with a Gothic doorway of eight recessed orders. Crossing a pass at 992m, we descend to **Logroño**, 24km S.

VITORIA TO LOS ARCOS (72km). Fork right onto the C132 from the N1 just E of Vitoria, with the MONTES DE VITORIA rising to the S, shortly passing (right) *Aberásturi*, its 12C Romanesque church retaining a good doorway.—The Romanesque church at hilltop *Estibaliz* (left) has been over restored.—*Anúa* (left), where *Sta. Lucía*, with an unusual early Gothic polygonal apse and door with carved capitals, is passed to the left, and later *Eguileta*, with a good Romanesque church. NE of Eguileta is *Erunchun*, where the church has an early Gothic porch and two Romanesque chapels. Crossing the *Puerto Azáceta*, the road descends to (27km) *Maestu*, with Transitional *N.S. del Campo* and ruined *S. Martin*, with an early Gothic doorway.—At *Leorza* and *Cicujano*, not far N, are Romanesque churches; at *Igoroin* there is a simple Cistercian Gothic church.—24km *Acedo*, where we turn right for (13km) *Los Arcos* (or continue 21km E to **Estella**); see Rte 4.—From Los Arcos the C121 continues SE via *Sesma* to (22km) *Lodosa*, on the Ebro, with a large church and ancient houses, from which we may approach **Calahorra** (see below) by crossing the river at *S. Adrián*, further SE.

The N1 leads SW from Vitoria (see Rte 1A), skirting the battlefield of 1813. After 25km diverge left onto the N232, shortly traversing *Zambrana*, with an old church and ruins of two castles, then (left) *Salinillas de Buradón*, with ruined walls and ancient castle, and later, *Briñas*, with a medieval bridge and a church with carvings by Matías el Francés, Vigarni's assistant.

19km **Haro** (8700 inhab.), an agricultural and vinous town at the confluence of the Tirón and Ebro, gave its title to Luis Méndez de Haro (1598–1661), the minister of Felipe IV. The *Ayuntamiento* dates from 1769, while notable among many ancient houses is the 16C *Casa de Paternina*. *Sto. Tomás* is a large hall-church with a Plateresque porch of 1516 by *Felipe de Vigarni*. Also containing features of interest are Gothic *S. Nicolás* and *N.S. de la Vega* (18C).—For *Sto. Domingo de la Calzada*, 20km SW, see Rte 4.

HARO TO LOGROÑO VIA LAGUARDIA (42km). This alternative road leads E through the fertile district of the Rioja Alavesa on the N bank of the Ebro, passing (6km) **Labastida**, with many old houses, the Romanesque fortress-chapel of *El Cristo*, with Renaissance additions, and a church with a 17C porch and 18C tower.—Near by are ruined *S. Martín de los Monjes* (12C) with curious rock-cut graves, the castle of *Toloño*, and remains of the Franciscan friary of *S. Andrés de Maya*, with a 13C cloister and ruins of the conventual aqueduct.—3km. To the right is *S. Vicente de la Sonsierra*, with a hilltop castle, a pilgrims' hospice, and in the well-vaulted church of 1520–50, a retablo by Damián Forment. Near by, Romanesque *Sta. María de la Piscina* was founded in 1136 by Don Ramiro of Navarra, son-in-law of the Cid.—Continuing E, we pass *Abalos*, birthplace of Martín Fernández de Navarra (1765–1844), the biographer of Cervantes (1819), with the *Pal. del Marqués de Legarda* and a 15C church. We shortly bear away from the wall of the SIERRA DE CANTABRIA to approach *Laguardia*; for which and the road on, see above.

7.5km **Briones**, well-sited on a hill, like Haro is reputed for its wine. Surrounded by walls and with a ruined castle, it retains several old mansions, notably the *Pal. de Marqués de S. Nicolás*. The hall-church, completed in 1546 to the designs of Juan Martínez, has an 18C Baroque tower and well-restored organ.—Some 3km NE stands *S. Vicente de la Sonsierra*; see above.—The castle and chapel of *Davalillo* are finely situated on a bend of the Ebro. At *Torremontalbo* are the remains of another castle.—From (15km) *Cenicero* a road crosses the river to *Laguardia* (11km NE: see above) via *Elciego*, birthplace of the chronicler Manuel Navarrete Ladrón de Guevara, Bp of Mondoñedo. Its parish church contains Churrigueresque retablos.—12km SW of Cenicero is *Nájera*; see Rte 4.—7.5km *Fuenmayor* (left) has a 16C hall-church. Shortly beyond Fuenmayor the road veers NE to approach **Logroño** (see Rte 4), also bypassed to the S.

Continuing E on the N232, at 13km *Agoncillo* is bypassed, with ruins of Roman *Egon* and a castle with four square towers.

At 24km the C123 leads S to (12km) **Arnedo** (11,750 inhab.), an old town with castle ruins, an aqueduct, and *S. Tomás* of c 1500.—*Quel* (4km E), also with a ruined castle, was the birthplace of Manuel Breton de los Herreras (1796–1873), the playwright.—12km W is *Arnedillo*, with hot springs, where in Janaury 1932 six demonstrating strikers were shot down by nervous Guardia Civil in retaliation for the murder of five civil guards at Castilblanco in Extremadura a week earlier.

Hence the C115 climbs across country to *Soria*, 60km SW, following the valley of the Cidacos, via (22km) *Yanguas*, with medieval walls, a Romanesque tower of 1146, Moorish castle, and ancient houses. *S. Miguel* has elaborately carved altar pieces.

11km **CALAHORRA** (17,850 inhab.; Parador) is an ancient town at the confluence of the Cidacos and Ebro, well-sited but largely ruinous, and any relics of its Roman walls have been demolished in the interest of modern development, mostly towards the NW.

The Celiberian stronghold of *Calagurris Nassica*, unsuccessfully besieged by Pompey in 75 BC, was taken by Afranius four years later after a famine so dreadful that it became proverbial. The see, founded in 1045, has been united with Logroño since 1890. Enrique de Trastámara was proclaimed King of Castile here by Du Guesclin in 1366.

Among Calahorra's natives were Quintilian (c AD 35–100); Aurelius Prudentius (fl. 348–410), the Christian poet; and Antonio Llorente (1756–1823), historian of the Inquisition.

The **Cathedral**, by the bridge, was restored in 1485 after a flood. The Cap. Mayor was built in 1621, and the main portal and façade and the Epifania chapel were later altered. The N door is a mixture of Gothic and Renaissance styles; the curious W Front with its oblong tower dates from 1680–1704. The Nave is pure late Gothic, with stellar vaulting springing direct from octagonal piers. There is a Churrigueresque retablo, with a martyrdom in high relief, in a chapel off the ambulatory; the Sacristy contains a mid 15C Custodia known as 'El Ciprés'.

The other churches are of slight interest. Late Gothic *S. Andrés* has a brick tower and curious W door; *Santiago*, of Classic design, is domed. In the *Carmelite convent* nearer the cathedral is a Flagellation by *Gregorio Fernández*.

12km. From *Rincón de Soto* (left) one may cross the Ebro and turn right to *Milagro*, with a Moorish castle; at *Aldeanueva de Ebro*, to the right at this junction, the parish church contains a 16C retablo by Pierre de Troas (Troyes) and Arnao de Bruselas.

11km **Alfaro** (8750 inhab.), where brick-built *S. Miguel* (16C) contains notable choir stalls and a Plateresque reja, preserves several ancient houses of Aragonese type, including the *Casa de los Frías* and the *Pal. Abatial*, built in the late 18C to plans by Ventura Rodríguez.

We reach the junction of the C101 at 5km, and 14km beyond enter **Tudela**, for which and the road on to **Zaragoza** see Rte 3.

7   Bilbao to Santander

107km (66 miles). N634. 34km **Castro Urdiales**—24km *Laredo*—31km *Solares*—18km **Santander**.

Maps: M 442.

BILBAO (433,100 inhab.; 115,000 in 1920), capital of Vizcaya, is a thriving industrial city at the centre of a conurbation with a population approaching a million. It derives much of its prosperity from the rich veins of haematite in the area, and from its position on the navigable Nervión. It can hardly be believed that in the late 18C Bilbao was considered by William Bowles (1705–80; the Irish author of an 'Introducción a la Historia Natural y de la Geografía Física de España', and for many years superintendent of the Spanish state mines), who had lived here for some years, to be 'one of the neatest towns in Europe'. Having suffered from bombardment and fire during the Carlist Wars, old Bilbao offers little of interest, but its natural situation is imposing. Its climate is temperate, but the prevalent *siri-miri*, or Scotch mist, makes it depressingly damp in winter, and the atmosphere is polluted.

Bilbao was founded in 1300 by Diego López de Haro and enjoyed an uneventful history until the 19C. Sacked by the French in 1808, it was besieged three times during the civil wars later in the century, which gave the town the name of 'Ciudad de los Sitios' (sieges). In June 1835 Don Carlos, the pretender, anxious to score a striking success, despatched the famous 'guerrillero' Zumalacárregui against Bilbao, where he was mortally wounded after seizing the heights of Begoña. A second assault that October was repulsed with the help of the British Auxiliary Legion. In 1873, during the second Carlist War, the inhabitants were also able to beat off the besiegers. In the Civil War it held out against the Nationalists, behind its 'Ring of Iron', until 19 June 1937, but the 20,000 shells which rained down on the city did not improve its appearance.

The old English words *bilbo* (cutlass) and *bilboes* (iron fetters) testify to the fame of Bilbao as an ironworking town, and one which has always had strong commercial ties with England, but it was not until c 1870 that the deposits of iron ore at Somorrostro, to the NW, were actively exploited. Meanwhile, in 1857, the Bank of Bilbao was established; in 1896 the first dry dock was constructed, and a revival of shipbuilding was initiated.

Bilbao was the birthplace of the composer Juan Cristóstomo de Arriaga (1806–26); Miguel Unamuno (1864–1936), author and philosopher; and José Antonio de Aguirre (1904–60), the Basque President from 1936.

The centre of old Bilbao, which lay entirely on the right bank of the Nervión until after 1874, when the new quarters which soon eclipsed it in size were laid out, is the Arenal, a promenade, to the E of which is uninteresting 18C *S. Nicolás de Bari*, containing statues by Juan de Mena. To the SW by the bridge is the unwieldy *Teatro de Arriaga*; to the N, beyond the *Puente de Begoña*, is the *Ayuntamiento* and the tree-planted *Campo de Volantín*. From the S side of the Arenal we may enter the adjacent arcaded PL. NUEVA, beyond the far corner of which is the *Museo Histórico*. Its archaeological collection contains a Cross from Durango and a Romanesque tympanum from Santurtzi. Adjacent is *SS. Juanes*. Further SW stands *Santiago*, mainly late 14C, with a fragment of a later cloister and modern W front and tower; the S porch is dated 1571.

Further S is *S. Antón* (15C, but spoiled by restoration), and Dominican *La Anunciación* (15C; altered in the 17C). On a height to the E (approached by a long flight of steps and a lift) is Gothic *N.S. de Begoña* (c 1511, with a modern tower and cloister), containing paintings by Luca Giordano, and the Pilgrimage to Begoña by Echena.

The *Puente del Arenal* crosses the Nervión into modern Bilbao and the Pl. de España, from which the Gran Vía de López de Haro extends to the W, to the N of which is *S. Vicente*, a 16C hall-church in the traditional style. Beyond (left) the *Diputación* is the Pl. Federico Moyúa, the oval hub of the town, from which the C. Elcano leads NW towards the *Parque de Doña Casilda de Iturriza* and the **Museo de Bellas Artes**.

On the ground floor are works by Q. Massys, C. Engelbrechtsen, and Mabuse, while the later Italian and Flemish Schools are also represented. The collection includes paintings by El Greco, Ribalta, Roelas, Ribera, Fr. Herrera the elder, Orrente, Zurbarán, Cano, Fr. Rizi, and Valdés Leal. Among the portraits are *Velázquez*, Felipe IV; *Carreño*, Doña Teresa Francisca Mudarra; *Claudio*

Coello, Carlos II; Maria-Anna de Neubourg; *Goya,* María Luisa de Parma, the poet Moratín, and engravings. Sculptures include a seated Virgin by Juan de Mena, and there are some good pieces of ancient furniture. Other rooms contain 19C Spanish paintings, and works by Sorolla, Solana, and Zuloaga.

From the far end of the Gran Vía the broad Av. de Sabino turns S to meet the N634 leaving the town to the W. Just beyond is the entrance to the motorway.

BILBAO TO PLENTZIA (26km). From the N end of the C. Elcano (see above) we cross the *Puente de Deusto* and soon fork right onto the Bl103 through *Asua,* to the E of which is the airport of *Sondika.*—7km E at *Zamudio* is a 16C hall-church and a tower-house.—To the N at *Lújua* are new university buildings.—Bear NW to pass *Erandio,* with a 15C church and tower-house. The sea is reached after traversing the residential districts of *Las Arenas* (at the E end of the *Puente Vizcaya*), *Neguri,* and *Algorta,* just N of which, at *Getxo,* is another medieval tower-house. The fishing port of *Plentzia,* now a small resort (as is contiguous *Gorliz*), has a church of some interest.—7km inland is the modernised 13C castle of *Butrón.*—The return to Bilbao may be made via *Mungia* (see p 117), further E.

BILBAO TO SANTURTZI. The industrial W bank of the Nervión may be followed by driving W on the N634 and, after crossing the Río Cadagua, forking right onto the C639. This threads its way through the port districts of *Baracaldo, Sestao* (with a tower-house) and the blast furnaces of *Los Altos Hornos, Portugalete,* and *Santurtzi.* Overlooking Portugalete is Gothic *Sta. María.* The river is spanned by the *Puente Vizcaya,* a lofty transporter bridge of 1893.

BILBAO TO REINOSA (132km). The C6318 leads SW up the valley of the Cadagua towards the Cantabrian highlands to (20km) *Güeñes,* with a 17C palace and Gothic church. 9.5km beyond is **Balmaseda** (7950 inhab.), a pleasantly sited town with three old bridges and two medieval churches.—14.5km *Villasana de Mena* (where in the church of the Franciscan nunnery is the tomb of a canon of Sevilla on which is depicted the Giralda as it was before the 16C alterations). Here a left-hand turn leads past Romanesque *S. Lorenzo* (c 1185–1200) at *Vallejo de Mena* to *Vigo-Siones,* with the richly carved 12–13C church of *Sta. María,* overlooked by the sierra rising to 1243m; to the N extend the MONTES DE ORDUNTE (1044m). At 16km we cross the C629 and, 10km beyond, reach **Espinosa de los Monteros,** the scene of the defeat of Blake by Victor in 1808, and headquarters of the Monteros de Espinosa, the personal bodyguard of the kings of Castile, established by Count Sancho García in honour of a huntsman of Espinosa who had saved his life. It retains a number of old houses, and the Plateresque hall-church has an unusual sanctuary.—At 11.5km *Cueva* lies to the left. Above Cueva the lane climbs steeply past a Romanesque sanctuary to a fine viewpoint.—The main road veers SW to (16.5km) *Soncillo,* where we turn NW to cross the N623 at 9km just S of the *Puerto del Escudo* (1011m). The N bank of the extensive *Embalse del Ebro* is skirted to approach **Reinosa,** 25km further W; see Rte 30.

BILBAO TO COLINDRES (FOR LAREDO) BY THE INLAND ROAD (c 80km). From *Güeñes* (see above) we bear right onto the C6210 through *Zalla,* with a tower-house. N of Zalla at *Avellaneda* the *Casa de Juntas,* containing a regional museum, is another medieval tower-house of a type commonly met with in this rugged district of hills and glens.—14.5km *Carranza,* with a tower-house and the bishop's *Pal. de Aedo,* beyond which we descend the valley of the Asón to meet the C629.—*Ramales de la Victoria,* to the SW, with a ruined palace, was the scene of Espartero's victory over Maroto in May 1843. Turning N, *Rasines,* birthplace of the architect Juan Gil de Hontañón (fl. 1500–26), is traversed, and also the fishing village of *Limpias* on the estuary. The coast road is met at *Colindres,* 4km SW of *Laredo;* see below.

The N634 (parallel to which a motorway is under construction) drives NW from Bilbao, climbing past *Abanto,* with ancient *S. Pedro,* and (19km) *Somorrostro,* centre of an extensive mining area.—To the right is *S. Julián de Muskiz,* with a ruined chapel, 15C castle, and 16C palace. The road winds above the rocky coast before descending to (15km) **Castro-Urdiales** (13,050 inhab.), a fishing port of Roman foundation (*Flaviobriga*). It is built partly on a peninsula on whose extremity stands 13–14C *Sta. María*, with unfinished towers, a solidly buttressed apse, and monumental brasses. Adjacent is a ruined Templar house. The Black Prince was nominal lord of the town in 1366–70. Antonio Hurtado de Mendoza (1586–1644), the poet and dramatist, was born here.—Prehistoric paintings have been discovered in a cave near *Sámano*, 3km S.

We continue to skirt the coast, turning abruptly S before crossing the Aguera, beyond which the road ascends through well-wooded country before climbing down steeply to approach (26km) **Laredo** (12,450 inhab. out of season), once described as a decayed seaport, with an extensive beach—a wide spit of sand jutting out towards Santoña on the opposite side of the bay. It has been developed into a summer resort of huge proportions. The ancient town, to the NE, retains some old houses and the remains of two monasteries. Charles V landed here in 1556 on his way from Flanders to Yuste, and presented two bronze eagle lecterns to the *Church*, a 13C building with double aisles. The *Ayuntamiento* is 16C.

Colindres, with ancient houses, on the estuary of the Asón, is passed.

At (9km) *Cicero* a road bears right for (5km) **Santoña** (10,350 inhab.), a resort lying beneath an imposing rock, and with a 13C church. It was the only Spanish fortress from which the French were not driven during the Peninsular War. Santoña was the birthplace of Juan de la Cosa (died 1509), the mariner and cartographer.—*Noja* is 12km NW. 8km further W, at *Bareyo*, are two Romanesque churches and, in the *Conv. de S. Sebastián de Anó*, the tomb of Barbara Blomberg (died 1598; mother of Don Juan of Austria). Born at Ratisbon, she had retired to the district in 1577, and after the death of Don Juan the following year lived at Colindres.—*Ajo*, N of Bareyo, preserves 14–16C houses.—Hence one may skirt the coast via *Somo*, or drive SW to rejoin the main road at *Solares*.

The N634 leads away from the coast through *Hoznayo*, with a 17C palace (as has *Villaverde de Pontones*, to the N), to approach (22km) *Solares* on the Río Miera, reputed for its mineral waters.—*La Cavada*, 5km SE, preserves an 18C cannon foundry, 4km W of which at *Liérganes*, are some 17C mansions. The foundry, established by 'Juan Curcio' of Liège, furnished the Crown with 939 large cannon during the years 1635–40.

SOLARES TO TORRELAVEGA (32km). This deviation may be followed by travellers wishing to bypass Santander to regain the Asturian coast further W. The road bears SW past *Sobremazas*, with the *Casa de los Cuetos*, and *Penagos*, near which is the Baroque *Pal. de Elsedo* (1710) with a remarkable chapel.—12.5km *Sarón*, S of which is Romanesque *Sta. María de Cayón*.

Some 16km further S, in the valley of the Pisueña, lies **Villacarriedo**, with the magnificent Baroque *Pal. de Soñanes*, built in 1722 by the Italian Cosimo Fontanelli round the ancient solar of the Díaz de Arce family; at nearby *Selaya* is the *Pal. de Donadío*, and other old mansions.

The N634 continues W through attractive country past (8km) *Castañeda*, with a Romanesque church with Gothic and 18C additions, to cross the N623 (see Rte 29) at *Vargas*. The road winds down to (11.5km) *Torrelavega* (see Rte 30), and leads W towards *S. Vicente de la Barquera*, at 4km passing the turning (right) for *Santillana del Mar*; see Rte 31.

At Solares we turn right for (8km) *El Astillero*, a shipbuilding centre in the days of wooden vessels, to follow the line of the bay past the airport of *Parayas* and *Muriedas* (with an ethnological museum in the *Casa Verde*) to approach the outskirts of **Santander**; see Rte 29.

II CASTILLA Y LEÓN

The autonomous region is almost conterminous with what was 'Old' Castile (*Castilla la Vieja*) and the ancient kingdom of León, with the exception of the provinces of Logroño and Santander, now known respectively as La Rioja and Cantabria. Its characteristic landscape is a limitless undulating plateau or *meseta*, scattered with earth-coloured villages, the skyline being only occasionally broken by a thin line of poplars, flat-topped hills, or distant mountain ranges. The soil is generally fertile; indeed, the area is one of the granaries of Spain, but the rainfall is scanty, although less so than in Castilla-La-Mancha. The main source of water is found in the Duero and its tributaries fed by the snows of the Cantabrian mountains to the N, the sierras of La Demanda and Cebollera to the NE, and Guadarrama and Gredos to the S.

The rolling *meseta* of León to the W is similar, bleak and wind-swept, and equally subject to violent variations in temperature. To the NW is the wide valley of the *Bierzo*, hemmed in by mountains abutting Galicia; to the S the Sierras de Gata and de Peña de Francia wall off Extremadura and the Tagus basin; to the W a stretch of the Duero forms the frontier with Portugal.

Historically, 'Old' Castile has been considered by the Castilians as the heartland of Spain, largely because in the medieval period its comparatively high population enabled it to dominate surrounding regions. Its early counts and kings were among the first to make any organised stand against the Moors, and it owes its name to the numerous castles (*castillos*) erected as successive bulwarks against Islam. Burgos was the first capital of the expanding Christian kingdom, before being superseded by Valladolid. Later conquests enabled the capital to be established further S, beyond the barrier range of the Guadarramas. Here also at an earlier period (from the last decade of the 5C) were those areas most settled by the Visigoths; whether it is coincidental that these provinces are among the most backward in Spain is open to question; as Antonio Machado has written 'wretched Castile, once supreme, now wrapped in tatters, despises what she does not know'. Valladolid is notoriously reactionary, as is Burgos, which during the 1960s is said to have provided almost as many candidates for the Academia General Militar as the whole of the Basque provinces and Catalunya combined.

Emerging from the Asturian highlands after the first Moorish advance, in the 9C Alfonso the Catholic of León overran the country as far S as the Tormes, although the capital was not established at León until c 910. Meanwhile León squabbled with Castile and Navarra (the former nominally subject to León), largely due to the unwise habit of Leonese kings dividing their territories between their sons. The Moors, taking advantage of this, pressed northward again in the 10C and were not driven out until the following century, after which León's re-population was undertaken.

Each of the provinces of Ávila, Palencia, Segovia, Soria, and Zamora has less inhabitants than it had in 1920.

8 Burgos

BURGOS (856m; 152,550 inhab.; c 9000 in 1800; 32,000 in 1920; 81,000 in 1960), the dour capital of the former kingdom of Castile and León, is distinguished for its cathedral, and illustrious for its historical associations as the residence of Fernando III (el Santo), Alfonso X (el Sabio; the Learned, but *not* Wise), and the Cid. Although now surrounded by rapidly growing suburbs, the old centre preserves several interesting monuments, while in the immediate vicinity are the *Cartuja de Miraflores* and the monastery of *Las Huelgas*. The climate of Burgos is more notorious for its extremes than that of Madrid.

It claims as its founder Diego Porcelos, who c 884, at the command of Alfonso III, built a castle on the bank of the Arlanzón as a check to the Moors. The city remained subject to the kings of León until 926, when its citizens elected two judges to govern them, among whom were Laín Calvo, who repelled the attacks of León and the Asturias, and Nuño Rasuro, his son-in-law. The first independent leader was Fernán González (c 950), who bore the title of count of Castile. Fernando I, his great-grandson, assumed the title of king, and by his marriage with Sancha, heiress of León, united the two crowns. In 1087 Alfonso VI removed the court from Burgos to Toledo (recaptured from the Moors two years earlier), and disputes as to precedence between the two ended only when, after the fall of Granada in 1492, the royal residence was transferred to Valladolid, and later to Madrid. In the 15C it was the main depot in N Spain for the export of wool.

Burgos was unsuccessfully besieged by Wellington in September/October 1812 (when Major Edward Somers-Cocks, one of Wellington's outstanding intelligence officers, was killed); but in 1813 the castle was blown up by the French prior to their retreat to Vitoria. From October 1937 reactionary Burgos was the temporary capital of Nationalist Spain after Franco was nominated Generalissimo there. In December 1970 the 'Burgos Trials' of dissident Basques brought notoriety to the place. It is a curious coincidence that Lady Holland, when visiting Burgos in 1804, remarked that prayers were then being said in the cathedral for the success of the royal arms against the Biscayans during some trivial commotion, which Godoy was supposed to exaggerate, 'that he may have the honor of quelling them and receive from the deputies of Biscay a good round sum to prevent the soldiery from committing excesses'.

Its most famous native was Rodrigo Díaz de Vivar (c 1043–99), known as El Cid (arabic Sidi) Campeador (surpassing in valour), whose true character, that of an unscrupulous mercenary leader, has been veiled in the romantic language of the 'Poema del mio Cid', an epic of Spanish heroism. Pedro I of Castile (1333–69), known alternatively as 'the Cruel' and 'the Lawgiver', was also born here, as were the *converso* bishop, Pablo de Santa María (c 1350–1435); the architect Diego Siloé (c 1495–1563); the blind musician Francisco Salinas (1513–90); and Francisco de Enzinas (hellenised to Dryander; 1520–52), the humanist and disciple of Luther.

From just W of the central *Puente de S. Pablo* spanning the Arlanzón, the Paseo de Espolón extends to the *Puente de Sta. Mariá*, named after the adjacent castellated gateway (the *Arco de Sta. María*), originally part of the 11C fortifications, the masonry of which may be seen at the rear. The decorative façade facing the river, with its flanking towers and turrets, was erected in 1536 to flatter Charles V, who is represented in company with Burgalese heroes.

Beyond the gate rises the ***Cathedral**.

The archiepiscopal see of Oca (36km NE) was transferred to Burgos in 1075 but the cathedral was not founded until 1221 when Fernando III, in honour of his marriage with Beatrice of Swabia, laid the first stone. By 1230 part of the church was sufficiently advanced to be used for services. The unusual Angevin vault of the only surviving original chapel suggests that the first architect may have been the Anglo-Angevin Ricardo, who was working at Las Huelgas before

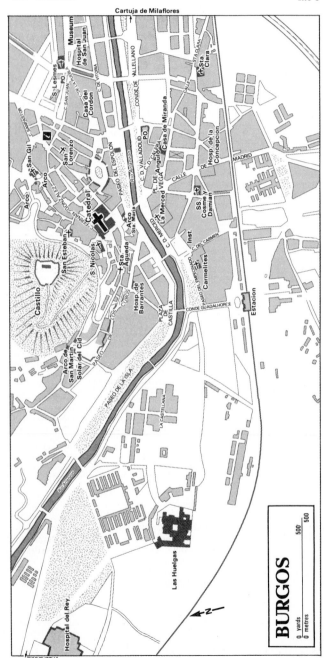

BURGOS

1203 and still living near Burgos in 1226. By c 1235 the master was Enrique, also architect of León cathedral, probably a Frenchman; at his death in 1277 the fabric, consecrated in 1260, must have been substantially complete. The upper stages and spires of the W towers were added by Juan de Colonia in 1442–58, and the Cap. del Condestable (1482–94) by his son, Simón de Colonia. The central lantern was not completed until 1568 by Juan de Vallejo from the designs (1540) of Francisco de Colonia, Simón's son.

The lower part of the W Front was unfortunately deprived of most of its decoration by an 18C restorer, but the transeptal façades are unaltered. The rose-window is flanked by two openwork spires, 90m high. The *Puerta Alta de la Coroneria* (N; closed), with statues of the Apostles (completed 1257), is surmounted by an arcade; beyond, reached down steps, is the Plateresque *Puerta de la Pellejería* (on the E side of the N transept), a profusely ornamented work of 1516 by *Francisco de Colonia*. After skirting the octagonal Condestable chapel and the cloisters, with a view of the *Puerta del Sarmental*, probably by Master *Enrique*, we regain the W front.

The Interior, 106m long with the Condestable chapel, is 58m wide across the transepts, but the effect of length is impaired by the intrusive central *coro*, which extends halfway down the nave. The main arcade of the nave is in the pure 13C style, but the unusual triforium, with five or six lights in each bay surmounted by a semicircular arch, was later rebuilt or cloaked with Flamboyant work. The ridge-ribs running along the length of the high vaults suggest English influence. The immense piers of the crossing, rebuilt to support the lantern, have Renaissance panels at their bases; the apse piers were decorated with scrollwork to match them. In the pavement below the *cimborio* a slab marks the tomb of the Cid and Jimena, his wife. He was originally buried at S. Pedro de Cardeña (cf.), but during the Peninsular War the tomb was rifled by Prince Salm-Dyck, and the bones were carried off to Sigmaringen. They were rediscovered and returned to Burgos at the instance of Alfonso XII, and were interred here in 1921.

The *Escalera Dorada* (1523), an imposing double staircase by Diego de Siloé, ascends to the Puerta Alta in the N Transept; the rose-window of the S Transept retains late Gothic glass. The Retablo of the altar mayor was designed by Rodrigo and Martín de la Haya, Domingo de Berriz, and Juan de Ancheta. It dates from 1562–80. Surrounding the Virgin of 1461 is a series of statues and reliefs, with smaller subjects in the predella below.—On the N side are three 14C tombs of *infantes*, including Don Sancho (brother of Enrique II), who was a prisoner in England in 1347.—At the back of the presbytery are reliefs of the Passion: the three in the centre are by Felipe Vigarni.

The *Coro*, enclosed by a grille of 1602, and decorated on the exterior with paintings by Juan Rizi of 1654–59, contains 103 walnut *Stalls* carved by Vigarni, the seats ornamented with box inlay. In the centre is the tomb (1260) of Abp Maurice (died 1238), an Englishman, with a wooden effigy covered with gilt and embossed copper, retaining some of its Limoges enamelling.

The Chapels are varied in period and style. Beginning in the NW corner, beneath the 16C clock with its jaquemart is the *Cap. de Sta. Tecla*, a profusely decorated work of 1734 with all the characteristic over elaboration of the followers of the Churrigueras. The *Cap. de Sta. Ana*, completed by Simón de Colonia in 1482, contains a *Retablo* by Gil de Siloé and Diego de la Cruz, unsatisfactorily restored, and the alabaster tomb of Bp Luis de Acuña (died 1495), by Diego de Siloé, and that of the archdeacon Fernando Díez (died 1492) by Simón de Colonia.

Beyond the N transept is the *Cap. de S. Nicolás*, with an Angevin octopartite vault, a 16C portative organ of ivory and ebony, and the Isabelline tomb of Pedro Fernández de Villegas (died 1536; a translator of Dante); the chapel of *La Navidad*, with its elliptical dome (1571); and two 13C chapels, one with the tomb of Bp Gonzalo de Hinojosa (1307–20), with carved mourners and reliefs.

At the E end, entered from the Trassagrario, is the opulent *Cap. del Condestable* (1494; by Simón de Colonia), built for Pedro Hernández de Velasco (died 1492), the hereditary Constable of Castile, with a reja of 1523 by Cristóbal Andino and an elaborate vault. The retablo of the main altar is by Vigarni and Diego de Siloé (1532); on the left is a Plateresque altar by Siloé and a triptych of the School of Gerard David; opposite are an Ecce Homo with a Dutch inscription, and inlaid stalls. In the centre is the tomb of the founder and his wife, Mencia de Mendoza (died 1500) of Atapuerca marble with figures of Carrara marble, carved by a Genoese master; the adjoining marble slab was intended for its base. Note also the small 17C organ, unusual in having no trumpets.

The *Cap. de Santiago* (completed 1534; by Juan de Vallejo), SE of the apse, has ribbed vaults which are outstanding examples of the period. The large *Cap. de la Presentación* in the S nave aisle contains the tomb (1524; by Vigarni) of Canon Lerma, rejas by Andino, and a Virgin by Seb. del Piombo. The *Cap. del Santisimo Cristo* is dedicated to a leather-covered image with articulated limbs, the 'Cristo de Burgos', at least as old as the 13C. In the SW corner of the transept is the *Cap. de la Visitación* (1442; perhaps by Juan de Colonia), containing the tomb (1447) of Bp Alonso de Cartagena (died 1456), son of Bp Pablo de Santa María.

The *Cloisters* (c 1300–24), housing the *Museo Diocesano* and several statues and tombs, are entered from the S transept through a door by Simón de Colonia. To the left are statues of Alfonso X and Violante of Aragón. The *Cap. de Sta. Catalina* (1316–54) in the E walk has a ribbed vault resting on finely carved corbels. It contains a collection of vestments, plate, and MSS, etc. The adjacent Chapel preserves, supported high on the wall, the 'Cofre del Cid', an iron-bound chest which the Cid is said to have filled with sand and pledged to the Jews as full of gold as surety for a loan of 600 marks. The *Chapterhouse*, adjoining, has a flat wooden ceiling of Moorish character, a Flemish 15C triptych, and a Crucifixion attributed to Mateo Cerezo. At the end of this gallery is a Romanesque tomb of 1150 from S. Pedro de Arlanza, and in the S walk, among others, that of Canon Diego Santander (1523) by Diego de Siloé.

A right hand turn off the C. de la Paloma (skirting the cloister) leads into the arcaded PL. MAYOR, with the *Ayuntamiento* on its S side. A short distance E is the *Casa del Cordón*, begun in 1482 by the Constable de Velasco, and named from the cord of St. Francis which connects the arms of Velasco with the royal arms and those of his wife. Fernando and Isabel received Columbus here in 1496, and here Felipe I died in 1506.—The lane skirting its S side leads to the former *Hosp. de S. Juan*, with a doorway of 1479; adjacent *S. Lesmes*, with a late Gothic S doorway, contains a fine retablo of c 1510. Near by is a Plateresque mansion (in the C. de Calzadas).

The C. S. Juan leads W past (left) Baroque *S. Lorenzo*, built on an octagonal plan. Further N, to the E of the *Arco de S. Gil*, steps ascend to *S. Gil* (1399, with later alterations), preserving retablos and tombs of interest, and two slate effigies with alabaster faces and hands, in a style peculiar to Burgos.

The C. Fernán González leads back towards the N front of the cathedral, passing several Plateresque mansions including the so-called *Pal. del Conde de Castilfalé*. Turn uphill to **S. Esteban** (1280–1350), with an imposing W Front.

The baptistry, left of the entrance, has good arcading and reliefs; the balustrade of the W gallery is effective late Gothic work; and the pulpit and the tomb beneath the organ gallery are notable specimens of Renaissance carving. The last chapel in the S aisle is covered with beautiful arabesques. The 14C cloister has been sadly mutilated.

Ascending behind the church we pass through the horseshoe gateway of the 14C *Arco de S. Esteban* to reach the *Castillo*. Little of it survived a fire in 1736 and the demolition of the fortifications by the French in 1813. Subterranean works have been excavated.

It was the residence of the early kings. Within its walls García IV of Navarra was confined by Fernán González, and Alfonso VI of León by the Cid. Alfonso VIII gave it in dower to his queen, Eleanor of England. Here Fernando III received Sta. Casilda, daughter of the Moorish king of Toledo, who was converted to Christianity. The marriage of the Cid and Jimena was celebrated here in 1074.

On descending the S slope of the hill and passing through the *Arco de Fernán González* (1592), turn right to reach the site of the 'Solar del Cid', his ancestral mansion, demolished in 1771, marked by a stele and two obelisks bearing shields, erected in 1791. Between this point and the cathedral stood the *Judería*.

Passing the Moorish *Arco de S. Martín* (14C), we descend to the left, and turn along the sheltered *Paseo de los Cubos*, the bastioned wall begun in 1276. The walled town is re-entered after passing the *Hospital de Barrantes* (founded 1627), with a gateway of 1661.

SW of this point is the *Paseo de la Isla*, in which is a re-erected Romanesque doorway from *Cerezo de Riotirón* (on the E boundary of the province) and an arcade of six Plateresque arches.

Passing (left) the old *Prison*, with an early Renaissance façade bearing the arms of Charles V, *Sta. Águeda* or *Gádea* is reached. In its predecessor Alfonso VI was forced by the Cid to swear that he had no part in the slaying of his brother Sancho at Zamora (cf.).

S. Nicolás, just NW of the cathedral (best seen in the afternoon), was begun in 1408. It is remarkable for the *Retablo* of the high altar (1505) by Francisco de Colonia, into the base of which are incorporated the canopied tombs of Alfonso Polanco (died 1490) and Gonzálo Polanco (died 1505) and their wives.

Just beyond and opposite the W front of the cathedral is the *Pal. de Castrofuerte*, with an early Renaissance portal and patio.

Crossing to the S bank of the Arlanzón by the *Puente de Sta. María* and following the C. de la Calera (left), where the *Casa de Angulo* has a turreted entrance and decorated windows, we reach the restored *Casa de Miranda* of 1545. This picturesque mansion, with its attractive patio and imposing staircase, now houses the **Provincial Museum**.

Rooms on the Ground Floor are devoted to the archaeology of the province, including mosaics from Clunia, Visigothic sarcophagi, a carved altar support from Quintanilla de las Viñas, and a stone recording the refounding of Lara (era 900; AD 862); also 14C polychrome sculpture and a collection of Gothic and Renaissance tombs, among the finest of which are those of Juan de Padilla (died 1492) by Gil de Siloé and of Antonio Sarmiento (died 1533) and his wife, attributed to *Rodrigo de la Haya* (1548). In the gallery round the patio are collections of carvings, capitals, and sculpture.—First Floor. Collections of Moorish and Mudéjar work, including a carved ivory case for a ball game (Córdoba; 10C); an ivory casket carved with fabulous beasts in Persian style (Cuenca; 1026), bearing added 12C Limoges enamelled plaques; and a copper reliquary casket from Silos (13C). Other rooms display ecclesiastical plate; the 14C Treasure of Briviesca; a late 12C Frontal from Silos with enamelled bronze figures of saints; and a 14C processional cross. Among paintings are a Virgin and Child of the School of Memling; Berruguete's Mass of St. Gregory; eight panels of the Passion from Oña (15C); a 17C retablo from La Merced; works by Jan Mostaert, Bayeu, Luca Giordano, and Juan Rizi (a portrait by Rizi shows Burgos and its vanished castle in the background); a watercolour view of Burgos in 1802; and Felipe IV and his family in the gardens of the Buen Retiro, Madrid. A collection of 16–17C Furniture, Ceramics, and more archaeological finds are also to be seen.

Among the churches in the S part of the town is *Sta. Clara* (SE of the museum), from which, turning W, the *Hosp. de la Concepción* (completed 1561) is passed to approach the C. de Madrid. Here, to the S beyond the railway, are remains of the *Agustinas*, with a late Gothic cloister.—The C. de la Concepción leads W past *SS. Cosme y Damián*, with a Plateresque doorway (and Plateresque mansion opposite) to the Renaissance *Instituto* (founded as the *Col. de S. Nicolás* in 1570), and a few steps further W, the Baroque church of the *Carmelitas*.—The C. del Carmen leads S to approach—again, beyond the railway—15C *Sta. Dorotea* and, to its W, 14C *SS. Pedro y Felipe*.—Regaining the river, turn right past the 15C doorway of *La Merced* to reach the Puente de Sta. María.

Two recommended short EXCURSIONS in the immediate vicinity of Burgos go to *Las Huelgas* and the *Cartuja de Miraflores*. The former is approached by forking left off the Valladolid road (N620) leading W along the S bank of the Arlanzón.

The *Monasterio de Las Huelgas*, a Cistercian nunnery, was founded by Alfonso VIII in 1187 on the site of a country residence (*huelga*, repose) of the Castilian kings at the request of his wife Eleanor (daughter of Henry II of England).

The convent, to which only ladies of the highest rank were admitted as nuns, was granted extraordinary privileges. The abbess was a princess-palatine, second only to the queen and as 'señora de horca y cuchillo' (gallows and knife) possessed powers of life and death over 51 manors. Several Castilian kings were knighted in the church, beginning with Fernando III in 1219, and in 1254 the future Edward I of England (aged 15), who here married Leonor, sister of Alfonso X. The Black Prince was lodged here after the battle of Nájera (1367).

The *Church* was built in c 1180–1230 in a plain English-looking Gothic style by the English or Angevin Master, Ricardo. It is entered by a cloister porch on the N side, adjoining the tower (with little castles crowning its buttresses), and with double wheel-windows. Within the porch are four tombs of c 1210–40. On either side of the high altar are kneeling figures of Alfonso VIII and Eleanor of England. The octopartite domical vaults of the crossing and chapels, of Angevin type, are notable. The pivoted pulpit is 16C. In the N aisle are the tombs of Enrique I (died 1217), Fernando de la Cerda (died 1275; the eldest son of Alfonso X), surmounted by a 15C sculptured Crucifixion, and Leonor (died 1244; daughter of Alfonso VIII and queen of Jaime I of Aragón). In the *Nuns' Choir* (the structural nave) at the E end of the Renaissance stalls is the double tomb of the founders, both of whom died in 1214, between those of their eldest daughter Berenguela (died 1246), wife of Alfonso IX, and Margaret of Savoy. Further E are the carved sarcophagi of Berenguela (1241–79; daughter of Fernando III and abbess of Las Huelgas) and Blanca (died 1325; daughter of Afonso III of Portugal). The S aisle contains tombs of royal ladies including (E end, opposite the cloister door) Constanza 'la santa' (died 1243; daughter of Alfonso VIII).

The *Claustro Mayor*, with wooden doors of Mudéjar craftsmanship, built in the mid 13C in Gothic style, contains recently exposed remains of polychromed Mudéjar stucco work in the vaults, dated to 1275. The *Sacristy* is entered through magnificent doors, perhaps from Sevilla. The early Gothic *Chapterhouse* of nine bays is vaulted from four shafted columns of markedly English appearance. Here are kept the '*pendón*' of Las Navas (in fact the tent flap of the Moorish king), flags from ships commanded by Don Juan of Austria at Lepanto, and several paintings.

In the *zaguán* is the *Museo de Ricas Telas*, a unique collection of early textiles, jewellery, and arms discovered in the royal tombs. Many types of Christian, Moorish, and Oriental stuffs and brocades are displayed, together with court costumes of Castile from the 12th to the 14C. The most remarkable exhibits are those in cases 8–11 from the tomb of Fernando de la Cerda, the only burial of the series left undisturbed by Napoleon's troops: they include his sword, spurs, belt (bearing English heraldry), and ring. Note the 'Cross of Las Navas' with its case of embossed leather.

The Romanesque *Cloister* of c 1187 is now entered, with its round arches on coupled shafts, and with stiff foliated capitals. At its NE corner stands the Moorish *Cap. de la Asunción* (c 1200). In a corner of the gardens, from which there is a view of the E end of the church, is the *Cap. de Santiago*. Andalusian in style, it is entered through a pointed horseshoe arch of brick. It contains the articulated *Statue of Santiago*, seated on a throne and holding a sword in the counter-balanced right hand. The statue is said to have been made to enable Fernando III to avoid receiving the accolade of knighthood (in 1219) from an inferior.

To the NW beyond Las Huelgas, approached through the grove of El Parral, is the **Hospital del Rey**, founded by Alfonso VIII for poor pilgrims. An elaborately decorated Plateresque archway of 1526 admits to the Renaissance courtyard, richly ornamented with shields and medallions. To the right is the hospice (*Casa de los Romeros*); to the left the church, with a restored 13C porch.

Some 3km from the centre, approached by turning E along the S bank of the Arlanzón past the Convent of the *Carmelitas Descalzas* and along the shady Paseo de la Quita, there turning right across the railway, is the *****Cartuja de Miraflores**. This Charterhouse was built in 1441–51 by Juan II on the site of a palace begun by his father Enrique III. Its *Church*, overlooking a garden patio, was designed in 1454 by Juan de Colonia, continued by his son Simón, and completed by Isabel the Catholic in 1488 as a memorial to her parents. The parapet and pinnacles were added in 1539. The late Gothic doorway (1486) admits to an interior divided in the Carthusian manner into three sections (from W to E, for the public, the lay brethren, and the monks).

In front of the high altar is the elaborate *Monument of Juan II and Isabel of Portugal*. Designed by Gil de Siloé in 1486, it was completed in 1493 and surrounded by a wrought iron screen by Fray Francisco de Salamanca.

The recumbent figures of the king and queen (who died in 1454 and 1496 respectively), carved in their robes of state, lie on the star-shaped tomb, its plan that of two intersecting squares. The face of Juan is regarded as a genuine although posthumous portrait. At the corners 16 lions support the royal arms; the intervening spaces contain New Testament subjects.

In a recessed arch on the left, entwined with vine leaves, is the *Tomb of the Infante Don Alfonso* (1453–68), their son, whose death opened the succession to Isabel the Catholic. Originally buried at Arévalo, his body was moved in 1492 to this tomb, made at the same time as that of his father. The kneeling statue much resembles that of Juan de Padilla in the Provincial Museum. The spectacled figure low down on the left is alleged to be a self-portrait of the sculptor, whose masterpiece this is. Gil de Siloé, assisted by Diego de la Cruz, also executed the *Retablo* of the high altar (1496–99), with kneeling statues of the king and queen at the foot. On either side are monks' stalls, carved in 1488 by Martín Sánchez; the officiating priest's stall is especially delicate. The stalls of the lay brethren's choir are by Simón de Bueras (1558); the figure holding a child in a chalice is St. Hugh of Lincoln.

The chapel contains an Annunciation by Berruguete, a triptych attributed to Juan de Flandes, and a Magdalen by Ribera. The stained glass was brought from Flanders in 1484, except that of the apse, which is Spanish work of 1657. The chapel of *S. Bruno*, near an Annunciation by Mateo Cerezo, contains a wooden figure of the saint by Manuel Pereira.

10km beyond Miraflores, S of *Cardeñajimeno*, is the convent of **S. Pedro de**

Cardeña, traditionally founded in 537 by Queen Sancha, but more probably in 917. It was the burial place of the Cid and Jimena. Babieca, his charger, was buried outside the gate. Their empty monument (cf. p 145) is in a side chapel, modernised in 1736. The restored church of 1447 was handed back in 1950 to the Cistercian order, having been used as a Fascist prison during the Civil War. Of the 11C buildings, the tower and cloister remain; some dependencies were destroyed by fire in 1967.

For roads from Burgos to **León**, **Valladolid**, **Madrid**, and **Soria**, see Rtes 9, 10, 12, and 13 respectively; for **Santander**, **Vitoria**, and **Logroño**, see Rtes 29, 1, and 4, in reverse.

9   Burgos to León

A.   Via Sahagún

192km (119 miles). N620. 6km. N120. 54km *Osorno*—22km *Carrión de los Condes*—44km *Sahagún*—26.5km. N601. 21.5km *Mansilla de las Mulas*—18km **León**.

Maps: M 441, 442.

This is the continuation of the main pilgrimage road to Santiago; see Rte 4. At 6km turn right off the Valladolid road. After 15km the C627 turns right to (18km) *Villadiego*, birthplace of Enrique Flórez (1702–73), the historian. It has a Romanesque church, fortified tower, and porticoed houses.—9km *Olmillos de Sasamón*, with a ruined 15C castle and a 16C hall-church containing a Renaissance retablo.

2km N lies **Sasamón**, Roman *Segisamo*, seat of a bishop in the 11C, where *Sta. María la Real* (13–15C) has a portal similar to that of the S transept of Burgos cathedral, and a dilapidated late Gothic cloister.

At (6km) *Villasandino* an ALTERNATIVE road, following more exactly the old road to Santiago, diverges left past *Villasilos*, with a hall-church of c 1550 (adjacent to which is *Villaveta*, whose church has fine stellar vaulting), to (10.5km) **Castrogeriz**, birthplace of the composer Antonio de Cabezón (c 1500–66). The earliest *fuero* now extant is that given to the town in 974. In the 16C it was the seat of the Council of Castile. Apart from a ruined castle, it contains a Transitional *Colegiata* (in its sacristy the remains of a 16C Flemish portative organ have been transformed into a cupboard); the early 16C hall-church of *S. Juan*, with a 12C tower (note fish-scale tiles) and cloisters; and *Sto. Domingo*, with 16C tapestries. Not far off are the ruins of the early 14C monastery of *S. Antón.*—Turning NW and then SW across the Pisuerga, the road approaches (26km) *Frómista*, on the N611 (see Rte 30), where restored Romanesque *S. Martín* (1035–66) has an octagonal lantern and twin turrets. *S. Pedro* contains 14–16C paintings; and *Sta. María del Castillo*, mainly Plateresque, a 16C Hispano-Flemish altarpiece of 29 panels. Bearing NW through (13km) *Villalcázar* (see below), the main route is regained 6km beyond, at *Carrión de los Condes*.

Villasandino has two star-vaulted hall-churches, one preserving an unpainted 16C organ possibly played on by Cabezón in his youth. We bear NW through *Padilla de Abajo*, with an interesting church of 1573, to (13km) **Melgar de Fernamental**, with a late Gothic church of cathedral proportions, enlarged in the 16C. It contains an organ of 1884 by Juan Otorel preserving part of the 17C instrument, restored in 1977; its 'chamade' is outstanding.

Crossing the Pisuerga and *Canal de Castilla*, we meet the N611 (see Rte 30) and turn left to (11km) *Osorno*, with a conspicuous

church tower and two chapels with artesonados. Its 17–18C organ
has been unsatisfactorily restored.

22km **Carrión de los Condes**, the seat of the cowardly Infantes de
Carrión, who married the daughters of the Cid and then maltreated
them, with dire consequences to themselves (cf. S. Esteban de
Gormaz). It was the birthplace of the poet Marqués de Santillana
(1398–1458). Shem Tov Ardutiel (Santob; c 1290–c 1369), compiler of
'Proverbios morales', was rabbi here. Romanesque *Sta. María del
Camino* has a notable façade, and interesting tombs; 12C *Santiago*
has a remarkable carved frieze. *N.S. de Belén* is Gothic. Of the
Benedictine *Conv. de S. Zoilo* there remain cloisters begun in 1537
by Juan de Badajoz and completed in 1604 with an upper storey by
Pedro Torres. The Classical hall-church of *S. Andrés* preserves stalls
from the nearby ruined abbey of *Benevivere*, founded in 1165.

At **Villalcázar de Sirga**, 6km SE, is **Sta. María la Blanca*, built by the Templars
early in the 13C. Its square E end and ridge-ribs suggest English influence. Its
porch is richly carved. In the S transept are the impressive royal tombs of Don
Felipe (died 1274; who was first married to Christina of Norway; cf. Covarrubias), and Leonor Ruiz de Castro, his second wife.

At *Nogal de las Huertas*, 7km NW of Carrión, are the scant remains of the
Benedictine *Conv. de S. Salvador*, with a nave and doorways of 1166. The
parish church contains an 11C wooden crucifix.—15km NW of Carrión on the
C615 are *Renedo de la Vega* (with the nearby ruins of Mudéjar *Sta. María de la
Vega*) and, 9km beyond, **Saldaña**, a picturesque village with a *Bridge* of 23
arches over the Carrión. Remains of its 11C *Castle*, and *S. Miguel* (16–18C) are
of interest. Near by *N.S. del Valle* contains an 8C Byzantine Virgin.

The main road shortly skirts *Calzada de los Molinos* and (15.5km)
Cervatos de la Cueza, both with churches preserving fine
artesonados. It then bears NW past *Terradillos de los Templarios* to
(27km) Sahagún.

Sahagún (i.e. S. Facundo) is a decayed and crumbling town from
which in 1780 Pablo de Olavide escaped to France from a prison of
the Inquisition. It was the starting point late in December 1809 of the
retreat of Sir John Moore's army to A Coruña. It possesses the ruin of
what was once one of the greatest Benedictine abbeys in Spain, the
retiring place of the kings of León; and also fragments of Mozarabic
S. Juan, founded by Alfonso III in 907 and rebuilt in 1213, but burned
in 1810 and 1835. The *Cap. de S. Mancio* retains the tomb of Alfonso
VI (died 1109) and of his Moorish wife, Zaida; in the treasury is a
custodia by *Enrique de Arfe*.—The early 12C Mudéjar brick tower of
S. Tirso (restored) and the 13C churches of *S. Lorenzo* and *La
Trinidad* are of interest. The *Franciscan Convent* preserves horseshoe
arches, and the *Santuario de la Peregrina* (1257) a good doorway,
and a chapel containing relics of Mudéjar stucco work.—See Rte 9B
for the C611 leading S.

We cross the Cea and at 26.5km meet the N601; turn right.—At
21.5km *Mansilla de las Mulas*, with a porticoed plaza and relics of its
former walls.—To the W after crossing the Esla is the Benedictine
abbey of *Sta. María de Sandoval*, with early ribbed vaults (c 1200) in
the church, lengthened in 1462.

12.5km NE is restored **S. Miguel de Escalada*, built in 913 by refugee
Mozarabic monks from Córdoba who used the horseshoe arch throughout, even
in the plan of the apses. A feature is the exterior gallery. The aisled nave is of c
930; the tower, 11C.—*Gradefes*, further up the valley of the Esla, has a
Romanesque church (begun 1177; under restoration) of a Cistercian nunnery.

18km **León**; see Rte 18.

S. Miguel de Escalada

B. Via Palencia

215km (133 miles). N620. 76km. N610. 11km **Palencia**—45km
Villalón de Campos—16km. N601. 67km **León**.
Maps: M 441, 442.

For the first 76km see Rte 10. We then fork right to **Palencia** (see Rte
30) and follow the N610 W.

An ALTERNATIVE route is that FROM PALENCIA TO SAHAGÚN (63km),
then following Rte 9A. The road (C613) leads NW across the fertile
but uninterestng TIERRA DE CAMPOS, the 'Campi Gotici' of medieval
writers, where the walls of most village houses are constructed of
earth and chopped straw or *tapia*, on a base of stone.—At 14.5km
Becerril de Campos is bypassed. It was the birthplace of the historian
and satirist Sebastián Miñano (1779–1845), and has five (two
ruinous) churches, including *Sta. María*, with an attractive choir
gallery.—7km **Paredes de Nava**, birthplace of the sculptor and artist
Alonso Berruguete (c 1480–1561) and Jorge Manrique (1440–79), the
soldier-poet. Late Gothic *Sta. Eulalia*, with a spired tower, contains a
retablo of 1560 by Inocencio Berruguete and Esteban Jordan, with
paintings by Alonso Berruguete. The church and its 'museum',
largely devoted to the Berruguetes, was gutted of its paintings by
thieves in November 1979. Its *Organ* (1793) by Tadeo Ortega (who
also constructed that in Sta. María, of 1791) is the most important
parish organ in the Tierra de Campos. (The region contains more

organs for its area than any other in Spain, many of them recently restored or being restored.)—*Frechilla*, 13km W, has a well-carved Baroque retablo and an imposing organ in its church.—16km *Cisneros*, which gave its name to the family of which Card. Cisneros (cf. Torrelaguna) was the most famous member. The curious early 16C Mudéjar church of *SS. Facundo y Primitivo* has notable ceilings; *S. Pedro* has a Mudéjar vault.—9.5km *Villada*, with three Baroque churches. 4km S, at *Villacidaler*, the brick church has a Plateresque retablo by I. Berruguete.—9.5km *Grajal de Campos*, with a 15C fort with corner towers (the earliest in Spain built to resist artillery), a palace of 1540, and an early 16C church containing a Christ by Juan de Juni.—Passing the Benedictine abbey of *S. Pedro de las Dueñas* (begun c 1110) we approach *Sahagún*; see Rte 9A.

The N610 bears W from Palencia through the TIERRA DE CAMPOS; see above.

At 11.5km the C612 forks left to (39.5km) *Medina de Rioseco* (see Rte 21A), at (12.5km) *Torremormojón*, with a ruined 14–15C castle, passing 5km N of **Ampudia**. The three square towers of its *castle* are surrounded by a well-preserved lower round-turreted curtain wall. It was besieged in turn by Comuneros and royalists in 1521. Its state rooms have artesonado ceilings. The *Gothic church* has a splendid tower known as 'La Giralda de Campos', a Plateresque retablo and good tombs.—Some 13km SW of Ampudia at *Villalba de los Alcores* is a 12C castle altered in the 15C; near by are the ruins of the once extensive Cistercian abbey of *Matallana* with a church begun in 1228.

Continuing W on the N610, at 10km *Baquerín*, with a finely carved retablo in its church, lies to the S.—4km *Castromocho* has two 16C churches of note, one containing a restored organ, and the other with a Burgundian roof.—6km NE is *Fuentes de Nava*, with two restored organs by *Tadeo Ortega*: that in *S. Pedro* of c 1788, that in *Sta. María* of 1790. Both churches are of interest.—4km NW of Castromocho is *Abarca*, with a brick Mudéjar tower (15C), and a beautiful restored organ by Tadeo Ortega (1778) in its church.—19.5km *Villalón de Campos*, noted for its cheese, has arcaded streets and an early 16C pillory (*rollo*).—At *Cuenca de Campos*, 5km S, 13C brick *S. Justo* has painted and gilded artesonado roofs and an altarpiece by Esteban Jordan, and there are good retablos in *Sta. María del Castillo* (c 1500) in the old fortress.—The main road makes a semicircle to the W. At 16km the C620 turns left to (45km) *Benavente* (see Rte 21B), and at 8.5km bypasses **Mayorga**, on the Cea, where on 20 December 1809 Sir David Baird's forces joined up with Moore's army only days before starting the retreat to A Coruña. Its brick Transitional *Church* contains a fine artesonado ceiling and 15C retablos.—10km *Albires* (to which there is a direct crossroad from Villalón), 9km beyond which we meet the road from Sahagún, 21.5km before reaching *Mansilla de las Mulas*; see Rte 9A.—For **León**, 18km beyond, see Rte 18.

10 Burgos to Salamanca via Valladolid and Tordesillas

240km (149 miles). N620. 76km. **Palencia** lies 11km NW—49km **Valladolid**—30km **Tordesillas**—85km **Salamanca**.

Maps: M 442.

The N620 bears W and then SW, following the valley of the Arlanzón.

At 13km it meets the extension of the A1 bypassing Burgos, and 7km beyond enters *Estépar*, with a fortified 13C church.

At 10km *Sta. María del Campo* lies 11km S. A picturesque village, it retains a battlemented gate and a 15C church dominated by a Plateresque tower designed by Diego de Siloé and Felipe Vigarni, and containing good tombs and stallwork.

At 15.5km the village of *Palenzuela*, 3km S, with a ruined castle, lies close to the Arlanza. The Plateresque hall-church of *S. Juan*, the 15C *Hospital*, the ruins of 13C *Sta. Eulalia*, and the monastery of *S. Francisco*, are of interest.—There is a large late Gothic church at *Tabanera de Cerrato*, 9km further S.

At 6km *Quintana del Puente*, with its ancient bridge, is bypassed.

Valbuena de Pisuerga, 8km N, has an 18C church with a Churrigueresque high altar. Close by is *S. Cebrián de Buena Madre*, with a Gothic church and imposing mansion.—At *Cordovilla la Real*, 6km W of Quintana, are a Plateresque church, a bridge of 1778, and remains of the abbey of *S. Salvador del Moral*.

We pass (right) the confluence of the Arlanza and the Pisuerga on approaching (11.5km) *Torquemada*, now bypassed, with an old *Bridge* of 25 arches, and restored *Sta. Eulalia*. Tomás de Torquemada (1420–98), the Inquisitor-general, was perhaps born here.

6km SE is *Hornillos de Cerrato*, with a ruined castle, on the road to *Baltanás*, 6.5km beyond. There the *Hosp. de Sto. Tomás* has a Baroque front, and a church containing objects of interest.—*Cevico Navero*, 12km further SE, has a church with Romanesque capitals and Transitional front, E of which are the ruins of the *Conv. de S. Pelayo*.

There are Romanesque churches at *Villamediana* (6km W of Torquemada with 13C walls; and at *Valdeolmillos*, 5km beyond.

At 13km *Reinoso de Cerrato*, with remains of a castle and Renaissance church, lies 4km E; at *Villaviudas*, 4km beyond, the Gothic church has a Churrigueresque altarpiece.

The main road soon bypasses *Magaz*, with castle ruins, beyond which the N610 bears right to (11km) **Palencia**; see Rte 30.—At 8km we bypass (left) the railway junction of *Venta de Baños* (7200 inhab.), 1km E of which is restored •*S. Juan Bautista* at **Baños de Cerrato**, built by the Visigothic king Recceswinth in 661 largely of material from the Roman temple at the hot springs which gave the place its name.

On the road to *Tariego de Cerrato*, to the S, is a medieval bridge over the Pisuerga, and 9km to the SE of Tariego is *Cevico de la Torre*. 6.5km beyond is the enormous castle and 15C church of *Alba de Cerrato*.—Some 7km E of Cevico, at *Vertavillo*, is a church consecrated in 1192. NE of Vertavillo is *Castrillo de Onielo*, the Celtiberian *Arcilasis*, with old walls and a Gothic church.

The N620 shortly passes (left) the partly Romanesque church (with a rebuilt nave) of the *Conv. de S. Isidro*, known locally as *La Trapa*, founded in 911.—8.5km *Dueñas*, scene of the first meeting between Isabel of Castile and Fernando of Aragón only a few days before their marriage in Valladolid (1469). In 13C *Sta. María* are Isabelline wall tombs, carved stalls, and a 16C Gothic retablo.—17km *Cabezón* (left) on the far bank of the Pisuerga, crossed by a bridge near which Bessières defeated the Spaniards under Cuesta in 1808, has castle ruins.—*Cigales*, 3km right of the main road, has a Renaissance hall-church by Juan de Herrera.

14km **Valladolid** (Rte 11A), also largely bypassed. *Arroyo*, with a Romanesque church, is passed en route to (11km) **Simancas**, Roman *Septimanca*. Its moated slate-roofed *Castle* has been the repository of national archives since they were transferred here in 1545. Some were used as kindling by Kellermann during the Peninsular War. Scholars intending to study should apply in advance; but generally on view are the marriage contract of the future Felipe II and Mary Tudor and that of Fernando and Isabel, among other important documents and autographs. Ramiro II defeated a Moorish force near here in 934. Hugh Roe O'Donnell (?1571–1602), Lord of Tyrconnel, died of poison at Simancas. The parish *Church* has a Romanesque W tower and a retablo by I. Berruguete and Bautista Beltrán (1563), painted by Jerónimo Vázquez; the lierne vault of c 1540 recalls English work. A *Bridge* of 17 arches crosses the Pisuerga here, which meets the Duero a short distance beyond, of which the proverb says: 'Duero tiens la fama y Pisuerga lleba el agua' (Duero gets the glory; Pisuerga brings the water), used with a much wider application.

19km **Tordesillas** (6800 inhab.; Parador), an important river crossing.

It was a centre of the Comunero rebellion, crushed in 1521 at the battle of *Villalar* (13.5km NW), where Juan de Padilla was defeated by the troops of Carlos V. Alonso de Castillo Solórzano (1584–1648), the author of picaresque stories and *entresmeses*, and the braggart Nationalist general, Queipo de Llano (1875–1951; cf. Sevilla), were born here. It was the Treaty of Tordesillas of June 1494 which agreed the line of longitude demarking the Spanish and Portuguese spheres of influence in the New World.

S. Antolín, above the picturesque bridge, contains a Crucifixion by Juni and the Alderete tomb (1550) by a local sculptor. Gothic *S. Pedro* and *Sta. María* are other notable churches, the latter with a handsome Herreran tower. In the town centre is an attractive arcaded *Plaza*.

On a commanding site above the river stands the **Conv. de Sta. Clara*, once a palace of Pedro the Cruel, although begun in 1340 by Alfonso XI. Juana la Loca (the Mad; 1479–1555), mother of the Emperor Charles V, died here after 49 years of semi-confinement, during which she is said to have occupied a small cell without windows. The story that she spent her time watching the coffin of her husband Felipe I (died 1506) is inaccurate.

The convent contains much fine Mudéjar work, including the Patio of S. Pedro, and a beautiful artesonado ceiling over the Cap. Mayor; also a 15C Flemish retablo and, in the chapel, the founder's tomb of 1435.

Note an early clavichord and a square virginal (by Hans Bos of Antwerp) brought here c 1560 by Mary of Hungary. One of the 18C organs had its pipes removed in 1950 by the sacristan, who sold them to a local plumber. The *little* portative organ was given to the church by Juana. It was restored in 1974 for an historical recording, on condition that it was afterwards dismantled, on the specific instructions of the then director of the Patrimonio Nacional.

For roads from Tordesillas to **Toro** and **Zamora**, and to **León** or **Astorga**, see Rtes 20 and 21 respectively; and for **Madrid**, Rte 21A in reverse.

Crossing the Duero, turn right past the Parador and bear away from the river to cross the lonely undulating plain to (29km) *Alaejos*, with a ruined castle and two Renaissance churches, of which *Sta. María* contains a retablo in part by Esteban Jordán, and artesonados. Its once-famous white wine is no longer produced.

12km due E lies **Nava del Rey**, where the great hall-church of *Los SS. Juanes* (16–17C), partly by Rodrigo Gil de Hontañón, has a splendid tower, and a retablo mayor by Gregorio Fernández. The *Capuchinas* contains sculpture by Carmona.

Carpio, 16km SE of Alaejos, was the home of the legendary hero Bernardo del Carpio, nephew of Alfonso 'el Casto'. SW of Carpio is *Fresno el Viejo*, where the brick 12–13C Hospitaller church of *S. Juan* contains a 15C Mudéjar tomb.—At *Cantalapiedra*, 27km S of Alaejos, the remarkable church is a former mosque, rebuilt in 1405 and altered in the 18C.

56km **Salamanca**; see Rte 26.

11 Valladolid to Madrid

A. Valladolid

VALLADOLID (320,300 inhab.; c 21,000 in 1800; 76,000 in 1920; 151,000 in 1960) stands on the plateau of Old Castile at a height of c 700m, on the left bank of the Pisuerga at its confluence with the Esgueva (here covered), and not far NE of its confluence with the Duero. The rapidly growing city of some industrial and commercial importance is the centre of the Castilian corn trade. It is also the administrative capital of Castilla y León. Although containing several fine old buildings, it is distinctly modern in appearance. Its layout is extremely confusing, and the sign posting of exits is exceptionally bad. Numerous buildings of secondary interest are spread over a large area, and Valladolid still gives the impression of being 'a large rambling city . . . run up in a hurry', to quote Henry Swinburne, who passed through in June 1776.

Valladolid's name has been derived from the Arabic *Belad-Walid* (land of the governor). A favourite seat of the Castilian kings from the 12C, it was not until after the conquest of Granada that it temporarily supplanted Burgos as the official capital. In 1560 Felipe II, although born here in 1527, finally established the court at Madrid. A brief renewal of importance under Felipe III ended with the accession of Felipe IV and the confirmation of Madrid as 'the only court'. Its thriving population rapidly declined to a mere 20,000. It suffered severely in the plague of 1647–52, and from the French in the Peninsular War, when many of its buildings were stripped of their treasures. It was a stronghold of the Falangists (led by Onésimo Redondo) during and after the Civil War, and remains reactionary.

Among its natives (or Vallisoletanos) were Pánfilo de Narváez (1478–1529), explorer of Florida and the lower Mississippi; Hernando de Acuña (1520–80), the soldier-poet; the artists Juan Pantoja de la Cruz (1553–1608) and Antonio de Pereda (1611–78); Anne of Austria (1601–66), wife of Louis XIII of France; Valentín Llanos Gutiérrez (1795–1885; author of novels written in England where he was exiled and married Fanny Keats); José Zorrilla (1817–93), the poet and playwright; and the poet—also long exiled—Jorge Guillén (1893–1984). Catherine of Lancaster, widow of Enrique III, died here in 1418; and Columbus in 1506.

Several roads converge on the riverside Paseo de Isabel la Católica or the Pl. de Zorrilla (with the Tourist Office) near its S end, adjacent to the Campo Grande.

From the N end of the Paseo take the C. de S. Quirce to the Pl. de la Trinidad past the *Pal. de los Condes de Benavente* (1518) and (left) massive *S. Nicolás* (from 1624, with early Churrigueresque fittings in its sacristy). Contemporary *S. Quirce* contains late 17C retablos. Some distance to the N is the *Conv. de Sta. Teresa*, founded by the saint in 1569, with a retablo by Cristóbal Velázquez and sculptures by Gregorio Fernández. The C. de Exposito leads S from the Pl. de la Trinidad (formerly at the centre of the *Judería*), passing near (right) the *Conv. de Sta. Catalina*, mainly 16C, where Juan de Juni (1507–77) is buried. It contains a Christ by Juni and another by Gregorio Fernández. Beyond is *S. Agustin* (founded 1407; altered by Diego de

Praves in 1625). Continue along the C. de Exposito to approach the **Casa de Fabio Nelli**.

Named after its owner (died c 1612), a Maecenas of Valladolid, the imposing late 16C building now houses a museum containing archaeological collections; Oriental textiles from the tomb of Alfonso (son of Sancho IV); panels from the retablo of S. Benito el Real (c 1420); Renaissance tiles from the Palace; and early 14C wall paintings from S. Pablo, Peñafiel.

Opposite are the *Pal. Valverde* (1503; altered 1763) and the old *Casa Fernández de Muras. S. Miguel*, designed by Diego de Praves, contains sculptures by Gregorio Fernández.—Turning NE along the C. Fabio Nelli, we pass the *Conv. de las Brigadas* (1637–95) with remains of the *Pal. de Butrón* (c 1570). Turn right on regaining the C. S. Quirce to approach the Pl. de S. Pablo, passing (right) the mid 16C *Palacio Real*, bought in 1600 by the Card.-Duke of Lerma, who sold it to Felipe III. It was briefly Napoleon's residence in 1809. The galleries of the patio are adorned with the busts of Roman emperors and the arms of Spanish provinces.

Opposite is the imposing façade of ***S. Pablo**, partly rebuilt by Juan

The West Front of S. Pablo, Valladolid

de Torquemada (1463) and altered by Lerma, whose arms are seen on the upper part, above the Gothic portal of 1492. The interior, restored since it was ruined by the French in 1809, contains tombs by Berruguete and Leoni, and two handsome transeptal doorways, transitional between Gothic and Plateresque.

For the *Casa del Marqués de Villena*, opposite its S side, see below.

To the NE of S. Pablo is the *Colegio de S. Gregorio, completed in 1496. Its splendid entrance façade, rich in heraldic ornament, has an elaborate portal flanked by *maceros* or mace-bearing wild hairy men, surmounted by an armorial tree. In the first court is a window with stucco decoration in the Moorish style; in the second is a rich Plateresque gallery surmounted by a frieze bearing the ox yoke and arrows of the Catholic Kings.

It now houses the *Museo Nacional de Escultura Religiosa, an important collection of cloyingly realistic 13–18C Castilian sculpture formed after the sequestration of church property in the late 1820s.

Among the more remarkable objects are remains of the colossal retablo carved by Alonso Berruguete in 1532 for S. Benito el Real, and other fragmentary retablos for the same church, and also stalls by Andrés de Nájera with details by Diego de Siloé and Guillén de Holanda; a Pietà by Gregorio Fernández (1617), and also his Magdalen, Baptism, Sta. Teresa (1627), a recumbent Christ, St. Peter enthroned, and his portrait by Diego Valentín Díaz; Pompeo Leoni, fragments of a retablo from S. Diego (1665); Juan de Juni, Entombment, reliquary bust of Sta. Ana, St. Anthony of Padua, the Baptist; attributed to Jorge Inglés, Retablo of St. Jerome; Nuño Gonçalves, Apostles; Alonso de Villabrille, Head of S. Pedro (1707), and bust of Mariana de Jesús; late 15C Flemish retablos from the Conv. de S. Francisco; and numerous other minor works. In the garden are re-erected arches from the Romanesque cloister of S. Agustín.

To the left of the entrance is the *Chapel* (1488; by Juan Güas), with fine lierne vaults and carved bosses. It contains a Renaissance retablo (coarsely retouched) carved by Berruguete in 1526 for the monastery of La Mejorada (Olmedo), and his first recorded sculpture. The kneeling gilt bronze statues are by Juan de Arfe after Pompeo Leoni (1608). Also notable are a Crucifixion by Antonio Moro; the Tomb of Bp Diego de Avellaneda by Felipe Vigarni; Death, once attributed to Gaspar Becerra, but probably not Spanish (in the antechapel); an Annunciation (1596) by Gregorio Martínez; and colossal statues of Sta. Mónica and Sta. Clara de Montefalco (17C). In the raised choir are Baroque stalls from S. Francisco.

Further along the street is the *Casa del Sol*, with a doorway of 1540, once the residence of the Conde de Gondomar, ambassador to the court of James I; and *S. Benito el Viejo* (1599).

To the NE is the *Conv. de Sta. Clara* (1495; its church interior transformed in 1747). To the E is the *Audiencia* (mainly 1562, with a late 15C patio), on the site of the Palace of the Viveros, where Fernando and Isabel were married in October 1469.—A few steps NE of the Audiencia is *S. Pedro*, by Rodrigo Gil de Hontañón; opposite the Audiencia is the early 17C *Conv. de Descalzas Franciscas*.

From the *Casa del Marqués de Villena* (see above; a mid 16C mansion with an Ionic patio) the C. de las Angustias leads SE, passing (right) a house on the SE corner of the Pl. de S. Pablo of c 1500 in which Felipe II was born. It provides a view (in a side street to the left) of the early 13C tower of *S. Martín*; the church contains a retablo of 1672, a group by Gregorio Fernández, and a Pietà by Juan

Detail of the portal of S. Gregorio, Valladolid

de Juni (in the sacristy). The neighbouring *Hosp. de Esgueva* preserves a polychrome Mudéjar ceiling.

Further on, opposite the *Teatro Calderón*, is *N.S. de las Angustias* (1604; by Juan de Nates, a pupil of Herrera), with an Annunciation over the high altar by Cristóbal Velázquez, and the theatrical 'Virgen de los Cuchillos' by Juan de Juni, so-called from the seven knives (symbolising the Seven Sorrows) which pierce her breast. Other sculptures are by Gregorio Fernández, and the statues on the front are by Francisco del Rincón.

Behind the theatre is the *Pal. Arzobispal*, formerly the mid 16C *Casa de Villasantes*. A few steps to the W is *La Vera Cruz*, begun in 1595 by Diego de Praves and altered in the 1670s. It contains a Descent from the Cross and Dolorosa by Gregorio Fernández, and a Christ at the Column in a Baroque retablo of 1693 by Alonso Manzano.

A short distance E of the theatre stands early 14C Gothic **Sta. Maria la Antigua**, with three parallel apses and early 13C campanile,

Lombard in form, but with northern mouldings. The retablo mayor is an exaggerated work by Juan de Juni (1556). To the N is the restored Romanesque cloister.

From behind the church, the C. de Don Juan Membrillo, containing several old mansions, leads E, and bearing left we approach *La Magdalena* (1566; designed by Rodrigo Gil de Hontañón), with a huge coat of arms on its façade, and containing a retablo by Esteban Jordán.—Further E is the *Conv. de las Huelgas*, its church of 1579–1600 containing the late 14C tomb of María de Molina (died 1321; wife of Sancho IV of Castile), and a retablo by Gregorio Fernández.

The C. de Colón, with the restored *Casa de Colón* (Columbus) containing an apology for a museum, leads S from La Magdalena. It passes (right; in the C. Card. Mendoza) the restored **Colegio de Sta. Cruz**, begun in 1487 in the Gothic style and completed in 1491 in the Plateresque style by Lorenzo Vázquez, the earliest Renaissance work in Spain. The windows of 1768 are insertions by Ventura Rodríguez. A group of the founder, Card. Pedro González de Mendoza, surmounts the entrance, beneath which is a chapel containing the Cristo de la Luz by Gregorio Fernández and a Mater Dolorosa by Pedro de Mena.

SE is *S. Juan*, with Baroque retablos. In the nearby C. Don Sancho Huelgas is the red brick **Colegio de los Ingleses**, founded by Sir Francis Englefield, who fled to Spain in 1559 where he died c 1596. At the instance of the Jesuit Robert Parsons, it was endowed with many privileges by Felipe II in 1590 as a seminary for English priests who were to re-convert their country. Its cloisters were built in 1614, but most of the edifice dates from 1680.

From the Pl. de Sta. Cruz, adjacent to the Colegio de Sta. Cruz, we turn N, passing the 17C *University*, with a façade by Narciso and Diego Tomé (1715). It attained its greatest influence in the 16–18Cs, although founded in the mid 14C.

To the W rises the **Cathedral**, begun in 1580, but probably not designed by Juan de Herrera, as previously assumed. It was left unfinished at the death of Felipe II in 1598. The exterior was unsuccessfully remodelled by Alberto Churriguera in 1729. Of the four projected towers the only one completed fell in 1841 and was rebuilt in 1880–85.

In the austere interior are some inlaid stalls, designed by Herrera for the Conv. de S. Pablo; the tomb of Count Pedro Ansúrez (died 1119); and a Transfiguration by Luca Giordano. The Retablo mayor is by Juan de Juni (1551). In the sacristy is a silver *Custodia* of 1590, the masterpiece of Juan de Arfe.—In the gardens are relics of 12–14C Sta. María la Mayor.

A short distance to the SW, beyond the Pl. de Fuente Dorada, is the **Plaza Mayor**, rebuilt after a fire in 1561 (which also destroyed an area to the NE), and the former site of spectacles, executions, and bull fights. Here in 1521 Charles V formally pardoned the Comuneros, and in 1559 Felipe II held the first of several *autos de fe*. In 1452 Ávaro de Luna, minister of Juan II, was beheaded in the Ochavo, NE of the *Ayuntamiento*.

George Borrow put up at the *Caballo de Troya* inn (remodelled) in the C. de Correos, NW of the Ayuntamiento.—A short distance further N is the *Conv. de S. Benito*, founded in 1389, with a cloister of c 1600; the Church of 1504 has a porch of 1572 by Rodrigo Gil de Hontañón. Opposite is the 16C *Casa Alonso Berruguete*. Close by is the *Conv. de Sta. Isabel*, its mid 16C church with Gothic vaulting and a retablo by Juan de Juni.

From the Pl. de Fuente Dorada, the C. de Teresa Gil leads S near (left) *S. Felipe Neri* (1658–75) and *El Salvador* (completed 1576), with a brick tower of 1618. Further along are the *Conv. de la Concepción* (1521), the 15C *Casa de las Aldabas*, birthplace in 1425 of Enrique IV of Castile, and the *Conv. de Porta Coeli* (1598–1614).

The C. del Salvador leads SE from the church to the **Colegio de los Escoceses**, founded at Madrid by Colonel William Semple in 1627 and transferred here in 1771. Of the original buildings only the Baroque façade survived a fire in 1929. Beyond it stands *La Gran Promesa* (built in the early 17C as the church of the Colegio de S. Ambrosio), containing altarpieces by Berruguete and a Christ by Esteban Jordán.—A short distance S is *S. Andrés*.

At the S end of the C. de Teresa Gil is the Pl. de España, from which the C. Miguel Iscar leads W across the site of the former *Morería* past the *Conv. de Capuchinos*. On the left, beyond a garden is the *Casa de Cervantes*, occupied by the author of 'Don Quixote' in 1605 (the year of publication of the first part, in Madrid). Adjacent is a rebuilt fragment of the *Hospicio de la Resurrección*, mentioned by Cervantes.

The *Pl. de Zorrilla* is soon reached, at the N apex of the CAMPO GRANDE, an extensive park within which are re-erected remains of the 12C cloister of the Templars of Ceinos de Campos. On the S side are the *Conv. de las Lauras* with a chapel of 1606; the *Conv. de S. Juan Letrán*, a Baroque work of 1675–1739; and, further W, the *Colegio de Agustinos* (1759; by Ventura Rodríguez), with the *Museum of the Philippine Mission*, an interesting collection of Oriental art and ceramics.

To the SW of the Pl. de Zorrilla are the *Colegio de Niñas Huérfanas* (1629) and adjacent *S. Ildefonso* (1618), and the *Conv. de Sancti Spiritus* (1520), with a retablo mayor by Esteban Jordán. Both Juan de Juni and Gregorio Fernández lived and died (in 1586 and 1636 respectively) in the C. Gregorio Fernández, leading W from the Campo Grande.

The C. de Santiago leads N from the Pl. de Zorrilla to the Pl. Mayor, passing the *Colegio de Dominicanas Francesas*, with a patio of 1506–47 and church of 1730, and *Santiago* (1490–1505), with a good tower, and a retablo by Berruguete.

To the W of the Pl. Mayor is Baroque *La Pasión* (1671), restored to house a *Museum of Sacred Art*. Beyond is the *Conv. de Sta. Ana*, a Neo-Classical rebuilding of 1780 by Francisco Sabatini, its church containing three religious paintings by Goya. Near by is *S. Lorenzo* (1512; altered 1621).

The Pl. del Poniente to the N abuts the Paseo Isabel la Católica.

At *Fuensaldaña*, 8.5km N, is a fine 15C castle retaining a 13C gateway.

B.   Via Villacastín

190km (118 miles). N403. 43km *Olmedo*—41km. NVI—25km *Villacastín*—22km *S. Rafael*—2km. A6—57km **Madrid**.

Maps: M 442.

The A6 motorway may be entered c 39km beyond Olmedo, at *Villacastín*, or just N of *S. Rafael*. The A6, the recommended road, especially in winter, pierces the Guadarrama range below the NVI, which climbs over the *Puerto de los Leones*.—The first exit on the far side of the sierra provides a convenient approach to the *Escorial* (9km S) for travellers wishing to visit it on the way to Madrid.

The N403 drives due S, at 11km crossing the Duero, and later its tributaries the Cega and Eresma. It passes through a district of flat-topped hills to approach (32km) **Olmedo**, bypassed, an old walled town once of importance. It gave its name to Lope de Vega's tragedy, 'El Caballero de Olmedo' (1641).

It was in the *venta* here that Gautier was so astonished to see a handsome girl suckling a puppy. She was a Pasiega (from the valley of the Río Pas, S of Santander) going to Madrid, as did many women from this region, to take up a situation as a wet nurse, and was afraid that her supply of milk might otherwise run dry.

Protruding from the remaining town *Walls*, best seen to the SW, skirting the Medina del Campo road, is 13C *S. Miguel*, built over a crypt, and with painted ceilings. Mudéjar *S. Andrés* has a restored retablo, the first important work by Alonso Berruguete (1514). *Sta. María* preserves remains of a Romanesque door and a curious reliquary retablo of 49 compartments. To the NW is the *Conv. de la Mejorada*, with a derelict late 15C Mudéjar chapel.

At *Iscar*, 16km NE, are a castle keep and Mudéjar brick church.

OLMEDO TO SEGOVIA VIA COCA (72km). A by-road leads SE to (20km) **Coca**, ancient *Cauca*, an Iberian town sacked by the Romans in 180 after a characteristically obstinate siege. The *Arco de la Villa* is the main relic of its medieval walls. The imposing *Castle* (restored) of *mampostería* and pink brick, with a typical cluster of bartizan turrets and defended by a deep dry moat, dates from the early 15C and belonged to the Fonseca family, dukes of Alba. It now houses a Forestry Commission School. *Sta. María*, with a 14-sided sanctuary, contains the 16C tomb of Bp Juan Rodríguez de Fonseca by Bartolomé Ordóñez.—20.5km **Sta. María la Real de Nieva** is named after its convent founded by Catherine of Lancaster in 1393. In the Gothic cloister Enrique IV convened the Cortes in 1473 when he rescinded the popular privileges granted during the previous ten years.—The C605 continues SE, at 4km passing a road to *Paradinas*, with a late Gothic hall-church.—At 22km the road forks, both leading to **Segovia**: the left approaches the Sanctuary of Fuencisla below the prow of the Alcázar; the right meets the N110 from Ávila, which enters the town from the W: see Rte 25C.

8km *Almenara de Adeja* lies to the right, where a Roman villa with mosaics has been excavated.—At 8km *Arévalo* is 12km SW; see Rte 21A.—18km *Martín Muñoz de las Posadas*, bypassed, has a palace of 1572 by J.B. de Toledo. It was built for the inquisitor Diego de Espinosa, whose tomb is in the church. At 2km the N403 turns right for **Ávila** (see Rte 23), 37km S, later passing through a district strewn with granite boulders.

The A6 motorway may be joined soon after this turning, and we meet the NVI, running parallel to it.—9km *Sanchidrián*, bypassed, has a church by Juan de Herrera.—At 20km the N110 from **Segovia** (37km NE) to **Ávila** (27km SW) is crossed; see Rte 16.—*Villacastín* has an *Ayuntamiento* of 1687, while *S. Esteban* is an imposing hall-church begun in 1529, containing a fine retablo mayor, interesting tombs, and a 16C organ. The motorway may be joined here as our route approaches the SIERRA DE GUADARRAMA, or just N of the old summer resort of *S. Rafael*, 22km beyond.

For the road and motorway from this point to Madrid see Rte 21A; for **Madrid** itself, Rte 40.

C. Via Segovia

195km (121 miles). N601. 50km *Cuéllar*—60km **Segovia**—N603.
28km—A6. 57km **Madrid**.

Maps: M 442.

The road leads S and then veers SE across the Duero, at 23km
passing the castle keep of *Portillo* (14–15C), to approach (27km)
Cuéllar (9050 inhab.), a shrunken town still dominated by its late
15C *Castle* (partly restored), with a courtyard of 1558. Some town
walls survive. Romanesque *S. Esteban* has a brick apse with
decorative arcading and contains Mudéjar tombs; *S. Martín* is
likewise Mudéjar Romanesque; and *S. Andrés* and the *Hosp. de
María Magdalena* retain features of interest. It was the birthplace of
Diego Velázquez de Cuéllar (1461/6–1524), the *conquistador*.

We turn S through pine woods, once much more extensive, and
cross the Cega, with a wide view of the SIERRA DE GUADARRAMA as
we approach it.—33km *Carbonero el Mayor*, where *S. Juan Bautista*
contains a retablo by disciples of Ambrosius Benson.

At 19km a right fork leads through *Zamarramala* to approach Segovia via the
Templar church of *La Vera Cruz*, with a fine view of the *Alcázar* commanding it;
see p 206. At Zamarramala itself is a mute 18C organ. All its pewter pipes were
removed in one hour in October 1978—the scandalous end of too many such
instruments 'conserved' by the ecclesiastical authorities.

The main road provides a panoramic view of **Segovia** from the NE as
we descend into the valley of the Eresma past the Parador (to the left)
to approach the Aqueduct; see Rte 25C.

For the road to **Madrid** via the *Guadarrama tunnel* see Rte 25A; for that via *La
Granja* and the *Puerto de Navacerrada* see Rte 25B: both in reverse.

12 Burgos to Madrid via Aranda

Total distance, 239km (148 miles). N1. 39km *Lerma*—44km
Aranda—40km *Boceguillas*—18km *Sto. Tomé del Puerto*—7km
Somosierra—91km **Madrid**.

Maps: M 441.

Some stretches of the N1, the main approach from the French border to Madrid,
have been improved in recent decades, but the road is still far from the standard
one might expect. Further improvements are promised and work is progressing.

The road climbs due S from Burgos to a height of 958m before
descending to a junction at 9.5km. For the left fork to *Soria* see Rte
13, in which the detours to *Covarrubias* and *Sto. Domingo de Silos*
are described. These places may as conveniently be visited from this
route, regaining the N1 at Aranda.

The N1 traverses the dull rolling plateau of Castile, with occasional
distant views of the SIERRA DE LA DEMANDA to the E, to approach
(29km) **Lerma**, an old town overlooking the Arlanza. Passing through
a gateway one may enter the old enceinte and ascend to the huge
Palace of the Dukes of Lerma, with its four corner towers. It was built
by Francisco de Mora in 1617 for the Card.-Duke of Lerma (c 1550–
1625) a favourite of Felipe III; in September 1804 it was visited by
Lady Holland. Sacked by the French during the Peninsular War, it is

now little more than tenements. It is connected by a covered walk to the *Colegiata de S. Pedro*, a hall-church of 1570–1616 containing the impressive bronze *Monument* (1603) to Abp Cristóbal de Rojas y Sandoval (Lerma's uncle), completed by Lesmes Fernández de Moral in the style of Pompeo Leoni.

Here in January 1722, in the presence of the Duc de Saint-Simon, took place the marriage of the 12-year-old Louise Elisabeth d'Orléans and the young Prince of Asturias (1707–24). As Luis I he reigned for eight months before dying of smallpox. Saint-Simon, who also caught smallpox, stayed at the priest's house at *Villalmanzo*, to the NE of Lerma. He was attended by John Higgens, an Irishman, and the King's doctor from 1717–29.

Continuing S, the road at 31km bypasses (left) *Gumiel de Hizán*, where what was a fine organ has been destroyed by restorers of the church, and its pipes stolen.—We descend into the valley of the Duero to enter (12km) **Aranda de Duero** (27,850 inhab.), also bypassed to the W, a growing town of little interest except for the church of *Sta. María*. Its restored *S Front* is an impressive work by Simón de Colonia, and bears the insignia of Fernando and Isabel. The interior, of unusual splendour, contains a pulpit attributed to Juan de Juni and a carved 14C font. *S. Juan*, to the W, has a good W tower and a S Doorway of eight recessed orders (c 1400).

At Aranda in 1518 Charles V, on his first visit to Spain, en route between Valladolid and Zaragoza, first met his younger brother Ferdinand of Austria. Ferdinand was on his way out of the country, never to return.

For *El Burgo de Osma*, 58km E, see Rte 16. For *Peñaranda de Duero* (19.5km NE) and the Duero valley from El Burgo to **Valladolid** see Rte 17.

ARANDA TO SEGOVIA VIA TURÉGANO (105km). The C603 turns right off the N1 just S of Aranda and bears SW.—At 31.5km the Cistercian abbey of *Sacramenia* (c 1200) lies c 7km NW; its 13–15C cloister was acquired by William Randolph Hearst in 1925 and later rebuilt at Miami beach.—*Fuentidueña*, 10km W of this turning, is dominated by a ruined castle and restored Romanesque church. It retains a ruinous medieval gate. The church of *S. Martín* has been removed to New York.—The Duratón is crossed at 7.5km and we turn S through pine woods to (16km) *Cantalejo*. (The Romanesque priory of *S. Frutos* of c 1100, enlarged a century later, dramatically sited above a loop of the Duratón some 18km NE, may be reached from here over rough by-roads.)—16km *Turégano*, with a Romanesque church and 15C *Castle* founded by Fernán González in the 10C. In the castle moat is the 13C church of *S. Miguel*.—At *Aguilafuente*, 12km NW, is a restored brick Romanesque church and a castle. 2km S of Aguilafuente, on the site of a Roman villa, an extensive Visigothic necropolis has been discovered.—The C603 circles to the W, at 24.5km meeting the N601 9.5km from **Segovia**; see Rte 25C.

From Aranda the N1 continues S across rolling hills, providing panoramic views as it approaches the barrier range of the SIERRA DE GUADARRAMA, rising to 2273m to the SE, and further SW to 2209m.— 40km *Boceguillas*.

BOCEGUILLAS TO SEGOVIA VIA SEPÚLVEDA AND PEDRAZA (70km). We turn right to approach (10km) spectacularly sited **Sepúlveda**, the ancient *Septempublica*. A characteristic small town in danger of being spoilt by uncontrolled building, it surmounts a craggy hill in a loop of the Duratón. It was seized by Fernán González in 940 and its *fueros* date from 1076. On 30 November 1808 Marshal Victor, while marching on Madrid, attacked the place. The 6000 Spaniards defending it fled in panic to Segovia. The *Arco de la Villa*, the last of the original seven town gates to survive, has been needlessly demolished to allow a freer flow of its slight traffic. At the W end of the Plaza stands the old *Ayuntamiento* (restored), from behind which steps ascend to *El Salvador*, dating from 1093, with a galleried portico (perhaps the earliest of its type) and a detached belfry. Beyond is *N.S. de la Peña*, with a Romanesque tympanum and tower begun in 1144. Among other churches are Romanesque *S. Bartolomé*; *S. Justo*, with a Mudéjar artesonado and 12C carvings in its crypt; and ruined

Santiago, with a brick apse and later S door.—The road shortly climbs steeply. We turn sharp left, with an extensive view towards the sierra, at 11.5km passing (left) the castle of *Castilnovo*, of Moorish foundation but largely rebuilt in the 15C.—At 13km ***Pedraza de la Sierra**, well-sited on a rocky outcrop, is 2km to the left. Entered by a fortified gateway and with a *Plaza* of great character, it is a picturesque partly walled village of some charm, but in danger of over exploitation. The *Castle* of the Condestable de Velasco, in which the sons of François I were held hostage after Pavia (with Ronsard's father as their majordomo), was acquired in the 1920s by Ignacio Zuloaga, the artist. Romanesque *S. Juan* retains a good, but tastelessly restored, tower; Romanesque *Sta. Maria*, in ruins, preserves what may be an arcade of brick horseshoe Mudéjar arches (? lacking their pillars). *N.S. del Carrascal*, in the valley below, also in ruins, has a derelict aqueduct near by.—Regaining the main road, at 5km Romanesque *N.S. de las Vegas* is passed, before we reach (5.5km) the N110. The ruined priory of *Sta. Maria de la Sierra* (c 1200) is to the left on approaching (right at 6km) *Sotosalbos*, with a fine Romanesque church.—19km **Segovia**; see Rte 25C.

At 18km (*Sto. Tomé del Puerto*) we reach the N110 turning SW direct to Segovia (see Rte 16) and shortly start the 7km climb by an improved road to the *Puerto de Somosierra* (1404m). This was the scene of the charge of Polish lancers on 1 December 1808 of whom some 57 were killed or wounded, when a force of c 12,000 Spanish troops defending the pass was scattered, allowing Napoleon and his army to enter Madrid a few days later.

The undulating road soon descends into the Lozoya valley and (17km) **Buitrago**, an ancient walled and now reservoir-moated village. Its 14C castle, altered in the 15C by the Marqués de Santillana, shows Mudéjar features as does the 15C church and brick-built *Hospital*.

The N1 again climbs. Off it at 6km the C604 leads right to (27km) *El Paular*; see Rte 25B.—3km *Lozoyuela*, bypassed.

The C100 forks left here through *El Berrueco* (N of which is the castle of *Mirabel*, overlooking a reservoir) and climbs across a mountain spur to (12km) **Torrelaguna**, Roman *Barnacis*, with relics of Moorish walls, a Gothic *Ayuntamiento*, and a *Pósito* (granary) of 1495. It was the birthplace of Card. Cisneros (1436–1517).—In a stalactite cave at *Patones*, to the NE, are Aurignacian carvings.—At *Uceda*, 8km E, is the ruinous mid 13C church of the *Virgen de la Varga*.—The C100 continues S, crossing the Jarama, to (10.5km) *Talamanca*, with a fine Roman *Bridge* (to the NW), relics of walls, a medieval church, and a Romanesque church with a brick apse.—The road drives due S past *Valdetorres*, with a late Gothic church (1625). The N1 can be rejoined 42km S of the detour by forking right after 6km.

The main road, climbing through a district of granite boulders, traverses *La Cabrera* after 7km. W of La Cabrera are the ruined *Conv. de S. Antonio.*—18km *El Molar*, with a 13C church.—At 24km we skirt *S. Sebastián de los Reyes* and adjacent *Alcobendas*. These are now scruffy dormitory suburbs of Madrid, which soon presents itself as it did to Michael Quin, who entered it from this direction 165 years ago, 'standing almost, like Palmyra, in the midst of a desert . . . no shady groves, no avenues, no country seats, bespoke the approach of a great capital'.

The N1 soon veers off to the right and turns S to join the N end of the Paseo de la Castellana, the main N–S thoroughfare of Madrid. The M30 or Av. de la Paz continues ahead to bypass the centre of the city, and a sharp lookout is necessary to follow directional signs. For **Madrid** see Rte 40.

13 Burgos to Soria

141km (87 miles). N1. 9.5km—N234. 33.5km. *Hortigüela.*
Covarrubias is 13km W.—12km *Salas de los Infantes.*—4.5km. **Sto. Domingo de Silos** is 13km W.—24.5km *Leonardo de Yagüe*—57km **Soria**.

Maps: M 442.

We follow the N1 S, at 9.5km forking left at *Sarracin*, close to the Italianate *Pal. de Saldañuela* (1530), incorporating a medieval tower, and the castle of *Olmos Albos*.

After c 11km, some 2km beyond *Hontoria de la Cantera*, an unmarked track to the left leads 3km to the ruined monastery of *S. Quirce*, with carved panels and Romanesque capitals in its interior.

8.5km *Cuevas de S. Clemente*, from which a minor road leads 12km to *Covarrubias*, but another approach 14km further SE is more interesting.—The road crosses the SIERRA DE LAS MAMBLAS (1374m) at the *Mazariegos pass* (1060m) and at 7km passes a left turn for (3.5km) **Quintanilla de las Viñas** (where the guide and key are collected) and the important Visigothic chapel of *N.S. de las Viñas*, not far beyond the village.

Only a square apse and transepts remain of what was once a three-naved building blending Asturian and Mozarabic styles, which may date from as early as the 7C. Certain carved stones, dated from the early 10C, are possibly from repairs taking place at that period. Of particular interest are the horizontal bands of carving on the exterior and the horseshoe arch of the sanctuary, its imposts resting on Roman columns and carved with angels supporting the sun and moon. Other Visigothic reliefs are also preserved here.—Further E on a height are the remains of a Celtiberian settlement. To the SE are ruins of a castle of Fernán González. Near *Campolara* are the relics of an Ibero-Roman city. Another Celtiberian fortress has been discovered to the W of the main road, to which we return and turn left.

7km *Hortigüela*. The much recommended DETOUR to Covarrubias and Sto. Domingo de Silos may conveniently be made from here, adding 26.5km to the route. The C110 leads W along the beautiful valley of the Arlanza, shortly passing the extensive and impressive ruins of the monastery of *S. Pedro de Arlanza*, the original resting place of Fernán González (died 970; see below). It was begun in 1080, but largely rebuilt in the 15C. The fortified tower is well preserved; note the shields high up at each corner. (There was a project to remove carvings and parts of the building to a higher site, with the construction of a reservoir further E.) Continuing up the valley, **Covarrubias** is entered. The attractive if somewhat over-restored village has remains of walls, a gatehouse of 1575, and an unusual 10C *Tower, with considerable batter. The *Colegiata* (14–15C) contains several well-carved tombs, among them those of Fernán González (to the left of the high altar), moved here from S. Pedro de Arlanza in 1841, and of his wife, opposite; also that of Christina of Norway (died 1262), who had been married for four years to Felipe, son of Fernando III. The beautiful 17C organ, containing some wooden pipes, has been restored. The Cloister is 16C. In the museum is a painted and carved triptych attributed to Gil de Siloé, what is thought to be an old Flemish copy of a lost Virgin and Child by Van Eyck, MSS and Vestments. 15C *Sto. Tomás*, restored, stands to the N of the village.

The BU903 leads S. At 11.5km turn left past *Santibáñez del Val* (near which are two 10C or 11C chapels, one, *Sta. Cecilia*, with a melon-domed sanctuary) to (7km) the village and monastery of **Sto. Domingo de Silos** (re-occupied since 1880 by Benedictines from Solesmes). It is famous for its beautiful two-storeyed cloister and for its school of Gregorian chant.

Founded at the beginning of the 10C, the former monastery of S. Sebastián had been sacked by the Moors, and its rebuilding was entrusted to Domingo, a monk from Cogolla. He remained there from 1041 until his death in 1073 and became its patron (not to be confused with Sto. Domingo de Guzmán; see below).

From the mid 18C church by Ventura Rodríguez we descend through a Romanesque doorway from its predecessor, and are escorted (do not be hurried) round the lower gallery of the *Cloister (c 1150), with its single secular cypress. The columns and capitals of varying and elaborate design (some worn) deserve close inspection, as do the corner pilasters decorated with reliefs recalling those at Moissac (N of Toulouse). Note also the 14C painted Mudéjar ceilings (in part restored). The upper storey was added in the late 12C. A vault at a lower level contains a *Museum*, with a painted Guzmán tomb, a Mozarabic silver chalice, ivory perfume cases, and a 12C copper retablo; also a rather nasty replica of the enamel frontal in the Burgos Museum. The old *Pharmacy* is of some interest.

STO. DOMINGO DE SILOS TO ARANDA (45km). From just W of Silos one may drive SW through an impressive gorge to (19km) *Caleruega*, birthplace of Sto. Domingo de Guzmán (1170–1221; founder of the Dominican Order), and down the valley of the Bañuelos to *Aranda*; see Rte 12.

Winding through a gorge to the E of Silos, at 13km the N234 is regained 4.5km S of *Salas de los Infantes*, itself only 12km SW of Hortigüela. A turning between the two leads 11km NE to *Vizcainos*. Both Vizcainos and adjacent *Jaramillo de la Fuente* preserve 12C churches.

Salas was famous for the legend of the Seven Infantes de Lara, killed by the Moors in 970. The tomb of their father, Gonzalo Bustos, is in the hall-church of *Sta. María* (1549). For the road from here to *Nájera*, see the sub-route on p 129, in reverse.

At 14km from Salas (or 9.5km from the Silos turning) the C111 climbs SW over the ridge of *El Cerro* (1130m) to (13km) *Huerta del Rey*, amid pine woods. About 7km beyond, to the right, are a rock-cut theatre at *Peñalba del Castro* and the extensive archaeological site of Roman *Clunia*. *Coruña del Conde*, further SW on the road to *Peñaranda de Duero* (see Rte 17), preserves a castle.

15km *S. Leonardo de Yagüe*, with a 16C castle. From here an attractive road with wide views leads S, climbing down to (19km) *Ucero* and, 15km beyond, *El Burgo de Osma*; see Rte 17.—The main road continues E through pine woods, with the SIERRA DE URBIÓN to the NW rising to 2229m, and crosses the *Puerto Mojón Pardo* (1234m) to approach (27km) *Abejar* (with a good 18C organ, the key of which is retained in Madrid!).—10km N is *Molinos de Duero*, with ancient houses. *Vinuesa*, 4km beyond, has several 18C mansions. (Molinos may also be approached by a direct road from Salas, which at *Duruelo*, c 16km NW of Molinos, passes only a few kilometres S of the source of the Duero.)—12km *Cidones*, S of which rises the *Peñón de Acenilla* (1433m) and the ridge extending E to the abrupt *Pico Frentes* (1380m).—At 13km a turning leads 2km to the Romanesque church of *La Mongia*, part of a ruined monastery.—We shortly meet the N122 and descend to **Soria**; see Rte 5.

Carving in the cloister at Sto. Domingo de Silos

14 Soria to Teruel

A. Via Calatayud and Daroca

230km (143 miles). N234. 91km **Calatayud**—41km **Daroca**—N330.
42km *Monreal del Campo*—56km **Teruel**.

Maps: M 442, 443.

Fork right 5km W of Soria, bearing SE across the high wind-swept
plateau, at 10km passing *Almenar de Soria* with its castle, to
approach (20km) the *Puerto Bigornia* (1100m), overshadowed to the
NE by the MONCAYO massif (2313m). The road then descends below
the SIERRA DE LA VIRGEN (rising to 1427m) parallel to the Rambla de
Ribota to bypass (32km) *Cervera de la Cañada*, where Gothic
Mudéjar *Sta. Tecla* was built by Mahoma Ramé in 1426.—*Aniñón*, to
the NE, has a characteristic Mudéjar church containing a good early
16C retablo.—5km *Torralba de Ribota* (left) has a church of the same
style as that at Cervera, begun in 1367.

A left turn on approaching Calatayud leads shortly to the site of Iberian *Bilbilis*,
later a Roman municipium. It was the birthplace of the poet Martial (AD 43–
104), who returned here to die after 35 years in Rome. It was the scene of a
victory by Metellus Pius over Quintus Sertorius in 73 BC. Its insignificant ruins
lie partly under a chapel on the *Cerro de Bámbola*.

CALATAYUD (17,650 inhab.), on the Jalón, is surrounded by
crumbling clay hills, some in the quarter called La Morería having
caves which are still populated.

It is probably of Moorish origin, being founded in the 8C by Ayub, a nephew of
Musa. Others claim that its former name may well have been *Qalat al-Yahud*,
castle of the Jews, and a Jewish tombstone dated 919 records their early
presence. Montaigne's mother, Antoinette de Loppes (López), was descended
from the Pazagon family, once prominent in the *Judería*, which lay between Sta.
María la Mayor and the W wall of the town.

Calatayud contains two collegiate churches: *Sto. Sepulcro*, to the NE,
once the Spanish headquarters of the Knights of St. John, was
founded in 1141 and rebuilt in 1613; *Sta. María la Mayor*, in the
centre, has a fine portal of 1528 and a lofty tower, octagonal in its
upper tiers. Several other churches have Mudéjar towers, including
late 15C *S. Andrés*; *S. Pedro Mártir*, with azulejos in its coro; and *S.
Martín*, with a charming patio. The *Conv. de Sto. Domingo*, E of the
town, has a three-storeyed patio, with part of the exterior enriched
with Mudéjar patterns.

Baltazar Gracián (1601–58), author of 'El Criticón' and other works, was born at
Belmonte de Calatayud, 12km SE.

For the road from Zaragoza to Madrid via Calatayud, and for the crossroad via
the *Monasterio de Piedra* to *Molina de Aragón*, see Rte 72.

The N234 leads SE up the valley of the Jiloca, thickly planted with
orchards, to (8km) *Maluenda*, with the important *Mudéjar church of
SS. Justa y Rufina* (c 1413) and *Sta. María*, with a Mudéjar tower and
rebuilt nave.—At (5km) *Morata de Jiloca*, to the right, 14C Mudéjar
S. Martín has unusual vaults. At 5km *Fuentes de Jiloca*, with a good
hall-church of 1580, is skirted, and the road later climbs to the *Puerto
de Villafeliche* (860m) to meet the N330 from Zaragoza on

approaching (23km) **Daroca**. For Daroca and for the road on to **Teruel**, 98km S, see Rte 73.

B. Via Almazán, Medinaceli and Molina de Aragón

256km (159 miles). N111. 35km *Almazán*—39km *Medinaceli* crossroads—NII. 15km.—N211. 60km *Molina de Aragón*—48km *Monreal del Campo*—1km. N234/330. 56km **Teruel**.

Maps: M 442, 443.

Driving due S, the road later traverses pine woods and crosses the *Alto de Lubia* (1080m) before entering the fortified town of **Almazán** (5750 inhab.) on the left bank of the Duero. Due to its position near the frontier of Aragón it played a vital role in the dynastic wars of the 14C. Together with several neighbouring fiefs, it was granted by Enrique de Trastámara to Bertrand Du Guesclin.

Passing the octagonal *Ermita de Jesús* (18C), we enter the town by the *Puerta de la Villa* which leads directly into the *Pl. Mayor*. Here is late 12C *S. Miguel*, with a remarkable *Mudéjar vault. Further W is the medieval *Pal. de Altamira*, with a Renaissance gallery overlooking the Duero. To the E is late Gothic *Sta. María*, not far from

Interior of the cupola of S. Miguel, Almazán

the twin-towered *Puerta de los Herreros*. In the centre is Renaissance *Santiago*. Other churches of interest are *S. Esteban* in the decayed SE quarter; *N.S. del Campanario*, further W, with the *Puerta del Mercado* beyond; and *S. Vicente*, to the NW.

For the roads SW to *Atienza* and *Sigüenza* see Rte 15.

Morón de Almazán (13.5km SE on the C116) has a plaza containing Renaissance mansions, dominated by the Plateresque tower (1540) of its church.

Continuing S, at 37km a right turn climbs to the former Moorish stronghold of **Medinaceli** (1201m). This is now a mere village perched above the Jalón valley, but it preserves several attractive old mansions. Of the Roman city of *Ocilis* there remains the 2nd or 3C *Triumphal Arch*, the only one with a triple archway to survive in Spain.

Almanzor, the scourge of the Christians, died here in 1002. After its reconquest in 1124 the family of La Cerda, dukes of Medinaceli, established themselves here, claiming Castile and León by right of descent from the Infantes de la Cerda, the sons of Alfonso X, 'el Sabio', who were dispossessed by their uncle, Sancho IV. Their imposing *Castle* still stands and the 16C church contains several of their tombs. The *Beaterio de S. Román* was formerly a synagogue.— For *Ambrona* see Rte 72.

Turn right on climbing down into the valley and follow the N11 (see p 435) across the *Puerto Esteras* (1138m). At 15km turn left onto the N211 for (22km) *Maranchón*, passing at *Aguilar de Anguita* the site of a Roman camp and prehistoric cemetery.

The castle and curtain wall of Molina de Aragón

21km SW is *Riba de Saelices*, with a Romanesque church door. N of Riba de Saelices is the *Cueva de los Casares* which contains prehistoric engravings.

38km **Molina de Aragón** is an ancient town incorporated with Castile in 1293 by the marriage of its lady, Doña Blanca, with Sancho IV. It preserves its 12–13C *Castle* with tall square towers and an extensive curtain wall, a medieval bridge, and notable churches: *S. Martín* is 12C, as are the ruins of *Sta. María del Conde*; *Sta. Clara* is Transitional; *S. Francisco* dates from 1284; while in *S. Gil* is the tomb of Doña Blanca.

12km *Castellar de la Muela* has a Churrigueresque church and a Romanesque chapel of interest.

At 11km a mountain road leads S through the SIERRA DE ALBARRACÍN to Albarracín via *Alustante*, with a fine church of 1400, and (37km) *Orihuela de Tremedal*, nestling among pine woods. The *Puerto Orihuela* (1650m) is crossed below the *Caimodorro* (1935m); to the E is the small spa of *Bronchales*; to the SW rise the MONTES UNIVERSALES (several peaks over 1800m), so-called from being the source of rivers which irrigate several parts of Spain, including the Tagus, the Turia, and tributaries of the Ebro. For (41km) *Albarracín* see Rte 73.

The N211 continues E across the SIERRA DE MENERA to enter the wide valley of the Jiloca and (25km) *Monreal del Campo*, founded in 1120 by Alfonso I of Aragón ('el Batallador') to keep in check the Moors of Daroca, who were not subdued until 1122.

The main road from Zaragoza to Teruel is met on the far bank of the river, where we turn S for (56km) **Teruel**; see Rte 73.

15   Soria to Guadalajara via Almazán and Atienza, for Madrid

170km (105 miles). N111. 35km Almazán—C101. 46km. Atienza lies 4km right—33km Jadraque—48km Guadalajara.

Maps: M 442.

This route follows the old road from Soria to Madrid, and is an alternative to the present main road via *Medinaceli*; see Rtes 14B and 72.

Follow the main road as far as *Almazán* (see Rte 14B), there turning SW across the high-lying *Altos de Barahona*, at 34km reaching crossroads.

The left turn leads to (25.5km) *Sigüenza* (see Rte 72), passing (right, after 18km) *Palazuelos*, with old walls and a 15C church. 2km beyond Palazuelos is the Romanesque church of *Carabias*.

12km. **Atienza** lies 4km to the right. The successor of Celtiberian *Tutia*, it is now a walled village dominated by castle ruins and containing seven medieval churches. Several were altered in the 16C, but many retain Romanesque features of interest.

A poor road leads W below the SIERRA DE PELA (1538m) to (57km) *Ayllón*, passing (14km) *Albendiego*, where the Romanesque church has remarkable windows of pierced stone and, later, *Campisábalos* and *Villacadima*, both with

Romanesque churches. A track to the right beyond Villacadima leads to *Tiermes*; see Rte 16.

The C101 bears S to (33km) *Jadraque*, with the 15C *Castle* of the Duque de Osuna, and a church containing alabaster tombs.—19.5km *Hita*, home of the archpriest Juan Ruiz (died 1353), the poet. It retains an old castle, a 12C gate, and the ruined monastery of *Sopetrán*.

At *Espinosa de Henares*, 11km N, the 16C church has an artesonado roof, and there are prehistoric and Roman remains near the chapel of *La Soledad*.—7km beyond is **Cogolludo**, with the Renaissance *Pal. de Medinaceli*, completed in the Florentine style in 1495, probably by Lorenzo Vázquez; also a 16C hall-church and ruined castle.—Some 13C W of Cogolludo is *Beleña de Sorbe*, with a 12C church, altered in the 16C. In the Henares valley to the S are the churches of *Mohernando*, with the tomb of the Eraso family, and, beyond, *Cerezo*, with an artesonado ceiling.

The N11 is met 22km S of Hita. Turn right there to approach **GUADALAJARA** (55,150 inhab.; 14,000 in 1920; 21,000 in 1960). Although it retains a few buildings of interest, it was severely damaged during the Civil War.

The 18C bridge over the Henares here has Roman foundations, but the Roman settlement of *Arriaca* has vanished. The Moorish town—*Wad-el-Hajarah* (river of stones)—was taken in 1085 by Álvar Fáñez de Minaya. During the 15–17Cs members of the house of Mendoza, Duques del Infantado, held their court here in almost royal state, and played the Maecenas. The third duke entertained François I (when a captive in Spain after Pavia); and in 1559 Felipe II and his third wife, Isabel de Valois, were married in the ducal chapel. In 1578 the historian Bernardino de Mendoza (c 1540–1604) was appointed ambassador to England. In the 18C Thomas Bevan from Melksham in Wiltshire, lured over from England with his fellow workers, was unable to revive the expiring manufacture of cloth here, a disastrous project initiated by Felipe V.

The most important monument is the splendid **Palacio del Infantado**, NW of the town centre. The Plateresque *Façade*, studded with bosses, has a portal crowned by a huge escutcheon supported by satyrs, lowered to its original position. Above the escutcheon is a row of Mudéjar windows. The *Patio* is effective, decorated with balustrades of twisted columns and the arms of the houses of Mendoza and Luna. Sacked by the French in 1809, and burnt out in 1937, the palace (begun in 1461 by Juan and Enrique Gūas, and completed in 1492)—thoroughly restored when not actually rebuilt—houses a singularly uninspired collection of paintings, mostly of religious subjects, perhaps the best of which is a S. Sebastián by Carreño.

Among churches, most of which have been rebuilt or restored, are *Santiago*, preserving 13–15C details; *S. Nicolás* (1691); *S. Gil*, partly 15C; *S. Esteban*; *S. Ginés*, containing mutilated Mendoza and Tendilla tombs; and *Sta. María de la Fuente* (15C), with a 13C Mudéjar tower. The former nunnery of *La Piedad* (1530), now the *Instituto*, contains a patio and staircase of interest. A mansion in the Pl. de Dávalos behind the Ayuntamiento retains a Renaissance patio and artesonado ceilings. The *Conv. de Carmelitas de Arriba* (1591) contains a Churrigueresque sacristy; the *Conv. de S. José* dates from 1615. In the crypt of 15C *S. Francisco* is the mausoleum of the Mendozas, whose 28 marble tombs (1696–1720) were rifled by the French in 1809.

For the road on to (21km) *Alcalá* and **Madrid**, 35km beyond, see Rte 72.

16   Soria to Plasencia via Segovia and Ávila

413km (256 miles). N122. 56km **El Burgo de Osma**—13km *S.
Esteban de Gormaz*—N110. 54km *Riaza*—74km **Segovia**—66km
Ávila—81km *El Barco de Ávila*—69km **Plasencia**.

Maps: M 442, 447.

This long but interesting route follows the N slope of the SIERRAS DE
GUADARRAMA, and DE GREDOS. It should not be attempted in winter
except in good weather.

For **Soria**, see Rte 5. The N122 leads SW, at c 29km passing (right)
Calatañazor, near where, according to tradition, Almanzor, the
scourge of Christian Spain, was finally defeated by the Leonese in
1002. The picturesque village retains walls and a ruined castle, and a
late Gothic church with Romanesque and earlier decoration and a
rare 16C organ.

27km **EL BURGO DE OSMA** (5050 inhab.) is a characteristic old
town with crumbling walls and arcaded streets. It has one of the
finest cathedrals in Spain for design and detail. Approaching the
cathedral, in the *Pl. Mayor* are the *Casas Consistoriales* of 1768 and
the *Hosp. de S. Agustín* with a façade of 1700. The C. Mayor runs S
past the 17C *Bishop's Palace*.

The *****Cathedral**, begun in 1232 to replace a church of 1110, was
completed by the end of the 13C; the Baroque *Tower* by *Domingo
Ondátegui* dates from 1744. The *S Portal*, enriched with statues of c
1300, is modelled on the Puerta del Sarmental at Burgos and is
probably by the same craftsmen.

The *Coro* contains stalls of 1589, and organ cases of 1641 (S) and 1787; the
Renaissance trascoro dates from c 1550 and the Gothic from c 1480. The reja of
the Cap. Mayor is by Juan Francés (1515) and the retablo by Juan de Juni and
Juan Picardo (1554). An ambulatory and E chapel were added in 1781 by Juan
de Villanueva. In the N Transept is the vaulted *Vestuario* (before 1281, beneath
the *Cap. de S. Pedro de Osma* of 1530–47), from which two Romanesque
windows opening onto the Cloister have been uncovered. The saint's *Tomb*, of
painted stone, is unique in its period (1258) for naturalistic treatment and
calculated lack of symmetry.

From the *Cloisters*, added in 1500–23, the *Museo* is entered. It contains a
panel attributed to Nicolás Francés, 16–18C vestments, and a piece of the
Persian silk shroud of the patron (1199); an illuminated Bible (13–14C), a 12C
Charter thought to be the earliest example in Castilian, and a copy of the
Apocalypse of Beatus of Liébana (1086). The *Sacristía mayor* (1780) and
Sacristía de Santiago (1551) contain good paintings; the former also preserves a
musical astronomical clock made in London.

S. Domingo de Guzmán (1170–1221), founder of the Dominican Order, took
orders as a canon regular in the cathedral chapter of Osma in 1194.

Beyond the W end of the cathedral a gate leads to the old bridge,
while the C. del Puente runs S to the *Carmelite Convent* (1607). From
the *Seminario* (1778) the C. del Marqués del Vadilla leads back to the
Soria road, on the far side of which is the former *University of Sta.
Catalina* (1555).

To the S are twin hills. One has a ruined castle; the other is the site of Roman
Uxama Argelae, which gave its name to the city.

16km due N lies *Ucero*, commanded by a well-preserved castle, and (3km
beyond) the picturesquely sited 12C Templar church of *S. Juan de Otero*, with
remains of the Templars' house.

The SO160 leads S and then SE to (15km) **Gormaz**, dominated by its huge

Moorish *Castle* (965; but altered in the 13–14Cs), with twin keeps and 21 other towers. It is well worth visiting for the views from its windswept walls. A road now climbs to the summit.—13km further E lies **Berlanga de Duero**, commanded by an impressive 15C *Castle* with a 13C curtain wall. The *Colegiata* is a notable hall-church of 1530 by Juan de Rasines. It contains good rejas and stalls and a Churrigueresque retablo.—7km beyond Berlanga is the curious 11C Mozarabic chapel of *S. Baudelio*, where horseshoe arches radiate from a central column to which a tribune with a gabled oratory is fixed. It retains the faded remains of 12C murals. (Some were until recently displayed in the Prado, Madrid, having been returned from the USA. They had found their way there in 1922, five years *after* the declaration of the chapel as a National Monument.)—The churches at *Caltojar* and *Bordecorex*, further SE, and *Andaluz* (dated 1114; 8km NE of Berlanga), have features of interest.

The N122 climbs W from El Burgo de Osma to cross the Duero by an ancient bridge of 16 arches at (13km) **S. Esteban de Gormaz**. The 12C churches of *S. Miguel* and *Del Rivero* both have exterior galleries. To the SW once stood the oak wood where the Infantes de Carrión are said (in the 'Cantar de mio Cid') to have abandoned their wives.—For the road W to *Aranda* see Rte 17.

A road forking left, immediately after the bridge, leads 35km S to **Tiermes** or *Termancia*, the extensive site of a partially excavated Iberian town, with its archaeological *Museum*. The main route may be regained near *Ayllón*, to the NW.

Turning right after crossing the Duero, the road later climbs out of a valley onto a plateau providing a panorama of the SIERRAS DE AYLLÓN and DE GUADARRAMA (further W) before descending to (36km) **Ayllón**, a partly walled village containing the *Contreras Palace* (1497), an irregular arcaded plaza, the church of *S. Miguel*, and the impressive ruins of *S. Juan*; those of the *Conv. de S. Francisco* lie to the NW.

16km NW is *Maderuelo*, on a ridge dominated by the church of *Sta. María*; *S. Miguel* is also basically Romanesque. A medieval bridge, sometimes submerged by the reservoir, leads to *La Vera Cruz*, from which Romanesque murals have been removed (and until recently displayed in the Prado, Madrid).

We shortly bypass *Sta. María de Riaza*, its church with a good artesonado ceiling, and continue SW to (20km) *Riaza*, a summer resort with a 16C church, 10km S of which is the winter sports development of *La Pinilla*.

At 11.5km the NI is met (see Rte 12). Turn left, then right after 5km, to skirt the N flank of the Guadarrama range.—At 15.5km a right fork leads 8km to *Pedraza de la Sierra*; see p 166.

At 22.5km, after passing (left) the ruined priory of *Sta. María de la Sierra*, we skirt (right) the village of *Sotosalbos*, with a fine Romanesque church.—After 8km a left-hand fork leads directly to (12km) *La Granja*; see Rte 25B.

The road shortly descends towards (11km) **Segovia** (see Rte 25C), with a good view of its *Aqueduct*, continuing ahead at the crossroads and bearing left towards (37km) *Villacastín*; see Rte 11B. On crossing the NVI and A6, a high-lying region of granite boulders is traversed, with a view S and SW towards the barrier ranges of the SIERRAS DE MALAGÓN and DE GREDOS, before descending to (29km) **Ávila**; see Rte 23.

The road circles to the right below the town walls, crosses the Adaja and turns left.

ÁVILA TO ARENAS DE S. PEDRO (80km). The C502 forks left 6km W of Ávila, shortly passing a turning to *Sotalvo*, with the 15C castle of *Aunquesospese*. At 16km it passes through *Solosancho*, in the plaza of which stands a carved granite boar from the remarkable fortifed site of *Ulaca*, 2km S.—We climb the *Puerto de Menga* (1566m) and cross the upper valley of the Alberche, at 28km reaching a right-hand turning (C500) for the *Parador de Gredos* (1580m), a centre for excursions into the sierra. The wild goats (*Capra Pyrenaica*) of this area have been saved from extinction.

Hoyos del Espino, some 18km W, in the upper valley of the Tormes, is the starting point for the easiest ascent of the CIRCO DE GREDOS, with *Almanzor* (2592m) further SW, the highest peak in the SIERRA DE GREDOS.—The road beyond Hoyos passes through or near several picturesque villages to regain the N110 at *El Barco de Ávila*, 36km W; see below.

The C502 climbs S to the *Puerto del Pico* (1352m), providing a magnificent *View SW, and zigzags steeply down the S flank of the range to **Mombeltrán**, crossing the often visible *Roman road* which climbed across the mountains here. *Mombeltrán castle* (1393), is ascribed to Juan Güas. Its *Hospital* is 16C. We later turn right to approach *Arenas de S. Pedro*; see Rte 49.—The C502, forking left, continues S, shortly crossing the Tiétar, to meet the NV 46km from Arenas and 7km W of *Talavera*; see Rte 50A.

The N110 leads W from Ávila along the narrowing valley of the Adaja, at 42km crossing the *Puerto de Villatoro* (1388m), with a view SW.—12km. *Bonilla de la Sierra*, c 5km N, has a 15C church covered by a pointed barrel vault of 16m span.—7km *Piedrahita*, with a former 18C palace of the Albas and a church with an 18C organ.

21km **El Barco de Ávila**, an old town with ruined walls, has a pleasant plaza, a late 15C castle (best seen from the bridge), an early 14C church with good rejas and 15C paintings, a Virgin by *Vigarni* and a relief by Vasco de la Zarza. Its 16C church contains an unrestored 18C organ with five rows of trumpets in 'chamade'.

EL BARCO TO BÉJAR (30km). The C500 climbs NW through attractive country, off which after c 4km a road forks right to *El Tejado*, beyond which are the extensive prehistoric ruins of *El Berrueco*, encircled by a wall.—Crossing the SIERRA DE CANDELARIO, we meet the N630 and turn left for *Béjar*; see Rte 27A.

Continuing SW from El Barco, at 17km we descend steeply from the *Puerto de Tornavacas* (1277m) into the long and narrow upper valley of the Jerte, and at 18km skirt the village of *Cabezuela del Valle*, with the *Panera* (1814m) rising to the S, and the *Camocho* (1826m) to the W, to approach (34km) **Plasencia**; see Rte 27A.

17 Soria to Valladolid via Aranda

204km (126 miles). N122. 56km **El Burgo de Osma**—13km *S. Esteban de Gormaz*—41km **Aranda de Duero**—40km *Peñafiel*—54km **Valladolid**.

Maps: M 442

For the road to (69km) *S. Esteban de Gormaz*, see Rte 16.

At *Berzosa*, 10km N, is a notable Romanesque church with an exterior gallery, characteristic of the region; and near *Alcubilla de Avellaneda*, c 22km NW, is the ruined monastery of *La Espeja*. The 16C church contains alabaster Avellaneda tombs.

A bypass has been constructed N of S. Esteban, which rejoins the main road just before a turning to *Rejas* (3km right) with two Romanesque churches.—17.5km *Langa de Duero* retains a medieval bridge, a castle keep, and a Gothic church. The Duero is crossed 8km further on at *La Vid*, with an Augustinian church begun in 1542.

An ALTERNATIVE road is that turning N before crossing the river to (7.5km) **Peñaranda de Duero**, dominated by a medieval square keep, and with a 15C carved stone pillory opposite its S Gate. Flanking the restored *Pl. Mayor* is the Renaissance *Pal. de los Condes de Miranda* (also restored), with Plateresque additions of c 1530 by Francisco de Colonia or Lorenzo Vazquez. The 17C *Pharmacy* may be visited. The *Colegiata* dates from 1732.—For *Coruña del Conde*, 12km NE, and *Clunia*; see p 169.

For **Aranda de Duero** see Rte 12.

The N122, cutting across a bend of the Duero, leads almost due W, off which a minor road skirts the river to (20km) *Roa de Duero*, above its right bank, with a large Plateresque *Colegiata* with remains of a Gothic porch and containing star-vaulting. Card. Cisneros, who had been twice regent, died here in November 1517 just before receiving his dismissal from Charles V; and here the guerrilla general Juan Martín Díaz ('El Empecinado'; 1775–1825) met his death.

Peñafiel (5200 inhab.) at the confluence of the Duratón with the Duero, is dominated by its remarkable *Castle*, built along an abrupt ridge flanked by ramparts dating from 1307, and with an imposing 15C keep. *S. Miguel* is ascribed to *Juan de Herrera*; *Sta. María* contains a 16C retablo; and the more interesting *Conv. de S. Pablo* (1324), Gothic Plateresque in style, retains an elaborate Mudéjar apse. The curious *Pl. del Coso*, to the S, surrounded by shuttered wooden loggias, should not be overlooked.

It is recommended to cross the river here and follow the far bank through (6.5km) *Pesquera de Duero* (15km N of which is the castle of *Encinas de Esqueva*), to approach **Valbuena de Duero**, with the partly restored Cistercian abbey of *Sta. María*, founded in 1190. It retains a splendid 13C and Renaissance cloister, and an impressive refectory with a pointed barrel vault.—Some 14km to the N is the derelict 15C castle of *Villafuerte*.

At *Olivares de Duero* return to the S bank to *Quintanilla de Onésimo*, with a star-vaulted 16C hall-church.—6km *Sardón de Duero*, near which is the Premonstratensian abbey of *Retuerta* (c 1200), with a notable chapterhouse.—The main road crosses the river after 11km to bypass (left) *Tudela de Duero*, with a hall-church of 1555, and shortly veers NW to approach **Valladolid**; see Rte 11A.

18 León

LEÓN (822m; 127,100 inhab.; 22,000 in 1920; 59,000 in 1950), former capital of the ancient kingdom, and now the thriving capital of its province, lies largely on the left bank of the Bernesga. Apart from its imposing cathedral, it preserves several other buildings to remind one of its medieval importance.

It derives its name from the Roman *Legio Septima*, the legion quartered here by Augustus to defend the plains from the forays of the Asturian highlanders. It resisted the Visigothic advance until 586, when it was taken by Leovigild; but although it fell to the Moors early in the 8C, León was recaptured by Ordoño I in 850, and Ordoño II (913–23) fixed his court here. In 996 it was assaulted and burned by Almanzor after a lengthy siege, but was recovered after the battle of Calatañazor (1002). Alfonso V rebuilt the walls in *tapia*, and assembled the Cortes here, and in 1037 Fernando I was crowned king of León and Castile in an earlier cathedral. The present walls were built by Alfonso XI in 1324, but after his death Pedro the Cruel removed the court to Sevilla, and León became a backwater, described as 'dull and decaying' by Ford in the 1830s.

Buenaventura Durruti (1896–1936), the anarchist, was born here.

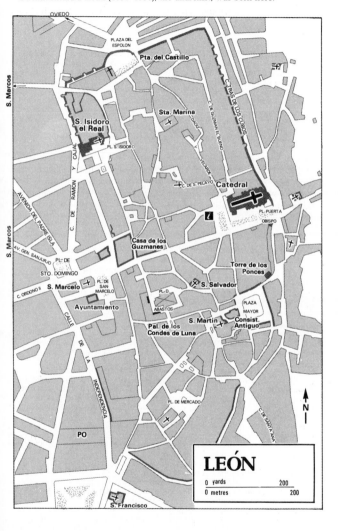

From the Glorieta de Guzmán el Bueno at a central point of the riverside *paseos*, the C. Ordoño II leads to the undistinguished Pl. de Sto. Domingo. To the right is *S. Marcelo* (founded in the 12C, but rebuilt in 1588–1625), containing sculptures by Gregorio Fernández. Behind it is the *Ayuntamiento* (1585), and almost opposite, the *Diputación* (1566; by Rodrigo Gil de Hontañón), formerly the *Casa de los Guzmanes*, with noteworthy patio and grilles. Behind it is the 16C

Pal. of the Marqués de Villasinta, and adjacent, the *Casa de Botines* (by Gaudí; 1894).

Continuing E, we shortly enter the Pl. de Regla, dominated by the *Cathedral, a remarkable example of the best type of French Gothic construction translated into Spanish, begun 1258 and completed c 1303.

Of the three cathedrals which preceded it, the second was built on part of the site of the palace Ordoño II (died 932, and buried in the cathedral) had constructed in the Roman thermae; the third, of which important remains have been discovered, dates from the 11C. The present building had been barbarously disfigured in the 15–17C, and Widdrington, who visited in 1843, suggested that a 'Junta of conservation and purification could be established in Spain without much difficulty, which might banish by degrees all those altar pieces and other works unworthy of preservation'. During the restoration of 1868–1900 many of the additions of previous centuries were removed. The roof was damaged by fire in 1966, but has been repaired.

The *W Front* contains three portals, separated by two narrow stilted arches supported by clustered shafts and adorned with sculptures in the manner of the transeptal porches at Chartres. On the central shaft of the main doorway stands the image of N.S. la Blanca, and in the tympanum is Christ between the Virgin and St. John, with the Last Judgement below. The side tympanums illustrate the lives of Christ and the Virgin.

The *W Towers* (65m and 68m high) are 13–15C; the openwork spire of the *S Tower* was built in 1458–72 by Joosken van Utrecht, who completed the *S Transept* in 1448. The three-storeyed *S Portal* has three 15C doorways, above which is a statue of S. Froilán, Bp of León in 990–1006. The Apse, with its flying buttresses, and the Plateresque wall of the sacristy, are best seen from the former Puerta del Obispo (now a plaza) to the SE. See below for the area to the S.

The interior is narrow in proportion to its length (90m long; 40m wide). The main arcade of the aisled nave, with its clustered piers, is surmounted by a graceful triforium and clerestory, the latter lighted by exceptional *Stained Glass* of every period from the 13C onwards; some of the finest fills the rose-windows of the W and transeptal fronts, and the apse.

The *Coro* contains two tiers of *Stalls* (1467–81) by Juan de Malinas and Diego Copín de Holanda, with remarkable misericords, and is surrounded by a *Trascoro* of c 1570–87 by Juan de Badajoz el Mozo, of carved and gilded alabaster, with painted figures by Esteban Jordán. The retablo of the Cap. Mayor, a modern composition, contains paintings by Nicolás Francés (after 1427); to the N is a Pietà by Roger van der Weyden.

In the E chapel is the 14C tomb of the Condesa Sancha de León, below which is represented the punishment of her nephew and heir, who was torn to pieces by wild horses for the murder of his aunt. Several tombs of miscellaneous bishops may be seen in the other chapels.

The Plateresque *Puerta del Dado* admits to the vestibule of the *Cloister* (14C, but unskilfully altered c 1540), entered through finely-carved doors, and now housing the cathedral and diocesan *Musem, tastefully installed in a series of rooms beyond the N and E walks. A Plateresque staircase of 1534 by Juan de Badajoz el Mozo ascends to the *Chapterhouse.*

Among the more notable objects displayed in this extensive but miscellaneous collection are the early 17C Chest of S. Friolán; a Crucifixion by *Juan de Juni*; Sta. Ana with the Virgin, attributed to *Gaspar Becerra*; a late 12C Crucifixion from Vallejo; a 14C Mudéjar Wardrobe; a 15C Sta. Catalina; a 13C Virgin and Child from Mansillas de las Mulas (one of numerous Romanesque examples); a 16C portative Organ; a 13C S. Isidoro; a Bible of 920; and an 11C Antiphoner with Mozarabic musical notation.

In The C. Card. Landázuri, N of the cathedral, is the hospice of *N.S. de Regla*, with the re-erected façade of the former palace of the Marqués de Prado at Renedo de Valdetéjar (1620). Adjacent is a gateway in the *Walls* of closely-spaced solid semicircular bastions or *cubos*, largely 11C but restored in 1324, and since degraded; only 31 of the original c 80 towers survive.

From opposite the cathedral, proceed NW to approach collegiate *S. Isidoro el Real*, with its Romanesque tower.

It was founded in the 11C by Fernando I (who died here in 1065) and Doña Sancha as a shrine for S. Isidoro of Sevilla (died 636; not to be confused with S. Isidoro Labrador, patron of Madrid). The imposing W narthex remains, begun by their son Alfonso VI and consecrated in the presence of Alfonso VII in 1149. Considerable alterations were made in the 16C. The Romanesque doorway, surmounted by a Renaissance coat of arms and a 16C equestrian statue of S. Isidoro, contains in its tympanum a 12C sculpture of the Sacrifice of Abraham. Further E is the *Puerta del Perdón*, depicting the Descent from the Cross (11–12C).

The interior, lighted by a large clerestory, contains massive pillars with richly sculptured capitals. from the N Transept opens a 12C chapel preserving fragments of contemporary paintings. The Cap. Mayor, a late Gothic work, by Juan de Badajoz, dates from 1513.

At the W end, entered by a separate doorway, is the *Panteón de los Reyes*, the burial place of the early kings of León and Castile. Here, in the 11C *Cap. de Sta. Catalina*, until desecrated by Soult's troops in 1808, rested the ashes of Alfonso V (died 1028), Fernando I (died 1065), his daughter Urraca de Zamora, and a score of other *Infantes*. The vault paintings, representing the Lives of Christ and the Apostles, the Signs of the Zodiac, and the Months, date from the penultimate decade of the 12C.

Dependencies include the *Treasury*, containing a 12C enamel casket; another of 1059 with ivory plaques; a 16C silver processional cross; an 11C agate chalice, etc.; the modernised Cloister; and a Library, most of the more valuable contents of which were burned by Soult, but it still possesses an illuminated Bible of 960. The vestibule preserves remains of 15C (? Florentine) frescoes.

On the E side of the plaza is a 14C palace.

Turning W (right, abutting the church), another section of the ramparts is passed.

Crossing the C. Padre Isla to reach a circular plaza, follow the main avenue to the NW to approach the former *Convento de S. Marcos* (now a luxury hotel, after being used as barracks). Founded in 1168 for the Knights of Santiago, whose scallop shells are in evidence, it was rebuilt in 1513–49 to the designs of *Pedro Larrea*. The sumptuous Plateresque façade (1533–41), also attributed to *Juan de Badajoz*, has a frieze of historical and mythological busts in high relief by *Juan de Juni*. Over the elaborate main door is an equestrian figure of Santiago. The nave of the *Church* (restored) is spacious and lofty; the *Stalls*, in a gallery above the entrance, were carved by Guillermo Doncel in 1537–43, but were clumsily repaired in 1723.

An *Archaeological Museum* is housed in the *Chapterhouse* (right of the entrance), with its artesonado roof. Among sculptures are an 11C ivory Christ, a 12C Crucifixion, a Virgin and Child from S. Miguel de Escalada, a 10C Mozarabic Cross from Santiago de Peñalba, medieval textiles, vestments, ironwork, arms, and Roman and Renaissance statuary. Among the antiquities here and in the *Sacristy* (which has an elaborate vault), are memorials to the Seventh Legion; finds from Corullón in the Bierzo; and monuments of the 3C AD, in which the horseshoe arch is depicted 500 years *before* the Moorish invasion.

Off the upper storey of the cloister opens the cell in which Francisco de Quevedo was imprisoned in 1640–43 by Felipe IV for his lampoons against Olivares; he died two years later, broken in health.

From the cathedral apse, one may follow a lane S to the massive *Torre de los Ponces*—recalling the Leonese family of which Juan

Ponce de León (?1460–1521), discoverer of Florida, was the most famous member—there turning right into the old *Pl. Mayor*. On its W side is the *Consistorio Antiguo* of 1677, behind which is 13C *S. Martín*, restored in the 18C and containing sculptures by Gregorio Fernández, and Luis Carmona.

The C. de la Azabachería leads W to the Pl. del Conde de Luna, with the *Pal. de los Condes* with a 14C doorway, Renaissance front with a tower, and unfinished patio.—*S. Salvador* (under restoration), a few paces to the NE, is in part mid 10C.

Further S in this area, where the ancient Judería stood, is the Pl. del Mercado, where *N.S. del Mercado* preserves an 11C apse.— Further SW are gardens, overlooked by *S. Francisco*, containing the Baroque retablo made for the cathedral in 1724. The C. de la Independencia leads N past a stretch of medieval walls to regain the Pl. de Sto. Domingo.

For roads from León to **Burgos**, see Rte 9; from León to **Madrid**, Rte 21: both in reverse. From León to **Astorga**, see Rte 36; to **Oviedo**, Rte 33 in reverse; for *Benavente* and **Zamora**, Rte 19.

19 León to Salamanca via Benavente and Zamora

198km (123 miles). N630. 70km *Benavente*—NVI. 6km—N630. 60km **Zamora**—62km **Salamanca**.

Maps: M 442

From *S. Marcos* in León (see above) we cross the Bernesga, and turn left, driving due S along the wide valley of the Esla.

33km. *Valencia de Don Juan*, 6.5km SE, until the end of the 14C known as Coyanza, has a 14–15C *Castle* of striking outline overlooking the Esla.

9km *Toral de los Guzmanes*, with remains of the 14C *Pal. de los Guzmanes*, and two partly Mudéjar churches.—12km *Villaquejida*, where the 16C chapel of *Sta. Columba* is paved with 5C Roman mosaic, now in a poor state.

Valderas, 16.5km SE, sacked by Lancaster in 1387, retains vestiges of its medieval walls.

20km **Benavente** (12,800 inhab., with a bypass). Only one tower survives of the stronghold of the Pimentel family, which was gutted by Moore's troops on their retreat to A Coruña. It had successfully resisted an Anglo-Portuguese attack in 1387 (in which Sir John Falconer, one of Lancaster's retainers, was killed). Before being dismantled in the 19C the 'vast shapeless pile, possessing the marks of great antiquity', completely dominated the town.

The remaining tower, now roofed by an octagonal artesonado taken from a ruined church in the vicinity, has been incorporated into a Parador. Cruciform *Sta. María del Azogue* (1170–1220) retains notable doorways, five apses, and a lofty tower; the main porch and Baroque retablo date from 1735. 13C *S. Juan del Mercado* preserves a good S Door; and the *Hosp. de la Piedad*, with its cloister, has a well-carved early 16C entrance.

Bearing SE, we shortly cross the Esla, spanned by a Roman bridge, and turn right.

At 29km, just beyond *Granja de Moreruela*, a track to the right leads c 3km to the impressive ruins of the Cistercian abbey of **˙Moreruela**, founded in 1131, and the first of that Order in Spain; its apse is particularly fine.

After 14.5km we meet the N525 (see Rte 39) after crossing an arm of the *Esla reservoir*, and continue due S to approach (22.5km) **Zamora**; see Rte 20.

Shortly after crossing the Duero, a left-hand turning leads 7km SE to hilltop **Arcenillas**, where the church contains 15 *˙Paintings* of the Life of Christ by *Fernando Gallego* (1490; restored 1971); another 20 were sold by the cathedral chapter of Zamora in 1712. Note also the fluted columns, and the 13C Crucifixion. (Key at No. 2 in the adjacent plaza.) The main road may be regained c 4km W.

The N630 continues S across the limestone hills of the TIERRA DEL VINO, at 24km passing *Valparaiso*, with the scanty ruins of an abbey where Fernando III was born in 1199.—At 16km we pass (left) a late 15C fortified palace at *Villanueva de Cañedo*, and cross a monotonous plateau to approach (22km) **Salamanca**; see Rte 26.

20 Tordesillas to Zamora via Toro (for Braganza or Miranda do Douro)

67km (41 miles). N122. 34km **Toro**—33km **Zamora**.

Maps: M 442

For **Tordesillas**, see Rte 10. The N122 drives due W, at 18km passing a road to *S. Román de Hornija* (7.5km SW), with an 18C church preserving part of the original structure founded by Chindasvinth c 750, and containing two Visigothic tombs.

16km **TORO** (9750 inhab.), possibly Roman *Arbucala*, stands on a long low hill with an extensive view S across the Duero, and was once a place of importance.

Juan II, son of Catherine of Lancaster, was born here in 1405. In 1476 Fernando the Catholic and Afonso V of Portugal fought an indecisive battle near by, but the Portuguese withdrawal put an end to the faction of La Beltraneja. Here in 1506 was held the Cortes by which the royal authority of Fernando was recognised after the death of Isabel. In 1645 the Conde-Duque de Olivares, the disgraced minister of Felipe IV, died here, after two years of exile.

The **˙Colegiata** (Sta. María la Mayor; being restored) built from 1160 to the 13C, is remarkable for its richly sculptured and painted W *Doorway* in almost perfect preservation. The N Doorway, the capitals of the chancel arch, and the 16-sided Tower are also notable, while the dome may be compared with those of the cathedral at Zamora, the *old* cathedral at Salamanca, and that of Plasencia. The tombs in the sanctuary include that of the warrior-bishop Alonso de Fonseca, who fought beside Fernando at the battle of Toro. The Sacristy contains a fine painting of c 1500 entitled La Virgen de la Mosca (the fly).

To the W stood the ancient *Judería*.

Among other buildings of interest are the *Colegio de los Escolapios*, with a Plateresque courtyard, near the *Pl. Mayor*, with a

Casa Consistorial of 1778 by Ventura Rodríguez. To the N is *Sto. Sepulcro*, with three Romanesque-Mudéjar apses. Near by is the *Torre del Reloj* of 1733. Among other churches are *Sto. Tomás Cantuariense* (much restored); *El Salvador* (13C Mudéjar); *S. Pedro del Olmo*, with a 14C brick nave and wall paintings; *S. Lorenzo*, a late 12C brick church with a retablo by Fernando Gallego and good tombs in its 15C sanctuary. *Sancti Spiritus* (1316–15C) contains the tomb of Beatriz of Portugal (died c 1410; wife of Juan I of Castile). The brick hermitage of *Sta. María de la Vega* (consecrated 1208), in the S suburb, has 15C wall paintings.

Only a portico remains of the mansion of the Marqués de Sta. Cruz de Aguirre, where the Cortes de Toro were probably held. The *Hospital* of c 1500 retains a good Gothic doorway. Off the Paseo de S. Francisco is a privately owned bullring of 1828 with wooden galleries.

At *Mixos*, to the NW, is a church of c 900 with Roman stones used as altars, and wall paintings.—*Villalonso*, c 12km NE, has a well-preserved castle.

Leaving Toro, the road briefly skirts the N bank of the Duero, which is regained at (33km) **ZAMORA** (58,550 inhab.; 18,000 in 1920; 35,000 in 1950; Parador). Once known as 'el bien cercada' (the well-walled), it retains relics of its ramparts and several Romanesque churches, including an imposing cathedral.

Zamora owes its importance to its position on the Duero, and was long a disputed frontier post. Taken from the Moors by Alfonso I in 748, it was attacked unsuccessfully in 939 by Abderrahman III, who is said to have lost 40,000 men in the breaches of its seven walls. From this originated the proverb, 'Zamora is not gained in an hour'. In 985 Almanzor captured and destroyed the place. It was rebuilt after 1065 by Fernando I, who bequeathed it as an appanage to his daughter Urraca. Her brother Sancho II (Fernando's successor to the Castilian throne) claimed Zamora, but the Cid (a foster brother of Urraca) refused to take up arms against her. In 1072 Sancho was lured to his death by Vellido Dolfos, who, pretending to lead the king to an unguarded postern in the W wall, stabbed him in the back.

Life in the convent of Sta. María in the late 13C is amusingly described by Peter Linehan in his study of the Spanish Church in that epoch (see Bibliography). In the 15C Zamora was captured by the Portuguese supporters of Juana la Beltraneja, but surrendered to Fernando the Catholic in 1476. In 1520 it was a stronghold of the Comuneros. It was the birthplace of the novelist and critic Leopoldo Alas ('Clarín'; 1852–1901; see Oviedo).

The C. de Sta. Clara enters the old town from the E, passing *Santiago* (c 1200) to approach the insignificant Pl. Mayor, with the *Old Ayuntamiento* of 1504. On the right is *S. Juan*, with an early Renaissance door and florid Gothic S window (bricked up).

The C. Ramos Carrión leads W past the Parador in the former *Pal. of the Condes de Alba Aliste* (15–16C), its imposing Renaissance courtyard carved with medallions and coats of arms. Further on is the *Hospicio* (1798). To the N is the *Hospital* completed in 1662. It hides *Sta. María la Nueva*, which preserves 8C capitals on its apse and contains a Christ by Gregorio Fernández. Behind the church is a *Museum of 'Pasos'*.

To the SW, in an area formerly the Judería, are *La Concepción* and Romanesque *S. Cipriano*. We shortly pass (right) *La Magdalena* (c 1165), its S doorway, with elaborately decorated recessed arches, surmounted by a rose window. Within are two canopied tombs, one—of María de la Cerda—with twisted columns and curious capitals.—*S. Ildefonso* (13–15C), S of its plaza, has a front of 1798 and a raised coro.

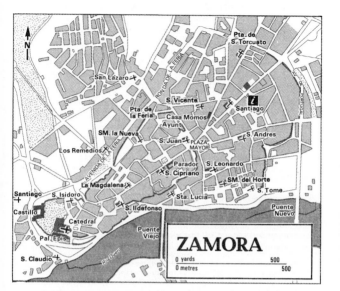

At the W end of the ridge stands the partly ruined *Castillo* (Urraca's stronghold), below which is the 12C *Ermita de Santiago*, said to mark the site of Sancho's assassination. The promontory is dominated by the *Cathedral*. This dates principally from the second half of the 12C (beg in 1151; consecrated 1174). The Gothic Cap. Mayor was added in 1506 and the N Front was classicised and the cloister rebuilt by Juan Gómez de Mora in 1591–1621.

Characteristic features are the massive *W Tower* with its widening tiers of round-arched windows and the Dome with corner turrets, similar to the Torre del Gallo at Salamanca, but with only one row of lights (cf. Toro). On the S side the centrepiece of the 12C façade is the *Puerta del Obispo* with scroll-like mouldings.

The interior is notable for its huge columns; the typical '*medio naranjo*', accentuated by the rib vault, of the dome; and the *Stalls* of c 1490, which have been attributed to Rodrigo Alemán. The execution of the carvings, particularly of the misericords, is extremely delicate and includes some indelicate satires on monastic life which were once nailed down by a bishop. The bishop's throne, the rejas, and iron pulpits, are notable. In the *Cap. del Cardenal*, at the W end, is a damaged Retablo by Fernando Gallego (1466), whose painting of Christ in Glory is on the Trascoro.

From the plain *Cloister* a staircase ascends to the *Museum*. This contains a silver custodia by Juan de Arfe (c 1515) and a remarkable series of 15–16C *Flemish Tapestries*, known as the 'Black Tapestries' (depicting the Coronation of Tarquin, the Parable of the Vine, the Trojan War, and the Hannibal series). They are badly displayed.

A walk descends across the ramparts behind the *Bishop's Palace* (S of the cathedral) and the legendary *Casa del Cid* (11–12C), with a view of the fine medieval *Bridge* of 17 arches. To the SW is *S. Claudio* (1100 and later), with a Romanesque door. One may descend SE past *Sta. Lucía* and a 16C palace to *Sta. María de la Horta* (12C and 1495), with a square tower. Beyond is *Sto. Tomé* and, to the N, remains of *S. Leonardo*, both with Romanesque fragments. Passing S.

Leonardo, one may ascend to the Pl. Mayor.—16C *S. Andrés*, a short distance E, contains a Monument to Antonio Sotelo attributed to Pompeo Leoni, wide vaults, and an artesonado roof.

The C.S. Torcuato leads NE from the Pl. Mayor, passing (left) the early 16C *Casa de los Momos*, with carved chains, *ajimez* windows, and a massive archway.—13C *S. Vicente* lies to the left a few steps beyond.—Further NE are 17C *S. Torcuato*, the *Hospital*, with a doorway of 1526, and the *Puerto de S. Torcuato*.

At *Hiniesta*, 8.5km NW, is an early 14C church with an immense vaulted porch.

For the road N to **Benavente** and S to **Salamanca** see Rte 19; for **Puebla de Sanabria** and **Ourense**, Rte 39; for *Arcenillas*, c 8km SE, see p 183.

ZAMORA TO FERMOSELLE (64km). The C527 leads SW to approach the N bank of the *Embalse de Almendra* on the Tormes. This flows into the Duero some 10km beyond *Fermoselle*, where there is a notable Gothic church. The Portuguese frontier may be crossed here at the *Barragem de Bemposta* (Customs); see *Blue Guide Portugal*.

ZAMORA TO MIRANDA DO DOURO (56km). Follow the N122 W to cross the Esla at 24km, there turning left through *Villacampo*, with a Mudéjar church and the *Puerta de S. Andrés*. The nearby ruins of the *Despoblado de Santiago* are of interest. Cross the Duero after 11km, and again at the Portuguese frontier some 20km further W, at **Miranda do Douro** (Customs); see *Blue Guide Portugal*. It was here on 28/29 May 1813 that Wellington, having ridden from Salamanca, was slung across the gorge in a 'kind of hammock' suspended by ropes to inspect some 60,000 Anglo-Portuguese troops. During previous weeks they had assembled within Portugal under the command of Gen. Graham. This composed the heavyweight left wing of his thrust across the Esla, the movement of which the next day was to outflank the French entirely, and which was perhaps the most successful single offensive manoeuvre of the Peninsular War. The immediate campaign culminated in the great victory at Vitoria (q.v.) only three weeks later.

ZAMORA TO BRAGANZA (114km). The N122 leads W.—At 12km a right-hand fork approaches (10km) *Campillo* and *'S. Pedro de la Nave*, a Visigothic church of exceptional quality (c 700; restored c 900), resembling those of the Asturias. Owing to the construction of the Esla dam, the church was moved from its original site in 1930–32 and rebuilt here.—Regaining the main road, cross the Esla at 12km and bear NW, later parallel to the Portuguese frontier, to (18.5km) *Fronfría*. About 7km E of Fronfría is a 12–15C castle, formerly Templar and later belonging to the Albas. The main road continues W parallel to the border with Portugal to (19km) *Alcañices*, formerly fortified, to reach Customs after 23km, near *S. Martin del Pedroso*. For **Braganza**, 30km beyond, see *Blue Guide Portugal*.

21 Madrid to León or Astorga via Tordesillas

A. Madrid to León

320km (199 miles). A6. 107km *Adanero* junction—NVI. 14km *Arévalo*—33km *Medina del Campo*—24km **Tordesillas**—C611. 46km **Medina de Rioseco**—N601. 38km *Mayorga*—58km **León**.

Maps: M 442.

For the **motorway** from Madrid to the Adanero junction see Rte 11B in reverse.

11km **Arévalo** (6600 inhab.), also bypassed, is entered by turning left. Once of importance, it is surrounded by fragments of former walls, contains several 16–17C mansions, and has remains of a royal residence in the 15–16C incorporated in the *Conv. de S. Bernardo el Real*. In the 1620s a colony of 600 Walloon artisans was established here and 74 textile workshops were in operation, but the manufacture later foundered. Among its churches are Romanesque *Sta. María*, with a tower surmounting a gate in the old walls; *S. Miguel*, with loopholed walls and a blunt tower; *S. Martín*, with a Romanesque doorway and two brick towers, behind which is a restored square; brick *El Salvador*; *Sto. Domingo de Silos*, containing work of all periods from Romanesque to Renaissance, and the *Conv. de S. Francisco*, founded in 1214.

Not far S is *La Lugareja* (or *Gómez Román*), a remarkable fragment of the brick 13C church of a former Cistercian nunnery.

Continue N past the *Castle* (now a grain silo) and cross a Mudéjar bridge, bearing right to regain the NVI.

The left fork (C605) leads 26km W to **Madrigal de las Altas Torres**, birthplace of Isabel the Catholic (1451–1504). The almost perfect circle of its ruinous *Walls* (c 1300) is strengthened by the towers which give the place its sobriquet. The walls are pierced by four gates at the cardinal points, of which the *Puerta de Cantalpiedra* (W) is in good preservation; others have been over restored. Gothic *S. Nicolás de Bari* has a brick tower and artesonado roof; *Sta. María del Castillo*, on the site of the Moorish citadel, is Romanesque, internally rebuilt in the 17C. The *Hospital Real* was founded in 1443. The *Conv. de las Agustinas* contains what remains of the *Palacio Real*—the alcove is shown where Isabel was born—with other dependencies. Outside the walls is the derelict Renaissance *Conv. de los Agustinos*, where Luis de León died in 1591.—The NVI may be regained at *Medina del Campo*, 26km N via the C610.

36km **Medina del Campo** (18,900 inhab.), the 'city of the plain', a railway junction and the centre of some of the finest corn-growing districts in Spain, is now a dull old place. It used to be *the* market town of Castile and its fairs were long famous.

The Treaty of Medina del Campo (1489) between Ferdinand of Aragón and Henry VII of England provided for true friendship and alliance between the signatory nations, the subjects of which might carry on commerce with, travel through, or remain in either kingdom 'without general or special passport'. Among natives of Medina del Campo were Bernal Díaz del Castillo (1492–1581) and José de Acosta (1539–1600), both historians of the conquest of Central America.

The 14C *Colegiata del S. Antolín*, S of the Plaza, contains carved retablos, that of the high altar being in part by Berruguete, but mainly by Juan Picardo, Juan Rodríguez, and Cornelis de Holanda. The Cap. Mayor is of 1503; and to the right of the entrance is a Baroque chapel.—Near by is the balconied *Casa Consistorial* of 1660. Adjacent, over an arch at the corner of the plaza, is the house in which Isabel the Catholic died in 1504. *S. Miguel* is a notable Mudéjar church with a brick tower and apse, and portal of 1582. *La Magdalena* was completed by Rodrigo Gil de Hontañón, and contains a Crucifixion by Esteban Jordán. The brick *Hospital* of 1591–1619 was designed in the style of Herrera. Among ancient mansions the most notable is the brick *Casa de Las Dueñas*, attributed to Andrés de Nájera, with Renaissance patio, staircase, and artesonado ceilings.—E of the town rises the brick *Castillo de la Mota* (restored), with bartizan turrets. It was built by Fernando de Carreño in 1440 for Juan II and altered in 1479. Caesar Borja was imprisoned there in 1504–06.

The brick church of *Villaverde de Medina*, 10km W, contains a retablo by
Gregorio Fernández.

24km **Tordesillas**; see Rte 10. For the road to *Benavente* and *Astorga*
see Rte 21B.
   We drive due N on the C611 to (18km) *Torrelobatón*. Its noble 15C
* *Castle* has a 45m-high keep and three drum towers.

12km E lies the village of *Wamba*, where Wamba, the king of the Visigoths, was
elected in 672. He took the oath on the tomb of his predecessor Recceswinth,
who is buried in the Mozarabic *Church* of c 928, remains of which are
incorporated in the 13C structure.

The main road continues N over the dreary PÁRAMO DE LA MUDARRA
to (27km) **Medina de Rioseco** (5050 inhab.), an interesting but
decayed town, the Roman *Forum Egurrorum*, guarded by old walls. It
has been reputed since the 14C for its cloth fairs. Blake and Cuesta
were defeated near here by Bessières (14 July 1808), who proceeded
to sack the place: nuns from the Conv. de Sta. Clara were selected for
a worse fate.
   The picturesque winding arcaded C. Mayor, or de la Rúa, runs
through the town from N to S. Near the centre is *Sta. María del
Mediavilla*, a hall-church of 1490–1520 by Gaspar de Solórzano, with
star-vaulting, and a tower of 1738. The Retablo Mayor by Esteban
Jordán (1590) was painted by Pedro de Oña (1603); the reja and
woodwork is from S. Francisco (see below). The N chapel has a
remarkable cupola in polychrome stucco of 1554 by Jerónimo del
Corral, Benavente tombs, an altarpiece by Juan de Juni, and a reja
by Francisco Martínez. The treasury contains a Custodia by Antonio
de Arfe (1585) and a cross by Pompeo Leoni. The late 18C organ by
Francisco Ortega has been restored.
   Santiago, to the NE, is a fine example of Plateresque, Renaissance,
and Baroque styles, by Rodrigo Gil de Hontañón. It has a Churrigueresque retablo, and a Mater Dolorosa by Juan de Juni.—At the
S end of the town *S. Francisco* (late Gothic; restored 1531) has
Plateresque retablos, a S. Sebastían and other terracotta statues by
Juan de Juni, tombs with bronze weepers by Andino (1539), and a
Renaissance organ loft.—*Sta. Cruz* is again restored, after its
(recently) restored vaulting collapsed.

8.5km NE is the early 16C castle of *Belmonte de Campos*, with a noble keep.
Some 15km E, reached by turning off the Palencia road (C612), is the castle of
Montealegre. N of Montealegre is the fortified church of *Meneses* (15C).

Bear NW from Medina, at 12.5km passing (6km W) *Aguilar de
Campos*, where *S. Andrés* is a good late 1C Gothic-Mudéjar church.
7km beyond this turning is *Ceinos de Campos*, with a Templar
church.—At 8km the N610 from Palencia joins the main route. For
the road beyond (10km) *Mayorga* see Rte 9B.

B.   Tordesillas to Astorga
via Benavente

328km (204 miles). A6. 107km *Adanero* junction—NVI. 71km
Tordesillas—84km *Benavente*—66km **Astorga**.

Maps: M 442, 441.

For the road to Tordesillas see Rte 21A; for **Tordesillas** itself, Rte 10.
At 21km *Mota del Marqués* also bypassed, has a ruined castle, the
hall-church of *S. Martín* by Juan Gil de Hontañón, and the
Renaissance patio of the *Pal. of the Marqués de Viesca*.

7.5km. *S. Cebrián de Mazote*, 5km E, has a restored Mozarabic
church of c 915, with marble columns and capitals.

8km NW of S. Cebrián, on a hill, stands depopulated *Urueña*, with restored
walls and castle, to the SE of which is a small Romanesque basilica with an
octagonal tower.—About 10km E is the Cistercian monastery of *La Espina*,
completed in the 14C and restored after a fire in 1731. It has a 17C cloister and a
hostelry of 1789.

6.5km. *Villagarcía de Campos*, 9km NE, has a castle and, in its 17C
church, an impressive alabaster retablo by Juan Sanz de Torrecilla
(1582). Padre José Francisco Isla (1703–81), author of 'Fray
Gerundio', was a novice (from 1719) at the Jesuit monastery here.

21.5km *Villalpando*, with 12C walls, retains the massive *Puerta de
S. Andrés* and Mudéjar *Sta. María la Antigua*.—14km. *Villalobos*,
6.5km E, was occupied by Lancaster prior to calling off the Anglo-
Portuguese campaign in León of 1387.

At 10.5km fork right to bypass **Benavente**, 3km NW; see Rte 19.

BENAVENTE TO PUEBLA DE SANABRIA (85km). The C620 drives due W up the
valley of the Tera, at 26km passing the 12C church of *Sta. Marta de Tera*. The
N525 from Zamora is met 25.5km beyond. *Puebla de Sanabria* is 23km further
W; see Rte 39.

We ascend the Orbigo valley to the NW through the country of the
Maragatos, with the MONTES DE LEÓN looming ahead. At 20km *Alija
del Infantado*, with ruins of a fortified 15C palace, is 7.5km E.

Some *Maragatos*, considered to be the descendants of the Berber highlanders
who entered Spain with Tarik and Musa, still inhabit the dreary moorland
villages W of Astorga; others live in the town itself. Both men and women are
handsome. The carrying trade of NW Spain was once largely in their hands. The
men wore a characteristic costume, notably zouave-like breeches, while the
jewellery worn by the women was of peculiar design; see below.

21km *La Bañeza*, bypassed, is of slight interest. There are several
churches in the vicinity with curiously designed belfries.

25km **ASTORGA** (869m; 12,750 inhab.), Roman *Asturica Augusta*,
was described as a 'magnificent city' by Pliny, but is no longer so.

It preserves *Roman Walls* more than 6m thick, battered and deprived of their facing
(partly restored on the SW and NE sides). Behind them the Spaniards defied
Junot for two months in 1810, the French in turn resisting Castaños for three
months in 1812. Napoleon personally followed Sir John Moore no further than
Astorga, there leaving Soult to carry on the pursuit (January 1809). Until the
early 19C, the carriage road from Madrid to Galicia came to an abrupt end at
Astorga.
It was the birthplace of Francisco Villagrán (1507–63), the conquistador and
governor of Chile.

At the NE corner of the town stands the imposing red and greenish-
grey stone *Cathedral, begun in 1471 probably to the design of
Simón de Colonia, and continued (nave and transeptal chapels) by
Rodrigo Gil de Hontañón in 1530–59. Between its W Towers (of
differing stone) is a Baroque portal (completed 1693) bearing reliefs
of the Life of Christ. The weathercock is a figure of Pedro Mato, a
well-known Maragato (see above).

The Baroque West Portal of the Cathedral, Astorga

The well-vaulted interior, lighted by a clerestory of 16C glass, contains a Retablo with 'compartments of marble sculpture in alto relievo, the figures as large as life', which much impressed Edward Clarke in 1760. This is the masterpiece of Gaspar Becerra (1562). The reja of 1622 and the stalls of 1551 display good walnut carving. The Gothic Cloister was restored in 1780. The *Sacristy* of 1722 contains a *Treasury*. The archives were destroyed by the French in 1810.

SE is the incongruous *Bishop's Palace* (1909), by Gaudí and Ricardo Guereta. It now houses a *Museum of the Pilgrimage Road*, with a collection of carved tombs; Roman capitals, stelae, and coins; fragments of mosaics, glass and terra sigillata; pilgrims' medals, gourds, sticks, and shells; polychromed statues, processional crosses, ecclesiastical plate, ceramics, and glass.

In the arcaded *Pl. Mayor* is the *Ayuntamiento* (1684) with a clock bearing two jaquemart figures in Maragato costume, before which on Corpus Christi and Ascension days the Maragatos used to dance the curious *cañizo*. Behind and to the right is Baroque *S. Julián*, with a late Romanesque doorway. To the NE of the Plaza is a vaulted Roman *Cryptoporticus* (known as the *Ergástula*).

Former Maragato villages in the neighbourhood include *Santiago Millas*, 11km SW on the LE133, *Val de S. Lorenzo* (to the W of this road), and *Castillo de los Polvazares*, 6km W.

For the road from León to **Ponferrada** via Astorga see Rte 35A.

22 Madrid to Salamanca via Ávila

205km (127 miles). A6. 78km *Villacastín* junction—N501. 29km **Ávila**—56km *Peñaranda de Brocamonte*—42km **Salamanca**.

Maps: M 442.

For the alternative road to Ávila via *El Escorial* see Rte 42.

For the road to the *Villacastín* junction see Rte 11B in reverse. Turn left to follow the N501 (N110) across a granite boulder-strewn region to approach **Ávila**; see Rte 23.

Leave Ávila by following either of the roads skirting the walls. They meet beside the *Puerta del Puente* at the W end of the town. Crossing the Adaja, turn right (retrospective views on climbing out of the valley) to traverse the rocky hills of LA MORAÑA.

At 5km a turning to the right leads c 7km to *Las Cogotas*, a type settlement of the Iron Age: an acropolis within concentric walls (6–3C BC).

19km. The ruined castle of *Narros de Saldueña* lies c 7km N.— 11.5km. *Fontiveros*, 9km to the right, was the birthplace of St. John of the Cross (1542–91; S. Juan de la Cruz), like Sta. Teresa, of Jewish ancestry. The church has a 12C nave and a 16C sanctuary by Rodrigo Gil de Hontañón.—*Madrigal de las Altas Torres* is 21km beyond; see Rte 21A.

We reach the plain of Salamanca at (20.5km) *Peñaranda de Bracamonte* (6250 inhab.), a decayed town with two large plazas, a granite hall-church (restored) with a curious altarpiece, and a Carmelite convent founded in 1669, with a pleasant patio.

The church at *Macotera*, 11km SW, has a fine artesonado ceiling. There is another impressive 15–16C church at *Santiago de la Puebla*, 4km beyond.

The direct road to Salamanca, 42km W, is of slight interest. The DETOUR via Alba de Tormes (11km longer) may be made by following the SA114, turning left off the N501.—30km **Alba de Tormes** is dominated by the *Torre de la Armería*, all that remains of the castle which gave the ducal title to the Álvarez de Toledo family. The most notorious member was Fernando, third Duke of Alba (1507–82), governor of the Spanish Netherlands. The Tower (restored in 1961) contains retouched frescoes of the battle of Mühlberg (1547), in which the duke saw action. Sta. Teresa (of Ávila; 1515–82) died in the *Conv. de Carmelitas Descalzas*, which she had founded here in 1571. Its church contains a Mater Dolorosa by Pedro de Mena and a fine tomb by Simón de Galarza. 12C *S. Juan* has curious Romanesque sculptures of the Apostles, and a good retablo of 1771; *S. Miguel* and *Santiago* have 13–15C tombs, the latter also with an artesonado ceiling; and there are good sculptures in *S. Pedro* (rebuilt 1577 and 1686). The *Conv. de Sta. Isabel* (1481) contains an artesonado and the tomb of Juan de las Vargas (died 1525). In *Las Benitas* are a 16C doorway and 15C tombs.—Not far S are the ruins of Gothic *S. Leonardo* (1429–82), with a later cloister.

Detail of the Carmelite convent, Alba de Tormes

After crossing the Tormes, here dammed, bear NW to (23km) Salamanca. On approaching the city we pass the two hills, *Los Arapiles*, which were the main bones of contention in the **Battle of Salamanca** (22 July 1812).

Here, in a lightning attack after several hours of manoeuvring, Wellington in three-quarters of an hour overturned the fortunes of the entire French campaign in the Peninsula. The British casualties were c 3180, the Portuguese lost 2040, and the French approx. 14,000. The victory would have been complete had not the Spanish force guarding the bridgehead at Alba de Tormes withdrawn contrary to orders, allowing the French to retreat across the river.

For **Salamanca** see Rte 26.

23 Ávila

ÁVILA (40,150 inhab.; 13,000 in 1920; 21,000 in 1950; Parador) is a 'provincial' capital famous principally for its impressive circuit of medieval walls and fine Romanesque churches. It stands on a spur above the river Adaja in the midst of a boulder-strewn plateau, overlooked by the SIERRA DE ÁVILA (1131m). Owing to its altitude its winter climate is severe, but in summer the well-watered valleys of the neighbouring mountains offer a pleasant refuge from the drought of the Castilian plain.

The foundation of Ávila 'de los Caballeros' is lost in antiquity, being ascribed in legend to Hercules under the name of *Abula*. Known to the Romans as *Avela*, it was later a bone of contention between Moors and Christians, but remained in Spanish hands after being re-fortified in the late 11C. It dates its decadence from the expulsion of the Moriscos by Felipe III.

The town's most famous native was Teresa Sánchez de Cepeda y Ahumanda (Sta. Teresa de Jesús, or de Ávila; 1515–82), of noble and Converso lineage. At the age of seven she attempted to escape with her brother to seek martyrdom at the hands of the Moors, and in 1534 she took the veil at the Carmelite convent of La Encarnación. She founded the first convent of Discalced (barefoot) Carmelites (S. José; see below) in 1562; was beatified in 1614 and canonised in 1622. She is the co-patron of Spain (with Santiago).

Also born here were the composer Tomás Luis de Victoria (1548–1611) and Sancho Dávila (1523–83), the military commander. Although born in Madrid, George (Jorge Ruiz) Santayana (1863–1932), the philosopher, spent his youth here.

The *old* enceinte should be entered on foot, as parking can be a problem.

From the C. S. Segunda, skirting the E side of the medieval town, we see the great castellated *Apse of the Cathedral* which forms a bastion in the •**Walls**. These were built in 1088–91 by Raymond of Burgundy, son-in-law of Alfonso VI, from the designs of Cassandra, a Roman, and Florian de Ponthieu. The walls are in a remarkable state of preservation. They have 88 *cubos* or cylindrical towers, and nine gates, the latter consisting simply of two towers close together, connected by an arch and battlemented walk.

A convenient entry is through the *Puerta del Peso de la Harina*, just N of the apse, next to the *Casa de la Misericordia*, with its 16C doorway. The granite •**Cathedral**, the greater part of which was begun in 1157, is in the earliest Gothic style. Its fortress-like appearance is largely due to Bp Sancho (1188), who kept Alfonso IX in sanctuary here during his minority. The N Doorway, with statues and carved tympanum, dates from the 13C; the inferior W Portal (1779) is flanked by two early Gothic towers, one unfinished, and guarded by two *maceros* or mace bearers, like wild men of the woods.

The interior, containing curious red and white mottled masonry, has a narrow aisled *Nave* with a blind triforium and a large clerestory; the glass is by *Nicolás de Holanda (1536)*. The *Trascoro*, facing the entrance, bears coarse but vigorous reliefs by Juan Rodríguez. The *Coro* contains a remarkable *Sillería* of 1547 by Cornelis, a Dutchman, and two gilt iron pulpits (15th and 16C), the older (S) by Juan Francés. The double-sided *Cap. Mayor* contains good glass of 1497 by Juan de Valdivielso; the Retablo Mayor (1508) was painted by Santos Cruz, Pedro Berruguete, and Juan de Borgoña. In the *Trassagrario* is the Tomb, by Vasco de la Zarza (1518), of Alfonso de Madrigal (1400–55; Bp of Ávila c 1450, nicknamed 'el Tostado', the swarthy), showing the polymath prelate writing. In the S Transept are several good tombs and the sepulchre of Bp Sancho Dávila of

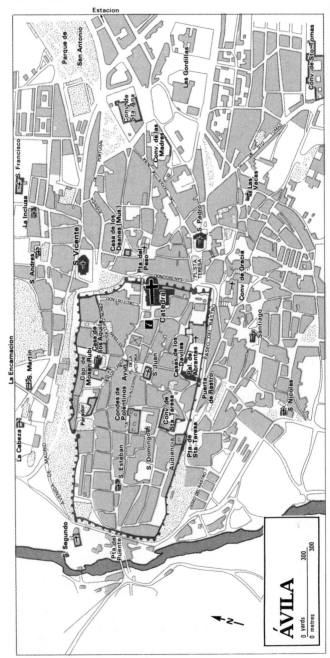

Sigüenza (died 1534); the glass in the transept is by Alberto de Holanda and Diego de Ayala (1538).

The *Sacristy*, entered from the S aisle, has a good octagonal vault, but bedaubed with paint and gilding. It contains Renaissance marbles, with terracotta groups of the Passion above. The Relicario preserves a silver monstrance by Juan de Arfe (1571). A Romanesque door on the S side of the nave admits to the partially restored 13C *Cloister*, which, Townsend observed, was worthy of attention 'for its exquisite neatness, and elegant simplicity'. The *Cap. del Cardenal*, on the E side, has good ironwork and painted glass of 1498 by Santillana and Valdivielso.

Turning right on leaving the cathedral, follow the C. del Tostado, where a mansion has curious heraldic devices, to reach the *Puerta de S. Vicente*. In this NE sector of the enceinte stood the Judería.

Just outside the gate is *S. Vicente, founded in 1307 where the saint and his sisters are said to have been martyred in 303. On the S side is a 13C portico with banded shafts protecting the 12C door, which has curious capitals, and an Annunciation on one of the jambs. The severe *W Front* (c 1170–90, with one tower partially completed in 1440) is remarkable for its double doorway surrounded by rich Romanesque sculpture. The central arched porch may be compared with that at Toro. The Romanesque interior is notable for the *Tomb* of the patron saints, a sarcophagus of c 1180 on an Italian-Gothic base covered by a canopy of 1465. Beneath the triple apse is a modernised crypt.

A short walk to the N are Romanesque *S. Andrés*, with good S and W doorways and 12C apse, and *La Inclusa*, with a Renaissance portal and sculptures ascribed to A. Berruguete.

Further N is the former convent of *S. Francisco*, with a restored star-vaulted chapel of c 1480, and another containing murals by Sansón Florentino (c 1500).—Further W is *La Encarnación*, founded in 1479, and the home of Sta. Teresa for 27 years. Closer to the town are *S. Martín*, with a Romanesque tower, and the chapel of *La Cabeza* (1210).

Some distance to the W, below the NE corner of the walls, is *S. Segundo*, a Romanesque hermitage (its interior altered in 1579) with a good roof and well-carved capitals on its apse. It contains the tomb statue of 1573 by Juan de Juni of S. Segunda, a muscular bishop of Ávila who is said to have hurled down a Moorish chief from the ramparts.

Further S are the old and new bridges across the Adaja. (The view of the walls is very fine from the Cuatro Postes on the hill to the NW, but the view *from* the walls is now spoilt by the erection of a hotel on this previously desolate slope.)

On the S side of the town are the restored Romanesque churches of *S. Nicolás* and *Santiago*, the latter with a 14C tower, and the abandoned hermitage of *S. Isidro*. Near Santiago is the *Conv. de la Concepción*, much altered in the 16C, with stalls of 1400.

The enceinte may be re-entered by the *Puerta del Rastro*, then passing some 15–16C mansions: on the right the *Pal. de Abrantes* and the *Casas de los Dávilas*; on the left the fortified *Torreón de Oñate* or *de Guzmanes*. Keeping to the left, the Baroque *Conv. de Sta. Teresa* is approached. Built on the site of her birthplace, the church contains a Christ by Gregorio Fernández, and a museum.

Just inside the *Puerta de Sta. Teresa* is the 15C mansion of the *Duque de la Roca* (now the Audiencia), with a front of 1541. The C. Jimena Blázquez leads N past Romanesque *Sto. Domingo* to the C. Vallespin. To the W in the C. Vallespin is *S. Esteban*, with an interesting early 12C apse. Turn E past the mansion of the *Condes de Polentinos* (1535; by Vasco de la Zarza), with a good doorway and

The walls of Ávila

patio, to approach the small *Pl. Mayor*. To the S is *S. Juan*, with the tomb of Sancho Dávila (see History). The left turn behind the modern Ayuntamiento leads to the Parador. Turn to the right off the street to approach the *Cap. de Mosén Rubí, a lofty cruciform chapel of 1516. It has tombs of interest and glass by Nicolás de Holanda. Further E is the *Casa de los Duques de Valencia* or *de los Aguilas*.

From the cathedral square, one can either continue E to the *Museo Provincial*, housed in the *Casa de los Deanes* a short distance E of the *Puerta del Peso*, or skirt the cathedral cloister to reach the *Puerta del Alcázar*. Beyond this stands **S. Pedro**, facing the Pl. de Sta. Teresa (the scene of *autos-de-fe*). This 11–13C building in some ways resembles S. Vicente. It has a good Romanesque apse and is notable for the beautiful *Rose-window* surmounting its plain W front.

The C. Duque de Alba leads NE to the *Carmelite Conv. de las Madres* (or *S. José*; 1615; by Francisco de Mora). It contains the tomb of Lorenzo de Cepeda (1580), brother of Sta. Teresa, and the monument of Bp Álvaro de Mendoza (died 1586), with a kneeling statue by Esteban Jordan. Beyond are the convents of *Sta. Ana* (16C; with remains of a church of 1350) and *Las Gordillas*, with the *Tower of María Dávila* (died 1511) by Vasco de la Zarza.

From just E of S. Pedro a short walk to the SE brings one to the *Conv. de Sto. Tomás*, founded by Fernando and Isabel and built in 1493 by Martín de Solórzano. It was damaged by fire in 1949.

Passing through cloisters, the church is entered beneath a depressed arch bearing the Coro; the high altar is raised on a similar arch at the E end. The retablo, the masterpiece of Pedro Berruguete (c 1499), illustrates the life of St. Thomas Aquinas. The *Sillería*, especially the canopies of the royal seats, are delicately carved in Flamboyant designs.

Below is the exquisitely sculptured white marble *Tomb of Prince Juan* (1478–97), only son of Fernando and Isabel, by Domingo Fancelli (1512). In the third N chapel are effigies by an unknown master of Juan Dávila and Juana Velázquez, attendants of the prince (1503). In the sacristy a plain slab marks the burial place of Tomás de Torquemada (1420–98), the Dominican inquisitor-general. During his 18-year control of the 'Holy Office' he was ultimately responsible for burning alive some 2000 heretics, mostly *conversos*, and mutilating in some way a further 17,000. The convent also houses some oriental antiquities.

The return to the centre may be made along the Carrera de Sto. Tomás to the W, passing near the 15C *Cap. de las Vacas* and the *Conv. de Gracia*.

For the road to **Salamanca** see Rte 22; for **Plasencia** or **Segovia**, Rte 16; for **Toledo**, Rte 24.

24 Ávila to Toledo

137km (85 miles). N403. 56km *S. Martín de Valdeiglesias*—39km *Maqueda*—14km *Torrijos*—28km **Toledo**.

Maps: M 447.

The N403 leads S, at 20km crossing the *Puerto de la Paramera* (1395m) before bearing SE and entering the upper valley of the Alberche and briefly skirting a reservoir.—At 20km *Cebreros* lies 8.5km E. It has a large granite hall-church and the ruined *Conv. de S. Francisco*.

16km *S. Martín de Valdeiglesias*, beneath an E spur of the thickly wooded SIERRA DE GREDOS, retains several old houses, an unfinished church by Herrera, and the restored *Castle of Álvaro de Luna*. The area is in danger of being spoilt by the erection of 'chalets'. See also Rte 49 for *Toros de Guisando*, to the W.

At 8km *Cadalso de los Vidrios*, with the 16–18C *Pal. de Villena*, lies 7km E.—12km *Almorox* has a notable church, its Cap. Mayor by Juan Gil de Hontañón.—8km *Escalona*, overlooking the sandy bed of the Alberche, with an imposing ruin of a *Castle* built in 1442 by Álvaro de Luna, and collegiate church. Juan Manuel (1282–1348), the chronicler and poet, was born in an earlier castle on this site.

11km *Maqueda*, its castle (now Civil Guard barracks) with a Mudéjar archway and battlements of Moorish tiles; *Sta. María* has a Mudéjar apse. It was here c 1422 that Rabbi Moses Arragel began his translation of the Bible, with commentary and illuminations.—Crossing the NV (see Rte 50A), the road bears SE to (14km) **Torrijos** (8050 inhab.). Its collegiate church of 1500 has a richly ornamented Plateresque portal. The semi-Moorish *Pal. de los Duques de*

Altamira by Juan de Herrera has four saloons decorated with arabesques and artesonado ceilings. Alonso de Covarrubias (1488–1564), the architect, was born at Torrijos.

16km SW is *La Puebla de Montalbán*, with a pleasant Pl. Mayor and a parish church with Renaissance arches and artesonado ceiling. For the road beyond see Rte 50B.

The main road passes at 5km just S of *Barcience*. On the façade of its imposing castle (1440) is carved a huge lion.—At 10km we cross the Río Guadarrama and a low ridge to approach (13km) **Toledo**; see Rte 43. For the road on to *Ciudad Real* see Rte 48B.

25 Madrid to Segovia

A.   Via the Guadarrama Tunnel

87km (54 miles). A6. 37km *Villalba* junction—20km *S. Rafael* junction—N603. 30km **Segovia**.

Maps: M 442.

The Av. Puerta de Hierro, the main exit from Madrid to the NW, shortly passes the 'Iron Gate' erected in 1753 at the entrance to a royal park. It crosses the Manzanares and, as the A6, bears uphill past several garden suburbs. At 16km the C505 forks left for *El Escorial*; see Rte 42. The road undulates across the bare exposed plateau—still largely a 'hideous, grassless, treeless, colourless, calcined desert', as described by Richard Ford, with no visible limit except the SIERRA DE GUADARRAMA rising to the N.
    At 37km the N601 branches right to (13km) crossroads just N of the village of *Navacerrada*; see Rte 25B.

The old main road (NVI) continues NW through the village of *Guadarrama* (with a ruined church incorporating an early mosque) before climbing steeply to the *Puerto de Guadarrama* or *de los Leones* (1511m), where a stone lion commemorates the opening of the road across the range in 1749. Napoleon himself led his army over the snowbound pass on Christmas Eve 1808 in an attempt to trap the British army under Moore (see Astorga).—At *S. Rafael* (24km) fork right onto the N603; see below.

The motorway runs parallel to and W of the NVI, at 9km reaching a junction before starting the gentle ascent to the *Guadarrama tunnel*, in fact two separate tunnels pierced through the range in 1964 and 1972; toll.

To the left is a gigantic *Cross* of reinforced concrete encased in stone rising to a height of 150m above the site of the **Valle de los Caídos** (the Fallen), which can be approached from this junction.
    The grandiose expiatory monument in the Fascist taste to those slaughtered in the Civil War of 1936–39 was inaugurated in 1959; political prisoners were employed in its construction. Built by Diego Méndez following the designs of Pedro Muguruza, this work of supererogation consists of a massive subterranean *Basilica* (250m long) entered by a vaulted passage hewn through the solid rock. Below the cupola lies the Falangist martyr José Antonio Primo de Rivera (1903–36), while in the crypt repose the remains of unknown victims of the war, ostensibly of every political conviction. Gen. Francisco Franco (1892–1975) also

chose to be interred here beneath a symbolically whited sepulchral slab near the altar.

The *Escorial* is 9km S of the motorway junction; but see Rte 42. The granite **Sierra de Guadarrama**, the ancient *Montes Carpetani*, stretches with its continuations from SW to NE, forming the frontier between the Castiles for a distance of c 100km. It is prolonged to the NE by the SIERRA DE AYLLÓN and to the SW by the SIERRA DE GREDOS. Several of its summits are over 2000m, and it culminates near its centre at *Peñalara* (2429m). Several areas on the lower slopes of the range have been disfigured during recent decades by the uncontrolled erection of chalets.

Shortly after traversing the Guadarrama tunnel leave the motorway and turn right onto the N603.—The exit for *Ávila* may be made at *Villacastín*, 21km further NW.

Crossing a ridge, with a wide view ahead of the Castilian plateau, we later pass a turning (left) to the huge square château of *Riofrío*, begun in 1752 by V. Rabaglio for Isabel Farnese. Part of the building houses a *Hunting Museum*; the estate, full of game, is an appropriate setting.

Segovia soon comes into view on the left, and is shortly entered; see Rte 25C.

B.   Via the Puerto de Navacerrada and La Granja

85km (53 miles). A6. 37km *Villalba* junction—N601. 13km *Navacerrada* junction—7km *Puerto de Navacerrada*—17km **La Granja**—11km **Segovia**.

Maps: M 442.

Although scenically the more attractive of the two routes described, during winter months heavy snowfalls make the Navacerrada pass liable to intermittent closure or accessible only with chains, which are obligatory. Notices to this effect are displayed at the exit to Madrid and on the NVI. For the main road to the village of *Navacerrada*, see Rte 25A.

An ALTERNATIVE road, only 8km longer, leads via Colmenar Viejo to the Navacerrada junction. The C607 is entered not far N of the Paseo de Castellana and later passes (right) a turning for the early castle of *Viñuelas*, which once belonged to the Order of St. John.—At 31km **Colmenar Viejo** (19,850 inhab.), now a dormitory town, is bypassed; its parish church is 14C, with Renaissance alterations.

At 17.5km *Manzanares el Real* lies 6.5km to the right, a centre for the exploration of the granite peaks of *La Pedriza*. The *Castle* of the Mendozas was built in 1435–80 by Juan Gúas for the Dukes of Infantado. It is distinguished by such Mudéjar features as honeycomb cornices, diamond point in plaster, and embedded stone balls.

At 9km turn right onto the N601 above the village of *Navacerrada*.

We climb through pine forests on the S slope of the Guadarrama range to (9km) the *Puerto de Navacerrada* (1860m).

At the pass, a popular centre for winter sports and starting point for excursions and ascents in the sierra, a good mountain road (C604) leads right to the *Puerto de los Cotos* (1830m), overlooked to the N by *Peñalara* (2429m), the highest peak of the range. It then descends into the wooded valley of the Lozoya. At

21km the Carthusian monastery of **El Paular** is reached. Abandoned and used as glass works, it has recently been reoccupied by Benedictines. Part of its dependencies have been converted into a hotel. It was founded by Enrique II in 1390 and built by Rodrigo Alfonso, architect of the cathedral at Toledo. The *Church* (1440), by the Moorish architect Abderrahman, has a painted alabaster retablo ascribed to Genoese sculptors of the 15C, a reja of 1599 by Juan Francés, and a main door and cloister (1475–1500) by Juan Güas. The *Cap. del Tabernáculo* is an extravagant Baroque work of 1724 designed by Francisco de Hurtado, with vaults painted by Palomino.—*Rascafría* lies 3km beyond, and the NI 25km further E, reached at a point 68km N of Madrid.

The N601 descends from the pass along the N flank of the range by a series of steep zigzags known as *Las Siete Revueltas*. After traversing the extensive pine forest of *Balsaín* (or *Valsaín*) it passes the remains of a palace built for Felipe II in 1566, but burnt down (deliberately, according to Saint-Simon) at the turn of the 18C.

17km **La Granja** (or, more correctly, **S. Ildefonso**) is a small town and summer resort lying at 1192m at the foot of the *Reventón* (2080m).

It was long reputed for its glassworks, which still flourish. In the original *Fábrica de Cristales* (under restoration) established here by Carlos III, were made the huge mirrors which adorn so many Spanish palaces, but the expense (and breakage) in their transport consumed any chance of profit. John Dowling, an Irishman who managed the works in the 1770s, also set up a cutlery manufactury there.

The ineffective Republican offensive of the last week of May 1937 near here was later described by Hemingway in 'For Whom the Bell Tolls', although he was in New York at the time.

A hermitage dedicated to S. Ildefonso and a shooting box built by Enrique IV c 1450 were presented by the Catholic Kings to the monks of El Parral in Segovia in 1477, and around the grange (*granja*) arose a village. Felipe V, the first Bourbon king of Spain, purchased the farm in 1720 and commissioned Theodore Ardemans to design a palace. The project was carried on by Francisco de Ortega and finished in 1723. A recasing of the whole structure was begun in 1735 by Juvara and completed by Sacchetti in 1739—the result being, according to Richard Ford, 'a theatrical French château, the antithesis of the proud, gloomy Escorial, on which it turns its back'. The gardens, laid out by René Carlier and Étienne Boutelou, were not finished until the reign of Carlos III.

Felipe V abdicated the throne here in Janaury 1724, only to resume it the following August; here in 1783 Carlos III received the Comte d'Artois (Charles X) when on his way to attack Gibraltar. Queen María Luisa is said to have preferred the apartments overlooking the courtyard in which her bodyguard exercised. In 1795 Godoy signed the treaty here which virtually handed Spain over to France. Here Fernando VII, during an illness in 1832, first revoked and then revived the Pragmatic Sanction of 1829 (by which the Salic Law had been abolished), a vacillation precipitating the Carlist Wars in the reign of his infant daughter, Isabel. And here in 1836 the Queen Regent Cristina was forced by mutinous sergeants to restore the democratic constitution of 1812.

In 1918 a disastrous fire destroyed the N wing of the palace and gutted most of the royal apartments, the chapel, and other dependencies, parts of which have since been restored. Another fire in August 1985 damaged the so-called Casa de los Príncipes.

From the *Puerta de Segovia* ascend the leafy Pl. del Palacio, flanked by outbuildings, to reach the rear façade of the **Palace**. The main façade, 150m long and with a handsome portico, fronts the gardens. The sparsely furnished apartments may be visited. Of more interest is the important collection of *Tapestries*, some brought from Brussels by Charles V, including St. Jerome at Prayer (16C), and some from cartoons by Goya. The *Chapel* contains frescoes by Bayeu and Maella, which suffered in the fire. By the high altar are the tombs of

Felipe V and his wife Isabel Farnese (died 1746 and 1766). The organ is by José Otorel (c 1850).

The formal *Gardens, including the plantation, cover 145 hectares. They contain 26 elaborate fountains, designed mainly by Frémin and Thierri, with the same reliance on classical mythology with those at Versailles; and they excel some of them in magnificence.

In the middle of the *parterre* SW of the palace is the *Fuente de la Fama*, with a high jet, and at the end is the *Baño de Diana*, of which Felipe V sardonically remarked 'it has cost me three millions and has amused me three minutes'. From the *Fuente de las Ranas* (Latona and the Frogs) c 200m SE, a walk passes the Pl. de las Ocho Calles with its eight fountains to cross the gardens to fountains on its W side. To the SW is the *Fuente de Andrómeda* and further in the same direction is El Mar, the artificial lake 50m above the palace, supplying the fountains with water. The *Casa de la Góndola* houses a pleasure boat of Carlos III.

The fountains play on certain days in summer only: check beforehand.

The N601 turns NW, shortly passing (right) the former royal domain of *Quita Pesares* (i.e. Sans-Souci), now an asylum, and near a 'Spanish Whisky' factory, before descending gently to the Pl. de Azoguejo and the Aqueduct of **Segovia**; see below.

C.   Segovia

SEGOVIA (50,750 inhab.; 16,000 in 1920; 32,000 in 1960; Parador 2km N, off the Valladolid road), a characteristic Old Castilian town, stands largely on a rocky ridge (1002m) between the rivers Eresma (N) and Clamores. The depression separating it from its unattractive modern suburbs to the E is spanned by its remarkable Roman aqueduct, which strides towards the medieval enceinte picturesquely girdled by ancient walls (sections still to be cleared of later accretions). Within the walls the Cathedral tower, among others, rises above a medley of narrow and irregular streets. Above its prominent W apex towers the romantically perched Alcázar.

Segobriga, a town of Iberian origin, rose to importance under the Romans who occupied it in 80 BC. Under the Visigoths it became the seat of a bishop. The Moors are believed to have introduced the cloth industry for which it was long reputed, but c 1085 it reverted to the Christians. It became a royal residence during the 13C (although the palace caved in in 1258, killing the dean of Burgos and hurting several bishops). Juan Gutiérrez, dean of Segovia, has been described as the 'eminence grise' behind English policy in the Peninsula during the last quarter of the 14C. It was also the home of the influential financier and last appointed court rabbi of Spain, Abraham Seneor, who in 1492 accepted baptism as Fernando Núñez Coronel.

In 1468 Enrique IV, repudiating his reputed daughter Juana la Beltraneja, publicly assumed his sister Isabel as his heir by leading her horse through the streets, and here in 1474 Isabel the Catholic was formally proclaimed 'Queen of Castile'. In the 14th and 15Cs the Cortes frequently met within its walls. In 1520 Segovia actively espoused the cause of the Comuneros, although its isolated Alcázar remained loyal.

A duel here in 1758 was the basis of Jovellanos's play 'El Delicuente honrado' (1774). The proposed establishment of an Economic Society in 1779 met with opposition and two years passed before it was formed, owing to the support of Campomanes. The society later suggested that all mayors and intendants should be forced to study political economy, a measure unfortunately not implemented.

Segovia was sacked by the French in 1808. An attempt was later made to restore its flagging woollen industry, but in 1829, when some improved machinery was introduced, it was immediately destroyed by the boetian handloom weavers.

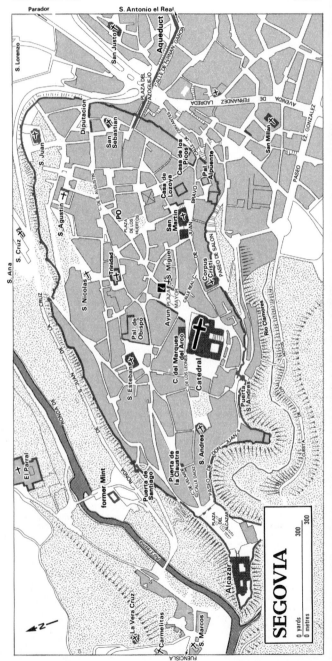

SEGOVIA

0 yards   300
0 metres   300

General Varela commanded the Segovia front during part of the Civil War. When he was minister of war in the Nationalist cabinet in 1942, 'N.S. de Fuencisla', the patron saint of the town, was named a full field marshal for her part in its defence. This apparently caused Hitler to remark that he would never visit Spain under any circumstances.

Segovia was the birthplace of Andrés Laguna (1499–1560), the Converso naturalist, botanist, and physician; Alonso de Ledesma (1562–1633), the 'Conceptista' poet; Diego de Colmenares (1586–1651), the city's historian; and Arsensio Martínez Campos (1831–1900), the reactionary general whose *pronunciamiento* at Sagunto in 1874 restored the Bourbon dynasty. The poet Antonio Machado (1875–1939) lived in the C. de Desamparados in 1919–31; cf. Soria and Baeza.

Most roads entering Segovia converge on the undistinguished *Pl. del Azoguejo*, crossed however by the immense *Aqueduct, one of the largest antique structures surviving in Spain. Known familiarly as 'El Puente', it is built of huge blocks of Guadarrama granite, without mortar. Of its total length of 813m, 274m are in two stages, while the height of its 165 arches varies from 128m downwards depending on the conformation of the ground. Note the slots in each stone, enabling it to be gripped by giant pincers and raised by block and tackle or crane.

The Roman aqueduct, Segovia, drawn by Edward Hawke Locker c 1813 (the abutting church of Sta. Columba was later demolished)

It probably dates from the time of Augustus and was restored under Trajan (98–117). It brings the water of the Riofrío to the city. Beginning near *S. Gabriel*, E of Segovia, it spans the intervening depression and intersects the city towards the Alcázar, the latter part of its course being subterranean. In 1071 35 of the arches were destroyed by the Moors, and they lay in ruins until 1483 when Isabel employed Juan Escovedo, a monk of El Parral, to rebuild them (letting him retain the scaffolding in lieu of payment). Apart from these and a few more modern restorations it is an untouched monument of ancient engineering genius. George Borrow waited under the 107th arch for the better part of an August day (1838) for his Spanish colporteur.

While the old town may be entered by car, it is more convenient to visit this area on foot, later driving round the walls, see below.

The pedestrian C. de Cervantes ascends NW from the plaza, continued by the C. de Juan Bravo. Bearing right, this passes the restored *Casa de los Picos*, a fortified 14C mansion which c 1500 received its remarkable façade, studded with faceted stones.— Beyond on the left, back from the street, is the 14C *Pal. de los Condes de Alpuente*, with two *ajimez* windows and decorated with plaster pargetting or *esgrafiado* work, still a favourite local style. Further on, steps lead down to the partly restored *Alhóndiga*, or public granary.

A Gothic house, called that of Juan Bravo (died 1521; a leader of the Comuneros), faces a plaza overlooked by the *Casa del Marqués de Lozoya* or *Mayorazgo de Cáceres*, with a 15C patio and a tower, among other restored mansions, and **S. Martín**, dating from the 12C. The church has an exterior gallery of local type and a tower partly rebuilt after a fire in 1322. It retains a good W portal and contains an alabaster tomb in the florid late Gothic chapel of the Herreras (? by Juan Güas).

From the S side of the plaza a lane descends to the tree-lined PASEO DE ISABEL II, flanked by a well-preserved section of *Wall*, strengthened by projecting *cubos*.

The main street next passes the former *Prison* (right; 1737), now housing the library and archives, and then (left) *Corpus Cristi*, originally a synagogue. In plan it resembles Sta. María la Blanca at Toledo, but it is much plainer in detail, and was damaged by fire in 1899.

The street ends in the *Pl. Mayor*, an irregular old square, partly arcaded. In it is a dilapidated 17C *Ayuntamiento*. *S. Miguel*, to the right, was designed by Rodrigo Gil de Hontañón (1588). The nearby Pl. de los Huertos is dominated by the pargetted tower of the 15C *Casa de Arias Dávila*.

The *Cathedral, the latest in Spain in the Gothic style, is basilican in plan, with no projecting transepts. It terminates on the E in a corona of seven polygonal chapels profusely adorned with pinnacles. The plain W front (requiring buttresses) overlooks a grass-grown forecourt. At the S angle of the W front rises a tall square tower terminating in a belfry chamber and cupola. Over the crossing is the cimborio, its design, like the tower, heralding the Renaissance. Its architects were Juan Gil de Hontañón and his son Rodrigo (died 1577), who, following the design of their cathedral at Salamanca, began work in 1525. It was completed c 65 years later. Both architects are buried under plain slabs near the cloister entrance. The previous 12C cathedral which stood near the Alcázar was wrecked by the Comuneros in 1520. Its Gothic cloister, built by Juan Güas in 1472–91, was re-erected on its present site by Juan de Campero.

The interior impresses by the wide span of its arches and the richness of its vaulting, but is disfigured by an ugly trascoro and respaldos (1784; by Ventura Rodríguez) and by tastelessly decorated chapels in the ambulatory. The smaller of the two organs (1702; by Echevarria) is untouched; the larger one, by Pedro Liborna de Echevarria, dates from c 1760. The choir stalls are from the old cathedral. A pierced Flamboyant balustrade takes the place of a triforium. Some windows retain stained glass by Pierre de Chiberry, a Fleming. The marble retablo mayor of 1775 is by Sabatini.

The nave is flanked by dark chapels. The first chapel in the N aisle has a mahogany reja; the fifth contains a retablo of 1571 designed by Juan de Juni and a triptych by Ambrosius Benson.

A fee is charged to enter the *Cloister* (see history, above) and *Museum* in the base of the tower. This contains the tomb of Don Pedro, the infant son of Enrique II, who was killed in 1366 by falling from a balcony of the Alcázar. The *Sala Capitular*, with a painted artesonado ceiling, is hung with Flemish tapestries from cartoons by Rubens; the series, with another, is continued on the stairs and in the *Archivo* above, a badly displayed collection of illuminated MSS, incunables, vestments, ornaments, and paintings including The Evangelists, by Ribera. The original Scale Drawings of the cathedral, on parchment, are of interest but are not normally on show. Here also is the case of a 17C Flemish harpsichord, possibly by Ruckers, which the guide insists is a 'clavicornio' of the 13C. It stood in the cloister until 1976, having long been used as a pigeon cote!

Almost opposite the cathedral entrance stands the *Casa del Marqués del Arco*, with a 16C patio. From there follow the street NW past *S. Andrés* (early 12C; modernised), with a Romanesque apse, passing several medieval doorways in the C. Daoiz, to reach the P. del Alcázar.

The **Alcázar**, occupying the W extremity of the ridge the old town straddles, and looking sheer down into the valleys of the Eresma and Clamores, is built possibly on Moorish or even Roman foundations. It is entered by a bridge spanning a dry moat cut into the rock.

Enlarged in 1352–58 by Enrique II, it was further extended by Catherine of Lancaster and her son, Juan II, in 1410–55. Prince Charles (later Charles I of England) was entertained here in 1623 and supped on 'certain trouts of extraordinary greatness'. It was a state prison under Felipe V, who in 1726 here confined his minister Ripperdá (1680–1737), who escaped two years later.

In 1862, when occupied by the artillery school, it was so seriously injured by a fire that, apart from the towers, most of what we see dates from a restoration begun in 1882.

Its conspicuous features are the *Torre de Juan II*, with its canopied windows and bartizan turrets, and the *Torre de Homenaje*, with seven turrets, its roof providing panoramic views. The most interesting rooms are the *Salón de la Galera*, with a Mudéjar frieze (an embellishment done for Catherine of Lancaster in 1412), the *Salón del Trono*, the *Salón del Solio*, decorated in 1456 by Xadel Alcalde, and the *Pieza del Cordón*.

The Pieza del Cordón, decorated with the cord of St. Francis, commemorates the story that Alfonso 'the Learned', having expressed the heretical opinion that the earth revolved around the sun, was so terrified by a thunderbolt that he immediately recanted and penitently assumed the cord. Also displayed are a 15C Flemish retablo, another by P. Berruguete, and some ancient armour and artillery.

A road descends E to the *Puerta de Santiago*, by which we reach the Paseo de S. Juan de la Cruz (formerly the Ronda de Sta. Lucía; see below). The Paseo de Don Juan II leads S, passing near the former *Malatero*, being restored to house a museum, and the *Puerta de S. Andrés*, a 12–13C gate bearing a tablet in commemoration of 'Don Pablo de Segovia', the picaresque hero of Quevedo's novel. Bear left at the gate to regain the Pl. Mayor after passing through the former *Judería*.

An alternative route from the Alcázar follows the C. Velarde, passing through the Romanesque *Puerta de la Claustra*, the survivor of four which once separated that quarter from the town, to approach *S. Esteban*; see below.

The C. Escudero descends from just W of the Ayuntamiento, passing the restored *Casa de Don Álvaro de Luna* (?12C), said to be the residence of Don Álvaro in 1445, and in the 16C the local tribunal of the Inquisition. To the right stands **S. Esteban** (13C), with a Romanesque exterior gallery and an imposing 12C *Tower* (rebuilt, and recently re-roofed). The *Bishop's Palace*, opposite, with curious reliefs on its granite façade, lacks an upper storey. There is talk of it being converted to house a provincial museum of religious art.

Following the C. de la Victoria to the E, passing (left) a lane descending to Romanesque *S. Quirce*, we skirt a Dominican convent in a fortified mansion built on Roman foundations, known as the *Casa de Hércules* from the figure on its tower. Beyond is *La Trinidad* (12C), with a characteristic exterior arcade. It contains an Isabelline chapel of 1513. *S. Nicolás*, to the E, retains its apse and some murals, but late Gothic *S. Agustín* lies in ruins. A lane later leads right past the over-restored *Casa de Apiroz* towards the 16C Herreran church of the *Seminario*.

The triangular Pl. del Conde de Cheste is soon entered, with the *Diputación* and other typical mansions with patios and sculptured doorways. They include the 14C *Casa de los Lozoya* and *Casa de Segovia*.—To the N in a lonely plaza is desecrated Romanesque *S. Juan de los Caballeros* (partly restored), with a good tower, triple apse, exterior arcade, and Gothic W door; it is used as a ceramic factory.—Just SW of the Pl. del Conde de Cheste is Franciscan *S. Sebastián*, just beyond which, from the N end of the Aqueduct, steps descend to the Pl. del Azoguejo.

Several interesting buildings lie outside the walled enceinte and are perhaps best visited by car. Driving N from the Pl. del Azoguejo, follow the wooded Paseo de S. Juan de la Cruz, shortly passing the *Hospicio*, formerly the Dominican *Conv. de Sta. Cruz*, founded by Fernando and Isabel (depicted above the W portal). Tomás de Torquemada was once prior. It was completed in 1492 by Juan Güas. Note the arrows and ox yoke on the exterior frieze of the apse.

A short walk to the E brings one to Romanesque *S. Lorenzo*, with a Mudéjar tower, three apses, and an arcade of coupled columns with good capitals. The plaza of this suburb has been restored. To the N, across the Eresma, is the *Conv. de S. Vicente el Real*.

The Paseo descends past (right) the former *Casa de Moneda* (in which all Spanish coins were minted from c 1586 until 1730). On the far bank of the river is the Hieronymite monastery of *El Parral* (partly restored), founded in 1447 by Juan Pacheco, Marqués de Villena, on a spot where he had fought three successful duels, and later reputed for its vineyards and gardens ('las huertas del Parral, paraíso terrenal'). It now accommodates only six or eight monks.

The *Church*, by Juan Gallego (1494; with a tower completed in 1529 by Juan de Campero) is entered through an unfinished portal. It contains the Plateresque tombs of the founder and his wife, and between them a retablo designed in 1528 by Juan Rodríguez and Diego de Urbina. The Cap. Mayor dates from 1472–85 (by Juan Güas and Bonifacio); the Coro from 1494.

In the side chapels (where pigs were penned in 1848) are the Gothic tombs of Segovian nobles. Beside the elaborate sacristy door is the tomb of Beatriz de Pacheco, illegitimate daughter of the founder. Two cloisters may also be seen, although the larger may be closed.

The Eresma is crossed a short distance W. Turn right further W to approach the remarkable Templar church of *La Vera Cruz* (c 1204–

08), with three apses and a sculptured W doorway. In the centre of the 12-sided nave is a walled chamber of two storeys built on the model of the Rotunda of the Holy Sepulchre in Jerusalem. It contains late 15C murals, and a retablo of 1516.—For *Zamarramala* see p 164.

Nearer the river to the W is *S. Marcos* (12C) and, right, the 17C *Carmelitas*, with the tomb of St. John of the Cross (cf. Fontiveros). It contains only his head and trunk; other limbs had been amputated and dispersed as relics.

Beyond is the *Sanctuario de Fuencisla* (1613; by Juan de Mora). Opposite rises the *Peña Grajera* (crag of the crows), the local Tarpeian Rock. Further N is a Baroque *Arco de Homenaje* (1704).

Crossing the *Puente de S. Lázaro*, the valley of the Clamores is followed by the Cuesta de los Hoyos, commanding an impressive *View of the 'prow' of the Alcázar and the walls. Later, the former *Matadero* on a rocky spur is passed. At the main crossroads turn left past (left) Romanesque **S. Millán**, perhaps founded in the 10C, with a good doorway, triple apse, and exterior arcades on both sides, with carved capitals. To the right further on is restored *S. Clemente*, passed before regaining the Aqueduct.

The most important building in the S quarter of the town is the **Conv. de S. Antonio el Real**, standing a short distance W of the road to La Granja before reaching the Plaza de Toros; it may also be approached by following the line of the Aqueduct to its termination, there bearing right. The convent was founded by Enrique IV in a country house, and rebuilt by Xadel Alcalde in 1455. The portal of the *Church* (1488), the ceiling of the chancel, and the painted wooden Calvary with figures by a Flemish sculptor, are remarkable. In the convent itself (ring at the interior door) the magnificent artesonados of the main *Cloister*, the *Sala Capitular*, and *Sala de los Reyes* (Sacristy), are all in a perfect state of preservation.

Not far E of the Pl. del Azoguejo stands *S. Justo*, with a good Romanesque tower and doorway, retaining some interesting but over restored murals. Near by *S. Salvador*, preserving Romanesque details, has a Baroque interior and 16C Flemish triptych.

The C.S. Francisco climbs S from the Aqueduct, passing the *Artillery School* (established 1764), partly in the dependencies of the *Conv. de S. Francisco* (founded in 1220), with a Plateresque patio. Continue S past *Sta. Eulalia*, to the E of which is the florid Gothic *Conv. de Sta. Isabel*; while to the W is *Sto. Tomás*, with Romanesque details.

For roads from Segovia to **Soria** and **Valladolid** see Rtes 11C and 16 respectively, in reverse. For the road to **Ávila** see Rte 16.

26 Salamanca

SALAMANCA (800m; 154,000 inhab.; 32,000 in 1920; 87,000 in 1960; Parador), standing proudly above the N or right bank of the Tormes, is famous for its two cathedrals and its university (the senior Spanish foundation). The area of the walled city was formerly rather larger than Oxford and Cambridge combined. Although it has suffered much from fire and sword throughout the ages, and more recently from unrestricted building in the immediate suburbs, central Salamanca has preserved numerous fine old buildings, weathered to a beautiful golden brown. It is architecturally one of the more interesting cities of Spain. The climate is often dry and sunny, but subject to violent extremes.

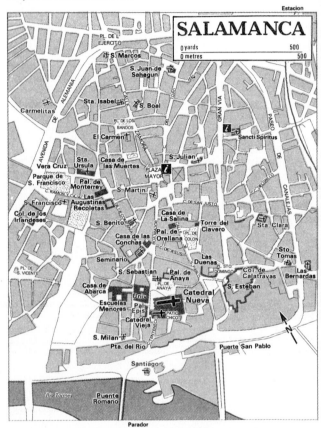

Salmantica was already an important Iberian city when captured by Hannibal in 217 BC. The defenders were disarmed, but the women, who had not been searched, supplied their men with weapons, enabling them to turn the tables on their captors and escape to the hills. Impressed by their resource, Hannibal allowed them to return unmolested. Under the Romans Salamanca was a station on the Vía Lata (later known as the Vía de la Plata) from Mérida to Astorga, and it flourished under the Visigoths. Taken by the Moors in 715, it was recaptured only in 1055, after 300 years of intermittent warfare which left the country between the Duero and the Tagus an uninhabited wilderness.

In 1085 Alfonso VI gave Salamanca to his son-in-law and daughter (Count Raymond of Burgundy and Doña Urraca) to repopulate; and c 1220 Alfonso IX of León founded the university. Despite this and other marks of favour the Salmantines were continually in rebellion against the central authority, until the culminating insurrection of the Comuneros in 1521 was crushed by Charles V. The marriage of his son, the future Felipe II, and María of Portugal was celebrated here in 1543, but the town and university, corrupted by the ultra-clericalism of the time, gradually decayed.

The final blow was struck by the French in 1811, when the entire SW quarter of the town, including numerous colleges and religious foundations, was demolished by Marmont to set up fortifications against Wellington, who in turn was obliged to besiege them. On 22 July 1812 Wellington, by his lightning victory of Salamanca (called Arapiles by the Spanish after the village and hills round which the battle centred, SE of the town; see last section of Rte 22) scattered the French, but the following winter they returned to pillage the place again.

In 1832 Colonel Badcock, a peninsular veteran, enquired why one sector of the town appeared in a more derelict state than he remembered it. He was told that the French had left a large deposit of gunpowder there, and that the Spanish garrison could find no better place to smoke than over the apertures of the store. The consequent explosion and devastation was as a matter of course blamed on the British!

Salamanca was the Nationalist HQ during the earlier part of the Civil War of 1936–39.

It was the birthplace of Fernando Gallego (c 1460–1550) and Antonio Carnicero (1748–1814), artists; Juan del Encina (1469–1529?), the playwright, poet and musician; José Churriguera (1660–1725), the architect; and Diego de Torres Villarroel (1693–1770), the satirist and poet, whose picaresque autobiography was published in 1743–58.

View of Salamanca from the west during the Peninsular War

Roads from Zamora and Valladolid converge a short distance N of the main avenue or *paseo* surrounding the old town, in the centre of which is the Pl. Mayor. Roads from Ávila, Plasencia, and Ciudad Rodrigo converge S of the river, here spanned by two modern bridges. Between them the Tormes is crossed by the *Puente Romano* (pedestrian only) of 26 arches. The 15 northernmost arches are mainly Roman work (rebuilt under Trajan and Hadrian); the rest date from 1499 to 1677. On the hill to the S stands the ungainly new Parador.

The *Plaza Mayor*, one of the largest in Spain, is a handsome square built in 1733 from designs by Alberto Churriguera, assisted by José de Lara and Nicolás Churriguera, while the *Ayuntamiento* on its N side was completed by Andrés García de Quiñones in 1755. The walks beneath its arcades are the fashionable promenades of the Salmantines. Two façades bear the busts of kings and—with one exception at the NE corner—worthies of Spain.

Immediately SW of the Plaza is 12C *S. Martín*, with a Romanesque N door and Renaissance S door (1586), both surmounted by a group of St. Martin dividing his cloak. Within are Gothic tombs and a retablo of 1731 by García de Quiñones.

The C. Mayor leads SW to the corner-sited *Casa de las Conchas (long under restoration), its architect now assumed to be Lorenzo Vázquez. Completed by 1483, its exterior is studded with shells, the badge of its builder (Dr Talavera Maldonado, whose son had married a Benavente), a knight of the Order of Santiago, their motif repeated on its grilles and elsewhere.—On the opposite corner is the Jesuit *Seminario* or **La Clericía** (begun in 1617 by Gómez de Mora, with a huge domed church (completed 1750; under restoration) and Baroque cloister.—Adjacent is the Renaissance *Conv. de S. Isidoro* (restored since being used as a bus station). For the area to the N see below.

A short distance S is the Pl. de Anaya, with on its N side *S. Sebastián* (1731; by Alberto Churriguera), the former *Colegio S. Bartolomé* (1765; by José Hermosilla), and another college with a patio by José Churriguera.

The plaza is dominated by the *Catedral Nueva, an imposing Gothic pile begun in 1513 by Juan Gil de Hontañón and completed by his son Rodrigo, assisted by Juan de Álava.

The N door carries a relief of Christ's entry into Jerusalem; further E is the rather ineffective façade of the transept, plastered with pinnacles; the E end is square, an unusual feature. The *W Front*, completed by 1531, is an extravagant example of late Gothic decoration, notably the central *Puerta del Nacimiento*, with sculptured panels attributed to Juan de Juni and Becerra. The *SW Tower*, modelled by Rodrigo on that of Toledo cathedral, was cased in masonry some years after the Lisbon Earthquake of 1755, which had weakened the structure. The central Cupola, begun in 1705 by José and Joaquín Churriguera, was not completed until 1733.

The well-proportioned interior (103m long; 49m wide) has its vault supported by finely moulded piers; a pierced balustrade (with bust medallions above and below) takes the place of a triforium. A gallery of Flamboyant tracery runs round the aisle and transepts at the level of the capitals of the main arcade. The interior of the cupola is elaborately carved.

The *Coro* (1733) contains stalls decorated by Alberto Churriguera. In the Trascoro, by Joaquín Churriguera, are figures by Juan de Juni. The Cap. Mayor (c 1588) retains Flemish glass and an Assumption by Gregorio Fernández. Note the organs, the smaller of 1588, and the huge Baroque instrument of 1745 by Pedro Liborna de Echevarria, with its trumpets in *chamade*.

From the *Puerta del Patio Chico* one may step out to obtain an interesting view of the exterior conical cupola of the *old* cathedral, with its scaly tiles. It was once crowned with a weathercock from which it took its name *Torre del Gallo*.

From a door in the S aisle steps descend into the *Catedral Vieja (consecrated 1160), celebrated in the Latin couplet: 'Dives Toletana, pulchra Leonina, sancta Ovetensis, fortis Salmantina'. In some ways it is one of the most interesting Romanesque churches in Spain. An entrance fee is charged.

Traditionally founded by Bp Jerónimo (died 1120), its building was certainly in progress in 1152–89, and in general lines it is typical of the transitional Romanesque of Southern France. Some of the windows on the N and W sides have been blocked. The beautiful *Dome* is unusual, and appears to owe its design to Byzantine tradition, the ribbed vault being raised on two tiers of arcaded lights, unlike the dark cupolas of Aquitaine, but with similarities of style to those of Toro and the old Chapterhouse at Plasencia. The main arcade is pointed, but the upper wall arcades are round-headed. The capitals are curiously and boldly sculptured, and some are surmounted by statues at the spring of the corner-ribs.

The main apse contains a curved **Retablo** containing 53 paintings by Nicolás Florentino (c 1445–66) with his fresco of the Last Judgement above; the lower frieze is attributed to Gallego. The *Cloister*, entered from the S transept, was begun in 1177. It has been largely modernised, although some early capitals survive. On its E side are the *Cap. de Talavera*, with a curious dome with a star-shaped *Vault*, and the *Cap. de Sta. Bárbara* (1350). The *Chapterhouse* contains a triptych of St. Catherine by Gallego among other paintings, and a curious carving of St. Hubert. On the S side is the *Cap. de S. Bartolomé*, erected in 1422 by Diego de Anaya, Abp of Sevilla (died 1437; founder of the Colegio de S. Bartolomé), whose *Tomb* is surrounded by a magnificent 16C *verja*. The vault is English in character, with tiercerons and ridge-ribs. The *Organ*, with a Mudéjar tribune, is one of the oldest surviving in Europe (1380; that at Sion in Switzerland is 1390). The soundboard is original. (Among the musical instruments preserved in the cathedrals are a set of shawms, but in the early 1970s their rarer cases were jettisoned by the ecclesiastical authorities as being of no consequence!) Note the painted doors (14C) and turrets.

Turn left on leaving to pass (right) the former *Bishop's Palace* (the Nationalist HQ during the Civil War), since 1987 restored to house both the municipal and cathedral *Archives*, and a *Diocesan Museum*. As yet this does not contain much of particular interest, apart from a wooden model of García de Quiñones' Ayuntamiento (1745).

Adjacent are the *Col. de S. Ambrosio*, with a façade of 1720 by Manuel de Lara Churriguera, and (further on) the *Col. de Carvajal* (1602). A lane descends behind the old cathedral to the site of the Puerta del Río, and to Mozarabic *Santiago* (founded 1145; restored), with a view of the *Roman Bridge* (see p 209).

Bear left when returning uphill, and then right along the C. Libreros past *S. Millán* (1480, with a Baroque doorway of 1635), to approach the *Patio de las Escuelas*. To the right is the old *Rectoral*, the former residence of Unamuno, and now preserving his Library; see below.

The Patio is dominated by the main entrance façade of the ***University** (before 1529) on its E side, a masterpiece of Plateresque art profusely adorned with escutcheons, medallions, and scrolls. The lowest medallions contain portraits of Fernando and Isabel, surrounded by a dedicatory inscription in Greek.

Founded before 1230 by Alfonso IX of León in emulation of the Castilian university of Palencia, Salamanca absorbed the sister foundation in 1239 when the crowns of Castile and León were united in the person of Fernando III. In 1254 Alfonso 'el Sabio' founded the law schools and the library, and from that date the university, acknowledged by Pope Alexander IV to be one of the four great universities in the world (with Paris, Oxford, and Bologna), grew in importance. In the 15–16Cs it had over 10,000 students and 25 colleges—four of them (S. Bartolomé, del Arzobispo, Cuenca, and del Rey) *Escuelas Mayores*, the preserve of aristocratic families; the rest *Escuelas Menores*. Columbus consulted the astronomical faculty which in the next century taught the Copernican theory, elsewhere regarded as heretical.

Among distinguished professors in the 15–16Cs were Luis de León (c 1527–91; the *converso* Biblical translator and poet); Francisco de Vitoria (died 1546; defender of the American Indians); Beatriz de Galindo, 'la Latina' (1475–1535; the first woman professor, who taught Queen Isabel Latin); Melchor Cano (died 1560); and Juan Ribera (died 1611; Abp of Valencia). Among the less distinguished was Diego Torres Villarroel. Abraham Zacuto carried out astronomical research for the bishop for several years prior to 1480.

Aristocratic prejudice and religious bigotry brought about its decline. William Dalrymple, who passed this way in 1774, remarked that most of the colleges appeared 'as if they had been lately wasted and ruined by a ravaging army'. They were so depleted in numbers that in some he found only the head of the house, with one or two students, and in many 'not above six or seven'. This decline was further precipitated by the destruction and demolition of colleges in 1811. But it later revived: Ford jocularly calling the town 'Bull-ford', numbering its students 'amongst the boldest and most impertinent of the human race, full of tags, and rags, fun, frolic, Licence, and guitars'. It is now attended by c 12,500 students.

The interior, built between 1415 and 1529, is less remarkable. Among some old furniture is a rare portative organ (16C), possibly used by Francisco de Salinas. On the N side of its patio is the *Lecture Room* or *Paraninfo*, with the pulpit from which Luis de León lectured. After five years of imprisonment by the Inquisition for his advanced ideas, his famous opening words to his expectant audience were: 'Dicebamus hesterna die . . .' (as we were saying yesterday). Here also took place the historic confrontation (12 October 1936) between Miguel de Unamuno (1864–31 December 1936), who had been Rector of the University for 14 years, and the Nationalist General Millán Astray, whose slogan, 'Viva la muerte' and 'Mueran los intelectuales', symbolised the military mind. On the E side is the *Chapel* (1767). The 16C *Staircase*, on the S side, adorned with reliefs of bull fights, etc., ascends to a gallery with an artesonado ceiling. Beyond a 16C iron gate is the *'Old' Library* (containing c 130,000 volumes, 462 incunables, and 2800 MSS).

In the centre of the Patio de las Escuelas is a statue of Luis de León. On its S side are the two Plateresque doorways of the **Escuelas Menores** (c 1500–33). The first door admits to Archives, the second to a patio with curiously weak-looking arches. The building contains a museum displaying paintings done by Gallego in 1494 and transferred to canvas.

The *Casa de Alvárez Abarca*, physician to Isabel the Catholic, on the W side of the Patio de las Escuelas, now houses the **Museo de Bellas Artes**, to be expanded.

Restored in 1973, and preserving an artesonado from Dueñas, the collection includes an *anon. Flemish* Captain and harquebusier, and a Knight of Malta; *School of Zurbarán*, Portrait of Fray Iñigo de Brizuela; *J.A. Beschey* (1710–86), Elevation of the Cross; *anon. Dutch* Landscapes; *Rigaud*, Francisco L. de Borbón, Jardín del Príncipe, Aranjuez; *Ranc*, María Ana Victoria de Borbon; *M. Carbonero*, The Condesa de Pardo Bazan; *Zubiaurre*, Luncheon; *Bacarisas*, View of Segovia; *Zuloaga*, a Segovian; *Echevarria*, Portrait of Unamuno, and his sculpted head by *Moisés Huerta*; and Hunting angels (Cuzco School). Some stelae are in the garden.

From the Pl. de Anaya follow the C. Tostado downhill and cross the C.S. Pablo to approach the Pl. de Sto. Domingo, passing (left) the Plateresque portal (1553) of the Dominican nunnery of **Las Dueñas**, founded in 1419. It contains a Mudéjar doorway and an attractive 16C **Cloister*, an irregular pentagon of two storeys (restored) with grotesque capitals.

A footbridge crosses to **S. Esteban*, assigned to the Dominicans when their previous home was destroyed by flood in 1256. It gave asylum to Columbus in 1484–86 when he was endeavouring to interest the university in his project of finding a passage to the Indies. Diego de Deza (later Abp of Sevilla and Grand Inquisitor; died 1497) recommended him to the queen. The present church, begun by Juan de Álava in 1524, has an imposing *W Front which rivals that of the University. It depicts the Stoning of St. Stephen (1610; by Juan Antonio Ceroni of Milan). Note, among other delicate sculptures, the upper frieze of children and horses.

The monastery is entered from beneath the arcade to the right, then up a staircase of 1533 in the NE corner of a cloister. From the upper storey one may reach the raised *Coro*, decorated with a feeble fresco of 1705 by Palomino. At the E end of the Church is an ornate retablo of 1693 by José Churriguera, with statues by Carmona, a Martyrdom of St. Stephen by Claudio Coello, and a 12C Limoges enamel Virgin. The Tomb of Fernando Álvarez de Toledo, the 3rd Duke of Alba (1507–82), has been moved to a chapel off the cloister. The Sacristy, by Juan Moreno, was begun in 1627.

Adjacent to the E is the *Col. de Calatrava*, a dignified building begun in 1717 by Joaquín and Alberto Churriguera, with a notable interior stair. Beyond, to the right, is *Sto. Tomás*, with a Romanesque apse (1179) dedicated to Thomas Becket four years after his assassination. Further E is the chapel of *Las Bernardas* (1552); while some distance to the S stands the former *Conv. de La Vega*, its garden containing ruins of a beautiful cloister of c 1160.

On returning to S. Esteban, bear right to reach the Pl. de Colón, passing (right) *La Trinidad* or *S. Pablo* (1677), containing good sculptures. No. 32 is the 16C *Pal. de Orellana*, No. 34 the *Casa de Abrantes*, with a 15C doorway. At the NE corner rises the *Torre del Clavero, with eight bartizan turrets, built in 1480 by Francisco de Sotomayor, 'clavero' or key warden of the Order of Alcántara. Restored, it contains the *Museo de la Ciudad*, with objects of local interest.

The C.S. Pablo leads past (left) the *Casa de la Salina*, now the *Diputación*, built for the Fonseca family c 1519–50. It has a majestic arched façade and a patio whose projecting gallery is supported by wooden consoles carved with remarkable figures.

Retracing our steps for a short distance, turn right uphill to regain the Casa de las Conchas. Follow the C. de la Compañía, in which *S. Benito* (rebuilt 1504) is passed on the right and, beyond (left), **Las Agustinas Descalzas**. Built in 1626–36 by Juan Fontana for a convent founded by the Conde de Monterrey, viceroy of Naples, it is decorated with Italian marbles and contains several paintings of the Neapolitan School, including a Conception by Ribera. Notable are the Kneeling Tomb Sculptures by Giuliano Finelli of the Conde de Monterrey and his wife, the sister of Olivares.

Opposite stands the imposing **Pal. de Monterrey** (begun 1540), with its floreated balustrade (restored).

The C. de Ramón y Cajal leads left past the Capuchin church of *S. Francisco* (1746–56; by Andrés García de Quiñones), with statues by Carmona, to enter the Parque de S. Francisco. On the left is the former *Colegio de los Irlandeses* (or *del Arzobispo*), founded in 1521 by Abp Alonso de Fonseca.

The Irish college itself was founded in 1592 for the training of c 30 priests, with James Archer as its first rector. Joseph Townsend, who visited the place in 1786, reported that the course lasted eight years, and that the students, who had no vacations, rose every morning at 4.30. Among its later rectors was Dr Curtis, who materially assisted Wellington during the Peninsular War by collecting military information in the area.

The building, by Pedro Ibarra and Alonso de Covarrubias, is entered by an Ionic portal with the Fonseca arms and a relief of Santiago (to whom it was dedicated) fighting the Moors. From the galleried patio, with medallions by Berruguete, a Plateresque doorway admits to the *Chapel* (by Juan de Álava) with a retablo of 1531, probably also in part by Berruguete.

The adjacent building, with a notable portal, is by Juan de Sagarviñaga (1790). *S. Blas*, opposite, of 1772, retains a Romanesque apse.

In the quarter N of the Monterrey palace is (right) the *Casa de las Muertes* (c 1545), built for Abp Fonseca, its façade decorated wth busts of himself and his nephews, and with skulls. Unamuno died in the adjacent house (cf. University).

Sta. Úrsula, opposite, has an apse crowned by a balustraded *mirador*; within is the Tomb of Abp Fonseca, by Diego de Siloé. Note the artesonados.—Beyond the convent is the *Cap. de la Vera Cruz*, once a synagogue, retaining a 16C doorway but rebuilt in 1713. It contains *pasos* by Gregorio Fernández and A. Carnicero, and sculpture by Juan de Juni.—Other sculptures of interest may be seen in the sacristy of the *Adoratrices* convent opposite, with relics of a 13C church.

Further N are the *Carmelitas* (founded by Sta. Teresa in 1570); *S. Juan Bautista*, with remains of a Romanesque cloister; and the 15C *Casa de Doña María la Brava*.—To the E is the Pl. de los Bandos, with *El Carmen* (1703) and two 16C mansions.

From its E side the C. de Zamora leads N to the *Conv. de Sta. Isabel*, founded in 1433, with tombs of the Solis family, a painting of St. Elisabeth of Hungary by Nicolás Florentino, and a notable artesonado over the Coro. The street ends at (left) *S. Marcos* (1202), one of the few round churches having no connection with the Templars or Hospitallers.

E of the C. de Zamora, and just S of Sta. Isabel, is the Pl. de S. Boal, its *Church* of 1740 by Alberto Churriguera, and the *Casa del Marqués de Almaza*, briefly Wellington's quarters in 1812; also two 15C mansions.

Turning right just N of S. Boal, one may work one's way E, passing the *Torre del Aire* (a survival of the Pal. de la Cuatro Torres), to the C. de España. Further E, behind the Tourist Office, is *Sancti Spiritus*, by Rodrigo Gil de Hontañón. It has a richly chased portal of 1541 by Berruguete and a retablo mayor of 1656. The roof over the Coro and some of the sculptures are notable.

In the same area but further S are the remaining arcade of the cloister of Gothic *Sta. Clara*; the *Col. de Josefinas*, with an early 16C patio, Romanesque *S. Cristóbal*, and (nearer the centre) *S. Julián*, rebuilt in 1582 but retaining a 12C tower and doorway. It contains a statue of S. Pedro de Alcántara by Pedro de Mena.

Don Juan (1478–97), the only son of Fernando and Isabel, died at the *Casa de las Cadenas* in the nearby C. de Pozo (cf. Sto. Tomás, Ávila).

For roads from Salamanca to **Valladolid**, **Zamora**, and **Ávila**, see Rtes 10, 19, and 22, in reverse; for roads to **Plasencia** and **Ciudad Rodrigo**, Rtes 27A and C.

SALAMANCA TO LEDESMA (37.5km) FOR FERMOSELLE. An alternative road along the N bank of the Tormes passes at 18km *Almenara de Tormes*, with a mid 12C church.—The C517 turns off the N620 just W of Salamanca. Fork right off the C517 after 28.5km at *Villarmayor* for **Ledesma**, an attractive old walled town with an arcaded plaza, a *Bridge* on Roman foundations, and relics of Roman baths. *S. Miguel* is part Romanesque; 13–16C *Sta. María* contains tombs of interest; the *Ayuntamiento* dates from 1606.

The SA302 continues NW, later skirting arms of the *Embalse de Almendra*. 3km beyond (48km) *Almendra* bear right on the C525 to cross the Tormes to approach (c 12km) *Fermoselle*; see p 186.—The left fork leads to *Vitigudino*, 26.5km S; see below.

SALAMANCA TO LUMBRALES (97km). The good but lonely C517 continues W from (28.5km) *Villarmayor* (see above) to (41.5km) *Vitigudino*, also bypassed. 7km SW of Vitigudino is the Iberian site of *Yecla de Yeltes* or *la Vieja*.—15km *Cerralbo*, with relics of a castle.—12km *Lumbrales*, with lead mines and several dolmens in its vicinity, retains relics of pre-Roman walls at *Las Merchanas*.— The C517 continues NW, passing S of *Hinojosa de Duero*, the old parish church of which is Romanesque, and peters out at *Muelle de Vega Terrón*, overlooking the Douro. There is talk of joining up with with N221 at *Barca de Alva*, between *Freixo de Espada-à-Cinta* and *Figueira de Castelo Rodrigo*; see Blue Guide Portugal.

From Lumbrales, the SA324 turns S to (10km) *S. Felices de los Gallegos*, with a part Romanesque church, fortified gate, and 16C keep. In March 1810 serious skirmishing took place at *Barba de Puerco*, on the Águeda further W, between Gen. Crauford's Light Division and French forces based on S. Felices.—The main road continues S parallel to the river to meet the N620 at (39km) *Ciudad Rodrigo*; see Rte 28.

27 Salamanca to Cáceres

A. Via Plasencia

216km (134 miles). N630. 74km **Béjar**—58km **Plasencia**—84km **Cáceres**.

Maps: M 447.

The N630 drives due S, at 8km passing (left) *Arapiles* and the site of the *Battle of Salamanca* (see p 192). The N630 follows approximately the line of the Via Lata (locally called the Camino de la Plata), the Roman road which ran from Mérida to Salamanca and Astorga. Fragments of its paving can be traced here and there.—At 10km *Alba de Tormes* lies 10km E; see Rte 24. Later passing near the *Embalse de Sta. Teresa*, to the E, the road starts to climb. The SIERRA DE CANDELARIO rises to the S and the SIERRA DE PEÑA DE FRANCIA (see Rte 27B) to the W. The road reaches a height of 1202m before descending past the road from El Barco de Ávila to approach Béjar.

4km to the left from a junction just before the town is the picturesque village of **Candelario**, with its balconied houses overhanging steeply climbing lanes. An unusual feature is the double lower doors to numerous houses. The ancient coiffure of the region may still be seen here. The Sierra rises to 2425m further S.

Béjar (938m; 17,300 inhab.), a small industrial town formerly reputed for its blankets, retains stretches of ancient Moorish fortifications restored in the 12C. It is dominated by the *Alcázar del Duque de Osuna*, a feudal palace with a 16C Classical patio, containing a local museum. *Sta. María* is early 13C; *S. Salvador* dates from 1554.—The C515 leads NW past the castle of *La Calzada*, of Roman foundation, and with remains of an ancient causeway, to (25.5km) *Santibáñez de la Sierra*; see Rte 27B.

The N630 circles to the SW to the *Puerto de Béjar* (1048m), beyond which a road leads 6km right to *Montemayor del Río*, with a Roman bridge, 15C castle, and 13C church. At 14km an abrupt right bend brings one down to *Baños de Montemayor*, a thermal resort since Roman times, with a leaning church tower.

5km. **Hervás**, 3km left, an attractive village lying among olive groves and cherry orchards, is known for its well-preserved *Judería*; *S. Juan* contains Baroque retablos. The main road may be regained to the W.

5km. *Abadía*, with a Templars' castle converted into a Cistercian abbey, retaining a 13C cloister of horseshoe arches (restored), lies 3km to the right. Near by are the remains of a 16C palace built for the Duke of Alba by Flemish and Italian craftsmen.

The road continues towards the fortified village of *Granadilla, c 14km beyond, on the banks of the *Embalse de Gabriel y Galán*, formed by damming the Alagón. The village itself, although deserted, has been partly restored and can be approached with difficulty by foot. Its fine castle dates from 1400.

16.5km. A road to the right leads shortly to *Caparra*, with a four-square Triumphal Arch and, in the valley, a Bridge, relics of Roman *Capera*.

Some 7km further W at *Guijo de Granadilla* is a bridge on Roman foundations. José María Gabriel y Galán (1870–1905), the regional poet, lived and died here.

At 18km, after passing the *Arcos de S. Antón*, a medieval aqueduct of 53 arches, we enter **PLASENCIA** (31,200 inhab.), an attractively situated provincial town on the N bank of the Jerte, which descends from the SIERRA DE GREDOS (see latter part of Rte 16) to join the Alagón.

It was founded by Alfonso VIII in 1189 on the site of Roman (?) *Ambracia* or *Dulcis Placida*, destroyed by the Moors, the pious founder giving it the motto 'Ut Deo placet'. In 1196 it was briefly recaptured by Almanzor and many of its inhabitants were sent to work on the mosque at Rabat.

Traces of ramparts survive, but most of the 68 semicircular towers or *cubos* have been built against, and are hardly recognisable as fortifications. The castle was destroyed during the Peninsular War. The river is spanned by the *Puente de S. Lázaro* (1498) and the *Puente Nuevo* (1512). Above the bridges rises the ornate but sombre Gothic *Cathedral*. It was begun in 1498 by Enrique de Egas and continued in 1513–37 by Juan de Álava, but remained unfinished. On the N side is the *Puerta del Enlosada*, in the style of Berruguete, dating from 1558.

Abutting it is a fragment of the former cathedral of c 1320–1400, its *Chapterhouse* with a 13C *Dome* of the type of the Torre del Gallo at Salamanca. Its *Cloisters* date from 1416–38. A remarkable spiral staircase ascends to a terrace.

The cathedral is notable for the size and unbroken shafts of the pillars and the delicacy of its vaulting. The *Cap. Mayor*, completed by Francisco de Colonia and Juan de Álava in 1522, contains a retablo by Gregorio Fernández (1626). To the left of the retablo is the tomb of Bp Ponce de León (died 1573) by Mateo Sánchez de Villaviciosa. The *Reja* of 1604 is the masterpiece of J.B. Celma, but perhaps the most striking feature of the church is the *Sillería* by Rodrigo Alemán (1497–1520). This is an elaborate and beautiful piece of carving, with sacred and profane, if not obscene, subjects juxtaposed.

Facing the cathedral and in the C. de Obispo Casas are some old mansions, including the *Casa de Deán*, which has a corner balcony. To the N is 13–14C *S. Nicolás*; opposite is the *Pal. de Mirabel*, with an attractive two-storey patio. *S. Ildefonso*, further NE, contains a fine effigy of Cristóbal de Villalba. *S. Martín* contains a 16C retablo by Juan de Jaén, with four paintings by Morales (1565).

In the Pl. de S. Nicolás is the *Casa de las Bóvedas* (1550) with a saloon decorated with frescoes of the battles of Charles V. *S. Vicente* (1464–74), adjoining, contains an armed but mutilated effigy of Martín Nieto (1597), a remarkable staircase of 1577, and good azulejos in the sacristy.

In the arcaded PL. DE ESPAÑA stands the 16C *Ayuntamiento*, with a good artesonado in its main hall.

At the end of the C. del Marqués de la Constancia is *Sta. Ana* (1556); to the N is *S. Salvador*, containing important monuments.

To the SE by the *Puerta del Sol* is *S. Pedro*. Near the *Puerta de Coria* is Romanesque *Sta. María Magdalena*.

For the road NE to **Ávila** see Rte 16, for *Yuste* and *Jarandilla*, Rte 49; both in reverse.

PLASENCIA TO TRUJILLO (83km). The lonely C524 climbs left off the N630 just S of the town, at 11km passing 5.5km SW of *Malpartida de Plasencia*, with a fine church.—At 17km we cross and briefly skirt the Tagus just below its junction with the Tiétar. The jagged gorge of the Tagus is overlooked by the ruins of the 12C Moorish castle of *Monfragüe*, below which late Neolithic paintings have been discovered. The road continues S, traversing a depopulated tract to *Trujillo*, seen from some distance away on its hill; see Rte 51.

The main road drives SW, at 7km passing a turning (right) to (11.5km) *Galisteo*, with remains of Moorish walls and castle, a medieval bridge, and the 13C Mudéjar apse of its church.—*Coria* lies c 26km further W; see Rte 27C.

At 9.5km the 12C castle of *Mirabel* and *Pal. del Marqués de*

The plaza, Garrovillas

Mirabel, lie 9km left. After 17km the *Puerto de los Castaños* (493m) is crossed. To the W at *Palancar* is a 17C monastery encircling the diminutive dependencies of its predecessor.—5km *Cañaveral*, with a Moorish tower, is entered and, 5.5km beyond, the road from Coria is met; see Rte 27C. The ruins of the Roman bridge of *Alconétar*, destroyed by the Moors in 1232, which would have been submerged, have been moved to a site near an arm of the huge *Embalse de Alcántara*, fed by the Tagus and spanned by a two-storey bridge carrying both road and railway.—A right-hand turning at 14km leads 10.5km to **Garrovillas**, with a curious white-washed *Plaza*. 15C *Sta. María* and *S. Pedro* are of interest, and there are several prehistoric sites in the vicinity.

The main road veers S to approach (26km) **Cáceres**; see Rte 51.

B.   Via La Alberca: the Batuecas

260km (161 miles). C512. 29km *Vecinos*, bearing left just beyond— 34.5km *Santibáñez de la Sierra*—C515. 10.5km. *Miranda del Castañar* lies 3km left.—turn right 3km after regaining the main route—11km **La Alberca**—SA201. 22km C512. 44.5km *Villanueva de la Sierra*—33.5km **Coria**—C526. 32km N630. 40km **Cáceres**.

Maps: M 441, 447.

This is a slow but beautiful and wild road through the SIERRA DE PEÑA DE FRANCIA as far as Coria. The range is said to have been named in honour of French colonists brought to Salamanca by Raymond of Burgundy in 1085.

An ALTERNATIVE road from Vecinos via *Tamames* is 11km shorter. From Tamames follow the SA204 SW through *El Cabaco*, 3km beyond passing the mountain road circling steeply up to the conical summit of the broken range (1732m), commanding a magnificent *View*. The convent there dates back to the early 15C.—7km *La Alberca*; see below.—El Cabaco is approached from *Ciudad Rodrigo*, 29.5km W, by the C515 via *Tenebrón* and *El Maíllo*.

The C512 drives SW from Salamanca, at c 30km forking left to approach a spur of the SIERRA DE LA PEÑA DE FRANCIA, with the peak of the range prominent to the SW. At *Santibáñez de la Sierra* the C512 meets the C515 from Béjar. Turn right here, following the gorge of the Alagón.—At 10.5km picturesque *Miranda del Castañar, with its castle and Romanesque church, lies to the left.— We shortly turn right, climbing steeply through wooded hills (views E) for (14km) *La Alberca*.—An ALTERNATIVE approach is to follow the road opposite the Miranda turning to (10km) *Sequeros*. After 4km turn left past *S. Martín de Castañar*, with medieval walls and a castle, to meet the SA202 below the *Peña de Francia* some 5km NW of La Alberca.

La Alberca, a large—and until the 1960s unspoilt—village of Moorish origin, preserves numerous ancient houses flanking cobbled streets, an arcaded *Pl. Mayor*, and a 17C church. The Ofrenda a la Virgen and the Loa (a mystery play) are performed here on 15–16 August, when local costumes and jewellery of curious design (cf. Astorga; the Maragatos) are displayed. A monument commemorates Maurice Legendre, whose pioneering study of the area was published in 1927.

After climbing steeply S to *El Portillo* (1240m), the road descends in zigzags into the rugged valley of *Las Batuecas*. With the three parallel valleys of *Las Hurdes*, Las Batuecas was notorious as late as the 16C as the haunt of savage and evil spirits, the latter exorcised by the foundation of a Carmelite monastery in the valley in 1599. Bowles reported that the holy fathers of the convent were 'seldom in a hurry to open their doors' to a distressed traveller, unless provided with a letter from the provincial or general of their Order. Some Hurdanos apparently worked on the cutting of the Panama Canal. The area was the subject of Buñuel's film 'Las Hurdes' ('Land without Bread') of 1932.

On meeting the C512 turn right to cross the Río Hurdano (feeding the *Embalse de Gabriel y Galán* to the SE) and a ridge, with the SIERRA DE GATA rising to the NW, to *Villanueva de la Sierra*.

A turning c 15.5km W climbs steeply to *Santibáñez el Alto* (653m), a curious village commanding panoramic views.—The C526 is met 14.5km further W; see Rte 27C.

At 7.5km bear right.—The CC204 leads SE to (9.5km) *Montehermosa*, where, at the Romería of S. Bartolomé (24 August), local costumes are displayed. *Plasencia* is 27.5km beyond; see Rte 27A.

26km **Coria**; see Rte 27C.

C.   Via Ciudad Rodrigo and Coria

249km (155 miles). N620. 89km **Ciudad Rodrigo**—C526. 88km **Coria**—32km N630. 40km **Cáceres**.

The N620 briefly follows the S bank of the Tormes to the W before veering SW, at 20km passing (right) *Barbadillo*. At nearby *S. Julián de Valmuza* Roman ruins and mosaics have been found.—3km *Calzada de Don Diego*, with a mansion of the Duque de Tamames. Beyond, the road continues SW across the undulating plateau to (66km) **Ciudad Rodrigo**; see Rte 28.

Turn S, with the SIERRA DE GATA rising to the SE to 1592m, at 14km passing *El Bodón*, scene of skirmishing during the Peninsular War (25 September 1811).—*Fuenteguinaldo*, 11km SW, was Wellington's HQ in August 1811. Near by are the extensive ruins and defensive walls of Iberian *Urueña*.—At 32km the *Puerto de Perales* (910m) is crossed, with *Jalama* rising to the W (1492m).

11km. The fortified village of *Gata*, 11km NE, has a good 16C church. The astronomer Abraham Zacuto lived here from c 1480 before emigrating to Portugal (see Salamanca University).

At the next junction there is a turning to *Santibáñez el Alto*, 14.5km E; see above.—*Hoyos*, 4.5km W of this crossroad, has a fine 15C church.—The road (C513) continues W below *Trevejo*, with an early 16C castle. Here a road climbs c 14km right to *S. Martín de Trevejo*, its church containing three paintings by Morales.—The main road circles to the NW to (c 16km) *Valverde del Fresno*, the nearest village to the Portuguese border, 17km SW. For *Penamacor*, 15km beyond, see *Blue Guide Portugal*.

The C526 continues to descend past (16km) *Moraleja*, from which the lonely CC214 leads 30km SW across the SIERRA DE LA GARRAPATA to *Zarza la Mayor*; see Rte 51.

15.5km **CORIA** (10,400 inhab.), a dilapidated episcopal town on the Alagón, preserves granite *Walls* incorporating material from Roman *Cauria*. Its 12C *Castle* has an imposing 15C pentagonal tower. The town was sacked by the French in August 1809. During the winter of 1812–13 it was the HQ of Sir Rowland Hill prior to his advance on Béjar at the start of the Vitoria campaign.

The rebuilding of the **Cathedral** as a church of single span (17m) was begun in 1496 by Martín and Bartolomé de Solórzano, and completed in 1570 by Pedro de Ibarra. It contains *Stalls* of 1489 and 1515 by Martín de Ayala, a reja of 1513 by Hugo de Sta. Úrsula, a Baroque retablo mayor by Juan and Diego de Villanueva (1749), an 18C organ by Verdalanga, and tombs designed by Diego Copín and Juan Métara. The tower was rebuilt in 1760; the cloisters date from 1473.

Below the cathedral a medieval *Bridge* on Roman foundations spans the old course of the Alagón.

After crossing the river, at 12km *Torrejoncillo*, once reputed for its cloth workers, is skirted. 10km beyond, the Moorish castle of *Portezuelo*, later reconstructed, is passed. After 10km the N630 is met by the Roman bridge at *Alconétar*, for which and the road beyond, see Rte 27A.

28 Ciudad Rodrigo to Fuentes de Oñoro (for Guarda)

24km (15 miles).

Maps: M 441.

CIUDAD RODRIGO (15,300 inhab.; Parador), an ancient and characteristic frontier fortress, was founded in 1150 by Count Rodrigo González Girón and strongly fortified by Fernando II (c 1190). Its later and more powerful defensive *Walls* are still standing, and the walk round them is recommended. The former *Alcázar*, begun in 1372, which dominated the bridge over the Agueda, in part houses the Parador.

The town suffered two sieges during the Peninsular War, the first in 1810, when it was taken by Massena and Ney. In January 1812 Wellington decided to secure the place as a base of operations, and a lightning attack surprised the garrison, but he was only master of the fortress after a costly 11-day siege in which Gen. Crauford (1764–1812) of the Light Division lost his life in the breaches. The Allies lost c 1100 men; the French c 530, but the garrison of c 1940 was taken prisoner. Wellington received an earldom, and the Spanish title of Duque de Ciudad Rodrigo. (The siege is described in detail in D.D. Howard's 'Napoleon and Iberia'.)

Cristóbal de Castillejo (c 1491–1550), the poet, was a native.

The ***Cathedral** is a beautiful Gothic building of c 1165–88, with 'Angevin' octopartite vaults of 1212–c 30. It was damaged in 1812 by the British bombardment from the *Tesones* (two knolls N of the town), but has been restored. It preserves three fine portals, notably the richly sculptured *W Doorway*. The jamb statues of saints stand on little replicas of the Torre del Gallo at Salamanca; beneath the Coronation of the Virgin in the tympanum are quaint carvings of the

Last Supper, etc. The doorway is preceded by a porch and steeple of 1765, a Baroque work by Sagarviñaga.

The solid-looking interior contains elaborate capitals and a wealth of sculpture. At the E end, the central one of the three apses was added in 1550. The *Choir stalls*, with their grotesque carvings by Rodrigo Alemán (from 1503) recalling those of Plasencia and Zamora, should be scrutinised. One organ, known as the 'Realejo', is 16C and has a beautiful 'jeux de regal'; the other is 17C.

On the N is a *Cloister* (begun c 1320) with remarkable capitals and other carvings. A Crucifixion in the NW corner bears the name of the builder, Benito Sánchez. On the Renaissance door leading into the garth are busts of a canon and of the architect, Pedro Güemez, who completed the N and E walks in 1538.

The *Ayuntamiento* (restored) facing the picturesque *Pl. Mayor* is one of several 15–16C mansions surviving. Another is the *Pal. de los Castros*, with spiral pillars, occupied by Wellington after the siege (near the E gate). Also of interest are the *Cap. de Cerralbo* (1588–1685), with an altar painting by Ribera; the church of the *Clarisas*, by Rodrigo Gil de Hontañón; *S. Pedro*; and *S. Agustín*.

Some 4km downstream stands the partly restored monastery of *N.S. de la Caridad*, with an imposing 16C façade and an 18C interior by Sagarviñaga. It was Marshal Ney's headquarters during his siege of Ciudad Rodrigo.

Near *Zamarra*, c 14km SE, are the remains of a large pre-Roman town.

For the road to **Coria** and **Cáceres**, see Rte 27C.

After crossing the Águeda, which frequently formed part of a fluctuating frontier during part of the Peninsular War, follow the N620 to the W. At 24km the village of **Fuentes de Oñoro** lies just left of the road. It gave its name to the bloody battles of 3–5 May 1811, when Massena attempted, ineffectually, to dislodge Wellington from before the Portuguese frontier fortress of *Almeida* (some 18km NW). His failure led to the marshal being deprived of his command.

The battles took place to the S and E. The French suffered heavily in crossing the rivulet of Dos Casas and in the fighting in the narrow stone-walled lanes of the village, losing c 2200; the Allied loss was c 1550.

The ruins of *Fort Concepción*, the pivot of Wellington's left wing, lie not far N of Fuentes de Oñoro, between the Dos Casas and the Portuguese border.

The frontier is crossed at (3km) *Vilar Formosa* (Customs). The improved N16 bears due W across the gorge of the Côa to (42km) **Guarda**, and the N332 leads NW to (15km) *Almeida*; see *Blue Guide Portugal*.

III   CANTABRIA; ASTURIAS; GALICIA

Cantabria, the former seaboard province of Santander, and also known as *La Montaña*, was until recently politically part of Old Castile. It is similar in many ways (although not so rich) to its neighbouring autonomy of the Asturias. Both are notable for their primitive churches, which have survived almost intact from the early Romanesque period. Their green valleys, with an Atlantic rainfall, are naturally fertile. Cantabria's orchards, fisheries, and the cattle of the upland pastures are sources of prosperity, as are the mineral deposits in the neighbourhood of Oviedo and Avilés, exploited since the last century. Until the coming of the railway the area, with a rock-bound coast and cut off from Castile by the Cantabrian mountains, was only entered with difficulty.

Asturias, formerly the province of Oviedo, takes it name from the Iberian tribe of the Astures, who put up a stout resistance against the Roman and Visigothic invaders of their mountain fastnesses. In 718 a small force of Moors, following the retreating Christians into these broken ranges, were ambushed in the glen of Covadonga and defeated, since when the Asturias claims to be the cradle of the Spains. In 1388 Juan I, at the request of John of Gaunt (who doubtless had in mind the newly-established title of Prince of Wales), conferred the title of Prince of Asturias on his eldest son before his marriage to John of Gaunt's daughter. The title has been borne by the heir apparent to the Spanish throne ever since.

Galicia, occupying the NW corner of the Iberian Peninsula, is divided into four provinces—*A Coruña, Lugo, Ourense*, and *Pontevedra*. It is a wild and mountainous country with great expanses of heath separated by swift rivers (often flowing in deep gorges), of which the main ones are the Miño and its tributary the Sil. The coast is exposed to the Atlantic and has been broken up into innumerable sandy bays and estuaries (known as *rías*), shaded by fir and eucalyptus forests, which are its most attractive natural features. The climate of the coast is rainy and temperate, and the lower valleys produce some of the best wine in Spain, although in relatively small quantities. The highlands on the borders of Castilla y León and the Asturias are subject to extreme cold, and snow lies on the peaks almost throughout the year.

Everything that can be is built of granite, down to the little farmyard storehouses (*hórreos*) like tiny chapels topped by a granite cross and festooned with golden maize, the vine props, and even the fences. These *hórreos* (from the Latin *horreum*) are raised on stone or wooden pyramidal pillars or '*pegollas*', looking like large mushrooms (called *tornarratas*), to keep vermin out. They are also found in the Asturias where they are usually square, while those in Galicia are normally rectangular, like a large elongated kennel on stilts.

Creaking oxcarts, whose heavy wooden axles emit a shrill whine as they are dragged slowly along the narrow lanes, are occasionally seen and heard. Often single cows are seen grazing by the roadside or being taken for a walk on a lead along the verge; and occasionally one may see women, wearing wooden clogs, balancing on their heads immense parcels of every description, milk churns, etc. Jardine, writing in the late 18C, remarked that perhaps the race was 'rendered short and thick by the custom of carrying burdens on their heads, particularly the women, who . . . often carry the men across the rivers on their heads in a basket'.

This kingdom, founded by the Suevi in the NW of the Peninsula in 409, lost its independence to the Visigoths in 585 and to the Moors in 713. After the disastrous raid of Almanzor at the end of the 10C which spread havoc over the whole of the kingdom of León, Alfonso VI was aided in the reconquest by Raymond and Henry of Burgundy. Henry was rewarded with the Duchy of Portugal (1095), which at that time extended from the N coast to the Douro and included what is now Galicia.

In 1128 Henry's son Afonso Henriques declared Portugal independent of Galicia and the countries thenceforward followed separate paths, the Spanish province becoming re-attached to León. Its ecclesiastical capital, Santiago de Compostela, was the object of one of the most frequent pilgrimages of the Middle Ages.

In language and customs the people of Galicia closely resemble those of northern Portugal; indeed their dialect is much nearer Portuguese than Castilian. Moreover, they share the Portuguese skill in improvisation, and their lyric poetry, brought to a high pitch in the works of Rosalía de Castro, is very like the Portuguese in inspiration. An increasing number of books are published in Galician.

Although the total population of Galicia has increased comparatively little during the last 50 years, the Gallegos are a prolific race and the country is apt to be overpopulated, its fertile area being small, so that it is not surprising that Galicia supplies a large number of emigrants not only to America and Northern Europe, but also to other parts of Spain. The populations of the provinces of Ourense and Lugo are lower than they were in 1920, but the ports of Vigo and A Coruña—261,000 and 231,000 respectively—have been growing rapidly.

Few of the villages of Galicia—unless very remote—are very attractive, and the houses built by the 'Americanos' (those who have returned home from abroad after accumulating capital) are usually characterless and garishly coloured. In recent years many signposts have been daubed over by reactionary Galicians wishing to perpetuate their dialect. The state of many of the roads in this province leaves much to be desired, but long-overdue improvements are slowly being effected in certain areas, including the building of a motorway between A Coruña and Tui.

29 Santander to Burgos

154km (96 miles). N623.

Maps: M 442.

SANTANDER (179,700 inhab.; 73,000 in 1920; 114,000 in 1960), capital of the autonomy of Cantabria, is largely a modern town lying along the N shore of its bay, looking S towards the Cantabrian mountains. The proximity of the fashionable seaside suburb of El Sardinero provides additional animation in summer, but Widdrington was not far wrong when he remarked in the 1830s that it was 'the only place in Spain of similar magnitude, where no artist, in any department, has left a memorial of his skill . . . .'

The name of Santander, Roman *Portus Victoriae*, is a corruption of S. Emeterio (martyred at Calahorra c 300), whose relics are preserved in the cathedral. In 1248 Fernando III set sail from here with a fleet to blockade Sevilla. In 1522 Charles V landed here on his second visit to Spain; and in 1623 Prince Charles (the future Charles I of England) embarked here after his visit to Madrid.

The town was sacked by Soult in 1808. In 1893 much damage was done when a cargo of dynamite exploded, killing 300 people; and a large area was destroyed by a fire in 1941. Isolated, Santander fell to the Nationalists in August 1937. Some 60,000 Republicans were captured; the usual proscriptions and executions followed. There has been much rebuilding in recent decades.

The Catholic and reactionary historian Marcelino Menéndez Pelayo (1856–1912) was born here, and in 1945 a university named after him was founded. Other natives were Joaquín Telesforo de Trueba (1799–1835), novelist and playwright, who emigrated to England in 1823 and remained there until 1834; the poet Gerardo Diego (1896–1987); José María de Pereda (1834–1906), the novelist, at *Polanco* on the Torrelavega road; and the artists Francisco Iturrino (1864–1924) and María Blanchard (1881–1932, in Paris). Benito Pérez Galdós (1845–1920), the novelist, had a summer villa here.

The waterside PASEO DE PEREDA extends from the *Puerto Chico* to the E to the Av. de Alfonso XIII to the W. Steps beside the Banco de España ascend to a vaulted passage beneath the cathedral. In the passage is the entrance to the impressive early Gothic *Crypt* (c 1300), now used as a parish church. Ascending steps to the left beneath another vault the entrance of the *Cathedral* is reached, a 13C building altered in the 16th and 18Cs, and largely rebuilt by 1955. The restored 14C *Cloister* survives on the S.

Just N of the junction of the Paseo and Avenida is the old arcaded *Pl. de Velarde*. From here the C. Juan de Herrera leads W to the *Ayuntamiento*, a short distance beyond which, in the C. Rubio, is the *Municipal Museum*, containing a well-displayed collection of paintings.

The ground floor is devoted to 'Pancho' Cossio, Francisco Iturrino, and María Blanchard; the first floor contains works by local artists; on the floor above are canvases by Nicanor Piñole, Eduardo Chicharro, landscapes by Agustín Riancho (1841–1929), Solana's 'Los Traperos', a St. Anthony of Padua (?) by Carreño, anon. Portraits of Floridablanca, and Carlos III, and several 19C portraits.

Some distance to the E, in the C. Casimiro Sainz (just N of the Puerto Chico) is the *Museo de Prehistoria*, containing extensive and important collections from Altamira and other sites in the province, including some huge stelae.

The Av. de la Reina Victoria, a prolongation of the Paseo de Pereda, leads to **El Sardinero**, with a *Casino* facing the fine sandy beach divided into two bays by a rocky promontory, the *Punta del Rastro*, whose flat top, laid out as gardens with tamerisk trees, commands the best view.

To the E is the peninsular of *La Magdalena*, conspicuous on which is the former royal palace, now a summer school. *International University* buildings lie not far NW of the Casino.

It was from a storage dump at Soto de la Marina, c 6km W of Santander, that in July 1980 7000 kilos of plastic explosives were stolen by members of ETA disguised as civil guards.

For the road from Santander to **Bilbao** see Rte 7 in reverse; for those to **Gijón**, and **Oviedo**, Rtes 31A and B; for **Palencia** Rte 30.

The N623 turns S from the W end of Santander before climbing to the SW up the valley of the Pas, at one time a district from which numerous wet nurses originated (cf. Olmedo).

28km *Puente Viesgo*, from which the prehistoric caves of *El Castillo* and *La Pasiega* may be visited. The road traverses several villages as it ascends through the CORDILLERA CANTÁBRICA, climbing steeply to (33km) the *Puerto del Escudo* (1011m), occasionally closed in winter. It provides a view SW over the *Embalse del Ebro*, on the N bank of which is the small spa of *Corconte*.

The road soon climbs again to cross the *Puerto de Carrales* (1000m) to approach (31.5km) *Escalada*, with a 17C palace and partly Romanesque *Colegiata*. Here we cross the upper Ebro.—14km to the W is the Mozarabic and 12C church of *S. Martín de Elines*.—At 11km a left turn leads to (6km) *Sedano*, to the E and SE of which are *Gredilla* and *Moradillo* respectively, both with Romanesque churches of interest, the latter dating in part from 1188.—The main road later climbs to the SE to (19.5km) the *Puerto de Páramo de Masa* (1050m) in the MONTES DE OCA.

20km *Sotopalacios*, with a ruined castle, shortly beyond which is *Vivar del Cid*, perhaps the childhood home of El Cid (Rodrigo Díaz de Vivar; c 1040–99; see Burgos). We pass near (left) *Fresdelval*, with an early 15C cloister and Renaissance patio of the former monastery, on approaching the N surburbs of **Burgos**; see Rte 8.

30   Santander to Valladolid via Palencia

255km (158 miles). N611. 27km *Torrelavega*—48km *Reinosa*—32km **Aguilar de Campóo**—27km *Herrera de Pisuerga*—25km *Osorno*—50km **Palencia**—10km. N620. 39km **Valladolid**.

Maps: M 442.

The stretch between Santander (see Rte 29) and Torrelavega is being improved by the construction of a motorway parallel to the N611. **Torrelavega**, an industrial town of 56,500 inhab., has an arcaded Pl. Mayor, and a tower-house of the Garcilaso de la Vega family near the old church.—For neighbouring *Santillana*, see p 229.

At 4.5km beyond Torrelavega picturesque *Cartes*, with the 15C *Torre de los Manriques*, lies to the right. Shortly beyond, at *Yermo*, is late Romanesque *Sta. María* (1203). The road later follows the narrow gorge of the Besaya, at 16.5km passing (left) 12C *S. Román de Moroso* at *Bostronizo* (*Arenas de Iguña*). Another church of interest is at *Silió*, to the E at 7km.

Bárcena, with old houses and a Romanesque church, is shortly bypassed to the W. The road winds SW through the *Hoces de Bárcena* to approach (16km) **Reinosa** (850m; 13,300 inhab.), a small industrial town and summer resort, where in May 1987 an incident involving police brutality brought the place into the limelight.

At *Bolmir*, to the SE, is a Romanesque church. There is another at *Retortillo*, on a height beyond. Material from the neighbouring Roman town of *Julióbriga*, the site of which is adjacent to the approach road, has been incorporated in it.

The C25 leads W from Reinosa past *Fontibre* and the headwaters of the Ebro, and the ruined 15C castle of *Argüeso* (right) on the SW flank of the sierra, here rising to 1491m.—The C628 ascends W past the tower of *Proaño* towards the ski slopes of *Alto Campóo* on the PEÑA LABRA (*Pico de Tres Mares*; 2175m).

6km **Cervatos** has a 12C *Church with remarkable Romanesque sculptures.—At 5km the *Puerto Pozazal* (987m) is crossed, and c 15km beyond, at *Cabria* (left), *S. Andrés* has a doorway dated 1222.

6km **Aguilar de Campóo** (6700 inhab.), also bypassed, perhaps Roman *Velliva*, is an old town of some charm, with remains of walls and two ruined castles on neighbouring hills. It was made a Marquisate by the Catholic Kings in favour of Fernández Manrique, who here received Charles V in 1517 and 1522 on his journeys between Valladolid and the coast. On the *Puerta de Reinosa* is an inscription in Castilian and Ladino. No. 17 C. del Puente is the *Casa Rectoral*, notable among several medieval houses. *Sta. Cecilia* (1041 and c 1200) and the *Colegiata de S. Miguel* contain tombs of interest. Not far W of the centre is the monastery of *Sta. María la Real* (c· 1180–1213), under restoration, with a Romanesque cloister; the church is being excavated.

A road leads N via *Cillamayor* to (15km) *Barruelo de Santullán*, SW of which is *Revilla*, all with Romanesque churches preserving features of interest.

AGUILAR TO CERVERA DE PISUERGA (25km). The P212 circles to the NW, skirting a reservoir near *Villanueva de Pisuerga*, with a remarkable Romanesque church portal, *Salinas de Pisuerga*, with a medieval bridge (?Roman), and *Villanueva de la Torre*, with an 11C church, to the N.—To the S of Salinas is Romanesque *Sta. María*.—Above **Cervera de Pisuerga** stands a Renaissance church containing a retablo of 1513 by Felipe Vigarni; 3km to the W is the well-sited Parador of *Fuentes Carrionas*.—To the W c 16km N of Cervera is *S. Salvador de Cantamuda*, with a 13C bridge and 12C church, where the altar slab has its original columns.—12km further N is the *Puerto de Piedrasluengas* (1313m); see Rte 32.

CERVERA TO HERRERA DE PISUERGA (39km). The C627 leads S, at 4km bearing left; *Pisón de Castrejón*, 9km W, has a church of 1100 with a 15C doorway. (The C626 continues 26km W to *Guardo* and *Cistierna*, 33km beyond, but the route is of slight interest.) The road climbs over a ridge, then descends past (11km) *Perazancas* and roadside *S. Pelayo* (containing wall paintings), and 5km beyond, passes a road (left) leading to the Romanesque churches of *Cozuelos de Ojeda* and *Vallespino de Aguilar*.—3km *Olmos de Ojeda* (right) has a monastic church with a 12C barrel vault and a signed doorway of 1190.—There is a good church of 1270 at *Santibáñez de Ecla*, 4km SE.—4km *S. Pedro de Moarves* has a portal containing a notable frieze of apostles.—The Romanesque church of *Villabermudo* is passed on approaching (13.5km) *Herrera de Pisuerga*; see below.

The N611 descends the valley of the Pisuerga, later passing (left) a turning for the monastery of *Sta. María la Real* at *Mave*, dating from 1208. Its church has apsidal murals, a Romanesque walnut altar, and a 17C cloister.—Among other Romanesque churches in the area are those at *Becerril del Carpio*, to the W; at *Gama* (SE); and, approached by the next turning left, at *Rebolledo de la Torre*, its porch with carvings dated 1186 by Juan de Piasca.

19km *Alar del Rey* stands at the head of the *Canal de Norte*, opened in 1759. At *Nogales*, on its outskirts, is a fine Romanesque church; while 3km SE is the abbey of *S. Quirce* (1147), with a dome of Persian type.

8km **Herrera de Pisuerga** preserves relics of its walls and a ruined castle. In the vicinity is a Visigothic cemetery, although the majority of Visigoths in Spain settled further SE.—The road shortly veers away from the river to bypass (25km) *Osorno*; see Rte 9A.

At 6km we pass (left) *Las Cabañas de Castilla*, with a brick church and a medieval tower of the Counts of Osorno, and later skirt *Marcilla de Campos*, with a Baroque church, to approach (11.5km) *Fromista*; see Rte 9A.

Many of the villages in the fertile but uninteresting TIERRA DE CAMPOS, the 'Campi Gotici' of medieval writers, which we now traverse, have houses constructed of consolidated earth and chopped straw or *tapia*, on a base of stone.

At (6km) *Piña de Campos*, with an unfinished Renaissance church and remains of a castle, a road leads 4km E to *Támara*, an old walled village. Here *S. Hipólito* (1334 and 15C) contains an extraordinary 17C organ supported by a single wooden pillar; stalls, lectern, and font of 1582, and a tower designed by Rodrigo Gil de Hontañón. The *Iglesia del Castillo* is 11C.—At *Santoyo*, 5km beyond, *S. Juan Bautista* has a retablo of 1570 and a beautiful 17C organ with human masks emitting the notes.—5km to the SE lies *Astudillo*, with 13C walls, the Mudéjar convent church of *Sta. Clara* (founded 1355; restored), and other late medieval churches.—**Palencia** is 30km SW.

6km *Amusco* has a large Romanesque church with a retablo of gilded wood statues and a Mudéjar pulpit. It was the birthplace of the poet and playwright Gómez Manrique (c 1412–c 1490).—At *S. Cebrián de Campos* (6.5km NW) the church has a 16C tower and notable retablos.

At 5km *Ribas de Campos* is 3km NW. There the priory of *Sta. Cruz* has an early Gothic church and Romanesque chapterhouse.— *Monzón de Campos* is shortly bypassed, dominated by its *Castle* (now a hotel) and the old *Pal. de Altamira*. Just beyond Monzón a road to the right leads to *Husillos*, the site of one of the oldest abbeys in Castile; the present buildings date from the 12C.

Fuentes de Valdepero, its 16C castle defended against the Comuneros in 1520 by Andrés de Rivera and the women of the village, is skirted to approach Palencia, which is also bypassed to the E.

PALENCIA (71,700 inhab.; 20,000 in 1920; 41,000 in 1950), (apart from a notable cathedral), is a somewhat characterless but rapidly growing provincial capital. It lies on the river Carrión not far N of its confluence with the Pisuerga, and is the centre of a rich area of cereal production.

Pallantia, a town of the Iberian Vaccaei, put up a strong resistance before submitting to Roman domination. In 457 it was taken by the Visigoths. Although the Moorish invasion extended to Palencia, in 921 it was again in Christian hands and in 1035 received its first bishop. In the 12–13Cs it was a residence of Castilian kings, and in 1208 the earliest university in Spain was founded here by Alfonso VIII, and attended by Domingo de Guzmán, later founder of the Domincian Order. In 1239 the university was removed to Salamanca. Catherine of Lancaster (aged 14) and the future Enrique III (in his 10th year) were married in the cathedral here in 1388. Punished by Charles V for its share in the Comunero revolt of 1520, Palencia gradually lost its importance. It was plundered by Gen. Foy in 1812.

The cathedral is conveniently approached by circling to the W of the centre, following the avenues skirting the river (which is crossed by an ancient *Bridge* of three arms), and turning E into the C. Salvino Sierra, S of which stood the Judería.

The ***Cathedral** was begun in 1321 and completed in the 16C, replacing an earlier church which had been built above the cave of St. Antoninus; see below. It has no W façade, but the transeptal portals are good, notably the *Puerta del Obispo* (S), richly sculptured by Diego Hurtado de Mendoza in the late 15C. Between this and the small portal (the usual entrance) rises a massive square tower by Gómez Díaz de Burgos (mid 15C).

The interior, with its double transepts and rows of chapels on the N side, contains interesting works of art. They are badly lit; light should be specifically requested for Vigarni's Retablo; see below. The main work of the nave (c 1450–1516) is by Bartolomé de Solórzano. The triforium has unusual tracery. The E end, including the E transepts and the apse with its chapels, dates from the 14C; the remainder, with a new Capilla Mayor, was added in the 15–16Cs. The trascoro, with sculptures and bas-reliefs, possibly by Simón de Colonia, contains a retablo by Jan Joest of Haarlem (1505), among others. A Plateresque staircase descends to the Visigothic *Crypt* (c 673, with a vestibule of c 1075) in which Sancho III Garcés, 'el Mayor', is said to have discovered the statue of 'S. Antolín', martyred at Pamiers in the 2C.

The Coro has a reja of 1571 by Gaspar Rodríguez and stalls of c 1400–25 by Luis Centellas, completed in 1560 by Pedro de Guadalupe. High in the S transept is a clock with figures of a knight and a lion to strike the hours and quarters. The 18C organ retains its beautiful Baroque case, but the instrument has been ruined by 19C restoration.

The Capilla Mayor has a reja by Cristóbal Andino and a beautiful five-tier Retablo of 1505 by Vigarni, with a Crucifixion of 1519 by Juan de Valmaseda. The 12 painted panels are by Juan de Flandes, who undertook to complete them in three years from 1506. On the outside of the trassagrario are 15–16C tombs, including the sepulchre of Fr Núñez, abbot of Husillos (1550). In the earlier Cap. Mayor, further E, are the tombs of Queen Urraca of Navarra (1189; high up on the left wall) and Inés de Osorio (died 1492). The vault dates from 1424.

In the Sacristy are a custodia of 1585 by Juan de Benavente and a diptych by Pedro Berruguete; in the Sala Capitular are some Brussels tapestries of 1530. The Cloister (1520; by Juan Gil de Hontañón) lost its tracery in the 18C.

Immediately N of the apse is the Hospital de S. Antolín, rebuilt in the 15C, with a doorway of 1580.—Cross the adjacent Pl. de Cervantes diagonally, and turn right past the 17C Cap. de las Dominicanas, with a cupola of 1742, to reach the late 18C Bishop's Palace. Turning right again, 16C Sta. Marina is passed to approach **S. Pablo.**

Founded by St. Dominic, it was begun c 1230 and rebuilt in the 14–15C. Of the two tombs of the Rojas family, that with kneeling figures of the Marqués de Poza (1577) and his wife is by Francisco Giralte. On the S is the Cap. de Zapata, with an altar of 1516. The retablo mayor dates from 1597.

From just E of the church the C. Mayor, in part pedestrianised, leads S to the Ayuntamiento, E of which is S. Francisco (13C, but much altered in the 17C), preceded by a graceful Gothic arcade.—To the S is the small Pl. Mayor, from the SE corner of which we may turn right to reach the Diputación. This houses the Museo Arqueológico, with a good Roman section, the Retablo of S. Millán (c 1400), and an early S. Sebastián (damaged) by El Greco.

The C. de Colón leads S past conventual Sta. Clara (1378–1400), containing tombs of the admirals of Castile and 16C marble effigies, to Plateresque S. Bernardo.—Turning N up the C. Mayor here, a lane (A. Fernández del Pulgar) leads left to S. Miguel (13C; damaged by fire in 1966), with a crenellated tower and unusual four-sided Cap. Mayor. The Cid and Doña Jimena were married in an earlier church on the site in 1074.—To the NE is a Jesuit church of 1598 with Churrigueresque altars and a natural wood retablo.

The N611 leads S from Palencia, shortly passing an exit (right) to Villamuriel de Cerrato, on the far bank of the Carrión, with an early Templar church.—The next left-hand turning leads to Baños de Cerrato; see Rte 10, and likewise for the N620 (met 9.5km from Palencia), bearing SW parallel to the Pisuerga to (39km) **Valladolid;** see Rte 11A.

31 Santander to Luarca

A. Via Gijón and Avilés

300km (186 miles). N611. 27km—N634. 36km *S. Vicente de la Barquera*—61km *Ribadesella*—N632. 39km **Villaviciosa**—30km **Gijón**—25km **Avilés**—70km. *Canero*—N634. 12km **Luarca**.

Maps: M 441, 442.

A beautiful, but—in the latter half—a slow and tiring road. The stretch between Santander (see Rte 29) and Torrelavega is being improved by the construction of a motorway parallel to the N611. This will bypass *Torrelavega*, which is of slight interest.

Bearing W at Torrelavega onto the N634, we shortly pass a right-hand turning for (4km) *Santillana del Mar (Parador). Still a picturesque old town, it is in grave danger of excessive exploitation (and it should be avoided at weekends and in the summer). It preserves numerous stone mansions, mainly 15–16C, and a fine *Ayuntamiento*. Famous in fiction as the birthplace of Gil Blas, of more interest is its Romanesque *Colegiata (late 12C), containing the tomb of Sta. Juliana, a 4C martyr (Santillana is a corruption of her name), a retablo of 1453, and a 17C silver altar frontal. The restored Cloister with its coupled columns and elaborate capitals was built slightly later than the church.

The 17C *Conv. de Regina Coeli*, near the town entrance, now houses a museum, mostly of religious art.

Some 2km SW are the *Cuevas de Altamira, a series of caves famous for their Magdalenian paintings of c 12,000 BC. The delineations of bisons, boars, deer, etc., painted in ochre and sometimes outlined by flint scratches or shaped to the natural protuberances of the walls, are remarkably lifelike. Although the caves were discovered in 1868, their entrance having fallen in at some remote date, the deteriorated paintings were not noticed until 1879. Some objects found here are displayed in the adjacent museum.

Note. The number of visitors has had to be very strictly limited to prevent the paintings being lost entirely to posterity, in spite of measures of preservation already in force.

SANTILLANA TO S. VICENTE DE LA BARQUERA (29km). This alternative road winds parallel to the coast via *Comillas*, a small resort overlooked by the *Pal. of the Marqués de Comillas*, several ugly seminaries, and a building known as 'El Capricho', by Gaudí. The main road is regained 8km beyond.

The N634 leads W from Torrelavega to (17km) *Cabezon de la Sal*.

At *Ruente*, 7km S, is the 15C *Casa del Rey*, briefly the residence of Charles V. Beyond Ruente the mountain road (C625) leads up the valley of the Saya, crossing the SIERRA DEL CORDEL at the Puerto de la Palombera (1260) for *Reinosa*; see Rte 30.

5km *Treceño*, birthplace of Juan de Herrera, the architect (1530–97), and of the didactic writer Fray Antonio de Guevara (c 1480–1525).— We descend to the coast, crossing the *ría* by the *Puente de la Maza* of 28 arches (1433), with views inland towards the Picos de Europa, to enter (14km) **S. Vicente de la Barquera**, a picturesque fishing port. Its arcaded streets overlooked by a battered castle, ruins of a 13C Franciscan convent, several 16–17C mansions, and 13C *N.S. de los Ángeles*, are of some interest.

The following 60km of coast are particularly beautiful, with the

SIERRA DE CUERA rising to the S, and the PICOS DE EUROPA behind. The Nansa is crossed at 8km, 3km beyond which is the turning to *Unquera*, a starting point for the exploration of the region, where the N621 leads inland to *Potes*; see Rte 32.—A track to the right leads to the *Cueva del Pindal*, containing paintings of the Altamira type.

At 22km the industrial port of **Llanes** (14,400 inhab.), with a 17C castle, medieval tower, and 15C church, is bypassed; inland the SIERRA DE CUERA rises to 1315m.—6km. *Celorio* (right), with ruins of the Romanesque monastery of S. *Salvador* (1071), and, 4km beyond, S. *Antolín de Bedón* (1251), are passed.—At 8km the main road continues W to (8km) *Llovio* (see Rte 31B); we bear right for (9km) the small port of **Ribadesella** (6850 inhab.), the birthplace of Darío de Regoyos (1857–1913), the artist. The town is attractively situated at the mouth of the Sella, on the far bank of which is the stalactite cave of *Tito Bustillo*, with prehistoric paintings.

From Ribadesella we traverse several villages retaining old mansions and medieval towers, and pass near the prehistoric site of *Picos del Castro*. At 17km (left) *Gobiendas*, with a 9C church, is bypassed; beyond it a by-road climbs to the *Mirador de Fito*, commanding extensive views.—4km *Colunga*.—The fishing village of *Lastres*, with a 15C *Colegiata*, lies 4km N.—At 10km *Priesca* is to the left, where S. *Salvador* dates from 921.—The road circles to the SW above a *ría* to (8km) **Villaviciosa** (15,850 inhab.), with several attractive streets in the old town. Charles V stayed at C. del Agua 31 on his first visit to Spain in 1517, having landed at *Tazones*, 12km N. *Sta. María* retains a 13C doorway with good sculptures.

Many villages in the area possess curiously primitive Romanesque churches. The most notable is that of *•Valdediós*, 9km SW, consecrated in 893. It is adjacent to the ruinous Cistercian church of *Sta. María* (1218), known as 'El Conventín'. Other examples are *•S. Juan de Amandi* (1134; restored 1755), with a semicircular arcade at its entrance and expressive capitals in its unusual apse; *Lugás*; and *Valdebarcena*, 2km, 5km, and 8km respectively S of Villaviciosa. Others are at *S. Andrés de Bedriñana* (9th and 16Cs), and *S. Lázaro de Lloraza* (11C), 3km N, and 8km NW.

The N634 may be joined 10km beyond Valdediós, 22km E of **Oviedo**; see Rte 31B.

The N632 winds over the hills, later passing the buildings of the *Universidad Laboral* before entering Gijón.

GIJÓN (256,450 inhab.; 57,000 in 1920; 111,000 in 1950; 185,000 in 1970; Parador), a rapidly growing and flourishing industrial centre, retains few monuments of interest. What remains of the old town stands on an isthmus between the hill of Sta. Catalina and the mainland. To the W is the modern harbour, laid out in 1892 and since enlarged, extending to the *Puerto del Musel* on the far side of the bay; to the E is the *Playa de S. Lorenzo*.

Roman and Visigothic *Gigia*, of which little is known, was only very briefly in Moorish hands, as they abandoned the coast after the reverse of Covadonga (q.v.). The town was destroyed by fire in 1395. The harbour, founded in 1552 by Charles V, sheltered the shattered remnants of the Armada in 1588. It was later resorted to by the English 'for filberts and chestnuts', and also exported a little coal. A new quay was built in 1766, extended in 1859, and again since. In 1808 Toreno and the Asturian deputies sailed from here to seek British support against the French invasion of Spain. In 1837 George Borrow entered Gijón 'barefoot and bleeding', having walked some 200 miles from El Ferrol under a continuous downpour of rain. The town was seriously damaged in 1934 and

1936, when the Nationalist-held barracks were under attack, and ferocious proscriptions followed its capture by the Nationalists in October 1937.

Among natives were Gaspar Melchor de Jovellanos (1744–1811), the poet and statesman; Caén Bermúdez (1749–1829), historian of Spanish art; and the Liberal general Evaristo San Miguel (1785–1862).

At the E end of the harbour is the Pl. del Marqués, with the 16C *Colegiata* and *Pal. del Conde de Revillagigedo* (15C; altered in 1702). From the Pl. del Marqués the C. del Instituto leads S to the *Inst. Asturiano Jovellanos*, founded in 1797. Its collection of old master drawings, formed by Caén Bermúdez, was destroyed in 1936.

In the Campo Valdés, beneath the E side of the hill, are the *Pal. de los Condes de Valdés* (1590), with two heavy towers, and *S. Pedro*, rebuilt in 1954. Near by is the 16C **Casa de Jovellanos** (restored), containing works by Asturian artists including Nicanor Pinolé, Florentino Soria, Adolfo Bartolomé, Evaristo Valle, Sebastián Miranda's carved Retablo de Mar, and an old wooden model of Gijón.

In the 'Pueblo de Asturias' on the right bank of the river Piles, are museums devoted to the ethnography of the region, the *gaita* (an instrument related to the bagpipes), ceramics, etc.

GIJÓN TO OVIEDO (29km). The A8 and A66 motorways provide the best approach. An exit at 22km leads c 10km to the Visigothic church of *Villardeveyo* (c 900), not shown on most maps. It has a rose-window above paired lights, an anticipation of Gothic tracery.—For **Oviedo** see Rte 33.

The A8 provides a faster route to *Avilés*, 25km W (see below), but the N632 may also be followed.

A DETOUR off the N632 may be made by turning right at 8km to the fishing village of *Candás*, and (11km) *Luanco*, with a clock tower of 1705, the *Pal. de los Pola*, and an early 18C church. At Luanco in 1786 Townsend spent ten days at the home of the Count of Peñalba, where 'the style of living resembled the old British hospitality; and the long oak tables surrounded by strong oak benches, were every day well covered'.—The *Cabo de Peñas*, Roman *Arae Sextianae*, lies 9km NW.—Turning SW, passing near *Manzaneda*, with a 12C Templar church, the main route is regained at (13.5km) Avilés.

After passing the great steelworks, built as a metallurgical centre for the area, **AVILÉS** (88,000 inhab.) is entered. According to Townsend, it possessed no manufactures in his time 'except of copper and brass pans for the surrounding villages, and some thread' for the inhabitants' own consumption.

It was the birthplace of Juan Carreño (1614–85), the artist; Pedro Menédez (1519–74), the mariner and *conquistador* of Florida; and the playwright and critic Francisco Antonio de Bances Candamo (1662–1740).

The conspicuous church of *La Merced* with its two tall towers, originally 14C, is now mainly modern. *S. Nicolás de Bari* (13–14C) contains the tomb of Menéndez, and the Cap. de los Alas, good retablos and tombs. Romanesque *S. Francisco* has a 9C relief; *Sto. Tomás de Cantorbéry* (restored) was one of the first churches dedicated to Becket. Among old mansions the *Pal. de Valdecarzano* (or *Baragaña*), in the C. Herreria, is outstanding, with an unspoilt front of c 1300; here Pedro the Cruel lodged in 1352. The *Pal. de Campoosagrado* has a 17C Baroque façade of three orders. In the Pl. de España are the *Ayuntamiento*, a long arcaded building of 1670, and other 17–18C mansions.

Continuing W, the resort of *Salinas* is skirted. S of it, at *Laspra*, is a hilltop church retaining 9C work.—At 13km the airport for the region is passed to the right. 5km beyond is *Sota del Barco*, with the old *Castillo de Don Martín*, on the right bank of the Nalón estuary.

8km upstream, on the far bank of the Nalón, lies **Pravia** (11,950 inhab.), with a *Colegiata* of 1715 and late 18C *Casas Consistoriales*.—A by-road leads N to regain the main road W of *Muros*. A lane forks right off this by-road to *Santianes*, the residence of the Asturian kings from c 750 to the foundation of Oviedo; the 17C church preserves remains of a basilica of 783.

Crossing the Nalón, we pass through *Muros de Nalón*, with the nearby *Valdecarzana palace*. Shortly beyond one may make a DETOUR to the fishing village of **Cudillero**, huddled around its harbour, with its *Ayuntamiento* in an old castle.

At 18km, *S. Martin de Luiña*, whose church contains interesting inscriptions and a late 17C retablo, beyond which the road becomes very much more hilly and winding and requires slow and cautious driving as each ridge approaches the rocky coast. They are referred to by Borrow as '*Las siete bellotas*' (the seven acorns—i.e. acorn shaped). After 34km we meet the N634 from Oviedo (see Rte 31B), and 12km beyond enter **Luarca**, a fishing port of 20,150 inhab., well-sited in a sheltered cove at the mouth of the Rio Negro. For the road W see Rte 34.

B. Via Oviedo

305km (189 miles). N634. 123km *Llovio*—81km **Oviedo**—101km *Laurca*.

Maps: M 441, 442.

For the road to *Llovio* see Rte 31A.

Here we turn inland, following the right bank of the Sella to (15km) *Arriondas*.—Just before the road enters the town, a left turn leads SE to (7km) *Cangas de Onis*, a pleasant centre from which to explore the PICOS DE EUROPA; see Rte 32.

The main road now ascends the valley of the Piloña to (16km) *Villamayor*, with ruined Romanesque churches and several old mansions.—5km *Infiesta*, in a deep valley with marble quarries, has a curious sanctuary to the S, where three chapels are sheltered by a cave. The mountains rise to 1420m to the SE.—14km *Nava*, retaining the fortified *Pal. de la Cogolla*; the famous 12C church, destroyed during the Civil War, has been reconstructed. We traverse well-wooded and undulating country, passing collieries among the apple orchards, to (14.5km) **Pola de Siero** (40,350 inhab.) and, 16km beyond, enter **Oviedo**: see Rte 33A.

The N364 climbs W through *Sograndio*, with a Transitional church, bypassing (left) *Caldas*. Near Caldas is the large Romanesque church of *S. Juan de Priorio* (late 11C).—2km to the right in the Trubia valley, entered at 12.5km, is restored *S. Pedro* (c 900).

The old 0424 leads S up the Trubia valley to (8km) *Tuñón*, with the abbey church of *S. Adriano* (891; restored 1108). After following a defile we reach (11.5km) *Caranga*, where the valley divides. The left branch leads to the churches of *Arroja* and (11km) pre-Romanesque *S. Miguel del Bárzana*; the right leads to (10km) *La Plaza de Teverga*, with a *Colegiata* of c 1070, and Romanesque churches at neighbouring *Riello* and *Villanueva*.

The main road later follows the Nalón valley to (13.5km) **Grado** (13,200 inhab.), where another *Pal. de Valdecarzana* and the 18C

Cap. de los Dolores are of interest.—Cave paintings may be seen above *S. Roman de Candamo*, 9km N.—The road crosses a ridge, bypassing (left) *Dóriga*, where two churches preserve Romanesque features, before descending to (12km) *Cornellana*, with 11C *S. Salvador*.

CORNELLANA TO CANGAS DE NARCEA (41km). The C635 follows the right bank of the Narcea to the S. At 12km turn right onto the 0410, later the C631. (9km S lies *Belmonte de Miranda*, with a ruined abbey.) The road shortly crosses to the left bank, and this is followed to (48km) *Corias*, with the monastery of *S. Juan* (rebuilt 1773), containing two cloisters and the tomb of its founder, Bermudo III (1072–37).—3km **Cangas de Narcea** (20,050 inhab.), hemmed in by steeply scarped mountains, retains a crooked bridge, and a collegiate church of 1642.— The road later climbs S onto the upland of *Las Branas*, inhabited by a curious unassimilated pastoral race, where primitive thatched cabins or *pallazas*, formerly the refuge of both man and beast but now mostly derelict, may occasionally be seen. At 34km we cross the *Puerto de Leitariegos* (1525m) in the CANTABRIAN CORDILLERA and zigzag down to (15.5km) *Villablino* in the upper valley of the Sil; see p 244.

9km *Salas* (9300 inhab.) has a 16C church containing the monument of 1582 by Pompeo Leoni to its founder, Card. Fernando de Valdés (Salas, 1483–1568); relics of the chapel of *S. Martín*, dating from a restoration of 951, are in the cemetery. At *La Campa* is the tower of the castle of *Miranda*.

The road now climbs steeply to (12km) *La Espina*.

LA ESPINA TO GRANDAS DE SALIME (90km). The C630 leads SW to (12km) **Tineo** (20,100 inhab.), with the 18C *Casa de Campomanes* and a monastic church and cloister opposite.—At 3km a turning leads right to the 12C monastries of *Obona* and *Bárcena* (c 4km W, and 10.5km beyond). The C630 winds its way across country to (32km) *Pola de Allande*, near the Romanesque church of *Célon*, which has 14C murals. It climbs to cross the *Puerto del Palo* (1146m) before descending into the valley of the Navia to (43km) *Grandas de Salime*, beyond its reservoir; the church has important Romanesque features. Here also is a small ethnographical museum.—The road goes on across the *Alto de Acebo* (1030m) to (27.5km) **Fonsagrada** (9400 inhab.), capital of this wild region.—At 39.5km is *Castroverde*, with remains of one of the finest medieval castles of Galicia; *Lugo* lies 33.5km further W.

From La Espina the main road descends steeply down the valley of the Ore to meet the N632 at 30km.—12km *Luarca*; see Rte 31A.

32   The Picos de Europa

Maps: M 442.

This mountain massif may be approached from several directions, perhaps most conveniently from the N634, skirting its N side, but also from the S near *Riaño*. Communications around Riaño may be interrupted by the construction of a huge reservoir which will submerge the town.

A. UNQUERA TO RIAÑO VIA POTES (95km). From *Unquera*, reached by turning off the N634 12km W of *S. Vicente de la Barquera*, follow the N621 SW beside the Deva, with a view of the conical *Peña Mellera*, to (11km) *Panes*, with a Mozarabic chapel of c 1000. To the right is the *Gorge of the Cares*, followed by the C6312; see B, below.

Bear left to penetrate the impressive *Desfiladero de la Hermida*, to whose steep sides chestnut trees cling wherever they can find a

hold.—At (12km) *La Hermida* the valley momentarily expands.—
7km. To the left is Mozarabic *Sta. María de Lebeña* (before 924),
with horseshoe arches and an exterior gallery.—At (7.5km) *Ojedo*,
with a Romanesque church, the C627 turns left, ascending to (28km)
the *Puerto de Piedrasluengas* (1313m), 38km N of *Cervera de
Pisuerga*; see Rte 30. There is a good 12C church at *Piasca*,
approached by turning right 8km from Ojedo.

1.5km **Potes** (291m), the village centre of the mountain-girt valley
of Liébana, is commanded by the *Torre del Infantado*.

From a branch of the N621 which turns W a lane leads left to *Sto. Toribio de
Liébana*, a monastic church of 1250 to which a Baroque chapel has been added.
The road continues W beside the Deva and below the E massif of the Picos,
Andara then to 2441m, to *Espinama*, overlooked to the S by *Coriscao* (2234m)
and (23.5km) *Fuente Dé* (1070m; Parador), below the *Mirador del Cable*
(1926m). Espinama is centre for the exploration of the high peaks of the central
massif, with the *Peña Cerredo* (2648m) rising to the NW.

The N621 climbs S from Potes up the Quivesa valley, and then winds
to the SW to (26.5km) the *Puerto de S. Glorio* (1609m), between the
PEÑA PRIETA MASSIF to the SE (2536m) and the *Coriscao* to the NW,
providing views on clear days.—The road descends steeply through
Llánaves de la Reina and gorges to (9.5km) *Portilla de la Reina*.—A
mountain road climbs N here to cross the *Puerto de Pandetrave*
(1562m) to *Sta. Marina de Valdeón*, from which a track descends to
the *Posada de Valdeón* in the Cares valley; see C, below.—The N621
follows the valley of the Yuso to the SW to (11.5km) *Boca de
Huérgano*, with castle ruins, to approach the *Riaño reservoir* under
construction.—The LE241 climbs S over a pass at 1316m for (29.5km)
Guardo.

B. UNQUERA TO ARRIONDAS VIA CANGAS DE ONIS (73km). The
C6312 leads W, at 11km following the gorge of the Cares parallel to
the coastal SIERRA DE CUERA to (23km) *Arenas de Cabrales*, reputed
for its strong goatsmilk cheese.—A road leads S here to *Camarmeña*,
below the central massif of the PICOS DE EUROPA, with the *Torre
Cerredo* rising to 2648m due S. From *Sotres*, to the SE, several tracks
ascend into the range.—3km *Carreña*, formerly a centre of pilgrimage and of the traditional dance called the 'corri-corri'; there are
several ancient mansions in the area. We now descend the valley of
the Gueña past (22km) *Abamia* (left), where heavily restored 12C
Sta. Eulalia contains tombs traditionally said to be those of Pelayo
and his queen; but see below.

Some 2km beyond adjacent *Corao* the left-hand turning leads in
7km to **Covadonga**, a commercialised hamlet occupying a beautiful
site. It is famous as the scene in 718 or 722 of the first reverse of the
Moors since 711, and the beginning of almost 800 years of intermittent warfare ending in the Christian reconquest of Granada in 1492.

The Moors had by 714 overrun the Asturias. They were resisted by guerrilla
bands, one of which, led by Pelayo or Pelagius, consisting of c 300 men, was
brought to bay by a small Moorish force. The Moors were ambushed and
defeated with heavy loss, and Pelayo was proclaimed king on the *Campo del
Rey* below the village (in fact he had already been so-designated). Having over
extended their communications in this mountain fastness, and seeking more
promising areas to conquer, the Moors later abandoned the N coast and turned
their attention to France (where in 732 they were decisively defeated near
Poitiers by Charles Martel). The Moorish evacuation of the Asturias enabled its
kings to consolidate their strength. By 754, under Alfonso I, the Asturians were
making counter raids, reaching as far S as Coria; by 856 León had been re-
settled, temporarily, although not definitively until after 1002.

The 16C *Colegiata* of Covadonga has a cloister containing two old tombs; in the rock wall opposite, above a waterfall, is the shallow cave where traditionally Pelayo and his band had their backs to the wall. It is now approached by a flight of marble steps. Adjoining is the chapel of the *Virgen de las Batallas*, the successor of one built by Alfonso I that was damaged by fire in 1777 and again in 1936. A recess in the cave contains the sarcophagus of Pelayo (died 737) and his wife Gaudiosa, and at the back of the chapel is the tomb of their daughter Ermesinda and her husband (Alfonso I; died 757). From the cave a tunnel leads to the terrace of the twin spired neo-Romanesque Basilica of *N.S. de las Batallas* (1877–1901), on a spur jutting out into the valley.

Beyond Covadonga the road climbs steeply SE through beautiful scenery to (12km) the small upland *Lakes of Enol* and *La Ercina*, from which a track climbs S, overlooked by the massif of the *Peña Santa* (2596m), the NW buttress of the Picos de Europa. The district is reserved as a National Park for the preservation of its characteristic fauna such as *izards* (the 'chamois' of the region), wild cats, ospreys, and vultures, etc. Some bears survive, but they are rarely seen.

Regaining the main road, at 4km we enter **Cangas de Onis** (6500 inhab.), the residence of early Asturian kings. It is notable for the chapel of *Sta. Cruz*, founded in 735 by Fávila on a Celtic tumulus, and for a picturesque 13C *Bridge* across the Sella.—3km NW at *Villanueva* (on the road to Arriondas, 4km beyond, on the N634) is the partly restored monastery of *S. Pedro*, founded by Alfonso I in 746 and rebuilt in 1687. Much of the existing building is 12C, including the apse, and it preserves a remarkable doorway whose capitals depict a bear hunt. This is perhaps a reference to the fact that when Fávila, Pelayo's son, was killed by a bear in 739, he was succeeded by Alfonso, his brother-in-law.

C.   CANGAS DE ONIS TO RIAÑO (62km). The C637 leads S up the valley of the Sella, later threading its gorge, the *Desfiladero de los Beyos*, before climbing steeply to several fine view points and zigzagging to (34km) the *Puerto de Pontón* (1290m). From here a mountain road climbs NE over the *Puerto de Panderruedas* (1450m) to the *Posada de Valdeón*; see p 234.—At 11km we meet the C635 from Oviedo to Riaño, 5km S.

The C635 climbs NW along the upper valley of the Esla, near its source, to (22km) the *Puerto de Tarna* (1490m), with the *Mampodre* (2190m) rising to the S. It then descends the valley of the Nalón, passing several reservoirs, to (47km) **Pola de Laviana** (15,350 inhab.), with silver-bearing copper mines. At 14km industrial **Langreo** (36,350 inhab.) is crossed, and **Oviedo** is entered 21km beyond.

Perhaps a more attractive road is that climbing SW just prior to Pola de Laviana, to (18km) *Cabañaquinta* in the parallel valley of the Aller. The valley is followed down to meet the N630 at 16km, and 24km S of *Oviedo*; see below.

33 Oviedo to León

A. Oviedo

OVIEDO (184,450 inhab.; 70,000 in 1920; 124,000 in 1960), the
ancient capital of the autonomous *Principado de Asturias*, and a
flourishing modern town, lies between the sea and the Cantabrian
mountains, near the centre of the Asturian coal and iron fields. Part of
the older town surrounding its Gothic cathedral, and the Asturian
Romanesque churches on Mount Narranco, compensate for the
ugliness of its industrial environs. The climate is moderate; the
rainfall heavy. The curious way in which the otherwise flat cider is
poured will be noticed.

Founded in 757 by Fruela I as a fortress to guard the pass of Pajares, Oviedo
became the capital of the Asturian kings in 810, when Alfonso II, 'el Casto' (the
chaste; died 843), a native of the town, removed his court here from Pravia. In
812 an episcopal see was established. With the re-occupation of León in 1002
the political importance of Oviedo evaporated, and its history was the uneventful record of the capital of a mountain province until the unresisting town was
sacked by Marshal Ney and Géneral Bonnet in 1809.
    As 'Vetusta' it was scene of the novel by Leopoldo Alas ('Clarín'; 1852–1901,
who held the chair of Law here in 1883) entitled 'La Regenta' (1885).
    Oviedo suffered severe damage and loss of life in the rising of the extreme
socialists in 1934, ruthlessly suppressed by Generals Goded and Franco, and
again in the siege of 1936–37.
    It was the birthplace of the liberal Conde de Toreno (1786–1843), a historian
of the Peninsular War; Ramón Pérez de Ayala (1881–1962), the novelist; and
Idalecio Prieto (1883–1962), the socialist politician.

In the town centre lies the sloping and well-wooded PARQUE DE S.
FRANCISCO laid out on the site of an old hospital. A few steps to the

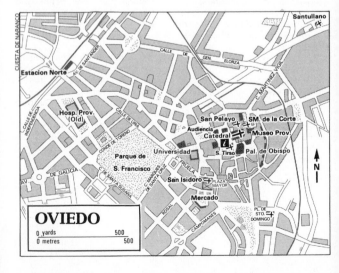

NW is the building of the *Hospicio Provincial* (1752; by Ventura Rodríguez), restored and converted into a luxury hotel.

From the E corner of the park, the C. de Fruela leads past the ex-Jesuit church of *S. Isidoro* to the diminutive *Pl. Mayor* and arcaded 18C *Ayuntamiento*.

S of the church is the Market, beyond which is the 18C *Pal. del Parque* or *Pal. de S. Feliz*. Some distance to the E is the convent church of *Sto. Domingo*, with a late 16C nave and a porch designed by Ventura Rodríguez.

Proceeding N from the Pl. Mayor and passing (left) the partly 14C *Casa de la Rúa*, the Pl. de Alfonso II is shortly reached, flanked to the E by the cathedral.

The **Cathedral* is a cruciform building begun in 1388, replacing the original church founded by Fruela I in 781 and enlarged by Alfonso II in 802. Nothing of the former remains except for the Camara Santa, restored since being dynamited in October 1934. Little appears to have been done since to clean the structure, black with grime. The crocketed W Front, with three deep porches (1512; by Pedro Bunyers) has an unfinished air owing to the absence of statues in the niches and the incompleteness of the N Tower, which has not been carried above the nave. Above the central doorway is a relief of the Transfiguration. The *S. Tower*, a feature of the landscape, is a masterpiece of Late Gothic detail, surmounted by an openwork pyramidal spire with flanking spirelets (1556).

The interior, although small (67m by 22m) is well proportioned and lighted. Clustered piers spring straight from base to vault, and their side colonettes are broken by simple foliage capitals. The triforium of the nave (1497) contains Flamboyant tracery, as does the clerestory. The chapels in the aisles were 'modernised' in the 18C. The *Cap. Mayor*, with brilliant glass, contains the Coro, but the retablo of 1525 by Giralte and Valmaseda has been clumsily repainted and regilt. The ambulatory, a 17C addition, at present displays photographs concerning the destruction and restoration of the treasures in the Cámara Santa; see below. The organ retains its 18C case only. In the *Sala Capitular* are the remarkable late 15C stalls saved from destruction and recently restored (see 'The Gothic Choirstalls of Spain', by D. and H. Kraus).

In 1786 Townsend was present when the 'Santissimo Sudario' (shroud) was shown to some thousands of peasants who had come in from the surrounding villages. Most had 'baskets full of cakes and bread, which they elevated as high as possible the instant the curtain was withdrawn, in the full persuasion that the cakes, thus exposed, would acquire virtues to cure or alleviate all disease'.

Opening off the N transept is the *Panteón del Rey Casto*, a tomb-chapel constructed by Alfonso II for the early kings of Asturias. The chapel was entirely rebuilt in the Baroque taste in 1712 when the inscription on the sarcophagi was obliterated; the attributions of burials are largely guesswork.

From the S transept steps ascend to the much-restored **Camara Santa**. The vault of the first chamber, remodelled by Alfonso VI (died 1109), is supported by six pilasters, each bearing two statues of Apostles, with curious capitals above. The tessellated floor resembles 9C Norman work in Sicily. The inner chamber, the Cap. S. Miguel, probably the identical structure raised by Alfonso II in 802, retains its rough semicircular vault and rude capitals.

In August 1977 several of the relics (saved from the French in 1809 at the cost of the more solid gold and silver plate) were stolen and smashed by a vandal. They were recovered and have since been painstakingly restored, and are again preserved here. They include an 11C coffer covered with silver plates adorned with reliefs and a border of Cufic writing; the Cruz de los Ángeles (808; a Maltese cross adorned with gold filigree and precious stones); the Cruz de la Victoria (908); a gold reliquary with agate inlay presented by Fruela II in 910; and two ivory diptychs (?11C).

The *Cloister* (c 1302–45 and 1487–97) contains 12–14C tombs; off it is the

Chapterhouse. The *Archives* contain the will of Alfonso II and an illuminated 12C MS (El Libro Gótico).

Turning left into the C. de Sta. Ana, we pass modernised *S. Tirso*, retaining its E window of c 815, to reach the entrance (right) of the *Pal. de Velarde*, dating from 1767 and containing a remarkable patio. Well restored, it has since 1980 housed the **Museo de Bellas Artes de Asturias**.

Notable are a triptych of the Adoration of the Magi, attributed to the Master of the Legend of the Magdalen (c 1520; formerly in S. Tirso); Juan Carreño, Portrait of Carlos II aged ten; Elias Vonck, Still life with fish; Dionisio Fierros, Mother and daughter; Pérez Villaamil, The cave at Covadonga in 1850; an anon. English male portrait, and M.J. Menéndez, Portrait of the Marqués del Vadillo. Several rooms are devoted to 19–20C Asturian artists, among them Augusto Junquera (1869–1942), Nicanor Piñole (1878–1978), Evaristo Valle (1873–1951); and Joaquín Vaquero (1900–).

A lane opposite leads to the 16–18C *Bishop's Palace*, built on the site of a castle erected by Alfonso II. From the lane one can get a glimpse of the exterior of the Cámara Santa, including part of Alfonso VI's work, and the tower of c 1080.—E of the cathedral is the *Conv. de S. Vicente*, rebuilt after 1493, with a cloister begun before 1550 by Juan de Badajoz but only completed in 1775. It houses the provincial **Archaeological Museum**, with an impressive collection of local antiquities. Also shown is the cell of the reformer Benito Jerónimo Feijóo (1676–1764); his tomb is in adjacent *Sta. María de la Corte* (18C).—Beyond is the convent of *S. Pelayo*. Further E, the C. del Paraiso follows the line of Oviedo's medieval *Walls*.

The C. de Martínez Vigil leads downhill to the NE to approach *Santullano or *S. Julián de los Prados*, a curious building with three square apses, founded c 830 by Alfonso II and containing remarkable *Murals* of a late Roman type.

At the NW corner of the Pl. de Alfonso II (W of the cathedral) is the 18C *Pal. de Heredia* and, adjacent, the mid 18C *Pal. de Camposagrado*, occupied by the *Audiencia*.—Beyond (left) is the *Toreno Palace* and, further W, the *University* (1604; by González de Bracamonte and Juan del Rivero), badly damaged in 1934.

On the CUESTA DE NARANCO, c 3km NW, reached by crossing the bridge immediately W of the Railway Station, are two remarkable pre-Romanesque churches. *Sta. María de Naranco* was built c 850 as the hall of a palace and converted to a church after 905. It is a rectangular structure with two external porches, and the flat buttresses peculiar to Asturian Romanesque. At either end is a vestibule, and underneath is a crypt. A feature of the interior is the series of shield-like medallions arranged as though hanging from the consoles above them.

Nearby *S. Miguel de Liŀlo* is a cruciform building founded in 848. One arm was later rebuilt. The curious stone tracery of the windows (seen through rusting protective netting) is noteworthy. The carvings on the column bases and the door jams reproduce grotesque designs common on late Roman consular diptychs, but the bordering arabesques are purely Visigothic.

For the roads from Oviedo to **Santander** and to **Luarca** see Rte 31B; for **Gijón**, 29km NE on the motorway, see Rte 31A; likewise for **Avilés**.

B. Via the Puerto de Pajares or the motorway

115km (71 miles) by the N630; 121km (75 miles) by the motorway, which provides a smoother and faster drive across the CORDILLERA CANTÁBRICA. The N630 is more likely to be blocked intermittently by snow at Pajares in winter; but as the main monument of interest—*Sta. Cristina de Lena*—is approached just before the N entrance to the motorway, the choice beyond is open.

Maps: M 441.

The road circles to the SW on leaving Oviedo, later following the valley of the Caudal to skirt (19km) the iron-smelting centre of **Mieres** (58,700 inhab.).

At 11km turn off the main road at *Pola de Lena* to follow a parallel road. This crosses the N630 further S to approach hilltop *Sta. Cristina de Lena*. (Before climbing the path uphill, enquire for the key at the house immediately beyond the bridge.) The curious cruciform structure of 912 (or possibly as early as c 845), richly decorated in the Visigothic style, has a chamber opening off each side, and a remarkable iconostasis.

The A66 motorway may be entered 6km S of this detour. The motorway ascends the flank of a ridge, with a fine view W towards the splintered crags of the *Peña Urbiña* (2417m). It passes through a series of tunnels beneath the main range of mountains, at 28km crossing the *Embalse de los Barrios de Luna* to skirt the reservoir. A winding by-road follows the far bank, while the C623 circles to the NW to (41km) *Villablino*.—After 18km the Río Luna is crossed. The motorway traverses an empty plateau to meet the N120 after 31km, where we turn left to (8km) **León**; see Rte 18. The motorway continues SE to meet the N630 9km S of León.

The N630 climbs steeply SE to (20km) the *Puerto de Pajares* (1379m; Parador) and shortly skirts (left) *Arbás*, with restored Romanesque *Sta. María* (c 1216; reconstructed 1716). To the E rises the *Braña Caballo* (2189m). The road circles to the S past (13km) *Villamanín*, with a Templar chapel and remains of a Roman causeway. After several short tunnels it skirts (13km) *La Pola de Gordón*. Leaving the mountains, we cross the *Alto del Rabizo* (1160m), with retrospective views of the Cantabrian range, and follow the left bank of the Bernesga to (33km) **León**; see Rte 18.

34 Luarca to A Coruña

A. Via Ribadeo and Villalba

212km (131 miles). N634. 52km *Ribadeo*—39km *Mondoñedo*—
34km *Villalba*—17km *Baamonde*—NVI. 47km *Betanzos*—23km **A
Coruña**.

Maps: M 441.

From *Luarca* (see last paragraph of Rte 31A) the road skirts the
seaward ridge of the SIERRA DE RAÑADOIRO, shortly bypassing
Puerto de Vega, where Jovellanos died in November 1811, persecuted by his political enemies.—21km **Navia** (9000 inhab.),
the birthplace of Ramón de Campoamor (1817–1901), the poet.

From the far bank of its ría the C644 follows the windings of the Navia valley,
much of it now filled with reservoirs, shortly passing the Celtic settlement of
Coaña, to (80.5km) *Grandas de Salime*; see p 233.

From approx. this point the shape of the *hórreos* (see Glossary)
changes from the square Asturian form to the oblong type of Galicia.
    At 26km we reach and cross the estuary of the Eo by the new
bridge to (4km) **Ribadeo** (9100 inhab.; Parador), with an 18C church
and two-towered castle.
    On the E bank of the *ría*, a fine natural harbour, lies *Castropol*
(5250 inhab.). Further S is *Vegadeo* (5150 inhab.), at the head of the
ría.

The N640 climbs SW along the left bank of the Eo to (45km) *Meira*. The steep
and winding but beautiful road later crosses the SIERRA DE MEIRA at the *Puerto
Marco de Alvare* (575m). The Cistercian monastery of *Mieres* was founded in
1144, but the church was not consecrated until 1258; its Renaissance cloister
now serves as the village plaza.—**Lugo** is 35km further SW; *Villalba* 34km W on
the LU120.

At 19km the N634 turns inland. For the coastal road beyond (5km)
Foz see Rte 34B.—11km **Lourenzá**, with a rebuilt Benedictine convent preserving the 10C founder's tomb and a palaeo-Christian
tomb. The 17C church, by Pedro de Monteagudo, has an imposing
early 18C Baroque façade by F. Casas y Nóvoa.
    9km **Mondoñedo**, a sequestered town of 6950 inhab., contains in
its lower part a notable *Cathedral*, begun c 1220, with four 16C
chapels at the E end. The W front retains Gothic features based on
the cathedral of Sigüenza, but was attractively cloaked in the local
Baroque style in 1705. Note the sculpted St. Jerome and his lion on
the façade. In the S Chapel is a wood carving of the Virgin and six
seraphim, said to have been brought from St. Paul's in London at the
Reformation. Note also the gilt and green Baroque organs (1759).
Antonio de Guevara, the didactic writer, was bishop here from 1537
until his death in 1545.
    Near the *Bishop's Palace* is a *Fountain* dated 1548. Adjoining *N.S.
de los Remedios* (12C; rebuilt 1738) is the *Hospital de S. Pablo*, with a
carved centrepiece of 1755. The *Conv. de los Picos* and the *Seminario*
are both 17C.

At *Alfoz*, 17km N on the LU160, are the castle of *Castro de Ouro* and
Romanesque *S. Martín*, occupying the site of the earlier cathedral (842–1112).

The main road climbs to (13km) the *Puerto de la Xesta* (545m) and crosses bleak uplands, with the SIERRA DEL XISTRAL rising to the NW to 1036m, to approach (21km) **Villalba** (16,650 inhab.). Here the picturesque *Torre de los Andrade* accommodates a Parador.—**Lugo** lies 35km S; see Rte 35B.

The NVI is met 17km SW, where we turn right for (47km) **Betanzos** and **A Coruña**, 23km beyond; see Rte 35A.

The Cathedral, Mondoñedo

B.   Via Ribadeo, Viveiro and Ferrol

265km (164 miles). N634. 52km *Ribadeo*—19km. C642.—5km *Foz*—
38km **Viveiro**—35km *Ortigueira*—55km **Ferrol**—NVI. 17km
Pontedeume—21km **Betanzos**—23km **A Coruña.**

Maps: M 441.

For the road from *Luarca* to *Foz* see Rte 34A.

Foz (8800 inhab.), on its estuary, is crossed. Inland is the 11C church
of *S. Martín de Mondoñedo*, with remarkable capitals and carved
stone retablo. Follow the coast to the NW, at 19km bypassing (left)
Sargadelos, known for its ceramics, and the home town of António
Raimundo Ibáñez, first Marqués de Sargadelos, the 18C economist.
In 1804 he established a factory of imitation 'Bristol ware', while
between 1845–62 it was producing a type of Toby jug, under the
supervision of a Staffordshire potter, Edwin Forester.

19km **Viveiro** (14,800 inhab.), reputed for its sardine fisheries, has
a 12-arched *Bridge* spanning the sandy mouth of the Landro. Four of
its ten *Gates* have survived, one (the *Castillo del Puente*; 1554)
bearing the escutcheon of Charles V. *Sta. María del Campo* is said to
date from the 9C; *S. Pedro* has Romanesque carvings. The *Franciscan Church* and that of *Valdeflores* are also of interest.—The road
bears N and then W to cross at 17km the *Ría del Barqueiro*, 7km N of
which is the rocky *Punta de la Estaca de Bares*, the northernmost
point of Spain.

18km **Ortigueira** (16,450 inhab.), a resort on the indented shore of
the *Ría de Sta. Marta*. On the far bank of the ría the coast runs out to
Cabo Ortegal, surrounded by dangerous reefs.—Beyond (9km) *Mera*
the road runs inland, off which, at 6km, the C646 forks right to
(12km) *Cedeira* (8050 inhab.). From Cedeira the coast may be
followed to (38km) *Ferrol*.

The C642 continues SW, at 14km passing near (left) the castle of
Moeche and crossing (7km) *S. Saturnino*, with the former *Conv. de
Sto. Domingo*. At 5km the 14C castle of *Naraio* is not far S.—6km
Xubia, with the Cluniac Romanesque church of *S. Martín.*

8km **Ferrol** (83,500 inhab.; Parador), Spain's most prestigious
naval base, with extensive modern dockyards, is of slight interest in
itself, although it retains a few 18C buildings and has a pleasant
alameda alongside the arsenal wall.

It was originally named from an ancient *farol* or light marking the entrance to its
land-locked harbour. It was chosen as a naval base by Felipe V in 1726, and
under Carlos III it became the site for the royal naval arsenal, in 1769–74 being
strongly fortified. In 1800 a squadron under Adm. Warren and Gen. Pulteney
attacked the port, but just as the garrison was on the point of surrender the
British troops re-embarked and the relieved Spaniards were left masters of the
bloodless field.

It was the birthplace of Genaro Pérez Villaamil (1807–54), the artist; Concepción Arenal (1820–93), the Spanish 'Elizabeth Fry'; Pablo Iglesias (1850–1925),
the socialist reformer; José Canalejas (1854–1912), the politician; and Gen.
Francisco Franco (1892–1975), the late dictator of Spain, descended from a
family of naval administrators.

About 2km NW of Ferrol is the curious church of *Chamorra*, surrounded by
megalithic remains.

The ría is now crossed by a bridge to (6km) **Fene** (6km S of *Xubia*).
Bear S to (11km) **Pontedeume** (8400 inhab.), with ruins of a fine old
Bridge, once with 58 arches, and of the *Pal. of the Counts of Andrade*
(1370–1400), as well as a 15C *Ayuntamiento*.

About 12km E, on the bank of the Eume, is the collegiate church of *Caaveiro*, a ruined fortified building probably of the 12C, but including some Baroque work.

A DETOUR inland may be made to the derelict Cistercian monastery of *Monfero, with grandiose 17–18C buildings preserving a curious slate and granite façade. It is approached by the LC152 circling E and SE from Pontedeume to (18.5km) the village of *Monfero*, from which the main route may be regained at *Betanzos*, 20km SW.

Passing near *S. Miguel de Breamo* (1187), the road later skirts the E bank of its ría to enter (21km) **Betanzos** where we turn right for (23km) **A Coruña**; for both, see the latter part of Rte 35A.

An ALTERNATIVE approach is by forking right across the ría c 13km S of Pontedeume, shortly passing the 12C monastic church of *S. Salvador* at *Bergondo*, and near the *Pazo de Lancara*, to meet at 10km the NVI 6.5km NW of Betanzos.

35 León to A Coruña or Santiago via Astorga, Ponferrada and Lugo

A. León to A Coruña via Lugo

323km (201 miles). N120. 46km **Astorga**—NVI. 59km **Ponferrada**—19km **Villafranca del Bierzo**—102km **Lugo**—74km **Betanzos**—23km **A Coruña**.

Maps: M 441.

The road as far as Lugo is a continuation of the main pilgrimage road to Santiago (see Rtes 4 and 9A), extended by Rte 35B.
  For **León** itself see Rte 18.
  Driving SW from León over the monotonous plateau, at 30km the Orbigo is crossed by a 13C *Bridge*.

It was the scene of the famous 'Paso de Honor' in July 1434 when, during the 30 days of the great jubilee of Santiago, Suero de Quiñones and his nine companions challenged every knight who disputed the pre-eminent beauty of his lady. In all 727 courses were run, one knight was killed and 11 were wounded before Suero consented to remove the iron collar he wore in token of his vow.
  There are important 13C tombs at the monastery of *Benavides*, 5km N.

17km **Astorga**; see Rte 21B.

The former pilgrimage road (LE142) ran due W from Astorga via (22km) *Rabanal del Camino*, with a Romanesque church and relics of a Templar house, and *Foncebadón*, 5km beyond, below a pass at 1500m. *Ponferrada* lies 28.5km further W.

The much-improved NVI, which is followed NW, climbs the lower slopes of the MONTES DE LEÓN to (20km) the *Puerto de Manzanal* (1225m), now rarely snowbound, and circles to the SW across the bald hills to descend into the valley of the Tremor.—20km *Bembibre* (bypassed) has a 15C church in a former synagogue, burnt down in 1934, and a castle of the Dukes of Frias. Crossing another ridge, the road descends towards (19km) Ponferrada, which may also be bypassed to the N.

PONFERRADA (53,750 inhab.; 9800 in 1920), now a growing industrial and mining town dominated by a huge slag heap, was Roman *Interamnium Flavium*. It was rebuilt in the 11C as a refuge for travellers and pilgrims on the road to Santiago. The old centre is approached by turning left on descending the long main thoroughfare, to reach the characteristic *Pl. Mayor*. In the square is the Baroque *Ayuntamiento* of 1692, with its squat towers. Adjacent is a medieval gate tower and near by is *N.S. de la Encina*. The imposing if over-restored *Templar castle* (12C and c 1340) on the site of the Roman castro, is a short distance beyond.

On the outskirts is *Sto. Tomás de las Ollas* (restored), with an oval apse and curious vault (c 930). It was a dependency of the early monastery of S. Pedro de Montes.

Some 21km S, approached by the LE161, and at a height of 1093m, stands Mozarabic *Santiago de Peñalba* (937); it is overlooked to the S by the *Cabeza de la Yegua* (2135m) in the *Sierra del Teleno*, rising further SE to 2185m.

From Ponferrada the C631 leads N and then NE, following the valley of the Sil, to (63km) **Villablino**, a coal-mining town of 14,500 inhab. situated in wild hill country below the *Puerto de Leitariegos*; see p 233.—The 12C abbey of *Sta. María de Sandoval*, restored in the 16–17C, lies on the road SE towards *Murias de Paredes*.

For the old road from Ponferrada to *O Barco* see Rte 36.

Ponferrada lies in the saucer-shaped valley of an ancient lake, now drained by the Sil, and known as the **Bierzo**. Almost cut off by mountains and with plenty of water, the area was a resort of medieval anchorites. In the 7C, led by S. Fructuosus (who later, c 656, became Bp of Braga and Metropolitan of Galicia), they built their hermitages in its remote valleys. Although harried by the Moors, the hermits returned in the 9C, and the ruins of their chapels and the convents which succeeded them abound. The Bierzo takes its name from *Bergidum*, where remains of Suevic fortifications may be seen on the summit of a hill above *Pieros*, just W of *Cacabelos* (on the old road from Ponferrada to Villafranca. In a rearguard action here on 3 January 1809 Gén. Colbert was killed by one of Moore's riflemen.

Cacabelos may be approached by turning N off the present NVI 10km W of Ponferrada. Just to the S of this turning is the monastery of *Carracedo*, founded in 990 and rebuilt in 1138, with remains of a 13C royal palace, 16C dependencies, and a tower of 1602.

10km **Villafranca del Bierzo** (Parador), an old village of some charm, stands above the confluence of the Valcarce and Burbia. It retains a round-towered *Castle of the Dukes of Alba* (16C), a collegiate *Church* rebuilt in 1726, with an artesonado ceiling, a large *Franciscan Convent* (founded in 1550 by Pedro de Toledo, viceroy of Naples), and several old mansions. It was the birthplace of Fray Martín Sarmiento (1695–1772), the scholar and Feijóo's assistant.

The beehives here were formerly made of hollowed tree trunks, about a metre high, and covered with slate. Southey relates a tale told him by an English traveller, who going behind a *posada* one moonlight night and seeing one, 'congratulated himself that the people there were so far advanced as to have made such a convenience . . . and was in a situation very unfit for making a speedy retreat when he took off the cover, and out came the bees upon him.'

At **Corullón**, 4km S of Villafranca, commanded by a medieval tower, are two 11–12C churches. *S. Miguel*, to the right on approaching the village, has a remarkable façade and apse; beyond, at a lower level, is *S. Esteban*. The road continues to climb above the valley to a fine viewpoint.

Passing through a short tunnel, the NVI ascends the valley of the Valcarce to the NW. This was the line of Sir John Moore's retreat in

January 1809, when hundreds of men (and women and children)
perished of cold after their excesses in the wine cellars of Ponferrada.
The road continues to climb steeply up the E side of the valley before
reaching the summit level between the SIERRAS DEL COUREL (SW)
and DE ANCARES (NE) at (28km) the *Puerto de Pedrafita do Cebreiro*
(1109m), where Moore's treasure chests containing 150,000 dollars
were hurled into a ravine, and Paget's rearguard beat off Soult's
pursuing cavalry.

PUERTO DE PEDRAFITA TO GUNTIN VIA SARRÍA (95km). From just beyond the
pass, the old pilgrimage road (LU634) diverges W through *Cebreiro*, where
primitive *pallazas* or thatched shepherds' cabins may be seen, to (39.5km)
Samos. The Benedictine abbey of *S. Julián*, rebuilt in the 16C, and the home of
the reformer Feijóo, was burnt out in 1951. The church (after 1734) survives,
with the Siren's fountain in the cloister.—12km **Sarría** (12,100 inhab.), Roman
Flavia Lambris, with remains of a castle, a Transitional church, and the Gothic
and Renaissance *Conv. de la Merced*, with important tombs.—The C546 leads
31km NW to *Lugo*.—The C535 continues W to cross the Miño at (15km)
Portomarín, a village reconstructed on a height above the *Embalse de Belesar*
(1963), the waters of which would have covered its few monuments, including
the fortified Romanesque church of *S. Juan* and 12C *S. Pedro*.—At 12.5km we
meet the N640 7km S of *Guntin*; see Rte 35A for the road beyond.

The gradual descent into Galicia from the Puerto de Pedrafita leads
through (19km) As Nogais (*Nogales*), with an old castle and pre-
Romanesque church, and (11.5km) *Becerreá*, with a ruined monastery of 1166 and the Romanesque church of *Oselle* to the NE. Later
the Neira valley is crossed and then a rolling plateau to (42.5km)
Lugo (also bypassed to the W).

LUGO (72,500 inhab.; 30,000 in 1920), a provincial capital, stands
above the valley of the Miño, spanned by a fine old *Bridge*. Modern
development has largely changed its character, and the walled
enceinte is not noticeable until close at hand.

Of Celtic origin, Lugo was known to the Romans as *Lucus Augusti*, and they
strongly fortified it. The medicinal springs below the *Santiago gate* were also
known to them, and the lampreys of the Miño (*Minius*, from the vermilion found
near it) were prized at the epicurian feasts of imperial Rome. The city was
sacked by the Suevi in 509 and captured in 714 by the Moors, but only remained
in their hands until 755. Sir John Moore's army halted here briefly (6–8 January
1809) before continuing its retreat through the sleet to A Coruña, and the place
was later sacked by both Soult and Ney. Its recent history has been uneventful.
Borrow stayed a week here in July 1837, where 30 of his Testaments were
disposed of in one day, the bishop himself purchasing two copies.

The late *Roman Walls, built of slate and stone, and the most perfect
of their kind surviving, are 9–12m high and over 6m thick. They
consist of 85 *cubos*, girding the town in a rough square rounded off at
the corners. Their circuit by car may be made in an anticlockwise
direction.

The NVI enters the enceinte at the leafy *Pl. de España*, just E of the
*Cathedral, standing at the SW corner. The cathedral's three towers,
which are a conspicuous feature, and the *W front* date from 1769–84.
They cloak the late Romanesque structure, begun in 1129 by Raimundo de Monforte; the sanctuary and transepts were completed by
1177, but work on the nave continued for another century.

The interior, modelled on that of Santiago, has a nave of nine bays with a
pointed wagon-vault, and very low aisles. The deep triforium is lighted by
round-headed windows, but towards the nave are two pointed arches in each
bay divided by coupled shafts. Off the N transept is a vaulted Romanesque
chapel with well-carved tombs. Note the retablos over the doors in the N and S

transepts, and the Rococo Lady Chapel. The ambulatory chapels were rebuilt in the 14C. The carved walnut *Silleria* in the Coro dates from 1624. The *Cloister*, on the S, is a spacious work of 1714 by Fernando de Casas y Nóvoa, who also designed the circular E chapel (1735).

The N door (note hinges) is surmounted by a figure of Christ above a pendant capital depicting the Last Supper. From this door a lane leads N past (right) the *Bishop's Palace* (16–17C, with a façade of 1743) to the picturesque arcaded *Pl. del Campo*, with its 18C fountain.

The Rúa Nueva leads ahead to *S. Francisco* (c 1510, with a Romanesque cloister of coupled columns altered in 1452), now housing the *Provincial Museum*, with archaeological and sculptural collections of interest. To the E is the 14C *Conv. de Sto. Domingo*; to the S is an area under excavation, where Roman mosaics have been uncovered (and may be displayed in situ).

To the NE of the Pl. de Sto. Domingo is the *Diputación* and, beyond, Baroque *S. Froilán*.—The C. de la Reina leads S from the plaza past 18C *Sta. María la Nova* to the arcaded *Ayuntamiento* of 1738 facing the Pl. de España.

For the road from Lugo to *Santiago* see Rte 35B.

The NVI leads N, at 13km veering NW; the road ahead (C641) leads 22km to *Villalba* (see Rte 34A). The main road ascends the Ladra valley to (14km) *Baamonde*, there meeting the N634, and bears W through (12.5km) *Guitiriz*, a small spa. It then descends past (28km) *Coirós*, with a 12C church, to approach **Betanzos** (11,400 inhab.).

The *old* town, on the site of Roman *Brigantium Flavium*, stands on a low hill defended by medieval gates. *Sta. María del Azogue* (1346–1447) has a fine doorway in the persistent local Transitional style. *S. Francisco* (after 1387) contains the *Tomb* of Fernán Pérez de Andrade, resting on white marble boars, its sides depicting hunting scenes. *Santiago*, rebuilt in the 15C, retains Romanesque work. Romanesque *S. Martín*, above the town, commands a view of the ría and the richly-wooded countryside.

At *Oza dos Rios*, 8.5km S, is a parish church of 1121; *S. Salvador* at neighbouring *Cines* dates back to the 10C.

For the road N to *Pontedeume* and *Ferrol*, and *Bergondo*, on the W side of the estuary, see the latter part of Rte 34B.

The road climbs through eucalyptus woods. At 6.5km a motorway to A Coruña may be entered.—At *Cambre*, just S of this, is *Sta. María* (1194).—Crossing the tidal Mero, either turn right or climb the hill of Elvina to enter A Coruña from the S: both roads converge at the S end of the harbour before reaching the Cantón Grande.

A CORUÑA (*La Coruña* in Castilian, famous in English history as *Corunna*, and also formerly known to British sailors as 'The Groyne') is an active commercial port with a population of 231,700 (64,000 in 1920; 128,000 in 1950; 206,800 in 1975). Its main industries are the curing, salting, and canning of fish, but it also has large petrol refineries. It stands on a neck of land separating the sandy bay of *Orzán* (W) from the *Ría de la Coruña*, but the interesting *old* town occupies only a spur of the headland jutting out into the Atlantic. The characteristic *miradores* or glazed balconies give many streets the appearance of huge conservatories.

A port founded here possibly by the Phoenicians was captured by the Romans in 60 BC and named *Ardobicum Corunium*. It fell into Moorish hands in the 8C and again in the 10C until the defeat of Almanzor in 1002. In 1386 the Portuguese briefly occupied the place; and in 1370 John of Gaunt landed here with an army of 7000 men to claim the crown of Castile in the right of his wife, daughter of Pedro the Cruel. Charles V embarked here for the Low Countries in 1520 after his first visit to Spain, as did Felipe II in 1554 on his way to marry Mary Tudor. In July 1588 the 'invincible Armada' of 130 ships with 2630 cannon and 27,500 men set sail from A Coruña to crush Elizabeth I. Less than a year later Drake and Norreys landed in the harbour, burned the town, and drove back a relieving force.

Hugh Roe O'Donnell, Lord of Tyrconnel, landed here in 1602 after the disaster at Kinsale. Melchor de Macanaz, the economist, persecuted by his political enemies, was imprisoned here from 1748, and was busily occupied in writing until shortly before his death in 1760.

It was long the port of disembarkation from the Falmouth packet, and here Edward Clarke (in 1760) and Robert Southey (in 1797), among other travellers, first landed in Spain. Arthur Jardine, author of 'Letters from Barbary', containing interesting observations on 18C Spain, was British Consul here in 1779–95. Alexander Humboldt sailed from here to Central America in May 1799.

On 16 January 1809 Sir John Moore's army, retreating before Soult, having previously destroyed all supplies (including 4000 barrels of gunpowder) they were unable to load onto transports, engaged in a gallant rearguard action on the heights of *Elvina*, in which the losses were c 900 on each side. Moore was mortally wounded and the command devolved on Sir John Hope, who successfully embarked the army, which by then consisted of about 15,000 men, on waiting transports.

In 1815–20 A Coruña was a centre of anti-monarchist agitation, in which Gen. Juan Porlier (1788–1815), one of the first Liberal martyrs 'pronouncing' against the king, was executed. In 1823 it was occupied by the French troops supporting Fernando VII. The 27-year-old civil governor and his wife were shot dead by the Nationalists within a few hours of the uprising here in July 1936.

A Coruña was the birthplace of Emilia Pardo Bazán (1851–1921), the novelist; Eduardo Dato (1856–1921), the conservative politician; Ramón Menéndez Pidal (1869–1968), the polymath; and Salvador de Madariaga (1886–1978), the Liberal statesman and exiled author. Picasso lived here in 1891–95.

While the life of the modern port centres on the lower town, the main interest and charm of A Coruña for the visitor lies in the picturesque **Ciudad Vieja** on the N spur of the harbour. The harbour had been fortified since the days of Enrique III, the principal strongpoint being the *Castillo de S. Antón* (now containing an archaeological collection), built on the site of a hermitage on the outermost reefs on the E side in 1589, and later accommodating Macanaz (see history). To the S stands the *Castillo de S. Diego*.

The old town is best approached from the *Cantón Grande* (in which, at No. 13, Sir John Moore died) by following the Av. de la Marina. From its far end one may climb to the *Pl. de Azcarraga*, on the S side of which is the 18C *Comandancia*. To the W is *Santiago* (early 12C) with a wide nave, two good doorways, one with a relief of Santiago at Clavijo, and a triple apse.

From the opposite corner of the plaza we approach *Sta. María de Campo* (c 1215–1302), badly restored, with one pointed and two round-headed arched doorways and rudely-carved capitals. To the E is the late Gothic *Conv. de Sta. Bárbara*, its gateway surmounted by a curious relief of St. Michael weighing souls (?1613). Just to the S is *Sto. Domingo*, 18C Galician Baroque, with a Churrigueresque retablo, beyond which is the *Jardín de S. Carlos*, in which is the granite *Tomb of Sir John Moore* (1761–1809). Some stanzas from Charles Wolfe's poem (published in 1817, describing his burial) are carved by the gate overlooking the harbour, as well as Galician verses by Rosalia de Castro.—To the E is the *Conv. de S. Francisco*, largely rebuilt in 1651, but with the remains of its 14C chapel. Beyond are the well-preserved *Ramparts*, with three sea gates (16–17C).

Returning to the Av. de la Marina, turn into the *Pl. de María Pita*, named after the city's heroine during the English attack of 1589. The plaza replaced a wall which formerly separated the *Ciudad Vieja* from the *Pescadería* or fishermen's quarter which once occupied the isthmus.

To the N of the plaza is the triple-domed *Ayuntamiento*, to the W of which are the 18C churches of *S. Jorge* and *S. Nicolás*. A little N, in the former *Real Consulado del Mar*, is the *Museo Provincial*, containing paintings by Goya and Ribera, Galician ceramics from the Real Fábrica de Capuchinas, etc. In the nearby church of *Las Capuchinas* (18C Baroque) is a S. Francisco by Zurbarán.

The C. Real, parallel to the Av. de la Marina, leads back to the Cantón Grande.

At the far N of the peninsula rises the so-called *Torre de Hércules* (101m), refaced in 1791, and still serving as a lighthouse. The original Roman *pharos* was probably rebuilt under Trajan by C. Servius Lupis, according to a damaged inscription on the rock (now covered). Edward Clarke remarked that the inscription referred to Mars, and was amazed that the Spaniards should be 'so perverse' as to give it to Hercules.

For the road S to **Santiago**, **Pontevedra**, and **Tui**, see Rte 38.

B. Lugo to Santiago

105km (65 miles). N640. 19km—C547. 31km *Melide*—55km **Santiago**.

Maps: M 441.

Cross the Miño and bear SW.—At 3.5km *Sta. Eulalia de Bóveda* lies c 9km W. This is a remarkable subterranean church of three aisles with a porch (4–5C), entered through a horseshoe archway and preserving curious paintings and carvings of religious dances.

Crossing a ridge, at 14.5km *Guntin* is entered, just beyond which turn right. The road ahead crosses the MONTES DE VACALOURA to (24km) *Taboada* and *Chantada* 13.5km beyond; see Rte 36.

13km. To the right is the Romanesque monastic church of *Vilar de Donas*, with a good doorway, paintings of 1386, and tombs of interest.—*Palas de Rei* is shortly reached as the road leads over rolling country to (19km) **Melide**. Here *Sta. María* has murals in its apse, and—to the W, just S of the town—12–14C *S. Pedro* has good tombs. The *Ayuntamiento* occupies a former Baroque chapel.

The DETOUR should be made to *Corredoiras*, 16km NW, from which a by-road leads E to (9km) **Sobrado 'de los Monjes'**. The imposing *Monastery*, long neglected, preserves a 13C kitchen and a sacristy of 1471 by Juan de Herrera. The Baroque *Church*, with a front of 1676 by Pedro de Monteagudo, was consecrated in 1708 and contains well-carved choir stalls. The *Cap. del Rosario* (1673) is by Domingo de Andrade; the adjacent late 12C *Cap. de la Magdalena* contains tombs of 1513. The *Hospedería* has a front of 1555, and a cloister of 1635. The *Great Cloister* was completed in 1744. Off it opens the restored 12C *Chapterhouse*; the *Claustro del Jardín* dates from 1753.

To the W, c 6.5km N of Corredoiras, is the 11–13C monastic church of *Sta. María de Mezonzo*, founded by S. Pedro Mezonzo, Bp of Compostela in 986 and author of the 'Salve Regina'.

The C547 winds W from Melide across wooded country through (17km) *Arzuá*. At 27km it skirts (left) the airport of Santiago to approach **Santiago** itself, 11km beyond; see Rte 37.

36   Ponferrada to Vigo via Ourense

260km (161 miles). NVI. 13km—N120. 44km *A Rúa* junction—27km
Puebla de Trives—23km *Castro Caldelas*—52km **Ourense**—30.5km
Ribadavia—55.5km *Porriño*—15km **Vigo**.

Maps: M 441.

For **Ponferrada** see Rte 35A.

PONFERRADA TO THE A RÚA JUNCTION VIA CRUCEDO (66km). The *old* main road,
now superseded (see below), follows the right bank of the Sil, at 6km crossing to
wind SW through (15km) *Carucedo*, where there is a small lake formed
originally by a Roman dike built as part of extensive works to exploit the
region's alluvial gold. The road shortly regains the Sil, here dammed, circling
to the W through the mountains to (29km) *O Barco* before joining the main route to
approach the *A Rúa* junction.

The new N120 veers SW off the NVI just beyond the turning to
Carracedo (see Rte 35A), later crossing the rocky valley of the Sil and
a ridge of mountains by a series of viaducts and tunnels to bypass *O
Barco* and *A Rúa*. Just W of A Rúa it reaches a junction.

A RÚA TO LALÍN VIA MONFORTE DE LEMOS (123km). The improved
C533 circles to the NW, following the banks of the Sil past (22km)
Quiroga, with the Romanesque church of the *Hospital*, and past
another early Romanesque church at *S. Clodio*, on the far bank.
There is a good restored Romanesque and Gothic church at *Torbeo*,
to the SW.—22km **Monforte de Lemos** (20,250 inhab.), an ancient
and picturesque town on the Cabe, crossed by a medieval bridge
below the castle-crowned hill which gave it its name, and which
successfully resisted capture by John of Gaunt's troops in 1386. Late
Gothic *S. Vicente del Pino* has a Renaissance doorway of 1539 and a
cloister with a three-storeyed gallery, the top one glazed. There are
two good Baroque churches near by. The immense *Col. del Cardenal*, or *Instituto* was formerly a Jesuit convent (1592–1616). The
Chapel, with two patios, contains an impressive 17C walnut retablo
by Francisco de Moure of Ourense, to the left of which is the kneeling
figure of Card. Rodríguez (1500). Paintings ascribed to Andrea del
Sarto, two early works by El Greco, and three of the School of
Santiago, may be seen. A *Museum of Religious Art* has been installed
in the *Conv. de Sta. Clara* (near the old bridge), containing works by
Gregorio Fernández and Pedro de Mena, and a collection of cult
objects.

MONFORTE TO OURENSE (49km). The C546 leads W. At 11km a lane bears left to
Romanesque *S. Fiz de Cangas*, passing the Romanesque abbey of *Ferreira* (12–
18C), containing the tombs of two armed knights and a well-carved apse.—To
the NW not far beyond this turning is *S. Miguel de Eiré*. After passing (left) a
turning to the Romanesque abbey church of *Pombeiro*, the road shortly bears
SW above the Miño to cross the Sil at their confluence. Both flow through
imposing gorges (views).—Turn left immediately after crossing the Sil to
approach (c 6km) *S. Estevó de Ribas de Sil*, an ivied convent begun in 1184
(although founded perhaps as early as 550 by S. Martín de Dume, from near
Braga in Portugal). The largest of its three cloisters has three storeys (1595).
There is a remarkable Baroque façade to the convent entrance.—Regaining the
main road, turn left and follow the bank of the Miño to (20km) *Ourense*; see Rte
39.

The C533 leads NW from Monforte, at 22km reaching a turning (left)
to the remains of the abbey of *S. Pelagio Diomondi* (c 1170),
approached by a rough road.—Shortly beyond this turning we pass

the important Romanesque church of *S. Esteban de Saviñoa* (or *de Ribas del Miño*), and descend into and cross the deep vine-terraced valley of the Miño; there is another Romanesque church at *Asma*, on the far bank.—11km **Chantada** (10,350 inhab.).

To the NE at *Pesqueiras* is *Sta. María* (1121); at *Taboada* (13.5km N) the church has a carved tympanum of 1190. NW of Taboada is *S. Pedro de Bembibre*, dated 1171.—SE of Chantada, off the Ourense road, at *S. Esteban de Chouzán*, the church is a relic of a double abbey of Benedictines founded c 1155 and altered in 1314.

The road climbs to cross the SIERRA DEL FARO and another ridge to approach (37km) *Lalín*, on the Ourense–Santiago road; see Rte 39.

At the A Rúa junction the N120 turns SW across the Sil, near a bridge of Roman foundation. Crossing a ridge, it descends in zigzags to the valley of the Bibéi, ascending steeply to (27km) **Puebla de Trives** (746m; 5300 inhab.), a summer resort. The road then descends into the gorge of the Navea before crossing the *Puerto de Cerdeira* (950m). To the S rises the *Cabeza de Manzaneda* (1778m).—23km *Castro Caldelas*, well-sited on a promontory at 793m (views), retains its 14C castle.

14km *Leboreiro*. On the river Mao 6.5km S of Leboreiro is the former Cistercian monastery of *Montederramo*, founded in 1124, with a domed church of 1607 and two cloisters (under restoration).—Regaining the main road, we climb across the ALTO DEL RODICIO (943m) and descend steeply to the NW.—A turning to the left at 12km leads to (5.5km) *Maceda*, with castle ruins, and beyond to the large Baroque church of *Los Milagros* (1713–68).

Beyond (5km) *Esgos*, the curiously sited rock-hewn church of *S. Pedro de Rocas* (10–12C) stands on a height 5km to the right.

19km **Ourense**; see Rte 39, and also for the road NW to Santiago.

OURENSE TO PONTE DE BARCA VIA CELANOVA (105km). The N540 leads SW from Ourense passing a Romanesque church at (10km) *Loiro*, and at *Vilanova de Infantes* an old tower and Baroque sanctuary.—26km **Celanova** (8050 inhab.), an interesting old town—see the C. de Abajo—lies in the centre of a rich agricultural region. It was the birthplace of the Galician poet Manuel Curro Enríques (1851–1908). The huge Benedictine *Conv. de S. Salvador* (now a college) presents a Baroque front to the characteristic *Pl. Mayor*. John of Gaunt and his court resided in an earlier convent on this site in the autumn of 1386. The *Church* (1681) contains a splendid retablo, late Gothic choir stalls, and 11C tombs. Of the two cloisters, the larger was begun in 1550 and finished in the 18C; the other (1611–1722) has a balcony or *paleiro*. Behind, in the garden, is the Mozarabic chapel of *S. Miguel* (c 940–70).—In the vicinity is the Celtic fort of *Castromau*.—For the crossroad from *Xinzo de Limia* to *A Caniza* via Celanova see Rte 39.
The N540 continues S, crossing the *Alto de Vieiro* to (16km) *Bande* and later, beside a reservoir, the ancient spa of *Baños de Bande* (Roman *Aquis Querquenis*), site of a 1C fortified camp. Near by is the remarkable Visigothic church of ***Sta. Comba**, on a Greek cross plan with a sanctuary of c 700 built to house the shrine of S. Torcuato, and restored c 872.—At 22km we reach crossroads: that turning right leads to *Entrimo*, its church with a remarkable Baroque façade; that to the left (a Roman road) crosses the Portuguese frontier 18.5km S at the *Portela do Homem* (750m; Customs), and after traversing the nature reserve of *Peneda do Gerês* at 24km reaches the N103 29km NE of **Braga**.
The N540 crosses the frontier 10km SW near *Lindoso*, with a rebuilt 14C castle, below which the numerous *espigueiros* (the Portuguese equivalent to the Galician *hórreos*; see Glossary) are a curious sight. The road descends the valley of the Limia to (31km) **Ponte de Barca**; see *Blue Guide Portugal*.

The N120 follows the right bank of the Miño to (30.5km) **Ribadavia**

(7050 inhab.), with relics of its castle, walls, and the palace of its counts. It has a quaint *Plaza*, an *Ayuntamiento* with elaborate ironwork; *Santiago* and *S. Juan*, preserving Romanesque work; Gothic *Sta. María*; *S. Ginés de Francelos* (of Visigothic type; c 800); and the convent church of *Sto. Domingo* (14–15C, but of earlier foundation).

The road now bears away from the river through (8km) *Melón*, with ruins of a 12C Cistercian abbey, and briefly turns N at (7.5km) *A Caniza* to cross the *Puerto de Fuentefria* (805m; views). A turning to the left not far beyond leads to late 13C *Sta. María* (on earlier foundations) at *A Franqueira* and at 22km passes the 11C castle of *Villasobroso*. To the N of Villasobroso is the spa of *Mondariz*, scattered among pine woods on the banks of the Tea.—7km **Puenteareas** (15,900), with its fine old *Bridge*, is crossed. 11km beyond is *Porriño*, on the N550; see Rte 38.

Here we climb NW over a ridge. On the far side is (15km) **VIGO**, a lively modern town of 261,350 inhab. (53,000 in 1920; 199,000 in 1970), attractively sited on the S shore of its deep land-locked ría. One of the more important ports on the Spanish coast, during recent decades it has grown rapidly as a commercial and industrial centre. Its quays are busy with factories curing and preserving fish. Vigo is protected from the full force of the Atlantic by the *Islas Cies*, while to the N is the ridge of hills above Cangas forming the *Morrazo peninsula*, reached by frequent ferries.

Roman *Vicus Spacorum* was early referred to as a bathing resort—in a song by the Galician '*joglar*' Martin Codax (early 13C). Drake raided the harbour in both 1585 and 1589. In October 1702 the Duke of Ormonde with Stanhope and Rooke attacked the French and Spanish treasure fleet, just returned from the River Plate. Fourteen ships were captured and most of the rest sunk, although the Comte de Château-Renaud escaped with some French vessels during the action.

The port was again attacked by the English in October 1719 under Lord Cobham, when the licentious troops plundered and set fire to the place. Cobham made a rich haul of arms before marching on Pontevedra, where he collected more booty. In 1936 Vigo's unarmed civilians were brutally attacked by Nationalist-led forces when the latter took over the town.

Vigo is visited less for its own interest, which is very slight, than for the beauty of the surrounding country. The old town, a network of steep narrow lanes with 16–18C granite houses, some tarred on the windward side to resist the damp, lies huddled below the hilltop *Castillo del Castro*. Neo-Classical *Sta. María* dates from 1816. Below, near the *Dársena del Berbés*, the fishing harbour, are a few old arcaded houses.

In the *Parque de Castrelos*, S of the town, is a *pazo* of 1670 housing the *Municipal Museum*, with collections of paintings and archaeology. E of the Museum is the Baroque *Pazo de Sto. Tomé*.

VIGO TO A GARDA (51km). The C550 bears SW, at 14km passing *Monte Ferro* jutting into the Atlantic, with the *Islas Cies* beyond, and skirts the extensive *Playa de América*.—At (7km) **Baiona** (10,150 inhab.), a resort of some character with a 12C church, the *Castillo de Monte Real*, on a fortified wooded promontory, has been converted to house a Parador.—Rounding *Cabo Silleiro*, the road runs due S along the rock-bound coast to (17.5km) *Oia*, with a ruinous monastery and Transitional *Church* of c 1246 with a façade of 1740 and 16C cloister.—12.5km **A Garda** (9550 inhab.), at the foot of the hill of *Sta. Tecla*, on which are the remains of a Celtic castro and an *Archaeological Museum*. Its summit provides a good view across the mouth of the Miño, on the far bank of which is the Portuguese town of *Caminha*. Here the road turns NE parallel to the river, traversing woods, to (28km) **Tui**; see Rte 38. Facing it is fortified *Valença do Minho*; see Blue Guide Portugal.

37 Santiago de Compostela

SANTIAGO DE COMPOSTELA (82,400 inhab.; 26,000 in 1920; 55,500 in 1950), well described by George Borrow as 'a beautiful old town, in every respect calculated to excite awe and admiration', and one of the goals of medieval pilgrimage, stands on a low hill in the midst of green countryside watered by the Sar and the Sarela. It contains a number of fine granite buildings and is dominated by the great cathedral.

Not all visitors have been charitable. Dalrymple, who passed that way in 1775, remarked that it swarmed with priests, 'who enjoy great incomes, live in luxury and every kind of dissipation'. It contains a University, and is noted for having one of the rainiest climates in Spain. It is also one of the few towns where mendicants or *pordioseros* are noticeable. The Airport is at *La Bacolla*, 11km E.

Legend relates that the body of St. James the Great (Santiago; St. Jacques in French), having landed in a stone coffin (sic) at Padrón (*Iria Flaviá*; 20km SW), was discovered in 813 by Theodomir, its bishop, directed by a star which appeared above a wood on the site where Santiago now stands (*Campus Stellae*). The chapel built by Alfonso II was enlarged by Alfonso III into a church in c 879–96, around which a town soon grew. This was destroyed by Almanzor in 997, who carried off the bells of Santiago to Córdoba, but the saint's tomb was spared. In 1090 the episcopal see was transferred from Iria Flavia to Compostela.

Diego Gelmirez, the first archbishop (1100–30; the see was elevated in 1120, when that of Mérida was abolished), in rebuilding the cathedral, incorporated the saint's bones in the foundations. The efficacy of the pilgrimage, although locally frequented as a result of Santiago's miraculous exploits against the Moors (as at Clavijo in 844, Coimbra in 1064, and in 1212 at Las Navas de Tolosa), became bruited abroad, and roads from the frontiers and seaports of Spain were made for the influx of pilgrims. The first recorded English pilgrimage to Santiago is that of Ansgot de la Haye of Burwell, Lincolnshire, c 1093. Chaucer's 'Wife of Bath' had been 'In Galice at seint Jame . . . '. Apart from numerous ecclesiastics, pilgrims or visitors of note during the medieval period included William X, Duke of Aquitaine (1137); Henry the Lion, Duke of Saxony and Bavaria (1182); Sir James Douglas (1330); Baron Rozmital, from Bohemia (1466); Anthony, Earl Rivers (1472); Jerome Münzer, from Nuremberg (1494); Andrew Boorde (1532); and William Lithgow (1620). A guide for pilgrims, known as the *Liber Sancti Jacobi* or *Codex Calixtinus*, was compiled in the mid 12C, possibly by Aymery Picaud. In 1168 the Order of Santiago was established, confirmed by Pope Alexander III in 1175.

The Church profited very considerably, and Santiago has been described by Peter Linehan as 'the anchorage of one of the great ecclesiastical pirates of the thirteenth century, Abp Juan Arias' (1238–67). In 1386 John of Gaunt, claiming the throne of Castile in the right of his wife, daughter of Pedro the Cruel, invaded Galicia and was crowned at Santiago. After the Reformation (when Erasmus poked fun at the cult) the pilgrimage waned, although it is still visited by the devout, particularly in Compostelan years (when 25 July falls on a Sunday), when it is promoted.

In 1809 the treasury was plundered by Ney, but the spoils were disappointingly meagre, the offerings of the pilgrims having been appropriated already by the clergy for their own use.

The spacious ***Plaza del Obradoiro**, immediately W of the cathedral, by which it is dominated, is a convenient point from which to explore the town. It is surrounded by imposing buildings: to the W is the *Pal. de Rajoy* (now the *Ayuntamiento*), built as a seminary in 1772; to the N is the huge ***Hospital Real**, erected by Enrique de Egas as a pilgrim hostelry in 1501–11, at the command of Fernando and Isabel.

In 1954 it was converted into a luxury hotel, the *Hostal de los Reyes Catolicos*. The main front of 1678, with its Plateresque portal, is crested by a series of well-

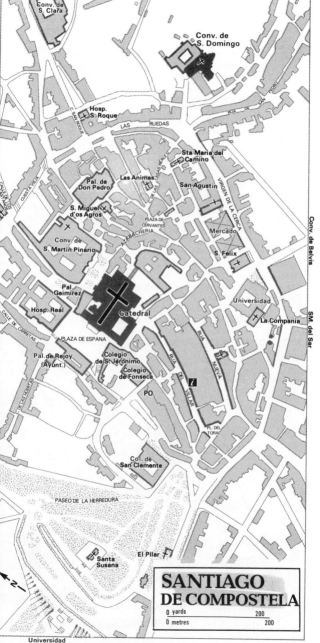

Conv. de S. Clara

Conv. de S. Domingo

Hosp. S. Roque

LAS RUEDAS

SAN ROQUE

RÚA DE SAN PEDRO

Sta María del Camino

Pal. de Don Pedro

Las Ánimas

CUESTA S. VIV.

CALLE DE S. ROQUE

San Agustín

S. Miguel d'os Agros

PLAZA DE CERVANTES

VIRGEN DE LA CERCA

Conv. de S. Martín Pinario

AZABACHERIA

Mercado

S. Félix

Conv. de Belvís

Pal. Gelmírez

Hosp. Real

CALLE DE CARRETAS

Catedral

Universidad

La Compañía

SM. del Sar

PLAZA DE ESPANA

Pal. de Rejoy (Ayunt.)

Colegio de S. Jerónimo

Colegio de Fonseca

RÚA NUEVA

RÚA DEL VILLAR

PO

i

CUESTA TRAPAS

PL. DEL TORAL

Col. de San Clemente

PASEO DE LA HERRADURA

Santa Susana

El Pilar

SANTIAGO DE COMPOSTELA

| 0 yards | 200 |
| 0 metres | 200 |

Universidad

designed mouldings. Within are two Renaissance patios, two later courtyards of the Doric order, and a *Chapel* with a reja of 1556 and a dome supported by pillars of late Gothic workmanship. The Sala Real was frescoed by Arias Varela in 1783.

On the S side of the square is the *Colegio de S. Jerónimo*, with a late 15C doorway (rebuilt in 1665) in the Romanesque style. Behind it is the *Col. de Fonseca*, founded by Abp Alonso III de Fonseca in 1525, and now a Library, with a Plateresque doorway and charming patio; its chapel and hall may be visited.

On the N side of the cathedral is the *Pal. Arzobispal* (1759–1854), occupying the site of the *Palace of Abp Gelmírez*. Parts of the earlier building survive, including the vaulted *Salón de Fiestas* and the *Kitchen*, which date from c 1120 and from the incumbency of Abp Arias.

The fabric of the *Cathedral remains substantially the same as it was after the rebuilding begun by Bp Diego Peláez c 1075 and continued by Abp Gelmírez and his successors, but practically the whole of the exterior was recased in the 17–18Cs. It was consecrated c 1128, but not completed until 1211. In plan it resembles that of St. Sernin at Toulouse, begun contemporaneously. It is curiously tufted with vegetation, as are many other buildings in this damp climate.

The imposing *W Front* or *Fachada del Obradoiro* (1750), by Fernando Casas y Nóvoa, is a masterpiece of the Churrigueresque style, the overcharged detail being disguised by the great mass of the general design, which is partly indebted to the façades in Cuzco. It is flanked by two towers, 70m high.

In the uppermost niche is a statue of the saint, above which is his ubiquitous

The Fachada del Obradoiro of the Cathedral, Santiago de Compostela

scallop shell. (The scallop or cockle, *venera* in Spanish and *vieira* in Portuguese, was formerly consecrated to Venus, and the venereal emblem was used as a charm against the Evil Eye by the Romans.)

The W entrance or *Portico de la Gloria* (see below) is approached by a quadruple flight of steps (1606), below which is a Romanesque *Crypt* of c 1175.

The S *Puerta de las Platerias* (1104), facing the Casa del Cabildo, displays some early work, but its two outer doors have been con-

Detail of the Puerta de las Platerias, Santiago de Compostela

cealed; one by the *Clock tower* (1680), the other by the E wall of the cloister, surrounded by a Renaissance balustrade. The marble outer shafts are carved with tiers of figures in niches; the jambs bear an inscription recording the erection.

At the E end is the *Puerta Santa* (1611), approached through an outer doorway with figures from the original coro.—On the N side is the *Puerto de la Azabachería* (jet carvers), modernised by Ventura Rodríguez in 1770. The circuit of the cathedral may be completed by turning through the vaulted passage beneath the Archbishop's Palace; see above.

The interior of the cathedral is 94m long, 60m across at the transepts, 17.5m across the aisles, and 22m high. Immediately within the W Front is the **Portico de la Gloria**, the masterpiece of Mateo (died 1217), the master of works in 1168. His kneeling figure is seen at the foot of the central shaft, which bears the Tree of Jesse and the figure of Santiago. The credulous knock their heads against that of Mateo to obtain a share of his talents.

Over the main doorway is Christ in glory, encircled by elders with musical instruments. The side doors symbolise the Synagogue (left) and the Heathen (right); the arches are supported by Apostles, etc. The columns rest on monsters. The carving is throughout admirable, and remarkable for the absence of the grotesque. The whole composition bears traces of polychrome painting of 1651 (cf. *Toro* and *Ourense*).

Within the church the Romanesque work is striking in its plainness, with carving on the capitals only. The general gloom is due to the absence of a clerestory, and the blocking up of the S windows. The triforium, with double-arched openings, is unusually deep and lofty. An octagonal *Cimborio* (1384–1445) replaces the original lantern tower. It is here that the *Botafumeiro*, the giant censer of 1602, is hung and swung. The organ has been gutted, and its case of 1705 contains an Italian electronic organ.

The *Cap. Mayor* has two bronze pulpits (1584; by J.B. Celma); the *High Altar*, in the Churrigueresque style (1656–1703), bears a silver shrine of 1715 with a seated *Statue of Santiago* (c 1211), embellished with precious stones, and likened by Ford to 'a spider in the middle of its web, catching strange and foolish flies'.

Behind, a stair is ascended by the devout wishing to kiss the mantle of the image, lit by a silver lamp, the gift of Gonzalo de Córdoba; in the small crypt below are exposed relics of Santiago and two of his disciples.

In the S transept, on the right of the entrance to the cloister, is a 10C tympanum depicting Santiago *Matamoros* (the Moor-slayer) at the battle of Clavijo, the earliest representation of the subject.

In the centre of the S aisle is an ante-room, off which (left) is the *Cap. de S. Fernando* (1521), and (right; partly visible through a reja) the *Cap. de las Reliquias*, with effigies of kings and queens of León, including Berenguela (died 1149; wife of Alfonso VII), Fernando II (died 1188), and Alfonso IX (died 1230).

Among the treasures adorning the modern retablo (replacing one destroyed by fire in 1921) are the jewelled Cross of Alfonso III (874), a silver-gilt statue of Santiago (Parisian work of 1304), and a Custodia by Antonio de Arfe (1546). On the wall are five mid 15C Nottingham alabasters.

The late Gothic *Cloister* was begun in 1521 by Juan de Álava and completed in 1509 by Rodrigo Gil de Hontañón. On its W side are the *Library* and *Sala Capitular*, with collections of tapestries; in the basement are archaeological collections.

Juan de Álava was also responsible for the *Sacristy* (1538), off the S transept.—Steps in the N transept mount to the *Cap. de la Corticela*, entered by a Romanesque doorway, and originally separate from the cathedral.

The chapels opening off the ambulatory contain the 13–17C tombs of miscellaneous cardinals, archbishops, and other ecclesiastics.

To the N, opposite the Puerta de la Azabachería, is the façade of the **Conv. de S. Martín Pinario**. Its *Church*, entered from the E, was designed before 1611 by Gines Martínez, but it is badly damaged by damp. It contains a huge Churrigueresque retablo of 1733 by Casas y Nóvoa, behind which is the coro, with stalls by Mateo de Prado (1639–47).—Opposite are the Gothic *Pal. de Don Pedro* (in which a small *Pilgrimage Museum* is projected) and, adjacent to the S, *S. Miguel d'os Agros* (1754), with a Gothic chapel.—To the NW is the *Conv. de S. Francisco*, with remains of a 14C chapterhouse; the church of 1742 has a monumental front of 1783.

Also in this northern quarter, beyond the line of former walls and once the *Judería* of Compostela, are the *Hosp. de S. Roque* (1577; front of 1647); and further N on the A Coruña road, the late 18C *Conv. de Sta. Clara*. It has a remarkable 'Plattenstil' façade by Simón Rodríguez, and in the domed church a Baroque altarpiece of 1700 by Domingo de Andrade and carved stalls.

To the NE is the **Conv. de Sto. Domingo**, containing an extraordinary *Staircase* by Andrade, consisting of three separate spirals, each ascending to a different floor; the *Church* has an apse of 1230, a 15C nave, and a portal of 1667 by Andrade.

Returning towards the centre by the C. de las Casas Reales, we pass (left) *Sta. María del Camino* (1770; with a 16C Gothic chapel), and (right) the late 18C *Cap. de las Ánimas*, with a relief of souls in Purgatory.

On reaching the triangular Pl. de Cervantes, one may follow the Preguntoiro S to the Pl. de Feijóo, to the E of which is *S. Félix*, altered in the 17–18Cs but retaining a 12C portal and early tombs.—N of the adjoining market place is *S. Agustín* (1648; by González Araujo), with a cloister of 1623.—To the S are the old buildings of the *University* (rebuilt in 1769–1805 by Melchor de Prado y Mariño), founded in 1532. Behind it is the Jesuit church of *La Compañía* (1583–1673).

To the E is the *Conv. de Belvis*, with a church of 1739 by Casas y Nóvoa.

SE of the town, just beyond the bypass, approached by the C. de Sar, is collegiate **'Sta. María de Sar** (c 1133–70), a curious building remarkable for the cant of its piers, probably caused by subsidence, although their inclination is so uniform that some have thought it intentional. The adjoining fragment of a beautifully sculptured *Cloister*, the finest example of carving in Santiago after the Pórtico de la Gloria, contains the 13–16C tombs of priors.

Immediately SE of the cathedral is the Pl. de la Quintana, flanked by the *Monasterio de S. Pelayo*; to the S is the *Casa de los Canónigos*. Adjacent is the small Pl. de las Platerías, with the *Casa del Cabildo* (1758; by Fernández Sarela). Off this leads the characteristic flagstoned and porticoed **'Rúa del Vilar**, in which No. 1 is the *Casa del Dean* (1752), also by Sarela. At its far end, in the Pl. del Toral, No. 2 is a late 18C mansion.—One may return by the arcaded **Rúa Nueva**, parallel to the E, passing 12C *Sta. María Salomé*, with a 15C front and tower completed in 1743.

A few steps W of the Pl. del Toral is the busy Puerta Fajera, beyond which is the Alameda. From the Alameda leads the shady *Paseo de la Herradura* (horseshoe), providing pleasant vistas. We pass, to the N, the classical front of the *Col. de S. Clemente*. The *Mirador*, to the W, commands a view over the new *University quarter*. On the summit of the hill stands 12C *Sta. Susana*, from which the Alameda may be regained, passing (right) *El Pilar* (1720).

SW, in *Baixo Sar*, is *Sta. María de Conjo*, with a Romanesque cloister and 17C church containing Churrigueresque retablos.—Further N is *S. Lorenzo de Transouto*, founded in 1217 and rebuilt c 1700.

38 A Coruña to Tui via Santiago and Pontevedra (for Oporto or Braga)

177km (110 miles). A9. 72km **Santiago**—N550. 20km *Padrón*—
37km **Pontevedra**—20km *Redondela*—28km **Tui**.

Maps: M 441.

The direct N550 is of little interest, winding up onto a typical stretch
of Galician upland with views over open heaths, and the motorway is
recommended. This will eventually be continued S from Santiago to
Tui, but the only section at present (1988) completed is that from
Pontevedra to a point W of Redondela, with a branch off to Vigo.

A CORUÑA TO SANTIAGO VIA CORCUBIÓN, MUROS, AND NOIA
(213km, without detours). This slow circuit may be followed by those
with plenty of time to spare, and the detour is preferable to many
stretches of the *Rías Bajas*, which are far more obviously populated.
A number of small fishing villages may be approached from the road
described, several of them retaining early Romanesque churches.

Climb SW from *A Coruña* (see last part of Rte 35A), passing *Oseira*,
with a late 12C church, at 35km crossing **Carballo** (25,700 inhab.) to
approach (28km) *Baio*, only 9km from the *Ría de Corme y Laxe.*—
From (8.5km) *Vimianzo*, once celebrated for its gold mines, and with
a restored castle and picturesque *pazo*, a by-road leads 18km NW to
Camariñas (7200 inhab.), on its ría. 5km N of Camariñas is *Cabo
Vilán*, the wildest point on this savage coast.—Opposite is *Muxía*
(7100 inhab.), commanded by *N.S. de la Barca*, reached by a by-road
passing near *Cereijo*, with a 12C church, *Ozón*, with an impressive
hórreo, and *Moraime/Molinos*, where Romanesque *S. Julián* has a
porch copied from the 'Gloria' at Santiago.

At *Cée* (24.5km SW from Vimianzo) fork right for adjacent
Corcubión, a small village on its ría, defended by two dismantled
forts.

13km beyond lies *Fisterra*, or **Finisterre** (5300 inhab.) where in 1837 George
Borrow was apprehended by the Justicia, who assumed him to be the Carlist
pretender! To the S is *Cabo* or *Cape Finisterre*, the 'Land's End' of Spain, known
to the Romans as *Promontorium Nerium*. Offshore, in 1747, Adm. Anson won a
battle against Adm. La Jonquière; and in 1805 Adm. Strachan overtook and
captured French ships fleeing from Trafalgar.

From Cée turn SE through (12km) *O Pindo*, above which the hill
(635m) provides the best view point over the coast.—13km *Carnota*,
with the longest *hórreo* in Galicia, beyond which we round a
peninsula to (16km) **Muros** (12,300 inhab.), with its narrow alleys and
arcaded streets and the Gothic *Colegiata de S. Pedro*. The N bank of
the ría is skirted to cross the Tambre just seaward of the 14C *Puente
Nafonso*, for **Noia** (14,150 inhab.).

The port, now silted up, was described by Froissart as 'the key to
Galicia'. A medieval bridge crosses the Traba. *S. Martín* (before
1434) has a good rose-window and 16C towers; *Sta. María a Nova* is
set in a picturesque churchyard with a curious chapel and several
calvaries; *S. Francisco*, begun in 1522, is Plateresque.

The C543 climbs NE and winds through wooded hills to (37km)
Santiago; see Rte 37.

The peninsula formed by the ridge of the *Sierra de Barbanza* (691m) extending
into the Atlantic SW of Noia is skirted by the C550, but only the N flank is

really attractive. Beyond (36km) **Sta. Eugenia/Ribeira** (24,550 inhab.) the banks of the *Ría Arousa* are too populated, and the views often spoilt.—The road bears NE through (8km) *Puebla del Caramiñal* (10,050 inhab.), *Boiro* (17,300 inhab.), 8km beyond, and after 10km bypasses (right) *Rianxo* (12,700 inhab.) to approach *Padrón*, 20km further NE; see below.

From **Santiago** (see Rte 37) follow the N550 SW, at 14km Passing Baroque *N.S. de la Esclavitud*, formerly a place of sanctuary for criminals.—**Padrón** (9950 inhab.), Roman *Iria Flavia*, and an episcopal see before Santiago, was the legendary landing place of the body of Santiago, which floated up the ría in a stone coffin; see Santiago. It was the birthplace of Camilo José Cela Trulock (1916–), the novelist, and here also the poetess Rosalío de Castro (1837–85) lived and died. The *Colegiata*, with a nave of 1714, contains the tombs of 28 bishops, while notable among old mansions is the *Casa del Obispo de Quito* (1666). The Ulla is crossed to *Puentecesures/ Enfesta* on a bridge built by Mateo of Compostela (cf. Portica de la Gloria) on foundations of the Roman *Pons Caesaris*.

PADRÓN TO PONTEVEDRA VIA CAMBADOS (80km). On crossing the Ulla fork left on a lamentable road (C550) through eucalyptus and pine woods to (25km) the port of **Villagarcía de Arousa** (30,200 inhab.). A good view over the ría may be obtained from the summit of *Lobeira* (290m) to the S. The road continues SW past **Vilanova de Arousa** (15,300 inhab.), birthplace of Ramón María del Valle-Inclán (1866–1936), the poet and playwright.—A causeway now approaches the *Illa de Arousa*.—11km **Cambados** (13,100 inhab.; Parador), with the *Pazo de Fefinañes* and the picturesque ruins of *Sta. Marina*.—On a height c 10km SE is the Romanesque abbey church of *Armenteira* (1181), with a good doorway and rose, and 18C cloister.—The C550 circles to the SW. Turn left at the neck of a peninsula, on which are the resorts of *O Grove*, 5km N, and *A Toxa/La Toja*, with thermal springs known to the Romans.—One may circle the peninsula, from the W coast of which there is a closer view of the *Isla de Sálvora* guarding the entrance of the *Ría de Arousa*; to the S is the *Isla de Ons*.

The main road bears round to the SE through (12.5km) the resort of **Sanxenxo/Sangenjo** (14,350 inhab.) and (11km) picturesque but unkempt *Combarro*, which was a typical Galician fishing village. Shortly beyond Combarro we turn below the monastery and Neo-Classical church of *Poio* to approach *Pontevedra*.

The N550 leads due S from Padrón through (16km) *Caldas de Reis* (8900 inhab.), with a Romanesque church containing tombs of the Camoens family, and the old *Torre de Doña Urraca*.

21km **PONTEVEDRA** (64,200 inhab.; 29,000 in 1920; Parador), at the head of its ría, and the provincial capital in spite of the pretensions of Vigo, retains an attractive and characteristic old centre of arcaded streets and ancient houses bearing escutcheons. For those who prefer to base themselves in a town for the exploration of the area it is a pleasant centre.

From the S end of *Puente del Burgo* one may circle to the right, shortly passing (left) 16C *Sta. María la Mayor*, with a front by Cornelis de Holanda, and a carved interior W doorway, to reach the Alameda. This is flanked to the E by the *Ayuntamiento*, and to the S by the ruins of the *Conv. de Sto. Domingo* (c 1331–83), consisting mainly of the E end of the church with five polygonal apses containing stone crosses, etc. Beyond, among gardens, is the *Diputación*.

The C. Michelena leads SE to the conspicuous round **Cap. de la Peregrina** (1792)—to the N of which is the Pl. de Ourense, and to *S. Francisco* (begun c 1274).—The Pasantería leads N from the square, descending a short distance to the diminutive *Pl. de la Leña*. Here, in a typical mansion of 1760, is the *Museum*, containing collections of ornaments from local churches, and prints and documents illustrating Galician history, etc.—To the N is Baroque *S. Bartolomé* (after 1686), with a Magdalen by Gregorio Fernández.

To the E, beyond the main road, is the Gothic *Conv. de Sta. Clara.* The granite lanes and little squares in the area W and NW of the museum deserve exploration.

The CIRCUIT of the *Morrazo peninsula* may be made by following the C550 to the SW through (7km) **Marín** (23,200 inhab.), with a harbour and naval training college; 12km *Bueu* (12,150 inhab.), with a small nautical museum; and right at 11km, *Hío*, with a Romanesque church.—Turning to the SE, we drive through (5km) **Cangas** (22,000 inhab.), with a church of 1542 and a view across the ría to Vigo, and then (5km) **Moaña** (17,850 inhab.). At 9km we pass below the new motorway bridge spanning the narrows of the ría, which may be crossed here to **Vigo**, to the SW (see last part of Rte 36), or **Redondela**, to the SE.

Continuing S from Pontevedra, at 11km the Verdugo is crossed W of a Roman bridge. On the far bank a road leads 4km E to the 15C castle of *Sotomayor.*—The head of the *Ría de Vigo* is skirted before entering (9km) **Redondela** (27,550 inhab.), with a Gothic parish church and the *Conv. de S. Lorenzo Justiniano* dating from 1501.

14km **Porriño** (13,700 inhab.), beyond which we descend the fertile valley of the Louro to (14km) **TUI/TÚY** (15,100 inhab.; Parador), an old frontier town guarding the passage of the Miño opposite *Valença do Minho.*

Once known as *Tude*, and of great antiquity, it was selected by Witiza as his capital c 700. It was briefly in Moorish hands (716–40), and the present town occupies a new site chosen by Fernando II in 1170. It suffered from earthquakes in the 16th and 18Cs. In 1809 Soult was frustrated in his attempt to cross the river here by the Portuguese garrison of Valença. In 1963, during the Salazar regime, Valença did not give asylum to Republic fugitives from Vigo. Attempting to escape across the International Bridge, they were handed back to the Natonalists, who shot them.

Bp Lucas (c 1160–1249), the credulous historian, was perhaps the most famous incumbent of the see, from 1239.

The fortress-like *Cathedral, partly restored, was begun c 1180 but the only 12C work remaining is the N Tower and doorway and the lower part of the chancel and transepts. Note the capitals in the S transept. The *Nave* (1218–39) is French in style. The *W Doorway* dates from 1225–87, but the upper part of the choir and the *W Front* were not completed until the 15C, although in characteristic Galician fashion their style appears to be some 200 years earlier.

The interior, with Renaissance rejas, is heavily braced as a precaution against earthquakes. The sillería of the coro is boldly carved. To the E of the S transept is the chapel of *S. Telmo* (the Blessed Pedro González; died 1240), the patron of the cathedral and of Spanish mariners, and the British sailors' 'St. Elmo', whose fire-balls clinging to the yards were regarded as a favourable omen. The kneeling figure is that of the founder, Bp Diego de Torquemada (1579); near by is the grave of Bp Lucas. The huge organ is gutted. The *Cloister*, to the S (1264; altered 1408–65), has been marred by the addition of an upper storey.

At the E end of the Alameda stands *Sto. Domingo* (1330–1415), with a good E end, two tombs of interest in the N transept, and reliefs in its cloister. The platform behind commands a good view across the Miño.

S. Bartolomé is Romanesque; Neo-Classical *S. Francisco* preserves remains of its Gothic predecessor; and the *Cap. de S. Pedro Telmo* is an example of the 18C Portuguese style.

For *A Garda*, 28km SW, see the last paragraphs of Rte 36. For the road skirting the Miño to the E see Rte 39.

The two-storeyed *Puente International* (333m long) was built by Eiffel, the French engineer, in 1885. The bridge may be crossed (Customs) to **Valença do Minho**, with its picturesque fortified enceinte, worth the walk not only for itself but for the view of Tui from its walls. For Valença and the S bank of the Minho see *Blue Guide Portugal*.

Monção lies 18km E; **Ponte de Lima** 38km S, and **Braga** 33km beyond; **Viana do Castelo** is 51km SW, and **Oporto** is 73km further S.

39 Zamora to Santiago via Puebla de Sanabria and Ourense

378km (235 miles). N630. 23km.—N525. 91km *Puebla de Sanabria*—84km **Verín**—30km *Xinzo de Limia*—39km **Ourense**—56km *Lalín*—55km **Santiago**.

Maps: M 441.

For **Zamora** see Rte 20. Driving N, at 25km the dammed Esla is crossed, near the ruins of the 13C *Puente de la Estrella*. Bear NW to (19km) *Tábara*, where the church of 1137 has a good tower and sanctuary rebuilt in 1761. The road crosses the *Portillo de Sazadón* (820m), a shoulder of the SIERRA DE LA CULEBRA, rising further to the W to 1238m.—At 35km we meet the C620 from Benavente and veer W through (5.5km) *Mombuey*, with a 13C church tower and spire. Ahead extends the SIERRA DE LA CABRERA (2124m).

At 26km **Puebla de Sanabria** (Albergue) is bypassed. It has a galleried *Ayuntamiento*, relics of walls and a mid 15C castle, and a late 12C church.

12km to the NW is the *Lago de Sanabria*, a deep lake with sulphur springs, the largest of several tarns on the S slope of the roadless SIERRA DE LA CABRERA. At *S. Martín de Castañeda*, on the lake's N shore, is a large triple-apsed church of c 1150 with a W front of 1571, the relic of a Benedictine monastery of 916. Another road skirts the S bank to the village of *Ribadelago*.

The C622 climbs S from Puebla de Sanabria to cross the Portuguese frontier (Customs) at 19km, descending to **Bragança** 20.5km beyond; see *Blue Guide Portugal*.

The N525 continues W, crossing the *Portilla de Padornelo* (1352m) and the *Portilla de la Canda* (1262m). It bypasses (left) *Pereiro*, with an important Romanesque church, before crossing the *Alto do Canizo* (1052m) to enter (49km from the Pueblo de Sanabria turning) *A Guadiña*.

21km N on the E bank of the *Embalse de Bao*, approached by the C533, is **Viana del Bollo** (6400 inhab.) an unspoilt old town with arcaded streets and a feudal keep.

The road bears SW over the hills to (36km) **Verín** (10,050 inhab.; Parador), on the Támega. The town is overlooked from the N by the fortified village and *Castle of Monterrey*, with its 13C church preserving well-sculptured features. On the adjacent hill is the parador.—At *Mijós*, 4km NE of Verín, is a 9C church containing murals.

The C532 leads S down the valley of the Támega to cross the Portuguese

frontier at (15.5km) *Feces de Abaixo* (Customs) and enters **Chaves** 10.5km
beyond; see *Blue Guide Portugal.*—*Vila Real* lies 64km further SW.

The N525 circles to the NW, crossing the *Alto de Estivadas* (849m)
and descending to (30km) **Xinzo de Limia** (10,550 inhab.).

XINZO DE LIMIA TO A CANIZA VIA CELANOVA (73km). The C531 turns NW,
crossing the *Alto de Forriolo* (842m) to (29km) *Celanova*; see p 250. On
approaching the town we pass the Romanesque church of *S. Munio de la Veiga*;
there is another at *Paizás*, NW of Celanova. The road continues down the valley
of the Arnoia through *Milmanda*, with an ancient bridge, ruined castle, and *Sta.
Maria de Alázar*, to cross the Miño just beyond (28.5km) *Cortegada.*—*A Caniza*
is 15.5km beyond; see Rte 36.
    The Portuguese frontier may be crossed 16km SW by skirting the river to
Ponte Barxas (Customs) for *São Gregorio*, and *Melgaço*, 10.5km beyond; see
Blue Guide Portugal.—The N bank of the Miño may be reached by a bridge just
before the frontier and followed to (35km) *Salvaterra de Miño* (9250 inhab.) and
Tui, 17.5km beyond; see last part of Rte 38.

The N525 continues N from Xinzo through (6km) *Sandiás*, with a
ruined castle. At 11km *Allariz* (5550 inhab.) is bypassed, with 12C
Santiago, and the 18C *Conv. de Sta. Clara* with tombs of several
children of Alfonso X.

To the W is *S. Martiño de Pazó* (10C; restored); at *Xunqueira de Ambia* (6km E
of the main road) is a church of 1164 with a 16C cloister and Renaissance stalls.

22km **OURENSE/ORENSE** (94,350 inhab.; 18,000 in 1920; 55,000 in
1950), an ancient town and modern provincial capital, stands on the S
bank of the Miño and its confluence with the Barbaña. Its characteristic older nucleus clusters around its cathedral.

It takes its name from its hot springs, the Roman *Aquae Urentes* or *Auronensis*.
In the 6–7C it was the capital of the Suevi, although disputed with the Vandals
and later the Visigoths. It was destroyed by the Moors in 716, and c 900 rebuilt
by Alfonso II. John of Gaunt held his court here during the few months of his
'reign' as king of Castile in 1386–87 (cf. Celanova). In May 1809 it was the
starting point of Soult's advance into Portugal after the embarkation of Moore's
column, and a few months later it saw his army in retreat, shattered by
Wellington at Oporto.
    It was the birthplace (at the *Pazo de Casdemiro*, not far NE) of Benito
Jerónimo Feijóo (1676–1764), the influential Benedictine reformer.

A bypass has been constructed to the W of the town. It crosses the
Miño a short distance downstream from the beautiful seven-arched
*****Bridge** of 1230, with a central span of 45m. Just to the S of the
bridge is *N.S. de los Remedios* (1522; rebuilt 1584).
    To the NE of the arcaded *Pl. Mayor* stands the *****Cathedral**,
founded in 572, rebuilt in 1132–94, and again in its present form in
1218–48. The façade, once covered with elaborate 13C decoration,
was badly restored in the 16–17Cs. The Portal beneath the narthex,
called *El Paraiso*, imitating the Pórtico de la Gloria at Santiago,
preserves some of its original painting. On the left is a crude fresco of
Cristóbalon or St. Christopher.

The long nave and aisles are 13C work. The transepts, with their boldly
sculptured doorways, the chancel, and ambulatory (1620), were rebuilt on 12C
foundations. The *Cimborio*, by Rodrigo de Badajoz, dates from 1505. The Coro
has a Plateresque reja and carved stalls of 1590. The Cap. Mayor has a retablo
by Cornelis de Holanda, beside which are reliefs of martyrdoms. In the N aisle is
the chapel of *S. Juan Bautista*, built in 1468 by the Conde de Benavente to atone
for damage wrought in the cathedral during the feud between his house and the
Condes de Lemos. Its window tracery shows English influence. The tomb of
Card. Quevedo y Quintana (died 1586) has a statue by Solá. A chapel to the E of
the N transept contains a Plateresque silver altarpiece.

Only a fragment survives of the 13C cloister, now used as a vestry. The *Sacristy* contains a copy of the Monterrey missal, the first book printed in Galicia (1494), Limoges enamels, early 18C silver altar frontals, and a Cross attributed to Enrique de Arfe, but spoilt by regilding and the addition of coarse gems.

To the S, adjoining the old *Bishop's Palace* (containing the provincial *Archaeological Museum*), is ancient *Sta. María la Madre*, restored in the 18C, with a 17C high altar by Moure.—Further S is *La Trinidad*, with a curious 16C towered front.

Above the cathedral to the E is the *Conv. de S. Francisco*, now barracks, but the *Cloister* of 1332, its 60 arches supported by coupled columns with capitals sculptured with foliage and figures, may be visited. (The church, with Gothic and Renaissance tombs in its triple apse, was rebuilt on a new site further N in 1928.)

For the N120 to **Vigo** see Rte 36; for the C546 to **Monforte de Lemos**, 49km NE, see p 249.

OURENSE TO SANTIAGO VIA A ESTRADA (115km). This alternative road turns off the N120 14km W of Ourense to follow the N541, which passes near several old churches in the wooded hills to the W. Among them are the 12C Templar churches of *Moldes* and *Boboras*, but they are not so easy to find.—At 14km **Carballiño** (11,050 inhab.), an ugly town, is bypassed, and the road climbs across the *Alto de Paraño* (800m), at 29km, just beyond *Soutelo*, turning right for (6km) *Cachafeiro*.—At *Acebeiro*, 7km NE, are the ruins of a Cistercian monastery founded in 1170.—From Cachafeiro follow the C541 NW through *Forcarei* (8000 inhab.) across fertile countryside in which are several Baroque *pazos*, to approach (26.5km) **a Estrada** (27,350 inhab.). The Ulla is crossed at (11km) *Puentevea* and **Santiago** is reached 14.5km beyond; see Rte 37.

The main road (N525) climbs to the N from Ourense. From it the N540 turns NE at 11km for (26km) *Chantada* and **Lugo**, 47km beyond.

At 11.5km the DETOUR of 9km to Oseira should be made by turning right off the N525 and up a wooded valley. The Cistercian monastery of ***Oseira**, founded in 1135 and completed in 1239, was largely rebuilt after a fire in 1552, although the church retains Romanesque and Gothic features. It received the sobriquet of 'the Escorial of Galicia' after receiving its Baroque additions.

Its main façade dates from 1708, at right angles to that of the *Church* (1637), flanked by two towers. There are three cloisters, that 'de los medallones' (reconstructed in 1553); the Gothic Patio 'de los pináculos'; and the 17C Patio 'de los Caballeros'. Between the first two an imposing monumental staircase of 1647 ascends to the upper floor, off which are the kitchens and refectory; it also provides access to the *Library* of 1776, retaining some of its original walnut cases.

The *Church* was consecrated in 1239; off it opens the low-vaulted *Sacristy*. The *Chapterhouse*, with palm-vaulting rising from twisted columns, is 14C; the *Choir* was added in 1675. The crossing and ambulatory, approached through two Baroque *retablos*, received polychrome decoration in the early 17C. Off the N transept is the 12C chapel of *S. Andrés*. Note the painted altars in other chapels. The work of restoration continues.

On regaining the main road turn N to climb across the *Alto de Sto. Domingo* (810m) and descend to (33.5km) **Lalin** (18,950 inhab.), the centre of a region known as the Deza.

15km *Silleda*, c 7km N of which (sign-posted), in a loop of the Río Deza, stand the picturesque ruins of the monastery of *S. Lorenzo de Caboeira**, with a Romanesque church of 1192.

16.5km *Valboa*, with the *Pazo de Oca*, with attractive formal gardens and moss-grown water tanks. —3km *Ponte Ulla*, shortly beyond which the road skirts the *Pico Sacro* (534m). Its summit, with the 11C cave chapel of *S. Sebastián*, commands a view of **Santiago**, which is now approached; see Rte 37.

IV MADRID; CASTILLA-LA MANCHA; EXTREMADURA

The *Comunidad* de **Madrid**, formerly part of New Castile, is now a separate autonomy; otherwise **Castilla-La Mancha** is conterminous with what was New Castile, but with the addition of Albacete, formerly part of the Reino de Murcia. It is perhaps the bleakest and least beautiful region of Spain, although its desolate, sun-scorched and windswept plateaux, almost treeless and almost rainless, have an attraction of their own. Its most characteristic area is *La Mancha*, the home of 'Don Quixote' and the scene of many of his adventures.

On the N and NE it is separated from Castilla y León and Aragón by the sierras of Gredos, Guadarrama, and the Montes Universales. In these latter, more scenically attractive uplands, rises the Tagus, and sluggish Guadiana, which runs W through broken country N of the *Serena* into Extremadura. Since the 1950s the Guadiana has been partly harnessed for projects of land reclamation associated with the 'Badajoz Plan'. To the S and SE rise the barrier ranges of the Sierra Morena and Sierra de Segura.

Toledo, its capital, was reconquered in 1085, and much of these extensive territories were then annexed by the Castilians, calling it Castilla 'la Nueva' (new). It was not until after the battle of Las Navas de Tolosa (1212) that, having erected many more castles to consolidate this advance, they were able to push into Andalucía.

Extremadura, often anglicised as *Estremadura*, comprises the provinces of *Cáceres* and *Badajoz*, representing the old districts of Alta Extremadura, the basin of the Tagus, and Baja Extremadura, the basin of the Guadiana, on which stood ancient Mérida. To the W is Portugal; to the S is the Sierra Morena. For centuries it was a no-man's land between the Christians of León and the Andalucian Moors.

Characteristic of the landscape are the extensive heaths of gumcistus. The soil is not infertile but the area is subject to drought. Agriculture, for long at a low ebb, has been stimulated in recent decades by widespread irrigation schemes, the construction of reservoirs, and schemes of afforestation. Sheep farming is still important to the economy, while herds of swine still find their food in the oak, chestnut, and beech forests.

Hernán Cortes (died 1547), conqueror of Mexico, and Francisco Pizarro (died 1541), conqueror of Peru, among many other *conquistadores*, were both Extremeños, and their fame encouraged the emigration of the more ambitious inhabitants from the province whose position was too remote to command any direct advantage from the wealth of the Americas. The population of every province in this huge autonomous area is less than it was in 1940.

40 Madrid

MADRID (3,158,800 inhab.; 729,000 in 1920; 1,096,000 in 1940; 2,177,000 in 1960), the political capital of Spain (and capital of its autonomous *Comunidad*), and the highest capital in Europe (646m), is situated almost exactly in the centre of the Iberian Peninsula on a bare and exposed upland plateau—still largely a 'hideous, grassless, treeless, colourless, calcined desert'—with no visible limit except the Sierra de Gaudarrama to the N. It has many of the characteristics of a cosmopolitan capital, but apart from its political significance (less since the inauguration of autonomies), its main attractions for the traveller are the unrivalled collections of the Prado Museum, among others of lesser importance.

Recent changes have increasingly tended to obliterate Madrid's national characteristics and peculiarities. Richard Ford (when describing Madrid 140 years ago) had reproached the unheeding Spaniards for doing their best 'to *denationalise* themselves, and to destroy with suicidal hand their greatest merit, which is in being *Spanish*; for Spain's best attractions are those which are characteristic of *herself*; here all that is imitated is poor and second-rate, and displeases the foreigner, who . . . hopes to find again in Spain . . . all that has been lost and forgotten elsewhere'.

It is certainly no longer the 'blanche ville aux sérénades' of Musset. The residential quarters which have grown up in every direction are impersonal, unlike the narrow winding streets of Old Madrid that are still to be found near the Puerta del Sol and in the SW quarter. On the W and S the low hills occupied by the town are skirted by the insignificant *Manzanares* (now canalised), 'a rivulet with the reputation of a river' as Cervantes called it, spanned by several handsome bridges. Its narrow banks are no longer white with the town's washing, as they were when first seen by Robert Southey in January 1796.

Dense traffic flows along Madrid's widened and once dignified tree-lined avenues. Underground carparks, one-way streets, and fly-overs proliferate, as do new banks, hotels, blocks of flats and offices, and suburban estates. An elaborate series of ring roads under construction promises to ease the communication problem caused by the town's extraordinary growth. The M30 or Av. de la Paz, skirting Madrid's E side, has now been completed. Its depressing shanty slums or *chabolas* have to a large extent been demolished and replaced by tower blocks. Industry occupies many outlying areas, except to the W where the 'green belt' of the Casa del Campo offers some slight protection from the encroaching metropolis. Considering what architectural riches some other Spanish towns have to offer, there are many who would agree with Ford that 'those who the soonest shake the dust off their feet, and remain the shortest time in Madrid, will probably remember it with most satisfaction'.

The climate, although hot and oppressive in summer, and cold but dry in winter, is not so trying as is sometimes represented. Spring, although it has many delightful days, can be rainy; autumn is usually fine. It is proverbial that the subtle air of Madrid 'which will not extinguish a candle, will put out a man's life', and even on sunny days there can be abrupt falls in temperature at sunset.

Although there are numerous prehistoric remains in the vicinity of Madrid, particularly near the terraced banks of the Manzanares and Jarama, and over 40 Roman sites in the area, the earliest mention of Madrid, as *Majrit* or *Magerit*, occurs in the mid 10C. It was merely an outpost of Toledo when captured by Alfonso VI of León in 1083, and its growth was gradual. It was walled in the 12C. Alfonso X granted it his *fuero real* in 1262. The Cortes met for the first time here in 1309 under Fernando IV, and again in 1335 under Alfonso XI. Enrique IV replaced the Moorish *alcázar* by a new palace c 1466 (burnt to the ground in 1734). François I of France was confined in Madrid after the battle of Pavia in February 1525 until the Treaty of Madrid in 1526.

In 1561 Felipe II decided to make Madrid the '*única corte*', and with the establishment of the seat of government the town's limits were extended. In 1625 it was surrounded by a *tapia* wall which, reconstructed in 1782, was only demolished late in the 19C. It maintained its rank as capital in spite of abortive attempts by Felipe III to prefer Valladolid, and Carlos III to prefer Sevilla.

In 1605 the first part of 'Don Quixote' was published at Madrid; and in the 17C the capital enjoyed a golden age, with Cervantes (died 1616), Lope de Vega (died 1635), Velázquez (died 1660), and Calderón (died 1681) living and working here. In 1623 Prince Charles Stuart (later Charles I), accompanied by the Duke of Buckingham, spent almost six months in Madrid when suitor for the hand of the Infanta Maria, sister of Felipe IV (as described by James Howell). The visit was celebrated with bull fights and *fiestas*, although political and religious differences prevented the match. Rubens visited Madrid for nine months from August 1628. In 1633 the building of the new Palace of the Buen Retiro was commenced, observed with interest by Arthur Hopton, the British envoy. In 1649 Madrid was visited by the Earl of Clarendon. In 1650 Anthony Ascham, Envoy from the Commonwealth, was assassinated here by embittered royalists.

Carlos III did much to improve Madrid, which lived up to its reputation as one of the filthiest of Europe's capitals. Baretti, in 1760, writes of the 'horrible stink' that gave him a headache immediately on entering its gates. In 1764 (the year Beaumarchais visited Madrid) the new palace on the site of the old was constructed. Street lighting was improved and the streets were paved after a fashion, several new ones being laid out and embellished. A number of important public buildings were built. Here in 1766 riots took place against an attempt by the king's Italian minister, the Marqués de Esquilache, to control the length of cloaks and the size of hat brims. In 1773 an elephant was brought to Madrid and promenaded through the streets, much to the public's consternation. In 1775 the Economic Society of Madrid was founded, in which year Thomas Pelham, 2nd Earl of Chichester, visited Madrid during the ambassadorship of Lord Grantham. According to the census of 1787, its population had by then risen to 156,000.

In 1808, at the start of the Peninsular War, the French entered the capital, when the abortive insurrection of the '*Dos de Mayo*' took place, after which Joseph Bonaparte, known as 'Tio Pepe' or 'Rey Plazuelas' (from the clearances he later made in the congested town) occupied the palace until ousted by Wellington in 1812.

Among visitors to Madrid during the first few decades of the 19C were John Philip Kemble, in December 1802; Victor Hugo, in 1811; Washington Irving (appointed to the American Legation in 1826; he remained in Spain until 1829); David Wilkie, who spent seven months here prior to May 1828; Richard Ford, for the first time, in 1831; George Borrow, in 1836; Théophile Gautier in 1840; Henry Southern, secretary to the embassy in 1833–39, was the probable author of 'Madrid in 1835'.

Often the scene of *pronunciamientos* during the 19C, Madrid proclaimed the Republic in 1931, and as the seat of government (until it was transferred to Valencia) the town underwent a protracted siege from October 1936 until March 1939. During the siege the University City, in the front line, was destroyed. The usual proscriptions took place on its occupation by the Nationalists. Under the dictatorship it was again the corrupt administrative capital of Spain. Little of historical moment has occurred since, although Madrid was the scene of the assassination of Adm. Carrero Blanco in 1973, of the lingering death of Gen. Franco in 1975, and of the abortive *coup* of February 1981 by Col. Tejero of the Guardia Civil.

In April 1979 Enrique Tierno Galván, a Socialist mayor, took office; May Day manifestations were again tolerated, replacing the military processions and political demonstrations of loyalty to the Fascist cause previously imposed on the populace.

Among natives of Madrid were Alonso de Ercilla y Zúñiga (1533–94), author of the epic poem 'La Araucana'; Lope de Vega (1562–1635); Tirso de Molina (Fray Gabriel Tellez; 1572–1648); Francisco Gómez de Quevedo y Villegas (1580–1645); Calderon de la Barca (1600–81); Francisco Santos (1623–98), author of 'Dia y Noche de Madrid', 1663; Ramón de la Cruz (1731–94); Nicolás and his son Leandro Fernández de Moratin (1737–80, and 1760–1828); Manuel José Quintana (1772–1857); Ramón de Mesonero Romanos (1803–82), *costumbrista* and topographer, who wrote a guide to Madrid in 1831; Juan Eugenio Hartzenbusch (1806–80); Mariano José de Larra (1809–37); Jacinto Benavente (1866–1954); José Ortega y Gasset (1883–1955); Gregorio Marañon (1887–1960); endocrinologist and author; Pedro Salinas (1892–1951); and Arturo Barea (1897–1957). Benito Pérez Galdos (1843–1920) lived most of his life in Madrid.

Among artists were Francisco Collantes (1599–1656); Francisco Rizzi (1614–85); Claudio Coello (1642–93); José del Castillo (1737–93); Luis Paret y Alcázar (1746–99); Leonardo Alenza (1807–45); Eugenio Lucas (1817–70); José Gutiérrez Solana (1886–1945); and Juan Gris (1887–1927).

Louis Blanc (1811–82), the French socialist, was born here. Domenico Scarlatti died in Madrid in 1757; G.-B. Tiepolo in 1770; and Luigi Boccherini in 1805. The English ambassadors Richard Fanshawe (1608–66), and Benjamin Keene (1697–1757) both died in office in Madrid.

Employment of Time. Visitors making a short stay in Madrid will probably start by making their first visit to the Museo del Prado. A day may be spent exploring the old town to the W of the Puerta del Sol and surrounding the Pl. Mayor, and seeing at least the exterior of the Palacio Real; a further day may be spent visiting the Archaeological Museum, and others, bearing in mind that several museums are only open during the mornings, or are closed for at least two hours for lunch. **Most museums are closed on Mondays**, and some may be closed in August. Several of the main shopping streets run from and parallel to the C. Serrano, an area perhaps best visited in the late afternoon.

Hours of admission to the main museums, etc. are listed below but are liable to change. Museums may open and close later during summer afternoons.

Madrid's streets were numbered in 1833, beginning at the end nearest the *Puerta del Sol*, with even numbers on the right and odd on the left.

Academia de Historia, Real (Gabinete de Antigüedades)	C. León 21	16.00–19.00 on prior appl.
America	Av. Reyes Católicos	—
Arqueológico	C. Serrano 13	09.15–13.45
Arte Contemporáneo	Av. Juan de Herrera	10.00–18.00 Sun 10.00–15.00
Artes Decorativas	C. Montalbán 12	10.00–15.00 Sat/Sun 10.00–14.00
Carruages (carriages)	Campo del Moro	10.00–12.45; 15.30–17.15 Sun 10.00–13.30
Cerralbo	C. Ventura Rodríguez 17	10.00–14.00; 16.00–19.00
Descalzas Reales	P. de las Descalzas Reales	Wed & Sat 10.00–1.30; 16.00–18.00; Fri 10.00–13.30 Sun 11.00–14.00
Ejército (Army)	C. Méndez Nuñez 1	10.00–14.30
Encarnación	Pl. de la Encarnación	Tue, Wed, Sat 10.00–13.30 & 16.00–18.00 Fri 10.00–13.30 Sun 11.00–14.00
Etnología	C. Alfonso XII 68	10.00–14.00; 16.00–19.00
Jardín Botánico	S. of Prado museum	10.00–18.00
Lázaro Galdiano	C. Serrano 122	10.00–14.00
Municipal	C. Fuencarral 78	10.00–14.00; 17.00–21.00 Sun 10.00–14.30
Naval	C. Montalbán 2	10.30–13.30
Numismatic	C. Jorge Juan 106	—
Palacio Real (also Library, and Armoury)	C. Bailén 8 Pl. de Oriente	09.30–12.45; 15.30–17.15 Sun 09.30–13.30
Prado (and Casón del Buen Retiro)	Paseo del Prado C. Felipe IV, 13	09.00–19.00 Sun 09.00–14.00
Reina Sofía, Centro de Arte	C. Sta. Isabel 52 (Atocha)	10.00–21.00
Romántico	C. S. Mateo 13	10.00–18.00; Sun 10.00–14.00
S. Antonio de la Florida		10.00–13.00; 16.00–19.00 11.00–13.30; 15.00–18.00 in winter and Sun morning only
S. Fernando, Real Academía de Bellas Artes de	C. Alcalá 13	09.00–19.00 Sun/Mon 09.00–14.00
S. Francisco el Grande		11.00–13.00; 16.00–19.00; closed Sun
Sorolla	C. Gen. Martínez Campos 37	10.00–14.00
Tapices, Fábrica de	C. Fuenterrabía 2	09.30–12.30; closed Sat/Sun
Valencia de Don Juan	C. Fortuny 43	—

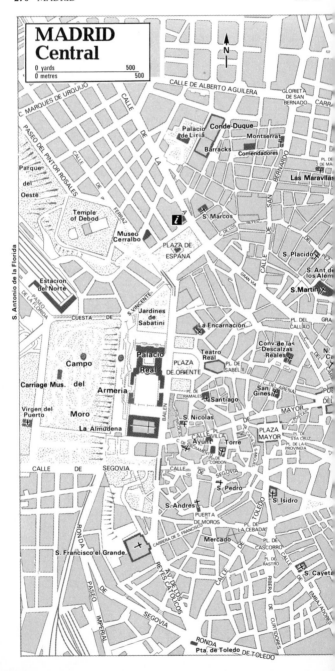

MADRID Central

0 yards 500
0 metres 500

N

CALLE DE ALBERTO AGUILERA

GLORIETA DE SAN BERNARDO

CARR

C. MARQUES DE URQUIJO

CALLE

PASEO DEL PINTOR ROSALES

CALLE DE FERRAZ

LA

Palacio de Liria

Conde-Duque

Montserrat

Barracks

Comendadores

PL. DE 2 DE MA

Las Maravillas

Parque del Oeste

Temple of Debod

Museo Cerralbo

PLAZA DE ESPAÑA

S. Marcos

C. DE LOS REYES

SAN

DEL

BERNARDO

S. Placido

PEZ

S. Ant de los Alem

GRAN VIA

S. Martin

S. Antonio de la Florida

Estación del Norte

PASEO DE LA FLORIDA

CUESTA DE

S. VINCENTE

Jardines de Sabatini

La Encarnación

PL. DEL CALLAO

PL. DEL GRA

Conv de las Descalzas Reales

N. Ca

Campo

del

Palacio Real

Teatro Real

PLAZA DE ORIENTE

PL. DE ISABEL II

C. DE ARENAL

San Ginés

MAYOR

PUI

DEL

Carriage Mus.

Armeria

PL. DE RAMALES

Santiago

S. Nicolas

CALLE DE SEGOVIA

PLAZA MAYOR

CUCHILLEROS

PL. DE STA CRUZ

Virgen del Puerto

Moro

La Almudena

BAILEN

PL. DE LA VILLA

Ayunt

C. DE SEGOVIA

PL. DE CORDON

Torre

CAVA DE S. MIGUEL

PL. DE LA PROVINCIA

CALLE

DE

SEGOVIA

CALLE

DE

SEGOVIA

S. Pedro

S. Isidro

TOLEDO

S. Andres

PUERTA DE MOROS

PL. DE LA CEBADA

RONDA

S. Francisco el Grande

CARRERA DE S. FRANCISCO

Mercado

PL. DE CASCORRO

PL. DEL RASTRO

S. Cayeta

RIBERA

DE

EMBAJADORES

CURTIDORES

AV. DE LOS REYES CATOLICOS

PASEO

DE

IMPERIAL

SEGOVIA

RONDA

Pta. de Toledo

DE TOLEDO

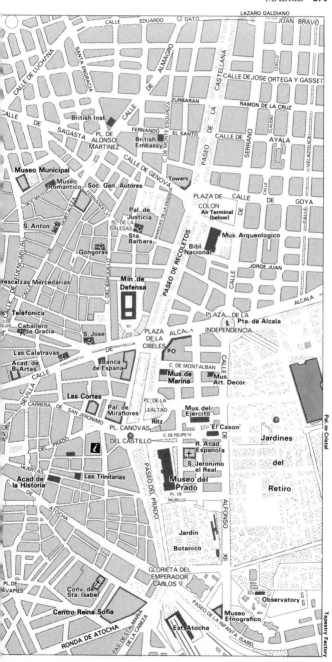

LAZARO GALDIANO
JUAN BRAVO
CALLE EDUARDO DATO
CALLE DE ALMAGRO
SANTA ENGRACIA
CALLE DE LA CASTELLANA
CALLE DE JOSE ORTEGA Y GASSET
COELLO
CALLE DE LUCHANA
ZURBARAN
RAMON DE LA CRUZ
CALLE DE SAGASTA
British Inst.
PL. DE ALONSO MARTINEZ
FERNANDO
EL SANTO
CALLE DE MONTE ESQUINZA
British Embassy
CALLE DE GENOVA
CALLE DE SERRANO
AYALA
CLAUDIO
VELAZQUEZ
Museo Municipal
Museo Romantico
Soc. Gen. Autores
Towers
PLAZA DE COLON
CALLE DE GOYA
FERNANDO VI
HORTALEZA
C. DE MATEO
Pal. de Justicia
Air Terminal (below)
CALLE
S. Anton
MARQUES DE LA ENSENADA
PL. DE LA SALESAS
Sta. Barbara
Mus. Arqueologico
FUENCARRAL
DE
CALLE DE BARQUILLO
Gongoras
Bibl. Nacional
PASEO DE RECOLETOS
JORGE JUAN
escalzas Mercedarias
Min. de Defensa
CALLE
ALCALA
Telefonica
Caballero de Gracia
S. Jose
PLAZA DE LA CIBELES
PLAZA DE LA INDEPENDENCIA
Pta. de Alcala
Las Calatravas
Acad. de B. Artes
Banca de Espana
ALCALA
PO
C. DE MONTALBAN
Mus. de Marina
Mus. Art. Decor.
SEVILLA
CALLE
Las Cortes
CARRERA DE SAN JERONIMO
Pal. de Miraflores
PL. DE LA LEALTAD
Ritz
Mus. del Ejercito
'El Cason'
Jardines
Pal. de Cristal
PL. CANOVAS
DEL PRADO
DEL CASTILLO
C. DE FELIPE IV
R. Acad. Espanola
S. Jeronimo el Real
del
HUERTAS
Acad. de la Historia
Las Trinitarias
Museo del Prado
PL. DE MURILLO
Retiro
C. DE ATOCHA
PASEO DEL PRADO
ALFONSO XII
Jardin Botanico
GLORIETA DEL EMPERADOR CARLOS V
PL. DE LAVAPIES
Conv. de Sta. Isabel
Centro Reina Sofia
PASEO DE STA. MARIA DE LA CABEZA
RONDA DE ATOCHA
PASEO DE LA INFANTA ISABEL
Observatory
Museo Etnografico
Est. Atocha
Tapestry Factory

A. From the Pl. de la Cibeles to the Puerta del Sol

The topography of Madrid can be best understood by taking the **Pl. de la Cibeles** as a focal point, where the C. de Alcalá intersects the main N–S thoroughfare between the Paseo del Prado and Paseo de Recoletos (extended further N by the long Paseo de Castellana). The plaza, congested with traffic, is named after the *Fountain of Cybele* (1780; by Francisco Gutiérrez and Robert Michel). To the SE is the **Pal. de Comunicaciones** (*Correos*, or General Post Office; 1913), a pretentious 'wedding-cake' edifice also facetiously known as 'N.S. de Comunicaciones' or even as the 'Casa de tócame Roque' (Do as you please).—To the SW is the *Banco de España* (1891, and since extended), built on the site of the palace of the Dukes of Béjar.

To the NW is the *Ministerio de Defensa* (or *Ejército*), which occupies the former *Pal. de Buenavista*, built in 1772 by Pedro Arnal and in 1805 given to Godoy. In 1841–43 it was the residence of Espartero; and in 1869–70 that of Prim (assassinated in 1870 near the corner of the C. del Marqués de Cubas, to the SW).

The C. de Alcalá leads gently uphill to the SW passing (right) *S. José*, completed in 1742, beyond which the Gran Via forks right; see Rte 40G.

Crossing this street and continuing up the N side of the C. de Alcalá, with a good retrospective view of the *Puerta de Alcalá* (q.v.; but with the skyline now dominated by a tower block at the NE corner of the Retiro park), the church of *Las Calatravas* (c 1686), with a Baroque retablo by Pablo González Velázquez, is passed, and then (No. 15), the *Casino de Madrid*, a club with an appropriately ornate entrance hall.

No. 13 is the building of the ***Real Academia de Bellas Artes de S. Fernando**, displaying a classical front of 1774 by Diego de Villanueva. It contains the works of art acquired by the Academy since its foundation in 1752 other than those canvases transferred to the Prado in 1902. The building has been restored recently, and its collections have been reformed, but many feel that the more selective assembly of paintings formerly on display was preferable to the quantity now to be seen.

Among these are the following portraits: *Esquivel*, His daughter, and of José Villaamil; *Andrés de la Calleja*, José de Carvajal y Lancaster, and Carlos III; *Mengs*, the Marquesa del Llano; *Louis Michel van Loo*, Barbara de Braganza; *Antonio Ponz*, Self-portrait; *José Vergara*, Self-portrait; *Batoni*, Manuel de Roda, and A Youth; *Madrazo*, Manuel García de la Prada, and Isabel II. *Goya*, 'La Tirana' (the actress Rosario Fernández), Juan de Villanueva (the architect), Leandro Fernández de Moratín, José Luis Munarriz (Secretary of the Academy), Godoy reading, Fernando VII on horseback, Self-portrait (1815), Self-portrait while painting, Burial of the Sardine, Scene in a madhouse, Bull-fight, Inquisition scene, and Penitents. *Esteve*, Young Godoy; *Carnicero*, Godoy, Principe de la Paz; *Zurbarán*, Blessed Alonso Rodríguez, and five Portraits of Mercederios (monks of the Order of Mercy); *Ribera*, Ecce Homo, St. Antony of Padua, Assumption of the Magdalen, and Head of the Baptist; *Murillo*, S. Diego de Alcalá, Resurrection, Ecstasy of S. Francisco de Asis, Magdalen; *Alonso Cano*, Crucifixion, and Jesus and the Samaritan woman; *Pereda*, The dream; and polychrome sculptures by *J. Gines*.

Valdes Leal, S. Pedro; *Pedro de Mena*, Mater Dolorosa; *Herrera el Viejo*, Presentation of the Virgin; *Carreño*, Mariana de Austria, and Magdalen; *Velázquez*, Felipe IV, and Mariana de Austria; *Vicente López*, King and Queen of the Two Sicilies, Carlos Maria Isidro de Borbon, María Francisca de Braganza, and Isidro González Velázquez; *Zacarias González Velázquez*,

Portrait of Ventura Rodriguez; *Carlos de Haes*, The Royal Palace and the Manzanares; *Eugenio Lucas*, Corrida de toros; *Rubens*, Susanna and the Elders, Hercules and Omphale, S. Agustin between Christ and the Virgin; *Martin de Vos*, Descent from the Cross, and Abundance; *W.C. Heda*, Still life; *B. Strigel*, Maximilian and his family (a copy); *Giovanni Bellini*, Christ; *Arcimbaldo*, Spring; *Hans Muelich*, Crucifixion; pastel portraits by *Faraona Olivieri*.

The central *Salon de Actas* is lit from eight oval windows in the ceiling; note also the carved plaques (some damaged); the *Chapel* contains a Crucifixion by *Morales*.

Other rooms contain a series of prints by *Picasso*; *José Alonso del Rivero*, Carlos III distributing land in the Sierra Morena; *Sotomayor*, The wedding, and Alfonso XIII; *Sorolla*, Beach scenes, etc.; *Cecilio Pla*, Beach scenes; *Vazquez Diaz*, The Baroja brothers; *E. Chicharro*, Self-portrait; *F. Labrada*, Female portrait; Still lifes by *Van der Hamen* and *P. Claez*; *Lucas Jordan*, Adoration of the shepherds; *Gaspar de Crayer*, Fernando of Austria (died 1641); *Snyders*, Boar-hunt; *Ribalta*, S. Juan de Ribera; *Ribera*, Burial of Christ (two examples) and Martyrdom of S. Bartholomew; *A. Cano*, Pietà, the Baptist, and the Virgin of Montserrat; and a collection of Silver.

In the same building is the **Calcografía Nacional**, where old engravings from original plates are for sale.

Adjacent is the *Hacienda* (Min. of Finance), built in 1769 as the Aduana (Customs House).

We shortly enter the E end of the **Puerta del Sol**, an irregular space—not a gateway—from which ten streets radiate. The historic heart of the town and a hub of activity, it has recently been spruced up, re-paved, and embellished with lamps which have been the subject of much criticism. On the S side, in the entrance hall of the unimposing *Police Headquarters* (*Seguridad*; 1786), is a stone slab indicating Kilometric Zero, from which distances in Spain are calculated.

Designed as the *Gen. Post Office* by Jacques Marquet, the Seguridad was later the *Min. de la Gobernación*. It is surmounted by a clock placed there in 1866, donated by its maker, Losada, a Spaniard resident in London.

At the E side of the plaza stood the chapel of the *Buen Suceso*, whose façade bore the figure of the sun which gave it its name; opposite was the emplacement of the fountain known as 'La Mariblanca'. It was adjacent to the *Librería S. Martín*, on the S side, that José Méndez Canalejas (1854–1912), the politician, was assassinated.

In the C. de Carretas, leading S, stood the well-known bar, *El Pombo*. To the W of the Seguridad stood the convent of *S. Felipe el Real* and the *Gradas de S. Felipe*, once a famous rendezvous, below which were the toy stalls known as the *Covachuelas*. Opposite the Seguridad stood the *Inclusa* (foundling hospital) or *Niños Expósitos*.

In the C. del Carmen, leading NW, stands *N.S. del Carmen* (1660; by Miguel Soria), the church of a convent built in 1575 on the site of a brothel.

The C. Mayor leads W from the W end of the plaza; see Rte 40C.

B.   From the Puerta del Sol to the Palacio Real

For the *Puerta del Sol* see above. The C. Arenal leads NW from its W end, shortly passing (left) **S. Ginés** (1465; rebuilt in 1645 and since restored), containing El Greco's 'Expulsion of the Money-changers'. Borrow's Testaments were once used at the Sunday school in this church. Below is a chapel formerly used by penitents during Lent for spiritual exercises and mortification.

The C.S. Martín, opposite, ascends to the Pl. de las Descalzas, and the *Convento de las Descalzas Reales, now containing a 'Museum of Religious art'. Visitors are conducted—do not be hurried—from the main cloister through an elaborately decorated hall.

The *Upper Cloister* is surrounded by chapels, containing a recumbent Christ by *Gaspar Becerra; Pedro de Mena*, Mater Dolorosa; *Zurbarán*, St. Francis; and *Brueghel the Elder*, Adoration of the Kings. The *Salón de los Reyes* preserves a Mudéjar frieze and a collection of portraits. Other rooms accommodate 17C Brussels' tapestries from cartoons by *Rubens*; religious works of the Flemish school, and a display of reliquaries. The main **Chapel** (1564; by J.B. de Toledo), approached from the lower cloister, contains the tomb of the foundress, Juana of Austria (daughter of Charles V), by Pompeo Leoni.

Tomás Luis de Victoria was choirmaster and organist here from 1586 until his death in 1611. By the late 18C matters had deteriorated. William Beckford complained, when he attended mass here, of the 'wretched music' and 'vile stink'.

Opposite is the new building of the *Monte de Piedad*, the municipal pawn office, established in 1703, and the *Caja de Ahorros* (Savings Bank; 1838), preserving a Baroque portal.

The C. de Arenal leads into the PL. DE ISABEL II, dominated to the W by the **Teatro Real** (1818–50; by Antonio López Aguado), opened as an opera house, inaugurated with Donizetti's 'La Favorita', and replacing the earlier *Coliseo de los Caños de Peral*. The metro rumbles below.

The building also accommodates the *Conservatory of Music*. Some rare Baroque viols were donated to the Conservatory in c 1960 to form the basis of a collection of musical instruments, but they were allowed to fall apart (the glue melting in the heat of the summer) and were later jettisoned as bits not worth keeping.

The short C. de Arrieta leads NW from the plaza to the tree-shaded **Conv. de la Encarnación** (early 17C; by Gómez de Mora). It preserves a few paintings of interest, and the retablo of the church is an Annunciation by Carducho. Its vaults are frescoed by Francisco Bayeu, and it contains a restored 18C organ.

A short distance further NW is the Pl. de la Marina Española, with the former *Pal. de Godoy* (1776; by Sabatini), conveniently near the Pal. Real; and adjacent *Pal. del Senado*, on the site of a late 16C Augustinian convent.

Immediately to the W is the C. Bailén. Below its far side are the *Sabatini Gardens*, on the site of former royal stables, overlooked by the N front of the Pal. Real.—For the *Carriage museum* and *S. Antonio de la Florida* see Rte 40L.

To the W of the Teatro Real are the **Pl. de Oriente**, cleared by Joseph Bonaparte in 1811, but dating in its present form from 1841 when it was levelled and trees planted. In the centre is an equestrian *Statue of Felipe IV*, modelled by Montañés after a painting by Velázquez, and cast at Florence by Pietro Tacca (with the help of calculations by Galileo). The statue—'a solid Velázquez', as Richard Ford called it—was presented to the king in 1640 by the Grand-duke of Tuscany and until 1844 stood in the Retiro. The reliefs on the pedestal are modern.

The 44 statues of Spanish kings and queens which embellish the gardens were intended, like those in the Retiro, for the top of the palace, but they were found to be too heavy.

To the SE of the plaza stands *Santiago* (1811; by Juan Antonio Cuervo); beyond which, in the C. de Santiago, George Borrow lived in 1837–38.

The ***Palacio Real** is an imposing late Renaissance building in a commanding position on a height that falls steeply to the W and N, but so exposed to the chill winter blasts from the Guadarrama range that it is said that its sentinels were constantly frozen to death. The four wings form a square around a central courtyard, while two projecting wings to the S flank the Pl. de Armas. Above a rustic basement of granite rise the upper storeys of Colmenar stone, the whole articulated by pilasters and Corinthian columns, crowned by a balustrade originally intended to support statues (see above). On the E façade is the *Puerta del Principe*, but the principal entrance is on the S side, facing the Pl. de Armas, separated by a railing from the Pl. de la Armería. The lower SW wing is occupied by the *Armería Reál*; see below.

In Richard Ford's opinion this was 'one of the finest armouries in the world' and of greater interest than the palace itself which, while admittedly a truly royal one, 'nothing is more tiresome than a palace, a house of velvet, tapestry, gold and bore . . . '. Ford repeats a story told of a young bodyguard at court who omitted to pay the usual salute to the Duque de Infantado. When excusing himself that he did not know his rank, he was told by his grace, more witty than most: 'my friend, the safe rule is to suppose everybody in the palace who looks like a monkey to be a grandee of the first class'.

The exterior façades are closely related to Mansart's garden front to the central block at Versailles as well as to Vanvitelli's work at Caserta, while the windows and entablature correspond exactly to Bernini's design for the Louvre. The courtyard is closer to the Farnese palace in Rome and the Ducal palace at Modena. The present palace, begun by Felipe V in 1738 by G.B. Sacchetti of Turin, and subsequently completed under Carlos III in 1764, replaced a previous palace (founded by Enrique IV c 1466 on the site, it is said, of a Moorish Alcázar), which burnt down on Christmas Eve, 1734.

A much more splendid scheme, designed by Felipe Juvara (died 1735) was abandoned by Felipe V on the score of expense. The main scheme of decoration was begun in 1753 by Corrado Giaquinto, who in 1761 was followed by Mengs and G.B. Tiepolo. It was of this palace that Napoleon remarked that his brother Joseph was better lodged than he himself was in the Tuileries. In 1812 Wellington, on entering Madrid shortly after his victory at Salamanca, took up temporary residence here.

Entering from the S courtyard, visitors are conducted round the apartments in groups by guides curiously fascinated by ceilings. Do not be hurried; see p 91–92. The tour starts at the foot of the *Grand Staircase*. Beyond lies the spacious central patio, which is surrounded by a porticus with statues of the Roman emperors of Spanish birth (Trajan, Hadrian, Theodosius, and Honorius). In a recess opposite the staircase is a statue of Carlos III as a Roman emperor. The Staircase, with a painted ceiling by Giaquinto, ascends to the guardroom, containing 16C Flemish tapestries and armour made for royal children (Felipe III when prince, and others); the ceiling is by Tiepolo. The adjacent *Salón de Columnas* contains busts of emperors from Herculaneum and 16C bronzes.

We proceed through the Saleta, Antecámara (with four portraits by Goya of Carlos IV and María Luisa, and a clock of 1786) and Rococo *Salón de Gasparini*, named after the Neapolitan artist who decorated it, with a fine marble floor and a profusion of chinoiserie stucco work.

From the adjacent Tranvia the *Salón de Carlos III* is entered, that king's bedroom in which he died. It contains his portrait by Maella and a vault painted by Vicente López in 1828. Next are the remarkable *Sala de Porcelana*, covered with modelled plaques by

Italian artists but made in the Buen Retiro factory (cf. the similar room at Aranjuez); and the *Sala Amarilla* (or Yellow Room), with a ceiling of 1829 by Luis López and a fine suite of chairs. The *Gran Comedor* of 1879 preserves the painted ceiling of the earlier Cuarto de la Reina, by Mengs, Francisco Bayeu, and others. From the Gran Comedor we enter the *Music Room*, containing a tintinnabulous collection of clocks, of which both Carlos IV and Fernando VII were amateurs. A gallery surrounding the patio is entered to reach a series of rooms at the NW corner of the palace, now housing a collection of paintings, among which are:

R1 *Van der Weyden*, Felipe I; *Bermejo*, Isabel la Catolica.—**R2** attributed to *Caravaggio*, Salome with the head of the Baptist.—**R3** works by *Goya*, including cartoons for tapestries, and two scenes of the making of gunpowder and shot in the Sierra de Tardieta during the Peninsular War; also paintings by *Vicente López*.—**R4**, furnished as the bedroom of Carlos IV, with two landscapes by *Luis Paret* (San Sebastián, and Pasajes).—**R5** *Velázquez*, Caballero de la Orden de S. Juan, and study of a white Horse (restored); attributed to *Herrera el Viejo*, Four doctors of the Church.—**R6** contains an old *copy of a Rembrandt* portrait, portraits of Felipe IV and Isabella de Bourbon attributed to *Rubens*, and smaller works of the Flemish school.—**R7** is dominated by *El Greco*, St. Paul, and five works attributed to *Bassano*.—**R8** is devoted to paintings by *M.-A. Houasse*, and also contains two by *Watteau*.—The next room displays *Ribera*, Portrait of Don Juan José de Austria on horseback; *Bartolomé González*, Portraits of Felipe III and Margaret of Austria; and, of historical interest, a View of the old Palacio de Buen Retiro, by *Del Mazo*.—Further rooms contain works of lesser interest and lead to one displaying collections of porcelain and glass.

The domed **Capilla Real** is approached. By Sacchetti and Ventura Rodríguez, it was completed in 1757. It has ceiling paintings by Giaquinto, an unfinished altarpiece by Mengs, and an organ by Jordi Borch.

Opposite the sacristy are two rooms containing reliquaries (one carved by Berruguete; and another given to Charles V by François I) and a shrine containing the bones of Fernando III (died 1252; canonised 1671).

The tour continues through several rooms on the E front, including the *Salón de Tapices*, entirely hung with tapestries; the *Salón de Armas*, containing the Triptych of Isabel the Catholic (1496; by Juan de Flandes and others); and another Tranvia, with a display of porcelain and miniatures, to enter a suite of 17 rooms left as they were by Alfonso XIII when sent into exile in 1931. The contents of his study characterise the man.

We return to the Cámara, its vault by Maella, and the adjacent *Salón de Grandes*, its walls covered with blue silk, to enter the *Salón del Trono*. It contains gilt bronze lions cast at Naples in 1651 by Finelli for the old Alcázar, which survived the fire of 1734. It was here that Ford saw Fernando VII lying in state, 'his face hideous in life, now purple like a ripe fig, dead and dressed in full uniform, with a cocked hat on his head, and a stick in his hand'. The mirrors, from the factory at La Granja, were designed by Ventura Rodríguez for the positions they occupy, but the intervening statues had been brought from Italy by Velázquez for Felipe IV. The two large clocks in ebony and bronze cases are English. The ceiling painting (1764; by G.B. Tiepolo, then aged 78) represents the Majesty of Spain, and illustrates provincial costumes; in the corners are stucco reliefs of the Seasons by Robert Michel. We return to and descend the Grand Staircase.

At the NW angle of the palace is the **Library**, possessing over 300,000 volumes and 4000 MSS, the archives of the royal house from

1479, and 265 *incunabula* (among them the Book of Hours of Isabel the Catholic). Among earlier librarians was the arabist José Antonio Condé (1765–1820). Other collections include maps, prints, engravings and drawings, and medals; also musical instruments (including some by Stradivarius) and scores, a selection of which are on display.

The palace also contains numerous *Tapestries*, beginning with several Flemish series (late 15C), among them those of the Passion, from designs by Van der Weyden; the Acts of the Apostles (1527; after Raphael); the Honours, the Apocalypse (Van Orley), and the Conquest of Tunis (Van Aelst and Willem Pannemaker), etc.

Near the entrance is the **Pharmacy**, containing retorts and other utensils, a distilling unit, Talavera ware, and jars from the Buen Retiro factory.

The nucleus of the **Armería Real**, installed in the S extremity of the W wing, was the collection of Flemish and German armour brought to Spain by Charles V and housed in a separate building by Felipe II, destroyed by a fire in 1884. It had been plundered in 1808, but most of the more precious objects have survived, including the MS catalogue of Charles V's armour. Artistically, the most remarkable pieces are those of the early 16C, when the rivalry between the German and the Italian armourers led to the production of decorative masterpieces, but from the point of view of general design armour had reached its culmination somewhat earlier, under Maximilian I and Felipe I (father of Charles V).

Only at Vienna is there a naturally formed body of arms and armour (as distinct from specific collections) worthy of comparison. In these two armouries alone is it possible to study complete suites or 'garnitures', each consisting of several suits for different purposes, and provided with spare parts. But this collection is neither well displayed nor adequately labelled, and its complete rearrangement is long overdue.

Among the more interesting exhibits are Charles V's suits of armour by Kolman Helmschmeid (1471–1532) and his son Desiderius (1500–c 1578), including (A 164) that worn at the battle of Mühlberg in 1547 and depicted by Titian in the equestrian portrait in the Prado. Among other historic pieces are the light armour worn by Charles at the taking of Tunis in 1535, on the Algerian expedition of 1541, and (A 188) that in Roman style (1546; by Bartolomeo Campi of Pesaro) presented to the emperor by Guid'Ubaldo II, Duke of Urbino; A 298, black and gold armour 'of Sebastián of Portugal', by Anton Pfeffenhauser of Augsburg; A 139, a gold-decorated suit by the Negroli brothers of Milan; A 291, armour made for Felipe III by Lucio Piccinino; A 16–17, tournament suits of Felipe I; M 10, steel turban and breastplate of Barbarossa, taken at Tunis; the parade armour of Felipe II; A 149, equestrian armour inherited from Maximilian I, designed by Hans Burgkmair and made by Kolman Helmschmeid, with scenes in cut, engraved, and inlaid steel; the arms of François I taken at Pavia; and the swords of Fernando the Catholic (G 21), Gonzalo de Córdoba (G 29), and Francisco Pizarro (G 35).

To the S of the palace is the unfinished cathedral of *N.S. de la Almudena*, an ambitious but commonplace edifice designed by the Marqués de Cubas and begun in 1880. A few steps beyond is the W extremity of the C. Mayor; see Rte 40C.

C.   S of the C. Mayor

The **Calle Mayor** leads W from the SW corner of the Puerta del Sol.
Off it to the left, after a short walk, is the Pl. Mayor (also approached
more directly by the C. Postas, in which the ancient *Posada del Peine*
is preserved).
The ***Plaza Mayor** is a spacious rectangle about 120m long and
90m wide, surrounded by arcades sheltering small shops and bars,
etc. In the centre is an equestrian statue of Felipe III (restored) by
Giovanni da Bologna and Pietro Tacca (1615).

The plaza's balconied houses were built in 1617–19 on a uniform plan by Juan
Gómez de Mora. On the N side is the *Casa Panadería*, which succeeded a
municipal bake house of 1590 (and which, with the exception of the porticus,
was rebuilt after a fire in 1672). From the bake house the king used to survey the
proceedings in the square below, which was formally inaugurated in 1620. Here
took place *autos-de-fé*, executions, fireworks, bullfights, festivals, and popular
demonstrations, including the tournament held in 1623 in honour of the Prince
of Wales, afterwards Charles I. Another was held to celebrate the public entry of
Carlos III into his capital in 1760, as described by Edward Clarke. Here too were
played the religious *autos* of Lope de Vega, among others.

A short distance to the SE of the plaza is the PL. DE LA PROVINCIA,
flanked by the brick façade of the *Ministry of Foreign Affairs*.
Erected in 1634 by J.B. Crescenzi to house the Audiencia, it once
contained the notorious *Carcel de Corte*, in which George Borrow
was briefly incarcerated in May 1838.
From the S side of the plaza leads the C. de Toledo, flanked for a
short distance by arcades. It continues S through the *barrios bajos*,
parts of which retain some of the character of Old Madrid. On the left
rises the pro-cathedral of **S. Isidro el Real** (1664), gutted in 1936, with
a Corinthian façade by the Jesuit Fr. Bautista. It is dedicated to S.
Isidro Labrador (died 1170), the patron of Madrid, who passed his life
as a labourer or servant. His silver shrine is preserved.

Some distance E, at 10 C. de la Magdalena, is the *Pal. de Perales*, by Pedro de
Ribera.

Just S of S. Isidro is the Pl. de Cascorro and, beyond, the Pl. de Rastro,
from which the *Ribera de Curtidores* leads downhill. This is the scene
of the ***Rastro***, a characteristic rag fair, particularly on Sunday
mornings when it tends to be overcrowded. Most of the 'antique'
shops in the area are also open at other times.
In the C. de Embajadores, to the E, is the remarkable front of *S.
Cayetano* (c 1690; by José Churriguera), burnt out in 1936.

Further SE, in the district of *Lavapiés*, that of the ancient *Judería*, is the
characteristic *La Corrala*, galleried tenements in the C. Mesón de Paredes. Near
it gardens have been laid out around the ruined church of the *Escolapios*.

To the W is the C. de Toledo, which descends steeply to the *Puerta de Toledo*,
begun in 1813 to the design of Antonio Aguado to commemorate the return of
Fernando VII from captivity at Valençay, and inaugurated in 1827. The street
continues downhill towards the **Puente de Toledo**, a massive stone bridge of
1718–35, crossing the canalised Manzanares on nine arches, and with Baroque
decorations by Pedro de Ribera.

On the opposite bank are several cemeteries, including (off the C. del Gen.
Ricardos) the walled *British Protestant Cemetery*, on land purchased in 1854,
but of slight interest (cf. Málaga). Remains of prehistoric settlements have been
found in the vicinity.

A short distance SW of S. Isidro, opening off the C. de Toledo, is the

Pl. de la Cebada, in which Rafael Riego (1785–1823) was hanged for his share in the Liberal rising of 1820.—Adjacent is a market, NW of which is the PL. DE PUERTA DE MOROS, from which the Carrera de S. Francisco leads downhill to the W to **S. Francisco el Grande**.

The original convent church (in which Doña Juana, wife of Enrique IV, was buried) made way for the present building, begun in 1761 by Friar Francisco Cabezas and completed by Sabatini in 1785. The dome—32m in diameter—was designed by Miguel Fernández. The church, intended in the mid 19C to be the national pantheon, for which it was soon found to be unsuitable, was restored in 1889 and elaborately decorated, but without much taste.

The interior (fee) is a rotunda, with a Cap. Mayor facing the entrance and three domed chapels on each side. The cupola and chapel ceilings are frescoed by Bayeu and others. In the first chapel to the left, with good carved doors, is Goya's St. Bernardino of Siena preaching (a somewhat academic work normally only lit up by the guides when satisfied that their presence is required in conductng visitors round the building; but light should be specifically requested). The stalls at the E end were brought from El Parral, Segovia; the Chapterhouse, reached from the third chapel on the left, contains stalls from El Paular (cf.). Miscellaneous paintings by Pacheco and other 18C artists line the cloister.

Returning on our tracks, before reaching the Pl. de Puerto de Moro, the church of *S. Andrés* is to the left. This is one of the oldest foundations in Madrid, although dating in its present form from the 17C. Its contents were destroyed in the Civil War.—Adjoining to the N is the *Capilla del Obispo* (1535), one of the town's few Gothic churches. It contains notable woodwork, Plateresque tombs, and a retablo mayor by Francisco Giralte.

The characteristic *Cava Baja* leads NE back towards the Pl. de Puerta Cerrada and the Pl. Mayor. The towering exterior of the W side of the plaza and steps ascending to the *Arco de Cuchilleros* from the C. Cava de S. Miguel are seen when approaching from this direction.

From the Pl. de Puerta Cerrada bear NE. S of the C. de Segovia; to the left is 14–15C *S. Pedro el Viejo*, with a Mudéjar tower and a retablo by José Churriguera.

The C. de Segovia descends steeply to the W and passes under a *Viaduct* sustaining the C. de Bailén to reach the Manzanares at the widened nine-arched **Puente de Segovia** (1584; by Juan de Herrera).—To the N of the bridge is the chapel of the *Virgen del Puerto* (1718; by Pedro de Ribera), rebuilt since its destruction in the Civil War. A good view of the W façade of the *Palacio Real* is obtained from here; see also Rte 40L.

The C. de S. Justo leads NW from the Pl. de Puerta Cerrada, passing (right) *S. Miguel*, a Rococo work of 1745 by the Italians Giacomo Bonavia and Guarino Guarini. Further on, to the left, are the *Bernardas Recoletas* (1671–1744). Beyond, facing the C. Mayor, is the former mansion of the Duque de Uceda, now housing the *Gobierno Militar*.

A few steps N of the C. Mayor here is *S. Nicolás*, with a 12C brick Mudéjar tower, the oldest building in Madrid.—Turn right (E) along the C. Mayor to approach the *Pl. de la Villa*. On the W side is the *Ayuntamiento* (1640–70; by Gómez de Mora), with a façade of 1787 by Villanueva fronting the C. Mayor. The towers and doorways are by Ardemáns.

Within are a handsome staircase and a room containing an allegorical painting by Goya, among other works.

To the S is the *Casa de Cisneros* of 1537, but much restored.

Opposite the Ayuntamiento is the restored *Torre de los Lujánes*, with a late Gothic portal. François I may have been confined here in

1525 before he was moved to the Alcázar.—Just around the corner in the C. del Codo is a door with a horseshoe arch.—The *Conv. de las Carboneras*, behind the tower, has a good relief over the entrance to its church of 1607.

Continuing E along the C. Mayor, we regain the Pl. Mayor by its NW entrance.

D.   W of the Paseo del Prado

From the *Pl. de la Cibeles* (see Rte 40A) we skirt the *Banco de España*, following the Paseo del Prado to the S, later reaching the **Pal. de Villahermosa** (1806; by López Aguado), reconstructed internally and restored to accommodate exhibitions of art. There is a project to use it as an extension to the Museo del Prado (on the SE side of the Pl. de Cánovas de Castillo). (It is very probable that shortly after the publication of this edition of the Blue Guide this building will house a proportion of the **Thyssen-Bornemisza Collection**, at present based at the Villa Favorita, near Lugano in Switzerland. The next edition of this guide will describe this collection.)

In the centre of the plaza is the *Nepture fountain* (1780; by Juan Pascual de Mena). On the SW side is the *Hotel Palace* (1912), built on the site of the former Medinaceli palace, demolished in the 1890s.

The Carrera de S. Jerónimo ascends gently NW towards the Puerta del Sol, passing (right) the **Pal. de las Cortes**, with its portico of Corinthian columns. This, with its modern extension, is the home of the *Cortes Españolas* (or Parliament).

Completed in 1850 by Narciso Pascual y Colomer, it is flanked by two bronze lions cast from cannon captured in the Moroccan campaign of 1860. They replaced stone lions, one of which was decapitated by a cannon-ball in the Revolution of 1854. Théophile Gautier, who did not admire the building, doubted whether good laws could be enacted in such a structure; and as to the statue of Cervantes in the triangular garden opposite, he remarked that while it was praiseworthy to erect a statue to the author of 'Don Quixote', they might have erected a better one while they were at it.

Ford maliciously retold the story of Fernando III, who, being a saint, escaped Purgatory when he died, 'and Santiago presented him to the Virgin, who forthwith desired him to ask any favour of beloved Spain. The monarch petitioned for oil, wine, and corn— conceded; for sunny skies, brave men, and pretty women— allowed; for cigars, relics, and bulls— by all means; for a *good government* —'"Nay, nay", said the Virgin, "that never can be granted; for were it bestowed, not an angel would remain a day longer in heaven"'.

Here, on 23 February 1981 took place the abortive coup against the government by Col Tejero of the Guardia Civil.

To the left further up the street is the former *Pal. de Miraflores* (c 1727; by Pedro de Ribera), now business premises.

A short distance N of the Pal. de las Cortes is the *Teatro de la Zarzuela* (1856), rebuilt behind its façade, which survived a fire in 1909.

From the Pl. de las Cortes the C. del Prado ascends SW past (right) the **Ateneo de Madrid**.

Founded in 1837, this once influential club, housing a good library and small concert hall, was for many years a hive of Liberal activity. Among its members have been an impressive number of political and literary figures.

The street continues to climb to the Pl. de Sta. Ana, on the E side of which is the mid 19C *Teatro Español*, damaged by fire in 1975. It was built on the site of the former *Corral de Comedias del Príncipe*.— George Borrow's Bible showroom and warehouse was situated in the adjacent C. Príncipe.

The C. de León turns S off the C. del Prado.—At No. 15 in the C. de Cervantes (left off the C. de León), dating from 1587, lived Lope de Vega intermittently from 1610 until his death in 1635; the house has been restored and furnished as it might have been in his time.— Cervantes (died 1616) was buried in the *Conv. de las Trinitarias* (the present building dating from 1696) in the C. de Lope de Vega, parallel to the S, but the site of his grave is not known. The site of the press where the first part of 'Don Quixote' was printed by Juan de la Cuesta in 1605 is marked by a plaque at C. de Atocha 85, reached by the C. de León.

At the intersection of the C. de las Huertas and the C. de León is the building, by Villanueva, of the **Real Academia de la Historia**, founded in 1738.

Among paintings to be seen here are portraits of Carlos IV and María Luisa by Goya, and his portraits of Fr. Juan Fernández de Rojas and of Josef de Bargas y Ponce; Angelica Kauffmann's portrait of the philologist Lorenzo Hervás y Panduro; and an anon. portrait of Isabel the Catholic (similar to that in the Pal. Real). Note the bust of Jovellanos by Monasterio. In an adjacent room is a reliquary-retablo from the Mon. de Piedra (1390) depicting angels playing musical instruments; note also the reverse side of the doors. Remarkable is the silver *Disc of Theodosius* (AD 393), discovered near Almendralejo in 1847. Among other antiquities are a painted map of Mexico City (1735); two paleo-Christian sarcophagi from Hellín; an illuminated document of García de Najera (1054), from Pamplona; and a caliph's linen head scarf from S. Esteban de Gormaz. The Library preserves some important MSS, including items from S. Millán de Cogolla, and S. Pedro de Cardeña. The collection of medals is also notable.

The C. de Atocha leads downhill to the SE towards the Glorieta de Emperador Carlos V, passing (right) the *Hospital de S. Carlos*, its SE wing begun by Sabatini but not completed until the 19C.—In the C. de Sta. Isabel, parallel to the S, is the main façade of the former *Hospital General de Atocha*, now housing the **Centro de Arte Reina Sofía**.

Commenced in 1758 from plans by José de Hermosilla adapted by Sabatini, work continued until the death of Carlos III in 1788. The building was threatened with demolition in the early 1970s, but its restoration was put in hand in 1980. The huge brick and stone edifice, four to five storeys above ground, built around a courtyard, was adapted by the Min. of Culture as a cultural centre and inaugurated in May 1986.

At present the remarkable building contains several rooms devoted to three simultaneous exhibitions of 20C and Contemporary Art. It is likely that the collections of the *Museo Español de Arte Contemporáneo* (see Rte 40L) will be transferred here in due course, among other cultural projects envisaged.

A short distance to the NW is the restored mid 17C convent church of *Sta. Isabel*, gutted in 1936.—To the SE is the *Estación de Atocha* (formerly known as *de Mediodía*), from the predecessor of which the first railway ran to Aranjuez in 1846; the line on to Alicante was inaugurated in 1851. A *Science Museum* is to be established here.

See also the latter part of Rte 40E, below.

E.   E of the Paseo del Prado

The long C. de Alcalá climbs E from the *Pl. de la Cibeles*, skirting the *General Post Office* (see Rte 40A) and (left) the *Café Lion* to approach the PL. DE LA INDEPENDENCIA, in the centre of which is the *Puerta de Alcalá* (1778; by Sabatini), erected to flatter Carlos III.—The C. de Serrano leads N; see Rte 40J. To the SE is the *Retiro Park*; see below.

The **Paseo del Prado** leads S from the Pl. de la Cibeles. This broad tree-shaded boulevard was laid out by Carlos III's minister the Conde de Aranda after 1767 and planted with rows of trees in the 1780s on the *pratum* (meadow) of *S. Jerónimo*, long the most fashionable promenade of Madrid. The most frequented part, once the animated scene of flirtation and elegant lounging described by so many travellers, was the *Salón del Prado*, which extended to the present Pl. de Cánovas del Castillo.

To the E stood the *Palace of the Buen Retiro*, which grew from a royal apartment abutting the church of S. Jerónimo (see below) to an extensive pile of buildings raised between 1632 and 1640, of which little survives. When Carlos III moved to his new palace on the W side of the town it became increasingly abandoned. The king established a porcelain factory in a hermitage in 1759, importing workers from Capodimonte; in 1767 the gardens were opened to the public. But in 1808 both the palace and gardens were converted by the French into a fortress, a citadel occupying the site of the factory. By the time Wellington had attacked the place in August 1812, and after Gen. Hill's destruction of its fortifications later that year, little remained except the *Casón*, the 'Hall of the Realms', and piles of rubble. (See 'A Palace for a King', by Jonathan Brown and J.H. Elliott, for a full description.)

No. 2 C. de Montalbán, the first street to the left off the Paseo del Prado, is the entrance to the **Naval Museum**, in the building of the *Min. de Marina*.

Among ship models are a Flemish galleon of 1593 and the three-decker 'S. Antonio' of 1799. Here also are the Chart of Juan de la Cosa (1500), the earliest known map to show America; the Code of Signals invented by the Marqués de la Victoria (1687–1772) and a Table designed by him for the instruction of his officers, a predecessor of the War Game. Among the portraits is that of Gabriel de Aristizabal, by Goya. There is a collection of navigational instruments, and among books displayed are the rare 'Arte de Navegar' of Pedro de Medina (1545) and the 'Breve Compendio' of Martín Cortés (1551). The library contains 15,000 charts, plans, and drawings, and a valuable collection of naval documents.

At No. 12 in the street is the ***Museo de Artes Decorativas**, consisting of five floors ranged around a central patio displaying representative examples of Spanish furniture of every period, while certain rooms are devoted to tapestries, embroideries, lace, and leatherwork; glass, and ceramics; silver, and ironwork, etc. Note the artesonado in R16 and the Manises tiled Valencian kitchen in R46.

Continuing down the Paseo del Prado, we shortly reach the Pl. de la Lealtad, in which rises the *Monumento del Dos de Mayo*.

On 23 March 1808 Madrid was occupied by the French under Murat; on the 2 May the populace, alarmed by the removal of the royal princes from the palace, rose in revolt. Murat, with his Mameluke troops, repressed the rising with ruthless severity and, after trial by court martial, executed hundreds of citizens on the Prado. Luis Daóiz and Pedro Velarde, whose medallion portraits appear on the obelisk, were two artillery officers who fell rather than surrender their guns. Jacinto Ruiz, a third officer, is commemorated by a statue in the Pl. del Rey. Although the revolt failed, it led indirectly to the intervention of the British and the eventual liberation of the Peninsula.

On the S side of the plaza stands the *Ritz Hotel* (1912), where on 20 November 1936 the anarchist leader Buenaventura Durruti died, having been mortally wounded near the Model Prison the previous day; the hotel had been converted into a hospital.

Turning left just beyond the hotel, we pass (right) the N entrance of the **Museo del Prado**; see Rte 40F.

Ascending the C. de Felipe IV, bear left to approach the **Museo del Ejército** (Army Museum), with its entrance on the N side of the C. de Méndez Nuñéz. The museum has been housed since 1841 in the 'Hall of the Realms', one of the few surviving buildings of the Buen Retiro palace (see above), and its dependencies.

Among military relics are a sword of the Cid, called 'La Tizona'; the sword of the Alcaide of Loja; weapons and the tunic of Boabdil; a miniature ivory triptych of Charles V, and his tent and furniture used on the Tunis expedition in 1535; the half-armour of Gonzalo de Córdoba with page and esquire to Isabel the Catholic, and a later Milanese set; the *boina* (beret) of the Carlist general Zumalacárregui, and souvenirs of Gen. Espoz y Mina and Gen. Narváez; the swords and pistols of Palafox; the coach in which Prim was assassinated, and the car in which Adm. Carrero Blanco was blown up in 1973.

Individual rooms are devoted to the expulsion of the Moors from the Kingdom of Granada; the insurrection of 1808 and Spanish exploits during the Peninsular War; the Guardia Civil; and the Civil War of 1936–39. Among other exhibits are numerous portraits, flags, colours, decorations, and uniforms; models of fortifications and bridges; armour; and a collection of lead soldiers.

A short distance to the SE is the **Cáson de Felipe IV** (restored, and with a new W front added in 1886), designed in 1637 by Alonso Carbonel as a dependence of the Buen Retiro palace and intended as a ballroom. The ceiling of the main saloon was decorated in fresco by Luca Giordano in 1692 with an Allegory of the Golden Fleece. The building is at present divided in two, the W end containing the post-Goya 19C collections of paintings of the Museo del Prado.

These include several portraits by *Vicente López*, notably of María Cristina de Borbon, the Duque del Infantado, Alejandro Mon, Señora de Delicado de Imaz, and Antonio Ugarte and his wife; *Alenza*, Self-portrait; *Alma-Tadema*, Pompeian scene; Landscapes by *Beruete* and by *Carlos de Haes*; *Casado del Alisal*, The surrender at Bailén; *Esquivel*, Portraits of Mendizabal, among others; *Gisbert*, The execution of Torrijos (cf. Málaga); *Eugenio Lucas*, Inquisition scenes, etc.; *Federico Madrazo*, Portraits, including Carolina Coronado, the Condesa de Vilches, and Tomas Owens O'Shea; *David Roberts*, The Torre del Oro, Sevilla, and the Castle of Alcalá de Guadaira; and representative examples of the work of *Tejeo*, *Regoyos*, and *Sorolla*, among other artists of the period.

In the E end of the building, approached by a separate entrance, is installed *Picasso*'s painting entitled 'Guernica' (first exhibited in Paris in July 1937), the eventual siting of which has been the subject of controversy, and very likely will be moved to the *Centro de Arte Reina Sofia*; see p 281. It was placed here in October 1981, elaborately protected by bullet-proof glass and, ironically, guarded by armed Civil Guards, no longer so much in evidence. The artist's preliminary sketches are displayed adjacent.

To the E, on the far side of the C. de Alfonso XII, extends the **Retiro Park** (119 hectares).

The site, already a royal domain in the time of Felipe II (who intended it as a country seat for Mary Tudor), was laid out in the 1630 by Olivares as a Buen Retiro or 'pleasant retreat' for Felipe IV; see above. Here in 1792 took place Vicente Lunardi's famous ascent by balloon. After the Revolution of 1869 the W side was built over, and in 1876 the rest became municipal property.

Entering the park from this point, one may approach the SW corner of the *Estanque Grande*, an oblong artificial lake, its E bank now regrettably overshadowed by a conspicuous monument dominated by an equestrian statue of Alfonso XII by Benlliure. To the SE of the lake is the *Pal. de Velázquez*, an exhibition hall of 1887 (restored). Contemporary with it is the *Pal. de Cristal*, to the S.

Near the SW corner of the park is the colonnaded *Observatory* (1790; by Juan de Villanueva), gutted by the French and recently restored. It contains a collection of astronomical instruments, etc.

A short distance SW of the Casón stands the building of the *Real Academia Española* (1894), founded in 1713 (78 years after the 'Académie Française'), its members being responsible for the revision and publication of the 'Diccionario de la Lengua'. Their first 'Diccionario de autoridades' (6 vols) was published in 1726–39.

Adjacent to the S is the conspicuous brick and white stone church of **S. Jerónimo el Real**, a Gothic building of 1505 with two lofty spires, but much restored. To the S are remains of a cloister of 1612. The church overlooks the **Museo del Prado** (see Rte 40F), the N entrance of which may be reached by steps descending through what was once the orchard of the Hieronymites.

Immediately S of the museum is the main entrance, by *Villaneuva*, of the **Jardin Botánico**, founded by Carlos III in 1774 with plants brought from the old botanical garden of Migas Calientes, near Madrid.

It suffered severely during the 19C, and since. Ford reported that it was once inhabited by a brood of boa-constrictors that had escaped from the menagerie in the Buen Retiro, which—until winter killed them off—bolted any unfortunate cat or dog that unwittingly strayed in to study botany. It was sadly depleted by a cyclone in 1866, and by the 1960s was in a deplorable state of neglect, with collapsed glasshouses and overgrown beds.

In 1978 its thorough restoration was undertaken under the aegis of Leandro Silva Delgado, and the gardens were re-opened to the public in December 1982. The *Library* preserves the botanical drawings of Celestino Mutis.

S of the botanical gardens is the Glorieta del Emperador Carlos V, SW of which is the new *Centro de Arte Reina Sofía* (see latter part of Rte 40D). To the SE in the Paseo de la Infanta Isabel is the building of the *Min. of Agriculture* (1893), shortly beyond which is the **Museo Etnología**, recently reformed, with changing collections from the Philipines, Morocco, and elsewhere.

A few minutes' walk further SE brings one to the *Panteón de Hombres Ilustres*, containing monuments to several 19C Spanish generals and politicians. Adjacent is the basilica of *N.S. de Atocha*, begun in 1873 on the site of a Dominican convent founded in 1523 by Hurtado de Mendoza, confessor of Charles V.

Near by, in the C. Fuenterrabía, is the **Real Fábrica de Tapices**, where the royal tapestry factory has stood since 1889. It is still in active operation and may be visited. It was established by Jacob Vandergoten of Brussels in 1720, and flourished during the reign of Carlos III, being supplied with numerous remarkable cartoons by Mengs, Bayeu, and by Goya in particular; cf. p 289.

F.   The Museo del Prado

The ***Museo del Prado**, on the E side of the *Paseo del Prado* and N of the botanical gardens (see Rte 40E), contains the national collection of paintings. It is *closed every Monday*, and on 1 January, Good Friday, 1 May, and 25 December. The usual entrance is at the N end, but there is another in the middle of the long W façade.

More than one visit is recommended for, as Richard Ford so rightly remarked, 'picture seeing is more fatiguing than people think, for one is standing all the while, and with the body the mind is also at exercise in judging, and is exhausted by admiration'.

The building (1785–1819), by Juan de Villanueva, was originally intended as a natural history museum, although never so employed. It was a headquarters of French cavalry during their occupation of Madrid. In 1819 Fernando VII assembled the paintings scattered among various royal palaces and installed them here. The origin of the collections owes much to the acquisitive tendencies of Charles V, whose enthusiasm for art was shared by Felipe II. These were augmented by Felipe IV, the patron of Velázquez, and Felipe V imported numerous works of art from France. Further additions were made by Carlos III. Several paintings suffered during the first decades of the museum's life in a mania of unscholarly restoration. An important acquisition was the collection of early paintings taken in 1836 from the suppressed monasteries in Madrid and the neighbourhood, and housed in the Conv. de la Trinidad until their removal to the Prado in 1872. Some hundreds of paintings were removed temporarily to Geneva late in the Civil War.

The 19C paintings in the collection are housed in the *Casón de Buen Retiro* (see p 283). It is expected that the *Pal. de Villahermosa* (NW of the adjacent Pl. de Cánovas de Castillo), recently devoted to temporary exhibitions, will form an extension of the museum: see p 280.

Meanwhile, the building of the Museo del Prado is still (1988) undergoing a thorough and long overdue modernisation, and several sections are at present closed to the public. It is hoped that its reorganisation will have been completed by the time the next edition of this guide is published, when the present description will be revised. The provisional distribution of the paintings of the major artists and schools is indicated here, and the more important paintings are listed, without attempting to describe the contents of each room.

A complete (unillustrated) catalogue is available at the bookstalls, together with several illustrated commercial guides. There is a cafeteria in the basement of the SE corner of the museum.

At present **RR52A** and **B**, on the right of the N entrance (GROUND FLOOR) contain temporary displays of *Bosch*, *Cranach*, *Van der Weyden*, *Patinir*, and *Dürer*, among others. **RR51A** and **B**, to the left, also contain temporary exhibits. **RR50** and **49** contain *14–16C Spanish* paintings. **RR53–57** (to the left) may contain *Zurbarán*. **RR75, 60, 61**, and **61B** are devoted to *Rubens*. **RR60A, 61A, 62A**, and **63A** contain paintings of the *17C Flemish* School; **62B, 63**, and **63B** display works by *Jordaens* and *Van Dyck*. The *Dutch* School is to be seen in **RR64–65**. **R66**, adjacent, contains drawings and several small works by *Goya*, whose 'Black Paintings' are in **R67**. (**RR71–73**, on the W side of this wing, will contain the sculptures of the collection, and the *Treasure of the Dauphin*, comprising 16–17C goldsmiths' work and carved crystals brought to Spain by Felipe V).

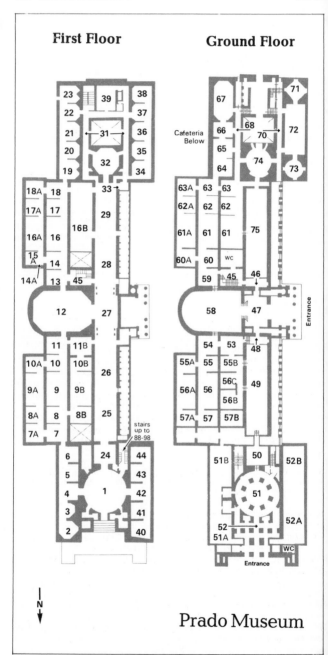

First Floor

Ground Floor

Prado Museum

Stairs adjacent to R66 ascend to the FIRST FLOOR, the S part of which is devoted to *Goya*, with some of his portraits in **RR35–38** and his cartoons for tapestries in **RR19–23**; but see also **RR32** and **39**. **RR28–29** are largely devoted to *17C Italian* paintings, **16B** to *Titian*, and **16–17** to the *Venetians*. *Zurbarán* is to be seen in **R17A**, *Murillo* in **16A**, and *Velázquez's* 'Las Meninas' in **R15**. More *Velázquez* is to be found in the adjoining rooms, particularly in **R12**, and **R27**, adjacent. **RR24–26** contain *Spanish 17C* paintings, including *El Greco*. **RR7–10**, **7A–10A**, and **8B–10B** are at present closed, but will display *16–17C Italian* paintings. **RR40–44** contain the *15C Flemish* School; **RR2–6**, *15–16C Italian* Schools. Very few French, and no English paintings are at present on show.

Spanish Schools; 14–15Cs: 1321, anon. Retablo from S. Benito (Valladolid; c 1420); 1332, the *Master of Arguis* (Huesca; c 1450), The legend of S. Miguel; 1336, *Master of Sigüenza*, Retablo of the Baptist and Sta. Catalina; 3039, *Fernando Gallego*, Martyrdom of Sta. Catalina; 2545, *Nicolás Frances*, Retablo of the Virgin and S. Francisco; 2670–71, anon. Retablo of S. Vicente; 2668–69, *Martín Bernat*, scenes from the life of Santiago; 618, *Pedro Berruguete* Auto de Fé presided over by Sto. Domingo de Guzmán, and others by the same artist.

16C: 1339, *Fernando Yañez*, S. Damián; 3110, *Juan de Borgoña*, Magdalen; 1925, *Alejo Fernández*, Flagellation; 843, *Vicente Masip (the elder)*, Martyrdom of Sta. Inés; 849, Calvary; 851, Visitation; 850, Descent from the Cross; 840 and 842, *Juan de Juanes (Juan Vicente Masip)*, Martyrdom and entombment of St. Stephen; 848, Ecce Homo; 846, The Last Supper; 855, Portrait of Luis Castelló de Vilanova; 690, *Juan Correa*, Nativity; 689, Visitation; 672, Virgin and Child with St. Ann; 3017, *Pedro Machuca*, Descent from the Cross; 2171, *León Picardo*, Annunciation; 2656, *Luis de Morales*, Virgin and Child, among others; 1036, *Sánchez Coello*, Portrait of Felipe II (recently attributed to *Sofonisba Anguisciola*); 1136, Prince Don Carlos; 1139, the Duchess of Savoy; 2935, *Juan de Flandes*, Raising of Lazarus; 2937, Ascension; 6897–6902, *Rodrigo de Osona, the younger*, Passion scenes; 809, *Doménico Theotocópulos*, better known as **El Greco**, Gentleman with his hand on his chest; 2644, Trinitarian friar; and several other portraits.

17C: 2804, *Francisco Ribalta*, Christ embracing St. Bernard; 1072, **Ribera**, St. Peter; 1100, St. Bartholomew; 1101, Martyrdom of S. Felipe; 1117, Jacob's dream, and several others; 3009, **Zurbarán**, Fray Diego de Deza; 656, Defence of Cádiz against the English; 1236, The vision of S. Pedro Nolasco; 1237, The apparition of S. Pedro to S. Pedro Nolasco; 1239, Sta. Casilda; 2803, Still life; 1241, The Labours of Hercules; 629, *Alonso Cano*, Christ sustained by an angel; 627, Virgin and Child, and several others.

Velázquez: 1177, Margarita of Austria, wife of Felipe III; 1178, Felipe IV; 1213, Triton Fountain at Aranjuez (and in comparison, 1214, *Del Mazo*, Calle de la Reina, Aranjuez); 1181, Conde-Duque de Olivares; 1170, Los Borrachos (the topers); 1171, Forge of Vulcan; 1192, Infanta María Teresa de Austria, daughter of Felipe IV, aged ten; 1200, Jester of Felipe IV, called 'Don Juan de Austria'; 1173, Las Hilanderas, a scene in the tapestry factory of Sta. Isabel at Madrid (damaged by fire in 1734); 889, View of Zaragoza, mainly by *Del Mazo* (the figures are probably by Velázquez); 1207, 1206, Menippus and Aesop, arbitrary titles for two strongly characterised types of low life in Madrid; 1208, Mars; 1189, Don Baltasar Carlos aged six; 1182,

Felipe IV; 1184, Felipe IV in hunting costume; 1188, Don Carlos, second son of Felipe III; 1191, Mariana de Austria, second wife of Felipe IV; 1186, Don Fernando de Austria, brother of Felipe IV; 1172, The Surrender of Breda (1625) or Las Lanzas, in which Gen. Spinola, a Genoese in the service of Spain, consoles the defeated Dutch leader, Justin of Nassau (the head of Velázquez himself is seen on the extreme right); 1180, Don Baltasar Carlos on horseback; 1198, Pablo de Valladolid, jester of Felipe IV; 1194, Montañes, the sculptor; 1193, Antonio Pimentel, Count of Benavente; 1178, Felipe IV on horseback at El Pardo; 1201, 2, 4, and 5, four dwarfs of Felipe IV: El Primo, with an open book, Sebastían de Morra, simply stolid, 'El Niño de Vallecas', more than half an idiot, and 'El Bobo de Coria'; 1179, Isabella de Bourbon, first wife of Felipe IV, on horseback; 1187, Infanta Doña María, sister of Felipe IV, afterwards Queen of Hungary; 1219, Felipe IV, armed; 2873, Madre Jerónima de la Fuente; 1167, Crucifixion; 1166, Adoration of the Magi (1619), an early work containing portraits of the artist's Sevillian contemporaries; 1196, Antonia Ipeñarrieta y Galdós, the child added after the death of the artist (?); 1224, Male portrait (probably a Self-portrait in c 1623); 1174, Las Meninas (1656).

Recently cleaned, it depicts the Infanta Margarita María attended by the maids of honour (*meninas*) Agustina Sarmiento and Isabel de Velasco. In the foreground are the figures of the dwarf Mari Bárbola and Nicolasito Pertusato, and in the background at an open door stands José Nieto, the queen's chamberlain. On the left is seen Velázquez engaged in painting the portraits of the king and queen, whose figures are reflected in the mirror at the back. The red cross of Santiago worn by the artist is said to have been added by Felipe IV himself.

888, *Del Mazo*, Margarita de Austria, daughter of Felipe IV; 2571, La Cacería del tabladillo en Aranjuez; 1221, Don Baltasar Carlos, son of Felipe IV, aged 16; 645, *Carreño de Miranda*, Pedro Ivanowitz Potemkin, the Russian ambassador; 650, The Duque de Pastrana; 642, Carlos II; 644, Doña Marina de Austria; 1126, *Rizzi*, Auto de Fé in the Pl. Mayor, Madrid; 978, **Murillo**, The Virgin appearing to St. Bernard; 973, Conception; 975, Virgin with a Rosary; 989, St. James the Great; 2845, Caballero de golilla; and many others by the same artist; 836, 837, Landscapes by *Iriarte*.

18C: 936, *Meléndez*, Still life, one of several; 2875, *Paret y Alcázar*, Masked ball; 2422, Carlos III dining before his court; 605, 606, *Francisco Bayeu*, Madrilenian scenes; 2440, *Maella*, Carlota Joaquina, Queen of Portugal and daughter of Carlos IV; 641, *Carnicero*, Ascent of the Montgolfier balloon over Madrid in 1792; 640, View of the Albufera de Valencia; 2649, Doña Tomasa de Aliaga; 2581, *Esteve*, Joaquina Téllez-Giron, daughter of the Duque de Osuna; 2876, Mariano S. Juan y Pinedo, aged 10; 2514, *Inza*, Tomás de Iriarte.

Goya: Portraits: 721, Francisco Bayeu, the artist; 727, Carlos IV; 728, María Luisa wearing a mantilla; 741, 742, La Maja desnuda, and La Maja vestida, certainly *not* the Duchess of Alba, an intimate of the artist, who is said to have served as model; 740, Doña Tadea Arias de Enríques; 734, Maiquez, the actor; 720, María Luisa on horseback; 2862, María Luisa wearing a bustle; 2448, Marquesa de Villafranca (died 1835); 729, Infanta María Josefa, daughter of Carlos III; 723, Self-portrait, c 1815; 726, Carlos IV and his family (one of the most satirical portrait groups ever painted); 2449, the Duke of Alba; 719, Carlos IV on horseback; 731, Infante Carlos María Isidro, son of Carlos IV; 722, Josefa Bayeu de Goya (?); 736, Gen. Urrutia;

2784, Gen. Ricardos; 739, the Duke of Osuna and his family; 737, Carlos III; 725, Equestrian portrait of Palafox; 3255, Floridablanca; 724, 735, two contrasting portraits of Fernando VII; 2898, Juan Bautista de Muguiro; 2899, The milkmaid of Bordeaux; 3236, Jovellanos; 2447, Doña María Antonia Gonzaga, Marquesa de Villafranca; 7020, the Duquesa de Alba and her dueña; and, recently acquired, the Marquesa de Sta. Cruz with a harp in her hand.

748, 749, The 'Dos de Mayo', and the Fusillade of the 'Tres de Mayo'; 2785, The Colossus or Panic; 744, a Picador; 3047, Bullfighting scene; and the so-called *Pinturas Negras* (black paintings), 14 murals designed for his country house on the banks of the Manzanares, 'La Quinta del Sordo'.

Some 50 *Cartoons for tapestries*, painted for the royal tapestry works of Sta. Bárbara between 1775 and 1792, the designs being reproduced for the royal palaces of Madrid, the Escorial, and El Prado. For many years the cartoons were stored in the cellars of the factory, but after repeated applications by successive curators of the Prado, they were at length unearthed, restored, and exhibited.

Among them are: 768, Picnic on the banks of the Manzanares; 769, Dancing at S. Antonio de la Florida; 773, The parasol; 780, The pottery seller; 798, The snowstorm; 804, Blind-man's buff; 799, The village wedding; 801, The stilt-walkers; 2857, Hunters; and 778, Blind man with a guitar.

Italian Schools; 14–15Cs: 15, *Fra Angelico*, The Annunciation; 2838–40, *Botticelli*, three of four panels of the story of Nastagio degli Onesti ('Decameron', V.8); 248, *Mantegna*, Death of the Virgin; 3092, *Antonello de Messina*, Christ supported by an angel; 296, **Raphael**, Holy Family with the lamb; 297, The Virgin with the fish; 301, Holy family, known as 'La Perla'; 299, Portrait of a cardinal; 298, Christ bearing the Cross, known as 'El Pasmo de Sicilia' (painted for Sta. Maria dello Spásimo, Palermo); 332, *Andrea del Sarto*, The artist's wife; 111, *Correggio*, 'Noli me tangere'; 112, Virgin and Child with St. John; 279, The Conde de S. Segundo; 280, A lady with her three sons; 18A, *Barocci*, Crucifixion; 288, *Giorgione*, Virgin and Child between St. Anthony of Padua and St. Roch; 50, *Giovanni Bellini*, Virgin and Child between two saints; 434, **Titian**, Virgin and Child between two saints; 408, Federico Gonzaga, Duke of Mantua; 415, Isabel of Portugal; 409, Charles V with his dog; 410, Charles V at the battle of Mühlberg, wearing the suit now in the Royal Armoury; 407, Self-portrait when an old man; 418, Bacchanal; 422, Venus and Adonis; 429, Adam and Eve; 412, A knight with a clock; 432, 'La Gloria', or the Apotheosis of Charles V (this painting was brought from Yuste to the Escorial together with the body of the Emperor); 240, *Lotto*, Micer Marsilio and his wife; 345, *Piombo*, Christ bearing the Cross; 346, Christ in Limbo; 502, *Veronese*, The finding of Moses, and several others by the same artist; 382, *Tintoretto*, Woman baring her bosom; 378, Man with a gold chain; 262, *Moroni*, A soldier; 34, *Bassano*, Last Supper.

17–18Cs: 147, *Gentileschi*, The finding of Moses; 2631, *Ludovico Carraci*, Venus and Adonis; 3090, *Reni*, Hipomenes and Atalanta; 211, S. Sebastián; 65, *Caravaggio*, David and Goliath; 63, *Cantarini*, Holy Family; 324, *Salvator Rosa*, View of Salerno; 48, *Batoni*, Sir William Hamilton; 49, Charles Cecil Roberts; 352, *Solimena*, Self-portrait; 475, 2462–3, Venetian and Neapolitan scenes; 4180–1, *Battaglioli*, two Scenes at Aranjuez; and several paintings by *Luca*

Giordano (known as *Lucas Jordan* in Spain), and *G.B.* and *G.D. Tiepolo.*

Flemish Schools: 2825, *Van der Weyden*, Descent from the Cross; 2540, Pietà; 1461, *Dirck Bouts*, Annunciation, Visitation, Nativity, and Adoration; 1921, *Petrus Christus*, Virgin and Child; 1557, *Memling*, Triptych of the Nativity, Adoration, and Presentation; 2643, *Gerard David*, Rest on the Flight into Egypt; 2056, **Hieronymus Bosch** (known in Spain as 'El Bosco'), Extraction of the Stone of Madness; 2822, Table of the Seven Deadly Sins; 2052, The haywain; 2823, The Garden of Delights; 2695, The crossbowman; 2048, Adoration of the Magi; 2049, The Temptation of St. Anthony; 1611, *Patinir*, Rest on the Flight into Egypt; 1614, St. Jerome and the lion; 1615, The Temptation of St. Anthony; 1616, Crossing the Stygian Lake; 2801, *Quentin Massys*, Christ shown to the people; 2095, *Huys*, Hell; 1933, *Ambrosius Benson*, Virgin and Child with St. Ann; 2182, *Joos van Cleve*, An Old Man; 1932, *Van Orley*, Virgin and Child; 3209, *Mostaert*, A Youth; 2567, *Reymerswaele*, Moneychanger and his wife; 2100, St. Jerome; 3232, *Coecke van Aelst*, Temptation of St. Anthony; 1393, *Brueghel the Elder*, The Triumph of Death; 6393, *Pieter Aertsen*, Going to market; 2110–1, **Antonio Moro** (*Anthonis Mor van Dashorst*), Maria of Austria, and Maximilian II; 2114, The artist's wife; 2108, Mary Tudor, second wife of Felipe II; 2118, Felipe II; 2109, Catalina of Austria; 2119, Woman with gold chains; 2107, Pejerón, the buffoon; 1624, *Frans Pourbus*, Marie de Médicis; 1954, *Van Somer*, James I of England; 2734–45, *Frans Franken the younger*, Old Testament scenes; 2045, 2816, *Brueghel the Younger*, Snow scenes (the latter being a copy of a lost painting by the Elder Brueghel); 1394, *Brueghel 'de Velours'*, Sight, one of several characteristic paintings; 1856, *Van Dalen*, Landscape; 1446, 1854–5, *Van Valckenbourgh*, Landscapes; 1443, *Momper*, Landscape with drying washing, and others; 1670, **Rubens**, The three Graces; 1669, The Judgement of Paris; 1685, Marie de Médicis; 1686, Felipe II on horseback; 1689, Anne of Austria; 1688, his copy of Holbein's Sir Thomas More; 1493, Polixena Spinola, Marquesa de Leganés; 1486, Henry, Count of Berg; 1487, Jacob Gaultier, with an archlute; 1488, Pal de Pont, the engraver; 1489, The artist with Sir Endymion Porter; 1495, Mary Ruthven, the artist's wife; 1483, Amalia de Solms-Braunfels; 1481, Diana Cecil, Countess of Oxford; 1549, *Jordaens*, His family in a garden; 2441, *Frans Luyck*, Mariana de Austria; 1347–8, *Van Alsloot*, Festival at Ommeganck; 1738–48, *Snayers*, Battle pieces; 1349, *Van der Meulen*, A general taking the field; 1813, *David Teniers*, The archduke Leopold William in his picture gallery, and numerous genre scenes.

Dutch School: 2808, *Rembrandt*, Self-portrait; 2132, Artemis; 2754–6, *Heda*, Still lifes; 2151, *Wouwerman*, Leaving the inn, and others; 2974, *Van der Hecke* (or *Koninck*), The Philosopher; 2121, *Van Ostade*, Rustic concert, and several others; 2978, *Van Goyen*, Landscape; 1728–9 *Ruisdael*, Woods; 6892, *Ter Borch*, Petronella de Waert; 2976, *Van Mierevelt*, Elisabeth von Bronckhorst; 2131, *Paul Potter*, Two cows and a goat; 2103, *Metsu*, Dead cock.

German School: 2179, *Dürer*, Self-portrait (1498); 2180, Male portrait (1524); 2177–8, Adam and Eve; 2183–4, *Amberger*, Jörg Zörer, the goldsmith, and his wife; 2219, *Baldung Grien*, The three Graces; 2220, The Ages of Man, and Death; 2175–6, *Cranach the Elder*, The

Hunt of Charles V and the Duke of Saxony in the Torgau (1544), with the castle of Hartenfels in the background; 2182, attributed *Holbein the Younger*, Portrait of an old man; 2820–21, *J. Ch. Vollardt*, Landscapes; 2200, **Mengs**, Carlos III; 2201, María Amalia of Saxony; 2186, María Josefa of Lorraine, archduchess of Austria; 2188, Carlos IV, when prince; 2189, 2568, María Luisa de Parma, princess of Asturias; 2190, Fernando IV of Naples; 2197, Self-portrait; 2198–9, Leopold of Lorraine, later Emperor, and his wife, Marie Luisa de Bourbon.

French School: 2788, *Nicolas Tournier*, Negation of St. Peter; 148, *Cecco del Caravaggio*, Woman with a pigeon; 2235, *Pensionante di Saraceni*, The bird-seller; 2304, *Poussin*, Landscape with St. Jerome, and others; 2254, Embarkation of St. Paula Romana at Ostia, and others; 1503, *Sebastien Bourdon*, Christina of Sweden on horseback; 2987, *Vouet*, Time vanquished by Youth and Beauty; 2337, *Rigaud* (copies of), Felipe V, and 2343, Louis XIV; 2353, *Watteau*, Rustic wedding; 2269, *Houasse*, View of the Escorial; 2387, Luis I; 2329, *Ranc*, Felipe V, and other royal portraits; 2282, *Van Loo*, Infante Felipe, Duque de Parma; 2283, The family of Felipe V; 2794, *Oudry*, The Conde de Castelblanco, and 2793, Lady Mary Josephine Drummond, Condesa de Castelblanco; *C.J. Vernet*, View near Sorrento; 2302–3, *Pillement*, Landscapes.

English School: 2979, *Gainsborough*, Isaac Henrique Sequeira, his physician; 3013, *Romney*, Master Ward; 3040, *Hoppner*, Mrs Thornton; 3012, *Lawrence*, Miss Carr; 3116, *Raeburn*, Mrs Maclean of Kinlochaline; and a few other portraits.

Notable also is 2226, Doña Concepción Aguirre y Yoldi, by *Wertmüller*. Another anon. painting of interest is 1940, The beheading of the Baptist.

G.   From the Pl. de la Cibeles to the Pl. de España; the Gran Vía

Ascending the C. de Alcalá from the *Pl. de la Cibeles* (see Rte 40A), turn right into the Pl. del Rey (off the S end of the C. Barquillo). Its W side is overlooked by the almost entirely reconstructed **Casa de las Siete Chimeneas**, on the site of the original 16C building attributed to Juan de Herrera. It was the residence in 1623 of Prince Charles Stuart, Buckingham, Sir Kenelm Digby, and Endymion Porter; of Sir Richard Fanshawe in 1664–66; and in the mid 18C of the Marqués de Esquilache. Together with a modern extension to the N, it now houses functionaries of the *Min. of Culture*.

The **Gran Vía** bears right off the C. de Alcalá. This important commercial thoroughfare was cut through a formerly congested area between 1910 and 1936, providing a direct route to the Pl. de España, to the NW. Many of the larger cinemas are in the Gran Vía.

At the W end of the parallel C. Caballero de Gracia is an *Oratory* of 1795 by Juan de Villanueva, near which Anthony Ascham was assassinated in 1650 (see history).

To the right of the junction known as the Red de S. Luis (from which the C. Montera descends to the Puerta del Sol) the Gran Vía is dominated by the *Telefónica* (1929). Before reaching this the C. de Hortaleza and C. de Fuencarral diverge to the NE and NW respectively. The Telefónica was used as a Republican observation post during the defence of Madrid.

A DETOUR may be made along the C. de Hortaleza to *S. Antón* (left), by Pedro de Ribera, and containing Goya's The last Communion of S. José de Calasanz (1820); apply at No. 53.—In the C. de Góngora, a little to the E, is the Baroque church of the *Mercedarias Descalzas*, better known as the *Góngoras*, founded by Felipe IV and completed in 1689.

Turn left shortly beyond S. Antón for the *Museo Romántico at No. 13 C.S. Mateo.

Established in 1924, it contains several portraits of the period c 1800–60, notably: *Esquivel*, Nazario Carraquieri, and Gen. Prim; *Vicente López*, the Marqués de Remisa; *Alenza*, Agustín Argüelles; and works by *Cabral Bejarano*, *Eugenio Lucas*, *Luis Ferrant*, and *Espalter*, among others. Also, among earlier paintings are *Goya*, St. Gregory the Great; *Carnicero*, Godoy; and *Zurbarán*, S. Francisco Xavier. A room is devoted to *Mariano José de Larra* (1809–37), a young romantic who committed suicide. The library contains autographs and books and journals published during the Peninsular War.

A short distance to the NW at No. 78 C. Fuencarral is the former *Hospicio de S. Fernando*, with its elaborate doorway and red brick front, erected in 1729 to the plans of Pedro de Ribera. It now houses the reformed *Municipal Museum. The archives and library formerly here are being moved to the restored buildings of the Conde-Duque barracks; see below.

The Basement contains archaeological collections, including two Roman mosaics unearthed in Carabanchel. Of particular interest is the Maquette of Madrid (5.20m by 3.40m; at 1:864) made by León Gil de Palacios and completed in 1830, which gives a better idea of the town's topography at the time of Ford and Borrow than many written descriptions.

Among the numerous topographical views on display are those by Juan de la Corte, Félix Castello, J. Leonardo, Manuel de la Cruz, José del Castillo, Andrés Ginés de Aguirre, José María Avrial, Fernando Brambila, Pharamond Blanchard, Perez Villaamil, Gonzalez Velázquez, Bayeu, Maella, et al. Among several portraits and sculptures, the marble Bust of Isabel I veiled, by Camillo Torreggiani, is a curiosity; another section is devoted to Buen Retiro porcelain.

The C. de la Palma runs W to *Las Maravillas*, founded in the 17C, but largely rebuilt by Miguel Fernández in 1770. N of Las Maravillas is the Pl. del Dos de Mayo, scene of the resistance to the French of Daóiz and Velarde; see p 282.

The C. de Fuencarral leads back from the Municipal museum to the Telefónica.

Continuing W along the Gran Vía, the third turning to the right leads shortly to domed *S. Martín* (1761), in which William Bowles (1705–80; q.v. Bilbao) was buried.

Further N is *S. Antonio de los Alemanes* (1626; formerly 'de los Portugueses'), containing frescoes by Carreño, Rici, and Luca Giordano.—Close by to the NW is S. Plácido (1661), with an imposing high altar containing an Annunciation by Claudio Coello and frescoes by Rici. This once-fashionable Benedictine convent was the subject of scandal in 1628, when the Inquisition assumed that the hysterical nuns were under the influence of Illuminism and witchcraft.

The Gran Vía bears NW at the Pl. de Callao and descends to the Pl. de España (formerly the Pl. de S. Marcial, on the site of the old S. Gil barracks), containing a *Monument to Cervantes* by Coullaut Valera (1927). A few steps to the NE is *S. Marcos* (1753; by Ventura Rodriguez).

The C. Princesa leads NW. On its right is the rebuilt **Palacio de Liria** (1956), residence of the Alba family and their protége, and housing Alba archives and collections.

The original building, erected in 1770, was seriously damaged by Nationalist bombing in November 1936, but a number of its treasures were saved and may be seen on prior application. These include the armour of the Conde-Duque de Olivares (died 1645), and of the 3rd Duke of Alba (died 1582), and portraits of the latter by *Titian*, *Sánchez Coello*, and others; also *Titian*, Portrait of the Duke of Mantua; *Fra Angelico*, Virgin of the Pomegranate; *El Greco*, Crucifixion; *Velázquez*, Infanta Margarita María; and works by *Palma Vecchio*, *Bronzino*, *Rubens*, *Rembrandt* (Landscape), *Ruysdael*, *Teniers*, and *Reynolds*. Also Brussels tapestries presented to the 3rd Duke by the city of Antwerp.

For the area to the NW see Rte 40L.

To the E of the Pal. de Liria is the huge **Conde-Duque Barracks**, founded in 1720 on the site of the palace of the Conde-Duque de Olivares. On its E front the portal of 1720 is by Pedro de Ribera. The barracks have recently been restored to house exhibition rooms and the library and archives of the Municipal Museum.

Further E, the C. del Cristo leads to the church of *Las Comendadores de Santiago* (1693; by Manuel and José del Olmo); and beyond, in the C. de S. Bernardo, the façade of *Monserrat* (1725).

To the N is the Glorieta de Ruiz Jiménez, which occupied the site of the *Quemadero* where heretics were burned by the Inquisition: large deposits of ashes and human bones were found near by in 1868.

The C. de S. Bernardo leads downhill, passing (right) the undistinguished buildings of the old *University*, formerly belonging to the Jesuits and in 1842 used to accommodate the faculties which moved from Alcalá de Henares to Madrid in 1836. Most faculties are now in the rebuilt *University City*; see Rte 40L.

The Gran Vía is regained a short distance NW of the Pl. de Callao.

H.   From the Pl. de la Cibeles to the Pl. de Colón

The Paseo de Recoletos leads N from the Pl. de la Cibeles (see Rte 40A) and takes its name from a former convent of the Franciscan Recollects. It passes over the site of the famous garden of the Regidor Juan Fernández and of the *old* English Cemetery. Following the W side of the avenue, we pass the *Café Gijón*, opposite which is the former residence (now a bank) of the Marqués de Salamanca (1811–83), the entrepreneur responsible for the development of the area to the NE; see Rte 40J.

The C. de Bárbara de Braganza climbs left, passing (right) the *Pal. de Justicia*, occupying the site of a convent of Salesian nuns founded in 1750 by Bárbara de Braganza, consort of Fernando VI. Their tombs, designed by Sabatini and sculpted by Francisco Gutiérrez, are in the adjacent Baroque church of **Sta. Bárbara** or **Las Salesas Reales**, with an elaborate façade of 1758 by Francisco Carlier and Francisco Moradillo.

Baretti considered it the 'grandest' of Madrid's churches. It altars were not, as elsewhere, 'adorned with little nosegays of natural or artificial flowers, nor is it hung with pretty cages of canary birds, that keep chirping the whole day long, to the great diversion of those who go to hear masses . . . '.

The E side of the paseo is dominated by a ponderous building of 1892 housing both the **Biblioteca Nacional** (facing the Paseo de Recoletos) and the *Museo Arqueológico Nacional*, with its entrance in the C. Serrano to the E. The former was founded by Felipe V in 1712 by adding the books he had brought from France to the Old Royal Library. It contains c 1,000,000 printed books, c 2000 incunables, and over 100,000 MSS, drawings and engravings, some of which are occasionally on display.

The ***Museo Arqueológico**, still being re-arranged, was founded in 1867 and installed in this building in 1895. Beneath the gardens to the left of the entrance is a *replica* of the *Altamira Caves* (q.v.).

The BASEMENT is largely devoted to the Prehistoric collections, including (**R2**) a skull and tusks of early elephants from Piñedo (Toledo), Torralba and Ambrona (Soria), and elsewhere; also artefacts found at the Cerro de S. Isidro (Madrid) in 1862, the first palaeolithic site excavated in Spain.—**R3** incised bones from the Cueva del Castillo (Puente Viesgo, Santander) and finds from other caves on the Cantabrian and Mediterranean coasts.—**R4** *Neolithic period.* Ceramics, and other artefacts from the Cueva de los Murciélagos (Granada), and Los Millares, including stylised slate idol-plaques, silex knives, and a cylindrical idol of alabaster (from Extremadura).—**RR6–7** *Bronze Age* and *Early Iron Age.* Ceramics from El Algar (Almería); arms and their moulds; shell, bone, and bronze necklaces; arms from a shipwreck near Huelva (9C BC); gold torques and spiral bracelets, etc.; gold vases from Axtroki (Guipúzcoa).—**RR8–9** Artefacts from the necropolis of Osera (Ávila) and from Numancia (Soria); the Celtiberian silver treasure from Salvacañete (Cuenca), among other finds.—**R10** contains material from the Balearics (Talayot culture), and three bronze bull's heads from Costix; **R11** displays artefacts from the Canaries.

RR12–18 contain material from elswhere besides Spain, including artefacts from the W Sahara, Egypt and Nubia, and Cyprus; Etruscan antiquities, and Greek and Roman ceramics; armour, etc.

GROUND FLOOR. **R19**, with finds from the necropoli of Tútugi, and Tugia; the Phoenician 'sphinx' of Balazote; the Treasures of Jávea (Alicante), Lebrija (Sevilla), Abengibre (Albacete), and Aliseda (Cáceres); and a reconstructed Iberian funerary monument from Pozo Moro (Albacete).—**R20** Sculptured frieze from a temple at Osuna; the Dama de Baza (4C BC; discovered in 1971), preserving much painted decoration; the Greco-Iberian Dama de Elche (? 3C BC); and female figures from the Cerro de los Santos (Albacete).—**RR21–23** are devoted to *Roman Spain*, including among sculptures a statue of Tiberius (from Paestum); a huge mosaic from Hellín; several bronze plaques; a Trajanic inscription from Cartagena; and the Madrid puteal; glass, jewellery, etc.—**RR24–26** contain late Roman mosaics and paleo-Christian sarcophagi.

RR27–29 display *Visigothic* material (6–8Cs). Notable is the 'Treasure of Gurrazar' (Toledo), including the votive crown of Reccesvinth (649–72), five other crowns, and several pendant crosses. Also an ivory crucifix offered in 1063 to S. Isidro at León by Fernando I and Doña Sancha; the 'Bote de Zamora' of ivory and silver, with Cufic inscriptions (964); the earliest known Astrolabe (Toledo, 1066); and a bronze Lamp from the Alhambra (1305). Adjacent **RR34–35** contain artesonado ceilings from the palace of the Duques de Maqueda (Torrijos, Toledo), and from Sevilla.

RR30–32 continue the display of *Hispano-Moresque* ceramics, azulejos, and lustreware, etc.—**R33** is devoted to the *Romanesque* and *Gothic* collections, with a representative collection of sculptures (including Nottingham alabasters), capitals, well heads, choir stalls (from Gradafes, León, furniture, ceramics, silverware, tombs, etc.

Those rooms on the FIRST FLOOR that have been re-arranged contain arms and armour and scientific instruments; Spanish and Italian Renaissance bronzes and sculpture, and ceramics; and collections of glass and porcelain, etc. Further rooms will be opened in due course. The *Library* and *Numismatic cabinet* are also on this floor.

Immediately to the N is the **Pl. de Colón**, on which stood the *Mint* (now transferred to No. 106 C. de Jorge Juan, near the Av. de Dr

Esquerdo, and containing a *Numismatic museum*). On the W side of the plaza is a monument to Columbus (1885), while to the E is a conspicuously ugly modern monument to the Discovery of America. Below the square is the *Air Terminus* for *Barajas*, Madrid's airport.

I. N of the Pl. de Colón and
W of the Paseo de Castellana

The Pl. de Colón (see above) is dominated to the NW by the twin *Torres de Jerez* (1976). Passing these, follow the Paseo de Castellana to the N, shortly reaching the C. de Fernando el Santo.

This ascends past (left) the cylindrical *British Embassy* (1966) to the *British Institute*, on the far side of the C. Almagro. The first director of the institute, from 1940, was Walter Starkie (1894–1976).

Some minutes' walk N brings us to a flyover, below which is a collection of contemporary *Outdoor Sculpture*.
  Turning left immediately beyond the flyover, and then right, at No. 43 C. Fortuny is the *Instituto Valencia de Don Juan, a private museum notable for its collection of Spanish ceramics.

Among these is the great Azulejo made in Granada in the reign of Yusuf I (1408–17), known by the name of Fortuny, the artist and a former owner; a fine series of Manises, Paterna, Teruel, and Andalucian wares; heraldic glazed panels from Sevilla (13C); and a remarkable collection of Hispano-Moresque lustre ware. Other collections include textiles, from Egyptian materials and Moslem stuffs of the 10C to 17C Spanish brocades; jewellery, seals, and harness ornaments; Buen Retiro, and Alcora pottery; Compostellan jet carvings. Among individual exhibits of note are the 14C 'Bote de Cuéllar' (an inlaid box from Granada); the Statutes of the Order of the Golden Fleece, illustrated by Simon Bening (1537); a 12C enamel book cover from Silos; an Iberian silver Helmet; an emerald Dragon offered by Hernán Cortes to N.S. de Guadalupe; and among paintings, an Allegory by *El Greco*, and *Velázquez*, Portrait of Quevedo (wearing glasses). The numismatic collection is also important.

By turning left at the N end of the C. Fortuny we reach at No. 37 Paseo de Gen. Martínez Campos, the **Museo Sorolla**. It displays the personal belongings of the artist (1863–1923) and representative paintings donated to the State by his widow. They are perhaps best viewed on sunny days.

For the area further N see Rte 40K.

J. The Barrio de Salamanca

This district, extending to the E of the Paseo de Castellana and N of the C. de Alcalá, is named after the Marqués de Salamanca, who after 1865 laid out the grid of streets beyond the crumbling boundary walls of Madrid, which were then demolished. The built up area was later greatly extended.
  Parallel to and E of the Paseo de Castellana is the *C. Serrano*, a fashionable shopping street running N from the Pl. de la Independencia. The C. Serrano, and the C. Velázquez and C. Principe de Vergara further E, are the area's main N–S thoroughfares. With its

wide avenues—many regrettably no longer tree-lined—it is a residential and commercial area partly inhabited by the equivalent of
Sloane Rangers.

Towards the N end of the C. Claudio Coello (by No. 104), running parallel to C.
Serrano, Adm. Carrero Blanco, President of the Spanish Government, was
assassinated by ETA in December 1973.
    The abduction of José Calvo Sotelo from his home at 89 C. Velázquez and
subsequent assassination (13 July 1936) precipitated the Spanish Civil War.

The C. Goya, leading E from the Pl. de Colón, is one of the main
thoroughfares forming the grid. Parallel to it, four streets to the N, is
the C. de José Ortega y Gasset (or Lista), leading E to the Pl. de
Salamanca, inaugurated in 1911. It passes near (in the C. Castelló)
the *Fundación March*, venue of some good exhibitions of art, etc.,
established by the banker and entrepreneur.
    SW of the junction of C. Serrano with C. Diego de León stands the
United States Embassy block (No. 75).
    Beyond, at No. 122 (right) is the *Museo Lázaro Galdiano*.
    The extensive collections of José Lázaro Galdiano (died 1948),
which he bequeathed to the State, are displayed on three floors.
Some attributions are problematical.

Rooms on the GROUND FLOOR contain some of the more notable antiquities and
works of decorative art, among them a collection of Limoges enamels, medieval
ivories, 10–11C Byzantine cloisonné enamels, Baroque and later jewellery,
Renaissance bronzes and plaques; and among individual items, a cup of
Matthias Corvinus (1462); gold earrings by *Benvenuto Cellini*; collar with
medallion of the 3rd Duke of Alba, by *Caradosso*; rock crystal cup surmounted
by an enamelled gold figure of Neptune, by the *Sarachi* of Milan (c 1600);
terracotta bust of Christ, by *Verocchio*; a dancing faun, by *Sant'Agata*; and
Leonardo da Vinci, St. John the Divine.

FIRST FLOOR. Byzantine ivories; ivory and silver tankard of Charles V; *Benvenuto Cellini* (?), enriched case in the form of a book, ordered by Pope Paul III
for Charles V; enamelled gold cup given by Archduke Albert to Gen. Spinola
after the surrender of Breda; ivory medallion of Ferdinand II; the 'Cup of Julius
Caesar' (Augsburg, mid 16C); Roman agate cup with Renaissance mountings;
and arms and armour (including reproductions). Among paintings: several early
Spanish pictures; *Lucas Gassel*, Landscape; *Pourbus*, Portrait; *Carreño*, Fernando de Valenzuela, Iñes de Zuñiga, Condesa de Monterrey, and the Conde
de Aguilar; anon. Italian portrait of the Duque del Infantado; *Sánchez Coello* (?)
Female portrait; *Pantoja de la Cruz*, Duchess of Savoy; *Antony Mor*, João III of
Portugal; *Reynolds*, Mrs Damer, Gen. Stringer Lawrence; *Gainsborough* (?),
Landscapes, and a portrait; portraits by *Vicente López*; and *F. Madrazo*,
Gertrudis Gómez de Avellaneda.

SECOND FLOOR. The Virgin of Mosén Sperandeu (Tarazona; 1439); *García del
Barco*, Triptych of Ávila; *P. Berruguete*, Self-portrait; *Bartolomé de Castro*, Sto.
Domingo, Annunciation, Nativity, Epiphany; the Virgin of Columbus (c 1540),
with the unfinished cathedral of Sto. Domingo in the background; *Gerard
David*, Virgin; *School of Bruges*, Virgin of the Beautiful landscape; *Joos van
Cleve*, Leonor of Austria (sister of Charles V); *Bosch*, St. John in Patmos, the
Vision of Tondal; *Dürer*, Virgin in a garden; *Ysembrandt*, Virgin; *Q. Massys*,
Triptych; *Master of the Half-lengths*, Virgin; portraits by *Van Orley* (?), and
Pourbus; *Mabuse*, Triptych; *Ludolf de Jongh*, Female portrait; *Rembrandt*,
Saskia (1634); Landscapes by *Wouverman*, *Hobbema*, *A. Cuyp*, and *Teniers*;
Velázquez, Góngora (1622), and Juana Pacheco; *Zurbarán*, S. Diego de Alcalá;
El Greco, S. Francisco with brother Leo, St. John and the Holy Woman, S.
Francisco, Mater Dolorosa; *Murillo*, Sta. Rosa de Lima; *Ribera*, S. Pedro;
Carreño, Carlos II; *Mengs*, Carlos III; portraits of Jovellanos; *Goya*, Descent
from the Cross, cartoon for a tapestry of Summer, the Conde de Miranda (1777;
the artist's first dated portrait), and other portraits and sketches; Portraits by
Maella, and *Esteve*; *Francis Cotes*, Female portrait; *Allan Ramsay*, Augusta of

Saxony; *Lawrence*, Master Ainslie; *Reynolds*, Lady Sondes; *Romney*, The widow; Landscapes by *Constable*, and Seascapes by *Bonington*; Watercolours by *Turner*; *Tiepolo*, Portrait of his wife, Cecilia Guardi; *Guardi*, The Grand Canal; also collections of 16–18C Miniatures and of clocks and watches, including Charles V's ivory hunting watch in the form of a cross, and the escritoire of Marie Leczinska.

THIRD FLOOR. *Pantoja*, Portraits of Felipe II, and Felipe III as a child; Portraits of Lope de Vega; *Mengs*, Self-portrait; and Portraits by *Esquivel*, and *Bayeu*. Renaissance and Baroque plaques; coins and dies; medals and medallions; swords, firearms, and powder flasks; cutlery; fans; Moroccan and Granadine fabrics; vestments and embroidery; and collections of azulejos.

For the area further N see below.

K.   Northern Madrid

The C. de María de Molina, immediately N of the Museo Lázaro Galdiano, leads E towards the Airport and W to the Pl. del Dr Marañón, from which the Paseo de Castellana continues N.

Bearing left between the museum and the plaza is the C. de Pinar with the *Residencia de Estudiantes*, founded in 1910, once administered by the influential *Institución Libre de Enseñanza*. At one time it counted amongst its residents Lorca, Buñuel, Dalí, and Alberti, and amongst its teachers, Ortega y Gasset and Unamuno.

The Castellana is overlooked from the E by the *Museo de Ciencias Naturales* (at present closed, and its important collections in an unpardonable state of neglect).

To the left further N is an extensive range of ministerial offices built on the site of the former Hipódromo or racecourse. Begun in the early 1930s, these *Nuevos Ministerios* were intended to accommodate all the ministries of the time, but with the mushroom growth of bureaucracy they now house a mere fraction.

Further N still, beyond a flyover and several new towerblocks (left) is the Pl. de Lima, to the right of which is the *Bernabéu Stadium* (home ground of the Real Madrid Football Club); to the left is the *Pal. de Congresos y Exposiciones*, embellished by a mural by Miró and containing a concert hall.

Still further N are the Pl. de Cuzco and, beyond, the Pl. de Castilla. From the latter the C. de Agustín de Foxá leads NE to the *Estación de Chamartín*, the new but uninspired main railway terminus of Madrid.

L.   Northwestern Madrid

A few paces NW of the NW end of the *Pl. de España* (see latter part of Rte 40G) at No. 17 C. de Ventura Rodríguez is the **Museo Cerralbo**, containing the collections of the 17th Marqués (died 1922).

Paintings here include: *Zurbarán*, Conception; *Tintoretto*, Male portrait (damaged); *Mengs*, the 12th Duke of Alba; *Van Dyck*, Marie de Médici; and genre scenes by *Eugenio Lucas*. In the chapel: *El Greco*, S. Francisco. The armoury contains some pieces of interest, and furniture and the minor arts are well represented.

To the W stood the *Montaña barracks*, destroyed during the Civil

War. Now laid out as gardens, this improbable site has been embellished since 1970 with palm trees and the *Temple of Debod* (4C BC), given to Spain by Egypt.

The Paseo de Pintor Rosales leads NW above the hillside PARQUE DEL OESTE, from which a cablecar (or *teleferico*) communicates with the *Casa del Campo*; see below.

The Cuesta de S. Vicente descends SW below the flyover SW of the Pl. de España to skirt the gardens of the *Palacio Real* (see Rte 40B), part of the so-called *Campo del Moro* (where the Moors established a camp in 1109), laid out in 1566 and open to the public since 1978. From the Paseo del Virgen del Puerto, skirting its W side, one may approach the **Museo de Carruajes**, containing a well-restored and displayed collection of coaches, funeral coaches, travelling carriages, sledges, etc., including the litter of Charles V; and collections of saddles (several being gifts from South American states), harnesses, bits, etc.

Of historical interest is the carriage built in 1832 in which Alfonso XIII and his English bride Victoria Eugenia (Ena) were returning from their wedding (31 May 1906), when an assassination attempt was made on them as they were driving along the C. Mayor. A bomb disguised as a bunch of flowers was hurled from No. 88 in that street, killing a number of guards and spectators but leaving the couple unharmed.

Further W, beyond the Manzanares, is the well-wooded **Casa del Campo**, a royal park (1721 hectares) laid out before 1623 and once surrounded by a wall.

One of the few open spaces remaining in the immediate vicinity of Madrid, its bosky heights provide panoramic views of the town, which was heavily bombarded from this quarter by the Nationalists during the Civil War. It contains a *Zoo* and amusement park, and is connected to the Paseo de Pintor Rosales (see above) by cablecar.

From the *Estación del Norte* (serving several suburban routes), N of the Cuesta de S. Vicente, the Paseo de la Florida leads NW, after some distance passing (right) *S. **Antonio de la Florida** (1797; by F. Fontana). The church is notable for the series of frescoes painted on its ceiling by Goya in 1798. It also contains the remains of the artist, brought from Bordeaux and buried beneath the cupola in 1919.

The main subject represents St. Anthony raising a murdered man from the dead in order to name his murderer and so save an innocent accused. The frescoes, secular in spirit, were received with enthusiastic admiration and won for Goya the post of first painter to the court. Some have seen in them an expression of the artist's cynical attitude towards the Church, for in his angels and other figures he is said to have mingled portraits of court ladies with those of less reputable models.

In 1928 a new church, a replica of the old, was built adjacent for the service of the parish.

Just to the NE, beyond the railway line (which may be crossed here) is the *Hill of Principe Pio*, with a small cemetery where lie the victims of the uprising of 3 May 1808.—A road climbs through the PARQUE DEL OESTE to regain the Paseo del Pintor Rosales not far NW of the *Temple de Debod*; see above.

The C. de la Princesa leads NW from the Pl. de España, passing the *Pal. de Liria* (see Rte 40G), eventually reaching (left) the Escorial-like *Air Ministry*, completed in 1951 on the site of the old *Model Prison*. It was near here that the anarchist leader Durruti was mortally wounded in November 1936.

Beyond is a memorial *Arco de la Victoria*, in the Fascist taste.

Just N of the arch are the *Instituto de Cultura Hispanica* and the **Museo de America** (in 1987 closed for a thorough reformation).

The museum contains the Oñate collection of Mexican and Peruvian terracotta vessels; the Larrea collection of over 600 Inca ceramics and other specimens of Tihuanaco culture; Maya sculptures from Yucatán; a monument to the Mexican chief Tizoc; the Treasure of Las Quimbayas; gold objects found in Colombia, etc. Also two Maya MSS—the Troana and the Cortesiano—and paintings on mother-of-pearl by Miguel González (1698) depicting the Conquest of Mexico; wax figurines of local types by Andrés García (c 1800), and numerous other collections. The re-opening of the museum is awaited with interest.

Some distance further NW, extending on both sides of the Av. de Puerta de Hierro, is the *Ciudad Universitaria*.

Founded in 1927, the new university was devastated in 1936–39, when it stood in the front line of the siege of Madrid. It has since been largely rebuilt on a new plan, but hardly a single building merits attention.

To the W of the Av. de Puerta de Hierro (which leads NW to the 'Iron Gate' of 1753, at the commencement of the N6) the Av. Juan de Herrera leads past the entrance to the *Museo Español de Arte Contemporáneo* (see below) and, not far beyond, the *School of Architecture*, adjacent to which the Isabelline Portal of the former Hospital de la Latina has been re-erected.—Further NW is the rebuilt *Pal. de la Moncloa* (1955), now the residence of the President of the Government (or Prime Minister).

The **Museum of Contemporary Spanish Art** was inaugurated in 1975, but the internal distribution has been much criticised and it is likely that the collections will be moved eventually to the *Centro de Arte Reina Sofía*; see Rte 40D. It is surrounded by gardens embellished with stone and rusting metal sculptures.

Although it pretends to be a national museum of contemporary art, much that is shown is hardly contemporary, and the collections are by no means representative of recent Spanish painting.

Among the more interesting works which may be on show are: *José María Lopez* (1883–1954), A chain of prisoners; *Ramón Casas* (1866–1932), El garrote vil; *Ignacio Zuloaga* (1870–1945), Torerillos de pueblo, The bleeding Christ, Cousin Cándida, Landscape at Alhama, Mountains of Calatayud, Nude, Portrait of his father; *José Gutierrez Solana* (1886–1945), The fishermen's return, Chorus girls, The *tertulia* in the Café de Pombo (1920), The display cases, The bullfight, Clowns, Portrait of Unamuno, Woman sewing, Funeral procession, The bishop's visit; *Valentín Zubiaurre* (1889–1963), Basque *bersolaris*; *Ramón Zubiaurre* (1882–1969), Shanti Andía; *Juan Echevarria* (1875–1931), several portraits; *Fernando Alvarez de Sotomayor* (1875–1960), portraits; *Julio González* (1876–1942), Two women; *María Gutiérrez Blanchard* (1881–1932), Breton women; *Pablo Ruiz Picasso* (1881–1973), Woman in blue, Los congrios (1940), The artist and his model (three examples, 1963); *Salvador Dalí* (1904–), Girl at the window, Girl's back; *Francisco Arias* (1912–76), Roman Circus at Mérida; *José Frau* (1898–1976), Fairy-tale landscape; *Francisco Gutiérrez (Pancho) Cossío* (1889–1970), Portrait of his mother, Tables; *Cirilio Martínez Novillo* (1921–), Landscapes; *Godofredo Ortega Muñoz* (1905–82), Landscapes; *Daniel Vázquez Diaz* (1882–1969), The cuadrillas, Eva; *Joaquín Sunyer* (1875–1956), María Dolores crocheting; *Rosario de Velasco* (1910–), Adam and Eva; *Hermenegildo Anglada-Camarasa* (1871–1959), Portrait of Sonia Klamery in 1914; *Joaquín Valverde* (1896–1982), Ayer; *Antonio López Torres* (1902–), Self-portrait; *Antonio López García* (1936–), Bride and groom; *Amalia Avia Peña* (1930–), Townscapes; *Antonio Zarco Fortes*, Man sleeping on a bench;

Carmen Laffont (1934–), The bride; *Enrique Brinkmann* (1938–), The tie; *Modesto Cuixart* (1925–), Omorka, Fernandina; *Francisco Farreras* (1927–), View of Cuenca; *Fernando Zóbel* (1924–84), Navacerrada; *José Hernández* (1944–), Venetian opera; *Rafael Canogar* (1935–), Painting No. 41; *César Manrique* (1920–), Lacran; *Lucio Muñoz* (1929–), Sequeros; *Ramiro Tapia* (1931–), Carnivorous plant; and representative works by *Antoni Tàpies* (1923–); *Alfonso Fraile* (1930–); *Eusebio Sempere* (1924–85); *Pablo Palazuelo* (1916–); *Joan Miró* (1893–1983); and *Juan Gris* (1887–1927).

Sculpture includes work by *Eduardo Chillida* (1924–); *Pablo Serrano* (1910–); *Amadeo Gabino* (1922–); *Martin Chirino* (1925–); and *Julio López Hernández* (1930–).

For roads from Madrid to **Tordesillas** and **León** see Rte 21; to **Ávila** and **Salamanca**, Rte 22; to **Segovia**, Rte 25; **El Escorial**, 42; **Toledo**, 43; **Cuenca**, 44; **Valencia**, 46; **Albacete**, 47; **Aranjuez** and **Bailén**, 48; **Arenas de S. Pedro** and **Plasencia**, 49; and **Talavera** and **Trujillo** for **Mérida**, Rte 50. For **Valladolid**, **Burgos**, and **Soria** via **Almazan** see Rtes 11B, 12, and 15, in reverse. For the **Environs of Madrid** see Rte 41.

41 Environs of Madrid

The only short excursion of any interest in the immediate vicinity of Madrid is that to *El Pardo*; see below. Although travellers preferring to base themselves on the capital may conveniently make day-trips to *El Escorial* (Rte 42), *Alcalá de Henares* (p 438), *Guadalajara* (Rte 15), and *Aranjuez* (Rte 48A), anything further afield (*Segovia, Ávila,* or *Toledo,* for example) can hardly be explored in any detail in this way. The roads to these destinations are often crowded at weekends, particularly when returning on Sunday evenings.

Drive NW from the C. Princesa and along the Av. Puerta de Hierro past (left) the *'Iron Gate'* erected in 1753 at the entrance of a royal park. Bear right onto the C601, parallel to the Manzanares, through scrubby woods to (13km) the village of **El Pardo**, founded by Carlos III.

It is divided by a plaza from the **Palace**, a square edifice with a tower at each corner and surrounded by a moat, with its principal entrance on the S side.

The present palace, which Edward Clarke considered 'an indifferent seat for an English country gentleman', is in fact a not-inelegant building with pleasant patios and colourful gardens. It was constructed on the site of a hunting lodge built in 1405 by Enrique III. This was replaced by a palace begun in 1547 by Luis de Vega for Charles V, and completed in 1558 by Felipe II, who adorned it with works of art. Many of these were lost when the S wing was almost entirely destroyed by fire in 1604. The present building by Francisco de Mora dates from the reign of Felipe III. Enlarged by Carlos III—it once had stabling for 800 horses and 1000 mules—it received its internal decoration under Carlos IV and Fernando VII. Here in 1766 Carlos III found refuge after the riots (or *motin*) raised in Madrid by his unpopular Italian minister Esquilachi, who attempted to prohibit the wearing of long capes and slouch hats, and the king spent many winters here hunting. It was the official residence of the late dictator; visiting VIPs now stay here.

Its interior, visited by guided groups, is less elegant, although certain formal reception rooms are attractively decorated, particularly one in the 'Chinese taste'. Several ceilings, with frescoes by various artists and stuccoes by Robert Michel, are of some quality. Some rooms are hung with tapestries (after Teniers or from Goya's cartoons).

Just N of the palace stands the ***Casita del Príncipe**, a 'cottage orné', built in 1786 for Carlos IV when Prince of the Asturias as a retreat from the stilted etiquette of his father's court.

From the entrance rotunda one may visit a series of well-proportioned and elegantly decorated and furnished rooms. The Yellow Room (left) and (right) a room with frescoes by Luca Giordano are particularly attractive, while a third contains frescoes by Gonzalez Pastor. Some portraits by Mengs and a series of Tiepolo pastels are notable.

On the hill to the W is the convent church of *Sto. Cristo*, with an Entombment by Gregorio Fernández and two paintings by Ribera.

About 3km SE is the *Pal. de la Quinta*, containing a collection of wallpapers.

42 Madrid to El Escorial

44km (27 miles). NVI. 16km—C505. 28km **El Escorial**.

Maps: M 447.

Drive NW from the C. Princesa and along the Av. Puerta de Hierro, past (left) the '*Iron Gate*' erected in 1753 at the entrance of a royal park, and follow the NVI NW. To the right is a racecourse; beyond, in the park of *El Pardo* (see Rte 41) is the small palace, originally a hunting box, of *La Zarzuela* (no adm.). Built by Carlos IV, it has been reconstructed on the site of an earlier building, from which a much-debased form of operetta, first performed here in the 17C, takes its name of *zarzuela*. It is now a residence of the Spanish royal family.

At 16km fork left, later crossing a ridge from which the Escorial comes into sight under the jagged sierra.—17km *Galapagar*, formerly the last intermediate halt of royal funerals. The present clergy house was Felipe II's residence during the building of the Escorial. One reason for the dearth of trees here is that in previous centuries they were felled for the production of charcoal for the kitchens and braziers of Madrid, and no one ever considered reafforestation.

The view of the Escorial as we approach it has radically changed in recent decades; the monastery no longer stands in comparatively splendid isolation and the lower slopes of the range are now disfigured by new buildings. The road skirts *El Escorial de Abajo* (with the railway station) and passes the **Casita del Principe** (or *de Abajo*), a miniature country house in the style of the *Casa del Labrador* at Aranjuez, built in 1772 by Juan de Villanueva for Carlos IV when prince. Among the elaborately decorated rooms are one in Pompeian style and another adorned with over 200 Buen Retiro porcelain plaques depicting mythological scenes.

The older town of **S. Lorenzo de El Escorial** (1030m; with a combined population of 14,900 inhab.) is dwarfed by the huge bulk of the adjacent monastery. Since 1792 it has formed a '*ciudad*' in itself. Its name is probably derived from the slag or *scoria* of old iron mines in the vicinity.

The ***ESCORIAL** includes a monastery, a church, and library; a royal palace and royal mausoleum. Like the Royal Palace in Madrid it is still conserved by the Patrimonio Nacional; see p 91–92. The granite-slated edifice is an austere composition, mainly Tuscan in style, and in plan a rectangular parallelogram 205m from N to S and 160m from E to W, with towers at each corner and loftier towers and the dome of its church rising in the centre. It has a certain grandeur of conception, summed up by Felipe II in his instructions to Herrera: 'Above all do not forget what I have told you; simplicity in the construction, severity in the whole, nobility without arrogance, majesty without ostentation'.

The reactions of visitors have been mixed. Edward Clarke (1760/61) found it 'a large confused stupendous pile'; Gautier considered it 'the dullest and most wearisome edifice that a morose and suspicious tyrant could ever conceive for the mortification of his fellow-creatures'; while Richard Ford suggested that it might 'disappoint at first sight, for expectations have been too highly raised; but this is the penalty which the credulous hope of travellers must pay, who will go on expecting too much in spite of illusion-dispelling experience'.

Admission. Tickets are obtained at the N and W entrances; there is no charge to enter the church.

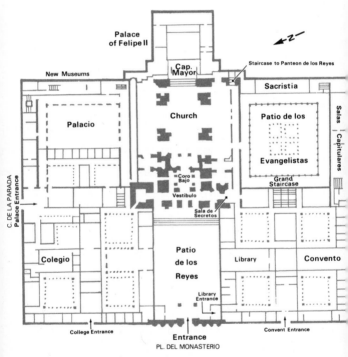

El Escorial

The Escorial was built in 1563–84 by Felipe II partly in compliance with the wishes of his father Charles V in constructing a royal burial place, and to fulfil a vow made at the battle of St. Quentin, fought in 1557 on St. Lawrence's Day (10 August). But the immediate inspiration was as likely to have been a similar foundation, the Jeronimite monastery at Belém near Lisbon, commenced in 1502 by his maternal grandfather, Manuel I, work on which was still in progress. The story that the groundplan of the structure is intended to represent the gridiron on which the saint was martyred is indifferently supported by the plan itself, although there are some sculptured gridirons on the main façade.

The first architect, Juan Bautista de Toledo (who had worked with Michelangelo on St. Peter's in Rome), was summoned from Naples in 1559, and the first stone was laid on 23 April 1563. After his death in 1567 work on the fabric was completed by Juan de Herrera on 13 September 1583. The monastery was planned to house 50 Hieronymite monks, but the number was increased in 1564 to 100, which caused changes to be made in the design. The *Palace*, in which Felipe II lived intermittently for 14 years, was intended as a simple appanage to the monastery, but on the lavish decoration and enrichment of the rest of the building vast sums were squandered. Distinguished artists from Italy and elsewhere were invited to cover its walls with frescoes and paintings. The rare books and MSS assembled in the *Library* made it one of the most valuable in the world. The *Church* was enriched with works of art and gold and silver vessels, and—the king being a relicomaniac—515 reliquaries enshrining (it is said) 7421 relics.

In 1671 the monastery and some of its contents were damaged by fire. In 1681 the description of the place by Francisco de los Santos was published (translated into English by George Thompson in 1760), and it was described again in 1764 by Andrés Ximenez.

In 1808 the building was plundered of its bullion by the French under La Houssaye, who left the relics in a pile on the floor; the exterior was also injured. In summer 1812 several thousand English and Portuguese troops were quartered here for ten days. Fernando VII attempted to repair the damage, and after his death many of the best paintings were removed to Madrid. It ceased to be a royal residence c 1861, and since 1885 the monastery has been occupied by Augustinian monks. The future Republican President Manual Azana 'lost his religious faith' at their college.

The principal entrance is in the centre of the main *W Façade*. The portal is surmounted by a colossal stone statue of St. Lawrence, by Monegro, with head, hands, and feet of marble. Pass through a vestibule to the *Patio de los Reyes*. It takes its name from the six huge statues of the Kings of Judah, also by Monegro, high up on the façade of the church. The 'plate of gold' on a pinnacle above the church is said to have been placed there to show that the colossal expense of building had not exhausted resources, but in 1949 the metal was found to be gilded bronze, engraved with prayers for protection against storms.

The **Church* or *Templo* (1578–81) is entered through a dark *Sotacoro*, a vestibule under the choir, which is supported by a flat vault (the *boveda plana*), a triumph of architectural skill. The interior, square in plan, with four massive fluted piers (8m square), conveys by its fine proportions, its bold vaulting, and its granite simplicity, an impression of grandeur, even if badly lit.

Around the walls are 42 subsidiary altars, with altar pieces by Navarrete, Zuccaro, Pellegrino, Tibaldi, Luca Cambiaso, Michiel Coxcie, and others. On the vaulting are frescoes by Luca Giordano. On the right is the marble Christ, carved by Benvenuto Cellini in 1562, and given to Felipe II by the Grand Duke of Tuscany in 1576. It was carried here from Barcelona on men's shoulders.

The *Cap. Mayor*, adorned with precious marbles, is approached by a flight of steps. The *Retablo*, 28m high, an elaborate design of marble and gilded bronze by Giacomo Trezzo of Milan, includes statues and medallions by Leone Leoni and his son Pompeo, and paintings by Pellegrino Tibaldi and Zuccaro.—On each side are the *Oratorios*, low chambers of black marble for the royal family, and on these are the so-called *Enterramientos Reales*, kneeling bronze-gilt groups by Pompeo Leoni. On the left are Charles V with his wife Isabel (mother of Felipe II), his daughter María, and his sisters Leonor and María. On the right kneel Felipe II, Ana (his fourth wife), Isabel (his third), and María, his first wife, with her son Don Carlos; Mary Tudor is conspicuous by her absence.

Reached from the SE corner, beyond the Antesacristia, is the *Sacristia*, with arabesque ceiling paintings by N. Granelo and Fabricio Castello, and paintings by Ribera, Luca Giordano, Titian, and others.

At the end of the room is the *Retablo de la Sta. Forma*. Behind it, in the Camarín, is preserved the host which is said to have bled at Gorcum in Holland in 1525 when trampled by Zwinglian soldiers. Bas-reliefs on the altar depict the miracle and the presentation of the wafer to Felipe II by Rudolf II of Germany. The painting, by Claudio Coello, depicts the reception of the relic in this sacristy. The heads are portraits: Carlos II, who erected the altar, kneeling in the centre; behind him are the dukes of Medinaceli and Pastrana; the prior is Francisco de los Santos, the historian of the Escorial; and low on the left is the artist.

The *Coro Alto*, overlooking the W end of the church, is closed to the public but permission to visit it may be obtained.

It contains 124 stalls, carved in seven sorts of wood, after Herrera's design. Although Felipe II, whose stall was at the SW angle, frequently joined in the devotions of the monks, it would have been in the *old* church that—according to the story—he received the news of the momentous victory of Lepanto (1571) without moving a muscle, and at the end of the service ordered a Te Deum to be chanted.

The *Choir*, decorated with frescoes by Cincinnato and Luqueto, that on the vault by Cambiaso, contains a wonderfully poised lectern, a rock crystal chandelier, and four organs (1578; by Gilles de Brebos of Antwerp), which until 1650 were the largest in the world. Badly modernised in the 1920s, they have been restored recently, but are musically uninteresting. Padre Antonio Soler was at one time organist and choirmaster here, and it is recorded that Lord Richard Fitzwilliam (1745–1816) was given harpsichord lessons by Soler when he was visiting the Escorial in 1772. In the Antecoros are kept 216 huge parchment choir books, some with illuminations by Andrés de León and his pupil Julián de la Fuente.

From the vestibule of the Antesacristia steps descend past the entrance of the **Panteón de los Infantes** (see below), and then the *Pudridero* (or rotting place, a vault where royal corpses remained for ten years before being committed to their final resting places), to reach the **Panteón de los Reyes**, an octagonal vault c 9m in diameter, directly beneath the Cap. Mayor. This chamber was left in bare and dignified simplicity by Felipe II; the marble and gilt enrichment, designed by G.B. Crescenzi and begun in 1617, was added by Felipe III and Felipe IV. The body of Charles V was transferred here c 1634 from the old church. Here lie all later Spanish monarchs, except Felipe V and Fernando VI with their queens, buried respectively at La Granja and Sta. Bárbara (Las Salesas Reales, Madrid). Opposite the entrance is an altar with a crucifix by Pietro Tacca. On six sides are horizontal recesses holding 24 black marble sarcophagi in antique style, each bearing the name of the occupant. Kings (including Isabel II) lie to the left of the altar; queens who have been the mothers of kings lie to the right (the last, Victoria Eugenia, wife of Alfonso XIII, was transferred here in 1985).

Felipe IV would lie in the niche destined for his corpse while mass was being celebrated over him, while his son (the moronic Carlos II) would gaze for hours at the mummified remains of his ancestors, which he had caused to be displayed.

The *Panteón de los Infantes* contains the tombs of princes and of queens ineligible for the royal vault. In the fifth chamber is the marble tomb, with a recumbent effigy, of Don Juan of Austria (1547–78), half-brother of Felipe II and victor of Lepanto. In the last is interred Don Carlos (1545–68), son of Felipe II.

From the Antesacristia one may enter the *Lower Cloister* (Claustro Principal Bajo) surrounding gardens in which is a Doric temple with statues by *Monegro*. The frescoes in the cloister are by Tibaldi. On the S side are the *Salas Capitulares*, with a Pompeian ceiling by Granelo and Castello. Among paintings here are: *after Velázquez*, Innocent X; *Ribera*, Holy Trinity; *Carducho*, Visitation; *Navarrete*, Martyrdom of Santiago and four other works; an early *El Greco* (?) of St. John the Baptist and St. John the Evangelist; and flower paintings by *Daniel Seghers*.—In the end room are collections of vestments, plate, and cult objects, and an alabaster St. John the Baptist by *Nicolás Vergara*.

At the SW angle of the cloister is the *Old* Church, containing three paintings attributed to Titian (Adoration, Ecce Homo, and Martyrdom of St. Lawrence). On the walls are the mortuary crowns of Spanish kings.

The *Escalera Principal*, doubtfully attributed to J.B. Castello, ascends from the W side to the *Upper Cloister*. Here the friezes by Luca Giordano depict the Battle, Siege, and Surrender of St. Quentin, and Felipe II and his architects planning the Escorial. Also by Giordano is the ceiling painting of 'St. Lawrence ascending into Heaven' (among his companions may be recognised the portraits of Charles V, Felipe II, and Carlos II).

On leaving the cloister, in which (Clarke reported in 1760) it was said that Felipe II's 'unquiet and perturbed spirit still nightly visits his favourite mansion, and stalks horrid round the long arcades and corridores of the Escurial', we pass through the 'Sala de Secretos', so-called from its peculiar acoustic properties, back to the vestibule at the main entrance of the monastery.

Stairs ascend to the **Library**, a long vaulted room with a marble floor. The frescoes by Tibaldi (ceiling) and Carducho refer to the liberal arts and sciences, in colours 'too gaudy for the sober books' in Ford's opinion. In the bookcases (made by José Flecha from the Doric designs of Herrera), the older books stand with their front edges bearing their titles turned outward, as arranged by Arias Montano (1527–98), the first librarian. Clarke relates that the illiterate Hieronymite monks into whose hands the library fell were inordinately suspicious of anyone showing sufficient interest as to copy anything, saying 'if you copy our manuscripts, the originals will then be worth nothing'.

Among the treasures, some of which may be on display, are: Missals of Charles V, Fernando and Isabel, and Felipe II; the Codex Aureus, with the Gospels in gold letters, made for the Emperor Conrad II and Heinrich III (early 11C); the Codex Albeldensis (976); a 15C Virgil, written in Spain; a 15C Apocalypse, with elaborate illustrations; and the Cantigas de Sta. María, by Alfonso el Sabio. The globe belonged to Felipe II.

The library, in spite of past vicissitudes, contains c 40,000 printed volumes. The *Biblioteca de Manuscritos*, shown by special permission, contains c 2000 Arabic MSS, among others.

The *Palacio Real* (visited in escorted groups; do not be hurried) is reached from the vestibule by the N portal, from which stairs ascend to the first floor. The rooms first shown are notable for their tapestries, mostly made in Madrid (after Teniers, Wouwerman, Goya, Bayeu, et al).

At this NE angle of the complex is a small suite of richly decorated private apartments known as the *Habitaciones de Maderas Finas (fine woods), for which a special entrance ticket should be requested. The quality of the cabinet work and the marquetry of the doors, floors, panelling, and furniture is incomparable. Work on these rooms, which should not be missed by the connoisseur, dates from the reign of Carlos IV, and was only completed in 1831.

The *Sala de las Batallas* is decorated with a huge fresco (1587; by Granelo and Castello) of the Battle of Higueruela (1431; against the Moors of Granada). The costumes, copied from an earlier work found in the Alcázar at Segovia, are of historical interest. Between the windows and at the ends of the room are other military and naval scenes.

We descend to the **Palace of Felipe II**, first entering the rooms of the Infanta Isabel (daughter of Felipe II). They contain historical relics, including a portative organ of 1575 by Gilles de Brebos, used by Carlos I at Yuste, and a 16C Flemish Virgin and Child. The room in which the king gave audience and received ambassadors has whitewashed walls, Talavera tiling, and contains two Brussels tapestries from the Spheres series (16C), several views of royal residences and battle pieces. In the adjoining room, with magnificent marquetry Doors (German), and a curious Sundial on the floor, are portraits by Pantoja.

Adjacent is the simple *Bedchamber*, but the austere monarch is said to have died in a small recess, from which his bed commanded a view (through movable shutters) of the high altar in the church. A copy of the Haywain, by Bosch (original in the Prado), Pantoja's Portrait of the king in old age, and works of the Flemish and German Schools are also displayed here, together with the litter that carried the king on his last painful journey to the Escorial.

Returning to the rooms of the Infanta Isabel, we descend to the **New Museums**, a series of vaulted rooms in which most of the finer paintings of the Escorial collection have been installed.

These include, in **RI**: *Patinir*, Landscape with St. Christopher; *Bosch*, Mocking of Christ, a copy of a panel from the Garden of Delights (original in the Prado), and two Temptations of St. Anthony from the School of Bosch; *Gerard David*, triptych of the Deposition; some restored studies of natural history by *Dürer*.—**RII** is largely devoted to paintings by *M. Coxcie*, while **RIII** contains *Titian*, Burial of Christ, St. Jerome, and an Ecce Homo; and *Veronese* (?), Annunciation.—**RIV** *Titian*, Last Supper (painted in 1564 for the refectory of the Escorial), mutilated and retouched; works by *Veronese*, *Bassano*, *G. Reni*, *Zuccaro*, and a St. Jerome by *Palma Vecchio*.—**RV** contains some outstanding paintings by *Ribera*, including St. Jerome, Jacob guarding Laban's flock, Aesop, St. Francis, and the Burial of Christ; and **RVI** *Velázquez*, Joseph's coat (painted in Italy c 1630); *A. Cano*, Virgin and Child; *Valdés Leal*, Nativity; *Carreño* (?), Carlos II as a child, and Mariana de Austria.

A subsidiary range of rooms is devoted to the *Architectural History of the Escorial*, with numerous designs, plans, engravings, models, etc., and a collection of tools and machines used in the construction of the monastery. At a higher level are three rooms containing further important paintings, including *Van de Weyden*, Christ on the Cross between the Virgin and St. John, and a copy by *Coxcie* of his Descent from the Cross (the original in the Prado); *El Greco*, St. Maurice and the Theban Legion (1582), and the 'Gloria de Felipe II'. Also preserved here are ten tapestries of the Conquest of Tunis by *G. Pannemaker* (completed 1554), and a 16C tapestry copy of *Bosch*'s 'Garden of Delights'.

Flanking the main courtyard are several dependencies of the monastery, including a range to the S added by Villanueva which spoils the original vista of the sierra.

The **Casita de Arriba** (smaller than that 'del Principe'), also by

Villanueva, restored and refurnished, is a short distance to the W of the monastery and may be visited.

In the town to the E is the restored 18C *Real Teatro de Coliseo.*

For the *Valle de los Caidos,* approached by a turning off the C600 8km N of El Escorial, see p 198.

EL ESCORIAL TO ÁVILA (63km). The C505 shortly climbs SW, passing a turning to the *Silla del Rey,* an eminence from which Felipe II used to view the gradual rise of the monastery. At 6.5km turn right at a junction.—The M562—an attractive by-road—turns left via (10km) *Robledo de Chavela,* its church containing a late 15C retablo probably painted by Antonio de Rincón, to *Navas del Rey,* 15km beyond; see Rte 49.—The main road ascends gradually through the SIERRA DE GUADARRAMA, at 19km bypassing (right) *Las Navas del Marqués* (1318m), with a ducal residence built by Pedro de Ávila, Marqués de las Navas. We traverse an extensive pine forest planted by the Duque de Medinaceli to cross the ALTO DE VALDELAVIA (1448m) and another lower ridge to approach **Ávila** from the E; see Rte 23.

EL ESCORIAL TO NAVALCARNERO (41km). The C600, which provides a convenient route bypassing Madrid for travellers wishing to drive direct to Toledo, leads SE past (14km) *Valdemorillo,* where the 12C church was altered by Herrera, to (8km) *Villanueva de la Cañada,* where in 1937 the poet Julian Bell (driving an ambulance) was killed during the battle of *Brunete,* but see Rte 49. (The rebuilt village of Brunete is skirted 6km further S.)—*Navalcarnero* is 13km beyond; see Rte 50A.—The C404 leads across the NV and circles to the E past (14km) *Batres,* with a 13–16C castle belonging to the Garcilaso de la Vega family. The N401, for Toledo, is reached 11km beyond.

43 Madrid to Toledo

70km (43 miles) N401.

Maps: M 444 or 447.

The first part of the road, of little interest in itself, has been improved by the construction of bypasses but is still liable to get clogged by commercial traffic.

From the S end of the Paseo del Prado follow the Paseo de Sta. María de la Cabeza to the SW and cross the Manzanares, traversing an industrial area.

To the W is *Carabanchel Alto,* where Teresa Cabarrús (1773–1835), later Mme Tallien, was born, when her father, the Conde de Cabarrús (1752–1810) was a minister of Carlos III. The notorious prison of *Carabanchel Bajo* is further to the NW.

At 13km *Getafe* is bypassed. Its hall-church of 1549–1645 by Alonso de Covarrubias contains paintings by Claudio Coello and a retablo by Alonso Cano. The *Hosp. de S. José* dates from 1527.—14km *Torrejón de la Calzada* has a 15C church; *Torrejón de Velasco,* to the E, a 17C church and remains of a castle.

10km **Illescas** (6050 inhab.) is skirted. In the C. Mayor is a house occupied by François I after his captivity in Madrid. 12C *La Asunción* (altered in the 16C) has a Mudéjar tower; the *Puerta de Ugena* is also Mudéjar. The *Hosp. de la Caridad* (1500; restored 1588) had five paintings by El Greco, last seen in the Prado.

Important excavations have recently taken place at *Carranque,* 7km NW of Illescas.

Cervantes was married in 1584 to Catalina de Salazar y Palacios (by whom his pastoral of 'Galatea' is said to have been inspired) in the church of *Esquivias,* 8km E.

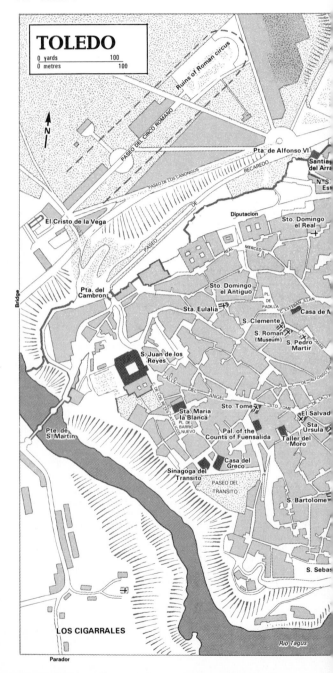

TOLEDO

0 yards   100
0 metres   100

N

Ruins of Roman circus

PASEO DEL CIRCO ROMANO

Pta. de Alfonso VI

Santiago del Arra

RECAREDO

N.S. Est

PASEO DE LOS CANONIGOS

El Cristo de la Vega

Diputación

Sto. Domingo el Real

PASEO   DE

Bridge

REAL   MERCED

Pta. del Cambron

Sto. Domingo el Antiguo

PL DE PADILLA

C. ESTEBAN ILLAN

Sta. Eulalia

S. Clemente

Casa de M

S. Roman (Museum)

S. Pedro Martir

S. Juan de los Reyes

CALLE

DEL   ANGEL

DE LOS REYES CATOLICOS

DE ALFONSO

C. STO. TOME

Sta. Maria la Blanca

DE BARRIO NUEVO

Sto. Tomé

C. STO. TOME

El Salvad

Sta Ursula

Pal. of the Counts of Fuensalida

Taller del Moro

Pte. de S. Martin

Sinagoga del Transito

Casa del Greco

PASEO DEL TRANSITO

S. Bartolome

S. Sebas

LOS CIGARRALES

Rio Tagus

Parador

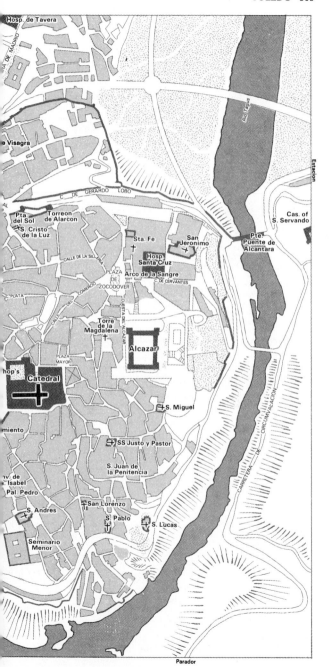

Hosp. de Tavera

VIA DE MADRID

e Visagra

Rio Tagus

Estacion

C. DE GERARDO LOBO

Pta. del Sol
S. Cristo de la Luz
Torreon de Alarcon

Cas. of S. Servando

Sta. Fe

San Jeronimo

Pte. Puente de Alcantara

CALLE DE LA SILLERIA

Hosp Santa Cruz

PLAZA DE ZOCODOVER

Arco de la Sangre
C. DE CERVANTES

C. PLATA

CUESTA DEL ALCAZAR

Torre de la Magdalena

Alcazar

CALLE DEL COMERCIO

PLAZA MAYOR

hop's

Catedral

S. Miguel

CARRETERA DE CIRCUNVALACION

miento

SS Justo y Pastor

S. Juan de la Penitencia

v de Isabel
Pal. Pedro

San Lorenzo

S. Andres

S. Pablo

S. Lucas

Seminario Menor

Parador

The dull road continues SW, after c 30km descending towards Toledo, passing (right) the *Hosp. de Tavera* (see p 312) to approach the *Puerta de Bisagra*.

TOLEDO (54,350 inhab.; c 25,000 in 1800; 31,000 in 1940; the population at one time was possibly as high as 200,000; Parador above the town to the SE), the ancient capital of Castile, and now of Castilla-La Mancha, is finely sited on a rugged bluff (529m) washed on all sides but the N by a loop of the impetuous Tagus in its deep gorge. In spite of a certain amount of modernisation, its steep and tortuous lanes or wynds and its outwardly plain houses with their nail-studded doors guarding hidden patios are still characteristic of its long Moorish occupation. A museum in itself, the town is tourist conscious and the main streets are disfigured by stalls overflowing with souvenirs including bogus antique Toledo ware.

Toletum, capital of the Carpetani, captured in 192 BC by the Romans, was described by Livy as 'urbs parva sed loco munita'. It was favoured by the Visigoths and by the middle of the 6C had been established as their capital. It was one of the few cities whose Roman walls was spared by Witiza. Wamba, who built the first castle, on the site of the Alcázar, is regarded as one of its first benefactors.

It was captured by the Moors in 712, and *Tolaitola* soon became a centre of trade, a high proportion of its population being either Jews or Mozarabic Christians. Both groups were allowed to worship undisturbed. A later attempt to confiscate the wealth of the Jewish community led them to appeal to the growing Christian power for assistance, and Alfonso VI, aided by the Cid, entered Toledo in triumph in 1085, styling himself 'Emperor' of Toledo.

The policy of religious toleration was maintained despite the interference of bigoted prelates, and the place prospered as the capital of the kingdom and the base of renewed assaults on Moorish bastions. It was the home of a famous school of translators, who did much to disseminate a knowledge of Arab science, medicine, and philosophy among the scholars of Christian Europe. Here, during the 12th and early 13Cs studied Robert Anglicus (c 1141), the first translator of the Koran into Latin; Daniel Morley, the mathematician and astronomer; and Michael Scot (c 1217), author of 'Abbreviatio Avicennae' and astrological and other works for Frederick II Hohenstaufen.

In the 16C it was a stronghold of the Comuneros revolt, and after their leader Juan de Padilla had been defeated at Villalar in 1521 the town was defended by his widow, María de Pacheco, and the archbishop, Antonio de Acuña.

In 1492 most of the Toledan Jews were forced into exile abroad, but its large *Converso* community stayed on (although Sta. Teresa's grandfather, a silk merchant of Toledo of *Converso* lineage, had moved to Ávila in 1465). The dead hand of the Inquisition, the transference of the court to Madrid in 1560, and the expulsion of the Moriscos in 1609 put an end to its prosperity, although the immemorial secret of forging steel weapons still remained the peculiar property of the 'Ciudad Imperial y Coronada'. Perhaps because of the prohibition of Arabic in 1580 (for the city had been bilingual before then; indeed, at the time of its capture in 1085 its indigenous Mozarab population was entirely Arabic-speaking) a very pure Castilian came to be spoken in Toledo.

The Archduke Charles, unsuccessful rival of Felipe V, considered making Toledo once more the capital; but the place lapsed into provinciality and made little mark on history in the 19C (when during the First Carlist War the royalists here were commanded by George Dawson Flinter, an Irish soldier of fortune). It briefly came into the news again in the summer of 1936, when its isolated Alcázar was under siege.

Among its natives were S. Ildefonso (607–67); Alfonso X 'El Sabio' (the Learned, *not* Wise; 1221–84); Juana 'la Loca' (the Mad; 1479–1555); Juan de Padilla (1484–1521); Garcilaso de la Vega (1503–36), the poet; Francisco Cervantes de Salazar (?1514–75), historian of Mexico; Sebastián de Covarrubias (1539–1613), the lexicographer; Francisco de Rojas (1607–48), the dramatist and author of 'La Celestina', of *Converso* descent; and Anselmo Lorenzo (1841–1914), the anarcho-syndicalist. Doménico Theotocópulos (1541–1614), better known as 'El Greco', settled in Toledo for life in c 1575.

Use of time. While it is preferable to spend at least two days in Toledo, time often presses, and the following plan of visit is suggested. (Visitors should be able to guide themselves by the principal buildings, most of which have their names clearly displayed, but as the naming of streets is erratic, an effort has been made to show accurately on the plan every twist and angle of the narrow lanes rather than to indicate their names.)

Morning: starting from the *Pl. de Zocodover*, and passing the Cathedral, visit the *Taller del Moro* and *Pal. de Fuensalida*; (*Sto. Tomé*); *S. Juan de los Reyes*; *Sta. María la Blanca*; *El Tránsito*; (the *House of El Greco*); *S. Román*. Any spare time may be devoted to the *Alcázar*, open all day. In the afternoon: the *Cathedral*; *Hosp. de Sta. Cruz* (museum); *Cristo de la Luz*; *Santiago de Arrabal*; and the *Hosp. de Tavera* (museum).

Although some of the main streets *may* be traversed by car, it is recommended that motorists park outside the old enceinte, either near the *Puerta de Bisagra*, or further W near the *Puerta del Cambrón*. The main points of interest are at no great distance from either. Little has changed since the late 18C, when Henry Swinburne observed that 'no stranger in his sober senses would venture up or down [the streets] in a carriage'.

Approaches. The roads from Madrid and Ávila converge near the *Puerta de Bisagra*, at a central point in the walls circling the N side of the town. This area is now also reached by a new road turning off the N400 from Aranjuez, approaching from the E and crossing the Tagus not far N of the *Puente de Alcántara*. Another road has been completed, which may be entered just S of the latter bridge. It circles above the N bank of the Tagus and, after narrowing S of the *Paseo del Tránsito*, leads to the *Puerta del Cambrón*. An exterior road (the Carretera de Circunvalación), circling through *Los Cigarrales* high above the S bank of the river, provides several spectacular views, and visitors with a car are recommended to drive round this road before entering Toledo, or at least before leaving.

The description has been divided into five sections, the first covering extramural Toledo in an anticlockwise direction, its bridges, the Cigarrales, and the Hospital de Tavera, etc.

A.   Outside the walls (by car)

The Pl. de Alfonso VI (a roundabout just W of the *Puerta de Bisagra*) provides a view of a long stretch of Moorish *Walls*. From here, follow the Paseo del Cristo de la Vega to the W, soon passing (right) the church of that name, to cross the Tagus and turn left.

El Cristo de la Vega is the frequently restored Mudéjar successor of the 4C basilica of Sta. Leocadia. A statue of the saint, by Berruguete, stands over the portal of 1770.—Extending from the church to the NE is the site of a *Roman Circus*.

The road passes the **Puente de S. Martín** (pedestrians only), of five spans, with a defensive tower at each end, the far one bearing an escutcheon and inscription dated 1690. It was begun in 1203 and restored at the end of the 18C. The story is told that during its construction the architect confided to his wife that when the timber centrings were removed the arches would fall. She forthwith set fire to them and, when the whole collapsed, the calamity was attributed to the 'accident'.

Just to the N on the far bank are the scanty remains of an ancient bridgehead known to romance as the *Baño de la Cava*. Here, according to the story,

Florinda or 'La Cava' (called Zoraide by the Moors), daughter of Count Julian, was bathing when seen from the terrace above by Roderic 'the Last of the Goths', who seduced her. Julian, who was governor of Ceuta, invited the Moors to assist him in avenging the outrage, but they, not stopping at the defeat of Roderic at the Guadalete in 711, swept N to occupy almost the whole peninsula.

The road which shortly forks left, known as the *Carretera de Circumvalación*, climbs through **Los Cigarrales** (from the Arabic *shagarăt*, the place of trees), an area dotted with villas often in extensive grounds. The best comprehensive views are commanded by these heights and from the Parador (the turning to which we shortly approach), from which a bird's eye view is obtained, although El Greco's well-known panorama was painted from the NW. The views are particularly striking towards sunset. We later descend towards a modern bridge over the Tagus. Near this on the far bank are the remains of the *Turbina Vargas*, waterworks on the site of the *Arteficio* devised by the engineer Juanelo Turriano in 1568, and, on the near side, relics of a Roman Aqueduct.

We now approach the pedestrian **Puente de Alcántara**, of two unequal spans, with a Rococo portal of 1721. Dating from 1259 and restored in 1484, it replaces a Moorish bridge (*el-kantara*, the bridge) of 871, itself the successor of a Roman structure destroyed in 854. At its W end is a square tower of 1484 bearing a statue of S. Ildefonso (to whom Felipe II dedicated the bridge in 1575) by Berruguete. Adjacent is the blocked *Puerta de Alcántara*, with remains of Visigothic work.

The road circles below the restored *Castle of S. Servando* (1384) and we turn left across the river, skirting a stretch of walls encircling the suburb of *La Antequeruela* to regain the Puerta de Bisagra.

To the E of this turning is the neo-Mudéjar *Railway Station*, overlooked by the modern buildings of the *Military Academy*. Beyond the station, to the left, is the restored '*Pal. de Galiana*', once a Moorish villa. Begun in the 11C, it preserves some 13C rebuilding and murals of c 1375. It stands on the *Huerta del Rey*, where at the Cortes held in 1085, the Cid denounced the Counts of Carrión to Alfonso VI for the outrages they had committed.

The shady PASEO DE MERCHAN, an alameda planted in 1628, extends NE from the Puerta de Bisagra to the unfinished **Hospital de Tavera** (or de *S. Juan Bautista*, or *de Afuera*, outside the walls). It was built in 1541–99 by Covarrubias and Bartolomé Bustamente for Card. Juan de Tavera (died 1545). A colonnade dividing the spacious classical patio leads through a handsome marble portal by Alonso de Berruguete to the chapel of 1624 by Gonzáles de Lara. Beneath the dome is the marble tomb of the cardinal, the last work of Berruguete, who died here in 1561 in the room under the clock.

The building contains a *Museum* founded by the Duchess of Lerma, a reconstruction of a noble mansion of the 16C with its contents, including some Flemish tapestries. The *Pharmacy* may be on view. The *Library*, with some bindings of interest, retains the archives of the hospital.

Among paintings are: works by *Luca Giordano* and *Bassano*; a 15C *Flemish Shipwreck caused by devils*; *Ribera*, Bearded Woman; *Tintoretto*, Holy Family; *Moro*, Marqués and Marquesa de las Navas; *Titian*'s copy of his Charles V at the Battle of Mühlberg; a fine secular Portrait by *Zurbarán* of the Duque de Medinaceli; *Carreño*, Card. Sandoval y Rojas, and the Duques de Ferias; and *El Greco*, S. Pedro, Baptism of Christ (his last work), portraits of Card. Tavera (restored), and a small polychrome wooden statue of Christ.

To the E in the suburb of *Las Covachuelas* are remains of a *Roman*

Amphitheatre.—Some distance to the W is the *Fábrica de Armas Blancas*, dating from 1777–83.

The manufacture of 'Toledo blades' is of unknown antiquity, being referred to in the 1C BC by Grattius Faliscus. Some peculiar virtue in the water and sand of the Tagus, used for tempering and polishing, is said to give the swords their pre-eminent quality, but more obvious is their damascened ornamentation. The custom of decorating arms and armour with gold incrustation was probably a Visigothic introduction, encouraged by the Moors. In the early 18C a former sword manufactory was apparently worked with the assistance of English tools, confiscated from English workmen who had been commissioned to raise water from the Tagus, and whose success raised the envy and jealousy of local engineers.

B. Puerta de Bisagra; Pl. de Zocodover; Hospital de Sta. Cruz; Alcázar

The enceinte is conveniently entered by passing round the *New* **Puerta de Bisagra**, a double gateway flanked by massive round towers dating from 1550. The roof tiles display the Imperial arms of Charles V.

The *Old* **Bisagra gate** or *Puerta de Alfonso VI* is a short distance W. It is the only 9C Moorish gate now surviving. Through it Alfonso VI and the Cid entered Toledo in 1085. Although it is partly built up and its arches and columns have been restored, its flanking towers are almost in their original state. Its name is derived from the Arabic *báb* (gate) and *sahra* (wasteland).

To the right is 13C **Santiago del Arrabal**, with a recessed brick façade and Moorish tower of c 1179. The interior contains unusual brick vaulting, a restored artesonado ceiling and arabesqued pulpit (14C).

The 16C door of *N.S. de la Estrella* is passed (right) as the C. Real del Arrabal circles to the E, shortly passing a turning to *Sto. Cristo de la Luz* (see Rte 43D), and ascends to the battlemented **Puerta del Sol**, a 12C Mudéjar gatehouse rebuilt in the 14C by the Hospitallers. The central structure, flanked by a square and semicircular tower, is decorated with interlaced arcades above. The tall outer Moorish arch is supported by two columns. Within this is a lower arch, above which is a 13C relief.—Adjacent is the *Torreón de Alarcón*.

Sta. Fé, with a 16C portal, is passed (left) on approaching the triangular PLAZA DE ZOCODOVER, deriving its name from the Arabic *sük ed-dawabb*, a horse market. Rebuilt when not restored since the Civil War, with its arcades and cafés it is still the centre of Toledan life and lounging as it was in the days of Cervantes.

On its E side is the rebuilt Moorish *Arco de la Sangre del Cristo*, from which steps descend to approach (left) the Hospital de Sta. Cruz.

In a lane to the left is the 16–17C portal of the *Conv. de Sta. Fé*. Its church has a Churrigueresque retablo and an 11C vaulted octagon from a Moorish palace.
Near by, in the C. de Cervantes, is the site of the *Posada de la Sangre* (rebuilt), where Cervantes is supposed to have written the novel 'La Ilustre Fregona'.

The ***Hospital de Sta. Cruz** is a remarkable Renaissance edifice built for Card. Pedro Mendoza in 1514 by Antón and Enrique de Egas, and continued by Covarrubias (1524–44). Above the ornate Portal (not by the Egas) is carved an Adoration of the Cross; the Mendoza arms adorn the patio. The Plateresque staircase, windows, and balustrade are notable, as are the Mudéjar artesonado ceilings. There is also a small patio containing Visigothic capitals from an earlier palace on this site. The lantern, destroyed in error by Republican bombs, has been replaced.

The great wards of the hospital, forming a cross of two storeys, now house the *Museo de Sta. Cruz, containing an extensive collection of Brussels' tapestries (including a series of the Life of Alexander the Great; early 17C), furniture, and ecclesiastical art originally assembled for an exhibition devoted to Charles V and his time.

In the wing opposite the entrance are the blue silk Standards of the Holy League and a smaller pennant flown at Lepanto (1571). Among paintings: an *anon.* 16C Hispano-Flemish triptych; *Morales*, Christ at the column; *Ribera*, Holy Family, and Descent from the Cross; *Orrente*, Self-portrait, and an Adoration; *Moro*, Calvary; an *anon.* Flemish diptych of the six children of Juana 'la Loca' and Felipe 'el Hermoso'; *Goya*, Crucifixion; *Pantoja*, Charles V; and among examples of the very uneven work of *El Greco*, Christ stripped of his raiment (a version of a painting in the cathedral), S. Nicolás; a fine Santiago, La Veronica, and an Assumption, finished in the last few months of his life. Among the sculpture note the Bust of Juanelo Turriano, the engineer, by *J.B. Monegro*; a marble Bust of a Cardinal, by *Nicolás de Busi*; and a polychromed wooden figure of St. Martin (16C).

The *Archaeological collection* is displayed in rooms surrounding the patio; these include Roman mosaics, one depicting fishing scenes (found near the Fábrica de Armas; see above); rope-worn marble Wellheads (early 11C), and baked clay Wellheads (14C); Mudéjar *tinajas* or storage jars; azulejos, carved beams, Visigothic capitals, etc. Collections of *Glass and Ceramics* may be seen in galleries on the floor above.

Below the Hospital and to the left is the *Conv. de la Concepción Francisca*, with a brick tower of c 1300. The gate at the left-hand corner admits to the *Cap. de S. Jerónimo*, a fine example of Mudéjar building on a small scale, with elaborate decoration and a domed ceiling inlaid with tiles (1422). The main church dates from 1484; the raised coro from 1573.

From opposite the Hospital, with a good view of the towering N front of the Alcázar, one may climb a lane zigzagging up to it. Alternatively, it may be approached by ascending from the SE corner of the Zocodover.

The massive **Alcázar**, with low towers at each corner, stands four-square on the highest point of Toledo.

The fort founded on this site by Alfonso VI after his capture of Toledo developed under his successors into a castle and royal palace, receiving the title of Alcázar in the reign of Fernando III. Charles V practically rebuilt it to its present dimensions. It has been thrice burned: in 1710, during the War of the Spanish Succession, by Count Starhemberg; in 1810 by the French on evacuating Toledo; and in 1887 by accident. In the 1780s its apartments were fitted up with spinning wheels and looms; from 1882 to 1936 it was occupied as a cadet school.

In 1936, on adhering to the Nationalists, the small garrison—most of the cadets being on summer leave—and a large civilian community were besieged under the commandant, Col. Moscardo, from 21 July to 28 September, when it was relieved by Gen. Varela. (No prisoners were taken by the Nationalists on entering Toledo, their Moroccan troops even killing the doctors and wounded militiamen remaining in its hospitals.) Gravely damaged by shell fire and mining, the ruined fortress was later virtually rebuilt.

The N façade was originally the work of Covarrubias (1535–51); the E façade, with Doric pilasters, exhibits the classic work of Herrera; the W façade, dating from the time of the Catholic Kings, has a portal added by Covarrubias. The central *Patio* (1559), surrounded by a Corinthian arcade of two storeys, contains a bronze group of Charles V as conqueror of Tunis, a copy of the original by Pompeo Leoni. At the S end is a wide state staircase designed for Charles V by Villalpando and Herrera; and it was of this that Charles exclaimed: 'When I climb it I feel myself to be truly Emperor'.

To the E are terraced gardens; a short distance to the SE is the late Mudéjar tower of *S. Miguel*.—To the W is the Mudéjar tower of *La Magdalena* (destroyed in 1936 and rebuilt in a different style), just beyond which is the *Corral de Don Diego*, with an interesting gateway, and remains of a 14C palace, with a well-preserved octagonal ceiling.

C. The Cathedral and the sector to the S of it

The narrow C. del Comercio leads SW from the Zocodover, later skirting the exterior of the cathedral cloister. Turn left here below the *Arco de Palacio* to enter the Pl. del Ayuntamiento, which is overlooked by the W front of the cathedral, best seen from its SW corner.

The *Cathedral, seat of the Primate of Spain, is mainly in the pure vigorous style of the 13C, with several later accretions. Its interior, although containing important paintings, and a number of fine features, is ostentatious to a fault. The Rev. Edward Clarke thoroughly disapproved of so much wealth 'so uselessly locked up . . . dormant riches, which a mistaken piety has so absurdly set apart for ever; which answers no rational purpose, and which neither serve to the glory of God, nor the good of man'.

The church on this site is said to have been founded in 587 by St. Eugenius, first bishop of Toledo under King Reccared. When they captured the city the Moors converted it into their chief mosque. When Alfonso VI took Toledo he guaranteed them the continued possession of their mosque, but during his absence in the following year Constance, his French consort, and Bernardo, the first archbishop, forcibly reclaimed it for Christian worship.
    Fernando III pulled down this building, and in 1227 laid the first stone of the present cathedral, French in inspiration, which was completed in 1493. The first architect was Maestro Martín (1227–34), succeeded by 'Petrus Petri' (died 1290), probably a Frenchman.
    In 1521 it was plundered by the Comuneros and in 1808 by the French under La Houssaye. Most of the treasures removed in 1936 have since been recovered

The W Façade, begun in 1418, consists of three portals: the central *Puerta del Perdón*; to the S, the *Puerta de los Escribanos* or *del Juicio*; to the N, the *Puerta de la Torre* or *del Infierno*. The bronze plates covering the door date from 1377.

The N Tower, 90m high, was begun in 1380 by Juan Alfonso, and continued by Álvar Martínez; the lantern and spire, encircled by three bands of horizontal rays symbolising the Crown of Thorns, were added in 1452 by Anequín de Egas.

The dome of the lower S Tower (1519; by Enrique de Egas) was designed by Jorge Manuel Theotocópulos (the son of El Greco) in 1631.

On the S Façade are the *Puerta Llana*, an incongruous design of 1800, and the *Puerta de los Leones* (1467; named from the shield-bearing lions on pillars in front of its deeply recessed portal), elaborately ornamented with sculptures and carvings by Anequín de Egas, Alfonso Fernández, and Juan Alemán. The bronze doors were begun in 1545 by Francisco de Villalpando, but the upper part was restored in the 18C.

The transeptal *Puerta del Reloj*, hemmed in by later dependencies on the N side, and also known as the *Puerta del Niño Perdido* or *de la Feria*, is the oldest door in the cathedral (c 1300).

The usual entrance is by the *Puerta de Mollete*, by the N Tower, which admits to the *Cloisters* (see p 317), but only the S walk of the lower cloister is public. Tickets are available for admission to the chapels, coro, sacristy, treasury, towers, etc., but these are likely to be closed between 13.00 and 15.30, although the rest of the cathedral is open all day.

Steps descend from the Renaissance *Puerta de la Presentación* (1568) into the dark *Nave* of seven bays. The double aisles are continued as a double ambulatory; the transepts do not project beyond the side walls, but terminate in portals beneath rose-windows. Eighty-eight piers formed of clustered shafts support the vaulting, and between the outer piers is a series of chapels.

The stained-glass windows date from 1418–1570, designed in the main by Jacob Dolfin (1418), Joachim of Utrecht (1429), Alberto de Holanda (1525), Nicolás de Vergara, and his sons (1550). The nave has a large clerestory and no triforium, but the transept has a triforium on its E side, and there is another in the chancel. The building accommodates ten organs, including one by Verdalanga and Echevarria (1755), and six portative or processional organs.

Beneath the cathedral extends a vast *Crypt*, with piers corresponding to those above.

The *respaldos* of the **Coro** are composed of elaborate 14C Gothic screens, the jasper pillars of which support an arcade of reliefs. On the trascoro, at the W end, are statues by Nicolás de Vergara. The reja which faces the Cap. Mayor is by Domingo de Céspedes (1547; originally silver-plated, but said to have been hastily and irrevocably coated with iron to preserve it from the French in 1808).

The walnut Stalls are regrettably badly lit. They are in two tiers; the tower, by Rodrigo Alemán (1495), is backed by 54 reliefs depicting the Conquest of Granada, of interest for the detail of costume and equipment. On the upper tier (completed 1543), the 35 stalls on the N side are by Vigarni; those on the S side and the archbishop's throne by Berruguete, who also carved the Transfiguration above the throne. The bronze and iron reading desks, with good reliefs, are by Nicolás de Vergara and his sons (1574); the lectern (1646; by Vicente Salinas) stands on a Gothic pedestal of 1425.

The **Cap. Mayor** was enlarged by Card. Cisneros in 1504. The remarkable reja (1549; by Villalpando) is flanked by two pulpits of gilt metal made from the bronze tomb prepared for himself by Álvaro de Luna, but broken up in 1449 by the Infante (later Enrique IV) in revenge for his defeat by De Luna at Olmedo. The huge Gothic *Retablo*, of carved, painted, and gilded larch, was completed in 1504 under the direction of Enrique de Egas and Pedro Gumiel.

Beneath Gothic canopies by Diego Copín on each side of the altar are the monuments of the Reyes Viejos (the old kings): on the left, Alfonso VII, Sancho II, and the Infante Sancho (son of Alfonso el Conquistador); also the Renaissance tomb of Card. Mendoza (1428–95; by Andrea el Florentino), with his effigy. On the right are monuments to Sancho II and the Infante Pedro (son of Alfonso VII).

The outer walls of the Cap. Mayor, begun in 1490 by Juan Güas, Anequín de Egas, and others, are embellished with statues (some old work reused) and reliefs in canopied niches in a setting of gilded foliage and arabesques. The theatrical Churrigueresque *Transparente*, described by Richard Ford as a 'fricassée of marble', is the work of Narciso Tomé (1732). It displays considerable technical ability although it is entirely out of harmony with its surroundings.

Opposite is the Gothic octagonal *Cap. de S. Ildefonso*, containing the mutilated monument of Card. Gil de Albornoz (died 1367), the tomb of his grand-nephew Bp Alonso Carrillo de Albornoz (died 1514; by Vasco de la Zarza), and, among others, that of Iñigo López Carrillo de Mendoza who died in 1491 at the siege of Granada.

To the S is the *Sala Capitular*, with an artesonado ceiling and Mudéjar portal of 1510. Its frescoes of 1511 are by Juan de Borgoña. Of the 'portraits' of archbishops only those after Card. Cisneros have any claims to authenticity.

To the N is the Flamboyant Gothic *Cap. de Santiago* (1450) erected by Count Álvaro de Luna, master of the Order of Santiago, as his family burial place. It is embellished with his crescent moon and Santiago's scallop. In the centre are the altar tombs with effigies of Álvaro (died 1453) and his wife, Juana de Pimentel. Their portraits also appear on either side of the central panel of the retablo.

A passage adjacent leads to the Plateresque *Cap. de los Reyes Nuevos* (1534; by Alonso de Covarrubias), with monuments (right) of Enrique II (died 1379) and his wife, Juana; and (left) Enrique III (died 1407) and his wife Catherine of Lancaster (died 1418; daughter of John of Gaunt). The kneeling statue by Juan de Borgoña is of Juan II (died 1454; buried at the Cartuja de Miraflores, Burgos). In the choir are statues by Jorge de Contreras of Juan I (died 1390) and his wife, Leonor; the altarpiece is by Maella.

The **Sacristia** (1616; by Nicolás de Vergara) has a ceiling fresco by Luca Giordano. The Christ stripped of his raiment, on the altarpiece, is an early work (1579) by El Greco, who also painted the Apostles round the walls. Here also are *Goya*, Christ taken by the soldiers; *Orrente*, Nativity; and *Bassano*, the Deluge.—The adjoining *Vestuario* contains *Bassano*, Nativity, and Circumcision; *El Greco*, St. Francis; *Giovanni Bellini*, Burial of Christ; and *Van Dyck*, Holy Family, and Clement VII.

Adjacent to the W is the *Cap. de la Virgen del Sagrario* (1606; by Nicolás de Vergara the younger), containing an ancient image, off which is the *Ochavo* (1630; by J.B. Monegro), containing reliquaries, to which the Treasury may be moved. This is at present in the *Cap. de S. Juan* below the N tower, a Renaissance chapel with an elaborate roof, constructed by Alonso de Covarrubias in 1537.

It contains a Sword said to have belonged to Alfonso VI, and another of Sancho IV; the cross and ring of Card. Cisneros; the silver-gilt Cruz de la Manga (16C; by Gregorio de Varona of Toledo); the Cross planted by Card. Mendoza on the captured Alhambra in 1492; and a silver-gilt Custodia (1524; by Enrique de Arfe), among other cult objects.

The **Cap. Mozárabe** below the S tower, erected in 1504 by Enrique de Egas, has a reja by Juan Francés (1524) and glass of 1513 by Juan de la Cuesta displaying the arms of Card. Cisneros, its founder. He also planned, defrayed, and headed in person the Oran campaign (1509), depicted in fresco on the W wall by Juan de Borgoña (1514).

Swinburne, badly served by his guide, remarked: 'Ask them anything about the Mozarabic chapel, and what is done there, they will tell you, as they did us, that mass is said there in Greek'.

The *Mozarabic liturgy*, the original national liturgy of the Spanish church, which is celebrated in this chapel, is of Visigothic origin. It is so-called because it was preserved by the Mozarabic Christians in the churches, including six in Toledo, allowed to them by the tolerant Moors. Not founded on the Roman use, and differing from it in various points, it is characterised by its simplicity and by the number and length of its hymns. Cisneros, who established the service here, did much to preserve the ritual from oblivion.

According to the story, the rival claims of the Visigothic and Roman ritual were subjected to trial by combat under Alfonso VI in 1086. The Mozarabic knight was victorious. An ordeal by fire was then demanded, which took place in the Zocodover, when the Mozarabic missal remained unconsumed in the flames and the Roman missal leaped beyond their range. Since neither was injured, both were adjudged authoritative.

The *Cloisters* have two storeys, the lower begun by Abp Tenorio (died 1399), whose tomb, by Fernán González, is in the *Cap. de S. Blas*, at its NE corner; the upper was added by Card. Cisneros. The frescoes on the walls are by Bayeu and Maella.

In the N walk is the **Cathedral Library**, preserving important MSS, notably musical, but special permission is required to view them. Little has changed since Edward Clarke remarked that 'they do not much care to show their library, and less to print a catalogue . . . less they should disclose how rich they are: politically apprehending, perhaps not without reason, that if others were let into the secret, they might possibly like to have a greater share in these treasures than would be agreeable'. Ford noted that although the library contained some fine things, 'nothing is more unsatisfactory than a hurried *looking* at books . . . and especially when a hungry and siestose canon is yawning at your elbow, and repenting of having unlocked the prison-door'.

The upper cloister is connected to the 18C *Archbishop's Palace* by an archway spanning the street; its Sala de los Concilios has a rich artesonado.

The restored *Ayuntamiento*, on the SW side of the plaza, built under the Catholic Kings, was altered in 1599–1618 by Jorge Manuel Theotocópulos.

Behind the E end of the cathedral is the *Posada de la Hermandad*. Its late 15C doorway is a relic of the prison of the Hermandad, a civic brotherhood established in the 13C to deal with robbers and murderers.—To the N, beyond the undistinguished *Pl. Mayor*, are the restored remains of a mosque on Visigothic foundations (27–31 C. de la Tornerías).
From the SE corner of the cathedral one may approach (SE) *SS. Justo y Pastor*, with a Mudéjar apse of c 1300, S of which is a relic of *S. Juan de la Penitencia* (1511), burnt in 1936. Lanes descend to late 13C Mozarabic *S. Lucas* (restored), to the W of which is *S. Pablo*, Renaissance with Gothic vaults. Further NW is *S. Lorenzo*, skirted by the quaint C. Bajada al Barco (which leads back to the cathedral).

From the S end of the Pl. del Ayuntamiento the C. de Sta. Isabel leads to the *Conv. de Sta. Isabel de los Reyes* (founded in 1477 in two Ayala Mansions), with a good artesonado and a stuccoed room of 1449.— Adjacent is Mudéjar *S. Antolín* (14C).—To the SE is *S. Andrés*, with a sanctuary of 1513 by Juan de Borgoña, a retablo by Francisco de Amberes, and Mozarabic ceilings.—Further S is the *Seminario Menor* in a 14C Mudéjar mansion with Plateresque additions.

SW of Sta. Isabel is 14C *S. Bartolomé*, with a brick apse. To the extreme S is Mozarabic *S. Sebastián*, founded c 602 and retaining Visigothic columns, although rebuilt in the 13C. To the W is *S. Cipriano*, rebuilt in 1613.

D.   SW Toledo: Taller del Moro; Sto. Tomé; Casa del Greco; El Tránsito; Sta. María la Blanca; S. Juan de los Reyes

From the S side of the Pl. del Ayuntamiento (by the cathedral) follow the street bearing W. It shortly passes (left) *Sta. Úrsula*, a Mudéjar work of 1360 altered in the 16C, to reach *El Salvador*, built on the site of a mosque. From its far side turn right to enter the *•**Taller del Moro**, part of a late 14C building consisting of one large and two small rooms, retaining some of its original decoration. It was once used as a workshop (*taller*) for the cathedral masons, and now houses a small collection of carved woodwork and azulejos, and a 12C inscription on stone in both Latin and Arabic.

It is also traditionally connected with the massacre known as 'The Day of the Ditch'. The Moorish governor (a renegade Christian) invited, it is said, the leading Christian nobles and citizens to a banquet here, admitting them one by one. As each entered his head was struck off and his body rolled into a ditch, until 400 in all were slain; thus the proverbial expression 'Noche Toledana' for a restless night (cf. Sala de la Campana, Huesca).

Adjoining—and approached across a garden—is the 15C *Palace of the Conde de Fuensalida*, in which Isabel of Portugal, wife of Charles V, died in 1537. The fine two-storey patio preserves some Mudéjar decoration.
Adjacent is **Sto. Tomé** (1300–20), its interior restored in the 18C, with a Mudéjar tower. The burial of Gonzalo Ruiz, Conde de Orgaz, took place in this church in 1323. El Greco's famous *•Painting* of the event, now cleaned, is displayed in an annexe.

The figures bearing the corpse represent St. Stephen and St. Augustine, who appeared at the ceremony to honour the count's piety in founding the church. The bystanders are portraits of distinguished citizens of Toledo at the time of its painting (1584–88) and include El Greco himself, Alonso de Covarrubias (6th and 4th from the right), and Diego de Covarrubias (above St. Stephen). The acolyte is said to be Jorge Manuel, the artist's son.

Turning SW along the C. de S. Juan de Dios, we shortly pass (left) the **Casa del Greco**, owing its name to the fact that the artist lived and died (1614) in part of the palace which formerly stood here. There are vaults of Roman masonry below the building, and the garden patio contains fragments of archaeological interest. The house (restored in a fake 16C style) contains a somewhat miscellaneous collection of paintings, among them, by *El Greco*: View of Toledo (not to be confused with the more famous 'Storm over Toledo' in the Metropolitan Museum, New York), Christ, Twelve Apostles, Crucifixion, St. Peter, St. Francis, and portraits of Juan de Ávila, Alonso de Covarrubias, and his son Bp Covarrubias.

Other works include: *Velázquez*, Four sketches; *Murillo*, Sta. Bárbara; *Carreño*, Mariana of Austria, Carlos II; *Pantoja*, Felipe II; *Herrera el Viejo*, St. Andrew, and other saints; *Zurbarán*, Lament of St. Peter; *Tristán*, Crucifixion; *Del Mazo*, Mariana of Austria.

Adjacent is the ***Sinagoga del Tránsito**, built in the Moorish style of 1366 for Samuel Levi, treasurer of Pedro the Cruel.

Despite the influence of Pedro's mistress, María de Padilla, who was well-inclined towards Levi, their connection was terminated by Pedro executing him and seizing his wealth. After the expulsion of the Jewish community Isabel the Catholic presented the building to the Order of Calatrava, and it was dedicated first to St. Benedict and later to the Death of the Virgin (*el Tránsito*). After decades of neglect, work on its restoration was started in the mid 17C at the instigation of Francisco Pérez Bayer, the Hebrew scholar.

The galleried interior has no aisles; the frieze displays the arms of Castile and León. The Moorish arcade above, the arabesques, and the Hebrew inscriptions in praise of God, of Don Pedro, and of Levi, should be noted. Several Jewish tombstones date from the 14C. The building also houses a small *Sephardic Museum and Library*, and a map indicates the situation of all Jewish communities in Spain prior to 1492.

The C. de los Reyes Catolicos leads NW through the former *Judería*, in which two synagogues remain of at least seven (in 1391), to approach (right) the former *Ibn Shoshan synagogue*, now ***Sta. María la Blanca**.

Founded in 1203 and rebuilt after a fire in 1250, it was at the instigation of S. Vicente Ferrer seized by the Christians in the first decade of the 15C. It was put later to a variety of lay uses, among them as a refuge for reformed prostitutes, a barracks and store (in 1791–98), and a carpenter's workshop.

The interior has double aisles, separated by octagonal pillars with capitals moulded in plaster and ornamented with fir cones, etc. Above are Moorish arches. On the bases of some of the columns, the altar steps, and the pavement, are ancient azulejos. The doors and ceiling are of larch. The sanctuary dates from c 1550; the retablo is by Bautista Vázquez and Nicolás Vergara the elder (1556).

A few paces beyond is ***S. Juan de los Reyes**, the church of a Franciscan convent founded by the Catholic Kings in commemoration of the dispersal of the La Beltraneja faction at Toro in 1476 (and, before the conquest of Granada, intended as their burial place; cf. Capilla Real, Granada). The first architect was Juan Güas, and the main structure was completed in 1492; the NW Façade, begun by Covarrubias in 1553, was not finished until 1610. The exterior of the apse is richly decorated, and hung with the fetters of Christian captives released during the final stages of the Granada campaign.

Detail of the frieze in the Sinagoga del Tránsito, Toledo

The two-storeyed *Cloister* of 1510 is among the richest examples of Florid Gothic in Spain. The *Church*, restored after being damaged by the French in 1808, consists of an aisleless nave flanked by chapels, around which it runs a frieze of Gothic lettering referring to its foundation. By the last pillars in the nave are openwork tribunes bearing the interlaced initials of Fernando and Isabel. In the shallow transepts are statues of saints, between which are the escutcheons of Castile and Aragón, surmounted by eagles' heads and surrounded by the emblems of the Catholic Kings. The Cap. Mayor of 1552 is by Felipe Vigarni and Francisco de Comontes. The pulpit, entered from a passage in the wall, is supported by a petrified palm stem.

A short distance further NW is the **Puerta del Cambrón**, 'the gate of the thornbush', the Moorish *Báb-el-Makara*. It was rebuilt by Alfonso VI, but in its present form, with four towers, it dates from a reconstruction in 1576.

To the E is the Neo-Classical *Asylum* (1793; by Ignacio Haan), commonly known as *El Nuncio* from an earlier one founded on the site by the Papal Nuncio in 1493.

E.   NW Toledo: S. Román;
Sto. Cristo de la Luz

From *S. Juan de los Reyes* (see above) follow the C. del Angel E to the N front of Sto. Tomé and turn left along the narrow C. Campana and C. de Alfonso XII to reach the small Pl. Padre Mariana. (This may also be approached from the NW side of the Ayuntamiento by following an alley across the C. Trinidad.)

The C.S Román leads left off the plaza past (right) 17C *S. Juan Bautista* and (left) Dominican *S. Pedro Mártir*, mainly 16C, with tombs (including that of the poet Garcilaso de la Vega; died 1536) and monuments from other buildings.

A few steps further brings one to **'S. Román**, consecrated in 1221. It has a Mudéjar tower (before 1166) and restored 13C murals. Probably built on the site of a Visigothic church later converted into a mosque, it combines Christian and Moorish elements in a way that makes it one of the more interesting and important Mudéjar churches in Toledo. It also houses a *Museum of Visigothic Art*, with a section covering the 6C Councils of Toledo and a lapidary collection.

A short distance downhill to the left is the imposing cloister of a convent, now a school.—Opposite the entrance is the *Conv. de S. Clemente* with a Renaissance doorway by Alonso de Covarrubias, beyond which is the Pl. de Padilla.

To the W is *Sta. Eulalia*, a Mozarabic church founded in 589 and retaining Visigothic columns and horseshoe arches.—A few paces to the N of the plaza is *Sto. Domingo el Antiguo* (1576; by Herrera and Vergara), the burial place of El Greco, with three paintings ascribed to his early period.

Turning E from the plaza along the C. Esteban Illán, we pass at No. 9 (if closed, apply next door) the **'Casa de Mesa**, with remains of an early 15C Mudéjar mansion. The interior, consisting of a saloon and smaller rooms, is exquisitely decorated in the Moorish style (after the school of Granada), with delicate and complicated relief work on the walls, fretted windows, friezes, and artesonados. Note the band of 16C azulejos around the base of the walls.

Continuing E, the *Instituto* (1799; the former *University*) is passed on the left. Beyond is *S. Vicente* (1595).

A lane to the N leads to the *Conv. de Sta. Clara*, with an altarpiece of 1623 by Luis Tristán. Beyond, to the left, is Baroque *Sto. Domingo el Real*, with a Gothic cloister.

On the SE side of the Pl. de S. Vicente are the 17C buildings of the *Conv. de las Gaitanas*. On the E side is a 16C doorway on which is carved the cord of St. Francis (on the façade of the present Post Office).

The Cuesta de las Carmelitas descends steeply to the NE to **'Sto. Cristo de la Luz**, formerly the miniature mosque of *Báb-el-Mardom*. It is one of the earliest examples surviving of Moorish architecture in Spain, built by Musa ibn Ali in 999 probably on the site of a Visigothic chapel, of which it incorporates some capitals.

The name refers to the legend that at the capture of Toledo Babieca, the Cid's charger, knelt before the mosque and refused to move until the wall was opened, when a recess revealed a crucifix and a still-burning lamp. The first mass in the reconquered city was forthwith celebrated here, and Alfonso VI hung his shield above the altar.

The interior is divided into nine square compartments, the remarkable vaults of which, formed by intersecting ribs, vary in design. In the middle are four low round columns with sculptured capitals, from which spring heavy horseshoe arches. The transept and apse were added in the late 12C and contain remains of wall paintings.

A few paces downhill brings one to the C. Real del Arrabal a short distance from the *Puerto de Bisagra*.

44 Madrid to Cuenca

A. Via Tarancón

164km (102 miles). NIII. 81km *Tarancón*—N400. 83km **Cuenca**.

Maps: M 444.

The NIII drives SE through new suburbs and across an uninteresting grey countryside, at 20km crossing the Jarama.

It was in the area SE from here that the *Battle of the Jarama* took place in February 1937. The Abraham Lincoln and British Battalions of the International Brigade saw action, but it resulted in a stalemate.

Chinchón (Parador), 26km S, may be approached from the next right-hand fork. (Although described here, it may be more conveniently visited together with Aranjuez in a day-trip from Madrid.) The M302 crosses the Tajuña at 16km and climbs to Chinchón, with a picturesque, if over-restored, *Plaza Mayor*, overlooked by a 16C church containing a painting attributed to Goya. Immediately SW of the plaza is a 17C Augustinian convent, well-restored to house the Parador. Remains of a castle lie further SW; there is another at *Casasola*, 4km NW. Quinine derives its name *Chinchona* after a Marquesa de Chinchón had discovered its properties. 'Chinchón', the local *aguardiente*, is based on aniseed.—5km SE is *Colmenar de Oreja* (5050 inhab.), a larger village, also with a characteristic plaza, and 16C church. From Colmenar a road leads 22km SW to *Aranjuez*, while the NIII may be regained 13km NE.

At 7km **Arganda** (22,050 inhab.) is bypassed. It has a transformed castle of 1400 and a church of 1525 with Churrigueresque altars.— The road descends to (11km) *Perales de Tajuña*. At Perales and in the area between it and Carabaña (11km E), prehistoric, Celtiberian, and Roman remains have been found. The 15C church at *Carabaña* contains a Renaissance retablo and good monuments.

The road climbs past the *Peñas Gordas* (794m) and bypasses (11km) *Villarejo de Salvanés*, with a 13C church and old castle keep. It descends into the valley of the Tagus, at 12.5km passing the ruined 11C castle of *Fuentedueña del Tajo*.—Ascending again, at 19.5km **Tarancón** (9600 inhab.) is bypassed. Its church has an elaborate but mutilated late Gothic façade.

It was the birthplace of Melchor Cano (1509–60), the theologian, and Agustín Fernando Muñoz (1808?–73), a guardsman with whom María Cristina contracted a morganatic marriage shortly after the death of Fernando VII, and who she created Duque de Riansares (after the neighbouring river).—Lorenzo Hervás y Panduro (1735–1809), the polymath, was born at *Horcajo de Santiago*, 20km due S.

For the road on to *Valencia* see Rte 46.

Turning left onto the N400, we now strike E to (26km) *Carrascosa del Campo*, sacked in 1808, and the centre of a depopulated region of the SERRANÍA. Its church has an ornate 16C portal.

13km N is **Huete**, ancient *Istonium* and Moorish *Webde*, with a ruined castle (besieged by the Almohads in 1172) and a 13C *Bishop's palace*. Among several churches, *S. Esteban* has a handsome coro, *S. Lorenzo Justiniano* a good façade, and *Sto. Domingo* a 15C tomb.

The road climbs through attractive wooded country past (11km) *Huelves*, with an early castle, to (39km) the *Puerto de Cabrejas* (1150m). It then descends into the valley of the Júcar, at 12km meeting the N320 from Priego (see Rte 44B), and 6km beyond enters Cuenca. See below for approaches to the *old* town.

   CUENCA (923m; 40,000 inhab.; 13,000 in 1920) is a modern but somewhat isolated provincial capital. Above it, romantically sited on a rocky spur, is the picturesque medieval nucleus, cut off from the Serranía de Cuenca by the deep defiles of the Júcar and its tributary the Huécar. Old walls and towers overhang both streams, and from its seven gates narrow lanes wind up towards the cathedral.

Roman *Conca* was given by Mutamid, king of Sevilla, to Alfonso VI as the dowry of his daughter Zaida. The city later rebelled but was subdued in 1177 by Alfonso VIII after a nine-month siege. Its influential *fueros* date from 1189/90. It was a centre of the wool trade in the medieval period. In 1808–11 Cuenca was three times sacked by the French, and in 1873–74 by the Carlists. In 1936 the cathedral library was set alight and 10,000 volumes perished, including the 'Catecismo de Indias'.
   Cuenca was the birthplace of Card. Gil de Albornoz (c 1310–67, died at Viterbo), the papal general; Alonso de Hojeda (c 1468–1515), a companion of Columbus and explorer of Guiana; Andrés Hurtado de Mendoza (c 1490–1561), viceroy of Peru; and Hernán Yáñez de Almedina (fl. 1500–20), the artist.

The easiest approach to the old town is to remain on the N400 and not fork right towards the modern town. On the N bank of the river is the 14C *Conv. de S. Antón*, with a 16C Plateresque doorway and church with an elliptical dome. Turn right across the *Puente de S. Antón* and bear left, skirting the gardens of the Pl. de Trinidad, and turn left. See below for the new town.
   On crossing the tributary Huécar the C. Palafox (later the C. Andrés de Cabrera and C. Alfonso VII) climbs up to the *Pl. Mayor*, entered by passing through the arches supporting the *Ayuntamiento* of 1760; see below.

To the SW are late 17C *La Merced* and the *Seminario*, with a 17C portal. Beyond is the *Torre de Mangana*, a relic of Moorish fortifications.

Modern Cuenca has few monuments of interest. Keep ahead at the Pl. de Trinidad to enter the main Avenida, in which are the *Beneficencia Municipal* of 1777 and, further on (right), the *Hosp. de Santiago*, a 15C foundation. At the end of the street is a triangular plaza flanked by 14C *S. Francisco* (or *S. Estebán*), containing 18C sculpture.
   The C. Aguirre leads S of the central PARQUE DE S. JULIÁN towards the *Puerta de Valencia*, adjacent to the riverside C. Tintes. After crossing the Huécar here one may climb up stepped lanes into the old town. Or turn right to follow the riverbank to a point below the *Casas Colgadas*, which may be reached from here, where another bridge re-crosses the Huécar to approach *S. Pablo*; see below.

To the right of the Pl. Mayor is the cathedral; ahead the *Conv. de las Petras*, with an elliptical church designed by Ventura Rodríguez and

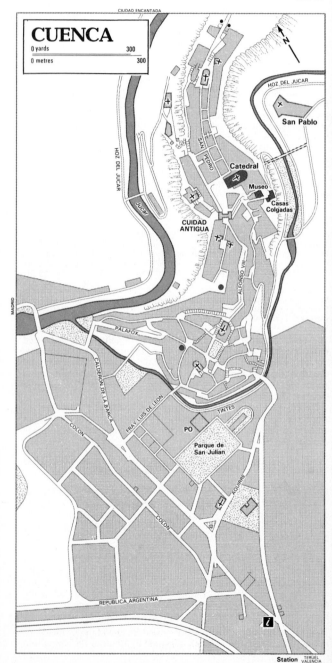

CIUDAD ENCANTADA

CUENCA

| 0 yards | 300 |
| 0 metres | 300 |

HOZ DEL JUCAR

San Pablo

HOZ DEL JUCAR

Jucar

SAN PEDRO

Catedral

Museo

Casas
Colgadas

CUIDAD
ANTIGUA

MADRID

ALFONSO VIII

PALAFOX

CALDERON DE LA BARCA

FRAY LUIS DE LEON

COLON

TINTES

PO

Parque de
San Julian

AGUIRRE

COLON

REPUBLICA ARGENTINA

Station   TERUEL
VALENCIA

Alejandro González Velázquez; to the SW an alley leads down to restored *S. Miguel*; another to the NW descends to the *Conv. de los Descalzos*, overlooking the Júcar gorge, and beyond to the chapel of *N.S. de las Angustias*.

The **Cathedral** (best seen in the morning) was founded by Alfonso VII. The W Front, clumsily rebuilt in the 1660s, has been tastelessly restored (after a plan made by Vicente Lampérez) since the partial collapse of the N tower in 1902, but the old doors with their bronze bosses survive.

The nave (c 1208–50), crossing, and the W part of the choir (1208) are simple Gothic work, containing features of Anglo-Norman character. The capitals and vault above the crossing are noteworthy. The apse is an elaborate late Gothic construction (1448–90; perhaps to the design of Anequín de Egas) with a strong suggestion of Moorish influence in the shape of the arches and the arrangement of the columns. The clerestory of the nave has widely spaced interior tracery, and in the rose-window of the N transept is good stained glass; little of the other glass merits attention. The 18C organ is by Julián de la Orden.

The modernised *Coro* has a reja and eagle lectern by Hernando de Arenas (1557) and 18C stalls. The high altar of 1785 is a commonplace classical composition by Ventura Rodríguez; the Virgin is by Pedro de Mena. The S transept contains 15–16C tombs of the Montemayor family. On the S side of the ambulatory are the Sagrario and *Sacristy*, with a remarkable vault, and sculptures by Pedro de Mena. The adjoining *Sala Capitular*, with a Plateresque portal and coarsely over-painted artesonado, contains carved walnut doors and stalls. The *Treasury* preserves medieval plate, a fine Byzantine diptych, and among paintings, two by El Greco, and a Crucifixion attributed to Gerard David.

The E chapel retains an outstanding artesonado. The large *Cap. de los Caballeros* contains two retablos by Hernán Yáñez, tombs of the Albornoz family, and a door of 1546 by Xamete, a Frenchman, also responsible for the Plateresque portal decorated with Christian and pagan motives at the end of the N transept.

The *Cloister* (1583) was designed by Juan Andrés Rodi; off it is the Mendoza chapel with the tomb of Diego Hurtado de Mendoza (died 1566), viceroy of Siena.

Opposite the 16C *Bishop's Palace*, SE of the cathedral, is a mansion housing the *Museo Provincial*, with archaeological collections of interest, including finds from Valeria (35km S) and Segóbriga (q.v.).

A lane leads to the *Casas Colgadas* (hanging houses), corbelled out over the gorge of the Huécar. They contain the tastefully designed private *Museum of Abstract Art*, opened in 1966 and since extended (and with a restaurant). It displays frequently changed exhibitions of representative works by contemporary Spanish artists.

Beyond, to the left, is the dizzy *Puente de S. Pablo*, a footbridge 105m long. It was thrown over the gorge in 1903, at a height of 45m, for the convenience of the Dominicans of *S. Pablo*, the 16C convent seen on the opposite bank.

It is worth continuing the ascent from the Pl. Mayor to the round 17C church of *S. Pedro* and beyond to the battered *Puerta del Castillo*, and descending steps to the right towards a wilderness of rocks for the sake of the *Views* of the old town, with its perpendicular cliffs of houses, and the Huécar far below.

For the '*Ciudad Encantada*' see Rte 45B.

Travellers wishing to regain the Valencia road may follow N420 bearing SW into the Júcar valley via (29km) *Baños de Valdeganga*, crossing the river alongside a hump-backed Roman bridge 4km beyond, to meet the NIII 32km further SW at *La Almarcha*.

CUENCA TO MOTILLA DE PALANCAR (69km), also on the Valencia road, but 47km
further SE; but see below. The N320 leads SE, at 8km reaching a turning (right)
for adjacent *Arcas*, with a Romanesque church (? Celtiberian *Arcavica*).

A DETOUR may be made by following a minor road (CU712) S from Arcas to
(25km) *Valera de Arriba* and the ruins of Roman *Valera*, important enough to
have a mint, and still under excavation. There are remains of a castle and
church on a wind-blown height. It was a bishop's see until the 8C. Another
church contains the alabaster tomb of Hernando de Alarcón (died 1582). The
main road is regained 14km E.

The N320 bypassing Arcas crosses the *Puerto de Tórdiga* (1200m) to (41km)
Almodóvar del Pinar, its church preserving good sculptures.—Here either bear
right to (20km) *Motilla* or fork left for (16km) *Campillo de Altobuey*, with the
Conv. de S. Agustín. At Campillo de Altobuey veer SE via *Puebla del Salvador*,
with a 16C church, to meet the NIII at (22km) *Minglanilla*.

B.   Via Guadalajara

209km (129 miles). NII. 31km **Alcalá de Henares**—25km
Guadalajara—N320. 57km *Sacedón*—90km N400—6km **Cuenca**.

Maps: M 444.

For the road to Guadalajara see Rte 72; for **Guadalajara**, Rte 15.

For an ALTERNATIVE but crosscountry road from Madrid to *Sacedón* follow the
NIII to (27km) *Arganda* (see Rte 44A), there turning N onto the C300 to (10km)
Loeches. Here are the palace and *Dominican Convent* (1636–64) to which in
1643 the Conde-Duque de Olivares retired disgraced by Felipe IV, and where
he was buried in 1645, having meanwhile been exiled to Toro.—The M211
leads E to (16km) **Nuevo Baztán**, an interesting early 18C experiment by Juan
de Goyeneche in land settlement and town planning, with an enormous *Church*
by José Churriguera, completed in 1722. The same architect was responsible for
the layout of the village, its plaza, and other public buildings (1709–13).—The
M253 leads down to cross the Tajuña for (16km) *Mondéjar*. Its parish church of
1516 has a tower of 1560. The beautiful doorway of ruined Gothic *S. Antônio*
(1487–1509) is one of the earliest in Castile to show Renaissance decorative
motifs. We continue E, at 9km forking left to meet the C200 and the Tagus at
13.5km.—**Pastrana**, 7.5km to the left, was the birthplace of Juan Bautista Maino
(1581–1649), the artist. The Gothic *Colegiata* contains a retablo by Juan de
Borgoña, the tombs of Ana Mendoza de la Cerda, Princess of Éboli, and her
family, good choir stalls, a rich treasury, and magnificent *Tapestries* woven in
the 15C to record the taking of Tangier and Arzila by the Portuguese, but some
have been cut down to fit round furniture. (Modern copies are displayed in the
Paço dos Duques at Guimarães, Portugal.) The ducal *Palace* at Pastrana (begun
in 1541) is being restored. Here the one-eyed princess was confined from 1581
until her death in 1592 on account of her liaison with Antonio Pérez, Felipe II's
secretary.—Turning right at this junction, the C204 bearing NE for (29km)
Sacedón forks left after 1.5km.—The right fork leads past the nuclear power
station of *Zorita da los Canes*. Near by is a restored castle surrounding a small
Romanesque church, and on the neighbouring *Cerro de la Oliva* are remains of
the Visigothic city of *Recopolis* (c 580).—4km beyond are the ancient walled
village of *Almonacid de Zorita* and adjacent *Albalate*, with a good 16C hall-
church with reticulated vaults.

From the Guadalajara bypass turn SE onto the N320 into the district
known as LA ALCARRIA. At 6km the monastery of *S. Bartolomé* at
Lupiana, founded in 1370, and the mother house of the Hieronymite
Order, lies to the left. The ruined church was completed in 1632, and
an impressive three-storeyed Renaissance cloister survives (the
dependencies are now private property, but may be visited on
application).

The village of *Horche* is shortly bypassed. It has a 15C church.—11km *Armuña de Tajuña*, with a ruined castle and fortified church.—7km to the SW is *Aranzueque*, with a Plateresque church. The N320 veers E through (6km) *Tendilla*, with an arcaded main street. About 4km beyond, to the right, are the ruins of the 17C *Conv. de la Salceda*.—Beyond (11km) *Alhóndiga* the road descends into the valley of the Tagus, crossed to enter (19km) *Sacedón*, its a Renaissance hall-church with fine Gothic vaulting.

To the N is the *Embalse de Entrepeñas*; 5km to the S, the bank of the extensive *Embalse de Buendia*, also known as 'El Mar de Castilla'. We wind over the hills and through (9km) *Córcoles*, with a 15C church and the ruined Benedictine monastery of *Monsalud*, of which the 13C Chapterhouse and tombs in the 16C cloister are noteworthy.—9km *Alcócer*, with remains of a castle and ramparts. Ungainly *Sta. María* has a Romanesque W doorway, nave of 1260, and a late Gothic crossing and sanctuary.—The road shortly bears SE across an arm of the reservoir, here fed by the Guadiela, to (26km) *Cañaveras*.

20km NE, spectacularly sited above the Escabas, is **Priego**, with a 16C church rebuilt after being set alight by Carlists.—3km beyond is the remote *Conv. de S. Miguel*, with 18C statues by Carmona.

The N320 crosses the SIERRA DE BASCUÑANA, rising to the E to 1388m, and meets the N400 after 46km, 6km W of **Cuenca**; see Rte 44A.

45 Cuenca to Teruel

A. Via Cañete

152km (94 miles). N420—71km *Cañete*—43km. *Ademuz* lies 6km S.—38km **Teruel**.

Maps: M 444.

The road leads SE. At 11km a by-road climbs E through pine woods to (10km) *Las Torcas*, and the first of a series of about 25 *torcas* or large sinkings in the ground due to the action of subterranean rivers: they vary from 45m to c 700m in width and from 10m to 75m in depth.

The main road climbs across the *Puerto de Rocho* (1150m), at 20km passing S of the ruined castle of *Cañada del Hoyo*, and 9km beyond *Carboneras*, with remains of a former Dominican convent, is bypassed.

A by-road circles SE from here to (23km) *Cardenete*, where the church has an artesonado roof 43m long; its castle dates from 1522.—18km further SE, on the W bank of the *Embalse de Contreras*, stands the ruined castle of *Enguidanos*.—17km NE of Cardenete, near *Villar del Humo*, are caves preserving prehistoric rock paintings.

The picturesque N420 veers NE past the marble quarries of *Pajaroncillo* (left) and follows the *Valley of the Cabriel*, here in an impressive pine-shaded gorge of tumbled rock.

31km **Cañete**, a small walled town, commanded by a mid 15C

castle of the Constable Álvaro de Luna. Beyond Cañete turn E
through broken country, at 43km reaching the turning for **Ademuz**,
6km S.

At the entrance of this ancient hillside village of narrow medieval alleys is a
curious twin-domed church, Romanesque on Moorish foundations.

The main road turns NE, with the *Javalambre* (2020m) rising some
distance to the E. The road threads the defile of the Turia, passing the
medieval tower of *Torre Alta* to (23.5km) *Villel*, with ruins of a castle
on an isolated peak. It was the birthplace of Francisco Tadeo
Calomarde (1773–1842), the reactionary minister of Fernando VII.
    The road provides a good view of the curious geological formation
of the surrounding hills as we approach (14.5km) **Teruel**; see Rte 73.

B. Via Albarracín

153km (95 miles). CU921. 30km. *La Ciudad Encantada* lies 5km
S.—35km. *Tragacete* lies 5km NW—43km **Albarracín**—TE901.
45km **Teruel**.

Maps: M 444.

This attractive alternative route crossing the *Montes Universales*—
not recommended in winter—is followed by turning right at the N
end of the *Puente de S. Antón* (see p 323). Drive N up the picturesque
valley of the Júcar past (21.5km) *Villalba de la Sierra*, there crossing
the river and climbing E through pine woods.

At 8.5km a right turn leads in 5km to **La Ciudad Encantada**, a geological
curiosity so-called from the fantastic forms into which the cretaceous rock has
been weathered: streets, buildings, monsters, and the like.—The by-road leads
S back to (25km) *Cuenca*.

The main road continues to follow the gorge of the Júcar through the
SERRANÍA DE CUENCA, at 35km turning right 5km SE of the characteristic mountain village of *Tragacete* to climb across the *Puerto de El
Cubillo* (1620m), and turning right again past (15.5km) the *Source of
the Tagus* (the *Tajo* in Spanish, which reaches the Atlantic at Lisbon).
The range is called the MONTES UNIVERSALES, being the source of
several Spanish rivers or tributaries of them.
    At 28km we meet the road from Orihuela del Tremedal (see p 173)
and 7km beyond, enter *Albarracín* (1200m), a well-sited and
picturesque but much shrunken Moorish city. From 1165 to 1333,
when it was annexed to Aragón, it was the capital of an independent
state.
    From the restored Pl. Mayor narrow rambling streets of timbered
houses with overhanging storeys ascend to the small *Cathedral*,
rebuilt c 1531 and internally classicised in the late 18C. It contains a
set of six 16C Brussels tapestries by François Geubels, a rock-crystal
Fish, and notable retablos, one by Joli.

SE of the town are the prehistoric shelters of *Callejón del Plou* and *El Navazo*,
with rock paintings.

The road skirts the Guadalviar, passing castle ruins, to meet the
N234 at 19km, 9km from **Teruel**; see Rte 73.

46 Madrid to Valencia via Motilla del Palancar

351km (218 miles). NIII. 81km *Tarancón*—104km. *Alarcón* lies to the right—14km *Motilla del Palancar*—81km *Requena*—71km **Valencia**.

Maps: M 444, 445.

For the road to *Tarancón*, bypassed, see Rte 44A.

At 9km a DETOUR may be made to **Uclés**, 6km E. Near Uclés, in 1100 Sancho, only son of Alfonso VI of León, was killed in battle against the Moors at a spot known as 'Sicuendes' (*siete condes*) from the seven counts who fell with the youthful *infante*. The village is dominated by an imposing *Monastery, founded in 1174 and sacked by the French under Victor in 1811. It is now a school.

The present buildings, begun in 1529 (Plateresque E front, adorned with the scallops of Santiago; and sacristy), were extended (N and W fronts) by Francisco de Mora, whose work here gave the place its sobriquet of 'el Escorial de la Mancha'. From the S front, with a Baroque portal of 1735 attributed to Pedro de Ribera, the central courtyard is entered, but enquire at the *portería* to visit the *Church*, containing 15–16C tombs, notably those of the Infanta Doña Urraca, and Jorge Manrique (died 1479), the poet. The refectory preserves a fine artesonado of 1548. Note the paintwork of the cupboards in the Plateresque Sacristy.

Two towers survive of the nearby castle.—The main road may be regained 7km SE.

13km *Saelices* (927m), just beyond which, 4.5km to the right, are the important Roman ruins of **Segóbriga**. They include a theatre and amphitheatre, and also remains of a 6C Visigothic basilica, but much of the site remains to be excavated. Adjacent is a small museum.

Puebla de Almenara, with conspicuous castle ruins, lies 15.5km beyond Saelices, on the by-road to *Belmonte*, 28km further S; see Rte 47.

The NIII continues SE from Saelices, at 12km passing *Montalbo*, with the ruins of a castle of the dukes of Gandia, to bypass (37km) *La Almarcha*. Beyond La Almarcha the NIII passes (right) the castle of *Garcimuñoz*, with a church within its walls. Jorge Manrique (q.v. Uclés) died fighting here.—At 29km we skirt the S end of the huge *Embalse de Alarcón*, fed by the Júcar and other streams, and 4km beyond (right) the village of **Alarcón**, well sited on a rocky ridge. Here are four derelict churches, 13–15C *La Trinidad* (restored), and a small 14C castle converted to house a Parador.

14km *Motilla del Palancar*, with a late 16C hall-church, stands on the crossroad between Cuenca and Albacete.

Villanueva de la Jara, 15km S, with a good 16C church and ruined fortifications, was the first base of the American 'Lincoln Battalion' during the Civil War.— *Iniesta*, 18km E of Villanueva, was the birthplace of Enrique de Villena (1384– 1434), an astrologer, and the first translator of complete versions of the 'Aeneid' and Dante's 'Divina Commedia' into Castilian.

At 28km *Minglanilla* is bypassed. There are salt mines to the S. The scenery becomes less bleak as we descend into the rocky valley of the Cabriel, skirting the S bank of the *Embalse de Contreras* through several short tunnels, to approach (38km) **Utiel** (12,050 inhab.). Surrounded by vineyards, Utiel has a church of 1548 and remains of walls.

The Baroque entrance to the monastery of Uclés

14km **Requena** (18,000 inhab.), bypassed, is an ancient town retaining some 15C houses and a ruined castle. Its churches were badly treated during the Civil War. They include *El Salvador* (1480–1533), with a Baroque interior, Isabelline doorway, and noble tower; *Sta. María* (c 1470; restored c 1730), also with a fine portal; and *S. Nicolás* (13C; altered 1787). The *Ayuntamiento* occupies the *Conv. del Carmen*, with a church in part dating from 1480.

REQUENA TO ALMANSA (83km). The N330 ascends S to cross the SIERRA DE MARTÉS to (36km) *Cofrentes*, at the confluence of the Cabriel and Júcar, dominated by a 14C castle. It ascends the valley of the Cantabán past the ruined castles of *Jalance*, *Teresa de Cofrentes*, and (25km) *Ayora* (6200 inhab.), to approach *Almansa* 22km beyond; see Rte 79.

31km **Buñol** (9100 inhab.), with a Moorish castle in which François I was briefly held, and a church containing sculptures by Ignacio Vergara.—There are castle ruins at *Macastre*, 6km S.

8.5km **Chiva** (6400 inhab.), commanded by ruins of a Moorish castle. Its church of 1733–81 has frescoes by José Vergara and retains the Romanesque belfry of its predecessor.

CHIVA TO L'ALCUDIA (46km). The C3322 runs across country to the SE via (25km) *Montroy*, on the Magro, with a ruined castle, and (17.5km) *Carlet*; see Rte 82.

CHIVA TO LIRIA (24km). The C3322 leads NE through (4km) *Cheste* (7000 inhab.), with a domed 18C church, later crossing the Túria to approach **Liria** (12,550 inhab.). As *Lauro* or *Edeta* this was the ancient capital of the Edetani. The *Ayuntamiento* occupies a Renaissance palace of the Dukes of Berwick and Alba. A municipal bakehouse, a medieval survival, and two other early houses retaining 16C azulejos may be seen. Among churches are 14C *La Sangre*, Gothic *El Buen Pastor*, and a Baroque *Parish church* of 1627–72 with a grandiose front by T.L. Esteve.

The C234 leads 43.5km NW from Liria to Chelva, later passing near the castle ruins of *Pueblo de Loriguilla*, and *Domeño*, with remains of a Roman fort, overlooking the Túria. *Chelva* is a secluded old town with a monumental Baroque church and the Roman aqueduct of *Peña Cortada*.

From Liria, the C234 leads SE to (30km) Valencia via *Benisanó*, a 15C stronghold retaining medieval walls, and (6km) *La Pobla de Vallbona* (7050 inhab.), with a Baroque church.—5.5km N of this road, approached by turning left after 6km, is *Bétera* (8750 inhab.), with a Moorish castle. About 12km further N, situated in pine-wooded hills, is the *Cartuja de Porta Coeli*, founded in 1272, with an early 15C aqueduct, a church altered in the 18C, and Gothic cloisters (14C; rebuilt 1479).

The NIII drives due E from Chiva, at 20km skirting (left) the airport, to enter the W suburbs of **Valencia**; see Rte 77.

Until the long-awaited section of. motorway circling to the W of Valencia is completed, travellers wishing to bypass the city to the S should turn off immediately after crossing the canalised Túria to join the N340 and A7.

47 Madrid to Albacete

249km (155 miles). NIV. 47km **Aranjuez**—16km *Ocaña*—N301. 60km *Quintanar de la Orden*—18km *Mota del Cuervo*—72km *La Roda*—36km **Albacete**.

Maps: M 444.

For the road to **Ocaña** see Rte 48A. **Ocaña** itself (5400 inhab.) is now bypassed.

Daniel O'Mahony, a general in the Spanish service during the War of the Succession, died here in 1714. In 1809, the Spanish were routed by Soult on the plain to the S and the town was sacked. It was also damaged during the Civil War, after which its gaol was the scene of the execution of c 2000 Republican prisoners.

To the S of the arcaded *Pl. Mayor* (1791) are remains of the Mudéjar *Pal. de Santiago* (15–16C). The *Pal. de Frías* is in the Isabelline style of 1500. A theatre occupies the former Jesuit church. Ruinous *S. Martín* to the NE retains a 16C tower; *Sta. María* (NW) has a Plateresque retablo and preserves ten 'processional' suits of armour (16–17C). The restored *Aqueduct* of 1578 was built by Herrera.

Tarancón lies 48km E; see Rte 44A.

The road leads SE across the monotonous plain of **La Mancha** for 60km to **Quintanar de la Orden** (8900 inhab.), noted for its Manchego cheese.

Sir Charles Wogan (1698?–1752?), a Jacobite soldier of fortune—who in 1719 rescued Maria Clementina Sobieska, betrothed to the Old Pretender, from confinement in Innsbruck—and a colonel in the Spanish service from 1723, was later governor of La Mancha, and from there corresponded with Swift, to whom he sent casks of wine.

Addicts of 'Don Quixote' may wish to visit the village of **El Toboso**, 9.5km S, home of the peerless Dulcinea.—19km SW of El Toboso is **Campo de Criptana** (13,300 inhab.), near which are several rebuilt hilltop windmills (at which the deluded Don tilted).—8km further W is **Alcázar de S. Juan**, a rail junction and busy wine centre of 25,550 inhab. Towards its W side are the restored *Torre de Don Juan de Austria* and adjacent red stone *Sta. María* (Romanesque). The town takes its name from a Moorish castle which later became the headquarters of the Military Order of S. Juan. (For *Argamasilla de Alba* see Rte 48A.)

18km **Mota del Cuervo** (5450 inhab.), with a ruined castle of the Order of Santiago.

Belmonte, 16km NE, the birthplace of Luis de León (1528–91), is overlooked to the E by a superbly sited and elegant *Castle* (1456). It was probably built by Juan Güas for the Marqués de Villena (but the triangular patio has been spoiled by a brick lining added by the Empress Eugenie). In the town, with an extensive curtain wall and three gates, *S. Bartolomé* (14C on Romanesque foundations) contains Pacheco tombs and well-carved choir stalls of 1545.—The church of *Villaescusa de Haro*, 6km beyond, has a fine Isabelline chapel, but it is not easy to get in.—The main road may be regained 10km S of Belmonte.

The N301 turns E and then SE again, at 19km bypassing *Las Pedroñeras* (6350 inhab.), and traverses a region of pine groves, at 19km reaching crossroads.

S. Clemente (6650 inhab.), 9km NE, has a charming 16C *Ayuntamiento* and *Pl. Mayor*, and well-vaulted *Santiago el Mayor* contains a notable Gothic alabaster crucifix, tastelessly displayed. Of interest is the squat *Torre Vieja* in the nearby Pl. de Carmen Martínez, among several other old buildings.

Villarrobledo (20,150 inhab.), 13km SW of the junction, with an *Ayuntamiento* of 1599 and *S. Blas* (16C), trades extensively in saffron, the region of Albacete being the world's main producer.

34km **La Roda** (12,550 inhab.) has a hall-church of 1564. 17km beyond we bypass *La Gineta*, with a 16C church, to approach (19km) Albacete.

ALBACETE (116,500 inhab.; 32,000 in 1920; 70,000 in 1950; Parador 3km S of the town, off the N430) is a dull provincial capital in the centre of a flat, uninteresting, but fertile plain.

Of Moorish origin (*al-basit*, the plain), it was near here in 1145–46 that two battles were fought between Christians and Moors, in the second of which Abu Ja'far, emir of Córdoba, was killed. Alcabete only attained its present importance after the malarial swamps surrounding it were drained by the *Canal de María Cristina* in the 19C. It became a centre for trade in saffron (q.v. Villarrobledo, above), sulphur, and wheat, and was long reputed for its *navajas* (clasp knives with spring blades) and *puñales* (daggers). It was for some time a HQ of the International Brigades during the Civil War.

Largely rebuilt, Albacete retains hardly a single old edifice, with the exception of *S. Juan Bautista*, a 16C hall-church completed by Diego de Siloé, but entirely restored since the Civil War. There is a *Provincial Museum*.

For roads to **Alicante** and **Murcia** see Rtes 79 and 80; for **Alcaraz** and **Úbeda**, Rte 82.

48   Madrid to Bailén

A.   Via Aranjuez and Manzanares

298km (185 miles). NIV. 47km **Aranjuez**—16km *Ocaña*—31km
Tembleque—26km *Madridejos*—17km *Puerto Lápice*—36km
Manzanares—30km *Valdepeñas*—69km *La Carolina*—27km *Bailén*.

Maps: M 444.

The much-improved road leads due S, at 13km passing (left) the
Cerro de los Ángeles, a low hill surmounted by a monument replacing another blown up in 1936. At 7km *Pinto* is bypassed. In the 15C
castle here Felipe II imprisoned the intriguing Princes de Éboli (cf.
Pastrana).—6km beyond is *Valdemoro*, where the 16C church contains paintings by Goya, Bayeu, and Claudio Coello.

At 3km *Ciempozuelos* (10,250 inhab.), Roman *Ischadia*, 4km E, has two
paintings by Claudio Coello in its church. It was the birthplace of the architect
Ventura Rodríguez (1717–85), and it was here that Eoin O'Duffy's Irish fascist
brigade saw action in February 1937.

The road descends to cross the Jarama, and at 18km enters Aranjuez,
first crossing the Tagus by a bridge of 1834; a bypass is under
construction to the W.
   ARANJUEZ (35,600 inhab.), a leafy oasis in the tawny Castilian
plateau and formerly a favourite pleasance of the Spanish court, is
reputed for its nightingales, asparagus, and strawberries. The town
itself, laid out in a grid, is of slight interest. It was formerly a horse-
breeding centre, but the *Caballerizas Reales*, or royal stables, are
now empty.

The PL. DE S. ANTONIO, close to the palace, is bounded on one side by the *Casa
de Oficios* or courtiers' quarters (1584–1762), on the other by the JARDIN DE
ISABEL II and the *Casa del Infante*. At the S end is a chapel by Bonavia, who also,
in 1749, completed the church of *Alpajés* (1680) at the far end of the avenue
extending E from the palace.

The **Palace**, in its present state, is a somewhat spiritless 18C building
in the style of Louis XIV; indeed Ford considered that it 'scarcely
deserves a visit'.

The summer residence built here in 1387 by Lorenzo Suárez de Figueroa,
Grand Master of the Order of Santiago, became royal property under Fernando
and Isabel. Charles V used it as a shooting box, and Felipe II, whose architects
were J.B. de Toledo and Herrera, enlarged it to a palace, but this was practically
destroyed by fires in 1660 and 1665. The present edifice is a reconstruction of
1715–52 by Pedro Caro, with two wings added in 1778. Felipe II had introduced
elms from England, and subsequent monarchs contributed to the embellishment of the palace and grounds.
   Late 18C travellers remarked that the local wild boar were so tame that they
were fed in the streets, while another exotic sight was of camels, imported
earlier in the century, carrying wood about the town. It was often visited from
Madrid, and here grandees 'appropriately mounted on asses, performed *bor-
ricadas* in the woods'—so wrote Ford—'for when a Madrileño on pleasure bent
gets amongst real trees, he goes mad as a March hare . . . '. Lady Holland had a
private audience with María Luisa here. The latter enumerated the children she
had had and those she had lost—six remained of 22—her favourite, Don
Francisco, bearing 'a most indecent likeness to the Prince of the Peace' (Godoy).
It was here that in March 1808 Carlos IV abdicated in favour of his son,
Fernando VII.

Schiller placed the scene of his 'Don Carlos' at Aranjuez.

From the W entrance, visitors are escorted through a long series of apartments containing frescoed ceilings and miscellaneous paintings, besides some fine chandeliers, clocks, furniture, mirrors, and inlaid woodwork. The most interesting room is the *Cabinet, plastered with plaques of Buen Retiro porcelain designed in the Japanese taste for Carlos III by Giuseppe Gricci of Naples c 1763. The mirrors made in the factory at La Granja (q.v.) add to the sumptuous effect. A small Museum of Costumes has been installed in the palace, which also includes a collection of fans and curious nursery furniture.

On its E side is the ornamental Parterre laid out in 1746 by Étienne Boutelou. From it two small bridges span the overflow canal (La Ría) to the JARDIN DE LA ISLA, designed by Sebastián Herrera in 1669. Its avenues and walks abound in ornamental fountains in the 18C taste; the main jet of the Fuente del Reloj serves as the gnomon of a sundial, and in a walk overlooked by the palace are surprise waterworks known as the Burladores.

A view of the palace at Aranjuez in 1773

The C. de la Reina, an avenue of plane trees and elms, leads E from the palace. It skirts the Jardin del Principe and passes (c 1.5km) the entrance to the *Casa del Labrador, built in 1805 for Carlos IV in emulation of the Petit Trianon at Versailles to the designs of Isidro González Velázquez.

Visitors are escorted round the apartments, elaborately decorated and furnished, containing several curious works in the minor arts, including a series of paintings of La Granja by F. Brambila (died 1842). The ceilings are frescoed by Vicente López, Maella, and others.
  The Sculpture Gallery, with a ceiling by Zacarías Velázquez, contains over 20 antique busts and hermae, Roman mosaics from Mérida, and a musical clock in the shape of Trajan's Column. In the Sala de María Luisa, with a ceiling by

Bayeu and Maella, are a table and chair of malachite presented by Prince Demidoff to Isabel II. The panelled walls of the *Gabinete de Platina* have bronze ornaments plated with gold and silver. Above the service staircase is a fresco by Z. Velázquez of the artist's wife and children on a balcony.

One may return to the town through the JARDÍN DEL PRINCIPE, between the C. de la Reina and the Tagus, laid out by Carlos IV before his accession.

Shaded by large trees and embellished by fountains, it has several sections. At its NW angle is the *Florera* or English Garden established by Richard Wall (1694–1778), an Irishman who served as Spanish Secretary of State in 1754–64. Here is the *Casa de Marinos*, built by Carlos III in connection with a scheme for improving the navigation of the river, a boat house in which may be seen several royal pleasure boats.

From 5km S of Aranjuez the N400 leads to *Toledo*, 42km SW; see Rte 43.

Just beyond this turning another leads due S past *Ciruelos*, with a late Gothic church, to *Yepes*, retaining old fortifications and reputed for its white wines; its church of 1552 contains paintings by Luis Tristán.—5.5km beyond is *Huerta de Valdecarábanos*, dominated by a 12C castle of the Order of Calatrava and with a mansion of 1539 with a Plateresque portal.—The main road may be regained 16km SE.

At 11km *Ocaña* (see Rte 47) is bypassed.—20km beyond is the troglodyte village of *La Guardia*, NE of which is the hermitage dedicated to the 'Sto. Niño', a Christian boy claimed to have been crucified here by Jews in 1490.

11km **Tembleque**, with an attractive wooden-galleried *Plaza Mayor.*—The road now traverses the monotonous steppes or *meseta* of **La Mancha**, exposed to wintry blasts and scorched in summer (see also p 331–32), at 26km bypassing **Madridejos** (9900 inhab.), with an imposingly buttressed bullring, and the hall-church of *El Salvador.*— 6.5km W is the castle of *Consuegra* (9650 inhab.), on a ridge studded with white 'pepper-pot' windmills (rebuilt).

17km *Puerto Lápice*, now bypassed to the E.—*Alcázar de S. Juan* lies 21km E; see Rte 47.

FROM PUERTO LÁPICE TO ALMURADIEL VIA DAIMIEL, ALMAGRO, AND CALZADA DE CALATRAVA (117km). This alternative route (N420) forks SW just S of the town to cross the Cigüela for (33km) **Daimiel** (16,250 inhab.), with Gothic *Sta. María* and classical *S. Pedro*. The town is also bypassed to the N for *Ciudad Real*, 31km SW; see Rte 48B. To the NW are the ornithological reserve of the TABLAS DE DAIMIEL and lakes known as '*Los Ojos del Guadiana*', the river winding its way W from here to Badajoz, and later forming the frontier with Portugal W of Huelva (cf. Ruidera). We turn onto the C417 SW of the town to (20.5km) *Bolaños de Calatrava* (9950 inhab.), with a restored castle, and bear SW to (4.5km) **Almagro** (8400 inhab.; Parador), a small town of some charm in the centre of the fertile CAMPO DE CALATRAVA, where Diego de Almagro (1478/9–1538), conqueror of Chile, is said to have been discovered as a foundling. In the characteristic *Pl. Mayor*, with its glazed upper floors, survives the *Corral de las Comedias*, a restored 16C theatre in which plays are to be seen in the season. To the NE of the town is the *Conv. de la Asunción*, with a Plateresque cloister; to the SW, the former *Franciscan* convent, well-restored to house the Parador. Among several other buildings flanking its unspoilt cobbled streets are those of its former '*university*' (1550), and the 16C chapel of *S. Blas*, built at the expense of Jakob Fugger and his nephews (who having leased the mines of Almaden, inaccessible to the W, had their offices here).—Turn right off the C415 SE of the town onto the C417, crossing a ridge to (8.5km) *Granátula*, the birthplace of Gen. Espartero (1792–1879), later crossing the Jabalón by a Roman bridge, to *Calzada de Calatrava* (5400 inhab.).

A short DETOUR from here is much recommended. Follow the CR504 to the SE over a ridge. Beyond on the left are the slight remains of the castle of *Salvatierra*, built near a Roman tower; to the right, approached by a rough but

passable track, are the imposingly sited 13th and 15C ruins of the fortress of
*Calatrava la Nueva, also comprising a conventual church with a rose-window,
and other dependencies (partially restored). The view S is very fine.

From Calzada de Calatrava follow the C410 SE to (30km) Viso del Marqués,
with a large *Palace* built for Álvaro de Bazán, Marqués de Sta. Cruz, begun in
1564 by J.B. Castello (el Bergamasco) and continued by Genoese architects.
The conventual church contains the tomb of Álvaro de Bazán and María
Figueroa.—The NIV is met at (6km) *Almuradiel*; see below.

11.5km (S of Puerto Lápice) *Villarta de S. Juan.*

The CR134 forks left here for (33.5km) **Argamasilla de Alba** (7000 inhab.), only
of interest because Cervantes is said to have written or at least conceived the
earlier chapters of 'Don Quixote' in the rebuilt *Casa de Medrano*, the former
prison. This is now generally accepted as the 'birthplace' of the Knight of the
Rueful Countenance; Don Rodrigo de Pacheco, a local *hidalgo*, was not
improbably the original of the immortal hero.
  Tomelloso (27,150 inhab.), the centre of the local wine trade, is 7km NE.—
Some 10km to the SE is the *Embalse de Peñarroyo*, to the E of which is the castle
of *Peñarroyo*, which is the scene of Don Quixote's adventure with the pup-
pets.—17km further SE is *Ruidera*, S of which is a series of small lakes known as
the *Lagunas de Ruidera*, where the Guadiana rises (q.v. Daimiel). At the head of
the uppermost lake is the *Cave of Montesinos*, apparently a Roman copper
mine; to the S extends the CAMPO DE MONTIEL, where Don Quixote sought
adventure.

24.5km **Manzanares** (17,400 inhab.; Parador S of the town), built on
the site of a castle erected after the battle of Las Navas de Tolosa
(q.v.), with a large late Gothic church and, to the SE, the 13C castle of
Peñas Borras. It was here that George Borrow met the famous blind
improvisor known as 'La Ciega de Manzanares' or the 'Manchegan
Prophetess', who used regularly to meet the Madrid diligence.

32km SE (beyond *La Solana*; 13,550 inhab.) lies *Alhambra*, of Roman origin,
where a paleo-Christian necropolis has been discovered, with a Moorish castle,
and a church, largely rebuilt, dating back to c 1217.

30km **Valdepeñas** (25,050 inhab.), bypassed to the W, is famous for
its wine, which should be sampled in one of its numerous *bodegas*.
The resinous flavour or *borracha* is due to the pitch with which the
interior of the wineskins is coated.

At *Villanueva de los Infantes* (6200 inhab.), 34.5km E on the C415, is the tomb of
the poet and satirist Francisco Gómez Quevedo y Villegas (1580–1645). There
are several places of interest in the area. At *Montiel* (14.5km SE), are the castle
ruins where Pedro the Cruel was assassinated in March 1369 by his half-brother
Enrique de Trastámara, after having been defeated in the field (and near the
scene of Don Quixote's liberation of the galleyslaves). There are remains of
castles at *Sta. Cruz de los Cáñamos*, to the S of Montiel; at *Almedina* (15km S of
Villaneuva), at *Puebla del Principe*, 7km beyond; and at *Villamanrique*, 7km W
of the last.

The NIV at 15km bypasses *Sta. Cruz de Mudela* (5150 inhab.), with a
15C church and an antimony mine once worked by the eminent 18C
printer Antonio de Sancha, to approach (17km) *Almuradiel*, a post
founded by Carlos III in 1768 to suppress brigandage in the Sierra to
the S.—For *Viso del Marqués*, 6km W, see above.

We begin the gradual ascent of the SIERRA MORENA, passing the
Venta de Cárdenas (which recalls Don Quixote's penance) to enter
the notorious *Desfiladero de Despeñaperros, a magnificent and
extensive rocky defile, often the scene of robbery in the past. Its
name signifies 'throw over dogs', meaning 'infidel houndes', according to Ford, who were here overthrown in the battle at Las Navas; see
below. Here, at the *Puerto del Rey*, according to John Talbot Dillon,
writing   in   the   late   18C,   a   toll   was   paid   'for   monkies,

parrots, negroes, and guittars unless played upon at the time: married women unless in company with their husbands or producing certificates . . . '. The well-engineered road traverses the pass in sweeping curves past (24km) *Sta. Elena* before reaching (9km) the insignificant village of *Las Navas de Tolosa*, celebrated for the victory of July 1212, when Alfonso VIII (miraculously guided across the sierra by Martín Alhaga, a mysterious shepherd) crushed the Almohads under Muhammad II al-Nasir.

At 3km **La Carolina** (15,050 inhab.) is bypassed. It was the most important of the settlements colonised in 1768 by Carlos III and his minister Pablo de Olavide (1725–1803) with Swiss and German immigrants in order to reduce the lawlessness of the Sierra Morena foothills. With the dismissal of Olavide it foundered, although Swinburne suggests that it was 'from eating unwholesome herbs, and drinking too much wine and brandy' that half the Germans died.

The C3217 leads across the hills to *Úbeda*, 51km SE; see Rte 84.

At 19km *Baños de la Encina* is 6km NW, with a fine *Castle* built in 968 by Hakam II.—*Linares* lies 11km SE; see Rte 84.

8km **Bailén** (15,800 inhab.; Parador), scene of the fortuitous 'victory' of 18 July 1808 of the Spaniards under Castaños over Gén. Dupont with 22,000 French, who unexpectedly capitulated four days later. Together with *S. Marcial* (cf.) it is celebrated in *Spanish* annals of the Peninsular War.

An anecdote is repeated that when Dupont delivered his sword to Castaños he said: 'You may well, General, be proud of this day; it is remarkable that I have never lost a pitched battle til now,—I, who have been in more than twenty, and gained them all'. 'It is the more remarkable', replied the sarcastic Spaniard, 'because I never was in one before in my life'.

For the road to **Baza** via **Baeza** and **Úbeda** see Rte 84; for **Jaén** and **Granada**, Rte 85; to **Córdoba** and **Sevilla**, Rte 90.

B.   Via Toledo and Ciudad Real

330km (205 miles). N401. 70km **Toledo**—34km *Orgaz*—86km **Ciudad Real**—CR512 and C401. 77km *Almuradiel*—NIV. 63km *Bailén*.

Maps: M 444.

For the road to **Toledo** see Rte 43.

TOLEDO TO MADRIDEJOS VIA MORA (70km). This crossroad (C400) forks left off the N401 c 7km SE of Toledo, after 15km passing *Almonacid de Toledo*, its ruined castle with an 11C keep within a double curtain wall.—5km *Mascaraque*, with slight remains of a 14C castle, and, 5km beyond, **Mora** (9500 inhab.), a thriving but ugly town with a 15C church with a Plateresque retablo. Its castle, built for Alfonso VII, commands a wide view.—Bypassing (right) *Manzaneque*, with a 14–15C castle, we cross a ridge and skirt the SW side of the *Embalse de Finisterre* to approach (30km) *Consuegra* (bypassed to the N), commanded by its conspicuous castle. For Consuegra and *Madridejos*, 8km E, see Rte 48A.

The N401 leads S to (25km) *Sonseca*.—5km W, at *Mazarambroz*, is a tower of a 14C castle and a church with a Mudéjar roof.—At *Casalgordo*, 4km S, are the slight remains of the Visigothic chapel of *S. Pedro de la Mata* (c 675), with a horseshoe-arched entrance.

The road bears SE to (9km) **Orgaz**, a pleasant little town with an arcaded *Plaza*, a large granite *Church* of 1762, the uncompleted last work of Alberto Churriguera, the imposing 14C *Castle* of the Pérez de Guzmán, and a Roman bridge. It was the birthplace of Juan Sánchez Cotan (1560–1627), the artist.—We climb olive-covered slopes and windmill-topped hills (views) to (9.5km) *Los Yebenes* (6000 inhab.), formerly a possession of the Knights of Malta. *S. Juan* has a 16C Mudéjar tower.—At 16km the castle of *Guadalerzas* lies to the left; to the W rise the MONTES DE TOLEDO. On crossing the SIERRA DE LA CALDERINA we descend SW towards the Guadiana to (36.5km) *Malagón* (7950 inhab.), with a Moorish castle and slight remains of Roman occupation.

A by-road leads SE to (20km) *Carrión de Calatrava*. After crossing the Guadiana a track to the right leads to the site of *Calatrava la Vieja*, with the extensive ruins of the former Moorish castle, later the original headquarters of the Knights of Calatrava. The Order was founded in 1158 to defend the S frontier of Castile but suppressed by the Catholic Kings, when its possessions were vested in the crown. The Nationalists claimed that in 1936 hundreds of their supporters were rounded up from villages in the province and thrown down a mineshaft here.— *Almagro* lies 18km SE of Carrión; see Rte 48A. *Ciudad Real* is 9.5km SW.

The N401 crosses the Guadiana 17km SW of Malagón and turns S to enter (7km) **CIUDAD REAL** (50,150 inhab.; 19,000 in 1920), a provincial capital which scarcely merits the (? ironical) praise of Cervantes, who called it 'imperial, the seat of the god of smiles'. Few would disagree with Gerald Brenan who condemned it as a 'dull, one-horse little place', but that was just after the Civil War.

It was founded as *Villa Real* by Alfonso X in 1252, and received the title of city from Juan II in 1420. It was one of the earliest towns to possess a *Hermandad*, or brotherhood, to protect its roads against robbers. Similar associations were established elsewhere in Spain (sometimes to protect citizens against the rapacious nobility), but the Catholic Kings developed the 'Santa Hermandad' as a general police force with para-inquisitorial powers—a precursor of the Guardia Civil.

Hernando Pérez del Pulgar (1461–1531), a hero of the siege of Granada, was born at Ciudad Real

Of the crumbling walls which formerly surrounded the city not much but the *Puerta de Toledo* survives, a gate in Mudéjar style built in 1328 to guard its N entrance. From here the C. Toledo, running SW, bisects the town, with the *Audiencia* on the left and the *Diputación* and 17C *La Merced* on the right, to approach the arcaded but otherwise undistinguished central *Plaza*. At its NE corner is the *Casa Consistorial* of 1869. To the W is the Paseo del Prado, with *Sta. María* (1490–1580), the former cathedral. It has good choir stalls and a retablo of 1616 by Giraldo de Merlo. The 17C tower was heightened in the 19C. Of an earlier church the blocked 12C W doorway survives.

To the NE is 14C *Santiago*, largely rebuilt. A short distance E of the central square is 14C Gothic *S. Pedro*, with a Flamboyant window, a Baroque retablo, and an alabaster wall tomb in the S chapel (c 1500).

At *Alarcos*, a site a few kilometres SW of the town, took place the battle of July 1195 in which Alfonso VIII suffered a serious defeat at the hands of the Moors. Near by is a hilltop chapel.

For *Almagro*, 26km SE on the C415, see Rte 48A. This DETOUR may be combined with ease with the main route, which follows the CR512 leading S to (38.5km) *Calzada de Calatrava*, for which and the road beyond see also Rte 48A.

Ciudad Real, like Mérida, 250km to the W, is the nearest large town from which the extensive, remote and depopulated area between them may be explored. It is bounded by the MONTES DE TOLEDO and SIERRA DE GUADALUPE to the N and the SIERRA MORENA to the S. The roads are few, not always of good quality, nor are there many monuments to see, but this is made up for by its spacious tawny grandeur. Further W, beyond Almadén and the parched sierras separating La Mancha from Extremadura, is the great deserted plain of LA SERENA, to the N of which the dammed Guadiana flows lazily to the W.

Its W districts are described in sub-routes from Rte 50B.

CIUDAD REAL TO CÓRDOBA VIA PUERTOLLANO (211km). The N420 drives SW past (18km) *Caracuel*, with a ruined castle.—3.5km beyond Caracuel a right fork leads 16.5km SW to *Almodóvar del Campo* (8250 inhab.), of ancient importance, with a much-altered 13C church and ruined castle. From here the main route is regained c 10km further SW.—The main road continues directly from this turning to (22.5km) **Puertollano** (50,200 inhab.), an ugly if remotely sited colliery town containing a large but over-restored church. We veer W before climbing out of the broad valley at (25km) the *Puerto de Pulido* (856m). The road now crosses the VALLE DE ALCUDIA, long a sheep pasturage in winter, climbing again across a series of ridges by the *Puerto de Niefla* (908m; views) in the SIERRA DEL REY, and then the *Puerto Valderreposa* (860m), to approach (36km) *Fuencaliente*, with prehistoric remains including the neolithic rock paintings of *Peña Escrita* and *La Batanera*.—12km *Azuel*, 19km NW of which is *Conquista*, a former estate of Pizarro, with bismuth mines.—7km *Cardeña*, 2km beyond which the CO510 turns off to the right, a beautiful but slow and winding cross country road which leads across the foothills of the SIERRA MORENA and down to (40km) *Montoro*; see Rte 90.—The N420, the easier road, descends from Cardeña towards the Guadalquivir valley and (37km) *Villa del Rio*, on the NIV 55km E of *Córdoba*; see Rtes 90 and 92.

CIUDAD REAL TO CÓRDOBA VIA ALMADÉN AND ALCARACEJOS (235km). Fork right off the N420 15.5km SW of Ciudad Real, at (30.5km) *Abenójar* bearing SW and twisting through the hills to enter the VALDEAZOGUES (Vale of Quicksilver) and at 41km passing the derelict furnaces of *Almadenejas*.—14km **Almadén** (9700 inhab.), Roman *Sisapo*, and the centre of the richest mercury deposits in Europe. Its name is a corruption of the Arabic words for 'the quicksilver mine'. The deposits were worked also by the Moors, whose castle of *Retemar* survives, but their serious exploitation dates from the 16C, when they were pledged by Charles V to the Fuggers of Augsburg (known in Spain as Los Fúcares; cf. Almagro) as a security for loans. The mines are to the W of the town. Mercury is found both in the virgin state and in cinnabar ore. The deepest shafts descend over 330m underground. Widdrington, in 1843, was one of the few English travellers who ever visited this remote area, although in 1753 William Bowles had made a report on the mines to the Spanish government (q.v. the translation by John Talbot Dillon in 1780).

At *Chillón*, 4km NW, is a ruined Moorish castle.—20km further W, at *Capilla*, are remains of a Templar castle and monastery.—*Cabeza del Buey* (7500 inhab.), 24km SW of Capilla, retains a few buildings of interest.—9km further W are the ruined Moorish castle of *Almorchón*, and the adjacent *Ermita de Belén* (formerly a Templar church), and, 23km beyond, *Castuera*; see p 344.

The C411 winds SW from Almadén to (30km) *Sta. Eufemia*, commanding extensive views, with ruined fortifications on a height to the W and a 14C church.—Although the main road continues due S to (25km) *Alcaracejos*, the following DETOUR of an additional 30km is recommended.

Turn W to (26km) **Belalcázar**, with an impressive ruined *Castle built in 1445 by Guitérrez Sotomayor. It is probable that the conquistador Sebastián de Benalcázar (or Belalcázar; c 1480–1551) was born here.—The C420 leads S to (8.5km) *Hinojosa del Duque* (8150 inhab.) where the Plateresque church contains a Churrigueresque retablo. (*Peñarroya* lies 31km SW; see Rte 54.)—We bear SE to (20km) *Alcaracejos*, with lead mines, a Plateresque church, and the ruins of the *Cerro del Germo*, a Visigothic basilica of the 6C.

11km E is **Pozoblanco** (13,900 inhab.), an old wool town and the birthplace of Ginés de Sepulveda (c 1490–1573), the theologian and adversary of La Casas.—*Dos Torres* (8km NW of Pozoblanco) has a late Gothic church and old houses; *Pedroche*, 10km NE, has ruined walls and 15C church with a tower by Hernán Ruiz.—**Villanueva de Córdoba** (10,550 inhab.), 21km E, is a curious remote old town with both Roman and Moorish remains.

The C411 leads S from Alcaracejos, crossing two ridges to reach (at 27km) the N432 just S of *Espiel* and 51km from **Córdoba**; see Rtes 54 and 92.

49 Madrid to Plasencia via Arenas de S. Pedro and Yuste

267km (166 miles). NV. 14km.—C501. 17km *Brunete* crossroads—
39km *S. Martin de Valdeiglesias*—73km *Arenas de S. Pedro*—65km
Jarandilla—10km *Cuacos*—**Yuste** is 2km right—8km *Jaraiz*—37km
Plasencia.

Maps: M 447.

Turn off the NV 14km SW of Madrid, at 7km passing *Villaviciosa de
Ordón*, with a castle of the Counts of Chinchón where Fernando VI
(died 1759) passed the last melancholy years of his life.

6km NE at the next right turning is *Boadilla del Monte*, fought over
in mid December 1936 (as described by Esmond Romilly, one of the
survivors) and again in mid July 1937 (when George Nathan,
commanding the Anglo-Saxon brigade, was killed). The *Pal. del
Infante Don Luis* (1776; by Ventura Rodríguez), and a Carmelite
convent of 1674 survive.

10km *Brunete* lies just N of the crossroads, fought over in mid July
1937, when tanks and planes were much in evidence. The atrocities
on both sides were revolting. The losses in the International Brigade
were particularly heavy, the Lincoln and Washington battalions
being obliged afterwards to merge (cf. *Villanueva de la Cañada*, 6km
N).

20km *Chapinera*, with a church built from the surplus material of
the Escorial, and a bishop's palace.—The road shortly descends to
the NW, crossing the upper valley of the Alberche, here dammed to
form the *Embalse de S. Juan*, and *Pelayos de la Presa*, with ruins of a
Cistercian abbey, partly 12C, with 15C cloisters and 16C church.—At
19km *S. Martín de Valdeiglesias* is bypassed; see Rte 24.

We shortly cross the N403 and pass (right) a turning to the 16C
monastery of *Guisando*, replacing its predecessor destroyed in a fire,
where in 1468 Isabel the Catholic was provisionally acknowledged to
be the successor of Enrique IV by the assembled Castilian nobles.
Adjacent are several of the crude granite-hewn animals known as
the '*Toros de Guisando*', probably marking the frontier of a Celtiberian tribe. Less than half those recorded a century ago have
survived.

The barrier range of the SIERRA DE GREDOS, the S flank of which
the route follows, rises steeply to the NW as several small resorts are
passed. Among them are (25km) *La Adrada*, with its castle ruins, and
Piedralaves, among pine woods, above which the sierra rises to
2009m. The road now veers SW parallel to the Tiétar, crossing a
number of its boulder-strewn tributaries, to meet the C502 (from
Ávila to Talavera) at 36.5km. Turn right here for (6km) **Arenas de S.
Pedro** (6600 inhab.), a summer resort and centre for excursions into
the foothills of the Sierra. It preserves several old houses, a large
Castle of c 1400, a Gothic bridge, 14C granite church, and the nearby
18C *Conv. de S. Pedro de Alcántara*, with a chapel by Ventura
Rodríguez guarding the relics of its patron (1499–1562), the Franciscan mystic canonised in 1669, who died here.

The C501 climbs through the woods to follow the flank of the sierra
at a higher level above the Tiétar, a district known as LA VERA, to
(20km) *Candeleda* (5300 inhab.). Above Candeleda rises the *Pico
Almanzor* (2592m), the highest peak of the range. The road—later
winding—continues to cross a number of *gargantas* or boulder-
strewn torrent beds, and the characteristic villages of (11km)

Madrigal de la Vera, (11km) *Villanueva de la Vera*, with an attractive plaza, *Valverde de la Vera*, with a restored plaza, and *Losar de la Vera*, with a 15C church, to approach (24km from Villanueva) **Jarandilla**, with a large church, and a castle (converted to house a Parador) in which Charles V lived while his quarters at Yuste were being prepared.

11km *Cuacos*, a village of ancient houses and with a 14C church containing an organ and woodwork from *Yuste*, 2km to the N.

The Hieronymite monastery of *•***Yuste** was founded in 1404. From February 1557 until his death in September the following year it was the place of retirement of the Emperor Charles V.

Some parts of the original dependencies, sacked in the Peninsular War, have been restored, for it was also virtually gutted in 1820, and fell into further decay after the suppression of the monasteries in the 1830s. No longer may one sleep 'the slumber of a weary insignificant stranger' in the room which the emperor died, as did Richard Ford when he rode that way in 1832. William Stirling (later Stirling-Maxwell), who so well described the ex-emperor's life at Yuste, visited it in 1849.

A short avenue of eucalyptus leads to the *Church* (1508). The two-storeyed *Cloister* may be seen but not entered. In the *Crypt* is Charles V's first coffin, in which his body remained for 16 years before being transferred to the Escorial (q.v.). A ramp, which the gouty monarch could mount on horseback, ascends to a terrace overlooking a fish pond. His apartments, which may be visited, are in the adjacent wing he had built in 1554. The view across the valley of La Vera, which so charmed the dying emperor, recalls his enthusiastic description: 'Ver ibi perpetuum' (here is eternal spring).

The monastery of Yuste, with the terrace overlooking the fish pond

From Cuacos the road winds SW, passing a turning to *Garganta la Olla*, the church of which contained another early 16C organ, taken from Yuste. After years of wilful neglect, in 1973 it was destroyed by the village priest and its smaller pipes were distributed among children as 'penny whistles' for correctly repeating their Catechism. (When this vandalism was reported to the bishop of Coria, the excuse given was that the church were responsible for the salvation of souls, not organs.)

8km **Jaraiz de la Vera** (8500 inhab.), with a 13C church. (From Jaraiz the NV may be approached by descending to and crossing the Tiétar on the CC914 to *Almaraz*, 32km S; see Rte 50A.) The C501 bears W to (37km) **Plasencia**; see Rte 27A.

50 Madrid to Mérida

A. Via Talavera and Trujillo

349km (217 miles). NV. 77km *Maqueda* crossroads—43km **Talavera de la Reina**—33km *Oropesa*—32km *Navalmoral de la Mata*—74km **Trujillo**—90km **Mérida**.

Maps: M 447.

The NV now bypasses the ugly dormitory towns of **Alcorcón** (140,950 inhab.) and **Mostoles** (150,250 inhab.). The alcalde of Mostoles was supposedly the first in Spain to 'declare war' on Napoleon in 1808. At 33km the NV skirts **Navalcarnero** (8050 inhab.), in the church of which Felipe IV married Anne of Austria in 1649.

The road traverses dull rolling country, with a view NW towards the SIERRA DE GREDOS, at 44km passing *Maqueda* (see Rte 24) and, 36km beyond, crossing the Alberche at its confluence with the Tagus to approach (7km) *Talavera*.

The battlefield of 28 July 1809 lay to the N here, the scene of the costly defeat of Victor and Jourdan by Sir Arthur Wellesley (created Viscount Wellington in recognition of this success), aided intermittently by Cuesta's Spaniards, who pillaged the baggage of their allies before making a precipitate retreat. The British casualties were c 5370 of a force of c 20,000; the French lost c 7270 of c 40,000.

Talavera de la Reina (64,850 inhab.; 22,500 in 1950), the ancient *Talabriga*, is a rapidly growing dusty town deserving a bypass. It has long been reputed for its porcelain (the display of which is ubiquitous), but it is not as 'full of nice bits for the sketch book' as it was in Ford's time.

The last town of consequence on the route of the Nationalist advance of Madrid in 1936, it fell to them on 3 September, after which their attention was drawn to the beleaguered Alcázar at Toledo. Talavera was the birthplace of Juan de Mariana (1536–1634), the historian, and probably of Jean Hyacinthe de Magellan (1723–90), who lived in England after 1764 and there perfected the construction of various scientific instruments.

By the Madrid road is the high-domed *Ermita del Prado*, with attractive azulejo decoration. In the arcaded *Pl. Mayor* is the *Arco de*

S. Pedro, a Roman gateway. Among the houses rise the *Torres Albarranas*, relics of the 10C Moorish wall. The 15C bridge over the Tagus is ruined. Near the river are derelict *Sta. María* (1400), with a rose-window of 1470, and the *Conv. de S. Jerónimo* (1369; altered in the 15–16Cs). Among convent churches are *S. Francisco*, with a Mudéjar tower; *Sto. Domingo*, with Renaissance tombs; Romanesque *S. Salvador*; and late Gothic *Santiago*, to the N, with a good W doorway of c 1400.

The NV bears away from the Tagus to approach (33km; bypassed to the N) **Oropesa**, the birthplace of the mystics Alonso de Orozco (1500–91) and Juan de los Angeles (1536–1609). The restored *Castle* of 1366–1402, now a Parador, commands a fine *View* N towards the SIERRA DE GREDOS.

OROPESA TO GUADALUPE (90km). The TO701 leads due S to cross the Tagus at (14km) *El Puente de Arzobispo*, with ceramic works. *Sta. Catalina*, burnt by the French and reconstructed in the 19C, contains well-carved stalls. The old *Bridge*, built in 1338 by Abp Tenorio and once fortified, was crossed by Wellington's army after the battle of Talavera.—The first left turning leads c 8km to the ruined fortifications of *Vascos*, of obscure origin but occupied by Romans and Visigoths, although probably abandoned in the 12C.—The TO702 leads S, later climbing to (36km) the *Puerto de S. Vicente* (807m), there meeting the C401 from Toledo; see Rte 50B, and for *Guadalupe*, 40km further W by the slow winding road.

The NV shortly bypasses (left) the village of *Lagartera*, reputed for its embroidered costumes and decorative straw hats, occasionally displayed.

At 28.5km another by-road (CC713) leads 72.5km S to *Guadalupe*, at 11km crossing the *Embalse de Valdecañas* on the Tagus. On the far bank stand six columns of a portico moved from the submerged ruins of Roman *Talavera la Vieja*.—Passing (right) *Bohonal de Ibor*, the road climbs past (25km) *Castañar de Ibor*, with castle ruins, and ascends the valley of the Ibor to (35km) *Guadalupe*; see Rte 50B.

After 2km the NV bypasses **Navalmoral de la Mata** (13,200 inhab.), where *S. Andrés* dates from the 13–15Cs.—After 1.5km the CC904 turns right, later crossing the Tiétar, for *Jarandilla de la Vera*, 34km N; see Rte 49.—At 5km the C511 turns NE direct to (52km) *Plasencia* through a district devoted to the cultivation of tobacco and dotted with drying-sheds.

To the left on a ridge rises the 13–16C castle of *Belvis de Monroy*. Beyond (10km) *Almaraz*, with a Gothic church with a Renaissance façade, a nuclear power station is skirted, surrounded by a circle of towers. The deep gorge of the Tagus is crossed by a *Bridge* (completed in 1537), the scene of Lord Hill's brilliant exploit in May 1812 in severing French communications.

Over 20 years passed before the bridge was reconstructed, and in times of flood travellers were occasionally obliged to wait for several days at a neighbouring *posada* before the river had subsided sufficiently to make the crossing.

After briefly following the S bank the well-engineered road climbs steadily, with magnificent retrospective *Views*, to (18.5km) the *Puerto de Miravete* (624m), at 13km passing *Jaraicejo*, with a handsome church. The road provides extensive vistas to the SW, with Trujillo on a height in the distance and, beyond, the pyramid of the *Sierra de Montánchez*.—We descend to cross the Almonte beside a picturesque earlier bridge, and bear S to (27.5km) **Trujillo**; see Rte 51.

TRUJILLO TO MÉRIDA VIA MONTÁNCHEZ (85km). The CC800 drives SW towards the characteristic outline of the *Sierra de Montánchez* (988m), at c 38km reaching the turning climbing steeply to the village of *Montánchez*. The hams of Montánchez, reputed in Extremadura, were much appreciated by Charles during his retirement at Yuste. The picturesquely sited town preserves the extensive remains of a Moorish *Alcázar* (views).—The N630 is reached further SW, 33km N of Mérida.

The NV veers S from Trujillo, at 14.5km passing *Sta. Cruz de la Sierra*, with prehistoric and Moorish ruins and a domed church, to cross the *Puerto de Sta. Cruz* (463m). At (22.5km) *Miajadas* the NV meets the C401 from Guadalupe; see Rte 50B.

MIAJADAS TO CASTUERA (67km). The C426 leads due S, crossing the Guadiana to (23km) **Don Benito** (27,800 inhab.), an ancient town with the Gothic hall-church of *Santiago*.—9.5km W is **Medellín**, Roman *Metellinum*, named after Metellus Pius (cf. Bilbilis). Once a flourishing town, and the birthplace of Hernán Cortés (1485–1547), conqueror of Mexico, it has never recovered from its sacking by Victor in 1809. The castle, partly restored, commands a fine view over the Guadiana, here crossed by a bridge of 1636.

6km to the E of Don Benito is **Villanueva de la Serena** (21,950 inhab.), birthplace of Pedro de Valdivia (1500–54), founder of Santiago de Chile, with a Gothic parish church, the *Conv. de S. Bartolomé*, and a Neo-Classical *Palace of the Order of Alcantara*.—The C420 bears SE, at 12km passing a turning (right) to (8km) *Magacela*, with a ruined castle.—26km **Castuera** (9050 inhab.), the main town of LA SERENA (see p 339, an arid and backward upland surrounded by mountains. It was once guarded against the Moors by the 'Siete Castillos de la Serena', seven forts at equal distance from each other in a semicircle 80km in length. The reactionary religious writer Donoso Cortés (1809–53) was born here.—6km SE on the road to *Cabeza del Buey* (see p 339) is the ruined castle of *Benquerencia de la Serena*.—16km SW is *Zalamea de la Serena* (6450 inhab.), which gave its name to Calderón's play 'El Alcalde de Zamalea' (c 1643). Zalamea's church tower incorporates part of a Roman temple.

From Miajadas the NV veers SW into the wide valley of the Guadiana, later crossing a low ridge to approach (53km) **Mérida**; see Rte 53.

B.   Via Toledo and Guadalupe

384km (238 miles). N401. 70km **Toledo**—52km *Navahermosa*—68km *La Nava de Ricomalillo*—22km the *Puerto de S. Vicente*—40km **Guadalupe**—35km *Logrosan*—44km *Miajadas*—NV. 53km **Mérida**.

Maps: M 447.

The road between Navahermosa and Logrosán—some 150km—is frequently slow and winding, and plenty of time should be allowed.

For the road to **Toledo** see Rte 43. On crossing the Tagus adjacent to the *Puente de S. Martín* turn right.—At 13km the well-preserved mid 15C castle of *Guadamur* is passed to the right. It has a solid square keep surmounted by six projecting turrets, and a lower wing with larger drum corner towers, between which thrust triangular towers, each topped by turrets. (In the mid 19C, at nearby *Guarrazar*, beside a fountain on the Toledo road, the Visigothic royal treasure now in the Archaeological Museum, Madrid, was discovered.)—3km *Polán*, with a battered castle similar to that at Guadamur.—16km *Gálvez*, with a 12th and 15C Mudéjar church.

Some 22km S of Gálvez, within a semicircle of mountains, is the ruined monastery of *S. Pablo de los Montes*.

At 9.5km we reach crossroads.—A worthwhile DETOUR is that to **Melque**, approached by turning right onto the C403 for 11km and then right again for 3km. The restored Mozarabic church of *Sta. María*, of c 862–930, displays several horseshoe arches within sturdy Cyclopean walls. The tower, built over a dome, is probably a later addition. Note the interior string courses and the rounded corners of the exterior. (Intending visitors should check about admission with the Museo de Sta. Cruz, Toledo.)—To the NW of the turning off the C403 is the large ruined castle of *Montalbán* (12C; possibly built by the Templars), with a huge entrance archway, and overlooking the ravine of the Torcón. Montalbán was the birthplace of Fernando de Rojas (1465–1541), the author of 'La Celestina'.

The castle of *Las Dos Hermanas* is passed on approaching (10.5km) *Navahermosa*. To the SW of Navahermosa at *Hontanar* are the ruined 14C *Torre de Malamoneda*, a ruined castle, and a hermitage.—Bear NW to (21.5km) *Los Navalmorales* and then veer SW along the foothills of the MONTES DE TOLEDO. At (46.5km) *La Nava de Ricomalillo*, where the road is joined by the C503 from Talavera, circle to the S to (22km) the *Puerto de S. Vicente* (807m), crossing the SIERRA DE ALTAMIRA, where the road from El Puente de Arzobispo is met; see Rte 50A.

The C401 winds down to cross the Guadarranque and climbs again, at 20km reaching a road turning left.

This leads 22km S to *Castilblanco*, overlooking the *Embalse de García de Sola*. Here, on the last day of 1931, the detested Guardia Civil were murdered by the villagers as they attempted to prevent a demonstration by Socialists against the civil governor of Badajoz.—16.5km further S is *Herrera del Duque*, with a castle and fortified church.—From *Valdecaballeros* (13km SW of Castilblanco) one may skirt the W bank of the reservoir, part of the dammed Guadiana, at 22km meeting the N430, which provides a comparatively rapid drive to *Mérida*, 113km W.

Continuing to wind across the wooded SIERRA DE GUADALUPE to the W from this turning, at 16km we reach a right-hand turning climbing below the disused railway viaduct to (4km) Guadalupe.

Guadalupe (640m; Parador; Hostel in the monastery precincts), an attractively sited village, retains arcaded cobbled streets, but it is spoilt by the religious souvenir industry. The place is dominated by the celebrated fortified *Monastery*, founded in 1340.

In June 1492, at a ceremony here in the presence of the Catholic Kings, Abraham Seneor, the eminent Jewish courtier and financier, accepted baptism as Fernando Nuñez Coronel. The monastery was sacked by the French in 1809 and abandoned in 1835, but since 1908 has been occupied by Franciscans.

Opposite the Parador (with a Mudéjar cloister) stands the restored *New Church* (1730). To the W, facing the picturesque *Pl. Mayor*, is the richly decorated façade of the old *Church* of 1389–1412, built by Juan Alfonso. Steps ascend to the doors, plated with bronze, new in 1433.

The nave is entered below a wide arch, to the right of which is a remarkable reja of 1514 by Francisco de Salamanca; the crestings over the aisle screens survive from the 15C. The *Cap. Mayor*, adorned with marbles, has a classical retablo by Juan Gómez de Mora, with paintings by Carducho and Eugenio Cajés. Above the high altar is the image of N.S. de Guadalupe (see below). The *Cap. de Sta. Catalina* contains the tombs of Prince Dinis of Portugal and his wife Joana (1461), and the *Cap. de Sta. Ana*, beside the entrance vestibule, the monument of Alonso de Velasco, by Anequín de Egas. The bronze Font is by Juan Francés (1402).

Adjacent to the church entrance is that to the *Monastery*. One is obliged to join a perfunctorily guided tour, but *take your time*. The *Mudéjar Cloister* (1402–12) of two storeys, entirely of brick with horseshoe arches, contains a central fountain surmounted by a pavilion of 1405 known as the *Glorieta* or *Templete*. This is capped with an octagonal spire of three diminishing stages, each with gables, blind-arcaded, and with a groundwork of green and white tiles. The cloister also contains the tomb of Bp Illescas of Córdoba, by Anequín de Egas (1458), and a 15C polychrome Calvary.

Adjacent is the *Old Refectory*, housing a collection of sumptuous 14–17C vestments and altar frontals, etc. That of Enrique II (No. 61) is outstanding.

The *Chapterhouse*, with a 16C arabesqued ceiling, contains a collection of 86 choir books, some with miniatures, missals, and bindings, and a 15C alabaster Virgin. Among the paintings, many deteriorated, are: attributed to *Isembrandt*, a Triptych; *Juan de Flandés*, Baptism; *Juan Correa*, Nativity; and a small painting by *Goya*.

The raised *Coro* of the church is next entered, with Churrigueresque Stalls of 1744 by Alejandro Carnicero, a 14C wooden Candelabrum, and remarkable organ cases.

Passing through the Antesacristia, the lavishly decorated *Sacristia (begun 1638) is entered. It displays—unfortunately badly lit—eight paintings of 1638–47 by Zurbarán, some illustrating the Life of St. Jerome; others are portraits of monks of his Order. In Widdrington's opinion, these paintings, 'untouched and uninjured', should have been moved to the Prado before they suffered the same fate as had the library, and where they might be *seen* to better advantage; nevertheless, it is remarkable to see such masterpieces still in the positions prepared for them. The study of Fray Gonzalo de Illescas seated at a table is outstanding. The windows and pictures are identical in size and are identically framed, and both wardrobes and mirrors form part of the design.

In the adjacent chapel are further paintings, including *Zurbarán's* Apotheosis of St. Jerome, and a Temptation of the saint (School of Zurbarán; also attributed to *Ribera*). Note the similarity of the temptress to the richly-clothed santas in the Sevilla Museum. A Turkish ship's lantern captured at Lepanto also hangs here.

From the adjoining *Cap. de Sta. Catalina* the octagonal *Relicario* of 1595, by Nicolás Vergara the Younger, is entered. The engraved silver-gilt box by Juan de Segovia (mid 15C), with earlier enamels, is of interest.—Red jasper stairs ascend to the *Joyero* of 1651, containing an ivory crucifix belonging to Felipe II, a Christ by Morales, paintings by Luca Giordano, and eight polychrome biblical figures by Luisa Roldán, including an enchanting Ruth.—In the *Camarin* (1696; by Francisco Rodríguez), seated on a hideous modern gyrating enamelled throne, is the gaudily-dressed smoke-blackened image of N.S. de Guadalupe.

Although not normally included in the tour, ask to see the *Gothic Cloister* (1502–24), now somewhat mutilated, round which the hostal has been installed. From its entrance one may walk round the exterior of the monastery, its solid bulk lightened by slender turrets, their pinnacles decorated with green and white tiles, to get back to the Pl. Mayor.

The heaths and hills around Guadalupe, rising to 1601m to the W, a height approached from the early 15C *Ermita del Humilladero* on the Oropesa road, provide several pleasant walks.

Regaining the C401, we climb to the *Puerto Llano* (642m; views) and traverse (17.5km) *Cañamero*, producer of the local turbid wine, to

approach (13.5km) **Logrosán**, in a valley below the W ridge of the
sierra. It has long been known for its rich deposits of lime phosphate
found in the hard black schist, whose sharp slaty rocks formerly
protruded uncomfortably in the village streets. 13–14C *S. Mateo*,
later altered, retains a good apse. Remains of a castle and relics of a
pre-Roman settlement may be seen on the hill of *S. Cristóbal* to the S.

20km *Zorita*. *Trujillo* (see Rte 51), 28km NW, is reached by the C524.

ZORITA TO CASTUERA (90km). The CC702 turns S just before Zorita for (19km)
Madrigalejo, where—en route from Trujillo—Fernando the Catholic died in
January 1516. The N430 is reached 11km beyond. Turning right here and then
left through *Acedera*, the Guadiana is crossed S of (9.5km) *Orellana la Vieja*,
with a castle containing a Renaissance patio. Continuing S, the Zújar is later
crossed (both rivers dammed to form reservoirs), and the lonely steppe of LA
SERENA is crossed to *Castuera*; see Rte 50A.

The C401 continues SW from Zorita to meet the NV at (24km)
Miajadas.—53km **Mérida**; see Rte 53.

51 Trujillo to Cáceres and Valencia de Alcántara (for Portalegre)

154km (95 miles). N521. 49km **Cáceres**—29.5km *Aliseda*—65.5km
Valencia de Alcántara.

Maps: M 447.

The more interesting road from Aliseda to Valencia de Alcántara
via Alburquerque, some 12km longer than the main route, is also
described.

TRUJILLO (9050 inhab.; Parador), an ancient and 'monumental'
town, one of the more interesting of its size in Spain, and dominated
by its castle, stands on a low hill skirted by the NV from Madrid to
Mérida. It is a convenient base from which to explore N
Extremadura.

Although it claims to have been founded by Julius Caesar, its name is a
corruption of *Turgalium*. It suffered the usual vicissitudes of the Reconquest,
falling to Giraldo Sempavor in 1165, and was refortified by Alfonso VIII after 1185.
It was retaken by the Almohads, and did not remain permanently in Christian
hands until after 1233.
    It was the birthplace of several *conquistadores*, among them Francisco Pizarro
(1476–1541), the brilliant but treacherous subjugator of the Incas; his half-
brothers Hernando (?1478–1557) and Gonzalo (1511/13–48); Francisco de
Orellana (1511–46), first explorer of the Amazon; and Diego García de Paredes
(1466–1530), the right hand of Gonzalo de Córdoba.
    Col John Squire (1780–1812), a military engineer employed on the con-
struction of the Lines of Torres Vedras and on bridging the Guadiana, died here.

The narrow streets of the old town are best explored from the
picturesque *Pl. Mayor**, overlooked to the N by well-vaulted *S.
Martín*, with good tombs and organ. Near the NE corner are the
solares of the *Duques de S. Carlos* and *Conde del Puerto*; to the S is
the *Pal. de Piedras Albas*; and further W, the 17C *Pal. de la
Conquista*.—Further to the SW is the *Pal. de Orellana-Pizarro*, with a
Plateresque patio.
    Behind the pharmacy at No. 14 C. Tiendas, leading S, stood the

Synagogue, the former entrance to which may be seen on request.—
Further S is 16C *S. Francisco*.

From the NW corner of the plaza one may ascend the Cuesta de la
Sangre to the right and through an arch, passing the 16C *Pal. de los
Chaves*, to *Santiago*.—A lane climbs right to the *Castle (under
restoration), with square Moorish towers and later additions. The
parapets provide extensive views. A lane to the left leads past the
rebuilt birthplace of Pizarro to approach *Sta. María* (15C), with an
over-restored older tower.—Further W is a restored arab cistern or
aljibe; several restored mansions, and the cemetery. Beyond the
cemetery is the best stretch of *Walls*, N of which is the *Conv. de S.
Francisco* (partly restored).

The castle at Trujillo from the west

Some distance to the E of the plaza (approached by car from the
Plasencia road) is the *Conv. de Sta. Clara*, transformed to house the
Parador. Several other stork-occupied towers and seigniorial mansions built by the returning *conquistadores* may be discovered in the
side streets of the town, which require some time and a stout pair of
shoes to explore in detail.

For the roads to *Montánchez* and *Plasencia* see pp 334 and 217.

The N521, formerly tree-shaded, leads due W, crossing olive groves
and pasture land. It skirts the SIERRA DE FUENTES on approaching
(49km) *Cáceres*, whose ancient towers dominate the growing modern town. The road circles N to the tree-lined Av. de España.

CÁCERES (65,750 inhab.; 20,000 in 1920; 40,000 in 1950) is a
pleasant provincial capital retaining a well-preserved medieval town
of considerable character.

Roman *Colonia Norbensis Caesarina*, on the Via Lata from Mérida to Astorga, was long a bone of contention between the Moors and Christians. Here in 1170 the militant Order of Santiago was founded, but it was not until 1229 that the town was finally conquered, by Alfonso IX.

Cáceres was the birthplace of several *conquistadores*, including Francisco Hernández Girón (?1505–53), later a rebel leader in Peru; and of José de Carvajal y Lancáster (1698–1754), minister of Fernando VI.

From the Av. de España the C.S. Antón leads NE, off which fork right past 15C *S. Juan* to approach the partially arcaded **Pl. Mayor**. This is flanked by the *Torre de Bujaco*, on Roman foundations; a Moorish tower; and to the SW by the *Ayuntamiento*.

Ascend steps on the SE side of the plaza to enter the **'Old Town**,

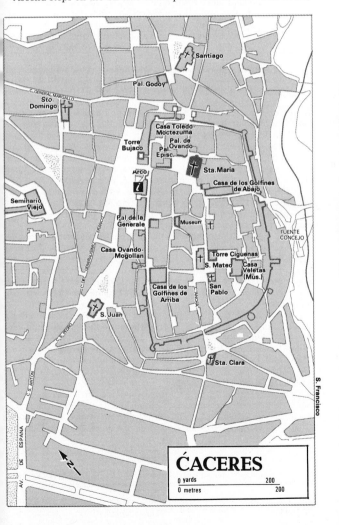

CÁCERES

0 yards   200
0 metres   200

S. Francisco

still surrounded by its partly Roman *Walls* with their gates and towers (much built against); their interior *adarves* may be followed except to the S and SE. The enceinte is traversed by narrow stepped lanes lined with the grim-looking *solares* of the *conquistadores* and their descendants. Almost any of its alleys will repay the unhurried wanderer, but the itinerary which follows takes in the more remarkable buildings. (If possible, a second visit should be made after dark, when its medieval atmosphere is more strongly felt.)

We approach the Pl. de Sta. María, passing (left) the *Pal. Episcopal*, built in 1587.—To the left is the *Pal. de Ovando*, with a Plateresque portal and fine patio.—At the N angle of the enceinte is the *Pal. de Toledo-Moctezuma*, once the residence of descendants of Juan Cano, a follower of Cortés and husband of the daughter of the last Aztec emperor.—To the E is the *Casa Carvajal*; to the W the *Pal. Mayoralgo*, with a 16C tower.—**Sta. María**, mainly 16C, has a tower designed by Pedro de Ibarra and a good retablo of 1551.

A lane leads NE from here to *Santiago*, a short distance beyond the walls, built by Rodrigo Gil de Hontañón in 1556. It has a fine reja and a retablo of 1563 by Berruguete.—To its W is the *Pal. de Godoy* (1594), with its corner balcony.

Turning S from Sta. María we pass (left) the remarkable *Pal. de los Golfines de Abajo* (late 15C) and, opposite, the 16C granite front of the *Casa de los Becerras*, between which a lane descends to the *Arco del Cristo*, the most complete of the Roman gates.—Ascending the Cuesta de la Compañía, the *Jesuit Church* and College of 1698–1750 are skirted to reach 15C *S. Mateo*, with a striking tower, and containing the tomb of the Marqués de Valdepuentes.

To the E is the 15C *Pal. de las Cigüeñas*, with a tower of 1477, and, opposite, the 17C front of the *Casa de Ovanda-Mogollón* or *Pal. de las Veletas*. It incorporates a mid 12C cistern, part of the Moorish Alcázar, and contains archaeological collections.

The C. Ancha descends S from the Pl. de S. Mateo past the *Casa de Ulloa*, *Casa de Paredes-Saavedra*, and *Casa de Sánchez de Paredes*, to the E of which is the 16C *Casa de los Pereros* (with exhibitions of contemporary art). Just beyond the walls is the *Conv. de Sta. Clara*, with a portal of 1614, from which the C. de Damas leads S to the great *Conv. de S. Francisco*, founded in 1472, with a fine late Gothic church and cloister.

In the C. del Olmos, parallel to and W of the C. Ancha, is the *Casa de Ovando-Pereros*.—Just NW of S. Mateo are the *Pal. de Roda*, the *Casa de Aldana*, the *Casa del Mono*, and the *Casa del Sol*.—Further W are the *Pal. de Golfines de Arriba* (15C, with a notable tower of 1515), and the *Casa Adanero*. Following the adjacent *adarve* skirting the walls we pass the 15C *Pal. de la Generala* to regain the steps by which we entered the enceinte.

To the N of the plaza is the *Abrantes palace* (16C, with an earlier patio), to the NW of which is *Sto. Domingo* (1524). SW of the church is the 16C *Casa de Galarza*, and S of the adjacent square, the *Pal. de la Isla*, W of which is the *Seminario Viejo* or *Col. de S. Pedro* (1604).

At *Cáceres el Viejo*, N of the town, stood the Roman camp of Q. Cecilius Metellus, dating from the war of 79 BC against Sertorius.

For the roads N to **Plasencia** and **Salamanca**, and **Coria** and **Ciudad Rodrigo**, see Rtes 27A and C, respectively; for that to **Mérida** and Sevilla, Rte 52.

The N523 leads 91km SW direct to *Badajoz*, traversing a remote and depopulated region of slight interest, and crossing three low passes.

CÁCERES TO ALCÁNTARA (63km) FOR CASTELO BRANCO, 78km beyond. The C523 forks right off the N521 13km W of Cáceres to (7km) **Arroyo de la Luz** (6600 inhab.), its church with a Retablo containing paintings by Morales, and a St. John by Pedro de Mena. A *Palace of the Counts of Benavente* is notable, while in the neighbourhood was ancient *Sansueña*.—At 17km *Garrovillas* lies 14km NE; see p 218.—The road turns W to (11km) **Brozas**, birthplace of several *conquistadores*, and of Francisco Sánchez de las Brozas ('el Brocense'; 1523–1601), the humanist. 16C Gothic *Sta. María* has a good tower and 18C retablos and rejas.

A ruined tower is passed to the right and we approach (15km) **Alcántara**, taking its name from its *Bridge (Arabic el kantara)* over the Tagus. It spans the gorge on six arches of uncemented granite, the two main arches 33.5m wide and 64m above the normal level of the river; the total length is 204m. It was built for Trajan by Caius Julius Lacer c AD 105. One of the arches, destroyed by the Moors in 1213, was rebuilt in 1543; the second arch from the right bank was blown up by Gen. Mayne in 1809, and temporarily repaired with woodwork. It was impassable from 1836, when the wooden arch was destroyed by the Carlists, until 1860, when the whole bridge was restored. A great dam holding back the waters of the *Embalse de Alcántara*, just W of the confluence of the Tagus and Alagón, has been constructed a short distance to the E, which spoils the otherwise impressive site. On the left bank is a small *Roman temple* with a memorial of the architect and, in the centre, a *triumphal arch*.

The town was once the headquarters of the military Order of Alcántara (transferred here from Ciudad Rodrigo in 1218), established to defend the frontier against the Moors, and has ruins of a castle. The 13C *Parish church* contains tombs of the Grand Masters of the Order and paintings by Morales. The *Church and Conv. de S. Benito* (1499–1577), begun by Pedro de Ibarra, with a dignified cloister and fine apse, is being restored.

Crossing the Tagus, at 11km we reach *Piedras Albas* (13km S of *Zarza la Mayor*; see Rte 27C), with Spanish Customs. The Portuguese frontier is 7km NW, here the Rio Erges, beyond which the road circles to the W to (60km) *Castelo Branco*; see Blue Guide Portugal.

From a point 5km S of Alcántara the CC220 leads 30km SW to meet the N521 27km from *Valencia de Alcántara*; see below.

The N521 leads due W from Cáceres to (29.5km) *Aliseda*, where the more interesting road (C521) to Valencia de Alcántara turns left for (43km) **Albuquerque** (6450 inhab.), a picturesque fortified town and centre of cork production. Inês de Castro was briefly exiled here c 1340. It fell to the Earl of Galway and Col John Richards (cf. Alicante) on 21 May 1705 after a short siege.

Its ruined *Castle* (1314), Gothic *Sta. María*, and *S. Mateo*, are of interest.

Some 12km E, perched above the N bank of the *Embalse de Peña del Águila*, reached by a poor road, is the castle of *Azagala*.—Badajoz is 45km due S on the C530.—To the W are the rock paintings of *El Risco de S. Blas*.—Some 13km NE, off the BA500, is the restored castle of *Piedrabuena*.

Follow the C530 NW to (34km) **Valencia de Alcántara** (8050 inhab.). In the vicinity are the remains of Roman *Julia Contrasta*. The walled town was captured in 1664 by the Anglo-Portuguese commanded by Major-Gen. John Burgoyne. Within the 13C castle is *N.S. de Roque Amador*. 13C *La Encarnación* has a Mudéjar doorway; its 17C organ has been converted into a chicken run.

The road bears SW, with the SERRA DE SÃO MAMEDE rising ahead, and shortly turns NW to reach the frontier at 12km (Customs).—At 9km *Marvão* is approached by climbing to the right; 1km beyond this junction a left turning climbs over the serra to (16.5km) *Portalegre*; the road ahead leads 8.5km to *Castelo de Vide*: see Blue Guide Portugal.

52   Cáceres to Sevilla via Mérida and Zafra

273km (169 miles). N630. 71km **Mérida**—27km *Almendralejo*—
27km **Zafra** is 6km SW—N432. 7km—N630. 64km *Sta. Olalla*—
71km **Sevilla**.

Maps: M 447, 446.

Drive S, with the SIERRA DE S. PEDRO to the SW and the SIERRA DE
MONTÁNCHEZ to the SE, at 14km passing the castle of *Herguijuelas*
to the left and, shortly beyond, castle ruins. At 16km there is a
turning to *Montánchez* itself; see p 344. Passing between the two
ranges we enter the broad valley of the Guadiana and approach
(41km) **Mérida**; see Rte 53.

20km SE, approached by a by-road skirting the left (S) bank of the Guadiana, is
the hilltop village of *Alange*, with a castle and three domed chambers of Roman
baths. It was near here in 1230 that Alfonso IX defeated a relief force of Moors
approaching Mérida. The valley beyond is being dammed.—*Almendralejo* is
21.5km SW.

Climbing out of the Guadina valley, we cross a ridge and at 27km
skirt **Almendralejo** (23,700 inhab.), birthplace of José de Espronceda
(1808–42), the poet. *La Purificación* dates from 1539.—At 15km
Villafranca de los Barros (12,450 inhab.) is bypassed. It has several
old houses and *Sta. María*, with a good Gothic façade.—Juan
Mélendez Valdés (1754–1817), the poet, was born at *Ribera del
Fresno*, 10km E.

12km *Los Santos de Maimona* (7550 inhab.) is just to the W, off the
road turning here to (6km) *Zafra*. Los Santos was a Roman site, where
the disc of Theodosius was found (now in the Real Academia de la
Historia, Madrid). Gothic *Los Ángeles* is notable.

Zafra (13,050 inhab.; Parador) was the Iberian *Segada*, and Roman
Julia Restituta, and called *Zafar* by the Moors. Manuel García (1805–
1906), the famous singing teacher, was born here.

In the town centre is the former *Alcázar*, later the residence of the
Dukes of Feria. Now accommodating the Parador, it was built for
Lorenzo Suárez de Figueroa in 1443, whose figleaf device appears on
this and several other buildings. It was gutted by the French in 1811.
The white marble patio was altered in the 16C.

In the adjoining chapel of *Sta. Marina* is the tomb (1601) of Lady
Margaret Harrington, erected by her cousin Jane Dormer, Duchess of
Feria and maid of honour to Mary Tudor. The tomb of the duchess
and of her husband, the Spanish ambassador to England, is in the
15C *Conv. de Sta. Clara*, S of the C. Mayor.—This leads right to the
arcaded *Pl. Grande* and adjacent *Pl. Chica* (both restored), an
attractive and characteristic area.

14C *N.S. de la Candelaria* contains 17C fittings, and paintings by
Zurbarán; the *Hosp. de Santiago* retains a good Gothic portal.

Ruins of a Moorish castle may be seen at *Medina de las Torres*, 10km S.

For the roads to **Jerez de los Caballeros** and to **Fregenal de la Sierra** see Rtes
55 and 56 respectively. For that from **Badajoz** to **Córdoba** via Zafra, Rte 54.

The N630 is regained 7km SE. At 12km it bypasses *Calzadilla de los
Barros*, with a good church, and, 6.5km beyond, *Fuente de Cantos*
(5350 inhab.), birthplace of Francisco de Zurbarán (1598–1664), its
parish church with a Baroque retablo.—Roman ruins lie c 4km SW.

We start to climb the N foothills of the SIERRA MORENA, at 15km passing a turning to *Montemolín*, 7km NE, with a Moorish castle and old houses.—6km *Monesterio* (6150 inhab.).

7km W at *Calera de León* is a medieval monastery of the Order of Santiago, with a Gothic church and two-storeyed cloister.—Some 7km S of Calera in the SIERRA DE TUDIA is the monastery of *Sta. María de Tentudía*, founded in the 13C, containing azulejos of 1518 by Niculaso Pisano and a Mudéjar cloister.

Crossing the *Puerto de las Marismas*, the easiest route through the convoluted sierra into Andalucía, at 22.5km a turning leads 9.5km NW to *Cala*, with castle ruins. After 2km we cross *Sta. Olalla*, also with a ruined castle.—15km SW is *Zufre*; see Rte 104.

At 31km we cross the dammed Rivera de Huelva, and 5km beyond the N433 from Aracena is met; see Rte 104. The road shortly starts to climb down from the sierra into the wide valley of the Guadalquivir, at 24km passing (right) the site of *Itálica* (see p 576). After 8km bear left across the arms of the river to enter **Sevilla**; see Rte 101.

53   Mérida to Badajoz (for Elvas and Évora)

61km (38 miles). NV.

Maps: M 447.

MÉRIDA (41,050 inhab.; 15,500 in 1920; Parador) has grown considerably in recent decades after centuries of vegetation. Once the capital of the Roman province of *Lusitania*, it contains more important Roman remains than any other town in Spain, but only recently has a museum worthy of the name to display these antiquities been inaugurated.

In 23 BC the legate Publius Carisius founded *Augusta Emerita* as a settlement for veterans of Augustus's Cantabrian wars. It flourished under the Visigoths, but in autumn 712 it was besieged by the Moors under Musa, and surrendered the following June. It was reconquered by Alfonso IX in 1230 and presented to the Order of Santiago, but the former metropolitan see was not restored owing to the opposition of the archbishop of Compostela, and Mérida never regained its former importance although granted the privilege of having a fair in 1300. The peripatetic Catholic Kings never even bothered to visit the place during their progresses through the peninsula. It put up a brief defence on 10 August 1936 when attacked by Yagüe and his Moors, before he turned on Badajoz.

It was the birthplace of Shemuel ha-Levi ben Yosef Nagrella (993–1056), the poet, rabbi, and general; Juan Pablo Forner (1756–97), the writer and polemicist; and José María Calatrava (1781–1847), the Liberal politician.

The NV from Trujillo bypasses Mérida to the E, to cross the Guadiana by a bridge of eight spans (1960), but fork right on approaching the town. This Av. de Extremadura skirts the slight remains of the NW end of the *Circus Maximus*, restored in 337–50, which once held 26,000 spectators. Excavations have laid bare some rooms in which the gladiators may have been housed. To the right is the *Acueducto S. Lázaro*.

To the right, just beyond gardens (left) is *Sta. Eulalia*. It dates from the 13C but preserves in the nave some Visigothic capitals from an earlier church on this site. The *Hornito* is claimed to be the oven in

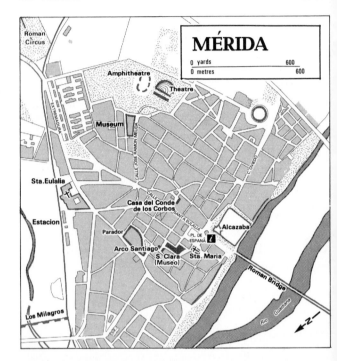

which the child martyr Eulalia (292–304) was roasted alive. The porch incorporates Roman material.

The Rambla opposite leads shortly to a junction of several little streets. The C. José Ramón Melida turns left to approach the *Museo Nacional de Arte Romana, the *Theatre*, and *Amphitheatre*.

The **Museum**, inaugurated in 1986 and still being arranged, is built in brick in a modern functional style over the site of the *Thermae*, the excavations of which are shown in situ. On the Ground Floor are most of the sculptures, including those of Augustus, Chronos, Isis, Ceres, Proserpina, and Mercury, and several examples of stelae, cippi, well heads, mosaics, lamps, bronzes, and murals. The First Floor is devoted to terra sigillata, ceramics, glass, jewellery, and numismatic collections. The Second Floor displays several other mosaics (against the walls), including boar-hunting and mythological scenes; epigraphical collections; a relief depicting a woman playing a form of lute; more stelae, and a number of busts (note the various forms of hair dressing).

To the SE is the *Theatre, dating from 24 BC, and one of the finest Roman monuments extant in Spain. The vomitoria or entrance passages, are remarkably well preserved, but the stage, with its elegant colonnade, has been largely rebuilt.—Adjacent is the **Amphitheatre** of AD 8, which had room for 15,000 spectators. Remains of a temple of Serapis and of a paleo-Christian basilica and necropolis have also been uncovered.

On returning along the C. José Ramón Melida, turn left along the main pedestrian street, passing near (right) the *Casa del Conde de los*

Corbos, built into a temple, preserving its peristyle of Corinthian columns, to reach the PL. DE ESPAÑA.

To its S is the **Alcazaba**, successively a Roman, Visigothic, and Moorish castle (in 835), an episcopal palace, a house of the Templars, and the residence of the 'provisor' of the Order of Santiago. It was gutted by the French in 1808. Within may be seen a restored courtyard. Steps descend to a huge cistern.

Skirt its N wall to the *Roman Bridge of 64 granite arches crossing the sluggish Guadiana. Dating from the time of Trajan, it was repaired in 686 and again in 1610. When two arches were broken down in 1812 to retard Marmont's attempted relief of Badajoz no move was made to repair them until after 1835.

On the sandbank upstream are relics of a Roman work called *El Tajamar*, built to protect the bridge piers from floods. The bridge that crosses the *Albarregas* (*Alba Regis*) a little downstream is built on Roman foundations.

Sta. María (on the W side of the Pl. de España), has Romanesque and Plateresque features. A few paces N is the former *Conv. de Sta. Clara*, containing a collection of antiquities, including Visigothic fragments, among which are some pre-Moorish horseshoe windows.—A short distance further N is the *Arco de Santiago*, a triumphal arch 13.5km high, stripped of its marble casing.—On the far side of the adjacent Pl. de la Constitución is the Parador, from which one may regain the central pedestrian street.

Some distance to the NW, to the right of the road to Cáceres just after crossing the railway, are the imposing remains of the Roman aqueduct of *Los Milagros*, ten arches of which still stand, now serving as the headquarters of the stork population of the Guadiana valley. It is possible that its red brick courses were laid to cushion the effects of earth tremors.

It once conveyed water from the *Lago de Proserpina* or *Charco de la Albuera* into the city. This lies to the NW, preserving a granite retaining wall and staircase towers.—A smaller reservoir, the *Albuera de Cornalbo*, near *Trujillanos* (reached by a road leading left off the NV 14km NE), has steps arranged in rows as though for a naumachia.

For *Alange*, 20km SE, see Rte 52; also for the road S to *Sevilla*.

Crossing the Guadiana, turn W below a ridge of hills beyond its S bank, at 24.5km passing a turning to *Montijo* (6.5km N), site of a minor battle between the Spanish and Portuguese in 1664, and the ancestral home of the Condesa de Montijo (1826–1920), from 1853 the Empress Eugénie, wife of Napoleon III.—At 16km inappropriately named *Talavera la Real* is bypassed, where *Sta. María de la Ribera* incorporates early Christian remains.

At c 14km we pass, on the far bank of the Guadiana, the village of *Sagrajas* (approached by a turning off the N523 from Badajoz to Cáceres). Near it took place the battle of *Zalaca* or *Sacrialis* (1086), in which Alfonso VI was severely defeated by Yusuf I, the Almoravid.

Badajoz, on its hill, is now approached. It is also bypassed to the S by the NV, which crosses the Guadiana by a modern bridge.—Fork right and either enter the town adjacent to the *Puerta de la Trinidad* (1680) or turn right just short of it to circle below the walls to reach the *Puente de Palmas*, a granite bridge designed by Herrera in 1596.

BADAJOZ (111,450 inhab.; 41,000 in 1920; 76,000 in 1950), the ancient capital of Extremadura, is mainly famous for the sieges it has sustained, particularly that of 1812, one of the more sanguinary episodes of the Peninsular War. The town itself is of slight interest, but has increased in size and importance since the 'Badajoz Plan' of harnessing the waters of the Guadiana has improved the economy of the area.

Badajoz, a name which has been derived from the Roman *Pax Augusta*, rose to prominence in 1009 when the al-Aftas Moors formed an independent principality at *Batatjoz* after the breakup of the emirate of Córdoba. The battle of Zalaca took place not far to the NE in 1086; see above. It was later subdued by the Almoravides, and was a focus of the struggle between Moors and Christians until finally secured in 1230 by Alfonso IX shortly before his death.

Its position on the Portuguese frontier has exposed it to many sieges: by the Portuguese in 1660; by the Allies in the War of the Spanish Succession (1705); by the French in 1808 and 1809. More important was Soult's siege of 1810–11, unsuccessful until the death of Rafael Menacho, who commanded the garrison. The perfidy of his successor, José Imaz, admitted the French and delayed for a year the relief of Andalucía. Beresford failed to recover the place in 1811.

On 16 March 1812 Wellington launched a surprise attack, and after dreadful carnage in the breaches the British forced their way into the fortress, which they then sacked. The defenders lost 1200 men out of 5000; the attackers 4760 out of 15,000.

It was again the scene of tragedy when captured by the Nationalists under Yagüe on 14 August 1936, when its Republican defenders—possibly 1800—were herded into the *old* bullring and massacred. Salazar's troops handed back to the Nationalists any refugees caught trying to escape across the border. An opponent of the Salazar regime, Gen. Humberto Delgado (1906–65) was murdered near here in strange circumstances, connived at by the Spanish authorities.

Badajoz was the birthplace of the *conquistadors* Pedro de Alvarado (1485–1541), lieutenant of Cortés; and Sebastián Garcilaso de la Vega (1500–59), protector of the Indians, who married an Inca princess; Luis Morales (1506–86), the artist; and Manuel Godoy, Principe de la Paz (1767–1851), favourite of Carlos IV and lover of his queen.

The town of Ladysmith, in South Africa, is named after a young girl of Badajoz, Juana María de los Dolores de León, rescued from the sack by Harry Smith (1787–1860), who married her. In 1846 he became governor of the Cape. Here in January 1836 George Borrow spent his first ten days in Spain, mostly in the company of the local gypsies, who are still in evidence.

From the *Puerta de Palmas*, adjacent to the old bridge, one may ascend to the unimpressive PL. DE ESPAÑA, in the centre of the old town. It is flanked by the **Cathedral** (1232–84), with a façade with Ionic columns (1619). The tower (1240–1419) was altered in the 16C.

The interior is blocked by the Renaissance coro of 1558, by Jerónimo de Valencia, with good carving on the organ galleries; the two 18C organs have been restored. The high altar of 1708 is Churrigueresque. The Chapel of the Duques de Figueroa contains notable tombs; while the bronze tomb slab of Lorenzo Suárez de Figueroa (died 1506; cf. Zafra), by Alessandro Leopardi of Venice, is on the N side of the Cloister of 1520, with its interlacing arches. The Chapterhouse contains paintings by Morales, Ribera, and Zurbarán.

Among other churches are: to the E, 17C *S. Andrés*, with a triptych by Morales; *La Concepción* (NE), with two re-touched paintings by Morales; and *S. Agustín*, to the N, with the grotesque 18C monument of the Marqués de Blai, a general of Felipe V.

The *Castillo* or *Alcázaba* at the NE end of the town, a mass of Moorish (c 1170) and later ruins, commands a good view. At its foot is the arcaded PL. ALTA. Further S is the Moorish *Torre Espantaperros* (meaning to frighten Christian 'dogs'; cf. Despeñaperros), with an *Archaeological museum*.

A few steps W of the Pl. de España is the *Diputación*, with a Museum containing paintings by Morales, Zurbarán, and others. Near by is the *Conv. de Descalzas.*—On the W side of the town is the *Conv. de Sto. Domingo*, adjacent to the Parque de Castelar and the wide Av. de Colón.

Beyond the river rises the fortified hill of *S. Cristóbal.*

The Portuguese frontier is 4.5km W of the far bank (Customs), with the fortress town of *Elvas* 10.5km further W, for which see *Blue Guide Portugal*; likewise for *Estremoz*, 41km beyond, and *Évora*, 46km SW of Estremoz.

BADAJOZ TO VILLANUEVA DEL FRESNO VIA OLIVENZA (64km). The C436 leads 26km SW to **Olivenza** (9900 inhab.), formerly a strongly fortified town, which was occupied by the Spaniards in 1801. Despite provision in the 1814 Treaty of Paris for its return to Portugal, this was never implemented. Some of its architecture is distinctly Manueline. The *Castle* dates from 1306. Among the churches the 15C *Misericordia* contains good azulejos of 1723; *La Magdalena*, some impressive spiral pillars; *Sta. María* is late 16C. The former *Hosp. de la Caridad*, founded in 1501, and the late 15C Doorway of the *Municipal Library* are of interest.

At 18km *Alconchel*, with a brick and stone castle, is passed, and the road veers SW to (20km) *Villanueva del Fresno*, 9km E of the Portuguese frontier (Customs). *Mourão* is 7.5km further W; see *Blue Guide Portugal*.

For *Alburquerque*, 45km N of Badajoz on the C530, see Rte 51.

54 Badajoz to Córdoba via Zafra

270km (168 miles). N432. 24km *Albuera*—52km **Zafra**—35km *Llerena*—31km *Azuaga*—32km *Fuente Obejuna*—16km *Peñarroya*—80km **Córdoba**.

Maps: M 447, 446 (for the sub-route *Llerena to Lora del Río*).

Bearing SE, at 24km we drive through **La Albuera**, scene of the bloody battle of 16 May 1811, which took place to the W of the village. In it Beresford defeated Soult, although he failed to relieve Badajoz. Under Beresford were 35,000 allied troops, of whom 9000 were British; Soult's army numbered 24,000. The casualties were almost 6000 (of whom 4160 were British), and between 7–8000 French.

LA ALBUERA TO JEREZ DE LOS CABALLEROS (50km). The N435 leads due S via (12km) *Almendral*, with a fortified church.—7km SE of Almendral is the well-preserved castle of *Nogales* (1438).—13km *Barcarrota*, birthplace of Hernándo de Soto (?1500–42), the *conquistador*. The old castle accommodates the bull-ring.—A good view of **Jerez de los Caballeros** (see Rte 55) is obtained as the road winds down the *Valle de Matamoros*.—*Fregenal de la Sierra* is 22km further SE; see Rte 56.

At 29km the short DETOUR may be made to hilltop *Feria*, 4km right, with a ruined 15C castle.—At *Salvatierra de los Barros*, c 10km W, is a ruined 13C castle.

23km **Zafra**; see Rte 52. The N630 is crossed at 7km and we continue SE, later passing (left) the ruined tower of *Villagarcia*, to approach (35km) **Llerena** (5100 inhab.). Llerena, with old walls, and a pleasant *Pl. Mayor*, has several interesting churches, notably *N.S. de la Granada*, with a fine tower, 55m high and topped by a *giralda*, and a two-storeyed exterior gallery. The 15C *Pal. de Luis de Zapata* has been restored.

In the late 1970s some 6400 carcasses were discovered near here which have been the subject of anthropological enquiry: were they the victims of cholera in the 14C, or of the Inquisition, who had a tribunal here?

LLERENA TO LORA DEL RÍO (92km). The C432 leads SE, at 5km skirting *Casas de Reina*. In the vicinity are remains of the theatre of Roman *Regina* and an extensive Moorish *Alcazaba*. The C432 enters the foothills of the SIERRA MORENA, here a mining district (lead, coal, and iron) of which the main centre is (22km) *Guadalcanal*. From 1728 Lady Mary Herbert and Joseph Gage drained its silver mines, as described by John Talbot Dillon. It was the

birthplace of Adelardo López de Ayala (1829–79), the statesman and dramatist.—*Alanis*, 11km beyond, has a 14C church and old fortifications. (The road
leading to *Fuente Obejuna*, 56km NE, is *not* recommended, although the
surface is good, winding through the wild and lonely ranges of the SIERRA
MORENA.

16.5km SW is **Cazalla de la Sierra** (5350 inhab.), with a number of 16–17C
houses, castle ruins, and several convents and churches, notably *N.S. de la
Consolación*, in the Gothic-Mudéjar style. On the outskirts is Baroque *N.S. del
Monte*.

25km **Constantina** (8100 inhab.), delightfully sited. Roman inscriptions survive, and there are castle ruins and a number of churches and chapels in various
states of decrepitude.—29km *Lora del Río*, on the Guadalquivir; see Rte 90.

The N432 turns due E from Llerena to (31km) **Azuaga** (10,100
inhab.), an ancient town (?*Municipium Julium*) with ruined castles.
In one called *Miramontes* the daughters of Trajan are said to be
buried.—At 11km we skirt *La Granja de Torrehermosa*, its church
with a Mudéjar tower of c 1500. At 21km the road bypasses **Fuente
Obejuna** (6800 inhab.), Carthaginian *Mellaria*, attractively sited on
the brow of a hill.

Its name recalls the play by Lope de Vega (1619) describing an incident which
had taken place here, when a cruel comendador of the Order of Calatrava was
assassinated by the villagers, a theme similarly treated by Tirso de Molina in 'La
dama del olivar'.

There are remains of 13–15C fortifications, and the church contains a
custodia by Enrique de Arfe.

The road gently descends the valley of the Guadiato, at 16km
passing through **Peñarroyo Pueblonuevo** (together 13,600 inhab.),
still the centre of a mining district (lead, iron, and copper), although
some buildings appear to be derelict.—*Hinojosa del Duque* is 31km
NE; see p 339.

7km *Belmez*, overlooked by its Moorish castle.—The road later
skirts the N bank of the *Embalse de Puente Nuevo*, at 41km passing
the ruined Moorish castle of *El Vacar*, and climbs over a shoulder of
the SIERRA MORENA.—*Cerro Muriano*, with copper mines and Iberian
settlements in the vicinity, is traversed and the road climbs down
steeply into the Guadalquivir valley to **Córdoba**; see Rte 92.

55 Zafra to Villanueva del Fresno via Jerez de los Caballeros (for Mourão and Évora)

84km (52 miles). N435. 9km—C4311. 31km **Jerez de los
Caballeros**—17km *Oliva de la Frontera*—27km *Villanueva del
Fresno*.

Maps: M 447.

19km *Burguillos del Cerro* retains a castle, possibly of Templar
foundation. The road follows the flank of the valley of the Ardila,
later crossing a ridge to descend to (21km) **Jerez de los Caballeros**
(10,200 inhab.), an attractive and characteristic old town, and the
birthplace of Vasco Núñez de Balboa (?1475–1519), the discoverer of
the Pacific. It is now a centre of the cork industry, and is reputed for
its hams.

It preserves remains of 13C walls and six gates, and a 14C *Castle* of the Knights Templar (Caballeros Templarios), who took the place from the Moors in 1229. Beside the castle is *Sta. María*, built in the 13C on a Visigothic site, but reconstructed in the 16C and later adorned in the Baroque taste.

Close to the *Clock Tower* is disused *La Vera Cruz*, now a wine vault. Slightly below the castle, on the saddle between the two hills on which the walled town was built, is the *Pl. Mayor*, with *Casas Consistoriales* of 1632, and **S. Miguel**, partly 15C but much altered, with a magnificent *Tower* of carved brick completed in 1756. Its Baroque S Doorway dates from 1719. The interior contains the Choir of the Order of Santiago, which succeeded the Templars.

Steep streets lead N to **S. Bartolomé**, mainly 16C but altered in 1739, with a W Front of azulejos in the Portuguese style, and a splendid *Tower* (1759), with interior vaulted ramps, its exterior of coloured stucco studded with azulejos and embossed, blue-glazed tablets. The baptistery is a late Gothic chapel. There are good effigies of Vasco de Jerez and his wife in the *Cap. de las Animas*.

To the SW, outside the walled town, is *Sta. Catalina*, the third of the so-called 'Torres Giraldinas'. Mainly 16C, the church contains a 17C retablo mayor and sculptures.

In the C. del Hospital, E of the Pl. Mayor, is the Gothic doorway of the roofless chapel of the *Hosp. de Transuentes*. To the NE the C. de Vasco Núñez de Balboa leads to the *Puerta de Burgo*, and is continued to the Pl. de Vasco Nuñéz, with the picturesque *Fuente de Caballos* beside the road.

Some 5km NW is the *Dolmen de Toniñuelo*, engraved with solar symbols.

The road winds through wooded country to skirt (17km) *Oliva de la Frontera* (6700 inhab.) and undulates NE parallel to the Portuguese frontier to bypass (27km) *Villanueva del Fresno*, there turning W to the frontier post (Customs).

Mourão lies 7.5km beyond, overlooking the Guadiana, which is to be dammed to the SW. For Mourão and for *Évora*, 55km further NW, see *Blue Guide Portugal*, and for *Monsaraz*, 12km NW of Mourão.

56 Zafra to Huelva

195km (121 miles). N435R. 42km *Fregenal de la Sierra*—41km *Jabugo* crossroads—44km *Minas de Riotinto* crossroads—23km *Valverde del Camino*—45km **Huelva**.

Maps: M 446.

The first two-thirds of this route are slow and winding, as the W extension of the SIERRA MORENA and the SIERRA DE ARACENA are crossed.

At 20km a left turning leads c 9km to *Valencia del Ventoso*, an ancient settlement with a castle of Moorish origin.—The road zigzags up to the *Puerto de la Granja* (575m) to (22km) **Fregenal de la Sierra** (5800 inhab.), birthplace of Arias Montano (1527–98), the humanist and first librarian of the Escorial, and of the politician Juan Bravo Murillo (1803–73). It was probably Roman *Concordia Julia Nertobrigensis*. Its castle dates from the 13C.

At *Segura de León*, 14km SE, are a 13C castle, 14C *La Asunción*, and the 17C *Ermita del Sto. Cristo de la Reja*.

15km *Cumbres de en Medio*.—4.5km E is *Cumbres Mayores*, with a late 14C castle. There are ruins of another castle 4.5km W, at *Cumbres de S. Bartolomé*.—The road winds across the sierra to meet and cross the N433 (see Rte 104) at 26km, before traversing the village of *Jabugo*, with a 17C church and with a reputation for its hams.

11km. *Almonaster*, 6km W, has castle ruins and a 16C church of interest.

11km. From this right-hand turning (H120) one may follow an ALTERNATIVE road (104km) to Huelva. This circles to the W via (39km) *Cabezas Rubias*, just S of which fork left through (15km) **Tharsis**, whose name recalls that of *Tartessos* or *Tarshish*, probably the Phoenician name for Andalucía. The copper mines here, exploited by Phoenicians and Romans, were—like those of Río Tinto— leased to Liebert Wolters. In private hands from 1829–66, when bought by a British company, they reverted to Spanish control in 1952. Hardly any trace of copper has been found in the ancient slag heaps, showing how perfect was the Roman system of smelting (cf. 'The Mines of Tharsis', by S.G. Checkland; 1967).—22km *Bartolomé de la Torre*, with an ancient castle, is passed, and the N431 is met 14km SE at *Gibraleón*, 16km from **Huelva**.

From the Cabezas Rubias fork another road bears right, winding through a broken depopulated region to meet the N431 at 66km, 7.5km E of *Ayamonte*; see Rte 103.

The main road continues to wind S, crossing the Odiel, and at 22km meets the C421 leading E to (8km) **Minas de Riotinto** which, with **Nerva**, 5km beyond, with a combined population of 13,800, is one of the oldest mining districts in the world. The mining area extends roughly from the Mérida–Sevilla highway to the *Minas de São Domingos*, beyond the Portuguese frontier. The Rio Tinto itself, its waters coloured by the copper and iron oxides washed into it, flows S through barren hilly country to reach and pollute the sea just E of Huelva.

The mines were worked probably by the Phoenicians, and certainly by the Romans, from Nerva to Honorius (AD 96–400). The workings were broken up by the Visigoths, and remained practically derelict until 1725 when they were leased by Felipe V to Liebert Wolters, a Swede, from whose successors they reverted to the crown in 1783. After nearly a century of indifferent success they were bought in 1873 by the Rio Tinto Company, largely a British concern. In 1954 the property reverted to Spanish ownership, but the British Rio Tinto-Zinc Corporation retains a one-third interest. D. Avery's study, 'Not on Queen Victoria's Birthday', gives the full history of the mines.

Nerva was the birthplace of Daniel Vázquez Díaz (1882–1969), the artist.

Zalamea la Real is bypassed as we follow the N435 S, circling to the W and then S again past (23km) *Valverde del Camino*. (At *Calañas*, 18km NW, is the chapel of *N.S. de España*, in which Roderic, the last 'king of the Goths', is said to be buried.)

25km *Trigueros* is bypassed. Near by are the rock carvings of the *Dolmen de Zancarrón de Soto*.—6km beyond Trigueros the A49 is reached 14km from the centre of **Huelva**; see Rte 103.

V CATALUNYA; ARAGÓN

Catalunya (*Cataluña* in Castilian; anglicised as *Catalonia*), comprising the four provinces of *Girona*, *Barcelona*, *Tarragona*, and *Lleida* (Lérida), is an ancient principality differing widely in character, climate, and language from the rest of the country; see also pp 93–94.

Separated from central Spain by the barren plains of the *Monègros* of eastern Aragón and by the mountains S of the Ebro, the Catalans have always looked upon the Mediterranean as their natural outlet. The soil of Catalunya is almost everywhere fertile, producing excellent wine, oil and fruit. Even where, as in the upland province of Lleida, the climate is less favourable, the hardworking peasantry surmounts the natural difficulties and 'make bread out of stones'.

There is little inertia here, and the capacity of the enterprising and mercantile Catalans to take advantage of modern industrial and commercial methods can be seen in the flourishing factories around Barcelona and many other towns. They mean business, and get on with the job.

Although the *Costa Brava*, the once attractive rocky coastline of the province of Girona, has changed radically during recent decades, and rarely for the better, inland and off the beaten track is some of the most beautiful countryside in Spain, of wooded hills and rich agricultural regions dotted with stone-built farms or *masias*, and endowed with a pleasant climate during most of the year.

Barcelona was recaptured from the Moors in 801, and the province was first governed by feudatories of the Frankish king, but the counts achieved effective independence in 874, and in 987 were recognised as sovereign princes after the brief recapture of Barcelona by Almanzor. The principality remained hereditary in the line of Wilfred 'el Velloso' (the Hairy; 857–902), whose descendants in 1137 acquired the throne of Aragón by marriage. Thenceforward the fate of the province was linked, even if tenuously, to that of Spain, but the Catalans clung obstinately to the partial independence embodied in their ancient *usatges* or code of rights. Both in 1640–43 and during the War of the Spanish Succession, Catalunya took the opportunity of rebelling against Castile, indicative of a desire for separation which has persisted. Even in the late 18C they would talk of making a journey *into* Spain, as they would of into France.

The futile wars of the 19C, hampering their commercial activities, frequently drove the Catalans to exasperation against the Madrid government and Carlism, republicanism, and anarchism were in turn supported by a resourceful people deprived of a peaceful safety valve. In 1879 the first newspaper to be written in Catalan, the 'Diari Català', was published; and during the following decades the voice of regionalism was heard increasingly. An alliance of Catalan parties, the SOLIDARITAT CATALANA, gained 41 of 44 seats in the 1907 elections for the Spanish *Cortes*. Attempts by the government to stop the growth of trade unions only precipitated outbreaks of violence, notably in July 1909 in Barcelona. The Spanish Anarchist party, the CNT, was later established, and kept up a running battle against the repressive measures of the authorities: by 1936 they counted 1,577,000 members.

Meanwhile, in 1888 and again in 1929 Universal or International exhibitions were held at Barcelona, symbolising the material prosperity of the Catalans. In 1931 a *Catalan Republic* was proclaimed under the presidency of Francesc Macià (1859–1933) after a plebiscite in which 592,961 voted for home rule and 3276 against, and Catalan autonomy was guaranteed by the new Spanish constitution, together with the official use of the Catalan language. (Its extensive literature is outlined in Arthur Terry's 'History of Catalan Literature'.)

During the Civil War Catalunya naturally supported the Republic; and for some years after, the effects of the disastrous struggle were felt more seriously here than in some other parts of the country—part of a deliberate policy of Nationalist (and Castilian) revenge. In 1940 Luis Companys, the President of the *Generalitat* from 1933, who had escaped to France, was turned over by the Nazis to Franco, and shot.

The recent prosperity of Spain has directed the natural energy of the Catalans back into its normal channel and, since the death of Gen. Franco, a certain measure of autonomy has again been introduced, the Generalitat being re-established in September 1977 under its president-in-exile, Josep Tarradellas. The Catalan language is now being used to an increasing extent, and place-names have reverted to their earlier form. Its population is now almost 6 million, more than double what it was in 1940, and it includes a large number of non-Catalans, mostly from the S of Spain, who have established themselves in Barcelona and other industrial centres (q.v. Bilbao), and who are known as *xarnegos*.

Aragón, to the West, comprises the provinces of *Huesca*, *Zaragoza*, and *Teruel*, extending over the middle Ebro basin from the Pyrenees to the Sierras of Javalambre and of the Maestrazgo to the S and SE. To the W, the Sierras de Cebollera, Moncayo, and the Montes Universales separate it from Castile. The barren Aragonese Pyrenees offer some impressive scenery, but from either bank of the Ebro extend sparsely inhabited semi-desert pasture lands, although hydroelectric schemes have increased the fertility of certain areas. These plains are subject to a Continental climate, with torrid summers and icy winters. Both the cold NW wind (*cierzo*) and the hot *bochorno* from the SE are robbed of all moisture by the mountains they traverse and rainfall is scanty.

It was in the Pyrenean fastnesses of the *Sobrarbe* that the Visigoths, driven there by the Moorish invasion, rallied, and eventually turned on the occupying Berbers. Zaragoza was recaptured by Alfonso el Batallador only a few years before Aragón became united with Catalunya in 1137. Their stubborn martial vigour, coupled with the trading capabilities of the Catalans, soon made the Aragonese respected throughout the Mediterranean. Like the Basques, they had their *fueros*, which strictly limited the powers of the king they elected, and they also appointed a *justiciar*, to whose authority any dispute involving their infringement was referred. The parchment on which these *fueros* were inscribed was in 1348 cut to threads by Pedro or Pere IV ('*el del puñal*'; him of the dagger); but the pertinacious Aragonese persisted in their rights even after the union with Castile until 1591, when Felipe II, enraged by Juan de Lanuza, the *justiciar* who had protected his scheming secretary Antonio Pérez, marched into Zaragoza, expelled the judge, and revoked their *fueros*. Some 61,000 industrious Moriscos left Aragón after 1609, and the region suffered in consequence.

The Aragonese have long had a reputation for obstinacy—so *testarudo*, that they were said (in the words of Richard Ford) 'to drive nails into walls with their heads, into which when anything is driven nothing can get it out'. For their resistance to the French during the Peninsular War see p 429.

The total population of Aragón has changed little during the last half century, although there has been a considerable drift from the provinces of Huesca and Teruel, while Zaragoza has increased from 575,000 to 828,500; the city of Zaragoza, now with 571,850 inhabitants, has increased by well over 100,000 in the last 20 years.

57 (Perpignan) Le Perthus to Barcelona via Figueres and Girona

A. Via the NII

164km (102 miles). NII. 26km *Figueres* junction—40km **Girona**—24km exit for the A7—26km *Calella*—21km **Mataro**—27km **Barcelona**.

Maps: M 443.

This route may be combined conveniently with the motorway (see Rte 57B) which provides suitable exits for most places of interest. It is certainly recommended to join the A7 S of Girona, unless making for any of the resorts on the coast between Blanes and Barcelona, which are described in the second half of this route.

For *Perpignan* and the road to the frontier at *Le Perthus* (Customs) see *Blue Guide France*.

The road climbs through the E foothills of the PYRENEES, here separating Roussillon from the Ampurdán/Empordà. Between 24 January and 10 February 1939 some 10,000 wounded, 170,000 women and children, 60,000 male civilians, and 220,000 men of the Republican army crossed the French frontier here during the closing stages of the Civil War, together with lorry loads of paintings from the Prado, en route to Geneva. Some 60,000 Republican troops were taken prisoner by the Nationalists.

6km *La Jonquera*, its church with a Romanesque door, is passed, to enter (19km; also bypassed) **Figueres** (30,400 inhab.), founded in 1267. It is dominated by the *Castillo de S. Fernando* to the NW, a fort laid out in the style of Vauban by Fernando VI, but seriously damaged in 1936 (now barracks). In its dungeon the Republican Cortes had their last meeting in Spain, on 1 February 1939.

Townsend, who in 1786 spent his first night in Figueres on 'three boards laid upon trestles to support a mattress', considered it a wasteful occupation building fortifications to keep people *out* of a country, and that the time and energy would have been better employed in 'mending roads, to invite strangers into Spain', an idea that has now taken root.

In 1701 Felipe V was married to Maria Luisa of Savoy in 14C *S. Pedro*, restored, with a Romanesque tower, octagonal lantern, 16C doorway, and modern windows. A few steps N of the tree-shaded Rambla in the centre, with the *Museo del Empordà*, is a meretriciously embellished *Museo-Teatro*, now accommodating a collection of works by the surrealist artist and exhibitionist Salvador Dali, born in Figueres in 1904.—To the W is a 15C palace.

Some 2km NE is *Vilabertran*, with an old palace and collegiate church (cons. 1101) with a good belltower.—*Peralada*, 3km beyond, was the birthplace of Ramón Muntaner (1265–1336), the Catalan chronicler. The Romanesque cloisters of the former Dominican friary and the capitals from S. Pere de Rodhes (see Rte 58B) in Gothic *N.S. del Carme* (founded 1206), are of interest. The 14C *Castle* contains an important library and works of art (previous authorisation to visit necessary).

Reached by a rough track c 15km NE are the remains of the monastery of *S. Quirze de Culera*, its church first consecrated in 935.

8km E is *Castelló d'Empúries*; see Rte 58B.—For *Besalú*, 24km SW on the C260, see Rte 59.—At *Lladó*, 5km NW off this road at 12km, is basilican *Sta. Maria* (1089).

The C252 forks left just S of Figueres for *Empúries* and *L'Escala*; see Rte 58B.—*Medinyà*, with a 14C church and early castle, and the castle of *Montagut* are passed before descending into the valley of the Ter. The river is crossed at its confluence with the Oñar at (40km) *Girona*. Turn left under the railway bridge and circle round to the central Pl. de Catalunya, built over the Oñar.

GIRONA (*Gerona* in Castilian; 86,600 inhab.; 18,000 in 1920; 32,000 in 1960), a provincial capital and growing industrial centre, retains a characteristic old centre of some charm.

Gerunda, a city of the Ausetani, was a Moorish possession from the late 8C until 1015. Its history is a tale of sieges for the most part successfully withstood, the most famous of which was the French assault of 1809 when a force of 35,000 commanded by Verdier, Gouvion St.-Cyr, and Augereau was kept at bay for seven months by the inhabitants aided by a small garrison and a few English volunteers. The women enrolled themselves into a company dedicated to Sta. Barbara, patroness of artillery. Eventually the commander, Mariano Álvarez de Castro (1770–1810), broke down under the strain of deprivation and the town surrendered, its food and ammunition exhausted.

It was here in 1802 that Lady Holland experienced for the first time the 'extreme derision and scorn with which a woman is treated who does not conform to the Spanish mode of dressing'.

It was the birthplace of the troubadour Cerverí de Girona (fl. 1250–80).

The narrow streets of the old town are best explored by foot. Cross the Onyar by the *Puente de Piedra* or at the PL. DE CATALUNYA, or from footbridges further N, providing a view of the once picturesque old houses overhanging the river.

Parallel to and E of the Rambla de la Libertat is the C. Ciutadans, with the *Ayuntamiento*, in part of 1642, and Tourist Office. Follow the C. Ciutadans to the N. It is extended by the C. Força to the foot of the cathedral steps, passing several restored medieval or Renaissance mansions. At the small square of Cort-Reial steps climb right to *S. Martí* (1610) and, beside it, the door of 1599 to the *Seminario*.— Another flight of steps ascends beside the church to the *Conv. de S. Domènec* (1253–1349). To the N stands the former *University* (1570) and, behind it, remains of a Cyclopean *Wall* rebuilt in the 3C. From here lanes leads to the *Pal. Episcopal*, with Renaissance windows. From beneath the palace a lane leads uphill to the ruins of the 14C *Torre de Gironella* (view).

The palace now contains the newly formed **•Museu Diocesano**. Notable exhibits are the Retablo de Púbol (1437) by Bernat Martorell, and Retablo de Cruïlles (1416) by Lluís Borrassà, among other paintings; a 12C painted beam from Cruïlles; 12–13C wall paintings; a MS copy of the Homilies of Bede with early 12C miniatures; and a 14C illuminated martyrology.

The Gothic **•Cathedral**, one of the finest buildings in Catalunya, stands at the head of a monumental staircase of 1607–90, flanked by the restored *Pia Almonia* (14C) and the *Audiencia* (1599).

The first church, founded by Charlemagne in 786, and desecrated by the Moors, was rebuilt in 1016–38, but the only important survival is the N Tower, called the *Torre de Carlemany* (1038–1117). It was with stones from a steeple of this old cathedral that the clergy of Girona celebrated Easter 1278 by bombarding the adjacent *Judería*.

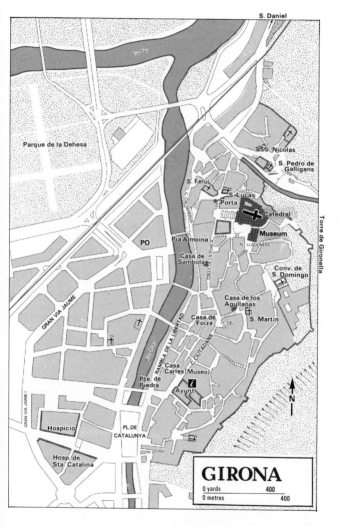

The present cathedral was begun when the apse chapels were constructed (1312–47; by Maitre Henri and Jacques Favran). The plan for the new nave, begun c 1350–86, its huge vault designed in 1416 by Guillermo Bofill, was considered unsafe by the chapter and was adopted only on the advice of a jury of 12 architects. The tower was built in 1581, and the W Front, to the designs of Pedro Costa, in 1733. The restored S Door was begun in 1394 by Guillén Morey; two of the original terracotta statues of the apostles by Antonio Claperós survive.

The interior is an apsidal hall surrounded by chapels and covered by Bofill's vault, the widest Gothic vault known (22m), 3.3m wider than that at Albi in Languedoc. The internal buttresses supporting it are 6m thick. Some windows retain glass of 1380 by Lluís Borrassà, and there is much of the 15C. The *Silleria* in the Coro, although altered in the 16C, preserves some original 14C stalls and a *Bishop's Throne* carved in 1351 by Maitre Aloy.

The *Cap. Mayor*, with a retablo of 1325 covered with silver plate and enamel, is surmounted by a remarkable wooden *Baldacchino*, also plated with silver, supported on shafts ornamented with enamelled escutcheons. The work was carried out by Maitre Bartolomé but altered in 1357 by Pedro Bernes of Valencia, who also made the whole of the lower range of the retablo.

To the left is the *Tomb of Bp Berenguer Argensola* (died 1408; by Pedro Oller), with a series of weepers. Among other tombs are those of Bernard de Pau (c 1457), in the first N chapel, probably by Lorenzo Mercadente de Bretaña; Count Ramón Berenguer II (died 1082), over the door of the sacristy, and his wife Ermesendis (died 1057), on the S wall nearly opposite, both dating from the 14C.

The *Chapterhouse* contains a small museum displaying a 13C Bible annotated by Charles V of France; an illuminated Apocalypse of 974; an alabaster statuette of ?Pedro IV of Aragón (c 1350, by Jaime Cascalls); the early 12C embroidery known as The Creation; and a collection of reliquaries and other cult objects.

The irregular Romanesque *Cloister* of c 1180–1210 has elaborately carved capitals.

Turn right at the foot of the steps and pass through the *Portal de Sobreportes* to (left) **S. Feliú**, its presbytery and nave dating from 1326. The steeple, truncated by lightning in 1581, was begun by Pedro Zacoma in 1368 and completed by Pedro Ramón in 1392. Embedded in the chancel wall are eight sarcophagi, two of them Roman (Rape of Proserpine, and Lion Hunt), the rest 4–5C. A sarcophagus above the altar contains the body of St. Felix of Girona (died 303); the retablo illustrates his life. In the domed *Cap. de S. Narciso* (1792) is a tomb of 1328; in the *Cap. de Sta. Afra* is a mid 14C alabaster Christ, perhaps by Jaime Cascalls.

To the E is Neo-Classical *S. Lucas* (1729), and beyond it are the so-called *Banys Àrabs*, recorded in 1194, but in their present form dating from the 13C.

From this point one may follow the *Paseo Arqueológico* which climbs through gardens providing a view of the fortress of Montjuïc (1653), which commanded the town until destroyed in 1809, and of the exterior of the cathedral.—At the far end of the paseo are the *Walls*, which may be followed for some distance along the perimeter of the old town.—On the hill above are more ruined forts blown up by the French.

To the N is Romanesque *S. Pere de Galligants*, completed c 1131, with an octagonal tower; the apse forms a bastion of the town wall; its cloister dates from c 1154–90. Slightly further N is the restored Romanesque chapel of *S. Nicolás* (late 12C).

A path leads up the valley of the Galligants to the monastery of *S. Daniel*, its late 11C church standing above a crypt containing the saint's shrine, with an effigy of 1345. The cloister of c 1200 has a late Gothic upper gallery.

The only buildings of interest in the new town are the *Hosp. de Sta. Catalina* (1666) and, opposite, the *Hospicio* of 1785 by Ventura Rodríguez. They are a short distance W of the Pl. de Catalunya.

GIRONA TO PALAFRUGELL (37km). The C255 circles to the NE, at first skirting the right bank of the Ter, with the wooded slopes of the SIERRA DE LES GAVARRES to the SE, to (25km) *La Bisbal* (7400 inhab.), with a 14C castle of the bishops of Girona. To the W is the monastic church of *S. Miquel de Cruïlles* (mid 12C), with a 10C cloister.—Driving E, we pass (left) *Vulpellac*, with a church of interest and a 14C castle.—5km N is **Ullastret**, with an important Iberian settlement with Cyclopean *Fortifications*; a small archaeological collection may be seen in the 14C hermitage.—*Peratallada*, E of this road, is a walled village.—Mozarabic *S. Julian de Buada* is close by.—8km *Palafrugell*; see Rte 58.

GIRONA TO S. FELIU DE GUIXOLS (36km). The C250 leads SE through (14km) *Cassà de la Selva*, its 15C church with a Renaissance front, to (7km) **Llagostera** (5050 inhab.), with remains of a 14C castle, 16C church, and old houses.—*S. Feliu* is 15km E, *Tossa* 19km S; see Rte 58.

For *Besalú* and **Olot** see Rte 59.

The NII drives due S. At 11km it passes (right) the airport and (left), 5km beyond, *Caldes de Malavella*, the 'Vichy Catalan', with medicinal springs, ruins of Roman *thermae*, and a medieval castle.

2km. *Sta. Coloma de Farners*, with a picturesque ruined castle (12–14C), lies 12km to the right.—22km further W, approached by a mountain road climbing into the SIERRA DE MONTSENY, is the small spa of *S. Hilari Sacalm* (801m).

At 6km beyond this turning an entry to the A7 Motorway is reached, the recommended road to **Barcelona**; see Rte 57B. For the continuation of the NII see below.

The C251 bears SW parallel to the motorway, skirting *Maçanet de la Selva*, with old houses and a ruined 12C castle, to (15km) *Hostalric*, a picturesque but dilapidated walled village above the Tordera valley, surrounded by plantations of cork-oaks.—6km *Breda* (right) is reputed for its pottery; its Gothic parish church retains a tower of 1068, and near by are the ruins of the Benedictine *Conv. de S. Salvador*. To the NW is the ruined castle of *Montsoliu*.—8km *S. Seloni*, its church (cons. 1106) with a Baroque front of painted plaster.—A tortuous road climbs NW to (22km) *Sta. Fé del Montseny*, among mountain lakes, passing the church tower of *Fogars de Montclús*.—The next right turning ascends 16km to the village of *Montseny*, with the range rising to its NE to 1709m. Winding through the centre of the massif, it descends the W slope beyond the *Collformic* (1145m) through *El Brull*, with a Romanesque church, and *Seva*, with an 11C church, to (26km) *Tona*; see Rte 60.—9km *Llinars del Vallès*, dominated by a castle of 1558, is passed as we emerge into the fertile valley of the Congost, to approach (11km) **Granollers**, an industrial town of 45,350 inhab., with a 14C church and ruined walls of 1377.—The ruined castle of *La Roca* stands 4km SE (beyond the A7); 8km SW, at *Montmeló*, are remains of a Carolingian church.—The A7 may be entered S of Granollers. A branch shortly bears off to approach the centre of **Barcelona**; see Rte 63.

The NII crosses a low ridge into the Tordera valley. At 12km *Blanes* lies 6km SE. *Lloret de Mar*, 4km beyond, is best approached from this direction; but see the latter part of Rte 58.

At 6km the road reaches the coast behind *Malgrat de Mar* and threads or bypasses a string of contiguous resorts of slight interest: *Pineda*, *Calella*, *S. Pol*, and **Canet** (8050 inhab.), retaining the medieval castle of *Sta. Florentina* and 15C *atalayas*.—19km **Arenys de Mar** (10,100 inhab.). Inland is *Arenys de Munt* with *S. Martí* of 1544.—Passing the so-called *Baños de Titus* and the hilltop *Torre dels Encantats*, we traverse *Caldes d'Estrac*, with a 13C church and ruined castle of *Nofre Arnau*, later passing near *S. Andreu de Llavaneres*, also with castle ruins.

9km **Mataro** (97,000 inhab.), the ancient *Iluro*, of which the Roman villa of *Torre Llauder* has been excavated, and now a manufacturing and ship-building centre. The railway from here to Barcelona was the first to be laid in Spain, in 1848. It was the birthplace of the architect Josep Puig i Cadalfalch (1867–1957). Relics of the walled medieval town lie inland, beyond which is *Argentona*, with an early 16C church and the ruined castle of *S. Vicente de Burriach* (15C).

The A19 motorway may be joined here for (28km) **Barcelona**, or one may continue to skirt the coast, at 8.5km passing a road running inland to *Villasar*, with a Gothic church, old castle, and several *atalayas*; and then *Montgat*, the castle of which put up a spirited defence against the French in 1808. Inland is *Tiana*, near which is the former *Cartuja de Montealegre* (founded 1344), commanding a wide sea view.

The outskirts of **Badalona** (229,800 inhab.), an industrial suburb of Barcelona, are entered. Excavations have brought to light part of the ground plan of Roman *Baetula*, together with finds dating from the 2C BC to the 4C AD. On the *Puntigal*, a cliff W of the town, is a carved inscription to Apollo. Near by is the ruined abbey of *S. Jerónimo de la Murta* (15C).

For **Barcelona** see Rte 63.

B.   Via the Motorway

168km, from the last entrance in France (104 miles). A7.

Maps: M 443.

The French A9 from Perpignan is recommended for travellers requiring a rapid route to Barcelona, or to bypass Barcelona. It has sufficient exits from which the major places of interest en route may be visited (see Rte 57A), and also to roads leading to many of the resorts of the Costa Brava; see Rte 58.

Climbing from *Le Boulou*, to the left on approaching Customs is a curious pyramidal construction (1976; by Ricardo Bofill) marking the frontier. The motorway crosses the NII climbing up the valley below to cross the border, here the E foothills of the PYRENEES.

The exit at 29km for *Figueres* should be taken for *Roses*, on the coast.—35km *Girona* exit; convenient also for *Palafrugell* and *Palamós*; the next one is best for *S. Feliu de Guixols* and *Tossa*.

At 28km from Girona the motorway veers SW along the valley of the Tordera, between the SIERRA DE MONTSENY to the W and the coastal SIERRA DE MONTNEGRE, and parallel to the C251; see Rte 57A.—At 40km *Granollers* is bypassed and 9km beyond we reach the A17 bearing left to (20km) central **Barcelona** (see Rte 63), passing a ruined castle at *Reixach*, once the stronghold of the Montcada family.

The city may be bypassed to the N, meeting the A2 motorway from Barcelona 25km further SW; see Rte 65B.

58 Portbou to Blanes: the Costa Brava

Maps: M 443.

Rte 58 is printed more as a convenient way to describe the area rather than one which should be methodically followed. Most of the resorts are more easily approached from the NII or A7 (see Rte 57). This 'Fabled Shore', as described in Rose Macaulay's delightful book, first published in 1949, has somewhat changed since then (during her drive along the Mediterranean coast and on to the Algarve she saw only one other GB car.)

Cerbère, on the French side of the frontier, is 47km SE of *Perpignan*, the main focus of traffic, from which we approach the Customs post and *Portbou*, once a fishing port, providing a panoramic view ahead of the rocky coast to the *Cabo de Creus*. The narrow winding road skirts the Mediterranean to (14km) *Llançà*, with a Baroque church.

A minor road hugs the coast to (8km) *El Port de la Selva*, overlooked by a 10C tower, and climbs steeply SE across a region of slaty terraced hills to high-lying crossroads.—From here there is a twisting descent to (13km) **Cadaqués**, with a 17C church containing a richly gilt organ case and the *Museo Perrot-Moore*, devoted to the graphic arts.—A lane leads to adjacent *Port-Lligat*, home of Salvador Dali.—A track leads NE to *Cabo de Creus* (the ancient *Aphrodision*); another circles SW to *Roses*.

The C252 bears SW from Llançà towards *Figueres*, passing the ruined castle of *Carmansó*.—At 9km turn left through *Vilajuïga*. From here a by-road ascends steeply into the SIERRA DE ROSES towards the very early Romanesque abbey of *S. Pere de Rodhes* (consecrated 1022; under restoration), and the nearby castle of *S. Salvador*. Both command extensive views.

The main road leads SE to (12km) **Roses** (8000 inhab.), occupying the site of the Greek colony of *Rhoda*. Visigothic remains have been found at *Puig de las Murallas*. The ruined *Citadel* (1543), once a fortified monastery (cons. 1022), which had undergone numerous sieges, was blown up by Suchet in 1814.

The C260 leads W across the EMPORDÀ PLAIN to (10km) **Castelló d'Empúries**, with a bridge over the Muga of 1354. Its 13–14C church, with a battlemented tower and early 15C doorway, contains an alabaster retablo of 1485 by Vicente Borrás. The 13C *Lonja*, restored; the *Conv. de Sta. Clara*, and disused *Sto. Domingo*, with a Renaissance and Baroque cloister, are of interest.

Continue S, inland from the sandy bay of the *Golfo de Roses*, to (9km) *S. Pere Pescador*.—About 9km W is the beautiful church (cons. 1066) of the Benedictine abbey of *S. Miquel de Fluvià*, with an 11C belfry and a front completed in 1533.—Continuing S from S. Pere, at 6km (*Viladamat*) turn left and left again to the village of *S. Martí*, and the important and extensive ruins of *Ampurias* or **Empúries**, the Greek and Roman port of *Emporion*, where Gnaeus Scipio landed during the Iberian expedition in the Second Punic War (218 BC).

Excavations have laid bare part of the harbour, fragments of the Roman wall and earlier Cyclopean wall, and the outline of several streets. There is a *Museum*, but most of the more important discoveries have been removed to Barcelona and Girona. A number of mosaic pavements remain in situ, and the site, on a gentle slope overlooking the bay, is impressive.

To the S is the resort of *L'Escala*, with an 18C church, from which one may circle the W flank of *Montgri*, passing the ruined late 13C castle of *Belcaire*. The hill is surmounted by a fine castle begun in 1294.— Turning left above the Ter, *Torroella de Montgri* (5650 inhab.) is entered. It has remains of walls and gates, a 14C church and *Ayuntamiento*, and medieval and Renaissance buildings.—5km E are the resort of *L'Estartit*, with a view of the offshore *Illes Medes*.

Crossing the Ter at Torroella, bear SE to (9km) *Pals*, an old village with ruined walls and towers, partly restored. Beyond, the road climbs E to (7km) *Begur*, near which are five *atalayas*.

Palafrugell lies 7km SW, but a by-road climbs down past *Fornells* to *Aiguablava* (Parador) and the sheltered village of *Tamariú*.

Further S are *Llafranc, Calella de Palafrugell*, and the botanical gardens on *Cap Roig*.

From **Palafrugell** (15,150 inhab.), with remains of Moorish walls and Baroque *S. Martín*, the C255 leads due S past *Mont-ras*, its church of 1599 with a fortified belfry known as the *Torre Simona*.— 8km **Palamós** (12,400 inhab.), founded in 1277, has a 14C church later altered and enlarged, and a small museum. The coast between here and *S. Feliu de Guixols*, 12km SW, has been irreparably spoilt, little attempt having been made to control the ruthless exploitation of its natural beauty. The road traverses *Platja d'Aro* to *S'Agaro*, with remains of a 14C cloister incorporated into the modern church.

S. Feliu de Guixols (15,500 inhab.), an old port whose staple industry was the export of the products of the surrounding cork-oak forest, is now a tourist centre retaining a paseo, a 14C church, near which are the 11C *Porta Ferrada*, and the Baroque *Arco de S. Benito* (remains of a vanished monastery). The *Museum* contains archeological collections, paintings, and sculpture.—The chapel of *S. Elm* on the hill to the SW was built as a landmark in 1452.

The C250 leads NW. At 6km *Romanyà de la Selva* is 4km N. Near by is the important megalithic monument known as the '*Cueva d'en Dayna*', on the S slope of the SIERRA DE LES CAVARRES (531m).—The C253 turns left 4km beyond this turning, bypassing *Llagostera* to meet the A7 c 18km SW; see Rte 52B.

The GE682 winds above the coast en corniche from *S. Feliu*, descending to (23km) **Tossa**, with relics of medieval walls, remains of a castle, a Baroque church of 1755, and a museum.—Beyond Tossa the road continues its serpentine course, but further back from the sea, to (9km) **Lloret de Mar** (10,450 inhab.), with the church of *S. Quirico* (1079). Beyond, it straightens out to bypass adjacent **Blanes** (20,350 inhab.), with a 14C church occupying an old palace. Turning right onto the B600, at 10km (from Lloret) we cross the NII, ascending the Tordera valley, and may join the A7 at 12km, just S of *Hostalric*. Alternatively, continue SW past the ruined castle of *Palafolls* to meet the NII behind *Malgrat*; see Rte 57A.

59   Girona to Ripoll via Olot

86km (53 miles). NII. 4km—C150. 16km *Banyoles*—14km **Besalú**—21km **Olot**—31km *Ripoll*.

Maps: M 443.

Driving N, we shortly fork left over the A7 and veer NW to **Banyoles** (12,450 inhab.), with the restored church of *Sta. María dels Turers*; conventual *S. Estebán*, its cloisters containing 12–16C tombs of abbots; and the *Pía Almoina*, begun in 1307 and containing an archaeological museum.—*Porqueres*, on the far side of the lake, preserves Romanesque *Sta. María* (cons. 1182).

The GE524, a picturesque by-road, leads W through (14.5km) *Mieres*, with a Renaissance church, and (9.5km) *Sta. Pau*, an ancient village with an early castle and 15C church, c 2km from which is the 9C *Santuario dels Archs*.—The road traverses a region of volcanic formation, cut by ravines known as *grederas*, to (9.5km) *Olot*; see below.

6km *Serinyà* has a 12C church. Near by is the *Cueva dels Encantats*, among others, containing paintings.—8km **Besalú**, an attractive old village, retains several relics of its past, including an over-restored, fortified *Bridge* (12th and 14Cs), some porticoed streets and squares, and ancient houses. Restored *S. Vicente* (1018–13C), the ruins of Romanesque *Sta. María* (?1055), the 11C *Hospital*, and the late 12C monastery of *S. Pedro*, are of interest, as is the recently discovered and restored *Mikwah* or *Jewish Baths* (11–12C) in the lower part, near the Fluviá. Among early 13C troubadours was Ramon Vidal de Besalú.—Some 2km N are remains of the late 11C monastic church of *Sto. Sepulchro*.

14km *Castellfollit de la Roca* has a Roman *Bridge* of two storeys. Near by are some curious basalt cliffs.

A road forking right leads through *S. Joan les Fonts*, with a Romanesque church, to join the C153. This climbs up the Vall de Bianya to (14.5km) *S. Salvador de Bianya*, with a church of 1170, and over the *Collado de Capsacosta* (870m) to meet at 9.5km the C151 6km S of *Camprodon*; see Rte 60 and for *S. Joan de les Abadesses*, 8km W.

7km **Olot** (25,050 inhab.) is an industrial town encircled by mountains. This was once a volcanic area—quakes in the 15C severely damaged the place. Olot was the birthplace of the composer Antonio Soler (1729–83). *S. Esteban* contains a Gothic retablo, and Christ carrying the Cross, by El Greco; the *Hospicio*, a small archaeological collection; and the *Torre Castany*, a museum of Catalan art, including *Ramon Casas'* 'La Carga' (police charging a crowd).

The C150 climbs 12km due W to cross the *Collado de Coubet* (1010m), with a fine view of the Pyrenees, from which a right turning crosses the *Collado de Santigosta* (1064m), climbing down directly to (11km) *S. Joan de les Abadesses*; see Rte 60.—The main road continues W, with the SIERRA DE STA. MAGDALENA (1526m) to the S, past *Vallfogona*, with remains of a castle and a church of 1756 retaining its 12C front, to (19km) *Ripoll*; see also Rte 60.

The C152 leads SW from Olot, at 8km turning left.

The C153 continues ahead, climbing in 13km to a pass at 1020m (views), and winding W across the mountains past *Rupit* and nearby *S. Juan de Fabregas*, both with Romanesque churches, before descending to (43km) *Vic*; see Rte 60.

The C152 turns SE down the valley of the Brugent, passing the castle of *Hostoles*, on a spur of the SIERRA DE FINESTRES, and *Amer*, with a Romanesque church, to (30km) *Anglès* (5050 inhab.), a walled village. Turn left there to regain *Girona*, 18km E, or continue S to (12km) *Sta. Coloma de Farners*; see Rte 57A.

60 (Perpignan) Camprodon to Barcelona via Ripoll and Vic

146km (90 miles) from the frontier at *Collado d'Ares*. C151. 18km *Camprodon*—14km *S. Joan de les Abadesses*—9km *Ripoll*. N152. 39km **Vic**—66km **Barcelona**.

Maps: M 443.

From *Le Boulou*, 21km S of *Perpignan*, turn right onto the D115, ascending the valley of the Tech through *Amélie-les-Bains* and

Prats-de-Mollo, there climbing across a pass at 1185m to reach the frontier at (53km) the *Collado d'Ares* (1513m; Customs).

The road now descends in sweeping curves past (10km) *Molló*, its Romanesque church with a remarkable tower. Shortly beyond, a mountain road turns left to *Beget* (c 12km) where 11C *S. Cristobal* has an early tower and contains an 11C Crucifixion.

8km *Camprodon* (950m) was the birthplace of the composer Isaac Albéniz (1861–1909). It has a 16C bridge with a defensive tower, and the restored monastic church of *S. Pedro* (cons. 904 and again in 1169).—*Llanars*, 2km NW, has a church consecrated in 1168.

The road follows the valley of the Ter to (14km) **S. Joan de les Abadesses** (800m), with a restored *Bridge* dating from 1130. The remarkable collegiate church of *ˑS. Joan* was founded in 887 by Count Wilfred 'el Velloso' (the hairy), whose daughter was the first of the abbesses. It was consecrated in 1150. In the N chapel is the strange wooden *Calvary* of 1250 known as 'las Brujas' (the witches). Note also the capitals and the 14C alabaster retablo in the S transept. The delicately columned cloister was begun in the 14C, and finished in 1445.—Ruined *S. Pol* has a Romanesque W door and trefoil apse.

9km **Ripoll** (12,200 inhab.), situated in the angle between the Ter and the Fresser, is known for its Benedictine Monastery, founded in 888 by Count Wilfred, and consecrated in 935 and 977. It was almost entirely rebuilt after a ravaging fire in 1835. The heavily restored *Church* (1032), with its square tower, is preceded by a narthex, protected behind a glazed 'conservatory', within which is the *ˑW Doorway* (1168). This is a remarkable example of Romanesque carving, with grotesque monsters and bands of sculpture illustrating the scriptures.

The plain interior has double aisles and massive square piers. It dates from the foundation; the short apsidal chancel and the apses on the E side of the transepts are slightly later. It contains the tombs of Counts Borrell II (died 992) and Ramón Berenguer III (died 1113). The *Cloister* is of two storeys, the lower Romanesque (c 1172–1206) with historiated capitals; the upper (c 1382–1408) with foliated capitals and carved abaci.

14C *S. Pedro*, restored, is a cavernous edifice with nave and aisles of nearly equal height.—The *Museum*, with miscellaneous collections, also contains numerous examples of firearms manufactured in Ripoll in the 16–18Cs.

For the N152 to *Puigcerdà* see sub-route of Rte 61, in reverse.

We follow the N152 down the valley of the Ter, at 15km passing (left) the castle of *Montesquiu*. Above are the ruins of the castle of *Besora*.

24km (also bypassed to the W) **VIC** (30,150 inhab.), the ancient capital of the Ausetani, is an episcopal town attractively sited in an amphitheatre of hills.

Its Parador is c 14km to the NE, overlooking the *Embalse de Sau* beyond *Tavernoles*, where *S. Esteve* is a well-preserved Lombardic church of 1078.

At the SE corner of the *Pl. Mayor* are a 16C *Palace* and the *Ayuntamiento* of 1509, with a tower of 1679. The C. de Riera descends towards the Neo-Classical **Cathedral**, a rebuilding of 1780–1803 by José Morató.

Of the former cathedral, consecrated in 1038, there remain the crypt, the tower called '*El Cloquer*' (1180), and the *Cloister*, although the last was taken down and re-erected in 1806. The N chapels also survive from the additions of 1633–80 by Jaime Vendrell; in the 6th is the silver sarcophagus (1728; by Juan de

Matons) of Bp Bernardo Calvó (died 1243). The gilt screen of the chapel dates from 1685. In the ambulatory is an alabaster retablo of 1427 by Pedro Oller and, opposite, the tomb of Canon Desputjol (died 1434), also by Oller.

The cathedral contains wall paintings by Josep Maria Sert, who had twice before decorated the church with murals (in 1900–15, and 1926–30). These earlier series were burnt in 1936 when the building was sacked. The present series were not quite completed at the artist's death in 1945; the lunettes above the cornice were painted by his pupil Miguel Massot from Sert's sketches.

The *Cloister* is of two storeys—the lower 12C, the upper of 1318–1400—is notable for its window tracery. Awkwardly placed in the centre is a *Monument to Jaime Balmes* (1810–48), the philosopher (1865). Off the NE corner is the *Chapterhouse* by Bartolomé Ladernosa, completed in 1360; further S, the domed *Cap. de Sta. María de la Redonda*, with a Baroque retablo.

The *'**Museo Municipal**, to the N, contains an impressive collection of early Catalan paintings.

Among them are examples of the art of *Ferrer Bassa* (1324–48), *Pere Serra, Jaime Ferrer I* and *II*, the *Maestro de Rubió* (c 1350), the *Maestro de Fonollosa* (c 1420), *Ramón de Mur* (1402–35; including his masterpiece, the Retablo of Guimerá), *Bernat Martorell, Jaume Huguet*, and *Juan Gasco*.

Notable among sculptures, besides several early Calvaries (including one from Erill-la-Val), is a carved retablo of 1341 from S. Joan de les Abadesses by *Bernat Saulet*. Other rooms display collections of embroidered vestments, and other fabrics, *guadamecils*, ceramics and glass, metalwork, coins, drawings, coffers (some ivory), furniture, and cult objects.

The cella of a 3C Roman *Temple* discovered during the demolition of the Moncada palace has been restored to house a lapidary collection.

Among churches of interest are *S. Justo* (late 15th and 17Cs); *Sta. Teresa*, completed in 1646, with a Baroque retablo; and *N.S. de la Piedad*, by José Morató, who also designed in 1753 the church of the 16C *Hosp. de Sta. Cruz*.

For the road NE to *Olot* see p 371.—At *S. Julià de Vilatorta*, 6km E, are castle ruins and a house of the Templars (cons. 1050), S of which, at *Vilalleons*, is a late 11C church.—There is another 11C church at *Sta. Eugènia de Berga*, 5km SE; at *Gurb*, 5km NW, is a ruined castle.

9km *Tona* (5100 inhab.) has a ruined castle and 11C church.—For the road climbing SE into the SIERRA DE MONTSENY see sub-route on p 367.

The N141C climbs SW across the *Puerto de la Pollosa*, providing several attractive views, via (19km) *Moià* to *Manresa*, 28km beyond; see Rte 64.—9km N of *Moià*, with a Baroque church, is *L'Estany*, its Transitional church of 1133 with a Romanesque cloister.—The B143 leads S from Moià, at c 17km passing near the 15C sanctuary of *S. Miquel del Fai*, overlooking the finest waterfall in Catalunya. 7km further S it bypasses **Caldes de Montbui** (10,150 inhab.), with hot springs. A barrel-vaulted Roman bath house survives. The parish church has a Baroque front of 1701 and contains a 12C Christ.

At 5km the old town of *Centelles*, bypassed, has an unfinished 18C castle. We thread the narrow wooded valley of the Congost and at 14km bear away from the old road to (11km) *Granollers* (see Rte 57A) through *La Garriga*. Here are 12C *Sta. María del Camí*, and *S. Esteban*, containing a retablo of the School of Huguet (c 1490).— *Llerona*, S of La Garriga, has a 12C church, and Romanesque *S. Feliu de Canovellas* is near by.

At 20km the motorway for **Barcelona** may be entered; see Rte 63.

61 (Bourg-Madame) Puigcerdà to Barcelona via Berga, Manresa and Terrassa

156km (97 miles). C1411. 48km *Berga*—49km *Manresa*—12km. BP1213. 18km **Terrassa**—A18. 29km **Barcelona**.

Maps: M 443.

For the N116 from *Perpignan* to (100km) *Bourg-Madame* and the N20 from *Foix* to (97km) *Bourg-Madame* see *Blue Guide France.*

With the recent completion of the *Túnel de Cadí* this route may grow in importance. It avoids the *Collada de Toses* (which may be snow-bound in December–March) between *Puigcerdà* and *Ribes de Freser;* see below.

Puigcerdà (1152m; 5850 inhab.), the frontier village, faces *Bourg-Madame* on the far side of the Raour, which is crossed by an *International Bridge* (Customs). Puigcerdà was founded in 1177 by Alfonso II as capital of the CERDANYA or CERDAGNE, a district divided between France and Spain by the Treaty of the Pyrenees (1659). The old town stands on a hill in the centre of a mountain-girt plain. The 15C *Ayuntamiento*, damaged in the Civil War, has been restored. Of *S. María* only the tower and a 14C doorway survive. 13C *Sto. Domingo*, restored, preserves its 15C grey marble front.

A 'neutral road' connects Puigcerdà with the village of **Llívia**, 4.5km NE, for the ancient *Julia Livia*, capital of the Cerdagne until 1177, due to a quibble in the Treaty of the Pyrenees (whereby the villages but not the towns of the Upper Cerdagne were ceded to France) occupies a Spanish enclave within France. The balconied streets are entirely Spanish in character and the church is fortified. Its *Pharmacy* is one of the oldest in Europe (c 1420).

PUIGCERDÀ TO RIPOLL (62km). The N152 turns left c 4km S of the town and climbs past the winter sports resort of *La Molina* to the *Collada de Toses* (1800m) before descending the upper valley of the Freser to (49km) *Ribes de Freser* (920m).—At *Queralbs* (1220m), 7km N, is a 10C church; further N, at *Núria* (2000m), approached by rack railway, is the sanctuary of *N.S. de Núria* (partly 11C).—Turning S, we pass a Gothic bridge and, at 10km, the ruined Romanesque church at *Campdevánol*, to enter *Ripoll* 4km beyond: see Rte 60.— W of Campdevánol is the early church of *S. Llorent*, beyond which the road climbs to (8km) *Gombrèn*, with medieval houses near the ruined castle and the Romanesque church of *Montgrony.*

Bearing SW from the N152 S of Puigcerdà, at 15km we climb steeply to the N entrance of the *Túnel de Cadí*, piercing the SIERRA DE CADÍ just W of the *Tosa d'Alp* (2531m).—At 13km *Baga*, with a ruined castle and Romanesque church, is bypassed to enter (3km) *Guardiola de Berguedà.*—9km E is *La Pobla de Lillet*, with a 12C Majesty in its church.

At 14km the C149 turns left across the *Embalse de la Baélls* to (16km) *Borredà*, from which a mountain road leads NE to (c 9km) *S. Jaume de Frontanyà*, Romanesque, with a lantern and lobed apse of c 1070.

3km **Berga** (13,550 inhab.), also bypassed, is a mining town with a ruined castle and the Gothic *Conv. de S. Francisco* (1333).—5km E is the Mozarabic church of *S. Quirze de Pedret* (late 10th and 12Cs).

A winding mountain road climbs W to (31km) *S. Llorenc de Morunys*, a former Benedictine church containing retablos by Pere Serra (1385), and Jaime Cirera (c 1425–50) and, in the chapel of *La Piedad*, one by Francisco Solives (1480).

We continue to follow the somewhat industrialised valley of the Llobregat through (8km) *Gironella.*—6km SW is *Caserres*, with the church and cloister of *S. Pedro* (c 1006).

The C154 leads across country to (57km) *Vic* (see Rte 60). At c 18km a left-hand turning leads to (4km) *Lluçà*, where the 11C Lombardic church of *Sta. María* has a 12C cloister.

22km *Balsareny*, with a 14C hilltop castle to the E.—10km. At *Santpedor*, 4km right, the church has a fine 12C tympanum and a Nottingham alabaster of St. Michael.

At (5km) *S. Fruitós de Bages* (to the left on the N141C) is the ruined monastery of *S. Benito*, with a lanterned church of c 1225, and an early Gothic Chapterhouse entered from a Romanesque cloister with a carved capital signed 'Bernardus'. Near by is a medieval bridge.

To the W is *Manresa*; see Rte 64.—The next turning to the left leads c 8km to *Rocafort*, where the remarkable Romanesque church of *Sta. María de Marquet* has a vault of horseshoe arches (late 10C).

The N flank of the serrated ridge of the SIERRA DE MONTSERRAT is prominent ahead (see Rte 64).—14km S of the Manresa turning, after passing through a short tunnel, turn left across the Llobregat onto the BP1213 for (18km) **TERRASSA** (155,600 inhab.), an industrial town which grew up next to ancient *Egara*. Its most interesting building (in the NW suburb of S. Pedro) is •**S. Miquel**, made up of two Romanesque churches and a baptistery. The marble columns of the square baptistery are Roman and support Roman and Romanesque capitals. The church was built before 450 but reconstructed in the 9C. The crypt contains 12C murals.

S. Pedro, with a curious triple-lobed apse (9C) and a 12C vaulted nave, contains important inscriptions; *Sta. María*, also with a 9C apse and nave consecrated in 1112, contains a painted stone retablo of the 10C and a late 12C mural devoted to Thomas Becket.

In the *Museum* are the Retablos of S. Pedro (1411; by Lluís Borrassà), and of SS. Abdon and Sennen (1460; by Jaume Huguet). The *Museo Soler y Palet* contains medieval paintings and sculpture and Catalan ceramics; the *Museo Biosca* preserves a collection of early textiles.

Among other old buildings are the *Torre del Palau* of the castle and the late Gothic *Casa Consistorial*. In the crypt of the modern church of *Santo Espiritu* is an alabaster tomb of 1544 by Martín Díaz de Liatzasolo. The *Cartuja de Vallparadis* (restored), also known as the *Castle of the Caballeros de Egara*, begun before 1110 but rebuilt after 1344, has a Gothic gallery of 1432.

From a point c 6km N of Terrassa, on a mountain rising to 1095m and riddled with caverns, the ruins of the Benedictine monastery of *S. Llorenç del Munt* may be reached. It was consecrated in 1064 and partly restored in the 14C.

Immediately S of Terrassa is an entrance to the A18 motorway driving 29km directly to central **Barcelona**; see Rte 63. At 10km it skirts (left) **Sabadell** (186,100 inhab.), also approached directly from Terrassa. Sabadell has a *Museum* of archaeology, ceramics, and Catalan paintings; also a collection of fans, parasols, and textiles.—The *Museo Sellarés y Pla* also preserves 15–19C textiles.—Just S of Sabadell is *Sta. María de Barbará*, with a late 11C Lombardic church containing murals of c 1200.

An ALTERNATIVE road is that passing under the A18 through (9km) **Rubí** (43,850 inhab.), there veering SE under the A7 to (5km) **S. Cugat del Vallès** (39,650 inhab.), on the site of Roman *Castrum*

Octavianum. The Benedictine abbey of *S. Cugat* (one of the oldest in Spain, said to have been founded by Charlemagne or Louis le Débonair) has an attractive *Cloister* of c 1190 by Arnal Gatell. The *Church*, with a notable W rose-window, contains the *Monument of Abbot Estruch* and 14–15C paintings. In the small museum is Pere Serra's Retablo de Todos los Santos (1375).—The road continues S through pine woods to circle round *Tibidabo* (352 m), there descending steeply into central **Barcelona**.

62 Puigcerdà to Lleida (Lérida) via La Seu d'Urgell and Bassella

184km (114 miles). C1313. 49km **La Seu d'Urgell**—51km *Bassella*—32km *Artesa de Segre*—24km. *Balaguer* is 2km W—28km **Lleida**.

Maps: M 443.

For *Puigcerdà* see Rte 61.

Travellers wishing to pass through *Andorra* from France may follow the N20 NW from *Bourg-Madame*, first crossing the *Col de Puymorens* (1915m) to meet the N22 at 30km, also approached by the N20 climbing S from *Foix* and *Ax-les-Thermes* (25km N); see *Blue Guide France.*—The N22 climbs to (6km) the frontier *Pas de la Case* (2091m; Customs) and then the *Puerto d'Envalira* (2407m), the highest road pass in the PYRENEES.—The road descends in sweeping zigzags to (11.5km) *Soldeu* and 6km beyond passes *S. Joan de Casellas*, a primitive Romanesque chapel, and then *Canillo*, with a good church tower.—6.5km *Encamp*, with a Romanesque belfry, is passed, and 5km beyond, *Les Escaldes* (above which is the isolated Romanesque chapel of *S. Miquel d'Engolasters*), which now merges with **Andorra la Vella** (1029m), the capital of the 'Neutral Valleys of Andorra', the last survivor of the former independent states of the Pyrenees.

Andorra, also known as the *Principality of Andorra*, occupies an area of 450km² in the upper basin of the Valira and has a population of 45,900 (5500 in 1930; 14,000 in 1958). The completion of a motorroad from France in 1931 and the establishment of hydroelectric power stations in the main valleys have robbed the state of most of its once-attractive isolation, when smuggling was the principal source of revenue. It now flourishes on a form of tourism, the streets of its capital lined with hotels, garages, and shops selling everything from souvenirs to untaxed luxury goods.

A long-standing dispute between the Counts of Foix and the Bishops of Urgell as to whom had the prior right to the suzerainty of the Andorran valleys was arranged in 1278 by arbitration or '*paréage*' to the effect that the inhabitants should be independent under a joint suzerainty, which still holds good. The French president and the bishop of Urgell each nominates a *Viguier* or vicar, mainly for judicial functions, while the administration is in the hands of a Council of 24 (elected every four years), who appoint a Syndic-General from among their number, but—as another writer has recently remarked—'Here, the attractive quaintness stops'.

The seat of this administrative council is in the 16C *Casa de la Vall*, where their archives were enclosed in a chest with six locks, one for each parish. To the N in the central square is a Romanesque church with gilded altars in the Catalan style.

The backcloth to the boom town is the upper valley, still preserving some wild scenery, approached by a road climbing N through the villages of *La Massana, Ordino*, and *La Cortinada* to (16km) *El Serrat*, surrounded by mountains rising to over 2900m.

Continue S from Andorra la Vella past the chapel of *Sta. Coloma*, with a round tower, 12C murals, and a horseshoe chancel arch.—7km *S. Juliá de Lória*, also with a Romanesque church tower, 4km beyond which the S frontier (Customs) is crossed 9km N of *La Seu d'Urgell*; see below.—A rough road leading W just S of the border leads c 9km to *Ars*, with another round-towered church.—To the right on approaching Urgell, at *Anserall*, ruined *S. Sadurni de Tabérnoles* (c 1040) has a curious apse and a Lombard tower.

From Puigcerdà follow the C1313 to the W, descending the valley of the Segre, with the SIERRA DE CADÍ to the S, rising at the *Cristal* to 2647m, shortly passing through *Bolvir*, with a Romanesque church, and (19km) passing *Bellver de Cerdanya*, with an old church and ruined castle.—At 7km a mountain road climbs 9km right to the small spa of *Lles*, NW of which is the Romanesque church of *Aranser*.—18km. To the right is *Estamariu*, with the half-ruined basilica of *S. Vicente*; beyond, there is an early belfry at *Bescaran*.

5km **La Seu d'Urgell** (10,200 inhab.; Parador), an ancient town of narrow streets, some arcaded, now surrounded by modern buildings, is called after its episcopal see founded in 820. The *Cathedral, dedicated to St. Odo, was built by Raimundus the Lombard in 1132–c 82. Notable are the W and S doors, apse, and cloister, one side of which has been destroyed. Unfortunately the interior is very dark. Ponce, a mid 13C bishop, had the reputation of being the father of ten children and a 'deflorator virginam', and was even more flagrant in satisfying his desires than was usual in that age. The *Museo* contains an 11C MS of the Apocalypse of Beatus de Liébana. From the cloister one may enter *S. Miquel* (1010–35). The 14C church of the former Dominican convent and the old *Casa Municipal* are also of interest.

For *Andorra la Vella*, 20km N, see above.

The road bears SW past *Castellciutat*, dominated by three forts, and later enters the gorge or *Garganta de Tresponts*, with cliffs some 600m high, to enter (23km) *Organyà*, with a Transitional church. At *Figols*, on the far bank of the Segre, is a Romanesque church of interest.—The road shortly skirts the W bank of the *Embalse de Oliana*, passing (6km) *Coll de Nargó*, with *S. Clemente* (c 1000).

The L511, a rough mountain road, climbs W via *Isona* to (60km) *Tremp* (see Rte 67B) over the *Collado de Bóixols* (1380m).

Cross to the left bank of the Segre S of the reservoir and traverse (15km) *Oliana*, its church door supported by two monolithic Doric columns, to meet the L301 for (25km E) *Solsona* at (7km) *Bassella*; see Rte 64.

At 16km *Gualter*, with *Sta. María* (completed c 1205), is bypassed. After 2km *Ponts*, with a ruined church of c 1100, is traversed to approach (14km) *Artesa de Segre*, with a 13C church.

ARTESA TO MONTBLANC (67km), a convenient road to follow if approaching *Poblet* and *Tarragona* from the N. The L302 (later the C240) turns S, at 15km bypassing **Agramunt**, where *Sta. María* (c 1163–1250) has a magnificent portal dated 1283 although in the Limousin Romanesque style.—15km *Tàrrega* (see

Rte 65A), where the NII is crossed.—At 10km we reach crossroads just NW of
Ciutadilla, with a ruined castle and monastery.—5km E are the castle and
Gothic church of *Guimerà*.—*S. Martí de Riucorb*, 7km W, has a Baroque church
with a belfry of 1774 by José Prat.—From *Maldà*, 2km beyond, with a ruined
14C castle, one may turn SE to regain the main road via (7km) *Vallbona de les
Monges*, with a nunnery founded c 1173 containing the tomb of Doña Violante,
queen of Jaime el Conquistador. The W tower, an octagon of c 1348, and the
cloister of c 1220–1445 are notable.—The A2 is crossed c 24km S of the
Ciutadilla crossroads, to *Montblanc*, 2km beyond, for which, and for *Poblet*, c
10km W, see Rte 65B.

Bearing SW from Artesa, at 10km *Cubells* is passed, with a Romanesque church door and 13–14C sculpture; and 14km beyond, Balaguer, 2km W on the far bank of the Segre, is also bypassed.
Balaguer (12,600 inhab.) has an arcaded *Pl. Mayor* and, among
several churches, that of *Sto. Domingo*, with a cloister of c 1323–50
by Jaime Fabre.—28km **Lleida**; see Rte 65A.

63 Barcelona and Environs

BARCELONA, capital of the ancient principality and modern autonomy of Catalunya and of its province, and with a population of
1,752,650 inhab. (959,000 in 1930; 1,527,000 in 1960), excluding
populous adjacent municipalities, is the most prosperous and
dynamic city of Spain. Many would agree with Rose Macaulay when
she wrote four decades ago of Barcelona: 'More, perhaps, than any
city in the world (Marseilles and Naples are near rivals) it gives an
impression of tempestuous, surging, irrepressible life and *brio*'. It is
also the most 'European' of Spanish cities.

The plain on which it stands is bounded on the NW by hills
culminating in that of *Tibidabo* (352m) and to the S by the isolated
hill of *Montjuïc*. The winter temperature is mild and the sultry
summer heat is tempered by sea breezes.

Carthaginian *Barcino*, founded by Hamilcar Barca c 230 BC, occupied a low hill
on which the cathedral now stands. It superceded an Iberian or perhaps
Phocaean settlement. Under the Romans it became the capital of *Layetania*, a
district of *Hispania Tarraconensis*, and in c 15 BC distinguished by Augustus
with the title *Colonia Julia Augusta Paterna Faventia Barcino*. It was destroyed
by the Franks in AD 263, but was then retaken by the Romans and defended by
a wall with 78 flanking towers. In 415 Ataulf, a Visigoth, made it his capital, and
Catalunya probably derived its name from *Gothalania*. In 713 it surrendered to
the Moors, but early in the 9C they were expelled by Louis le Débonair (son of
Charlemagne), who appointed a dependent count to govern the Spanish
marches.

In 874 Wilfred 'el Velloso' (the hairy), Count of Barcelona, was given
independence by Charles 'le Chauve' (the bald), and his descendants prospered. In 985 Almanzor attacked and burnt the town, but was driven out the
same year by Borrel II.

Ramón Berenguer I (1018–25) compiled the 'Usatges', the Catalan equivalent
to the *fueros* or privileges of Aragón and the Basque provinces. In 1137 Ramón
Berenguer IV, by his marriage with Petronila, daughter of Ramiro 'el Monje'
(the monk) of Aragón, united the kingdom to his domains and assumed the title
of King of Aragón. In 1259 the Consejo del Ciento (Council of the 100), founded
by Jaume I, promulgated the 'Consulat del Mar', the earliest code of European
maritime laws, which served as a model for other Mediterranean states.

The marriage in 1474 of Fernando of Aragón and Isabel of Castile (a kingdom
with a far higher population) marked the virtual end of the independence of
Catalunya, but an attempt by Felipe IV to ignore the *usatges* in 1640 drove the
Catalans to seek the assistance of France (the War 'dels Segadors' or harves-
ters). In 1705 they espoused the cause of the Archduke Charles against

Felipe V, the nominee of Louis XIV in the War of the Succession. The city was taken and sacked by Marshal Berwick in 1714, and its privileges abolished. Between 1718 and 1797 its population grew from 35,000 to 115,000. It was occupied by the French from 1808 to 1813.

Throughout the 19C it was a focus of unrest, declaring itself as a matter of course opposed to any constituted Castilian authority, in 1827 and 1868 supporting the Carlists. In 1835 it was a centre of anti-monastic agitation, while in the early years of the present century it was a hotbed of both corrupt electoral practices and of anarchist plotting. Anticlericalism and outbreaks of violence occurred in 1908–09, particularly during the 'Setmana Tràgica' of July 1909, and again in the immediate post-war period in reaction to the repressive governorship of Martínez Anido. Some 1000 citizens died for 'political' reasons in 1917–23, including over 100 anarchists gunned down by *pistoleros* for 'trying to escape' from confinement, under the so-called *Ley de Fugas*. By 1920 Barcelona's population (88,000 in 1818) had risen to 706,000. In 1923 Gen. José Primo de Rivera, then Captain-General of Catalunya, published in Barcelona his *Pronunciamiento* declaring the establishment of a military dictatorship. In 1929 a prestigious International Exhibition was held here. (There had also been one in 1888.) Catalunya remained a centre of disaffection, and on 14 April 1931 the Catalan Republic was proclaimed by Francesc Macià, although there was a reaction in October 1934, and autonomous institutions were suspended.

In 1936 (the year Alban Berg's Violin Concerto received its world première in Barcelona) Gen. Goded arrived from Majorca to raise the garrison for the Nationalists, but the attempt failed after violent street fighting, and it was not until 26 January 1939 that Nationalist forces under Gen. Yagüe entered Barcelona. Meanwhile it had been indiscriminately bombed by the Italians (1300 were killed in the raid of 18 March 1938 alone). Anti-clericism was again rampant during this period, and most of the churches of Barcelona were gutted by fire. From 24 January 1939 there was a mass exodus towards the French frontier, and those that remained suffered from ruthless proscriptions, many thousands being executed by the Nationalists.

The Generalitat was re-established in September 1977, and the city and Catalunya now materially flourish. Barcelona will host the Olympic Games in 1992.

Among those born in Barcelona are the writers Juan Boscan (1487/92–1542); Antonio Capmany (1742–1813); Joan Maragall (1860–1911); Eugeni d'Ors (1882–1954); Josep Carner (1884–1970); and Carles Ribas (1897–1902); among artists, Antoni Viladomat (1678–1755); Francisco Javier Parcerisa (1803–75); Santiago Rusiñol i Prats (1861–1931); Ramón Casas i Carbó (1866–1932); and Joan Miró (1893–1983); and the architect Lluís Domènech i Montaner (1850–1923); also Francisco Pi y Margall (1824–1901), President of the first Spanish Republic; Francesc Ferrer (1854–1909), the radical reformer; and Frederic Mompou (1893–1987), the composer.

Ramon Llull (1233–1316), the influential poet, author, and theologian, although born in Palma de Mallorca, came from a noble family of Barcelona.

Employment of Time. For the hurried visitor the principal objects will be the '*Barri Gòtic*', *Sta. María del Mar*, and the nearby *C. Montcada* and its museums, the *Drassens (Museu Marítim)*, *Museu d'Art de Catalunya* and *Military museum* on Montjuïc, Gaudí's '*Sagrada Familia*' and the *Monestir de Pedralbes*. Most museums are closed on Mondays.

A complex reorganisation of the museums of Barcelona is at present in progress, so check with tourist offices for the whereabouts of some collections, and for times of admission. The collection of late 19th and early 20C paintings in the *Museu d'Art Modern* is to be moved to the *Palau Nacional* on Montjuïc, for instance, and the *Casa de Caritat* will serve as the hub of several museums, such as those devoted to *Numismatic collections* and the *Post*; the *Graphic Arts*, and *Papermaking*; *Theatre, Cinema*, and *Photography*; *Contemporary art*, etc.

Although Barcelona has plenty of hotels, travellers are advised to ensure, if possible, that their hotel is reasonably near the 'Barri Gòtic', for many of the newer establishments are some distance away, and time can be wasted in travelling to the centre. Note that the Catalan for street is *Carrer* not Calle, and that *Avinguda* is Catalan for Avenida.

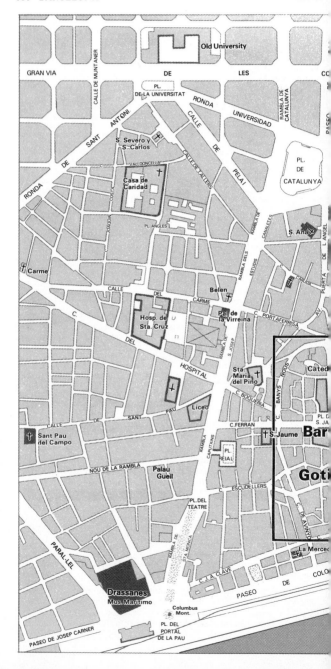

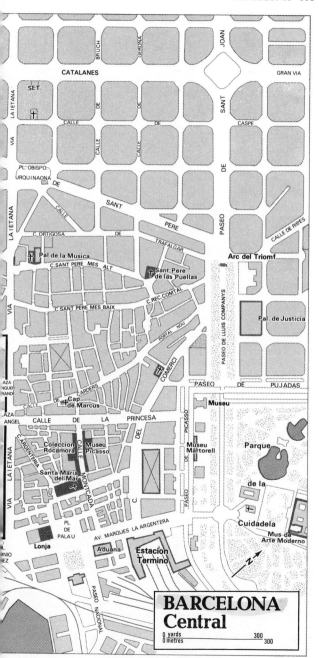

BARCELONA
Central

| 0 yards | 300 |
| 0 metres | 300 |

Arqueológico	Montjuïc	09.30–14.00; 16.00–19.00, except Sun
Arte de Catalunya	Pal. Nac., Montjuïc	09.00–14.00
Arte Moderno	Parque de la Ciudadela	09.00–14.00; 16.00–19.30 Shut Sun
Cathedral museum		11.00–13.00
Ciudad, Historio de la	Pl. del Rei	09.00–14.00; 15.30–20.00, except Sun
Marés, Federico	adjacent to cathedral	09.00–14.00; 16.00–19.30 Shut Sun
Maritimo		10.00–14.00; 16.00–19.00 Shut Sun.
Militar	Montjuïc	10.00–14.00; 16.00–19.00 Shut Sun.
Miró/Contempory Art	Montjuïc	11.00–20.00
Música	Diagonal 373	09.00–14.00
Pedralbes, (? also Cerámica)		10.00–13.00
Picasso	C. Montcada 15	09.00–14.00; 16.00–20.30 Shut Sun
Rocamora Collection (textiles and costumes)	C. Montcada 12	09.00–14.00; 16.30–19.00

The city may be divided conveniently into five sections: the *Barri Gòtic*; the *Ramblas*; NE of the Via Laietana; *Montjuïc*; and the *Eixample*.

A.   The Barri Gòtic

This is the nucleus of Barcelona. The city grew around it and was in turn surrounded by defensive walls (demolished 1868) containing an area of just over 10 hectares. The approximate line of the walls lay along the Paral.lel to the SW—commanded by the fortress of Montjuïc—the Rondas de Sant Pau, de Sant Antoni, de la Universitat, and de Sant Pere. To the NE it was defended by the Ciudadela.

It was at a gate in these walls that in 1775 Philip Thicknesse was obliged to wait 'above half an hour, no person being admitted to enter from twelve till one, though all the world may go up; that hour being allotted for the guards &c. to eat their dinner'.

The only wide street was the Rambla, until the Via Laietana was driven through the town as part of the grandiose 'Plan Cerdà' of 1859, named after Ildefons Cerdà, when the new town or *Eixample* (extension) was laid out on a grid pattern beyond the old, connecting it with outlying communities.

The Av. Diagonal intersects this grid. To the N is an extensive and fashionable residential and shopping district climbing the lower slopes of Tibidabo and Vallvidrera.

The narrow congested alleys of the Barri Gòtic are best visited on foot (but beware **Hazards**). This area is specifically that enclosed by the 4C *Walls*, considerable sections of which may still be seen. There was an ambitious and well-conceived project to uncover and restore their almost complete circuit as derelict houses abutting them were demolished, but this may take some time to come to fruition.

The Avinguda de la Catedral provides a good view of the W Front of the Cathedral, the huge square bastions of the walls to the right, and, beyond them, the cylindrical gate towers on Roman foundations facing the Pl. Nova.

The ***Cathedral** or **La Seu** was begun in 1298, but the W Front (the design by the French master, *Carlí*, is still preserved) was not completed until 1892, its openwork spires harmonising well with the older work.

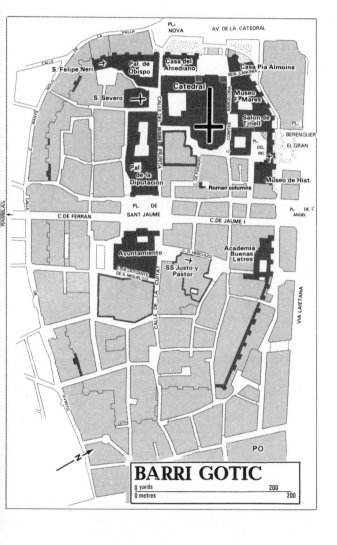

The original church, possibly built on the site of a pagan temple, was desecrated by Almanzor in the 10C; of its rebuilding by Ramón Berenguer II in 1058 nothing remains but the *Puerta de S. Severo* in the S transept and the entrance to the *Cap. de Sta. Lucia* outside the SW corner of the cloister. The *Puerta de S. Ivo* (above which are reliefs depicting the combat of the Knight of Vilardell with a dragon) is flanked by inscriptions relating to the building of the present church, finished as far as the W end of the coro in 1329 (with Jaime Fabre of Mallorca as master of the works from 1317 to 1339). The W end and cloister were built between 1365 and 1448 under Bernard Roca, Bartolomeu Gual, and Andrés Escuder; the octagonal towers above the transepts date from 1389; the clock tower is slightly older.

The fine proportions of the well-lit interior can now be appreciated. Behind two massive 15C columns supporting the cimborio (1422) is the *Trascoro*, decorated with marble reliefs by Bartolomé Ordoñez and Pedro Vilar. On either side, above the rows of chapels, is a deep triforium surmounted by a rather inadequate clerestory, many windows of which contain 15C glass.

The *Coro* (after 1390) contains high *Stalls* surmounted by canopies carved by Michael Lochner and Friedrich (completed 1490); the lower stalls, of 1457, are by Matís Bonafé. Lochner's *Pulpit* is reached by a stair by Pere Ca-Anglada, who also designed the *Bishop's throne*. The coats of arms on the upper tier of stalls are those of the Knights of the Golden Fleece who assembled at the first and last Chapter of the Order held here in 1519 by Charles V. They include the royal arms of Sweden and Poland and the devices of the Prince of Orange.

Most of the side chapels are closed by well-wrought grilles and contain 16–18C retablos, few of which are in good condition although that by Bernat Martorell (3rd chapel in the Ambulatory) is notable. Remarkable among tombs is that of Bp Ramón de Escales (died 1398), completed by Antoni Canet in 1409, in the last chapel of the ambulatory. Beneath the *Organ* (1539) in the N transept are two carved Moor's heads. From the foot of the altar steps a staircase descends to the apsidal crypt (by Jaime Fabre; 1339), containing a marble tomb with bas-reliefs by Giovanni Pisano.

Above the Gothic door of the *Sacristy* (containing the *Treasury*) are the wooden sarcophagi of Ramón Berenguer I (died 1025) and his wife Almodis. The *Cloister*, with its irregular arches and curious capitals, contains the *Pabellón de S. Jorge* (its vault boss carved by Joan Claperós), adjoining which is a pool with an enclosure for the 'Capitoline geese' kept here as a reminder of Roman greatness in Barcelona. The *Chapterhouse* on its W side (c 1400; by Arnau Bargués) contains paintings, notably a Pietà by Bermejo. The Romanesque door of the *Cap. de Sta. Lucia* (1257) is seen on leaving the cloister by the SW door.

Facing the W side of the cloister is the *Casa de l'Ardiaca* (or Archdeacon's house) of 1510, now occupied by city archives, with a charming courtyard and Renaissance doorway.—To the left is the *Palacio del Bisbe* (bishop's), which incorporates some Romanesque parts of the original palace begun in 1255.

Adjacent *S. Sever*, by Jaume Arnaudies, was completed in 1705, with Baroque decoration.—A passage between the two last leads to *S. Felip Neri* (1721–52), with Neo-Classical altars of 1778.—A museum devoted to footwear may be visited in this plaza.

Skirt the Cathedral Cloister to pass the Gothic *Puerta de Sta. Eulalia*, and—at the angle of the cloister and apse—the *Puerta de la Pietat*, with a sculptured Pietà in its tympanum. To the right is the *Casas de los Canonges* (restored). Turn down the narrow C. de Paradis. At No. 10 (the *Centre Excursionista de Catalunya*; founded in 1876), in a house built on the highest point of the old settlement, stood a Corinthian temple dedicated to Augustus. Four columns remain in situ and may be seen from the vestibule.

The passage shortly enters the **Plaça de S. Jaume**, the heart of the quarter, on the site of an ancient cemetery.

To the right stands the **Palau de la Generalitat**, the seat of the ancient parliament of Catalunya. The entrance in the C. Bisbe Irurita, spanned by a footbridge, is in the plain façade of a building of 1425 by Marc Safont, surmounted by a medallion of St. George (Sant Jordi) and the Dragon carved in 1418 by Pere Johan. The façade fronting the plaza, by Pere Blai, was not built until c 1596. It was here that Macià, the first President, announced the *Catalan* Republic (14 April, 1931).

From the courtyard a flight of steps with an elaborate balustrade ascends to an arcaded gallery. From here one may enter the *Pati dels Tarongers*, an upper courtyard overlooked by finely carved windows and curious gargoyles. On the right is the *Cap. de S. Jordi* (1434; by Safont). Opening off the gallery of the main patio is the classical *Salón de S. Jordi*.

On the opposite side of the square is the *Casa de la Ciutat* or *Ajuntament de Barcelona*, with a façade of 1847. Companys proclaimed the Spanish Republic on 14 April 1931 from here. On the NE side is the façade of the old Gothic town hall of 1402, by Arnau Bargués, bearing sculptures by Jordi de Déu.

Among the richly decorated rooms on the first floor is the *Saló de Cent*, where councillors were elected, a Gothic chamber 27m long, dating from 1373, entered by a Renaissance doorway with twisted columns. The *Saló de Cròniques* is decorated by paintings by Josep Maria Sert of the Catalan expedition to the East under Roger de Flor. The *Chapel* of 1410 was the original home of the retablo 'dels Consellers' painted by Luis Dalmau in 1445; see p 397.

To the S of the Ajuntament, in the shadow of its simple but incongruous modern extension, stands the 15C *Palau de Centellas*, with its patio.—To the N, the C. Hèrcules leads to *S. Just i Pastor*, a restored building of 1360 claiming to occupy the oldest ecclesiastical site in Barcelona.

A passage opposite leads to the late 14C *Palau Palamós*, with an attractive patio.

A parallel alley to the S leads to C. del Subteniente Navarro and (left) part of the exterior *Town Wall* which has been exposed.—Continuing N, we cross the C. de Jaume I at the PRAÇA DE L'ANGEL, just N of which is the *Plaça de Berenguer el Gran*, also displaying a stretch of the 4C walls buttressing the chapel of *Sta. Àgata* and the old palace.

These may be approached by retracing our steps and turning right and right again past the 15–16C *Casa Clariana-Padellás* (brought from the C. de Mercaders earlier this century and re-erected on this site). In it is the *Museu d'Història de la Ciutat*.

Subterranean galleries display in situ the extensive remains of the Visigothic and Roman town. Excavations are continuing, particularly on the 4C Christian basilcia and 11C cathedral. The first and second floors are devoted to the history and development of the city from the 16th to the 19C; collections of plans and drawings; sections devoted to its craft guilds, and the minor arts, etc. The **Chapel of Sta. Àgata** may be entered from the first floor. It was built by Bertrán Riquer in 1319, has an octagonal belfry, and contains the retablo of the Epiphany by Jaume Huguet (1466).

Adjacent to the museum is the *Plaça del Rei*, on the site of the old palace of the counts. Across the N corner are stairs ascending under a lofty arch to the *Saló del Tinell*, the great hall of the *Palau Reial Major*, with a span of 17m, completed in 1370 by Guillem Carbonell. In 1716 it was converted into the conventual church of *Sta. Clara*, and in 1940 it was purchased by the municipality and restored. In the earlier part of the palace are remains of murals of c 1300. Fernando

*The ancient walls of Barcelona, seen from the Pl. de
Berenguer el Gran*

and Isabel received Columbus here on his first return from the New
World (June 1493). The building is surmounted by an unusual tower
of 1557 consisting of five superimposed galleries, known as the
Mirador del Rei Martí.

Leaving the plaça, turn right towards the apse of the Cathedral to
follow the C. dels Comtes past the *Palau del Lloctinent*, completed in
1557 by Antoni Carbonell for the viceroy of Catalunya. Off the
dignified courtyard ascends a staircase with a superb coffered
ceiling. The building houses the *Archives of the Crown of Aragón*
(founded in 1549), comprising over four million documents dating
back to AD 448.

No. 10 in the street houses the *Museu Marés in former conventual
dependencies. The museum contains the important collections
formed by the sculptor Frederic Marés (1896–) and donated by him
to the city.

The ground floor contains over 400 medieval polychromed wood sculptures,
well-displayed and described. Among 10–16C stone sculptures in the Crypt, a
Romanesque portal from the destroyed church of Anzano (Huesca) has been
incorporated into the building. Some Roman remains are also displayed in
situ.—The first floor contains over 1000 examples of Spanish sculpture from the
early Middle Ages to the end of the 19C, remarkable both for their range and for
their quality.—The 2nd and 3rd floors constitute a museum of bygones illustrating everyday life, including collections of locksmith's work; costumes,

fans, parasols, purses, combs, scissors, jewellery, watches, sticks, braces; games, dolls, and playing cards; the *Sala del Fumador*, with a collection of pipes, snuff boxes, match boxes (15,000 specimens), cigarette papers; and minor religious art, reliquaries, and ex-votos. The collection of Arms and Armour is housed in the *Military Museum* on Montjuïc.

The W Front of the cathedral is regained on passing the 15C *Casas de la Canonja y de la Pia Almoina* (1546), containing the cathedral archives, incorporating on its far side more Roman wall.

Just N of the Pl. Nova is the building of the *College of Architects*, with a frieze designed by Picasso (1960). To the left, in the C. de Cucurulla, is the 16C *Casa Bassols* (housing the Cercle Artistic).— The Av. del Portal de l'Angel leads directly to the Pl. de Catalunya. It passes near (right, at C. Montsió 3) *'Els Quatre Gats'*, a famous avantgarde artistic rendezvous at the turn of the century.

B.   The Ramblas

These are best visited from the *Pl. de Catalunya*, a hub of activity lying between the old town and the new. The tree-lined **Ramblas**, a busy thoroughfare and promenade, lead from its S corner to the harbourside Pl. del Portal de la Paz. Their name is derived from the Arabic *raml*, sand, for they occupy the site of the Riera de la Malla, a seasonal torrent whose channel was used in the dry season as a road. Nevertheless, by 1366 a covered sewer existed along its length.

The *Rambla de Canletas* is succeeded by the *Rambla dels Estudis* (also known as 'dels Ocells' from the bird market held there). On the right is the *Església de Betlem* (1681–1732; by Josep Juli), a former Jesuit church, gutted in 1936.

One may turn down the C. del Carme (opposite the arcaded *Palau Moia* of 1790) towards the former **Hospital de la Sta. Creu**. The courtyard entered first contains a collection of ancient surgical instruments from the Acadèmia de Medicina of 1764. In the chapel is a Baroque altarpiece.—Opposite stands the *Casa de Convalescència* of 1638, the exterior of which, to the W, is decorated with statues by Lluis Bonifas of 1677.—Within the Hospital may be seen some remarkable azulejos by Llorens Pasoles (1684) and Ramón Porcioles (1665). Off the Gothic *Cloister* is the *Biblioteca de Catalunya*, housed in the great wards built in 1415 around a central courtyard. The *Church*, altered in the 18C, contains a group representing Charity, by Pere Costa. The main front of the building is best seen from the C. de Hospital, S of the courtyard.

Further W, at the junction of the C. de Hospital with the C. del Carme, is Romanesque *S. Llàtzer* (Lazarus), relic of a leper hospital founded c 1150.

In the *Rambla de S. Josep* (or *de les Flors*), with its flower market, is the **Palau Virreina** (1778), so-named because it was once the residence of the widow of the viceroy of Peru, Manuel Amat. It houses a *Postal Museum* and other miscellaneous collections, and is the site of occasional exhibitions.

Nos 61–65 in the Rambla are the *Gran Teatre del Liceu*, an operahouse rebuilt after a fire in 1861. In 1893 two anarchist bombs were thrown into the auditorium by Santiago Salvador, killing 20. This was in reprisal for the execution of Paulí Pallàs, who had failed to assassinate Gen. Martínez Campos.

The C.S. Pau leads right through a poor and populous district to **S. Pau del Camp**, the oldest church in Barcelona, founded before 977 by Guibert Guitard for Benedictine monks. It was restored in 1127 and again since the Civil War. The 13C façade is notable for the capitals of the entrance, probably from an earlier building, and for the symbolic carvings on the tympanum. The plain interior is in the shape of a Greek cross, with a central octagon tower and three apses. The diminutive *Cloister* has arches of three and five lobes supported on twin columns. The 14C *Abbot's house* is now the rectory.

Just beyond lies the Paral.lel, once considered the 'Montmartre' of Barcelona but now a somewhat depressed and seedy area.

The *Rambla dels Caputxins* ends at the Pl. del Teatre, where Nos 3–5 in the street are the *Palau Güell* (1889; by Gaudí). It houses the *Museu de les Arts de l'Espectacle* (theatre museum), with its entrance in the adjacent Nou de la Rambla.

The *Rambla de Sta. Mónica* ends at the *Pl. del Portal de la Paz*, in the centre of which rises the ugly *Columbus Monument*, a column 52m high, erected in 1890 from the designs of Gaietà Buigas.

To the right are the ***Drassens**, the remarkable medieval covered shipyards, restored to house the ***Museu Marítim**.

The collections include numerous ship models; photographs and drawings illustrating the history and sociology of the maritime settlements of Catalunya; maps, navigating instruments, and figureheads (among them the 'Blanca Aurora', a portrait of the owner's daughter). A full-size replica of the *galera* 'La Real', which fought at Lepanto in 1571, was built here in 1971 to celebrate the quatercentenary of the battle.

Part of the old town *Wall* may be seen in the Paral.lel, on the far side of the Drassens.—To the right is the *Estació Marítim*, and ahead floats a replica of the *'Sta. María'*, surprisingly diminutive, in which Columbus set sail in 1492 on his first voyage of discovery.

From here one may follow the palm-lined but otherwise undistinguished PASSEIG (PASEO) DE COLOM on the site of the old sea wall.

Behind the *Capitania General*, further N, is the former convent of *La Mercè* (1775; by Josep Mas), preserving a façade of 1516 from demolished S. Miquel.—At 28 C. Ampla is the *Palau Sessa-Larrard* (1778; by Josep Ribes), one of several notable mansions in the area.

From just N of La Mercè, the C. de Avinyó and (left) the C. Rosa and C. Escudellers lead back to the Ramblas through the '*barri Xines*' (the red-light district) of Barcelona, a colourful cosmopolitan port area of narrow alleys and innumerable bars, crowded night and day by those seeking and offering diversion at a price.—Just to the N before reaching the Ramblas is the arcaded *Pl. Reial*, with a palm-shaded garden. From its N end one may follow the C. Ferran to the right past Gothic *S. Jaume* (1394), built on the site of an ancient synogogue, and left into the C. Banys Nous, to the left of which, until 1834, were *Jewish Baths*. After crossing the pedestrian C. Boqueria, turn left into the *Pl. de S. Josep Oriol*.

The W side of the square is dominated by ***Sta. Maria del Pi** (1322–1486; restored since the Civil War), with a Romanesque door. It stands on the site of an earlier building named after a pine tree that grew in the Pl. del Pi. The W portal and rose window are well designed, as is the octagonal tower. The *Sacristy* contains an Adoration by Antoni Viladomat (1678–1755), buried in the church. The *Chapterhouse*, by Bartomeu Mas, was completed in 1468.

By following the C. Petritxol N and crossing the C. Portaferrisa, we enter (via the C. del Bot) the *Pl. de la Vila de Madrid*, where excavations of a Roman road and tombs are displayed in situ.—A

short alley leads N into the C. Sta. Anna. The conventual church of
Sta. Anna, founded in 1146 but altered in later years, has a portal of c
1300. The interior has been restored since being gutted in 1936.
Adjoining is a two-storeyed *Cloister* (15C). Passing this, the C.
Rivadeneyra leads directly into the Pl. de Catalunya.

C. NE of the Via Laietana

From the Av. de la Catedral the C. Tapineria leads past the Pl. de
Ramon Berenguer el Gran to the Pl. de l'Angel; see p 385. Crossing
the Via Laietana here, cut through the old city after 1908, follow the
C. Bòria and the C. de Corders. In the latter (right) is the façade of the
12C *Capella de Marcús* (restored), with external blind arcading.

Turn right here across the C. Princesa into the **C. Montcada**,
containing several interesting medieval mansions. No. 15, the *Palau
Berenguer d'Aguilar* (possibly by Marc Safont), now houses the
Museu Picasso, to be extended, an important but still unrepresenta-
tive collection of the works of Pablo Ruíz Picasso (1881–1973),
donated by the artist to Barcelona in 1970. It shows the successive
stages of his development during his years in Málaga (1889–90), La
Coruña (1891–95), and Barcelona (1895–1904).

GROUND FLOOR: Early drawings and sketches, including the artist's father, *José
Ruiz Blasco*; a Self-portrait; and Landscapes (1896–97); nude studies; a copy of
Velazquez's portrait of Felipe IV; Portrait of Tía Pepa; sketches for 'Science and
Charity', and the final work (1897). Note also the storage jars in situ in R11.
  FIRST FLOOR: 'La Chata'; Lola, the artist's sister; and figure studies in the
manner of Toulouse-Lautrec; Menu for 'Els Quatre Gats' restaurant (1900; see p
387); preliminary sketches for 'El clam de las Verges', and carnival themes; The
kiss; Margot; 'Desemparats' (Mother and child, 1903); The madman (1904);
Señora Canals (1905); studies for 'La Vida'; 'La Salchichona'; Harlequin (1917;
the model was Léonide Massine); and El paseo de Colón; a series on the theme
of 'Las Meninas' of Velázquez (58 works in all; 1957); studies of Doves at
windows; Ceramics (1948–57); and Portraits of Jaume Sabartés (1881–1968),
donor of many works to the museum.
  SECOND FLOOR: Portrait of Dora Markovitch; Head of a young girl; Youth;
Head of a goat; Toad; and Hen; Illustrations for the Metamorphoses of Ovid
(Skira, 1931); Portraits of Françoise Gilot; Fauns and Centaurs, etc. Jacqueline
Picasso donated an additional 41 pieces of pottery in 1981.

Opposite, in the 14C *Palau dels Marqués de Lllió* (No. 12), is the
Museu Téxtil i d'Indumentària (or Manuel Rocamora collection,
named after its founder), a remarkable collection of over 4000 items,
of fundamental importance for the study of Spanish costume. Additional sections are devoted to dolls, shoes, fans, socks and stockings,
purses and wallets, and handkerchiefs.

Continuing down the C. Montcada, we pass three more 15C
mansions (Nos 14, 23, and 25), and No. 20, the 17C *Palau Dalmases*,
with a Baroque courtyard and staircase, to reach the finest church in
Barcelona after the cathedral, *Sta. Maria del Mar*, with a good W
portal.

Begun in 1329 and completed in 1383, it displays the wide nave typical of
Catalan Gothic (apparently designed by Jaume Fabre, the second architect of
the cathedral). The E door dates from 1542; the N tower was completed in 1495,
and the S not until 1902. The aisles are as high as the nave and are very narrow.
The chapels are lighted by good stained glass, notably that of the Last
Judgement (1494; by Senier Desmanes of Avignon), and the Coronation of the

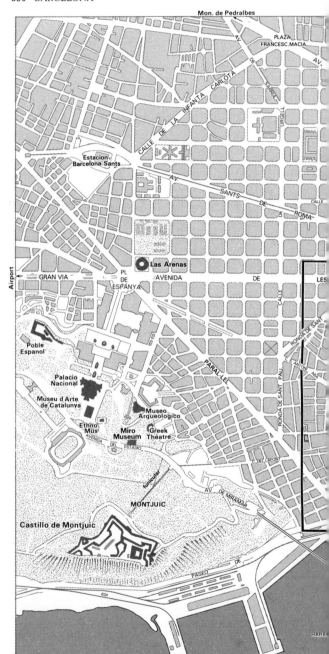

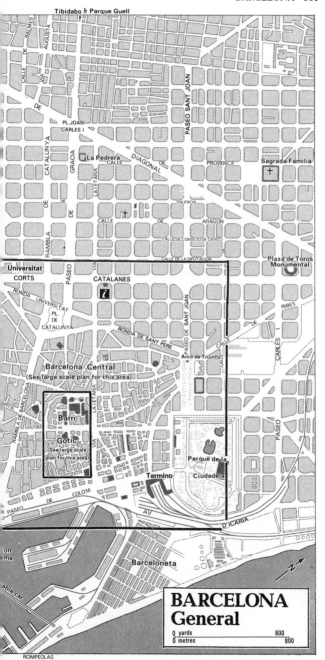

Tibidabo & Parque Guell

CALLE DE BALMES
VIA AUGUSTA
CALLE DE
PASEO SANT JOAN

PL. JOAN
CARLES I

La Pedrera
GRACIA
CALLE DIAGONAL DE
PROVENCA
Sagrada Familia

DE
LA LETANA
DE

CALLE
VALENCIA
DE
ARAGON

RAMBLA
CALLE DE CONSEJO DE CIENTO
CALLE DE LA DIPUTACIÓN

Plaza de Toros
Monumental

Universitat
CORTS
PASEO
VIA
CATALANES

RONDA UNIVERSITAT
PL.
DE
CATALUNYA

RONDA DE SANT PERE

PASEO DE SANT JOAN
RIBES
DE
CARLES

Arco de Triunfo

Barcelona Central
(See large scale plan for this area)

RAMBLA DE BARCELONA
LA LETANA
VIA

Barri
Gotic
(See large scale
plan for this area)

Parque de la
Ciudadela

Termino

PASEO
DE COLOM
AV
D'ICARIA

Barceloneta

ROMPEOLAS

BARCELONA
General

0 yards	800
0 metres	800

Virgin in the W rose. Gutted in 1936, it lost its Baroque fittings and now shows its original simple lines, but several chapels have been disfigured since by tasteless modern statues. On each side of the chapel beneath the organ (N side) is a curious little tomb.

Leaving by the S front, turn left into the Pl. del Palau. On the right is the **Casa de la Llotja** or *Exchange*, built to the design of Joan Soler i Faneca in 1774–94 on the site of the *Consolat de Mar*, the Gothic exchange hall of 1392, by Pere Arvey. This has been preserved and may be entered from the courtyard opening off the C. Consolat.

On the SE side of the plaza is the *Escola Nàutica*, behind which the Passeig Nacional skirts the port quarter of **Barceloneta**, a regularly planned suburb laid out by the Marqués de la Mina in 1755. In Barceloneta, *S. Miquel del Port* (1755; by Francesc Paredes and Pere Màrtir Cermeño), contains sculptures by Pere Costa.—Beyond is an insalubrious beach.—The recently extended quay or breakwater, leads to the *Torre de S. Sebastià*, from which a cablecar crosses the harbour to *Montjuïc*.

On the far side of the Pl. del Palau is the *Duana Vella*, built in 1792 for the Comte de Roncali and now housing the *Govern Civil*.—The Av. del Marquès de l'Argentera leads NE past the Railway Station of *Barcelona Termini* or *de França* to approach the PARC DE LA CIUTADELLA, laid out after 1869 on the site of the citadel built in 1715 by Felipe V. The park still contains a small group of buildings which were left standing, including a chapel and the old *Palau Reial* (formerly the *Arsenal*) to which two wings were added in 1915. It was the seat of the Catalan Parliament in 1932–39.

Since 1945 it has accommodated the **Museu d'Art Modern**, largely devoted to the school of Catalan art of the final decades of the 19C and the Madrid school of the early years of the 20C, although certain sections and the patios contain contemporary works. It is expected that the collection will be moved to the Palau Nacional on Montjuïc in due course.

Several rooms contain the works of *Nogués, Pidelassera, Sunyer, Canals, Fortuny* (including his huge 'Battle of Tetuan'), and *Sert* (with sketches and models of his work in the cathedral of Vic). *Dali* (Portrait of his father), *Miró*, and *Tàpies* are only represented by one work each. The collection contains few individually important paintings; but noteworthy are *Sorolla*, Portrait of Elena and María; and *Zuloaga*, My Cousins.—The first floor, on which some furniture of the period is displayed, also houses a *Numismatic collection*, which may be inspected on advance application.

Behind the museum are a *Zoo* (with an albino gorilla) and an *Aquarium*. The park also contains an ornamental *Cascade* (by Josep Fontserè; assisted by the youthful Gaudí).—Further W is the *Museu de Geologia* or *Martorell*, with important mineralogical collections, to the N of which is the *Museu de Zoologia*, housed in a building by Lluis Domènech i Montaner, run up for the Exhibition of 1888.

A short distance W of the park is *S. Agustí Vell*, with a 17C portal and one walk of a 14C cloister.

To the NW of the park, flanking the Passeig de Lluis Companys, is the *Palau de Justícia*, completed in 1908, and, beyond, a brick *Arc de Triomf* erected for the Exhibition of 1888.

Before reaching this, one may turn left down the C. Baixa de S. Pere, off which (right) is the convent church of **S. Pere de les Puelles** (mid 10C). It has suffered many partial destructions and alterations since it was built on the site of S. Sadurní, a foundation of 801. The main rebuilding took place in 1147 but the E end dates from 1498.

The C. Alta de S. Pere may be followed for some distance to reach (right) the exotic *Palau de la Música Catalana* (1908; by Domènech i Montaner), in which Pau Casals' orchestra gave its first performance, in 1920; and beyond, the pargetted *Casa de Gremi de Velers* (1763; by Joan Garrido), built for a guild of silk weavers.

Crossing the Via Laietana, one can regain the Av. de la Catedral is regained to the S, or follow the pedestrian C. Comtal opposite, to approach the Pl. de Catalunya.

D. Montjuïc

The **Montjuïc**, a hill rising steeply above the harbour, derives its name either from *Mons Jovis* or *Mons Judaicus* (with an ancient cemetery of Barcelona's Jewish community). In 1937 Benjamin Britten and Lennox Berkeley composed a suite of Catalan dances entitled 'Montjuïc'.

In 1929 the park on the N slope of the hill was occupied by an International Exhibition, planned on a grandiose scale, as—further S—are the projected facilities for the Olympic Games of 1992. Several buildings erected in 1929 remained as a permanent attraction, among them the *Palau Nacional*, the *Poble Espanyol* (Spanish village), and the *Estadi* (stadium), near which another is being constructed for the 1992 Olympic Games. Between the Palau Nacional and the Pl. d'Espanya are several exhibition halls in which the city's numerous trade fairs are held.

Approaches. The main places of interest may be reached with ease by car from the Pl. d'Espanya; or from the Pl. del Portal de la Paz by a road climbing to the Miramar (the W terminus of a cablecar crossing the harbour). Further W, beyond a new luxury hotel designed by Ricardo Bofill, is the intermediate funicular station for the Castell (its lower station is at the W end of the Nou de la Rambla), which may also be approached by road.

At the E end of the Montjuïc stands the **Castell** or *Citadel*, erected in 1640 during the War 'dels Segadors' and extended in 1694.

It was surprised and captured by Lord Peterbrough in 1705, during the War of the Succession. In 1808 French troops under Gén. Dufresne (who had entered in the guise of allies) suddenly evicted the Spanish garrison and made themselves masters of Barcelona. Espartero bombarded the city from here during the insurrection of 1842. On 13 October 1909 Francesc Ferrer, the radical reformer, was shot here, as was Lluis Companys on 15 October 1940. During the Civil War it was used as a prison.

It was handed over to the municipality in 1960, since when a **Museu del Exercit** or *Military Museum* has been installed in its cavernous casemates.

Of particular interest are the numerous plans and models of the castles of Catalunya displayed in R4, while R6 contains the arms collection of Frederic Marés (q.v. Museu Marés). Other rooms are devoted to the early military history of Catalunya, and to the fortress during the War of the Succession and in the Peninsular and Carlist Wars (in Catalunya). Steps ascend to the roof, providing panoramic views over the city and port.

Descending from the citadel, turn left along the Av. de Miramar to reach the **Fundació Joan Miró** (1975; by Josep Lluís Sert), an open-plan building incorporating the *Centre d'Etudis d'Art Contemporani*, with exhibition halls, book and print shop, library and documentation centre, auditorium, and archives (containing over 5000 drawings), ranged round a series of internal and external patios. A representative collection of the art and sculpture of Joan Miró (1893–

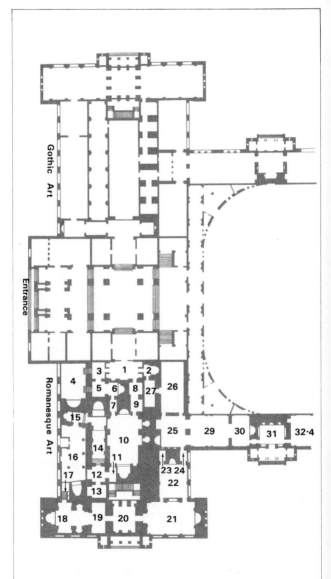

Museu d´Art de Catalunya

1983) is displayed; note also Chillida's 'Meeting-place', and Calder's Fountain of Mercury (1937).

Beyond is the **Palau Nacional**, a mausoleum of a building, but housing the *Museu de Arte de Catalunya, one of the most important collections of Romanesque art in the world.

At present the collections are divided into three main sections: Romanesque; Gothic; and Renaissance, Baroque, and Neo-Classical. The series of rooms to the right of the entrance vestibule incorporate reconstructions of numerous murals from remote villages in the Catalan Pyrenees. Most of them had been covered by later fittings, and some were actually being removed from the country when their transport to Barcelona was undertaken in 1919, although the building was not used as a museum until 1934.

Among the more outstanding exhibits are:

R1 Visigothic and pre-Romanesque capitals and stone carvings.—**R2** Apse from the chapel of the castle of Marmellar (mid 12C).—**R3** Mural of the Stoning of Stephen from S. Joan de Boí (11C).—**R4** Apse from S. Pere, la Seu d'Urgell; paintings from S. Joan de Boí; polychrome wooden Christ in Majesty.—**R5** 12C frontals from S. Quirze de Durro.—**R6** Apse from Ginestarre de Cardós; 12C Christ on the Cross.—**R7** Photographs of early churches and the process of transferring the paintings.—**R10** Apse painting from Argolell; wall painting from S. Quirze de Pedret; apse, with the parable of the Wise and Foolish Virgins (12C); paintings from the chapel of the castle of Orcau.—**RR11–12** 12C wood carvings, including the 'Battlo' Majesty, with a tunic decorated with Islamic motifs.—**R13** A series of 12–13 wooden seated Virgins, including one from Ger; 12C altar frontal from S. Sadurní de Tavernoles.—**R14** Pantocrator, from the apse of S. Climent de Taüll (note foreshortening); pine sedilia from the same church.—**R15** Apse from Sta. Maria de Taüll; frontal from the same.— **R16** Aisle painting from Sta. Maria, and four figures from a Descent from the Cross (12C); wooden Crucifixion dated 1147; 12C wooden Virgin from a Calvary from Durro; wooden St. John and the Virgin from Erill la Val.—**R17** Capitals from Tavernoles (12C).—**R18** Apse from Esterri de Cardos (12C), and frontal from the same church.— **R19** Eight wooden Virgins.—**R20** Wooden Crucifixion of S. Pere (13C).—**R21** Apse from Sta. Eulalia, Estaon; 12C altar frontal from Mosoll; altar frontal from the Vall d'Aran (early 12C); 12C altar from the chapel of Encamp (Andorra); frontal from Avià (13C); reconstruction of a baldacchino with 12–13C fragments from Tosas (Lleida).

Between RR21 and 22 are four columns and capitals from the cloister of S. Pere de les Puelles, Barcelona (12C).—**R22** Apse from S. Miquel d'Engolastres (Andorra), consecrated 1163; three polychrome figures from Vilanova de l'Aguda; polychromed female saint from S. Martí Sarroca (13C); four panels from a group of the Virgin and Magi, with heads in relief (13C).—**R23** Keystone from Ripoll.—**R25** A collection of capitals. It is advisable to visit RR 29–34 before returning to R25 and leaving through RR26–27.

R29 Navarro-Aragonese frontals (12–13C).—**R30** Apses from Toses (Girona).—**R31** Apse from Andorra la Vella (13C), and a collection of bronze and copper crucifixes, censers, croziers, chests, etc., many enamelled.—**R32** Retablo of S. Miquel by the *Master of Soriguerola*.—**R33** murals of the assault on Palma de Mallorca by Jaime I, and the battle of Porto-Pi, both from the Palau d'Aguilar in the C. Montcada; artesonado panels from Aragón (c 1400); wooden reliquary chest with stucco reliefs (13C shrine of S. Candido, S. Cugat del Vallès).—**R34** Baldacchino from S. Sadurní de Tavernoles.

Detail from the apse of S. Climent de Taüll

R26 Paintings from the Chapterhouse of the monastery of Sigena (q.v.), and five tombs from Sta. María de Matallana (Valladolid).—**R27** Chivalric scenes (c 1200).

Cross the entrance vestibule to enter the E wing and **R40**, the first of over 20 rooms devoted to Gothic paintings and sculpture. Among the more striking works are: **R43** *Pere García de Benabarre*, Salome with the head of the Baptist (from S. Juan Bautista, Lleida), etc.; *Gonçal Peris* and *Jaume Mateu*, Jaime I el Conquistador; and a remarkable collection of sculptural fragments, Nottingham alabasters, ecclesiastical plate, etc.—**R52** frontal of Sto. Domingo de Guzmán (c 1315, from S. Miguel, Tamarite de Litera); panels from Mahamud (Burgos, c 1300); *Joan de Tarragona*, Retablo from the castle chapel of Sta. Coloma de Queralt; *Rómulo de Florencia*, Retablo de S. Vicente (Estopanyà, Huesca); *Arnau Bassa* and follower, Annuciation and Epiphany; *Serra brothers*, Retablo of S. Esteban (Sta. María, Gualter), and *Serra family*, Retablo of the Virgin, and Annunciation (Sigena); *Pere Serra*, Virgin and Child and angel musicians (Sta. Clara, Tortosa).—**R53** *Jaume Ferrer II*, the Retablo de S. Jerónimo (c 1457), including also SS. Martin and Sebastian; *Pere García de Benabarre*, Virgin and Child with S. Vicente Ferrer, and donors; *Guerau Gener* and *Lluís Borrassà*, Nativity.—**R54** *Master of Castellfollit*, Retablo of SS. Pedro and Andrés; *Jaume Cirera*, S. Miquel liberating souls; *Joan Mates*, Retablo of S. Sebastián; *Master of Sta. Basilissa*, Retablo of S. Julián and Sta. Basilissa; *Bernat Martorell*, Retablo of S. Vicente, and the Retablo of S. Juan Bautista and S. Juan Evangelista; *Follower of Marçal de Sax* and *Pere Nicolau*, Retablo of Sta. Bárbara.—**R55** *Joan Reixac*, Retablo of Sta. Úrsula.—**R59** *Bartolomé Bermejo*, Christ descending into Hell.—**R60** *Lluís Dalmau*, the Verge dels Consellers (1445); *Jaume Huguet*, Retablo de S. Miquel, Retablo de S. Vicente, and the Retablo of S. Agustín.—**R61** *Master of la Seu d'Urgell*, Annunciation.—**R63** the *Master of Frankfurt*, triptych of the Baptism of Christ; *Pedro Berruguete*, S. Gregory; *Ayne Bru*, Beheading of S. Cucufate (from S. Cugat).

Other rooms contain *Tintoretto*, Portrait of the Marqués de Sta. Cruz; *El Greco*, SS. Pedro and Pablo; *Ribalta*, Portrait of Ramon Llull; *Velázquez*, S. Pablo; *Zurbarán*, the Immaculate Conception; *Ribera*, Martyrdom of S. Bartolomé; and several works by *Antoni Viladomat*.

The museum is undergoing extensive reorganisation and some rooms may be closed temporarily. The collections from the present Museu d'Art Modern, among others, will be transferred here in due course.

A short distance to the NW is the **Poble Espanyol** (or 'Spanish Village'), a picturesque architectural anthology contrived for the Exhibition of 1929, reproducing life-size replicas of façades of characteristic buildings and plazas from provincial towns and villages throughout Spain. It is planned to refurbish and re-vitalise it as a *Museum of Traditional Arts and Industries*.

Not far E of the Palau Nacional, lower on the hillside, is the ***Museu d'Arqueologia**, with notable prehistoric and Greco-Roman collections.

Left of the vestibule are **RR1–3**, displaying Palaeolithic material.—**R4**, Neolithic, with exhibits from the Cueva de la Fou de Bor at Bellver (Lleida), the Cueva Fonda at Salomó (Tarragona), etc.—**R5** is devoted to the Megalithic culture; **RR6–8** to the Bronze Age culture of El Agar, and **R9** to the Hallstatt period.— **RR10–14** contain Hellenic and Carthaginian objects from the Balearic islands, including notable jewellery.

In **R15** is a scale model of part of the excavations at Empúries, objects from which are in **RR16–17**, among them Greek vases, glassware, fragments of painted stucco, and a statue of Asclepios (4C BC). Other important sculptures are a bronze panther's, head (6C BC), the Venus d'Empúries, and a head of Artemis of the school of Scopas. Among exhibits of technical interest are the fittings of a Roman military catapult.

A series of rooms contains minor objects from the Classical periods: **RR18–19**, Greek and Etruscan vases; **R20**, Iberian culture; **R21**, Roman bronzes, and a mosaic of Bellerophon; **RR22–23** Roman glass and pottery.—Returning through these rooms, we enter **R24**, with exhibits of Roman religious life, and then **R25**, its walls displaying with mosaics of racing chariots found at Barcelona and Girona. The dome contains a reproduction of the mosaic covering the early Christian mausoleum at Centcelles (Tarragona).—In **R27** is a reproduction of a kitchen, while **R28** is arranged as an atrium. **R29** exhibits the Venus of

Badalona.—**R33**, with furniture from early Christian and Visigothic tombs.—
Additional material is displayed in the N wing.

Adjacent to the E is a *Greek Theatre*, built for the 1929 Exhibition. To
the SW is the *Museu Etnològic*, containing collections from Africa,
Spanish America, the Philippines, and Japan.

A long flight of steps descends from the N front of the Palau
Nacional to the Pl. de Carles Buïgas, just W of which is the ***German
Pavillion**, designed by Ludwig Mies van der Rohe for the 1929
Exhibition, reconstructed in 1986 on its original site.

The Av. de la Reina María Cristina leads towards the two towers at
the entrance to the Fair Grounds and the *Pl. d'Espanya* beyond.

E.   The Eixample

The extension or 'new town' was laid out after 1859 on a grid plan,
the project of Ildefons Cerdà, and is of slight interest except for a few
individual buildings. These are spread out over an extensive area
and some are best visited by car.

From the N corner of the *Pl. de Catalunya* the wide **Passeig de
Gràcia** leads NW to meet the *Diagonal* at the PL. DE JOAN CARLES I.
At the lower end of the Passeig (No. 43, left) stands the *Casa Batlló*
(1907), by Gaudí. Adjacent is the *Casa Amatller*, by Puig i Cadafalch.
Three buildings to the S is the *Casa Lleó Morera*, by Domènech i
Montaner. These monuments of the Modernist period of Catalan
architecture are known as the 'Manzana de la Discòrdia'.

Turning right in the C. de Aragó, in the third block is *La Concepció*
(1293–1448, with an oblong cloister of c 1400), brought to this site
when the monastery of Jonqueres in the old town was demolished in
the 1870s.

Returning to the Passeig and turning right, we come to Gaudí's
Casa Milà, popularly known as 'La Pedrera' (the quarry), completed
in 1910.

To the right in the **Diagonal** (No. 373) is the *Palau Quadras* (1904;
by Puig i Cadalfalch), housing the *Museu de la Música*, with a
representative collection of early instruments (notably guitars) and
modern reproductions.

Continuing E along the Diagonal, bear left along the C. Provença
to a plaza above which rears the unfinished **Templo de la Sagrada
Família**, one of the more extraordinary of Catalan churches. George
Orwell thought it was 'one of the most hideous buildings in the world
. . . [with] four crenellated spires exactly the shape of hock bottles'.

Begun by Francesc de Paula Villar i Lozano in 1882 and continued by Antoni
Gaudí i Cornet (1852–1926), its most obvious features are the curious spires,
over 100m high, the stalactite canopies over the triple porches of each façade,
and the luxuriant carving over the whole surface. Making our way through a
builder's yard, we may visit a small exhibition in the crypt of plans and models
for the building, work on which was practically abandoned between 1936 and
1954. Work has since been resumed, causing further controversy, the argument
being that any attempt to follow Gaudí's original designs would be contrary to
his conception of the finished work, for he would invariably make changes
during building operations, rarely conforming to the prototype. Whether there
is sufficient support for this misguided scheme remains to be seen: uncompleted, it could have remained both a monument to its architect and an assertive
symbol for a vital city.

Some other examples of Gaudí's work—apart from the *Palau Güell* (p 388) and those in the Passeig de Gracia—are listed below: *Casa Calvet* (1904), at 48 C. de Casp; *Casa Vicens* (1885), 18–24 C. de les Carolines; the *Colegio de les Teresianes* (1894), 95–105 C. de Ganduxer; the *Torre Figueres* (1902), 16–20 C. de Bellesguard; the *Parc Güell* (1900–14), off the C. d'Olot; and the gates, walls, and pavilions of the *Finca Güell* (1887), 77 Av. de Pedralbes.

Some distance N of the Sagrada Familia is the *Hospital de S. Pau* (1912), by Lluís Domènech i Montaner, with its multicoloured cupolas, and with the rebuilt façade of Baroque *Sta. Marta* (1747), brought from the old city.

The Diagonal leads W from the Pl. de Joan Carles I to the PL. DE FRANCESC MACIÀ.

From here the C. Infanta Carlota Joaquima turns S to the *Estació Central Sants*, and the *Parc de l'Espanya Industrial*, embellished with curiously ugly towers, from which the C. de Tarragona bears SE past the *Parc de Joan Miró* to the *Pl. d'Espanya*.

The Diagonal continues W past (left) the glass-fronted *Torres Trade* (1969; by J.A. Coderch de Sentmenat and M. Valls i Vergés) at 86–94 Gran Via de Carles III, to reach the Pl. de Pius XII. Beyond are several faculty buildings of the **Ciutat Universitària** and (right) the entrance to the gardens of the *Palau de Pedralbes* (1929), presented by the city to Alfonso XII and later the residence of visiting dignitaries. It was Negrín's HQ during the latter part of the Civil War.

The Av. de Pedralbes leads NW from the Pl. de Pius XIII to the ***Monestir de Pedralbes**, one of the more interesting and attractive buildings in Barcelona, founded in 1326 by Elisenda de Montcada (died 1364), queen of Jaume II.

The imposing Catalan Gothic *Church* contains good choir stalls and beautiful stained glass, while in the choir lies one half of the foundress's richly carved alabaster tomb. On the far side of the wall, in a small chapel off the cloister, the other half may be seen, less elaborate, and of stone. Off the impressive three-storeyed *Cloister*, with clustered columns supporting ogival arches—26 on each side— is a vaulted Chapterhouse of c 1419, with a finely carved keystone and good glass, and containing a small museum. In the *Cap. de S. Miquel* are important murals by Ferrer Bassa (1346).

Near the entrance within the monastery wall, the façade of a demolished monastery from Breda (near Hostalric) has been reconstructed.

The ***Museu de Ceràmica**, formerly in the Palau Nacional on Montjuïc, has recently been transferred to Pedralbes. It provides a comprehensive view of Spanish decorative pottery from the 13C to the present; the collection of 16–18C lusterware is outstanding.

Rooms are devoted to Moorish and early Catalan ware (23 pieces having been found in Palma de Mallorca in 1937); ceramics from Paterna, Manises, Teruel, and Barcelona; lusterware from Manises, and also from Barcelona, Reus, and Muel; collections of decorative tiles, *zocalos*, dados, ad plaques.

The *Museu d'Arts Decoratives* will also be moved to this site in due course.

Some distance to the NE at the main crossroads of the suburb of *Sarrá* stands *S. Vicente*, rebuilt in 1379 on the site of a church founded in 980.

For **S. Cugat del Valles** and **Terrassa** see the latter part of Rte 61; for **Montserrat** and **Manresa**, Rte 64; for **Vic** and **Ripoll**, and for **Girona**, see Rtes 60 and 57, in reverse; for **Lleida** and **Tarragona** see Rtes 65 and 66.

64 Barcelona to Bassella via Montserrat, Manresa, Cardona, and Solsona

164km (102 miles) including the ascent to the monastery of
Montserrat. A2 and A17. 31km *Martorell* junction—C1411. 23km
Monistrol. **Montserrat** is c 9km SW.—15km **Manresa**—C1410. 32km
Cardona—20km **Solsona**—25km *Bassella.*

Maps: M 443.

The motorway bearing NW and skirting the Llobregat is followed to
the *Martorell* junction; see Rtes 65A and B. Here turn right, with a
* *View* of the MONTSERRAT MASSIF ahead, and right again off the NII
into the Llobreqat valley to *Monistrol.*

View of the Montserrat massif

Turn left here and climb in steep zigzags to the **Monastery of
Montserrat**. There are several spectacular views of the mountain on
the ascent.

Remarkable for its unusual physical appearance, the mountain of ***Montserrat**,
rising to 1238m, is an isolated ridge of reddish sandstone and conglomerate
running from SE to NW. Its serrated summit (the ancient *Mons Serratus*) thrusts
up at irregular intervals a series of barren pinnacles formed by erosion and
separated by fissures of varying depth. Further down, below a bewildering
chaos of buttresses, gorges, and hanging boulders, the range has been worn
into terraces, owing to the varying hardnesses of its rock strata.

The origin of the **Monastery**, according to legend, dates from 880, when an
image of the Virgin (which had been brought from Barcelona in AD 50 by St.
Peter and hidden in a recess of the mountain at the time of the Moorish
invasion) was discovered fortuitously by shepherds. Gondemar, Bishop of Vic,

attempted to remove it to Manresa, but on reaching the ledge where the monastery now stands it refused to proceed further. The chapel erected there was reinforced by a nunnery, in 976 replaced by a Benedictine convent.

Centuries of prosperity ensued, especially under the auspices of the Spanish popes Benedict XIII (Luna) and Alexander VI (Borja), the former in 1410 raising the abbot to the dignity of a mitre, with independence of episcopal authority. It was twice visited by the Catholic Kings in 1493. From 1499 it was the seat of a printing press, one of the earliest in Spain. In 1522 Ignacio Loyola kept vigil here. Felipe II's largess enabled the church to be rebuilt. Several English travellers passed this way in the 18C, among them Thicknesse and Swinburne in 1775, Townsend (1786), and in 1802 Lady Holland. During the Peninsular War the abbey was sacked by the French under Suchet, after having been fortified by the *somatenes* or Catalan guerrillero. Ford visited it in 1831, but in 1835 the monastery was suppressed and the image was removed to Esparraguera until reinstated in 1874. In December 1970 some 300 Catalan artists, writers, and intellectuals briefly shut themselves up here, issuing a manifesto in solidarity with the Basques during the 'Burgos trials'. The Montserrat legend inspired Wagner's 'Parsifal'.

Visitors expecting some serene sanctuary in the mountain fastness will be disillusioned: the commercialisation of the cult is at once apparent. On either side of the entrance to the basilica are the *aposentos* for lodging pilgrims. To the left of the courtyard are fragmentary remains of the old monastery, consisting of one walk of a *Cloister* (after 1476), a 17C belfry (unfinished), and a Romanesque doorway. Ahead is the cloister built under Fernando VII that precedes the façade (1900) of the *Basilica*, a commonplace Renaissance building of 1560–92. Above the high altar is the dark-complexioned 12C wooden Virgin and Child—blackened by the smoke of candles smouldering over the centuries—seated on a silver throne (1947) in the centre of the *Camarín*. This sumptuous oval chamber in the apse (1880) is approached through the *Sacristy*, containing the treasury, mostly modern gifts. Several museums are housed in the dependencies, together with a library of over 200,000 volumes. The *Escolania* or music school is behind the church.

Numerous signposted footpaths lead from the monastery into the massif itself, affording views of its fantastic rock formations and over the plains of Aragón and Catalunya. From *Los Degotalls* and *S. Jerónimo* (or *S. Geroni*) there is a magnificent *View of the Pyrenean* chain from the Canigou as far W as the Maladetta. The majority of the hermitages—mostly ruined—scattered over the mountain are of slight interest.

From Monistrol, where the Llobregat is crossed by a Gothic *Bridge*, turn onto the C1411 for (15km) **MANRESA** (67,000 inhab.), ancient *Munorisa*, an industrial town above the left bank of the Cardener. Immediately below the ruins of 18C *S. Ignacio* is the cave in which Loyola is said to have written his 'Spiritual Exercises' (1522); its cloister houses the *Municipal Museum*.

Crowning a rocky bluff is **Sta. María de la Seu**, most of which dates from a reconstruction begun in 1328 by Berenguer de Montagut but not completed until the mid 16C. The tower dates from 1590; the ugly W front from the 19C. The interior, although the main vault is exceeded in width by that of Girona, shows the greatest breadth across nave and aisles of any church with aisles and clerestory. It preserves notable stained glass. In the S nave aisle is a Retablo of 1394 by Pere Serra. On the N side is a cloister and restored baptistery, part of the original building of 1020.

In the town are *Sto. Domingo* (1318–1438) and 16C *N.S. del Carme*.

The road winds up the valley, passing potash mines at (15km) *Súria* (6850 inhab.), to (17km) **Cardona** (6600 inhab.; Parador), commanded by its *Castle*, incorporating the Parador. The castle's

Chapel (1040) contains tombs of the Dukes of Cardona, the first
Constables of Aragón. The town, which was given the right to hold a
market as early as 986, and with a parish church consecrated in 1397,
is perhaps better known for its *Salina*, nearer the river. This is an
extraordinary surface deposit of salt, famous since antiquity, which
may be visited on application to the director of the workings.
(Objects carved in rocksalt are liable to melt if transferred to damper
climates.)

The road continues to climb, with extensive views N towards the
PYRENEES. At 12km it passes near the 16C sanctuary of *El Milagro*,
with a Baroque retablo by Carlos Morató (1768), before descending
to (18km) **Solsona** (6250 inhab.), Roman *Setelix*, made a bishopric in
1593, and the birthplace of the artist Francisco Ribalta (1563–1628).

The town retains relics of ramparts and a ruined 12–13C *Castle*.
Near the *Bridge* (replacing one of 12 arches destroyed in the Civil
War) stands the dark single-naved *Cathedral* of 1163, rebuilt in the
14–15C. It contains 15C stall work against the apse wall.

It is said that the **Museo Diocesano** in the adjacent 17C *Bishop's Palace* houses
the 11–12C frescoes from S. Quirze de Pedret; the 13C decorations of a wall
tomb from S. Pau de Caserras by the Master of Llusanés; 12C panels from the
altar of Sagars; the 13C retablo of S. Jaume de Frontanyà, and the Last Supper
by Jaume Ferrer I. Sculptures include fragments from the cathedral; capitals
from S. Pedro de Madrona; a 14C tomb of an abbot of Serrateix; and the tomb of
Hugo de Copons (died 1354) from Llor.

At *Olius*, c 6km NE, are a church consecrated in 1079 and a 13C
watermill.—A lonely road leads SW from Solsona, later descending
past *Montfalcó Murallat* (see p 403) to (53km) *Cervera*.

The main route descends into the Segre valley to meet the C1313
at (25km) *Bassella*; see Rte 62.

65   Barcelona to Lleida (Lérida)

A.   Via Martorell and Cervera

162km (100 miles). A2 and A7. 31km *Martorell* junction—NII. 38km
Igualada—37km *Cervera*—12km *Tàrrega*—44km **Lleida**.

Maps: M 443.

Bearing NW and skirting the Llobregat, follow the motorway past
(18km) *Molins de Rei*, and (right) the castle of *El Papiol*. There is a
16C castle at *Pallejá*, on the far bank of the river. From the viaduct
spanning the Llobregat there is a view (right) of the *Pont del Diable*,
an ancient bridge restored in 1768 but almost destroyed during the
Civil War. Here is a *Triumphal Arch*, erected (according to a modern
inscription) by Hannibal in honour of Hamilcar Barca A.U.C. 535 (218
BC).

Turn off the A7 and bypass **Martorell** (15,950 inhab.) with
museums of slight interest, to follow the old but improved main road,
providing a good view of the MONSERRAT MASSIF (see Rte 64).—
Skirting (37km) **Igualada** (31,550 inhab.) the the road ascends the
valley of the Anoia.

At 8km the C1412 leads 18km N to *Calaf*, with ancient ramparts and a ruined Moorish castle. A by-road turns right to *Rubió*, which has a fortified church with a late 14C retablo.

At 15km *Sta. Coloma de Queralt* lies 12km S, where 13C *Sta. María de Belloc* contains the tombs of Sta. Coloma; Pedro VI, lord of Queralt, and Alamanda de Rocaberti, made by Pedro Aguilar of Lleida and Pedro Ciroll, a local master, in c 1350–70.

At **Cervera** (14km) (6450 inhab.) are the huge decaying buildings of the *University*, by Luis Curiel, established in 1717 on the suppression of those of Lleida and Barcelona, but moved back to Barcelona in 1841. Here in 1760 Joseph Baretti, on entering its portals without first begging permission from the obstreperous students, was hissed at and stoned. It now contains a small ethnological *Museum*.

Cervera's *Dominican Church* has a good cloister; the *Ayuntamiento* (Francisco Puig; 1688) contains a collection of paintings. *Sta. María* (c 1200–1487) has an octagonal tower of 1431 by Pedro de Vallebrera, and a notable altarpiece and tomb (1382), both by Jordi de Deu. Among other buildings are the 11C *Puerta de S. Martín*; the round church of *S. Pere le Gros*; *S. Antonio*, with a Baroque doorway; and the remains of Gothic *Sta. María Magdalena*.

6km NE, on a hill near the village of *Les Oluges*, stands *Montfalcó Murallat, 15 houses enclosed by a huge wall with only one gateway; and near by, the ruined Moorish castle of *Sta. Fé*.—The L311 leads 14km N to *Guissona*, with a 14–17C church and a late Gothic mansion of 1515; off this road is *El Llor*, with a Romanesque church and later castle.—There is also a medieval castle at *Florejacs*, c 10km W of Guissona.—To the NW of Cervera, also approached by a turning off the L311, are *Montcortés*, with a Renaissance castle; *Concabella*, and *Pelagalls*, with Romanesque churches and *Les Pallargues*, with a medieval castle.

12km **Tàrrega** (11,050 inhab.)—where begins the monotonous LLANO D'URGELL—has a parish church with 17C Gothic star-vaulting.—*Verdú*, 5km S, has a 14C castle and a church with a Romanesque portal and rose-window.—3km *Vilagrassa*, with a good Romanesque church doorway, NE of which is *Anglesola*, with 12–14C statues in its church.

At 8km the road bypasses *Bellpuig* where the parish church contains the elaborately sculpted *Tomb of Ramón de Cardona*, Viceroy of Sicily (died 1522), with his armed effigy by Giovanni di Nola (1531).

1km further S, in what was a 13C Franciscan convent (refounded by Ramón de Cardona in 1507), is a degraded three-storey *Cloister*, late Gothic below, Renaissance above, with a newel staircase.

The NII now crosses a rich area of orchards, and the hilltop cathedral of Lleida comes into view, the town being reached at 33km.

LLEIDA (Lérida; 106,800 inhab.; 38,000 in 1920; 62,000 in 1960), is a busy but—apart from its Old Cathedral, *La Seu Vella*—a not very interesting provincial capital dominated by its fortress hill. Its older centre is crossed by two long streets running parallel to the Segre.

Ancient *Ilerda*, a key city of Roman Catalunya, has often been the theatre of sieges and war. It was held for Pompey by Afranius and Petreius, who were defeated by Caesar. Soon afterwards it became a municipium and the seat of a university. Such was its remoteness, however, that the recusant youth of Rome used to be threatened with exile there. Its Moorish occupation ended with the victory of Ramón Berenguer V in 1149. The university was re-established in 1300, its pupils including Vicente Ferrer and Calixtus III (Alfonso Borja).

In 1640 it declared for Louis XIII and after an unsuccessful siege by Gen.

Tomb of Ramón de Cardona at Bellpuig

Leganés was taken by Felipe IV. The Grand Condé was unable to recapture it in 1644. During the War of the Succession it was sacked by Berwick and Orléans in November 1707; and Felipe V, the claimant whom they supported, was routed at Almenar (21km N) by Stanhope on 27 July 1710, and barely escaped with his life.

In the Peninsular war the citadel was surrendered to Suchet in 1810, who drove the defenceless citizens on to the glacis, where they were exposed to the fire of both sides until the governor capitulated.

In August 1936 its New Cathedral was set alight when Durruti's column moved up to the front. Gen. Yagüe and his Moors entered the place on 3 April 1938.

Lleida was the birthplace of the composer Enrique Granados (1867–1916, who drowned when the 'Sussex' was torpedoed by a German submarine); and of Salvador Seguí (1885–1923), the syndicalist leader.

Opposite the N end of the principal *Bridge* (on Roman foundations)

spanning the Segre stands an old gateway leading to the arcaded Pl.
de Paeria, with an *Archaeological and Historical Museum*. To the E is
the Pl. S. Joan; to the W, turning towards the pedestrian C. Mayor, is
the *Ayuntamiento*, with a 13C front. On the N side, further on, is the
'New' Cathedral, a plain Corinthian building of 1761–90 designed by
Pedro Mártir Cermeño. It was gutted in 1936, but was later struc-
turally restored. The *Museu Capitular* contains 15–16C tapestries.—
Opposite is the *Hosp. de Sta. María* (1454–1512), housing a local
museum.—*La Sangre*, some distance beyond, has a Plateresque
portal.

To the N of the Catedral Nova is *S. Llorenç* (1270–1300), with a 15C
tower and 14–15C retablos. It is said to occupy the site of a Roman
temple converted into a mosque. At its W end is a Baroque extension.

The *Museu Diocesà* in the C. del Bisbe contains several 13C
painted frontals; the abbess's throne from Sigena (c 1330); a 14C
retablo from Castelló de Farfanyà and later retablos by members of
the Ferrer family, notably a panel by Jaume Ferrer II of a knight
hunting. Sculptures include a late 14C series of reliefs from Corbins,
a 13C frontal from Buira and fragments from the Seu Vella.

The C. Tallada climbs E. N of it is 13C *S. Marti*; to the S the
Instituto, in a 15C convent with an 18C patio. The street reaches
gardens to the W of the **Castle**, *La Zuda*, mid 13C and enlarged in
1341 by Simón de Navers. The *Puerta del Léon* in the outer wall of
1826 leads to the fortifications erected by the French during the War
of Succession.

Within these is the *Seu Vella* or ***'Old' Cathedral**, dominated by its
tower. It was used as barracks between 1707 and 1948 and has since
been gradually restored.

Appalling damage was done during the 240 years of military occupation.
Partitions separated the crossing from the nave, which was at one time used for
machine gun instruction; the aisles were converted into dormitories, with a floor
added just below the level of the capitals, below which were stables; the
kitchen and canteen were contained in the cloister!

The Seu Vella is a remarkable example of the transitional style.
Begun in 1203 by Pedro Decumbro for Pedro II, it was consecrated in
1278, although the cloister was still unfinished in 1350 and the
octagonal tower (by Carlos Galter of Rouen) was not completed until
1416.

The roofs are of stone, and for this reason the building was once
used as a magazine. The *S Doorway* (called the *Porta dels Fillols*) is
the finest of the three portals; its outer porch was built by the
Flemings Bartolomé de Bruselas and Esteban de Gostant in 1386.

The curious *Capitals* within repay examination, as do the details of the carvings
in the cloister. On the S side of the presbytery is the tomb of Archdeacon
Berenguer de Barutell (died 1432); on the walls opposite are restored line
drawings of c 1300 of New Testament scenes. The cathedral has five apses, but
only three with bays in the nave. Over the crossing is an octagonal lantern rising
on conical squinches. Both the transepts and W Front have rose-windows. The
Cloister, to the W, is entered from the *Puerta de los Apóstoles* and has 12
traceried windows. The five traceried bays on its S side provide a *mirador*
overlooking the plain.

For roads from Lleida to **La Seu d'Urgell**, **Vielha** and **Huesca** see Rtes
62 and 67A, B and D, respectively, in reverse; for **Zaragoza**, Rte 69;
for **Alcañiz**, Rte 70; and for **Tarragona**, Rte 66.

B.   Via the Motorway

170km (105 miles). A2 and A7. 31km *Martorell* junction—22km
Villafranca del Penedes exit—18km A2. **Santes Creus** exit—22km
Montblanc and **Poblet** exit—53km *Lleida* exit—6km **Lleida**.

Maps: M 443.

For the road to the *Martorell* junction, see Rte 65A. The A7 bears SW,
at 6km passing (left) *Gelida*, where the church is built into the ruins
of a castle said to be of Roman foundation, and 16km beyond
bypasses *Vilafranca del Penedes*; see Rte 66.—At 18km veer W onto
the A2 for 18km.

The Cistercian abbey of *Santes Creus, 6km N, still surrounded by
its ancient walls, may be conveniently visited from here. Founded in
1150, it was moved to this site in 1158 by Ramón Berenguer IV. It was
badly damaged in the anticlerical rising of 1835 and restoration is still
in progress.

In the courtyard is the *Cap. de Sta. Lucía* (1741). The re-consecrated *Church* of
1174–1221, with its rose window and massive square piers, contains tombs of
members of the House of Aragón, among them: Pere III (el Gran—died 1285—
by Master Bartomeu and Guillem d'Orenga); and Jaume II—died 1327—with
his wife Blanche d'Anjou, by Jaume Lorana de Montmeló and Bertrán Riquer,
with effigies by Francesc Muntflorit; also the tomb of Roger de Lauria (died
1304), the admiral who destroyed the fleets of Charles d'Anjou in 1284, and of
Frederick of Sicily in 1299. In the *Coro* are the tombs of Ramón and Guillermo
de Moncada, who fell at the taking of Mallorca in 1229. The central lantern is
dated c 1314; the tower was added in 1575.
     The *Cloister* also contains several notable tombs and has a six-sided fountain
pavilion on its S side. The S walk was designed in the 1330s by Raynard
'Fonoyll', an Englishman (cf. Montblanc). The *Chapterhouse, Dormitory,* and
other conventual dependencies are of interest, as are the remains of the *Palace*
of Pedro III and Jaume II, and the *Old Cloister* of 1163. The *Abbot's Palace* (c
1570–90) is now the *Ayuntamiento.*

10km due W of the same exit from the A2 is **Valls** (18,850 inhab.),
birthplace of Narcís Oller (1845–1930) the novelist, and of Roberto
Gerhard, the composer (1896–1970). It retains one or two picturesque
streets, ancient ramparts, a ruined castle, and a wide-naved church
of the Girona type (1570).—7km further W, at *Alcover*, is a Romanesque church known as 'La Mezquita'.—*Montblanc*, 17km NW, is
reached from Valls by a road climbing across the *Coll de Lilla* (580m;
views); the A7 can be regained 11km N via *El Pla de Sta. María*,
which has a cruciform Romanesque church.
     The A7 bears NW and then W, at 22km reaching the exit for
Montblanc (5300 inhab.), 2km S, a decayed town with remains of
gates and *Ramparts* of 1372. *Sta. María*, begun in 1352 by *Raynard
'Fonoyll'* (cf. Santes Creus), has a Plateresque portal of 1668; *Romanesque S. Miquel* has been restored. Other ancient buildings include
the *Casa Aguiló*, with a Romanesque front and Gothic windows; the
Hosp. de Sta. Magdalena, with a 16C cloister; and a medieval *bridge*
over the Francolí N of the town.
     Poblet can also be visited from here by following the N240 W for c
4km, then forking left through *l'Espluga de Francolí*, which has a
Gothic *church* with a doorway of 1297 and the medieval *Hosp. de S.
Juan.*
     At 6km we reach the once wealthy and powerful monastery of
Poblet, or *Sta. María de Poblet*. It was founded by Ramón

Berenguer IV in 1149 and populated by Cistercian monks from Fontfroide near Narbonne.

It takes its name not from the legendary hermit, Poblet, but from a poplar grove (*populetum*). It was favoured by the kings of Aragón, some of whom chose it for their burial place (cf. Santes Creus), but the brotherhood of Poblet became in time the preserve of the sons of the aristocracy and a den of dissipation. Its abbots ruled their lands with inflexible severity. Swinburne tells the story that their immense lordships served 'as so many nurseries and seraglios for them, where the wives and daughters of their vassals are humbly devoted to their pleasures'; and continues, 'some years ago, a set of wild young officers, who owed the fathers a grudge, carried thither a bevy of common strumpets drest out like ladies, and contrived matters so, that while the men of the party went up into the hills to see prospects, the females were left to be comforted by the Bernadines. The hot-livered monks employed the time of absence to the best advantage, but smarted so severely for the favours they obtained from the good-humoured nymphs, that for many months afterwards the chief dignitories of the house were dispersed about the neighbouring towns, under the care of the barber-surgeons'. Not surprisingly, in 1835 the 'constitutionalist' Catalans suspected the abbey to be a nest of Carlism, and a mob from the adjacent villages invaded it, burning the library and archives and smashing the monuments.

Now admirably restored, the monastery and 18C dependencies are again occupied by Cistercians.

Philip, Duke of Wharton (1698–1731), Jacobite, and ex-president of the 'Hell-Fire Club', died there in abject poverty; as Duke of Northumberland, he had visited Madrid in 1726 to urge a Spanish descent on England in favour of the Stuarts.

To the right on entering the outer gate is the *Cap. de S. Jorge* (1442). Passing through the inner *Puerta Dorada* (1499), to the left is the Romanesque *Cap. de Sta. Catalina*, dating from the time of Ramón Berenguer IV. In front is the elaborate W Front of the *Church* (1716), flanked by tall watch-towers; on the left is the castellated *Puerta Real* (1309); on the right are the ruins of the 18C *Abbot's Palace*. On entering the monastery (conducted tour), to the right, above the huge wine vaults, is the *Pal. del Rey Martín*, begun by Martín I (1395–1410) as a retreat for his old age. Additions were made in 1632.

Next to the beautiful late Romanesque and Gothic *Cloister* are the *Refectory*, the *Kitchen*, and the finely proportioned Gothic *Chapter-house*. On the N side of the cloister is the *Glorieta*, a hexagonal fountain pavilion very similar to that at Santes Creus. The *Upper Cloister*, seen from the Dormitory, is still derelict.

From the S side of the cloister we enter the *Iglesia Mayor* (begun after 1166), cathedral-like in its dimensions. It contains tombs of members of the House of Aragón which stand on either side of the crossing on depressed arches and which were built by Pedro IV in 1367. The tomb chambers beneath were inserted in 1661 by the Duke of Cardena y Segorbe.

On the N side are the tombs of Jaume I (died 1276); Pere IV (died 1387) and his two wives; Fernando I (died 1416); and Martín I. On the S are those of Alfonso II (died 1196); Juan I (died 1395); and Juan II (died 1479)—with their respective wives. After 1835 parts of the broken tombs were removed to Tarragona, but all that survived has now been returned. The remains of the kings and queens were reburied here in 1952, and the tombs restored and embellished with effigies by Federico Marés.

The high altar of 1529 is by Damián Forment. The *Sacristia Nueva*, on the S side of the church, dates from c 1705–34.

Other dependencies of interest are the *Library* and *Archives* beyond the NE corner of the cloister, and the enormous *Dormitory*, a vaulted hall 87m long, reached by steps directly from the church. Behind the apse are ruined cloisters and the Romanesque *Cap. de S. Esteban*, not on view.

At *Milmanda*, 2km S, there is a castle which was the summer residence of the abbots.

3km NW is *Vimbodi*, the main centre of the rioting against the monastery in 1835. Its church contains retablos taken from the monastery. The N240 can be regained just beyond Vimbodi and passes under the A2 before reaching (11km) *Vinaixa*, where there is an early 14C church. Turn left to (3km) *L'Albi*, with a palace of 1600. Just N of L'Albi the motorway can be rejoined (20km W of the Montblanc exit).—At 33km the turning for **Lleida** (6km N) is reached, the Old Cathedral conspicuous on its hilltop.

The N240 continues NW from Vinaixa to (15km) *Les Borges Blanques* (5150 inhab.), wrecked during the fighting of January 1939, to approach **Lleida**, 24km beyond; see Rte 65A.

For the road W to **Zaragoza**, see Rte 69.

66   Barcelona to Tarragona

106km (66 miles). A2 and A7. 53km *Vilafranca del Penedès* lies 2km right; the A7 may be regained 2km beyond. At 21km one should turn off onto the N340 skirting the Mediterranean to visit one or two monuments of interest en route to (3km) **Tarragona**, which may also be entered 26km beyond this turning; see below.

Maps: M 443.

BARCELONA TO EL VENDRELL VIA SITGES (72km). This ALTERNATIVE coastal route can be followed by taking the C246 leading SW across the Llobregat and at 13km skirting Barcelona's airport at *Prat*.—This road passes through pine woods behind the beaches to approach (14km) **Castelldefels** (24,700 inhab.), with a Romanesque church and the keep of its former castle, before climbing to the corniche of the COSTAS DE GARRAF.—The resort of (6km) **Sitges** (11,850 inhab.) was the birthplace of Joaquim Sunyer (1874–1956) the artist. Santiago Rusiñol had a studio here, now the *Museo del Cau Ferrat*. In the *Casa Llopis* there is a collection of Empire and Restoration furniture. The chapel of the *Hosp. de Juan Bautista* contains a retablo by Jaime Forner (1544).—7km **Vilanova i la Geltrú** (43,850 inhab.), where the church of the old quarter contains a Renaissance retablo, and in the restored castle of *La Geltrú, the Museo Balaguer*, a collection of antiquities and paintings, including an Annunciation by *El Greco*. The road skirts several small resorts and turns inland at 15km, below the 12C castle of *Calafell* to join the N340 at 3km, just S of **El Vendrell** (11,650 inhab.). This was the birthplace of the 'cellist Pau (Pablo) Casals (1876–1973) and of the revolutionary Andrés Nin (1892–1937).—The main route described is joined 3km W.

For the road to (31km) the junction for *Martorell*, see Rte 65A. This avoids the climb made by the N340 to the *Puerto de Ordal* (453m).

At 20km the A7 bypasses **Vilafranca del Penedès** (25,000 inhab.), made a free town to attract settlers after being taken from the Moors in 1000, and now the centre of a fertile wine-growing district. It contains a few old mansions, including that of the barons of Rocafort and a palace of the kings of Aragón. *Sta. María* (before 1285) has been much altered. The *Conv. de S. Francisco*—now a hospital—contains a retablo by Luis Borrassá. The chapel of *S. Juan de los Hospitalarios* was begun in 1307. A *Museu dei Vi* (wine) may be visited.

There is a notable 12C Romanesque church at *S. Martí Sarroca*, 11km NW, with a retablo by Jaime Cabrera.—At *Olèrdola* (c 7km S) are the ruins of a castle, possibly the stronghold of *Carthago Vetus*, the first Punic settlement in Catalunya, but the existing walls are those built by Cato in 197 BC. *S. Miquel* has a chapel consecrated in 925, with nave and transepts of 991 and vaults and lantern completed in 1108.

The A7 is rejoined SW of Vilafranca and followed for 22km. There, either turn off to join the N340 or continue ahead through *Sta. Margarita*, with a Romanesque church, and (15km) *L'Arboc*, where *S. Julián* has a façade of interest, to (8km) *El Vendrell*; see above.

At c 5km after entering the N340 from the motorway (or c 8km from El Vendrell) the road passes round the *Arco de Barà*, a 2C Roman arch with a span of 5m and four fluted pilasters on either face; it was built astride the old *Via Maxima* by L. Licinius Sergius Sura, a friend of Pliny the Younger. It was damaged in the Civil War but has been restored.

The road later skirts *Altafulla*, with ruined castles, one on the cliff edge, and *Tamarit*, with a restored 12–13C castle, a late Romanesque church, and the *Torre de Mora* (1562).—On approaching Tarragona the road passes the so-called *Torre de los Escipiones*, a square monument almost 9m high. On one face there are two mutilated male figures in high relief and traces of an inscription. It dates from the latter half of the 2C AD, and therefore probably does not commemorate the brothers Scipio who were killed at Anitorgis (Alcañiz) in 212 BC.

Those entering Tarragona directly from the motorway, will first pass (right) the *Acueducto de les Ferreres*, part of the Roman aqueduct that brought water to Tarraco from the river Gaiá. It was destroyed by the Goths and although partly restored in the 18C the water channel has disappeared. Two tiers of arches (25 above; 11 below) remain. It is 24m high and 217m long.—To the right, immediately after crossing the Francoli, are the remains of the 4–5C baptistery of *Centcelles*, in which mosaics are preserved.

TARRAGONA (109,100 inhab.; 28,000 in 1920; 42,000 in 1960), a provincial capital, stands on a limestone hill overlooking the sea just E of the Francoli. It is a centre for the export of Tarragona wine. On the far bank of the river are extensive oil-cracking installations. In the old town, surrounded by Cyclopean walls and partially dismantled more recent fortifications, stands its cathedral, of considerable architectural interest.

The Carthaginian fortress of *Tarchon*, built on the site of the Iberian stronghold of *Cosse*, became under the Romans one of the more important cities in the peninsula. At first occupied by Publius and Gnaeus Scipio, *Tarraco* was made the capital of *Hispania Citerior* or *Tarraconensis* by Augustus and named *Colonia Julia Victrix Triumphans*. The emperor himself wintered here in 26 BC after his Cantabrian campaign. The fertile plain and sunbaked shores ('aprica littora') were praised by Martial, as were its wines by Pliny.

The city was damaged by Visigothic invaders in the early 5C, but later regained its prosperity. (Hermengild was beheaded here by his Arian father, Leovigild, for adhering to the Roman faith.) In 714 it was razed by the Moors, and remained practically deserted until 1089, when the former archbishopric, which had been transferred to Vic, was re-established. In 1118 the city was granted to Robert Burdet, a Norman adventurer.

Tarragona joined the revolt of 'Els Segadors' in 1640 and was reduced in 1643, its commercial importance passing to Barcelona and Valencia. It was captured and burnt by the British in 1705, during the War of Succession. By 1775, when visited by Swinburne, it had 'contracted to a very trifling city', covering 'only a small portion of the Roman enclosure'. In 1811 it was one of the few cities in Spain that offered serious resistance to the invading French and, when it was eventually taken by Suchet, ruthlessly sacked. The retreat of Sir

John Murray before Soult's approach to Tarragona in 1813 was described by
Napier as 'an operation perhaps the most disgraceful that ever befell the British
arms'. The monks of Grande Chartreuse migrated here in 1903, where they
established a liqueur factory. Nationalist troops entered the town in January
1939, which experienced the usual proscriptions.

TARRAGONA

The N340 climbs to the SE perimeter of the enceinte and follows the
Rambla Vella, parallel to the wider tree-lined *Rambla Nova*, separating it from the new town.

Between the S extremity of the walled area and the beach (beyond the railway
line) is a relic of the 2–3C Roman *Amphitheatre*, long used as a quarry, into
which has been built 12C *Sta. María del Milagro*.

The C.S. Hermengild leads right, off the SE end of the Rambla Vella,
past a tower to the Pl. del Rei, flanked by the *Museo Arqueológico,
built against the Roman walls, the foundation of which may be seen
in the museum basement. The Ground Floor contains an extensive
collection of Roman sculpture and mosaics. There is a mosaic of fish
on the stair. The First Floor has smaller artefacts, including ceramics,

terra sigillata, busts, and a notable Sarcophagus depicting the Rape of Proserpina.

Passing to the E of late 16C *La Sangre*, turn right through one of the original gateways in the Cyclopean walls and follow the Paseo de S. Antoni past the *Portal de S. Antoni*, adorned with 18C trophies, to the N entrance of the ***Paseo Arqueológico**. This walk passes between the 3C BC walls and the fortifications erected under the direction of English engineers during the War of the Succession. It is adorned with antique fragments (including a bronze statue of Augustus presented by Italy in 1936) and provides a close view of the finest stretch of the surviving 3C BC ***Wall** and its Roman superstructure.

From the SW end of the paseo, turn left through the *Portal del Roser* into the Pl. Pallol. The Roman gateway may have been the entrance to the *Forum*. Turn left immediately and follow the Baixader Roser to the *Archbishop's Palace* (1814–27), which incorporates a considerable section of the walls and a tower. Turning round the N wall of the cathedral cloister we pass, in a courtyard (left), the chapel of *S. Pau*, fabled to be built on the spot where St. Paul preached in AD 60. It appears to have been partly rebuilt by 1243, but the W front with its square door, round windows, and elaborately corbelled cornice, is probably older.

The C. Coques skirts the E side of the cathedral, its exterior cluttered by dependencies. Note the remains of a Romanesque church built into a house at the corner of the C. Sta. Tecla. The *Casa de los Concilios* dates from 1584.

The ***Cathedral**, or *La Seu*, was begun in 1171 on the site of a mosque, which may have occupied the site of a Roman temple. It was well adapted for defence against the possible return of the Moors: the apse has the simplicity of a bastion. Work continued throughout the 13C and the building was consecrated in 1331.

The unfinished *W Front* has two stages, with a huge rose-window between buttresses intended to be surmounted by pinnacles. In the niches of the *Gothic Portal* (1289) are statues by Barthélemy 'le Normand' of prophets and apostles, and the tympanum is filled with elaborate tracery. The statues on the flanking buttresses are by Jaime Cascalls of Zaragoza (1375). The doors themselves are dated 1510. On either side are smaller Romanesque doors, that on the S with a relief of the Passion; above the other is an early Christian sarcophagus. Over each door is a wheel window. The *Tower* of 1292, square below and octagonal above, and the eight-sided cimborio, are best seen from the E end of the church.

The interior (103m long; 45m accross the transepts; 32m across the nave) is dark and severe. It has massive piers with delicately carved bases and capitals. The nave is almost twice the height of the aisles. Some of the stained glass in the clerestory and transepts is by Juan Güas. The walnut *Sillería* in the Coro is by Francisco Gomar and his son (1478); the restored *Organ* of 1563 was designed by Jaume Amigó of Tortosa, carved by Jerónimo Sancho and Pedro Ostris, and painted by Pere Serafí.

To the N, in the chapel of *El Sto. Sepulcro*, there is a marble Christ by Francisco Gomar on a Roman sarcophagus. In the second chapel on the N side is the Italian Renaissance tomb of Abp Pedro de Cardona (died 1530) and an altarpiece ascribed to Lluís Borrassa; in the wall between the fourth and fifth chapels is the tomb of Abp Juan Terés (died 1603) beneath a Corinthian pavilion by Pedro Blay.

The *Baptistery*, to the SW, dates from 1341. The chapel of *S. Miquel* (1360) has a retablo of 1432 by Ramón de Mur, and beyond it the Baroque chapel of *Sta. Tecla* (1765) is by José Prats.

The transepts are lighted by a low octagonal cimborio, and on the E side of each transept is a small Romanesque apse. On the right, between the S transept and the Cap. Mayor, is the Romanesque *Puerta de Sta. Tecla*. The *Cap. Mayor* (1171–1226) contains a notable Retablo of 1434 by Pere Joan de Vallfogana and Guillermo de la Mota, behind which is the Romanesque apse. On the N side of the Cap. Mayor, near a Byzantine doorway, is the *Cap. de los Sastres* (tailors: c 1360–80), with a relief of the Virgin. The adjacent round-arched double doorway leads to the cloister and has some expressive sculptures on its far side.

The *Cloister* of c 1215 is disfigured by unattractive grilles placed within each arch. Most of the capitals are foliated but some have quaint reliefs, including one of a cat's funeral conducted by rats, rudely interrupted by the awakening of the 'deceased' (end of second bay going E). The old *Chapterhouse* (SE corner) contains figures of saints of c 1330. On the E side is the *Cap. de Sta. Magdalena*, with curious reliefs depicting her life (16C). In the W wall are embedded Roman sculptural fragments and a small Moorish arch with a Cufic inscription, including the date 349 (AD 960). At the SW corner is the *Cap. del Sacramento*, with a doorway brought in part from the Roman forum. The tomb of its founder is by Pedro Blay (1590). There are some 16C statuettes and bronzes on the altar.

The *Museo Diocesano*—in the old and new Chapterhouses—comprises a collection of 14–15C retablos, sculpture and plate, archbishops' portraits, the 15C tapestry known as 'La Bona Vida', and cult objects. The cathedral archives were burnt by Suchet.

A gate just outside the S transept leads to Romanesque *Sta. Tecla la Vella.*

The *Camarería* in the Pl. de la Seu dates from the 14C. There are Roman fragments and a Hebrew inscription built into the front of No. 6 in the nearby lane of the Escribanias (the Judería lay between the cathedral and the E wall of the town).

Descending the cathedral steps, the picturesque arcaded *C. Mercería* (left) leads to the Pl. del Foro.—The C. Mayor leads downhill past the C. Cavallers, in which the *Museu de Castellarnau* (at No. 4) contains miscellaneous collections, to reach the Pl. de la Font, named after the well situated there. At its W end is the *Ayuntamiento* of 1862. The plaza is on the site of the *Roman Circus*—some of its arches may still be seen built into the houses of the Pl. de los Cedazos (a few steps NE), in the Pescadería to the E and in neighbouring alleys.

The *Portalet* leads from the E end of the Pl. de la Font to the Rambla Vella, and beyond to the Rambla Nova. The extensive remains of the *Roman Forum* have been uncovered three streets to the S of Rambla Nova.

From the W end of the Rambla Nova the Av. Ramón y Cajal leads W for some distance to the *Museu Paleocristià*, in a Romano-Christian necropolis of the 3–6C. The remains of a basilica and two crypts may be visited here.

For *Valls* (20km further N along the N240) and for the road to *Montblanc* see Rte 65B. For **Reus** and the roads S to **Valencia** see Rte 76.

67 The Central Pyrenees

A. (St. Béat or Luchon) Vielha to Lleida via Sort and Tremp

242km (150 miles). N125 from *St.-Béat.* 8km *Fos*—3km frontier—N230. 10km *Bossòst*—16km *Vielha*—C142. 46km *Esterri d'Àneu*—C147. 30km *Sort*—43km *Tremp*—58km *Balaguer* crossroads—C1313. 28km **Lleida**.

Maps: M 443.

Note: Hikers and mountaineers should refer to the paragraph on p 95 with regard to frontier posts, etc. Both this route and several others in the Pyrenees are likely to be snow-bound during part of the winter, and information concerning the state of the road should be sought.

For *St.-Béat* and *Luchon* see *Blue Guide France.* The frontier is crossed at the rebuilt *Pont du Roi*, 3km S of *Fos* (Customs), where the road enters the **Vall d'Aran**, that of the upper Garonne (Garona) river. Until the completion of a road in 1924 this valley was connected with the rest of Spain only by bridlepaths. Although N of the watershed, it remained part of Spain because of an omission in the Treaty of Corbeil (1255), perpetuated in the Treaty of the Pyrenees (1659; cf. Puigcerdà). Practically independent until the 18C, it was annexed to France by Napoleon in 1808, but finally recognised as Spanish in 1815.

At 10km *Bossòst*, overlooked by a ruined castle, has a good 12C church; here also is a Customs post for travellers crossing the steep *Coll del Portillón* (1293m) from *Luchon*, 18km W.—The road climbs SE through *Aubert*, with a Romanesque church containing murals, and below *Vilac*, with a 13C church, to (16km) **Vielha** (971m; Parador), a delightfully placed village, within a circle of mountains. It preserves several old houses and a massive church with an octagonal tower and ornate interior.

For the road S through the tunnel to *Pont de Suert*, see Rte 67B.

The road continues E, at 6.5km passing (right) *Arties* (Parador), and (3km) *Salardú*, picturesquely sited and retaining remains of ramparts and a castle; its 13C church contains a 12C Christ. The *Casa de Berentete* (1580) is notable.—At *Unyá* (NE) is the 14C fortified *Casa de Bastete*, and a 12C church.—*Tredòs*, later passed, has had the murals from its 12C church removed to New York. The road climbs through (7km) *Vaqueira*, a winter sports development, with *Beret* at a higher level to the NE, to reach (9.5km) the *Puerto de la Bonaigua* (2072m), with the *Pico de Moredo* (2760m) rising to the NE, and the *Saboredo* (2764m) to the S.

The road now descends in sweeping curves to (20km) *València d'Àneu*, its church, with a broach spire, containing wall paintings; and 3km beyond, *Esterri d'Àneu*.

In the upper valley of the NOGUERA PALLARESA, to the NE, are the churches of *Isabarre*, Romanesque, with murals, and *Isil*, dating earlier than 1095.

Continuing down the valley, at 6km *Espot* is 6km W (1340m). A mountain road from here climbs into the *Parque nacional de Aigües Tortes* and the deserted craggy peaks of the SIERRA DELS ENCANTATS, well described in Robin Fedden's 'The Enchanted Mountains' (1962).

4km *Escaló*, near which is the 11C monastery of *S. Pedro de Burgal*.—8km *Llavorsi*.

A minor road leads N up the VALL DE CARDÓS through *Ribera de Cardós* and (right) *Esterri de Cardós*, both with Romanesque churches, to (19km) *Tavascan*.

The C147 turns SW to (8km) *Rialb*, at the foot of the VALL DE LLESSUI.—*Surp*, to the N, has a Romanesque church.—4km **Sort** (720m) has a ruined castle and remains of fortifications and is the village capital of this mountainous district of PALLARS.

The C146 climbs steeply SE from here past *Vilamur*, with a Romanesque church, to (21km) the *Collado del Canto* (1725m), before descending to meet the C1313 6km SW of *La Seu d'Urgell*; see Rte 62.

Continue down the valley through (12km) *Gerri de la Sal*, with a Romanesque church consecrated in 1149, and thread the impressive *Desfiladero de Collegats* to (16km) *La Pobla de Segur*.

The C144 leads NW up the valley of the Flamicell to *Senterada*, c 19km N of which is the Romanesque church of *Cabdella*, with remains of 13–14C murals.— The road climbs NW of Senterada to (15km) the *Collado de Perves* (1325m), descending past *Viu de Llevata*, with a 12C monastic church, to (16km) *Pont de Suert*; see Rte 67B.

The C147 now skirts the W bank of the *Embalse de S. Antoni*, passing the village of *Talarn*, its church containing a restored 18C organ. —15km **Tremp** (5600 inhab.), the principal town of the valley, with remains of old walls and a church dated 1642 with Gothic vaulting.

The C1412 leads SE, climbing to (19km) *Isona*, where there is a richly sculptured 12C church portal. A track leads NE to the Romanesque basilica of *Abella de la Conca*, with a retablo by Pere Serra (c 1375). Also near Isona are *Llordá*, with an early castle and church of 1040; and *Covet*, off the road to *Artesa de Segre* (38km S), its church with a remarkable carved doorway dated 1100.

To the right, on reaching the *Embalse dels Terradets* c 10km S, are the ruins of the 11C castle of *Moror*. To the N are remains of an Augustinian sanctuary within a fortified precinct. It has a 12C Romanesque cloister with arches, now blocked, and its church once contained important apse paintings, now removed to Boston.

On crossing the Noguera Pallaresa S of the reservoir, we enter the defile of the *Portell dels Terradets*, which cuts through the SIERRA DEL MONTSEC.

At 11km the old road (L904) makes a long swing to the W through (10km) *Àger*, with a ruined *Colegiata* and other churches.—19km S, beyond the *Collado del Àger* (912m) near *Avellanes*, there is the Premonstratensian monastery of *Sta. Maria de Bellpuig* (1166), with a Romanesque cloister and 14C church.— *Balaguer* is 19km further S.

The new road winds due S above the E bank of the river, here dammed, and crosses the Segre just S of their confluence. At 35km the C1313 is reached 2km from the *Balaguer* crossroad; see Rte 62. **Lleida** is 28km further SW.

B.   Vielha to Lleida via Benabarre

163km (101 miles). N230. 40km *Pont de Suert*—59km *Benabarre*—
64km **Lleida**.

Maps: M 443.

From *Vielha* (see Rte 67A) the road climbs steeply SW for 8km to
enter the *Túnel de Vielha*. It emerges 5km S, below an E spur of the
Pico de Aneto (3408m; the highest peak in the Pyrenees), part of the
barren *Maladeta* massif, and descends the upper valley of the
NOGUERA RIBAGORÇANA.

At 21km the C144 climbs W across the *Collados de Espina* (1407m) and *de
Fadas* (1470m) to meet the C139 at (32km) *Castejón de Sos*, 14km S of
Benasque; see p 418.—The HU940 soon turns left off this road for *Roda de
Isábena* (see below), c 28km SW.—At 4km the churches of *Barruera* and *Durro*. At 22km is the spa of *Caldes
de Boí* (1740m). At 16km the Romanesque churches of *Erill la Val* (left), with a
slender tower; and right, *Boí*, containing reproductions of the original murals
(now preserved in the Museu d'Art de Catalunya, Barcelona) and with a six-
storey tower. High up on the valley side to the E, the remarkable little
Lombardic basilicas (both consecrated in 1123) at *Taüll* have also had their
murals preserved in Barcelona: *S. Climente* is at one end of the village and *Sta.
Maria* is at the other, the latter with a curious octagonal dome and leaning
tower.

The Romanesque tower of S. Climent, Taüll

2km *Pont de Suert*, close to which are the ruins of the monastery of *Labaix*.

For the C144 climbing SE across country to (41km) *La Pobla de Segur*, see Rte 67A.

The road skirts the W bank of the *Embalse de Escales*, passing through several short tunnels, to (15km) *Sopiera*. Near by, E of the reservoir, is the monastery of *Alahón*, founded in 835. The sacristy of the church (consecrated 1123) has 14C murals.

At 22km the road turns W, away from the river, with the *Montsec* (1329m) to the S, through *Tolva*, with a church consecrated in 1130. At 22km we enter *Benabarre* (782m), with a castle and old houses.

From here a by-road leads 30km almost due N to **Roda de Isábena**. At 19km *Lascuarre* (2km W of the road) has a fine mid-16C church. The small *Cathedral of Roda* dates from 1067 and has a 12C cloister; its organ (c 1500; modernised c 1600) is still playable. The *Bishop's Palace* is a 15C mansion.—Near *Calvera*, c 15km further NE, is the 11C monastic church of *Obarra*.

For *Graus*, 21km NW, see Rte 67C.—The N230 turns S across country to (39km) *Alfarràs*—on the C148 from Binéfar to Balaguer via (14km E) *Castelló de Farfanya*, with a ruined castle and 14C church.—Continuing S, the road skirts (4km) *Almenar*. Near here, on 27 July 1710, Stanhope routed Felipe V's army, commanded by the Marqués de Villadarias.—21km **Lleida**, its cathedral-crowned hill conspicuous from afar; see Rte 65A.

C.   (St.-Lary) Bielsa to Barbastro

134km (83 miles). D929. 19km *Túnel de Bielsa*—HU640. 13km *Bielsa*—34km *Ainsa*—C138. 50km *El Grado* junction—18km **Barbastro**.

Maps: M 443.

From *St.-Lary* (see *Blue Guide France*) the road climbs to the SW—passing Customs at 15km—and after 4km enters the *Túnel de Bielsa*; then descends to (13km) *Bielsa*, the main village (1053m) of the upper Cinca valley. It retains its 16C *Ayuntamiento*, but was damaged prior to its capture by the Nationalists on 6 June 1938; 4000 Republican troops escaped to France over the *Puerto de Bielsa*.—11km NW is the *Parador Monte Perdido*, at the far end of the Valle de Pineta, overlooked by *Monte Perdido* to the W (3355m) and the four summits of the *Marboré* (3248m).

The road continues through the *Desfiladero de las Devotas* to (23km) *Escalona*, from which a mountain road climbs NW towards the impressive *Garganta de Añisclo* in the *Parque nacional de Ordesa*.—11km **Ainsa**, the walled capital of the old mountain kingdom of Sobrarbe, stands on a height above the modern village at the confluence of the Cinca and the Ara. It has a picturesque porticoed *Pl. Mayor* surrounded by dark grey, slate-roofed schist houses, a tiny *Colegiata* (12C, with later additions) and to the W, the remains of a palace.

The C138 leads NW to (6km) *Boltaña*, overlooked by slight ruins of its castle, and with a *Colegiata* of 1544. The road continues through the gorge of *Jánovas* to (35km) *Torla*; see p 423.

The C140 leads SE, then climbs NE. At 11km it passes (left) a road ascending to the monastery of *S. Victorian*, a 9C foundation with an 18C church.—The C140 continues E from this turning to cross the *Collado de Foradada* (1020m) to meet (at 19km) the C139 between *Graus* and *Benasque*; see p 418.

From Ainsa the main road skirts the *Embalse de Mediano*, and passes a track to the 11C church of *S. Martín de Buil*. It then climbs above the reservoir to (c 32km) to the ALTO DE PINO (857m). 7km beyond this it passes *Naval*, with a ruined castle and 16C church.—11km *El Grado*, with a 15C *Colegiata*, stands above the S end of its reservoir, from which a road leads E through *La Puebla de Castro*, Roman *Labitolosa*. The Romanesque church here contains a retablo of 1303. The road continues, via (17km) *Graus*, to *Benabarre*, 21km SE; see Rtes 67B, and 67D.

18km **Barbastro**; see Rte 67D.

D.   Lleida to Huesca via Barbastro

123km (76 miles). N240. 50km *Monzón*—20km **Barbastro**—55km **Huesca**.

Maps: M 443.

An ALTERNATIVE, more southerly, route via *Fraga* and *Sariñena* (135km) is first described. For (27km) *Fraga*, see Rte 69.
From the far bank of the Cinca turn right onto the C1310, skirting the river to (22km) *Chalamera*, overlooked by a Transitional hermitage. Veer W, at 7km passing 5km SW of *Alcolea de Cinca*, birthplace of the novelist Ramón Sender (1902–82).—11km *Vilanueva de Sigena*, just beyond which (left) is the **Conv. de Sigena** (partly restored), founded in 1188 by Alfonso II of Aragón and Sancha of Castile.

Within a picturesque group of dependencies stands the church, with a good Romanesque doorway. Opening off the S transept is a Mudéjar chapel dating from 1354, and off the N transept the chapel of *S. Pedro*, containing the tombs of Pedro II and knights who fell at Muret (SW of Toulouse) in 1213. In other parts of the church are the sepulchres of prioresses and of the convent. It was severely damaged during the Civil War and only fragments of the important paintings (c 1321–47) have survived (now in the Museu de Art de Catalunya, Barcelona).

2km *Sena*, with a 16C *Ayuntamiento*.—14km *Sariñena*, c 15km SW of which is the abandoned *Cartuja de las Fuentes*, with a huge church and conventual dependencies dating from 1732, although founded in 1510.—The road now turns N, at 13km passing 10km W of *Peralta de Alcofea*; its early 13C church has a notable carved portal.—11km *Sesa*, with a late Romanesque church; 6km *Novales*, with a 12C church; 6km *Albero Alto*, whose Gothic church has a Plateresque retablo; 7km *Monflorite*, with a ruined church of 1176.— 7km **Huesca**; see Rte 68.

The N240 leads NW to (39km) *Binéfar* (7800 inhab.). —12km E is *Tamarite de Litera*, where the *Colegiata*, a ruinous basilica in the Poitevin style, has a 14C lantern and additions of 1619; the ruin of *S. Miquel* has Romanesque doorways.
The industrial town of (11km) **Monzón** (14,850 inhab.), at the confluence of the Sosa and the Cinca, is overlooked by a dismantled Templar castle. *S. Juan* is 15C; *S. Francisco*, 13C; and the

Colegiata was rebuilt c 1500. Monzón was the birthplace of Joaquín Costa (1846–1911), the political writer.

14km N, at *Fonz*, are a ruined 12C castle, 14C *Hospital*, old houses, and a late 15C church preserving good woodwork.

A by-road (HU874 and then HU850) leading direct to Huesca turns left and then right on crossing the Cinca; at 18km it passes *Berbegal*, with a Romanesque *Colegiata*; 6km *Laperdiguera*, with a Gothic church, and tower of 1553; 8km *Pertusa*, with a collegiate church of 1575 designed by Juan de Herrera and covering a circular crypt; and 5km *Antillón*, with a Romanesque church. The C1310 is joined at (22km) *Monflorite*; see above.

20km **Barbastro** (14,550 inhab.), an ancient city destroyed by Pompey but rebuilt and renamed *Brutina* by Decius Brutus. In 1064 it was taken from the Moors by Guillaume de Montreuil, an ally of the Catalans and Aragonese, and sacked. It was the birthplace of Lupercio de Argensola (1559–1613), poet and statesman; of his brother Bartolomé (1562–1631), poet and historian; and of Gen. Antonio Ricardos (1727–94).

The *Cathedral*, with a separate, six-sided tower, was built in 1500–33, probably on the site of a mosque, to the designs of Juan de Segura. Its notable vaulting is sustained by six pillars. It contains retablos by Damián Forment and his pupils (c 1560–1604), and stalls of 1594, now placed around the apse. There are also some Baroque additions.

The new *Ayuntamiento* cloaks a late 15C building by Farag de Gali, the Moor.

BARBASTRO TO BENASQUE (96km). Follow the C138 NE for 9km, then turn right across the Cinca onto the HU904. It winds through several tunnels and impressive gorges, skirts the W bank of the *Embalse de Barasona*, and passes a medieval bridge before entering (25km) *Graus*, with an arcaded plaza, a number of old houses, and Romanesque *S. Miguel*.—The early 13C church at *Capella*, 5km NE, has a retablo of 1527 by Pedro Núñez, a Portuguese; the road from *Benabarre* to *Roda de Isabena* is met 7km beyond; see p 416.

The C139 ascends the valley of the Esera, crossed by several medieval bridges, and passes the attractively sited village of *Perarrúa*, with its ruined castle. At 26km there is a turning for *Ainsa* (Rte 67C).—22km *Castejón de Sos*, (for the road to *Pont de Suert*), beyond which the road ascends the VALLE DE BENASQUE past *Villanova*, with a curious 16C retablo in its church, to (14km) *Benasque* (1138m). Here there are a 13C church, some picturesque old houses, and a gloomy castle with ravines on three sides.—A mountain road continues NE, passing a turning for (6km) the winter sports resort of *Cerler*, and then peters out at the head of the valley, dominated by the barren MALADETA MASSIF, with the *Pico de Aneto* (3408m), the highest peak in the Pyrenees, rising to the E; the *Pic des Posets* (3371m), the second highest, to the W; the *Pico Periguero* (3222m) to the NW; the *Pico de Sauvegarde* (2738m) to the NE. The *Puerto de Benasque* or *Port de Vénasque* (2448m), an opening on this frontier ridge, lies just to the E of the last.

23km NW of Barbastro is the Moorish-looking village of *Alquézar, the Roman *Castrum Vigetum*. It has a picturesque *Pl. Mayor*, a fine 12C *Castle* and a *Colegiata* of 1532 by Juan de Segura. This contains a 17–18C organ, paintings by Alonso Cano, 15C retablos and a 13C wooden Crucifixion, and is abutted by remains of a Romanesque cloister.—The main route can be rejoined 18km SW, via *Adahuesca*, with a Romanesque church.—*Bierge*, 6km N, also has a Romanesque church, containing murals.

The N240 leads W, at 6km passing (right) the 14C monastery of *Pueyo*.—At 25km *Casbas* lies 5km N, with a Cistercian monastery which was badly damaged in 1936.—7km. The Romanesque and 15C church of *Sta. María del Monte* at *Liesa* (3km right) contains 13C murals. More important are those of c 1305 at *S. Miguel de Foces* (1259), SE of *Ibieca*, 3km further N.

SANGÜESA **419**

4km *Siétamo*, near the front for some time during the Civil War, preserves the 14C *Pal. de Aranda*, birthplace of the Conde de Aranda (1719–98), minister of Carlos III and 'hammer of the Jesuits'.

At 6km *Loporzano* (2km right) the late Gothic church of *S. Salvador* contains a Plateresque retablo from Monte Aragón.—The 16C church at *Barluenga*, 5km further N, has an artesonado ceiling and 13C murals.—At *Sta. Eulalia la Mayor*, c 5km NE of the road to Barluenga, there is a Romanesque chapel and ruined 12C monastery.

The road passes (right) the ruined monastery of *Monte Aragón*, burial place of Alfonso el Batallador (died 1134); it was largely rebuilt by Sofí in the late 18C.—7km **Huesca**; see Rte 68.

E.   Pamplona to Huesca

162km (101 miles). N240. 39km. *Sanguesa* is 5km S—6km. *Leyre* is 4km NE—45km *Puente la Reina de Jaca*—44km *Ayerbe*—28km **Huesca**.

Maps: M 443.

The N240 bears SE some 5km S of *Pamplona*; see Rte 2.

At 8km the NA234 turns left to (6km) *Artaiz*, with several towerhouses and a Romanesque church with remarkable carvings, and *Urroz*, 4km beyond, also with a church of interest; *S. Miguel* at *Aoiz*, 7km further E, contains a retablo by Ancheta.

Some of the Pyrenean valleys of Navarra may be explored from here by ascending the VALLE DEL IRATI through *Oroz-Betelu* to (26km) *Arive*, beyond which extends the *Forest of Irati*.—From Arive, follow the NA202 across the ridge to the E to (24km) *Escároz*; 2km N is *Ochagavía*, its church containing a late 16C carved retablo. Near by are the castle of *Ezperun* and the 13C Romanesque basilica of *Muskilda*.—The road continues NE to the frontier at (19km) the *Puerto de Larrau* (1573m). At 9km a road climbs over the ALTO DE LAZAR (1129m; views) into the parallel *Valle de Roncal* for (10km) *Isaba*; see below.

The N240 continues SE parallel to the SIERRA DE IZCO past *Monreal*, with the monastery of *S. Cristóbal*; and *Idocín*, birthplace of the guerrilla general Francisco Espoz y Mina (1784–1836); then over the low *Puerto Loiti* (724m), at 19km reaching a turning (left) for (3km) *Lumbier*, ancient *Illumberri*.

From Lumbier the NA211 climbs NE over a ridge to (22km) *Navascués*, its parish church with a fine Gothic doorway and a well-preserved Romanesque chapel.—The road continues N up the VALLE DE SALAZAR to (23km) *Escároz*; see above. Alternatively cross the *Puerto Las Coronas* (950m), to the E, for *Burgui* in the *Valle del Roncal*; see below.

At 6km from the Lumbier turning we reach a junction 5km N of *Sangüesa*: a recommended DETOUR, passing (right) the ruined castle and walls of *Rocafort* (Roman *Sancossa*).

Sangüesa is a small but ancient town on the left bank of the Aragón. By the bridge stands *Sta. María la Real* (mainly 13C), with a slender octagonal tower and spire, and an impressive sculptured *Doorway* (signed by Leodagarius in c 1170). Among other churches are Romanesque *Santiago*, with a battlemented tower; *S. Salvador*, 14C Gothic with a Romanesque door; *S. Francisco*, and *El Carmen*, both with Gothic cloisters. The *Ayuntamiento* occupies part of the former castle of the princes de Viana. To the S is the *Pal. de Vallesantoro*, an imposing Baroque mansion. Among other buildings of interest are the 15C palaces of the counts of Guaqui, of the Dukes of Granada, and the *Casa de Paris*.

7km E is the medieval castle of *Javier*, birthplace of S. Francisco Xavier (1506–52), containing murals depicting the Dance of Death.—8km W is *Aibar*, an old town of arcaded streets and Gothic doorways, dominated by its church and with slight ruins of a castle.—*Sta. María* at *Cáseda* (8km S of Aibar) contains a retablo of 1580 by Ancheta.

SANGÜESA TO ZARAGOZA VIA THE 'CINCO VILLAS' (150km). The C127 leads SE past the chapel of *S. Adrián*, formerly belonging to the Templars, and climbs to (13km) **·Sos del Rey Católico** (Parador), an ancient walled town now being restored. Here the *Pal. Sada* was the birthplace of Fernando the Catholic (1452–1516); it was altered in the 16–17Cs. Among several other mansions in its narrow streets is the Gothic *Pal. de Camporreal*.—*S. Esteban* (11–13C) has frescoes in its apse and contains a notable font, and a crypt and doorway carved c 1190. The street ascends the *Castillo de la Peña Feliciano*, with a tall clock tower.

Sos is one of the so-called CINCO VILLAS, the others being *Sádaba*, *Ejea de los Caballeros*, *Uncastillo*, and *Tauste*. These were raised to the rank of towns by Felipe V for their services in the War of Succession.

From Sos the road climbs SE over a ridge to (24km) **Uncastillo**, medieval in appearance, where Romanesque *Sta. María* has a Gothic tower with bartizan turrets and a pinnacled spire, a Plateresque cloister, and on its W front, an early carved tympanum of the Magi identified as the source of the whalebone relief in the Victoria and Albert Museum, London. Note also the apse and the well-carved S porch. *S. Andrés* is Renaissance in style; *S. Juan* preserves 13C murals.

Turn SW and continue past the remains of the Roman aqueduct of *Los Bañales*, to (16km) **Sádaba**, with an imposing early 13C *Castle* and the very slight remains of a *Synagogue*.—The 2C tomb of the Atilia family, known as the *Altar de los Moros*, can be found by turning right off the direct road to Sos immediately after crossing a canal, and following the lower track.

From Sádaba climb SE onto the plateau of LAS BÁRDENAS REALES for (22km) **Ejea de los Caballeros** (15,850 inhab.), now the largest of the five towns, and once walled. The fortified Romanesque church of *S. Salvador* was consecrated in 1222.—The road follows the left bank of the Arba to the SW to (26km) **Tauste** (7250 inhab.), where the Mudéjar church has a good tower of 1243 and carved and painted 16C retablos.—The N232 may be entered 14km SW on the far bank of the Ebro, 50km from **Zaragoza**; see Rte 71.

From the Sanguesa turning, the N240 continues E over a ridge, to reach, at 5km, a good new road, climbing 4km to the Cistercian monastery of **·S. Salvador de Leyre**, with a very ancient church, a burial place of the kings of Navarra. The *Crypt*, with its curious stunted piers, belongs to the work consecrated in 1057. The apsidal sanctuary and its aisles are of 1098. To these was added a single nave (late 13C) with later ribbed vaults. Its 17–18C dependencies were restored in 1950.

The main road skirts the N bank of the *Embalse de Yesa* past hilltop *Tiermas*; at 19km it reaches the C137 turning N up the once remote VALLE DE RONCAL.

The road first threads the gorge of the Esca to (14km) *Burgui*, with the ivy-clad ruins of the monastery of *Burdaspal*, and (11km) **Roncal**, with a medieval bridge, numerous ancient houses, and a hilltop church. The local cheese is good.—The road continues to (7km) *Isaba*, with a fortified church containing a retablo of 1540 and mid-18C organ; then climbs steeply NE along the frontier ridge to (26.5km) the *Collado de la Piedra de S. Martín* (1760m; Customs). SE of this rises the *Pic d'Anie* (2504m).—Just S of Roncal a road climbs E (views), and later drops steeply into the VALLE DE ANSÓ at (16km) *Ansó*, with a late Gothic church.—The N240 may be rejoined at *Berdún*, 25km S; or one may continue E over another ridge to *Hecho*, in the parallel valley. 2km N of Hecho is the 9C monastery of **·S. Pedro** at **Siresa**, its church begun in 1082.—*Puente la Reina de Jaca* is c 30km S.

Just beyond the E extremity of the reservoir, a road to the right leads c 9km above its far bank (on the road to *Sos*, 28km SW) to the

Detail from S. Salvador, Ejea de los Caballeros

abandoned village of *Ruesta*.—The main road continues E along the N bank of the Aragón past (17km) *Berdún*, on its outcrop, and, 9km beyond, *Puente la Reina de Jaca*.

Although the main route now turns S (see below), *Jaca* (21km E), and *S. Juan de la Peña* may be conveniently visited from this point. The C134 continues up the valley of the Aragón.—At 10km turn right for (4km) **'Sta. Cruz de la Serós**. It has a curious Romanesque *Church* with a tall square tower of c 1095; its neighbour, *S. Caprasio*, is dated 848.—A passable track climbs steeply for 6km to the 'old' monastery of **'S. Juan de la Peña**, huddled beneath a huge overhanging cliff. Near by stood the city of Pano, destroyed by the Moors in the 8C. The monastery was founded before 858, several times burned, and plundered by Suchet in 1809. It retains its Romanesque *Church*, encircled by a fortified wall.

It is said that during the Dark Ages the chalice of Roman origin, now in Valencia

Cathedral, was preserved here, which gave rise to the romances of the Holy Grail. In 1071 S. Juan was the site of the introduction of the Roman rite into Spain by the legate of Alexander II. In 1770 a pantheon for the heroes of Aragón was constructed in the interior, decorated with reliefs. Steps descend from the entrance to the *Crypt*, above which is the courtyard, crossed to reach the *Church*, its three apses under the impending rock. On the far side is the partially restored Romanesque *Cloister* (note the capitals), to the left of which is the *Cap. de S. Victoriano* (1433).

The road continues to climb to a *Mirador*, providing a fine view of the PYRENEES, and past the Baroque-fronted *'New' Monastery* of 1693–1714, also destroyed by Suchet's troops.—From just N of *Bernués* (12km E) the road turns N over the *Puerto de Oroel* (1080m), below the *Oroel* (1769m), and descends to (16km) *Jaca*; see Rte 68.

The N240 climbs to a pass at 684m in the SIERRA DE LA PEÑA and descends parallel to the Gállego; it later threads a gorge past (left) the detached perpendicular cliffs known as *Los Mallos* (the ninepins) *de Riglos*.—34km *Murillo de Gállego*, with a 12C church. 1km beyond, a turning leads 4km right to *Aguero*, its 13C parish church containing a restored 18C organ. Well-sighted *Santiago*, an unfinished building of c 1200 with finely carved archivolts and capitals is reached by a track to the right before entering the village.

The next left turn leads to the 12C *Ermita de Sta. María* at *Riglos*, containing Romanesque murals.

9km *Ayerbe*, with its *Ayuntamiento* in a 15C mansion, and the *Torre de S. Pedro* (12C).

7km NE is the village of *Loarre*, with a spired Romanesque church.—Beyond, on a rock outcrop commanding a wide view, is the remarkable *Castle of Loarre (11–13C; restored). Its curtain wall encloses an impressive Romanesque church with well-carved capitals. (Check first in the village if the guardian is there.)

At 12km a conspicuous ruined castle is passed at *Plasencia del Monte*; near by the ruined villages of *Anzano* and *Castejón de Brecha* have late Romanesque chapels with fine carvings.—2km *Bolea* (5km N) has a notable hall-church of 1556 by Bartolomé de Barazábal.

14km **Huesca**; see Rte 68.

68 (Pau) Somport to Zaragoza via Jaca, and Huesca

260km (161 miles), from *Pau*. N134. 33km *Oloron-Ste.-Marie*—55km *Puerto de Somport*—N330. 32km **Jaca**—C134. 18km *Sabiñánigo*—C136. 51km **Huesca**—N134. 71km **Zaragoza**.

Maps: M 443.

For the roads from *Pau* to the *Puertos de Somport* and *del Pourtalet* see Blue Guide France. Both passes are likely to be snow-bound in winter.

An ALTERNATIVE route from Pau to Sabiñánigo (113km) is that over the *Puerto del Pourtalet* from *Laruns* (37km due S of *Pau*) or from adjacent *Eaux-Bonnes*; the D934 climbs round the E flank of the pyramidal *Pic du Midi d'Ossau* (2884m) to the *Puerto* (1794m; Customs), providing a splendid retrospective view. The frontier is marked by a dry stone wall.—The C136 descends SE past (left) *Formigal*, (11km) *Sallent de Gállego* (1305m), with a church of 1537 by Juan de Segura, and (6km) *Escarilla*, with a fortified church and old bridge.—A mountain road climbs NE through the *Garganta del Escalar* to the *Balnario de Panticosa*, to the N of which rises the *Grande-Fache* (3005m); the *Vignemale* (3298m) is further E.—The main road leads S, skirting a small reservoir and passing (left, on a precipitous rock) the monastery of *Sta. Elena*. —15km *Biescas*, with a Templar Church.

From Biescas the C140, a winding mountain road, climbs E across the *Puerto de Cotefablo* (1423m) to meet (23km) the C138 just S of *Torla* (1113m), an old village of smoke-blackened 13C–16C houses. The HU360 climbs NE, from which a track forks left to *Bujaruelo*, passing the chapel of *Sta. Elena* in a wooded gorge. Above Bujaruelo is the frontier *Port de Gavarnie* (E; 2270m). The HU360 passes below the *Tallon* (2848m) into the VALLE DE ORDESA, at the far end of which rises *Monte Perdido* (or *Mont Perdu*; 3355m).—From *Broto*, with a 12C chapel, S of the turning for Torla, the C138 circles SE to (33km) *Boltana*; see Rte 67C.

The C136 continues S, at 7km passing W of *Olivàn* and *Lárrede*, both with early Romanesque churches with Mozárabic features, to reach *Sabiñánigo*, 8km beyond; see below.

From the **Puerto de Somport** (1632m; Customs), the Roman *Summus Portus*, the road descends past ruins of a hospice dated 1108, and the winter sports development of *Candanchu*. The pass was used by 'al-Gáfaqī's Moors in 732 to invade France; but they were repulsed by Charles Martel at Poitiers. It was later one of the main routes across the Pyrenees of pilgrims to Santiago. After Candanchu the road passes the S entrance of the 8km-long *Somport rail tunnel* (1928), and (12km) *Canfranc*, overlooked by the *Collarada* (2886m), and with a castle built by Felipe III.

At 14km a track leads E to (c 7km) *Acin*, near which is the remote 11C chapel of *N.S. de Iguacel*.

6km **JACA** (820m; 11,100 inhab.), an ancient frontier fortress and a base from which the Christians reconquered Aragón from the Moors. Like Huesca it bears the heads of four sheiks on its coat of arms.

It was taken by M. Porcius Cato in 194 BC and surrounded by a wall, fragments of which still remain. It was overrun by the Moors c 716, but was recaptured definitively c 810. Its *fueros*, confirmed in 1063 by Sancho Ramírez IV of Navarra, are amongst the oldest in Spain.

The town stands above the left bank of the Aragón on a hill surrounded by ramparts; the E side has been laid out as a promenade with fine mountain views. The *Citadel* was constructed after 1592. The massive ****Cathedral**, to the E, was founded in 814, but the present building dates mainly from 1063 (and has been considerably altered since). The chapels and side vaults are by Juan de Segura (c 1530); the nave vault by Juan de Bescós (1596), with well-carved corbels. The silver shrine (1731) of Sta. Orosia, the patroness, lies below the altar, below the octagonal cupola of the crossing, and in front of the deep central apse. The apse is flanked by chapels closed by 12C wrought-iron screens. The Plateresque portal of the *Cap. de S. Miguel* (on the S side) and the *Sacristy* doorway (1523) are by Giovanni Moreto. The 17–18C organs have been restored.

The *Diocesan Museum* contains Romanesque murals from S. Juan Evangelista at Ruesta (q.v.), and from the apses of the hermitages of Bagüés, Osia, and others.

The *Ayuntamiento* in the C. Mayor dates from 1545. At the E end of this street stands a Benedictine *Convent* containing the sarcophagus of Sancha (died 1096), daughter of Ramiro I of Aragón. Just S of the Ayuntamiento is the 15C *Torre del Reloj* (restored). The church of *El Carmen* retains a late 17C façade and tower.

The medieval *Puente de S. Miguel*, on the old pilgrims' road,

crosses the Aragón W of the town.—*Sta. Cruz de la Serós* is 4km to
the left of the C134, 11km W of Jaca; see Rte 67E, and also for *S. Juan
de la Peña.*

Follow the N330 E to (18km) **Sabiñánigo** (9100 inhab.). Petroleum
deposits were found near by in 1979. The Gállego is crossed and
skirted to the S.—See above for the road from the *Puerto del
Pourtalet.*—A new road ascends to the *Puerto de Monrepós* (1262m;
views), then descends past (32km) *Arguis* and its small reservoir.—
The road later skirts the villages of *Nueno, Igriés,* and *Yéqueda,* all
with Romanesque churches, the first with a 16C brick tower.

At 22km **HUESCA** (41,450 inhab.; 14,000 in 1920; 23,000 in 1960),
a provincial capital, stands on a hill in the centre of its *hoya* or *huerta,*
irrigated by the Isuela, fed from the barren foothills of the Pyrenees.

Osca, the capital of the Vescitani, was chosen by Quintus Sertorius as a
headquarters against the partisans of Sulla, and here he established a university
in 75 BC. It was overrun by the Moors in 789 but was recaptured in 1096 by
Pedro I of Aragón, and was his capital until Zaragoza was taken 22 years later.
The four heads on the city's arms are those of Berber sheikhs killed at its siege.
As a Nationalist outpost it suffered severely in 1936–38.

The Coso Alto and the Cosa Bajo follow the line of the old enceinte to
the SW and S; here are the brick Baroque façade of *S. Vicente el Real*
(18C) and the brick churches of *Sto. Domingo* (1696) and *S. Lorenzo*
(further E; 1624). The C. Goya ascends N of the latter to **S. Pedro el
Viejo,** the oldest church in Huesca. Begun c 1134 by Mateo de
Agüero, but not completed until the 13C, it has a slender, six-sided
tower, and its nave and aisles each end in an apse. The grotesque
capitals in the Romanesque *Cloister* (many restored) are also of
interest. In a chapel on the S side is the tomb of Ramiro II of Aragón
(el Monje, the monk; died 1137); in another is a 14C painted
Crucifixion.

From the adjacent Pl. de los Fueros de Aragón, to the N, turn left,
then right to approach the **Cathedral**. It is a late Gothic building, well
restored and cleaned, begun in 1497 by Juan Olózaga, and completed in 1515. It incorporates much of an earlier church, begun in
1278, of which the W portal (1313) was part; above it is Olózaga's
florid frontal surmounting a curious brick Mudéjar gallery. The tower
is octagonal.

The aisles are much lower than the nave. The *Retablo* of the High Altar is the
masterpiece of Damián Forment (1520–34); in the *Cap. Mayor* is a tomb by
Forment for one of his pupils. In the first S chapel, under a cupola of 1646, is the
armoured effigy of Vicencio Lastanosa (1665). In the *Sacristy* is a custodio of
1601 by José Velázquez; in the archives, silver panels from a retablo of 1367.
From the N aisle a doorway leads into the *Cloister,* retaining two Gothic walks
(1411–59) and curious wall tombs. Battered fragments of the original Romanesque cloister are visible in the yard below.

In the *Parroquia,* entered through the *Bishop's Palace,* is the Retablo
de Monte Aragón (1512), attributed to Gil de Morlanes the Elder. The
palace has 15C timber roofs. The *Museo Diocesano* contains primi-
tives collected from churches in the region.

In the Pl. de la Catedral are the *Ayuntamiento* of 1578 and the *Col.
de Santiago,* the latter with a façade of 1612 by Mendizábal, and
containing some panels from the retablo of Sigena.—The C. Quinto
Sertorio leads N to the Pl. de la Universidad, on the W side of which is
the *Museo Provincial* in a building once occupied by the *University*
(refounded by Pedro IV in 1354).

Detail from S. Pedro el Viejo, Huesca

Below the adjacent *Instituto*, once the *Pal. de los Reyes*, is the *Sala de la Campana*, a vaulted 12C chamber named from a stratagem of Ramiro II. In 1136 he summoned his insurgent nobles to consult on the casting of a bell which would be heard throughout Aragón. As each entered the palace his head was struck off and his body flung into the vault (cf. Taller del Moro, Toledo). The *Sala de Doña Petronilla* is a late 12C chapel.

On the ramparts to the NW, near the bridge over the Isuela, is the Gothic convent church of *S. Miguel* (c 1200–1350).

For roads from Huesca to **Pamplona** and **Lleida** see Rtes 67E and D, in reverse.

The N123 leads SW and passes (19km) *Almudévar*, where the 18C church contains retablos by Gabriel Joli.—At 27km the Gállego is crossed and the road veers S parallel to it, crossing the dreary LLANOS DE VIOLADA to (26km) **Zaragoza**; see Rte 71.

69   Lleida to Zaragoza

146km (90 miles) by the A2 motorway; 142km by the NII.

Maps: M 443.

As there is very little of interest along the road across the monotonous MONEGROS the motorway is recommended, being the most rapid, although more expensive, route.

Most of this desert area was in Republican hands until March 1938 when their forces were pushed back to Lleida. George Orwell's experiences on the Aragón front in the SIERRA DE ALCUBIERRE, S of Huesca, are vividly described in 'Homage to Catalonia'.

The NII leads SW from **Lleida** (see Rte 65A), at 11km bypassing *Alcarràs*, with remains of ramparts, and crossing a ridge between the Segre and Cinca, descends steeply to (16km) **Fraga** (11,200 inhab.). The town is reputed for its figs and famous for the obstinacy of its inhabitants. The 12C church of *S. Pedro* has a late Gothic vault and tall tower and spire; beneath one of the altars is a remarkable 14C carving of the Three Living and the Three Dead, re-used as a frontal.

There is an important Roman site at *Pilaret de Sta. Quitera*, 4km NW. The C1310 follows the W bank of the Cinca before veering NW to *Sariñena*; see sub-route of Rte 67D.—For *Mequinenza*, 20km S, see Rte 70.

After crossing the Cinca the road climbs briefly to the inhospitable and sparsely inhabited salitrose region of LOS MONEGROS. At 25km it crosses the motorway to (2km) *Candasnos*, its church with an imposing early 16C altarpiece, and 18km beyond, *Bujaraloz*, on a crossroad between *Caspe* (33km S; see Rte 70) and *Sariñena* (40km N).—Off this road, 15km N, is the ruined castle of *Castejón de Monegros* and a 14C church enlarged in 1591.

At 18km W of Bujaraloz a road of some interest leads across country directly to (c 100km) *Cariñena*, 47km SW of Zaragoza. The Z700 turns SW. At 14km turn left to (4km) **Velilla de Ebro**. A track leads uphill from the village for c 1km to the extensive ruins of the Roman colony of *Julia Lepida Celsa*, still being excavated, with a small site museum.—Rejoin the main road, cross the Ebro and turn right to meet (4km) the N232; then turn left for (15km) *Azaila*, just beyond which, to the right, are the hilltop ruins of an Iberian and Roman fortress (somewhat over restored) and cemetery.

From just N of Azaila follow the C221 W to (23km) *Belchite*, the scene of serious fighting in 1936–38. A new town has been built adjacent to the ruins of the old, deliberately left standing as a macabre monument to the horror of Civil War.—Continue W, at 19km skirting *Fuendetodos*, a poor village, where the birthplace of Francisco Goya (1746–1828) has been preserved.—24km *Cariñena*, off the N330; see Rte 73.

The NII continues W from this turning, crossing an area forming the front during the fighting of 1936–38. Bear NW through (33km) *Alfajarín*, with a ruined castle and chapel, and a Mudéjar church with a brick front and octagonal tower (1486; by Andalla de Brea and Mahoma Muferriz).—20km **Zaragoza**, see Rte 71.

Travellers bypassing Zaragoza can join the motorway just before reaching *Alfajarín*, or just before crossing the Gallego, in the NE suburbs of Zaragoza.

For the roads NW, see Rtes 3 or 6 in reverse; for that to **Madrid**, see Rte 72.

70   Lleida to Teruel via Alcañiz

279km (173 miles). NII. 29km (bypassing *Fraga*)—C231. 24km *Mequinenza*—34km *Caspe*—29km **Alcañiz**—N420. 79km *Montalbán*—84km **Teruel**.

Maps: M 443.

This is a slow, crosscountry route, occasionally hazardous in winter, in which two sub-routes—described immediately below—are incorporated.

LLEIDA TO ALCAÑIZ VIA GANDESA (154km). The N230 leads S from Lleida, soon crossing the A2.—At (c 21km) *Sarroca de Lleida*, the cave paintings beside the Río Set near *El Cogul* are c 12km E.—The Romanesque church of *Torrebesses*, with a 14C stone retablo, is passed to the E as the road ascends SE.—17km *La Granadella*, with a Baroque church tower. Turn SW to (24km) **Flix** (5000 inhab.), on a loop of the Ebro, with a Moorish castle.—8km *Ascó*, with a ruined castle, 10km beyond which the road meets the N420; turn right for (11km) *Gandesa*.—For Gandesa, **Tortosa** (41km S) and for the road to **Alcañiz** (62km W), see Rte 74. At a road junction 47km W of Gandesa and 15km SE of Alcañiz, the N232 turns S to (59km) *Morella*; see Rte 75.

MORELLA TO TERUEL VIA CANTAVIEJA (149km). This route first winds through the hilly MAESTRAZGO, where the going has never been easy. The CS844 leads SW to (15km) *Cinctorres*, with a church of 1758 containing three panels by Bernardo Serra dated 1441.—The road crosses the *Puerto de las Cabrillas* (1320m) to (21km) *La Iglesuela del Cid*, with an arcaded *Ayuntamiento* and several old mansions.—*Villafranca del Cid* (9km SE), is a walled village with a 13–14C *Ayuntamiento*.—Follow the TE800 NW to (13km) **Cantavieja** (1299m), with the *Muela* (1779m) rising to the N and the *Tarayuela* (1738m) to the S. The old town retains much of its wall, a picturesque, arcaded plaza, and a huge parochial church of 1664–1746.—A road passes through the arch of an octagonal church tower to *Mirambel*, 15km NE, also walled; 7km N of it, at *Olocau del Rey*, are 16C public buildings and a Gothic church.—Continue W from Cantavieja and cross (11km) the *Puerto de Cuarto Pelado* (1612m), the first of several N spurs of the PEÑARROYA MASSIF (2024m), to (38km) *Allepuz*.—At (15km) *Cedrillas* are castle ruins, 10km beyond which we cross the *Puerto de Cabigordo* (1602m) to (26km) **Teruel**; see Rte 73.

The NII leads SW from **Lleida** (see Rte 65A) to bypass (27km) *Fraga* (see Rte 69). After crossing the Cinca, turn left, soon passing under the A2, to (26km) **Mequinenza**. Here a castle dominates the confluence of the Segre and Ebro. It was captured by Alfonso I in 1133 with a fleet built at Zaragoza, but not definitively held until 1149, by Ramón Berenguer IV of Barcelona. It was of importance during the War of the Succession; was sacked by the French in 1811; and has been virtually rebuilt since the Battle of the Ebro (between late July and late December 1938). A dam has been built to the W.

The route now follows a new road, later skirting the S bank of the Ebro.—34km **Caspe** (8350 inhab.), an ancient town built along a ridge above the Ebro, and on the Roman road from Tarragona to Zaragoza.

Here in 1412 the 'Compromise of Caspe' settled the problem of the Aragonese succession by placing on the throne a member of a junior branch of the

Castilian house of Trastámara. In 1936 the insensate Guardia Civil used the wives and children of local trade union members as a human barricade when confronting the advancing Republican columns.

The hilltop *Colegiata*, a Romanesque and Gothic building of the 13–14Cs, was severely damaged during heavy fighting here between the International Brigades and the Nationalists, to whom it fell on 17 March 1938.

At *Fabara (6km N of *Maella*; 21km SE of Caspe) is the finest example of a Roman funerary monument in Spain.

The C231 continues SW from Caspe across broken country to (29km) **Alcañiz**; see Rte 75.
    Turn left 3km W onto the N420 to (14km) *Calanda*, in the centre of an olive-growing district. It has a 17C church and was the birthplace of the film director Luis Buñuel (1900–83).—15km *Alcorisa*, with the *Pal. de Lalinde*, the *Pl. de los Arcos*, and *Sta. María*, of some interest.—The road beyond crosses the steppe-like desert or TIERRA BAJA of Teruel and at 31km the *Puerto de las Traviesas* (1180m) to (16km) *Montalbán*. Here there is a fine *Pl. Mayor* and a Mudéjar-Gothic *Church* (c 1210–14C), ornamented with polychrome bricks.
    Turn left 3km beyond. The N211 continues due W, later crossing the *Puerto Minguez* (1270m) and *Puerto de Bañón* (1269m) to reach the N234 at (50km) *Caminoreal* 7km N of *Monreal del Campo*; see Rte 14B.—The road now climbs over the SIERRA DE S. JUST by a pass at 1400m. At 22km it bears W over the *Puerto del Esquinazo* (1370m).—*Aliaga*, 18km SE, with a medieval castle surrounded by a curtain wall with towers, was the *Laxia* of Ptolemy.
    The road later veers S and follows the valley of the Alfambra to (59km) **Teruel**; see Rte 73.

71   Zaragoza

ZARAGOZA (anglicised as *Saragossa*; 571,850 inhab.; c 40,000 in 1800; 140,000 in 1920; 304,000 in 1960). Capital of the autonomy of Aragón and of the ancient kingdom, it is a sprawling industrial town, largely on the S bank of the Ebro. The present city surrounds its crumbling old centre, from which rear up the towers and multi-coloured domes of its two cathedrals.

Celtiberian *Salduba* was favoured by Augustus and called *Caesaraugusta*, later corrupted by the Moors to *Sarakusta*. It was always a free city, and became the seat of assizes, and of a mint. From 466 it was in the hands of the Visigoths. Early in the 8C it fell to Berber allies of the Moors. In 777 the Berbers requested aid from Charlemagne at Paderborn in their quarrel with the Caliph of Córdoba, but in the following year they refused to admit his troops within their gates and the retreating army was attacked by the Basques in the Pyrenean pass of Roncesvalles.
    In 1115 or 1118 it was recaptured by Alfonso I, el Batallador. In 1137, with the marriage of his niece to Ramón Berenguer IV of Barcelona and the extension of territory taken by Fernando el Conquistador, Zaragoza became the capital of a great maritime power. Fernando of Aragón married Isabel of Castile in 1469 and was able to maintain the political equality of his kingdom and to insist on the observance of the ancient *fueros* of Aragón. But in 1590, when Antonio Pérez took refuge there from the anger of Felipe II, the king forced the Justiciar, Juan de Lanuza, to flee, revoked the *fueros*, and re-introduced the Inquisition.
    On 20 August 1710 Stanhope won a battle at *Torreno*, to the S, which gave the Archduke Charles the mastery of Zaragoza.

On 25 May 1808, at the start of the Peninsular War, Gén. Lefebre met with unexpected resistance when attacking the place. The citizens, organised by the peasant leader Jorge Ibort, placed themselves under the command of José de Rebolledo Palafox y Melci (1776–1847), an Aragonese noble, and resolutely withstood the assault. This began in earnest on 15 June and the French would have forced an entrance at the Portillo but for the bravery of Augustina de Aragón (Byron's 'Maid of Saragossa'), who when her lover fell at the side of his gun, seized the match from his hand and continued firing. On 13 August the French defeat at Bailén (q.v.) temporarily relieved the town and Lefebre was forced to retire. In December Zaragoza was again invested, this time by an army of 30,000, commanded by Lannes, Mortier, Moncey, and Junot. Fire and pestilence broke out, and the French were obliged to take each house by storm as tiles were hurled at them from the roofs. It was not until 20 February 1809 that it surrendered, a mass of smoking ruins.

When Ford passed through in 1831 he condemned the place as a 'dull, old-fashioned, brick-built town', of which, with the present rage for demolition, there is not much surviving.

In 1923 its archbishop was assassinated. Gen. Franco was the first commandant of the Military Academy established there in 1928. In 1933 a general strike here lasted for 57 days, a revolutionary committee of workers being led by Durruti. In 1936 Nationalist troops were in control of the town before the trade unions were able to organise resistance, and there was severe repression.

The city has grown rapidly in recent decades. It is expected that the U.S. air base there will be suppressed.

Among natives were Avempace (died 1138), the Almoravid philosopher; Jerónimo de Zurita (1512–80), the historian; Ignacio Luzán (1702–54), poet and critic; Ramón de Pignatelli (1734–93), the engineer; and the artists Francisco and Ramón Bayeu (1734–95, and 1746–93, respectively).

A.   The Old Centre

The PL. DE ESPAÑA, at the N end of the wide arcaded *Paseo de la Independencia*, remains a hub of activity. It is a central point on the *C. del Coso*, which follows the line of the old city wall.

From just E of the plaza the narrow C. de Don Jaime I leads N through the old town. W of it is an area of pedestrian alleys. On the left is Baroque *S. Gil*, with a Mudéjar tower of c 1350 and a retablo by Ancheta.—In the C.S. Jorge (right) is Mudéjar *SS. Juan y Pedro*, with a brick tower; and the *Conv. de la Enseñanza*, built on the site of the Lanuza palace, razed on Felipe II's orders. The *Judería* was also in this area. Just S of the church was the *Roman Theatre*, now under excavation.

To the left in the C. Espoz y Mina is *Sta. Cruz* (1680; by Agustín Sanz); opposite, at No. 23, is the former *Pal. de los Pardo*, with a Renaissance patio. It was restored to house the *Museo Camon Aznar*, with an extensive collection of paintings assembled by the art historian (1898–1979), who was born in Zaragoza.

Among the more important works, are: *Massys*, S. Jerónimo; *Andrea del Sarto*, Four saints; *El Greco*, Still life, The Magdalen, an Annunciation (with his son), and a polychromed wooden sculpture of Christ; *Zurbarán*, Crucifixion, and Still life; *Ribalta*, S. Luis Beltrán; *Ribera*, Archimedes, and Head of a saint; *Morales*, Ecce Homo; *Valdes Leal*, Apostle's head; *Rembrandt*, Male portrait; *Hals*, Male portrait; *Wouwerman*, Equestrian scene; *Van Dyck*, sketch for the portrait of Endymion Porter and the artist in the Prado; *Velázquez*, sketch for a head of a Menina; *Giaquinto*, Joseph's Dream; *Goya*, Self-portrait wearing spectacles, Inquisition scene, and three Bull-fighting scenes—also, in a separate room, his Engravings; *Lucas*, Landscapes, and other works; *Chardin*, The kitchen; and later 19C and 20C paintings of varying merit. Notable among the sculptures is a bronze Head of Unamuno by *Pablo Serrano*.

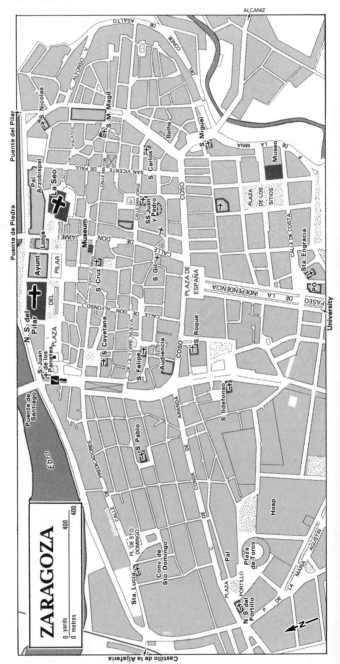

ZARAGOZA

0 yards   400
0 metres   400

The large *Pl. del Pilar* is a few steps to the N, its far side dominated by the Lonja, Ayuntamiento, and N.S. del Pilar to the W; to the E by the *Pal. Arzobispal* (1787) and the old Cathedral, or La Seo. It is worth walking round the narrow alleys encircling the latter to see the *Muro Mudéjar*, a wall covered by a mosaic of brick and azulejo tiles at the NE angle. The adjoining apse shows traces of Romanesque work.

The *Seo was erected as a mosque on the site of an older church. This was reconstructed after 1119 and has since been considerably altered, particularly after the extensive rebuilding by *Charles de Mendivi* in the mid 16C. In 1318 it was appointed the metropolitan church of a new archbishopric detached by Pope John XXII from that of Tarragona. Its archives and library have been systematically pillaged. The building is at present (1988) being very thoroughly restored and cleaned, and the description below may well be superseded in some details.

The main NW façade was built by Julián de Yarza in 1683; the tall tower beside it by J.B. Contini in 1690. The *Cimborio* was erected by Pedro de Luna (Benedict XIII) in 1412 and rebuilt by Juan Botero in 1520.

The building is almost square, with double aisles and a row of external chapels on all four sides. Its slender pillars support a lofty pointed vault with foliated keystones. The marble floor is designed to mirror the vault plan.

Facing the SW entrance is the Plateresque *Trascoro* (1557; by Arnau de Bruselas and Tudedilla), decorated by Juan Sanz and with plasterwork by Juan de Bruselas. In the centre is an 18C baldacchino with twisted columns by Juan Zábalo. The *Coro*, with a 16C grille, contains 15C stalls. The *Cap. Mayor* has an alabaster retablo begun in 1431 by Pere Johan, and continued by Hans de Suabia between 1467 and 1477. The lantern above it is by Gil Morlanes (1488). The interior cupola of the cimborio was completed in 1520 by Enrique de Egas.

To the left of the altar are the tombs of Abp Juan de Aragón (died 1475; brother of Fernando the Catholic) and of Pedro López de Luna, the first archbishop.—The black slab on the wall marks the burial place of the heart of Don Baltasar Carlos (the *infante* so often painted by Velázquez), who died of smallpox at Zaragoza in 1646. The organ of 1413 was rebuilt in the 18C. Notable in the *Cap. de S. Miguel* is the tomb, with its mourners, of Abp Lope Fernández de Luna (died 1382), by Pere Moragues.

The *Sacristy* contains a Plateresque custodia of 1541, probably designed by Damián Forment, an English chasuble from old St. Pauls, London, and a collection of cult objects. The *Chapterhouse* normally contains paintings by Ribera, Zurbarán and Goya, and an important collection of 15–18C tapestries.

Walking W, on the right is the *Puente de Piedra*, with seven pointed arches, rebuilt in 1437 and several times restored. Further W is the *Lonja, a plain rectangular hall of 1551 by Gil Morlanes the Younger and Juan de Sariñena, Gothic in plan and Plateresque in ornament, with an impressive cornice. Within, the 24 Ionic columns and pilasters are encircled by a band of curious ornamentation, its frieze recording the erection of the building.

Beyond the *Ayuntamiento*, the plaza is flanked by the unwieldy bulk of **N.S. del Pilar**, built to enshrine the cult image of Zaragoza, and also patroness of the Guardia Civil. (In 1931 the local Guardia 'endeared' themselves to the strikers by firing on the train evacuating their wives and children.)

Legend relates that Santiago, when preaching in Spain in AD 40, saw a vision of the Virgin, who descended on a marble pillar supported by angels and commanded him to build a chapel in her honour. This chapel was replaced by a church in the 13C, largely destroyed by a fire in 1434, only the high altar and coro surviving. In 1681 Francisco Herrera el Mozo began the present building, which was further remodelled by Ventura Rodríguez and José Ramírez in 1754–66.

The central dome is surrounded by ten cupolas roofed with multi-
coloured tiles. The four slender yellow-brick towers were not
completed until 1903. A Romanesque tympanum from the earlier
chapel has been built into the S front.

The interior is divided into three aisles of seven bays each, but the square piers,
faced with Corinthian pilasters, are too ponderous for the height of the vaults.
The *Coro* is a Renaissance work of 1564 by Juan de Moreto, a Florentine who
sculptured the three rows of stalls following designs by Étienne d'Obray.
Moreto was also responsible for the organ case (1529). The reja of 1579 is by
Juan Celma; the High Altar of 1515 by Damián Forment.
    Near the E end of the church is the oval *Sta. Capilla*, surrounded by
broccatello marble columns, where, protected by a silver reja, is the cult image.
During the Civil War, it was reported to have been hit by a Republican bomb,
which 'miraculously' did not explode. The outer dome was frescoed by
González Velázquez; one of the spandrels is by Goya (the Virtues); the rest by
Francisco Bayeu.

At the far end of the plaza rises the *Torreon de la Zuda* (containing
the Tourist Office), part of the residence of Alfonso el Batallador.
Adjacent to it is *S. Juan de los Panetes*, with a Churrigueresque
portal of 1720 and a 13C brick tower. A few steps further W are the
insignificant remains of 3C *Roman Walls*.
    Walk S past the covered *Market* and turn left past Baroque *S.
Cayetano* (1681–1704; by Villanova); it contains the tomb of Juan de
Lanuza. Then turn right for the C. de la Torre Nueva (named after a
90m-high leaning tower dating from 1504; needlessly demolished in
1894; see frontispiece).—On the SW side of the adjacent plaza is *S.
Felipe* (1691; by Miguel Jiménez) and the *Pal. de los Condes de
Argillo*, the latter with a patio of 1663 and now housing the *Museo
Pablo Gargallo*, devoted to that sculptor (Maella 1881–Reus 1934).
    Turn E along the C. de Candalija, in which is the 15C *Casa Fortea*,
to enter the small Pl. de Sas. The C. Alfonso I leads back to the Coso.

B.   Western Zaragoza

From this point in the Coso, walk W past (left) 18C *S. Roque*, with
brick towers, and (right) the *Audiencia* (1537), formerly the mansion
of the Condes de Luna, a family to which Benedict XIII and the
wicked count in Verdi's 'Il Trovatore' (1853) belonged. The Audiencia is also known as the 'Casa de los Gigantes' from the colossal
figures guarding the entrance.
    Follow the C. de Conde de Aranda to the W. The second street on
the right leads to **S. Pablo**, the most interesting church in Zaragoza
after La Seo. It was founded after 1266, has a 13C Mudéjar tower,
and was enlarged in the 16C. The wooden retablo mayor of 1529 is
by Damián Forment; in a chapel behind it, there is another retablo in
his style. The organ of 1572 is undergoing restoration.
    Regaining the C. de Conde de Aranda, turn right and follow the
street—several minutes' walk—to the *Puerto del Portillo*, passing
(left) *N.S. del Portillo* (1731) to approach, beyond the recently laid-
out gardens, the E side of the castle of *La Aljafería*. This has six
heavily restored towers and the whole is surrounded by a dry, brick-
walled moat.

It was once the palace of the Berber sheikhs and later the residence of the kings of Aragón. It is named after its builder, Ahmad Abu Yac'far ibn Suleyman, a member of the Banu Hud dynasty. It was sporadically the seat of the Inquisition between 1485 and 1759; was used as barracks from 1772, although partly destroyed by Suchet in 1809; and was later used as a hospital, then as a prison, before being re-occupied by the military. It suffered extensive destruction and vandalism during this period and is now being thoroughly restored, when not rebuilt, as the future seat of the Cortes of Aragón.

Notable are the Moorish arches of the N portico of the central *Patio de Sta. Isabel*; the Oratorio and *mihrab* of the Mezquita; the Staircase of 1492; the *Salón del Trono*, its artesonado ceiling with the ensignia of Fernando and Isabel and pendant ornaments; the Sala de Sta. Isabel, probably the birthplace of Isabel of Portugal (1271–1336), daughter of Pedro III of Aragón; and the *Torre del Trovador*, said to have been the prison of 'Manrico' (cf. Audiencia).

C. Southwestern Zaragoza

From the *Puerta del Portillo* follow the Paseo de María Agustín, circling to the SE past the *Puerta del Carmen* (1782; by Agustín Sanz), to enter the oval Pl. de Aragón.

A short distance to the SW are the buildings of the *University*, founded in 1474, its former site flanking the Corso E of La Seo.

By turning N along the Paseo de la Independencia, we soon pass (right) the Plateresque *Portal of Sta. Engracia*, built by the *Gil Morlanes* (father and son) in 1519.—From here the C. de Costa Canalejas leads E to the Pl. de los Sitios, on the far side of which is the **Museum**.

The Ground Floor is devoted to the *archaeological collections*, including important material from Azaila, Botorrita (Iberic script on bronze), Vellila de Ebro, and Bilbilis; a notable collection of Roman mosaics, several from Zaragoza itself, but also from Estada (NE of Barbastro), Fraga and other sites; note especially the Orpheus mosaic. Sections follow which are devoted to the Visigothic and Moorish occupations of the province.

The First Floor contains *Paintings*, including panels by *Jaime Serra* from the Retablo of Sto. Sepulcro; the Retablo of Sta. Cruz de Blesa by *Miguel Jiménez* and *Martín Bernat*; a statue of the Guardian Angel by *Gil Morlanes*, polychromed by *Bernat*; and another statue of S. Onofre, attributed to Damián Forment; S. Pedro Nolasco by *Jusepe Martinez*; and several anonymous 17C Magdalenas.

Among more modern works are *Goya*, Dream of S. José, and Portraits of Ramón de Pignatelli, the Duque de San Carlos, Carlos IV, María Luisa, and Fernando VIII; *Vicente López*, Calomarde; *Esquivel*, Juan Lombia; and representative paintings by Francisco Bayeu, and Eugenio Lucas, and *David Wilkie's* Augustina de Aragón. Also works by Sorolla, Zuloaga, Rusiñol, Chicharro, and Natalio Bayo.

Another section is devoted to Aragonese ceramics.

A few minutes' walk to the NE brings one to 14C *S. Miguel*, with a Mudéjar tower of c 1260 and altar piece of 1519 by Damián Forment and Gabriel Jolí.

The Coso is a few paces to the N, in which, to the W below Nos. 126–32, are the *Baños Judios* of c 1250. Beyond this we regain the Pl. de España.

In the E quarter of the enceinte, between the C.S. Vicente de Paul and the Coso, are three churches of slight interest: *S. Carlos* (1570), with decoration of 1723 and containing a S. Francisco Borja by Ribera; *La Magdalena*, 14C, with a Mudéjar tower; and Churrigueresque *S. Nicolás*, further N.

A short stretch of *Roman wall* may be seen flanking the Coso as it approaches the Ebro, here crossed by the *Puente del Pilar*.

About 10km N, on the E bank of the Gállego, is the *Cartuja de Aula Dei* (1567), restored after 1809. For the time being it may be visited by males only; the frescoes by Goya in the church have been repainted.

For roads from Zaragoza to **Pamplona**, **Logroño**, **Huesca**, and **Lleida** see Rtes 3, 6, 68, and 69 respectively, in reverse; for **Calatayud**, **Daroca**, and **Alcañiz** see Rtes 72, 73, and 74.

72 Zaragoza to Madrid via Calatayud, (Siguenza) and Guadalajara

322km (200 miles). NII. 87km **Calatayud**—84km *Medinaceli* crossroads—17km *Alcolea del Pinar*—(**Sigüenza** is 20km NW)—78km **Guadalajara**—25km **Alcalá de Henares**—31km **Madrid**.

Maps: M 442.

Although improved in parts, this is *not* a good road considering its importance; in several sections the going is slow. The NII, leading SW, is soon joined by the bypass, and crosses the SIERRA DE LA MUELA.—At 34km *Épila* is 9km right, where in 1384 Pedro IV defeated a league of Aragonese nobles. The Baroque church contains the tomb of Lope Jiménez de Urrea (died 1475), viceroy of Sicily.—4km N of Épila, at *Rueda de Jalón*, is the Moorish castle of *Rota*.

At 17km the road skirts *La Almunia de Doña Godina*, with relics of Moorish fortifications. There are Celtiberian and Roman remains in the vicinity. To the N is the chapel of *N.S. de Cabañas*, with 12C frescoes and an artesonado ceiling.—The next turning to the right leads 4km to *Ricla*, on the far bank of the Jalón, with a Mudéjar belfry to its 16–18C church.

At 8km *Tobed* lies 15km SE, its church of 1359 with Mudéjar decoration incorporating the Islamic confession in Arabic.—At *Mesones*, c 16km NW, is a palace of the antipope Benedict XIII (Pedro de Luna; c 1330–1423); he was born in the huge 14C palace at *Illueca*, in the parallel valley to the W.

The road now climbs to the *Puerto de Morata* (708m) and winds through the hills, crossing two more ridges before descending to (19km) **Calatayud**; for this and for the valley of the Jiloca to the SE see Rte 14A.

CALATAYUD TO MOLINA DE ARAGÓN (75km). The C202 climbs SW to (26km) *Nuevalos*, picturesquely sited at the S end of the *Embalse de la Tranquera*, 3km S of which is the monastery of *Piedra*, founded in 1194 by Cistercians from Poblet, and moved to its present site on the opposite bank of the Río Piedra in 1218. It was damaged in the anti-clerical rising of 1835 but has been restored and converted into a hotel.

The *Church* was refaced in the 17C, but the *Cloister* and *Staircase*, with its 14C–15C vault, was not altered. The other dependencies are also of interest. Not the least of the charms of Piedra is its delightful situation in a wooded valley with several pools and waterfalls.

The road continues S, at 18km passing the old village of *Milmarcos*, and 16km beyond meets the old road from *Embid* (14km NE), with a well-preserved castle.—4km *Rueda de la Sierra*, its 12C church with a late Gothic chapel, 8km beyond which is *Molina de Aragón*; see Rte 14B.

From Calatayud, the NII continues W up the valley of the Jalón past (7km) *Terrer*, with a Mudéjar church, to (7km) *Ateca*, with two imposing towers—one (13C) above a converted mosque, the other belonging to the *Ayuntamiento*, formerly a castle.—14km *Alhama de Aragón*, Roman *Aquae Bilbilitanae*, an old spa whose springs were rediscovered by the Moors, who built the towering Alcázar.—Other castles are passed at (6.5km) *Cetina* (left) and (8km) *Ariza*, SW of which is the site of an Iberian town.

At 6.5km *Monteagudo de las Vicarias* is 9km NW, encircled by remains of ramparts, with a 15C castle and 16C church with a late Gothic doorway.—The road goes on over a pass at 1082m to (23km) *Morón de Almazán*; see Rte 14B.

At 7km (left), after passing a Parador, is **Sta. María de la Huerta**, with the impressive remains of a great Bernadine *Monastery*, with a huge, sexpartite, vaulted Gothic *Refectory* (1223). Its well-proportioned *Church*, begun in 1179, contains the grave of Abp Rodrigo Jiménez, who fought at Las Navas de Tolosa (q.v.), and a two-keyboard 18C organ. The rose-window has been restored. Off the S transept is an octagonal chapel of 1750. The N transept contains the tomb of the Cid's grandson, and the 13C *Cloister* is entered from here. A monumental 17C staircase ascends to the *Upper Cloister* (1547) and that of the hostelry (1582–1637).

Beyond (11km) *Arcos de Jalón*, with a medieval castle, the road threads a gorge, at 17km reaching the crossroads below **Medinaceli**, on a commanding height to the NW; see Rte 14B.—The road veers S, climbing to the *Puerto Esteras* (1138km) and turns W past (17km) *Alcolea del Pinar* (1205m).

A minor road turns right off the NII c 5km beyond the Medinaceli crossroads through (5km) *Torralba*.—3km to the N, near *Ambrona*, is a *Museo Paleontologico*, covering an excavated site displaying in situ the remains of elephants which roamed the area some 300,000 years ago.—The road continues W from Torralba, descending the upper valley of the Henares and passing N of *Guijosa*, an old walled town with a 13C church, to approach (17km) **Sigüenza**; see below.

The NII continues W, then SW across the high-lying plateau, at 14km passing (left) the 14C castle of *La Torresaviñan*; and c 5km N, *Pelegrina*, with a ruined castle and Plateresque church.

The DETOUR to *Sigüenza*, an additional 17km, should be made from Alcolea del Pinar by turning right onto the C114, which is followed for 20km.

SIGÜENZA (1070m; 5300 inhab.; Parador) is an attractive old cathedral town built on a steep slope rising like an amphitheatre above the upper valley of the Henares, and dominated by the former castle of its bishops.

Its name is derived from Celtiberian *Segontia*, said to have been founded by fugitives from Saguntum at *Villa Vieja*, a short distance NE. The diocese was re-established c 1124 and a university college was founded here in 1477. It suffered from its position as a Nationalist salient during 1936–37; the cathedral was shelled by them when capturing the place.

The ALAMEDA, laid out in 1804 'for the solace of the poor', lies below the town, near the river. To the W is the *Humilladero*, a Gothic Chapel with a Renaissance doorway; to the N is *N.S. de los Huertos* (1524); to the E rises grandiose *S. Francisco* (1615); and S of this is Baroque *S. Roque*, in the street of that name, the main artery of a model suburb laid out by Bp Diaz Guerra during the last two decades of the 18C on plans supplied by Luis Bernasconi.

The C. de Medina leads uphill from S. Francisco to the early Gothic **Cathedral**, begun c 1150, consecrated in part in 1169, but reported to be in a state of disrepair in 1253. It has been much altered since. It is a plain building in a mixture of styles including French influences—its second and third bishops were Frenchmen. The central lantern, a later addition, has been restored after damage in the Civil War.

The *W Front* is divided by massive buttresses and is flanked by low towers, and has a fine round-arched door. On the left is the *Chapterhouse* of 1527. The *S Front* is flanked by a slender tower of 1300 and has a 13C rose above Bernasconi's classical portal inserted in 1797.

The nave vault is supported by massive clustered piers. The *Sillería* dates from 1490; the trascoro and altar from 1665–88. Against the coro is the Retablo de la Virgen de la Leche (milk; 1514). The *Cap. Major* contains the tomb of Abp Bernardo of Toledo, the first bishop of Sigüenza; the retablo of 1611 is by Giraldo de Merlo. The N pulpit is dated 1495; the S pulpit of 1573 is the masterpiece of Martín de Valdoma.

On the N side is the Portal of the *Cap. de la Anunciación* (1516), an effective combination of Gothic, Renaissance, and Mudéjar ornament. The adjoining chapel has a Plateresque portal similar to that of the *Sacristy* and a panelled ceiling by Covarrubias (1535) with heads set in medallions; it contains some Nottingham alabasters of c 1400.

To the S of the choir is the *Chapel of the Arce Family* in which is the charming semi-recumbent figure of Martín Vázquez de Arce (c 1495), known as **'El Doncel de Sigüenza**. He was killed at Granada in 1486. The *Cap. de S. Marcos* contains a 15C triptych by Fernando del Rincón; that of *Sta. Librado* preserves the mausoleum of Don Fadrique de Portugal (bishop in 1512–32), but it has

El Doncel de Sigüenza

been drastically restored since 1936, and six 16C Italian panels. Off the late Gothic *Cloister* to the N (1507; by Alonso de Vozmediano), a chapel displays 17C Flemish tapestries.

Opposite the cathedral is a **Museum** containing: El Greco, *Annunciation*; Zurbarán, *Immaculate Conception*; and works attributed to Salzillo, Morales and Pompeo Leoni. There is also a collection of curious bronze crucifixes. The patio houses 15C figures of Adam and Eve.

The C. de Román Pascual, W of the cathedral, passes the *Col. de S. Bartolomé* or *Seminario Mayor* (1651; enlarged 1761), and crosses the C. del Card. Mendoza to reach the Renaissance *Casa de la Inquisición* at C. de la Yedra 2. This street leads to the C. del Peso (right), in which are the late 16C *Casa del Pósito* and remains of the town walls, and is continued by the C. del Hospital, where the *Hosp. de S. Mateo*, founded in 1445, has two reliefs over the doorway.

The restored *Pl. Mayor*, S of the cathedral, is surrounded by porticoes and balconies mostly designed by Francisco Guillén (1498 onwards). On the S side is the *Ayuntamiento* of 1512 by Juan de Garay.—To the E the *Puerta del Toril* leads into open country across the 17C bridge and aqueduct called *Los Arcos* (view).

The C. Mayor climbs steeply S, past the picturesque Travesaña Baja (right) and ruined *Santiago* (12C), to the **Castle**, rebuilt in the 12C and 14–15Cs on the site of the Moorish Alcázar, and recently rebuilt to house the Parador. The C. de Jesús leads to *S. Vicente* (12–13C); near by is the 15C *Casa del Doncel*.

The C. Bajada de S. Jerónimo descends to the *Seminario Menor* and the *Pal. Episcopal* of 1625, built to house the university, closed in 1837.

The C204 bears SW to rejoin the NII 29km SW of Alcolea del Pinar, where turn right. Another right turn 6km before meeting the main road leads 16km W to *Jadraque*; see Rte 15.

The C204 continues SE after 2km. At 12km this leads past (3km right) *Valderrobollo*, with a small Romanesque church and what remains of the monastery of *Ovila*, much of which has been removed to the USA.—9km further SE is *Cifuentes* (hundred fountains), with a large ruined castle of 1324, Renaissance convents, and *El Salvador*, with a notable door of c 1268 and rose-window.—The N end of the huge *Embalse de Entrepeñas* is 15km S; see Rte 44B.

At 20.5km a by-road leads left past the *Pal. de Ibarra*. Near here Roatta's Italian Fascists were routed in March 1937.–9km **Brihuega**, a fortified town impressively sited on a hill above the Tajuña. On 10 December 1710 Stanhope was taken prisoner here by the Duc de Vendôme, whose army, having made a forced march from Talavera, took Stanhope's troops by surprise. Starhemberg's army of 13,000, arriving later, was then heavily engaged at *Villaviciosa*, 5km NE. Although the result of the battle was indecisive, the Austrians were obliged to retreat to Catalunya.

The *Puerta de Cozadón* at Brihuega survives, together with four Romanesque churches including *Sta. María de la Peña* and *S. Felipe* (restored). Near by is a conspicuous building designed as a cloth factory by Carlos III. The so-called *Cuevas Arabes* are worth visiting.

6km *Trijueque* is bypassed, with remains of 13C fortifications and a 16C church; 3.5km beyond is *Torija*, with a Renaissance church and ruins of a once-famous 13C castle, blown up in 1811.

At 19km **Guadalajara** is bypassed; see Rte 15.—We cross the Henares and skirt the river, at 16km passing *Meco* (4km right), where the church has star-vaulting (1560), and contains three Churrigueresque retablos, and paintings by Juan Correa.

The road bypasses *Alcalá de Henares* at 5km.

ALCALÁ DE HENARES (137,150 inhab.; 100,600 in 1975; 57,350 in 1970; and still growing rapidly) is now little more than a dormitory town of Madrid. It has been long famous for its University and as the birthplace of Cervantes.

Roman *Complutum* stood further S, on the opposite bank of the Henares (where there are also ruins of a Moorish castle called *Alcalá la Vieja*), but there are no visible remains. Here also St. Fructuosus (later Bishop of Braga and Metropolitan of Galicia) founded the monastery of Compludo c 650. The Moors built a castle (*Al-Kalat*) on the present site, which was captured in 1118 by the bellicose Abp Bernard of Toledo, who also acquired the surrounding territory. Abp Tenorio raised the walls (in part restored) and built a bridge over the Henares in 1389. In 1508 Card.-Abp Francisco Jiménez de Cisneros (1436–1517) founded the university, which soon had 10,000 students; and here in 1514–17 were printed the six volumes of the famous Complutensian Polyglot Bible (in Latin, Greek, Hebrew, and—in part—Chaldaean).

With the transference of the university to Madrid in 1837 and the confiscation of the wealth of the monasteries the importance of Alcalá declined rapidly. But even by the mid 18C its decay had set in. Baretti records that 'out of nineteen or twenty colleges . . . two-thirds are absolutely unhabitable'; and the walls of the Col. de Málaga, once with four or five courtyards, were falling into their cellars, and 'spiders form their webs in the clefts of the broken steps of the principal staircase'.

It was from the prison here that Juan March, a millionaire convicted of fraud in 1932, bribed his way free; Andrés Nin was held here in June 1937 before being taken away by the Communists and murdered.

Apart from Miguel de Cervantes y Saavedra (1547–1616) its natives include Juan Ruiz (c 1283–c 1350), author of the 'Libro de buen amor'; Catherine of Aragón (1485–1536); the Infante Fernando (1503–64), brother of Charles V, who became Ferdinand I of Austria in 1521, and who, after the Peace of Augsburg in 1555, invited Loyola to send Jesuits to Vienna to combat the spread of Protestantism; Francisco de Figueroa (1536–1617), the poet; Antonio de Solis (1610–86), the historian of Spanish America; Juan Martín Díaz (1775–1823), 'el Empecinado', the guerrilla general; Eugenio Lucas (1817–70), the artist; and Manuel Azaña y Díaz (1880–1940, in Montauban), the Republican president in 1936–39 (who also translated Borrow's 'The Bible in Spain', some G.K. Chesterton, and Voltaire into Spanish).

In the town centre is the Pl. de Cervantes, E of which, in the Pl. de S. Diego, stands the **Col. Mayor de S. Ildefonso**, once the headquarters of the university. It is a magnificent Renaissance building begun in 1498 by Pedro Gumiel, rebuilt in 1543–83 by Rodrigo Gil de Hontañón and restored after severe damage during the Civil War.

The Plateresque *Façade (1537–53) bears Cisneros' arms, supported by swans (*cisnes*) and the Franciscan cord, and is decorated with medallions of the Doctors of the Church. Of the three interior Patios, the first (1676), of three storeys, bears the statues and the coats of arms of the founder and of S. Tomáas de Villanueva; the second was destroyed; the third, called 'El Trilingüe' (after the schools of Latin, Greek, and Hebrew which once surrounded it), dates from 1557 and is by Pedro de la Cotera. The *Paraninfo* or Great Hall is entered from here, with a painted ceiling and Plateresque galleries (1519). The *Chapel*, Gothic in design and Plateresque in ornamentation, contains the mutilated Carrara marble tomb of Card. Cisneros and that of Francisco Vallés, Felipe II's physician.

To the S of the plaza are the deteriorated façades of former colleges. Together with convents and their dependencies these now house a variety of organisations; some are still used as barracks.

Among the very few of interest are, in the C. de los Escritorios, the *Iglesia Magistral*, founded in 1136, but the present building (1509; by Pedro Gumiel) was gutted by fire during the Civil War and has been largely rebuilt.—Little remains of the former *Palacio Arzobispal* (begun 1209; partially restored after a destructive fire in 1940) apart from a pair of *ajimez* windows and a massive tower. Most of the existing edifice dates from the rebuilding commenced c 1375 by Abp Tenorio and continued in 1422–34 by Abp Contreras; the façade and patios were decorated by *Alfonso de Covarrubias* in 1524–34 for Abps Fonseca and Tavera. It now houses *National Archives*.

At No. 48 in the arcaded C. Mayor, running E–W, is a house built in 1955 on the site of one of several claimed to be where Cervantes was born; it contains a *Cervantine museum and library*.

Rebuilt defensive *Walls* are passed on leaving the town to rejoin the NII before entering or bypassing **Torrejón de Ardoz** (75,600 inhab.; 21,000 in 1970), where Narváez defeated Espartero in 1843. Baroque *S. Juan Evangelista* contains Claudio Coello's Martyrdom of St. John. The early 17C *Casa Grande*, at No. 2 C. Madrid, once in Jesuit hands, has been restored and contains a collection of icons.—To the NE of the town is a US air base, the subject of controversy.

The road skirts (left) *S. Fernando de Henares* (19,600 inhab.), S of which stands a former palace (1749) built for Fernando VI. Carvajal later established a cloth factory here which at one time employed several English and Irish artisans.

To the N is the airport of *Barajas*, passed before entering the E suburbs of **Madrid**: see Rte 40.

73 Zaragoza to Valencia via Daroca and Teruel

330km (205 miles). N330. 86km **Daroca**—N234. 98km **Teruel**—85km *Segorbe*—34km *Sagunto* crossroads—4km A7. 23km. **Valencia**.

Maps: M 443.

The road leads SW from *Zaragoza* (see Rte 71) parallel to the W bank of the Huerva, passing on the far bank at 19km the Celtiberian site of *Botorrita*, and 9km beyond, *Muel*, with a Roman fountain, now in the *Ermita de N.S. de la Fuente*, in which are saints painted by Goya in 1771. (Goya was born at *Fuendetodos*, 24km SE; see p 426.)—10km *Longares*, its hall-church of c 1580 with a 14C tower and an untouched 16C organ. At 5km we pass (right) the Baroque sanctuary of the *Virgen de las Lagunas*, to approach (4km) **Cariñena**, reputed for its wines (considered 'most excellent' by Baretti, who passed that way in 1760). The church tower is a relic of a fortress of the Knights of St. John. The *Cap. de Santiago* is a former mosque and contains an 18C organ.

At 6km *Paniza* is bypassed, with a 15C church and a Mudéjar belfry, beyond which we climb to the *Puerto de Paniza* (915m).—16km *Mainar*, with a notable 16C church tower. At 15km the road is joined by the N234 from *Calatayud*; see Rte 14A.

2km **Daroca** (787m), lying in the most fertile part of the valley, between the SIERRA DE STA. CRUZ (1423m) to the W, and the SIERRA DE CUCALÓN (1492m) to the SE. It is a town of great antiquity, surrounded by a *Wall* (13–16C) with 114 towers. The neighbouring hills are crowned with ruined castles. It was subject to floods, and a 700m-long drainage tunnel (*La Mina*) was dug in 1560 by Pierre Bedel (cf. Teruel), its N entrance a short distance SE of the *Puerta*

Alta. The *C. Mayor*, flanked by old houses, leads W from this past the 15C *Casa de la Cadena* and 13C *Casa de Trinitarios*. Uphill to the right is the *Pl. Mayor* and the *Colegiata de Sta. María*, begun in the 13C, altered in 1458–79, and rebuilt c 1587. Its Mudéjar tower dates from 1441 and it retains a doorway with 13C reliefs. It contains a *Museum of Ecclesiastical art*, including a custodia of 1388 and several 15C retablos.

The ancient *Ayuntamiento*, close by, is now the gaol.

Among churches of interest are Gothic *S. Andrés*; Romanesque *S. Juan*, *S. Miguel*, and *Sto. Domingo de Silos*, with a Mudéjar tower and a notable Retablo by Bartolomé Bermejo. At the far end of the C. Mayor is the *Puerta Baja*, roofed with glazed tiles and flanked by 14C turrets.

The N234 bears SE up the Jiloca valley past (26km) *Calamocha*, with a Moorish bridge and tower, to (9km) *Caminoreal*, and 7km beyond, *Monreal del Campo*; see Rte 14B.—To the SE the SIERRA PALOMERA rises to 1529m; to the SW the foothills of the SIERRA DE ALBARRACÍN (1935m).—Cross the *Puerto de Singra* (1000m); and at 38km a right-hand turn leads to (27.5km) **Albarracín**; see Rte 45B.

18km **TERUEL** (916m; 25,950 inhab.; 12,000 in 1920; Parador 2km N), a provincial capital. It is largely brick-built, with restored remnants of castellated walls and Mudéjar towers just visible among the blocks of the modern town, and rises above the banks of the Turia in its well-wooded vega, surrounded by fissured hills and precipitous cliffs of barren red clay. Its climate in winter is severe.

Celtiberian *Turba* was destroyed by the Romans as a reprisal for Hannibal's sack of Saguntum. It became a centre of Moorish influence and large numbers of Moors continued to live there after its reconquest in 1171. Jews also formed an important part of its population until 1486, when survivors were expelled after a pogrom. During the Civil War Teruel was held by the Nationalists until 14 December 1937, when it was taken and sacked by the Republicans, to be recaptured a fortnight later. At one time during the battle the temperature fell to 18°Celsius below zero. The fighting here over a period of two months cost the Nationalists approximately 14,000 dead, 16,000 wounded, and 17,000 sick, apart from those within the town, 9,500 of whom were killed or taken prisoner. Republican casualties have been estimated at half as much again.

From the Zaragoza road, a bypass veers right to avoid the town centre, which can be entered by forking left past Gothic *S. Francisco* (1401) and ascending to a paseo overlooked by the Mudéjar tower of *S. Salvador*. Pass through this and turn left to 18C *Sta. Teresa*; then right, to the central Pl. Mayor. At the far end of this is the **Cathedral**, built in 1248–78, altered in 1596–1614, and which received Churrigueresque additions c 1658–85. The central lantern of 1538 is by Martín de Montalbán. The nave is roofed by a remarkable painted *artesonado* of c 1260–1314. The retablo mayor of 1538 is by Gabriel Jolí.

By passing below the Mudéjar tower the *Bishop's Palace*, with a Renaissance entrance and patio, is reached.—The C. de los Amantes, flanking the *Ayuntamiento* in the *Pl. Mayor*, leads to *S. Martín*, with a Mudéjar *Tower* (restored in 1591 by Pierre Bedel, and again recently). Near this is the *Puerta de la Andaquilla* and a provincial *Museum*.

Turn NE along the C. 22 de Febrero to 17C *S. Miguel*. Beyond it is **Los Arcos de Teruel**, a remarkable aqueduct built by Pierre Bedel, a French engineer (cf. Daroca) in 1537–58.—Ruinous *La Merced*, in the suburb below, has a good brick tower.—A short stretch of *wall*

survives to the E of S. Miguel, and further SE is the polygonal tower
known as the *Castillo de Ambeles*.

The C. de S. Miguel leads S past the porticoed *Casa de la
Comunidad* and other old houses behind the cathedral, beyond
which turn right towards a triangular arcaded plaza from which the
stepped C. de Hartzenbusch leads to **S. Pedro**. This restored Gothic
church with a Mudéjar tower was refitted in the Churrigueresque
style in 1741 but retains an altar piece by Gabriel Jolí and a 14C
cloister.

In an adjacent chapel are said to be the remains of the 13C 'Lovers of Teruel'
(Isabel de Segura and Juan Diego Martínez de Marcilla), who died of grief at
being separated and were buried in one tomb. The popular legend has inspired
many dramas, perhaps the best known being those by Tirso de Molino (1635)
and by Hartzenbusch (1837).

A few steps to the S is *S. Andrés*, with a rebuilt tower and the tomb of
Sánches Muñoz, the antipope Clement VIII, elected at Avignon in
1423.

One may leave the town by crossing the viaduct immediately S of
the line of the old fortifications, bearing left to regain the main
road.—For roads to **Cuenca**, see Rte 45, in reverse.

The N234 climbs across the SIERRA DE CAMARENA at (16km) the
Puerto de Escandón (1242m), and 7km beyond skirts the chilly
upland town of *La Puebla de Valverde*, with relics of Moorish walls.

LA PUEBLA DE VALVERDE TO CASTELLÓ DE LA PLANA (126km). The C232 winds
across hilly country to (19km) **Mora de Rubielos** (where the 15C *Colegiata* was
burnt during the Civil War), with a restored *Castle*, altered c 1490.—14km
Rubielos de Mora, a village retaining numerous old houses; and 19km beyond,
Cortes de Arenoso, with a late 15C Valencian triptych in its church, are passed
to cross (31km) the *Puerto El Remolcador* (1018m) for (10km) *Lucena del Cid*. To
the NW rises the *Peñagolosa* (1814m). From Lucena, an old hill town with a
ruined castle (of the Duques de Híjar) and the 3C BC Celtiberian tower at
nearby *Los Foyos*, the road descends to (14km) **Alcora** (8000 inhab.), famous for
its ceramics factory, established by the Conde de Aranda in 1727.—19km
beyond is *Castelló*; see Rte 76.

The main road continues SE across country, later descending
through the rugged SIERRA DE ESPIÑA by a new stretch avoiding the
steep *Cuesta de Ragudo*. At 50km it bypasses *Viver*, with an old
tower containing numerous Roman inscriptions. Near by were the
Republican fortifications which stopped a Nationalist advance on
Valencia in July 1938.—3km **Jérica**, with ruined walls, Moorish
castle, and a small *Museum*. *S. Roque* (1395) contains a retablo by
Lorenzo Zaragoza; the *Parish church* has an elaborate Renaissance
portal; and *El Socorro*, 16C paintings and tombs of the Coverio family
(1600–09).

At 10km **Segorbe** (7650 inhab.), also bypassed, an ancient city of
Roman origin (*Segobriga Edetanorum*) with remains of walls, stands
in a side valley above the Palancia, commanded by two castles.

The ugly *Cathedral* (1483–1534; but entirely 'modernised' in 1795)
has been largely restored, as has its 15C cloister.

Works by Vicente Masip, Juan de Juanes, and Jacomart may be seen in the
Museo Diocesano, a miscellaneous collection of ecclesiastical art assembled
from churches in the area devastated during the Civil War. It also contains a
good Limoges enamel triptych, while other works are displayed in the octagonal vaulted *Chapterhouse*.

Some 5km W are the ruins of the *Cartuja de Valdecristo*, founded in 1385.

The road soon leaves the hills to cross the fertile *huerta* of Sagunto, at 20km passing its fortified acropolis, to meet the N340. Turn right to join the A7 23km N of **Valencia**; see Rte 77. For **Sagunto** see Rte 76.

74 Zaragoza to Tortosa via Alcañiz

207km (128 miles). N232. 57km *Azaila*–46km **Alcañiz**—15km. N420. 47km *Gandesa*—N230. 42km **Tortosa**.

Maps: M 443.

The road leads SE from *Zaragoza* (see Rte 71), roughly parallel to the Ebro; at 20km it passes a by-road leading 29km due S to *Belchite* (see p 426); 22km beyond, just after *Quinto*, the left fork (on crossing the river at 2km) leads to *Velilla de Ebro*; see p 426.

The N232 veers S to (15km) *Azaila*; see also p 426.

AZAILA TO GANDESA VIA CASPE (101km). This crosscountry road (C221) leads E on a plateau overlooking the Ebro to (18km) *Escatron*, where, turning right along a track on the far bank, is the abbey of *Rueda*, founded in 1182 by Alfonso II and abandoned in 1835. The church of 1238 has an early 14C cloister, recently restored (enquire at Escatron if the guardian is likely to be there).—28km *Caspe*; and 21km, *Maella*; see Rte 70.—The N420 is reached 27km beyond and 7km W of *Gandesa*; see p 427, and below.

At 14km *Híjar* is bypassed, its church restored after being gutted in 1936.—At *Albalate del Arzobispo*, 10km SW, are ruins of a fine castle of c 1310 incorporating a Mudéjar chapel.

33km **Alcañiz** (11,650 inhab.; Parador), ancient *Anitorgis*. In 212 BC Hasdrubal defeated the Scipios here. It is commanded by its *Castle*, which has a pointed barrel-vaulted 12C chapel and later porch. Its tower contains murals. The main building of 1728 now houses the Parador, adjacent to which an earlier fortress and church have been excavated.

Flanking the *Pl. Mayor* are the Renaissance façade of the *Ayuntamiento*, the adjoining arcaded 14C *Lonja* (restored), and grandiose *Sta. María* with a monumental Baroque portal. *N.S. del Carmen*, with a Baroque retablo and concha, and the *Bridge*, are also of interest.

Alcañiz was the birthplace of the influential journalist Francisco Mariano Nifo (or Nipho; 1719–1803).

Climbing SE from the valley of the Guadalope, we reach a road junction at 15km and turn left. For the N232 bearing right to *Morella*, see Rte 75.—To the N is the *Cueva del Charco de Agua Amarga*, with remarkable rock paintings.—The N420 now traverses a particularly attractive district, with wide views SE towards the hills known as the PUERTOS DE BESEIT, at 15km crossing the Río Matarraña, where near *Mazaleón*, 7km left, are Iberian sites.—At 7km the road passes near that of *S. Antonio* on approaching **Calaceite**, with a Baroque church and a picturesque *Ayuntamiento* and *Pl. Mayor*.

25km *Gandesa*, the centre of the Battle of the Ebro in the summer of 1938. A late 12C porch in the Limousin style survives. (Some 2 million of the 5.4 million vines in the region were destroyed during the fighting.)—For *Móra d'Ebre*, 24km further E, see Rte 76.

The road climbs SE over the SIERRA DE PANDÓLS (703m), descending to reach the Ebro at (27km) *Xerta*, the scene of fighting during the Carlist Wars. It retains an ancient *azud* or wheel to raise water from the river to irrigation channels.

14km **TORTOSA** (31,200 inhab.; 47,200 in 1975; Parador), a dull old town, retaining some walls and commanded by its castle. It lies on both banks of the Ebro, here 220m wide, allowing small sea-going vessels to use its quays.

Roman *Dertosa Julia Augusta* was sufficiently important to posses a mint. It remained in Moorish hands, despite an attempt in 809 to capture it, until it fell to Ramón Berenguer IV in 1148 after a long siege, aided by a Genoese contingent and the Knights Templar. In 1413–14 it was the site of a disputation between Christians and Jews, prompted by Jerónimo de Santa Fé (himself an apostate), which was to precipitate numerous anti-semitic reactions throughout the kingdom. In 1708 it was taken by the French under Orléans; and in the Peninsular War it surrendered to Suchet in 1811. In the Civil War the Ebro formed the front for several months, and Tortosa suffered serious damage before the Nationalists entered it on 18 April 1938.

The ferocious Carlist general Ramón Cabrera (1806–77), known as the 'Tiger of the Maestrazgo', was born here; in 1849 he retired to England and is buried at Virginia Water; also, the composer and musicologist Felipe Pedrell (1841–1922). Adrian Dedel (died 1523), the Dutch tutor of Charles V and inquisitor-general of Aragón, was Bishop of Tortosa from 1516 until his election to the papacy as Adrian VI in 1522.

Commanding the N end of the town is the *Citadel*, an extensive ruin in which the Parador is now housed. It provides panoramic *views* over the rich plain to the SW, ringed by mountains, with the *Caro* (1434m) due W. The ancient *Judería* was to the W, below the castle hill.

The **Cathedral** was founded in 1158 on the site of a mosque built in 914, but the present building was begun in 1347 by Benito Dalguayre. The massive unfinished façade was added in 1705–57.

The double *Ambulatory*, with its pierced stone screens, is very fine. The reliefs on the pulpit and the iron choir screen deserve notice. The *Cap. de Sta. Cinta* (1672–1719) is embellished with precious marbles; in the *Cap. de Sta. Candia* are the tombstones of the first four bishops (1165–1245). The *Sacristy* is said to contain a Moorish ivory casket. The 13C–14C *Cloister* is entered through a portal at its W side.

Opposite the main entrance is the restored 14C *Bishop's Palace*. A few old houses may be seen in the C. de de la Rosa and in the C. Moncada, where stands Baroque *La Purísima*. The old *Ayuntamiento* has a front of 1768. To the right is the *Col. de Sto. Domingo*, housing the *Museo Municipal*. Close by is the *Conv. de S. Luis*, founded in 1544, with a Renaissance front by Juan Anglés, and a three-storeyed patio enriched with 38 busts of the kings and queens of Aragón.

The 14C open *Lonja* has been rebuilt in the park S of the railway bridge.

The A7 motorway can be joined 11km SE, and the N340 2km beyond; see Rte 76.

75 Alcañiz to Castelló de la Plana via Morella

180km (112 miles). N420. 15km. N232. 59km **Morella**–35km. C238. 71km **Castelló de la Plana**.

Maps: M 443.

For **Alcañiz**, see Rte 74.—At the junction 15km SE turn S.

At 1km the TE300 turns left, passing (11km) the attractive village of *La Fresneda*, with arcaded streets and ancient houses, before reaching *Valderrobres* 11km beyond. This is an old town with a 12C church, an impressive ruined *Castle* of the kings of Aragón (c 1400), and a 17C *Ayuntamiento*.—There is some fine scenery among the mountains further S, as at *Beceite* or the *Embalse de la Peña*.—The main route can be rejoined 26km SW at *Monroyo*.

26km *Monroyo*.

9km SE, off the TE302 to Valderrobres (see above), is *Peñarroya de Tastavins*, with a good 14C Mudéjar church and another church of 1556.—7km SW of Peñarroya is the Gothic *Castillo de Herbés*, a noble fortified mansion.—A rough road continues SW to meet the N232 at the *Puerto de Torre Miró* (1259m), 11km N of Morella.

The main road winds and climbs 21km S to this same pass, providing several views over the wild, depopulated, rugged region of the MAESTRAZGO. Morella, on a commanding height 11km ahead, is the 'capital' of the region, and a good base from which to explore it. This approach passes a Gothic *Aqueduct* (c 1273–1318).

MORELLA (1004m), identified as the Roman *Castra Aelia* and the winter quarters of Sertorius, is an ancient frontier fortress of steep arcaded streets. Its dominating *Castle* is well worth the stiff climb for the extensive *Panorama* over the surrounding hills of the Maestrazgo. It was held by Cabrera (cf. Tortosa) from 1838 until its capture by Espartero in 1840.

The 14C *Town Walls* are well preserved and include 14 towers and four gates. Among the latter is the *Puerta de S. Miguel* of 1360. *Sta. María la Mayor* (1265–1330) has carved doorways of c 1355–80 and a raised *Coro* of 1426 by Pedro de Segarra, who also built the belfry. The vault beneath the coro was added in 1440 and the winding staircase in 1470. The trascoro is by José Beli, an Italian. In the *Cap. Mayor* is a retablo of 1677, and Churrigueresque decoration of 1685 by Vicente Dolz, who was also responsible for the stalls of 1672. Some of the windows contain glass of 1386 by the Valencians Juan Gascó and Pedro Ponc. The 18C *Organ*, with a beautiful tone, has been restored. The *Sacristy* contains a Visitation by Joan Reixach, and S. Roque by Ribalta; vestments of 1410, and other cult objects.

S. Juan dates from 1479. A former *Franciscan Convent* retains a cloister of c 1290 and a church consecrated in 1390, with Neo-Classical additions of 1800. *S. Miguel*, by José Palau, was completed in 1729.

Among the civic buildings the most interesting are the *Ayuntamiento* of 1361–1414, with 17C alterations, and the *Almudin* of c 1260.

For the road from Morella to *Teruel*, see p 427.—To the NW, off the CS840, are the caves of *Morella la Vella*, containing prehistoric paintings.—The road goes on to (12km) *Forcall*, an ancient place of arcaded streets, with a 13C church and Baroque belfry (1760).—4km further W is *Todolella*, with an old castle.—6km N of Forcall stands the castle of *Ortells*, and 6km beyond (on a rough road) is *Zorita del Maestrazgo*, where the rock-cut chapel of *N.S. de la Balma* has a Churrigueresque portal and verja of 1510.

Leaving Morella, the N232 bears E, with good retrospective views, to cross the *Puerto de Querol* (784m), and zigzags steeply down past (right) the 18C *Santuario de Vallivana*.

At 24km (from Morella) a by-road turns right for (7km) **Catí** an ancient village damaged during the Civil War. The 13C parish church contains an altarpiece of 1460 by Joan Reixach. The Italianate *Ayuntamiento* dates from 1427; the *Casa Abadia* from 1378; the *Casa del Delme* is early 15C; and the *Casa de Miralles* (c 1455) is by Pedro Crespo of Santander.

The main road follows the Rambla de Cervera. Turn right after 11km.—*Vinaròs* is on the coast 29km further E; see Rte 76.

5km **S. Mateo**. The *Iglesia Arciprestal* has a nave and apse of 1360 and an octagonal tower and doorway of 13C. The Plateresque retablo mayor is by Pedro Dorpa, a pupil of Damián Forment. The Gothic *Ayuntamiento*, the *Casa de Borull*, and the Plateresque *Pal. de Villores* are also notable.

A by-road leads SW via (11km) *Tirig*. In the vicinity and in the *Barranco de Valltorta* are prehistoric wall paintings.—11km *Albocácer*, with 13C *S. Juan*, the *Parroquia Alta*, and remains of a Templar castle.—17.5km further W is the walled village of *Benasal*.—The main route can be rejoined 13km E of Albocácer.

The C238 continues S from S. Mateo parallel to the coastal ridge of the *Atalayas de Alcalá* to (19km) *Cuevas de Vinromá*, with pre-historic shelters containing rock paintings.—21km, *Cabanes*, 3km W of which is a *Roman Arch*.—17km *Borriol*, with a ruined castle. Beyond this the road circles to the SE below the motorway to (9km) **Castelló de la Plana**; see Rte 76.

VI VALENCIA; MURCIA

The old kingdom of **Valencia**, now an autonomous *Comunidad*, comprises the provinces of *Valencia, Alicante*, and *Castellón*. It was finally taken from the Moors by Jaime el Conquistador in 1238, but the indigenous Morisco population was allowed to remain, to cultivate the land in peace until 1609. In that year a high proportion of them were expelled by Felipe III, leaving only enough old men to hand down to the Valencians the system of irrigation which they had developed to perfection.

This *riego de las aguas* (unharmed by the Civil War) is literally the life blood of the kingdom. The water, flowing down from the snows of the mountain barrier that wards off the rigours of the Aragonese or Castilian winters, is divided up skillfully among canals, channels, and irrigation drains. The *huertas* of the maritime strip, thus fertilised and vivified by almost continual sunshine produces an unending series of crops: fruit, wine, oil, hemp, almonds, and, in the marshy districts, rice; and mulberries were once grown for what was long a flourishing silk industry.

Whether the Valencians deserve the invidious reputation with which Ford and others have saddled them, is a matter of dispute. The populations of both the provinces of Alicante and Valencia have doubled in size since 1930, and their capitals have grown from 71,000 to 246,000 and from 316,000 to 775,000 respectively.

Murcia, an ancient kingdom, now autonomous, is one of the driest parts of Spain. In climate, tropical productions, and general aspect its maritime region resembles Spanish Africa. It is subject to violent changes of temperature and to the scourge of the *leveche*, a parching wind from the Sahara. The soil, naturally fertile, is made luxuriantly productive by skilful methods of irrigation, while Cartagena, the principal port, is the outlet for the products of a district rich in minerals.

Under the Romans Murcia was included in *Hispania Tarraconensis*; under the Moors it was first part of the emirate of Córdoba, but later became independent. It was occupied by Castile in 1243.

For its size its population is high: 955,500.

76 Tarragona to Valencia

A.   Via the N340

261km (162 miles). N340. 85km *Amposta*—32km *Vinaròs*—7km **Benicarló** (*Peñiscola* is 8km S)—66km **Castelló de la Plana**—42km **Sagunto**—29km **Valencia**.

Maps: M 443.

For **Tarragona**, see Rte 66.

TARRAGONA TO GANDESA (87km). The N420 leads W to (13km) **Reus** (79,250 inhab.), the principal market for the wines and other products of the Priorato. Much of the commerce of the town dates from 1750 when an English settlement was established there. The inhabitants distinguished themselves in 1835 by their cold-blooded acts of murder in the anti-monastic rising. It has since often been the centre of industrial disturbances. Gen. Prim (1814–70); Mariano Fortuny (1838–74) the artist; and the architect Antoni Gaudí i Cornet (1852–1926) were born here. The *Casa de la Ciudad* and several old mansions, including the 17C *Casa de Bofarull*, are of interest. *S. Pedro* has an altar by the Austrian Perris Ostris and a tower of 1562 by Benito Otger of Lyon.

The road starts to climb steeply into the sierra to the W to (22km) the *Puerto de la Teixeta* (546m), shortly after which a by-road turns left to the restored castle of *Escornalbou* on its commanding height. It incorporates remains of an Augustinian house founded in 1162, notably the Transitional church of 1165–1240 and a Romanesque cloister.—11km *Falset*, with a former *Medinaceli palace*, and noted for its lead mines. The vineyards of Priorato flourish here, taking their name from the priory of *Scala Dei*, a Charterhouse founded in 1163, whose ruins lie c 25km N (NE of *La Villel Baixa*).—The road later descends to (17km) *Móra la Nova*, taken by the Nationalists on 7 November 1938 at the end of the Battle of the Ebro (in which total losses on *each* side were probably in the region of 50–60,000).—On the far bank of the river is *Móra d'Ebre*. Approximately 10km S are the ruined Moorish castle of *Miravete*, later held by the Templars and Hospitalers.—*Gandesa* is 24km W of Móra; see p 442.

The T320 skirts the E bank of the Ebro soon passing a turning for (7km) *Tivissa*, near which is an Iberian settlement. Later, at *Rasquera*, there is a turning for the baths of *Cardó*, accommodated in a 17C monastery below the SIERRA DE CARDÓ (941m). The road eventually enters *Tortosa*; see Rte 74.

The old main road from Tarragona to Valencia is here described as a convenient way to include the several resorts strung out along the coast rather than as a recommended route. A pleasanter, but more expensive, drive is on the motorway (see Rte 76B), which is provided with several convenient exits.

The N340 skirts an industrial area with cracking plants and crosses the undulating CAMPO DE TARRAGONA, bypassing **Salou** (16,450 inhab.), ancient *Salauris*. Jaime el Conquistador set sail from here in 1229 to conquer Mallorca.—18km **Cambrils** (11,150 inhab.). The sierra (rising to 720m) approaches the coast and the landscape changes.—At 15km *L'Hospitalet de l'Infant*, taking its name from a hospice founded here in 1314, is passed, and then a nuclear power station, beyond which we cross the motorway.—17km *L'Ametlla de Mar* is 2km left. The road circles W past the castle of *Perelló* with a view of the extensive delta of the Ebro, which projects c 25km E of the original coastline. Dotted with lagoons and intersected by canals, the delta is largely devoted to market gardening and the cultivation of rice, and the production of salt.

At 28km the C235 leads right, to **Tortosa**, 13km NW; see Rte 74.

To the W rises the mountain range known as the PUERTOS DE BESEIT (*Caró*; 1434m); to the SW, the ridge of *Montsiá* (762m).

The road soon crosses the Ebro, bypasses **Amposta** (14,650 inhab.), and then passes (16km) **S. Carles de la Ràpita** (10,050 inhab.). Carlos III once planned to establish a great Mediterranean port here, sheltered by a lobe of the delta, but the project was abandoned after his death in 1788.

21km **Vinaròs** (17,750 inhab.), a fishing port on an open bay, is noted for its sturgeons and lampreys. (The Duc de Vendôme, Felipe V's commander at Villaviciosa in 1710, is said to have died here in 1712 from a surfeit of the local fish.) In April 1938 the Nationalist forces reached the Mediterranean at Vinaròs, cutting Republican Spain in two. The N232 climbs inland from here to **Morella**, 64km W; see Rte 75.

7km **Benicarló** (16,650 inhab.; Parador), once fortified. It has an 18C octagonal church tower and a dome covered with blue azulejos.

The imaginary dialogue in Azaña's 'La Velada de Benicarló' took place here.

The CS850 leads inland 7km to *Calíg*, and 7km beyond, *Cervera del Maestre*, both with medieval churches; near the latter are the ruins of the castle of *Montesa*.

A brief DETOUR may be made to (8km) **Peñiscola**, a fortified sea-girt promontory jutting out into the Mediterranean. Until comparatively recently it was only accessible from the mainland by a narrow sandspit, but the pressures of tourism have converted it into a 'picturesque' resort. It has been over exploited and many of its views have been obliterated by the erection of tower blocks.

A Phoenician settlement, it was named *Tyriche* from its resemblance to Tyre, and was later known to the Greeks as *Chersonesos*. Jaime el Conquistador took it from the Moors in 1234 and gave it to the Templars. Here, from his deposition by the Council of Constance in 1417 until his death in 1423, lived the schismatic pope Benedict XIII (Pedro de Luna, or 'Papa Luna'). In 1811 it withstood for 11 days a siege by the French under Suchet.

The over-restored **Castle** still contains imposing Gothic rooms. To the left of its entrance are the stables; to the right the guardhouse. Vaulted stairs ascend to a central platform. Above the stables is a vast hall and an adjacent chapel. Steps descend to the *Sala de Conclave*.

The parish church dates from 1739.—The main road is regained 6.5km NW, 6km from Benicarló.

The N340 and A7 turn away from a coastal ridge, with the *Atalayas de Alcalá* rising to the W, at 17km bypassing *Alcalá de Chisvert*, its 18C church with an octagonal belfry. The coast is regained at (26km) *Oropesa (del Mar)*, with castle ruins.—Several other resorts have been developed along the shore in recent decades on either side of *Benicasim*, bypassed. Behind these rises the pine-covered limestone ridge known as the DESIERTO DE LAS PALMAS, rising to 728m, hidden in which is an 18C monastery. The forest was damaged by fire in August 1985.

22km **Castelló de la Plana** (124,500 inhab.; 34,000 in 1920; 75,000 in 1960): although a provincial capital and a centre of citrus export, it is of slight interest. Several of its churches were gutted in 1936.

It was refounded here after its recapture from the Moors by Jaime I in 1233; the former town was further N. After fierce fighting in its suburbs the Nationalists took the place on 14 June 1938.

The diminutive Pl. Mayor, just W of the C. Mayor, is commanded by an octagonal belfry of 1604 adjacent to rebuilt *Sta. María* (1409–1549). The *Ayuntamiento* dates from 1716. The C. Caballeros leads N, in which a *Museum* contains paintings by *Ribalta*, *Ribera*, *Bermejo*, and others, and a collection of ceramics from *Alcora* (19km NW; see p 441).

6km E is the port of *El Grau*.

Continuing S, at 6km **Vila-real** (38,550 inhab.) is bypassed, founded on a grid plan in 1272 by Jaime I. Its principal church (1759) has an octagonal brick tower.

The C223 leads 14km W to **Onda** (17,400 inhab.). At 7km it passes N of *Betxi*, birthplace of Antonio Ponz (1725–92), author of the 18 vol. 'Viaje de España' (1784–94), the first important topographical guide to large areas of Spain. The parish church of Onda is 18C; *La Sangre* retains a Romanesque doorway. Here also is a ruined castle and ceramic museum. Beyond rises the SIERRA ESPADÁN (1101m).

6km SE of Vila-real is **Burriana** (25,100 inhab.), with remains of walls and a 16C church. Its adjacent port is mainly concerned with the export of oranges from the extensive groves in this area.

At 13km **Nules** (11,050 inhab.) is skirted; and 14km beyond is the ruined castle of *Almenara*, once a key to Valencia. Here Jaime I defeated the Moors in 1238.—On a neighbouring height there are remains of a Roman camp and temple.—A further succession of resorts and *playas* line the coast.—At *Benavites*, 3km SW, is a medieval tower incorporating a number of inscribed Jewish tombstones.

Ahead rises the acropolis of **SAGUNTO**, the town of which (55,300 inhab.) is entered at 9km.

Almost certainly an Iberian foundation, the name may come from a colony of Greeks from the island of Zacynthus, who are said to have allied themselves with Rome in the 3C BC. Excavations have exposed masonry of the type common at Emporion, which tends to confirm this. In 219 BC Hannibal attacked Saguntum and after a siege of eight months entered its citadel. Although recaptured by the Romans five years later, it never regained its importance—its red pottery and sailcloth were then reputed. It fell into decay, being later known simply as 'Muri veteres' (old walls).

The Moors, who built an alcázar on the castle hill, called it *Murbiter*, and the name *Murviedro* was in use until 1868, when the old name was revived. It put up a stubborn resistance to the French in 1812 until isolated by Suchet's defeat of Blake on the plain of Valencia. In 1874 it was the scene of Martínez Campos's *pronunciamento* which restored the Spanish Bourbons.

From the main road turn right past *S. Salvador*, a rebuilt Gothic church with a Romanesque door. Follow the C. Mayor past the Moorish *Puerta Ferrisa* and *S. Miguel*, with a doorway and azulejos of 1746, to the *Pl. Mayor*. Its arcades are partly supported by Roman columns taken from the ruins.

At the SW corner of the plaza is *Sta. María*, built in 1334 on the site of a mosque, and altered during the 18C. The N door has Gothic sculpture.—To the SE, in the C. de Tras Sagrario, are remains of the so-called *Temple of Diana*.

The C. del Castillo ascends to the **Roman Theatre** and a small museum. The theatre, long used as a rope-walk, was damaged by Suchet's troops in 1808, but still remains one of the better preserved theatre ruins still existing. It dates from the late 2C AD. The auditorium comprises 33 rows of seats divided into three tiers, still discernable, but the topmost gallery was destroyed in 1812. Little remains of the buildings of the stage and the orchestra except their foundations.

Continuing the ascent, a drawbridge is crossed to enter the **Castillo**, a series of fortified works occupying the ridge which dominates Sagunto.

Excavations carried out intermittently since 1921 have uncovered stretches of the Roman and pre-Roman masonry, but practically all the walls above ground level are of Moorish construction or later. To the left of the Pl. de Armas are further excavations, including a circular medieval mill resting on Roman foundations, with a large section of Iberian walls revealed beneath it.

Insignificant remains of a *Roman circus* lie beyond gardens N of the town centre; further N, near *Los Valles*, an Iberian sanctuary of Bacchic type has been discovered.

The most convenient approach to Valencia (27km S) is by the A7. At 5km it passes the ruined hilltop castle of *Entenza*. Below this, *Puig*, with a huge monastery, was the scene of Jaime el Conquistador's victory of 1238, which gave him the mastery of Valencia; the Gothic church contains the tomb of Bernard Guillén de Entenza, Jaime's uncle. For **Valencia** itself—the first view of which is an immense car cemetery—see Rte 77.

The old road continues past (4km) Entenza, through **Puçol** (11,550 inhab.), bypasses (left) *Puig*, and crosses several suburban villages, including *Meliana*, its Baroque church containing fine azulejos; and later reaches (left), the former monastery of *S. Miguel de los Reyes*, founded in 1371 and re-dedicated in 1546 for monks of the Hieronymite order. The church and dependencies date from c 1590–1644 and are from plans of Alonso de Covarrubias. It has been a prison since 1859.

Valencia is entered just E of the *Puente de S. José*.

B. Via the Motorway

260km (161 miles). A7. 74km **Tortosa** exit—107km **Castelló de la Plana** exit—56km **Sagunto** exit—23km **Valencia**.

Maps: M 443.

This is the recommended road, avoiding numerous villages and less interesting resorts, but with enough exits from which to approach the coast or interior.

Enter the motorway either due N or NW, before the airport. It runs more or less parallel to the N340 as far as the exit for **Tortosa**, 11km NW; see Rte 74. On crossing the Ebro (just beyond this exit), the A7 follows the valley to the W of the *Montsiá* ridge (762m). It bypasses (left) *Amposta*, before reaching the exit for (27km; right) *Ulldecona* and (11km SE of the A7) *Vinaròs*.

Ulldecona (5250 inhab.) has a ruined castle and a Gothic church with an octagonal tower and retablo by Sariñena.—A by-road ascends the valley of the Cenia to the W to (c 31km) the ruins of the Cistercian abbey of *Benifazar* (1276), with a nave of 1430–1518, a 13C chapterhouse, and a cloister completed in 1379. Further N rise the ranges known as the PUERTOS DE BESEIT (*Encanadé* to the NW; 1396m).

At 19km **Peñíscola** rises beyond the isthmus 6.5km SE. The motorway again runs parallel to the N340, bypassing (17km) *Alcalá de Chivert* before reaching (44km) the N entrance for **Castelló de la Plana**.—It circles W of *Vila-real*, with the SIERRA ESPANDÁN rising to the SW, and crosses extensive citrus groves, to follow the coast.—At 55km **Sagunto**, reached by an exit 7km S of the town, is bypassed, and **Valencia** is entered 23km beyond; see Rte 77.

The long-awaited Valencia bypass will bear SW from the Sagunto exit, circling to the W of *Paterna*, *Manises*, and *Torrent*, to rejoin the present A7 20km S of Valencia.

77 Valencia

Central Valencia is not easily approached, having a confusing system of one-way streets. On reaching the S bank of the Turia, park as near as possible to the NE side of the old city.

VALENCIA (744,750 inhab.; 247,000 in 1920; 504,000 in 1950) is the third largest town in Spain and still growing. The ancient capital of its kingdom, and now of the autonomy, it lies 4km inland from the port of *El Grao* in the midst of a fertile huerta watered by the Turia, now canalised around the S side of the city. It enjoys a fine climate, although in summer it is sultry. Two medieval gates have survived the demolition of the walls in the 1870s and there has been much more destruction in recent years in the interest of modernisation. Many of its churches were disfigured in the 17–18Cs and were seriously damaged in 1936. Much of the former enceinte has a down-at-heel appearance and has changed little since Augustus Hare condemned it over a century ago as 'a very concentration of dullness, stagnation, and ugliness'.

The Roman consul Decius Junius Brutus founded the city on the site of a Greek settlement c 139 BC and settled the defeated soldiers of the Lusitanian general Viriatus there. It was sacked by Pompey after his defeat of Sertorius in 75 BC, but was rebuilt as the Roman colony of *Valentia Edetanorum*. It fell to the Visigoths in 413, and to the Moors in 714.

In 1012 a grandson of Almanzor declared the city's independence, but it was retaken by the Almoravides in 1092. Meanwhile Alfonso VI of León, smarting under his own defeat at Zalaca in 1086 (q.v.), allied himself with the deposed king and despatched an army of Christians and Moors under The Cid to besiege it. After 20 months it was surrendered in 1094 and The Cid ruled it until his death in 1099. Jimena, his widow, was expelled two years later and the Moors re-occupied the place until the advance of Jaime el Conquistador in 1238.

For 400 years Valencia was one of the most flourishing cities of Spain. In 1407 the *Taula de Cambis* or bank of exchange and deposit was established; and in 1474 one of the first Spanish printing presses was set up (that of Benedict Monfort produced some imposing works in later years). But in the 17–18Cs its prosperity suffered severely after the expulsion of the Moriscos by Felipe III; and Felipe V slighted it for resisting his succession. In 1762 it was still a maze of 428 'streets', mostly unpaved, and the system of night watchmen (*serenos*) established by Joaquín Fos in 1777 was the first of its kind in a Spanish town. By 1800 its population was c 80,000.

In 1808 the citizens of Valencia rose against the French and under the government of Padre Rico repulsed the attack of Moncey; but in 1812 they capitulated to Suchet. In 1871 the mid-14C battlemented walk was pulled down to give employment to the poor. Valencians took an active part in the Republican movements of 1868, 1869, and 1873. In 1932–36 Valencia was the scene of extremist revolutionary activity, and it was a seat of the Republican government during the Civil War. It fell to the Nationalists on 30 March 1939.

It was from the Sto. Domingo barracks here that Gen. Milans del Bosch ordered his tanks onto the streets in the abortive coup of February 1981. The city experienced severe flooding in October 1982.

Prominent natives include the preacher Vicente Ferrer (1350–1419), one of many named after the saint martyred in Valencia in 304; Juan Luis Vives (1492–1540), friend of Erasmus and tutor of Mary Tudor; Luis Beltrán (1525–81), apostle of the Indies; Guillén de Castro (1569–1631), the playwright; the artists Vicente Juan Masip ('Juan de Joanes'; c 1510–79), Mariano Salvador Maella (1739–1819), Agustín Esteve (1735–c 1820), and Joaquín Sorolla (1863–1923); the engraver Tomás López Enguidanos (1773–1814); Ignacio Vergara (1715–76), the sculptor; Francisco Pérez Bayer (1714–94), the Hebraist and educationalist; Antonio de Cavanilles (1749–1804), the botanist; Vicente Salva (1786–1849), the bibliographer; and the novelist Vicente Blasco Ibáñez (1867–1928).

The Valencians indulge themselves with fireworks at their several *fiestas*. For example, during the *Fallas of S. José* in mid March they erect elaborate structures promoted by the toy manufacturers and set them alight in the streets to honour their patron saint.

The following description of the city is divided into three sections: the N half; the S part; and the *Museo de Bellas Artes*.

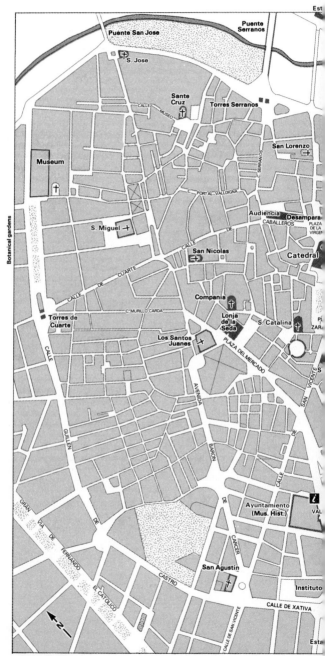

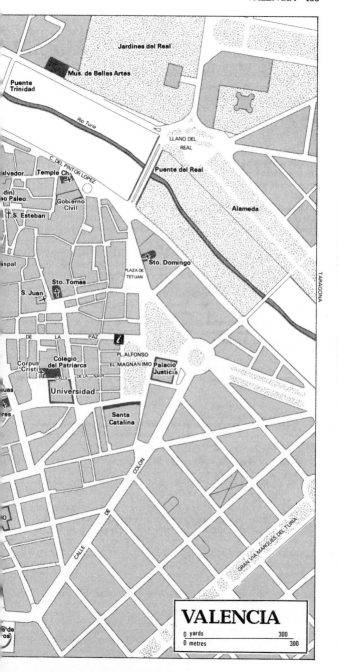

Jardines del Real

Mus. de Bellas Artes

Puente Trinidad

Rio Turia

C. DEL PINTOR LOPEZ

LLANO DEL REAL

Puente del Real

alvador

Temple Ch.

dini
o Paleo.

T.S. Esteban

Gobierno Civil

Alameda

aspal

Sto. Domingo

Sto. Tomas

PLAZA DE TETUAN

S. Juan

DE   LA   PAZ

PL.ALFONSO

Corpus Cristi

Colegio del Patriarca

EL-MAGNANIMO

Palacio Justicia

CALLE   DE LA   NAVE

uas

Universidad

res

Santa Catalina

COLON

CALLE   DE

GRAN VIA MARQUES DEL TURIA

TARAGONA

s de
os

VALENCIA

0 yards	300
0 metres	300

A. Northern Valencia

From the W end of the *Puente del Real* over the Turia—completed in 1598 and restored in 1683—follow the Paseo Pintor López NW past the *Gobierno Civil* and the *Temple* church. Both were originally parts of the Templars' Convent; the present building, of 1770, contains frescoes by José Vergara.

From the W side of the *Gobierno Civil*, follow a street past *S. Esteban* (1472–1515), decorated in the Churrigueresque style in 1689 by J.B. Pérez, to the old *Almudin* or public granary (14C; altered 1517). This is now occupied by the *Museo Paleontológico* with collections of extinct S. American fauna.—A few paces N is 16C *El Salvador*, with a 13C tower.

Continue past the Almudin to the circular Pl. de la Virgen. On the E side, connected to the cathedral by a bridge, is the chapel of *N.S. de los Desamparados* (the helpless; 1667). Of unpretentious exterior, its elliptical interior has been lavishly decorated by Vicente Gasco (1756); but the frescoes of 1701 by Palomino are weak. The present image is a copy of the original, carved in 1416 for the first lunatic asylum in Spain.

A walk around the cathedral, below the bridge, passes the *Pal. del Marqués del Campo*, and near the only genuine Gothic mansion surviving in the city, the *Casa del Almirante* (No. 14 in the C. del Palau, leading E). The *Archbishop's Palace* is connected to the cathedral by a vaulted footbridge. Adjacent is the 13C *Puerta del Palau*.

The Pl. de Zaragoza, S of the cathedral, provides a good view of the *Miguelete* or *Micalet* (1381–1429), with its octagonal bell tower. The *Cathedral itself stands on the site of a former mosque, occupying that of an early church, overlying a Roman temple of Diana. The present building was designed by Arnau Vidal and begun in 1262; was continued by Nicolás de Autun (or Ancona?; fl. 1303), and extended in 1480. Its first archbishop was Rodrigo Borja (Borgia; afterwards Pope Alexander VI). Its interior was partly Corinthianised in 1744–79 by Antonio Gilabert.

The *Portal 'de los Hierros'* adjoining the Miguelete is an unsuccessful Baroque experiment begun by the German Konrad Rudolf in 1703 and completed largely by Francisco Vergara in 1713. Skirting the W side of the cathedral, we regain the Pl. de la Virgen, where beneath a rose-window is the *Puerta de los Apóstoles* (1354; restored in the 15C), with mutilated sculptures. Here, since the 10C at least, the 'Tribunal de los Acequieros' or 'de las Aguas' took place: a court established to settle disputes connected with the irrigation of the *huerta*, presided over by eight peasant judges. No oaths were taken nor records kept (probably because the judges were illiterate), but their decisions were final.

The interior of the cathedral was vandalised in 1936. The sanctuary, decorated in Churrigueresque style by J.B. Pérez, contains walnut *Stalls* of 1604 carved by *Domingo Fernández Ayarza* and organs of 1513. On the N side is a late Gothic pulpit.

The 18C casing of the six southernmost columns of the nave have been removed to display the original Gothic masonry and ogival arches. Above these the old brick roof can be seen. Over the crossing is the cimborio (14C; but completed in 1430 by Martín Llobet), its windows filled with sheets of alabaster. The *High Altar* (accidentally burned in 1469 during a ceremony in which a dove bearing lighted tow represented the Holy Ghost) was restored in 1498 and modernised in 1862. The door panels of 1506 were painted by Hernán

Yáñez and Fernando Llanos. The baldacchino is made up from part of the destroyed trascoro.

Above the font to the left of the main door is a Baptism by Vicente Masip the Elder; on the other side a chapel contains the tombs of Diego de Covarrubias (died 1604) and his wife.

A passage leads to the old *Chapterhouse* (1369) with an octagonal vault. It contains chains taken from the port of Marseille by the Aragonese fleet in 1423, and the tomb of Abp Pérez de Ayala (died 1496). In the Gothic niches of the S wall there are alabaster reliefs of 1424 by the Florentine Giuliano (?da Poggibonsi). Above the altar is an agate chalice with gold handles and jewelled bands, claimed to be the 'Holy Grail'. It was brought here in 1437 from S. Juan de la Peña (q.v.). Of Roman origin, it bears traces of alterations in the 9C, 15C and 16C. Paintings by Juan de Joanes and others of the Valencian School are displayed along the walls, together with an Incredulity of St. Thomas by Andrés Marzal de Sax.

The first chapel in the right aisle has a reja of 1647 and part of the original alabaster high altar. Paintings by Maella and Goya in the next chapel illustrate the life of S. Francisco Borja. In the S transept is the tomb of Ausias March (died 1459), the Catalan poet. The panels from the organs, carved in 1513 by Luis Muñoz to designs by F. Yáñez, are now in the Ambulatory. Off this is the well-vaulted *Sacristy*, entered beneath a Christ bearing the Cross by Ribalta.

In the third chapel of the left aisle as we return is the tomb of St. Louis d'Anjou, Bishop of Toulouse (1274–97), and a S. Sebastían by Orrente. Leading off this chapel is the *Treasury*, containing a gold *Portapaz or ciborium by Benvenuto Cellini, embellished with coloured enamels; a pyx by Bartolomé Coscolla (1398); parts of the retablo of SS. Cosmas and Damian by Yáñez and Llanos; a Bible annotated by S. Vicente Ferrer; Renaissance jewellery, and cult objects.

The pedestrian C. Navellos leads N past Churrigueresque *S. Lorenzo*, designed by José Mingues, with a fine tower, to reach the Turia. Turn left to the **Torres de Serranos**, a town gate of 1398 by Pedro Balaguer, and to the *Puente de Serranos*, the oldest bridge in Valencia, rebuilt in 1518. Despite Swinburne's remark in the 1770s that the river contained 'scarce enough water . . . to wash a hand-kerchief', it was subject to sudden floods and has been canalised recently to the W and S of the city, and its former bed has been partly laid out with gardens.

From the Pl. de los Fueros, just S of the gate, the C. de Roteros leads W to *Sta. Cruz*; its Classical façade is by Gaspar de Santmartí. Further W are the dependencies of the *Conv. del Carmen* (suppressed 1835), now the *Escuela de Bellas Artes*, with remains of 13C work and a Renaissance cloister.

The C. de Serranos leads SW to the Pl. de Manises, flanked by 16C–17C mansions, and the Baroque tower of *S. Bartolomé* (rebuilt by J.B. Pérez in 1683). On the S side is the old *Audiencia or *Pal. de la Generalidad*, a restored building of 1481–1510 by Pedro Compte. The tower by Gaspar Gregori dates from 1518–79. Two rooms on the entresol have elaborate ceilings of 1535; on the first floor the *Salon de las Cortes* is embellished with mural canvases of 1593, mainly by Juan Sariñena, Vicente Mestre, and Francisco Pozzo, representing the assembly of the Provincial Estates. Below runs a dado of azulejos (1574), and above is a gallery supported on elaborately carved shafts (1566). The artesonado ceiling was completed in 1566.

The C. de Caballeros has several señorial houses and curious patios. It leads W, passing (left, in the C. Abadia) **S. Nicolás**, built on the site of a mosque in the 14C, enlarged in 1455, and transformed by J.B. Pérez in 1693. Its vault has a fresco of 1697 by Dionis Vidal, aided by his master, Palomino. The tower was added in 1755.

The church contains a Crucifixion by Rodrigo de Osona the Elder (1476), a Last Supper and eight smaller paintings by Macip, and other works of his school; in the *Sacristy* are heads of Christ and of the Virgin by Macip, and a 15C chalice.

The C. de Caballeros is extended by the C. de Cuarte, leading to the **Torres de Cuarte**, the second survivor of the town gates. It was built in 1441–60 by Pedro Bonfill in the style of the Castel Nuovo at Naples, and retains marks of the French sieges of 1808 and 1812.

Beyond (right) is the JARDÍN BOTÁNICO, founded in 1633 and moved here in 1802; further W (left) is *S. Sebastián* (1739), remarkable only for its azulejos.

From the Torres de Cuarte, the C. Murillo Carda leads SE to the *Pl. del Mercado* (formerly the scene of bullfights, tournaments, and executions). On the N side is *Los Santos Juanes*, built in 1368, rebuilt by Vicente García in 1603–28, and with a Churrigueresque front added in 1700. The interior, gutted in 1936, has been restored.

Further W is *S. Joaquín* (1771; by José Puchol), containing sculptures by Ignacio Vergara.

NE of the Market is the ***Lonja de la Seda** (Silk Exchange), built in 1498 by Pedro Compte and Juan de Iborra. A low square tower divides the Gothic façade into two parts, one with an ogee-crowned doorway, windows with elaborate tracery (restored), and the escutcheon of Aragón; the other half has square-headed windows and an elaborate upper gallery of 1498–1548 begun by Compte.

Inside is the *Salon de Contratación, its roof supported by eight twisted columns and 16 pilasters without capitals. A door on the left admits to the spiral staircase ascending to an upper room containing a magnificent artesonado ceiling of 1427 made by Juan Llobet and Andrés Tanón for the Sala Daurada of the old Ayuntamiento.

Behind the Lonja is *La Compañía*, containing a Conception (1578) by Juan de Joanes.

A pedestrian alley (C. de Trench) leads left from the S end of the Pl. del Mercado. It passes (right) the circular Pl. Redonda to 14C *Sta. Catalina*, with a hexagonal tower (1705) by J.B. Viñes. The Pl. de Zaragoza can be reached a short distance beyond.

B.   Southern Valencia

From the Pl. de Zaragoza the C.S. Vicente leads SW past *S. Martín*, a Gothic shell of 1372 masked by Baroque decoration. Over the doorway (1740; by F. Vergara) is a bronze equestrian statue of the saint dividing his cloak (1494; attributed to Piers de Backer, a Fleming).

An alley just S of the church leads past the 18C **Pal. del Marqués de Dos Aguas**, a remarkable Baroque mansion with a grotesque *Portal. Built in 1744, it is supported by crouching figures designed by Hipólito Rovira and carved in white translucent alabaster by Ignacio Vergara. The palace contains a *Ceramic Museum* complementary to that in the Ayuntamiento. The tiled kitchen is notable.

In the area just to the N, and on either side of the C. de la Paz, was the ancient Judería of Valencia.

Turning S, we pass *S. Andrés* (1602–84), with a Baroque doorway attributed to J.B. Pérez.—A few steps to the E is part of the *University* (founded in 1499), occupying an early 19C building enclosing a Doric courtyard.

One of the treasures of its Library is a copy of 'Les Trobes', the first book of any consequence printed in Spain. In the chapel (1737) there is a retablo (1516) by Nicolás Falcó.

To the N stands the **Col. del Patriarca** (1586–1610; by Guillem del Rey) with a two-storeyed Renaissance patio. It was founded by Juan de Ribera (1533–1611), a persecutor of the Moriscos; he is buried in the S transept of the adjoining church. On the right of the entrance is the dark *Cap. de la Concepción*, with 16C Flemish tapestries and paintings by Sariñena. The *Museo* on the first floor contains works by Macip, Morales, El Greco, Ribalta, Correggio, Piombo, and Dirk Bouts (a small copy of his triptych at Granada).

At the SW corner of the building is **Corpus Cristi**, with a Vision of S. Vicente Ferrer by Ribalta in the first N chapel; also a Last Supper by the same artist above the high altar of 1603.

A few minutes' walk to the SW brings one to the PL. DEL PAÍS VALENCIANO, on the W side of which is the *Ayuntamiento* (1763), with a modern façade.

It contains the *Museo Histórico*, and *Archaeological* and *Ceramic collections*. The latter comprise good representative examples of Paterna and Manises wares and interesting pieces recovered in the excavation of early kilns.

Further S is the *Estación del Norte*. Almost opposite it is a former *Jesuit college* surmounted by a Baroque cupola of 1721. To the W is *S. Agustín* (14C; restored).

The C. Barcas and then the C. Pintor Sorolla lead E from the Pl. del País Velenciano to the Pl. Alfonso el Magnanimo. On its E side stands the *Pal. de Justicia* (1768–1802; by Felipe Rubio), which served as a customhouse until 1828, and then as a tobacco factory until 1910.—Continuing N, skirting the Glorieta de Gómez Ferrer, we reach the triangular Pl. de Tetuán.

On its E side is **Sto. Domingo**, founded in 1239, with a church of 1781 containing frescoes by José Vergara. The tower has a double spiral staircase. The Gothic *Cap. de los Reyes* (1437–62) by Francisco Baldomar and Pedro Compte has a ribless vault and contains the tombs of Rodrigo Mendoza (died 1554) and his wife. The late 15C Gothic *Cloister* and *Chapterhouse* may be viewed with a permit from the adjacent *Capitanía*.

A short distance W from the SW corner of the plaza is *Sto. Tomás*, with a Baroque façade (1736) by Ignacio Vergara. Just beyond stands restored *S. Juan del Hospital*, built in 1316 by the Knights of St. John of Jerusalem. The interior has remains of decoration (1685) by J.B. Pérez.—Close by is the early Gothic *Chapel of the Knights* and, on the other side of the street, the priests' hospice of 1356, with an 18C staircase and good azulejos.—Further on is the Churrigueresque *Cap. del Milagros* (1686), with azulejos of c 1700. A few paces NW are remains of the Moorish *Baños del Almirante* (11C–12C).

Immediately N of the Pl. de Tetuán is the *Puente del Real*.

C. The Museo de Bellas Artes

On crossing to the N bank of the bed of the Turia by the Puente del Real and turning left, we skirt the JARDINES DEL REAL to reach the dependencies of a Baroque convent (designed by J.B. Pérez) now housing the *Museo de Bellas Artes*.

It is particularly rich, as might be expected, in paintings of the Valencian School, largely collected from suppressed convents. From the vestibule we enter the *Cloister*, containing reliefs and other sculptures of various periods. In the floor of **R6** is set a large mosaic of the Nine Muses from Moncada; near by crouches the 5–4C BC Iberian Lioness of Bocairente. Other rooms and galleries display medieval sculpture and more modern works, including several by Mariano Benlliure (1862–1947).

R24 (on the First Floor) is the first of a range devoted to medieval painting.—**R25** *Jaime Bacó*, or *Jacomart*, Santiago and S. Gil; *Maestro del Grifo*, Altarpiece of the life of S. Vicente Ferrer (c 1500); *Felipe Pablo*, Panels from the retablo mayor of Sto. Domingo (1523), with scenes from the life of St. Dominic; *J.J. de Espinosa*, Jerónimo Mos.—**R28** *Rodrigo de Osona the Younger*, Christ before Pilate; *Rodrigo Osona the Elder*, Pietà; attributed to *Juan Reixach*, Panels and predella of the retablo of the Virgin, from Portacoeli.—**R21** *Maestro de Bonastre*, Annunciation; Altarpiece of Fray Bonifacio Ferrer (c 1400), formerly attributed to *Lorenzo Zaragoza*, but more likely the work of an Italian painting in Spain; *Maestro de los Marti de Torres* (?Gonzalo Pérez), Altarpiece of S. Martín, Sta. Ursula, and S. Antonio Abad; *Maestro de Gil y de Pujades*, History of the Cross, formerly attributed to *Pedro Nicolau*.—**R30** *Hieronymus Bosch*, Triptych (Passion Scenes); *Pupil of Fernando de Llanos*, Holy Family (c 1500); *Pinturicchio*, Virgin and Child with Bp Juan Borja, the donor.—**R33** Altarpiece from the Ermita de Puebla Larga, attributed to the *School of Andrés Marzal and Pedro Nicolau* (c 1430); *Maestro de Artés*, The Last Judgement (c 1500).—**R32** *?Nicolás Falcó*, with sculptures by *Damián Forment*, Retablo from the Conv. de la Puridad; *Maestro de Perea*, Adoration (c 1491); *Maestro de Martínez Vallejo*, Virgin and Child.

R34 contains several works by *Juan de Joanes*: El Salvador (two examples) Mystic betrothal of Sta. Inés with the Ven. Agnesio (c 1553), Ecce Homo, SS. Vicente Ferrer and Vincente Martyr.—**R35** *Nicolás Borrás*, Holy Family.—**R36** *Hernán Yáñez de la Almedina*, Resurrection.—**R37** *Ribalta*: S. Isidro Labrador, S. Juan Evangelista, S. Agustín, Last Supper, S. Bruno, S. Pablo, S. Pedro.—**R39** *Van Dyck*, Francisco de Moncada.—**R40** *El Greco*, The Baptist; *Ribera*, S. Sebastián; *Murillo*, ?Portrait of an unknown man.

RR41–46 and **55–56** form the upper gallery of the cloister: *Damián Forment*, carved alabaster altarpiece; *Gaspar Requena* and *Pedro Rubiales*, altarpiece from the Conv. de la Puridad (1540); *J.J. de Espinosa*, St. Peter of Nola interceding for two friars; *Velázquez*, Self-portrait; *Goya*, Children's games, Portraits of his brother-in-law (Francisco Bayeu), of Joaquina Candado (Goya's housekeeper), and of Rafael Esteve (the Valencian engraver); *Orizonte*, Landscapes; *José Avrial*, Pl. de la Paja, Madrid; *Vicente López*, Portraits of Carlos IV, Josefa Ortiz, and Manuel Monfort.—The second and third floors contain a miscellaneous collection of more modern works.

There is little of interest to see in the immediate vicinity of Valencia. Its port of *El Grao*, 4km E, has remains of the medieval shipyard or *Atarazanas* (five arcaded ranges begun in 1331 and rebuilt in 1410).

Not far S of the NIII (for Madrid), before reaching the airport, is *Alaquàs*, with the *Pal. de la Casta* (1584), a huge hollow square with towers at the angles: its Baroque church of 1694 has a retablo of 1600 with sculpture by Esteve Bonet and paintings by Cristóbal Lloréns.— Further S is **Torrent** (51,750 inhab.). Its *Ayuntamiento* incorporates a castle keep and a church containing Gothic paintings and a Baroque retablo.

N of the NIII are **Manises** and **Paterna** (on the far bank of the Turia), with a combined population of 57,350 inhab. The former was famous under the Moors for its metallic lustreware and is still a centre for the manufacture of majolica and glazed tiles. Green and blue pottery is produced at Paterna, which retains an old *Palace* and medieval watch-tower.—12km NW of Manises is *Ribarroja del Turia*, with a medieval castle, and near by, the extensive ruins of Roman *Pallantia*, known as *Valencia la Vella*.—**Burjassot** (35,700 inhab.), E of Paterna, is a former centre of silk production and has subterranean granaries (1573) in the Arab style covered with a flagged walk. The 15C *Castillo del Patriarca* has artesonado ceilings; and the church contains early paintings.

For roads from Valencia to **Madrid**, see Rte 46; for **Teruel** and **Zaragoza**, Rte 73; for **Tarragona**, Rte 76: all these in reverse. For **Alicante** and **Murcia**, see Rte 78; for **Almansa**, **Albacete**, and **Úbeda**, Rte 82.

78   Valencia to Murcia via Alicante

A.   Via the N332 and the Coast

265km (164 miles). N332. 40km. *Cullera* is 2km NE—25km **Gandía**—25km. **Denia** is 8km E—8.5km *Gata*. *Jávea* is 8km E—21.5km *Calpe*—11km **Altea**—10.5km *Benidorm*—10km *Villajoyosa*—32km **Alicante**—N340. 24km **Elche**—33.5km **Orihuela**—24km **Murcia**.

Maps: M 445.

This route can be easily combined with Rte 74B. The A7 should be taken from a point just before Altea to Alicante.

VALENCIA TO CULLERA VIA THE COAST (40km). The V15 crosses the canalised Turia to the SE of the centre and skirts sand hills through *El Saler*. It passes the freshwater lagoon of **La Albufera** (Arabic *el-buhera*), bounded on its landward side by rice fields. Between the lagoon and the sea is the narrow pine-clad bar called LA DEHESA, pierced by two outlets. It abounds in waterfowl and fish, particularly eels, but the area is in grave danger of being spoiled by coastal developers. The title of Duc d'Albufera was bestowed on Marshal Suchet in 1812.—At 18km a Parador is passed, then several small villages are traversed before we turn left to the *Faro de Cullera* on its rocky headland and follow the bay to the centre of old **Cullera** (20,350 inhab.), dominated by its ruined castle. The road crosses the Júcar at its mouth to meet the N332 2km beyond.

The N332 drives S from Valencia, bypassing *Silla*, with an 18C church and *Ayuntamiento* in its former castle. It then veers SE, skirting the lagoon of **La Albufera** (see above) to (32.5km) **Sueca** (24,350 inhab.) and crosses the Júcar just W of *Cullera*; see above.

18.5km *Tabernas de Valldigna* (right) is known for its strawberries. Beyond it the ruined *Castle of S. Juan* is passed before entering (14km) **Gandía** (48,550 inhab.). This ancient town, 4km from the mouth of the Serpis and the resort of *Grao de Gandía*, provided the ducal title for the Borja family. It was the birthplace of the Catalan poet Ausias March (1395–1459). Parts of its walls survive. The *Pal. de los Duques* (16C and 18C) was the birthplace and residence of S. Francisco Borja (1510–72), the fourth Duke of Gandía and a superior of the Jesuit Order. It is now a Jesuit college and contains some azulejos of note, including a Manises tiled floor of the Elements. The first Jesuit college in Spain was established at Gandía in 1547. Close by is the 14C–16C *Colegiata* and to the SE the *Ayuntamiento* (1781). The *Escuelas Pías*, at the S end of the town, was founded by Francisco Borja in 1546; it was rebuilt in 1788. *S. José* contains Baroque altars and the *Conv. de Sta. Clara* has paintings by Pablo de S. Leocadio.

8km **Oliva** (20,100 inhab.), birthplace of the author and savant Gregorio Mayans y Siscar (1699–1781), has a notable 16C palace. —At *Pego*, 9km S, there is an early 17C church with a tower of 1700 and good retablos.—A mountain road beyond Pego crosses the jagged sierra to the *Coll de Rates* (540m;

view) before descending to (43km) *Callosa* (see below). The huerta S of Oliva is rich in orange groves, and it is also known for its muscatel grapes, dried to make Valencia *pasas* (raisins).

At 10km one can turn left to follow the coast road to *Denia*; or alternatively at *Ondara*, 7km beyond. Ahead rises the conical peak of *Mongó* (753m). **Denia** (21,900 inhab.), situated between this isolated mountain and the sea, is an Iberian foundation and was probably colonised by Greeks; the latter called it *Hemeroskopeion* from its position commanding the coast (or *Artemision*, after the temple of Artemis which stood below the castle hill).

Its present name is derived from Roman *Dianium*, whose harbour, now silted up, was chosen by Sertorius as a naval base. Its prosperity increased under the Moors, and the Aragonese captured it only after having erected a castle on the hill of *S. Nicolás* (1244). In the 11C it was the residence of the Jewish poet Isaac ben Reuben. A decline set in with the expulsion of the Moriscos. It was twice besieged in 1707–08 during the War of the Succession and twice bombarded during the Peninsular War. In 1813 the French garrison was blockaded here for eight months.

Little remains of ancient Denia apart from battered ramparts and castle ruins. The *Ayuntamiento* of 1612 was restored in 1877; *Sta. María* dates from 1734.

A road climbs round the SE flank of the *Mongó*, easily climbed for the view; in clear weather it is possible to see the Balearic island of Ibiza, c 135km E. The road then descends steeply to (10km) **Jávea** (10,900 inhab.; Parador), between the *Cabo de S. Antonio* and *Cabo S. Martín*. The town, once walled, retains some old houses and a fortified *church* (1513) designed by Domingo de Urteaga. An interesting modern church in the shape of a ship's hull is nearer the port. There are stalactite caves in the neighbourhood. Much of the local building stone is quarried from the tide-washed rocks.—Further SE rises the *Cabo de la Nao*, the nearest point of the mainland to the Balearics.

The main route may be regained at *Gata*, 8km W of Jávea; or at *Calpe*, 14km S, beyond *Moraira*, a small resort with a ruined castle.—8.5km *Gata de Gorgo*. —*Jávea* (see above) is 8km E.

Follow a short defile to (11km) **Benissa** (7050 inhab.), with a fortified church, and veer S towards the *Peñon de Ifach*, rising dramatically from the sea to 332m. At its base is (10km) **Calpe** (8050 inhab.), a village with a Mudéjar church, but spoiled by development.—The road crosses the SIERRA DE BERNIA, which here juts out into the sea, to (8km) *Olla de Altea*, where the motorway is joined.

A road climbs inland to (10.5km) *Callosa de Ensarria* (7100 inhab.); 10km beyond, on the steeply ascending C3313, is the *Castle of Guadalest*, perched picturesquely on a crag above its village, and entered only through a rock-hewn tunnel.—4km S of Callosa is *Polop*, with a ruined castle, from which one may descend to the coast at *Altea* or *Benidorm*, 11km S.

At 3km **Altea** (11,150 inhab.), an attractively sited resort, dominated by its blue-domed church. It is protected from the S by the SIERRA HELADA and from the N and W by more conspicuous ranges (BERNIA, to the N at 1129m; CAMPANA, to the W at 1410m; and the SIERRA DE ALTANA to the NW, rising to 1558m).

The N332 continues SW to (10.5km) **Benidorm**—also bypassed— now with a resident population of 25,000 (12,000 in 1970), which rises dramatically during the long season. It was once a small port for fishing and for goods smuggled into Alicante. The old village standing on a promontory defended by a castle and fortifications now commands a disenchanting view of hotels and apartment blocks strung out along the *playas*, the stamping ground of package tourists throughout the year.

10km **Villajoyosa** (20,750 inhab.), another resort which belies its name, retains a Gothic church and some walls. To the NW rises the SIERRA DE CABEZÓN (1207m).—At 17km a left fork leads along the shore to (10km) *Playa de S. Juan* (9800 inhab.), 7km E of Alicante.

Ahead, on a commanding height, is the *Castillo de Sta. Bárbara* (see below), skirted as we cross the E suburbs to approach the waterfront of (15km) Alicante.

ALICANTE (245,950 inhab.; 63,000 in 1920; 102,000 in 1950), a provincial capital and once the strongest fortress in the kingdom of Valencia, is an active and growing commercial port, but contains few buildings of interest. It is still visited for its pleasant winter climate; in summer, although torrid, it is not scourged by the parching *leveche* of Murcia.

It is said to occupy the site of Roman *Lucentum* but it played only a small part in history until 1706, when it was attacked from the sea by Sir John Leake and defended by Gen. Daniel O'Mahony. In December 1708 it was besieged by Felipe V's French troops, commanded by d'Asfeld, who in the following March blew up the castle together with the English garrison—commanded by Gen. John Richards.

It was long the residence of an English merchant colony, importing 'all sorts of bale goods, corn, and Newfoundland cod', and exporting wine and barilla. It was garrisoned by English troops throughout the Peninsular War. In 1844 an insurrection led by Pantaleón Bonet was brutally quelled and the ringleaders shot without trial. The last (6th) Earl Powerscourt died here in 1875.

During the Civil War Alicante was a Republican centre. José Antonio Primo de Rivera (1903–36), founder and martyr of the Falange, a reactionary fascist organisation, was incarcerated in the Dominican convent (then a prison). After a hurried trial he was shot by the local bosses before the sentence could have been commuted by the Government. The poet Miguel Hernández (1910–42) was allowed to die of neglect in Alicante's gaol during Franco's regime.

It was the birthplace of Gabriel Miró (1879–1930), the novelist.

Most roads converge on the palm-lined EXPLANADA DE ESPAÑA skirting the harbour, parallel to which a tessellated promenade has been laid between these trees. The Pl. Puerto del Mar at the E end leads into the old BARRIO DE STA. CRUZ to the Pl. del Ayuntamiento, with the *Ayuntamiento* itself, a Churrigueresque building of 1696–1760 with two square towers.—Turn left and pass through an archway to the pedestrian C. Mayor; just N is **S. Nicolás de Bari** (1616–62), with a well-proportioned dome and galleries surrounding the apse and sides. The interior is a good example of the Herreran style, gutted in 1936 but now restored. The *Cloister* and a chapel left of the entrance contain Churrigueresque decoration.

The C. Jorge Juan leads E from the Ayuntamiento, from which steps ascend to Gothic *Sta. María*, with a Baroque W front and towers of 1720.—The neighbouring *Casa de la Asegurada* houses a collection of abstract art and sculpture donated to the city by Eusebio Sempere (born in 1924 at Onil, 31km NW).

The C. Jorge Juan skirts the Paseo Ramiro to reach the Paseo de Gomiz, and the entrance to the *ascensor* to the **Castillo de Sta. Bárbara**, extensive fortifications crowning the summit of an isolated hill dominating the town and providing panoramic views. The lower *Castillo de S. Fernando*, rebuilt during the Peninsular War, is now a ruin. A path leads down the hill's N and W slopes to Sta. María. The castle can also be approached by car from a turning off the Valencia road.

The modern town lies W of the Rambla Méndez Núñez. Parallel to it, further W, is the Paseo de Federico Soto, at the N end of which is the circular Pl. de los Luceros. W of this is the *Diputación*, housing the *Museo Arqueológico*.

ALICANTE TO CARTAGENA (110km). The N332 bears left off the N340 after 7km to (13km) **Sta. Pola** (12,000 inhab.), near which are the remains of the necropolis of *Ilici*, which has yielded a quantity of Iberian and Roman relics. (Offshore is the small island of *Tabarca*, with restored 18C fortifications.) The road beyond, after skirting salt pans (the haunt of flamingos), passes numerous coastal developments, including (17.5km) *Guadamar* (5700 inhab.), which overlooks the mouth of the Segura and (13.5km) **Torrevieja** (12,300 inhab.), seriously damaged by the earthquake of 1829.—After (25km) **S. Javier** (12,650 inhab.), with an *Airforce Academy*, the road skirts the W shore of the MAR MENOR, a shallow salt lagoon c 19km long and 11km broad. It has several small islands and is separated from the Mediterranean by narrow spits of land flanked by dunes. On the S spit is the extensive modern development of *La Manga*; just beyond is the *Cabo de Palos*.—This can be approached by turning left at 19.5km, 3.5km before entering **La Unión** (14,250 inhab.), the centre of an unattractive mining region whose zinc and silver-laden lead mines were worked by both Carthaginians and Romans. Turn W here parallel to the coastal ridge to (11km) *Cartagena*; see Rte 80.

The N340 bears right after 7km and skirts the airport. At 17km **ELCHE** or **Elx** (164,800 inhab.; 12,300 in 1920; 73,000 in 1960), is bypassed to the S. Its main curiosity, when entered from the E, is the exotic **Palm Forest**, the only example of its kind in Europe, which extends around three sides of the old nucleus on the E bank of the Vinalopó; see below.

Probably of Iberian origin, it was an important settlement of the Graeco-Phoenicians called *Helike*; to the Romans it was known as *Colonia Julia Ilici Augusta*. The 'Dama de Elche' (now in the Archaeological Museum, Madrid), a remarkable stone bust discovered at *La Alcudia* (S of the centre) in 1897, is attributed to an Iberian sculptor of the 5C BC. A mosaic floor with Latin inscriptions was found on the same estate in 1959. Elche was a centre of anarchism during the early stages of the Civil War, and later a Communist HQ.

In the centre of the old town is blue-domed *Sta. María*, begun in 1673 but reconstructed after 1936. It retains its Baroque portal by Nicolás de Busi.—To the W and S are two towerhouses.—To the N is the 15C *Pal. de Altamira*, and beyond it a park with a small *Museum* containing a life-size stone lioness of the 4C BC.

The 17C *Ayuntamiento*, in the Corredora S of Sta. María, has a vaulted gateway incorporating part of the original building of 1444.—*El Salvador*, to the SE, contains a good 18C retablo.

A few minutes' walk E of the latter is the *Huerta del Cura*, with the curious *Palmera Imperial*, an old male palm with seven smaller stems clustered round the main trunk; it is so-named after a visit by the Empress Elisabeth of Austria. The Huerta is one of a series of separate plantations (*palmerales* or *huertas*), many unenclosed, with over 125,000 date palms (18–24m high) planted alongside canals of brackish water which are fed by a reservoir further up the Vinalopó.

Only the female palms bear fruit (about November); they are fertilised, often artificially, by the pollen of the male trees, which flower in May. Besides the fertile date palms, the male trees and barren female trees are valuable for their 'palms' or *ramilletes*, used on Palm Sundays. The branches intended for this purpose are bound up and concealed from the light so that they become bleached; each tree can produce about ten 'palms' every fourth year.

9.5km **Crevillente** (20,950 inhab.), with a reputation for its hemp-fibre mats.

At 9km a brief DETOUR S leads through *Cox*, with a ruined castle, and **Callosa**

de Segura (14,500 inhab.), with a Gothic hall-church of 1553, the main road being regained just before Orihuela.

12km **ORIHUELA** (50,100 inhab.), an old cathedral town astride the Segura but largely rebuilt after the earthquake of 1829. Unfortunately, more recent building has caused much of its unspoilt atmosphere to be dispersed. It claims to be the Visigothic *Orcelis*, but the name is more likely to be derived from Roman *Aurariola*. It is the 'Oleza' of Gabriel Miró's novels and was the birthplace of the poet Miguel Hernández (1910–42; cf. Alicante). Its *Huerta*, irrigated by the Segura, is notably fertile, as attested by the proverb: 'Llueva ó no llueva, trigo en Orihuela' (Rain or no rain, corn in Orihuela).

Bearing left off the N340 the centre is approached through a palm grove which leads past a gate adjacent to the *Col. de Sto. Domingo*, with a fine façade. This former *University* was begun in 1552 by Juan Anglés for Bp Loaces and continued by Agustín Bernaldino in the 17C. The stairs and refectory (with good azulejos) and the two cloisters are of this period. The adjoining Baroque *Church* (1659) by Pedro Quintana has a richly decorated ceiling.

The C. de S. Juan leads past the *Conv. de S. Juan* to the C. de Loaces, and then crosses the Segura. It soon reaches the Glorieta de Gabriel Miró and a park providing a view of the ruined *Castle* on its height and of the hillside *Seminario de S. Miguel* (18C).

Just N of the Glorieta, the C. de S. Pascual leads left. After crossing another bridge turn left to *Sta. Justa* (1319–48) with a dome and tower of c 1500 and unfinished Baroque front.—Beyond is the *Salesas*, bearing headless statues by Santiago Baglietto, a Genoese, and containing paintings by Vicente López and others.—*El Carmen*, set back in a small square, contains a Virgin by Salzillo.—To the N is *Santiago*, with a late Gothic front and nave, and a transept of 1554–1609.

The C. de Santiago is prolonged beyond *N.S. de Monserrate* (1748) and past (right) the *Capuchinos*, with a retablo by Esteve Bonet and a statue of S. Félix de Cantalicio by Salzillo, to reach the Murcia road.

From Sta. Justa one can approach the C. Mayor, at the E end of which is the 18C *Pal. Episcopal*, with a shady courtyard. Opposite it stands the *****Cathedral** (1305–55), with a remarkable transept (c 1500) having a vault with spirally twisted ribs. The N front (c 1550) is attributed to Jerónimo Quijano; the W and S doorways (*Puerta de la Cadenas* and *Puerta de Loreto*) are Gothic. The ambulatory chapels were added after the church was raised to cathedral rank in 1564. It contains a fine sillería, an untouched organ of c 1720, and good rejas, but many of its paintings were lost in the 1829 earthquake.

To the E is a small two-storey *Cloister* (open to the street), transferred here from the damaged *Conv. de la Merced* after the Civil War. The *Diocesan Museum* contains a Temptation of St. Thomas by Velázquez and Alonso Cano, works by Morales and by Ribera, and a processional Custodia.

To the N and in the C. Sta. Lucía (further E) are a number of old buildings. The C. Alfonso XIII leads back to the C. de Loaces, passing the Public Library and Archives, housed in the former *Palace of the Conde de Luna*. It also contains the curious *paso* known as 'La Diablesa', by Nicolás de Busi. To the E of this quarter, near the river, is *La Trinidad*, with a relief (1580) over the W door.

At 19km the main road skirts *Monteagudo*, a rocky height crowned

by a Moorish castle incorporating Roman remains, to enter **Murcia**
5km beyond; see Rte 80.

B.   Via the Motorway

256km (159 miles). A7.

Maps: M 445.

The motorway, a faster route, is entered c 12km S of Valencia, but
another entry is planned from the V15 leading SE from the city
towards *El Saler*. It will eventually be joined by the bypass circling to
the W from a point not far S of Sagunto.

The motorway bears away from the N332 to cross the Júcar, and
meets it again SW of *Cullera* to run roughly parallel to it, but further
inland, to a point 10km NE of *Alicante*. A bypass to Alicante is under
way which will meet the N340 not far E of *Elche*; beyond this follow
the main road to *Murcia*.

The A7 is provided with exits to most of the main resorts on this
coast: *Gandía*, *Oliva*, *Denia* and *Jávea*, *Benissa* (for *Calpe*), *Olla de
Altea* (for *Altea*), *Benidorm*, *Villajoyosa*, and *Alicante* itself.

C.   Via Xàtiva, and Alcoy

244km (151 miles). N340. 57km **Xàtiva**—50km **Alcoy**—55km
Alicante—82km **Murcia**.

Maps: M 445.

This is a slower road—particularly between Xàtiva and Alicante—
but more interesting and providing numerous attractive views.

The N340 drives S before circling to the W around *Silla*; at 22km it
passes 3km W of *Benifaio*, with two Moorish towers, and then
bypasses *Alginet*, its *Ayuntamiento* in a 16C palace.—11km
L'Alcudia.

8.5km SE is **Alzira** (38,350 inhab.), Roman *Sucro* and Moorish *El Gezira*,
originally on an island of the Júcar. *Sta. Maria* and *Sta. Catalina* are part Gothic;
S. Agustin contains old paintings; the *Ayuntamiento* (1561) contains a good
artesonado.—Further E, in a valley of the SIERRA DE LA MURTA, are the ruins of a
Hieronymite convent.

The main road skirts (10km) **Alberique** (8950 inhab.), with a church
dated 1701, and crosses the Júcar 5km beyond; it passes castle ruins
(left) before reaching the turning for *Xàtiva* (7km beyond).—For the
road (N430) to *Almansa*, 56km SW, see Rte 82.

6km **XÀTIVA**, or **Játiva** (23,900 inhab.), a well-sited town which
in Ford's estimation was 'one of the most picturesque towns in Spain,
not excepting Granada'. It has been famous for paper making since
1150 and must have been one of the first places in Europe where
paper was manufactured.

Xàtiva was of Phoenician origin, and called *Saetabis* by the Romans. It was also
known for its linen handkerchiefs, whose manufacture had been introduced
from Tyre. It was captured by the Moors in 714 and fortified. Jaime el
Conquistador re-captured it in 1244. The Infantes de la Cerda, heirs to the

Castilian throne, after being dispossessed by their uncle, Sancho IV, were imprisoned in the castle in 1284; as was Caesar Borja in 1504–05, and the Duke of Calabria in 1512–22.

The Borja family, prominent in Italian history as the Borgias, moved here from Borja in Aragón in the 14C. Alfonso Borja (1377–1458), later Pope Calixtus III, was Abp of Valencia; his nephew Rodrigo (1431–1503), the notorious Alexander VI, was the father of Caesar, Lucretia and Juan (who was father of S. Francisco Borja; cf. Gandía).

Xàtiva resisted the accession of Felipe V, but its English garrison under Col Campbell eventually surrendered to d'Asfeld's troops in 1707. The castle was sacked and its name was changed to S. Felipe; the older name was revived in 1834.

José or Jusepe de Ribera (1591–1652, in Naples) was born here, although he spent most of his life in Italy where he was known as 'Lo Spagnoletto'.

From the Alameda ascend to the parallel C. Moncada, the main street of the old town, in which are several typical Valencian houses and the Conv. de Sta. Clara. The C. de la Puerta de Sta. Tecla goes on to the Colegiata (1596), with rich marble decoration and a 15C triptych by Jacomart. Opposite is the Plateresque façade of the Hospital, with Gothic flights of angels over the door. The Museo Municipal (C. José Carchano) contains archaeological collections.

On the W hill, above the walled-up Puerta de la Aljama, is the Mozarabic Ermita de S. Feliú, with a round-headed doorway, six antique columns, and a 15C retablo. Above rise the extensive ruins of the Castle, mostly 15C, on a site originally fortified by the Iberians and commanding panoramic views. (Legend relates that Hannibal's wife, Hamilce, bore him a son here while he was besieging Saguntum.)

The N340 climbs S through picturesque country, at 11km passing 5km W of Benigánim, with a mosque converted to a church.—14km Albaida (5550 inhab.), with a triple-towered palace.

ALBAIDA TO VILLENA (45km). The C320 leads 9km W to **Ontinyent** (28,350 inhab.) in the upland valley of the Clariano; it retains a few fragments of its once formidable walls and a good 16C church.—Follow the C3316 S, following a defile, and skirting (10km) Bocairent, with paintings by Juan de Joanes in its church.—The road continues SW, gently descending the wide valley of the Vinalopó, at 7km passing Bañeres (3km SE), with a Gothic church and castle ruins, to approach Villena; see Rte 79.

From Albaida the road climbs SE to the Puerto de Albaida (620m), with fine views to the E on our descent, before passing (13.5km) Muro de Alcoy.—Ruins of a Templar castle at Lorcha lie c 18km NE. The C3311 winds E via (12km) Planes, with castle ruins, to Pego, 29km beyond; see Rte 74A.

5.5km **Cocentaina** (445m; 9950 inhab.), with an imposing turreted Palace of the Dukes of Medinaceli; Sta. María, with paintings by Nicolás Borrás; and the Conv. de Clarisas containing good sculptures.

Moncabrer, to the W, is the highest point in the SIERRA DE MARIOLA (1352m).

At 6km **ALCOY** (545m; 66,400 inhab.), a picturesquely situated and flourishing town on a promontory between the Molinar and Barchell, contains several Valencian Baroque churches. It manufactures paper, and cotton and woollen goods, and is known for its peladillas (sugared almonds). In July 1873 its mayor was murdered in a workers' revolution, and in the Civil War it was an Anarchist stronghold.

On or near St. George's Day in April a sham fight between 'Moros' and

'Cristianos' takes place to commemorate a battle of 1227, when St. George (*not* Santiago) came to the aid of the Christians defending the place.

The C3313 climbs E (retrospective views) and descends to (15km) *Benasau*, 4km SW of which is the walled village of *Penáguila*. It then continues E over the *Puerto de Confrides* (966m) to (21km) *Guadalest*; see p 460.

The N340 climbs S.

At 8km the A210 leads W to (9.5km) **Ibi** (20,000 inhab.—9km further W are crossroads; 2km N of this is *Onil*, with a palace (1539); 2km to the S is *Castalla*, with a ruined castle and late Gothic churches.—*Biar* is 10km beyond; see Rte 79.

At 6km the road crosses the *Puerto de la Carrasqueta* (1042m), commanding spectacular panoramic *views as it zigzags down to (13km) **Jijona** (8800 inhab.) an old hill town with an imposing castle and Gothic church. It is famous for its *turrón*, a nougat-like confection of ground almonds and honey. (*Turrón de Alicante* has whole almonds and is much harder.)

The road descends the barren valley of the Torremanzanas to meet, at 19.5km, the N332 8.5km NE of **Alicante**; see Rte 78A.

79 Albacete to Alicante

168km (104 miles). N430. 14km *Chinchilla*—58km **Almansa**—9km. N330. 29km *Villena*—18km. *Elda* is 2km SW.—40km **Alicante**.

Maps: M 445.

For **Albacete**, see Rte 47.

The N430 bears SE and passes (right) the turning to the Parador to approach (14km) a rugged hill rising some 280m from the plateau, on which is perched the ancient town of **Chinchilla de Monte Aragón** (968m), bypassed by the main road but reached by a road climbing left.

Chinchilla is somewhat dilapidated, but the old streets leading off the Pl. Mayor towards the *Castle* (15C) are lined with houses in Gothic and Mudéjar styles. The 18C *Ayuntamiento* has a front of 1590, and the old *Prison* opposite bears inscriptions of 1605 and 1637. Unfinished *Sta. María del Salvador*, largely built c 1440, has an apse with remarkable Plateresque decoration of c 1540, a reja of 1503, and 17C woodwork in the Sacristy. To the E is the ruinous *Conv. de Sto. Domingo* (14C), with a disfigured Gothic cloister. To the W are the *Col. de N.S. de las Nieves* and the *Hosp. de S. Julián* in the C. de los Benefactores below the castle. There was a Republican Artillery School at Chinchilla during the Civil War, and also at Almansa; see below.

The road now climbs E across a range of hills to (24km) the *Puerto Los Altos* (960m) in a barren steppe-like landscape.

At 22km a road leads N to (10km) *Alpera*, c 5km N of which is the *Cueva de la Vieja* among other caves, containing prehistoric rock paintings. There are remains of an Iberian town on the *Puntal de Meca*.

To the NE of this turning rises the *Mugrón* (1209m), dominating the area. At 6km the road passes (right) the *Embalse de Almansa*, a reservoir confined by a large masonry dam constructed by the Moors. At (6km) **Almansa** (950m; 20,400 inhab.) the Duke of Berwick

defeated the English partisans of the Archduke Charles—
commanded by Galway, Minas, and Tyrawly—on 25 April 1707. The
town, also bypassed, is dominated by a *Castle* of Moorish origin but
rebuilt in the 15C, standing on an isolated limestone hill. The *Parish
church* (late 15C) has a good tower and a Renaissance portal; the
adjoining *Pal. of the Condes de Cirat* is a robust work of 1575 (façade
and patio). Behind this, the *Conv. of the Agustinas* has a Baroque
door (1704). In the Nationalist repressions after the Civil War 36
citizens of Almansa were tried with the former civil governor of
Albacete and 32 were shot.

Near *Montealegre del Castillo* (22km SW), rises the *Cerro de los Santos*, ancient
Ello, where Graeco-Phoenician(?) sculptures of the 4C BC have been discovered
(now in the Archaeological Museum, Madrid, and museums at Albacete,
Murcia, Yecla, and Valladolid).

At 9km turn right onto the N330; for the N430 continuing E for
Valencia, see Rte 82 in reverse.—At 15.5km **Caudete** (7700 inhab.) is
5.5km right; its *Parish church* and the chapel of the *Pal. del Rosario*
have good retablos.

13km **Villena** (28,750 inhab.), an ancient town with several old
mansions in its narrow streets, dominated by a 15C *Castle*—but of
Moorish origin—with a large square tower. *Santiago* (1511) contains
unusual spirally-fluted columns, a polychromed wooden retablo
(1540) by Jerónimo Quijano, and a W door of interest. *Sta. María* is
16C. The *Ayuntamiento*, dating from 1707, houses an *Archaeological
Museum* containing the Bronze Age gold treasure discovered near
here in 1963.

Biar, 8km E, is commanded by a 13C concentric *Castle* with a large dungeon; its
Church has a sculptured portal (1519) and an imposing tower by Blas Aparicio
completed in 1733.

At 11km **Sax** (7350 inhab.), bypassed, has a castle ruin strikingly
perched on a rock pinnacle. The road continues down the valley of
the Vinalopó, veering SE to bypass (7km) **Petrel** (20,600 inhab.), with
a ruined Moorish castle. Contiguous to the W is **Elda** (53,150 inhab.),
an industrial town and the birthplace of Juan Sempere y Guarinos
(1754–1830), the literary critic. It retains a ruined *Alcázar*, and a
green-domed church.

Monóvar (11,150 inhab.), 7km SW of Elda, has a Moorish castle and a church
dated 1750. It was the birthplace of the author 'Azorín' (José Martínez Ruiz;
1873–1967).

At 12km the road forks left through a barren hilly district before
descending into flatter country to approach the industrial outskirts of
(28km) **Alicante**; see Rte 78A.

The right-hand fork passes through (2km) **Novelda** (20,950 inhab.), birthplace
of Adm. Jorge Juan y Santacilia (1713–73), author of numerous works on
astronomy, history, geography, and nautical subjects, and a member of the
Royal Society.—2km NW stands the curious triangular tower of the *Castillo de
la Mola*.—From the junction 6km S, the left fork leads to **Elche** (11km); the right
to (12km) *Crevillente*; for both, see Rte 78A.

80 Albacete to Cartagena, via Murcia

195km (121 miles). N301. 61km *Hellin*—43km *Cieza*—30km
Murcia—49km **Cartagena**.

Maps: M 445.

For **Albacete**, see Rte 47.

The N301 leads SE across a dreary plateau, with the rocky *Peñas
de S. Pedro* in the distance to the SW; and then crosses a range of
hills. At 51km it skirts *Tobarra* (7800 inhab.), with a ruined castle and
Franciscan *Convent*, and 10km beyond it enters or bypasses **Hellín**
(23,200 inhab.), ancient *Illunum*, known to the Romans for its sulphur
mines. These lie to the S and were re-discovered in 1564. Hellín was
the birthplace of Melchor de Macanaz (1670–1760), the political
economist hounded by the Inquisition. It contains a 16C–17C hall-
church.

The C3212 leads W to (36km) *Elche de la Sierra*, from which mountain roads
climb through a picturesque region W and NW (C415) to (38km) *Fábricas de
Ríopar*, and across a pass (1480m) below the summit of *Almenaras* (1798m) in
the SIERRA DE ALCARAZ. *Alcaraz* (see Rte 82) is a difficult 55km beyond.—The
remote town of **Yeste** (877m; 5850 inhab.), with a late Gothic church (c 1600)
and 16C *Ayuntamiento*, is 35km W of *Elche de la Sierra*, beyond the *Embalse de
la Fuensanta*.

At 9km the road passes near prehistoric paintings in the rockshelter
of the *Cuevas de Minateda*, and 3km beyond, a turning to *Jumilla*,
26km E; see Rte 82.—Crossing a ridge of hills into the province of
Murcia, at 31km we enter **Cieza** (30,350 inhab.) on the Segura; on
the far bank are the ruins of a Moorish castle.

At 21km **Archena** (11,950 inhab.) stands 4km to the W, on the right
bank of the river; it has remains of *Roman* and *Moorish baths*. It was
a Russian tank base during the Civil War.—The church at *Ulea*, 5km
NW of Archena, has a fine Mudéjar roof.

The Segura valley (Valle de Ricote) above Archena was the last enclave in
Spain to be inhabited by un-Christianised Moors, who left in 1505. Remains of
their fortress towers have survived. The conforming Moriscos remained here for
four years after the general expulsion in 1609, which so depopulated and
impoverished large areas of the country.

The main road bypasses (right) *Lorqui*, Roman *Ilorci*, near which
Publius and Gnaeus Scipio were killed by Carthaginian forces in 211
BC.—9km *Molina de Segura*, 3km W of which is *Alguazas*, with a
16C church with a Mudéjar ceiling, and a palace of the Bishops of
Murcia (1351).

After crossing its dusty outskirts (a bypass is under construction), at
12km we enter the city centre of **MURCIA** (284,600 inhab.; 142,000
in 1920; 218,000 in 1950). Dominated by its cathedral, and the capital
of its autonomy, Murcia, lying on both banks of the Segura, is
surrounded by a fertile *huerta*. It has a less dilapidated air than it had
two decades ago and much new construction has taken place in the
suburbs. It subsists largely on the produce of its market gardens and
the canning of its considerable fruit crop. Less important now is the
production of silkworm gut, an industry fomented by the *Estación
Sericícola* at *La Alberca*, 5km SW. Its climate is erratic: the torrid
summer is often affected by the parching dust of the *leveche*, while
winter nights are occasionally chilled by sudden frosts.

Little is known of Murcia before its rebuilding by the Moors early in the 8C on the foundations of an older town (Iberian or Roman?). It was named *Mursiyah*, and the river, the ancient *Tader*, was called the *Sekhurah*. In 1224, at the disintegration of the Almohade empire, it became the capital of a small Moorish kingdom. This was overrun by Fernando III in 1240, although its rebellious population was not subdued until 1243, when the town was settled with Catalans.

In 1707, during the War of the Succession, the city was saved from the Archduke Charles by its bishop, Luis de Belluga, who laid the environs under water and beat off the assailants with a small peasant force. In 1800 its population was already c 40,000. In 1810 it was sacked by Sebastiani; and in 1829 and 1879 it suffered from earthquakes and floods. In 1936 the churches, with the exception of the Cathedral and S. Andrés, were looted and burnt.

Among eminent Murcians were Ibn al-'Arabi (1165–1240), the Sufi mystic; Pedro de Orrente (1588–1645), the artist; Francisco Salzillo or Zarcillo (1707–83), the sculptor; and the Conde de Floridablanca (1728–1808), minister of Carlos III and prime mover in the expulsion of the Jesuits from Spain.

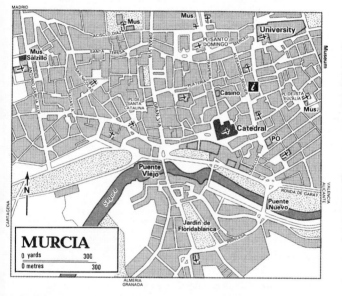

The Gran Via crosses the city from N to S, reaching the Segura at the Pl. de Martínez Tornell or El Arenal. The river is spanned by the *Puente Viejo* (1718–42).

There is little of interest on the S bank. The road continues past the Pl. del Camachos (1756), where bullfights once took place, to the *Jardin de Floridablanca*, at the far end of which is the restored *El Carmen* (1721–69), containing the Cristo de la Sangre by Nicolás de Busi, a predecessor of Salzillo.

To the W of the Arenal is the Paseo del Malecón, flanked by a *Botanical Gardens*. To the N of this, in the Plano de S. Francisco, is the *Audiencia* of 1628, originally the corn exchange. Parts of it are of an earlier building (1554–75). Beyond it is the market, behind which is the *Conv. de las Verónicas* with a Baroque front if 1755.

To the E of the Arenal are the gardens of the Glorieta de España, flanked by the *Ayuntamiento*, and beyond, the *Bishop's Palace* (1748), with a graceful patio.—A short passage between the two leads to the Pl. Card. Belluga, dominated by the cathedral.

The *Cathedral was originally a plain Gothic building of 1394–1465, but additions in the 16C and the construction of an entirely new front after a destructive flood of the Segura in 1735, have completely altered its external appearance.

The Baroque W Front, pyramidal in design, was built in 1736–54, following designs by Jaime Bort. It has Corinthian columns below and Composite above, with figures of saints in flowing drapery. The N portal, the elegant Italianate Puerta de las Cadenas (1515), is ascribed to Juan de León and Francisco Florentino. On the N side rises the imposing 90m high Tower of diminishing storeys. It was begun in 1521 by Francisco and Jacobo Florentino and received its second stage in 1526–46 by Jerónimo Quijano, but it was not completed until 1765–92 by Juan de Gea, José López, and Ventura Rodríguez. The summit can be reached by an easy ramp and spiral staircase and provides fine panoramic views; apply for entry at the Diocesan Museum.

At the SE corner of the cathedral is the octagonal Vélez Chapel, completed in 1507 and recalling the Manueline style; it bears large escutcheons and carved chains, the emblem of the Vélez family. The S Puerta de los Apóstoles is a restored doorway (c 1440) by Alonso Gil. Beyond it is the Plateresque Junterones Chapel (1529) by Quijano. (The valuable jewels of the Virgen de la Fuensanta, placed in the cathedral for safe keeping, were stolen in January 1977.)

The interior is Gothic in effect, with rich ogee arches in the aisles, but Plateresque and Renaissance decoration has also been incorporated. The Coro, blocking the nave, contains Stalls of 1571 from the abbey of S. Martín de Valdeiglesias, W of Madrid. The Cap. Mayor has a reja of 1497. On the left is an urn containing the entrails of Alfonso X. In the Cap. de los Junterones (fourth in S aisle) the altarpiece is an early 16C Italian Nativity.

The remarkable Cap. de los Vélez (fifth in the ambulatory), with a beautiful screen and rich vaulting, is a fine example of Plateresque decoration at its most lavish. The domed Sacristia Mayor, entered by a Plateresque door at the base of the tower in the N ambulatory, is by Jacobo Florentino, with woodwork of 1527. The Baptistery, in the N aisle, is a Renaissance chapel of 1541.

Off the N transept is the Diocesan Museum containing the sculptured Retablo de las Musas, a re-used sarcophagus front (3–5C); S. Jerónimo by Salzillo, and other sculptures; the double Retablo of St. Lucy and the Virgin by Barnaba de Módena; a collection of charters, including that of Sancho IV authorising the transfer of the see from Cartagena to Murcia (1291); a custodia (1677) by Antonio Pérez de Montalto; and other cult objects.

For the area E of the cathedral, see below.

From the N side, the pedestrian Trapería leads N past (right) the fin de siècle Casino with a lavishly decorated ballroom.—The street is crossed by the Platería (see below); to the left is the Renaissance mansion known as the Casa de los Salvages. Beyond it is unfinished Sto. Domingo (1543–1742; restored) and the Pl. Sto. Domingo.

The Gran Via Alfonso X continues N between the Conv. de Sta. Ana (right), with a church of 1728, and the Baroque front and dome of the Conv. de Sta. Clara, its church (c 1755) containing works by Salzillo.—Beyond it is the Museo Arqueológico.

The C. de Acislo Díaz leads W from Sta. Clara to Jesuit S. Esteban (completed in 1569) with a figure of S. Francisco Xavier by Busi, and the adjacent patio of the former Casa de la Compañía. Opposite is S. Miguel (c 1676) with a retablo mayor (1731) by Jacinto Perales and Francisco Salzillo, and other sculptures by the latter and by his father, Nicolás Salzillo.—A lane to the right leads further on to the 13C Ermita de Santiago (restored), the oldest church in Murcia.

The Platería (see above) leads W from the Trapería, passing near (left) S. Bartolomé, containing Salzillo's Virgen de las Angustias

Exterior of the Capilla de los Vélez, Cathedral of Murcia

(1741), to the Gran Via.—On the far side (left) is *Sta. Catalina* (1594 and later) with figures by Nicolás Salzillo.—From the plaza behind the church pass into the adjoining Pl. de los Flores, where *S. Pedro* has a retablo by Roque López.

From the Pl. de S. Pedro the C.S. Nicolás leads NW to sumptuous *S. Nicolás* (1743), containing a St. Anthony in Capuchin dress by Alonso Cano.—Follow an alley to the left just beyond the church, then turn right, and second left, to *S. Andrés* (1630–1762); adjoining it is the round *Ermita de Jesús* of 1696.

It now houses the **•Museo Salzillo**, an impressive collection of *pasos*, figures carried in Holy Week processions, by Francisco Salzillo (1707–83).

The first rooms contain works other than pasos: small statues of saints, a child Jesus, and a Nativity or Belém, consisting of over 1500 miniature figures. The chapel has been arranged so as to display the *Pasos* in the encircling side chapels, and comprise realistically coloured life-size groups representing the events of Holy Week. With those of the Nativity they betray Salzillo's Neapolitan origins by their resemblance to the popular *presepi* of the churches of Naples. The figures of St. John and St. Veronica, and of the Last Supper, are the most successful. Behind the altar is the 16C or early 17C image of Jesus the Nazarene, the only work *not* by Salzillo.

From the square immediately N of the cathedral, walk NE into the C. de Alejandro Seiquer (with the Tourist Office opposite) and turn N, passing (right) *S. Lorenzo*, with six domed bays, by Ventura Rodríguez, only completed in 1810.—Behind the church there is a market, just N of which is *La Merced*, an early Rococo work of 1727 notable for a series of early 17C paintings of the Order of Mercedarians by L. Suarez and C. Acebedo, two local artists. The dependencies now house the *University*.

Skirt the S side of the market, a short distance to the E of which, in the C. de Obispo Frutos, is the *Museo de Bellas Artes*, containing paintings by the Murcian school, a S. Jerónimo by Ribera, and more recent works.—From a few steps S, the C. Mariano Vergara leads back towards the cathedral past *Sta. Eulalia* (1779) with a museum adjacent, and the *Conv. de S. Antonio* (partly 16C). At the C. de Isidoro de la Cierva turn left past the Post Office. An alley just beyond, to the left, leads to 18C *S. Juan Bautista*, with a statue of S. Isidoro by Busi and others of the school of Salzillo. Adjoining are the 18C mansions of the Floridablanca and Saavedro Fajardo families.

The riverside gardens are regained a short distance to the S near the *Puente Nuevo*. Turn right along the Av. de Teniente Flomesta to the former *Col. de S. Isidoro*, founded by Card. Belluga in 1724. Behind it is the elliptical Rococo chapel of *S. Juan de Dios* (1745–81). Further along the avenue is the former *Seminario de S. Fulgencio* (1592–1701), now the *Diputación*, beyond which we regain the *Glorieta de España*.

For roads to **Orihuela**, **Elche**, and **Alicante**, see Rte 78A in reverse; to **Almería**, Rte 81.

The N301 bears SW, soon passing a left turn to the chapel of *La Fuensanta* (1694; by Toribio Martínez de la Vega) and the monasteries of *Sta. Catalina del Monte* (16C) and *La Luz* (18C), dominated by the ridge known as the *Cresta del Gallo* (518m).—The road climbs to (12.5km) the *Puerto de la Cadena* (340m), then descends to cross a *huerta* of citrus groves to (36.5km) Cartagena.

CARTAGENA (167,950 inhab.; 97,000 in 1920), a naval base in ancient times, was the strongest fortress in Spain, but it retains few relics of its past. It is still the main channel for the export of minerals from the surrounding hills (cf. La Unión), and its harbour, beautifully situated, is the safest on the Spanish Mediterranean coast. Its narrow entrance is guarded by the forts of *Galeras* (W) and *S. Julián* (E). Cartagena was seriously damaged in the Civil War, and the *old* town has a somewhat decrepit appearance in contrast to its modern suburbs.

Founded, or more probably rebuilt, by Hasdrubal, son-in-law of Hamilcar Barca, in c 243 BC, *Carthago Nova* became the centre of Carthaginian influence in Spain. Its gold and silver mines, worked by slaves, were an important source of wealth. In the Second Punic War the port was the principal objective in Spain of the elder Scipio Africanus; his siege and capture of it in 210–209 BC are described by Livy and by Polybius. It remained important under the Romans, and was nicknamed *Spartaria* from the abundance of esparto grass in the area; but its official title was *Colonia Victrix Julia Carthago Nova*.

The harbour was of little use to the Visigoths, but at the time of the Moorish invasion a duchy of uncertain extent under Theodomir seems to have maintained a partial independence under the suzerainty of the Caliph. Moorish

Kartajanah was taken by Fernando III in 1242, but was reoccupied by the Moors until 1265, when it fell to Jaime el Conquistador.

In 1585 it was raided by Francis Drake, who carried off its guns to Jamaica. Swinburne, who visited the place in 1775, considered that the arsenal had hardly sufficient equipment 'to fit out a frigate', and 'were it not for its celebrity ... scarce deserves a minute's attention from a curious traveller'. Widdrington, some fifty years later, also found it much decayed, containing only a corvette for sale which no one would buy. In 1873 the Communists held out for over six months against the Republic at Madrid. Although eventually subdued by bombardment, their resistance contributed to the final discredit of the government.

Russian tanks and other equipment were landed here during the Civil War, and the Nationalists bombed the place. In March 1938 the Nationalist cruiser 'Baleares' was sunk by Republican destroyers based in Cartagena. The Nationalist ship 'Castillo de Olite' was also sunk off Cartagena during the last few weeks of the war, with the loss of 1200 lives, while attempting to land troops here. Isidoro de Seville (c 560–636), the encyclopedist, and Fernando Garrido (1821–83), the socialist revolutionary, were born here.

The centre is approached by skirting the high-walled arsenal to reach the C. Real; this leads to the *Ayuntamiento* and the *Muelle de Alfonso XII*, the principal quay (on which stands Isaac Peral's *Submarine* of 1888). In front extends the harbour, its entrance protected by two breakwaters. On the quay to the right are Harbour Offices and barracks; adjoining these is the entrance to the *Arsenal* (no admission). This was built in 1733–82 and is overlooked and protected by the *Castillos de la Atalaya* (W) and *de Galeras* (SW).

To reach the *Castillo de la Concepción*, the highest point in the town, ascend the C. de Aire (roughly parallel to and E of the pedestrian C. Mayor). (The summit can also be reached by car from the Muralla del Mar.) C. de Aire climbs through a derelict area past 13C *Sta. María la Vieja*, the *Catedral Antigua*, in ruins since the Civil War. Roman inscriptions have been discovered among the foundations of the ruined fortress (rebuilt by Alfonso X) which occupies the probable site of the Roman arx.

It commands a panoramic view of the town, harbour, and surrounding heights, each crowned by a fort. The ruins of dismantled forts—*de los Moros, de Despeñaperros*, and *S. José*—on lower hills to the NE, may also be seen.

From the N end of the C. Mayor follow the C. Tomás Maestre and the C. Sta. Florentina to the **Archaeological Museum**. A *National Museum of Underwater Archaeology* has also been established in Cartagena, at C. Dique Navidad 6.—The *Torre Ciega*, a Roman monument N of the station (left beyond bridge over railway), has fragmentary decoration. The 4C–5C necropolis of *S. Anton* has recently been excavated; and part of a Roman amphitheatre has been discovered on the site of the Pl. de Toros.

The N332/342 leads NW, later crossing a ridge of hills before descending to (32.5km) *Puerto de Mazarron*; see Rte 81.

81   Murcia to Almería via Lorca and Vera

219km (136 miles). N340. 7km *Alcantarilla*—55km **Lorca**—18km *Puerto Lumbreras*—47km *Vera*—92km **Almería**.

Maps: M 445, 446.

From the right (S) bank of the Segura follow the N340 W to bypass

(7km) **Alcantarilla** (24,600 inhab.). 2km NE, on the far bank of the
Segura, is the Jesuit monastery of *La Nora*, its name derived from the
noria or Arab irrigation wheel for raising water. Originally Hieronymite, its Baroque church contains a St. Jerome by Salzillo.—At
Alcantarilla itself is the *Museo de la Huerta* containing local furniture, ceramics, textiles, and other artefacts.

ALCANTARILLA TO CARAVACA (63km). The C415 bears NW to (27km) **Mula**
(14,750 inhab.), with the hilltop 15C–16C castle of the Vélez. Its churches were
ruined in 1936. It was the birthplace of Ginés Pérez de Hita (c 1544–c 1619),
historian of the wars of Granada.—30km *Cehegin* (13,650 inhab.), with a
mid-16C *hall-church* and the *Ermita de la Concepción* with a Mudéjar roof
(1556).—6km *Caravaca*; see Rte 83.

The main road follows the valley of the Guadalentín, with the SIERRA
DE CARRASCOY (1066m) further S. It bypasses (16km) *Librilla*, a
village which was once the headquarters of the Murcian gipsies, and
which is divided by a ravine.—7km **Alhama de Murcia** (13,150
inhab.), a spa of very ancient origin, lies below its Moorish fort.—
12km **Totana** (18,550 inhab.), noted for its *tinajas* or water jars, has a
Church (before 1587) with a 17C Baroque portal, Mudéjar roof, and
16C retablo.

Aledo, a medieval village 9km NW in the SIERRA DE ESPUÑA (1585m), has ruins
of a castle held by the Knights of Calatrava between 1085 and 1160, although in
the midst of Moorish territory. Its wine is notable.
   The C3315 leads 29km SE to *Mazarrón* (10,250 inhab.), an ancient centre of
lead and iron mining, with a ruined castle of the Vélez and a Mudéjar church.
The small resort of *Puerto de Mazarrón* is 6.5km beyond.—The N332/342 leads
W from Mazarrón between the metal-bearing SIERRA DE ALMENARA (881m) to
the N, and coastal ridges, to meet the C3211 from Lorca 12km N of *Aguilas*; see
below.

The main road continues SW, S of the SIERRA DE LA TERCIA (989m), to
(20km) **LORCA** (61,900 inhab.). The old centre, N of the modern
suburbs, is somewhat decayed but several of its older buildings are
being restored.

The *Eliocroca* or *Ilucro* of the Romans and the *Lurkah* of the Moors, it was
reconquered in 1244 by Alfonso X and remained a Christian redoubt against the
Moors of Granada. In the late 17C and early 18C its school of painting enjoyed
some reputation. When Townsend passed through Lorca in 1778 he compared
its public walks to those of Oxford, 'but upon a more extensive scale, and more
beautiful'. Lorca is still supplied with water from the *Embalse de Puentes* (15km
NW); the original reservoir, built in 1791, burst its dam in 1802 and flooded the
town. Most of its churches were looted during the Civil War, and a Republican
artillery school was established there. It was the birthplace of the Carlist
general Rafael Maroto (1783–1847).

In the E suburbs, before crossing the Guadalentín, is 18C *S.
Cristóbal*. In the C. López Gisbert is the *Casa de los Guevara*, its
portal with wreathed spiral columns (1694); the *Casa de los Musso
Valente*, opposite, has a fine portal and patio (1600).—Not far W
stands domed *S. Matéo* (18C) and the 16C *Pal. de S. Julián*.—Beyond
(right) is the *Hosp. de S. Francisco*, its chapel containing Churrigueresque retablos with paintings of c 1759 by Manuel Caro.

Further W is El Carmen (1712; with Rococo plasterwork); beyond it is the *Ermita
de Gracia* (16C), and higher up to the right, the *Calvario*.

To the E is the Corredera, with the 16C portal of the *Rosario* church,
the *Bishop's Palace*, and several old houses.—Uphill is the Pl. de
Santiago, with its 17C church. The closely-built quarter on the slope

contains Renaissance houses, the remains of Gothic *S. Ginés* (13C), and 15C *S. Jorge*.

Its **Castle** (restored) is partly Moorish (12C) but the *Torre Alfonsina*, in bad repair, is 15C Spanish.—Below, from W to E, are ruined *S. Pedro* (15C and 18C), *Sta. María* (Gothic, with a doorway of 1596), and Baroque *S. Juan Bautista*.

In the restored *Pl. Mayor* are the *Ayuntamiento* (17–18C), flanked to the N by the large **Colegiata de S. Patricio**, with Baroque decoration, begun c 1550 but not completed until 1776; the sculptures on the main front date from 1627–1710. The S portal is an elegant work of c 1600. The Baroque tower was completed in 1772. The ironwork of the sanctuary, including the lectern of 1716, are notable; and the unusual Christ (1749) is by Manuel Santiago España, a Guatemalan.

For the road from Lorca to **Granada**, see Rte 86.

The C3211 leads SE to cross the *Puerto Purías* for (37km) **Aguilas** (20,250 inhab.), a small port practically deserted for centuries on account of raids by Barbary pirates. It was refounded on a regular plan by the Conde de Aranda in 1765. It lies between two bays, with its ruined castle on a rocky headland.—The main route can be regained by following the N332 SW over the silver-bearing SIERRA ALMAGRERA to (32km) *Cuevas de Almanzora* (8450 inhab.), a small mining centre with a *Castle* (1507, but later altered) built by the first Marqués de Vélez as a protection against corsairs.—*Vera* is 6km S; see below.

ALTERNATIVELY, turn left off this road 11km from Aguilas and skirt the coast via *Mojácar*.—16km *Villaricos*, where remains from the Carthaginian and Moorish occupation have been found; inland is the *despoblado* of *Almizaraque*, on a hill which has yielded late Neolithic finds.—Cross the Rio Almanzora but note that several *ramblas* or *barrancos* along the coast here are dry much of the year and bridges are sometimes broken by floods, so it may be necessary to cross on the riverbed. It was off the coast here in 1967, near the village of *Palomares*, that thermonuclear bombs were jettisoned by the Americans, causing an international scandal.—10km *Garrucha*, with a small harbour and 16C coastal fort. Beyond this the road crosses the mouth of the Aguas. At 5.5km a road turns by the Parador for Mojácar with the SIERRA CABRERA (960m) to the W; the road ahead leads to (22km) *Carboneras*, where a by-road turns inland to (37km) *Níjar*; see below.—**Mojácar**, a picturesquely sited hilltop village of flat-roofed, white-washed houses, has been developed as a tourist resort and has already lost much of its attraction.—The main route can be regained 14km W and 13km SW of *Vera*; see below.

The N340 leads SW from Lorca to (18km) *Puerto Lumbreras* (8550 inhab.; Parador), where the N342 for Baza and Granada turns NW; see Rte 86.—Continue SW, parallel to the SIERRA DE ENMEDIO (856m), to (24km) **Huércal Overa** (12,300 inhab.), with a good 18C church and ruined fortifications.

At 6km the C323 winds up the Almanzora valley via (c 45km) *Purchena* to (44km) *Baza*. Several marble-cutting works are passed en route; the main quarries are at *Macael*.

17km **Vera** (5350 inhab.), the ancient *Baria*, was destroyed in an earthquake in 1512. Its church dates from 1524, and the *Ayuntamiento* is also 16C. The area is rich in antiquities.—*Garrucha* is 10.5km SE; see above.

A road to *Mojácar* (see above) turns off the N340 at 13km, and climbs through the hills, with the SIERRA CABRERA to the S (960km) and the long ridge of the SIERRA DE LOS FILABRES to the N, here rising to 1301m.—22km *Sorbas*, picturesquely sited on a rock above the Río de Aguas.

A mountain road circles to the SE and then SW to (36km) **Níjar** (11,000 inhab.), with its potteries, below the SIERRA ALBAMILLA (1387m).—*Almería* is 33.5km further SW.

27km *Tabernas*, with a ruined Moorish *alcazaba*, the most import- ant in the province after that of Almería. Beyond it the road descends the rambla past (7km) '*Mini Hollywood*', a centre for the production of 'Spagetti Westerns' in the surrounding wilderness.—For the road turning NW from here to **Guadix** and **Granada**, see Rte 88A.

After passing through the orange groves of Rioja, the N324 and C332 (see Rte 88C) meet at (12km) *Benahadux*, NW of *Pechina*, and near the Iberian and Roman town of *Urci*. **Almería** is 12km due S; see 88A.

82 Valencia to Úbeda via Almansa, Albacete and Alcaraz

388km (241km). N430. 51km *Xàtiva* crossroad—56km **Almansa**— 72km **Albacete**—N322. 79km *Alcaraz*—53km *Puente de Génave*— 77km **Úbeda**.

Maps: M 445, 446.

For the road to the junction 5km NW of *Xàtiva*, see Rte 78C.

The N430 bears SW up the valley of the Cañoles, bypassing (5km) **Canals** (11,250 inhab.), birthplace of Alfonso Borja (cf. Xàtiva), with its castle.—At 6km (right) rise the imposing ruins of the castle of *Montesa*, once the headquarters of the Military Order of Montesa, founded in 1318 after the suppression of the Templars.

12km *Mogente*, with a Moorish castle (and the site of one of the first '*paradores*', set up at the turn of the 19C by the Marqués de la Romana). At neighbouring *Les Alcuses* are the ruins of a 5C BC Iberian settlement. To the S rises the SIERRA GROSSA (832m); to the NW the SIERRA DE ENQUERA (858m).

14km *Fuente la Higuera*, 4km left, was the birthplace of Juan de Joanes (Vicente Juan Macip; c 1506–79), who painted the retablo in its parish church. The road continues SW via (15.5km) *Caudete* (see Rte 79) to *Yecla* (16.5km beyond); Rte 83 can be followed from here.

At 10km we meet the Madrid–Alicante road, and 9km beyond, reach *Almansa*. For Almansa and for the road to *Albacete*, see Rte 79 in reverse.

The N322 turns SW off the Albacete bypass and crosses the plateau; the *Peñas de S. Pedro*, foothills of the SIERRA DE ALCARAZ massif, rise to the S to 1257m.—Beyond (28km) *Balazote*, where the curious Phoenician 'sphinx' (now in the Archaeological Museum, Madrid) was found, the road climbs up the valley of the *Jardín* to (43km) the *Puerto de los Pocicos* (1058m). Turn left 8km beyond the pass for **Alcaraz** (963m), a picturesquely sited old village dominated by the ruins of its extensive *Castle*, taken from the Moors in 1213 and rebuilt in 1507. Below it are the remains of Gothic *Sta. María*. In the village are *La Trinidad* (1544), with a good S doorway and ruined cloister, and the adjacent *Torre del Tardón* (1568). Further along the main street is 16C *S. Miguel.* The *Plaza* is flanked by the *Ayunta-miento* (1588). Several of these buildings were designed by the native architect Andrés de Vandaelvira (1509–75).

Shortly after rejoining the main road, the C415 turns right, later crossing the CAMPO DE MONTIEL for (55km) *Villanueva de los Infantes* and (34km beyond) *Valdepeñas*; see Rte 48A.

The road continues SW above the Río Guadalmena, with the main ridge of the SIERRA DE ALCARAZ rising to the SE to 1798m at the *Almenaras.*

At 51km, just before entering *Puente de Génave*, the J700 turns left to approach (16km) the hill village of *Orcera.* 7km beyond is the ancient but restored castle of *Segura de la Sierra*, overlooked to the S by the *Yelmo* (1809m).—A mountain road turns S 5km W of *Orcera*, later skirting the W bank of the *Embalse del Tranco* and ascends the upper Guadalquivir—between the SIERRA DE SEGURA (1964m) and the SIERRA DE CAZORLA (*Blanquillo*; 1830m). At 66km crossroads are reached 8km N of the Parador of Cazorla. *Cazorla* itself, 17km W, is on the far side of the ridge crossed at the *Puerto de las Palomas* (1290m); see Rte 84.

After crossing the *Puente de Génave*, the road descends the valley of the Guadalimar, at 19km passing 5km N of *Beas de Segura* (9150 inhab.), and at 18km crossing *Villanueva del Arzobispo* (8850 inhab.).—The high-lying village of *Iznatoraf* is passed (right) before entering (9.5km) **Villacarrillo** (12,100 inhab.), with an 18C *Ayunta-miento* and a church ascribed to *Vandaelvira.*—The road now follows the S slope of the LOMO DE ÚBEDA, with magnificent *Views across the Guadalquivir valley and of the· SIERRA DE CAZORLA beyond. At 22km it skirts *Torreperogil* and enters **Úbeda** 10km beyond: see Rte 84.

At *Sabiote* (4.5km N of Torreperogil) there is a Moorish castle converted into a palace in 1543.

83 Almansa to Baza via Caravaca, for Granada

364km (226 miles). C3223. 36km *Yecla*—C3314. 28km *Jumilla*—46km *Calasparra*—23km *Caravaca*—C350. 81km *Huéscar*—C3329. 28km *Cúllar Baza*—N342. 22km **Baza**.

Maps: M 445.

A good—if little used—crosscountry route, this road avoids the coast, and can as easily be followed from *Fuente la Higuera* if approaching from Valencia; see Rte 82.

From **Almansa** (Rte 79) turn S to (36km) **Yecla** (25,300 inhab.), notable for its wine. It has a ruined castle and the churches of *La Asunción* (1512), with a curious frieze of heads on its tower, and *S. Francisco* (damaged in 1936), containing an image by Salzillo. The *Casa de la Cultura* contains Iberian sculpture and other archaeologi-cal collections from the Cerro de los Santos. The *Ayuntamiento* (1687) with a 16C tower adjacent, contains paintings by Andrés Ginés de Aguirre (1727–c 1800), born in Yecla.

Bear SW across the *Puerto de Jumilla* (800m) to (28km) **Jumilla**

(20,650 inhab.), also known for its wine, and with a Moorish castle with a 15C keep added, late 15C *Santiago* and several Renaissance houses. To the S is the ancient vaulted chapel of *El Casón* and (c 6km beyond) the monastery of *Sta. Ana*, containing Salzillo's Christ at the column.

We follow the wide valley to the SW and at 23km cross the N301, to reach *Calasparra* (8700 inhab.) in the valley of the Segura, of Iberian origin and with a ruined castle.—Continue up the valley of the Argos. At 18km turn right along its tree-shaded approach to (5km) **Caravaca** (20,450 inhab.), where an apparition of the Cross is said to have taken place in 1232, twelve years *before* the town was occupied by the Christians. The Cross was stolen in 1935. Near the main square of the lower town is the hall-church of *S. Salvador* (1534–1600). From the square, narrow streets climb steeply to the restored *Castle*, once a Templar stronghold. It includes the church of *Sta. Cruz* (1617), with an unusual *Portal* (1722) of red and grey stone, somewhat Mexican in style. Caravaca was the birthplace of the artist Rafael Tejeo (1798–1856).

At *Moratalla*, 14km N, there is another fine but unfinished church begun in 1521 by Francisco Florentino, and a well-preserved medieval castle.

At 7km SW of Caravaca the road forks right, to cross a pass at 1100m; to the N rises the SIERRA DE TABILLA (2081m). At 50km the remote, high-lying village of *Puebla de Don Fadrique* is overlooked from the SW by the *Lobos* (1798m), and further W by the *Sagra* (2381m). Turn S here and skirt the SIERRA DE JUREÑA to (24km) **Huéscar** (10,200 inhab.), with a good late 16C hall-church.

The C3329 leads past (7.5km) *Galera*, near which is the Iberian necropolis of *Tútugi* (60 BC). It meets the N342 20.5km further S at *Cúllar Baza*, 22km NE of **Baza**; see Rte 86.

VII   ANDALUCÍA

Andalucía (anglicised as *Andalusia*), the great southern autonomy, stretching from Murcia on the E to the Portuguese frontier on the W comprises the eight provinces of *Almería, Granada, Jaén, Córdoba, Málaga, Cádiz, Sevilla,* and *Huelva.* Physically it consists mainly of the wide basin of the Guadalquivir, the *Wadi el Kebir* (great river) of the Moors and the *Baetis* of the Romans, which rises in the province of Jaén and enters the Atlantic at Sanlúcar. On the N, Andalucía extends up the S slopes of the Sierra Morena; on the S the valley of the Guadalquivir is separated by the Penibetic mountain system from the sun-drenched Mediterranean.

Except in the desert maquis of the *Sierra Morena* and the alpine regions of the *Sierra Nevada* the soil of Andalucía is extremely fertile. The southern districts especially produce luxuriant crops of oranges and lemons, vines, olives, as well as tropical plants such as palms and sugar-cane. Its mineral wealth includes lead, copper, and coal deposits (in the Sierra Morena); among them the anciently exploited mines of Rio Tinto, Tharsis and Linares. The sherry of Jerez de la Frontera needs little commendation.

Andalucía, whose name is derived from the brief Vandal occupation (409–29), has been identified with the *Tarshish* of the Bible (*Tartessos*). As the Roman province of *Baetica* it purveyed luxuries of every sort to the connoisseurs of imperial Rome. From 711 to 1492 it was the gradually diminishing centre of one of the most highly developed civilisations of the Middle Ages: the Western Moorish empire. This was rarely united under one ruler, and internecine strife among the emirs of Córdoba, Jaén, and Granada led to their collapse before increasing pressure from the Christian kingdoms of northern Spain. The expulsion of the Moriscos in 1609, little more than a century after the fall of Granada, was followed by a rapid decline in commercial and agricultural prosperity (only six Morisco families were allowed to remain in every village of more than a hundred houses, so that their skills would not be lost).

The effects of eight centuries of Islamic supremacy may be detected in numerous Arabic place-names, in local expressions, in the Andalusian pronunciation of Spanish, and in a tendency towards oriental exaggeration for which the region is sometimes reproached. Most of Andalucía was settled from the N before 1300. In the former kingdom of Granada (Málaga, Granada, and Almería), however, different traditions were once perceptible, but these are now less noticeable, except in certain isolated districts. Very different is the *Costa del Sol,* now an international playground: for while material prosperity has been brought to the region, this has destroyed most of its former character.

The largest increases of population have been in the provinces of *Sevilla* (1,478,000, compared with 792,000 in 1930); *Málaga* (1,025,000 compared with 610,000), and *Cádiz* (988,000 compared with 512,000); that of *Jaén,* however, is now less than it was in 1930. All the provincial capitals have grown very considerably during the last few decades.

84   Bailén to Baza via Baeza, and Úbeda

162km (100 miles). N322. 14km **Linares**—at 7km turn right onto the
C326 for (16km) **Baeza**—N231. 9km **Úbeda**—10km *Torreperogil*—
J314. 23km *Peal de Becerro*. *Cazorla* is 14km E.—C323 11.5km
Quesada—31km *Pozo Alcón*—43.5km **Baza**.

Maps: M 446.

For **Bailén**, see Rte 48A.—14km E is **Linares** (55,100 inhab.), an ugly
town with rich lead and copper mines worked partly by English
companies which had imported their machinery. It was the birthplace of Andrés Segovia (1894–1987), the guitarist.

It retains a few old houses and a good *Ayuntamiento. S. Juan de
Dios* has a notable Baroque façade; *Sta. María* contains Plateresque
chapels. The *Museo Arqueológico* displays finds from *Cástulo* (6km
S), an Iberian settlement where Scipio Africanus defeated the Carthaginians in 208 BC.

Continuing E, cross the Guadalimar and turn off the main road to
Úbeda, which leads past (17km) *Canena*, with a *Castle* of the Order
of Calatrava (modernised in the 16C and again recently) and the
Churrigueresque chapel of *La Yedra*.

At *Ibros* there are slight remains of a Cyclopean fortress near the
Callejon de Peñones, 5km beyond which is **BAEZA** (15,050 inhab;
20,000 at the end of the 15C), Roman *Vivatia*.

It was briefly occupied after the battle of Las Navas de Tolosa in 1212 and
sacked by Fernando III in 1239. Its Economic Society was established in 1774, a
year earlier than that of Madrid. The barracks of the Guardia Civil here were
once a stud farm. It was the birthplace of the sculptor Gaspar Becerra (1520–70);
and Antonio Machado, the poet, lived here in 1913–19.

The main axis of the town is the C. de S. Pablo, part of the road from
Úbeda to Jaén, in which are several good buildings, including the
Plateresque *Casino* (No. 18) and Gothic *S. Pablo*. Pablo de Olavide
(1725–1803), promoter of the repopulation of the Sierra Morena, is
buried here. In this he was prompted by Col Thürriegel, a Bavarian,
but his projected reforms caused him to be hounded by the Inquisition. At the SW end is the PASEO, an attractive arcaded plaza, and
(left) the *Torre de Aliatares*, a relic of 13C fortifications. At the far end
of the paseo are the *Arco del Pópulo*, the Renaissance *Casa del
Pópulo* (c 1530), and near the beginning of the Jaén road, the *Fuente
de Leones*.

In the S quarter are the ruins of *La Compañia* (17C) and *Sta. Cruz*,
with a Romanesque doorway. In the street to the right is the former
University (16C). Adjacent is the *Pal. de Benavente* or *de Jabalquinto*, with an imposing Isabelline façade, 16C cloister, and monumental staircase. The *Fuente de Sta. María* dates from 1564. Close to
the last are the former *Ayuntamiento* (*Pal. de Cabrera*) and the
former **Cathedral**, rebuilt in 1567–93 to the designs of Andrés de
Vandaelvira. Survivals of the earlier building on the site are the
Isabelline *Puerta del Perdón* and the *Puerta de la Luna*, with a
horseshoe arch. It contains some good retablos, stallwork of 1635,
and a custodia (1714) in the Baroque *Sacristy*. Remains of a mosque
have been discovered in the cloister. The bishopric founded here in
1228 was transferred to Jaén only twenty years later.

Parts of the town *Walls* remain, and the track skirting them
provides a magnificent *View* over the surrounding country; on clear
days Jaén can be seen to the SW.

Detail of the Palacio de Jabalquinto, Baeza

From S. Pablo the C. del Rojo leads NW to *Sta. Ana* and **S. Andrés** (1500–20), the latter with a Plateresque portal bearing the arms of Bp Suárez. The tower was completed in 1535; the N portal in 1560; and the Cap. Mayor (c 1562) was designed by Vandaelvira. The choir has stalls from destroyed Sta. María del Alcázar and a large triptych.

Further on is the 17C church of the *Descalzos*.—The C. de S. Francisco leads downhill past the ruins of *S. Francisco* (1546; by Vandaelvira). Beyond are the Renaissance *Hospital* and the

Ayuntamiento (1559), with a notable Plateresque front and loggia, and containing a huge Custodia.

BAEZA TO JAÉN (48km). The N321 descends SW through olive groves (extensive views), passing (right; 5km) *Begijar*, with a medieval castle converted into an episcopal palace. Cross the Guadalquivir by the ramped *Puente del Obispo* (16C). To the S rises the SIERRA ALMADÉN (2167m).—At 29km *Mancha Real* (8000 inhab.) is 2km S and has a large 16–17C church. The road then veers W to (19km) **Jaén**; see Rte 85.

9km **ÚBEDA** (29,050 inhab.; Parador), a picturesque old town preserving a number of imposing old mansions.

Briefly occupied in 1212, it was definitively captured in 1234. Francisco de los Cobos (c 1480–1547), secretary to Charles V, and José Elbo (1804–44), the artist, were born here; and St. John of the Cross (S. Juan de la Cruz) died here in 1591.

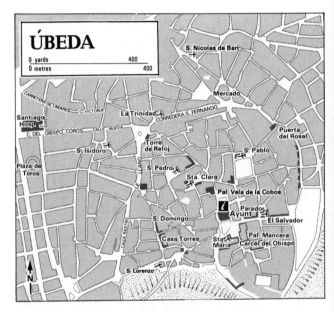

On entering the town from the W we pass (left) the huge *Hosp. de Santiago* (1575; by Vandaelvira), with a colonnaded patio, a staircase preserving its original frescos, and a reja of 1576 in its chapel (badly damaged in the Civil War). The central triangular plaza includes the medieval *Torre de Reloj*, with a 17C cupola. To the NW in the C. del Obispo Cobos is *S. Isidro*, with a Gothic doorway. From Baroque *La Trinidad* to the NE, the Corredera de S. Fernando descends, passing (left) the *Market*. Behind it the street climbs to **S. Nicolás de Bari** (15C), with a S doorway (1509) and W portal (1566) by Vandaelvira. Inside are the *Cap. del Deán Ortega*, with an entrance of 1537 and reja of 1596. Note the highly-patterned esparto carpets or *ubediés*, for which the town is noted.—Further uphill to the NW is the curious 16C *Casa de los Salvages*.

The C. de la Cava leads S from the central plaza, passing the square towers of the old town *Wall* embedded in houses to the left. Through a breach in the wall we reach the *Pal. de la Rambla*, a balconied Renaissance mansion with a patio by Vandaelvira.—From further down the street the *C. del Condestable Dávalos* leads to the *Casa de las Torres* (or *Pal. Dávalos*), with a two-storeyed patio of 1540. Not far E is disused *Sto. Domingo*, with a Gothic choir vault and artesonado roof to the nave.

S of the Casa de las Torres is ivy-clad *S. Lorenzo* (view adjacent), where we turn E through a picturesque plaza, pass through gates, and bear half-right to the striking PL. VÁZQUEZ DE MOLINA. To the N is the *Ayuntamiento*, the former *Casa de las Cadenas*, built by Vandaelvira for Felipe II's secretary; it has an imposing front and patio.

Sta. María de los Reales Alcázares, opposite, although masked by classical façades, is mainly late 15C; it has notable rejas by Maestro Bartolomé and part of a Gothic cloister. Note also the arabesque ceilings painted blue.—Close by are the 16C *Cárcel del Obispo* and the *Pal. de Mancera*, with a square tower.—To the S is the site of the *Alcázar*, with remains of its walls.

Beyond the Ayuntamiento is the *Pal. de los Ortegas*, with a restrained 17C front (now housing the Parador).—*El Salvador*, built in 1559 by Vandaelvira from designs by Diego de Siloé, contains statues from *Berruguete's* retablo (destroyed during the Civil War), a reja of 1557, and a chalice saved from its looted treasury. In the circular crypt is the grave of the founder, Francisco de los Cobos.

Behind the church are the ruins of the *Hosp. de Ancianos.*— Further E, the REDONDA DE MIRADORES provides panoramic * Views.

To the N is the *Pl. Mayor*, with the porticoed *Escuela de Artes* (once the Ayuntamiento) and **S. Pablo**, with a 13C W front and a polygonal apse (1380) with a mirador. The side façades date from 1490 (N) and 1511; the Plateresque tower from 1537. Stucco vaults were added in 1763, but the *Cap. del Camarero Vago* has a good doorway (1536) and retablo (1538).

In the C. Rosal and C. Montiel, to the NE, there are old mansions with attractive façades. One—the *'Casa Mudéjar'*—contains a museum. The C. Rosal leads down to a 14C Mudéjar *Town Gate*.

W of the SW corner of the Pl. Mayor, in a lane to the left, is the *Pal. de Vela de los Cobos*, with unusual balconies and an open loggia above.—Further NW is *Sta. Clara*, with a Gothic doorway, and beyond that, *S. Pedro*, partly Romanesque.

ÚBEDA TO GUADIX (114km). The C325 descends steeply S to cross the Guadalquivir, then climbs the far side of the valley to (23km) *Jódar* (11,700 inhab.) with a ruined Moorish castle and 17C church. The road continues S through the mountains of the SIERRA ALMADÉN, with the *Mágina* (2167m) to the W. At 29km it leaves *Huelma* (5850 inhab.) 5km W, to cross the *Cuesta los Gallardos* (1180m). At (14km) *Guadahortuna* fork left, crossing two other ridges to meet the N342 at 35km, 13km W of **Guadix**; see Rte 86.

The main route continues E to (10km) *Torreperogil*, then turns right to cross the valley of the Guadalquivir to (23km) *Peal de Becerro* (5700 inhab.), near which is the Iberian necropolis of *Tugia* (6–3C BC).

14km E is **Cazorla** (790m; 10,250 inhab.), a picturesque town with two medieval castles and a ruined Plateresque church. The Treaty of Cazorla in 1179 prescribed the limit of Aragonese expansion into Andalucía.—A sinuous mountain road climbs E past the castle of *La Iruela* to cross the *Puerto de las Palomas* (1290m; views) into the upper valley of the Guadalquivir and (25km) the Parador; see p 477.

Beyond Peal the road climbs SE into the mountains, passing through
the walled town of (11.5km) **Quesada** (7450 inhab.), with a small
museum devoted to the local artist Rafael Zabaleta (1907–60).—
Crossing the craggy *Puerto de Tiscar* (1183m; views), the winding
road slowly descends to (31km) *Pozo Alcón* (6100 inhab.), a remote
town, visited by the indefatigable Samuel Cook (later Widdrington)
in 1830, who then travelled N across the SIERRA DE SEGURA to Orcera
(q.v.). From Pozo Alcón the road turns S and circles around the W
extremity of the *Embalse del Negratin* (view to E, of the *Jabolcón*;
1492m) to approach (43km) **Baza**; see Rte 86.

85   Bailén to Granada via Jaén

130km (80 miles). N323. 37km **Jaén**—93km **Granada**.

Maps: M 446.

Drive due S to cross (13km) the Guadalquivir and bypass *Mengíbar*
(8050 inhab.) and ascend the valley of the Guadalbullón to (24km)
Jaén, with the *Jabalcuz* (1614m) rising further S.

JAÉN (95,800 inhab.; 33,000 in 1920; 65,000 in 1960; Parador) is
now largely a modern provincial capital of little intrinsic interest,
although the older town to the SW still retains a number of characteristic narrow straggling lanes. Its walls have practically disappeared but it is still dominated by its castle (see below). Much of its
prosperity is derived from the production of olive oil. Its climate is hot
in summer, but windy.

Jaén, identified with Roman *Aurinx*, was the centre of the small Moorish
principality of *Jayyan*, which fell to Fernando III in 1246. On 7 September 1312
Fernando IV died suddenly here, 30 days after the unjust execution of the
brothers Juan and Pedro Carvajal, who had summoned him to meet them before
God's judgement seat on that day: thus his surname 'El Emplazado' (the
summoned). It suffered severely in an earthquake in 1712, and in 1808 it was
sacked by the French. It was the birthplace of the grammarian Ibn Malik (died
1274).

The Av. de Madrid, entering the town from the N, passes the Parque
de la Victoria. A short distance NW, in the Paseo de la Estación, is the
Museo Provincial, containing a good *Archaeological collection*,
including a palaeo-Christian sarcophagus from Martos, and a 'bull'
capital from Bruñel-Quesada; on the upper floor are paintings,
including a Christ at the column by Pedro Berruguete, and 19–20C
works of slight merit.

Some distance S is the Pl. de la Constitución; beyond its NE corner
a street leads to the 17C *Conv. de Bernardas* by J.B. Monegro. The
ALAMEDA, further E, provides a good mountain *View.

A short distance SE of the plaza is *S. Ildefonso*, with a façade by
Ventura Rodríguez. The building is internally 14C Gothic and
contains Baroque retablos: that of the high altar is by Pedro and José
Roldan.—From the SW of the plaza the Pescadería leads past the
former *Casa de Vilches*, with an arcaded Renaissance front, to the PL.
DE S. FRANCISCO; on the N side is the *Diputación*, with a 17C loggia.

Opposite is the Renaissance **Cathedral**, built mainly on the plans of
Andrés de Vandaelvira (1534). Its noble W front is flanked by two
towers each 62m high, added in 1667–88 by Eufrasio López de Rojas,
which are its best feature.

A Gothic sanctuary of 1519 was demolished except for its E wall and the rebuilding did not start until 1540. Vandaelvira's work included the *Sacristy* (1555–79), but much of the church, notably the S front, was built by Juan de Aranda in 1634–54; the lantern was completed by Pedro del Portillo in 1660; the Sagrario, by Ventura Rodríguez, as late as 1764–1801. It was presumably in the previous church on this site that the Constable Miguel Lucas de Iranzo, Conde de Quesada, was murdered in 1473.

The walnut *Coro*, completed 1530, was sculptured by Gutierre Gierero (a German), López de Velasco, and Jerónimo Quijano; the trascoro bears a Holy Family by Maella. The 18C organs incorporate remains of one probably played by Francisco Correa de Arauxo. In the *Sacristy* are 16C reliquaries and a custodia by Juan Ruiz. The *Museo* contains paintings by Ribera and Valdés Leal, and other examples of ecclesiastical art; in the *Sala Capitular* is a retablo by Pedro Machuca.

From the W front the C. Maestra leads NW past the *Bishop's Palace* into the older town, passing (right) the *Casino Primitivo*, incorporating the *Pal. del Condestable*, decorated in the 15C by Moorish artists from Granada.—A right fork leads to S. Bartolomé (15–16C), with an artesonado roof.—The left fork continues N to S. Juan, with an early tower; to its E is a picturesque fountainhead of 1648 and the *Conv. de Sta. Clara*, with an artesonado roof in its church.

A lane to the right beyond S. Juan leads to Mudéjar *S. Andrés*, with a vaulted cupola and a chapel of 1515 closed by a beautiful *Reja* by Maestro Bartolomé of Úbeda.—Beyond is the *Conv. de Sta. Teresa* (*Hospicio de Mujeres*), beneath which extensive remains of 11C *Moorish Baths* have been discovered.—Alleys to the right lead to the so-called *Casa de la Virgen* (c 1500) and to the *Hosp. de S. Juan de Dios*, with a Renaissance doorway. The C. Sto. Domingo bears left past the *Conv.* (now *Hosp.*) *de Sto. Domingo*, with a doorway of 1587 by Vandaelvira, to Gothic *La Magdalena*, built on the site of a mosque. It contains a retablo by Jacobo Florentino; the cloister walk incorporates Roman tombstones in its walls.

Beyond is the *Puerta de Martos*, and remains of ramparts on the Córdoba road. Near by is the early 16C *Casa del Cadiato*, and the *Casa de los Priores* (in the C. de Hospitalico, uphill to the left).

Returning to S. Juan, the C. de Almendros Aguilar leads S, later passing the curious *Arco de S. Lorenzo*, with a 15C chapel in Moorish style and a vaulted sacristy; and then *La Merced*, to reach the C. Juan Montilla.

This leads SW past (left) the surviving *Conv. de Carmelitas Descalzas*, a nunnery founded in 1615, which preserves the original MS of the 'Cántico Espiritual' of St. John of the Cross.—Opposite is a stretch of town *Wall* and two towers, beyond which is the former *Carmelite convent*.

On a craggy height to the W is the impressive **Castillo de Sta. Catalina**, recently enlarged to accommodate the Parador. It is served by a good road, providing panoramic views. The castle stands on Moorish foundations, but was almost completely rebuilt after the Reconquest. Beside the tall keep is the 14C *Cap. de Sta. Catalina*, in one of the towers of the curtain wall.

JAÉN TO CÓRDOBA (107km). At **Torredonjimeno** (13,050 inhab.), 17km W, follow the N324 NW of (25km) *Porcuna* (7350 inhab.), Roman *Oulco*, once the centre of Mithraic rites. Boabdil was held prisoner here in the castle of the Knights of Calatrava.—14km *Cañete de las Torres*, with ruins of a Moorish castle; 7km beyond is **Bujalance** (8570 inhab.), with a seven-towered castle built for Abderrahman III in 935. The town was notorious for its *gaitero* or bagpiper, who charged a peseta to start playing and ten to stop.—The NIV is met 11km further NW (see Rte 90) 33km E of **Córdoba**.

JAÉN TO LUCENA (109km), FOR MÁLAGA. The N321 turns left at (17km) *Torredonjimeno* (see above) for (7km) **Martos** (22,050 inhab.), Roman *Colonia*

Augusta Gemella or *Tucci*. The old prison (1577) is now the *Ayuntamiento*, with a fine classical gateway. *Sta. María de la Villa* (restored) is of slight interest. To the E is the precipitous *Peña de Martos*, down which the Carvajal brothers were hurled; cf. Jaén.—The road winds through the hills to (24km) *Alcaudete*, see Rte 91.—At 7km W, turn left through broken hilly country to (19km) **Priego de Córdoba** (20,100 inhab.), a picturesque town containing a number of extravagantly Baroque churches. These are best visited on foot from the central plaza. It was the birthplace of Niceto Alcalá Zamora (1877–1948), President of the Spanish Republic in 1931–36. A short distance NE of the plaza is the *Castle*, and further on, *La Asunción*, with a magnificent stuccoed *Sagrario* (1782) and a verja (1575) at the W door.—To the E is the *Cap. de S. Nicasio* (1771; known as 'La Aurora'), with remarkable plasterwork and a Baroque retablo; and *S. Francisco*, with a curious marble and plaster front decorated with geometrical patterns, with good retablos and a Christ at the column by Montañés.—In the street running S from the main square are the *Colegio*, with a noble front, the *Cap. de las Angustias* (1775), and *El Carmen*, with a Neo-Classical tower.— Beyond is the *Fuente del Rey* (1782; by Alvarez Cubero), with over 180 jets; higher up is the *Fuente de la Salud* (1753).—From above the fountains one can turn back towards the centre past twin-towered *N.S. de las Mercedes*, with another interior of Baroque stucco. On the E side of the main plaza is the *Hosp. de S. Juan de Dios*, with a Doric patio (1637) and Baroque church.—To the N, and W of the castle, is the *Lonja*, with a Doric patio; near by is *S. Pedro*, with a polychrome stucco Camarín. The nearby *adarves* provide expansive panoramic views.—In the upper town is the half-ruinous *Virgen de la Cabeza*.

A mountain road leads S to (55km) *Loja*; see Rte 89A.

The C336 winds through the hills to the W from Priego to (8km) *Carcabuey*, dominated by its castle, and on to (22km) **Cabra** (20,100 inhab.), the ancient *Aegabrum*, a rambling old town whose marble quarries furnished many of the columns for the Mezquita at Córdoba. The ruined *Castle*, *S. Juan* (once a mosque and containing colonnades of stilted arches), and *Sto. Domingo* (1550) are of interest. Cabra was the birthplace of the blind minstrel Mukkaddam Ibn-Muafa (9–10C), originator of the zagal stanza and a forerunner of the troubadours; and of the author Juan Valera (1824–1905).—For *Lucena*, 9km SW, see Rte 93.

The N323 circles to the SE from Jaén, passing (13km; right) the ruined castle of *La Guardia*; and threads the narrow valley of the Guadalbullón before climbing through rugged country and bearing E to avoid the *Puerto de Zegri* (crossed by the old road).—At 50km *Iznalloz* (6700 inhab.) is 4km E of the road and has a hall-church of 1549.—9km NE of Iznalloz is *Piñar*, with a ruined castle.

The road veers SW past the *Embalse del Cubillas* and enters the fertile *vega* of **Granada**, providing a fine view of the city with the SIERRA NEVADA in the background; see Rte 87.

86   Lorca to Granada via Baza and Guadix

222km (138 miles). N340. 18km *Puerto Lumbreras*—N342. 98km **Baza**—48km **Guadix**—58km **Granada**.

Maps: M 446.

For **Lorca**, see Rte 81. Turn NW by the Parador at (18km) *Puerto Lumbreras*, briefly skirting the Rambla de Nogalte. The Moorish tower here was the legendary scene of a bloody battle before the reconquest of Granada. In October 1973 the rambla was the site of devastating floods. The road climbs to (29km) *Vélez Rubio* (839m; 6600 inhab.), with a notable church dated 1753.

The C321 climbs N past the *Cueva de los Letreros*, with prehistoric wall paintings, to (6km) **Vélez Blanco**, with an impressive *Castle* built by Italians in

1506–15 on a polygonal plan. Its Renaissance interiors were removed to New York in 1903 and have been re-erected in the Metropolitan Museum.

The main road leads W up the Rambla de Chirivel, with the SIERRA DE MARÍA (1948m) to the N, to enter the province of Granada at (27km) *Las Vertientes* (1130m).—20km *Cúllar Baza* (see last part of Rte 83), beyond which we cross the HOYA DE BAZA to (22km) **Baza** (20,900 inhab.), Roman *Basti* and Moorish *Bastah*. It was reconquered in 1489 after a six-month siege and some of the Christian cannons are preserved as posts on the Alameda. Nothing remains of the Moorish Alcazaba, but the town retains a few characteristic balconied streets. The only building of any interest is the Gothic *Colegiata* (1529–61), begun by Pedro Urrutia, with an 18C brick tower. In 1971 an extraordinary 4C BC statue, somewhat similar to the 'Dama de Elche', was found at Baza and is now in the Museo Arqueológico, Madrid.—To the NW rises the *Javalcón* (1492m), in which are cave dwellings.—For the road NW to Úbeda, see Rte 84, in reverse.

The road climbs briefly (views NE) before bearing SW through a curious country of pointed sandy hillocks on which only esparto grass will grow, and later descends to cross the valley of the Gor, with the HOYA DE GUADIX extending to the NW and the distant summits of the SIERRA NEVADA coming into view to the SW.

48km **Guadix** (949m; 20,200 inhab.) was the Moorish *Wadi-Ash*, replacing the Iberian and Visigothic city of *Acci* to the SE.

It was once important for its silver mines and more recently for steel knives and esparto mats. According to Brenan a gang of young terrorists took possession of the town early in the Civil War and assassinated anyone they felt deserved death. When the Nationalists eventually marched in they celebrated their victory by a still larger purge: 'One may take it as a rule that in class wars it is the side that wins that kills most'.

It was the birthplace of the Sufi poet Shushtari (c 1212–69, at Damietta); possibly of Pedro de Mendoza (died 1537), founder of Buenos Aires in 1537; of the dramatist Antonio Mira de Amescua (c 1574–1644); and of Pedro de Alarcón (1833–91), author of 'The Three-cornered Hat' (produced as a ballet by Diaghileff in 1919, with music by Manuel de Falla, and décor by Picasso) and other works.

Besides the Moorish *Alcazaba*, which overlooks the town, the only building of any interest is the red-sandstone *Cathedral*, a hall-church designed by Diego de Siloé in 1549, with an apse by Juan de Arredondo added in 1574, and completed in 1701–96 by Vicente de Acero and Gaspar Cayón. The Renaissance *Pl. Mayor*, damaged in 1936–39, has been tastelessly reconstructed. The *Church* of the *Conv. de Santiago* (c 1540) has a Plateresque porch and artesonado ceilings.

The curious looking *°**Barrio de Santiago** comprises numerous dwellings cut into the tufa, behind the simple entrances of which extend several rooms, sometimes on two storeys. Only a few are inhabited by gypsies. There is a similar cave district at *Benalúa*, 6km NW.
For *Lacalahorra*, c 17km SE, see Rte 88A.

The road winds through the tufa landscape to (6km) *Purullena*, also with numerous troglodyte homes, but the village is spoilt by an excessive display of pottery to tempt the passing tourist.—At 7km the N324 diverges right for *Úbeda* (see p 483) or *Jaén*.

We continue W above the valley of the Fardes past *Diezma*, with magnificent panoramic *°Views* S towards the SIERRA MORENA massif, dominated by the *Mulhacén* (3482m); see Rte 87.—The road enters more wooded country on climbing to (22km) the *Puerto de la Mora* (1390m), and winds downhill before crossing the *Puerto del Lobo* (1120m; views). Just before reaching the pass there is a turning (right) to (3km) *Víznar*, where, in an unidentified grave, lies Federico García Lorca, shot by the Falangists of Granada on about the 18 August 1936 (see Ian Gibson, 'The Death of Lorca').

The *vega* of Granada soon opens out to the W as the road descends steeply in sweeping curves, passing (left) the 14C *Puerta Fajalauza*, in the outer city wall, and (right) *S. Cristóbal*, to enter **Granada**; see below.

87   Granada and the Sierra Nevada

Granada (682m; 246,650 inhab.; 104,000 in 1920; 155,000 in 1960; 214,000 in 1975; Parador), the last possession of the Moors in Spain, is an ancient city situated on the slopes and at the foot of three low mountain spurs descending from the S and E towards the broad and fertile *vega* to the W. To the SE stretches the snowy SIERRA NEVADA massif.

On the central and highest spur, which presents a precipitous face towards the town, rise the walls and towers of the **Alhambra**. The depression occupied by the Alameda de la Alhambra separates this, on the S, from the *Monte Mauror* (on which are the Torres Bermejas). On the N it is separated from the lower hill of the *Albaicin* by the gorge of the Darro, a mountain stream which flows through the city (partly in a covered channel) to join the Genil to the S, which irrigates the *vega*. The Airport is c 15km to the W.

During recent decades this region has found a new prosperity based on improved irrigation and intensive agriculture, and on tourism, and the city has expanded considerably.

Its *gitanos* (gypsies), who settled here in the 16C, are a characteristic element in the population.

The Iberian settlement of *Elibyrge* (5C BC) was known as *Illiberis* by the Romans and Visigoths. Granada only emerges from obscurity as a Moorish city. It grew in importance as Moslem fortunes waned at Córdoba and Sevilla, and finally capitulated to the Christians in 1492.

For c 60 years after the fall of the Ommeyads of Córdoba in 1031, Granada was the capital of an independent kingdom under the family of the Zirites. It was later subject to the Almoravides, and then to the Almohades. On the decline of the latter, Ibn Hud, a descendant of the Moorish kings of Zaragoza established an independent authority in southern Spain in 1235, extending from Algeciras to Almería. On his death in 1238 he was succeeded by his rival Mohammed Ibn-Yusuf Ibn-Nasar (commonly known as Ibn el-Ahmar), who, when Jaén was captured by Fernando III in 1246, removed his capital to Granada. As Mohammed I (died 1272) he founded the Nasrid dynasty, which reigned there for 250 years.

Ibn el-Ahmar found it politic to remain on friendly terms with Castile (and even assisted Fernando III in the capture of Sevilla). He devoted his attention to the development and improvement of his kingdom, which under his successors reached its peak in material prosperity. Refugees from towns captured by the Christians flocked to this last redoubt, bringing with them their handicrafts and their industry. Trade and commerce flourished and the arts and sciences were fostered. During this period the population rose to c 200,000, over four times that of contemporary London. To Yusuf I (1334–54) and Mohammed V (1354–91) are ascribed the principal parts of the Alhambra. The decline of the emirate of Granada, weakened by internal dissensions and threatened by the proselytising enthusiasm of the Catholic Kings, may be dated from the reign of Muley Hassan (1462–85), who lost Alhama in 1482.

The romantic story has often been told of how Muley Hassan, captivated by the charms of Isabel de Solis, a *muladi* (a Christian converted to Islam) known by the Moorish name of Zoraya, aroused the jealousy of his first wife Ayesha for the future of her young son Abu Abdallah (Boabdil). A feud arose between the Abencerrages (who supported Ayesha) and the Zegris (who supported Zoraya). Ayesha fled with Boabdil to Guadix, where he was proclaimed king ('el Rey Chico'). After various vicissitudes Boabdil succeeded in dethroning his father (unpopular for imposing heavy taxes on the population) and his uncle Al-Zagal (who had also ruled for a time in Málaga and at Granada). But in 1483 at Lucena, and again in 1488 at Loja, Boabdil fell into the hands of the Spaniards, and only regained his liberty by accepting terms which held him passive while the Catholic Kings made further inroads into Andalucía. By the end of 1489 the emirate was reduced to the city of Granada and the mountainous Alpujarras to the S. A Christian expedition was sent there to cut off any possible aid from N Africa and a royal camp was established at Sta. Fé. Granada was indolently besieged over a period of eight months, during which time its surrender was negotiated for generous terms. The capitulation took place during the first few days of 1492. Ferdinando and Isabel wore Moorish costumes when they received Boabdil's surrender and officially entered the city on 6 January. Boabdil and his followers retired to the Alpujarras and left for Morocco some 21 months later. The repopulation of the conquered land was then put in hand, although perhaps three-quarters of the land available was given away in royal grants.

The capture of Granada was hailed as a triumph throughout Christendom, even being celebrated at old St. Paul's in London by a 'Te Deum'. However, the town fell on evil days, largely due to religious intolerance. Within three months an edict was published in Granada expelling all Jews from the Crowns of Castile and Aragón. In 1609 it was the turn of the Moriscos, which robbed it of its most industrious citizens.

Its university was founded in 1526.

By 1800 its population had fallen to c 40,000. During the Peninsular War it was pillaged by the French. In 1831 a certain Mariana Pineda was executed here merely for the 'crime' of possessing an embroidered banner of the Liberals.

During a long period of stagnation the exotic attraction of the Alhambra increasingly brought Granada to the notice of travellers, through both the writing of Washington Irving and Richard Ford, and through the works of a number of British and foreign artists, among them David Roberts, George Vivian, and J.F. Lewis. With the increasing influx of visitors the town revived and became more tourist conscious.

In 1936, following the military coup of 20 July, Granada experienced a bloodbath when the Nationalists killed indiscriminately anyone with liberal sympathies. The flower of her intellectuals, lawyers and doctors, including the poet Federico García Lorca, were among the 4000 assassinated in the city and its immediate surroundings during the Civil War (a mere 572 were formally recorded in the month of August 1936 alone). Granada lived up to its reputation for being reactionary and its citizens irascible.

The name Granada is derived from the Moorish *Karnattah*, and has no connection with the Spanish word for pomegranate—*granada*—although the fruit—stalked and proper—has been adopted as the canting coat of arms of the city.

Among Granadinos of note were Moses ben Jacob ben Ezra (c 1055–c 1138), the Jewish poet; Johannes Leo 'Africanus' (Hassan ibn Mohammed el-Wezaz; 1494–1552), the explorer; Fray Luis de Granada (1504–88), the preacher and religious writer; Diego Hurtado de Mendoza (1503–75), historian and humanist; Alonso Cano (1610–67), artist and sculptor; Francisco Martínez de la Rosa (1787–1862), the author; Angel Ganivet (1865–98), the philisophic novelist; and Manuel Gómez Moreno (1870–1970), the Arabist.

Note. As package tours appear to take priority, individuals are advised to book well in advance. A pension can often provide reasonable alternative accommodation. Motorists are advised not to use their cars except in the main streets.

The following description of Granada has been divided into five sections: the *Alhambra* and *Generalife*; the *Capilla Real, Cathedral* and surrounding area; NE Granada (the *Albaicin*); S Granada; and the *Sierra Nevada*.

The C. de los Reyes Católicos has been taken as the base line. It runs from the Puerta Real (an irregular square retaining the name of

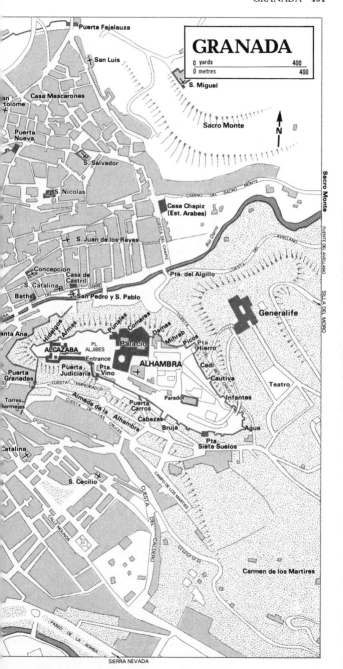

GRANADA

0 yards	400
0 metres	400

Puerta Fajalauza

San Luis

S. Miguel

Casa Mascarones

Sacro Monte

an
tolome

Puerta
Nueva

S. Salvador

N

S. Nicolas

CAMINO DEL SACRO MONTE

Casa Chapiz
(Est. Arabes)

Sacro Monte

CUESTA DEL CHAPIZ

Rio Darro

FUENTE DEL AVELLANO

S. Juan de los Reyes

AVELLANO

CUESTA DEL

SILLA DEL MORO

Concepcion
S. Catalina

Casa de
Castril

DARRO

Pte. del Algillo

Baths

DE

San Pedro y S. Pablo

Generalife

nta Ana

Hidalgos
Armas

Puntles

Comares

Damas

Mihrab

CUESTA DE

Picos

ALCAZABA

PL.
ALJIBES

Palacio

Pta
Hierro

Puerta
Granadas

Entrance

Puerta
Judiciaria

Pta.
Vino

ALHAMBRA

Cadi

Cautiva

Teatro

CUESTA

EMPERADOR

Torres
Bermejas

Almeda de la Alhambra

CUESTA DE LAS CRUCES

Puerta
Carros

Parador

Infantes

Catalina

Cabezas

Bruja

Agua

Pta
Siete Suelos

S. Cecilio

CAMPO DE LOS MARTIRES

CUESTA DEL CALDERO

CALLE MOLINOS

Carmen de los Martires

PASEO DE LA BOMBA

SIERRA NEVADA

a vanished gate) to the Pl. Nueva, below the W promontory of the Alhambra. The description begins at a central point where the Gran Vía de Colón leads N from the Pl. de Isabel la Católica.

A. The Alhambra and Generalife

Admission. While entry to the hill of the Alhambra itself is free, most of the buildings may only be visited, at stated hours, with two-day tickets obtained near the entrance to the enceinte. An early start is recommended, before the bus loads arrive. A second visit in the evening or towards sunset can be rewarding. Some parts described may be closed for restoration.

The *Hill of the Alhambra*, the 'Red Fort' (*Al Qal'a al-Hambra*), is a steeply scarped ridge rising abruptly from the valley of the Darro to the N and W; it rears above the trees of the Alameda to the SW; to the NE it is cut off by the *Cuesta del Rey Chico*—a ravine perhaps partly man-made—from the *Cerro del Sol*, on whose slopes rises the Generalife. The Moorish palace 'of the Alhambra' covers only a small part of its plateau, which, already fortified by nature, is encircled by a line of walls and towers closely following the configuration of the ground.

The direct approach road ascends from the *Pl. Nueva* (see p 502) by the steep Cuesta de Gomérez to the *Puerta de las Granadas*, surmounted by three open pomegranates. This was erected c 1536 (from designs of Pedro Machuca) on the site of the Moorish *Báb el-Ajuar*, a gate in the wall which once united the Torres Bermejas (see below) with the Alcazaba. Beyond the arch is the ALAMEDA DE LA ALHAMBRA, thickly planted with elms, where a footpath ascends to the left to the *Puerta de la Justicia*, the main pedestrian entrance to the enceinte. (Cars are directed by a roundabout route to the *Puerta de Coches*—formerly *de los Carros*.) The footpath passes the Renaissance *Pilar de Carlos V*, a wall fountain designed by Machuca and carved by Nicolas del Corte in 1545.

Paths lead SW up to the **Torres Bermejas** (Vermilion Towers) on *Monte Mauror*, a fortified outwork perhaps earlier than the Alcazaba, restored in the 16C.—To the SE (beyond the Alhambra Palace hotel) is the *Carmen de los Mártires* in the grounds of a former monastery of which St. John of the Cross was once prior.

The **Puerta de la Justicia** is a gate-tower built in 1348 by Yusuf I, with a horseshoe archway and vaulted passage making three bends so as to obstruct a hostile entrance.

Ascending through the gate we pass (right) the *Puerta del Vino*, so-called from its use as a wine store in the 16C; it is one of the oldest parts of the Alhambra, dating from the late 13C. We next reach the *Pl. de los Aljibes* (cisterns), so-called from the immense reservoir constructed by the Catholic Kings below part of it. The ticket office is to the right.

The E side of the plaza is dominated by the incongruous *Pal. of Charles V*, which masks the *Pal. of the Alhambra* behind it to the N. To the W is the *Alcazaba*, which it is convenient to visit first. A parapet to the N provides plunging views over the Darro towards the Albaicín quarter.

The **Alcazaba** was the Moorish citadel from the 11C, although little survives from that period; most of the exterior walls and towers date from the time of Ibn al-Ahmar (1238–72). It occupies the precipitous extremity of the hill and was formerly divided from the rest of the plateau by a depression now occupied by the cisterns below the Pl. de los Aljibes. Its E wall is strengthened by the *Torres Quebrada* and *del Homenaje*; on the N side is the *Torre de las Armas*; and at the NW angle, the *Torre de la Vela*, on which Card. Mendoza hoisted the Christian flag on 2 January 1492. It commands panoramic views over the town and the *vega* beyond, and of the SIERRA NEVADA to the SE.

The ***Palace of the Alhambra** is the most remarkable monument of Maghribian Moorish art surviving in Spain. It is built—partly on artificial foundations—close to the N edge of the hill and exhibits a simple exterior in contrast to its highly ornamented interior. Notable are the variety of its ceilings, with their stalactite pendentives and honeycomb cupolas; the lace-like diapers in plaster that cover many of the walls above a dado of richly coloured azulejos; and its several courtyards surrounded by elegant arcades of stilted or horseshoe arches supported by slender marble columns and spandrels of delicate tracery. A large part of the ornamentation is provided by inscriptions in Cufic characters or the more decorative Naskhi script, mainly pious sentiments or eulogies of the builder: 'Walà ghalìba ill'Allah'—God alone is Conqueror—frequently occuring.

The palace dates mainly from the 14C. Ibn el-Ahmar (1232–72), founder of the Nasrid dynasty, took up his residence here, but little remains of his 13C palace. Its principal builders were Yusuf I (1334–54), to whom the Court of Myrtles is due; Mohammed V (1354–91), responsible for the Court of the Lions; and Mohammed VII (1392–1408), who decorated the Tower of the Infantas. The Catholic Kings repaired and strengthened the edifice, but Charles V demolished part of it to provide a site for his Renaissance palace.

An explosion of powder outside the walls in 1591 damaged the Court of the Lions and the adjoining Sala de los Mozárabes. These were repaired, but the structure and decoration of the various other dependencies gradually deteriorated from centuries of neglect. Henry Swinburne, who visited the place in 1775, observed that the one-armed governor, who lived in one small corner of the palace spent most of his time drinking wine rather than looking after the structures. It was visited by Chateaubriand in 1807. In 1812 the French, under Sebastiani, attempted—unsuccessfully—to blow up the building when they retired from Granada.

In 1829 Washington Irving spent three months in the palace, where he began his romantic tales and sketches of the Moors and Spaniards in which he immortalised Francisca de Molina, 'Tia Antonia', who started to tidy up the dilapidated fabric. In 1831 Richard Ford spent the first of two summers there. It was visited by George Borrow on 30 August 1836. W.G. Clark, in 1849, complained of his guide that he would keep up a running commentary of the very smallest talk, 'recklessly confusing dates and facts, nations and personages; and for any special absurdity audaciously appealling to the authority of *Vasindon Eerveeen* . . . '. Intermittently, from 1828, haphazard attempts at repairing the damage was initiated, when it was not being pillaged by governors. Serious modern restoration did not begin until 1862, and continues.

From the vestibule we pass through the *Mexuar* or council chamber (converted into a chapel in 1544, but now restored). Off this there is a small oratory. Adjacent is the *Patio del Cuarto Dorado*, from which a 16C arch admits to the *Cuarto Dorado*, decorated in the Mudéjar style by the Catholic Kings.

To the E is the *Patio de los Arrayanes* (myrtles) or *de la Alberca* (of the pond), an open court down the centre of which extends a narrow fish pond between myrtle hedges; at each end is a graceful arcade supported by six columns and containing alcoves with stalactite vaulting. Above the S arcade is another gallery, with pierced woodwork, part of the building demolished to make room for the Pal. of Charles V. The E side of the patio has been restored, and in parts rebuilt, after a destructive fire in 1890.

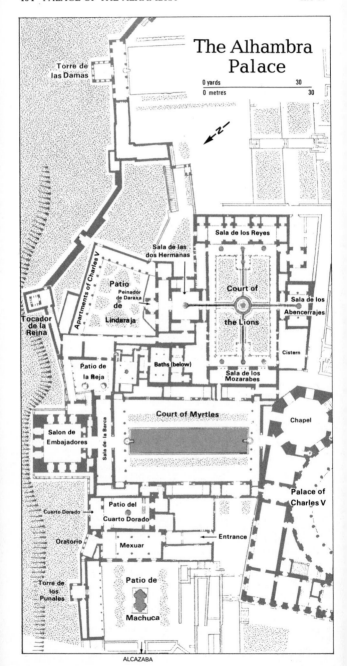

The Alhambra Palace

Torre de las Damas

0 yards 30
0 metres 30

Sala de los Reyes

Sala de las dos Hermanas

Apartments of Charles V

Patio de Lindaraja

Peinador de Daraxa

Court of the Lions

Sala de los Abencerrajes

Tocador de la Reina

Cistern

Patio de la Reja

Baths (below)

Sala de los Mozarabes

Court of Myrtles

Chapel

Salon de Embajadores

Sala de la Barca

Palace of Charles V

Cuarto Dorado

Patio del Cuarto Dorado

Oratorio

Entrance

Mexuar

Torre de los Punales

Patio de Machuca

ALCAZABA

At its N end is the *Sala de la Barca*, also damaged in the fire, said to be so-named from the form of its ceiling, which is shaped like the inverted hull of a boat (*barca*), but as likely from the Arabic *baraka*, a benediction. On the far side is the richly decorated **Salón de Embajadores** (ambassadors), the largest and one of the finest rooms in the palace. It occupies two storeys in the interior of the *Torre de Comares* and forms a square of 11m, with an intricately wrought dome of coloured larchwood 23m above the floor.

This was the audience chamber, with a throne occupying the recess facing the entrance. Above a dado of azulejos, the walls are covered by a polychrome veil of interlaced patterns and inscriptions stamped upon the plaster, one naming Yusuf I as the builder. In the thickness of the walls there are deeply recessed windows commanding views which in his time prompted Charles V to comment: 'Ill-fated was the man who lost all this'.

Near the far end of the patio (from which the octagonal crypt of Charles V's chapel can be visited) a door admits to the *Sala de los Mozárabes*, which suffered severely in the explosion of 1591. This is the antechamber to the **Patio de los Leones**, an open-air court (28m by 16m) begun in 1377, which is surrounded by an arcade of stilted arches supported by 124 white marble columns, the elaborate capitals of which retain traces of colour. At each end a graceful pavilion projects into the court, each with *media naranja* cupolas. The walls within the arcades are decorated with plaster fretwork patterns, but the ceilings are modern.

In the centre is a *Fountain* resting on the backs of 12 diminutive lions carved in grey marble. Around the edge of the basin runs an inscription in thanksgiving for its plentiful supply of water. (Gautier claimed to have camped in this courtyard for four days, keeping his bottles of sherry cool in the fountain.)

On its S side is the *Sala de los Abencerrajes* (see Granada's history), with a stalactite roof and inlaid larchwood doors; the decoration of the walls is a 16C restoration. To the E is the *Sala de los Reyes* (or *de la Justicia*), with elaborate *media naranja* vaulting and stalactite arches. In the main alcoves are ceiling paintings on leather, attributed to Christian artists of the late 14C. Ten Moors seated in council appear on the central alcove ceiling; the others depict chivalric and hunting scenes.

On the N side of the patio is the **Sala de las Dos Hermanas** (of the two sisters), named after the twin slabs of white marble in the pavement. Perhaps part of the harem, this room is unequalled for the beauty and richness of its decoration. The window opposite the entrance retains its Moorish shutter, the only one to survive in the palace. The *Honeycomb Dome*, the largest and most elaborate of its kind, is said to contain over 5000 cells. Off this opens the *Sala de los Ajimeces*, named after the windows on its N side; beyond is the *Mirador* or *Peinador de Daraxa*, overlooking its patio. To the E, a window looks down on the *Patio de la Sultana*, with its four cypresses.

A corridor on the W side leads to the *Apartments of Charles V*, two rooms 'modernised' c 1527, in which Irving took up his quarters in 1829.

A modern corridor leads to the *Peinador* or *Tocador de la Reina* (the queen's dressing room), a belvedere at the top of the *Torre del Peinador* (where the sultanas of the harem were succeeded by Elizabeth of Parma, wife of Felipe V). Encircled by an outer gallery is a pavilion embellished with Italian paintings (1539–46) by Julio de

Aquilés and Alexander Mayner. On the outside are scenes from
Charles V's expedition against Tunis. In one corner there is a
perforated marble slab through which perfumes may have been
wafted from below.

Stairs descend from a gallery adjacent to the Apartments of
Charles V to the small *Patio de la Reja* (or *de los Cipreses*), with a
fountain and four cypresses. On its E side is the *Sala de los Secretos*,
one of several small chambers from which a door admits to the *Baths*;
in the innermost room two marble baths survive. The vaulted roofs
are pierced by star-shaped openings, once perhaps filled with
coloured glass. The decoration of the *Sala de las Camas*, the reposing
room, dates from 1843–66.

The adjoining *Patio de Lindaraja* is a relic of the Moorish inner
garden, planted with cypresses, orange trees and box edgings. Cross
this to enter the main gardens of the palace. To the left is the *Torre de
las Damas* (previously known as the *Casa Sánchez*), in which Richard
Ford and his family lived during the summer of 1833. Opposite is a
large pool fed through two stone lions.

Several of the towers of the enceinte surrounding the E side of the
Alhambra hill have been restored, and some retain their original
decoration. Among them are the *Torre del Mihrab*, next to a small
mosque (c 1350); the battlemented *Torres de los Picos* (c 1300), below
which is the *Puerta de Hierro*; the *Torre del Cadi*; the fine *Torre de la
Cautiva* (the captive); and the *Torre de las Infantas* (its sumptuous
decoration, of the reign of Mohammed VII, showing signs of decadence). The *Cuesta de Rey Chico* is now spanned by a footbridge
allowing direct access to the *Generalife*; see below.

Those wishing to make a circuit of the walls should continue past the *Torre del
Agua* at the SE extremity of the enceinte, where the aqueduct from the Darro
enters the Alhambra. On the following stretch there are the remains of several
towers blown up by the French in 1812, including the *Puerta de los Siete Suelos*
(of seven floors), where Boabdil is said to have left the Alhambra in 1492, after
which it was walled up at his request.

In the centre of the gardens is the former *Conv. de S. Francisco*,
founded in 1495 and several times altered. In 1929 it was converted
into a Parador, recently enlarged and meretriciously furnished.
Within its church rested the bodies of Fernando and Isabel until their
transference to the Capilla Real.—Further to the E is *Sta. María*, on
the site of a mosque, designed by Herrera but built on a smaller scale
by Juan de Orea in 1581–1618. Its retablo (1671) is by Juan López
Almagro.

The *Palace of Charles V* was begun in 1526 by Pedro Machuca
(died 1550) and building operations progressed slowly for over a
century until finally abandoned, leaving the roof unfinished. In the
early 18C part of the structure was used as a powder magazine in
spite of the experience of 1591 (see Alhambra history).

On three sides, each 63m in length, are elaborate façades over a
basement of rusticated masonry. Above this is an upper storey with
Ionic pilasters between the windows. The S portal was completed in
1554, with sculptures by Niccolo di Corte; the W portal by 1563, with
sculptures by Juan de Orea and Antoine de Leval, and additions
above the portal by Juan de Minjares (1586–92). The circular *Patio*,
30m in diameter, was completed in 1616, and bullfights once took
place here. Its arcade of 32 Doric columns of conglomerate stone—
originally intended to be marble—come from a quarry near Sta. Fé
and support an upper storey with Ionic columns separating recesses

intended for sculptures. At the NW angle is a staircase; at the NE angle an octagonal *Chapel* (c 1540–99), designed to be surmounted by a dome. Its retablo, of Genoese marble, dates from 1546; the painting of the Magi from 1630.

The building accommodates two museums at present (1988). Although new museum premises have been built to the E of the Alhambra, there appears to be considerable conflict or confusion of interests: whether other collections in the city will be moved here or whether these will be moved elsewhere is undecided; and until the dispute is resolved the museums are given only summary descriptions.

On the ground floor is the ***Museo Nacional de Art Hispano-Musulman**, an extensive collection of material from the area, much of it from the Alhambra itself. It includes the 'Alhambra Vase', one of the finest existing specimens of 15C Hispano-Moresque ware. Among other exhibits are a Córdoban marble ablution bowl (10C) with curious carvings of eagles and of lions devouring gazelles. Also on display are numerous examples of Moorish ceramics, stucco work, and glass; tombstones; carved wood; carved capitals; fountainheads; bronzes; fabrics; and a variety of other objects of the period.

On the upper floor is the **Museo de Bellas Artes**. Selected items include a Carrera marble Fireplace depicting Leda and the Swan; the Limoges enamel Triptico del Gran Capitán (c 1500) by Nardon Pénicaud; a polychrome wooden Entombment by Jacobo Florentino; wooden relief from stall work by Diego de Siloé; a Portal from vanished S. Gíl by Siloé and his School; stalls from the Conv. de Sta. Cruz (1590) by Juan de Orea and Francisco Sánchez; and polychrome busts by Alonso Cano, Pedro de Mena, and Diego de Mora. Paintings include works by Juan Sánchez Cotán, Juan de Sevilla, Pedro Bocanegra, Van der Hamen, Mateo Cerezo, Estéban de Rueda, and Morales. 19C–20C paintings include works by José Gutierrez de la Vega, José Roldan, Vicente López, Madrazo, Villaamil, Fortuny, and Zubiaurre.

Partial view of the Generalife, Granada

Further up the Alhambra mountain spur stands the *Generalife, once the summer palace of the sultans. It can be approached either directly from the Alhambra gardens by a footbridge or by road to the entrance to its gardens. An avenue of clipped yews and cypresses leads up to the inner gate, passing an *Open-air Theatre* (1953).

The name (pronounced Heneralif) is derived from the Arabic *Jennat al-Arif*, meaning garden of Arif (the architect); but the builder of the palace, the original work of which dates from 1250, is unknown. An inscription records that it was decorated in 1319 for the Sultan Abul Walid.

Down the centre of the luxuriantly planted *Patio de la Acequia* (49m long) stretches a narrow aqueduct bordered by fountain jets. In the middle of its flanking arcade is a *mirador* with good, but damaged, plaster ornamentation; beyond is an arcade of five arches (restored), commanding attractive vistas. Adjacent is the *Patio de los Cipreses*, also with a pool and fountain jets. To the N is a gallery on two levels built in 1586, and on the slope behind, an upper garden. A belvedere of 1836 can be reached by climbing the successive terraces. One of the more delightful descents is by the *Camino de las Cascadas*, where runnels of water forming miniature cascades flow down conduits in its balustrades.

Still higher, and outside the limits of the garden, is a knoll known as the *Silla del Moro*, providing good views. There are remains of what was perhaps a mosque; and in the area there are traces of Moorish reservoirs.

B.   The Capilla Real and Cathedral

From the Pl. de Isabel la Catolica follow the Gran Via briefly and take the second left turning, to pass (left) the remarkable painted façade (an addition of 1729) of the *Casa del Cabildo Antiguo*. This was originally the *Madresa* or university of the Moors, built in 1349; it contains an octagonal Moorish room with a dome, and the *Sala de Cabildos* (1513) with a Mudéjar ceiling.

Opposite is the entrance to *Capilla Real* (fee), and next to it the Plateresque *Lonja* or Exchange (1522), built against the wall of the Sagrario and like the façade of the chapel, with its open-work balconies and pinnacles designed by Enrique de Egas. The late Gothic *Capilla Real was built by Egas in 1506–21 as a mausoleum for the Catholic Kings, superseding that of S. Juan de los Reyes at Toledo (q.v.), already partially completed. Flanking the Plateresque portal (1527) by Juan García de Pradas are statues by Nicolás de León, a French sculptor.

Until the chapel was completed the remains of Isabel (died 1504) and Fernando (died 1516) rested in the church of S. Francisco (see above).
    The *Sacristy* is entered first, containing the *Treasury* and important paintings, mainly from the collection of Isabel. These include: Roger van der Weyden, Nativity, and Pietà; Master of the Legend of St. Lucy, Mass of St. Gregory; Memling, The Holy Women, The Virgin, Pietà, Descent from the Cross, Virgin and female saints; Botticelli, Christ in the Garden; Dirk Bouts, The Virgin, Virgin and angels, Head of Christ; Pedro Berruguete, St. John on Patmos; and several anon. 15C works of good quality.
    In glass cases are the sceptre and crown of Isabel; her mirror converted into a custodia; an illuminated missal written for the queen by Francisco Flórez (1496); embroideries worked by Isabel; the sword of Fernando; banners used at the conquest of Granada; and a Tapestry of the Crucifixion between the sun

and the moon by Marcos de Covarrubias, and an altar cross.—A staircase ascends to the raised *Choir* at the W end of the chapel, with Plateresque stalls by Jacobo Florentino, but completed by Martín Bello in 1521. Some of the choir books have illuminations by Lorenzo Florentino (c 1545).

In the **Chapel** itself a superb *Reja*, designed by Juan de Zagala and Juan de Cubillana and made by Maestro Bartolomé of Baeza in 1520, separates the nave from the chancel. Here stand the white marble *Royal Monuments*, executed in the style of the Italian Renaissance with recumbent figures and elaborate sculptured decoration by Domenico Fancelli of Florence. They were made in Genoa and completed in 1517. Here also is the slightly higher monument (designed by Bartolomé Ordóñez; 1520) of Felipe I (El Hermoso, the Handsome; died 1506) and Juana (La Loca, the Mad; died 1555; cf. Tordesillas), the parents of Charles V. When descending to the small

The reja and tombs in the Capilla Real, Granada

vault below to view their simple leaden coffins Charles remarked 'small room for so great glory'. The candle to be kept perpetually lit before Isabel's tomb, in accordance with her will, has been replaced by a dim electric light bulb.

The *Retablo* is by Felipe Vigarni (1522), at the foot of which are kneeling statues of the Catholic Kings, remarkable as portraits (perhaps by Siloé). Below, in painted panels, are depicted their conquest and conversion of the infidel. The Relicarios or side altars (1632) are by Alonso de Mena. In the N transept is a retablo of 1521 by Jacobo Florentino el Indaco, incorporating some of his paintings and also paintings by Pedro Machuca; and a fine triptych by Dirk Bouts.

The adjacent cathedral can be entered from the Gran Via. The main W entrance is usually closed.

The construction of the **Cathedral** was begun in the Gothic style by Enrique de Egas in 1521, succeeded in 1528 by Diego de Siloé, who continued it in the early Renaissance style. On his death in 1563 the work was taken over by Juan de Maeda. Although consecrated in 1561 its vaults were not completed until 1704 and work on the W front lasted until 1714. Twiss remarked (in 1773) that the interior had been recently 'entirely encrusted with the finest marbles . . . and enriched with bronze gilt', but executed in a 'wretched and despicable manner'. Many will agree that this ungainly edifice is (in the words of John Harvey) 'one of the world's architectural tragedies, one of the saddest of wasted opportunities'.

The heavy W Façade, with massive pillars bearing figures of the Apostles, was designed just before his death in 1667 by Alonso Cano and built by José Granados. (Cano was buried in the cathedral, of which he had become a minor canon.) Over the *Puerta Principal* is a relief by José Risueño (1717) and over the side doors are reliefs by Michel and Louis Verdiguier (1783). The Doric lowest stage of the *N tower* (the S was never built) is by Juan de Maeda (c 1576); the Ionic and Corinthian upper stages by Ambrosio de Vico (c 1610).

The *Sacristy* contains a Crucifixion by Montañés, the Virgin appearing to St. Julian by Pedro de Moya, an Annunciation by Cano, and his carved Conception.—The adjoining Sala Capitular leads to a Churrigueresque oratory with a carved Virgin and Child by Cano, and an altarpiece attributed to Pedro Duque Conejo.

The *Nave* (from which the Coro has been removed and the 16C stalls placed in the sanctuary) has double aisles off which are side chapels. The groined roof is supported by huge pillars with engaged Corinthian columns. The Organs (1746) are by Leonardo de Ávila, but the acoustics of the building are bad and produce a five-second echo.

The almost circular *Cap. Mayor* has a dome supported by a double tier of Corinthian columns. Beside the entrance arch are kneeling statues of the Catholic Kings by Pedro de Mena Medrano (1677); above these are marble pulpits (1717) by F. Hurtado Izquierdo. The glass here and in the ambulatory is by Theodor de Holanda and Jan van Kampen. The seven paintings between the columns of the upper tier are by Cano, numerous of whose paintings and sculptures are to be seen in several of the chapels. Notable are three paintings by Ribera in the retablo of the Altar de Jesús Nazareno, in the S aisle.

The *Treasury* in the basement of the tower (NW corner) contains a Custodia presented by Isabel, a green set of Mudéjar vestments of 1544, and other cult objects.—The Renaissance *Sagrario*, abutting the S aisle, was built as a parish church by F. Hurtado Izquierdo in 1759 on the site of a mosque which had been used as a church until the middle of the 17C. It contains a notable Renaissance font, and the *Cap. del Pulgar*. Hernán Pérez de Pulgar (1451–1531) secretly entered Granada by night in 1490 and pinned to the mosque door a parchment bearing the words 'Ave Maria', for which exploit he was honoured by burial close to the royal vault.

Several works by Bocanegra, Diego de Pesquera, Juan de Sevilla, Juan de Mora, Alonso de Mena, et al. embellish other chapels of the cathedral.

Opposite the W front of the cathedral is the *Archbishop's Palace*, largely 17C. It was severely damaged by fire on 31 December 1982, when several paintings by Cano and Valdes Leal were said to have been destroyed.—The *Curia*, to the N, was completed in 1544 and was the seat of the university until 1679. It was designed by Diego de Siloé, but its portal is by Juan de Marquina and its Doric patio by Sebastián de Alcántara.

Immediately to the SW is the once picturesque *Pl. de Bibarrambla*, the scene of jousts, bullfights, and fiestas, and containing a 17C fountain brought from the demolished Conv. de S. Agustín.

The Moorish gate (*Bab ar-Ramla*, the sand gate) became known as the *Puerta de las Orejas* because the hands and ears (*orejas*) of malefactors were displayed here. (In 1621 a platform collapsed here at a festival and it was later said that the mob tore earrings from the ladies involved in the disaster, an episode which gave rise to yet another fable.) Removed in 1873, the gate was reconstructed in 1935 in the alamedas of the Alhambra.

Leading E from the SE angle of the plaza, the *Zacatin* crosses the *Alcaicería*, the former Moorish silk bazaar. It was burnt down in 1843 and later rebuilt in a crude attempt to copy the original style. The C. de S. Jerónimo leads NW from the N side of the cathedral, passing (left) *SS. Justo y Pastor* (late 16C, with a Baroque doorway), W of which, in a former Jesuit college, was the main University building from 1796.—To the right are the *Conv. de la Encarnación* (1524) and the college of *S. Bartolomé* (16C).—Beyond (left) is the Renaissance *Pal. de Caicedo*.

To the left on reaching the C. de Gran Capitán is **S. Jerónimo**, founded by the Catholic Kings, but long neglected. Its church was completed in 1547 by Diego de Siloé and its portal in 1590 by Martín Díaz de Navarrete and Pedro de Orea. It contains the remains of Gonzalo de Córdoba (died 1515), 'El Gran Capitán'. Siloé was also responsible for the doorways of the Gothic cloister. A second patio (1520) is a curious mixture of Moorish, Gothic, and Renaissance motifs.

Turning N along the C. de S. Juan de Dios we pass (left) the *Hosp. de S. Juan de Dios*, founded in 1552 after the death of the saint commemorated in its name.

Juan de Dios, or de Robles (1495–1550), was a native of Montemor-o-Novo in Portugal, and of Jewish lineage. He devoted his life to the succour of captives, foundlings, and the sick, and founded the Order of Charity (*Caridad*), approved by the Pope in 1570. He was canonised in 1691.

Over the portal is a kneeling statue of S. Juan by José de Mora. The Baroque *Church* (1738–59) with a front by José Bada, contains a Churrigueresque retablo.

Continue N, cross the Av. de la Constitución and skirt gardens to reach the former **Hospital Real**. This imposing Renaissance building, with fine Plateresque windows, was begun in 1511 by Enrique de Egas and was completed in 1536 by Juan García de Prades. It has recently been converted to house part of the *University*.

About 1km N, approached by the C. Real de Cartuja, E of the University, is the *Cartuja, founded in 1506 on an estate granted to Gonzalo de Córdoba and moved to its present site in 1516.

Around the *Cloisters* are the Gothic *Refectory* (begun 1531), *Chapterroom* and later *Chapterhouse* (completed 1567), the latter containing martyrdoms by Sánchez Cotán and Vicente Carducho. The Church contains paintings by Bocanegra and a screen (1750) with paintings by Cotán separating the monks' choir from that of the lay brothers. The *Sagrario* by Hurtado Izquierdo (1704–20) is richly embellished with marble, jasper, and porphyry, and has a fresco by Palomino in the cupola. The Churrigueresque **Sacristy** (1725–c 1783), designed by Izquierdo, continued by Luis de Arévalo and decorated by Cabello, is an extreme example of the style, extravagantly adorned with brown and white marbles and stucco, with its door and cupboards inlaid with silver, tortoiseshell, and ivory (by José Manuel Vázquez), and with a statue of St. Bruno (by José de Mora) on the high altar.

The Aceros de S. Ildefonso leads S from the University—passing *S. Ildefonso* (1555), designed by Siloé, and close to restored *La Merced* (1530)—to the Pl. del Triunfo.

The Gran Via, which was cut through a congested part of the old town at the beginning of this century, is a few paces to the SW; it can be avoided by turning SE through the mutilated 11C *Puerta de Elvira*, once the main gate of Granada, and following the narrow C. de Elvira S. This passes (right) *S. Andrés* and later *Santiago* (both c 1525; by Rodrigo Hernández), and (left) the doorway (1654) by Cano of the *Church of the Hosp. de Corpus Cristi*, to reach the Pl. Nueva.

C. Northeastern Granada (the Albaicín)

At the NW end of the Pl. Nueva is the *Audiencia* (formerly the *Chancillería*) built c 1531, with a façade (1587) by Juan de la Vega, and a balustrade added in 1762. It contains an arcaded patio and a stalactite ceiling (1578) over the staircase .

At the E end of the plaza is **Sta. Ana** (1548; by Siloé), with a graceful tower (1563) and Plateresque portal (1547) by Sebastián de Alcántara and his son Juan. It contains statues by José de Mora.

From the N side of the church the Carrera del Darro leads E along the right bank of the Darro. The **Albaicín**, the oldest part of Granada, is on the hill to the N; its name derives either from the Arabic *Rabad el-Bayyazin*, the quarter of the falconers, or from the fact that it was settled by Moors from Baeza after that town had been sacked by Fernando III. Bounded by the C. de Elvira on the W (see above) and by a partly suriving wall on the N, it is now a poor but characteristic area of narrow crooked alleys. It has a few churches of minor interest and numerous Moorish houses whose unpretentious exteriors occasionally veil interiors and gardens (*carmenes*) of considerable charm.

Following the Carrera del Darro, with the Alhambra looming high above, we pass, at the second bridge, a fragment of masonry on the far bank which is a relic of the 11C Moorish *Bridge of the Cadi*. It formed the ancient approach to the Puerta de las Armas of the Alhambra. At No. 31 in the Carrera are remains of 11C *Moorish Baths*. Uphill from here is the *Conv. de la Concepción* (1523), with a church of 1644.—Continuing E, we pass the *Conv. de Sta. Catalina de Zafra* (1540), incorporating a Moorish house.

The *Casa de Castril* (No. 43) has an elaborate Plateresque façade (1539), probably by Sebastián de Alcántara, and patios with carved wooden columns. It now houses archaeological collections, including Punic alabaster vases from Almuñécar, stone bulls from Arjona

(Jaén), a 9C lamp from the mezquita of Medina Elvira, and collections of cinerary urns, metalwork, ceramics, and other artefacts.

SS. Pedro y Pablo, opposite, was largely completed in 1576 by Juan de Maeda, and has a main portal by Pedro de Orea, but the tower and sacristy were not finished until 1593. Note its artesonado ceiling.

A short street climbs to *S. Juan de los Reyes* (c 1520; by Rodrigo Hernández) which incorporates the 13C minaret (altered) of the mosque of Ataibin, which became the first Christian church in Granada.

The Carrera del Darro is extended by a paseo—providing a neck-breaking view of the Alhambra—to reach the *Puente del Algíllo*. From here the *Cuesta del Rey Chico* climbs up the ravine between the Alhambra and Generalife.

Turn N to ascend the *Cuesta del Chapiz*, in which No. 14 is the 16C *Casa de Chapiz*, restored to house a school of Arabic studies.

The *Camino del Sacromonte* leads E. The *Cuevas* opening off it have long been inhabited by gypsies, who will endeavour to extort what they can from the tourist. On the hilltop stands the *Conv. del Sacromonte*, enlarged since the original building was completed in 1610. Human remains uncovered in neighbouring caves in 1594 were credulously assumed to be the bones of S. Cecilio and his fellow martyrs. Abp Pedro de Castro, whose tomb is in the church, founded the convent on the site of the discovery.—By following a line of Moorish walls *S. Miguel el Alto* (see below) can also be approached from here.

The Cuesta del Chapiz, still climbing, circles to the NW, off which a footpath zigzags up (right) to the high-lying *Ermita de S. Miguel el Alto*, built in 1673 on the site of a Moorish tower. Its chapel, rebuilt in 1815, provides a magnificent *View of Granada.

On reaching 16C *S. Salvador*, built on the site of and incorporating remains of the principal mosque of the Albaicín, turn left to follow alleys climbing to Gothic *S. Nicolás*, by Rodrigo Hernández (rebuilt after a fire in 1932). Its plaza commands a remarkable *View of the Alhambra.

Bear NW from the church to approach the *Puerta Nueva* and turn left along the Cuesta de la Alhacaba, skirting a stretch of the town *Walls*. We turn left at the W end of these and after a short distance pass (left) the *Conv. de Sta. Isabel la Reál*, founded by Isabel in 1501, with a domed church and a florid Gothic portal ascribed to Enrique de Egas. The convent is on the site of the *Palace of Dár al-Horra*, a residence of Moorish princesses; there are restored remains of it in a parallel alley to the N.

To the S is the *Casa del Gallo*, mentioned by Irving. Continuing S, we reach *S. José*, on the site of a mosque pulled down in 1517, but whose minaret is incorporated in the tower. Some 10C work has been exposed, including the oldest horseshoe arch in the city (S wall). The church was built in 1525 by Rodrigo Hernández and added to in 1544. It contains good artesonados, a red marble retablo designed by Ventura Rodríguez, and sculptures by José de Mora and Siloé.

Continue downhill to regain the Pl. Nueva.

D. Southern Granada

Immediately S of the Pl. de Isabel la Católica is the *Conv. de las
Carmelitas Descalzas*, founded in 1582. Beyond it the C. S. Matías
leads downhill to *S. Matías*, completed in 1550 and containing a
notable retablo (1750) by Blas Moreno.—Retracing one's steps, take
the second right turn to approach the *Casa de los Tiros*, a Mudéjar
mansion of c 1505, named after the muskets (*tiros*) projecting from
the upper windows of its façade. It houses the Tourist Office and a
museum of local history.

Continue SE along the C. de Pavaneras and turn right down the C.
de Carnicería to *Sto. Domingo* (1532), with a raised choir and Gothic
vaults.—Further downhill is the Pl. de los Campos Eliseos, in which is
the entrance gate to the *Cuarto Real de Sto. Domingo*, a late 13C
Moorish palace, with one surviving tower. It is said to retain magnifi-
cently decorated rooms untouched by the restorer, but admission is
difficult to obtain.

To the SW is the Pl. de Mariana Pineda and the *Diputación* (1764),
with a curious red and grey façade and quaint figures of soldiers
facing the CARRERA DEL GENIL (formerly *Paseo de Invierno*, or winter
promenade), with its plane trees. On its W side is *N.S. de las
Angustias* (1671) by J.L. Ortega, with a portal by Bernardo and José
de Mora, and containing statues (1718) by Pedro Duque Cornejo.

Further SE is the PASEO DEL SALÓN, the summer promenade,
shaded by elms. To the SW is the *Puente de Genil*, replacing an older
bridge spanning the river to the PASEO DEL VIOLÓN.

Turning NW from the Diputación, the (Pl. de) Puerto Real is soon
reached. To the W is *S. Antonio Abad* (1656), with a Baroque dome of
1747 and containing statues by Pedro de Mena.

Turning right at the Puerto Real, we pass (right) the Pl. del
Carmen; on its N side is the *Ayuntamiento*, incorporating a patio of
1622 and remains of a Carmelite convent. An alley to its W leads to
the *Casa del Carbón, originally a khan (early 14C), later an
alhóndiga (granary), a theatre, and in the 17C a coal-weighing office.
It is a remarkable example of the type of hostelry once ubiquitous in
Moorish Spain, and a rare survival.

Turn into the main street and then right to return to the Pl. de
Isabel la Católica.

E. The Sierra Nevada (by car)

The Paseo de Salón (see above), extended by the PASEO DE LA
BOMBA, ends at the *Puerta Verde*. Here, on the far bank of the Genil,
is the *Conv. de S. Basilio*, its church (1776) by Luis de Arévalo. Follow
the GR420 E, ascending the narrowing valley on a good mountain
road which later climbs in a series of zigzags to (35km) the Parador
and the Solynieve winter sports development.—The road continues
to climb past (right) Radio-telescope installations to a point below the
Pico Veleta (3398m), and continues to the base of the *Mulhacén*
(3484m), the highest summit. A difficult road descends the S face of
the massif to *Capileira*; see Rte 88C.

The snow-clad **Sierra Nevada**, part of the Penibetic mountain system which separates inland Andalucía from the Mediterranean coast, is c 80km long, extending from the *Montenegro* (NW of Almería) to the spur descending to *Padul*, due S of Granada. Much of the W end of the massif is now a nature reserve.

For roads from Granada to **Jaén**, and **Baza**, see Rtes 85 and 86, in reverse; for **Almería**, **Málaga**, **Córdoba**, and **Antequera** (for **Sevilla**), see Rtes 88, 89, 91, and 94.

88   Granada to Almería

A.   Via Guadix

171km (106 miles). N342. 58km **Guadix**—N324. 113km **Almería**.

Maps: M 446.

For the road to *Guadix*, see Rte 86 in reverse.

The N324 ascends SE, with the E ridge of the SIERRA NEVADA ahead. At 14.5km it passes **Lacalahorra** (3km right), dominated by a 16C *Castle* with domed angle towers, built in 1513 by Lorenzo Vázquez for Rodrigo de Vivar y Mendoza, Marqués de Cenete (the legitimised son of Card. Mendoza). Unfortunately much of its Italian Renaissance style decoration has been gutted, but it is still worth making the short detour.

At 22km *Fiñana*, with a ruined castle, is bypassed as the road descends parallel to the Rio Nacimiento, at 26.5km veering E, away from the old road, to (8km) *Gergal*, with prehistoric remains and a well-preserved medieval castle.—Due N rises the *Calar Alto* (2168m), the highest summit of the SIERRA DE LOS FILABRES, with its *Observatory*. At 18km we meet the N340 from Murcia in the Rambla de Tabernas and turn right for Almería; see latter part of Rte 81.

24km **ALMERÍA** (140,750 inhab.; 51,000 in 1920; 87,000 in 1960; 120,000 in 1975), although a rapidly spreading provincial capital, retains much of its older centre of narrow streets and pealing paintwork huddled below the castle hill. Its winter climate is warm and dry, but in summer the hot inland winds raise the shade temperature to 36°C (97°F).

Roman *Portus Magnus*, as Moorish *Al-Mariyat* attained such prosperity (and with a population of perhaps 150,000) that it was said that 'Cuando Almeríra era Almería, Granada era su alquería' (When Almería was Almería, Granada was but its farm). Between c 1035–91, from the fall of the Caliphate to its subjugation by the Almoravides, it was the most important capital in Moorish Spain. Under Ibn Maimün its pirates were as dreaded as those of Algiers.

Momentarily captured by Alfonso VII in 1147, Almería was not finally taken until 1488 by Fernando the Catholic. In 1490 its Moorish inhabitants were expelled with the excuse that they were plotting rebellion, and its importance declined. It revived with the opening of the railway in 1899 with the export of ore from neighbouring mines, but the city again stagnated in the 1920s, as decribed by Gerald Brenan. It was long a Republican base, and was the scene of an international incident on 31 May 1937 when in retaliation for two Republican bombs being dropped on the 'Deutschland' anchored off Ibiza, the 'Admiral Scheer' and a squadron of four German destroyers fired 200 shots into the town.

The Carretera de Granada reaches the centre of the town at the *Puerta de Purchena*. From this plaza the *Paseo de Almería*, the main shopping street, leads S to meet the usually dry rambla a short distance N of the port. The harbour is skirted to the W by the tree-lined ANDEN DE COSTA.

The C. de las Tiendas leads SW from the Puerta de Purchena past *Santiago*, with a tall 16C tower, and 18C *Sta. Clara*, to the Pl. Vieja (right). Further S stand the *Episcopal Palace, Seminary*, and the fortress-like **Cathedral**.

Construction of the present Cathedral began in 1524. It stood on the site of the great mosque, converted into a cathedral in 1490, but was shattered by the earthquake of 1522. It is remarkable for its four massive towers and Corinthian façade (1550–73) by Juan de Orea. The interior contains elaborately carved walnut stalls by the same artist. In the chapel behind the high altar lies the tomb of Bp Diego Fernández Villalán, the founder.

Between the cathedral and the Paseo de Almería stands 18C *Sto.*

The curtain wall of the Alcazaba, Almería

Domingo (restored). *S. Pedro* to the N, and *S. Juan* to the S, occupy the sites of mosques.

From the Pl. Vieja one can climb W to reach the extensive Moorish *Alcazaba (being restored), which dominates the town. It was built in the 10C by Abderrahman III and later enlarged, but was wrecked by the earthquake of 1522. The principal remains are the *Keep* erected by Fernando and Isabel, and a mosque converted into a chapel. The colourful gardens are a welcome relief from the dusty streets below. A curtain wall with towers links the castle with the neighbouring height of *S. Cristóbal*, crowned by an ugly monument on the site of a chapel built by the Templars after 1147.

The *Airport* of Almería is 7km E. Beyond it a road circles to the *Cabo de Gata* (agate cape), with caves famous for their crystals. The coastal SIERRA DE LA GATA rises to the NE.

For the road bearing NE from Almería to **Mojácar**, **Lorca**, and **Murcia**; see Rte 81 in reverse.

B.   Via Motril

183km (113 miles). N323. 67km—N340. 4km *Motril* crossroads—59km *Adra*—53km **Almería**.

Maps: M 446.

On crossing the Puente de Genil, turn right along the Paseo del Violón, passing further W the *Ermita de S. Sebastián*, once a mosque. Roman walls have been uncovered in this area. A short distance beyond (right) is the *Alcázar de Genil*, on the site of and incorporating relics of a mid-14C Moorish palace.

The road bears SW and passes (5km) the *Airport*. It then climbs gently to (10km) the low *Puerto del Suspiro del Moro* (860m), the watershed between the Genil and the Mediterranean. The name derives from the story that when Boabdil (see Granada history) turned to take his last look at Granada his mother reproached him with the words, 'weep not like a woman for what you could not defend as a man'.

At 5km the road skirts *Padul* and descends the valley of the Lecrin, with its almond, lemon, and orange groves. There is a view of the *Caballo* (3013m), the nearest high summit of the SIERRA NEVADA range, as the improved road passes *Durcal* and other villages. At 20km we reach the turning for *Lanjarón* (6km E; see Rte 88C).

After 10km the valley of the Guadalfeo is entered and the ruined castle of *Vélez de Benaudalla* is passed on the left. There is a view of the sea ahead as we approach (17km) the N340. Turn left here past (4km) **Motril** (40,500 inhab.). Its collegiate *Church* has a Gothic nave and Renaissance transeptal sanctuary.

The road skirts the coast, its shores defended by ancient *atalayas*, and bypasses the resorts of *Calahonda*, *Castell de Ferro*, and *La Rábita*. The SIERRA DE LA CONTRAVIESA and its foothills rise to the N.

59km **Adra** (17,400 inhab.), Phoenician *Abdera*, an ancient port with ruins of a Moorish castle.—At 4km *Berja* (11,150 inhab.) lies 13km inland, with lead mines in the vicinity.—After 7km the road bears away from the coast across the dreary CAMPO DE DALIAS. *Dalias* itself, a town of 33,000 inhab., is 8km N, below the massif of the SIERRA DE GÁDOR (*Morrón*; 2236m).

At 29km roads ascend steeply to the hill villages of *Enix* and *Félix*, both enjoying extensive views. **Roquetas de Mar** (18,900 inhab.), 5km S, is one of several resorts in the area.—3km *Aguadulce*, beyond which the road skirts the rock-bound coast to approach (10km further E) **Almería**, dominated by its *Alcazaba*; see Rte 88A.

C.   Via the Alpujarras

211km (131 miles). N323. 40km—C333. 6km *Lanjarón*—9km *Orgiva*—7km. C332. 58km *Ugijar*—23km *Laujar de Andarax*—56km. N340. 12km **Almería**.

Maps: M 446.

For the first 40km see Rte 88B.—6km **Lanjarón**, an attractive small town with a ruined castle, commanding good views, and well-known for its mineral springs. It is perched on a shelf at 720m, below the *Caballo* (3013m), amid terraces of figs, oranges, peaches, and pomegranates.—9km *Orgiva* (5000 inhab.), also picturesquely situated, overlooks the Guadalfeo and faces the SIERRA CONTRAVIESA. It retains a fortified mansion of the Condes de Sástago, and a Baroque church.

From here two roads cross the **Alpujarras**, a hilly and previously inaccessible region between the sunny S flank of the SIERRA NEVADA and the SIERRA CONTRAVIESA. In their beautiful and sometimes impressive valleys, abounding in numerous mineral springs, flourishing vines and a variety of fruits.

By the Treaty of Granada the Alpujarras was assigned to Boabdil and his followers, with his seat at Andarax, but he only remained there until the autumn of 1493, when he crossed over to Morocco, as did 6000 of the principal families during the next decade. In 1499 the rural Morisco population was presented by Card. Cisneros with the alternative of Christian baptism or exile. Many rose in revolt, and Fernando the Catholic was obliged to spend the following year restoring order. During the next few decades several attempts were made to suppress their language, dress, and customs. They were hounded by the Inquisition: by 1560 Moriscos accounted for over 85 per cent of those punished by tribunals. Legislation against them tightened further, and by December 1568 the Second Rebellion of the Alpujarras was under way. Vigorous counter measures were put into effect by the Marqués de Mondéjar and his rival the Marqués de Los Vélez (the latter being defeated the following May). By March 1570 it was decided that the only way to pacify the region was by mass deportation of the inhabitants and their dispersal throughout the country. But this was not entirely effected, and large numbers of Moriscos congregated in S Castile.

ORGIVA TO MECINA BOMBARÓN VIA TREVÉLEZ (60km). The GR421 turns N to follow the S flank of the Sierra Nevada, a good but narrow road commanding numerous extensive views S. At 16km it bears away from neighbouring *Pampaneira* and *Capileira* (supposedly repopulated by Gallegos), and climbs again to (19km) *Trevélez* (1476m), known for its snow-cured ham and for its witches. The *Mulhacén* (3482m) rise to the NW.—The road turns S and then NE to (19km) *Bérchules*, 2km beyond which it joins the main route 4km from *Mecina Bombarón*; see below.

From Orgiva continue SE and fork left at 7km.

The C333 climbs over the *Puerto Camacho* (1219m; views), crossing the SIERRA DE LA CONTRAVIESA and later descending steeply via (36km) *Albuñol* to (8km beyond) *La Rábita* on the coast. In the *Cueva de los Murciélagos*, near Albuñol, important neolithic remains were discovered in 1857.

The C332 ascends the valley of the Guadalfeo through (35km) *Cádiar*
and 3km beyond meets the more northerly road before reaching
(4km) *Mecina Bombarón*.—After 5km it skirts **Yegen**, the occasional
home of Gerald Brenan in the 1920s, as described in 'South from
Granada'. Among his visitors were Lytton Strachey, Carrington,
Leonard and Virginia Woolf, Roger Fry, David Garnett, Bertrand
Russell, and Augustus John.—11km *Ugijar*—23km *Laujar de
Andarax*, a high-lying village, beyond which we descend the valley
of the Andarax, with the *Sierra de Gádor* to the S, through (20km)
Canjáyar.—At 28km we pass near the prehistoric necropolis of *Los
Millares*, and *Gádor*, with Moorish ruins, to meet the N340 12km N of
Almería; see Rte 88A.

89   Granada to Málaga

A.   Via Loja

127km (79 miles). N342. 53km **Loja**—N321. 74km **Málaga**.
Maps: M 446.

Driving NW and then W, at 11km **Sta. Fé** (11,300 inhab.) is bypassed.
The original settlement was run up by Fernando and Isabel during
the siege of Granada. Three of the four gates surmounted by chapels
still stand. It was here in April 1492 that the Catholic Kings promised
Columbus certain privileges should his exploratory voyage bear fruit.

Not far to the N lie two estates granted by the Cortes (from the confiscated
property of Godoy) to the Duke of Wellington after the victory of Salamanca.
One, the *Soto de Roma*, had been owned previously by Ricardo Wall, the
minister (of Irish origin) of Fernando VI and Carlos III. It included part of the
village of *Fuentes Vaqueros*, birthplace of the poet Federico García Lorca (1898–
1936; he lived there until 1912; cf. Viznar). In 1933–43 almost all of this estate,
which had been let to small-holders, was sold to them at a very low figure. The
other property, the *Molino del Rey*, still in the possession of the family, is further
NW, near *Illora*, beneath the bleak wall of the SIERRA DE PARAPANDA.

The road skirts the *Airport* of Granada and passes (9km) *Láchar*, with
a curious but neglected castle-palace of the Duques de S. Pedro de
Galantino, which retains several horseshoe arches.

At 13km picturesque *Montefrio* (8450 inhab.), in the sierra 26km N, has an
abandoned church of the type of the Capilla Real, Granada, designed by Diego
de Siloé.

10km **Loja** (20,000 inhab.), now of slight interest, was once of military
importance as the key to Granada. It guarded the entrance to the
vega, but was taken in 1488 by Fernando and Isabel, aided by the
English archers of Sir Edward Woodville. Gen. Ramón Narváez
(1800–68), the rival of Espartero, was born here.
    The town is dominated by the walls of the ruined Moorish
Alcazaba. Early 16C *Sta. María* is built on the site of a mosque. *S.
Gabriel*, completed in 1566 from designs by Siloé, has a good
artesonado.

To the NE is the gorge of *Los Infiernos*, which contains the Genil; to the NW the river forms the *Embalse de Iznájar*.

The *old* road to Málaga forks left shortly after Loja to cross the *Puerto de los Alazores* (1040m) to *Colmenar*. Apart from offering plunging views of Málaga on its eventual steep corkscrew descent, it is not particularly recommended.

The *new* road veers left at 17km and meets (22km) the N331 from Córdoba just before crossing the *Puerto de las Pedrizas* (780m). The rapid descent down the valleys of the Cauche, then the Guadalmedina, passes through several tunnels and skirts (right) the estate of *La Concepción* in the lower valley. This is remarkable for its tropical vegetation and incorporates Roman remains from Málaga and Cártama in a 'Grecian temple'.

For **Málaga**, see Rte 97.

B.   Via Motril and Nerja

159km (99 miles). N323. 67km *Motril* crossroads—N340. 2km *Salobreña*—15km *Almuñécar*—22km *Nerja*—21km. *Vélez Málaga* is 4km N—32km **Málaga**.

Maps: M 446.

For the road to the coast 4km W of *Motril*, see Rte 88B.

The N340 leads W through a region of rich vegetation, with sugar-canes, palms, and tropical plants. The coastal scenery, particularly between Almuñécar and Nerja, is impressive, the road climbing high above the shore; but it demands careful driving.

2km **Salobrena** (8350 inhab.) retains its Moorish castle (restored), below which nestles the old town. Beyond this the road starts to climb.

15km **Almuñécar** (16,400 inhab.) is a good example of a coastal resort ruined by unrestricted exploitation, and now offering little more than dirty beaches. It was the site of Phoenician *Sexi*; there are Phoenician and Roman ruins at *Cueva de Siete Palacios*, and a ruined aqueduct.

The road now climbs steeply to its highest point, with sheer cliffs towards the sea where the SIERRA DE ALMIJARA reaches the sea. It then descends past *Maro*, where there is a turning to the stalactite *Cueva de Nerja*, containing Palaeolithic paintings.

The resort of **Nerja** (11,600 inhab.) (bypassed) has a Parador planned to overlook the bay from an isolated height; it has been inexorably encroached upon by more recent uncontrolled development.

Frigiliana, with an orchid farm, is perched on a hillside 6km inland and approached by a picturesque road.

At 8km *Torrox* (4km inland) has a population of 10,050. It is of Roman origin and was possibly the birthplace of Almanzor (940–1002), the scourge of the Christians.

13km *Torre del Mar*, 4km inland from which is **Vélez-Málaga** (41,950 inhab.) with an old upper town with ruins of a Moorish castle. *Sta. María* preserves considerable remains of a mosque; *S. Juan Bautista* contains sculptures by Pedro de Mena. The sanctuary of *N.S. de los Remedios* (1640) is also of some interest. Joaquín Blake

(1739–1827) was born here; he was a Spanish general of Irish descent and a great loser of pitched battles during the Peninsular War.—See below for the road from *Alhama de Granada*.

There is an old fort between *Almayate* and *Benajarafe*, but there is little else of interest on this stretch of coast, with its continuous chain of resorts following the example set by Torremolinos, the climate being their chief attraction. Málaga eventually comes into view set against its mountain background. The road enters its sprawling E suburbs, including once-fashionable *La Caleta*, to reach the Paseo del Parque of **Málaga** itself: see Rte 97. (If approaching from this direction, it is convenient to visit the old *English Cemetery* just N of the Av. de Pries in Caleta; see p 537.)

C.   Via Alhama de Granada

136km (84 miles). C340. 53km **Alhama**—19km *Ventas de Zafarraya*—C335. 28km **Vélez Málaga**—4km. N340. 32km **Málaga**.

Maps: M 446.

This attractive crosscountry route forks right off the N323 5km SW of Granada. It passes the Airport and (4km beyond) *Gabia la Grande*, with remains of a 5C *Baptistry* and the 15C tower known as *El Fuerte*.

At (8km) *Malá* we reach hilly country, with the SIERRA DE PERA to the S. At 18km the road descends above the *Embalse de los Bermejales*, with a fine view ahead of the SIERRA DE ALMIJARA (*Maroma*; 2068m).—The road then climbs over a ridge into the valley of the Alhama, in which, at 16km, are the *Baños de Alhama*. The *Baño de la Reina* may date from Roman times; the Moorish *Baño fuerte* is so-called from the heat and strength of its water.

The road climbs behind (2km) **Alhama de Granada** (960m; 6050 inhab.), perched on a cliff high above the river. Its *Church* (c 1500–26) was built by Pedro de Azpeitia and Enrique de Egas and has a tower added by Siloé.

The romantic capture of this 'key' to Granada in 1482 was the subject of a ballad by Byron ('Ay! de mi Alhama!'). The posada here was condemned by Ford as being 'truly iniquitous; diminutive indeed are the accommodations, colossal the inconveniences'. In 1884 the area was devastated by an earthquake.

The road climbs again, closer now to the Sierra, and bears NW along a valley to (19km) *Ventas de Zafarraya*; it then turns abruptly left through a cleft in the ridge and descends the S flank of the range in sweeping curves, passing some distance from several villages perched on its slopes, to (28km) **Vélez Málaga**; for this, and for the road to **Málaga**, see Rte 89B.

90 Bailén to Sevilla via Córdoba, Écija and Carmona

251km (156 miles). NIV. 27km **Andújar**—81km **Córdoba**—51km **Écija**—54km **Carmona**—38km **Sevilla**.

Maps: M 446.

For **Bailén** see Rte 48A. The NIV bears SW down the wide valley of the Guadalquivir to (27km) **Andújar** (35,500 inhab.) also bypassed. It was perhaps the Iberian *Iliturgis* and has a *Roman bridge* of 15 arches at the SW angle of the walled area. Part of its industry is the manufacture of the once ubiquitous *alcarrazas* or *jarras*, porous pottery vessels for drinking water.

The town retains fragments of a Moorish castle. In the central Pl. de España are the *Ayuntamiento*, some Renaissance mansions, a Baroque fountain, and the late Gothic church of *S. Miguel*, with an 18C tower. To the W is *S. Bartolomé* (c 1500), also with an 18C tower, and star-vaulting. *Sta. María* is a Gothic hall-church built on the site of a mosque, with a Plateresque façade (1559), a reja by Maestro Bartolomé, and a painting by El Greco.

Some 35km N in the SIERRA MORENA is the hilltop sanctuary of *Sta. Maria de la Cabeza* (founded 1277). It has restored dependencies, which until 1 May 1937 formed an isolated Nationalist outpost, the stubborn defence of which made headlines.

At 23km *Lopera* is 7.5km S, with a castle of Moorish origin. In the fighting of December 1936 the poets John Cornford and Ralph Fox were killed here, the former the day after his 21st birthday.

3km **Villa del Río** (6800 inhab.), bypassed, has a Moorish palace converted into a church, a *Roman Bridge* E of the town, and an 18C bridge over the Arroyo del Diablo.

At 9km **Montoro** (10,100 inhab.), 2km N, is perched above the Guadalquivir, crossed by a 16C bridge. In the town centre is Gothic *S. Bartolomé*, built of red sandstone, with a fine tower. A short walk uphill by an adjacent alley leads to *Sta. María* (being restored), containing some curious Romanesque capitals, unique in Andalucía.

We cross the Guadalquivir at (32km) *Alcolea*, where in June 1808 Gén. Dupont defeated a Spanish force only a few weeks before his capitulation at Bailén (q.v.). The town was also the scene of Marshal Serrano's dispersal of the troops of Isabel II on 28 September 1868, which precipitated her abdication.

14km **Córdoba**; see Rte 92. A bypass has been built circling S of the city.

CÓRDOBA TO CARMONA VIA LORA DEL RÍO (106km). The C431 leads W past the turning for *Medina Azahara* (see Rte 92) parallel to the foothills of the SIERRA MORENA.—25km *Almodóvar del Río* (6400 inhab.), Roman *Carbula*, with its picturesque restored Moorish *Castle*.—At 30km **Palma del Río** (17,350 inhab.) is 3km S on the far bank of the Guadalquivir, near its confluence with the Genil. The town has a few relics of its past, including the restored *Conv. de S. Francisco* (1492), now a hotel.—6km *Peñaflor*, Roman *Ilissa*, retains an old tower.—18km beyond is **Lora del Río** (18,050 inhab.), a rambling old town with a ruined Moorish castle and Churrigueresque *Ayuntamiento*.—By crossing the river here and turning right, a rough road can be followed SW directly to (27km) **Carmona**; see below.

Some 9km W of Lora there are slight remains of Roman *Arva*.—11.5km further W is *Villanueva del Rio y Minas*, 9km N of which are the remains of the Roman temple of *Munigua* (at the *Castillo de Mulva*).

Crossing the Guadalquivir at Córdoba, the road bears SW to (29km)
La Carlota (8150 inhab.), or ⅃ of the new towns largely repopulated
by Swiss and Germans during the reign of Carlos III (cf. La Carolina).—
22km **ÉCIJA** (34,700 inhab.), on the left bank of the Genil, is a very
ancient town displaying an imposing series of tall steeples studded
with azulejos. Notorious for its grilling heat in summer, Écija is
known as 'La Sarten (frying pan) de Andalucía'.

Roman *Astigi* became the seat of a bishop under the Visigoths, but its walls
were built by the Moors. It was retaken by Christian forces in 1263. It was
Ferrant Martínez, the bigotted archdean of Écija, who incited the anti-semitic
riots at Sevilla in 1391 which spread throughout Spain. It was also once the
headquarters of a famous band of outlaws, 'los Siete Niños de Écija'.
    Luis Vélez de Guevara (1579–1644), poet, playwright, and satirist, was born
here.

The church of *Sta. Ana* (c 1763) in the Conv. de Terceras, near the
bridge, has a picturesque corbelled tower decorated with azulejos.—
From a point further W the C. de Cervantes turns right towards the
Pl. Mayor, passing near *La Merced*; its retablo (1615) has carvings by
Felipe Vázquez. At the SE corner of the plaza is *Sta. Bárbara* (1790;
by Ignacio Tomás), with a battlemented belfry.

Just to the S the **·C. de los Caballeros** runs E, lined with mansions
and palaces. Among the most notable are the *Pal. de Peñaflor*, with a
Doric portal of 1721 and a galleried front with frescoed paintings; No.
41, the Renaissance *Pal. de Torres Cabrera* (c 1530); and No. 47, the
Pal. de la Marquesa de Alcántara, with a balconied Baroque portal.

To the S of the Peñaflor palace is *S. Gil*, founded in 1479 but altered
in 1770 and with a tower built in 1779. To the N of the palace the
great tower of *S. Juan* (1745) rises above its ruined church.

Further N is *S. Pablo* (1728–76), to the W of which is *Sta. Cruz*
(1776–1836), with a brick tower and containing an early Christian
sarcophagus and arabic inscriptions recording the setting up of
public fountains in 929 and 977. The latter were the gift of Princess
Subh, a Basque by birth, and mother of Hisham II.

Beyond the walls to the N is *La Concepción* (1684), with a twin-
towered front of 1745.—In the NE of the town *Sta. Florentina* has a
good Baroque S doorway (1759); to the S of it is the Churrigueresque
Conv. de Descalzos (1718–70).

From the NW corner of the Pl. Mayor a street leads past (right) the
Isabelline front of the *Conv. de las Teresas* (which occupied a 14C
Moorish palace) and the Isabelline *Hosp. de la Concepción* (1598).
Some distance further W, beyond the *Puerta Cerrada*, is *El Carmen*,
with a tall tower of 1637.

Just SW of the Pl. Mayor, beyond a smaller square, is *Sta. María*
(1778), with a splendid tower of 1717 and good retablos and tombs. In
front is a Baroque *triunfo* of 1766. Near by is the *Conv. de S.
Francisco*.

Return to the S perimeter of the town and turn right to pass (left)
the *Conv. de la Victoria*, with a brick steeple of 1757; and (right)
Gothic *Santiago* (c 1500; restored), with an Isabelline retablo, a
Crucifixion by Pedro Roldán, and a Renaissance patio.

To the right on leaving the town is the *Pl. de Toros*, on the site of a
Roman amphitheatre and near a Roman necropolis.

ÉCIJA TO UTRERA, FOR JEREZ AND CÁDIZ (79km). Fork left just W of Écija onto the
N333 for (39km) **Marchena** (16,150 inhab.), also with a bypass, an ancient town
granted by Fernando V to the house of Ponce de León, dukes of Arcos. The
more interesting part is to the N within the *Moorish walls*, where the palace of
the dukes once stood. The Gothic church of *S. Juan* (partly restored)

has a carved cedar *Coro*; and the tall tower of *Sta. María* is covered with
azulejos in the Portuguese manner. In the newer town are *S. Agustín* and *S.
Sebastián*, with Baroque details.

At 7km the road joins the N334 and turns right through (9km) *El Arahal* (see
Rte 94). Beyond this it forks left for (24km) **Utrera** (38,100 inhab.), Roman
Utricula. It is the centre of an agricultural and cattle-rearing district and is
renowned for its bulls. It was the birthplace of Rodrigo Caro (1573–1647), the
antiquary and poet; and of the dramatists Serafín (1871–1938) and Joaquín
(1873–1944) Álvarez Quintero.

On the NE outskirts is *N.S. de la Consolación*, its plain W front with a 16C
portal and slender tower; inside there are notable stalls, a carved retablo, and a
Mudéjar artesonado ceiling.—15C *Santiago*, by the Pl. Mayor, has a Flamboyant W door.—*Sta. María de la Asunción*, to the SE, dates from 1369 and has
a Gothic nave, Plateresque coro, and tall 18C tower; it also contains the tomb of
Diego Ponce de León.—Remains of its Moorish *Alcázar* have been restored.

The *Castle of Las Aguzadero*, c 21km SE, beyond *El Coronil*, dates from
1381.

The A4 motorway can be joined 14km W of Utrera; the N333 continues SW to
meet the NIV at 18km via *El Palmar de Troya*.

The NIV leads W from Écija through (15km) **La Luisiana** (6100
inhab.), another of Carlos III's colonies (cf. La Carolina and La
Carlota). 5km beyond, it skirts (left) the Infantado *Pal. de Moncloa* to
cross a deserted region before reaching (34km) Carmona, on a height
overlooking the plain.

CARMONA (22,900 inhab.; Parador) (Roman *Carmo*; Moorish
Karmuna) was captured by Fernando III in 1247. When taken by the
Nationalists in 1936 700 of its citizens were executed.

Immediately outside the Roman *Puerta de Sevilla* (2C; altered by
the Moors) is *S. Pedro*, begun c 1466. It has a rich interior and a tower
of 1704 in imitation of the Giralda at Sevilla.—Above it is the
imposing ruin of the *Alcázar de Abajo*, a Moorish fortress on Roman
foundations. Here one enters the old town, passing *S. Bartolomé*,
which retains a Gothic sanctuary and a S doorway with dog-tooth
ornamentation.

Uphill to the left is the *Pl. Mayor*, with the *Juzgado* of 1588 and the
Ayuntamiento, which contains several Roman mosaics.—Further on
is Churrigueresque *El Salvador* (1720) by Diego Romero and his sons.
To the left is late Gothic *Sta. María* (1424–1518), on the site of the
principal mosque, of which a patio survives. The *Sanctuary* (1551)
contains a high altar with a terracotta frontal; in the baptistery
is a 15C triptych by Alejo Fernández; in the coro, good 17C
woodwork.

Beyond the *Puerta del Sol* (SE of Sta. María) is the *Pal. del Marqués
de los Torres* (1755). To the N are the *Ayuntamiento Viejo*, with a
front of 1697; the *Conv. de Descalzas* (founded 1620); and *La
Trinidad* (1748).—Further E are *Sta. Clara* (1460), with artesonados
and a blocked Gothic W doorway; the polychrome brick chapel of *La
Caridad* (1510); and, at a higher level, *Santiago*, its steeple adorned
with azulejos and with a sanctuary of c 1350.—The street descends to
the *Puerta de Córdoba* (late 2C), altered by the Moors and provided
with Renaissance fronts in 1668.—In the valley below is a ruined
Roman Bridge of five arches.

The top of the hill is dominated by the extensive ruins of the
Alcázar de Arriba, an early fortress with an imposing entrance gate.
It was converted by Pedro the Cruel into a luxurious palace but was
abandoned after the earthquake of 1504. Part of it is the site of the
parador, commanding views over the valley of the Corbones.

From the Alcázar it is possible to return to the *Puerta de Sevilla*
through a picturesque quarter of cobbled lanes, passing the ruins of

Renaissance *S. José* and Gothic and Mudéjar *S. Felipe* (1473; by Martín García).

Also of interest is *Sto. Domingo* (or *Sta. Ana*; c 1522), now serving as a cemetery chapel, with a Renaissance nave and vaulted Gothic sanctuary; and higher, in the N suburb, 14C *S. Blas*, rebuilt in 1727.

Immediately W of the town (at the fork of the Sevilla and Alcalá de Guadaira road) turn sharp right and then left, where between two Roman roads is the important *Roman Necropolis* (2C BC–4C AD), with a small museum of glass, ceramics, cinerary urns, and bronzes, including a very modern-looking woman's Head in marble.

The subterranean, rock-hewn family tombs, approached by narrow stairways or perpendicular shafts, are generally arranged in groups. In front of each is a crematorium; and a few have vestibules. The more interesting are those called 'del Olivo', 'del Columbario', 'de Prepusa', and 'de Póstumo'. (This last has the Triclinio del Elefante, a stone figure of an elephant, and a circular domed mausoleum.) The remains of a temple-tomb c 30 paces long, with columns surrounding a galleried patio, have also been excavated, and is known as the 'Tumba de Servilia'. Close by are some prehistoric tumuli.

The C432 leads SW to (23km) *Alcalá de Guadaira* (see Rte 94) via *El Viso del Alcor*, with an old *Ayuntamiento*; and *Mairena del Alcor*, with a 15C castle.

The NIV continues W towards **Sevilla**, passing the *airport of S. Pablo* before entering its NE suburbs; see Rte 101.

91 Granada to Córdoba via Baena

166km (103 miles). N432. 52km *Alcalá la Real*—27km *Alcaudete*—26km *Baena*—61km **Córdoba**.

Maps: M 446.

Bear right off the N342 NE of Granada near (10km) *Atarfe*, passing the ruins of *Elvira* (perhaps Roman *Illiberis*), where there are traces of an acropolis, a subterranean aqueduct, and other remains.

In this area in 1319 the Moors defeated and killed the Infantes Pedro and Juan (uncles of the youthful Alfonso XI)—Pedro's skin is said to have been stuffed and placed over the gate of Elvira; also among those slain was a 'Lord of Ilkerinterrah' (England). The defeat was avenged in 1431 by Juan II and Álvaro de Luna at the battle of La Higueruela, named after the little fig tree under which the king bivouacked.

At 17km *Illora* (7km SW) has a ruined castle and a church containing Roman columns, possibly from Elvira.—At 4km *Moclín* (4.5km E) has a well-preserved Moorish fortress.—Another ruined castle is soon passed to the right on a ridge before the road descends to (21km) **Alcalá la Real** (20,800 inhab.), commanded by a Moorish castle and the ruins of *Sta. María*. Alcalá also contains one or two other churches of slight interest and a 16C abbot's palace. The sculptor Martínez Montañés (1568–1649) was born here.

The road climbs again to the *Puerto del Castillo* (940m) and winds through the hills to (27km) **Alcaudete** (12,050 inhab.), with a ruined Moorish castle. Turn W here.

26km **Baena** (17,000 inhab.) is dominated by a ruined Moorish castle with an unusual dome. In the upper walled town, known as the *Almedina*, there are several Renaissance mansions, Gothic *Sta. María* (restored since being burnt in the Civil War), and the *Conv. de* *la Madre de Dios.* The last is in Mudéjar style, with artesonados, and has a carving of the Annunciation in its late Gothic porch.

In the lower town are *S. Bartolomé* and (further E) *N.S. de Guadalupe* (c 1540), with an octagonal artesonado in its Capilla Mayor. Baena was the birthplace of José Amador de los Rios (1818–78), the historian of Spanish literature.

19km *Castro del Río* (7500 inhab.), on the Guadajoz, was long a centre of anarchism. It has a ruined castle and an *Ayuntamiento* preserving the prison of Cervantes, whose son was born here; *La Asunción* has a Plateresque doorway.

At 8km *Espejo*, Roman *Ucubi*, is skirted; it is dominated by the Mudéjar castle of the Dukes of Osuna.

34km **Córdoba** (see below), with the Sierra beyond.

92 Córdoba and Medina Azahara

CÓRDOBA (279,400 inhab.; 73,000 in 1920; 190,000 in 1960; Parador) lies largely on the N bank of the broad but shallow Guadalquivir, in a plain overlooked to the N by the SIERRA DE CÓRDOBA, a wooded spur of the Sierra Morena. Now a provincial capital, it was once the magnificent capital of Moorish Spain. It contains comparatively few memorials of its departed greatness, but among them are its remarkable *Mezquita* or mosque, its Moorish bridge, and the palace at *Medina Azahara* (c 10km W). The narrow and labyrinthine older streets are frequently flanked by houses with flower-decked patios, and it has a character of its own unlike Sevilla or Granada. The last 60 years have seen a new wave of prosperity and a great expansion of the city. Its climate is extremely hot in summer and it has abundant rain in winter, which is sometimes frosty.

Roman *Corduba*, an Iberian town of importance, was made a Roman colony by the consul Marcus Marcellus in 152 BC. It enjoyed the title of *Colonia Patricia* and the dignity of being the capital of *Hispania Ulterior*. After the battle of Munda (45 BC) it was punished by Julius Caesar for supporting Pompey; but under Augustus it became the flourishing capital of the province of *Baetica*, and the largest city in Spain. Its bishop, Hosius (257–337), presided in 325 over the Council of Nicea. During the Visigothic period (5–8Cs) it was the seat of a bishop subordinate to Toledo. To most of *Baetica* it was re-annexed to the Byzantine Empire under Justinian c 534, but it was taken by Leovigild in 572.

On invading Spain the Moors soon made themselves master of Córdoba, aided by its disaffected Jewish inhabitants. In 758 Abderrahman I (died 788), the surviving scion of the Ommayyads of Damascus, established an independent emirate centred on Córdoba and governed most of the Peninsula. Under his successors, notably Abderrahman III (912–61) and Hakam II (961–76), the city attained its peak of wealth, luxury, and culture. Under Hisham II (976–1012), the titular caliph, the powerful minister Almazor (died 1002) added to the city's military renown.

By the beginning of the 11C internal dissensions and a Berber revolt reflected its decline; and the Ommayyad dynasty came to an end in 1031 with the abdication of Hisham III. The caliphate split up into numerous petty kingdoms, or *taifas*, and the city passed to the Almoravides in 1094, and to the Almohades in 1149.

When Córdoba was captured by Fernando III in 1236 many of its inhabitants fled, and its decline was hastened by Christian indifference to industry, trade, and agriculture. At least one inquisitor, Diego Rodríguez Lucero, used the threat of accusation of heresy to procure its most beautiful women.

It remained a dull provincial capital for several centuries and its provincial nobility spent most of their time in each other's houses enjoying 'genteel refreshments, merry good-natured conversation, and some low card-playing', according to Swinburne (1775). He added that as a class he wondered 'how they ever learned to read or write, or having once attained so much, how they contrived not to forget it'. According to Twiss, a high proportion of their carriages and furniture came from England.

The city fell to the Nationalists early in the Civil War, and the proscriptions were severe. A reaction came in the municipal elections of April 1979 when it was the only town in Spain to return a Communist mayor.

Under the Moors Córdoba was reputed for its silversmiths' work and for Córdoban leather, from which the word 'cordwainer' for shoemaker is derived ('His schoon of cordewane', wrote Chaucer); and leather goods are still produced here, including the stamped, printed or gilded work known as *guadamecil* ware.

Among eminent natives were Seneca the Elder (died AD 39); his son Seneca the Younger (died 65) and grandson, Lucan (39–65), author of the 'Pharsalia'; Ibn 'Abd Rabbih (860–940), the poet; the historians Ibn Faradi (962–1012) and Ibn Hayyán (988–1076); Ibn Hazm (994–1064), statesman and philosopher; Ibn Guzman (c 1078–1160), the poet; Averroes (1126–98), the philosopher; Moses Maimonides (1135–1204), the rationalist Jewish rabbi; Pero Tafur (c 1410–c 1484), author and traveller; Ambrosio de Morales (1513–91), the historian; the poets Juan de Mena (1411–56), Luis de Góngora (1561–1627), and the Duque de Rivas (1791–1865); and among artists, Pablo de Céspedes (1538–1608), Juan Valdés Leal (1631–91), and Juan Antonio de Frías y Escalante (1633–70).

Garcilaso de la Vega (El Inca; 1539–1616) died here.

After describing the approaches to central Córdoba, the description of the city is divided into three parts, plus an excursion to Medina Azahara. *Visitors should not attempt to enter the maze of streets of the old town by car.*

From the Madrid road (off which a bypass circles to the SE), there are two alternative approaches: following the Av. de Libia through its E suburbs, passing (right) Mudéjar *El Carmen* (1580), with a retablo of 12 paintings by *Valdés Leal*. The road then skirts the N bank of the Guadalquivir by the *Ermita de los Mártires*, E of which is *N.S. de la Fuensanta* (1641).

The road passes the Pl. del Potro before reaching the *Puente Romano* and (right) the *Mezquita*. A short distance beyond the bridge are (right) the walls of the *Alcazar* and then the new bridge, at the far end of which roads diverge to Sevilla, Málaga, and Granada.

The second approach is by the Av. de Carlos III, which forks right at the E entrance of the city and circles N, passing (left) the Ronda del Marrubial with its long stretch of *walls* and towers.—On the right is the *Conv. de S. Cayetano*, founded by St. John of the Cross and completed in 1614.—Beyond, we pass (left) the *Torre de la Malamuerta*.

The Av. del Brillante climbs NW from the next junction towards the N suburbs and the Parador.

The road turns left after passing (right) the Railway station and the N end of the Jardines de la Victoria, and follows avenues S to meet the riverside road by the new bridge. Watch out for the turning if wanting to turn left here, otherwise you will be sent across the river.

The road to *Medina Azahara* (see Rte 92D) leads W from a central point of the Jardines de la Victoria, the E side of which is a convenient point from which to enter the Barrio de la Judería.

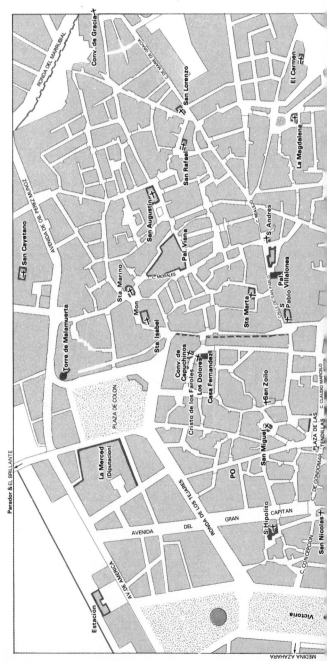

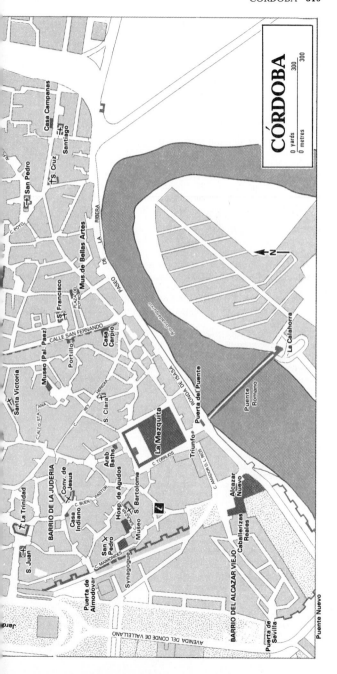

CÓRDOBA

0 yards 300
0 metres 300

Casa Campanes

Santiago

S. Cruz

San Pedro

C. POYO

Mus. de Bellas Artes

PASEO DE LA RIBERA

St. Francisco

PLAZA DEL POTRO

CALLE SAN FERNANDO

Portillo

Casa Carpio

Museo (Pal. Paez)

Santa Victoria

RONDA DE ISASA

Puerta del Puente

La Calahorra

RÍO GUADALQUIVIR

Puente Romano

C. REJ

S. Clara

CALLE STA. ANA

C. HEREDIA

La Mezquita

Arab Baths

Conv. de Jesús

Triunfo

C. TORRIJOS

BARRIO DE LA JUDERÍA

C. BUEN

C. PASTOR

Casa Indiano

La Trinidad

Hosp. de Agudos

S. Bartolomé

Museo

Alcázar Nuevo

C. AMADOR D. L. RIOS

San Pedro

Caballerizas Reales

S. Juan

C. MAIMONIDES

Synagogue

Puerta de Almodóvar

BARRIO DEL ALCÁZAR VIEJO

Puerta de Sevilla

AVENIDA DEL CONDE DE VALLELLANO

Jard

Puente Nuevo

A.   The Judería, Mezquita, Alcázar
and Museo Arqueológico

The *Judería* may be entered by the *Puerta de Almodóvar*, a Moorish gate in the *Walls*. A section of the walls, running S towards the Alcázar, has been restored and is skirted by gardens.

The whole area repays a visit after dark, when the strongly shadowed lanes and lantern-lit patios are displayed to great effect.

Turn right after passing through the gate; No. 18 in the C. Maimonides is a diminutive *Synagogue* (1315) in the Mudéjar style.—Beyond (left) is a small *Museum* housed in a 16C building.—Turn E to pass the partly restored *Hosp. de Agudos* (left) and then (right) the *Cap. de S. Bartolomé* (c 1275), with Gothic vaults, a frieze of Moorish alicatados, and a 15C pavement.—To the N is *S. Pedro de Alcántara* (1696; by Luis de Rojas).—Turn SE for the C. Torrijos and the NW corner of the mezquita.

The *Mezquita or mosque also contains—like a fly in amber—the cathedral. Originally the great mosque of the Ommayyad caliphs, ranking among the largest and most sumptuous of Moslem shrines, it forms a rectangle of 174m by 137m, and is surrounded by a massive battlemented wall 9m–18m in height, strengthened by solid square buttresses. Twenty-one doorways once admitted to the mosque and its forecourt, but several have been blocked up or destroyed, and those that survive have been restored and redecorated almost too completely.

Above the N wall rises the *Belfry* (93m high), a tapering square tower of five storeys surmounted by a figure of St. Raphael. It was begun in 1593 by Juan Ruiz the Younger to replace a minaret, but was not completed until 1664 by Gaspar de la Peña. It was repaired after the earthquake of 1755. (The mezquita is closed to the public during services, which are usually held at its SE corner, entered from the adjacent street.)

Its construction extended over two centuries, and four distinct stages are evident. When the Moors first settled in Córdoba they used half the Visigothic church of *S. Vicente* as a mosque. Later they bought the other half, cleared the site, and in 785 started building a new mosque. It was divided by columns into 11 vertical aisles running N and S, and 10 or 11 narrower cross aisles running E and W. This, completed in 796, forms only the NW quarter of the present edifice. With the increase in the Moslem population it was extended to the S by Abderrahman II (833–48), who added seven more cross aisles. A second and much greater extension was made in 961–66 of no less than 14 cross aisles, almost doubling the area by extending it to the present S wall, where the Mihráb was established in its present position.

Up to this point the mosque had retained a symmetrical groundplan, with the entrance and the mihráb at opposite ends of the main axis, a central aisle wider than the others. The third and last extension, completed by Almanzor in 990, comprised an additional eight vertical aisles to the E, without any compensating extension to the W, for the nature of the site no longer enabled it to be pushed further S.

After the reconquest, the Christians converted the mosque into the church of *La Asunción*; chapels were built against the interior walls; and the N front, previously open to the forecourt, was filled up, leaving as the main entrance the Puerta de las Palmas. Some years later a number of columns were removed from the SW part of the mosque to make way for a chapel with a coro and high altar, situated approximately where the second mihráb stood, and where the Cap. de Villaviciosa is now.

In 1523 the cathedral chapter, backed by the authority of Charles V against the more enlightened opposition of the city council, began the erection of the incongruous cruciform church that now occupies the centre of the mosque. The structure was designed by Hernán Ruiz the Elder and completed almost a century later.

The construction of this Renaissance building, 55m long, with a Coro and Cap. Mayor, a transept 15m across, and a lofty and richly decorated roof, involved the removal of about 60 columns. When in 1526 the emperor saw for himself the mischief he had unwittingly been induced to permit, he reproved the chapter with the words: 'You have built here what you or anyone might have built anywhere else, but you have destroyed what was unique in the world'. (This, in spite of the fact that he had in the same year approved of the destruction of part of the Alhambra at Granada to provide room for his palace.)

The present vaulting of the mosque dates from 1713, but in the principal aisle a portion of the original flat wooden ceiling, carved and painted, has been restored to view. Restorations have rescued and revealed several other features of the original mosque, both within and without, but much work still needs to be done.

At the base of the belfry (see above) is the *Puerta del Perdón*, which although built in 1377 is entirely Moorish in style. Its exterior is decorated with delicately carved arabesques and exhibits the escutcheons of Córdoba and the royal crown. The bronze-plated doors, bearing both Cufic and Latin inscriptions, admit to the *Patio de los Naranjos*, with palms, orange trees, and fountains—a characteristic court of ablutions and vestibule to the mosque. The N ends of the 19 interior aisles were once open to the court, so that the lines of trees appeared to continue the rows of columns (an arrangement which it was once proposed to restore).

Opposite is the *Puerta de las Palmas*, a Moorish doorway above which is a square attic added in 1531. Inside, we find ourselves in the subdued light of a forest of columns, with arched alleys and cross alleys extending in unusual vistas. The columns average c 4m in height, but are uniform neither in material nor in style.

The majority originate in Spain (Córdoba, Sevilla and Tarragona), but some come from as far afield as Narbonne and Nîmes, Carthage and other Roman towns in N Africa, and even Constantinople. Several varieties of marble, jasper, breccia and porphyry were used. Most of the shafts are smooth, though a few are spiralled; the capitals are mainly Byzantine or Moorish, but Roman and Visigothic examples can be seen in the older parts.

The present pavement of marble slabs is more than a foot above the original floor. The roof is low (c 12m), and is supported above the columns by a double row of Moorish arches, composed of alternate voussoirs of white stone and red brick. The wooden ceiling was probably originally all of *alerce* (larch), transported from Morocco. To the right of the entrance is a font support from the original Visigothic church.

Although the first *mihráb* has vanished, the site of the second, beyond the present coro, is distinguished by its fine arches and dome. Adjoining to the E is the elevated *Cap. de Villaviciosa* (regrettably inaccessible), a Mudéjar chapel of 1371 (restored 1892). The unprotected inscriptions on tombstones on the W wall have been defaced by graffiti and several of the columns have been similarly mutilated. The chapel may have been the second *maqsura*, or elevated platform on which the caliphs would pray on Fridays. To the E is the *Cap. de S. Pablo*, enclosed by 16C rejas, in front of which is the tomb of Pablo de Céspedes (died 1608), the artist of the retablo.

At the end of the aisle is the *Third Mihráb*, dated 965, its vestibule surrounded by interlaced arches on marble columns; the walls covered with coloured mosaics; and the roof formed by an octagonal cupola. The Mihráb itself is an octagonal recess c 3.3m in diameter

with carved marble walls. Its arches are supported by coloured
columns and the whole is roofed by a single block of marble,
hollowed to form a shell-shaped dome. The pavement is worn by the
knees of pilgrims circling seven times in imitation of the practice at
Mecca, although its alignment in fact lies W of the true direction of
Mecca.

A side chamber to the E, formerly the *Cap. de la Cena*, has been
restored to its original state, as have chapels to the W, which
constituted the third *maqsura* or caliph's gallery.

Off the Chapterhouse, to the E, is the *Treasury*, with a Gothic Custodia by
Enrique de Arfe (1518), a Crucifix attributed to Alonso Cano, a 14C Mudéjar
reliquary, and other cult objects. In the crypt below are altar frontals and
illuminated choirbooks.

The *Coro* of the degenerate church erected in the middle of the mosque was
completed in 1539 and contains elaborately carved Churrigueresque stalls by
Pedro Duque Cornejo (1677–1757); the Pulpits are by Michel Verdiguier (1760).
In the Cap. Mayor (1547–99) there is a retablo of 1628 by Alonso Matías
containing paintings by Palomino. The chandelier is of massive silver; the 17C
organ is mute. Bp Leopold of Córdoba (died 1557), natural son of the Emperor
Maximilian and half-brother of Felipe I, is buried in the transept. (Leopold also
had a natural son, called Maximilian, later Abp of Compostela; died 1614.)

In the C. de Torrijos, skirting the W side of the Mezquita, is the Portal
(1512) of *S. Jacinto*, part of the former Casa de Expósitos or Foundling Hospital (La Cuna).—Further S is the former *Episcopal palace*,
parts of which date back to the 15C. It occupies the site of the Roman
and Visigothic governors' residences and the alcázar of the caliphs. It
has recently been restored.

The street ends at the Churrigueresque *Triunfo*, a monument to S.
Rafael, by Michel Verdiguier (1781); according to Jardine some of his
other works had been destroyed the night after their erection by the
barbarous populous, to the great mortification of the Corregidor who
had commissioned them.

The C. Amador de los Ríos leads W to the **Alcázar Nuevo**, on the
site of a palace begun for Alfonso X in the late 13C, enlarged in 1328
and occupied by the Inquisition in 1482–1821. The interior contains
architectural remains of the Roman and Moorish periods (mosaics
and baths, the latter dating from 1328), and a Sarcophagus of c AD
200.

Further W, beyond an area of narrow lanes, is the 10C *Puerta de Sevilla*.

S of the Triunfo is the *Puerta del Puente*, a Doric archway of 1571 designed by
Hernán Ruiz, erected on the site of the Moorish *Bâb el-Kantara*. Beyond it is the
238m-long **Bridge** known as the *Puente Romano* (its 16 arches rest on Roman
foundations), spanning the Guadalquivir. It is the successor of a bridge ruined
by the Visigoths and rebuilt by the Moors in the 8C, and has been restored
several times since. At its far end is the crenellated *Torre de la Calahorra* (1369),
with a small museum containing several Roman mosaics.

Downstream are the remains of *Moorish Mills*. The northernmost mill
incorporates fragments of an Almohade palace built over the river which until
1492 housed the great wheel that raised water for the Alcázar gardens. These
are now crossed by the riverside Av. del Alcázar.

Returning to the Triunfo, skirt the S and E walls of the Mezquita and
turn half-right at its NE corner.—11C *Moorish Baths* survive between
Nos 4 and 6 in the C. Velázquez Bosco, a few paces to the NW.—On
reaching the C. Rey Heredia turn right, then left before reaching the
Conv. de Sta. Clara (with a minaret of c 1000), to approach a small
plaza overlooked by the elaborate Renaissance portal (1545) of the
Pal. de Jerónimo Paéz, designed by Hernán Ruiz the Elder, which
now houses the ***Museo Arqueológico**.

To the right side of the first patio are rooms devoted to prehistoric material, including figurines, ceramics, and arms, and several carved stone lions from the Iberian period; other rooms contain extensive collections of Roman mosaics (from Alcolea; and one of Romulus and Remus); a Bull from Cabra (2C); a silver hoard from Pozoblanco (98 BC); Roman sarcophagi, and epigraphical material; *terra sigillata* and other wares, glass, tiles and bronzes.—Note the Mudéjar cupola over the staircase. The first floor has a remarkable collection of Moorish capitals, bases, and wellheads; Arabic inscriptions; pottery from Medina Azahara; and an inlaid bronze Stag (now hornless), originally added by Abderrahman III to a fountain given to him by the Byzantine emperor Constantine VII (945–59). The museum is being extended into the adjacent building, in the foundations of which further Roman artefacts have been discovered.

By turning right along the C. Alto de Sta. Ana we enter the C. Angel Saavedra, near the site of *Jewish baths* (on the far side, left). Turn right again, passing (right) the *Pal. del Marqués de Fuensanta*, with a front of 1551, to reach the central, café-thronged PL. DE LAS TENDILLAS.

A short distance to the SE is *La Compañía* (1569; by Alonso Matís, a Jesuit), with a Baroque retablo by Pedro Duque Cornejo. Further S is Neo-Classical *Sta. Victoria*, begun in 1701 by Baltasar Graveton and completed by Ventura Rodríguez in 1788.

Turning W from the plaza, the C. de Conde de Gondomar leads towards the octagonal tower (completed in 1496) of *S. Nicolás*. It contains artesonados of 1580, Baroque retablos, a baptistery of 1554 by Hernán Ruiz the Younger, and a Renaissance door to its sacristy.—The C. de S. Felipe leads S, passing (right) the 16C *Gobierno Militar*, attributed to Alonso Berruguete, to *La Trinidad* (17C) and the remains of a small minaret (c 840). The latter survives from the mosque which became the conventual church of *S. Juan* (1576).—A few steps S of La Trinidad is the *Casa del Indiano*, with a 15C Moorish façade. Just E of it is the *Conv. de Jésus Crucificado* (1496–1588), with artesonado ceilings and a patio containing Roman, Visigothic, and Moorish capitals.

The *Puerta de Almodóvar* can be regained a short distance to the W.

B.   Eastern Córdoba

Proceed SE from the archaeological museum or follow the C. de Card. González from the SE corner of the Mezquita, to reach the C. de S. Fernando. Near the S end of its W side are the 15C *Casa de los Marqueses del Carpio* and the *Portillo*, an archway opened in the wall which once divided the ALMEDINA, or W part of the city, from the ALARQUÍA.

Opposite, an archway leads to a small plaza and the front of the *Conv. de S. Francisco*, founded by Fernando III. It is now a Churrigueresque building and contains a St. Andrew by Valdés Leal.—To the S, the C. de S. Francisco leads to the PL. DEL POTRO, with another monument to St. Raphael by Verdiguier, and the *Fountain* adorned with a colt (*potro*), mentioned in 'Don Quixote'. Cervantes is supposed to have lodged at an adjacent inn (restored). The nearby *Posada de la Herradura* is another similar survival.

On the E side of the plaza is the **Museo de Bellas Artes**, with a Plateresque portal, established in an old hospital.

The ground floor contains miscellaneous 19–20C paintings and sculptures. In the corridor are two heads in fresco (c 1280) from the Mezquita. On the floor above are representative works by Alejo Fernández, Pablo de Céspedes, Ribera, Murillo, Morales, Zurbarán, and Alonso Cano, and two portraits by Goya (of Carlos IV and of María Luisa). There are also several paintings by members of the Córdoban family of Castillo Saavedra, including some by Antonio del Castillo (1616–68), a pupil of Zurbarán.—The other side of the courtyard is devoted to the Córdoban artist Julio Romero de Torres (1885–1930), mostly portraits of local 'Nell Gwyns'.

A DETOUR to the E follows the C. Coronel Cascajo from the Pl. del Potro for some distance past the characteristic *Bodegas Campos* to (right) *Santiago*. It retains the 10C minaret of a former mosque and an artesonado of 1635. Opposite is the *Casa de las Campanas* (14C Mudéjar) and the neighbouring 15C *Casa de los Caballeros de Santiago*, with two Mudéjar patios.

Retrace your steps to the *Conv. de Sta. Cruz* (founded 1435), and bear half-right past *S. Pedro* (13C; on the site of the earlier Mozarabic cathedral, but extensively altered in the 16C) to approach the Pl. Mayor.

The C. Armas leads N from the Pl. del Potro to the brick-built *Pl. de la Corredera* or *Pl. Mayor* of 1683, restored after the removal of an unsightly market house. From its NW corner, bear half left along the C. de Claudio Marcelo to the *Pl. de las Tendillas*, or turn N to *S. Pablo*; see below. (Behind the *Ayuntamiento*, in the next street leading right beyond the NW corner of the Plaza Mayor, a late Roman temple has been excavated.)

C. Northern Córdoba

N of the Pl. de las Tendillas is *S. Miguel*, 13C but altered in 1749. From the NE corner of the plaza bear right along the C. Alfonso XIII past (left) Baroque *S. Zoilo* (1740) to Romanesque *S. Pablo*, founded in 1241, but with a Baroque façade of 1706. It contains Mudéjar capitals and ceiling (1537) and a Gothic chapel of 1409 with a Baroque camarín.

The C. de S. Pablo leads E near (left) *Sta. Marta* (completed in 1471) with a Gothic portal, and right, the *Pal. de los Villalones* (1560), and the Plateresque *Casa de Hernán Pérez de Oliva* (1542), to *S. Andrés* (13C, but largely rebuilt in 1733).

Some distance further E is 14C *S. Lorenzo*, with a good rose-window and a tower added in 1555. To its NW is *S. Agustín* (14C, later altered).

From opposite S. Andrés, a short walk N brings one to (right) the 17C **Pal. del Marqués de Viana**, with numerous patios and now open to the public as a *museum*.—Further N are Gothic *Sta. Marina*, with a Renaissance tower; opposite this is a *Monument to Manuel Rodríguez* ('Manolete'; 1917–47), the bullfighter, born in Córdoba, and who died in the ring at Linares.—Near by is the *Conv. de Sta. Isabel*, founded in 1491, with a simple front of 1576.

From the Puerta del Rincón to the SW, turn S and ascend steps to the right to the Plateresque front of the *Casa de los Fernández de Córdoba* and *Los Dolores*; opposite is the 17C *Conv. de Capuchinos*, with Mudéjar doors. The adjacent plaza contains the picturesque *Cristo de los Faroles*, which should be visited a second time after dark.—From the W end of the plaza turn right into the large PL. DE COLÓN.

At its NE end is the *Torre de Malamuerte* (1408). It owes its name to a garbled tradition that it was built as the price of a pardon from Enrique III by a knight who had murdered his wife. In fact it is linked by an underground passage to the *Casa del Conde de Priego*, where Fernando Alfonso de Córdoba and his wife and household were murdered in c 1455; the tragedy was dramatised in Lope de Vega's 'Los Comendadores de Córdoba'. In the 18C the tower became the observatory of the astronomer Serrano; and later a powder magazine.

At the NW side of the plaza is the highly-coloured Baroque building of the **Conv. de la Merced**, restored recently to house the *Diputación*.

From the SW side the busy Ronda de los Tejares leads SW to the JARDINES DE LA VICTORIA. The C. Cruz Conde turns left off the Ronda to the central plaza. The broad Av. del Gran Capitán also leads S, passing *S. Hipólito* (1348), with the nave added in 1736 and the tower begun in 1773. It contains an Ecce Homo by Valdés Leal and, in the choir, the sarcophagi of Alfonso XI (died 1350) and his father Fernando IV (died 1312).

D.   Medina Azahara (by car)

Follow the C431 W from a mid-point of the *Jardines de la Victoria* for c 8km; then turn right and later left, to reach the extensive palace complex of ***Medina Azahara** (or *Medinat*, or *Az-Zahra*) (normally closed Tuesdays).

Excavations have traced the line of the rectangular boundary wall, and the site of many of the principal buildings, several of which have been reconstituted, and others are in the process of restoration. A small display of fragments may be seen near the entrance, but most of the more important objects found are in the Archaeological Museum in Córdoba.

Building began c 936 under the aegis of Abderrahman III, for his favourite wife Zahra or Zahara (Flower). Its construction—allowing for exaggeration—employed 10,000 men with 2600 mules and 400 camels for 25 years; and the description of its size, luxury, and splendour by the Arab historian El-Makkari recalls the 'Arabian Nights'. It included not only a magnificent palace with gardens and fish ponds, but also a great *Mosque* (set at an angle just outside the SE angle of the main enceinte), baths, schools of learning, and other dependencies. Marble, jasper, and other costly materials were used lavishly, and of its 4300 columns some were brought from Carthage and other ancient cities (cf. the Mezquita). It had a garrison of 12,000; there were stables for 2000 mounts; and 4000 servants waited in the palace.

But in 1010 all this magnificence was destroyed by rebel Berbers, and for centuries the site was marked only by scattered debris.

The sensational discovery in 1944 of the *Royal Apartments*, retaining the fallen materials of their arches and roofs, has been followed by a meticulous reconstruction which enables one to appreciate the architectural magnificence of a mid-10C Moorish *Throne room*. A line of *Walls* to the W of the main garden complex has also been restored, together with several dependencies. The line of the direct road from Córdoba, and of water conduits from sources in the hills above, has also been discovered.

The neighbouring *Conv. de S. Jerónimo* (c 1408) was built with masonry from the palace; the church was rebuilt c 1794.—What remained of a country house of Almanzor at *Alamiría*, further W, was destroyed in 1926.

The road climbs N into the wooded hills. A left-hand turning leads c 5km to an Almohade mosque of c 1200, converted into the chapel of *Sta. María de Trassiera* and standing within a ruined castle.—Continuing NE from the crossroad the *Ermitas of Val Paraíso* are approached, dating from c 1709 but of slight interest.—One can continue the diversion by turning downhill from a point further NE (due N of Córdoba), passing a road to the left to the 15–18C convent of *Sto. Domingo de Scala Dei*, of which Fray Luis de Granada (1504–88) was Prior.

For roads from Córdoba to **Sevilla, Málaga, Granada**, and **Zafra** (for **Mérida** or **Badajoz**), see Rtes 90, 93, 91 and 54, the last two in reverse, and 90 in reverse for **Bailén**.

93 Córdoba to Málaga via Lucena and Antequera

176km (109 miles). NIV. 15km—N331. 57km **Lucena**—53km **Antequera**—51km **Málaga**.

Maps: M 446.

The N331 bears left off the NIV 15km S of Córdoba. At 14km it bypasses *Fernán Nuñez*, its ducal palace with an old tower, and castle ruins.—4km *Montemayor*, with a Mudéjar castle of the Dukes of Frías; 4km beyond this the town of *La Rambla* lies 4km W, with Renaissance churches and a ruined castle.

At 6km **Montilla** (21,800 inhab.) is 3km E, perched on two hills. It is possibly the site of Roman *Munda Baetica*, where Caesar defeated the sons of Pompey in 46 BC.

It was the birthplace of Gonzalo Fernández y Aguilar (1453–1515), known as Gonzalo de Córdoba, who earned the title 'El Gran Capitán' by his brilliant campaign against the French in Italy in 1495–98. In 1502–04 he expelled them from Neapolitan territory, and was the first of a long line of Spanish viceroys in Naples.

There is a Medinaceli palace near by, and the Mudéjar *Conv. de Sta. Clara* is of some interest.

The surrounding district, including the SIERRA DE MONTILLA, is known for a delicate white wine quite unlike the type of sherry to which is given the name '*amontillado*'. The latter is a blended wine of Jerez, whereas '*Montilla*' is the classical Córdoban table wine.

8km **Aguilar** (12,600 inhab.), among olive groves and vineyards, with a hilltop plaza, a ruined Moorish castle, and a parish church of some interest.

At 21km **Lucena** (30,100 inhab.) (also bypassed) is renowned for its apricots, olives, and pottery. It was populated during the Moslem period almost entirely by Jews and had one of the earliest Talmudic schools in Europe. They were driven out by the Almohades unless they converted to Islam, and many settled in Christian territory. Luis Barahona de Soto (1548–95), the poet and author of a treatise on hunting, and Hurtado Izquierdo (1669–1728, at Priego), the architect, were born here.

Among its churches are 15C *S. Mateo* in the Pl. Nueva, with good artesonados, a Renaissance high altar, and an exuberant Baroque *Sagrario*; *Santiago*, previously a synagogue, with a Gothic doorway and curious Baroque turret; the *Agustinas Recoletas*, with a Baroque portal; and further N, *S. Francisco*, with an octagonal lantern, Baroque retablo, and a charming patio. Another patio, with curious wall paintings, is in the *Hosp. de S. Juan de Dios*; its church contains a fine retablo, as does the chapel of the *Cristo de Sangre*.

21km SE is **Rute** (10,150 inhab.), near remains of a Visigothic city.—For *Cabra*, 9.5km NE, see p 486.

The road winds through the hills, descending into the valley of the Genil at (22km) *Benameji*, with castle ruins, a Baroque church, and a Renaissance palace of 1553.—At 24km we reach the Antequera bypass, but continue ahead for 7km into the town.

Antequera (35,750 inhab.; Parador), a straggling old town containing several churches and mansions of carved brick, lies at the foot of the *Sierra de Chimenea* (1369m) and the red limestone natural curiosity of *El Torcal.*

Originally a Roman station (*Anticaria*), it was taken from the Moors in 1410 by the Infante Fernando (afterwards Fernando I of Aragón), who was thenceforth known as 'el de Antequera'. Gunpowder is said to have been used for the first time in Spain on this occasion.

The 13C *Torre Mocha* of the ruined Moorish castle commands a fine view. The old *Puerta de Málaga* forms the *Ermita de la Virgen de Espera*, adjacent to which is *Sta. María la Mayor*, a hall-church of 1550 with an interesting W front, an artesonado roof, and a 14C retablo.—Mid-16C *S. Sebastián* has a brick steeple of 1709. Among other churches are *S. Juan Bautista* (1489–1584); *S. Pedro* (1522–74); *S. Francisco* (1507); and *S. Agustín*, with well-carved stalls. The *Pal. de Nájera* houses a small collection of antiquities. The *Arco de Sta. María de los Gigantes* (1585), erected in the Pl. Alta, incorporates Roman inscribed stones.

A few minutes' walk NE is the *Cueva de Menga*, a double dolmen; close by is another dolmen, the *Cueva de Viera*; a third, the *Cueva del Romeral*, stands on the *Cerrillo Blanco* in the vega.

ANTEQUERA TO RONDA (93km). Turn NW and then W on the N342 to (33km) *Campillos* (see Rte 95), and then due S onto the C341 to skirt the *Embalse del Guadalteba-Guadalhorce*. At 16km the road passes below hilltop **Teba**, a picturesque walled town. In 1330 Sir James Douglas, en route to Jerusalem with the heart of Robert Bruce, fell here in battle against the Moors. The casket containing the heart—which Douglas flung before him as though to lead the way into the thickest of the fight—was recovered, and Bruce's heart now rests in Melrose Abbey, Scotland.—At 4km the MA442 to *Alora* via the *Garganta del Chorro* turns left—a longer but interesting alternative route to *Málaga*, see p. 531.—Continue SW across country to (40km) *Ronda*; see Rte 96.

The main road is regained 3km E of Antequera, where, climbing to the SE it meets the N321 from Granada at (13km) the *Puerto de las Pedrizas* (780m). For the road beyond, see the latter part of Rte 89A.

94 Granada to Sevilla via Antequera and Osuna

263km (163 miles). N342. 53km **Loja**—27km *Archidona*—19km **Antequera**—N334. 48km *Estepa*—24km **Osuna**—41km *El Arahal*—31km **Alcalá de Guadaira**—20km **Sevilla**.

Maps: M 446.

For the road to *Loja*, see Rte 89A. Bear right at the bifurcation 17km beyond. After 10km the road bypasses **Archidona** (10,050) on the slope of a curiously shaped hill. Of interest are *Sto. Domingo*, the *Col. de Escolapios*, and a small octagonal *Plaza*.

The Guadalhorce is soon crossed, in a pleasant valley studded with white farmhouses, and we approach the conspicuous *Peña de los Enamorados* (880m), an abrupt rock from which a Moorish maiden and Christian knight are said to have hurled themselves to escape the pursuing vassals of her father (as told in Southey's ballad of 'Leila and Manuel').

At 14km the bypass of **Antequera** is reached; drive ahead to enter the town; see Rte 93.

From its W side, bear NW through (32km) *La Roda de Andalucía* and after 9km turn left away from *Casariche* (4.5km right), where Roman mosaics have been found, to (7km) **Estepa** (9800 inhab.), Iberian *Astapa* or *Ostippo*. In 207 BC its natives are said to have rivalled the Numantians in their stubborn resistance to the Romans. Its *Castle* commands a wide view, and Gothic *Sta. María*, early 17C *La Asunción*, *El Carmen*, the mid-18C tower of *La Victoria*, and the Baroque *Pal. de los Cerverales* are of interest.

At 24km **OSUNA** (16,050 inhab.), long famous for carnations which once covered the slope of its hill, retains a number of attractive streets and imposing old mansions. Swinburne somewhat unfairly condemned it as 'a large stinking town'; in fact it is now still one of the more *un*-spoilt towns of its size in Andalucía and deserves exploration.

This was Roman *Urso*, honoured with the title of *Colonia Gemina Urbanorum* and garrisoned by two legions from Rome itself. The Moors, who called it *Ushuna*, lost it to Fernando III in 1240. The last duke of Osuna united in his person 50 titles of nobility and enjoyed a huge income, but was totally ruined by his extravagance in attempting to compete with other European aristocrats.

In the town centre is the PL. DE ESPAÑA, with the *Ayuntamiento*, partially but soberly modernised. To the N is the *Market* with its patios. Continuing N, we pass (right) *Sto. Domingo* (1531), with Renaissance and Baroque retablos; and the *Audiencia*, with a Doric patio; and opposite, *N.S. de la Victoria* (1584), with a tall steeple. A few steps beyond is the late 18C *Arco de la Pastora*.

Opposite Sto. Domingo is the C. S. Pedro, retaining several imposing Baroque mansions including the *Pal. de Gomera* and the *Cabildo Eclesiástico* (1773), with a model of the Giralda at Sevilla above its portal. In two streets further S are the *Pal. de Puerto Hermoso* or *Juzgado*, with its Salomonic columns; the *Conv. de Sta. Catalina* (16C, with 18C dados); and the steeple of *S. Carlos el Real* (1664).

On returning to the main plaza (just S of which is the *Pal. de los Cepedas*), continue E, ascending to the *Torre Cartigines*, which contains a small Archaeological collection.—Continue the ascent to the hilltop, dominated by the old *University* with its cloister and blue-tiled turrets. It was founded in 1549 but suppressed in 1820. To the E are remnants of a Roman fortress.

To the W, overlooking the town, is the *Colegiata* of 1539. The entrance is now through the restored Plateresque patio on the N side. One is led first to the private chapel and lugubrious pantheon of the Dukes of Osuna, the first of whom received his title from Felipe II in 1562. In the Sacristy, with a carved wooden ceiling, there are four saints painted by Ribera, a Christ by Juan de Mesa, and a St. Jerome attributed to Pietro Torregiano. Other rooms contain cult objects, some Flemish paintings, and a Christ by Morales. The *Church*, an impressive building recently restored, contains two marble pulpits, a rare portative organ (late 16C), a retablo by Sebastián Fernández, and a restored Crucifixion by Ribera.

To the N, downhill and opposite the entrance to the Colegiata, stands the convent of *La Encarnación* (1549), with a Baroque church and steeple (1775). It also contains a collection of ecclesiastical art (note the pelican in the Sagrario, a polychrome alabaster Christ, and a S. Francisco de Paula by Juan de Mesa); but of more interest is the tiled dado or *zocalo* surrounding both the 18C cloister and the gallery above. Note the section depicting the Alameda de Hércules in Sevilla.

The road continues due W, at 17km bypassing *La Puebla de Cazalla* (11,000 inhab.), a wine-growing centre.—20km SW of it is **Morón de la Frontera**, (28,000 inhab.) temporarily an American base. It is commanded by the extensive ruins of its Moorish castle, built on the foundations of a Roman fort. Steep and often stepped streets radiate from the central *Ayuntamiento*. To the E is *S. Ignacio* or *La Compañia*, and late Gothic *S. Miguel*; to the S is the *Hospital* in a former convent, and the *Posada Lecilla*, with a relief of the Giralda on its portal (1744); to the W is *N.S. de la Victoria*, with an artesonado roof and round tower with a hexagonal belfry.

At 7km *Marchena* is 7km NE; see p 513.—After 4km *Paradas* is bypassed to the right, its Renaissance church tower studded with azulejos.—5km *El Arahal* (16,200 inhab.) has two churches of interest and the 15C *Hosp. de la Caridad*.

Continue NW down the valley of the Guadaira past (28km) *Gandul*, with a Moorish castle and prehistoric remains, to **Alcalá de Guadaira** (45,600 inhab.), Phoenician *Hienippe*, also bypassed.

The Moorish *Castle*, which surrendered to Fernando III in 1246, retains its subterranean corn magazines, several cisterns, its inner keep and a huge donjon added by the Spaniards, who carried out extensive works in the 15C. In 1332 Alfonso XI presented it to Doña Leonor de Guzmán, and it was later used as a state prison. The bridge over the Guadaira is on Roman foundations.

An industrial area is crossed before entering central **Sevilla** from the E, a short distance NE of the *Alcázar*; see Rte 101.

95   Antequera to Jerez via Olvera and Arcos

170km (105 miles). N334. 7km—N342. 68km *Olvera*—71km **Arcos de la Frontera**—30km **Jerez de la Frontera**.

Maps: M 446.

For **Antequera**, see Rte 93.

Drive NW and at 7km turn left for (27km) *Campillos* (7200 inhab.); its parish church has a Baroque façade.

A recently built road leads W to (41km) **Olvera** (9500 inhab.), whose remote valley was once ill-reputed as a refuge for bandits and *mala gente* in general: 'mata al hombre y vete a Olvera' (kill you man and fly to Olvera). In the darkest recesses of a posada here in 1851, George Cayley encountered a Cambridge friend on honeymoon, his wife disguised as a younger brother, and they had ridden thus all the way from Cartagena!

The imposing *Church* and remains of a castle dominate the town from a rocky crag.

From just E of the town one can reach the precipitously perched village of *Torre-Alháquime* by a minor road leading S. Beyond it is (15km) *Setenil*, one of the more curious villages in the area, many of its troglodyte dwellings huddled beneath impending rocks. The diminutive 'old' *Ayuntamiento* has an artesonado ceiling.

The main road crosses several ridges, with the SIERRA DE LIJAR to the NW (1051m) and SIERRA MARGARITA (1173m) to the SW, to (20km) *Algodonales*. Just beyond it the road is joined by the C339 from Ronda, 37km SE.—*Zahara 'de los Membrillos'* (of the quinces) perched below its ancient castle (once a Moorish stronghold) is c 7km S, off the road to Ronda, and commands superb views.

At 26km we pass **Villamartín** (12,250 inhab.), reputed for its '*pajarete*' wine, and skirt the N bank of the *Embalse de Bornos*, passing (12km) *Bornos* (7650 inhab.), with a Moorish castle and two monasteries.—To the NW is the Roman site of *Carisa Aurelio*, under excavation.

At 13km **Arcos de la Frontera** (25,150 inhab.; Parador), an attractive steep-streeted town of Iberian foundation, stands on a sharp ridge above a loop of the Guadalete. It was known to the Romans as *Arcobriga* and to the Moors as *Medina Arkosh*.

The Moors were dislodged from this almost impregnable stronghold by Alfonso X in 1264. In 1780 a colony of English officers of the 99th Regiment of Foot were confined here on parole for three months after the capture of a naval convoy, as described by Richard Croker.

The main thoroughfare climbs past the former *Conv. de S. Francisco* (17C), the *Hosp. de S. Juan de Dios* (c 1600), and the *Pal. de Águila*, with an Isabelline Mudéjar front, to the fortified *Pal. of the Dukes of Osuna* in a small plaza on the right. Here stands 15–16C **Sta. María de la Asunción**, with a good W front, and an unfinished tower of 1758 by Vicente Bengoechea. A hall-church with star-vaulting, it contains 15C murals, a retablo mayor by Jerónimo Hernández, and stalls of 1744.

Opposite the S door, and once part of the adjoining *Castle*, is the *Ayuntamiento*, with a Mudéjar artesonado. A *mirador* commands a plunging *View* over the *tajo* above the Guadalete, with lesser kestrels (Falco naumanni) wheeling above the cliff. Adjoining is the Parador. The former *Hosp. de la Encarnación* (1529), N of Sta. María, has a late Gothic portal.

Continue along the main street past the Isabelline front of the *Misericordia chapel*, founded in 1490, to *S. Pedro*, built on the edge of the cliff on the site of the Moorish fortress. It contains a retablo of 1542 by Fernando Sturm and others, and paintings by Zurbarán and Pacheco.

Retracing our steps, we can turn sharply downhill by the picturesque Cuesta del Socorro, passing *S. Agustín*; to our left is a second cliff (the *Peña Vieja*) dominating the N loop of the river. Continue downhill to the *E Gate*, beyond which is the *Asilo de la Caridad*, a charming Baroque work of 1764 with good brick detail and a patio.

From Arcos, the N342 undulates W across the LLANOS DE CAULINA through vineyards and olive groves. At 19km it passes the Moorish *Torre de Melgarejo*, reconstructed in the 14C, and (5km) crosses the A4 6km before entering **Jerez**; see Rte 102A.

96 Málaga to Arcos via Ronda

181km (112 miles). N340. 9km. C344. 27km *Coín*—64km **Ronda**—
C339. 17km. C344. 14km *Grazalema*—18km *El Bosque*—32km
Arcos.

Maps: M 446.

A longer, but interesting, ALTERNATIVE route to Ronda is first
described, via *Alora* and *Ardales* (c 130km, with short detours).
Follow the MA402 due W up the valley of the Guadalhorce for
19km.—**Cártama** (10,000 inhab.) is 3km SW, on the far side of the
river, which was once navigable up to this point. This was Roman
Cartima, and Carter, writing in the 1770s, remarked that its ancient
remains had been barbarously treated, with Roman statuary 'jammed
into the walls of houses to keep off carts'. There are also the ruins of a
Moorish castle here.

Keep on the MA402, later the C337, following the left bank of the
river and circle N to cross it at (19km) **Alora** (12,350 inhab.). Its
ruined castle, on twin peaks, has been converted into a cemetery.
The parish church (1600) has a wooden roof supported by cylindrical
columns.—Follow the W bank of the river to the N through its
characteristic sub-tropical vegetation for c 16km.—At this point one
can cross to visit the defile of the **Garganta del Chorro**.

The MA444 climbs W, off which a byroad turns left up into the still
remote MESA DE VILLAVERDE.

Off this road, by clambering down an unsignposted path to the left, one can visit
the remains of the basilical Mozarabic church of *Bobastro, cut into the
sandstone, with a curious sanctuary of horseshoe plan (c 898–917). The road
continues to climb along a narrow ridge past the high-lying reservoir supplying
the hydroelectric works below the *garganta*, and c 1km beyond comes to an
abrupt halt. On the summit to the right are the slight remains of the fortress
founded in 884 by Omar Ibn Hafsun (views).

The main road continues W along the S side of the *Embalse del
Conde de Guadalhorce* to *Ardales*, with castle ruins. Turn N here to
meet the MA452 S of *Teba* (see p 527), where turn left for **Ronda**.

The main road turns right off the coast road 9km SW of Málaga,
bypassing *Churriana* and the luxuriant *Hacienda de la Consuela*.—
29km **Alhaurín el Grande** (14,300 inhab.), noted for its marble
quarries, and the home of Gerald Brenan for several years before his
death in January 1987. He had formerly lived at Churriana.

7km **Coín** (20,950 inhab.), 15km beyond which the C344 bypasses *Tolox* (5km SW), with the *Torrecilla* (1919m) rising to the
SW. The road skirts picturesque *Alozaina* (right), and climbs to
(15km) the *Puerto de las Abajas* (820m) for (8km) *El Burgo*. There it
bears W and climbs again to the *Puerto del Viento* (1190m) and
passes the slight remains of an Aqueduct on approaching (26km)
Ronda.

RONDA (750m; 30,750 inhab.), one of the more picturesquely sited
towns of Spain, lies within an amphitheatre of limestone hills and
stands on a rocky bluff or shelf whose sheer walls fall on three sides
to a depth of 120m. In the midst of the town itself is the extraordinary
Tajo, the 75–90m wide gorge of the Guadalevín which separates the
modern quarter of the *Mercadillo*, founded by the Christians after the
reconquest, from the Moorish *Ciudad*. Below the latter, to the S, is the
Barrio de S. Francisco.

Substructures discovered in the foundations of Moorish buildings may be remains of Roman *Munda*, but the present town owes its importance to the Moors. Owing to its almost impregnable position, it remained the capital of an isolated Moorish kingdom until 1485, when it was surprised and captured after a secret march by Fernando the Catholic. In its siege *metal* cannon balls were used by Spanish artillery for the first time.

The *Maestranza*, a corporation of knights formed here in 1493 for the supervision of bullfighting, became the model for later societies of the kind throughout Spain. Pedro Romero's name is inseparable from the *Plaza de Toros*, for this 18C matador is credited with the invention of the classical bullfighting style of the School of Ronda. The Rondeños, who maintain their reputation as horse breeders, were once the most redoubtable smugglers of the SERRANÍA, but have lost their unenviable notoriety as masters of knife play.

Owing to the proximity of Gibraltar, Ronda was often visited by officers of the garrison—it was a salubrious summer residence for their families—and by English tourists during the 19C and since, but the *Hotel Reina Victoria* (1906), once British-owned, no longer retains its Edwardian atmosphere. Mementos of Rainer Maria Rilke, who was one of its more famous guests, are preserved.

During the first month of the Civil War a mob from Málaga threw 512 live prisoners of the Republicans over the cliff; from 16 September 1936 it experienced the usual Nationalist proscriptions.

Vicente Martínez de Espinel (1550–1624), musician, poet, and author of the 'Life of Marcos de Obregón' was born here. He is alleged to have invented the ten syllable line called *espinela*; and also to have added the fifth string to the guitar. Francisco Giner de los Ríos (1839–1915), the educationalist and founder of the influential *Institución Libre de Enseñanza* was also born here.

In the SERRANÍA DE RONDA the wild goat (*capra pyrenaica*) is protected; to the SE are groves of a species of pine (*Abies pinsapo*), unique examples of this prehistoric tree. Ronda is also known for its fruit, especially cherries, peaches, and apples.

At the NW edge of the town is the Alameda, laid out in 1806 and commanding a fine view to the W. To the S is the elegant *Plaza de Toros* (1784), the second oldest surviving in Spain after that at Sevilla. It has an exceptionally wide ring of 66m diameter.

The *Puente Nuevo* (1740–88), beyond the *Ayuntamiento*, has a single span of 33.5m. It provides the finest prospect of the *Tajo* or gorge of the Guadalevín, with the river foaming along its rocky bed 90m below; its main stream has been harnessed to drive the turbines of a small power station. José Martín Aldehuela, the architect, was killed by falling from the parapet while inspecting the work. An earlier bridge, of 1735, had collapsed, killing some 50 people.

Beyond the bridge is the *Ciudad*, an intricate Moorish town of tortuous lanes and tiny houses, many with walnut doors. The C. Tenorio leads right to the *Campillo*, a plaza (view) from which a rough track, forking almost immediately, descends into the gorge.

The branch on the right passes the *Arco de Cristo*, a Moorish gateway of c 1300, and leads down to the *Upper Mill*; from here there is an extraordinary upwards *View of the Tajo and its bridge.—The left path descends to the *Lower Mills*, where one can cross the river and work one's way downstream to steps climbing up to near the *Hotel Reina Victoria*. It is also possible to retrace one's steps from the Lower Mill and take a path to the right which ascends gently to the gateway between the Alcazaba and the Barrio de S. Francisco.

From the Campillo, the Ronda de Gameros leads to the *Casa de Mondragon*, whose two patios are decorated with moulded brick arches and glazed tiles. A gallery with a Moorish roof commands a plunging view of the valley.

Further on, in the attractive *Pl. de la Duquesa de Parcent*, is the 16C hall-church of *Sta. María la Mayor*. It was originally a mosque and its 13C *Mihrab* has been discovered; its tower is the former

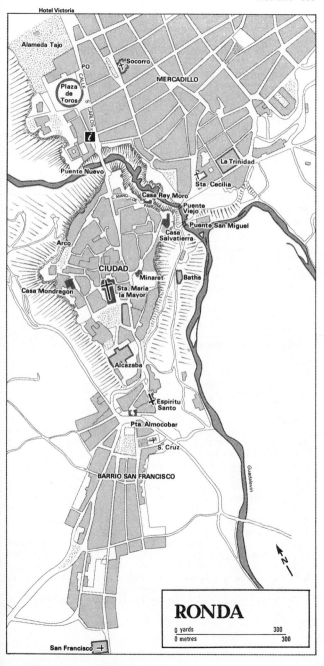

Hotel Victoria

Alameda Tajo

Socorro

MERCADILLO

Plaza de Toros

CALLE S CARLOS

PO

i

Puente Nuevo

La Trinidad

Sta. Cecilia

Casa Rey Moro

C. MARQ. DE PAREZOS

Puente Viejo

Puente San Miguel

Arco

Casa Salvatierra

CIUDAD

Minaret

Baths

Casa Mondragon

Sta. Maria la Mayor

Alcazaba

Espiritu Santo

Pta. Almocobar

S. Cruz

BARRIO SAN FRANCISCO

Guadalevin

N

San Francisco

RONDA

0 yards	300
0 metres	300

minaret.—Further S, beyond the *Alcazaba* blown up by the French in 1809, and 15C *Espiritu Santo*, is the suburb of *S. Francisco*, with the curious Moorish *Puerta de Almocobar*.

Returning to the Alcazaba, follow the C. Méndez Núñez. Near the corner of the C. del Marqués de Salvatierra (right) stands the minaret of the destroyed church of *S. Sebastián*. Near by, at No. 6 C. del Gigante, are remains of a 14C Moorish house.

Downhill to the right is the *Casa del Marqués de Salvatierra*, with its Renaissance façade; the figures supporting the pediment over the portal show colonial influence.

Further down the hill is a Renaissance archway, the *Puente Viejo* of 1616, on Roman foundations, and the *Puente S. Miguel*, both bridges affording good views of the Tajo. By the river (right) are remains of *Moorish Baths*.

Keeping to the right on re-ascending the hill, the so-called *Casa del Rey Moro* is passed, built in 1709 on earlier foundations. Its terraced garden commands another fine view of the Tajo. The *Mina de Ronda*, a subterranean stairway cut in the solid rock, climbs down from here to the river bed.

Excursions from Ronda include the stalactite *Cueva de Gato*, and the *Cueva de la Pileta*, with Palaeolithic rock paintings. The latter is beyond *Benaoján*, c 14km SE, reached by turning left off the C339 2km NW of Ronda. The ruins of *Ronda la Vieja*, the site of Roman *Acinipo*, include the *frons scenae* of its theatre; it is approached by turning right off the same road c 5km further NW.

For the road to *S. Pedro de Alcántara*, 49km SE on the coast, see Rte 97.

RONDA TO ALGECIRAS OR GIBRALTAR (102km). The C341 bears SW through olive groves and orchards and over the hills to (37km) **Gaucín**, picturesquely sited on a cleft ridge. Its Moorish castle provides a distant view of Gibraltar, with Africa looming behind. Guzmán el Bueno (see Tarifa) was killed at Gaucín in 1309.— After crossing the Guadiaro, at 23km **Jimena de la Frontera** (8400 inhab.) stands on a hill to the right above the Hozgarganta. Its Moorish *Castle*, captured in 1431, is entered through a triple horseshoe-arched gateway in which Roman tombstones have been incorporated.—2km *Almoraima*, with a 17C convent, 7km NW of which is the village of *Castellar de la Frontera*, with a large Moorish *Castle*.—Descending through cork woods the N340 is reached at 10km, with a view of oil refineries, and of *Gibraltar* 10km beyond, to the SE; *Algeciras* is 10km SW.

The main route descends into the valley of the Guadiaro NW of Ronda, and climbs through the hills. At 17km turn left onto the C344; the road ahead leads past *Zahara* to (20km) *Algodonales*; see Rte 95.

At 14km **Grazalema**, ancient *Lacidula*, has a good Gothic church and was well-described by Ford as a 'cut-throat den . . . fastened like a martlet's nest to the face of a mountain'; it was also the subject of Julian Pitt-Rivers' sociological study 'The People of the Sierra' (1954). It has the reputation of having one of the highest rainfalls in Spain.

The main road climbs W over the *Puerto del Boyar* (1103m), below the *Pinar* (1654m), before descending to (18km) *El Bosque*, with a Gothic church.

A DETOUR of an additional 23km can be made by turning back for 4km and following the C3331 SW past *Benaocaz*, with a church tower possibly that of a mosque, a Baroque *Ayuntamiento*, and ruined fortification. The road then descends to **Ubrique** (16,750 inhab.), long famous for its leatherwork, from there bearing NW to *El Bosque*.

The C344 leads due W across the hills to (32km) **Arcos**; see Rte 95.

97   Málaga to Algeciras via Marbella: the Costa del Sol

A.   Málaga

MÁLAGA (502,250 inhab., including *Torremolinos*; 150,000 in 1920; 275,000 in 1950; 361,000 in 1970; 408,000 in 1975; Parador), a provincial capital with an important harbour, is surrounded by luxuriant sub-tropical vegetation and backed by a semicircle of sunny hills. The products of its fertile *vega* are muscatel grapes (exported as raisins or as Málaga wine), oranges and lemons, sugar-cane, and a variety of other fruit and vegetables.

Its main attraction is its climate (written up by Edwin Lee in 1854), and it was long a favourite winter resort. Francis Carter, who had lived there for some years in the mid 18C, condemned the inhabitants for their love of dissipation', and 'as their traffic is lucrative, and their property extensive, each seems to vie with his neighbour in show and expence, and every one endeavours to move and maintain himself in a sphere above him; the mechanic appears a tradesman; the shop keeper, a merchant; and the merchants, nobles'.

Townsend, when he visited Málaga in 1787, was told that the heat in summer was such that the inhabitants remained indoors until the evening; but after dark the young people would bathe for hours in the sea, the sexes strictly segregated. To prevent intrusion, the girls were guarded by sentinels with loaded muskets. Nevertheless, the determined would go disguised as a female attendant, and in that character pass unobserved.

During recent decades the mushroom growth of adjacent resorts on the *Costa del Sol* has brought Málaga increased prosperity as the main city on the coast, with an airport 9km SW.

The Phoenician foundation of *Malaca* is referred to by Strabo, but the city later transferred its allegiance from Tyre to Carthage. On the advance of Scipio Africanus in the Second Punic War (218–201 BC) it made terms with the Romans and became a Roman municipium. It later maintained a brisk trade with Byzantium and was the seat of a bishop before the Moorish invasion, when after the battle of the Guadalete in 711 it fell to Tariq. It flourished as the principal port for Granada, but in 1487 it was captured by Fernando the Catholic after a dreadful siege followed by wholesale confiscations and autos-da-fé. With the expulsion of the Moriscos after their insurrection in 1568, the city lost much of its former prosperity. It was here in 1620 that the traveller William Lithgow was tortured by the Inquisition and 'Layd on the Racke'.

In 1810 it was taken by Sebastiani. It was a depot for delinquents or *presidarios*, who on their return after imprisonment on the African shore, were let loose on the town. In the opinion of William Mark, the British Consul there in the early 19C, this practice gave it a good claim to be entitled the sink of Spain in respect of vice and the almost total demoralisation of the lower classes.

In 1831 it was the scene of the unsuccessful rising of Gen. Torrijos, who with his 52 companions was captured at Alhaurín and executed by the absolutist governor, Gen. Moreno.

As early as the 1840s it claimed to have an ultra-civilised hotel, owned by a Mr Hodgson, where pale ale and Stilton cheese might be had for the asking. Here, wrote Ford, the bells which were hung would 'ring the knell of nationality' . . . while vague rumours were abroad that 'secret and solitary closets were contemplated, in which, by some magical mechanism, sudden waters are to gush forth . . . '. By 1850 there were c 120 permanent English residents in Málaga, many engaged in the wine trade, and it was visited annually by some 300 English travellers, a number wintering there. Augustus

Hare considered it the dearest place in Spain because it was the most Anglicised.

The Liberal proclivities of the town showed themselves again in 1868 and 1873 in insurrections against the central government. Both in 1931, when it became a Republican stronghold, and in 1936, extremists pillaged and burnt many of its convents and churches, and also looted private houses (cf. Ronda). It was shelled by a Nationalist flotilla, before being entered by Italian and Nationalist troops on 8 February 1937. The proscriptions which followed were particularly ferocious: several thousand republican sympathisers were killed, as were many of the refugees fleeing along the coast to the E. (1000 were killed by the 'Reds' prior to its fall; some 3500 were executed by the Nationalists in the following week; and during the next 7½ years another 16,950 were 'legally' sentenced and shot.) It was here that Arthur Koestler was captured before being imprisoned at Sevilla. Among the prosecuting lawyers was Arias Navarro, who had been imprisoned there for six months, and whose career culminated in being Franco's last Prime Minister, in 1973–76.

Among Malagueños were the Jewish philosopher Ibn Gabirol (Avicebron; c 1021–c 1057); Serafín Estébañez Calderon (1799–1867), author of many descriptions of Andalucian types and customs, a *Costumbrista*; Andrés Borrego (1802–91), the historian and journalist; Antonio Cánovas del Castillo (1828–97), the statesman; Pablo Ruiz Picasso (1881–1973), the artist (at Pl. de Merced 6); and the poets Emilio Prados (1899–1962) and Manuel Altolaguirre (1905–59), both of whom went into exile during the Civil War.

Most roads approaching Málaga eventually converge on the palm-shaded PASEO DEL PARQUE. This park skirts the inner harbour, laid out on land reclaimed from the sea, and is conveniently near most sights of interest. Beyond the Pl. de la Marina to the W, it is extended by the Alameda Principal to the *Puente de Tetuán*, spanning the seasonal torrent of the Guadalmedina (the river of the city) which is now regulated to prevent flooding.

In the C. Atarazanas, parallel to and N of the Alameda Principal, and built into the wall of the *Mercado* erected on the site of the Moorish arsenal, is a white marble horseshoe *Gateway*, built for Yusuf I (1333–54).

From just NW of the Pl. de la Marina the C. Marqués de Larios, the main thoroughfare of the older town, leads N to the PL. DE LA CONSTITUCIÓN. On the N side is the *Consulado* of 1782 by J.M. Aldehuela, with a pleasant patio. Adjacent is domed *Sto. Cristo* (17C), containing the tomb of *Pedro de Mena* (1628–88), the sculptor.

Further N is *Santos Martires*, with a tower of 1548 and a Baroque interior; to the SW is *S. Juan*, with a tall tower, completed in 1598 but altered in 1770.

From the NE corner of the square, the C. Sta. María leads to the **Cathedral** (also approach direct from the Paseo del Parque). It is a nondescript building, mainly Corinthian in character, begun by Diego de Siloé in 1528 and continued by Diego de Vergara the Elder (from 1549) and Younger (after 1588). Having been partially destroyed by an earthquake in 1680, it was not completed until 1719. The façade by José Bada, however, was not finished until 1788. (Bada was also responsible for the Baroque façade of the *Bishop's Palace*, opposite the W front.)

The W front, adorned with Corinthian columns and coloured marbles, is flanked by two towers, only one of which (domed) has been carried above the second storey, leaving the other an ugly stump. Carter found its N and S entrances 'immensely heavy, ill-shaped, and void of beauty', while the interior perspective was 'obstructed by a heavy, massy stone choir'; indeed, it displayed a 'want of symmetry, and frequent deviation from the rules of architecture'. In contrast his contemporary, Twiss, considered the cathedral 'one of the handsomest and neatest in Spain'.

The dark interior, with its overcharged vaulting, is ineffective, and the paintings in the chapels are of little interest. The *Cap. de los Reyes* (S of the ambulatory) contain statuettes of Fernando and Isabel by José de Mora (1681). The *Coro*, begun by Vergara the Younger in 1592, was not completed until 1662. By far the best thing in the church is the *Silleria* of the choir, made by various hands working between 1592 and 1658, and including figures by Pedro de Mena and Alonso Cano. The huge Organ of 1785 by Julián de la Orden, partly restored, is still half mute. The contents of the treasury disappeared in 1936.

Adjacent is the separate *Sagrario*, with a Plateresque retablo by Balmaseda. Incorporated into its N wall is the worn Isabelline portal of the Gothic church which formerly stood here, erected on the site of a mosque.

The C. S. Agustín leads NE to (right) the *Pal. de Buenavista* or *de Luna* (c 1550) housing the **Museo de Bellas Artes**.

In a patio adjacent are Roman mosaics from Cártama. Paintings include works by Morales and Luca Giordano; Ribera, Martyrdom of St. Bartholomew, Zurbarán, St. Benedict, and St. Jerome; Murillo, St. Francis de Paula; Antonio del Castillo, Adoration; and Pedro de Mena, Apparition of the Virgin to St. Anthony. The upper floor contains 19C paintings, including some by Sorolla, and by Muñoz Degrain (Picasso's master), among them his Basque drunkard; and a very few early works by *Picasso* (before the family moved to A Coruña in 1891).

Turn right on leaving to pass 17–18C *Santiago*, with a Mudéjar tower of 1545, before reaching the Pl. de la Merced. Turn S along the Alcazabilla to pass the slight remains (partially built over) of a *Roman Theatre*. At the S end of the street is the *Aduana* or *Customs House* of 1788–1829.

To the E is the entrance to the **Alcazaba**, a huddle of ruins which have been rather too thoroughly 'restored', but which incorporate several Moorish gates. A pleasant climb through gardens brings one to the main buildings arranged around patios, in which a *Museo Arqueológico* has been installed. Among the collection of statuary, mosaics, azulejos, plasterwork, and ceramics, is a maquette showing the possible distribution of the original buildings.

It is connected by a double wall with the *Gibralfaro* (*Jebel Faro*, mountain of the lighthouse). The castle, at a higher level to the E, was rebuilt by Yusuf I on the site of the Phoenician fortress; below it is the Parador. Zigzag walks through the gardens climb up the S slope to the summit of the hill (which can also be ascended by road) for the view.

At the E end of the PASEO DEL PARQUE is the *Fuente de Neptuno*, said to have been presented to Charles V by the Republic of Genoa (1560). Just beyond it is the *Hospital Noble*, a seamen's hospital founded by Dr Noble (1799–1861), an English physician who died at Málaga.

Immediately behind it is the *Plaza de Toros*. Highrise buildings now effectively block off much of the sea view.—The lighthouse on the old mole, commenced as early as 1588 and extended in 1900, commands a view of the harbour.

A few minutes' walk further E, beyond the *Plaza del Toros*, is (left) the ***English Cemetery**, in the tree-shaded centre of which is the Anglican church of St. George.

This, the first Protestant cemetery in Spain, was founded in 1830 by the British consul, William Mark (1782–1849), who had lived in Málaga since 1816 and had been consul since 1824. One of the first graves in it was that of Capt. Robert Boyd, a partisan of Torrijos (see history).

Previously, according to Ford, bodies of such heretics were buried upright in the sand below low water mark, but the orthodox fishermen feared that their soles might become infected. David Roberts, the artist, who visited the cemetery in 1833, was 'captivated by the views': he would be less captivated now.

The original walled enclosure, later much extended, contains some of the earlier graves, many embellished with shells. Among those buried here, including four victims of World War II washed ashore on the coast, are Mr Hodgson (see p 535); the poet Jorge Guillén (1893–1984); and in a common grave, 62 survivors of the German training ship 'Gneisenau', which in 1900 sank outside Málaga harbour.

It may be convenient to list here all the other British Cemeteries in mainland Spain, which have been laid out in a number of unlikely places. With certain exceptions, they have not been visited by the Editor, but some may contain sepulchral monuments of interest, or the remains of people of interest or eminence. The list does not include the battle sites of the War of the Spanish Succession, the Peninsular War (in which some 40,000 British dead were buried where they fell), or the First Carlist War (of which the plot on the N slope of Monte Urgull at S. Sebastián survives). They are listed in approx. date order: Cádiz (1832); Cartegena (1846); Valencia (1849); Tarragona (1850); Madrid (1853); Alicante (1854; transferred to a new plot in 1962); Sevilla (1855); Pasajes de S. Juan (mid 19C); Puerto de Sta. María (1866); A Coruña (1870); Huelva (1874); Águilas (1883?); Villagarcía (1914–18?); Bilbao (1929; but containing remains transferred from another site, including a grave dated 1806); Almería (1973). There are others at Jerez de la Frontera, and Linares.

The Editor would be grateful for any further information which might be of interest concerning them.

For roads from Málaga to **Granada**, and **Córdoba**, see Rtes 89, and 93, in reverse; for **Ronda**, Rte 96.

B. Málaga to Algeciras via Marbella

133km (82 miles). N340. 13km *Torremolinos*—16km *Fuengirola*—27km **Marbella**—11km *S. Pedro de Alcántara*—17km *Estepona*—36km *S. Roque. La Línea* (for **Gibraltar**) is 7km S.—13km **Algeciras**.

Maps: M 446.

The route follows the **Costa del Sol**, a narrow coastal strip skirting the Mediterranean and sheltered by the SIERRA BERMEJA and its extensions. The climate well justifies the name given to this region by its exploiters. Accessible only with difficulty as recently as 1930, this coast has become an increasingly popular holiday (and residential) area in recent decades; but with popularity it has lost almost all its original charm, as newer and more sophisticated pleasures have supplanted the delights of remoteness. New hotels, restaurants, clubs, villas, marinas, urbanisations, shops, and blocks of flats continue to spring up every day, and motorists are warned against dust clouds blown from building sites and unfinished works when passing through the congested resorts strung out along the shore. No longer can one describe Torremolinos—as did Rose Macaulay only 40 years ago—as 'a pretty country place, with . . . the little Sta. Clara hotel'; or S. Pedro de Alcántara as a 'half-ruined hamlet'.

The easiest way out of Málaga is to drive due W on the new road, which later bears S across the Guadalhorce, skirting the airport and passing (left) a turning to the Parador of (13km) *Torremolinos*, now with a bypass.

From contiguous *Benalmádena* (13,600 inhab.), a road climbs 17km W into the SIERRA DE MIJAS (1150m), to *Mijas* (14,800 inhab.).

This formerly unspoilt village was the subject of Ronald Fraser's study 'The Pueblo' (1973). Its Republican mayor remained concealed in his own house for 30 years after the Civil War, as described in the same author's 'In Hiding'.

16km **Fuengirola** (29,150 inhab.), partly bypassed, was the Phoenician *Suel*. It has remains of an old castle and was originally a small fishing port basking beneath the sierra. It was the scene of Gen. Blayney's disastrous expedition against the French in 1810, who made his dispositions 'with the utmost contempt of military rules', and was captured. Several *atalayas*, which served to guard the coast from Algerine pirates, may still be seen as we approach to the town—first skirting several smaller resorts.

The most fashionable part of the COSTA DEL SOL centres on (27km) **Marbella** (60,150 inhab.; 12,000 in 1960), formerly surrounded by orange groves and sugar plantations; the older town preserves a 15C palace and fragmentary walls.

Francis Carter, who passed that way in 1773, remarked that although the town lay in an 'exceedingly pleasant' position, its inhabitants 'bear the character of an uncivil inhospitable people, many of them descendants of the Moors, who still resent the ill-treatment of their forefathers'. Those who have gained from recent changes are no doubt now reconciled.

The sophisticated marina of *Puerto Banús* is passed on the way to (11km) **S. Pedro de Alcántara**, with ruins of a Moorish castle. Just beyond (left) are remains of a Roman villa destroyed in an earthquake in 365, and of a Visigothic basilica.

S. PEDRO DE ALCÁNTARA TO RONDA (49km). The much improved C339 climbs in a long series of sweeping curves through the foothills of the SIERRA BERMEJA, not passing through a single village, to reach the upland SERRANÍA and *Ronda* itself; see Rte 96. The road commands several fine views, but requires careful driving.

17km **Estepona** (23,550 inhab.), once a quiet fishing port, to the NW of which rises *Reales* (1450m), the highest point in the SIERRA BERMEJA. As recently as 1912 the road ended here. Albert Calvert's car was stuck in the deep sand; but 'the whole population, quite savage, and some stark naked, came to the rescue with ropes', and pulled it out.—The *Rock of Gibraltar* is seen ahead.—At 11km a mountain road climbs steeply to (26km) *Gaucín* (see p 534), off which at c 10km a turning leads 14km to the picturesquely-sited hill town of *Casares*, with a ruined castle.

At 10km we cross the Guadiaro and pass the fashionable *Sotogrande* development, before climbing to (10km) the *Puerto del Higuerón* (151m).

A left turning here leads S along a ridge to *La Línea*, with a good view of the sheer N face of the *Rock of Gibraltar* on the descent.

9.5km **La Línea de la Concepción** (56,600 inhab., known as *Llanitos*), was long a frontier town trafficking with Gibraltar and a favourite resort of sailors. It was once fortified, but now only the ruins of the castles of *S. Felipe* and *Sta. Bárbara* remain. They were erected by Felipe V in 1731 to guard both shores, but were dismantled by the British in 1810 at the request of the Spanish to make them untenable by the French. Beyond is the Spanish Customs, and the Neutral Ground on the isthmus, here c 550m wide.

For the **Rock of Gibraltar**, see Rte 98.

S. Roque (19,050 inhab.), 5km SW of this turning, and 7km NW of La

Línea, was founded in 1704, and has an early 18C church containing a good 18C organ (restored). It was the birthplace of Luis de Lacy (1775–1817), the Spanish general and Liberal martyr of Irish descent. Rochfort Scott, writing in the 1830s, repeats an anecdote concerning some garrison wives who walked out to S. Roque from Gibraltar wearing trousers, much to the astonishment of the locals; and the famous bandit José María robbed one fair wearer of such 'inexpressibles' merely to show his wife, and make her laugh!

At 3km the C3331 turns right for *Castellar* (17km N) and *Jimena de la Frontera*; see p 534.

To the left here, near the *Cortijo del Rocadillo*, on the far bank of the Guadaranque, stood *Carteia*, originally an Iberian settlement. It was later colonised by the Greeks, and in 206 BC occupied by the Romans. In 171 BC it was sacked by Scipio Africanus the Younger and re-peopled with the illegitimate descendants of Roman legionaries and Spanish women. The younger Pompey fled to here after his defeat by Caesar at Munda (45 BC). The once important city was used as a quarry for centuries. Although its site was still of interest to Francis Carter in the 1770s, little now remains, and the area is surrounded by oil refineries.

At 5km the C440 turns right, climbing NW into the sierra to (51km) *Alcalá de los Gazules* (5900 inhab.), a picturesque old town of Moorish aspect. It has a ruined fortress and 15C church studded with azulejos.—*Medina-Sidonia* is 24km further W; see Rte 99.

5km **Algeciras** (85,400 inhab.; 19,500 in 1920), although of historical importance, is an ugly town of very slight interest. The views across the bay towards Gibralter are impressive. Some arches of a Moorish aqueduct survive some distance inland beside the railway.

Algeciras is the terminus of regular ferries to Tangiers and Ceuta, and also of the railway from Madrid.

Roman *Portus Albus* was the 'Green Island' (*el Gezira el-Khadra*) of the Moors, whose name is preserved in the offshore *Isla Verde*. The successful assault on it by Alfonso XI in 1344 was reckoned among the greatest achievements of Christian chivalry; presence at the siege was a title to knightly fame. Chaucer records of his knight that 'in Gernade at the sege eek hadde he be of Algezir' (Prologue, 56–7). But in 1379 it was sacked in a Moorish raid. The town was rebuilt by Carlos III on a slightly more regular plan. It was the base of floating batteries during the siege of Gibraltar in 1779–83.

An international conference took place here in 1906 in an endeavour to settle several political problems. During the winter of 1927–28 W.B. Yeats convalesced briefly at the *Reina Cristina* hotel, one of the few relics of a more expansive era.

Pomponius Mela, the geographer, was born at *Tingentera*, on the bay of Algeciras, in the 1C AD.

For the road on to **Cádiz**, see Rte 99.

98 Gibraltar

GIBRALTAR is a British Crown Colony 5.86km2 in extent, situated on a 4km long peninsula jutting S from the Spanish mainland at *La Línea* (see above), and E of the horseshoe *Bay of Algeciras*. Its main physical feature is the massive grey limestone ridge or *Rock* rising some 426m from the Mediterranean at Highest Point. N of it is a sandy isthmus, the so-called 'Neutral Ground', on which an airstrip has been constructed, which extends to the W. Its population in 1985 was 28,850, including 20,000 British Gibraltarians, and 3400 non-British; the rest are members of the families of British armed forces (who are themselves not included in this figure).

It is still a British naval base and fortress, guarding the W entrance of the Mediterranean, and has been so since 1704. Its sovereignty has been long disputed, to the extent that for several years, until February 1985, it was isolated from land communication with Spain in a Spanish attempt to force the territorial and political issues at stake. These have yet to be resolved. Meanwhile Gibraltar again flourishes, and may be visited with ease.

Calpe, the Greek corruption of the Phoenicians' name for their trading station on the rock, was the northern bastion of the *Pillars of Hercules*, commanding the STRAITS OF GIBRALTAR. Beyond this point no other trader was allowed to venture until the decline of Phoenician power. The southern pillar was formed by *Abyle* (*Monte Hacho*, beside Ceuta), and both were fabled to have been raised by Hercules or Heracles when on his expedition to seize the cattle of Geryon (cf. the Isla de León). Heracles was the Greek counterpart of the Phoenician deity Melkarth. The W entrance of the Strait was between *Capes Trafalgar* and *Spartel*, beyond which lay the lost continent of Atlantis and the Islands of the Hesperides. The strong surface current, setting in from the Atlantic at an average rate of 4km per hour, combined with the prevalence of NW winds, made navigation difficult in the days of sail, and the Romans do not appear to have ventured beyond the *Fretum Gaditanum* until the 2C BC.

The Moorish name for the straits was *Bâb ez-Zakak* (the narrow gate) and the rock bears the name of its Berber conqueror, Tariq ibn Zeyad, who landed here in April 711: *Gebel Tarik*, the mountain of Tariq. It was first taken from the Moors in 1309 by Guzmán el Bueno, but in 1333 they regained it and it was not until 1462 that Gibraltar was finally recaptured by the Duke of Medina Sidonia. In 1552 its fortifications were strengthened by Giambattista Calvi, a Milanese, to protect it from the raids of Barbarossa.

On 24 July 1704, during the War of the Spanish Succession, Sir George Rooke and Sir Clowdisley Shovell suddenly attacked the fortress. They found it garrisoned by only 150 and took it in the name of the Archduke Charles of Austria, but hoisted the British flag. It was besieged by the French and Spanish in the following winter; and by the Spanish in 1727 (among the wounded on the Spanish side was the Duke of Wharton; cf. Poblet), although the Treaties of Utrecht (1713) and of Sevilla (1729) had confirmed British possession.

William Green, created a baronet in 1786, was responsible for the improvement of Gibraltar's fortification during the years 1761 to 1783. The last and most famous siege lasted from September 1779 to March 1783, when Gen. George Augustus Eliott (Baron Heathfield; 1717–90) was governor. For a last great assault (September 1782) the Spanish and French constructed floating batteries, which it was claimed, could neither be burnt, sunk, or taken, yet were totally annihilated by British gunners using red hot shot. José Cadalso, the poet and satirist, was killed during the siege, a fortnight after being promoted to colonel. Mozart wrote an 'Ode to Calpe' commemorating its spirited defence.

During several outbreaks of yellow fever during the early decades of the 19C, encampments were established on the isthmus. In 1909 a boundary fence was erected along its N side roughly parallel to the 18C Spanish Line. This was considered a further encroachment on her territory and a Spanish protest was registered. In 1938 work on an aircraft landing strip was begun.

As a naval base Gibraltar played a vital but passive role in both World Wars. In 1939–45 its defences, especially underground, were enormously strengthened. In 1940 the women, children, and the elderly were evacuated, mostly to England and Northern Ireland. In November 1941 the aircraft carrier 'Ark Royal' was torpedoed and sunk only 40km from Gibraltar.

The explosion, when unloading, of the ammunition ship 'Bedenham' (27 April 1951) caused more damage to buildings than in air raids during the war.

A referendum, in which almost 96 per cent of the electorate voted, took place in Gibraltar in 1967; 12,138 people wished to retain the link with Britain, and only 44 supported a change to Spanish sovereignty (Franco was still dictator). But progressive restrictions were enforced by the Spanish government, who closed the frontier in June 1969. It was not until 5 February 1985 that it was opened again, and during the rest of that year some 2,260,000 crossed into Gibraltar by land.

Meanwhile, constitutional changes were taking place. A measure of self-government was established by the formation of a House of Assembly in 1969, presided over by a Chief Minister (although the Governor is still responsible for matters of defence, internal security, and foreign affairs). The first mayor (in

1955) was Joshua Hassan, whose party won the 1984 election with eight seats; the opposition had seven. He retired in 1987.

As a result of changes in Britain's defence policy, the Royal Naval Dockyard was closed down in December 1984 and converted into commercial ship repair yards under Gibraltar Government ownership; the Naval Base is still operational. Its commodious enclosed harbour, formed by huge moles, protect it from SW winds, but there are now few ships at anchor, since fleets and flotillas have become largely superfluous.

The indigenous population is a somewhat mixed race, including many of Genoese descent, small Jewish and Indian communities, and a declining number of Moroccans. Over 19,000 are ostensibly Roman Catholic in spite of the attempts of S.H. Rule to convert them to Methodism in the 1830s. English is the official language, but Spanish is widely spoken. The Gibraltarians are now largely engaged in licit trade, but the smuggling industry—with considerable connivance on both sides—had long been a major cause of resentment on the part of the Spanish government. The Rock, still symbolising imperialist power and inviting uncomplimentary comparisons, has long been a thorn in their flesh. Henry Francis Cary (1772–1844), the translator of Dante, was born here.

'The Rock of Contention', by George Hills, is a good historical study up to 1974; both Richard Ford's and George Borrow's descriptions are critical.

Although British currency is used, the Gibraltar Government issues stamps, and its own 1, 5, 10, and 20-pound notes. Spanish money is accepted except in government offices and in post offices. British Airways and charter companies operate scheduled services from Gatwick or Manchester to Gibraltar; and it is expected that other lines will be inaugurated. Tangier is served by plane, hydrofoil, and catamaran. Local travel agents can give full information, together with facilities for excursions, etc. There are also bus services to parts of Andalucía.

The usual EEC regulations apply with regard to Identity Cards, Passports, and other documentation.

The main points of interest can be visited in a drive of two hours, for which a taxi can be hired by those without their own transport.

On crossing the frontier (Customs) and the airstrip, a roundabout is reached directly below the almost sheer wall of the *N Face* of the Rock, in which the *Upper Galleries* have been pierced; see below.

For travellers wishing to make a *circuit* of the Rock before entering the town, this is first described.

Turn left (E) of the roundabout to skirt (left) the *N Front Cemetery* (Christian and Jewish). Beyond this is the site of the *Devil's Tower*, demolished to provide a free field of fire.—A second left turn leads to the *Eastern Beach*.—The Catalan Bay Road circles S to *Catalan Bay* village (also with a beach), and passes below the E flank of the Rock, conspicuous on which is the extensive slope of the rainwater *Catchment System* of whitewashed galvanised iron. This still provides Gibraltar with most of its water, although some is imported by tanker from Morocco, and desalination plants have been constructed. The water drains into reservoirs with a capacity of 15 million gallons, hewn from the solid rock.

Sandy Bay is next passed, from which a tunnel (no adm.) runs due W through the Rock to the dockyards. The road enters a short tunnel below the SE flank of the ridge to approach the flatter *Europa Point*, the S extremity of the Rock, with its *Trinity House lighthouse* (1838). To the W extend old fortifications, and the slight remains of the Mudéjar chapel (a former mosque) of *Our Lady of Europe*. From here there are two alternative roads N.

The *Keightley Way tunnel* passes below the *Wind Mill Flats* to skirt two beaches and the *Parson's Lodge battery* to reach *Rosia Bay*, where one or two characteristic old houses survive. Nelson's body was brought ashore here from 'H.M.S. Victory' after Trafalgar.—

Mounted on the left a short distance beyond is the remaining 100-ton gun, delivered in 1822 from Armstrong so that Gibraltar might not be out-ranged by those supplied by them to the Italian fleet.—The Rosia road later skirts the *Dry Docks* to approach the *Southport Gates*; see below.

The Europa Road climbs past the former *Naval Hospital* (1745) towards the *Rock Hotel*, from which roads zigzag up the W flank of the Rock; see below. To the left are the *Alameda Gardens*, laid out by Sir George Don (1754–1832) during his governorship on what was previously a scorched area known as the *Red Sands*. Below the gardens, famous for their tree-geraniums, are the *Ragged Staff Stairs*, a weak sector of the earlier defences, where Rooke landed in 1704.—The road descends near the lower station of the cablecar and skirts the *Trafalgar Cemetery*, with graves of British naval officers who fell in that battle, to reach the *Southport Gates* at the S end of *Main Street*; see below.

Driving ahead from the roundabout just S of the airstrip, one can follow the Queensway between the *Line Wall* and the *Harbour*; the Line Wall road, skirting the inner side of the fortifications; or Main Street. All of these converge further S on the Southport Gates. Buildings of interest in the town can be approached from *Main Street*. At the N end is *Casemates Square*, dominated to the SE by the *Moorish Castle*; see below.

At a central point is the R.C. *Cathedral of St. Mary the Crowned* (*Sta. María la Coronada*), built on the site of a mosque. It was enlarged c 1550, reconstructed from 1787 after being seriously damaged in the Great Siege, and completed in 1820, when the tower was added.

Bomb House Lane, opposite, leads (right) to the *Museum.

It contains an interesting collection of paintings, watercolours, lithographs and prints of Gibraltar, including: View of the ruins, by Capt. Thomas Davis (1793); Views by Lieut. Frederick Leeds Edridge (1830–34); by Capt. J.M. Carter; by J.W. Peard (1838); by H.A. West; by L.H. Irving (1852); by Ph. Benucci (1826); watercolours of wild flowers of Gibraltar by Madelene S. Pasley (1876); and the MS and watercolours of the 'Journal of the Siege', by Capt. J. Spilsbury. Other sections are devoted to the tunnelling and boring of galleries in the N Face of the Rock in 1782–85 carried out by Henry Ince; collections of arms and ammunition used at the Siege (including hollow shot, and furnaces for the heating of red hot shot); models; maps and plans of the siege; a maquette of Gibraltar made in 1865 at 1:600 (50ft = 1 inch); the flora and fauna of Gibraltar; archaeological collections, including Roman, Visigothic, and Moorish capitals (probably from Carteia); sections concerning the Calpe Hunt, established by Adm. Fleming in 1817; Trafalgar; the 'Mary Celeste' (found drifting unmanned, and brought into Gibraltar in 1872); philatelic collections; and anchors and other nautical artefacts. The basement contains remains of *Moorish baths* in situ.

A few paces beyond is a small square, on the E side of which is the Anglican *Cathedral of the Holy Trinity*, a neo-Moorish building of 1820–32. It was raised to cathedral status in 1842 and contains the tomb of Sir George Don (died 1832), governor since 1814.—On the S side of the square is the *Line Wall house*, in which Prince George of Cambridge resided in 1838, and now the *Gibraltar Government Tourist Office*.

By skirting the cathedral and crossing Main Street here, one can climb to the building of the *Gibraltar Garrison Library* (1804). It was founded in 1793, a project of Col John Drinkwater (historian of the

Great Siege), Gen. Sir Robert Boyd, and Maj.-Gen. Charles O'Hara, the then Lieut.-Governor.

Continuing S in Main Street, we pass (left) the *Supreme Court* buildings of 1820; and right, the *King's Chapel*, adjacent to the **Convent** (since 1728 the residence of the Governor). These were dependencies of a Franciscan monastery of c 1531. The chapel comprises the E parts and N transept of the original church. Its restoration was completed in 1954 after being damaged by the explosion of 1951.

Among monuments are those to Sir Peter Durand, military architect and chief officer of Ordnance for Gibraltar and Minorca until 1715; to Sir Robert Boyd (died 1794), buried in the King's Bastion; to Lieut.-Gen. Colin Campbell, acting Governor, 1811–14; to Gen. Charles O'Hara, Governor in 1795–1802; and to several officers killed at Barosa or who died of plague.

The front of the Convent was replaced in 1864, when the present porch was built.—Opposite is the early 19C *Guard House*, the frequent venue of stilted ceremonious spectacles.

The street ends at the *Southport Gates*, in a wall which extends up the W slope of the Rock.

The **Rock** itself can be explored by ascending Europa Road past the *Rock Hotel* up Engineer Road and then zig-zagging up Queens Road and Cave Branch Road to *St. Michael's Cave*—an impressive hollow in the Rock, with stalactites and stalagmites, and well described by George Borrow. It is now commercialised as an attraction.—It is possible to ascend to *Highest Point* (426m). Further N there is a pedestrian road skirting the W flank of the Rock, passing the upper station of the Cable Car.

Descending NW, we reach the *Apes' Den*. There are two packs of semi-wild tail-less macaque monkeys (*Macacus sylvanus*), probably brought over from N Africa as pets by officers of the garrison in the early 18C. (Hold on to your hats, cameras, and handbags, for which they have a penchant.)

The road continues N to the *Upper Galleries*, tunnelled in the Rock during the last two decades of the 18C, and extended during the Second World War. From the embrasures, the plunging views over the isthmus to La Línea are impressive. The rock-hewn galleries, which descend to a chamber known as *St. George's Hall*, contain models of late 18C artificers, gunners, and officers.—The return can be made by Willis's Road, descending directly to the town past the *Moorish Castle*. This dates back to 725, but only its keep (1333) survives.

For roads from Gibraltar to **Málaga**, see Rte 97 in reverse; for **Algeciras** and **Cádiz**, Rte 99.

99   Algeciras to Cádiz

134km (83 miles). N340. 22km *Tarifa*—50km *Vejer*—29km *Chiclana*—23km **Cádiz**.

Maps: M 446.

From *Algeciras* (see latter part of Rte 97) the road climbs SW over two coastal ridges (the more westerly rising to 340m), providing views across the *Straits of Gibraltar* towards the coast of Morocco between

Ceuta and Tangiers; and retrospective views of the *Rock of Gibraltar*. At 22km it enters **Tarifa** (14,150 inhab.), also bypassed. It is the most southerly town on the Spanish mainland, and the *Punta Marroquí* is only 15km (9¹/₄ miles) from the African shore. It was off here in 1801 that Adm. Saumarez defeated a French and Spanish squadron under Linois.

Tarifa occupies the site of Punic *Josa* and Roman *Julium Traducta*. It is named after Tarif ibn Malik, leader of the first band of Moors despatched by Tariq to Spain in 711. Captured by Sancho IV in 1292, it was defended against counter attacks by Alonso Pérez de Guzmán. On the Moorish side was the traitor Infante Don Juan (Sancho's brother), to whom Guzmán's young son had been entrusted as a page. Juan brought the boy beneath the walls and threatened to kill him if Tarifa was not surrendered forthwith. Guzmán contemptuously tossed him a dagger and withdrew, preferring 'honour without a son, to a son with dishonour'. On hearing the cry of horror from the battlements when the boy was murdered, Guzmán stoically observed: 'I feared that the infidel had gained the city'. The king honoured him with the surname 'el Bueno', and he became the founder of the house of Medina Sidonia.

In December 1811, when garrisoned by British troops, a determined French attack was successfully repulsed.

The older town of narrow winding lanes retains parts of its crumbling Moorish *Walls* pierced by horseshoe arches. Between the town and the sea is the Alameda. The Moorish *Castle* lies to the E, and a Cufic inscription records that it was built in 950–60, but the *Torre de Guzmán* is more modern than that from which the hero flung his dagger.

S. Mateo, built on the site of a mosque, has blocked 15C windows, quaint gargoyles, and a Baroque W front. It contains a Visigothic tablet, dated 674, found a few kilometres away.

The road briefly skirts the shore before veering inland.

At 15km a left turn crosses a low ridge to (7.5km) a hamlet close to the beach of **Bolonia**, sheltered by the *Punta Camarinal* to the N. Here are the extensive remains of Roman *Baelo Claudia*; a theatre, three temples, forum, market, basilica, baths, and two necropoli have been excavated. Closer to the shore are the remains of a tuna-salting factory.

The main road crosses a marshy plain, possibly the one where Wallia the Visigoth defeated the Vandals in 417, driving them out of Spain over to Africa; and where Alfonso XI crushed the united armies of Yusuf I of Granada and Abul-Hassan of Fez in 1340. In this battle the first cannon used in Europe were brought into action, having been transported from Damascus by the Moors.

At 15km the fishing village of *Zahara de los Atunes* lies 10.5km SE; from it a by-road leads N to *Barbate*; see below.—Inland is the drained *Laguna de la Janda*, where in 711 Tariq first encountered Roderic 'the last of the Goths', who was defeated shortly afterwards on the banks of the Guadalete S of Jerez.

At 19km the road passes below the white Moorish-looking town of **Vejer de la Frontera** (12,100 inhab.), with a partially restored *Castle*, a Gothic *Church* with a rose-window, and the former *Conv. de las Monjas*, which may have been built on the site of a Roman temple.

10km SE is *Barbate*, with the slight remains of a fortification on the shore. To the W is the CABO DE TRAFALGAR (*Tarif al-Gar*, cape of the cave), off which on 21 October 1805 Nelson with 27 ships of the line and four frigates, defeated the allied French and Spanish fleet (33 ships of the line and seven frigates) under Villeneuve and Gravina. Both the British and Spanish commanders were mortally wounded.

21km NE of Vejer is *Casas Viejas* or Benalup de Sidonia, the scene of skirmishing in 1811 and where an anarchist rising took place in 1933. There are prehistoric paintings in the *Cueva del Tajo de las Figuras*, 8km further SE. Approximately 5km beyond are the ruins of the 18C Carmelite convent of *S. José*, abandoned in 1835.

The C343 leads 27km N (from Vejer) to **Medina Sidonia** (14,850 inhab.), a well-situated but decaying town. This was Roman *Asido*, and later the seat of the Guzmán family, dukes of Medina Sidonia. The seventh duke (1550–1615) was commander-in-chief of the Invincible Armada. Leonor de Guzmán, mistress of Alfonso XI and mother of Enrique de Trastámara, fled here from Alfonso's son, Pedro the Cruel; and here in 1361 Pedro may have put to death his own wife, Blanche de Bourbon.

The town retains part of its rampart wall, the Moorish *Arco de la Pastora*, the ducal *Palace*, and Renaissance *Ayuntamiento*. 15C *Sta. María* has a doorway and tower completed in 1623, and a retablo carved by J.B. Vázquez; *Santiago* is 16C. Ford hardly considered it worth visiting, for it was like so many such hillfort towns which, 'glittering in the bright sun . . . appear in the enchantment-lending distance to be a fairy residence', but which in reality were 'dens of dirt, ruin, and poverty'; and in many cases the same stricture applies today.

Arcos is 37km N; *Jerez*, 30km NW; *Alcalá de los Gazules*, 24km E; and *Chiclana*, 21km W.

Leaving Vejer by the main road, at 14km we pass (2.5km W) **Conil** (13,400 inhab.), a tunny-fishing port, with a *Torre de Guzmán*.—16km **Chiclana de la Frontera** (36,500 inhab.). A knoll to the E of here was the scene of the brief but bloody *Battle of Barrosa* (5 March 1811), in which Gen. Graham defeated the French under Victor.

The beach of *Sancti Petri*, 9km W of Chiclana, is protected by an island on which are remains of a 13C castle built on the ruins of a classical temple.

The road crosses the *Caño de Sancti Petri* on a causeway (see below) between salt pans to meet (5km) the former main road circling the bay of Cádiz from Puerto Real. Turn left towards the ISLA DE LÉON and (3.5km) **S. Fernando** (72,100 inhab.), a headquarters of the Spanish naval authorities founded in 1776, and with an *Observatory* of 1793. Its *Ayuntamiento* is by Torcuato Cayón. In 1810 the Cortes Constitutionales held their first meeting here, in the *Teatro de las Cortes*. To the NE is the arsenal of *La Carraca*, founded in 1790. It was the birthplace of Francisco Serrano (1810–85), general and politician; Juan van Halen (1788–1864), the Liberal general and adventurer, was also born on the island.

The town shared the name of Isla de León until 1813, when, in honour of the resistance of the Spanish under Diego Alvear y Ponce de León to the French assaults on Cádiz in 1810–12, it was re-christened S. Fernando. The island was granted in 1459 to the Ponce de León family, but reverted to the Crown in 1484. At the N end of the island is the rocky peninsula which is the site of Cádiz. The causeway, or *Puente Zuazo*, is reputed to have been originally a bridge-aqueduct built by Cornelius Balbus the Younger of Cádiz, destroyed by the Moors in 1262 and restored or rebuilt by Sánchez de Zuazo in the 15C. Near the bridge is the modernised *Castillo de S. Romualdo*, built by Moorish engineers in 1328 for Alfonso XI, and of interest for its regular rectangular plan and heavy square towers. The island was also the legendary pasture of the red cattle of Geryon, which were stolen by Hercules; at Torre Gordo there stood a Phoenician temple to Melkarth.

Passing the watch-tower at *Torre Gordo*, the road follows the narrow sand spit N. Swinburne reported that the winter storms were such that 'two men coming into town with provisions were swept off the isthmus by a sudden swell of the waves, and never heard of more'. The defensive forts of *Cortadura* and *Puntales* are later passed. Beyond the latter appears the peninsula of *Trocadero*, from which the direct road from Sevilla crosses the bay by a bridge built in 1971. The road then passes through the outer suburbs of modern **Cádiz**, passing (right) domed *S. José* (1783) before reaching the old fortification (1639); see below.

100 Cádiz

CÁDIZ (156,700 inhab.; 76,000 in 1920; 115,000 in 1960; Parador) is a provincial capital, one of the principal ports of Spain, and one of the oldest towns of Europe, but retains little air of antiquity. With tall white houses characterised by their *miradors* and roof terraces (*azoteas*), and narrow intercrossing streets, *old* Cádiz was likened by Ford to a 'sea-prison'. But it has a certain faded charm of its own, preferable to the modern suburbs strung out along the isthmus to the S. It stands on an isolated rock and is surrounded by sea walls except at its S entrance and towards the harbour.

The Phoenician settlement of *Gaddir* (an enclosure) was known to the Greeks as *Gadeira*. It is said to have been founded as early as 1100 BC and in the 7C BC it was a market for the tin of the Cassiterides and the amber of the Baltic. About 501 BC it was occupied by the Carthaginians. In 237 BC Hamilcar Barca landed here before his conquest of the Mediterranean coast of Spain. Julius Caesar, whose first magistracy was a Spanish quaestorship, recognised the importance of *Gades*, and as dictator endowed its inhabitants with Roman citizenship and the city with the title of *Julia Augusta Gaditana*. It also had the monopoly of the salt-fish trade with Rome. But with the fall of Rome, it sank into obscurity, and was of slight significance to the Visigoths and Moors.

In 1031 it was harried by Norman pirates. When Alfonso X reconquered *Jeziret Kádis* in 1262 he found the place almost depopulated, and re-colonised it with Christians from the Cantabrian coast.

With the discovery of America, Cádiz flourished again. In 1522, under Sebastián Elcano, one ship, the 'Victoria', with a surviving crew of 21, limped into harbour after circumnavigating the globe (cf. Sanlúcar). On several occasions in the 16C it repelled the attacks of Barbary pirates, but was less successful when in 1587 Drake here 'singed the King of Spain's beard'. In 1596 the 2nd Earl of Essex, with 6800 men, captured 13 men-of-war and 40 galleons in the inner bay and sacked the town. In this action Sir Walter Raleigh, Lord Effingham, Sir Francis Vere, Sir Conyers Clifford, Lord Thomas Howard, Sir George Carew, Sir Christopher Blount, Sir John (who was killed) and Richard Wingfield, and the young poet John Donne all took part; and William Alabaster, the poet, was chaplain to Essex. Later retaliatory expeditions in 1625 (led by Lord Cecil, accompanied by the 3rd Earl of Essex) and in 1702 were failures.

Between 1720 and 1765 it enjoyed the monopoly of the Spanish-American trade. In the British Factory here, unlike that at Lisbon, Irish Catholics predominated. Alexander O'Reilly (c 1722–94), a Spanish general of Irish descent, was governor of Cádiz in 1775–88 and did much to improve the town, which had been described earlier as being 'insufferably stinking'. It was blockaded by a British fleet from February 1797 to April 1798, and was bombarded by another squadron in 1800. At that time the population was as high as c 70,000.

In 1805 it saw the return of a shattered fleet after the battle of Trafalgar, off the cape to the S. Throughout the Peninsular War Cádiz was the seat of the Spanish Cortes. In 1810–12, under the Duque de Albuquerque, it resisted the French until relieved by Gen. Spencer. It was during the siege that the Liberal Constitution of March 1812 was proclaimed. In 1820 Rafael Riego defended the standard of Liberalism here, and the movement was only arrested in 1823 when Trocadero fell to another French army under the reactionary Duc d'Angoulême. (He had been invited into Spain to support the despotic regime of Fernando VII.)

In 1883 14 militant anarchists were garrotted here in the Mano Negra (Black Hand) conspiracy, on the pretext that they planned to massacre the whole of the Andalucian upper class.

There is a local phenomena called the *Solano*, an unpleasantly dry E wind, which in the words of C.A. Fischer (1802), disarmed the *gaditanas* and caused all the senses to be 'involuntarily inebriated'; when 'an irresistible instinct becomes authorised by example and is excited by solicitation'. To moderate this ferment of the blood, the sexes would go seabathing, the women strictly guarded by cavalry.

Cádiz was the birthplace of Lucius Cornelius Balbus (or Balbus Maior; fl. 40 BC), the first provincial to be a Roman consul; his nephew Balbus Minor constructed a dockyard at Cádiz. Other natives were Columella (fl. AD 40), the agricultural writer; Ibn Tufail (c 1105–85), the philosopher; José Celestino Mutis (1732–1808), the botanist; José Cadalso (1741–82), the author; Antonio Alcalá Galiano (1789–1865), author and politician; Juan Alvarez Mendizábal (1790–1853), the Jewish financier responsible for the expropriation of Spanish monasteries in 1836; Francisco Javier Isturiz (1790–1870), the Liberal politician; the Republican leader Emilio Castelar (1832–99); Segismundo Moret (1838–1913), the Liberal statesman; and Manuel de Falla (1876–1946), the composer.

John Brackenbury, the British Vice-Consul in 1822–40, was responsible in 1832 for the establishment of a Protestant Cemetery in the suburb of S. José (cf. Málaga).

The old town is entered by the *Puerta de Tierra*, constructed by *Torcuato Cayón* in 1755, but a large section of the defensive wall in this area was destroyed by an explosion of submarine mines in 1947.

Bearing right past the railway station, we reach (left) the Pl. de S. Juan de Dios, flanked by the Neo-Classical *Ayuntamiento*.—Ahead, the Av. Ramón de Carranza leads to the *Diputación*, built in 1773 as a *Custom House* by Juan Caballero.

In the pedestrian C. S. Francisco, parallel to the W, is *S. Agustín*, with a façade of 1647.

Beyond the Diputación is the Pl. de España, from which the C. Antonio López leads left to the PL. DE MINA, once the garden of a Capuchin convent. At its SE corner is the **Museo Provincial** (still undergoing reformation).

It contains paintings by Alejo Fernández, Rubens, Van Orley, Frans Franken, Alonso Cano, Luca Giordano, Murillo, Ribera, and Zurbarán; royal portraits by Carnicero, and Lawrence, Adm. Ignacio María de Álava (?). More important are the series of *Saints* by Zurbarán, formerly in the Cartuja at Jerez (q.v.) These are: St. John the Evangelist, St. Luke, St. John the Baptist, three of St. Bruno (one 'in extasy'), St. Lawrence, St. Mark, St. Matthew, St. Anthelm (Bp of Belley), St. Hugh of Grenoble, Blessed John Houghton (prior of the London Charterhouse), St. Hugh of Lincoln, and Card. Albergati.

The *Archaeological collections* include a few relics of Phoenician Gaddir, including a sarcophagus, Greco-Phoenician in style, and other finds from the necropolis at Punta de la Vaca; and the Mariquita del Marmolejo, a headless Roman statue from Lebrija, once worshipped as a Virgin.

A short way down the C. Rosario, leading off the S corner of the plaza, is the *Sta. Cueva*, a late 18C elliptical chapel by Torcuato Benjumeda. It contains three frescoes of religious subjects by Goya.

From the W side of the plaza, the C.S. José leads past (right) the *Pl. de S. Antonio*, with its 18C church, a plaza which Rochfort Scott (writing in the 1820s) referred to as 'a kind of treadmill, that fashion has condemned her votaries to take an hour's exercise in after the fatigues of the day'. The street leads to *S. Felipe Neri* (1719), in which the Cortes sat in 1811–12. It contains a Conception by Murillo and a terracotta head of St. John attributed to Pedro Roldan. Adjacent is the **Museo Historico**, with souvenirs of 1810–12, and the remarkable wooden *Maquette of Cádiz* in 1777.

In the C. del Sacramento, the next cross street, is the *Torre Vigía de Tavira*, an old semaphore tower or observatory, which according to Twiss, contained instruments 'chiefly made in London by Mr Dolland and Mr Bird'.—In the next street to the S is the *Hosp. de Mujeres*, with a patio of 1740; its chapel contains an Ecstasy of St. Francis by El Greco.

The C. del Sacramento leads left (SE) to the Pl. Castelar (or Candelaria), from the SE corner of which the C. de Santiago leads to Baroque *Santiago*, the adjacent 18C *Bishop's Palace* and the *Pl. de la Catedral*. At the far corner of the last is the *Arco de la Rosa*, a medieval town gate.

The **Cathedral** (*Nueva*), with a conspicuous dome of glazed yellow tiles, is a Baroque building begun in 1722 by Vicente Acero, continued intermittently after 1753 by Torcuato Cayón, but not completed until 1860. Townsend (1787) considered it 'a disgrace to taste', while Ford compared it to 'a stranded wreck on a quicksand'. It was for this cathedral that Haydn composed 'The Seven last Words from the Cross'. De Falla (died 1946) is buried in the crypt. It contains stalls of 1702.

The friable nature of its masonry has necessitated extensive restoration, but even in 1776 Swinburne had ominously remarked that in one chapel the work was so coarsely done and 'the squares . . . so loosely jointed and ill fitted, that in a few years the facing will be quite spoilt'.

The adjacent **Museum** contains a Custodia by Antonio Suárez (1674), with a car of 1740; another known as 'El Cogollo', attributed to Enrique de Arfe, the jewel-encrusted Custodia 'del Millón' (1721), and other cult objects; also paintings by Ribera, Morales, Valdés Leal, Alejo Fernández, Zurbarán, and Murillo (including a copy of the latter's Conception, attributed to Clemente de Torres).

To the SE is *Sta. Cruz*, the *Catedral Vieja*, with a massive tower. Built after 1265, it was so severely damaged in the English sack of 1596 that in 1602 it had to be virtually rebuilt. It contains a retablo mayor of c 1650.

Further SE is *Sta. María*, with azulejos painted in Delft in 1679 by

Armenian artists.—To the S is the former *Prison* (*Cárcel Real*: 1794), now being restored for other purposes.

Some minutes' walk to the W of the cathedral brings one to *Sta. Catalina*, containing the Marriage of St. Catherine, the last work of Murillo. He fell from the scaffolding when the painting was almost finished, and died in Sevilla from his injuries soon afterwards. Here also is a Calvary carved by Salzillo.—At the SW corner of the ramparts is the *Puerta de la Caleta*, from which a causeway leads out to the *Castillo de S. Sebastián*, with a square tower of 1613 built on Phoenician or Carthaginian foundations.

Circling N, the huge former *Hospicio* (1772; by Torcuato Cayón) is passed, and then (left) the fort of *Sta. Catalina* (1599), to reach the modern parador or *Hotel Atlantico* and the sea-flanked PARQUE GENOVÉS. The road later passes late 18C barracks, converted to house the *University*, and the residence of the Military Governor (1760), to reach *El Carmen* (1764), containing the grave of Adm. Gravina (1756–1806). He was the commander of the Spanish fleet at Trafalgar and died of wounds received in the battle.

We skirt the *Alameda*—once 'as much resorted to by ladies of easy virtue as our St. James's Park', noted Twiss; and the only place in Spain where he had seen 'bare-faced licentiousness and libertinism'— and bear SE to regain the Pl. de España.

For roads from Cádiz to **Algeciras**, and to **Jerez** and **Sevilla**, see Rtes 99 and 102, in reverse.

101 Sevilla

SEVILLA (anglicised as **Seville**; 645,800 inhab.; c 96,000 in 1800; 206,000 in 1920; 302,000 in 1940; 442,000 in 1960; 590,000 in 1975) is the fourth city of Spain, a provincial capital and the capital of the autonomy of Andalucía. It stands largely on the left bank of the Guadalquivir, but has extended considerably in recent decades. Its Cathedral, the Alcázar, and several museums and churches are remarkable. Its streets ans plazas, shaded by orange trees, are an attractive feature, but there is perhaps less justification now than there was that 'quien no ha visto Sevilla no ha visto maravilla'; but certainly when George Borrow lived there in the late 1830s, he considered it 'the most interesting town in all Spain', standing beneath 'the most glorious heaven . . . '.

Many of the older houses have an entrance porch (*zaguán*) with open-work iron gates (*cancela*)· and windows protected by iron gratings. From these is derived the old phrase '*comer hierro*' (to eat iron) used of the cloaked gallants wooing their *novias* caged within.

A less attractive feature is the increase in petty crime.

Ubiquitous in Sevilla is 'El Nodo' (the knot), a rebus seen both carved and painted. It comprises a double knot (*madeja*) between the syllables NO and DO, and is to be read as 'no m'ha dejado' (it has not deserted me), commemorating the fidelity of Sevilla to Alfonso X.

Roman *Hispalis*, Moorish *Ishbiliya*, was originally an Iberian settlement. Julius Caesar, who entered it in 45 BC, gave it the title of *Colonia Julia Romula*, and in the early imperial epoch it was one of the leading towns in the flourishing province of *Baetica*. Under the Visigoths (5–8Cs) it belonged to the kingdom of which Toledo became the capital. Hermengild, viceroy of Sevilla, abjured the Arian heresy and was put to death as a rebel by his father Leovigild in 586. But when the orthodox creed triumphed he was canonised together with

SS. Leandro and Isidoro, brothers and successive archbishops (and protectors of the city).

After the defeat of Roderic on the Guadalete in 712, Sevilla was captured by the Moors under Musa, the lieutenant of Tariq. It was later incorporated into the Caliphate of Córdoba, and rivalled the capital both in material prosperity and as a seat of learning. When the western caliphate broke up, Sevilla proclaimed her independence (1023) under the family of the Abbadites. They were in turn dispossessed by the Almoravides in 1091 and by the Almohades in 1147, under whom the city enjoyed a new period of prosperity, and many fine buildings, including the Giralda, were erected.

In 1248 it was reconquered by Fernando III, who died (and was buried) there in 1252. He divided among his followers (many from Burgos, Palencia, and Valladolid) the possessions of those numerous citizens who sought voluntary exile. Sevilla remained faithful to Alfonso X when his son Sancho revolted, and later became a favourite royal residence, especially of Pedro the Cruel (1350–69).

The discovery of the New World in 1492 raised Sevilla to the pinnacle of its fortune. Sebastian Cabot was employed as a cartographer here in 1512–16. In 1526 Charles V and Isabel of Portugal were married here. But during the reign of Felipe IV its prosperity declined, partly due to the plague of 1647–52, when some 60,000 died. The city also suffered from the rivalry of Cádiz under the first Bourbon kings; and later from the loss of the Spanish colonies. From 1808–12 it was occupied by the French under Soult (when a thousand canvases of varying quality were removed from the city); and in 1843 it was bombarded by Espartero.

It adhered to the Republican government at the commencement of the Civil War, but was seized by the Nationalist Gen. Queipo de Llano by a fortuitous *coup de main*. From here he made his notorious braggart broadcasts. The subsequent proscriptions were excessive, and the repression brutal.

With the autonomy of Andalucía, Sevilla again flourishes in several ways, and at present there is much talk concerning the forthcoming quincentenary celebration of the Discovery of America.

Among Sevillanos were the writers and historians Bartolomé de las Casas (1484–1566); Lope de Rueda (1500–65); Pedro de Cieza de León (1518–54), historian of Peru; Fernando de Herrera (1534–97); Mateo Alemán (1547–1615), author of 'Guzmán de Alfarache'; the humanist Argote de Molina (1548–98); Rodrigo Fernández de Ribera (1579–1631), author of the satirical 'Los anteojos de mejor vista'; Francisco de Rioja (c 1583–1659); Diego Jiménez de Encisco (1585–1634?); Nicolás Antonio (1617–84), the bibliographer (Sevilla had been dominated by the Cromberger family of printers in the first half of the 16C); Alberto Lista (1775–1848); Joseph Blanco White (1775–1841), the theological writer of Irish descent and author of 'Letters from Spain' (written under the pseudonym of Don Leucadio Doblado), who lived in England from 1810; Pascual Gayangos (1809–97), the Arabic scholar; Gustavo Adolfo Bécquer (1836–70); Antonio Machado (1875–1939); Vicente Aleixandre (1898–1984); and Luis Cernuda (1902–63).

Among artists: Francisco Pacheco (1571–1654); Francisco de Herrera the Elder (el Viejo; 1576–1656), and the Younger (el Mozo; 1612–85); Diego de Velazquez de Silva (1599–1660); Bartolomé Esteban Murillo (1618–82); Juan de Valdés Leal (1622–90); José Gutierrez de la Vega (1791–1865); Antonio Esquivel (1806–57); José, Joaquín, and Valeriano Dominguez Bécquer (1805–41, 1817–79, and 1834–70 respectively); and Manuel Cabral Bejarano (1827–63).

Among composers: Cristóbal de Morales (c 1500–53); Francisco Guerrero (1528–99); Joaquín Turina (1882–1949); and Manuel García (1775–1832), the singer and composer of *tonadillas*, and father of Malibran and Pauline Viardot.

In 1828 David Wilkie painted a portrait of Washington Irving in Sevilla; here two years later, Richard Ford spent his first winter in Andalucía; George Borrow spent his last months in Spain (1839–40) at No. 7 Plazuela de la Pila Seca (which lay near the old Puerta de Jerez); Julian Williams, a great collector of paintings, was British Vice-Consul here for many years of the second quarter of the 19C.

Sevilla (through Beaumarchais, who had visited Madrid in 1764) supplied the background to Mozart's 'Le Mariage de Figaro' (1786) and to 'Don Giovanni' (1787); to Rossini's 'Barbiere di Siviglia' (1816); and to Bizet's 'Carmen' (1875). Byron's 'Don Juan' (1818) was a local *hidalgo*.

Semana Santa, and the **Feria**. Sevilla is crowded and prices are raised for these events. The latter is usually held on the *Prado de S. Sebastián* from 18–23 April, but is postponed if the dates clash with Easter. Although originally a cattle market (founded 1848) it was a characteristic scene of merrymaking in reaction to the inhibiting solemnity of Easter. Bullfights take place in the late afternoons and fireworks at night; in the *casetas* (wooden or canvas huts run up for the occasion) revelry continues into the early hours.

The mariolatrous ecclesiastical functions of *Semana Santa* (Holy Week) are now grossly commercialised, and one cannot do better than to quote Alexander Jardine's remarks when writing of such spectacles over two centuries ago: 'Any details of their religious or superstitious ceremonies, I should think rather unworthy of your attention'. On Palm Sunday, on the Wednesday, on Maunday Thursday, and Good Friday frequent processions take place, organised by the various *cofradias* or brotherhoods. Clad in the forbidding hooded dress of penitents (*nazarenos*), they traverse the streets to converge on the Ayuntamiento, accompanying elaborately adorned Baroque carved groups or *pasos* representing saints, scenes from the Passion, or one of Sevilla's numerous Virgins. These floats are borne on the shoulders of as many as 30 men and are a curious relic of an age in which the visual impact of the paraphernalia of religion was essential to the propagation of the Faith. Halts are frequent, and monotony can soon set in, while the *saetas*—ostensibly spontaneous exhibitions of religious fervour—are usually sung by professionals as part of the pageant.

The following description of Sevilla is divided into five sections: the *Cathedral*, *Alcázar*, and *Barrio de Sta. Cruz*; W Sevilla; S Sevilla; N Sevilla; and *Triana* and the *Cartuja*.

S. Pablo Airport is c 12km NE.

A.   The Cathedral, Alcázar and Barrio de Sta. Cruz

Several roads converge on the roundabout of the *Puerta de Jerez*, at the S end of the Av. de la Constitutión. The E side of the avenue is dominated by the *Cathedral and its dependencies, crowned by numerous pinnacles and graceful flying buttresses; the distinctive *Giralda* towers above its NE angle. Although it is the largest *Gothic* church in the world, its exterior has a reprehensibly neglected appearance. Although open during normal hours, most chapels, etc. may only be seen at certain times, and for a *fee*.

After the conquest of 1248, the mosque begun by Yusuf II in 1171 was dedicated to Sta. María de la Sede, and continued to be used, but as a Christian cathedral. In 1401 the chapter resolved to erect on its site an entirely new building, an ambitious project begun the following year and practically completed by 1506. The name of its first architect is not recorded, but he was probably a Frenchman acquainted with the details of St.-Ouen at Rouen, and may have been Charles Galter (in Spain generally known as Carlí); he also worked at Barcelona and Lleida. At any rate Galter was in charge of the works here from the 1430s until his death in 1454.

The design is remarkable for its eclecticism and for the knowledge shown of French Gothic and of developments in Aragonese and Castilian architecture. The lantern collapsed in 1511, and was rebuilt in 1519 by Juan Gil de Hontañón. Later earthquakes weakened the fabric, and in 1888 part of the central roof fell in. The Sala Capitular, the principal sacristies, and the Cap. Real, were added in the 16C, largely by Diego de Riaño and Martín Gainza.

The *Puerta Mayor* in the centre of the W façade dates from 1887, flanked by two portals embellished with statues by Lorenzo Mercadante (1467) and Pedro Millán (c 1500). The *Puerta de la Lonja* or *de S. Cristóbal* on the S side, was completed in 1895. On the E façade are the *Puertas de la Campanillas* and *de los Palos*, both with sculptures by Miguel Perrín (1523), a Frenchman trained in Italy.

The **Giralda**, 94m high, was originally the minaret of the mosque. The lower part, 16.5m square and with walls 2.5m thick, was begun in 1184 in stone by *Ahmed ibn Baso*, and completed in brick by Ali de Gómara in 1198. The four sides are relieved by elegant balconied *ajimeces*, flanked by panels of diapered brickwork (*ajaracas*). On the N side there are some faded paintings by Luis de Vargas. The Renaissance open bellchamber and the diminishing stages above were added in 1568 by Hernán Ruiz. On the pinnacle is an oscillating bronze figure of La Fé (Faith) cast by Bartolomé Morel in 1568 from a model by Diego de Pesquera. This is the vane or *giraldillo* from which the tower takes its name.

The ascent of the Giralda is made in a succession of easy ramps rising to the stage or *cuerpo* 'de Campanas'. It has 24 bells, the oldest, of 1400, surviving from the first public clock set up in Spain.

The first Christian knight to ascend the minaret after the conquest was Lawrence Poore, a Scotsman. In 1839 George Dennis outclimbed most travellers, for not content with the prospect from the belfry, he shinned up an iron post, squeezed through a grating, and 'standing only on a small projecting stone, and clinging to the walls for support', found himself immediately below the figure of Faith herself. It was from here that 'Dr Disillusion' in Fernández de Ribera's 'Los anteojos de major vista' saw the world.

Continuing the anticlockwise circuit of the building, we pass the *Puerta del Oriente* and skirt dependencies surrounding the Patio de los Naranjos; this is also entered from the N by the Moorish *Puerta del Perdón*, retaining its Mudéjar bronze doors, but altered in 1522 when terracotta statues and a relief over the horseshoe arch were added by Miguel Perrín. The top storey is comparatively modern. (The arcades opposite were formerly the haunt of Sevilla's *escribanos* or scrivenors.)

The **Patio de los Naranjos**, the picturesque but neglected court of the old mosque, retains the fountain at which the Moslems performed their ritual ablutions. To the W is the *Sagrario*, also entered from the cathedral, but now used as a parish church; it was designed in 1616 by Miguel de Zumárraga and continued by Lorenzo Fernández de Iglesias. Its retablo (1669) contains sculptures by Pedro Roldán and comes from the destroyed Conv. de S. Francisco.

The E wing of the patio contains the **Biblioteca Colombina**, under restoration after the roof collapsed in 1985.

It was founded in 1552 from the bequest of Fernando Colón of the MSS of his father, the great Columbus, and over 3000 volumes collected by himself. With these are the chapter library of c 60,000 volumes, including illuminated missals, and other rare MSS and autographs. The Columbus MSS include the treatise drawn up by the navigator to prove that his projects were not antagonistic to Scripture, and his annotated copy of the 'Tractatus de Imagine Mundi' by Card. Pierre d'Ailly.

The 19C *Puerta de los Naranjos* is on the S side of the patio, but the usual entrance to the cathedral is by the *Puerta del Lagarto* (lizard). This is partly concealed by an archway of Mudéjar stuccowork belonging to the adjoining chapel, which contains six Visigothic capitals.

The portal is named after the stuffed crocodile (replaced by a replica) hanging in the vestibule, an unconventional present which accompanied a request from the Sultan of Egypt for the hand of the daughter of Alfonso X in 1260. The elephant's tusk, also there, is said to have been unearthed in the amphitheatre at Italica.

Notwithstanding the immense area and the towering clustered

columns of the interior, rising to a balustraded gallery, the first
general impression is one of solemn grandeur rather than of great
size. The enormous proportions are only realised as the eye becomes
accustomed to the gloom. The ground plan is a nave with double
aisles, off which open side chapels. The transepts do not project
beyond the side wall; in the centre are the Cap. Mayor and Coro. The
original brick floor was replaced by the present marble paving in
1793. Most of the windows contain stained glass, the earliest by
Cristóbal Alemán (1504), and others by Arnao de Flandes and his
brother, and by Carlos de Bruges.

At the E end is the **Cap. Real**, completed in 1575 by Juan de Maeda on the site
of an earlier royal burial chapel. Above the *Reja* (1771) by Van de Bovart is
Fernando III on horseback, receiving the keys of Sevilla. The chapel is
embellished with statues by Pedro Campana (1554; a Dutch artist). On the left
and right are the 19C tombs of Alfonso X and of Beatrice of Swabia, his mother
and wife of Fernando III, whose remains are in a silver and bronze shrine of
1717 in front of the altar. In the altar there is a much-restored image of the
Virgin said to have been presented to Fernando by Louis IX of France.
   Steps descend to a vault containing Fernando's original coffin and those of
Pedro the Cruel and his mistress María de Padilla, and of the Infante Fadrique
(cf. Alcázar); an ivory statuette (the Virgen de las batallas), said to have been
carried by Fernando III on his saddlebow; and other relics. In the Sacristy is a
Mater Dolorosa by Murillo.
   The chapel to the N contains a retablo by *Zurbarán*.
   Opposite the Cap. Real is the Cap. Mayor, with a *Reja* (1533) by Francisco de
Salamanca and Sancho Muñoz, a huge and elaborate Gothic *Retablo*, begun in
1482 by Pieter Dancart (a Flemish sculptor) and completed by other hands in
1525; wings were added in 1564. In the centre is the late 13C Virgen de la Sede.
Salamanca was also responsible for the iron pulpits. The *Sacristía Alta* behind
the Cap. Mayor has an artesonado ceiling and contains early paintings by Alejo
Fernández. Numerous terracotta statues embellish the exterior walls of the
chapel.
   The **Coro** has a *Reja* (1523) by Francisco de Salamanca and contains Gothic
Stalls by Nufro Sánchez and Dancart, a lectern by Bartolomé Morel (1570) and
organ cases dating in part from 1478. The organs were modernised at the turn of
the century and again since, but produce a five-second echo. (The building also
houses a very rare 'English' claviorgan of 1787 which deserves restoration.)
   On the *respaldos* of the coro are alabaster shrines, one on the S containing a
Conception by Montañés; on the *Trascoro* is Pacheco's Surrender of Sevilla.
Between this and the Puerta Mayor is the *Tombstone of Fernando Colón* (1488–
1539; son of Columbus), 'who', remarked Richard Ford (repeating Bourgoing),
'would have been considered a great man had he been the son of a less great
father'.
   At the SE corner of the cathedral is the *Sala Capitular*, an eliptical saloon with
a fine ceiling and adorned with marble reliefs of 1587. The frescoes by Pablo de
Céspedes may have been retouched by Murillo, who painted the eight ovals
between the windows and the Conception above the bishop's throne, above
which also is a 'portrait' of Fernando III on copper by Pacheco. Vestments are
displayed adjacent.
   To the W is the Plateresque *Sacristía Mayor*, containing the *Treasury* and two
paintings of the Virgin by Zurbarán; Pedro Campana, Descent from the Cross;
Pacheco, Conception, and others; also a Custodia by Juan de Arfe (1587) and a
bronze candelabrum, the *Tenebrario* (1562; by Pedro Delgado and B. Morel to
designs by Hernán Ruiz), used during the Easter ceremonies. Notable among
numerous relics and other cult objects on display are the Alphonsine Tables, an
elaborate reliquary in the form of a triptych bequeathed by Alfonso X; a cross
said to have been made from the first gold brought back from the New World by
Columbus; a head of the Baptist, by Montañés; and the keys of Sevilla
presented to Fernando III on its surrender (the silver gilt key given by the Moors
is inscribed 'May Allah render eternal the dominion of Islam in this city'; on the
iron gilt key surrendered by the Jewish community are the words 'The King of
Kings will open, the King of all the earth will enter').
   The adjacent *Sacristía de los Cálices*, entered through a chapel in which is a
Dolorosa by Pedro de Mena, contains Goya, SS. Justa and Rufina; Murillo, Head
of Christ, S. Fernando, Holy Family, and St. Frances Dorothea; Morales, Pietà;
Valdés Leal, Deliverance of St. Peter, Luis Tristán, Trinity; Alejo Fernández,

Interior of the Cathedral, Sevilla, by John Horder

Adoration, St. Peter, and others, and a Crucifixion by Montañés on the altar.

In the S Transept is the *Monument of Christopher Columbus* (Cristóbal Colón; 1451–1506) by Arturo Mélida (1891), brought with his remains from Havana in 1899 after the loss of Cuba.

In the next three side chapels (respectively) are the Plateresque tomb of Abp Hurtado de Mendoza (1509; by Domenico Fancelli); the Gothic tomb of Abp Juan de Cervantes (died 1453; by Lorenzo Mercadente 'de Bretaña'), and a

Marriage of the Virgin by Valdés Leal; and as we turn N, an Adoration by Luis de Vargas. Near the entrance to the Sagrario is a retablo by Pedro Villegas de Marmolejo.

In the first chapel of the N aisle is Murillo's Vision of St. Anthony of Padua (repaired since the kneeling figure of the saint was cut out of the canvas in 1874, to be recovered in New York some three months later). Above it is a Baptism by Murillo; also Jordaens, Circumcision, and Nativity; Valdés Leal, Scenes from the life of St. Peter; Pacheco, Conception; Zurbarán, SS. Justa and Rufina.—The next chapel contains the *Cenotaph of Bp Baltasar del Río* (died 1540), with a Genoese marble altarpiece and a terracotta relief of the Virgen de Granada, by Andrea della Robbia.—The next three chapels contain Juan de la Roelas, Santiago riding over the Moors; Herrera el Mozo, Apotheosis of S. Francisco, and Valdés Leal, Virgin presenting the chasuble to S. Idlefonso; and a Virgin and Child, by Alonso Cano.—The last chapel before regaining the Puerta del Lagarto contains a retablo by Ferdinand Sturm (1555), depicting the old Giralda in the lowest panel on the left.

Immediately NE of the Giralda is the *Archbishop's Palace* (1717), with a Baroque central feature; to the S is the irregular *Pl. del Triunfo*. On its SW side is the **Lonja** or Exchange, designed by Herrera and completed in 1598 to accommodate the vociferous merchants who formerly conducted their business in the Patio de los Naranjos; its main entrance is on the W.

From its arcaded patio a red marble stair (1787) ascends to the *Archivo de Indias*, founded in 1785, a collection of c 36,000 files of documents relating to the discovery of America and to the history and administration of Spain's American colonies. A changing exhibition of maps and other material is usually on view.

Further S is the old *Chapterhouse* (1770), in which a *Museum of Contemporary Spanish Art* has been installed.

On the S side of the plaza is the ***Alcázar**, the Mudéjar residence of Spanish kings for almost seven centuries. It is the successor of a more extensive Moorish citadel and palace, probably on the site of the Roman praetorium. Much of the present building dates from 1366, when Pedro the Cruel employed Moorish architects for his restoration or rebuilding, incorporating fragments from the previous edifice. Subsequent additions, alterations, and restorations (rarely happy) mingle Christian with Moorish motifs, and impair its claim to be a true monument of Moorish architecture.

Pedro the Cruel lived here with María de Padilla, and here caused the assassination in 1358 of his half-brother Fadrique, Master of the Order of Santiago. He also murdered his guest, Abu Said of Granada, for the sake of his jewels. One of these, an uncut ruby, presented by Pedro to the Black Prince in 1367, was worn by Henry V at Agincourt and adorns the Imperial Crown of Great Britain.

Isabel the Catholic constructed an oratory on the upper floor. Charles V (who was married to Isabel of Portugal in the Hall of the Ambassadors in 1526) added several rooms and laid out the garden. Felipe IV restored the palace c 1624; and Felipe V, who lived here in morbid seclusion for two years, built the pillared *Apeadero* and dug the fishpond c 1733. The offices over the Bath of Padilla date from the reign of Fernando VI. The palace was damaged by earthquake in 1755 and by fire in 1762, and was neglected until crudely restored in the 19C. The upper floor, which is of slight interest, and no longer on view, contains state apartments.

Passing through the *Puerta del León* (named after the lion in glazed tilework over its narrow archway), adjacent to the curtain wall of 1176, we enter the outer courtyard, formerly the *Mexuar* of the Moorish palace and now the *Patio de la Montería* (after the Monteros de Espinosa; see p 140). On the left is the *Sala de Justicia* (c 1345) and beyond is the *Patio de Yeso*, a relic of the Almohade palace.

Three arches lead to an inner court flanked by the principal façade of the Alcázar proper. To the right is the *Cuarto del Almirante* and the *Casa de Contratación*, founded by Isabel in 1503 as the official centre for organising expeditions and regulating relations between Spain and her recently discovered territories overseas. A vestibule hung with 17–18C tapestries communicates with the *Sala de Audiencia* and *Chapel*; the latter has an artesonado ceiling. On the end wall, and painted for this position, is the Virgin of the Seafarers by Alejo Fernández. The portraits to the right beneath the Virgin's cloak are said to be of Columbus and the Pinzón brothers. The frieze beneath the ceiling displays the arms of Admirals since the institution of the office in 1248.

The central part of the main façade (1364) is decorated with arabesques. Above these is a cornice surmounted by a row of windows with cusped arches, flanked by open galleries with marble columns and Moorish arches. A rectangular cartouche bears, in Cufic, the words 'God alone is Conqueror', the motto of the tributary Nasrid king of Granada, Mohammed V, who sent his craftsmen to carry out the work.

A passage to the left in the *Vestibule* leads to the *Patio de las Doncellas* (maids-of-honour), surrounded by an arcade of cusped arches on coupled marble columns, with open arabesques above. The columns, in the Renaissance style, and the upper storey date from a mid-16C restoration, in which Charles V's motto recurs frequently. The 14C azulejos, stucco work, and friezes should also be noted. On the far side is the 16C *Salon de Carlos V*, with a fine coffered ceiling. Adjoining it are the three *Apartments of María de Padilla*. The most splendid room in the Alcázar is the 10m square *Salon de Ambajadores* (of the Ambassadors), with a *media-naranja* dome; its walls, arches, and doorways are covered with elaborate and intricate Moorish decoration. Charles V was responsible for the incongruous balconies and Felipe II for the frieze of royal portraits. The *Comedor* or dining room is adjacent.

Pass through the *Apartment of Felipe II* to the small *Patio de las Muñecas* (dolls), named from two minute medallion faces at the spring of one of the smaller Moorish arches of the arcade. The upper floor dates from 1856. Adjoining are the *Bedroom of Isabel*, the bedroom of her son Juan (born here in 1478), and the so-called *Dormitorio de los Reyes Moros* (off the Patio de las Doncellas).

A passage from the smaller patio leads back to the entrance vestibule.

Turn right along a gallery to the *Patio de María de Padilla*, altered c 1732, and the site of the Gothic palace built after 1248. In the basement is a vaulted gallery with the alleged *Baños* (where the gallants of Don Pedro's court are said to have drunk María's bathwater in homage, one excusing himself lest 'having tasted the sauce, he might covet the partridge').

The first of the apartments here normally contains a magnificent series of *Tapestries* (under restoration) recording Charles V's Tunis Expedition of 1535.

The cartoons were drawn by Jan Vermayen, who accompanied the emperor as 'war artist' throughout the campaign; the tapestries were woven by Willem Pannemaker of Brussels, and completed in 1554. They were exhibited in London in connection with the marriage of Felipe II and Mary Tudor. Of the 12 panels, two are copies made in Madrid in 1740 shortly before the originals

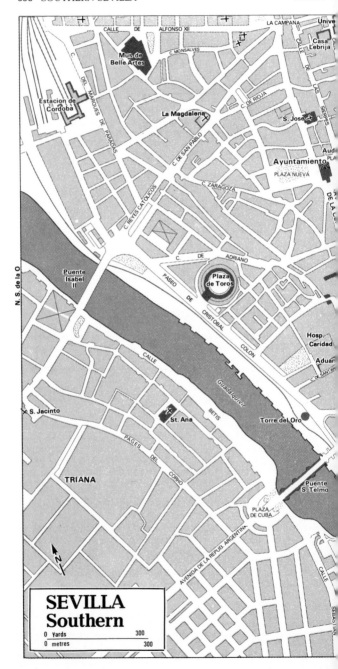

SEVILLA
Southern

| 0 | yards | 300 |
| 0 | metres | 300 |

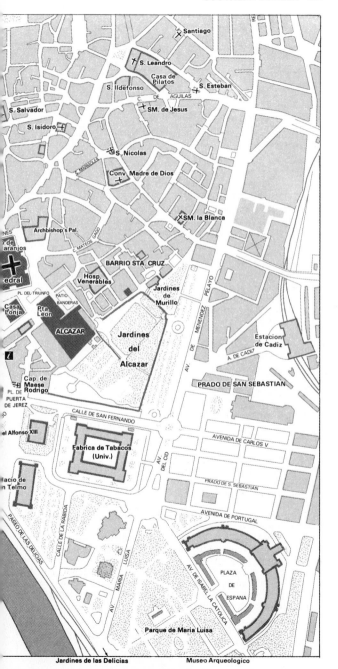

disappeared. On the Map of the Mediterranean, the figure leaning against the column represents Vermayen.

Beyond the apartments is the vaulted *Salón del Emperador*, which retains its Gothic form and has a dado of azulejos (1579) painted by Cristóbal de Augusta.

The **Gardens**, with their orange groves, palms, roses, brick walks with 'surprise water-works', box and myrtle hedges, etc., although neglected, form a pleasant oasis in the centre of the city. In the lower garden is a neo-Moorish pavilion (1543) by Juan Hernández and a labyrinth. A gateway of c 1500 from Marchena was re-erected here in 1913 and serves as an entrance to the *Huerta del Retiro*. Pass through the 18C *Apeadero*, a hall of marble columns, and the *Patio de Banderas*, with its orange trees, to regain the SE angle of the Pl. de Triunfo.

Turn right past the *Diputación*, and right again, to enter the **Barrio de Sta. Cruz**, the former *Judería*. The whole area evokes the 'Romantic' view of Sevilla, and could provide the characteristic scene for many operas and dramas. With its maze of alleys, *patios* and *plazuelas*, it is pleasant to wander through (although commercialised) by day or night, although an area further N is less sophisticated. Here also was the home of Blanco White; and of Washington Irving in 1828; while Murillo was buried in the former church of Sta. Cruz, destroyed by Soult.

The decrepit *Hospicio de Venerables Sacerdotes* has an azulejo decorated patio and a late 17C chapel containing works by Valdés Leal and murals by Lucas Valdés.—A short distance further NE is *Sta. María la Blanca*, a synagogue until 1391 and rebuilt as a Baroque church in 1659. It contains a Pietà by Luis de Vargas, a Last Supper by Murillo, and an Ecce Homo by Morales.

B.   Western Sevilla

The Av. de la Constitución leads N past the Cathedral to the **Ayuntamiento**, between the PL. DE S. FRANCISCO and the larger PL. NUEVO to the W. The Ayuntamiento was designed and built from 1527 by Diego de Riaño, completed c 1564, and restored in 1891. The elaborate ornamentation of the exterior, notably the E façade, is a masterpiece of the Plateresque style, but its unkempt condition reflects an all too frequent lack of interest in caring for Sevilla's monuments. The chapel dates from 1571.

From the N end of the Pl. de S. Francisco the narrow pedestrian *C. de las Sierpes*, formerly a favourite promenade, leads N past (left) the Baroque chapel of *S. José*. It is attributed to Pedro Romero (c 1690) and has a portal of 1766.

From the CAMPANA (the busy junction of streets at the N end of the Sierpes), the C. Alfonso XII leads W. A short walk brings one to (left) the ***Museo de Bellas Artes**, occupying the former *Conv. de N.S. de Gracia* or *de la Merced*. It is built around three patios, and was completed by Juan de Oviedo in 1612. The nucleus of the collection consists of paintings rescued by the exertions of Dean Manuel López Cepero from convents suppressed in 1836.

Among the more important works on display are Torrigiano's St. Jerome; Franz Frutet, Triptych of the Crucifixion; Marten de Vos the Elder, Last Judgement; El Greco, Portrait of his son; Alonso Cano, S. Francisco Borja; Tristán, Conception; Ribera, Santiago Peregrino, and Sta. Teresa; and in the **Church**, works by

Herrera the Elder, Montañés, and Zurbarán, including the latter's St. Hugh and Carthusian monks at table, and the Apotheosis of St. Thomas Aquinas (in which is depicted Charles V, with Zurbarán behind him); and Murillo, St. Thomas of Villanueva.

On the cloister wall are a series of charming Female saints by the School of Zurbarán. In the upper cloister are several works by Valdés Leal, and in an adjoining room Velázquez, The Virgin presenting the chasuble to S. Ildefonso, and Portrait of Cristóbal Suárez de Ribera. Of historical interest are a series of eight paintings depicting the celebrations of the accession of Fernando VI and Barbara de Braganza in 1747. Notable are Goya's Portrait of José Duarzo, a Still Life by Meléndez, and a series of Portraits by Esquivel. Among recent acquisitions is a Calvary by Lucas Cranach.—Other rooms are devoted to 19–20C painting, including several by Gonzalo Bilbao (1860–1938). Another section contains foreign works, including Cornelio Schut, Portrait of Fray Domingo Bruselas, and two battle scenes.

From the SE angle of the adjacent Plaza runs the C. Monsalves, where stood the house in which Richard Ford lived during the winter of 1831–32. To the right is the C. Fernán Caballero, where No. 14 was the home of the novelist 'Fernán Caballero' (Cecilia Böhl von Faber; 1796–1877).

Further S is **La Magdalena** (1704; by Leonardo de Figueroa), with a Mudéjar cupola, frescoes by Lucas Valdés, a Baroque retablo containing a carved Magdalen, and two paintings by Zurbarán in the Cap. Sacramental

The C.S. Pablo leads SW to the *Puente Isabel II* (1852; or *de Triana*; see Rte 101E). Before reaching the bridge, turn left along the Paseo de Cristóbal Colón and skirt a *Market*, perhaps on the site of the prison in which the sculptor Torrigiano died in 1522 under the ban of the Inquisition. We next pass the *Plaza de Toros* (1763; by Vicente Sanmartín), and the oldest in Spain.

The fourth turning to the left beyond the bullring leads to the *Hospital de la Caridad* (for the sick and aged poor), with a colourful façade; the arches in its grounds are remains of the medieval *atarazanas* built by Alfonso X, occupying the site of earlier Moorish shipyards.

Don Miguel de Mañara (1626–79), a profligate noble, turned from the frivolities of life and joined the fraternity of the Caridad. Its function was to provide Christian burial for executed criminals and he devoted the rest of his life and fortune to the establishment of this hospital. It was completed in 1674 from plans by Bernardo Simón de Pineda. Murillo, a friend of Mañara, is said to have designed the five large azulejos on the façade of the chapel. Mañara is buried at the foot of the high altar.

Six of the series of paintings executed for the chapel by Murillo in 1660–74 remain; five others were carried off by Soult—one is now in the National Gallery, London. Note also the Deposition by Pedro Roldán, and two cadaverous paintings (improved by recent cleaning) by Valdés Leal flanking the W door; his portrait of Mañara can be seen in the Chapterhouse.

Further S is the riverside **Torre del Oro**, a twelve-sided battlemented tower built in 1220. It was known to the Moors as the 'golden tower' after the colour of its azulejos. The round uppermost stage and the lower windows with balconies date from 1760. It contains a small *Naval Museum*.—The Puerta de Jerez is reached by turning E along the C. de Caballerizes.

C.   Southern Sevilla

On the N side of the Puerta de Jerez is the *Cap. de Maese Rodrigo* (c 1514; by Antón Ruiz and Martín Sánchez), part of the *Antiguo Seminario*. It contains a retablo by Alejo Fernández, a good artesonado, and azulejos.

To the SW the *Puente S. Telmo* crosses the river to *Triana*; see Rte 101E.

The Av. de Roma leads S past the grandiose *Hotel Alfonso XIII* to the *Pal. de S. Telmo* (1682–1796), with a Churrigueresque portal (1734). Its present appearance is due to Leonardo de Figueroa and his son Matías.

It was originally a naval college, where, according to William Jacob (1809), 'pretentions' were made 'to teach geography, algebra, geometry, and trigonometry; but having neither books, nor instruments, nor professors possessing any knowledge, their progress is very trifling'.

To the NE, in an area built over, abutting the SW wall of the Alcázar, stood the Plazuela de la Pila seca, where at No. 7 George Borrow lived in 1839–40.

On the S side of the C.S. Fernando, leading SE, is the huge bulk of the former *Fabrica de Tabacos, completed in 1766 to the designs of the Flemish engineer Sebastian van der Borcht. At one time 10,000 *cigarreras* were employed here, but 'Carmen' has left only a romantic memory, for the building now houses the *University*. These *cigarreras* were said by Ford to be 'more impertinent than chaste', and were obliged to undergo 'an ingeniously-minute search on leaving their work, for they sometimes carry off the filthy weed in a manner her most Catholic majesty never dreamt of'.

Beyond is the open PRADO DE S. SEBASTIÁN, still the scene of the annual *Feria*, and previously the *Quemadero*, site of the Inquisition's autos-de-Fé.

To the S of the University is the PARQUE DE MARÍA LUISA, until 1893 part of the grounds of S. Telmo. In 1929 a Spanish-American exhibition was held within and beside these riverside gardens, and some of the buildings erected for it remain.—To the E is the *Pl. de España*, within an immense hemicycle of buildings now accommodating the *Capitanía General* and the *Gobierno Civil*.

To the S is the **Museo Arqueológico**.

The **Basement** contains material from the Paleolithic period onwards, including: campaniform vases from Écija; idol plates or pendents (c 2000 BC) from the Cueva de la Mora (Jabugo), and owl-like idols from Morón; arrowheads, some of rock crystal; funerary stelae (8C BC) from Carmona; bronze fibulae; artefacts from Carambola, including replicas of the gold Tartessian treasure (8C BC) and a seated statuette of Astarte; bronze plaques and pectorals from Punta de Vaca of Punic or Phoenician origin (7C BC); Phoenician ceramics from Río Tinto; Punic amphorae, metal and bone objects, and bronze ex-votos.

The **Ground Floor** has an impressive collection of stone Bulls and stone Lions from Bornos, Estepa, and Utrera (2–3C BC), also reliefs of two soldiers from Estepa (1C AD); mosaics; a puteal from Trigueros, and Heads of Paris and Minerva, among others; bronze objects and figurines; statues from Italica, and the mosaic of Cacchus (Écija; 3C); statues of Diana and Mercury, both Roman copies of Hellenistic originals, together with one of Venus, from Italica; glass and sculpted fragments from Italica; ex-votos of feet; terracotta lamps; funerary inscriptions and stelae; cinerary urns; artefacts and capitals from Carteia; a collection of large statues and busts (in the central oval); glass and jewellery; a female head from Mulva (2C) and material from Munigua (near Villanueva del Río y Minas); paleo-Christian sculptures, sarcophagi, and capitals; material from Medina Azahara; and Moorish tiles, jars, well heads, woodwork, and other Islamic artefacts.

On the opposite side of the gardens is the **Museo des Artes y Costumbres Populares**. Near the entrance is a Map of Sevilla of 1771.

The main entrance to the University building, Sevilla, formerly the Tobacco factory

R1 displays a range of Costumes, purses, waistcoats, rosaries, jewellery, hatpins, rattles, and *grilleras* (cricket cages).—**R2** Costumes worn at Carnival and Corpus, including those used for the Dance of the Seises in the cathedral; frilled and flounced *flamenco* dresses, and examples of the *mantas* and *sayas* of Tarifa.—**R3** Musical instruments, including *zambombas*.—**R4** Agricultural instruments, including a *trillo* with its seat; saddles and stirrups; branding irons; basketwork, including esparto *redendels* for drying grapes; shepherds' carvings; firearms; ceramics, and bull sculptures by Mariano Benlluire.—**R5** Ecclesiastical plate.—**R6** Embroidery and lace, and a collection of *camisas* or chemises.—**R7** individual rooms displaying different types of furniture, including a '*casita de Feria*'; note the Mudéjar box.—**R8** Ceramics, mostly late 19C.

In the **Basement** are a series of alcoves and rooms displaying weights and measures; tinware (*hojalateria*) candleholders; wine and oil presses; implements for cleaning and softening leather; copper and brasswork; ceramics, including *tinajas* or large earthenware storage jars, *búcaros* or waterjugs, and *botijos* or pitchers; Pharmacy jars and ware from Triana, showing Japanese influence, and an extensive collection of azulejos, some with metallic lustre.

D. Northern Sevilla

Bear NE from the Pl. de S. Francisco, and then right, past the S side of *S. Salvador* (1671–1712), built on the site of the first grand mosque of Sevilla. Its tower incorporates part of the minaret erected in 1079 after an earthquake. It contains sculptures by Montañés and a Baroque retablo mayor of 1779.

To the right, a short distance further E, is *S. Isidoro*, perhaps the oldest church in Sevilla (c 1360), with a high altarpiece painted by Roelas.—During the winter of 1830–31 Richard Ford lived in a house which stood in the Pl. S. Isidoro.

A short distance to the SE is *S. Nicolás* (1781), and S of that, *La Madre de Dios*, its church probably designed by Hernán Ruiz the Younger and completed in 1572 by Pedro Díaz de Palacios. It contains a notable artesonado and effigies of the widow and daughter of Hernán Cortes, who are buried here.

In the C. de Aguilas, N of S. Nicolás, is the ***Casa de Pilatos**, the property of the Duque de Medinaceli. This Mudéjar mansion was begun c 1480 for Pedro Enríques de Rivera and completed by Pedro Afán de Rivera (1504–71), Duque de Alcalá and viceroy of Naples. Under the third duke, a patron of art, the house was the intellectual centre of Sevilla. (Its name is derived from the popular belief that the founder's son—Fadrique, first Marqués de Tarifa—copied it from Pilate's house when he visited Jerusalem in 1519.)

Beyond the Plateresque portal and entrance courtyard is a beautiful patio with marble columns and graceful arcades embellished with azulejos. At its angles are Roman statues from Italica and in the arcades there are 24 busts, some antique. Several rooms contain fine azulejos and aresonados, while the dome and carved ceiling over the staircase are also notable. On the first landing is a copy by Alonso Cano of Murillo's Virgen de la Servilleta.

S. Esteban, further E, has Gothic and Mudéjar remains and several works by Zurbarán (dispersed parts of a former retablo).—*Santiago* (1789), to the N, contains Baroque retablos.

The C. Caballerizas leads NW from the Casa de Pilatos between (right) *S. Leandro* (c 1600; with retablos by Montañés), and *S. Ildefonso* (rebuilt 1794–1841), containing a fresco of c 1375 from another church, a relief by Montañés, and figures from a retablo of 1637.—Continue NW to enter a plaza: opposite its N end is the belfry of Gothic *S. Pedro*, rebuilt in the early 17C, in which Velázquez was baptised. It contains a retablo by Felipe de Ribas and paintings by Roelas and by Campana.—To the N is *Sta. Ines*, with a Gothic chapel and 17C organs.—To the E is *Sta. Catalina*, with a Mudéjar tower of c 1350 and a chapel with a fine artesonado of c 1400.—To the NE is the *Conv. de Terceros*, with a retablo by Francisco de Ribas and the early 18C *Cap. Sacremental* by the Figueroas.

The C. Gerona leads NW from Sta. Catalina to the *Pal. de las Dueñas*, a Mudéjar residence of the Alba family. To the W of the palace is *S. Juan de la Palma*, a former mosque, with a Gothic doorway and a minaret of 1085.

Skirting the E side of the palace, we pass (right) the *Conv. del Socorro*, with a retablo by Montañés. Just beyond is *S. Marcos* (14C Gothic), with a Mudéjar portal, and on the site of a mosque; on the base of a minaret rises a tower of c 1350.—Adjacent to the NE is *S Isabel* (1609; by Alonso de Vandaelvira), with retablos by Montañés, López Bueno, and Juan de Mesa.—To the E is **Sta. Paula**, founded in 1475, the Gothic portal of which exhibits the arms and motto of the Catholic Kings and glazed terracotta embellishments of Niculoso Pisano surrounding medallions by Pedro Millán. It contains good artesonados and azulejos, several late Gothic tombs, sculptures by Montañés and Alonso Cano, and a S. Jerónimo by Ribera.

The C. de S. Luis leads N from S. Marcos through a poor area, passing (left) Baroque *S. Luis* (1732; by the *Figueroas*), and beyond (right) *Sta. Marina*, with a Mudéjar tower, but to all appearances gutted.—Further N (left) is *S. Gil*, with remains of 13–14C work; and in the adjacent *Basilica de la Macarena* is the 'Virgen de la Esperanza' (ascribed to Pedro Roldán or to his daughter Luisa; 'la Roldana'), one of the cherished cult images of Sevilla.

The neighbouring *Puerta de la Macarena* (named after a Moorish princess) was rebuilt in 1795.—To the E is a well-preserved stretch of **Walls**, part of the Almoravide re-fortifications of c 1100. Together with those of the Alcázar gardens they are all that remain of the ramparts which once included 166 towers and 12 gates, mostly destroyed in the mid-19C rage for demolition.—Beyond the gate is the *Hosp. de Cinco Llagas* (of the five wounds) or *de la Sangre* (the blood), with a classical façade.

Although founded in 1500, work was not begun until 1546, to a design by Martín Gainza; after his death it was continued by Hernán Ruiz and completed in 1613 by Ascencio Maeda. Its medallions have been ascribed to Torrigiano.

The C. Relator leads W, not far S of S. Gil, to approach the N end of the ALAMEDA DE HÉRCULES. It passes N of *Omnium Sanctorum*, with Gothic portals, pentagonal apse, and partially Moorish tower. The promenade was laid out by Asensio de Maeda in 1574; at its N end are two antique columns bearing statues of Julius Caesar and Hercules by Diego de Pesquera (1574).

A short distance to the NW, approached by the C. Calatrava, is the ***Conv. de S. Clemente el Real**, founded by Fernando III on the site of a Moorish palace, but rebuilt in the 18C. The earlier church has a huge and impressive artesonado ceiling and azulejos of 1588, while the walls higher up have frescoes of c 1700 by Lucas Valdés. The Plateresque high altar is by Felipe de Ribas. On its N side is a monument to María of Portugal, wife of Alfonso XI. On the right of the entrance is a statue of the Baptist by Gaspar Nuñez Delgado.

To the S, the C. de Sta. Clara leads past (left) the battlemented *Torre de Don Fadrique* (1252), a relic of the palace of the brother of

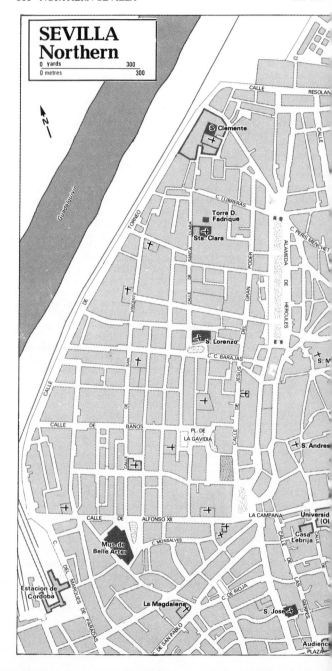

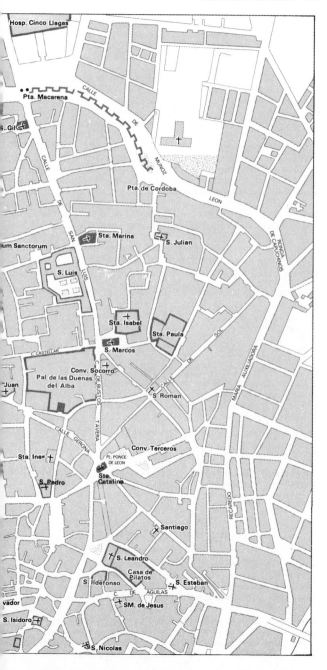

Alfonso X. Entered from No. 40 in the street is *Sta. Clara*, founded in 1260, with an orange-shaded patio and a doorway of 1622. It contains an artesonado, a retablo by Montañés and his school, and azulejo dados.

Continue S to pass (left) **S. Lorenzo**, rebuilt in the early 17C but retaining traces of Gothic and Mudéjar work. In the adjoining chapel there is the image of 'Jesús del Gran Poder' (1620; by Juan de Mesa). The church contains a retablo by Montañés with figures by Felipe de Ribas, and paintings by Pedro Villegas de Marmoléjo (1520–97), who is buried here. The Baroque retablos flanking the high altar are by Fernando de Barahona; later chapels contain paintings by Pacheco.

Continuing S, we enter the Pl. de la Gravida, a short distance SW of which is *S. Vicente* (14C, but largely rebuilt in the 18–19Cs). It contains a retablo mayor by Cristóbal de Guadix, a Descent from the Cross carved by Andrés de Ocampo, and the 'Virgen de los Remedios', by Villegas de Marmoléjo.

Turn SE across the plaza and the adjacent squares to reach the busy junction of LA CAMPANA, and there turn·E to (right) the C. de Cuna.—To the N is 14–15C *S. Andrés*, with Mudéjar chapels.—A few steps further E—until its removal to the *Fábrica de Tabacos* (see Rte 101C)—stood the University. Since 1771 it had occupied a Jesuit convent built in 1579 and demolished in the 1970s. It was raised to the rank of university in 1502, having been established as a school by Alfonso X in 1256.

The adjacent **University Church** (restored) contains works by Montañés, Roelas, Juan de Mesa, and Alonso Cano. In the left transept is the tomb of Lorenzo Suárez de Figueroa (died 1409); in the right transept are the effigy (1606) of the humanist Arias Montano and a monument to Gustavo Adolfo Bécquer, who with his brother Valeriano is interred in the crypt. In the nave are the Italian Renaissance tombs (1520; by the Genoese Antonio Aprile and Pace Gagini) of Pedro Enríquez and his wife, Catalina de Rivera.

On the right, going down the C. de Cuna, is the *Pal. de la Condesa de Lebrija*. It has three patios containing Roman mosaics pillaged from Itálica, and an artesonado over the staircase brought from the destroyed palace of the Dukes of Osuna at Marchena.

Among the mosaics is an octagonal one around a fountain; other bits of mosaic have been 'framed'. The rooms display a jumble of artefacts collected from Itálica, but the building is otherwise of slight interest.

At the S end of the street is *S. Salvador* (see above), a few paces NE of the Pl. de S. Francisco.

E.   Triana and the Cartuja

Roman *Trajana*, on the right bank of the old Guadalquivir (now a backwater) has been known since antiquity for its potteries, and later for the manufacture of azulejos. It now lies on the left bank of the *new* Guadalquivir, its N end united to the rest of the city by a broad artificial causeway, and further S by bridges. It had a large gypsy population, but is now little more than a residential suburb. Nationalist atrocities here in 1936 were particularly abhorrent.

From the convenient approach of the *Puente de Isabel II* (W of the Plaza de Toros) the C. de la Pureza leads S to Mudéjar-Gothic **Sta.**

Ana (1280). Its architect probably worked previously on Burgos cathedral, for the vault plan of Burgos (with the unusual English features of a longitudinal ridge rib) has been followed. Its Plateresque retablo contains paintings by Pedro Campana and others; in the left aisle is a painting of SS. Justa and Rufina (the virgin martyrs, who were potters in Triana in the 3C), attributed to Fernando Sturm; on the trascoro is the Virgen de la Rosa, by Alejo Fernández. Near the end of the right aisle is a terracotta tomb (1503) by Niculaso Pisano.

The **Cartuja** is approached by crossing to the W bank of the new course of the Guadalquivir and turning right immediately beyond the bridge. It is likely that the approach will be changed or improved by 1992, for part of the site is being laid out to accommodate the *Féria*.

The Cartuja was founded in 1401 as a charterhouse, but had been used as a pottery from 1841 until its removal to a new site off the Mérida road in 1980. It was long controlled by the English firm of Pickman and Son and its owner built two 'willow-pattern' summerhouses in its adjacent olive groves (now vanished). Extensive remains of its dependencies were altered for use as warehouses and workshops. *Sta. Maria de las Cuevas* remains intact; it contained the body of Columbus (died 1506), brought from Valladolid, from 1507 to 1542. The body was then taken to Haiti, and in 1796 to Havana, before being returned to Sevilla in 1899 (cf. Cathedral). The painting by Zurbarán of St. Hugh and Carthusian monks at table (now in the Museo de Bellas Artes) was painted for the Cartuja.

For roads from Sevilla to **Cádiz, Huelva**, and **Aracena**; see Rtes 102–4; for **Osuna, Antequera**, and **Granada**, and for **Carmona, Écija**, and **Cordoba** for **Bailén**, see Rte 94, and 90, in reverse, and likewise Rte 52 for **Mérida**.
For **Santiponce** and **Itálica**, see first part of Rte 104.

102 Sevilla to Cádiz

A. Via the Motorway and Jerez de la Frontera

129km (80 miles). A4. 84km—**Jerez** is 6km W.—The A4 may be regained 6km SE.—33km **Cádiz**.

Maps: M 446.

The A4 bears S from Sevilla, at 17km skirting *Dos Hermanas* (57,550 inhab.). (The NIV may also be followed, but as there is little to see en route there is little advantage except in cost.)
At 11km *Los Palacios y Villafranca* (24,350 inhab.) is bypassed to the right; *Utrera* is 14km E; see p 514.—22km. To the left is *Las Cabezas de S. Juan* (12,500 inhab.), where Col Rafael Riego 'pronounced' against the government, precipitating the Liberal revolution of 1820 (cf. Cádiz).—*Lebrija* is 13km SW; see Rte 102B.
The mountains of the SERRANÍA DE RONDA are visible in the distance to the SE. At 34km turn off the motorway to enter *Jerez*.
JEREZ DE LA FRONTERA (175,650 inhab.—Jerezanos; 65,000 in 1920; 131,000 in 1960), formerly called *Xerez*, was probably the Roman *Asido Caesaris*, corrupted by the Moors into *Sherish*; the suffix 'de la Frontera' (of Moslem Spain) dates from 1380. The old

town, with its narrow winding lanes, retains a number of attractive old mansions with their flower-filled patios shaded by orange trees and palms, but is mainly visited for its *bodegas*.

Jerez was captured from the Moors in 1264 by Alfonso X. Its white wines, known in England as sherry, were first exported to England in the reign of Henry VII. Many of the *bodegas* are owned by descendants of English families who have since intermarried with their own and with Jerez society. In the 1830s much ecclesiastical property in the area was sold off—land worth 20 million reales, where there were only 51 monks. Later in the century there was agricultural unrest, particularly in 1892 when the town was invaded by some 4000 sickle-brandishing Anarchists. At the turn of this century W.J. Buck (co-author of 'Wild Spain', and 'Unexplored Spain') was the British Vice-consul here.

Sherry. The *Bodegas*, lofty one-storey buildings with impressive rows of wine butts, are a characteristic feature of Jerez, and at most of the important establishments visitors are courteously shown round and given an opportunity to taste the various types of sherry. Among the principal shipping firms are Messrs Williams and Humbert, González Byass, Pedro Domecq, Sandeman, and Harvey.

The main sherry vineyards are some distance to the N, NW, and W of the town, and in the vicinity of *Sanlúcar de Barrameda*, further NW. At the vintage in September the small white grapes are crushed at the vineyards in the *lagares*, or presses, large wooden trays 50cm deep. The grapes are first trodden and afterwards subjected to hydraulic pressure (mechanisation has largely superceded the treading). The must produced is left in casks to ferment, thus converting the sugar in the grapejuice into alcohol. About two months later, when fermentation has ceased and the lees have fallen to the bottom of the cask, the clear new wine is racked off into clean casks, and it is then either stored in a *bodega* to mature alone or is used to refresh one of the *soleras*. These are the mother wines that are never moved. When some of the wine is taken out for making up blends or for shipping, younger wine is used to refresh the *solera* and to be 'educated' by the older wine and its impregnated cask.

Several kinds of sherry are used in making up shipping blends (e.g. *Amontillado, Fino, Palo Cortado, Oloroso*); and several kinds are used for blending in the *bodegas*: *color*, made by boiling down three butts of must to make one butt of '*vino de color*'; 'P.X.', made by sun drying the small sweet grape of that name until it is almost a raisin and then pressing it and adding a little wine alcohol to arrest the fermentation; and *Moscatel*, made in the same way, but from Muscat grapes. Sherry is generally shipped to England in butts (108 gallons), hogsheads (54 gallons), or quarter casks (27 gallons)—c 490, 245, and 122 litres, respectively, and bottled there.

Among books concerned with the subject are those by Rupert Croft-Cook, Julian Jeffs, and M.M. González Gordon—each entitled 'Sherry'.

The centre of Jerez is entered from the motorway by the Av. Alcalde Álvaro Domecq. After passing (left) *Sto. Domingo* (restored since burned in 1936) it continues as the C. Larga to the PL. DEL ARENAL, planted with palms. Beyond the plaza is the **Alcázar**, a medieval fortress-palace once belonging to the Duque de S. Lorenzo, and partially restored. (The *bodegas* of González Byass and of Pedro Domecq are to the W and NW respectively.)

To the N is the **Colegiata**, or *S. Salvador* (1696–1765), on the plans of *Torcuato Cayón*, with an elaborate sculptured portal; the isolated belfry is in a Moorish-Gothic style. The sacristy contains Zurbarán's 'Sleeping Girl'. Steps descend to a small plaza and to the Baroque doorway of the *Bertemati palace*.

SE of the Pl. del Arenal is *S. Miguel*, a Gothic building of c 1430–1569. Its W front is masked by an ornate classical façade of 1701, embellished with azulejos. The elaborately decorated transepts and bold pillars of the main arcade are noteworthy. The retablo mayor, completed in 1647, is by Montañes and José de Arce; that of the sagrario is a Rococo work of c 1750.

The C. Consistorio leads N from the Plaza del Arenal to the **Casa**

del Cabildo Vieja, formerly the *Ayuntamiento* (1575; by Andrés de Ribera). Its façade has a frieze of bold sculpture, but is marred by a later balustrade. It houses a small *Archaeological collection*, including a Greek helmet of the 7C BC found on the banks of the Guadalete (which flows a short distance SE of the town).

In the adjacent Pl. Asunción is *S. Dionisio*, a Moorish-Gothic church founded by Alfonso X but internally transformed in 1731 and with a Rococo retablo mayor; its Mudéjar *Torre de la Atalaya* dates from 1449, each side with different decoration.

From a short distance N the C. Francos leads NW, passing near several churches of slight interest, among them (right) *S. Marcos* (c 1480), with a front of 1613; and *S. Juan* (left, further along), of c 1423, with Mudéjar vaulting, to reach *Santiago*, a heavily restored Gothic church of c 1500 with a tower of 1663.

From here the C. de la Merced leads SW to the 16C *Hosp. de la Merced*. Turn left just beyond through the Pl. del Mercado, S of which is *S. Mateo*, with notable vaulting. Follow the C. Cabezas to Mudéjar *S. Lucas*, altered in 1730.—Further E is the *Casa de Ponce de León*, with a Renaissance patio and oriel (1537).

For **El Puerto de Sta. María**, 14km SW, see Rte 102B.

Follow the C. de Arcos, leading E from the centre, and turn right onto the C440 (for Medina Sidonia). After 5km we reach the **Cartuja de Jerez**, founded in 1477 by Álvaro Oberto de Valeto. It was derelict between 1835–1948 and has been heavily restored since. The Gothic church's richly decorated Baroque façade (1667) can be seen from the entrance, but—at present—this and most of the other dependencies may be visited by males only, the discriminatory illegality of which is to be circumvented by the cultural authorities.

Below the Cartuja flows the Guadalete, on the banks of which the Visigoths were dispersed in battle by the Moors under Tariq in 711 at the beginning of their occupation of the country.

The A4 can be re-joined here, circling to the SW. At 20km it bypasses (left) **Puerto Real** (23,900 inhab.), Roman *Gaditanus*, rebuilt by Isabel the Catholic in 1483. Its most interesting building is 16C *S. Sebastián*.—*Chiclana* is 16km further S; see Rte 99.

The motorway is extended along a peninsula on which the fort of *Trocadero* resisted the Duc d'Angoulême's troops in 1823. Near by are the shipyards of *Matagorda*. The road then crosses the bay by a bridge completed in 1971 to enter the suburbs of (13km) **Cádiz**; see Rte 100.

B.   Via Sanlúcar de Barrameda and El Puerto de Santa María

141km (87 miles). A4. 50km. C441. 13km *Lebrija*—34km **Sanlúcar**—CA602. 23km **El Puerto de Sta. María**—21km **Cádiz**.

Maps: M 446.

For the first 50km, see Rte 102A.

Here turn SW to (13km) **Lebrija** (25,350 inhab.), the *Nebrissa Veneria* of Pliny and Moorish *Nebrishah*. It is a well-sited town surrounded by walls and dominated by a castle overlooking the

Marismas of the Guadalquivir. It was the birthplace of Antonio de
Nebrija (1444–1522), the lexicographer and humanist. *Sta. María,*
orginally a mosque, has an early 19C tower modelled on the Giralda
at Sevilla and a cedar and mahogony retablo carved by Alonso Cano
(1636).

34km **Sanlúcar de Barrameda** (48,400 inhab.), the ancient *Luciferi
Fanum,* lies at the mouth of the Guadalquivir. It is the principal depot
for the *manzanilla* wine produced on the neighbouring sandhills.

Re-conquered in 1264, it was granted to the family of Guzmán el Bueno, but
reverted to the crown during the reign of Felipe IV in view of the growing
importance of the transatlantic trade. Columbus sailed from here in 1498 on his
third voyage to America, and in 1519 Magellan weighed anchor here with five
ships and a combined crew of c 240 men; only only one ship, the 'Victoria',
commanded by Sebastián Elcano, returned after circumnavigating the globe.
Wyndham Beawes, author of a ponderous 'Civil, Commercial, Political, and
Literary History of Spain', was long the British Consul here until his death in
1780.

The *Castle* commands a good view, and two gates of the town walls
are preserved. *Sta. María de la 'O'* (14C), has a Mudéjar portal and
alfiz, an artesonado ceiling and a screened private pew. Further
along the main street, with its bars serving *manzanilla,* is domed *Sto.
Domingo* (16C), well-vaulted and with a stone retablo. *S. Francisco*
was founded in 1517 on behalf of Henry VIII as the *Hospital of St.
George* for English sailors. Opposite is *S. Nicolás.* On the Cuesta de
Belén is the former *Montpensier palace,* with fantastic decoration on
its Gothic arcades, and the restored *Medina Sidonia palace.*

Chipiona (12,500 inhab.), 9km SW, ancient *Turris Coepionis,* has a
lighthouse marking the river mouth.—16km S is *Rota* (20,560 inhab.),
temporarily the site of a US base which it is planned to suppress.

The CA602 leads SE from Sanlúcar directly to (23km) **El Puerto de
Sta. María** (55,750 inhab.), the Roman *Portus Menesthei.* It is a wine-
exporting town at the mouth of the Guadalete, with a Moorish castle,
and several sherry *bodegas,* including those of Messrs Terry, and
Osborne (Duff Gordon).

Twiss mentioned that in 1773 he met the Marqués de la Cañada here, a
gentleman of Irish extraction, whose name was Tyrry, and who had a fine
library of English books and a collection of paintings. Henry Rumbold (1617–
90), the diplomat, was consul here and at Cádiz in 1660–63. Washington Irving
stayed at No. 57 C. de los Reyes Católicos in 1828, when writing 'The
Alhambra'. Rafael Alberti (1902–), the poet, was born here.

NE of the centre is the 16C *Conv. de la Victoria* (now a prison). Keep
to the right bank of the river to reach the *Hosp. de S. Juan de Dios.*
Behind it the C. José Navarrete runs inland, passing the restored
Castillo de S. Marcos, with an attractive mansion opposite.

Adjacent is the *Iglesia Mayor Prioral* or *N.S. de los Milagros* (1265;
rebuilt in the 17C), with a Renaissance S portal.—Further W is the
Casa del Marqués de Purullena, now gutted of its ballroom, but
previously the best of the town's mansions; and *S. Francisco,* with a
Baroque retablo and sculptures by Juan de Mesa.—Nearer the river
is the 18C *Concepcionistas.* The domed church of the *Conv. de
Capuchinas,* in the C. Larga, has a Baroque retablo. There is a
fortified church just E of the port.

Crossing the Guadalete, at 8km turn right at the main crosroads N
of *Puerto Real* (see Rte 102A) to cross the bridge (1971) for (13km)
Cádiz; see Rte 100.

103 Sevilla to Ayamonte via Huelva (for the Algarve)

155km (96 miles). A49. 51km. *La Palma del Condado* is 4km N; *Bollullos* is 3km S—27km. *Moguer* is 7km S—14km **Huelva**—N431. 63km *Ayamonte*.

Maps: M 446.

The alternative but slower N431 leads W parallel to and N of the A49, although most of the places of interest are easily approached by the new road.

Crossing both arms of the Guadalquivir, the road ascends the far bank past (right) *Castilleja de la Cuesta*. In the *Conv. de las Irlandesas* here, Hernán Cortés (1485–1547), the conquistador of Mexico, died. A small 18C Moresque castle built on the site of his house in the C. Real contains souvenirs of his exploits. Castilleja occupies the site of Iberian *Osset* and Roman *Julia Constantia*. Its ruins served as a quarry for the building of *S. Juan de Aznalfarache*, further S and now a transpontine suburb of Sevilla, with Roman walls and a ruined castle.—At *Valencina*, 4km NW, is the large chambered tomb of the *Cueva de Matarrubilla*.

At 15km *Umbrete* (right) has an azulejo dome to its church; and at *Bolullos de la Mitación* (left) an 11C mosque has been converted into a chapel.

At 5km **Sanlúcar la Mayor** (7750 inhab.) is 3km right. It was the Roman *Solis Lucus* and has a ruined *Alcázar*, a tower embellished with azulejos, and the Mudéjar churches of *Sta. María* (13C, on the site of a mosque), and fortified *S. Pedro* (12C).

Aznalcázar (8.5km SW) has a church with ornamental battlements and spire, and the shell of a castle. From here the road continues W, crossing the Guadiamar by a Roman bridge to (4.5km) *Pilas* (9800 inhab.), where Murillo had a house.—6.5km further S, at *Villamanrique de la Condesa*, there is a palace.

The main road descends to cross the Guadiamar and continues W across undulating country. At 33km it reaches crossroads 4km S of *La Palma del Condado* (9000 inhab.), with a Plateresque church and an *Ayuntamiento* with a portal decorated with azulejos.—For *Valverde del Camino*, 29km NW, see Rte 56.

The H612 leads S via (3km) *Bollullos par del Condado* (11,900 inhab.) and (9km) *Almonte* (12,950 inhab.) to (15km) *El Rocío*. (Almonte can also be reached by a direct road from Sevilla via *Pilas*; see above.) El Rocío, close to the NE edge of the MARISMA, is known for its now commercialised Whitsun pilgrimage.—The road continues SW, off which there is a turning to the *Pal. de Doñana*, within the **Nature Reserve of the Coto Doñana**, extending S to the Guadalquivir; enquiries about visiting the reserve can be made by telephoning 955 430432.—At 16km we reach the Atlantic at the *Torre de la Higuera*, from which the C442 turns NW behind the coastal dunes; at 22km it passes a Parador 6km before reaching *Mazagón*; see below.

At 9km **Niebla** is 4km right, on the bank of the Río Tinto. This was Roman *Ilipla*, which is now an interesting but decayed town containing several Moorish houses, a castle, and ruinous but complete *Walls. Its bridge is a well-preserved Roman structure. *Sta. María de la Granada* has Mozarabic details (10C) and a good tower. Close to it is the *Hosp. de N.S. de los Ángeles*, with its cloister.

Niebla was taken from the Moors in 1262 after a siege of almost ten months.

The district was made a *condado* in favour of Juan Alfonso de Guzmán on his marriage with Doña Beatriz, daughter of Enrique II, in 1396.

At 14km crossroads are reached 7km N of **Moguer** (10,100 inhab.), a decayed port beyond the far bank of the Río Tinto. It was the birthplace of the poet Juan Ramón Jiménez (1881–1958) and his donkey 'Platero' (there is a small museum in his house). In the Pl. Mayor are the Neo-Classical *Ayuntamiento*, and *N.S. de la Granada*, with a Giralda-type tower; in the *Conv. de la Esperanza* (rebuilt 1482) there are good azulejos and a Baroque altarpiece. On the N outskirts of the town is the *Conv. de Sta. Clara*, founded in 1348, with brick buildings in a Mudéjar-Gothic style. Its church contains an unusual series of choir stalls in Granadine style on a base of azulejos, tombs of the Portocarrero family, 15C painted doors, and a Sienese diptych, among other works.

7km further SW is the village of **Palos de la Frontera**, where the church of *S. Jorge* (1473) has remains of murals, an iron pulpit, and 14–15C alabasters.

It was from the former port of Palos that Columbus (Cristóbal Colón) set sail on 3 August 1492 in the 'Sta. María' on his first successful voyage of discovery; he returned here the following March. His second voyage also started from Palos, in September 1493. In May 1528 Cortés also landed here after the conquest of Mexico. It was thanks to two well-to-do citizens of Palos—Vicente and Martín Pinzón—that Columbus was able to obtain crews for his ships; the Pinzón brothers commanded the 'Niña' and the 'Pinta' in 1492.

3.5km beyond is the Franciscan monastery of *La Rábida*.

In 1491 Columbus sought refuge here when his lengthy negotiations to get the support of the Catholic Kings for his scheme had broken down; the decision was reversed the following year, partly due to the influence of the prior, Juan Pérez de Marchena, who had been Isabel's confessor.

The convent's dependencies (restored 1892) date in part from the 14C (e.g. the apse of the church). The artesonado roof of the nave, the 15C Mudéjar cloister, and the room in which Columbus lodged, are of interest. Murals by Vázquez Díaz were painted on the sacristy walls in 1930.

13.5km SE is *Mazagón*, with a Parador 6km beyond.

Huelva can be approached by crossing the mouth of the Tinto c 5km SW of La Rábida, and passing through unattractive industrial areas.

At 5km beyond the turning for Moguer, the bypass for *Ayamonte* turns right; the left-hand turning leads into the centre of Huelva.

HUELVA (127,800 inhab.; 34,000 in 1920; 75,000 in 1960) is a provincial capital and a flourishing port. It stands above the confluence of the navigable Odiel and the polluted Tinto, and is of commercial importance as the main channel for export from the rich pyrite mines inland. Extensive oil refineries have been established to the S, near *La Rábida* (see above). Its fisheries are also considerable.

Huelva preserves few traces of antiquity, although it occupies the site of Roman *Onuba* and probably of an earlier Phoenician settlement. It was re-captured from the Moors c 1262; a disused aqueduct N of the town is probably of Moorish construction. It suffered severely in the earthquake of 1755 which shattered Lisbon. The original railway and pier for the export of minerals were constructed by George Barclay Bruce in 1873–76. Few of its natives have risen to eminence, but Major William Martin, Royal Marines, 'The Man who never was', is buried here. He was already dead when washed ashore carrying fake despatches which successfully mislead the German high command prior to the North African landings in the Second World War.

The most interesting building surviving the earthquake is 16C *S. Pedro*, with a good tower, and incorporating fragments of a mosque. A *Museum* has been installed at Alameda de Sundheim 13, not far E of the central Av. de Martin Alonso Pinzón. It is largely devoted to the archaeology of the region, in particular to *Tharsis* (q.v.), but also contains a section on the fine arts. The *Ayuntamiento* and the *Diputación* are in the Av. de Martin Alonso Pinzón. Also near the centre is *La Concepción*, with two paintings by Zurbarán and good stalls; and *Sta. María de Gracia* (1500). Near the N end of the town is the *Conv. de la Merced* (restored after long use as barracks) with an unusual façade of 1605.

The main road is rejoined due N of Huelva. At 14km it circles round *Gibraleón* (9100 inhab.), dominated by its ruined castle; 2km beyond this the C433 turns right for *Tharsis*, 37km NW; see p 360.

At 19km *Cartaya* (9100 inhab.) is bypassed, once a Phoenician settlement, with a ruined castle.—7km beyond is **Lepe** (14,050 inhab.), Roman *Leptis*, with a Gothic church.—At 10km *Isla Cristina* (16,350 inhab.), 5km to the S, is a centre of sardine and tunny fishing on an inlet behind its beach.

10km **Ayamonte** (16,100 inhab.; Parador) lies on the E bank and near the mouth of the Guadiana, here almost 1km wide. This has formed the frontier with Portugal since 1267, apart from a few slight modifications 30 years later. The town was originally re-conquered by Sancho II of Portugal in 1238.

In addition to its Moorish *Castle*, it contain several buildings of interest: *N.S. de las Angustias*, with an attractive façade and Mudéjar roof; the convent church of *S. Francisco* (1527), with a good tower and ceilings rich in Mudéjar detail; *El Salvador*, also with a good tower; and the 16C *Conv. de Sta. Clara.*

Car and pasenger ferries link Ayamonte with *Vila Real de Sto. António*, further S on the far bank. There is a project to span the Guadiana here with an International Bridge.

Tavira is 22km W; for *Faro* (13km beyond) and the *Algarve* in general, see *Blue Guide Portugal.*

104 Sevilla to Rosal de la Frontera via Aracena (for Serpa and Beja)

157km (97 miles). N630. 9km *Santiponce* and *Itálica*—26km. N433. 55km *Aracena*—28km *Cortegana*—39km *Rosal de la Frontera.*

Maps: M 446.

After crossing the two branches of the Guadalquivir, and passing (right) the *Cartuja* (see last part of Rte 101), turn N onto the Mérida road.

The church of *Santiponce* is soon reached. It belonged to the *Conv. de S. Isidoro del Campo*, founded in 1298 by Guzmán el Bueno as a Cistercian house but transferred in 1431 to the Hieronymites. It contains a retablo of 1613 with sculptures by Montañés, who carved the effigies on the tomb of Guzmán and his wife. In a second Mudéjar church, added in c 1350 by the founder's son, is the latter's tomb.

This was the first resting place of the body of Cortés (cf. Castilleja de
la Cuesta) before its removal to Mexico. In the two-storeyed Patio de
los Muertos are 15–16C murals, and a frescoed dado of 1436 in the
Patio de los Evangelistas.

About 1km N (watch out for directional signs) are the ruins of
Italica, founded in 206 BC by Scipio Africanus as a home for
veterans. Under Hadrian it became a *colonia* and enjoyed considerable prosperity in the 2–3Cs. It claims to be the birthplace of three
Roman emperors: Trajan (c 53–117), Hadrian (76–138), and Theodosius (c 346–95), but the latter may have been born at Coca
(Segovia).

Italica was abandoned by the Visigoths in favour of Sevilla and its
remains used as a quarry. But the *Amphitheatre, built for 40,000
spectators, still retains a few rows of seats, underground passages,
and dens; and according to 18C travellers, wheat was later grown in
it. There are also traces of a *Forum*, two *Thermae*, a *Theatre*, and a
grid of streets.

Among the mosaics to be seen (surrounded by rusting barbed wire, and entirely
unprotected from the elements) are a colourful one of Birds; another of Neptune
(discovered in 1970); that in the so-called *Casa de Planetario*; and several with
geometric patterns. Others were grubbed up by pigs or removed by dilettante
during the course of centuries (cf. Pal. de la Condesa de Lebrija, Sevilla). Most
of the smaller antiquities have been removed to the Archaeological Museum in
Sevilla, although there is an apology for a museum at the site entrance.

The road climbs the foothills of the SIERRA MORENA. At 16km turn
left onto the N433 and ascend the upper valley of the Guadiamar. For
the road ahead, see Rte 52 in reverse.

At 38.5km *Zufre* (9km right) is perched spectacularly on a ridge overlooking the
Ribera de Huelva. Its 16C church is built on the site of a mosque, and relics of
Moorish walls are also evident.

17.5km **Aracena** (682m; 6150 inhab.), dominated by a Moorish castle
(12C; later partly reconstructed by the Templars). The tower of late
13C *N.S. de los Dolores* was the minaret of the former mosque. The
church has a good doorway and polygonal apse. Below, in Herreran
La Asunción, is a carving by Montañés. But the main attraction of the
place, apart from its pleasant climate and surroundings, is the nearby
Gruta de las Maravillas, a large stalactite cavern.

At 10km a left turning approaches (5km) *Alájar*, close to the *Peña
de los Ángeles*. In a cave here, called the *Sillita del Rey*, Felipe II is
supposed to have visited Arias Montano.

The N435 (see Rte 56) is crossed after 7km just N of *Jabugo*, and
10km beyond we pass beautifully sited *Cortegana* (5600 inhab.),
Roman *Corticata*, with an old castle enlarged in the late 15C and a
Gothic church of some interest.

14km *Aroche* (ancient *Aruci*), to the S, is bypassed, in a district rich
in prehistoric remains. The town still has its walls, a Moorish castle,
and an 18C church.

The road now descends the valley of the Chanza to (25km) *Rosal
de la Frontera*, the frontier village (Spanish Customs), and crosses
into Portugal 3km beyond.—For *Serpa*, 34km W, and *Beja*, 29km
beyond, see *Blue Guide Portugal*.

Grazing bulls near Aracena

Index of Artists and Architects

Among the principal Spanish artists, sculptors and architects (and including certain foreign artists working in Spain), together with their dates, are:

583

Index

To keep the index a reasonable length, only topographical entries
have been included, and only Barcelona, Granada, Madrid, Sevilla
and Toledo are subindexed. Places only mentioned in passing are
excluded, as are churches, monasteries, chapels and castles, etc. in
the vicinity of places indexed.

NOTES

NOTES

NOTES

NOTES

NOTES

NOTES

NOTES